Modelling, Simulation and Optimization

Edited by
Dr. Gregorio Romero Rey
Dra. Mª Luisa Martinez Muneta

Modelling, Simulation and Optimization,
Edited by Dr. Gregorio Romero Rey and Dra. Mª Luisa Martinez Muneta

This is a reprint of the book published in 2009 by In-Teh

Republished by InTech
Janeza Trdine 9, 51000 Rijeka, Croatia

Edition 2014

Technical Editor Zeljko Debeljuh

Cover Designer Dino Smrekar

Additional hard copies can be obtained from orders@intechopen.com

Modelling, Simulation and Optimization,
Edited by Dr. Gregorio Romero Rey and Dra. Mª Luisa Martinez Muneta
p. cm.
ISBN 978-953-307-048-3

For EU product safety concerns:
IN TECH d.o.o., Prolaz Marije Krucifikse Kozulić 3, 51000 Rijeka, Croatia,
info@intechopen.com or visit our website at intechopen.com.

Preface

Computer-Aided Design and system analysis aims to find mathematical models that allow emulating the behaviour of components and facilities. The high competitiveness in industry, the little time available for product development and the high cost in terms of time and money of producing the initial prototypes means that the computer-aided design and analysis of products is taking on major importance. On the other hand, in most areas of engineering the components of a system are interconnected and belong to the different domains of physics (mechanics, electrics, hydraulics, thermal...). When developing a complete multidisciplinary system, it needs to integrate a design procedure to ensure that it will be successfully achieved.

Engineering systems require an analysis of their dynamic behaviour (evolution over time or the path of their different variables). This is especially important in automotive products, railway dynamics, machine tools, robotics and aeronautics. Modelling a complete system with particular attention to detail in the specific component intended for analysis enables concepts relative to the component to be analysed as well as their influence on the rest of the system [i][ii].

The purpose of modelling and simulating dynamic systems is to generate a set of algebraic and differential equations or a mathematical model. This always leads to a description of the represented system that is never ambiguous.

In order to perform rapid product optimisation iterations, the models must be formulated and evaluated in the most efficient way. Automated environments contribute to this. Freeing engineers of the tedious task of producing equations is vital. In addition, this automation prevents the inevitable human error and leads to a rapid evaluation of the different alternatives of a particular component. One of the pioneers of simulation technology in medicine defines "Simulation" as a technique, not a technology, that replaces real experiences with guided experiences reproducing important aspects of the real world in a fully interactive fashion [iii].

In the following chapters the reader will be introduced to the world of simulation in topics of current interest such as medicine, military purposes and their use in industry for diverse applications that range from the use of networks to combining thermal, chemical or electrical aspects, among others...

Chapter 1 presents an overview of the state of the art of 3D applied to diagnostic tools, capturing techniques and models manufacturing, emphasizing their use in orthodontics. In addition, some clinical cases, treated using the above-mentioned technologies, are presented and discussed. Chapter 2 develops a three-dimensional computational model of the abdominal aorta and renal branches to show the ability to predict the unsteady flow patterns throughout the cardiac cycle. In order to solve the complex changes in the velocity gradients, induced by the pulsatile cardiac waveform, the grid will be sufficiently dense to make a proper calculation of the gradients possible. Chapter 3 discusses a conceptual bipedal model with symmetry and asymmetry applicable to both healthy subjects and stroke patients for Sit-To-Stand (STS) manoeuvre, by using synthesized reference trajectories and optimal feedback controller design. Chapter 4 develops a new strategy for autonomous grasping in a Virtual Environment (VE), based on the knowledge of a few object attributes like size, task, and shape, implementing a semi-intelligence algorithm, which makes a decision about how to grasp the selected object from among others.

Chapter 5 attempts to generalize the case of the ground stations located in urban areas with a high density of mobile radio systems in which it is necessary eliminate intermodulation interference, since these signals are unpredictable, and to reach conclusions in advance before a final decision about location and operation frequency up to device selection for implementing the ground satellite station. Chapter 6 creates a virtual environment that is assumed to accept the just-in-time characteristics of a threat signal as inputs, pass them through a simulator system and then produce a false target and realistic images that abide by the current sensor technology limitations and the prevalent laws of physics. Chapter 7 develops a new method to evaluate the risk of trajectory failure by using experimental data measurements, which consist of defining a metric (or distance) able to compare trajectories with each other in order to evaluate the handling loss risk and determine the limit states or the critical sections which govern the intersection between Vehicle, Infrastructure and Driver in the safety trajectory space.

Chapter 8 proposes a control strategy design method that accounts for the essential features necessary in the guidance and control of Autonomous Underwater Vehicles (AUVs), minimizing energy consumption and incorporating under-actuation, to be implemented onto a real vehicle and not only in numerical simulations. Chapter 9 investigates a methodology for the shape optimization problem for fluid flow systems, finding an optimal shape with two or three dimensions that satisfies certain requirements like reducing the drag force on the wing of a vehicle or reducing the viscous dissipation in hydraulic valves, pipes and tanks. Chapter 10 studies the factors that determine the quality and energy requirement of ploughing, the impact of body parameters, working modes and speed, as well as soil properties on it and to find technical solutions to improve ploughing efficiency.

Chapter 11 presents the methodology to model, simulate and optimize the interoperability and the use of control equipment in an electrical substation to train operators by means of a virtual reality environment, allowing navigation into the virtual electrical substation, interaction with the elements and including the behavioural laws associated with it. Chapter 12 performs a simulation of an electric arc furnace installation in order to design the installation for reactive power compensation, harmonic currents filter and load balancing, all to improve the efficiency of the entire installation. Chapter 13 presents a method that allows a better control of the temperature in the heating process of an electrical resistance, in the sense of reducing the time to reach the preset temperature value in the case of applying a step signal to the standard input of the controller. Chapter 14 simulates the useful utilization of regenerative energy destined to reduce overall energy Consumption, from braking energy which is temporarily saved in an Energy Storage System (ESS) until the correspondent power consumer is connected to the overhead line. Chapter 15 presents a model and a simulator to address the missing tools in the field of modelling and simulating Chip Design Processes

(CDPs), regarding resources and design artefacts within a CDP in a generic manner, their also being applicable to any other engineering or production process.

Chapter 16 presents a Direct Numerical Simulation (DNS) methodology, coupled with accurate numerical schemes and proper combustion models, for the analysis of non¬premixed reacting flows, allowing a comprehensive simulation of the physical process. Chapter 17 discusses and presents the applications of a simulator in the form of case studies by addressing several major optimization issues of Elemental Chlorine Free (ECF) bleaching, like the optimal splitting of the ClO2 charge between the different D stages or the impact of extraction stage pH, among other phenomena, and may be used effectively by mill personnel for pollution abatement and process optimization assessments.

Chapter 18 presents an application of the 9-velocity lattice gas model as an alternative and innovative approach to the wind field estimation problem in two dimensions with well known steady and non-steady laminar and turbulent flow situations; as a particular case, it is able to reproduce the typical surface layer quasi-logarithmic wind profile. Chapter 19 investigates numerically the flow and transport phenomena in a test cell with its south side partially shaded by trailing plants and the cover shaded by a shelter, and solves numerically by a finite volume numerical model the two dimensional unsteady transport equations for the velocities, turbulence, energy and spectral intensity of radiation.

Chapter 20 studies the different behaviours of the production line that would lead to a lack of productivity, according to the production axis, by indicating the losses that are incurred by problems in the production planning; the quality axis, by indicating in which measure the quality problems affect the productivity, and the maintenance axis, by taking into account the losses due to maintenance operations, based on statistical and probabilistic methods. Chapter 21 discusses the modelling and representation of a warehouse and presents an overview of "discrete-event simulation" and its derivate "trace-driven simulation" describing their features as well as two different ways (longitudinal and transversal analyses) to model the problem in order to employ these techniques in an effective manner.

In chapter 22, a well-established evolutionary optimization technique denominated Particle Swarm Optimization (PSO) is applied to problems in the urban water industry and, although originally it was designed to deal with continuous variables, the PSO variant considered in this chapter overcomes three typical weaknesses in this optimization technique. Chapter 23 discusses both how to model context-aware telematic application specific abstractions for large scale vehicular networks and how to simulate interactions between moving vehicles and static nodes using broadcasting and relevance back propagation algorithms over Bluetooth and WiFi networks. Chapter 24 describes a network model of maritime networks to investigate the impact of several network services designed to provide traffic engineering by using statistically and empirically valid modelling and simulation based on the mathematical analysis and the results of the simulation matching well with a real world example. Chapter 25 presents a search and rescue simulation for a partially flooded city making use of novel approaches in the areas of modelling, simulation, and optimization, pre-processing the model to make it suitable for simulation applications running quickly and efficiently, and using a hierarchical multi-agent planning and execution algorithm. Chapter 26 proposes an early restoration for lifeline systems after earthquake disasters focusing on two issues: an allocation problem as to which groups will restore which disaster places and a scheduling problem as to what order is the best for the restoration, applying a Genetic Algorithm Considering

Uncertainty (GACU). Chapter 27 presents a summary of how to use intelligent computational modelling for time series forecasting and the importance of the correct choice of the fitness function, by using three methodologies to adjust the parameters of an Artificial Neural Network (ANN) - a Modified Genetic Algorithm, a Particle Swarm Optimization and the GRASPES Method.

Chapter 28 introduces the data-driven fuzzy modelling method to an audience applying experimental modelling (e.g. scientists, engineers, medical scientists or machine diagnosis specialists, etc.) and makes a novel contribution to the field of experimental modelling.

Chapter 29 gives an overview of current research work related to the modelling and simulation of human behaviour in panic situations and presents the new 'SimPan' reference model as an innovation in this area. Chapter 30 briefly presents an overview of the most important elements of the PLAMAGS Project (Programming LAnguage for Multi-Agent Geo-Simulations), such as Virtual Geographical Environments (VGEs) and scenarios, as well as the specification of objects, agents and their behaviours.

We hope that after reading the different sections of this book we will have succeeded in bringing across what the scientific community is doing in the field of simulation and that it will have been to your interest and liking.

Lastly, we would like to thank all the authors for their excellent contributions in the different areas of simulation.

Dr. Gregorio Romero Rey

Dra. Mª Luisa Martinez Muneta

Universidad Politécnica de Madrid (Spain)

[i] Gordon G. (1969). Systems simulation, Prentice-Hall.

[ii] Bekey GA. (1977). Models and reality: some reflections on the art and science of the simulation, Simulation 29(5), pp.161-164.

[iii] Gaba D. (2004). The Future of Simulation in Healthcare. Qual. Saf. Health Care 13, pp.2-10.

Contents

Three-dimensional diagnosis and visualization supports in orthodontics based on Reverse Engineering and Solid Free-form Fabrication techniques

Alida Mazzoli[1], Michele Germani[2], Roberto Raffaeli[2] and Antonio Gracco[3]
[1] Department of Materials and Environment Engineering and Physics, Università Politecnica delle Marche, Via Brecce Bianche, 60131 Ancona (Italy)
[2] DT&M Group, Department of Mechanics, Università Politecnica delle Marche, Via Brecce Bianche, 60131 Ancona (Italy)
[3] Department of Orthodontics, Università di Ferrara, Via Montebello 31, 44100 Ferrara (Italy)

1. Introduction

Diagnosis means the art or act of identifying a disease from its signs and symptoms (Merriam Webster Dictionary, 2009). The maxillofacial region, extending from the base of the skull to the hyoid bone, is one of the most anatomically complex regions of the body. This area contains elements and organs belonging to a number of different systems that can be affected by a variety of local and systemic pathologic processes. Diagnostic imaging has assumed a central role in the evaluation of this region. New trends in dentistry include digital and three-dimensional (3D) imaging. The ultimate reward of the technologic imaging advancements is the digital representation of the patient's anatomy, as it exists in nature (anatomic truth). Oral and maxillofacial radiology provides the dentist with diverse diagnostic equipments. Current and evolving methods include computed tomography (CT), tomosynthesis (Badea et al., 2001), tuned-aperture CT (TACT) (Webber et al., 1997), localized, or "cone-beam", CT (Heiken at al., 1993) and magnetic resonance imaging (MRI) (Olt & Jakob, 2004). Although oral and maxillofacial radiology is nowadays widely accepted as a routine technique for dental examinations, the equipments are rather expensive and, furthermore, the radiation dose required to enhance both contrast and spatial resolution can be unacceptably high. A solution to this problem is partially given by the use of maxillofacial dedicated cone-beam CT equipments, which can provide images of sufficient quality for the specific diagnostic needs at significantly reduced absorbed radiation dose (Mah et al., 2003). Much effort has focused recently on computerized diagnosis in dentistry (Beers et al., 2003; Cousley at al., 2003). The study and monitoring of facial appearance is particularly important in the field of dentistry and reconstructive maxillofacial surgery. Usually, most of the 3D systems for dental applications found in literature rely on obtaining an intermediate solid model of the jaw (cast or teeth imprints) and then capturing the 3D information from that model (Williams et al., 2004; Alcaniz et al., 1998). User interaction is needed in such systems to determine the coordinates of specific reference points on a dental cast. Other systems for dentistry are under development in order to replace traditional approaches in diagnosis, treatment planning, surgical simulations and prosthetic replacements (Yamani et al., 2000; Halazonetis, 2001). Moreover, there is another class of machine technology, called Solid Free-form Fabrication (SFF), originally developed for industry that is getting a great amount of attention in the medical sector during the last few years (Sykes et al., 2004; Wohlers, 2004). SFF manufactured anatomical models find applications particularly in oral, maxillofacial and neurological surgery. In dentistry SFF can be used mainly for assisting diagnosis, planning treatment and manufacturing implants. The effectiveness of models manufactured by SFF has been demonstrated in various surgical procedures (Erben et al., 2002). In the following study, the reader is presented with an overview of the state of the art of 3D diagnostic tools in orthodontics, 3D capturing techniques and models manufacturing by SFF, emphasizing their use in orthodontics. Moreover some clinical cases, treated using the above-mentioned technologies, are presented and discussed.

2. 3D tools in orthodontics

The discipline of orthodontics is concerned with the face and the ability of the clinician to modify its growth. Orthodontists achieve their goals by manipulating the craniofacial skeleton, with particular emphasis on modifying the dentoalveolar region, the temporomandibular joint and the sutures. This article trace the way in which three-dimensional (3D) tools in orthodontics has developed their usefulness today, and the way in which they may develop in the future.

2.1 Radiographic tools

The cephalogram is the standard used by orthodontists to assess skeletal, dental, and soft tissue relationships. This approach, however, is based on two-dimensional (2D) views used to analyze 3D objects. Cephalometry was defined by Moyers (Moyers et al., 1988) as a radiographic technique for abstracting the human head into a measurable geometric scheme. Cephalometric radiography is used to describe the morphology and growth of the craniofacial skeleton, predict growth, plan treatment, and evaluate treatment results. Most of these tasks require the identification of specific landmarks and the calculation of various angular and linear variables. Two types of errors occur with this approach: errors of projection and errors of identification (Baumrind et al., 1971). Errors of projection are caused because the images are a 2D representation of a 3D object. X-ray beams are nonparallel and originated from a small source, leading to radiographs that are imperfect enlargements affected by the distances between the focus, the object, and the film (Adams, 1940; Bjork & Solow, 1962). Errors of identification are the errors of identifying specific landmarks on the images and are considered by many investigators as the major sources of error in cephalometrics (Hixon, 1956; Mitgaard et al., 1974). Despite several improvements in 3D cephalometric research (Swennen & Schutyser, 2006) this technique still remains time-consuming, exposes the patient to radiation and does not define the soft tissues. Current and evolving diagnosis tools include computed tomography (CT), tomosynthesis (Badea et al.,

2001) , tuned-aperture CT (TACT) (Webber et al., 1997), localized, or "cone-beam", CT (Heiken et al., 1993) and magnetic resonance imaging (MRI) (Olt et al., 2004). From the first commercial Computerized Tomography (CT) scanner appeared in 1972, in the early 1980s researchers began investigating 3D imaging of craniofacial deformities. Shortly after, the first textbooks on 3D imaging in medicine appeared and were based on the principles and applications of 3D CT and MRI-based imaging. 3D imaging has evolved into a discipline "dealing with various form of visualization, manipulation and analysis of multi-dimensional medical structures" (Ududpa & Herman, 1991) and new trends in dentistry include digital imaging and 3D imaging of the maxillofacial regions. Since the 1980s, the quality and speed of CT imaging has changed dramatically. Nowadays with improved techniques and imaging programs it is possible to produce images, which can be rotated and cut at any level. The last generation dental CT scanner are now available for clinical practice and uses the principle of tomosynthesis or cone-beamed CT, so called because of the shape of the x-ray beam, as for example the NewTom QR 9000 Volume Scanner (QR Srl, Verona, Italy) (Mozzo et al., 1998). It uses a cone-shaped x-ray beam that is large enough to encompass the region of interest. This type of beam uses the x-rays very efficiently, thus reducing the absorbed dose to the patient. This type of beam also allows for the acquisition of the image data in one revolution of the x-ray source and detector without the need for patient movement. These attributes make this system more efficient than others, and thus it can be applied for specific purposes in the maxillofacial region. As for regards the MRI, it is good for 3D imaging of soft tissues but the accuracy of the data is not sufficient for specific procedures such as for example the precision milling of prostheses, as it does not properly differentiate between air and bone. However, for soft tissues it is excellent, and can be useful in imaging of temporomandibular joints. It is also useful in the management of tumours of the head and neck region and for imaging the brain for neurological problems.

2.2 3D capturing techniques

Optical surface scanning was first tested in 1981 to produce a non-invasive 3D image of the face. The system was modified, improved, and re-tested (Arridge et al., 1985; Moss et al., 1987; Aung et al. 1995). Since that time, the system has also been developed to scan models of the teeth. In 1996, the hand-held scanner was designed to make the system mobile (McCallum et al., 1996). This can be used for scanning many parts of the body. The recent introduction of a probe that records the 3D co-ordinates of any point means that many of the hard tissue points used by Farkas (1994) can now be recorded. Over the years, the value of the 3D system in the diagnosis and management of patients has been demonstrated. 3D material has been obtained on various types of craniofacial anomalies such as cleft palate, hemifacial microsomia, and cherubism (Moss & James, 1984; McCance et al., 1997).

Technologies used for the measurement of the surface of objects with micro to macro sizes can be divided fundamentally into two groups: systems based on laser scanning and systems based on white light projection. The used equipment is different, however they are based on the same principle: triangulation.

Laser scanning systems employs lasers to project a spot, a line, multiple lines, or patterns onto a surface, whereas a light sensor, usually a camera, acquires the scene. The three elements laser, light sensor and object surface form a triangle. When the geometrical disposition of the laser and the light sensor are known, the distance of the object surface to the laser scanning device can be easily determined by triangulation. To measure surface areas the laser spot, line, multiple lines or pattern have to move over the area (i.e. scan the surface). For this process, different methods can be used, e.g. mirrors systems, electro-mechanical systems, hand operated systems.

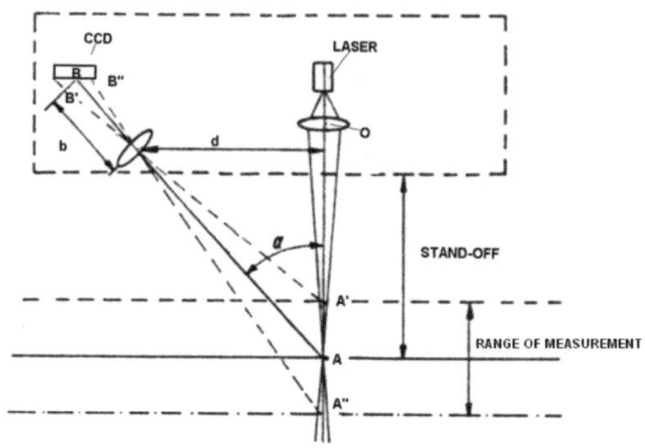

Fig. 1. The concept of laser triangulation

3D measurement systems based on white light employ projectors instead of laser light sources, to project light patterns onto the surface. The measurement principle remains the same: triangulation. A triangle is formed by projector, camera and object. In this case, to cover entire surface parts, surface areas are illuminated by the employed projector. Special codes are used to determine the origin of the light source, e.g. binary codes and colour codes. The two different technologies result in different surface scanning devices with diverse characteristics. Some examples are laser profilers mounted on CMM, portable coded light projection surface digitizer, portable laser scanners and hand held surface digitizers. Medical sciences are also interested in the 3D scanning technologies because of their high accuracy, fast acquisition and non-contact characteristics. A good example of the advantages of optical 3D measurement technologies in the medical field can be found in orthodontics. In fact, the 3D measurement of dental casts brings many advantages and new opportunities. Several 3D scanners specially designed for these applications are available on the market and are later on described in detail. They allow a precise, full automatic and fast 3D scanning of full dental casts, dies/stumps, inlay preparations, bridge preparations, bites/antagonists, wax-ups and superstructures. The acquired data can be useful for many reasons, as for example: 3D databases of dental casts accessible in a local area network reduce storage costs and give easy and instantaneous access to a patient's teeth profile (Gracco et al., 2005), 3D software solutions allow a simplified design of caps, crowns, inlays and bridges from the scanned data (Raffaeli et al., 2005). Reverse engineering systems in orthodontics are generally used for computer aided dental restoration and diagnosis and treatment planning.

2.2.1 Computer aided dental restoration

An accurate measurement of 3D models of the teeth is the basis of the entire process. As for regards the clinical requirements, the non-contact optical method is obviously the ideal approach. In the CEREC system (Otto et al., 2002; Luthardt et al., 2002), a probe was designed in order to acquire the optical impression of the selected tooth. However, it can only detect the depth of the cavity and not the complete 3D shape of the tooth. Other CAD/CAM systems available on the market, as for example IVB 3D Jena (http://www.ivb-jena.de) and 3Shape (http://www.3shape.com), tended to rely on in vitro shape measurement, mostly using a laser scanning technique to measure the shape of the model rather than the original tooth. The above because laser scanning is actually a point-wise method in principle, which allows only one height data point to be measured or recorded at a single instant. The use of a particular mechanical positioning setup, though, makes the point-wise scanning a rapid process of possibly within a fraction of a second, and it brings certain restrictions in the meantime that prohibits its direct application in an intra-oral environment. Fig. 2 shows the example of the 3D dental scanner 3Shape D-200 (3Shape A/S, Denmark), some sample data of 3D scans, as well as an example of digital design of dental restorations.

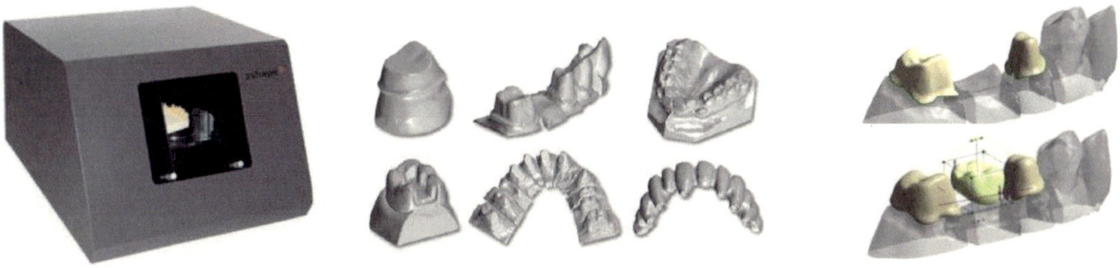

Fig. 2. 3Shape D-200 Dental 3D Scanner (left); sample measured data (center); 3Shape DentalDesigner software examples (right)

2.2.2 Diagnosis and treatment planning

Hard and software solutions are well-suited for orthodontic applications in which fast and accurate 3D scanning of full dental casts are essential. 3D orthodontics software currently under development includes functions as: storage, research and analysis (http://www.3shape.com) and for the orthodontic treatment planning and the correct placement of appliances (http://orthocad.com). As for regards the first aspects, 3D databases accessible in a local area network (LAN) reduce storage costs and give easy and instantaneous access to the patient's teeth profile. Moreover, scanning and software solution are often integrated with such 3D databases. In fact are often available software packages for the analysis of the patient's dentition in order to assess the efficiency of an orthodontic treatment. In such an application, an intuitive interface allows the user to set references points on the scanned casts in order to measure paths, angles and available space for orthodontics treatments. Different measurement tools are available, user is allowed to pick point on the cast 3D model or on 2D cross sections and measure distances. This also allows for easy comparisons among 2D cross sections. Moreover, analysis algorithms allow the user to measure the teeth size and position amid compare this data with statistics of population's standard mouth anatomy. Graphic reports allow the practitioner to compare two dental casts in order to analyze growth and dental treatment efficiency. In Fig. 3 are shown some functions of the software 3Shape Orthoanalyzer (3Shape A/S, Denmark).
As for regards the orthodontic treatment planning and the correct placement of appliances, the systems available on the market allow the orthodontist to make accurate measurements

for the treatment planning while at the same time eliminating plaster model storage and retrieval issues. Moreover, allow practitioners to simulate treatment strategies and select and execute the most appropriate treatment plan that includes precise positioning of orthodontic brackets as shown in Fig. 4.

(a)

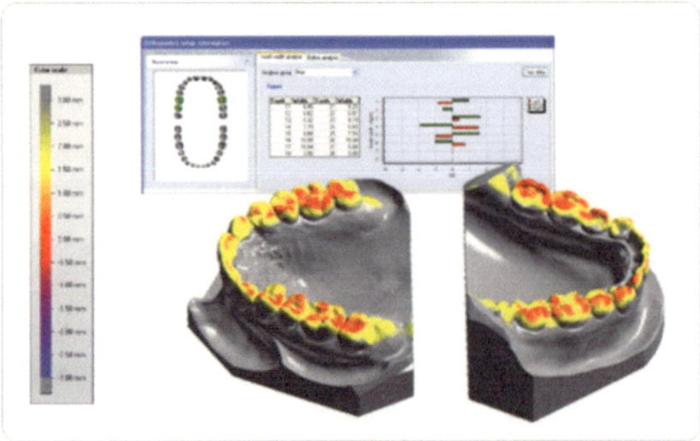

(b)

Fig. 3. Specific functions of the software package 3Shape Orthoanalyzer for storage (a), research and analysis (b) purposes in orthodontics

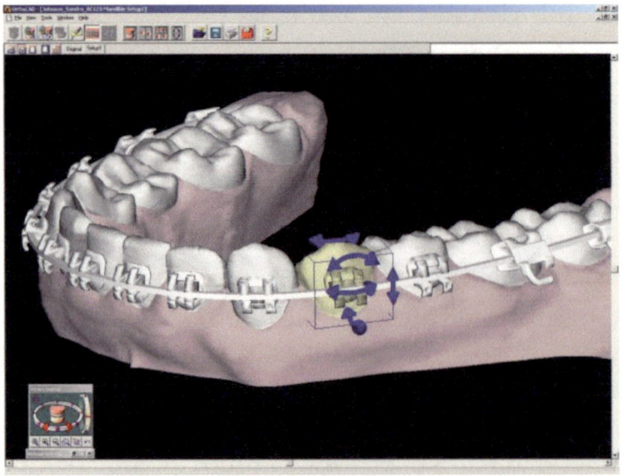

Fig. 4. Specific functions of the software Orthocad (Cadent Inc., USA) that uses computers to make an indirect bonding set-up for bracket placement

Lingual orthodontic treatment is an alternative to the traditional vestibular treatment, and is designed to satisfy those patients who wish to have their teeth aligned but do not want

labial brackets. Due to the difficulties in positioning, indirect bonding techniques have been developed to transfer brackets location from a physical model by bonding trays. A solution based on a new three-dimensional CAD system, called CADental, has been proposed to virtually design trays both for the requirements of lingual and vestibular appliances. It has been implemented using a geometrical modelling kernel, within a low-cost commercial CAD system (Rhinoceros 3.0, by Rhino3D). It allows the positioning of the brackets and the definition of a suitable bonding tray in a very short time, verifying, at the same time, the accuracy of the result in order to avoid errors and iterations.
The CADental software tool has been developed for an easy interfacing with 3D shape acquisition systems used to scan impressions and plaster casts, and with the rapid prototyping machines used to build physical models and trays (Fig. 5). During the implementation stage particular attention was dedicated to the development of a user-friendly interface suitable to non-expert users of 3D CAD modelling systems. The functionalities have been strongly automated and the user interface has been based on semantic entities linked to the operator's traditional way of working.

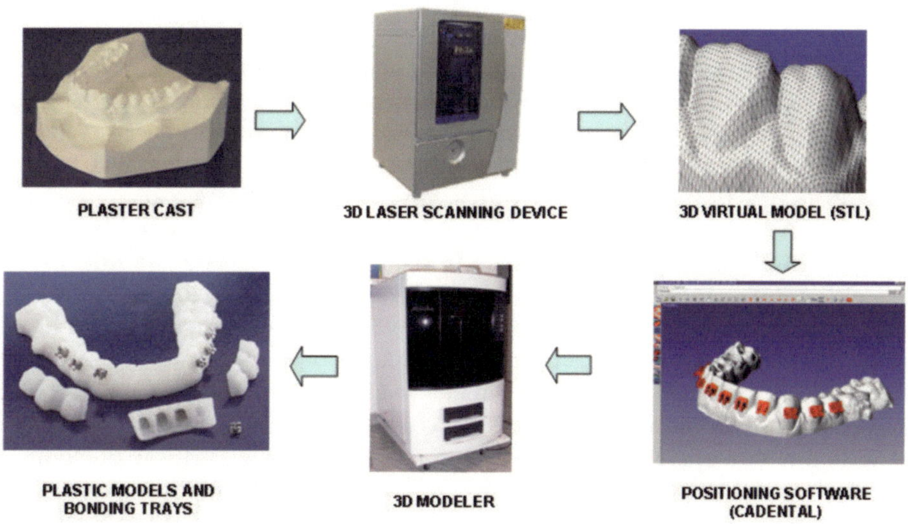

Fig. 5. Plaster casts or impressions scanning to obtain 3D virtual models. CADental software allows the manufacturing of the Tweed support, analyse and measure models, positioning of the brackets, creations of virtual set-ups and bonding trays. Models and trays can be manufactured in medical Acrylonitrile Butadiene Styrene (ABS) plastic

A successful large scale operation to mass produce a customized device brings together the best of reverse engineering hardware and software. Case in point, the company, Align Technology of California, manufactures clear, molded, removable thermoplastic shells called aligners to do the work of permanent metal braces (Melkos, 2005). The process is based on a series of scans collected during the layer-by-layer destruction of the study model poured from an actual patient dental impression. Surface data from the scanning process are analysed and processed to create the sequence of progressive orthodontic arrangements that will achieve the end goal of straightening or repositioning the teeth. The data are sent to a stereolithography machine to produce all the models required for the complete set. Then a thermoformed shell is made for each step in the treatment and the set is shipped back to the local dentist. Patients wear the removable device for only two weeks before moving to the next. This reverse engineering technology not only allows custom manufacture of the aligners at various stages of treatment but makes a simulation of the orthodontic correction process possible, using the patient's own data set. Optical modelling processing finds and application also in order to reduce the stress caused to patients by conventional methods of modelling using CT or MRI for extraoral defects and body areas. In fact the selected body part could be digitized using optical 3-coordinate measuring technology, providing an extensive data record. With such a technology, the patient's physical and psychological stress may be reduced. Diverse application were found in literature and describes for example a technique for optical modelling of facial prosthesis (Runte et al., 2002; Cheah et al., 2003), ocular prosthesis (Reitemeier et al., 2004) and ear prosthesis (Ciocca et al., 2004).

2.3 Solid Free-form Fabrication (SFF) techniques

SFF technologies, originally developed for industry, have been receiving a great amount of attention in the medical sector in the last few years. Medical SFF is defined as the manufacture of dimensionally accurate physical models of human anatomy derived from medical image data using a variety of SFF technologies. SFF-manufactured anatomical models find applications particularly in oral (Lee et al., 2006), maxillofacial (Winder et al., 2005) , neurological surgery (Muller et al., 2003; Mazzoli et al., in press) and orthopaedics (Minns et al., 2003). In medicine, they are mainly used for assisting diagnosis, planning treatment, and manufacturing implants (Petzold et al., 1999). SFF models' effectiveness has been shown in various surgical procedures (Erben et al., 2002). Patients find the medical models helpful for informed consent. Medical modeling is an intuitive, user-friendly technology that facilitates diagnosis and surgical planning, allowing surgeons to rehearse procedures readily and, moreover, improves communication between doctors and patients. Furthermore, SFF-manufactured models can be used in the reconstruction of post-traumatic defects, tumoral resections, and other complex craniofacial defects. SFF technologies can be of benefit in the pre-operating estimation of the quantitative surgical outcome, in the reduction of the operating time and in the production of more predictable results. Currently, the SFF techniques used in medical applications are 3D printing (3D-P), stereolithography (SLA), selective laser sintering (SLS), fused deposition modeling (FDM), laminated object manufacturing (LOM) (Berry et al., 1997; Leong et al., 2003; Liu et al., 2006) and electron beam melting (EBM) (Mazzoli et al., in press). Each of these different techniques builds up a model, layer by layer, using different processes and materials. 3D-P creates models by spraying liquid binder through ink-jet printer nozzles on to a layer of metallic or ceramic precursor powder. SLA by tracing a lower power ultraviolet laser across a vat filled with resin. SLS by a heat fusible power by tracing a modulated laser beam across a bin covered with the powder. FDM by heating thermoplastic material, extruded through a nozzle positioned over a computer controlled x–y table. LOM by a heat-activated, adhesive coated paper, tracing a focused laser beam to cut a profile on sheets positioned on a computer controlled x–y table. EBM consists of a layer-based direct manufacturing process of complex parts by melting metal powder with an accelerated electron beam. As for the materials 3D-P uses a wide selection of powder materials, SLS fine thermoplastic powder, SLA UV-sensitive resins, LOM thin sheets of material such as paper, FDM thermoplastic filaments and EBM fine metallic powder.

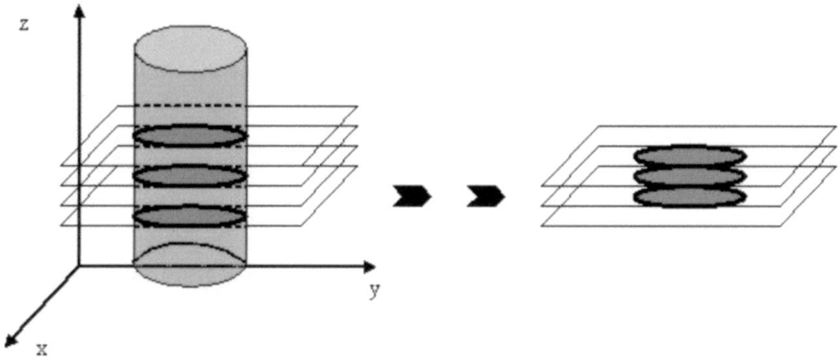

Fig. 6. The concept of layered manufacturing

The dimensional accuracy is a major concern for the clinical application of 3D medical models and was previously studied and assessed, under specific conditions, by some of the authors (Mazzoli et al., 2007). Techniques were developed to represent the data in 3D on a 2D screen. Given the visualization provided by sophisticated software packages, the fabrication of physical models may seem superfluous. However, even if the display of a 3D volume on a 2D screen provides useful information to the clinicians, as later on discussed in the presentation of some clinical cases treated at the Department of Orthodontics of the University of Ferrara, it does not provide with a complete understating of the patient's anatomy. In short, there are several visualization issues that are being addressed but not yet resolved by virtual models. For the above mentioned reason the construction of physical model is often necessary. An anatomical model can be manufactured using SFF techniques by the following steps:

1. acquisition: patient scans with X-ray CT or MRI imaging;
2. design: segmentation to delineate and extract the surface as triangles or polygons (creation of the 3D CAD solid model of the anatomy);
3. converting: convert the CAD model to STL format;
4. pre-process: slice the STL file into thin cross-sectional layers (generated by a dedicated software);
5. building process: construct the model one layer atop another by a selected SFF process;
6. post-process: clean and finish the model.

Specific scanning protocols are required to generate precise anatomical physical models. The type of scanner will need to be determined in order to check that the image reconstruction software can translate the data and also the kind of scan (i.e. axial or helical). The recommended slice thickness is 1.0 mm or less. The scan spacing: should be 0.5 mm or at least one-half the smallest dimension of interest. The resolution should be 512 x 512 or higher. The Field of View (FOV) should be chosen so that object imaged should fill the field of view without extending beyond it. The position of the long axis of the object to be scanned should be parallel to the bore of the scanner. Generally, scans should start just off the object and finish off the other side of the object (so that the entire object is imaged). Objects to be scanned should not be taped down or placed on similarly dense objects that will show up in the scan. If significant variations in material densities exist within the object to be scanned, distortion can be experienced (artifacts). In the case of metal artifacts, the distortion can be severe. The scan protocol can and should be adjusted to take into account the presence of artifacts. Moreover, the scan protocol should take in account any gantry tilt angle. It is advisable to avoid gantry tilt when acquiring a CT data set, otherwise, sophisticated mathematical algorithms are required to successfully correct the data. From the image data, the reconstruction software is then used to extract part contours and/or surfaces (segmentation), as the case may be. Segmentation may be carried out by image tresholding, manual editing or autocontouring to extract volumes of interest. One of the simplest methods of tissue segmentation applied to the images is CT number tresholding. A CT number range is identified by either region of interest (ROI) pixel measurements or pixel intensity profiles, which is representative of the anatomy to be modelled. As a matter of fact thresholding is the first action performed to create a segmentation mask on a set of digital images. The ROI can be selected by defining a range of grey values. The boundaries of that range are the lower and upper threshold value. All pixels with a grey value in that range will be highlighted in a mask. The selection of a proper threshold value is the major source of errors in this stage. In fact, low threshold value will yield too big models, while too high threshold value will cause fine structures not to be reproduced. This makes it impossible to find a "correct" threshold value. A solution for the threshold problem is to work with local thresholds for different regions of the model. Final delineation of the anatomy of interest may requires 2D or 3D image editing to remove any unwanted details. A number of software packages are available for data conditioning and image processing for the SFF of anatomical models, including MIMICS by Materialise NV (http://www.materialise.com), BioBuild by Anatomics Pty Ltd (http://www.anatomics.com/about/index.html), 3D Doctor by Able software Corporation Ltd (http://www.ablesw.com/) and Analyze by Mayo Clinic (http://www.mayo.edu/bir/Software/Analyze/Analyze.html). The clinical cases presented in this study were modelled using the software MIMICS that provides a comprehensive range of data interpretation and image processing to interface with SFF technology. As previously mentioned the SFF techniques currently used in medical applications are 3D printing (3D-P), stereolithography (SLA), selective laser sintering (SLS), fused deposition modeling (FDM), laminated object manufacturing (LOM) and electron beam melting (EBM). The above-mentioned techniques will be afterward described in detail.

2.3.1 3D Printing (3D-P)

3D-P uses a technology similar to the ink-jet printing. As shown in Fig. 7, parts are built upon a platform situated in a bin full of powder material. An ink-jet printing head selectively "prints" binder to fuse the powder together in the desired areas. Unbound powder remains to support the part. The platform is lowered, more powder added and levelled, and the process repeated. When finished, the green part is sintered and then removed from the unbound powder. No external supports are required during fabrication since the powder supports overhangs. 3D-P advantages include speedy fabrication and low material costs. Limitations on resolution, surface finish, part fragility and available materials are its disadvantages. The problem of the accuracy of the final parts is due to the stair-stepping effect in the X-Y plane, because of the print-head raster-scanning on the layers. Moreover, 3D-P parts have a ribbed and little rough appearance due to layering beads of plastic and are not suitable for extensive functional testing.

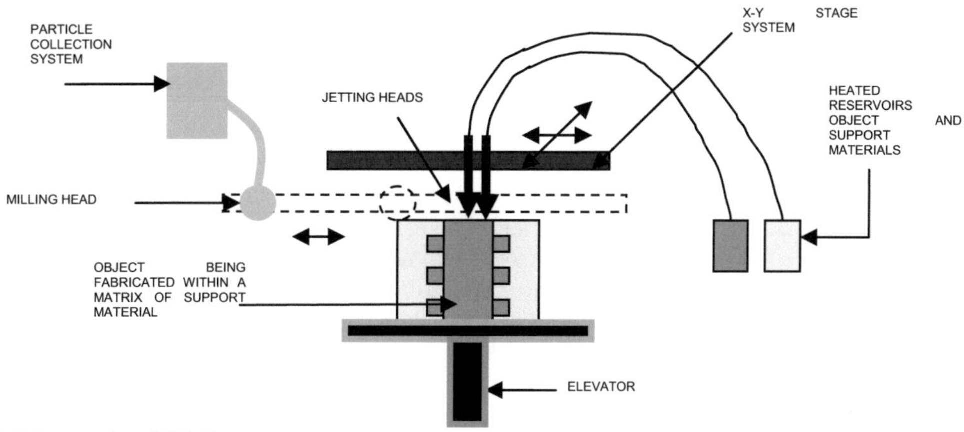

Fig. 7. Schematic of 3D-P

2.3.2 Stereolithography (SLA)

Patented in 1986, stereolithography started the SFF revolution. The technique builds three-dimensional models from liquid photosensitive polymers that solidify when exposed to ultraviolet light. As shown in Fig. 7, the model is built upon a platform situated just below the surface in a vat of liquid epoxy or acrylate resin. A low-power highly focused UV laser traces out the first layer, solidifying the model's cross section while leaving excess areas liquid. The movement of the laser light on the surface of the resin is controlled by a movable mirror, using the data from the CAD system. Next, an elevator incrementally lowers the platform into the liquid polymer. A sweeper re-coats the solidified layer with liquid, and the laser traces the second layer atop the first. This process is repeated until the prototype is complete. Afterwards, the solid part is removed from the vat and rinsed clean of excess liquid. This part is called "green part". Supports are broken off and the model is then placed in an ultraviolet oven for complete curing. In Fig. 8 is represented the schematic diagram of SLA.

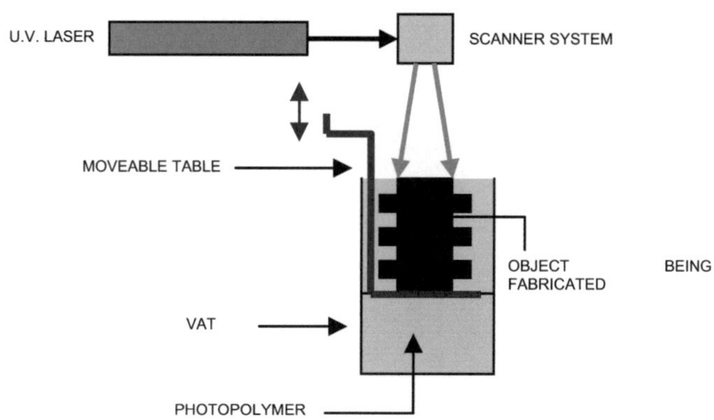

Fig. 8. Schematic of SLA

SLA can produce surgical templates out of sterilizable USP Class VI resin. Advantages of SLA process include high part-building accuracy, smooth surface finish, fine building details and high mechanical strength. Moreover, selectively colour-changing materials for biomedical applications are available, providing superior visualization by highlighting selected features in different colour. Disadvantages of this process include expensive equipment and material cost, wet materials handling and post-processing of the manufactured parts.

2.3.3 Selective Laser Sintering (SLS)

Developed by Carl Deckard for his master's thesis at the University of Texas, selective laser sintering was patented in 1989. The process is somewhat similar to SLA in principle as can be seen from the figure below. In this case, however, a laser beam is traced over the surface of a tightly compacted powder made of thermoplastic material. The powder is spread by a roller over the surface of a build cylinder. A piston moves down one object layer thickness to accommodate the layer of powder. Excess powder in each layer helps to support the part during the build. Heat from the laser melts the powder where it strikes under guidance of the scanner system. The CO_2 laser used provides a concentrated infrared heating beam. The entire fabrication chamber is sealed and maintained at a temperature just below the melting point of the plastic powder. Thus, heat from the laser need only to elevate the temperature slightly to cause sintering, greatly speeding the process. A nitrogen atmosphere is also maintained in the fabrication chamber in order to prevent the possibility of explosion in the handling of large quantities of powder. After the object is fully formed, the piston is raised to elevate the object. Excess powder is simply brushed away and final manual finishing may be carried out. No supports are required with this method since overhangs and undercuts are supported by the solid powder bed. This saves some finishing time compared to SLA. However, surface finishes are not as good and this may increase the time. No final curing is required as in SLA, but since the objects are sintered they are porous. Depending on the application, it may be necessary to infiltrate the object with another material to improve mechanical characteristics. Much progress has been made over the years in improving surface finish and porosity. The method has also been extended to provide direct fabrication of metal and ceramic objects and tools.

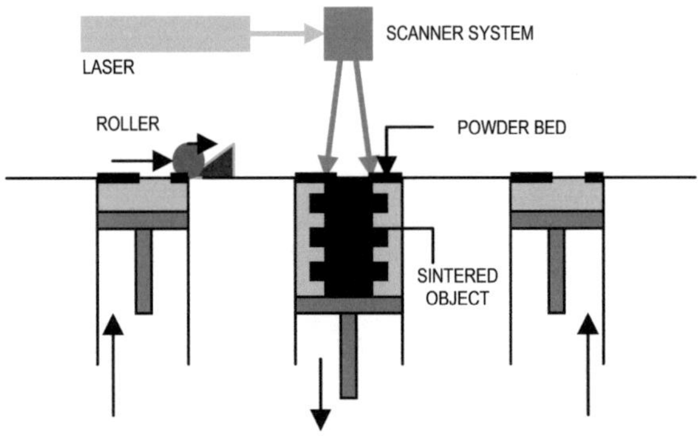

Fig. 9. Schematic of SLS

Advantages of SLS include high part accuracy, material versatility, easy post-processing and no support needed. Disadvantages include that SLS manufactured parts have little rough grainy and porous surface finish which is not as smooth as SLA but acceptable for most of applications but parts can be easily primed and finished to smooth level. The larger shrink rates of SLS increase the tendency for the prototype to warp, bow or curl subject to the part geometry. SLS features detail is not as crispy and sharp as produced by SLA.

2.3.4 Fused Deposition Modelling (FDM)

In this technique, filaments of heated thermoplastic are extruded from a tip that moves in the x-y plane as described in the figure above. The controlled extrusion head deposits very thin beads of material onto the build platform to form the first layer. The platform is maintained at a lower temperature, so that the thermoplastic quickly hardens. After the platform lowers, the extrusion head deposits a second layer upon the first. Supports are built along the way, fastened to the part either with a second, weaker material or with a perforated junction. FDM method produces models that are physically robust. Wax can be used as the material, but generally models are made of ABS plastic. Just out of the machine, models may have a fairly rough surface finish, but they can easily be cleaned up. Because of the use of a single well-defined thread to build the model, this is the only one of the processes where it is relatively easy to change colour; in fact the ABS fibre is available in a range of bright primary colours. Alternatively, models can be painted. Moreover, FDM provides a high level of visualization by highlighting selected features in a different colour. FDM can produce models out of medical grade ABS, which is sterilizable and translucent and meets all FDA USP Class VI requirements for temporary use inside the body.

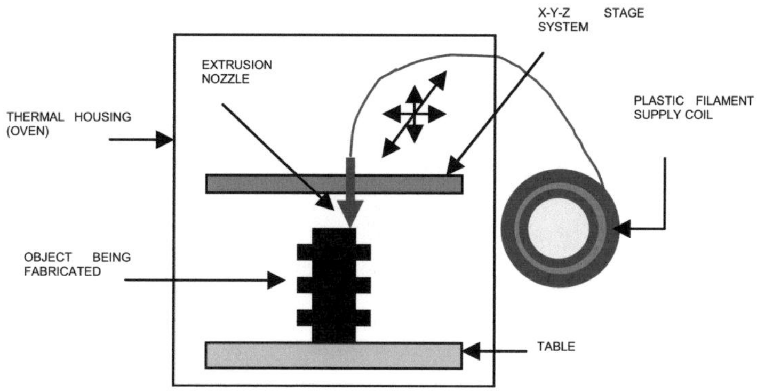

Fig. 10. Schematic of FDM

Advantages in using FDM include the speed and safety of the machine. The machine does not use any toxic materials, so it can be installed in an office environment. The build time for the machine is faster than the SLA. There is no part clean-up needed for a part made by FDM. Disadvantages include that surface finish of the parts is inferior to those produced using SLA or SLS, due to the resolution of the process which is dictated by the filament thickness. Accuracy is relatively low and is difficult to build parts with complicated details; poor strength in vertical direction and slowness for building a mass part.

2.3.5 Laminated Object Manufacturing (LOM)

In this technique, developed by Helisys of Torrance, CA, layers of adhesive-coated sheet material are bonded together to form a prototype. The original material consists of paper laminated with heat-activated glue and rolled up on spools. As shown in the figure below, a feeder/collector mechanism advances the sheet over the build platform, where a base has been constructed from paper and double-sided foam tape. Next, a heated roller applies pressure to bond the paper to the base. A focused laser cuts the outline of the first layer into the paper and then cross-hatches the excess area (the negative space in the prototype). Cross-hatching breaks up the extra material, making it easier to remove during post-processing. During the build, the excess material provides excellent support for overhangs and thin-walled sections. After the first layer is cut, the platform lowers out of the way and fresh material is advanced. The platform rises to slightly below the previous height, the roller bonds the second layer to the first, and the laser cuts the second layer. This process is repeated as needed to build the part, which will have a wood-like texture. Because the models are made of paper, they must be sealed and finished with paint or varnish to prevent moisture damage, but because the raw material (paper) is cheap, LOM is particularly suitable for large models given that the manufacturing speed is very fast. Disadvantages include that it is hard to make hollow parts due to the difficulty in removing the core and there are serious problems with undercuts and re-entrant features. Other problems are the great amount of scrap so that the machine must be constantly manned and parts need to be hand finished. Moreover, given that the laser cuts through the material, there is a fire hazard which means that the machines need to be fitted with inert gas extinguishers. The drops of molten material, which form during the cutting process, need to be removed also.

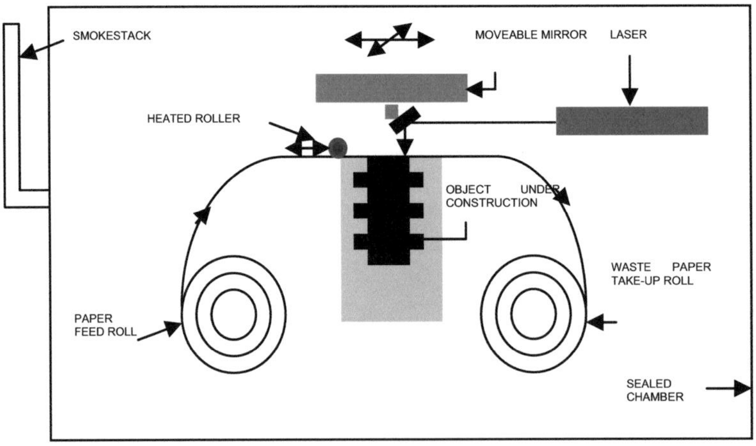

Fig. 11. Schematic of LOM

2.3.6 Electron Beam Melting (EBM)

Electron beam melting (EBM) is a type of rapid prototyping for metal parts. It is often classified as a rapid manufacturing method. The technology manufactures parts by melting metal powder layer per layer with an electron beam in a high vacuum. Unlike some metal sintering techniques, the parts are fully solid, void-free, and extremely strong. EBM is also referred to as Electron Beam Machining. High speed electrons (.5-.8 times the speed of light) are bombarded on the surface of the work material generating enough heat to melt the surface of the part and cause the material to locally vaporize.

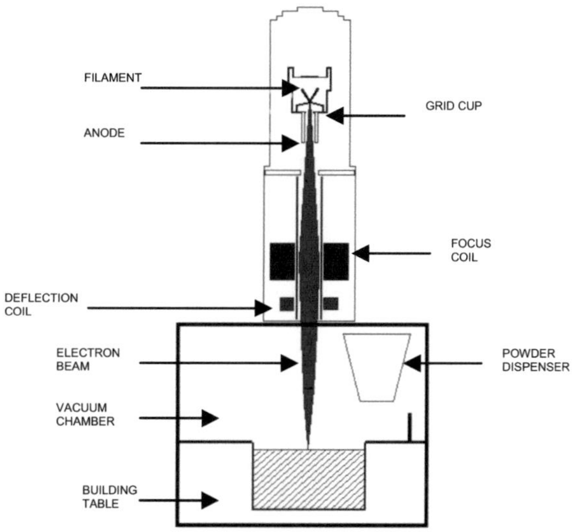

Fig. 12. Schematic of EBM

EBM does require a vacuum, meaning that the workpiece is limited in size to the vacuum used. The surface finish on the part is much better than that of other manufacturing processes. Only shoot-peening process to control residual stresses by compressing surfaces and polishing to reduce roughness may be needed as secondary finishing operations. EBM can be used on metals, non-metals, ceramics, and composites.
Some of its benefits include: ability to achieve a high energy level in a narrow beam, vacuum melt quality can yield high strength properties of the material, vacuum environment eliminates impurities such as oxides and nitrides and permits welding in refractory metals and combinations of dissimilar metals. Some apparent disadvantages of electron beam technology are: requires vacuum which adds another system on the machine which cost money and must be maintained, electron beam technology produces gamma rays while in operation and requires electrically conductive materials.
In the following section some clinical cases, treated with the aid of RE and SFF processes, will be presented and discussed.

3. Application of RE and SFF in clinical cases

Several clinical cases in the field of orthodontics, supported by the use of RE and SFF techniques, are provided in this section. In fact, the quality of service, in terms of improvement in patient satisfaction, is an increasingly important objective in all medical fields, and is especially imperative in orthodontics due to the high numbers of patients treated. All the cases are related to patients clinically treated at the Department of Orthodontics of the University of Ferrara (Italy).

3.1 Application of RE techniques

3.1.1 Evaluation of the post-extractive facial edema

A RE-based approach was also used in the evaluation of the post-extractive facial edema, after the unilateral extraction of completely impacted mandibular third molars on 40 patients. Range camera Comet Vario Zoom (Steinbichler Optotechnik GmbH, Germany) together with the processing software PolyWorks (InnovMetric Software Inc., Canada) were used to carry out computerized analysis of the 3D images obtained in this morpho-volumetric study of post-extractive edematous swelling as shown in Fig. 13. The acquired data and analysis revealed no statistically significant gender-related difference in edemal volume at any post-operative stage analyzed. Both male and female patients, however, showed a significant increase in volume (mean volume: 28,766.96 mm^3) two days after surgery. Furthermore, on the seventh day after surgery, the edematous swelling was reduced to levels similar to those recorded immediately following extraction in both males and females.

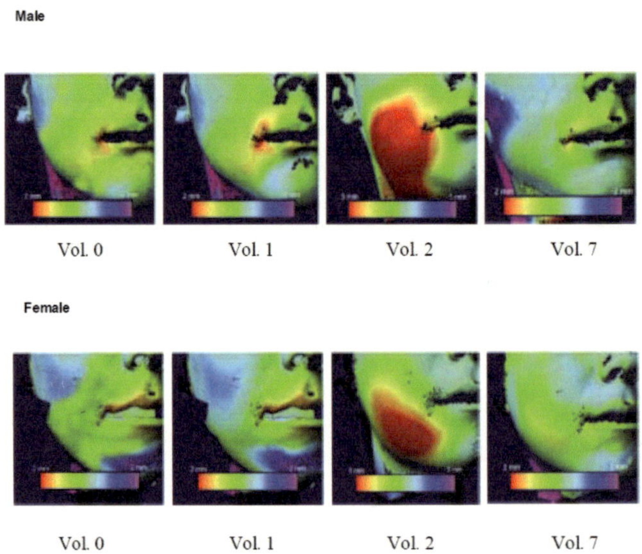

Fig. 13. Intermediate colours indicate the edematous distance and volumes

3.1.2 Evaluation of palatal morphologic and volumetric changes after the use of a rapid palatal expander (RPE)

RE systems and software were employed to evaluate the palatal morphologic and volumetric changes after the use of a RPE appliance in four children patients (aged 7-8 years) in mixed dentition with a posterior crossbite, a skeletal Class II malocclusion and with narrow maxillary arches (Mazzoli et al., 2008). The patients were treated using the Haas RPE in order to solve the maxillary contraction. For each patient three measurements were done: pre-treatment (T_1), after expansion therapy (T_2), and six months after the removal of the expander (T_3) without no contention. Traditionally, treatment stability was evaluated with calipers and compasses, which register just linear measurements and depend on the ability of the operator without providing precise 3D measurements.

In the above cited study a Roland Picza system (Roland DG Mid Europe Srl, Acquaviva Picena, Italy) was used to scan casts with a resolution of up to 0.05 mm and a scanning step up to 0.02 mm. The obtained data were managed using the software Rapidform (INUS Technology Inc., Korea), an advanced 3D scan data processing software, and Rhinoceros (McNeel, Seattle), a modeling software for designers. The base palatal volume was delimited by the gingival margins and by a vertical plane connecting the distal aspect of the last permanent molars. All tests confirmed the hypothesis that the measurements at T2 and T3 were significantly different from those at the start of the treatment supporting the effectiveness of the RME treatment. In Fig. 14 are showed the cross-sectional superposition of the recordings at T1, T2 and T3 reporting the variations in palatal transverse diameters between the above selected couples of teeth in one clinical case.

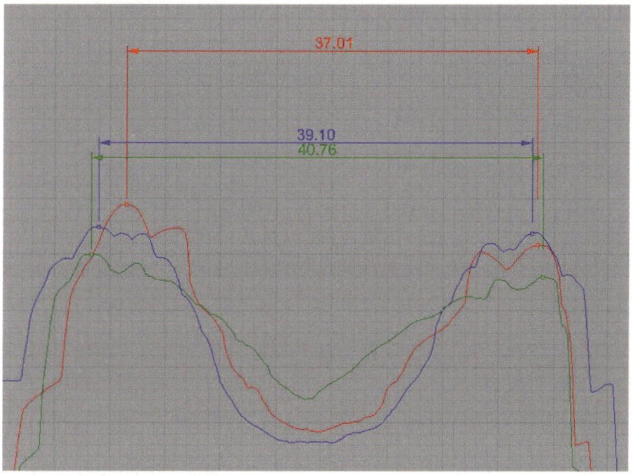

Fig. 14. Cross-sectional superposition of the recordings at T1 (red), T2 (green) and T3 (blue) reporting the variations in palatal transverse diameters between the outer side cusps of the first primary molars (54-64)

3.1.3 Evaluation of 3D Technologies in Dentistry

A study has specifically aimed to evaluate Reverse Engineering (RE) and Rapid Prototyping (RP) in order to define an ideal chain of advanced technological solutions to support the critical processes of orthodontic activity (Gracco et al., 2008). Information technology can provide a meaningful contribution to bettering treatment processes, and we maintain that systems such as CAD, CAM and CAE, although initially conceived for industrial purposes, should be evaluated, studied and customized with a view to use in medicine. Advantages to using such systems to carry out many of the stages in orthodontic processes currently performed by hand, such as the design and manufacture of corrective appliances and the production of virtual models of the dental arches, and also to determine the feasibility of their use in the planning and simulation of corrective and implantological treatment and in the design and manufacture of fixed and mobile prostheses. Two types of test were employed to study the acquisition systems, the first aimed at evaluating the system usability and the time required for scanning, and the second designed to compare the resolution and accuracy of the systems. To the former end a standard procedure of measurement which could be employed with both specific and general purpose systems, all used in conjunction with a suitable automatic positioning device, was established. The resolution and accuracy of the various acquisition systems were compared via the acquisition of a single view of a significant portion of the same plaster model. The CAD system was employed to measure the dimensional and morphological parameters directly using the triangulated point cloud, without further elaboration. The dimensional reference data were calculated from a measurement carried out by a coordinate measurement machine with contact sensors. This comparative study analyzed rapid prototyping systems and defined suitable methodologies of evaluating the fundamental components of an RE/RP manufacturing for application in the orthodontic field. The preliminary results demonstrate that replication of a plaster model is plagued by problems linked to the size of detail to be reproduced, which is similar to or finer than the fabrication layer of the various additive technologies studied, and therefore results in poor quality reproduction of tooth morphology.

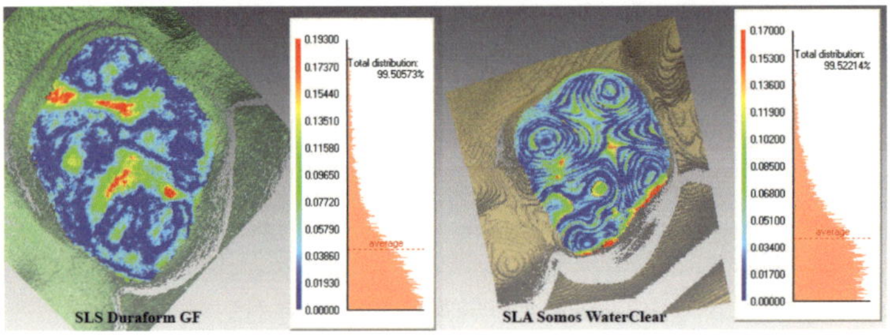

Fig. 15. Colour map of morphological analysis on tooth top: errors are due to surfaces grooves and fabrication layers

3.2 Application of 3D anatomical modelling and SFF techniques

3.2.1 Implant-prosthetic rehabilitation

46-year- old Caucasian female (S.F.) showing a partial edentulism referred to the left side of the lower half-arch and a lack of the upper maxillary dental elements, with the exception of the 1.7 and 1.8, due to a pre-existing trauma. Both the edentulous areas showed a high degree of bone resorption with a considerable height and thickness reduction of the alveolar ridge. Such a decrease of available bone tissue made the implant-prosthetic planning phase rather problematic and needed to be widened by CT surveys. In particular, the closeness of the inferior alveolar nerve was critical in the selection of the more suitable dental implants in terms of typology and size. For the above reason 3D renderings, using the software MIMICS, of the two maxillary arches was implemented highlighting the left portion of the inferior alveolar nerve as shown in Fig. 16.

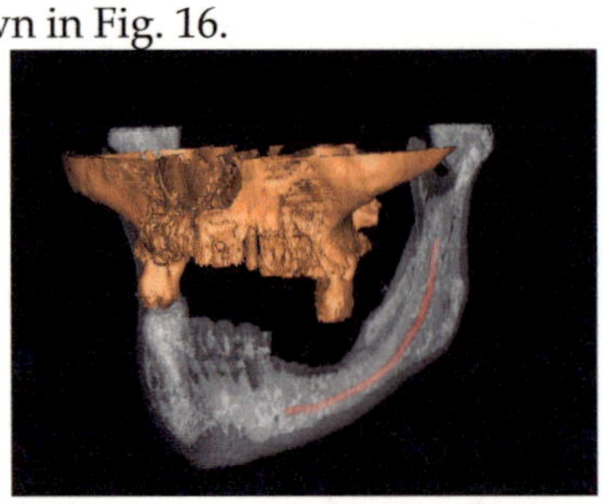

Fig. 16. 3D rendering of the maxillary arch. Highlighted in red the left portion of the inferior alveolar nerve

3.2.2 Impacted dental elements

23-year-old Caucasian female (P.S.) showing a total bone impaction of the elements 1.3 and 2.3. Conventional diagnostic tools used in dentistry (inspection and percussion) and radiographic tools (orthopanoramic and TeleRx) were not useful in order to precisely recognize the position of the impacted elements. In particular, it was not possible to identify the anteroposterior spatial relation of the impacted teeth. The 3D rendering and physical model of the maxillary arch irrefutably highlighted the palatal impaction of both the elements.

16-year-old Caucasian female (B.E.) showing a limited bone impaction of the element 2.2 and total impaction of the 2.3. In order to perform the surgical planning for the extraction of the element 2.3, later on an initial phase of alignment and levelling out of the upper maxillary arch, the critical aspect regarded the high level of contiguity between the impacted elements. The 3D rendering and SLA physical model of the maxillary arch (showed in Fig. 17) removed any doubt regarding the hypothetical root resorption relatively to the element 2.2 and simplified the treatment planning for the extrusion of the ectopic element 2.3.

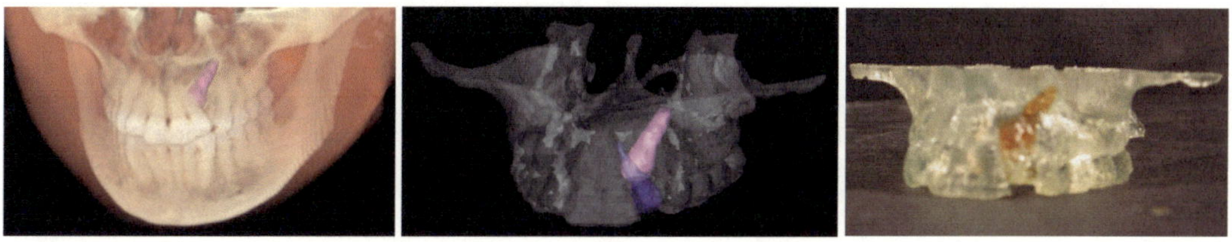

(a) *(b)* *(c)*

Fig. 17. (a) volumetric rendering, (b) detail and (c) SLA model of the maxillary arch confirmed the hypothetical root resorption relatively to the element 2.2 and simplified the treatment planning for the extrusion of the ectopic element 2.3

9-year-old Caucasian female (V.C.) showing a supernumerary tooth totally impacted (mesiodens) between the elements 1.1 e 2.1. The 3D rendering and physical model of the maxillary arch was manufactured in order to facilitate the oral surgery. In fact, the conventional radiographic tools were not helpful in the definition of the vestibular or palatine position of the mesiodens.

16-year-old Caucasian male (M.A.) showing a partial impaction of the 1.3, agenesis of the 1.5 and total impaction of the 1.7. Previous orthodontic treatments enabled the incomplete extrusion of the element 1.3 followed by a freezing of the same because of an infraocclusion of the tooth. The 3D rendering and the SLA model highlighted the impaction of the 1.3 on the vestibular cortical portion of the maxillary arch.

3.2.3 Joint-related diseases

16-year-old Caucasian female (S.M.) showing a dental class 1 with contracted arches, lower-front dental overcrowding and deep bite. From the objective examination of the stomathognatic apparatus the presence of left- hand joint-related sounds were noticed. The patient reported about the lack of pain and functional limitations. The 3D model of the mandible, manufactured in polyamide by SLS, showed an abnormal shape of the left-condyle: hypoplasic and flat.

3.2.4 Evaluation of the position of foreign bodies

18-year-old Caucasian female (P.D.) showing a radiopaque foreign body in the median area between the apices of the elements 1.2 e 2.1. Later on a trauma the patient refers about the lost out the 1.1 and immediately implanted. A second trauma caused the definitive avulsion of the element. Firstly, the patient was orthodontically treated in order to gain space and then was examined by a CT survey. The 3D rendering and SLA model of the upper maxilla allowed an accurate identification of the position and size of the foreign body as shown in Fig. 16. It was recognized as a rectangular block (4.67 × 8.03 × 3.77 mm), positioned in the vestibule, that determined an inflammatory resorption of the cortical portion of the vestibule itself. Later on the acquisition of the above described information, the avulsion was planned and executed and the foreign body was removed. It was determined to be gutta-percha. Contextually, autologous bone grafting was performed in order to fill the gap. An implant-prosthetic rehabilitation will be performed on the patient.

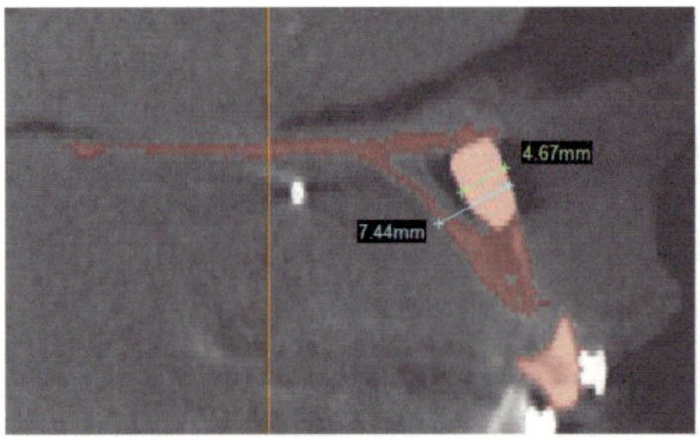

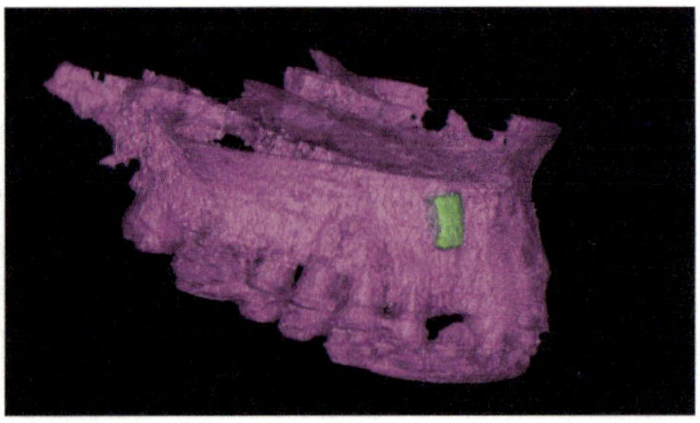

(a) *(b)*

Fig. 18. 2D evaluation (a) and 3D rendering (b) of an upper maxilla showing the presence of a radiopaque foreign body

3.2.5 Upper airways span monitoring

30 pediatric patients were selected and are currently under treatment by RPE (Rapid Palatal Expander), an orthopaedic appliance that widens the upper jaw by separating the midpalatal suture. The patients were monitored by cone-beam CT (CBCT) before the positioning of the RPE. The only one of them that has already completed the therapeutic treatment was subjected to another CBCT scan after the removal of the RPE. Contextually, the volume of the upper airways was modelled before and after the treatment and the volume augmentation was evaluated as shown in Fig. 19. In this case the estimated augmentation of the volume of the upper airways is equal to the 26.44%.

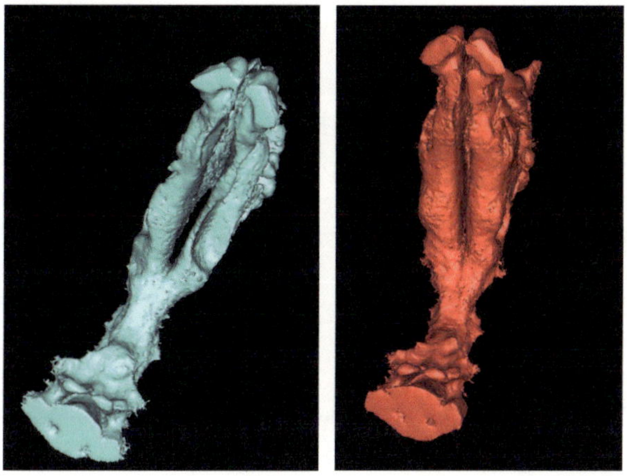

Fig. 19. 3D rendering of the upper airways relative to a RPE treated patient. Before (left) and after (right) the treatment is noticeable the augmentation of the volume of the upper airways.

4. Conclusions

Reverse Engineering and Solid Free-form Fabrication techniques have been substantially applied in medicine, however, their application in dentistry, and particularly in orthodontics, is not much widespread. This paper has discussed RE and SFF techniques and their usability in orthodontics. After presentation of RE and SFF technologies, the current and potential use in dental application are discussed showing some treated clinical cases. It is clear that the use of RE techniques and SFF models in dentistry will be expanded in the future with the ongoing research based on the development of new materials and technologies. A number of application examples are discussed, which demonstrate that RE and SFF techniques are playing a more and more important role in dental application.

5. References

Adams, J.W. Correction of error in cephalometric roentgenograms. *Angle Orthodontist*, 10, (1940) 3-13, 0003-3219

Alcaniz, M., Montserrat, C., Grau, V., Chinesta, F., Ramon, A. & Albalat S. An advanced system for the simulation and planning of orthodontic treatment. *Medical Image Analysis*, 2, 1 (1998) 61-77, 1361-8415

Arridge, S., Moss, J. P., Linney, A. D. & James, D. R. Three dimensional digitisation of the face and skull. *Journal of Maxillofacial Surgery*, 3, 13 (1985) 136-143, 0301-0503

Aung, S. C., Ngim, R. C. K. & Lee, S. T. Evaluation of the laser scanner as a surface measuring tool and its accuracy compared with direct facial anthropometric measurements. *British Journal of Plastic Surgery*, 48, (1995) 551-558, 0007-1226

Badea, C., Kolitsi, Z. & Pallikarakis, N. A 3-D imaging system for dental imaging based on digital tomosysnthesis and cone beam CT. *Proceedings of the IX Mediterranean Conf on Medical and Biological Engineering and Computing*, pp. 739-741, 953-184-024-5, Pula

(Croatia), June 2001, Faculty of Electrical Engineering and Computing (FER), Zagreb

Baumrind, S. & Frantz, T.C. The reliability of head film measurements. 1. Landmark identification. *American Journal of Orthodontics*, 60, (1971) 111-27, 0002-9416

Beers, A.C., Choi, W. & Pavloskaia E. Computer-assisted treatment planning and analysis. *Orthodontics & Craniofacial Research*, 6, S1, (2003) 117-125, 1601-6335

Berry, E., Brown, J.M., Connell, M., Craven, C.M., Efford, N.D., Radjenovic, A. & Smith, M.A. Preliminary experience with medical application of rapid prototyping by selective laser sintering. Medical Engineering & Physics,19, (1997) 90-96, 1350-4533

Bjork, A. & Solow, B. Measurements on radiographs. *Journal of Dental Research*, 41, (1962) 672-683, 1544-0591

Cheah, C.M., Chua, C.K., Tan, K.H. & Teo, C.K. Integration of laser surface digitizing with CAD/CAM techniques for developing facial prostheses, part 1: design and fabrication of prosthesis replicas. *International Journal of Prosthodontics*, 16, (2003) 435-441, 0893-2174

Ciocca, L. & Scotti, R. CAD-CAM generated ear cast by means of a laser scanner and rapid prototyping machine *Journal of Prosthetic Dentistry*, 92, (2004) 591-595, 0022-3913

Cousley, R.R., Grant, E. & Kindelan J.D. The validity of computerized orthognathic predictions. *Journal of Orthodontics*, 30, 2 (June 2003) 149-154, 1465-3125

Erben, C., Vitt, K.D. & Wulf, J. The Phidias validation study of stereolithographic models. *Phidias Newsletter*, 8, (March 2002) 15-16

Farkas, L. G. (1994). *Anthropometry of the head and face*, Raven Press, 0-444-00557-9, New York

Gracco, A., Buranello, M., Siciliani, G. & Guarneri M.P. Traditional vs. virtual gipsoteque in dentistry. *Mondo Ortodontico*, 5, (2005) 29-34, 0391-2000

Gracco, A., Mazzoli, A., Raffaeli, R. & Germani, M. Evaluation Of 3D Technologies In Dentistry. *Progress in Orthodontics*, 9(1), (2008), 26-37

Halazonetis, D.J. Acquisition of 3-dimensional shapes from images. *American Journal of Orthodontics and Dentofacial Orthopedics*, 119 (2001) 556-560, 0889-5406

Heiken, J.P., Brink, J.A. & Vannier, M.W. Spiral (helical) CT. *Radiology*, 189, 3, (December 1993) 647-656, 0033-8419

Hixon, E.H. The norm concept and cephalometrics. *American Journal of Orthodontics*, 42, (1956) 898-919, 0002-9416.

Lee, S.J., Jang, K.A., Spangberg, L.S.W., Kim, E., Jung, Y., Lee, C.Y. & Kum, K.Y. Three-dimensional visualization of a mandibular first molar with three distal roots using computer-aided rapid prototyping. *Oral Surgery, Oral Medicine, Oral Pathology, Oral Radiology & Endodontics*, 101, (2006) 668-674, 1079-2104

Leong, K.F., Cheah, C.M. & Chua, C.K. Solid freeform fabrication of three-dimensional scaffolds for engineering replacement tissues and organs. *Biomaterials*, 24, (2003) 2363-2378, 0142-9612

Liu, Q., Leu, M.C. & Schmitt, C. Rapid prototyping in dentistry. Technology and applications. *The International Journal of Advanced Manufacturing Technology*, 29, 3-4, (2006) 317-335, 0268-3768

Luthardt, R., Weber, A., Rudolph, H., Shhone, C., Quass, S. & Walter M. Design and production of dental prosthetic restorations: Basic research on dental CAD/CAM technology. *International Journal of Computerized Dentistry*, 5, (2002) 165–176, 1463-4201

Mah, J.K., Danforth, R.A., Bumann, A. & Hatcher D. Radiation absorbed in maxillofacial imaging with a new dental computed tomography device. *Oral Surgery, Oral Medicine, Oral Pathology, Oral Radiology and Endodontics*, 96, 4 (October 2003) 508-513, 1079-2104

Mazzoli, A., Germani, M. & Moriconi, G. Application of optical digitizing techniques to evaluate the shape accuracy of anatomical models derived from computed tomography data. *Journal of Oral and Maxillofacial Surgery*, 65, 7, (2007) 1410-1418, 0278-2391

Mazzoli, A., Germani, M. & Raffaeli, R. Direct fabrication through Electron Beam Melting technology of custom cranial implants designed in a phantom-based haptic environment. *Materials & Design*, in press, doi: 10.1016/j.matdes.2008.11.013, 0261-3069

Mazzoli, A., Germani, M. & Raffaeli, R. Reverse Engineering Techniques to Evaluate Palatal Morphologic and Volumetric Changes After the Use of a Rapid Expander. *Proceedings of the XVII IASTED International Conference on Applied Simulation and Modelling*, pp. 106-111, 978-0-88986-731-4, Corfù (Greece), June 2008.

McCallum, B. C., Fright, W. R., Nixon, M. A. & Price, N. B. A feasibility study of hand-held laser surface scanning. *Proceedings of Image and Vision Computing NZ (IVCNZ'96)*, pp. 103-108, Auckland (New Zealand), October 1998, Lower Hutt, Wellington

McCance, A. M., Moss, J. P., Fright, W. R., Linney, A. D., James, D. R., Coughlan, K. & Mars, M. Three dimensional analysis techniques — part 4. Three dimensional analysis of bone and soft tissue to bone ratio of movements in 24 cleft palate patients following Le Fort I osteotomy: a preliminary report. *Cleft Palate-Craniofacial Journal*, 34, (1997) 58-62, 1055-6656

Melkos, A.B. Advances in digital technology and orthodontics: a reference to the Invisalign method. *Medical Science Monitor*, 11, 5, (2005) 39-42, 1234-1010

Merriam-Webster Dictionary (2009). On line: http://www.merriam-webster.com/home.htm.

Minns, R.J., Bibb, R., Banks, R. The use of a reconstructed three-dimensional solid model from CT to aid surgical management of a total knee arthroplasty. A case study. *Medical Engineering & Physics*, 25, (2003) 523-6, 1350-4533

Mitgaard, J., Bjork, A. & Linder-Aronson, S. Reproducibility of cephalometric landmarks and errors of measurement of cephalometric cranial distances. *Angle Orthodontist*, 44, (1974) 56-61, 0003-3219

Moss, J. P., Linney, A. D., Grindrod, S. R., Arridge, S. R. & Clifton J. S. Three-dimensional visualization of the face and skull using computerized tomography and laser scanning techniques. *European Journal of Orthodontics*, 9, (1987) 247-253, 0141-5387

Moss, J. P. & James, D. R. An investigation of a group of 35 consecutive patients with a first arch syndrome. *British Journal of Oral and Maxillofacial Surgery*, 22, (1984) 157-169, 0266-4356

Moyers, R.E., Bookstein, F.L. & Hunter W.S. Analysis of the craniofacial skeleton: Cephalometrics, In: *Handbook of orthodontics*, 247-309, The Yearbook Publishers, 0-8151-6003-8, 1988, Chicago

Mozzo, P., Procacci, C., Sacconi, A., Martini, P.T. & Andreis, I.A. A new volumetric CT machine for dental imaging based on the cone beam technique: prelminary results. *European Radiology*, 8, (1998) 1558-1564, 0938-7994

Muller, A., Krishnan, K.G., Uhl, E. & Mast, G. The application of rapid prototyping techniques in cranial reconstruction and preoperative planning in neurosurgery. *Journal of Craniofacial Surgery*, 14, 6, (2003) 899-914, 1049-2275.

Olt, S. & Jakob P.M. Contrast-enhanced dental MRI for visualization of the teeth and jaw. *Magnetic Resonance in Medicine*, 52, 1 (July 2004) 174-176, 0740-3194

Otto, T. & Nisco, S.D. Computer-aided direct ceramic restorations: A 10-year prospective clinical study of Cerec CAD/CAM inlays and onlays. *International Journal of Prosthodontics*, 15, (2002) 122–28, 0893-2174

Petzold, R., Zeilhofer, H.F. & Kalender, W.A. Rapid prototyping technology in medicine—Basics and applications. *Computerized Medical Imaging and Graphics*, 23, (1999) 277-284, 0895-6111

Raffaeli, R., Germani, M., Mandorli, F. Innovative technologies to support positioning of corrective appliances in orthodontic treatments, *Proceedings of the XIV IASTED International Conference on Applied Simulation and Modelling*, pp. 48-53, 0-88986-467-5, Benalmàdena (Spain), June 2005, Acta Press, Calgary

Reitemeier, B., Notni, G., Heinze, M., Schöne, C., Schmidt, A. & Fichtner, D. Optical modeling of extraoral defects. *Journal of Prosthetic Dentistry*, 91, 1, (2004) 80-84, 0022-3913

Runte, C., Dirksen, D. & Delere, H. Optical data acquisition for computer-assisted design of facial prostheses. *International Journal of Prosthodontics*, 15, (2002) 129-132, 0893-2174

Swennen, G.R. & Schutyser, F. Three-dimensional cephalometry: spiral multi-slice vs cone-beam computed tomography. *American Journal of Orthodontics and Dentofacial Orthopedics*, 130(3), (2006) 410-416, 0889-5406

Sykes, L.M., Parrott, A.M., Owen, C.P., Snaddon, D.R. Applications of rapid prototyping technology in maxillofacial prosthetics. *International Journal of Prosthodontics*, 17, 4 (July-August 2004) 454-459, 0893-2174

Udupa, J.K. & Herman, G.T. (1991). *3D imaging in medicine*, CRC Press, 0-8493-3179-X, Boca Raton

Webber, R.L., Horton, R.A., Tyndall, D.A. & Ludlow, J.B. Tuned. Aperture Computed Tomography (TACT2). Theory and application for three-dimensional dento-alveolar imaging. *Dentomaxillofacial Radiology*, 26 (1997) 53–62, 0250-832X

Williams, R.J., Bibb, R., Tahseen, R. A technique for fabricating patterns for removable partial denture frameworks using digitized casts and electronic surveys. *Journal of Prosthetic Dentistry*, 91, 1 (2004) 85-88, 0022-3913

Winder, J. & Bibb, R. Medical rapid prototyping technologies: state of the art and current limitations for application in oral and maxillofacial surgery. *Journal of Oral and Maxillofacial Surgery*, 63, (2005) 1006-1015, 0278-2391

Wohlers, T. (2004). Wohlers report 2004. *Rapid Prototyping, tooling and manufacturing. State of the industry.* Annual Worldwide progress report, Wohlers Associates Inc., 0-9754429-0-2, Fort Collins, Colorado

Yamany, S., Farag, A.A., Tasman, D. & Farman, A.G. A 3-D reconstruction system for the human jaw using a sequence of optical images. *IEEE Transactions on Medical Imaging*, 19, 5 (2000) 538-547, 0278-0062

2

Computational Fluid Dynamics simulations: an approach to evaluate cardiovascular dysfunction

Eduarda Silva, Senhorinha Teixeira and Pedro Lobarinhas
University of Minho
Portugal

1. Introduction

The cardiovascular system is an internal flow loop with multiple branches in which blood circulates to transport nutrient and waste throughout the body. The heart is responsible to pump blood through the cardiovascular system consisting of a complex network of three types of vessels: arteries (distribution system), capillaries (diffusion and filtration system) and veins (collection system). To accomplish their function of distribute blood through the body, the vessels are not rigid but elastic tubes that constrict or dilate (Ku, 1997; Taylor & Draney, 2004).

Blood flow in the cardiovascular system is a transient phenomenon as a result of the cyclic nature of the heart. This means that, at a given point, the velocity and pressure conditions do change with time. In fact, in the circulatory system the velocity assumes a pulsatile behavior, varying between zero, when the aortic valve is closed, and high velocities during the systole (Taylor & Draney, 2004).

Although blood flow is normally laminar, the pulsatile nature of the flow makes possible the transition to turbulence, when the artery diameter and velocities are large, like the aorta. The branches, curves and others asymmetries that are present in the vascular system also create a tri-dimensional flow characterized by asymmetries in the velocity patterns, complicated secondary motions and even flow separation from and reattachment to the wall, causing recirculation zones (Ku, 1997; Boron & Boulpaep, 2003). These hemodynamic characteristics of blood flow have long been thought to play an important role in the pathogenesis of atherosclerosis. Diseases of the cardiovascular system are manifold and afflict millions of patients worldwide including cases of: coronary artery disease, ischemic gangrene, abdominal aortic aneurysms and stroke. Many of these disfunctions are the end result of atherosclerosis, characterized by plaque accumulation within the walls of the arteries (Taylor & Humphrey, 2009). When the plaque accumulation is significant and blocks blood flow through the artery, the local restriction is known as an arterial stenosis. Stenosis induces perturbations in the blood flow and, consequently, turbulence can occur in regions where the flow is usually laminar.

Atherosclerosis can affect all arteries of the body, but there are clear evidences that there is a predisposition to be localized at branches and bends within the cardiovascular system. This

observation reinforced and led to the now widely accepted hypothesis that there is an intimate relation between the complex velocity patterns and shear stresses and the location of atherosclerosis (Taylor & Humphrey, 2009).
The application of computational techniques has become an important tool in the investigation of blood flow in arteries, distinct from experimental techniques due to the ability to simulate velocity and pressure fields in virtual models of the cardiovascular system, predict the outcomes of interventions, and improve treatment strategies (Taylor & Draney, 2004; Chen & Lu, 2004). Furthermore, when compared to experimental investigations, computational methods are often less time-consuming and costly. Computational fluid dynamic (CFD) codes and commercial packages are nowadays very robust and they can be used in a variety of field applications from a simple two-dimensional flow case to complex three-dimensional unsteady flows. Also, with the increase of hardware capability, the use of CFD is becoming even more attractive.
CFD simulations of blood flow became the cutting edge tool to investigate cardiovascular dysfunctions. While advanced imaging and diagnosis equipments available today enable the physician to view the flow through arteries, CFD studies can go much further by quantifying phenomena difficult to describe using experimental and *in vivo* techniques including wall shear stress (WSS), mass transport, and stagnation regions (Taylor & Draney, 2004; Nanduri et al., 2009). Current application of CFD simulations of blood flow is largely focused on two major research areas: blood flow in both healthy and atherosclerotic arteries. The objective of the first approach is to compute with high accuracy the various hemodynamic patterns to better understand the vascular physiology and the mechanisms that contribute to the pathogenesis of atherosclerosis (Carneiro et al., 2008b). Alternatively, the CFD techniques can be used to understand the growth of the plaque, to predict rupture risk of the plaque and test novel or patient-specific intravascular devices prior to *in vivo* implementation (Kagadis et al., 2008).
In order to compute accurately blood flow, the CFD model needs to be developed bearing in mind the special requirements of this particular application. As mentioned before, blood flow can be firstly characterised for its unsteadiness. For this reason, the computational model needs to be able to compute complex gradient of velocities that can be extremely variable along the cardiac cycle. Also, blood itself should be modelled as a two-phase non-Newtonian fluid, because it is, in fact, a suspension of a large variety of cells in plasma. Another particularity of human vascular system is the flexibility and motion of the arteries wall. Gathering all these complex characteristics in a unique CFD model is a demanding aim and, since 1970s, many groups have developed and utilized these techniques without completely achieving a full realistic model. Still, enormous progress has been done mainly due to an increase in computational capabilities and to the development of more complex and adequate numerical methods. Nowadays, each research group are oriented to understand the impact of one or two of the above characteristics but not all (Nanduri et al., 2009). In this book chapter, special insight is given to the importance of generating more accurate and realistic geometries and the demand for robust grid generation techniques. The grid generation is a major problem and often takes more person-hours to construct the grid than it does to construct and analyze the physical solution.
A tri-dimensional computational model of the abdominal aorta and renal branches is presented. The model was developed using Fluent 6.3.26 as the CFD tool and results will show the ability to predict the unsteady flow patterns throughout the cardiac cycle. The

abdominal aorta and renal branches were selected in this study for being a region where atherosclerotic disease is likely to occur (Wood, 1999). In order to solve the complex changes in the velocity gradients, induced by the pulsatile cardiac waveform, the grid has to be sufficiently dense to make possible the proper calculation of the gradients. On the other hand, the grid cannot be so dense that the solution is impractical to obtain. Therefore, different grids were developed to compare element types and grid generation strategies. For all of them, the quality of the mesh and the accuracy of the solution were studied.

One of the advantages of using computer models is the flexibility and the reduced costs in testing alternative configurations and simulation parameters. For these reasons, after developing the entire model, parallel studies were developed to infer on the simplifications validity and to study alternative parameters regarding the geometric domain.

Finally, a general overview of additional pertinent issues is given to elucidate on the different possible strategies to optimize the model. The CFD models should be held as a permanent work in progress. There are always additional phenomena that can be included and, by increasing the grade of complexity, a better understanding on the biomechanics of blood flow will be achieved.

2. Blood flow in arteries: review of computational models

The relationship between blood flow in arteries and, the sites where atherosclerosis develops, has motivated much of the research on blood flow in the past four decades (Berger & Jou, 2000). There are many branches from the aorta to the major arteries, each of them divided again in smaller arteries and so on until the capillary bed, that have been, for a long time, pointed out as initial predilection sites to manifest atherosclerosis (O'Brien & Ehrlich, 1977). A brief description of the main studies and the most relevant achievements will be presented to give an overview on the tremendous advances that have been made in this field. Firstly, special attention will be given to studies in healthy arteries, followed by CFD models to evaluate stenosed arteries.

The first attempt to model flow in normal blood vessels remotes the decade of 1950s. Womersley (1955) analyzed the equations of viscous motion for laminar flow of a Newtonian and incompressible fluid in as infinitely long and straight circular pipe. The main issue was to calculate the velocity and flow rate in arteries according to the pressure gradients measured by McDonald (1955). The physiologic pressure obtained by McDonald was represented as a Fourier series to compute the velocity profiles. The main simplifications of this study were: the assumption of a rigid circular tube to represent large arteries and the assumption of a periodic pressure gradient only function of time, whereas it is generated by a pulse wave of finite velocity. To improve these limitations, in 1957, the same author included the wall motion in his model, expressed by equations for a thin, uniform and linearly elastic wall. The Womersley analysis was useful to gain a general understanding of the relevant forces involved in arteries flow (Ku, 1997). In 1977, O'Brien and Ehrlich presented an idealized model of the trifurcation flow in renal arteries. Renal arteries are bilateral side branches that form a trifurcation branch with the abdominal aorta. The geometry was assumed as two-dimensional and straight-sided, instead of curved and three-dimensional. Despite of being a very simplified model, it showed, at that early stage, the complexity of the unsteady flow patterns at a trifurcation and the relation to the development of atherosclerosis. The comparison of steady and unsteady results demonstrated that the WSS and recirculation were highly related and time-dependent through the cardiac cycle. The finite-difference calculations presented in this study may not be quantitatively highly accurate but they seem to present a very valid qualitative tendency of flow patterns. The limited computational resources at this stage forced this study to be two-dimensional, which may exclude certain features of the flow, such as secondary motions and circumferential variations of shear stress, features that may be critical to atherogenesis and plaque growth.

Avolio (1980) used the linear form of the Navier-Stokes equations to model wave propagation in the human arterial system. A multi-branched model of the human arterial system with 128 segments was constructed based on anatomical branching structure. The arterial segments were represented by uniform elastic tubes and characterized by electrical transmission-line properties. The work by Avolio (1980) represented significant improvements compared with previous electrical analogue models but it has been demonstrated that the complete blood flow patterns, such as secondary motion, cannot be obtained with a simpler 1D method.

Until fairly recently, the computational models used to predict blood flow were restricted to one or two dimensions. The transition to three-dimensional models, as a result of increasing computational hardware capability, had an enormous impact on the understanding of vascular hemodynamics since the problem could be described more properly than using 1D and 2D methods. Perktold & Rappitsch (1995) describe regions where separation and recirculation are expected to occur in a carotid artery bifurcation. The simulations used the time-dependent, three-dimensional, incompressible Navier-Stokes equations for non-Newtonian fluids. The complex rheological behaviour of blood was approximated using a shear model, where the apparent viscosity was expressed as a function of the shear rate. In this investigation, the effect of the distensible artery wall was also studied and it was described as a coupled fluid-structure interaction because the fluid motion and the wall motion are coupled. The velocity profiles, WSS distribution and the zones of reversed flow were obtained throughout the cardiac cycle. These results were compared with previous studies from the same authors, in which an independent ring model was used, and they shown that the coupled fluid-structure was more realistic and with influence on the flow dynamics. However, a relation between the results and atherogenesis was not established.

Later, Rappitsch & Perktold (1996) proposed a numerical analysis for an axisymmetric domain in order to study the influence of the flow patterns, such as WSS and reversed flow, on the mass transport.

Steinman et al. (1996) showed good agreement between measurements of blood velocity profiles obtained by MRI (Magnetic Resonance Imaging) and numerical simulations. So far, no direct comparisons between MRI measurements and numerical simulations have been made previously and this study was important to remark the validity of numerical modelling in providing an accurate solution that can easily match MRI *in vivo* results.

The application of the finite element method to qualitatively and quantitatively assess the blood flow field in abdominal aorta was described in the investigation by Taylor et al. (1998a, 1998b). The velocity profiles were obtained under resting and exercise conditions. It was noted that under resting conditions, a recirculation zone was formed along the posterior wall of the aorta, immediately distal to the renal vessels. Low values of time-averaged WSS were present in this location and these low shear areas are hypothesized to be more susceptible to cholesterol accumulation and atherogenesis. Under moderate exercise conditions, all regions of low WSS and high oscillatory shear index were eliminated. The investigations proved that exercise is one important mechanism increasing blood flow and WSS and it can represent a protection from atherosclerosis (Taylor et al., 2002). Following a different approach, Shipkowitz et al. (1998, 2000) and Lee & Chen (2002, 2003) developed numerical procedures based on finite volume method to simulate the flow in the abdominal aorta and its peripheral branches. Shipkowitz et al. (1998) compared the influence of assuming an axial uniform or a fully developed axial velocity profile in the inlet boundary condition and reported similar results for both. Lee & Chen (2002, 2003) demonstrated that a steady inflow may fairly describe the time-averaged blood flow behaviour when compared with a corresponding pulsatile case. Carneiro et al. (2008a) evaluated whether branches located upstream in the abdominal aorta lead to more complex flow patterns downstream.

Although numerous studies of blood flow have been conducted, only in the last decade they started to be based on realistic anatomies, acquired from computed tomography (CT) or MRI. It is well established that CFD simulations of blood flows require accurate reconstruction of geometry via imaging techniques. Cebral et al. (2002) developed a method for detail assessment of vessel anatomy and flow rate from MRI angiographic data. More recently, Kagadis et al. (2008) and Nanduri et al. (2009) presented cardiovascular models reconstructed from CT scan and they use them to conduct CFD simulations. These models can have a significant impact in medical interventions for being able to characterize non-invasively blood flow in patient-specific models.

For healthy vessels, blood flow is typically laminar but the presence of vascular diseases can generate turbulence during part of the cardiac cycle. He & Jackson (2000), in their studies on fundamental aspects of turbulence dynamics, observed that turbulence intensity is attenuated in accelerating phases and increased in decelerating phases of the cardiac cycle, mainly associated with the radial propagation of turbulence.

Turbulent flow in stenosed pipes has also been numerically studied to analyze which turbulence model could be more suitable in predicting flow profiles in stenosis region. One example of this investigation was carried out by Varghese & Frankel (2003). They simulated pulsatile turbulent flow in a rigid wall stenosed tube. The goal of their study was to predict, through direct numerical simulations, the flow features downstream of a stenosis under both steady and pulsatile conditions. The conclusions of this study indicated that the acceleration of the fluid through the stenosis resulted in WSS magnitudes that exceeded upstream levels, but WSS levels accompanied the flow separation zones that formed immediately downstream of the stenosis.

Li et al. (2007) developed a simulation model including fluid-structure interaction (FSI) and a turbulence model with realistic boundary conditions in a vessel with different degrees of stenoses. To reach this objective, the investigators performed a coupled simulation process through two commercial packages, Fluent and Abaqus, for the flow modeling and wall deforming calculation, respectively. This work shown that severe degree of stenosis causes a higher pressure drop across the vessel constriction, resulting in both higher blood velocities and peak WSS. Another relevant observation of this study pointed out the intimate correlation that exists between the increase of stenosis degree and the characteristics of the wall vessel displacement. The incorporation of wall vessel displacement mechanisms in the stenosis progression, and consequent atherosclerotic plaque rupture, brought new trends in numerical analysis in stenosed vessels.

3. Implementation of a Computational Model

The development of a computational model for a cardiovascular application involves different stages. First of all, it is essential to define the anatomic region of interest and create the computer model of the region. The computer model should be representative of the anatomic region and of the complex hemodynamic. Associated with a model there is always a set of assumptions and simplifications.
The second step is the generation of a suitable grid for the geometric domain. In third place should be the acquisition of a computational solution by solving the governing equations and the extraction of relevant hemodynamic information.

3.1 Mathematical equations

The mathematical description of pulsatile blood flow is possible by applying mass and momentum conservation. The mass of fluid is conserved, which means that the rate of increase of mass inside the element is equated to the net rate of flow of mass into the element across its faces. This relation is given by the mass conservation or continuity equation:

$$\frac{\partial \rho}{\partial t} + \rho \frac{\partial u_i}{\partial x_i} = 0 \tag{1}$$

where ρ stands for density, *t* for time, x_i *(i = 1, 2, 3)* or (x, y, z) are the three-dimensional Cartesian coordinates and u_i or (u_x, u_i, u_z) are the Cartesian components of the velocity vector *u*.
The law of conservation of momentum (Newton's second law of motion), which states that the rate of change of momentum of a fluid particle equals the sum of the forces on a fluid particle can be written as:

$$\rho \frac{\partial u_i}{\partial t} + \rho u_j \frac{\partial u_i}{\partial x_j} = -\frac{\partial \rho}{\partial x_i} + \rho \frac{\partial}{\partial x_j} \mu \left(\frac{\partial u_i}{\partial x_j} + \frac{\partial u_j}{\partial x_i} - \frac{2}{3} \delta_{ij} \frac{\partial u_l}{\partial x_l} \right) \tag{2}$$

Where μ stands for viscosity (White, 2003).

3.2 Numerical Solution

Fluent is a general purpose computer program for modelling fluid flow and it has been used in the present implementation. It solves the conservation equations for mass and momentum using a control volume based on finite difference method. The governing equations are discretized on a curvilinear grid and Fluent uses a nonstaggered grid storage scheme to store the discrete values of dependent variables (velocities, pressure and scalars).
The first step of this method is to divide the domain into discrete control volumes. The boundaries (or faces) of control volume are positioned mid-way between adjacent nodes. Therefore, each node is surrounded by a control volume or cell. The physical boundaries should coincide with control volume boundaries (Versteeg & Malalasekera, 1995).

A portion of a grid 2D used to subdivide the domain is shown in Figure 1, where it is possible to observe the common notation used to identify each node, its neighbours and its surfaces.

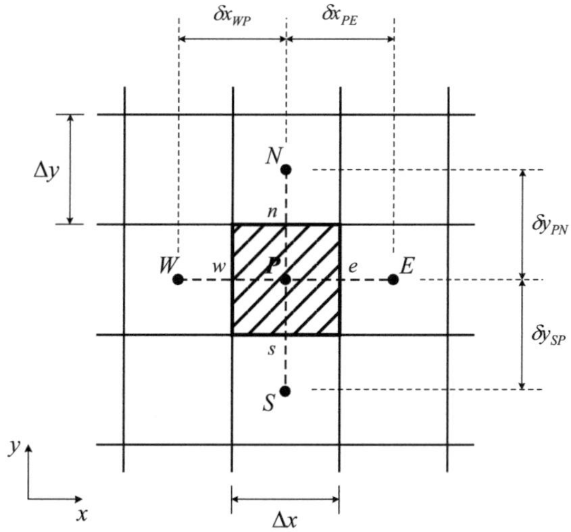

Fig. 1. A typical control volume (CV) and nomenclature used for the discretisation of equations in a 2D domain.

The integral form of the generic conservation equation for property ϕ, over a finite volume V of cross-sectional area S, is:

$$\int_{CV} \frac{\partial(\rho\phi)}{\partial t} dV + \int_{CV} div(\rho\phi v) dV = \int_{CV} div(\Gamma grad\phi) dV + \int_{CV} S_\phi dV \quad (3)$$

Equation 3 is re-written as integrals over the entire bounding surface of the control volume by using Gauss divergence theorem:

$$\int_{CV} \frac{\partial(\rho\phi)}{\partial t} dV + \int_A \rho\phi v \cdot n\, dA = \int_A (\Gamma grad\phi) \cdot n\, dA + \int_{CV} S_\phi dV \quad (4)$$

where vector n is the outward unit normal to surface element dA, and A is the cross-sectional area of control volume face (Versteeg & Malalasekera, 1995). Assuming that the density of fluid, velocity components and source term are known ϕ is the only unknown. The net flux through the CV boundary is the sum of integrals over the four (in 2D) or six (in 3D) CV surfaces:

$$\int_A f\, dA = \sum_j \int_{A_k} f\, dA \quad (5)$$

where f is the component of the convective $(\rho\phi v \cdot n)$ or diffusive $(\Gamma grad\phi \cdot n)$ flux vector in the direction normal to CV surface.
The simplest approximation to the integral is the midpoint rule. The integral is approximated as a product of the integrand at the cell-face centre (which is itself an approximation to the mean value over the surface) and the cell-face area (Ferziger & Peric, 2002):

$$F_e = \int_{A_e} f\, dA = \bar{f}_e A_e \approx f_e A_e \qquad (6)$$

Since the value of f is not available at the cell face centre *e*, it has to be obtained by interpolation of nodal values of the solution. This interpolation must have at least the same order of accuracy as that of the integration scheme. In order to preserve the second-order accuracy of the midpoint rule approximation of the surface integral, the value of f_e has to be computed with at least second-order accuracy.
For the temporal discretization of the first term in the conservation equations, the implicit Euler scheme has been used.
The integration of the differential equations in each control volume yields a finite-difference equation that conserves each quantity (velocities, pressure and scalars) on a control-volume basis. The integral conservation equation applies to each CV, as well as to the solution domain as a whole. This basic characteristic makes the finite volume method suitable for this type of application.
The discretized equations are solved sequentially and the SIMPLE algorithm has always been used in the present application. This type of algorithm is based on using a relationship between velocity and pressure corrections in order to recast the continuity equation in terms of a pressure correction calculation. In this way, the calculated velocity and pressure fields satisfy the linearized momentum and continuity equations at any point.
The system of algebraic equations for each variable is solved using a Line Gauss-Seidel procedure (LGS). To speed up the convergence achieved by the LGS procedure, Fluent uses a Multigrid acceleration technique by default to solve the pressure equation.
Fluent does not solve each equation at all points simultaneously and so an iterative solution procedure is used with iterations continuing until the convergence criteria specified has been achieved.
The new calculated values of a given variable obtained, in each iteration by the approximate solution of the finite difference equations are then updated with the previews values of the variable using an underrelaxation technique. The user can choose the best relaxation factors for each variable in order to achieve a better convergence.

3.3 Boundary Conditions

Numerical simulations were carried out assuming a Newtonian and incompressible behaviour on the fluid. The fluid was set as water-liquid but the viscosity was assumed as 0.0035 kg/ms and density 1056 kg/m^3, which are the properties of blood.
Simulations in this study were run for a pulse cycle raging from velocities close to zero, during the diastole, to a maximum velocity of 0.35 m/s, during peak systole, according to a representative suprarenal blood flow waveform calculated by Taylor & Draney (2004).

Using a representative and common abdominal aorta diameter (D=0.022 m) and considering the assumed fluid properties (viscosity and density), the mean Reynolds number is Re=730. For this reason, the flow was firstly modelled as laminar.

3.4 Geometry and Grid

In order to capture accurate local fluid dynamics in the abdominal aorta and renal branches, the geometry must be representative of the native anatomy. In this study, the geometry was constructed based on two different models proposed by Shipkowitz et al. (1998) and Lee & Chen (2003), both of them deduced from statistical data. The complete geometric domain of the idealized abdominal aorta model is presented in Figure 2.

Fig. 2. Illustration of the abdominal aorta model with the renal arteries.

In the present computational model, the major simplifications are associated with the assumption of rigid and straight arteries, which neglects the walls motion and curvature. Also, blood was considered as a Newtonian fluid.

In a finite volume approach it is necessary to discretize the domain using a grid (mesh). The accuracy of the CFD solution is governed by the number of cells and choice of which element type to use in the grid. In a previous study, four different grids were developed in order to compare the performance of different element type and mesh generation strategies (Fig. 3) (Silva et al., 2008). It is relevant to establish a relation between grids and accuracy in the results obtained in Fluent simulations.

It is relevant to point out that the grid has a noticeable effect on CFD results and for this reason the automatic grids (tetrahedral) are usually not adequate and they may compromise the validity of results.

4. Grid Optimization

Generating a grid requires a good understanding about element types, the appropriate distribution of elements over the domain, the strategy to use in the decomposition of the domain and the necessity of boundary layers. In this study, four different grids were obtained, using Gambit, in order to compare the performance of different element types and mesh generation strategies.

Regarding the element type, the first approach was the tetrahedral grid because tetrahedral elements can easily adapt to complicated geometries and, for this reason, the grid can be

obtained quick and automatically (Grid (1)). However, the homogeneous distribution of the elements did not seem adequate because it is essential to have high dense grid in the bifurcation regions where the flow becomes more complex. Actually, an optimal grid is often non-uniform: denser in areas where large variations occur from point to point and coarser in regions relatively stable. Consequently, in a new grid, a combination of tetrahedral and hexahedral elements was used. This allows high grid quality to be achieved throughout the domain and an appropriate distribution of each element type - hybrid grid (Grid (2)). Although the element distribution was improved, still all bad quality elements were located in the tetrahedral grid. For this reason, special efforts were made in order to divide the domain in different volumes. In each of them it was possible to generate hexahedral grids (Grid (3)).
In this study, as atherosclerosis lesions are expected to be located along the walls, it is important to characterize the flow patterns near the walls. In this way, boundary layers were implemented along the walls in order to capture the fluctuations in the flow field caused by the bifurcations. Since there is one plane of symmetry, the geometry can be divided in two equivalent parts which reduces significantly the computational time (Grid (4)).

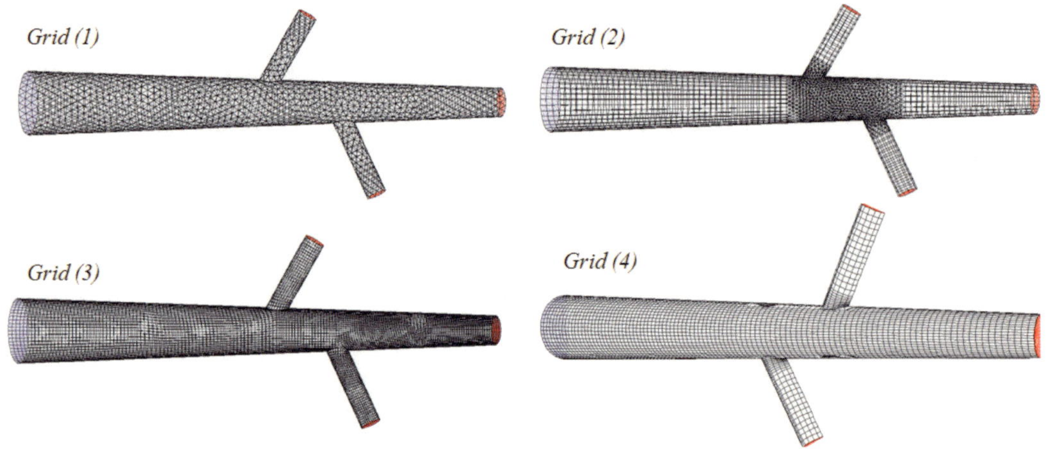

Fig. 3. Overview of the four different grids generated.

4.1 Grid Quality

Skewness is usually considered a parameter to evaluate mesh distortion and it has a significant impact on the accuracy of the numerical solution. Highly skewed cells can decrease accuracy and destabilize the solution.
Figure 4 illustrates what skewness represents for a 2D face. It is the angle between the area vector and the vector connecting the two cell centroids. An angle of zero indicates a perfectly orthogonal mesh which means that optimal quadrilateral meshes will have vertex angles close to 90 degrees, while triangular meshes should preferably have angles of close to 60 degrees and have all angles less than 90 degrees (CD-adapco STAR-CCM+, 2000-2006).

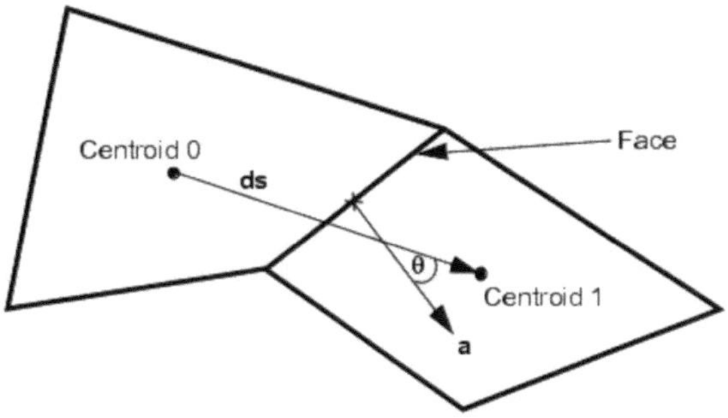

Fig. 4. Illustration of the skewness for a two-dimensional face (Adapted from CD-adapco STAR-CCM+, 2000-2006).

The quality of each grid was studied according to properties of skewness. In order to do this, two skewness measures were calculated, EquiAngle Skew and EquiSize Skew. For both properties, smaller values are more desirable (Table 1). In quantifying the quality of each grid, values of EquiAngle Skew and EquiSize Skew of 0–0.25 are considered excellent, 0.25–0.5 are good and 0.5–0.75 are fair. Grid (1) shows very high quality and the elements seem to adapt very well to the geometry. However, as explained before, the distribution of elements over the domain is not satisfactory. Furthermore, the use of hexahedral elements reduces the number of cells and, consequently, the CPU time. Grid (2) represents a good progress in terms of distribution, but the quality was reduced. A closer look on the bad elements (outside the interval 0-0.75) shows that all of them were located in the tetrahedral grid. Grid (3) is an entirely hexahedral grid. The implementation of this grid involves the partition of the domain in 8 volumes. The objective is to split the model into areas that can be meshed separately, while creating a uniform combination and allowing the lowest value of skewness possible. However, as smaller and more intricate volumes are created, the resulting elements tend to be smaller. Consequently, the quality is compromised, especially near the walls. This is the reason why the quality of Grid (3) is reduced. The same happens in Grid (4), due to the boundary layers implementation (which means a concentration of small elements near the walls). However, in order to evaluate grids, not only skewness properties should be compared, but also the accuracy of the computational solution.

Grid (1)	
EquiAngle Skew (0-0.75)	99.97%
EquiSize Skew (0-0.75)	100%
Grid (2)	
EquiAngle Skew (0-0.75)	99.95%
EquiSize Skew (0-0.75)	99.98%
Grid (3)	
EquiAngle Skew (0-0.75)	99.93%
EquiSize Skew (0-0.75)	99.93%
Grid (4)	
EquiAngle Skew (0-0.75)	99.83%
EquiSize Skew (0-0.75)	99.83%

Table 1. Grid quality evaluation for the four grids based on parameters of skewness.

4.2 Grid Accuracy

So far, the comparison between grids was made in terms of element type used, strategies of grid refinement and parameters of quality. However, it is also important to establish a relation between grids and the accuracy obtained in CFD simulations. A steady simulation was defined with a constant inlet velocity of 0.35 m/s, representing the maximum velocity of pulsatile profile.

Figure 5 shows the axial velocity contours in the axial plane 90 mm downstream the inlet boundary. This cross-section divides the abdominal aorta and the left renal branch. It is important that the grid imposes a smooth transition between the velocities near the walls, at abdominal aorta and renal artery, and the central flow. Grid (1), Grid (2) and Grid (3) show a very asymmetric and non-uniform distribution of axial velocities, principally in the renal wall. The external contour of the cross-section in Grid (1) proves that the tetrahedral elements cannot represent properly the circular geometry.

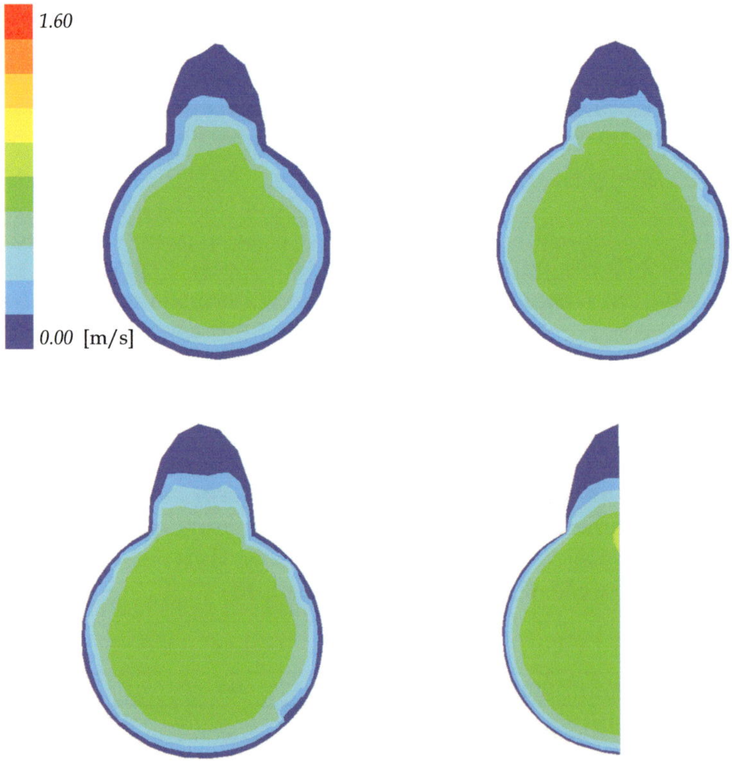

Fig. 5. Axial velocity contours at the axial plane 90 mm downstream the inlet boundary.

The implementation of boundary layers in Grid (4) shows a good effect in terms of a smooth transition from zero to maximum velocities and also improves the symmetry (this was proved for an equivalent grid in which the symmetry assumption was neglected). For being a good quality grid, with good parameters of symmetry and acceptable number of cells, Grid (4) was selected after the grid generation process.

4.3 Grid Density

To demonstrate the quality of the computational solution, it is essential to prove that the CFD results are grid independent. In other words, the results in terms of flow distribution are not dependent on the grid and they are only a consequence of the simulation parameters. Once the optimal grid generation strategy is achieved, different grids with different densities should be generated. The purpose is to evaluate if the solution converges to a value when the number of elements tends to infinite, which demonstrates that the results are independent on the grid, although the accuracy increases with the number of cells. Although accuracy increases with finer grids, the CPU and memory requirements to compute the solution and postprocessing also increase. Equilibrium must be established between the solution accuracy and computational time. In order to overcome the computational limitations, a variety of parallel paradigms have been implemented to parallelize the CFD codes and consequently speedup the computational jobs compared to the speed of a single computer.

5. Results

5.1 Velocity Profiles along the cardiac cycle

The axial velocity profiles, secondary motion and recirculation in abdominal aorta and renal branches were obtained and results are showed in Figure 6. The four different times illustrate the different phases of the cardiac cycle: acceleration phase (0.13 s), peak systole (0.25 s), deceleration phase (0.4 s) and diastole (0.8 s).

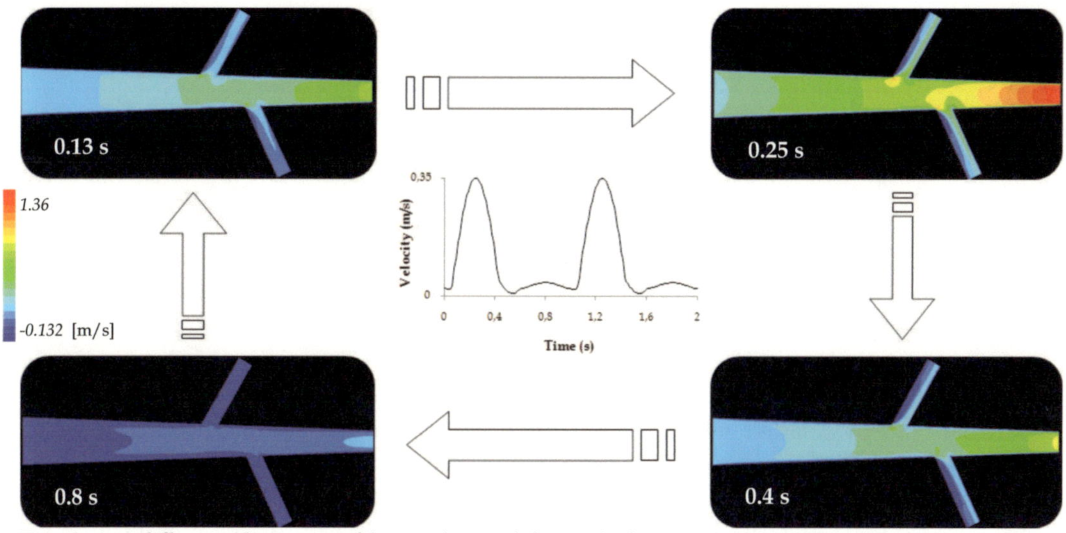

Fig. 6. Axial flow velocity profiles at the mid-frontal plane at 0.13 s, 0.25 s, 0.4 s, 0.8 s.

Comparing the velocity profiles, it can be concluded that the flow patterns are highly different along the cardiac cycle. The flow in the two renal arteries is also slightly different since they are not symmetric and geometrically the branching angles are different as well.

Flow results at renal branches proved the occurrence of flow separation since flow divides into two streams: maximum velocity at the distal wall of the bifurcations and slower moving fluid on the proximal wall (Fig. 7). Also, flow separation is more noticeable in the peak

systole and deceleration phases and it drops at the diastole phase. These blood flow patterns may be related to the development of atherosclerosis plaque at this location.
The present characterization of velocity fields, under laminar conditions, enables the comprehension of the abdominal aorta and renal arteries hemodynamics.

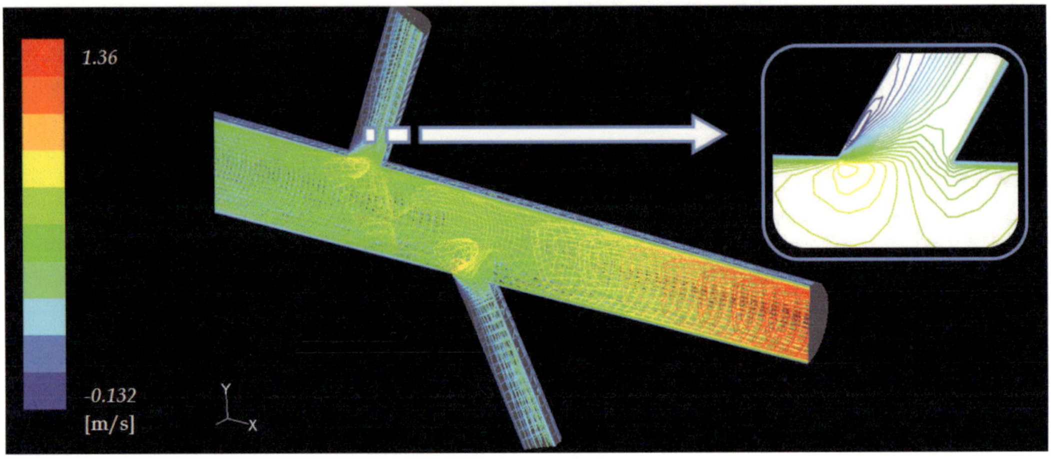

Fig. 7. Detail on the recirculation region at peak systole.

5.2 Shear-Stress analysis at wall boundaries

As blood flows across the endothelium, WSS is generated to retard the flow. Therefore the WSS (τ) represents the force acting tangential to the surface due to friction.
In laminar flows the WSS only depends on the velocity gradient at the wall, and the fluid dynamic viscosity. For no-slip wall conditions, generally applied in these studies, the properties of the flow adjacent to the wall/fluid boundary are used to predict the shear stress on the fluid at the wall. In a laminar flow, the WSS is therefore defined by the normal velocity gradient at the wall as (Fluent 6.2, 2005):

$$\tau = \mu \frac{\partial v}{\partial n} \tag{7}$$

Since the blood flow is highly skewed, the distribution of the WSS must be measured along the cardiac cycle by detailed velocity profiles very close to the wall (Wootton & Ku, 1999).
The distribution of WSS through a line along the abdominal aorta, proximal and distal renal walls is illustrated in Figure 8. The results show that WSS in the abdominal aorta wall tends to increase along its length and especially in the neighborhood of the renal branch. At the renal walls, the WSS distribution along the proximal wall deviates significantly from that found along the distal wall: low WSS at the proximal wall and high WSS at the distal renal wall.
The appearance of this low WSS in the proximal wall coincides with the presence of recirculation. Along the distal wall the WSS reaches a maximum in the entry of the bifurcation and tends to decrease along the distance.

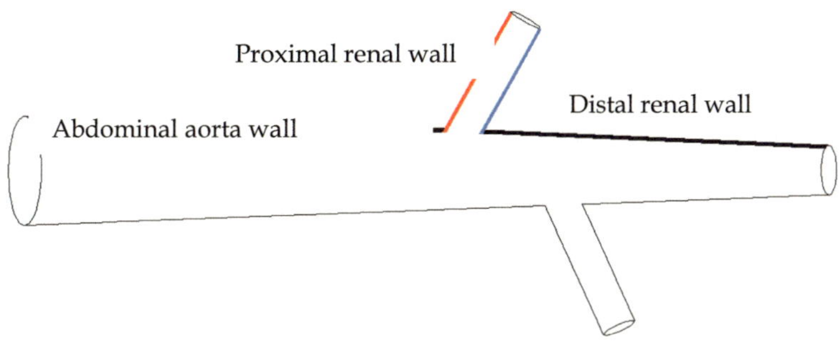

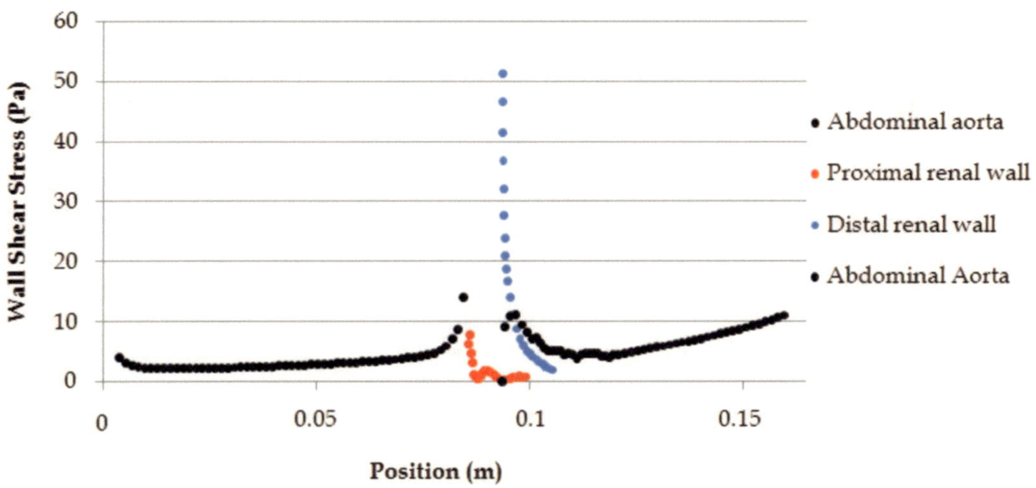

Fig. 8. WSS along abdominal aorta, proximal and distal renal arteries.

5.3 Fully developed inlet velocity

Two different configurations on the inlet velocity boundary condition were studied, either a uniform velocity or a fully developed velocity profile, both of them based on a physiologic velocity profile at peak systole.

Considering that, for laminar flow, the velocity inside a tube varies according to the equation:

$$u = \frac{\Delta p}{4\mu}\left(R^2 - r^2\right) \tag{8}$$

From Equation 8, the maximum velocity corresponds to r=0 and it can be written like:

$$u_{\max} = \frac{\Delta p R^2}{4\mu} \tag{9}$$

Assuming that the maximum velocity is twice the average velocity and combining this relation with Equation 9, results:

$$u = \frac{u_{\max}}{R^2}\left(R^2 - r^2\right) \tag{10}$$

Equation 10 can be written for rectangular coordinates, instead of cylindrical coordinates, in which yz coordinates correspond to the nodes coordinates in the inlet face (White, 2003):

$$u = u_{\max}\left(1 - \left(\sqrt{\frac{y^2 + z^2}{R}}\right)\right)^2 \tag{11}$$

In the uniform velocity configuration the velocity was set to 0.35 m/s, while in the fully developed flow the velocity varies along the inlet face according to equation 11 and assuming that u_{max} is 0.7 m/s.

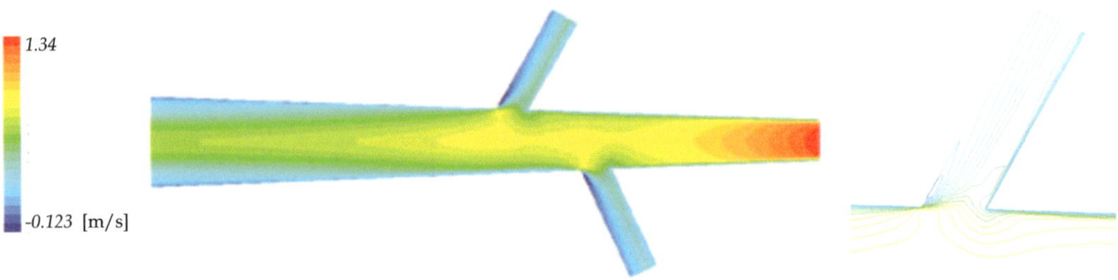

Fig. 9. Axial velocity profiles and iso-velocity lines at the mid-frontal plane for uniform (a) and fully developed (b) inflows.

The velocity contours show similar velocity distributions for both uniform and fully developed boundary condition (Fig. 9). The highest and lowest velocities are in the same range and they are found in the same locations. However, as expected, different flow patterns are obtained, specially, in the upstream portion before the bifurcations. Futhermore, the recirculation length is approximately the same in both cases. It seems that, apparently, the change in the inlet velocity does not affect the fluid dynamics in the complex regions.

5.4 Computational model based on *in vivo* anatomic images

The previous characterization of velocity fields and WSS distributions, under laminar condition, enables the comprehension of the abdominal aorta and renal arteries hemodynamics in idealized models. Afterwards, some investigations were made in order to infer about the sensibility of the model to the geometric domain. The impact of using *in vivo* anatomic images (obtained by CT) was analysed.

The computational method described herein was used to develop a model of the abdominal aorta and renal branches obtained from CT images of a normal adult subject. Our purpose is to compare the computational results obtained from a realistic and an idealized anatomic geometry.

CT scans the body and produces an image of each slice. The information from CT scan can be saved in a standard digital format called DICOM (Digital Imaging and Communications in Medicine). This is a universal file type, developed to facilitate data exchange between hardware, independently of manufacturer (Graham et al., 2005). The 2D images produce by CT systems can be assembled to produce complete 3D representations of scanned components with 3D image segmentation and volume rendering software. In the current project Mimics was used to produce the 3D model. To obtain a 3D model from 2D CT images, some steps were followed:

- After loading the CT images in Mimics, the first step was to segment the images, by applying filters of gray values, in order to select only the specific tissues of interest. In this case, the pixel range used to select the arteries is also the pixel range for other tissues (Fig. 10) For this reason the dynamic region growing tool was used to segment the CT images based on the connectivity of gray values in a certain pixel range.
- The final 3D object was constructed based on the previous image segmentation. This volume was exported as STL file to a Computing Aided Design (CAD) software, such as SolidWorks.
- The 3D model obtained directly from rendering the CT images had too much interference in its surface, which disable the appropriate mesh generation. Consequently, a second model was constructed in SolidWorks, using the first model as source for dimensions, curvature and bifurcation axes.
- The model obtained was then exported to Gambit as an ACIS file (version 10.0) and it was automatically meshed with tetrahedral elements.

The results presented here are very preliminary and comparisons can only be performed in a rough qualitative manner. Velocity contours are shown in Figure 11. The flow fields are highly different in terms of magnitude and patterns: the maximum velocity is no longer found in the outlet face but in the neighborhood of the right artery. Also, the abdominal aorta curvature seems to have a decisive impact in the flow fields.

The differences found between these two models do not compromise the validity of the previous results, mainly, because the procedure of 3D model generation from CT images needs to be improved and more carefully understood. On the other hand, the comparison between these two models should be seen as a suggestion to the importance of using *in vivo* data.

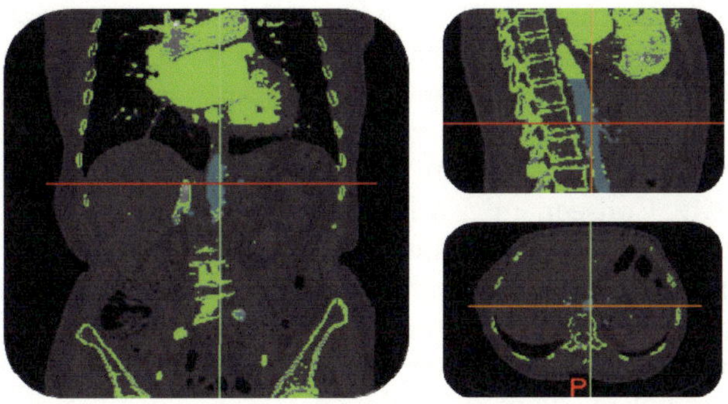

Fig. 10. Two-dimensional CT images and the result of the image segmentation.

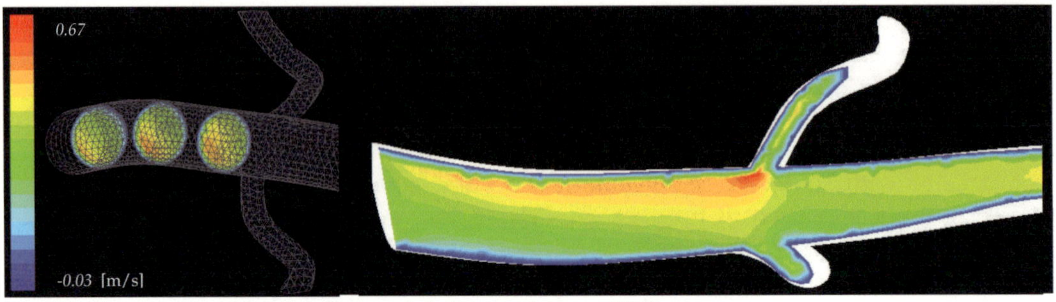

Fig. 11. Velocity profiles for the model obtained from CT images

6. Model Optimization

A model is, by definition, an approximation to reality. There are several reasons that contribute for this outcome; one of the most important is limitation in computational capacities. The closer the model gets to the real behaviour of the structure it is trying to emulate, the more complex it gets. Therefore there is, currently, no model that perfectly mimics the blood flow and blood vessels performance. Instead, there are different models that better contribute to the understanding of different phenomena. This topic on model optimization attempts to give an insight on the different paths that can be followed to increase the accuracy (and, inevitably, the complexity) of a model of cardiovascular structures. It is important to understand that when a research aims to give a deeper knowledge on a phenomenon through the application of computational models it is, most commonly, obliged to neglect some aspects. This is why this topic is crucial. It portraits the approaches that are made depending on the goal of the research. Each of the following points represents one of the parameters for which CFD has been perfected, thus contributing to the progress of the state-of-the-art.

6.1 Compliance of arterial walls

Various computational models, with rigid or compliant tubes, have been used to quantify flow and wall mechanical behaviors. It has been found that artery stiffness, stenosis geometry are the dominating factors affecting blood flow and artery motion.

FSI is a relatively new technique used in numerical problems to provide a better understanding on the blood flow characteristics because it includes the flow impact on structures (mainly artery walls) and on the local hemodynamics features. However, modeling the human circulatory system remains a very difficult process because of its geometrical complexity. Consequently, a large number of special assumptions have to be considered to simulate blood flow accurately. Since, a high majority of the studies represent trunked regions of arterial tree, it is necessary to take into consideration the link between local and global blood flow phenomena. As a result, to perform more realistic numerical simulations, the challenge in the geometric modeling approaches consists in the setting of proper coupling conditions to obtain quantities such as the flow rate, and the pressure at the interfaces between different model structures.

Chakravaty & Mandal (2000) have performed important studies on blood flow in a deformable stenotic artery and their aim was to validate a method of coupling wall deformations with fluid flow. Mandal (2005) simulated similar conditions while setting the fluid to have a different model for the fluid viscosity (Generalised Power Law non-Newtonian model). The methods employed by Mandal provided excellent results with look upon to fluid characteristics, like, fluid velocity, WSS and pressure gradients with respect to changes in stenosis shape and degree of narrow. However, their method could not provide the stress distributions across the wall as this was set to deform governing set of equations, rather than actually creating a wall model itself. Li & Kleinstreuer (2005) modeled blood flow with FSI in a stent, which then expanded within an aneurysm sac. The blood was set to have non-Newtonian properties. This work presented a three-dimensional view of the critical stresses within the stent and aneurysm as well as potential risks resulting from different flow pressures. Within our group, the effect of the artery wall deformation upon the flow patterns is also being investigated. The prime goal of this study is the development of numerical models able to predict the blood flow in the region of abdominal aorta under deformable boundaries. The simulations are being performed using adaptative dynamic meshes into Fluent (Ferreira et al., 2009).

6.2 Multiphase

Most CFD models are developed considering blood as a single-phase fluid and, as seen before, these models can accurately predict the flow patterns in three-dimensional models. Although blood behaves as a non-Newtonian fluid under certain conditions due to the rheological properties of a red blood cell-plasma suspension, it was shown that the Newtonian assumption is reasonable (Shipkowitz et al., 1998) for large arteries studies. Even though, it would be relevant to evaluate the spatial and temporal distributions of red blood cells and identify regions where adhesion and deposition to the artery walls occur. Several studies had already introduced multiphase models to study blood flow.
Following this multiphase characteristic of blood flow, some studies have presented results for a CFD models consisting of a continuous plasma phase and a dispersed RBC phase (Huang et al., 2009; Jung et al., 2009). In terms of numerical methods, Navier-Stokes equations are solved with the particular increment of a volume fraction for each phase, as well as mechanisms for the exchange of mass, momentum, and energy between the phases. Although the multiphase blood flow models proved to be in close agreement with the single-phase models, new insights were obtained about the flow characteristics that promote the migration of the cells to the arterial walls.

6.3 Microscale CFD models

The numerical simulations presented herein provide relevant information on the three-dimensional velocity profiles and they show the complex hemodynamics of blood flow in arteries. These numerical flow fields can be used to identify critical flow regions and, therefore, can be used as a powerful tool to optimize the medical devices design. However, these macroscale flow patterns do not fully describe the implications of the complex flow field to the blood cells. It is important to predict and avoid the occurrence of mechanical damage and/or destruction of platelets and red blood cells due to cardiovascular diseases or the implantation of medical devices. For these reasons, several studies are currently focused in investigating the mechanical loading on blood cells due to microscale flow structures. Liu et al., (2006) are focusing their research efforts in modeling blood flow at a cellular scale. Recently they proposed numerical methods able to compute red blood cells deformation and aggregation, cell-cell interactions and even cell migration. Quinlan and Dooley (2007) proposed a model able to compute flow-induced stress on a single red blood cell due to turbulent blood flow. This information can ultimately be useful for blood damage prediction in the design of medical devices.

7. Conclusion

The blood flow patterns presented so far were obtained with a very good quality grid, which was developed after sequence refinements and according to the computational facilities available. It is not expected that further refinements in the mesh will result in substantial differences in the solution.

The velocity profiles reveal the presence of reversed flow throughout the cardiac cycle, especially at deceleration period. The recirculation was found at the proximal wall of the renal branches and along the posterior wall of the abdominal aorta. It has been shown that the presence of recirculation in the renal arteries is coincident with the location of low WSS. These blood flow patterns may be related to the localization and development of atherosclerosis plaque at this location. More studies need to be performed in order to establish a direct correlation between these regions and the location of vascular diseases. Even though, some studies have indicated that low WSS usually occur in regions of high probability of plaque localization (Taylor et al., 1998b). The plots of velocity patterns and WSS distribution obtained in the present work are in good agreement with previous computational and *in vivo* studies (Taylor et al., 1998b; Lee & Chen, 2002).

In this study, the inlet velocity was assumed as uniform pulsatile according to a suprarenal velocity profile obtained by Taylor & Draney, 2004. However, it is possible that velocity profiles become fully developed by the time they reach the abdominal aorta. For this reason, the two configurations were tested and the results were similar for both constant and fully developed inflow.

8. References

Avolio, A. (1980). Multi-branched model of the human arterial system. *Med & Biol. Eng. & Comput*, Vol. 18, 709-718

Berger, S. & Jou, L. (2000). Flows in Stenotic vessels. *Annu. Rev. Fluid Mech.*, Vol. 32, 347-382

Boron, W. & Boulpaep, E. (2003). *Medical Physiology,* W. B. Saunders Company, 9781416023289, Philadelphia

Carneiro, F.; Silva, A.; Teixeira, S.; Teixeira, J.; Lobarinhas, P. & Ribeiro, V. (2008a). The Influence of Renal Branches on the Iliac Arteries Blood Flow, *Proceedings of the ASME 3rd Frontiers in Biomedical Devices*, 0791838234, Irvine, California, June 2008

Carneiro, F.; Ribeiro, V.; Teixeira, S. & Teixeira, J. (2008b) Numerical study of blood fluid analogous in the abdominal aorta bifurcation, *Proceedings of 4th International Conference on Comparing Design in Nature with Science and Engineering,* 97818456412072426, Algarve, June 2008, WIT Press, Southampton

CD-adapco STAR-CCM+, 2000-2006

Chakravarty, S. & Mandal, P. (2000). Two-dimensional blood flow through tapered arteries under stenotic conditions. *Intern. J. Non-Linear Mech.*, Vol. 35, 779-793

Cebral, J.; Yim, P.; Lohner, R.; Soto, O. & Choyoke, P. (2002). Blood flow modeling in carotid arteries with computational fluid dynamics and MR imaging. *Acad. Radiol.* Vol. 9, 1286-1299

Chen, J. & Lu, X. (2004). Numerical investigation of the non-Newtonian blood flow in a bifurcation model with a non-planar branch. *Journal of Biomechanics*, Vol. 37, 1899-1911

Ferreira, A.; Teixeira, S.; Teixeira, J. (2009). Contributions to the study of blood flow in the abdominal aorta and its branches. *ASME International Mechanical Engineering Congress & Exposition*, Lake Buena Vista, Florida, November 2009

Ferziger, J. & Peric, M. (2002). *Computational Methods for Fluid Dynamics*, Springer, Berlin, Germany.

Fluent 6.2 User's Guide, (2005). Fluent Inc.

Graham, R.; Perriss, R. & Scarsbrook, A. (2005). DICOM demystified: A review of digital file formats and their use in radiological practice. *Clinical Radiology*, Vol. 60, 1133-1140

He, S. & Jackson, J. (2000), A study of turbulence under conditions of transient flow in a pipe. *J. Fluid Mech.*, Vol. 408, 1–38

Huang, J.; Lyczkowski, R. & Gidaspow, D. (2009). Pulsatile flow in a coronary artery using multiphase kinetic theory. *Journal of Biomechanics*, Vol. 42, 743–754

Jung, J.; Lyczkowski, R.; Panchal, C. & Hassanein, A. (2009). Multiphase hemodynamic simulation of pulsatile flow in a coronary artery. *Journal of Biomechanics*, Vol. 39, 2064–2073

Kagadis, G.; Skouras, E.; Bourantas, G.; Paraskeva, C.; Katsanos, K.; Karnabatidis, D. & Nikiforidis, G. (2008). Computational representation and hemodynamic characterization of *in vivo* acquired severe stenotic renal artery geometries using turbulence modeling. *Medical Engineering & Physics*, Vol. 30, 647–660

Ku, D. (1997). Blood flow in arteries. *Annu. Rev. Fluid Mech*, Vol. 29, 399–434

Lee, D. & Chen, J. (2002). Numerical simulation of steady flow flieds in amodel of abdominal aorta with its peripheral bramches. *Journal of Biomechanics*, Vol. 35, 1115-1122

Lee, D. & Chen, J. (2003). Pulsatile flow fields in a model of abdominal aorta with its peripheral branches. *Biomedical Engineering Applications, Basis & Communications*, Vol. 33, 1305-1312

Li, Z. & Kleinstreuer, C. (2005), Blood flow and structure interactions in a stented abdominal aortic aneurysm model, *Medical Engineering & Physics*, Vol.27, 369-382

Li, M.; Beech-Brandt, J.; John, L.; Hoskins, P. & Easson, W. (2007). Numerical analysis of pulsatile blood flow and vessel wall mechanisms in different degrees of stenoses. *Journal of Biomechanics*, Vol. 40, 3715-3724

Liu, W.; Liu, Y.; Farrell, D.; Zhang, L.; Wang, X.; Fukui, Y.; Patankar, N.; Zhang, Y.; Bajaj, C.; Lee, J.; Hong, J.; Chen, X. & Hsu, H. (2006). Immersed finite element method and its applications to biological systems, *Comput. Methods Appl. Mech. Engrg.*, Vol. 195, 1722–1749

Mandal, P. (2005), An unsteady analysis of non-Newtonian blood flow through tapered arteries with a stenosis, *International Journal of Non-Linear Mechanics*, Vol. 40, 151-164

Nanduri, J.; Pino-Romainville, F. & Celik, I. (2009). CFD mesh generation for biological flows: Geometry reconstruction using diagnostic images. *Computers & Fluids*, Vol. 38, 1026-1032

O'Brien, V. & Ehrlich, L. (1977). Simulation of unsteady flow at renal branches. *Journal of Biomechanics*, Vol. 10, 623-631

Perktold, K. & Rappitsch, G. (1995). Computer simulation of local blood flow and vessel mechanics in a compliant carotid artery bifurcation model. *Journal of Biomechanics*, Vol. 28, 845-856

Quinlan N. & Dooley P.(2007). Models of Flow-Induced Loading on Blood Cells in Laminar and Turbulent Flow, with Application to Cardiovascular Device Flow. *Annals of Biomedical Engineering*, Vol. 35, 1347–1356

Rappitsch, G. & Perktold, K. (1996). Computer simulation of convective diffusion process in large arteries. *Journal of Biomechanics*, Vol. 29, 207-215

Shipkowitz, T.; Rodgers, V.; Frazin, L. & Chandran, K. (1998). Numerical study on the effect of steady axial flow development in the human aorta on local shear stresses in abdominal aortic branches. *Journal of Biomechanics*, Vol. 31, 995-1007

Shipkowitz, T.; Rodgers, V.; Frazin, L. & Chandran, K. (2000). Numerical study on the effect of secondary flow in the human aorta on local shear stresses in abdominal aortic branches. *Journal of Biomechanics*, Vol. 33, 717-728

Silva, A.; Teixeira, S. & Lobarinhas, P. (2008). The influence of different grid approaches on a cardiovascular computational model, *Proceeding of the 17th IASTED International Conference on Applied Simulation and Modelling 2008*, 9780889867482, Corfu, Greece, June 2008, ACTA Press, Calgary

Steinman, D.; Frayne, R.; Zhang, X.; Rutt, B. & Ethier, C. (1996). MR measurement and numerical simulation of steady flow in an end-to-side anastomosis model. *Journal of Biomechanics*, Vol. 29, 537-542

Taylor, C.; Hughes, T. & Zarins, C. (1998a). Finite element modeling of blood flow in arteries. *Comput. Methods Appl. Mech. Engrg.*, Vol. 158, 155-196

Taylor, C.; Hughes, T. & Zarins, C. (1998b). Finite element modeling of three-dimensional pulsatile flow in the abdominal aorta: relevance to atherosclerosis. *Annals of Biomedical Engineering*, Vol. 26, 975-987

Taylor, C.; Cheng, C.; Espinosa, L.; Tang, B.; Parker, D. & Herfkens, R. (2002). *In vivo* Quantification of Blood Flow and Wall Shear Stress in the Human Abdominal Aorta during Lower Limb Exercise. *Annals of Biomedical Engineering*, Vol. 30, 402-408

Taylor, C.; Draney, M. (2004). Experimental and computational methods in cardiovascular fluid mechanics. *Annu. Rev. Fluid Mech.*, Vol. 36, 197–231

Taylor, C.; Humphrey, J. (2009). Open problems in computational vascular biomechanics: Hemodynamics and arterial wall mechanics. *Comput. Methods Appl. Mech. Engrg.*, In Press, Corrected Proof, Available online 15 February

Varghese, S. & Frankel, S. (2003). Numerical Modeling of pulsatile turbulent flow in stenotic vessels. *Journal of biomechanical engineering*, Vol. 125, 445-460

Versteeg, H. & Malalasekera, W. (1995). *An introduction to computational fluid dynamic. The finite volume method.* Longman Scientific & Technical, 9780131274983 Harlow, UK

White, F. (2003). *Fluid Mechanics*. McGraw-Hill, 9780072831801, New York

Wood, N. (1999). Aspects of fluid dynamics applied to the large arteries. *J. Theor. Biol.*, Vol. 199, 137-161

Wotton, D.; Ku, D. (1999). Fluid Mechanics of Vascular Systems, Diseases, and Thrombosis. *Annu. Rev. Biomed. Eng.*, Vol. 01, 299-329

3

Asymmetrical Bipedal Modeling for Biomechanical Sit-to-Stand Movement

Asif Mahmood Mughal and Kamran Iqbal
University of Arkansas at Little Rock
USA

1. Introduction

Human bipedal model are symmetrical as well as asymmetrical depending upon nature of movement, task and orientation of the body. A bipedal model with a full symmetry of limbs is redundant due to the physiological equilibrium. Asymmetrical models are applicable to both healthy subjects and stroke patients for sit-to-stand (STS) maneuver. Healthy subjects usually donot behave with an exact symmetry on both extremities for STS due to seating position, sitting posture, seat and age related variables. On the other hand stroke patients with paraplegic limbs exhibit complete asymmetrical behavior in the right and left limbs, with one side of limbs moving significantly slower than the other side. Several researchers provided many computational solutions to model human bipedal design. Anderson and Pandy (2001) studied the bipedal modeling and neuro-musculoskeletal system with 3D modeling and combined it with optimization theory to simulate the dynamics of motor task. They also further elaborated this model with 23 degrees of freedom for mechanical linkages actuated by 54 muscles. In this study, they simulated results for repeated gait cycles and computed the minimal metabolic energy per unit traveled by using SD/Fast. Few other researchers also developed bipedal models such as Jalics et al. (1996) presented a 2D bipedal model with 5 links as 7 segments for locomotion control, and, Spong et al. (2006) presented a model for almost linear bipedal robot. In order to avoid redundancies, a 3-link model was more successful with no constraints or nonzero open loop eigenvalues as discussed by Iqbal and Pai (2000). This model does not provide analysis of right and left extremities especially for stroke patients and was developed for the sagittal plane movement simulation, postural stability and balance recovery after perturbation. The particular biomechanical model consists of a foot segment or the base of support (BoS), lower leg, upper leg, and a head arm and trunk (HAT). The assembly of three links represents a triple inverted pendulum model, which is intrinsically unstable and consistently needs control effort in the shape of joint torques to maintain a stable posture. Roberts and McCollum (1996) presented a Hamiltonian based mathematical model of human body similar to Hemami and Jaswa's (1978) inverted pendulum model. The 4 link rigid body model was further developed by Barin (1989) with a head link and this rigid body model is now being taught in biomechanics courses. Several text books have provided the detail explanation of this model with free body diagram, Lagrangian approach and estimation of these different variables among several age groups.

Recently 2 segment and 4 segment models were also used for postural stability with PID controllers by Iqbal and Roy (2004). Main contributions towards biomechanical studies are computational modeling schemes for simulation purposes and experimental validations. Analytical models are complex in nature and computationally expensive. But, these models can be used for variety of analysis, controller design and experimental studies where computational models lack in general.

In this chapter, we will discuss a conceptual bipedal model with symmetrical angles in sagittal and frontal planes. Asymmetry exists in the model due to asymmetrical connection of feet to the ground, and asymmetrical references to the ground for translational and rotational variables. With only one foot connecting to the ground, and other free foot makes a unconstrained model which is simple to use but less realistic. We present two modeling schemes in this chapter namely unconstrained model, and constrained model. This bipedal model consists of two feet, two lower limbs (shanks), two upper limbs (thighs), a pelvic junction, and a head-arm-torso (HAT) segment in both 2D and 3D spaces. The constrained models have both feet connected to the ground; which produces holonomic constraints to maintain a physical balance between two legs in x, y and z axes. For each model, Maple environment generates nonlinear ODEs in the state space formulation, which can be transferred to Matlab for simulation purposes. We prove the stability of these models with Lyapunov's indirect method, and also provide simulation results for regulated STS maneuver. We simulate these models for human STS transfer with synthesized reference trajectories, and optimal feedback controller design. Our results of angular profiles, feedback torques and some physiological variables indicate the usefulness of these modeling schemes for the study of biomechanical movements.

2. Conceptual Bipedal Model

The general structure of a bipedal model includes 2 foot segments, 2 lower legs (shanks), 2 upper legs (thighs) connected with pelvis through a 2-DoF joint. Pelvic segment is connected with a segment consist of head, arm, and trunk (HAT). Both feet are on x-axis, and each segment length is along y-axis. In sitting position thighs are along z-axis, and along y-axis at standing position as shown in Fig 1. There are 7 joints in the systems connecting in yz or sagittal plane with x as axis of rotation representing joint angles θ_1-θ_6 and θ_9. Hip-pelvic and pelvic-HAT joints can also move the limbs in xy or frontal plane with z- axis of rotation, and these angles will be modeled with Euler angle representations shown as φ_7, φ_8 and φ_{10} in Fig 1. These joints are represented as either revolute or universal joints in Maple's DynaFlexPro environment; Mughal and Iqbal (2007) discussed these joint types in details. A revolute joint connects two bodies with a fixed reference frame and allows a single relative rotation of the two frames; all other relative rotations and translations are prevented by this joint type. With this joint type an input torque can be specified as a variable, which will appear in dynamic equations. A universal joint allows two relative rotations, about orthogonal axes, of the two connected frames; all other relative motions of two frames are prevented by this joint type. It provides two rotational variables in dynamic equations for two orthogonal axes but a drawback is that input torques cannot be specified directly for these rotational variables.

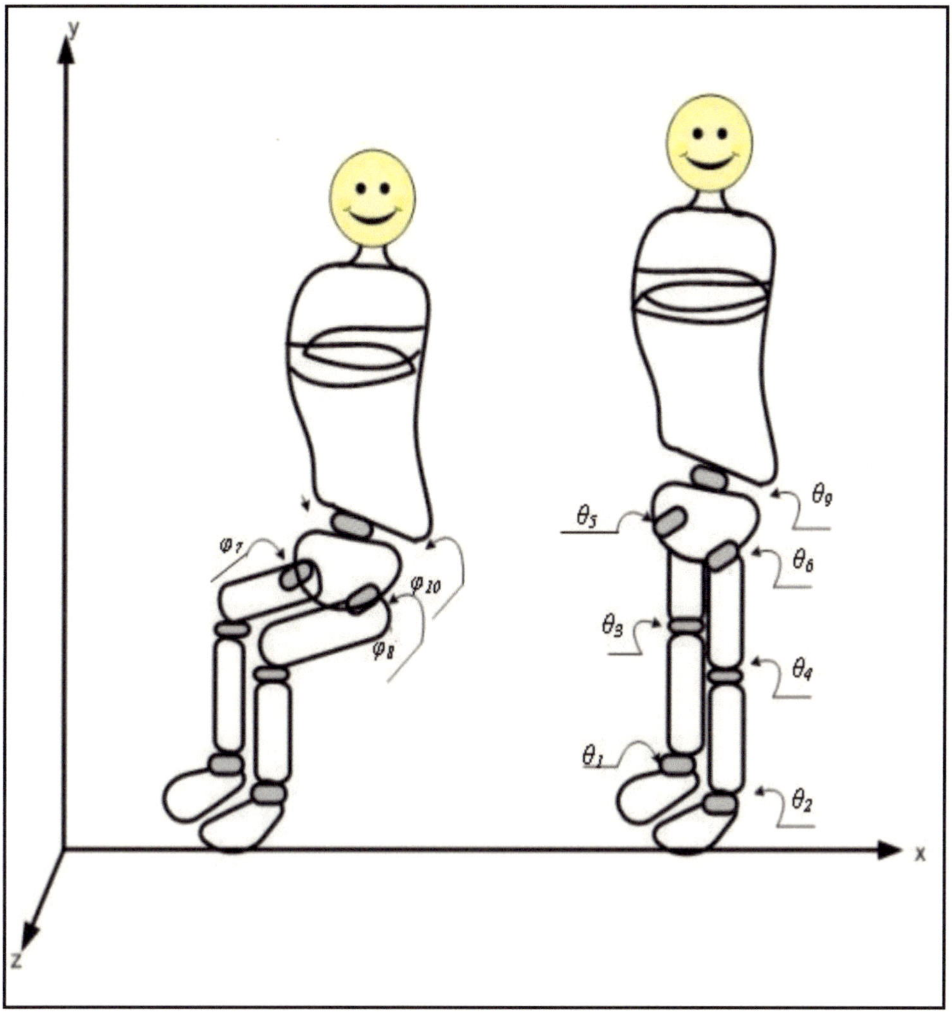

Fig. 1. Bipedal rigid body model, with sagittal plane angles θ_1-θ_6 and θ_9, frontal plane angles φ_7-φ_8, φ_{10}. The sagittal plane angles are shown in standing posture along x-axis and frontal plane angles are shown in sitting posture along z-axis. A small arrow in angle points towards its placement.

3. Unconstrained Bipedal Model

In this scheme, we joined right foot as a weld joint to the ground and left foot is a free foot without any joint. An 8-segmented biomechanical bipedal model in DynaFlexPro-ModelBuilder (GUI) environment is shown in Fig 2. J1 and J2 are the revolute joints from feet to lower limbs (Shank), J3 and J4 are the revolute joints from lower limbs to upper limbs (Thigh) representing sagittal plane angles θ_1 to θ_4 in Fig 1.These joints allow motion in yz plane or through axis of rotation along x-axis and are represented as x_1-x_4 variables in the system of equations with T1-T4 torque drivers (not shown in the figure). J5 is an universal joint with two angular movements in yz plane with rotation along x-axis with sagittal plane angle θ_5 (x_5) and in xy plane with rotation along z-axis as frontal plane angle φ_7 (x_7). There is no built-in torque driver in the universal joint, so there is an "Applied Moment" driver T57 at this joint to supply torques with two components T5 and T7 in x-and z directions respectively. There is a universal joint J6 on the left upper limb and pelvis segment which represents sagittal plane angle $\theta 6$ (x6), frontal plane angle $\varphi 8$ (x8) and a torque driver (applied moments) T68 with two components T6 and T8 for their respective angles. Similarly, pelvis-HAT joint J7 is also a universal joint with applied moment driver T910 supplying torques to sagittal plane θ_9 (x_9) and frontal plane φ_{10} (x_{10}) joint angles. This scheme has only one path for rotational variables to the ground i.e. R-tree and same path for translational variables to the ground i.e. T-tree.

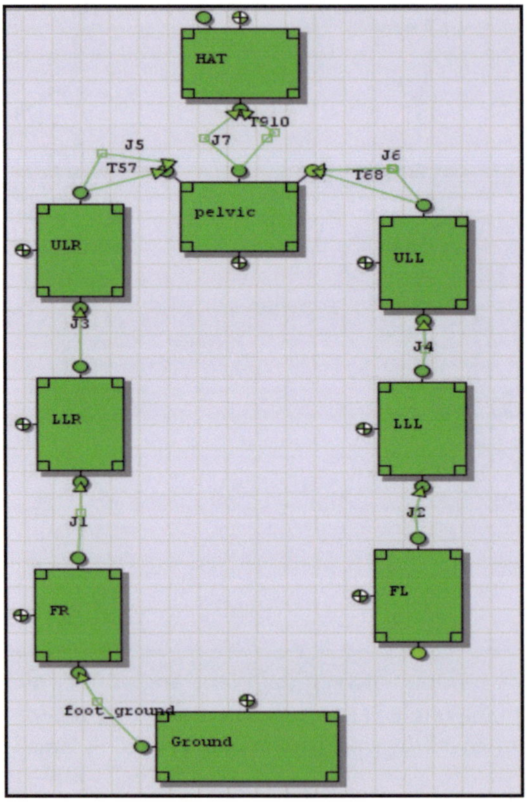

Fig. 2. Free foot rigid body model in Maple's GUI with T-Tree and R-Tree through joints

This model also does not move from its position for a normal gait due to the restriction of a weld joint. The system has 10 degrees of freedom and it is modeled using 10 generalized coordinates coupled by 0 algebraic constraints.

3.1 Mathematical Modeling for Free Foot Model

Let $\vec{x}(t)$ be the vector of joint angles and $\vec{\tau}(t)$ be the vector of joint torques.

$$\vec{x}(t) = \vec{x} = [x_1 \quad x_2 \quad \cdots \quad x_{10}]^T$$
$$\vec{\tau}(t) = \vec{\tau} = [T_1 \quad T_2 \quad \cdots \quad T_{10}]^T \tag{1}$$

This modeling scheme generates equations of the following form

$$M(\vec{x}, \dot{\vec{x}}) \cdot \ddot{\vec{x}} = F(\vec{x}, \dot{\vec{x}}, \vec{\tau}) \tag{2}$$

Where $M = M(\vec{x}, \dot{\vec{x}})$ is a 10 x 10 inertia matrix, $F = F(\vec{x}, \dot{\vec{x}}, \vec{\tau})$ is a 10x1 vector which contains external load, quadratic velocity terms and torques. The system of equations can also be represented as

$$\ddot{\vec{x}} = M^{-1} \cdot F = f(\vec{x}, \dot{\vec{x}}, \vec{\tau}) = f \tag{3}$$

Eq (3) represents the system in 10x1 nonlinear state-space formulations with 10 nonlinear functions. This system can be linearized for controller design and analysis as

$$\begin{bmatrix} \ddot{\vec{x}} \\ \dot{\vec{x}} \end{bmatrix} = [A] \cdot \begin{bmatrix} \dot{\vec{x}} \\ \vec{x} \end{bmatrix} + [B] \cdot \vec{\tau}$$
$$A = \begin{bmatrix} A_1 & A_2 \\ 0 & I \end{bmatrix}, B = \begin{bmatrix} B \\ 0 \end{bmatrix} \tag{4}$$

where A_1, A_2 and B_1 matrices are all 10x10 matrices given as

$$[A_1]_{ij} = \left.\frac{\partial f_i}{\partial \dot{x}_j}\right|_{x=x_e, \tau=u_e} \qquad [A_2]_{ij} = \left.\frac{\partial f_i}{\partial x_j}\right|_{x=x_e, \tau=u_e} \qquad [B]_{ij} = \left.\frac{\partial f_i}{\partial \tau_j}\right|_{x=x_e, \tau=u_e} \qquad i,j=1..10 \tag{5}$$

Linearization points i.e. standing posture joint angles x_e and joint torques u_e give the equilibrium position where $\ddot{x} = 0$ in Eq (5). It is important to note that here we are using $\vec{x} = \Delta\vec{x}$, where $\Delta x_i = x_i - x_{ei}$ and $\vec{\tau} = \Delta\vec{\tau}$ where $\Delta\tau_i = \tau_i - u_{ei}$ for linearization at equilibrium point. In this model, all joint angles are local or relative between two respective bodies, gravity is in negative y-axis and height in positive y-axis, so all joint angles are zero at standing posture due to collinear body frames. However, we solve for u_e at these angles to obtain $\ddot{\vec{x}} = 0$. This model produces pairs of eigenvalues in right and left half planes and thus is an unstable model, which requires a controller design to stabilize this system.

$$\vec{\tau}(t) = -K \cdot \begin{bmatrix} \dot{\vec{x}} \\ \vec{x} \end{bmatrix} + u_e \tag{6}$$

This torque input can be used with nonlinear model for stable postural movement; however, this torque to the nonlinear model requires additional feedforward torque component $u_e = [0\ 0\ 0\ 0\ 0\ 0\ 93.478\ 0\ 0\ 0]^T$ to stabilize the system at $\ddot{\vec{x}} = 0$.

3.2 Simulation and Results

We simulate the unconstrianted model with linear quadratic regulator (LQR) based controller design. We use the physical values from de Leva (1996) for this simulation. Fig 3 shows the angular profiles of free foot model with desired reference trajectories synthsized by Mughal and Iqbal (2008a) for STS movement. Angular profiles of knee and hip-pelvis sagittal angles follow the reference trajectories very closely and symmetrically, and these are only profiles starting from non-zero initial conditions. Ankle and pelvic-HAT sagittal angle also follow reference trajectories and settle within 2 secs. However, frontal angles took longer time to settle and hip-pelvic frontal angles show difference from reference trajectories.

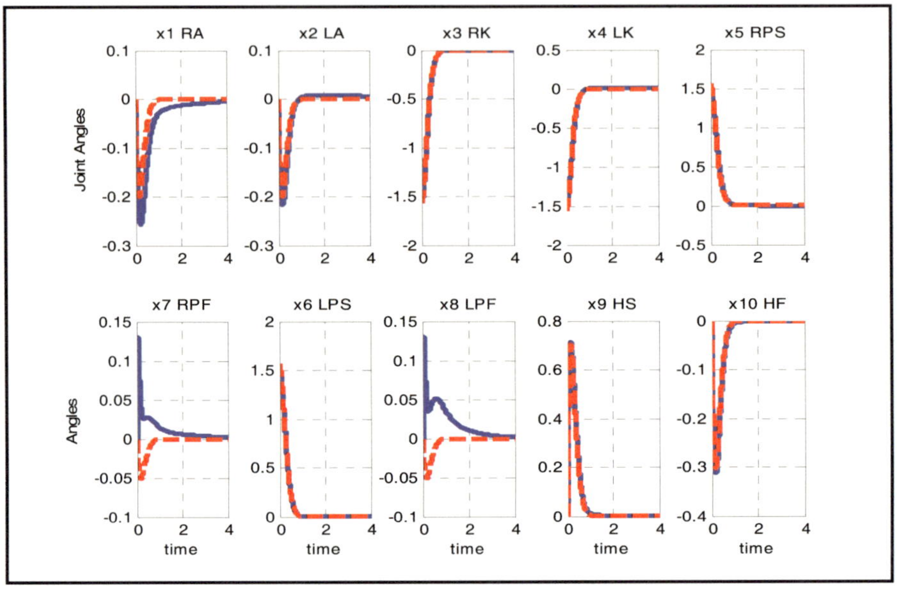

Fig. 3. Movement profiles of joint angles in radians (solid blue lines) and their reference trajectories (dashed red lines) R=Right, L=Left, A=Ankle angle, K=Knee angle, P= Pelvic-Hip joint angle, H=HAT-Pelvic joint angle, S=Sagittal plane, F= Frontal plane

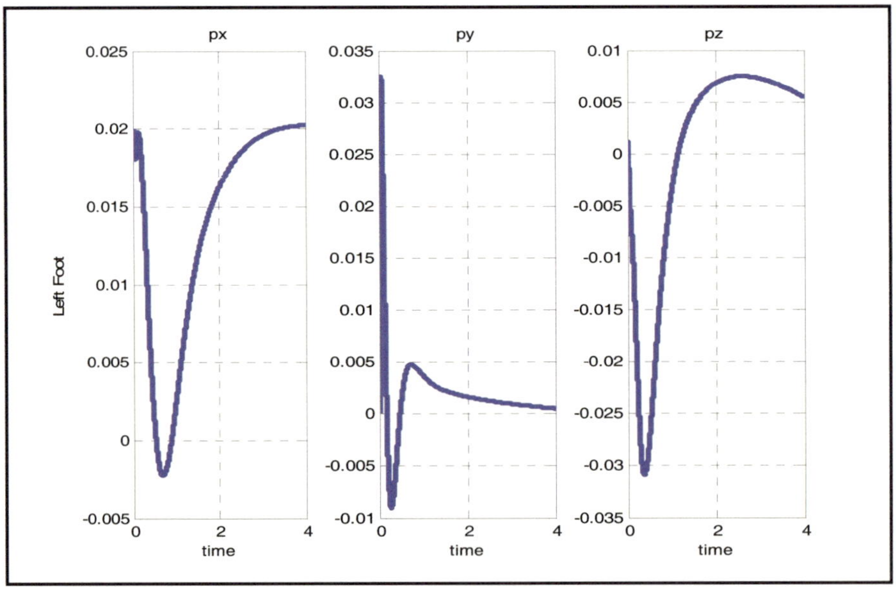

Fig. 4. Movement of a left foot positions in x, y and z direction (m) for a free foot model

Figure 4. shows the movement of a left foot with in a free foot model with LQR design to control joint angles only. The movement of left foot is very small but still it is moving significantly which is not very realistic for ordinary STS movement.

4. Constrained Bipedal Model

The model discussed in Sec 3 is without any geometric restrictions on physical body or in other words without any algebraic constraints. Although free foot is more related to stroke patients than a healthy subject, yet its movement can also violates some physiological constraints in healthy subjects. This model doesn't provide any control over the position of left (free) foot which is not a very applicable controlled bipedal model. Connecting each foot to the ground as a weld joint will generate irresolvable holonomic constraints in bipedal case due to lesser DOF in the system, so we now model with a 6-DoF joint for a left foot.

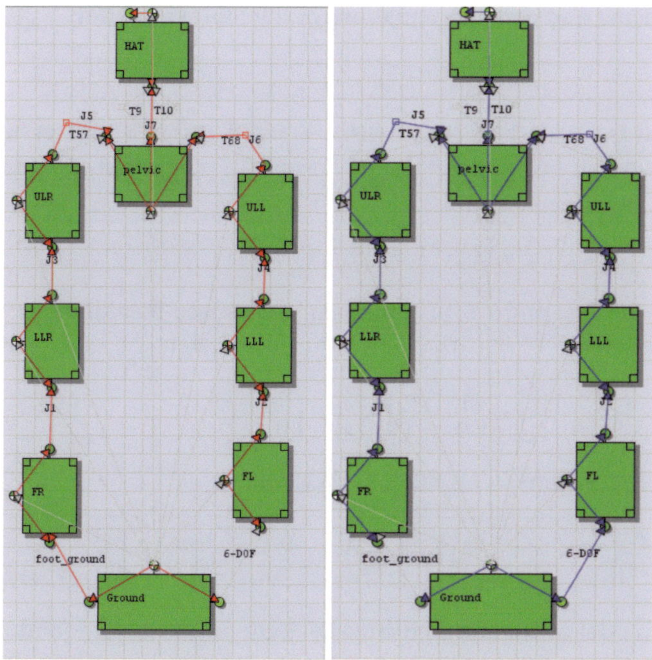

a) R-Tree of the Model b) T-Tree of the Model

Fig. 5. Bipedal model with a weld joint in right foot and a 6-DOF joint in left foot with different R & T tree for state variables.

Model shown in Fig 5 is similar in joint angle and torque definition but differ in T-tree and R-tree and 6-DOF joint for left foot. We join one foot with ground as weld joint and other as a 6-DOF joint, which introduces more variables of translation in the model. Adopting the different T-tree (reference of translational variables to the grouns) and R-tree (reference of rotational variables to the ground) for the model will result in three translational variables of left foot position to appear in the state equations. Fig 5a shows the bipedal model with R tree and Fig 5b shows the T-tree of the same model. This configuration and the additional three variables will results in three holonomic (algebraic) constraints in the system. This scheme is better than free foot scheme because of holonomic constraints which are the part of a physiological human model. This model does not move from its position for a gait cycle due to the restriction of a weld joint. The system has 10 degrees of freedom and it is modeled using 13 generalized coordinates coupled by 3 algebraic constraints.

4.1 Mathematical Representation

Let $\vec{z}(t) = [\vec{p}(t) \quad \vec{x}(t)]$ be the vector of left foot position variable $\vec{p}(t)$ and joint angles $\vec{x}(t)$, and $\vec{\tau}(t)$ be the vector of joint torques, where

$$\begin{aligned} \vec{p}(t) &= \vec{p} = [p_1 \quad p_2 \quad p_3]^T \\ \vec{x}(t) &= \vec{x} = [x_1 \quad x_2 \quad \cdots \quad x_{10}]^T \\ \vec{\tau}(t) &= \vec{\tau} = [T_1 \quad T_2 \quad \cdots \quad T_{10}]^T \end{aligned} \tag{7}$$

This modeling scheme also generate equations of the following form

$$M(\vec{z},\dot{\vec{z}}) \cdot \ddot{\vec{z}} = F(\vec{z},\dot{\vec{z}},\vec{\tau}) \tag{8}$$

Where $M = M(\vec{z},\dot{\vec{z}})$ is a 13 x 13 inertia matrix, $F = F(\vec{z},\dot{\vec{z}},\vec{\tau})$ is a 13x1 vector which contains external load, quadratic velocity terms and torques. The system of equations can also be represented as

$$\ddot{\vec{z}} = M^{-1} \cdot F = f(\vec{z},\dot{\vec{z}},\vec{\tau}) = f \tag{9}$$

Eq (9) represents the system in 13x1 nonlinear state-space formulations with 13 nonlinear functions. This system can be linearized for controller design and other analysis as

$$\begin{bmatrix} \ddot{\vec{z}} \\ \dot{\vec{z}} \end{bmatrix} = \begin{bmatrix} A_1 & A_2 \\ 0 & I \end{bmatrix} \cdot \begin{bmatrix} \dot{\vec{z}} \\ \vec{z} \end{bmatrix} + \begin{bmatrix} B_1 \\ 0 \end{bmatrix} \cdot \vec{\tau} \tag{10}$$

Where A_1, A_2 are 13x13 matrices and B_1 is a 13x10 matrix as

$$[A_1]_{ij} = \left.\frac{\partial f_i}{\partial \dot{z}_j}\right|_{z=z_e,\tau=u_e} \qquad [A_2]_{ij} = \left.\frac{\partial f_i}{\partial z_j}\right|_{z=z_e,\tau=u_e} \qquad [B]_{ij} = \left.\frac{\partial f_i}{\partial \tau_j}\right|_{z=z_e,\tau=u_e} \qquad i,j=1..10 \tag{11}$$

We linearize the model at standing posture i.e. joint angles z_e and joint torques u_e are the equilibrium position where $\ddot{\vec{z}} = 0$ from Eq (10). In this model, all joint angles are local or relative between two respective bodies, gravity is in negative y-axis and height in positive y-axis, so all joint angles are zero at standing posture due to collinear body frames. However, we solve for u_e at these angles to obtain $\ddot{\vec{z}} = 0$. This model produces pair of eigenvalues in right and left plane and thus an unstable model, which requires a controller design to stabilize this system.

4.2 Holonomic Constraints

Holonomic constraints are represented as closed forms of nonlinear algebraic functions and in bipedal model; these constraints represent the closed form of distance between the two ankle joints in x, y, z- directions. In this model, there are three holonomic constraints for position variables and three for velocity variables, which are also Scleronomous constraints i.e. doesn't depend on time explicitly. The position constraints for this bipedal system are represented as

$$\begin{aligned} -p_1 + C_1(\vec{x}) &= 0 \\ -p_2 + C_2(\vec{x}) &= 0 \\ -p_3 + C_3(\vec{x}) &= 0 \end{aligned} \tag{12}$$

Vector form representation of position and velocity constraints are given as

$$\begin{aligned} -\vec{p} + \vec{C}_p(\vec{x}) &= 0 \\ -\dot{\vec{p}} + \vec{C}_v(\vec{x}) &= 0 \end{aligned} \tag{13}$$

First and third constraints represent that the distance between feet should be equal to pelvic length in x and z directions respectively, because of one weld joint, and no frontal movement in ankle and knee joints. Second constraints maintain that the length of both legs should be equal in y-direction for any movement. Velocity constraints are the time derivatives of position constraints. These constrains are useful because these require to be satisfied during any movement profile to maintain the physiological distance between right and left feet. On the other hand it also adds zero eigenvalues in open loop system equal to number of position and velocity constraints. Also, this system requires a special controller which doesn't violate the constraint surface(equations) during the movement.

4.3 Decoupling of Linearized System

A linear system given in Eq(10) represents a 26th order system with 3 left foot position and velocity variables, 10 joints angles and velocities and 10 input torques to the joints. The order of state variables are given in Eq (7) and it has 20 pairs of nonzero eigenvalues in left and right half planes and six zero eigenvalues due to six holonomic (position and velocity) constraints in the system. It is challenging to find a controller design which doesn't violate the constraints during movement simulation. Iqbal et al. (1994) discussed the decoupling of constraints for bipedal model with only frontal plane angles, De Sapio and Khatib (2005) presented a decoupled controller design for holonomic constrained systems and furthermore, Hemami and Wyman (2007) discussed in details about decoupled design schemes for rigid bodies. We decouple the constrained system from unconstrained system to find the better control strategy for required task. Eq (13) shows us that in constraints equations left foot position and velocity variables occurs explicitly, while joint angle variables are used as nonlinear functions. So, we change the order of state variables for decoupling as

$$\begin{bmatrix} \vec{p} \\ \dot{\vec{p}} \\ \vec{x} \\ \dot{\vec{x}} \end{bmatrix} = [R_{26}] \cdot \begin{bmatrix} \vec{p} \\ \vec{x} \\ \dot{\vec{p}} \\ \dot{\vec{x}} \end{bmatrix} \tag{14}$$

Where R_{26} is a rotation matrix and linearized system will take a form as follows

$$\begin{bmatrix} \ddot{\vec{p}} \\ \dot{\vec{p}} \\ \ddot{\vec{x}} \\ \dot{\vec{x}} \end{bmatrix} = \begin{bmatrix} A_p & A_{px} \\ A_{xp} & A \end{bmatrix} \cdot \begin{bmatrix} \dot{\vec{p}} \\ \vec{p} \\ \dot{\vec{x}} \\ \vec{x} \end{bmatrix} + \begin{bmatrix} B_p \\ B \end{bmatrix} \cdot \vec{\tau} \tag{15}$$

Now, we decouple the constrained (translational) system from unconstrained (rotational) system, which is to separate the $\vec{p}, \dot{\vec{p}}$ from $\vec{x}, \dot{\vec{x}}$ variables. As $A_{xp} = 0$, and 20 x 6 matrix so we can decouple the systems as

$$\begin{bmatrix} \ddot{\vec{p}} \\ \dot{\vec{p}} \end{bmatrix} = A_p \cdot \begin{bmatrix} \dot{\vec{p}} \\ \vec{p} \end{bmatrix} + B_p \cdot \vec{\tau}$$
$$A_p = \begin{bmatrix} 0 & 0 \\ I_3 & 0 \end{bmatrix} \quad B_p = \begin{bmatrix} B_2 \\ 0 \end{bmatrix} \tag{16}$$

and

$$\begin{bmatrix} \ddot{\vec{x}} \\ \dot{\vec{x}} \end{bmatrix} = A \cdot \begin{bmatrix} \dot{\vec{x}} \\ \vec{x} \end{bmatrix} + B \cdot \vec{\tau}$$
$$A = \begin{bmatrix} A_{11} & A_{12} \\ I & 0 \end{bmatrix} \quad B = \begin{bmatrix} B_3 \\ 0 \end{bmatrix} \tag{17}$$

Where A_p and B_p are 6x6 and 6x10 matrices respectively with structures given in Eq (16). Similarly, A and B are 20x20 and 20x10 matrices respectively with structures given in Eq (17). A_{px} is a nonzero matrix which represents linearized form of constraints and will impose restriction on controller design. The joint torque vector is computed from a decoupled optimal controller design scheme. We discussed this scheme in Mughal and Iqbal (2009) with details of decoupling conditions to satisfy the holonomic constraints.

$$\vec{\tau}(t) = -K \cdot \begin{bmatrix} \dot{\vec{x}} \\ \vec{x} \end{bmatrix} - K_p \cdot \begin{bmatrix} \dot{\vec{p}} \\ \vec{p} \end{bmatrix} + u_e \tag{18}$$

This torque input can be used with nonlinear model for stable STS movement

4.4 Simulation and Results

We simulate the nonlinear model given by Eq(8) with decoupoled optimal controller design of Eq(18). We simulate the nonlinear model with reference trajectories at all joint angles and their respective velocities as well as left foot position and velocity variables. An error e(t) computed from output of nonlinear model with respect to desired (reference) response is an input to the feedback controllers as given in Eq (17). We use synthsized reference trajectories for angles and translational variables for entire STS movement as discussed in detail by Mughal and Iqbal (2008a). The output of this controller in addition to static torques u_e drives the nonlinear model, and stabilizes it from sitting to standing posture. Fig. 6 shows the profiles of ankle, knee hip-pelvic and pelvic-HAT joint angles. Blue solid lines represent the angular profiles and red dashed lines represent the reference trajectories in this simulation. It is clear that angular profiles follow the reference trajectories especially knee angles which has different position at sitting and standing positions. Fig. 7 shows the movement profiles of left foot translational variables, and it is evident that only joint torque controller can regulate the foot position effectively. Holonomic constraints from Eq(13) generates the refrence trajectoris for left foot translational variables from anuglar reference tarjectories, which shows almost negiligible movement in foot during entire STS task. There is no seperate control law for the foot position control and it is totally dependent upon joint angles. This shows that holonomic constrainst not only maintain physiological balance in the model but also useful for the movement coodination between joint angles and foot position. Fig. 7 also shows that three position based holonomic constraints from Eq(12) are not violated, which ensure the physiological balalnce during the movement. This model is more realsitic from unconstrianted model for STS movement of healthy subjects and stroke pateients due to imposed physiological (holonomic) constraints. It still has one weld or 0-DoF joint which doesn't allow any movement in the right foot, but other foot is tracked as 6-DoF joint and its translational movement is indirectly regulated.

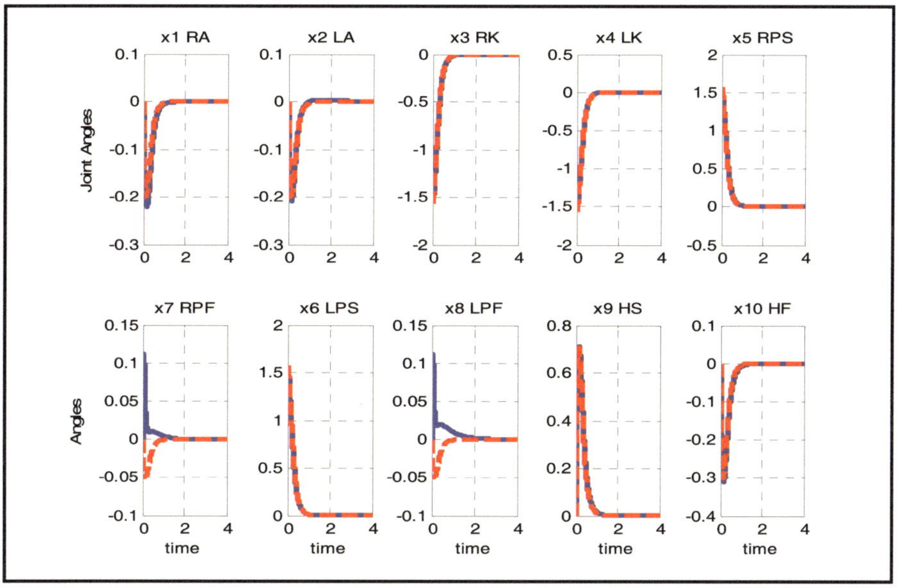

Fig. 6. Movement profiles joint angles in radians (solid blue lines) and their reference trajectories (dashed red lines). R=Right, L=Left, A=Ankle angle, K=Knee angle, P= Pelvic-Hip joint angle, H=HAT-Pelvic joint angle, S=Sagittal plane, F= Frontal plane

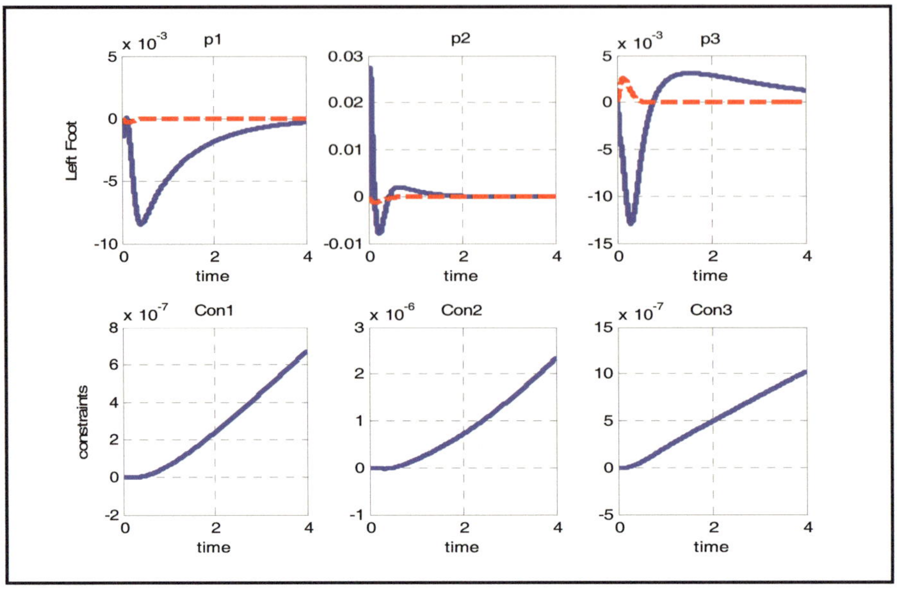

Fig. 7. Movement of a left foot position (m) in x,y,z directions (blue solid lines) with reference trajectories (red dashed lines) and constraints violation during movement

5. Symmetrical Angular Tree Model

Asymmetrical model with both R-tree and T-tree from different foot cannot produce symmetrical torques,which are required to study for healthy subjects. Now, we purpose a design with symmetry along R-tree or for joint angles and their respective torques, and asymmetry is only caused by T-tree and feet connection to the ground.

5.1 Twist Joint and Modeling Equations

Weld joint is not an ideal joint and though it restricts motion, yet an additional number of constraints don't allow us to work in this scheme. Now, we model a right foot with a revolute joint representing twist with y-axis as axis of rotation, which allow moving one end of foot in y direction connecting toes (other end) to the ground. Generating R-tree and T-tree with twist will bring twist variables in state equations with only 5 constraints but this model is redundant as compare to number of degrees in the system and not very different to previous model in Sec 4. So, we model a twist-joint right foot and a free left foot with a T-tree from it instead of pelvic joint.

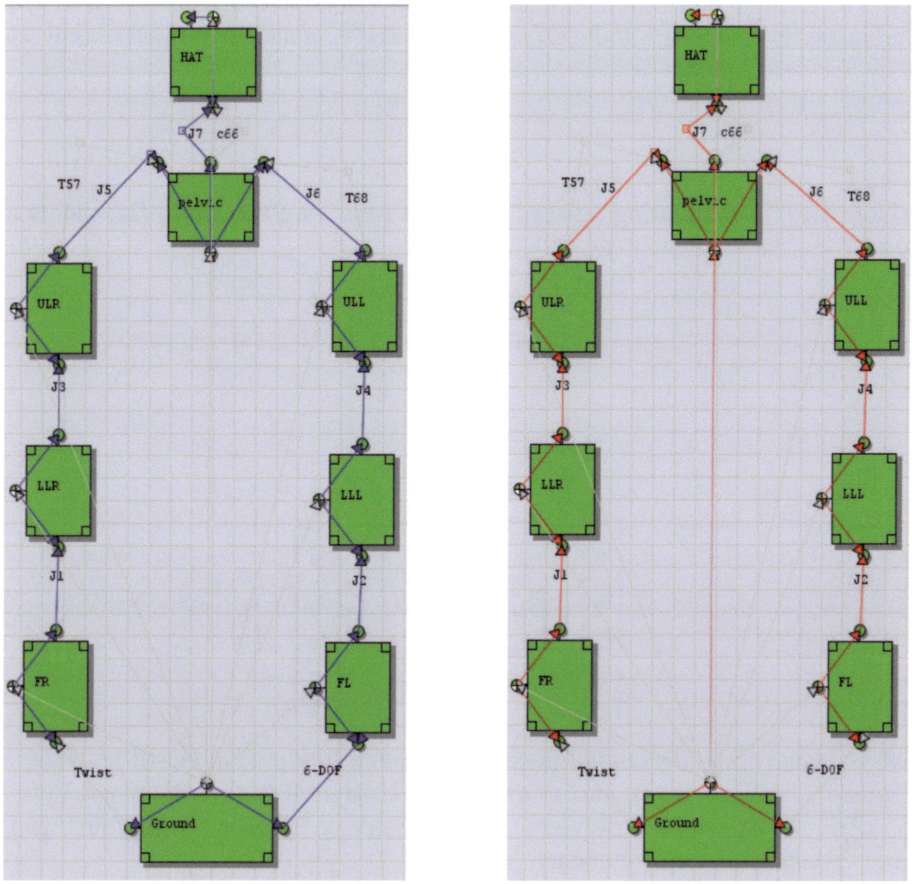

a) T-tree (blue lines) b) R-Tree (red lines)

Fig. 8. Bipedal Model with a 6-DoF left foot and a twist joint in a right foot

Fig 8 shows a model with different R-tree and T-tree from ground to each frame in the model. This create a model with a symmetry as well as asymmetry with 5 reactions as five holonomic constraints with 16 generalized (position) coordinates in the system. The structure of state space formulation remains the same, whereas left foot translational variables and pelvic rotation variables ζ_p, η_p, ξ_p. appear in the formulation. This model has similar structure of model with 13 generalized coordinates discussed in Sec 4 with three additional pelvic rotational variables. A general structure of nonlinear model is given as

$$\begin{bmatrix} \ddot{\vec{p}} \\ \ddot{\vec{x}} \\ \ddot{\vec{r}}_p \\ \dot{\vec{p}} \\ \dot{\vec{x}} \\ \dot{\vec{r}}_p \end{bmatrix} = f\left(\vec{p}, \vec{x}, \overrightarrow{r_p}, \dot{\vec{p}}, \dot{\vec{x}}, \dot{\vec{r}}_p, \vec{\tau}\right) \quad (19)$$

Where $\vec{p}$ is a vector of left translational foot position variables for p_1, p_2, and p_3 in x, y, and z direction respectively similair to Eq (7) and Eq(16) and $\vec{r}_p$ is a vector of pelvic angles.

$$\vec{r}_p = \begin{bmatrix} \zeta_p \\ \eta_p \\ \xi_p \end{bmatrix} \tag{20}$$

Linearizing Eq (19) at standing posture and after rotation given in Eq (21) yields a linear state space formulation given in Eq (22).

$$\begin{bmatrix} \dot{\vec{p}} \\ \dot{\vec{x}} \\ \dot{\vec{r}}_p \\ \vec{p} \\ \vec{x} \\ \vec{r}_p \end{bmatrix} \rightarrow \begin{bmatrix} \dot{\vec{p}} \\ \vec{p} \\ \dot{\vec{r}}_p \\ \vec{r}_p \\ \dot{\vec{x}} \\ \vec{x} \end{bmatrix} \tag{21}$$

$$\begin{bmatrix} \ddot{\vec{p}} \\ \dot{\vec{p}} \\ \ddot{\vec{r}}_p \\ \dot{\vec{r}}_p \\ \ddot{\vec{x}} \\ \dot{\vec{x}} \end{bmatrix} = \begin{bmatrix} A_p & A_{pr} & A_{px} \\ A_{rp} & A_r & A_{rx} \\ A_{xp} & A_{xr} & A_x \end{bmatrix} \cdot \begin{bmatrix} \dot{\vec{p}} \\ \vec{p} \\ \dot{\vec{r}}_p \\ \vec{r}_p \\ \dot{\vec{x}} \\ \vec{x} \end{bmatrix} + \begin{bmatrix} B_p \\ B_r \\ B \end{bmatrix} \cdot \vec{\tau} \tag{22}$$

Now we obtained three decoupled linearized system, one translation of left foot, one for pelvic rotational joints and the one for joint angles in sagittal and frontal plane. Both A_p and A_r represents the 6th order linearized system matrices for foot translational and pelvic rotational system respectively given as

$$\begin{bmatrix} \ddot{\vec{p}} \\ \dot{\vec{p}} \end{bmatrix} = A_p \cdot \begin{bmatrix} \dot{\vec{p}} \\ \vec{p} \end{bmatrix} + B_p \cdot \vec{\tau} \tag{23}$$

$$\begin{bmatrix} \ddot{\vec{r}}_p \\ \dot{\vec{r}}_p \end{bmatrix} = A_r \cdot \begin{bmatrix} \dot{\vec{r}}_p \\ \vec{r}_p \end{bmatrix} + \vec{\tau} \tag{24}$$

The other system is for only joint angle both in sagittal and frontal plane with similiar sturcuture and varaibles given in Eq(17) given as

$$\begin{bmatrix} \ddot{\vec{x}} \\ \dot{\vec{x}} \end{bmatrix} = \begin{bmatrix} A_1 & A_2 \\ 0 & I \end{bmatrix} \cdot \begin{bmatrix} \dot{\vec{x}} \\ \vec{x} \end{bmatrix} + \begin{bmatrix} B \\ 0 \end{bmatrix} \cdot \vec{\tau} \tag{25}$$

This modeling scheme has 5 holonomic constraints and this decoupling separates the joint variables from other variables and doesnot decouple all holonomic constraints in one subsystem so that the other subsystem is free of holonomic constraints. A full system is 32nd order with only 10 zero eigenvalues, and the system in Eq (23) has 6 zeros eigenvalues and these are due to three position constraints between feet. The pelvic rotational system in Eq (24) has only two zero eigenvalues due to pelvic angular constraints. The system in Eq (25) has also two zero eigenvalues one due to a symmtrical angular constraints in right and left limbs. Controller design becomes difficult due to holonomic constraints and symmetry because both of these add singularities to the system. This controller gain matrice in Eq(26) are obtained by satisfing stability requirements of linear decoupled models and holonomic constraints.

$$\vec{\tau}(t) = -K \cdot \begin{bmatrix} \dot{\vec{x}} \\ \vec{x} \end{bmatrix} - K_p \cdot \begin{bmatrix} \dot{\vec{p}} \\ \vec{p} \end{bmatrix} + -K_r \cdot \begin{bmatrix} \dot{\vec{r}}_p \\ \vec{r}_p \end{bmatrix} + u_e \tag{26}$$

5.2 Simulation and Results

We simulate the nonlinear system given in Eq (19) with a decoupled controller designs for three linear models and further into sagittal and frontal plane by using hybrid physiological cost optimization method. We use decoupled optimal controller design scheme which is complex in nature due to many analytical neceassary conditions from algebric constraintrs. We discueed these schemes in detail in Mughal and Iqbal (2008b), for decoupling conditions, hybrid physiological cost optimization and reference torques u_e. In this chapter we only focus on bipedal modeling with different possiblities without discussing the details of controller design scheme. Fig. 9 shows the angular profiles for sagittal and frontal angles for nonlinear model Eq(19) with feedback optimal controller design given by Eq(26). The magnitude of frontal plane angles shown in Fig. 9 are less as compare to results in Fig. 6 but still not following the desired response as sagittal angles do. We have three more variables of pelvic angle in state space and Fig. 10 shows the profiles of 3 left foot variables p_1, p_2, and p_3 and three pelvis angular variables (due to R-Tree) ζ_p, η_p and ξ_p. First three position holonomic constraints provides reference trajectories for a left foot position and we selected an arbitrary reference profiles for pelvic joint variables. These variables shows the movement which are more closely related to frontal plane angles. This overall scheme shows improved profiles due to more control over the STS movement with more variables for cost optimizations, and a twist joint. There are some differences in the right and left ankle trajectories and overall angles in sagittal plane are symmetrical in response.

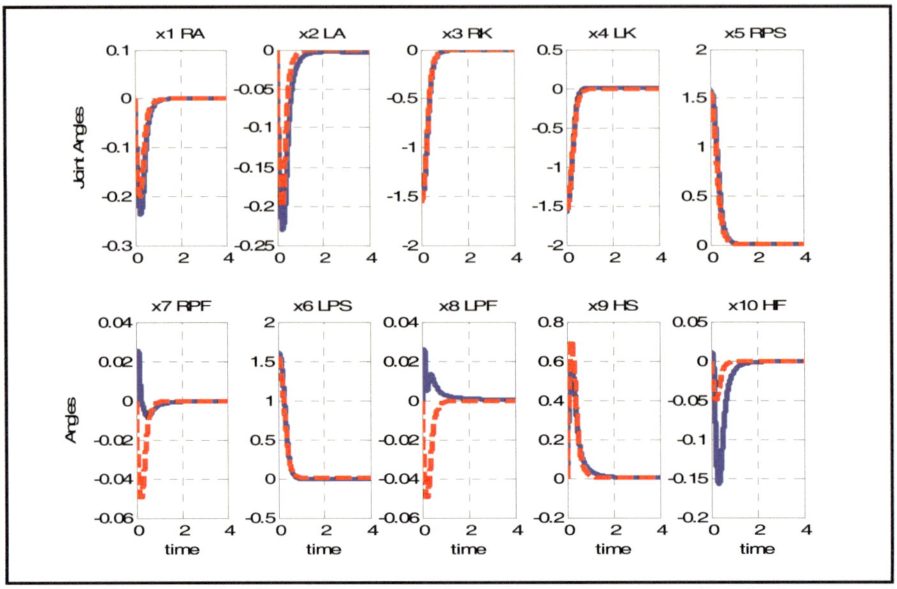

Fig. 9. Profiles of joint angles in radians with three decoupled controller designs, a twist joint in right foot and a free left foot

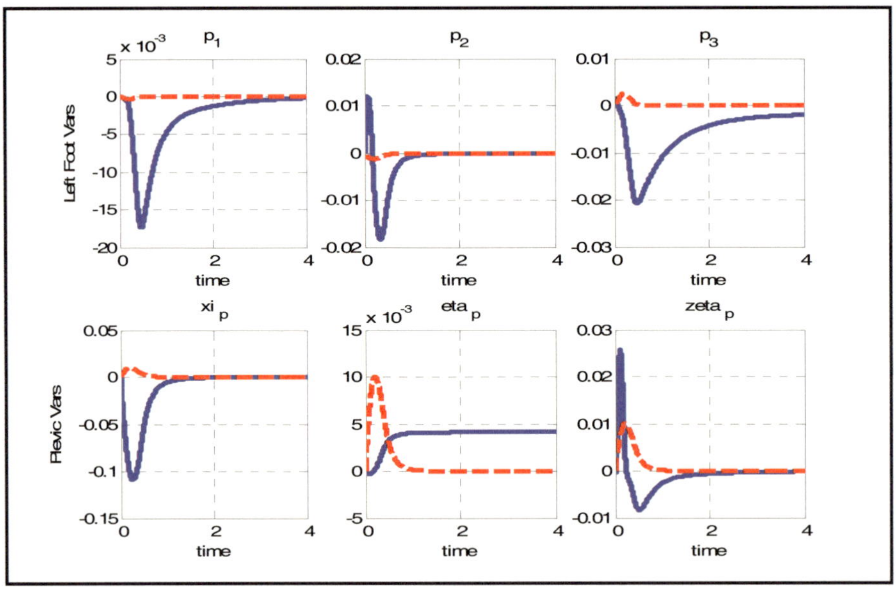

Fig. 10. Profiles of left foot (m) and pelvic joint state variables (radians) given by Eq (6.14) with reference profiles (dashed red lines)

Figure 11. shows the profiles of CoM movement and head movement in x, y and z axis. x-CoM and x-head positions settles at ½ distance between the feet, y-CoM settles at length reaching midway in pelvic height and y-head settles at total body height, initially it goes little down and this shows that the head for a small time goes down and then raises up in order to perform STS movement. Whereas, both z-CoM and z-head settles to 0 at steady state, that is a person in sitting or standing posture with a right foot on origin and a left feet on x-axis. Left foot position profiles in Fig 10 also explain the movement of CoM and HP during the movement which are not significantly large in magnitude but does affect the movement profiles. Similarly pelvic rotation angles specifically ζ_p, and ξ_p also account for their profiles during this task with small amount of torque components in the system. These physiological results of kinematic variables of CoM position and head position show the relavancy and applicability of this modeling scheme for STS manuver.

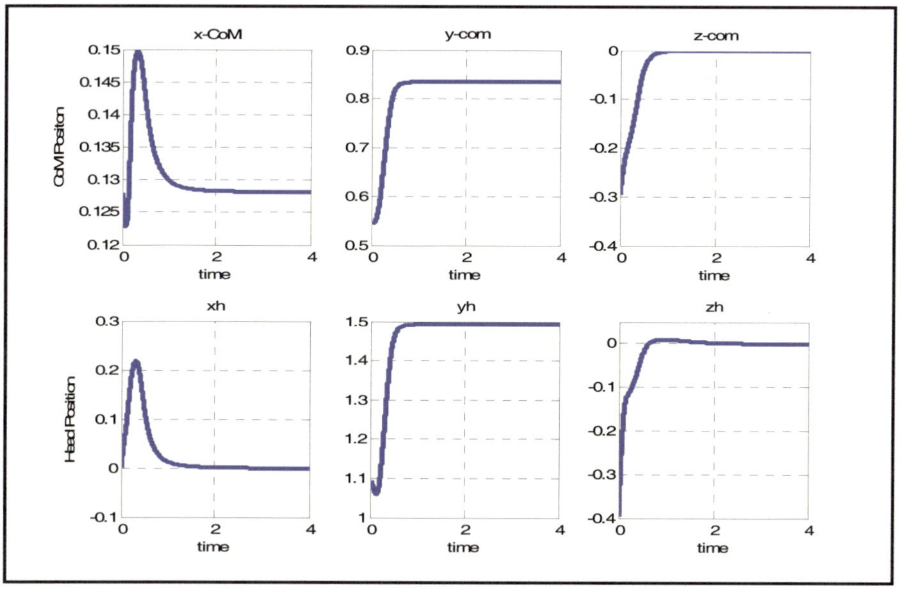

Fig. 11. CoM and HP profiles (m) during STS maneuver for system given by Eq (6.10)

6. Symmetrical Translational-Tree and Rotational-Tree Model

Creating a symmetrical model has many limitations and constraints due to the redundancy in the bipedal design. If we join both feet as weld joint and try to work with any T-tree or R-tree configuration, this model has many constraints and at stable standing (equilibrium) position, model has singularities and so unsolvable. Using the same scheme discussed in Section 3 and 4, and joining both as the weld (0-DOF) joint, instead of a free or 6-DOF left foot, generates 6 algebraic constraints with 10 generalized coordinates and with 4 general degree of freedom, this model is redundant and a singular linear matrix is unsolvable at standing posture. Now, we introduce another scheme in order to obtain computable symmetrical model. Feet as weld joints has no degree of freedom and it generates only reaction variables and in other words in a close chain system, there are either 3 or 6 reaction variables depending upon R-tree or T-tree configuration. With both weld feet in this scheme generates 12 holonomic constraints with 16 generalized coordinates and this system cannot be linearized at standing posture. The reason for asymmetrical torques at both right and left side comes from an engineering model, which starts solving for torques starting from right ankle and reaches to left ankle at the end. We now introduce a model with symmtrical R-tree and T-tree with aysmmtrical joint beteen ground and feet. In this case we try to reduce asymmtry due to engineering modeling schemes by allowing more variables in the system.

6.1. Feet Joints and Pelvic Variables

Now, we model a right foot with a revolute joint representing tilt with z-axis as axis of rotation, and a left foot as a revolute joint representing twist with y-axis as axis of rotation. This twist and tilt allows to move a feet in z and y direction and generates less constraints.

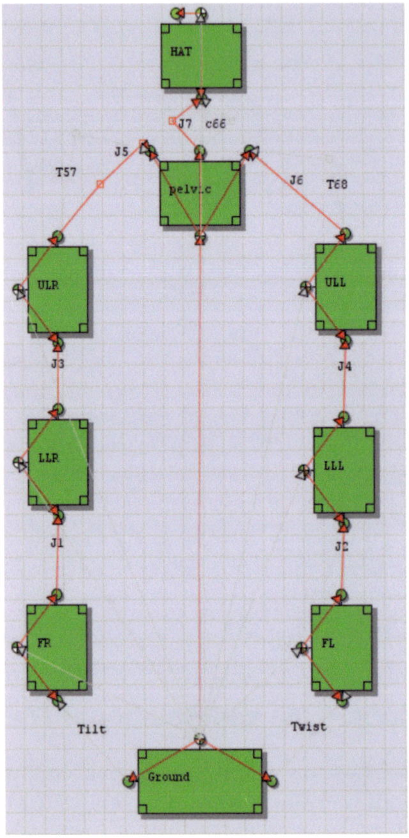

Fig. 12. 3D bipedal model with tilt and twist in both feet, and R-tree and T-tree from pelvis center and 6 additional state variables.

Generating R-tree and T-tree with twist and tilt will bring either twist or tilt variables in state equations with only 5 constraints but this model is still asymmetrical and redundant as compare to number of degrees in the system. Twist and tilt allows more movement and produces fewer constraints but for devloping a symmetrical model, we need to generate symmetrical behavior for right and left ankle, knee and hip-pelvic behavior with similar configuration of R-tree and T-tree. Removing R-tree and T-tree from tilt and twist joints of both right and left feet respectively, and adding pelvis position variables for translational and rotational degrees generates a symmetrical model as shown in Fig. 12. Both R-tree and T-tree join pelvis with the ground and follow the path symmetrical for left and right limbs till ankle joints. There are tilt and twist joints at right and left foot respectively and these joint variables does not appear in state equation because no T-tree and R-tree in these places. Allowing T-tree from pelvis generates three translational DoF in state equation as x_p, y_p, z_p for position of pelvis in x, y, and z directions. Similarly, R-tree through pelvis generates three rotational DoF to the state equation as ζ_p, η_p, ξ_p angular variables. There are 10 angular variables in sagittal and frontal planes and the system has 16 generalized (position) DoF with 10 constraints. There are also 10 reaction variables of 3 Ground Reaction Forces (GRF) and 2 Moments in each foot. In a right foot with a tilt joint, reaction moments are in y and x direction, whereas in left foot reaction moments in x and z direction for twist in the foot.

6.2 Modeling Equations and Decoupling

This above modeling scheme has 16 generalized coordinates for position variables and state space system is as follows

$$\begin{bmatrix} \ddot{x}_p \\ \ddot{y}_p \\ \ddot{z}_p \\ \ddot{\vec{x}} \\ \ddot{\zeta}_p \\ \ddot{\eta}_p \\ \ddot{\xi}_p \end{bmatrix} = f\left(x_p, y_p, z_p, \vec{x}, \zeta_p, \eta_p, \xi_p, \dot{x}_p, \dot{y}_p, \dot{z}_p, \dot{\vec{x}}, \dot{\zeta}_p, \dot{\eta}_p, \dot{\xi}_p, \vec{\tau}\right) \tag{27}$$

Eq (27) shows three translational coordinates x_p, y_p, z_p, and three angular coordinates ζ_p, η_p, ξ_p of pelvis with their respective derivatives for velocities and accelerations. There is a vector $\vec{x}$ for 10 joint angular coordinates with 7 in sagittal plane and three in frontal plane with exactly same configuration as discussed in previous sections. A torque vector $\vec{\tau}$ represents 10 joint torques for their respective joint angles in sagittal and frontal plane. At sitting position y_p is at combined foot and shank length and at standing posture y_p is at foot, shank and thigh length. Similarly, at sitting position z_p is at negative of thigh length along negative z-axis and zero at standing posture, whereas x_p remains at zero for sitting and standing posture. Rotational angles with respect to ground are at zeros at sitting and standing positions for pelvic center. For sake the of simplicity we represent three translational coordinates as $\vec{d}_p$ vector and three angular coordinates as $\vec{r}_p$ for pelvis as follows

$$\vec{d}_p = \begin{bmatrix} x_p \\ y_p \\ z_p \end{bmatrix} \tag{28}$$

$$\vec{r}_p = \begin{bmatrix} \zeta_p \\ \eta_p \\ \xi_p \end{bmatrix} \tag{29}$$

We linearize this model at standing posture to obtain a state space formulation as follows

$$\begin{bmatrix} \ddot{\vec{d}}_p \\ \ddot{\vec{x}} \\ \ddot{\vec{r}}_p \\ \dot{\vec{d}}_p \\ \dot{\vec{x}} \\ \dot{\vec{r}}_p \end{bmatrix} = [A] \cdot \begin{bmatrix} \dot{\vec{d}}_p \\ \dot{\vec{x}} \\ \dot{\vec{r}}_p \\ \vec{d}_p \\ \vec{x} \\ \vec{r}_p \end{bmatrix} + [B] \cdot \vec{\tau} \tag{30}$$

A and B are 32x32 and 10x32 order state space matrices by linearizing Eq(27) at standing posture. Now we rotate the state space formulation for decoupling the system into joint angles and pelvic translation variables as shown in Eq (31)

$$\begin{bmatrix} \dot{\vec{d}}_p \\ \dot{\vec{x}} \\ \dot{\vec{r}}_p \\ \vec{d}_p \\ \vec{x} \\ \vec{r}_p \end{bmatrix} \rightarrow \begin{bmatrix} \dot{\vec{d}}_p \\ \dot{\vec{r}}_p \\ \vec{d}_p \\ \vec{r}_p \\ \dot{\vec{x}} \\ \vec{x} \end{bmatrix} \tag{31}$$

$$\begin{bmatrix} \ddot{\vec{d}}_p \\ \ddot{\vec{r}}_p \\ \dot{\vec{d}}_p \\ \dot{\vec{r}}_p \\ \ddot{\vec{x}} \\ \dot{\vec{x}} \end{bmatrix} = \begin{bmatrix} A_P & A_{xP} \\ A_{Px} & A_x \end{bmatrix} \cdot \begin{bmatrix} \dot{\vec{d}}_p \\ \dot{\vec{r}}_p \\ \vec{d}_p \\ \vec{r}_p \\ \dot{\vec{x}} \\ \vec{x} \end{bmatrix} + \begin{bmatrix} B_P \\ B \end{bmatrix} \cdot \vec{\tau} \tag{32}$$

Now we obtained two linearized system, one for pelvic variables as

$$\begin{bmatrix} \ddot{\vec{d}}_p \\ \ddot{\vec{r}}_p \\ \dot{\vec{d}}_p \\ \dot{\vec{r}}_p \end{bmatrix} = \begin{bmatrix} A_d & A_{dr} \\ A_{rd} & A_r \end{bmatrix} \cdot \begin{bmatrix} \dot{\vec{d}}_p \\ \dot{\vec{r}}_p \\ \vec{d}_p \\ \vec{r}_p \end{bmatrix} + B_P \cdot \vec{\tau} \tag{33}$$

$$\begin{bmatrix} \ddot{\vec{x}} \\ \dot{\vec{x}} \end{bmatrix} = \begin{bmatrix} A_1 & A_2 \\ 0 & I \end{bmatrix} \cdot \begin{bmatrix} \dot{\vec{x}} \\ \vec{x} \end{bmatrix} + \begin{bmatrix} B \\ 0 \end{bmatrix} \cdot \vec{\tau} \tag{34}$$

Eq (33) has a 12th order decoupled system for $\vec{d}_p$ and $\vec{r}_p$ coordinates and Eq (34) is same as Eq (17) decoupled system. It is difficult to have an optimal controller design for a full 32 order system because A matrix has 20 zero eigenvalues pairs due to 10 generalized holonomic constraints or in total 20 position and velocity constraints for a state space system. For a decoupled optimal controller design, this scheme must follow the analytical necessasry conditions to satisfy the holonomic constraints. It is important to note that this sytem has many constraints and this is not possible to decouple a entire constrainted systems from unconstraiunted system. A linear controller design has two gain matrices for each model given in Eq(33) and Eq (34).

$$\vec{\tau}(t) = -K \cdot \begin{bmatrix} \dot{\vec{x}} \\ \vec{x} \end{bmatrix} - K_{dr} \cdot \begin{bmatrix} \dot{\vec{d}}_p \\ \dot{\vec{r}}_p \\ \vec{d}_p \\ \vec{r}_p \end{bmatrix} + u_e \quad (35)$$

6.3 Simulation for Linear System

We now simulate a system in Eq (30) with controller design given by Eq(35). There is further decoupling of angular components into frontal and sagittal planes to get a better design scheme. Fig. (13) shows the response of state variable vectors in simulated with a linear plant of Eq (30). Sagittal angular profiles behaves as desired as right and left knee angles change from $-\pi/2$ to 0 and right and left hip-pelvic sagittal angles changes from $\pi/2$ to 0 in STS maneuver. Right and left ankle angles and pelvic-Hat sagittal angle also settles at zero starting from the same value. Right and left hip-pelvic frontal angles are not affected by the controller and remain at very low zero value, and pelvic-HAT frontal angle settles at 0.008 rads. For pelvis DoF x_p, y_p η_p and ξ_p are also not affected by the controller and remains at starting values. Change are observable in z_p and ζ_p profiles, where, z_p settles at 0.25.

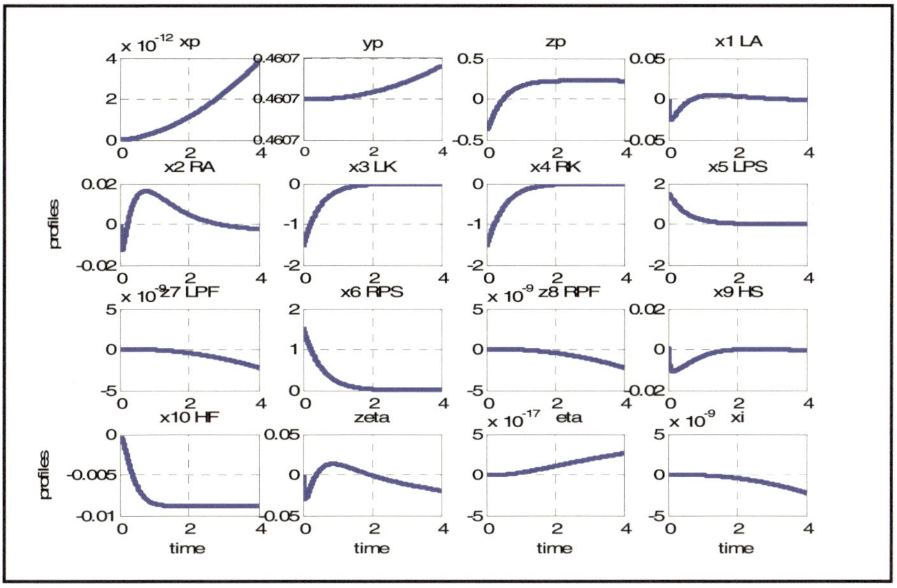

Fig. 13. Movement profiles pelvic variables and joint angles for linear symmetrical model R=Right, L=Left, A=Ankle angle, K=Knee angle, P= Pelvic-Hip joint angle, H=HAT-Pelvic joint angle, S=Sagittal plane, F= Frontal plane

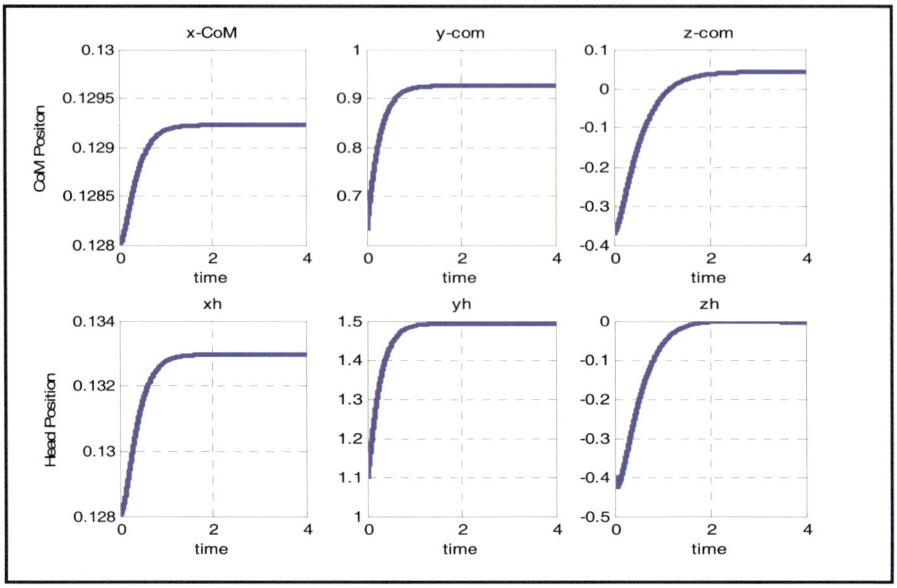

Fig. 14. CoM and HP profiles (m) for a linearized 32nd order model for STS maneuver

Figure 14. shows the CoM and HP profiles for this simulation of STS maneuver and it shows changes in x-axis for both profiles. Because of tilt in the right foot, CoM position and head frame in x-direction settles at slightly different values. Settlement of z-CoM at 0.05 instead of 0, is due to z_p settling at nonzero value. However, y and z axis profiles of head position shows the physiological correctness of STS maneuver, which can also be verified from knee and hip-pelvic sagittal angular profiles. Besides physiologically correct STS maneuver due to angular profiles and movement of head, this model has lot of limitations as many variables doesn't take any affect due to controller design. y_p doesn't move from sitting position, frontal angles doesn't show properly regulated performance. Due to 20 zero eigenvalues in 32nd order system and the rank of controllability matrix is only 4, which shows that the controller design doesn't regulate the states. An advantage of decoupling of a system is that it increase rank of decoupled system as compare to full order system. Symmetrical distribution of left and right side limbs for torques or gain scheduling may require either very high gains or some other design scheme to control the nonlinear plant.

7. Stability Analysis of Nonlinear System

The nonlinear unconstrained system or a nonlinear constrained system are stable with feedback controller design The nonlinear system for both constrained and unconstrained system is given as (36) representing either of Eq(3), Eq(9), Eq(19) or Eq(27).

$$\ddot{\vec{x}} = M^{-1} \cdot F = f(\vec{x}, \dot{\vec{x}}, \vec{\tau}) = f \tag{36}$$

After linearization this can be represented as Eq (37) same as either of Eq(4), Eq(10), Eq(22) or Eq(30).

$$\Delta\dot{x} = A\Delta x + B\Delta u$$
$$A = \left.\frac{\partial f}{\partial x}\right|_{x=x_e, u=u_e} \qquad B = \left.\frac{\partial f}{\partial u}\right|_{x=x_e, u=u_e} \tag{37}$$

$$A\Delta x + B\Delta u = 0 \rightarrow x \rightarrow x_e, u \rightarrow u_e \tag{38}$$

The nonlinear representation after Taylor's series approximation is given as

$$\dot{x} = Ax + Bu + g(x) \tag{39}$$

We adopt Lyapunov's Indirect Method to check for the stability of nonlinear system. According to this method, a stability point is tested for the stability of origin i.e. in the small neighborhood of equilibrium point a nonlinear system is approximated as linearized system provided the following condition holds.

$$\lim_{\|x\| \rightarrow 0} \frac{\|g(x_e, u_e)\|}{\|x\|} = 0 \tag{40}$$

g(x) can be determined as a difference between output of linearized system in MATLAB and a nonlinear system, and this term given by Eq(40) is zero. This leaves the stability to be determined by *A* and *B* matrices. In this bipedal model, eigenvalues of *A* matrix for an open loop system are in pair in right and left half planes, and thus a unstable system. If all the eigenvalues are in left half plane then this system is an asymptotically stable system. The controller designs for unconstrained system and constrained system with either LQR, H_2 or H_∞ optimization stabilizes the system and places all the eigenvalues in left half plane. However, in the case of decoupled controller design, this should also meet the additional criterion to satisfy the holonomic constarints.

8. Conclusion

A free foot model provides a simple model with no holonomic constraints. Designing control design schemes is relatively easy. Simulation results in Fig.3 and Fig. 4 display well controlled results settled within 2 seconds at steady state values. The left foot moves up to 3 cm in z direction which is also due to the more frontal angles movement. The free foot model does not impose restrictions on the left (free) foot to be on ground or any physiological constraints to be satisfied. In this case, the free foot model does not provide more physiological relevancy even though there is a well-behaved head position profiles for STS maneuvers. The second model with three holonomic constraints has more physiological relevance due to three holonomic constraints on the left foot position. These holonomic constraints maintain the distance between two feet in x, y, and z directions and due to these there are six eigenvalues of the system at zero. Decoupling the constrained system from the unconstrained system provides more flexibility on controller design. However, this scheme generates higher torques due to high controller gains to satisfy the holonomic constraints during simulation. Symmetrical systems with holonomic constraints are redundant with lots of singularities, which make system more complex, and an optimal controller design becomes a difficult task. On the other hand asymmetrical systems have singularities only due to holonomic constraints and an optimal controller design scheme for a nonlinear model is easily achievable.

In sec 5, we allow a twist joint instead of a weld joint which provides a model similar to the model in sec 4, with additional variables of pelvic joints. This also increases the size of the system to the 32nd order from the 26th order system with total of 5 holonomic (position) constraints and 10 joint torques. A twist in left joint allows with symmetrical R-tree to both feet from the pelvic joint, but does not provide symmetrical torque. Allowing for a symmetrical T-tree produces a model with no holonomic constraints like a free foot model which does not serve the purpose very well. A tilt in the right foot also provides a similar system but with a twist joint we achieved better results and thus provided this design scheme. It also explores the possibility of active torque components to this modeling framework, which requires the adaptation of fewer active components for better angular profiles. A weld joint or 0-DoF joint may not be a good assumption for STS which also adds more constraints to the system. On the other hand a twist or tilt joint provides better assumption with one less holonomic constraint to the system. A full symmetrical model discussed in Sec 6 has 20 singularities for a 32nd order system and decoupling allows improving the controllability of the system by improving rank of decoupled controllability matrices. Linear decoupled controller designs which fulfill all the necessary conditions for a large nonlinear system in Eq (30) is not very easily achievable. In this study we provide results of linear systems which show the applicability of symmetrical design with tilt and twist joints in the right and left feet respectively. Allowing both weld joints or both tilt and both twist joints result in overall singular system which is not available for further analysis and controller design.

In future research, other controller design schemes which solve this system may result in more effective designs. Also, additional controllers to optimize twist and tilt will provide an additional measure to achieve specific results. Effects of twist and tilt joints can also be useful to study instead of weld joint (0-DoF) at the left foot (model in sec 3 and 4) without pelvic joint variables. There are several other schemes which have potential for analysis and controller design, like a full symmetrical model with nonlinear controller design. More controller inputs other than only joint torques such as control over twist and tilt joints or control of pelvis frame with external controller design may result in better understanding of the symmetrical model. This modling scheme with physiological cost optimization (Mughal and Iqbal 2008c), will also produce a better design of the STS maneuver. These schemes provide an overall mathematical and analytical framework with optimal controller design to further study the human voluntary movement (like STS) for specific and required applications. There are myriads of possibilities and including all of these in a one model will results in much large and complex system, which may also be a redundant for a simple voluntary movement task.

9. References

Anderson, F. C. & Pandy, M. G. (2001). Dynamic Optimization of Human Walking, *Journal of biomechanical Engineering*, Vol. 123, (October 2001).

Barin, K. (1989). Evaluation of a generalized model of human postural dynamics and control in the sagittal plane, *Biological Cybernetics* Vol. 61, (1989) pp 37-50.

De Sapio, V. & Khatib, O. (2005). Operation space control of multi-body systems with explicit holonomic constraints, *Proceedings of the 2005 IEEE International conference on robotics and automation*, Barcelona Spain, April (2005).

Hemami, H. & Jaswa V. C. (1978). On the three link model of the dynamics of standing up and sitting down, *IEEE transaction on Systems Man and Cybernetics*, Vol. 8, (1978) pp115-120.

Hemami, H. & Wyman B. (2007). Rigid Body Dynamics, Constraints, and Inverses, *Journal of Applied Mechanics*, Vol. 4, (Jan 2007), pp47-56.

Iqbal, K. & Pai Y. (2000). Predicted region of stability for balance recovery: motion at the knee joint can improve termination of forward movement, *Journal of Biomechanics*, Vol. 33, (2000), pp1619-1627.

Iqbal, K.& Roy, (2004). A. Stabilizing PID Controllers for an inverted pendulum-based biomechanical model with position, velocity, and force feedback, *ASME Transactions on Biomechanical Engineering*, Vol. 126, (2004), pp838-843.

Iqbal. K., Kallel, H. and Hemami, H., (1994). Linear decoupling controllers for constrained dynamic systems, *International Journal of Control*, Vol. 60, (October 1994), pp607-616.

Jalics; L, Hemami, H. & Clymer B. (1996). A Control Strategy for Adaptive Bipedal Locomotion, *Proceedings of the 1996 IEEE International Conference on Robotics and Automation*" Minneapolis, MN, (April 1996).

de Leva, P., (1996), Adjustments to Zatsiorsky-Seluyanov's segment inertia parameters, *Journal of Biomechanics*, Vol. 29, (1996), pp. 1223-1230.

Mughal A. & Iqbal K. (2008a). Synthesis of Angular Profiles for Bipedal Sit-to-Stand Movement, *40th IEEE Southeastern Symposium on System Theory*, New Orleans, LA, USA, (March 17-18, 2008).

Mughal A. & Iqbal K. (2008b). Biomechanical bipedal model with asymmetrical reference trajectories for sit-to-stand task, *2nd International conference on Electrical Engineering*, Lahore, Pakistan, (25-26 March 08).

Mughal A. & Iqbal K. (2008c). Physiological cost optimization for bipedal modeling with optimal controller design, *International Conference on Computational & Experimental Engineering and Sciences*, Vol. 235, pp 1-6, Honolulu, HI, USA, (17-22 March 2008).

Mughal A. & Iqbal K. (2009). Controller Design by Decoupling of Angular Planes for Bipedal Sit-to Stand Movement, *11th Intl. IASTED Conf. on Control and Application*, Cambridge, UK, (13-15 July 09).

Mughal, A & Iqbal, K. (2007). Human bipedal biomechanical modeling with DynaFlexPro, SAE transactions on Digital Human Modeling for Design and Engineering", Seattle, WA, USA, (June 12-14, 2007).

Roberts, P & McCollum, G. (1996). Dynamics of sit-to-stand movement, *Biological Cybernetics*, Vol. 74, (1996).

Spong, M, Hutchinson, S. & Vidyasagar, M. (2006). Robot Modeling and Control", John Wiley and sons Inc. (2006).

4

Virtual Human Hand: Autonomous Grasping Strategy

Esteban Peña Pitarch
Uviversitat Politecnica de Catalynia
Spain

1. Introduction

Several researchers have spent time and effort studying grasping under different points of view, grasping objects in virtual environments (VE) is one of them. Now that the grasping strategy in VE has been solved, the next step is grasping any object in a VE, with minimum interaction with the user. In this chapter, we develop a new strategy for autonomous grasping in a virtual environment, based on the knowledge of a few object attributes like size, task, and shape. When the object is input a VE, the user chooses the object from among others, chooses a task inherent to the object selected, and then we implement a semi-intelligence algorithm, which makes a decision about how to grasp the selected object. When the system makes a decision, it determines whether the object is in the workspace of the hand. If it is then grasps, if is not, the virtual human (VH) moves to closer to the object so that it is now graspable. Simulation in VE is becoming more relevant every day and becoming a tool for designing new products. In the grasping area, grasping objects in a VE is commonly used by several researchers, but they don't pay attention to autonomous grasp. Autonomous grasp is an interesting problem, and its application in VE can help teach grasping to people with some diseases like ictus or those with amputations. It can also be used in robotics to teach the robotics hand to grasp.

2. Basic Concepts

For basic concepts, we introduce definitions from the literature Kapandji (1996), Tubiana (1981), Tubiana et al. (1996).
Free Motion In free motion, the hand moves freely in space. The basic free motions possible for the hand are:

- *Opening*: Fully extending the fingers and the thumb until the hand is fully open, as in the anatomical position.
- *Closing*: Fully flexing until the hand is closed in a fist with the thumb overlapping the index and middle fingers.
- *Clawing*: The motion that reaches the terminal position of metacarpophalangeal (MP) extension, interphalangeal (IP) flexion.
- *Reciprocal*: The motion that reaches a terminal position of MP flexion, IP extension.

Twelve variations of these motions are observed if the terminal position of each motion is the starting point of each other motion.
Resisted Motion Resisted motion is that performed by the hand against an external resistance, for the purpose of exerting force on an external object and sometimes changing its position.

- *Power grip*: Gripping an object against the palm (primarily isometric motion).
- *Precision handling*: Manipulation of an object by the thumb and fingers, not in contact with the palm (primarily isometric motion).
- *Pinch*: Isometric compression between the thumb and fingers.

3. Grasping Parameters

Before grasping the object, the VH needs do some actions first. We classify these actions as pre-grasp, grasp, and after-grasp. To concentrate only on grasp, we consider the object and the VH in position, meaning that the object is in the workspace of the hand. Pre-grasp actions are:

- *Hand Position:* The position of the wrist respect to the object.
- *Hand Orientation:* The hand has adequate orientation for the grasp.

These two pre-grasp actions need to work together. If we consider each separately, a good position with a bad orientation, results in an inability to grasp the object, and good orientation with a bad position results in the object not being reachable. In our algorithm both actions are doing in same time.
In this dissertation, after-grasp actions are considered in terms of the final position of the object.
Grasp involves operations related to the hand and the object, and we consider grasp touch, pull, push, etc. If we take the definition from a dictionary, one of the definitions is to take hold of or seize firmly with the hand. We extend this definition to include touch, pull, etc., ultimately amplifying the concept of grasp.
Parameters for the object and the hand are considered in the new step called grasp.

- *Object Attributes:* In the virtual environment, the object was built with techniques of computer-aided geometric design, and the basic attributes there are known. Other attributes, such as temperature, are described below.
- *Hand Orientation:* Hand orientation is related to hand shape. An adequate lecture of object attributes can give all possible options for grasp, with axes, planes, etc. Hand surface and object surface can give the hand orientation relative to the object.
- *Hand Position:* Hand position is similar to hand orientation and follows the same procedures for positioning the wrist as in the function of the object attributes.
- *Task:* This parameter can help the virtual human decide how to grasp the object.
- *Object Initial Position :* In some operations we need to know the initial position.
- *Object Final Position :* In some operations we need to know the final position.
- *One or Two Hands :* This parameter is related to several of the attributes discussed above.
- *Finger Number :* The number of fingers to use, depending on the type of grasp, object shape, etc.

- *Object Weight :* Object weight can be derived from the object shape if we know the density.
- *Object Stability:* For any small movement close to the position of equilibrium, the object stays in the equilibrium position.
- *Hand Anthropometry:* Virtual humans like real humans, have different-sized hands.

4. Relationship between Grasping Parameters

In this section, we establish the relationship between parameters and demonstrate that they need work together sometimes. To show this relationship, we present Figure 1. This figure shows the relationship independent of the dominant hand; for our VH, the dominant hand is usually the right hand.

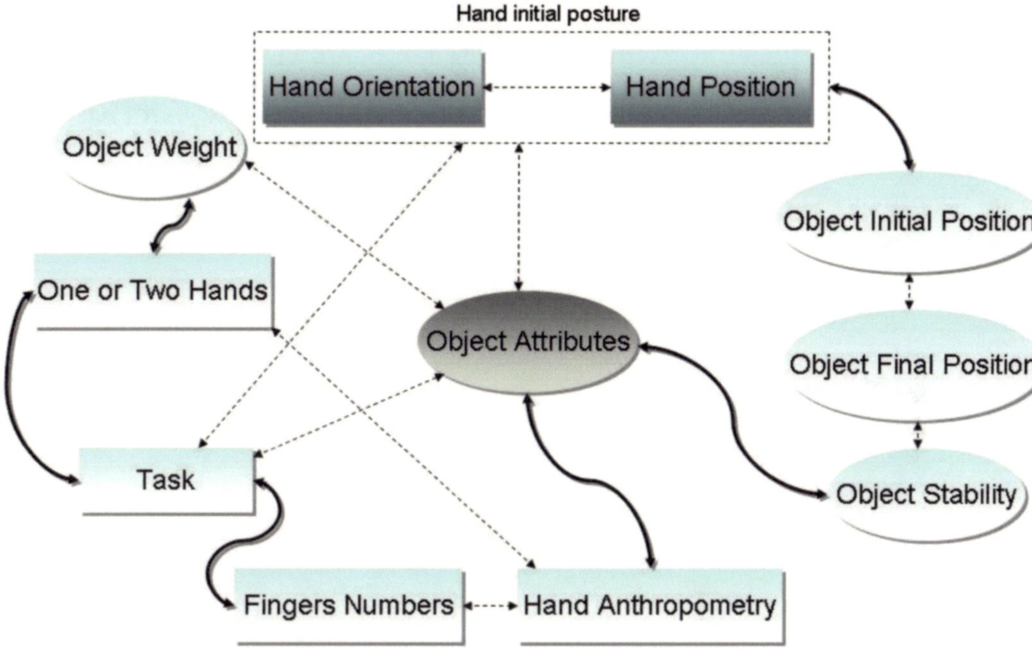

Fig. 1. Relation between grasping parameters

In this figure, fill arrows indicate functions between parameters that connect, arrows with dashed lines show relationships, the elliptic shapes are for the object, and rectangular shapes are for the hand. Hand orientation and hand position are related and closed with a dashed rectangle; both parameters work together, and we classify both as hand initial posture.
Hand initial position is a direct function with object initial position; they each depend one the other, e.g. in order to perform some action with the object, knowledge of the hand becomes necessary and with this first approximation we can know if the object is reachable or not. These parameters are related to object attributes, i.e., the object attributes permit different actions and depend on the hand initial position. In a similar way, the task can be done in relation with the hand initial position, i.e., if the object is not in the workspace, the task cannot be done.

The object weight, also relates to the object attributes, in the virtual environment, if we know the geometry and the density of the object we can know the weight with the geometric relation $W = V_0.\gamma$ in absolute terms, where W is the weight, V_0 is the volume, and γ is the specific weight .
The number of fingers and hand anthropometry are related, and the hands are used during the action too.
Object stability is a function of the object shape; a tall glass is less stable than a short glass when it is sitting on a table.
When the action is to do some particular task, the action is related directly to whether one or two hands are used or how many fingers are used. In the section below, we describe some tasks in which we can see this relation.

5. Parameters and Relationship

5.1 Object Attributes

Figure 2, shows the object attributes from engineering design. Attributes inherent to the object are volume, mass, inertia center, and inertia matrix. Some commercial programs call these characteristics, but we call them attributes. Inertia center is the center of mass (COM). Other attributes are:

- Temperature
- Fragility
- Surface shape

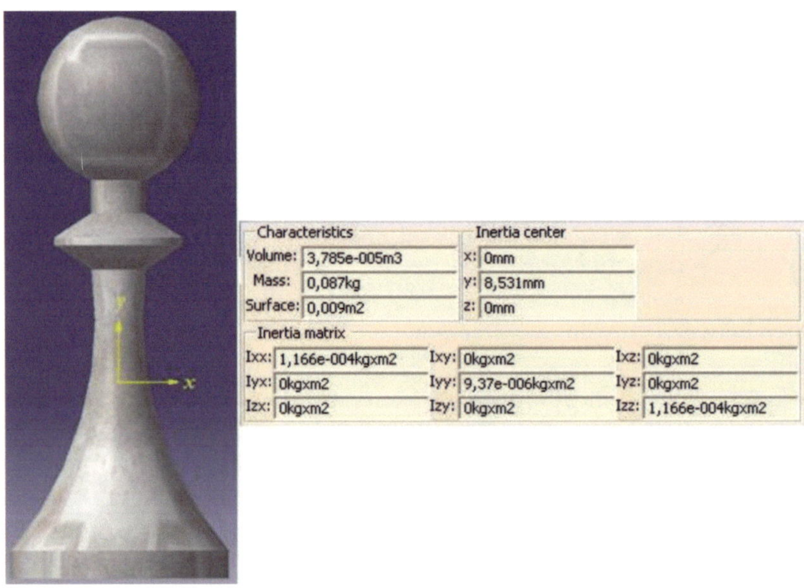

Fig. 2. Object with some attributes information

Temperature: When the objects have a temperature, this attribute can help decide what type of grasp is required.. For example, when grasping a mug, if the object are is filled with hot coffee and the action is to move we do not can grasp the side.

Fragile: If the object is fragile, this attribute can help decide what type of grasp is required.
Surface Shape: In a virtual environment, when we use the B-rep form found in the references Hoschek & Lasser (1993), Farin et al. (2002), Zeid (2005), and Wang & Wang (1986) , we show the definition of the object shape. In domain M in the plane with parameters (u,v), there is continuously differentiable and locally injective mapping $M \to S$, which takes points (u,v) in M into $\Re^3$. Then every point in the image set S can be described by a vector function $\mathbf{X}^i(u,v)$, where $i = 1,\ldots,n$ and n is the number of object, and represents the object i selected by the user. $\mathbf{X}^i(u,v)$ is called the *parametrization* of the surface S for the object i, and u,v are called the parameters of this representation; see Figure 3.

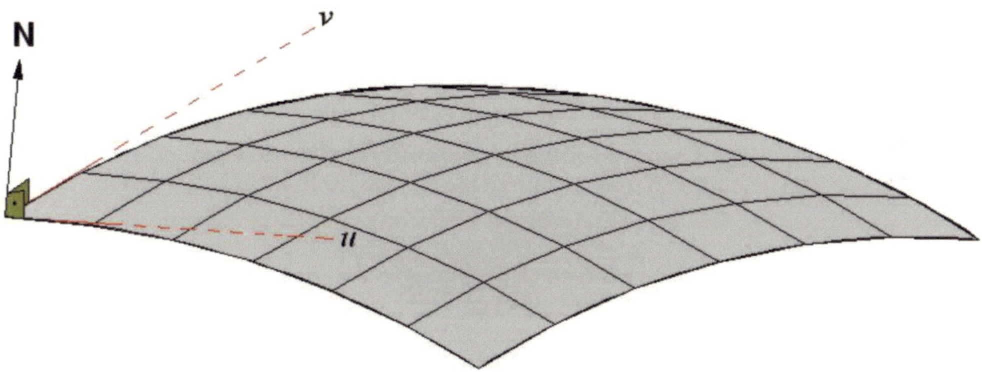

Fig. 3. Parametric surface

A parametrization is *regular* if for every point of S, the normal vector is defined:

$$\left| \frac{\partial \mathbf{X}^i}{\partial u} \times \frac{\partial \mathbf{X}^i}{\partial v} \right| \neq 0 \tag{1}$$

If $\left| \frac{\partial \mathbf{X}^i}{\partial u} \times \frac{\partial \mathbf{X}^i}{\partial v} \right|$ has a zero at the point $\mathbf{P}(u_0,v_0)$, then the surface has a *singularity* at $\mathbf{P}$.
The *tangent vector* to a surface curve $\mathbf{X}^i(u(t),v(t))$ can be computed as

$$\dot{\mathbf{X}^i} = \frac{\partial \mathbf{X}^i}{\partial u}\dot{u} + \frac{\partial \mathbf{X}^i}{\partial v}\dot{v} \tag{2}$$

In particular, the tangents to the parametric curves are given by

$$\mathbf{X}^i_u = \frac{\partial \mathbf{X}^i}{\partial u}\ (lines\ v = const.), \quad \mathbf{X}^i_v = \frac{\partial \mathbf{X}^i}{\partial v}\ (lines\ u = const.) \tag{3}$$

The two vectors $\frac{\partial \mathbf{X}^i}{\partial u}$ and $\frac{\partial \mathbf{X}^i}{\partial v}$ uniquely determine the plane, which is tangent to the surface at the point $\mathbf{P}(u,v)$.
The *unit normal vector* to the surface can compute for the object, using the vector product, as

$$\mathbf{N_o} = \frac{\mathbf{X}^i_u \times \mathbf{X}^i_v}{|\mathbf{X}^i_u \times \mathbf{X}^i_v|} \tag{4}$$

Usually we assume that the hand size is defined by two parameters, $HL = 190\ mm$ (Hand Length) and $HB = 90\ mm$ (Hand Breadth). With these two parameters and the object size, we can know if the virtual human can grasp the object as a whole or if it needs to search for parts of the object for grasp, i.e., one cannot grasp a whole chair, but we can grasp the back of the chair.

5.2 Hand Orientation

For hand orientation, we use the theory for two oriented surfaces. In this case the hand surface is oriented with the object surface, and the hand can be the right, left, or both hands. For simplify, we refer in this case to the right hand; the same equations can apply for the left hand or both hands. One surface M_H, where the subscript H indicates the hand surface, is orientable if the mapping of $M_H \to S^2$ is *regular*, and the vector normal is defined in Equation 4. If we change to other coordinates (u_1, v_1), shown for the hand in Figure 4, the new parametric representation is

$$\mathbf{Y}^j_{u_1} \times \mathbf{Y}^j_{v_1} = \frac{\partial(u,v)}{\partial(u_1,v_1)} \mathbf{X}^i_u \times \mathbf{X}^i_v \tag{5}$$

where $j = 1,2$, 1 for the right hand, 2 for the left hand, and for the corresponding unit vector:

$$\mathbf{N}_H = \epsilon \mathbf{N}_o \tag{6}$$

where

$$\epsilon = sign\left|\frac{\partial(u,v)}{\partial(u_1,v_1)}\right| \tag{7}$$

The orientation in the new parametrization is the same if the **Jacobian** of the transformation is positive, and is opposed if it is negative.

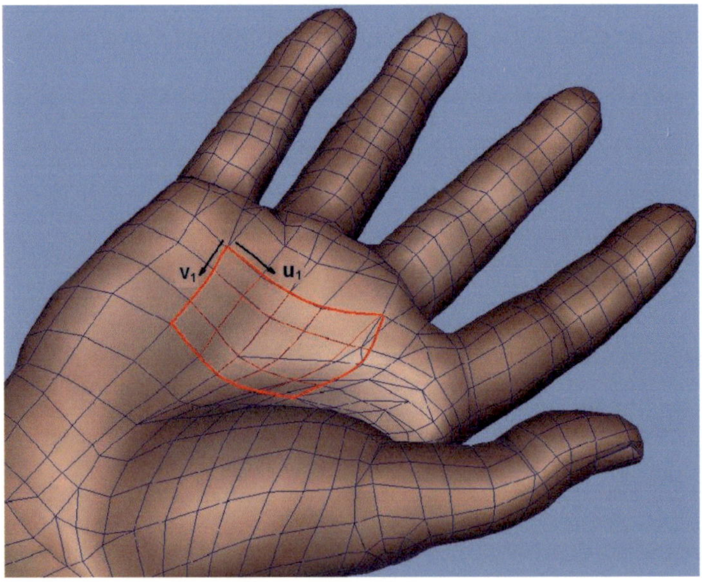

Fig. 4. Parametric surface for the hand

5.3 Hand Position

To consider the hand position with respect to the object, we refer this position with respect to the wrist. For us the global position for the hand is given by the position of the wrist. The point of reference for the object is the COM.

When the object enters the virtual environment, we know the position of COM. That is information inherent with the object; the position of the wrist is also known in each moment.

The coordinates of COM are $\mathbf{x}_c^i = [x_c^i \; y_c^i \; z_c^i]^T$, and the coordinates of the wrist are $\mathbf{x}_w^j = [x_w^j \; y_w^j \; z_w^j]^T$. We can locate the hand (wrist) with respect to the object with the linear transformation:

$$\mathbf{x}_w^j = A\mathbf{x}_c^i \tag{8}$$

where A is a transformation matrix. Figure 5 shows the wrist position with respect to the center of mass in pre-grasp action.

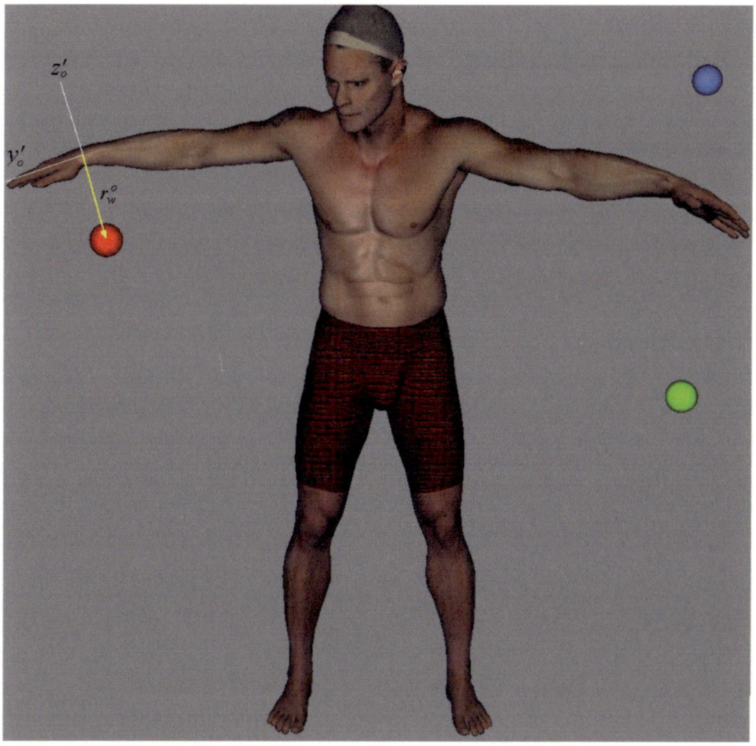

Fig. 5. Hand position respect the object

5.4 Task

The task is the most important attribute, and many times it decides for itself how to grasp the object; i.e., when grasping a mug containing drink, the usual response is to grasp the handle; when moving the mug, we can grasp the handle or the top. The *task* in the dictionary (Oxfort English Dictionary) is *a piece of work assigned or done as part of one's duties.* Follow this definition and the definition of task analysis.

Task Analysis: Task analysis is the analysis or a breakdown of exactly how a task is accomplished, such as what sub-tasks are required.
We divide tasks and sub-tasks into elemental actions, i.e., open the door is a task, and the elemental action is pulling or push. This elemental action can also be used for other tasks, like moving a joystick in a machine.

5.4.1 Elementary Actions

Pull: To pull is to apply force so as to cause or tend to cause motion toward the source of the force. This action can be done with one, two, three, or four fingers. We define this as PL_i, where $i = 1 \ldots 4$ and PL_1 means pulling with one finger and so on.
Push: To push is to apply pressure against for the purpose of moving. The number of fingers used is the similar as for pulling, but we add the use of the palm. We define this as PS_i, where $i = 1 \ldots 5$ and PS_3 is pushing with three fingers.
Pinch: A pinch is isometric compression between the thumb and the fingers. The number of fingers to used is defined as PI_i, where $i = 1 \ldots 4$ and PI_2 is pinching one object with the thumb and two fingers.
Power Grasp: A power grasp is the gripping of an object against the palm. We define this action as PG.
Precision Handling: Precision handling is the manipulation of an object by thumb and fingers, not in contact with the palm. We define this action as PH_i, where $i = 1 \ldots 4$ and PH_4 is precision handling with the thumb and four fingers.
Touch: To touch is to cause or permit a part of the body, especially the hand or fingers, to come into contact with so as to feel. We consider this action is transformed with the index. We define TO for touch.

5.5 Object Initial Position

The point of reference for object initial position is the center of mass (COM) of the object; this point is independent of the type of grasp, but the wrist position is referred to this point. In Figure 5 we can see the object position with respect to the wrist. This position in the global coordinates of the virtual environment (VE) tells the system where it is with respect to the global coordinates of the virtual human. Object initial position is defined by:

$$\mathbf{x}_c^i = [x_c^i \; y_c^i \; z_c^i]^T \tag{9}$$

5.6 Object Final Position

Knowledge of final position permits us to know a priori if the virtual human can do the task; if it cannot do the task, we need add some actions like walking, advancing the body, etc. To tell the system to add actions, a check of the workspace helps us determine the reachability of the action. In some tasks, i.e., moving a joystick in a machine to elevate the load, the object is fixed in the base and only moves with the constraints of spherical joints; the final position is always the same as the initial position.
We can use equations similar to those used for determining hand position to determine object final position. We know the object initial position relative to COM $\mathbf{x}_c^i = [x_c^i \; y_c^i \; z_c^i]^T$, and we know the object final position relative to COM $\mathbf{x}_f^i = [x_f^i \; y_f^i \; z_f^i]^T$, both with respect to the global coordinates. The relationship between the initial and final position is:

$$\mathbf{x}_f^i = B\mathbf{x}_c^i \tag{10}$$

where B is a transformation matrix.

5.7 One or Two Hands

This parameter is a function of the shape of object. Shape provides information about the size and the weight of object, which determine if one hand or both hands are used or if the action is not performed.

5.8 Number of Fingers

For touching, a virtual human only needs one finger, but for precision handling, the virtual human may need one, two, three, four, or five fingers for grasp. This parameters is a function of the shape and weight of the object.

5.9 Stability

Analysis of stability for some objects helps us to determine whether or not the object in a particular position can be touched. An example is a tall bottle. If the virtual human touch the top of the bottle and it is not stable the botlle can lose stability and fall. Falling not is the final reaction when we touch the object.
From the statics equilibrium, we can calculate if the object's position is stable, unstable, or neutral equilibrium; this is interesting to know for the actions of pulling, pinching, or touching. The general case with one degree of freedom for the object, defined by independent coordinate s, is

$$\frac{dV}{ds} = 0, \ \frac{d^2V}{ds^2} > 0 \ stable\ equilibrium$$

$$\frac{dV}{ds} = 0, \ \frac{d^2V}{ds^2} < 0 \ unstable\ equilibrium$$

$$\frac{dV}{ds} = \frac{d^2V}{ds^2} = \frac{d^3V}{ds^3} = \cdots = 0 \ neutral\ equilibrium$$

where V is the potential energy of the object.

5.10 Hand Anthropometry

We give the hand anthropometry for a 95th-percentile human hand related to the hand length and breadth. This parametric length for each bone permit the simulation of almost all the population.

6. Mathematical Model

We have defined task in elemental actions, and these actions are related to some parameters. In this section, we write each elemental action and show the equations in the function of parameters.

$$Pull(OS, HO, HP, T, OIP, OTH, FN, ST, HA)$$

$$Push(HO, HP, T, OIP, OFP, OTH, FN, ST, HA)$$

$$Pinch(OS, HO, HP, T, OIP, OFP, FN, HA)$$

$$Power\ grasp(OS, HO, HP, T, OTH, FN, HA)$$

$$Precision\ handling(OS, HO, HP, T, FN, ST, HA)$$

where:

OS= Object Shape, and the mathematical function is $\mathbf{X}^i(u,v)$

HO= Hand Orientation, $\mathbf{Y}^j(u_1,v_1)$

HP= Hand Position, $\mathbf{x}_w^j = A\mathbf{x}_c^i$

T= Task, user chooses the task

OIP= Object Initial Position, $\mathbf{x}_c^i = [x_c^i \; y_c^i \; z_c^i]^T$

OFP= Object Final Position, $\mathbf{x}_f^i = [x_f^i \; y_f^i \; z_f^i]^T$

OTH= One or Two Hands, a function of OS and represented by, $OTH = f(OS)$

FN= Finger Number, $FN = f(OS)$

ST= Object Stability, dV

HA= Hand Anthropometry, HL, HB

6.1 Pull

Pulling is a function of the object shape because in order to do this action we need to know a priori if is permitted to pull or not. For example, we can pull a door even though it is a big object, but we cannot pull a wall even though it is a similar object shape. The shape of the object can give us additional information, such as which parts of the object to pull.
It is also a function of hand orientation and hand position that if the object is outside the workspace of the hand, the virtual human cannot do this action. However, if the virtual human moves, he can reach the object.
As discussed earlier, task is the most important, because it can determine whether or not the action is pulling.
Object initial position is related to the workspace and hand position, i.e., object and hand position are two parameters that work together to define the object reachability.
When pulling, humans use one or two hands; for realistic actions, virtual humans use similar behavior and sometimes pull a door using two hands and pull a joystick using only one hand.
In similar way, we can use a determinate number of fingers; for pulling a door with two hands, the virtual human uses all the fingers, and for pulling a joystick and two fingers are sufficient.
Object stability helps determine if a small variation in the equilibrium position causes the object to lose the equilibrium; or not, e.g., pulling a 1.5-liter bottle of water by the top can cause the bottle to fall, and this is not the final position that the virtual environment is looking for.
Hand anthropometry helps to pull an object and can tell the system which part to pull, e.g., for a door, the handle.

6.2 Push

Knowledge of hand orientation, hand position, task, and object initial position are similar for the action of pull.
If we know object final position in pushing, we can see if this action can completed without additional actions, like walking or moving the virtual human.
The other parameters considerations for pulling apply here.

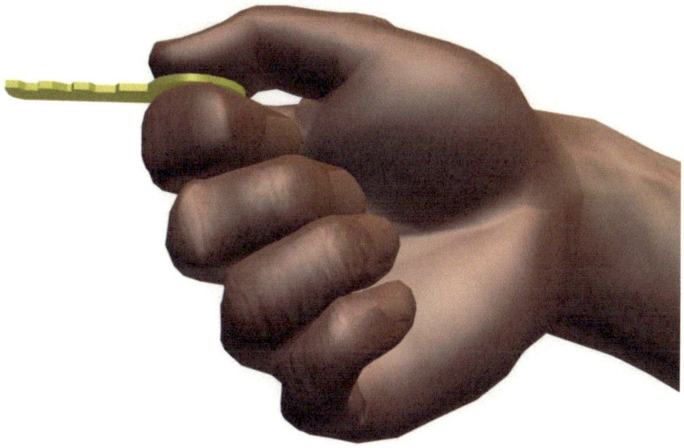

Fig. 6. Lateral pinch

6.3 Pinch

Let me explain why pinching is function of the parameters shown above. Picture 6 shows a lateral pinch for a key; the virtual human is using the thumb and the index finger laterally.
To pinch a key, is the object shape was analyzed first, then the hand orientation and hand position with respect to the object and then the object initial position and final position were considered. If the action were putting the key in a lock and rotating it ninety degrees to open or close the door, the final position for the object is the lock. Finger number in this case, following our definition above, is PL_1 because only one finger and the thumb is used and pinching always uses the thumb. Finally, the hand anthropometry was considered because in some cases the object with respect to the hand is too big for pinching, in this case, the object and the hand are in good proportion.

6.4 Power Grasp

In the object shape function, if the object is so big compared to the hand anthropometry that the virtual human cannot grasp the whole object, it can look for a part to grasp, e.g., a frying pan was designed for power grasping the handle. Shape can tell us the possibles parts for grasping.
All the other parameters have a similar role, which we describe above for the other basic functions.

6.5 Precision Handling

Precision handling is similar to power grasping with respect to the function parameters. The only remarkable difference is that in this case normally we only use one hand, and do not use the palm. In the function of the action relative to the object, the virtual human can use one, two, or more fingers. At this time the number of fingers to use is related to the object shape and the task to perform.

7. Grasping Strategy

We have defined all the parameters that work in grasping, and in this section we present the process of grasping. Figure 7, presents a flowchart of grasping. The objects are in the virtual environment, and the user chooses one object from among several. Each object has attached

information about several attributes, like task, shape, position of center of mass, etc.; these attributes help the system make a decision. Some objects can do different tasks, e.g., if the object is a mug, the task can be moving or drinking. Therefore, in this first approximation the user chooses the task inherent to the object.
Once the user chooses a task, the system helps make a decision about how to grasp because the system knows the attributes of the object and the task. But maybe the object is not in the workspace of the virtual human; if this is true, we need to tell the virtual human approximatelyhow to put the object in the workspace of the hand.

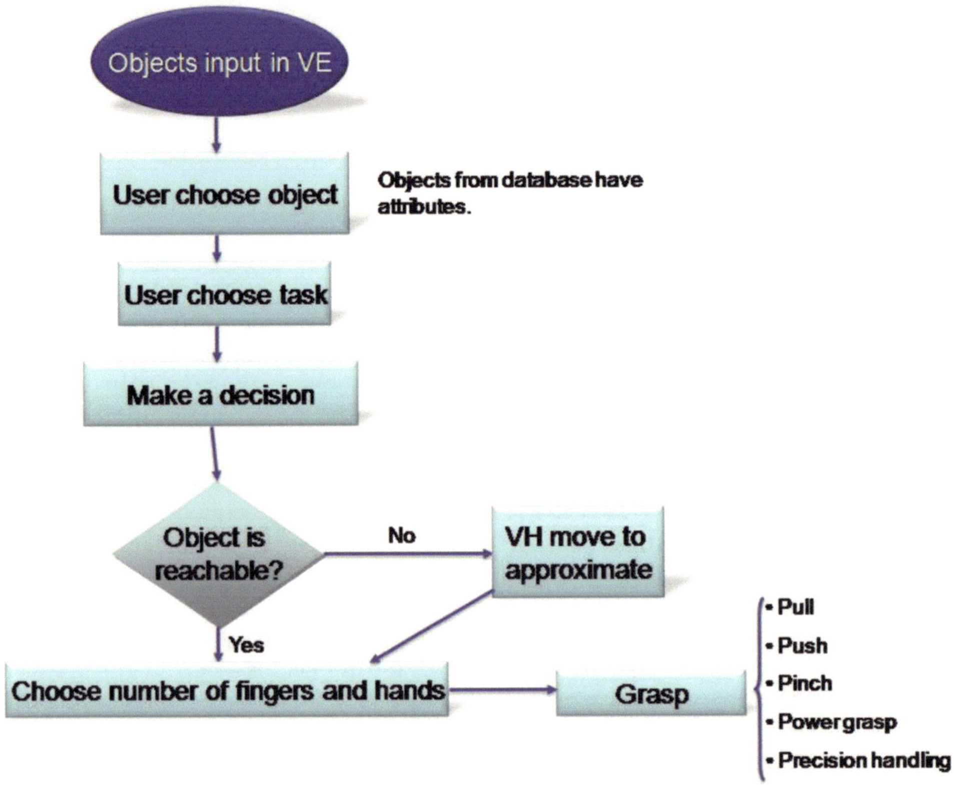

Fig. 7. Grasping flowchart

With the types of grasp and the shape of the object, the next step is to calculate the number of fingers and hands to use for grasping the object, and then grasp.
This is a heuristic definition for grasping. In the next section, we explain the semi algorithm for grasping the object.

7.1 Objects Input in the Virtual Environment

When the objects are in the virtual environment and the user choose one object to grasp, the system reads all of the attributes and saves them in a file with the extension "*.txt", which allows the file to be used in any code of language. Figure 2 shows an object with attributes like center of mass (COM) or, in this case, Inertia center, volume, mass, characteristics, and Inertia matrix.

7.2 User Chooses Object

This action occurs when there are many objects in the virtual environment; if virtual environment has only one object, the virtual human will know the object. One example is that the virtual human is taking a breakfast, and the objects on the table (virtual environment) are a coffee mug, cereal bowl, and spoon. The user chooses a coffee mug, and this inherently has all the properties with the center of mass, of course can change position of center of mass is function of quantity of coffee. For this the object, there are two reasonable tasks, drinking or moving. If the task chosen by the user is drinking, once the virtual human has drunk, it will put the coffee mug back on the table in the same position. During this process, the position of the wrist of the virtual human is known, the position of the center of mass is known, and we can calculate the hand orientation for performing this action.

7.3 User Chooses Task

This action is mentioned above, and the preceding section has an example of the task and how the user chooses.

7.4 Making a Decision

Inputs in a simple associator are task, weight, shape, temperature, etc., and output pattern is type of grasp, i.e. pinch, pull, etc. When VH take a decision there is based in a system linearly separable.

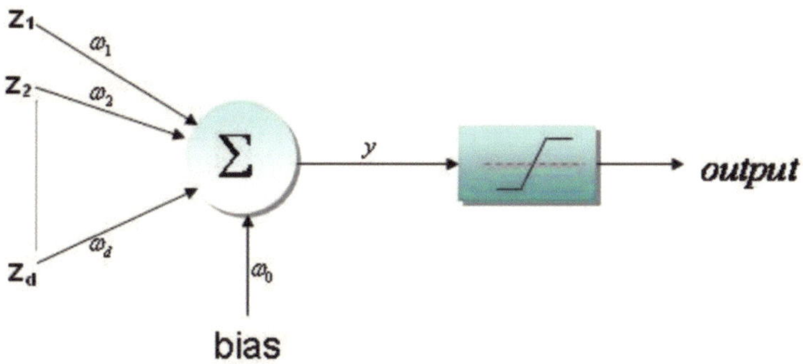

Fig. 8. Single perceptron

Figure 8 show a single perceptron from the works Hagan et al. (1996), Haykin (1999),Anderson (1997) where the input vector is $\mathbf{z} = [z_1, z_2, \ldots, z_d]^T$, bias is b, the weight vector considering each input is $\mathbf{w} = [\omega_1, \omega_2, \ldots, \omega_d]^T$, and the weight for the bias is ω_0.
In our case we choose apply these networks for a classification problems, in which the inputs are binary images of attributes like task, shape, temperature, and density. The output of the perceptron is given by

$$\mathbf{y} = g(\sum_{j=1}^{d} \omega_j \phi_j(z) + \omega_0) = g(\mathbf{z}^T \text{Œ}) \tag{11}$$

where Œ denotes the vector formed from the activations $\phi_0, \ldots, \phi_d$, and the function of activation in this case is a symmetric saturating linear (satlins), because this are a linearly separable. The input/output relation is:

$$g(a) = -1 \qquad a < -1$$
$$g(a) = a \qquad -1 \leq a \leq 1$$
$$g(a) = 1 \qquad n > 1$$

7.5 Determining Whether Object is Reachable and Approximating

The answer to this question can be found in Chapter four, where the analysis of workspace for the hand was studied. When checking the workspace for each finger with respect to the wrist position, the virtual human can know if the object with respect to the wrist position is reachable or not. If the object not is reachable, the virtual human can perform some actions to approximate, like walk and reduce the space to a convenient distance between the wrist and the center of mass of the object.

7.6 Choosing Number of Fingers and Hands

Based on object shape and hand anthropometry, we can determine if the use of one hand is adequate or if the use of two hands is required. Based on the geometric primitives for a regular basketball and one person with a 185 mm hand length, the ball cannot be grasped with one hand; two hands are required. Some objects are designed to grasp with both hands. Normally, if the object to be grasped is based on the primitive geometries for a sphere, cylinder, or box, if the dimensions for grasp are greater than the hand length, it automatically requires two hands.

$$If\ D > HL,\ then\ use\ two\ hands$$

where D is the side dimensions to grasp, and HL is the hand length.
To determine the number of fingers to use for a grasp, parameters like object shape, hand anthropometry, type of grasp, and task are used . We define elemental actions, and each elemental action shows the number of fingers to use. Power grasp and touch do not need the number of fingers defined; normally a power grasp uses five fingers and touch uses the index finger. Other grasp types are a function of parameters mentioned earlier. For precision handling, a primitive sphere is a function of the shape, or better if the radius of equator of sphere is ρ we can define the number of fingers how:

$$If\ 1 <= \rho <= 20\ mm\ then\ PL_1$$
$$If\ 20 <= \rho <= 40\ mm\ then\ PL_2$$
$$If\ 40 <= \rho <= 60\ mm\ then\ PL_3$$
$$If\ 60 <= \rho <= 90\ mm\ then\ PL_4$$

where the subscript 2 means the thumb and two fingers, and subscript 3 means thumb and three fingers, and so on.
We can use the same relationship for pinching. Pulling and pushing are also a function of size of the object; normally, to push a door we use all the fingers, but sometimes if we know the door, we use two or three fingers. For this analysis, we always use five fingers, similar to pulling.

7.7 Grasp

The last action is grasping. Grasping is function of the parameters founded above and forward and inverse kinematics. For several reasons, we prefer to explain the action of grasping in the next chapter and work in several examples demonstrating how this theory works in a virtual human. The output of grasp in this flowchart is the type of grasp and how the grasp uses all the parameters shown in this chapter. Figure 9 shows a type of grasp based on the task and other parameters. The positions of fingers are determined as a function of all the parameters defined for grasping, i.e., when grasping a mug to drink from the side, the object in this position has a cylindric shape and the virtual human knows the COM. Based on this, we can calculate the hand position and orientation and the position for all the fingers. In the case shown in Figure 9, the task is drinking, the beverage contained in the mug is hot, and the weight is light. In this case, the decision is to grasp for a handle, and the virtual environment knows the position of the handle. The handle has a known shape, and we can calculate the number and position of fingers.

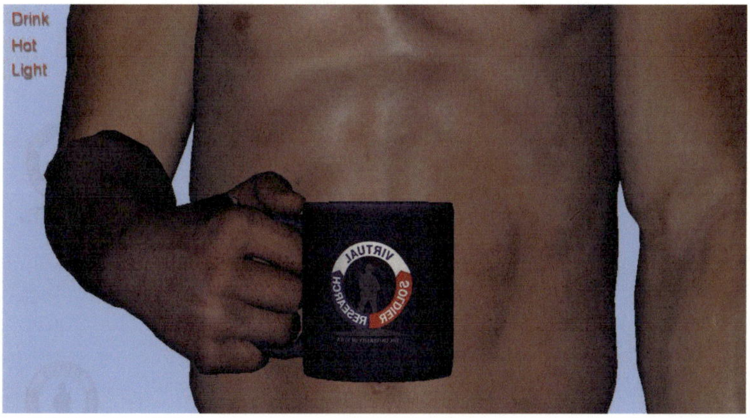

Fig. 9. Grasping a mug

8. Grasp Examples

Our approximation for to grasping is based on the movement of fingers. There are two types of movements. For grasping with power, the movement described, each finger except the thumb, is circular. For the second, when grasping with precision, the movement of fingertips, including the thumb, approximates a circle. Based on these approximations, we can simulate all the human grasping proposed by Buchcholz et al. Buchcholz et al. (1992). Pinching is a particular case of grasping with precision. Pulling, pushing, and touching we are considered positioning finger problems. For the first approximation of power grasping we can apply forward kinematics and calculate all the angles for every finger. For a cylinder with radius ρ , Figure 10 depicts cross-section of the cylinder and the schematic phalanx bones. The angles θ and q_i are obtained from the geometry relationship. This example is considered a power.
Where angle q_j for each finger, and subscript is $j = II \ldots V$ where subindex II is for the index, III middle, IV ring, and V small. These angles are for the proximal phalanx respect to the metacarpal bones for each finger. Similar for q_k, where $k = II \ldots V$, the subindex mean the same fingers related before and the angles are between proximal phalanx to medial phalanx. For q_l, where subscript is $l = II \ldots V$ are referred to angles between middle phalanx and distal

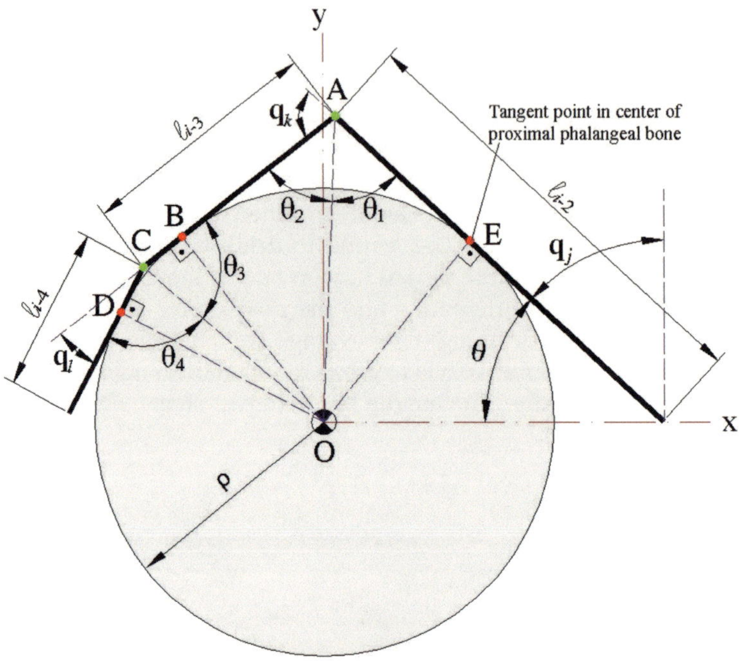

Fig. 10. The geometry relationship of finger segments

phalanx. All of these angles are calculated for geometry and changed from local to global with the transformation matrix developed in Appendix A.

For the second movements, we can calculate the fingertip position for each finger when grasp any object with precision and after applying inverse kinematics. Figures 11 and 12 depict the fingertip positions.

The angles β and α depend on the diameter of the ball. From the observation when people grasp a ball with radius $\rho = 27.5\ mm$, $\alpha = 0$ and $\beta = 60^o$. Also we impose that the middle finger stays in its neutral position. Therefore, we can determine the fingertip positions for the thumb, index, and ring fingers with respect to the wrist (global) coordinate system, and the small finger stays in the neutral position.

The inverse kinematic solutions depend on the initial values of the design variables for both iterative and optimization-based methods. Table 1 presents the solutions (q_i in degrees) for the index finger with the Newton-Raphson method, where the global coordinate is $[-11.22 \quad 152.341 \quad 77.4]$ in mm, the hand breadth is 200 mm, and the local coordinate is $[-7.3 \quad 59.9887 \quad 77.4]$ in mm.

From Table 1 it is shown that the convergence for Newton-Raphson method is very fast when the initial angles are close to the solution. For the first set of initial values, the solution for joint DIP (q_4) is negative and is in the range of motion. The negative angle for this joint represents hyper-extension. However, usually, we can observe that humans never grasp this sphere by DIP hyper-extension.

In practice, some joints in the fingers are coupled, i.e., the movement of one joint depends on the motion of another joint. For example, each finger except the thumb has two coupled joints. The distal interphalangeal joint (DIP) depends on the proximal interphalangeal joint (PIP) and

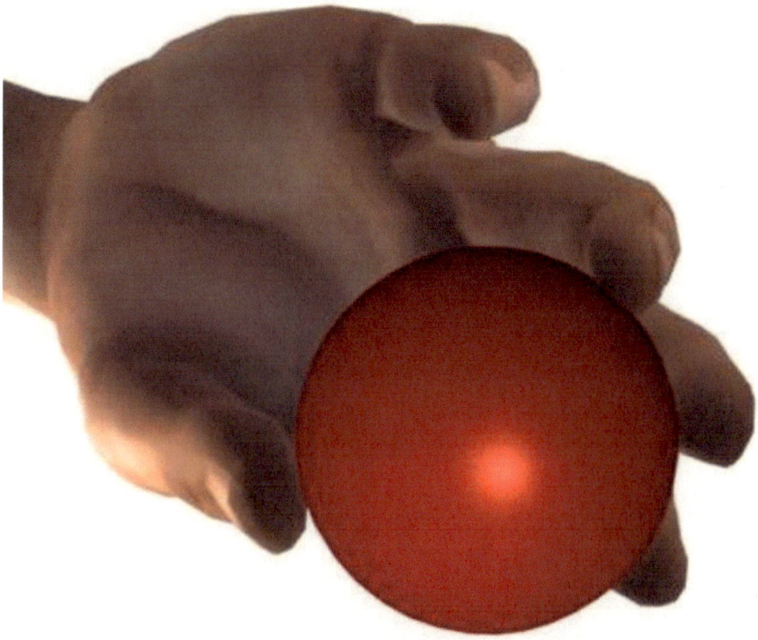

Fig. 11. Grasping a sphere

Initial	$q_1 = 0$	$q_2 = 30$	$q_3 = 30$	$q_4 = 10$
Iteration=7	$q_1 = 6.95$	$q_2 = 39.3$	$q_3 = 30$	$q_4 = -7.65$
Initial	$q_1 = 0$	$q_2 = 0$	$q_3 = 0$	$q_4 = 0$
Iteration=10	$q_1 = 6.95$	$q_2 = 42.3$	$q_3 = 10$	$q_4 = 26.6$
Initial	$q_1 = 0$	$q_2 = 10$	$q_3 = 10$	$q_4 = 0$
Iteration=7	$q_1 = 6.95$	$q_2 = 42.3$	$q_3 = 10$	$q_4 = 26.6$

Table 1. Index joint angles with Newton-Raphson method

the relationship is defined in the literature Rijpkema & Girard (1991), where the superscript i identifies the finger, beginning with the index finger and the last ending with the small finger.

$$q^i_{DIP} = \frac{2}{3} q^i_{PIP} \tag{12}$$

For the thumb, we can find a similar relationship:

$$q_3 = 2(q_2 - \frac{1}{6}\pi) \tag{13}$$

$$q_5 = \frac{7}{5} q_4 \tag{14}$$

The subindex shown above can found in Chapter 3.
When we impose the joint coupling function in Equation 12 to the index finger, it will have 3 DOF because q_4 is a function of q_3 . The result is shown in Table 2. The solution is the same for all different initial q_i values.

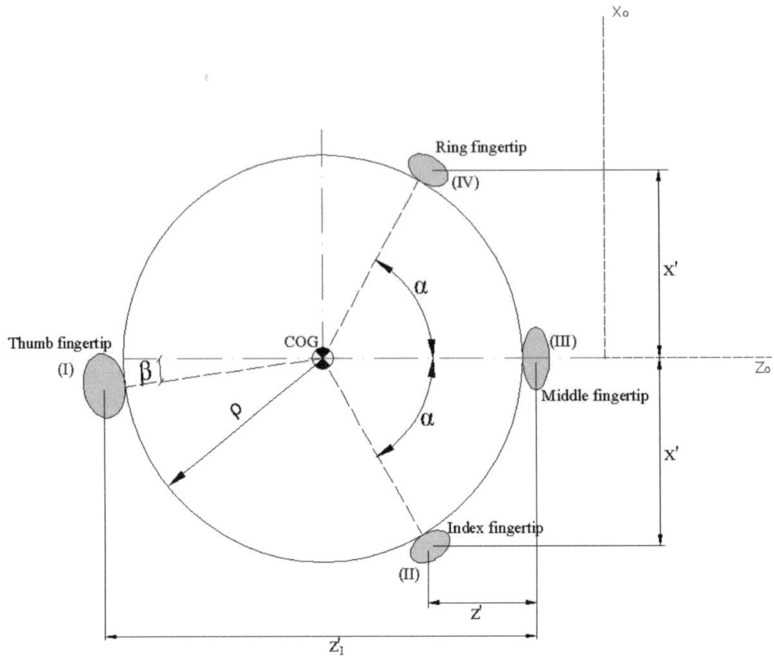

Fig. 12. Equator section with position of fingertips used

Initial	$q_1 = 0$	$q_2 = 0$	$q_3 = 0$	$q_4 = ---$
Iteration=9	$q_1 = 6.95$	$q_2 = 39.3$	$q_3 = 20.13$	$q_4 = 13.42$
Initial	$q_1 = 0$	$q_2 = 30$	$q_3 = 30$	$q_4 = ---$
Iteration=7	$q_1 = 6.95$	$q_2 = 39.3$	$q_3 = 20.13$	$q_4 = 13.42$
Initial	$q_1 = 0$	$q_2 = 10$	$q_3 = 10$	$q_4 = ---$
Iteration=9	$q_1 = 6.95$	$q_2 = 39.3$	$q_3 = 20.13$	$q_4 = 13.42$
Initial	$q_1 = 0$	$q_2 = 40$	$q_3 = 40$	$q_4 = ---$
Iteration=7	$q_1 = 6.95$	$q_2 = 39.3$	$q_3 = 20.13$	$q_4 = 13.42$

Table 2. Index joint angles with the Newton-Raphson method including joint coupling

Another approach for finger inverse kinematics is the optimization-based method. The hypothesis is that the feasible space is small for fingers during grasping. The problem will be: Given a point $\mathbf{x}^p$, find the joint angles $\mathbf{q}^i$ to minimize $\left\|\mathbf{p}^i - \mathbf{x}^p\right\|$, and the joint angles should lie in the limits as constraints. Therefore, the formulation is as follows

$$\begin{aligned} &Find: \mathbf{q}_i \\ &Minimize: \left\|\mathbf{p}^i - \mathbf{x}^p\right\| \\ &Subject\ to: q_j^{iL} \le q_j^i \le q_j^{iU} \end{aligned} \tag{15}$$

A gradient-based optimizer Gill et al. (2002) is implemented to solve this problem.

Table 3 shows the predicted joint angles for the optimization problem with different initial values. The results show that the optimization problem always has a feasible solution regardless of the initial values. It also shows that and they are the same for all different cases and the final solution is more reasonable than those obtained from the Newton-Raphson method.

Initial	$q_1 = 0$	$q_2 = 30$	$q_3 = 30$	$q_4 = 10$
Solution	$q_1 = 6.95$	$q_2 = 39.22$	$q_3 = 24.54$	$q_4 = 6.24$
Initial	$q_1 = 0$	$q_2 = 0$	$q_3 = 0$	$q_4 = 0$
Solution	$q_1 = 6.95$	$q_2 = 39.36$	$q_3 = 23.37$	$q_4 = 8.47$
Initial	$q_1 = 0$	$q_2 = 10$	$q_3 = 10$	$q_4 = 0$
Solution	$q_1 = 6.95$	$q_2 = 39.22$	$q_3 = 24.56$	$q_4 = 6.22$

Table 3. Index joint angles with the optimization-based method

9. Making a Decision

In this section we provide an example applying the Support Vector Machine (SVM) presented in the last chapter. The example shown here can be extended to any case, without losing generality. This example consists of putting an object in our virtual environment, in this case a mug. If there are more objects in the virtual environment, the user chooses the mug. Based on the functionality of mug, it has only two associated tasks, one is drinking and the other is moving. The user in this case chooses between these two tasks. In this case, to simplify the example, the known input parameters for this object are as follows, the others are 0:

$$Task \begin{cases} Drink = 1 \\ Move = -1 \end{cases}$$

$$Temperature \begin{cases} Hot = 1 \\ Normal = -1 \end{cases}$$

$$Weight \begin{cases} Heavy = 1 \\ Normal = -1 \end{cases}$$

We can add all the parameters, inherent to the object and described in Section 5.6, such a shape, hand orientation, number of fingers, etc. The problem become a classification problem between two classes.

$$y = hardlim\mathbf{g}(W^T\mathbf{p} + b)$$

If we choose $x = 0$, axis for classification and $b = 0$ the bias, the weight input vector is

$$W^T = [1,0,0,0,0,0,0,0,0,0].$$

The output, or decision, is to grasp the side or grasp the handle. In this case, we found a problem: if the mug is hot and the task is move, the virtual human cannot grasp the side of the mug. For this reason, we need to connect these outputs to another preceptron and build another output. Figure 13 shows the proposed network connected in parallel for the problem of output that is not consistent with the inputs. In this case, the perceptrons connected in parallel are $p = t - 1$, where t is the number of types of grasp inherent to the object in the function of the task.

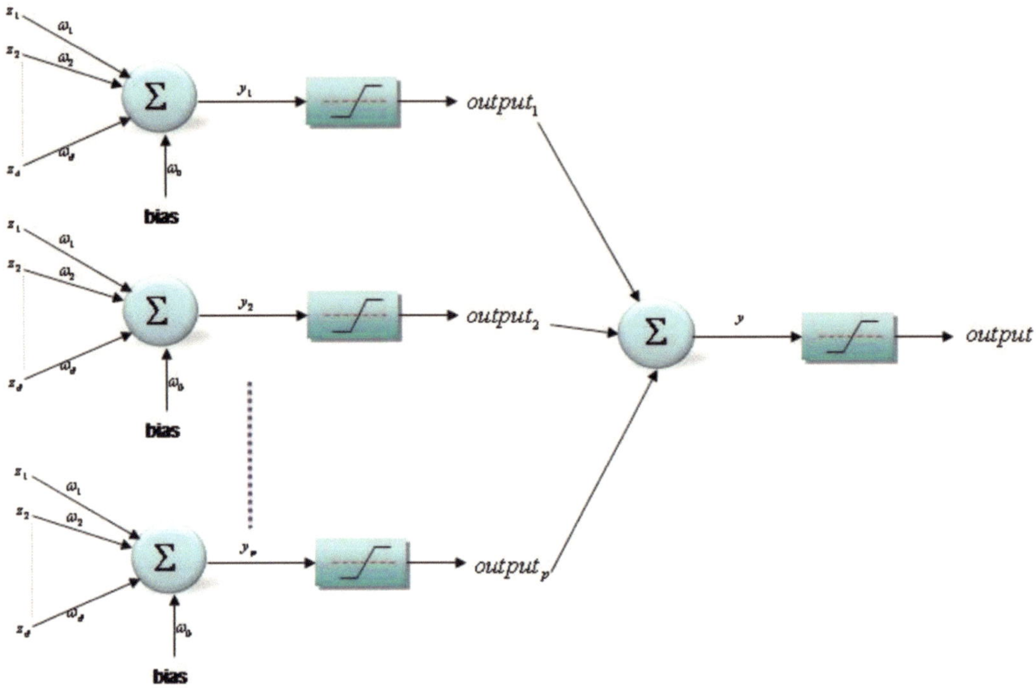

Fig. 13. Perceptrons connected in parallel

10. Choosing Number of Fingers and Hands

In this example, the parameters for grasping are any of the three ways to grasp a mug: by the side, top, or handle. The dimensions of the side to grasp are smaller than the hand length, and the virtual human uses only one hand. For the number of fingers to use, the parameter used for the first two types is $\rho = 80\ mm$. From Chapter 5, the number of fingers is PL_4, which means the thumb and four fingers. When the decision is to grasp the handle, the parameter is $\rho = 50\ mm$ and the finger number is PL_3, that is, index, middle, ring, and thumb. This grasp is shown in 8.

11. Grasping

The last action is grasping, once the user chooses the object among others in the virtual environment and the task, some objects only has designed for one task, or only there is one object in the virtual environment, if there is more than one choice. After, the algorithm take automatically makes a decision, choosing the number of fingers and hands, calculating the wrist position and orientation, and calculating the angles of every joint in our 25-DOF model. Wrists are connected with the upper body, and with this information $Santos^{TM}$ can grasp with his whole body in a realistic posture.
Figure 14 shows the results of applying the task-oriented object semi-intelligent system for grasping a mug. For this example, the three parameters drink, normal, and light, are choosen randomly, without lost generality. We can leave it so the user chooses the task. Once the decision is to grasp the handle, this is the result.

Fig. 14. Grasping a mug

Other types of grasp for different types of tasks and parameters for a mug are shown in Figures 15 and 16. Figure 15 makes a decision shows a grasp with power, and Figure 16 grasp shows grasping the top with precision.
Similar process and results are shown in Figures 17 and 18 for a joystick. In this case, there are only two tasks and the parameters are inherent to the joystick.

12. Conclusions

We have presented a novel theory for grasping based on the objects and their functionality. When the object is selected for the user, it is associated with more parameters, which we describe below. After the user chooses the task, the virtual human, if the object is feasible, grasps with the type of grasp calculated as a function of the mathematical model. The new concept in this chapter is that the virtual human can grasp autonomosly without the user once the task is chosen. Support Vector Machine (SVM) theory, for a perceptron, was applied for this autonomous grasp. The position and orientation of the hand or hands was calculated in reference to the center of mass of the object. Angles for each finger were calculated with the equations of forward and inverse kinematics for the novel 25-DOF hand model.

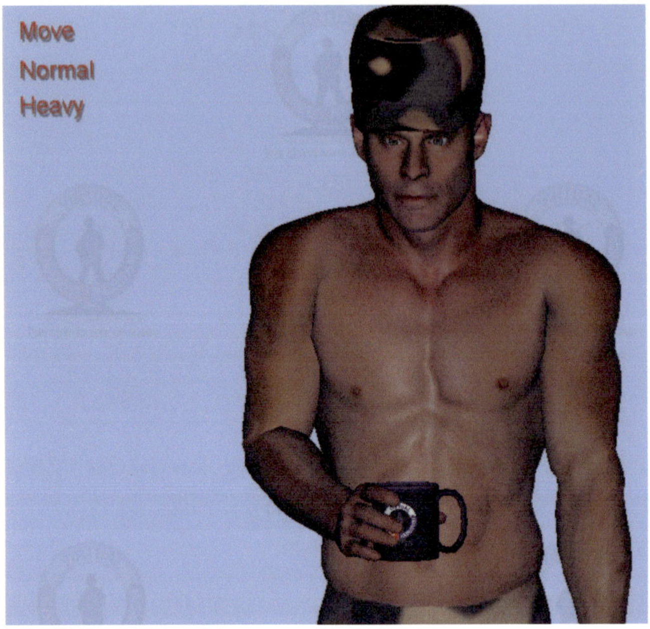

Fig. 15. Grasping a mug; power grasp

Fig. 16. Grasping a mug; precision grasp

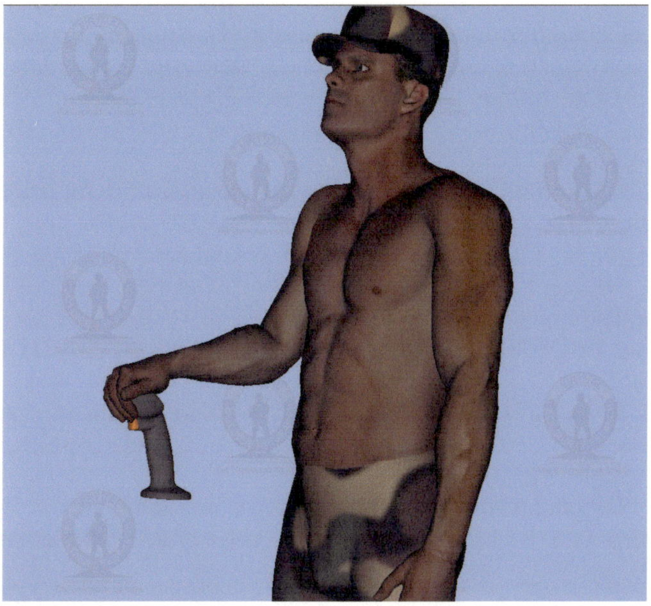

Fig. 17. Grasping a joystick; power grasp

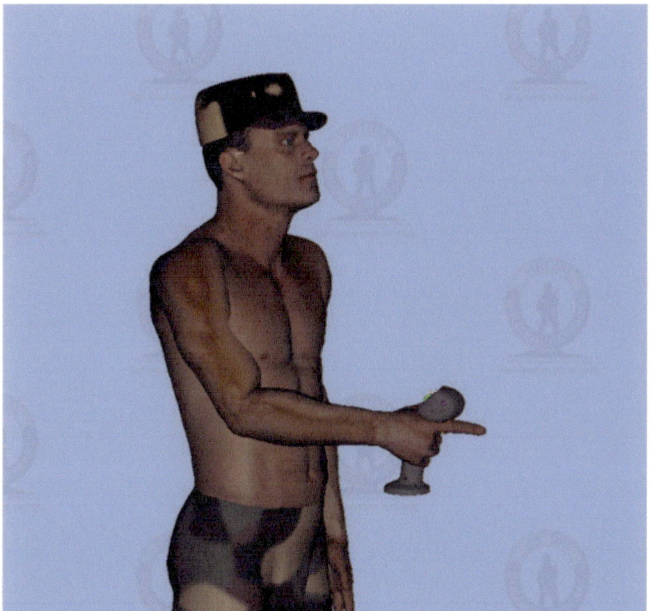

Fig. 18. Grasping a joystick; power grasp

13. References

Anderson, J. A. (1997). *An Introduction to Neural Networks*, Bradford Book, third edn.

Buchcholz, B., Armstrong, T. & Goldstein, S. (1992). Anthropometric data for describing the kinematics of the human hand, *Ergonomics* **35**(3): 261–273.

Farin, G., Hoschek, J. & Kim, M.-S. (2002). *Handbook of COMPUTER AIDED GEOMETRIC DESIGN*, Elsiever, 1 edn.

Gill, P., Murray, W. & Saunders, A. (2002). Snopt: An sqp algorithm for large-scale constrained optimization, *SIAM Journal of Optimization* **12**(4): 979–1006.

Hagan, M. T., Demuth, H. B. & Beale, M. H. (1996). *Neural network design*, Boston : PWS Pub.

Haykin, S. (1999). *Neuronal Network. A Comprensive Foundation*, Prentice Hall international, Inc., second edn.

Hoschek, J. & Lasser, D. (1993). *Fundamentals of COMPUTER AIDED GEOMETRIC DESIGN*, AK Peters, 1 edn.

Kapandji, I. (1996). *Fisiologia articular. Miembro superior*, Medica Panamericana, Madrid, 5 edn.

Rijpkema, H. & Girard, M. (1991). Computer animation of knowledge-based human grasping, *Computer Graphics* **25**(4): 339–348.

Tubiana, R. (1981). *The hand. Volume I*, W.B. Saunders Company, 2 edn.

Tubiana, R., Thomine, J. & Mackin, E. (1996). *Examination of the hand and wrist*, Martin Dunitz, 2 edn.

Wang, W. & Wang, K. (1986). Geometric modeling for swept volume of moving solids, *IEEE CG and A* **86**: 8–17.

Zeid, I. (2005). *Mastering CAD/CAM*, McGraw-Hill, Higher Education, 1 edn.

5

Intermodulation Interference Modelling for Low Earth Orbiting Satellite Ground Stations

Dr. sc. Shkelzen Cakaj
Post and Telecommunication of Kosovo (PTK), Republic of Kosovo

1. Introduction

Microsatellites in Low Earth Orbits (LEO) have been in use for the past two decades. Low Earth Orbit satellites are used for public communication and also for scientific purposes. Low Earth Orbits vary with the type of satellites and their primarily purposes. Low Earth Orbit scientific satellites have very wide application, including Earth's surveillance and astronomy applications. These satellites provide opportunity for investigations for which existing techniques are either difficult or impossible to be applied. Thus, it may be expected that such missions will be further developed in the near future especially in fields where similar experiments by purely Earth-based means are impracticable (Cakaj & Malaric, 2007).
Ground stations have to be established in order to communicate with such satellites, and the quality of communication depends on the performance of the satellite ground station, in addition to that of the satellite. Usually, these scientific satellites communicate with ground stations at S-band. Before the implementation of the ground station the analyses related to environmental factors have to be considered, especially in urban areas (Keim et al., 2004). Among these factors which could disturb ground station's performance is the intermodulation interference because of permanent presence of ground station uplink signal. At the ground stations located in urban areas with high density of mobile radio systems it is not easy to eliminate intermodulation interference, since these signals are unpredictable. Intermodulation products generated by radiofrequency (RF) signals present in the front end of the satellite ground station and uplink satellite signal are potential to disturb, especially in urban areas. Each case specifically should be studied with on site respective experimental investigations. These intermodulation products are caused because of eventual non-linearity at the low noise amplifier (LNA) used at the downlink of the ground station. The most influent are the third order of intermodulation products. Thus, only third order of intermodulation products is further considered.
Modelling process approach is an attempt to generalize the case and to make conclusions in advance before final decision about: location, operation frequency up to device selection for the ground satellite station implementation. Thus, interference of intermodulation products caused by uplink signal and any other radiofrequency signal presents in the front end of the ground station's receiving system is mathematically analyzed and then further modelled.

Based on the modelling concept, the intermodulation interference calculator is introduced as a main application point of this chapter.
In order to better understand the problem of intermodulation interference at satellite ground stations, the general aspects of satellite communications, orbits, artificial satellites and satellite ground stations are briefly explained.

2. General aspects of satellite communications

The basic resources available for satellite communications are *orbits* and *radio frequency spectrum* (RF). The typical satellite communication system comprises of a *ground segment, space segment* and *control segment*. The link which transmits radio waves from the ground station to the satellite is called *uplink*. The satellite in turn transmits to the ground station by the *downlink*. The ground segment consists of all the ground stations. The function of the *ground segment* (one or more ground stations) is to receive or transmit the information to the satellite in the most reliable manner while retaining the desired signal quality. The *space segment* consists of one or more artificial satellites. In case of more satellites they are organized in a network called *constellation*. The *control segment* consists of all ground facilities for control, monitoring and tracking the satellite.
There are two typical concepts of ground stations: single antenna system with the duplexer and double antenna system. At the single antenna concept, the separation of the transmission and reception is achieved by means of duplexer (Maral & Bousquet, 2002). Since, the discussion in this chapter is related to the satellite ground station performance, the typical ground satellite station architecture is presented in Fig. 1.

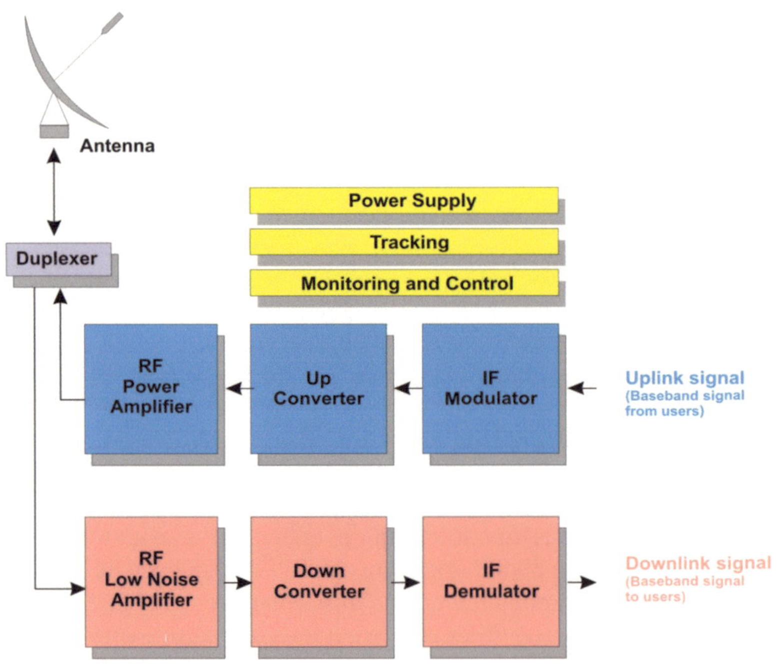

Fig. 1. The typical satellite ground station architecture

The *coverage area* (footprint) is defined as a region on the Earth from where the satellite is seen under a minimum predefined elevation angle (Cakaj et al., 2007). The communication between the satellite and a ground station is established only when the satellite is visible from the ground station. Before the implementation of ground station, analyses related to environmental factors have to be considered, especially in urban areas. Rain effects, the impact of intermodulation interference, and contact time duration under low elevation angles, are some of the aspects which should be considered due the final decision on the design of the ground station (Cakaj & Malaric, 2007).

The functionality of ground station can be disturbed because of the interference, since interference may be considered as a form of noise. Effects of interference must be assessed in terms of what is tolerable disturbing level to the end user receiver. Interference effect to the end user receiver will depend on the amount of frequency overlap between the interfering spectrum and the wanted channel passband (Richharia, 1999).

Aspects of intermodulation interference impact on performance of the low Earth orbiting satellite ground stations are further analyzed within this chapter and then closed with modeling concept of appropriate interference.

3. Orbits

The path of the satellite's motion is an *orbit*. The orbit lies in the *orbital plane*. In order to describe the satellite's movement within its orbit in space, a few parameters are required to be defined. These are known as *space orbital parameters* schematically presented in Fig. 2 and defined under below items a), b), c) and d) (Maral & Bousquet, 2002; Richharia, 1999; Roddy, 2006).

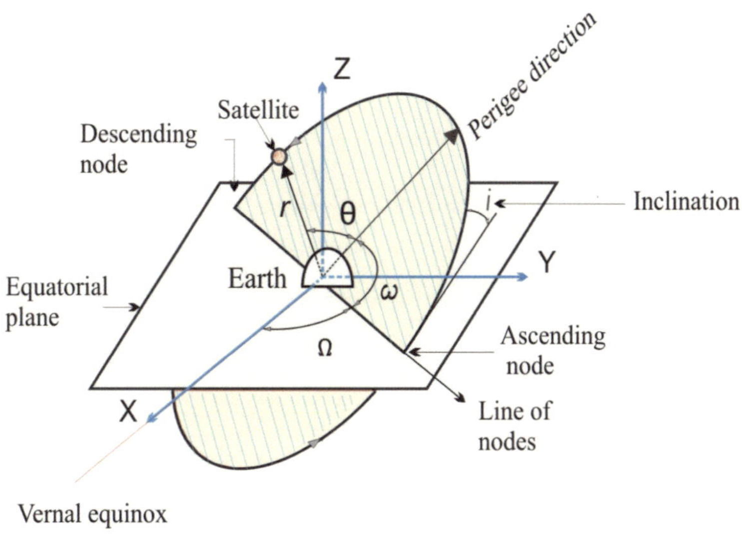

Fig. 2. Space orbital parameters

a) *The position of the orbital plane in space.*
This is specified by means of two parameters - the *inclination i* and the *right ascension of the ascending node Ω*. Inclination i represents the angle of the orbital plane with respect to the Earth's equator. The right ascension of the ascending node Ω defines the location of the ascending and descending orbital crossing nodes (these two nodes make a *line of nodes*) with respect to a fixed direction in space. The fixed direction is Vernal equinox. Vernal equinox is direction of line joining the Earth's and the Sun's center on the first day of the spring (Maral & Bousquet, 2002).
b) *Location of the orbit in orbital plane.*
Normally an infinite number of orbits can be laid within an orbital plane. So, the orientation of the orbit in its plane is defined by the *argument of perigee ω*. This is the angle, taken positively from 0° to 360° in the direction of the satellite's motion, between the direction of the ascending node and the direction of perigee (Maral & Bousquet, 2002; Richharia, 1999; Roddy, 2006).
c) *Position of the satellite in the orbit.*
The position of the satellite in orbit is determined by the angle θ called the *true anomaly,* which is the angle measured positively in the direction of satellite's movement from 0° to 360°, between the direction of perigee and the position of the satellite (Maral & Bousquet, 2002; Richharia, 1999; Roddy, 2006).
d) *The shape of orbit.*
The shape of orbit is presented by the *semi-major axis a* which defines the size of orbit and the *eccentricity e* which defines the ellipticity of an orbit. The orbit is a trajectory within an orbital plane with a maximum extension from the Earth center at the *apogee* (r_a) and the minimum at the *perigee* (r_p) as presented in Fig. 3 (Richharia, 1999).

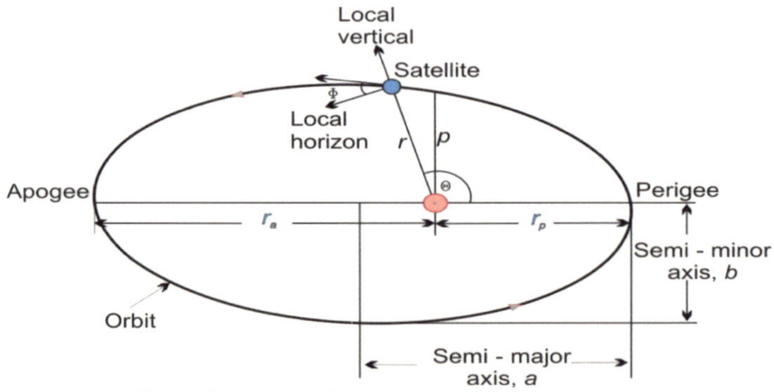

Fig. 3. Major parameters of an elliptical orbit

The eccentricity is defined as the ratio of difference to sum of apogee (r_a) and perigee (r_p) raddi as in Eqn. 1.

$$e = \frac{r_a - r_p}{r_a + r_p} \tag{1}$$

Applying geometrical ellipse features yield out the relations between semi major axis, apogee and perigee as:

$$r_p = a(1-e) \tag{2}$$

$$r_a = a(1+e) \tag{3}$$

both, r_p and r_a are considered from the Earth's center. Earth's radius is $r_E = 6378\,\text{km}$. Then, the highs of perigee and apogee are:

$$h_p = r_p - r_E \tag{4}$$

$$h_a = r_a - r_E \tag{5}$$

Orbits with zero eccentricity are called *circular orbits*. The circularity of the orbit simplifies the mathematical analysis, since then it is:

$$e = 0 \Rightarrow r_a = r_p = a \tag{6}$$

The movement of the satellite within its circular orbit is represented by *orbital time, radius, altitude* and *velocity*. Circular orbits are presented in Fig. 4, and mainly are categorized as:

- GEO (Geosynchronous Earth Orbits)
- MEO (Medium Earth Orbits) and
- LEO (Low Earth Orbits)

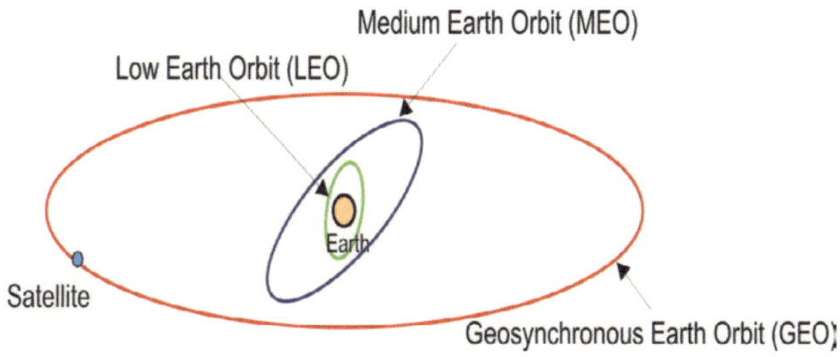

Fig. 4. Satellite orbits

3.1 Orbit and ground station geometry

In Fig. 5, the position of a satellite within inclined orbital plane with respect to the ground station is presented (Cakaj, 2008). The Earth rotates from East to West. This is known as *eastward direction*, the opposite is called *westward direction*. An orbit in which satellite moves in the same direction as the Earth's rotation is known as *prograde* or *direct orbit*. The inclination of a prograde orbit always lies between 0° and 90° (consider Fig. 2). Most satellites are launched in a prograde orbit because the Earth's rotational velocity provides part of the orbital velocity with a consequent saving in launch energy (Maral & Bousquet, 2002; Richharia, 1999; Roddy, 2006).

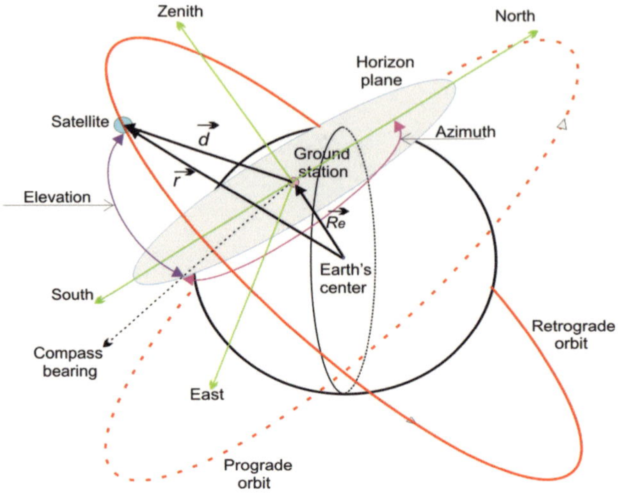

Fig. 5. Orbit and ground station geometry

An orbit in which the satellite moves in opposite direction to the Earth rotation is called *retrograde orbit*. The inclination of a retrograde orbit always lies between 90° and 180°. The position of the satellite within its orbit considered from the ground station point of view is defined by *Azimuth* and *Elevation* angles as presented in Fig. 5 (The *Azimuth* is the angle of the direction of the satellite, measured in the horizon plane from geographical north in clockwise direction. The *Elevation* is the angle between a satellite and the ground station horizon plane). From Fig. 5 yields:

$$\vec{d} = \vec{r} - \vec{R}_e \tag{7}$$

where, $\vec{r}$ is the satellite radius vector, $\vec{R}_e$ ground station radius vector and $\vec{d}$ is the satellite to ground station range vector.

Theoretically, the position of the orbit is fixed in space (or slowly varying), while the location of the ground station rotates with the Earth. Because of the Earth's motion the satellite's coverage areas on Earth change, especially for LEO satellites which move too fast over the Earth, as it is presented in Fig. 6 (http://www.noaa.gov, 2005).

Fig. 6. LEO satellite and coverage area

The main goal is to establish the communication between the satellite and the ground station. Since LEO satellites move too fast over the ground station, then the communication between the satellite and ground station depends on how long the satellite can be seen from the ground station. This in fact brings the problem on finding the look angles and range of the satellite from the ground station (refer to Fig. 5) (Roddy, 2006; Cakaj et al., 2007). Further, this is clarified through Fig. 7.

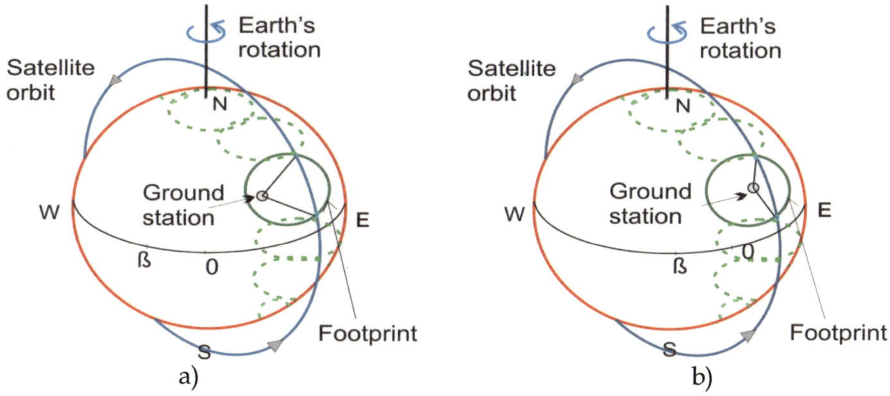

Fig. 7. Satellite passes for an Earth rotation angle of β per orbit

Because of Earth's rotation around its N-S axis for angle β the ground station changes the position relatively to orbital plane, so the pointing (azimuth and elevation angles) from the ground station to the satellite is not identical for the both satellite passes (see a) and b) in Fig. 7). Hence the communication duration between the satellite and the ground station is not constant and varies for each path over the ground station (Cakaj et al., 2007).

4. Artificial satellites

An artificial satellite is manufactured object dedicated to continuously orbit the Earth, or other body in space. The original objectives of artificial satellites were to serve low-cost communication relays and to provide new opportunities on investigation and development of new radio techniques.

Recently, especially with escalating cost of large satellites, attention is turned to smaller satellites so called *microsatellites*, which are taking also a new role, including science missions (Karoll et al., 1998).

An artificial satellite essentially consists of two main functional units: *payload* and *bus (platform)*. The primary function of the *payload* is to provide communication by repeater and antenna system. The *bus* provides all the necessary electrical and mechanical support to the payload. The bus consists of several subsystems. An artificial satellite (space segment) is presented in Fig. 8 (http://www.noaa.gov).

Fig. 8. Artificial satellite

Every satellite (especially, microsatellite when is dedicated for scientific purposes) carries special instruments that enable it to perform its mission (for example, a satellite that studies the universe has a telescope, a satellite that helps forecast the weather carries cameras to track the movement of clouds) (Essex et al., 2007; Grillmayer, 2004). There are six main types of artificial satellites, classified as follows (Oberright, 2004; Parrington, 1991).

- *Scientific research satellites*
- *Weather satellites*
- *Communications satellites*
- *Navigation satellites*
- *Earth observing satellites*
- *Military satellites*

Scientific research satellites gather data for scientific purposes. These satellites during performing their missions gather information about the composition and effects of the space around the Earth, record changes in Earth and its atmosphere and, still others observe planets, stars and other distant objects. Most of these satellites operate in low altitude orbits (LEO). Scientific research satellites also orbit other stars and planets (Mars, Moon, etc). Usually, these satellites communicate with ground stations in S-band.

Weather satellites are dedicated for analyses related to weather forecast. Weather satellites observe the atmospheric conditions over large areas. Their instruments measure cloud cover, temperature, air pressure, precipitation etc. Most of these satellites operate in low altitude orbits (LEO) and in S-band. These satellites always observe the Earth at the same local time. These weather data collected under constant sunlight conditions, then can be easier compared.

Communication satellites serve as relay stations, receiving radio signals from one location and transmitting them to another. A communication satellite can relay several television programs or very large number of telephone calls, and data services at once. Communication satellites are usually launched in a high altitude; such is geosynchronous orbit (GEO).

Navigation satellites enable operator of aircraft, ships, and land vehicles anywhere on Earth to determine their location with high accuracy. The satellites send out radio signals that are picked up by a computerized receiver carried on aircrafts, ships, or land vehicles.

Navigation satellites operate in networks in medium and low Earth orbits (MEO & LEO).
Earth observing satellites are used to map and monitor our planet's resources and ever-changing chemical-biological life. They follow LEO orbits. Under constant illumination from the Sun, they take pictures in different colors of visible light and non-visible radiation. Scientists use Earth observation satellites to locate mineral deposits, determine the location and size of freshwater supplies identify sources of pollution and study its effects, etc. (Oberright, 2004; Parrington, 1991).
Military satellites include weather, communications, navigation and Earth observing satellites used for military purposes.

4.1 Low Earth Orbit (LEO) satellites

LEOs are just above Earth's atmosphere, where there is almost no air to cause drag on the satellite and reduce its speed. Less energy is required to launch a satellite into this type of orbit than into any other orbit (Richharia, 1999). Satellites that point toward deep space and provide scientific information generally operate in this type of orbit. The Hubble Space Telescope, for example, operates at an altitude of about 610 km with an orbital period of 97 minutes (Difonzo, 2000). LEO altitudes range from 275km up to 1400km limited by Van Allen radiation effects (sensors, integrated circuits and solar cells can be damaged by this radiation) (Zaim, 2002). Satellites in these orbits have an orbital period of around (90-110) minutes. For satellites this is a short flyover period, which means that the antenna at the ground station must follow the satellite very fast with high pointing accuracy. The communication duration time between the satellite and the ground station takes (5-15) minutes 6-8 times during the day (Zee & Stibrany, 2000; Keim & Scholtz 2006). Mismatch in pointing will lead to a decrease of received signal strength and further to a reduction of the communication quality.
LEO satellites have very wide applications, from remote sensing of oceans, through analyses on Earth's climate changes, Earth's imagery with high resolution or astronomical purposes. These satellites provide opportunities for investigations for which alternative techniques are either difficult or impossible to be applied by means on Earth.

4.2 Constellation

The constellation is a system of low (medium) Earth orbit (LEO or MEO) identical satellites, launched in several orbital planes with the orbits having the same altitude. The satellites move in a synchronized manner in trajectories relative to Earth. The application of low Earth orbit satellites organized in a *constellation* is an alternative to wireless telephone networks. Satellites in low orbits arranged in a constellation, work together by relaying information to each other and to the users on the ground.
In case the satellites within a constellation are equipped with advanced on-board processing, they can communicate directly with each other by line of sight using inter-satellite links (ISL). If the ISL is between satellites in the same orbit, it is called intra-plane ISL, and if it is between satellites in adjacent planes it is called inter-plane ISL (Difonzo, 2000). The GPS (Global Positioning System) constellation is presented in Fig. 9 (htpp://www.gps.gov). This constellation is organized in 6 orbital planes of 4 satellites per plane (24 satellites). Each satellite circles the Earth twice a day.

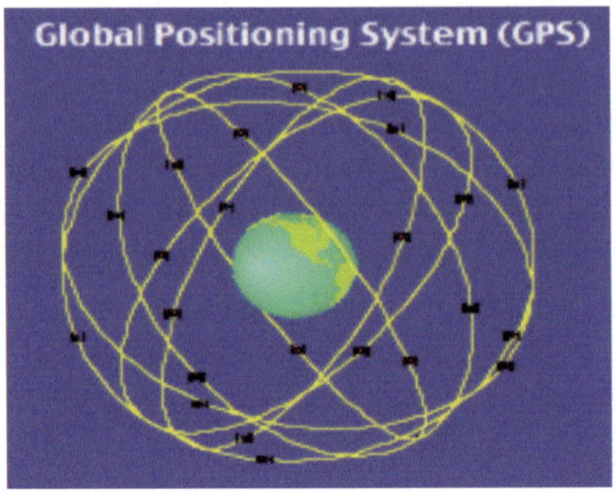

Fig. 9. GPS constellation

5. General aspects of interference

Interference may be considered as a form of noise. Effects of interference must be assessed in terms of what is tolerable disturbing level to the end user receiver. Interference effect to the end user receiver will depend on the amount of frequency overlap between the interfering spectrum and the wanted channel passband. From the technical and practical point of view, the following classification of interference should be considered (Richharia, 1999). These two scenarios in Fig. 10 are presented.

- *Co - channel interference*
- *Out - of - band interference*

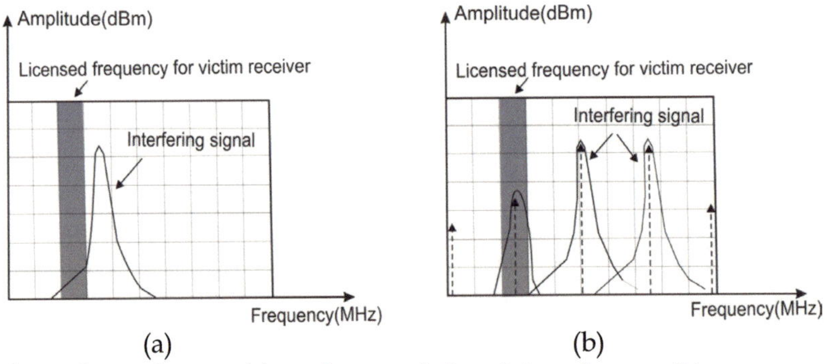

Fig. 10. Co-channel interference (a), and out - of - band interference (b)

The receiver hit by interference is called *victim* receiver. The *co-channel interference* occurs when the victim receiver is disturbed by the system or equipment operating at the same frequency as the victim receiver. This is caused by unexpected legal or illegal (unlicensed) signals. Applying strictly the ITU recommendations on emitted power and frequency planning it is possible the co-channel interference to be controlled and minimized. More problematic is *out-of-band interference*. This interference occurs when the victim receiver is hit by signals which are generated by equipment which does not operate in the same frequency as the victim receiver. The phenomenon of generating other signals from one or more signals is called *intermodulation* (Richharia, 1999).

These new generated signals can unexpectedly fall within a victim receiver licensed passband (Fig. 10b). In case the generated intermodulated signal is too strong, it will not only interfere but it could completely block the desired receiving signal (Cakaj, et. al., 2005) Through modelling process, the problem can be analyzed and avoided in advance.

5.1 Intermodulation interference

In satellite communication systems the intermodulation noise is generated by nonlinear transfer characteristics of devices. Toward the uplink, the intermodulation noise is mainly generated because of the high power amplifier (HPA) nonlinearity. Related to downlink performance, especially in urban areas (presence of GSM, UMTS, WiFi, WiMax networks) intermodulation should be considered because of the low noise amplifier (LNA) nonlinearity. Disturbance introduced due to nonlinearity is known as *intermodulation interference.* These interference sources are statistically independent.
The nonlinear transfer characteristic may be expressed as a Taylor series which relates input and output voltages (Roddy, 2006).

$$e_0 = ae_i + be_i^2 + ce_i^3 + \ldots \tag{8}$$

Here, a, b, c, and so on are coefficients depending on the transfer characteristic, e_0 is the output voltage, and e_i is the input voltage, which consists of the sum of individual carriers. Intermodulation interference components can be classified as:

- *Harmonic Products*
- *Intermodulation Products*

Harmonic products are single tone distortion products caused by device nonlinearity. When a non-linear device is stimulated by a signal at frequency f_1, spurious output signals can be generated at the harmonic frequencies $2f_1$, $3f_1$ ... N f_1. The order of the harmonic products is given by the frequency multiplier; for example the second harmonic is second order product. Harmonics are usually measured in dBc, which means dB below the carrier (fundamental) output signal.
Intermodulation products are multi-tone distortion products that result when two or more signals at frequencies f_1, f_2, ... f_n are present at the input of a nonlinear device. The spurious products which are generated due to the non-linearity of a device are related to the original input signals frequencies. Analysis and measurements in practice are most frequently done with two input frequencies. The frequencies of the two-tone intermodulation products are (Anritsu, 2000) :

$$Mf_1 \pm Nf_2 \quad \text{where } M,N = 0,1,2,3,\ldots..$$

The order of the distortion product is given by the sum *M+N*. The second order intermodulation products of two signals at f_1 and f_2 would occur at $f_1 + f_2$, $f_2 - f_1$, $2f_1$

and $2f_2$. The third order intermodulation products (component ce_i^3 of Eqn. 8) of the two signals at f_1 and f_2 would be $3f_1$, $3f_2$, $2f_1+f_2$, $2f_1-f_2$, f_1+2f_2 and f_1-2f_2. These are presented in Fig. 11 (Anritsu, 2000).
Mathematically intermodulation product calculation could result in "negative" frequency, but it is the absolute value of these calculations that is of concern. Broadband systems may be affected by all non-linear distortion products. Narrowband circuits are only susceptible to those in the passband. Bandpass filtering can be an effective way to eliminate most of the undesired products without affecting in band performance (see Fig. 11), but third order of intermodulation products are usually too close to the fundamental signals to be filtered out.

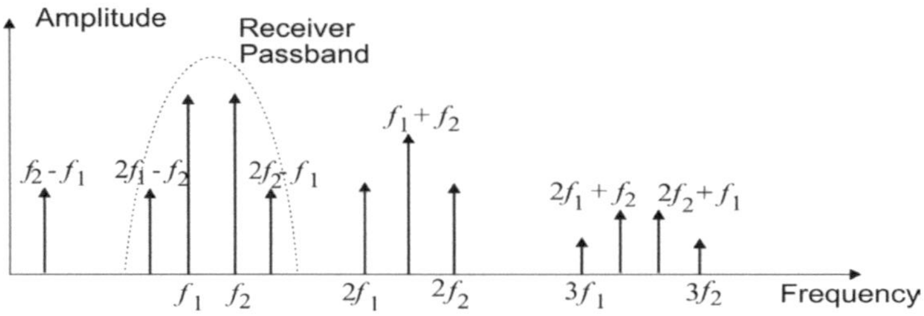

Fig. 11. Second and third order intermodulation products

Thus, the third order (and to a lesser extent fifth order) products contribute the major proportion of the intermodulation noise power. The closer the fundamental signals are to each other, the closer third intermodulation products will be to them. Filtering becomes very hard if the intermodulation products fall inside the passband. These unwanted intermodulation products can occur in receivers and may coincide with the operating frequency of the receiver in which case the wanted signal can be masked. The level of these products is a function of the *power received*. Further, out-of-band intermodulation products transmitted from the ground stations or satellites result in interference to other systems, also. To minimize such harmful emissions, international radio regulations restrict such out-of-band transmissions from ground stations to very low levels (Maral& Bousquet, 2002; Richharia, 1999; Roddy, 2006).

5.2 Intermodulation interference by uplink signal

The quality of communication depends on satellite ground stations performance. (Elbert, 2000; Landis & Mulldolland, 1993). The performance of a ground station could be disturbed by intermodulation interference because of permanent presence of uplink signal and any other RF (radio frequency) signal present in front end of receiving system. At ground stations located in urban areas with high density of mobile radio systems it is not easy to eliminate intermodulation interference signals since these are unpredictable. Each specific case specifically should be studied with on site respective experimental investigations.
Satellite ground station in urban area should be designed so that, at the receiver input, the level of the signal received from the satellite via the main beam of the ground station antenna exceeds the in-band noise by an adequate margin. But, the unwanted out-of-band inputs, as intermodulation products, generated by the ground station uplink signal and any

other radio frequency signal in front of low noise amplifier (for example: signals from nearby mobile system base stations), even though they are received via sidelobes in the ground station's antenna pattern, they could be higher and mask the wanted signal (Cakaj, et. al. 2008). Thus, within this chapter the interference of intermodulation products caused by uplink signal and any other radiofrequency signal present in the front end of the ground station's receiving system is analyzed and then modelled. Modelling process approach is an attempt as much as possible to generalize the case and based on that to make conclusions in advance before final decision on location, operation frequency up to device selection for the ground satellite station implementation.

In Fig. 12 it is presented the experiment set up which enables to check the intermodulation disturbance at the receiving satellite ground station. The double antenna ground station system is considered in order to clearly show up the presence of uplink signal. In Fig. 12, in front end, the GSM 1800 signals are considered, since they are close to S-band which is usually used for communication with LEO satellites. The similar procedure could be used in case of any other radio signal presence, also (Cakaj, et. al. 2005; Cakaj, et. al. 2008).

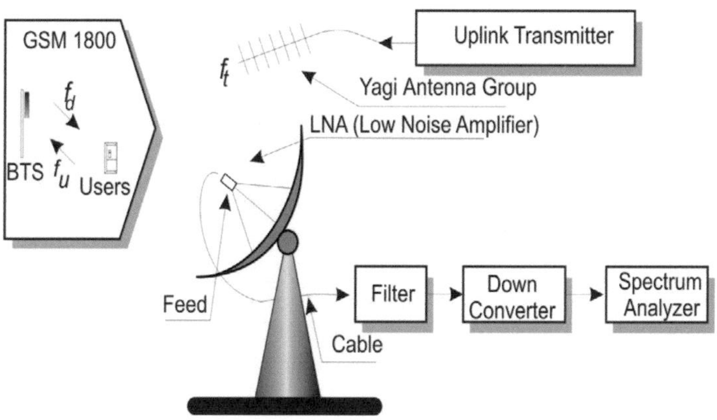

Fig. 12. Intermodulation scenario at satellite ground station

The presence of intermodulation products, at ground station, near the downlink frequency f_r caused by GSM 1800 and uplink signal f_t are expected because of eventual non-linearity of the Low Noise Amplifier (LNA) used in the front end at the downlink of the ground station. By the non-linearity of the low noise amplifier, the intermodulation products will be generated from the uplink signal at frequency f_t on one hand and GSM signals at frequencies (f_u, f_d) on the other (Cakaj, et.al., 2005).

Based on ITU-R F.382-6 (1.7GHz - 2.1GHz) frequency band for mobile systems at 1710MHz - 1785MHz is for the uplink and at 1805MHz - 1880MHz is for the downlink. The last channel frequency for uplink is 1781.4 MHz and for downlink it is 1876.4 MHz. The difference between the upper edge of the band and the last frequency within a band is called *Guard Band* (GB). Therefore, in our case the Guard Bands are:

$$GB_u = 1785MHz - 1781.4MHz = 3,6MHz \tag{9}$$

$$GB_d = 1880MHz - 1876.4MHz = 3,6MHz \tag{10}$$

For a particular case, considering uplink transmit frequency $f_t = 2055$ MHz and downlink receive frequency $f_r = 2232$ MHz, signals present at the front-end of the low noise amplifier (LNA) of the receiving system at the ground station are presented in Fig. 13 (Cakaj, et. al., 2005).

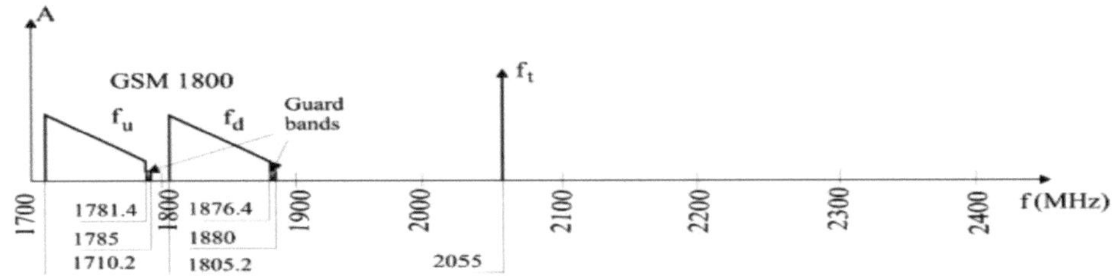

Fig. 13. Signals present at frontend (LNA) of the downlink

In order to clarify process, the first, few medium and the last one GSM 1800 channels with respective uplink f_u and downlink f_d signal frequencies are presented in Table 1.

Channel	f_u	f_d
512	1710.2MHz	1805.2MHz
521	1712.0MHz	1807.0MHz
523	1712.4MHz	1807.4MHz
586	1725.0MHz	1820.0MHz
632	1734.2MHz	1829.2MHz
868	1781.4MHz	1876.4MHz

Table 1. Frequency table of GSM 1800 uplink and downlink signals

Intermodulation products generated by signals at frequencies f_t and f_u fall too far on the frequency domain from the receiver's downlink frequency f_r, therefore they will not be treated. Third order intermodulation products generated by frequencies f_t and f_d are $2f_t \pm f_d$ and $2f_d \pm f_t$. Products $2f_t - f_d$ are worth further analysis, because they are only ones which fall in the frequency domain near the receiver's frequency f_r. These intermodulation products which appear at the LNA's output (respectively at the filters input) in frequency domain (RF) are presented in Table 2 (based on Table 1) and further in Fig. 14.

f_t	f_d	$2f_t - f_d$
2055MHz	1805.2MHz	2304.8 MHz
2055MHz	1807.0MHz	2293.0MHz
2055MHz	1807.4MHz	2292.6 MHz
2055MHz	1820.0MHz	2290.0 MHz
2055MHz	1829.2MHz	2280.8 MHz
2055MHz	1876.4MHz	2233.6 MHz

Table 2. Third order intermodulation products

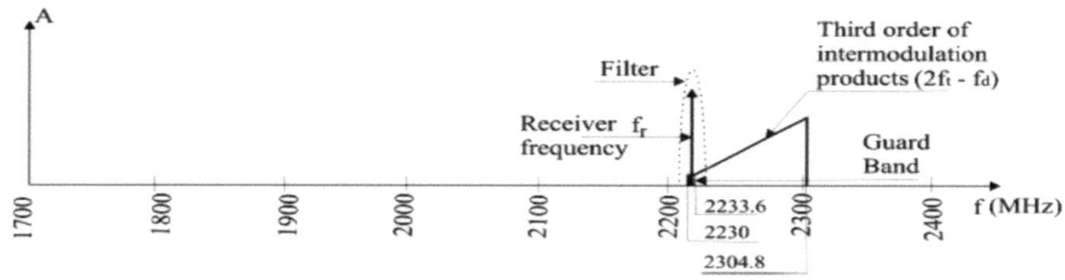

Fig. 14. Third order of intermodulation products

These signals will be faced with filter before going into the downconverter (see Fig. 12). The situation behind the filter and in front of the downconverter is presented in Fig. 15.

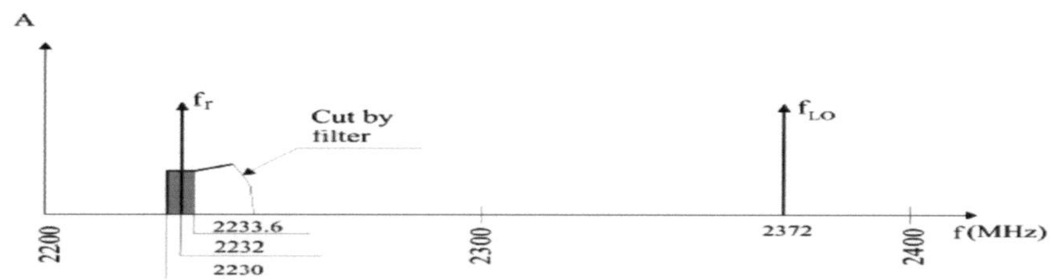

Fig. 15. Signals in front of downconverter

From Fig. 15 it is clear that the filter has substantially attenuated a considerable number of interference contributions from intermodulation products. Let us consider local oscillator frequency of the downconverter as f_{LO} = *2372MHz*. If all signals presented in Fig. 15 in RF domain mirror into IF domain (intermediate frequency is 140MHz) with frequency f_{LO}, the spectrum in Fig. 16 follows (Cakaj, et. al. 2005). From Fig. 16 it is obvious the presence of intermodulation products behind the downconverter and in front of the demodulator as well. The question is: are these products disturbing the desired signal!

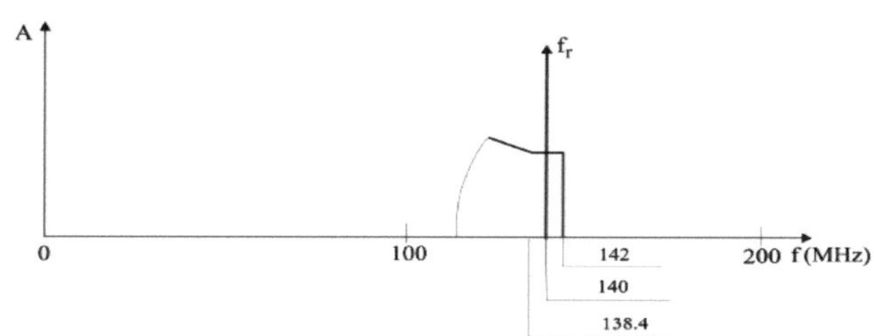

Fig. 16. Downconverter output

Further considering IF frequency as $f_{IF} = 140\,\text{MHz}$ and the receiving bandwidth $B = 100\,\text{KHz}$, than at IF output of the downconverter or as IF input of the demodulator, the bandwidth is:

$$139.95\text{MHz} < f < 140.05\text{MHz} \tag{11}$$

From Table 2 the intermodulation products (third column) are mirrored in IF band by local oscillator of frequency 2372MHz. The mirrored intermodulation products are: 67.2MHz, 79MHz, 79.4MHz, 82 MHz, 91.2MHz and 138.4MHz. No one of these intermodulation products fall within a frequency range under Eqn. 11, so there is no intermodulation interference. The upper edge of the frequency which can eventually disturb is 138.4MHz which one for the case of bandwidth of 100 KHz is too far in IF frequency domain. For the particular case above discussed, the receiving bandwidth of few 100 KHz will still be safe.

5.3 Interference modelling

Generally, if spurious signals generated as intermodulation products behind low noise amplifier *fall within a passband* of a receiver and *the signal level is of sufficient amplitude*, it can degrade the performance of the receiver. So, the receiver's operation will be disturbed if two above conditions are fulfilled. Based on this concept, and the above discussed particular case, it is built the intermodullation interference modelling which enables the interference calculation caused by any radio source of frequency f_x and satellite uplink signal of frequency f_t (Cakaj, et. al., 2008). Only third order of intermodullation products is considered. Among third order of intermodullation products are considered only components of frequencies $2f_x - f_t$ and $2f_t - f_x$. Fig. 11 and Fig. 16 tell us that these products could fall within a receiver's passband. Other intremodullation products of frequencies, $3f_x$ $3f_t$, $2f_x + f_t$ and $2f_t + f_x$ usually fall too far from the passband and practically are eliminated by filtering. Thus these products are not treated in modelling concept.

The amplitudes of intermodullation products of frequencies $2f_x - f_t$ and $2f_t - f_x$ are respectively $3A_x^2 A_t$ and $3A_t^2 A_x$, (these yields out from trigonometry) where A_x is amplitude of any radio signal of frequency f_x in front of low noise amplifier which is potential to cause intermodulation with uplink satellite signal of frequency f_t and amplitude A_t. Thus, third order of intermodullation products is characterized by:

$$f_{i1} = 2f_x - f_t, N_{i1} = 3A_x^2 A_t \tag{12}$$

$$f_{i2} = 2f_t - f_x, N_{i2} = 3A_t^2 A_x \tag{13}$$

where f_{in} is intermodualtion interference frequency of amplitude N_{in} for $n = 1,2$ behind the low noise amplifier. Since, the analyses are related mainly to the frequency domain, in order to simplify the case it is supposed that there is no amplification on overall system chain. Usually, the amplitude A_x is too low in front of low noise amplifier since it is limited by ITU rules about radiated power and consequently it is expected that the amplitude $N_{i1} = 3A_x^2 A_t$ will not disturb the receiver. The most dangerous component is $N_{i2} = 3A_t^2 A_x$ since the amplitude A_t is of high level because this is amplitude of uplink signal which has to overcome too high attenuation toward the satellite. The reference checking point is downconverter's IF output or demodulator's IF input. So, the intermodulation interference is checked around intermediate frequency f_{IF}. The mirroring into intermediate frequency is achieved by downlink local oscillator frequency f_{LO}. All frequencies are mirrored by f_{LO}, including intermodulation products and desired receiving signal of frequency f_r. Thus, it is:

$$f_{IF} = f_{LO} - f_r \tag{14}$$

For a receiver with bandwidth $B = 2\Delta f$, the receiving passband at IF input is from $f_{IF} - \Delta f$ up to $f_{IF} + \Delta f$ where f_{IF} is intermediate frequency which usually is 140MHz or 70MHz. Thus, the receiver could be disturbed if the intermodullation product mirrored at IF, falls within frequency band at IF input, mathematically expressed as:

$$f_{IF} - \Delta f \leq f_{in} - f_{LO} \leq f_{IF} + \Delta f \tag{15}$$

By substituting f_{IF} form Eqn. 14 to Eqn.15 yields out,

$$(f_{LO} - f_r) - \Delta f \leq f_{in} - f_{LO} \leq (f_{LO} - f_r) + \Delta f \tag{16}$$

Then further, if we substitute f_{in} from Eqn. 12 and Eqn. 13 at Eqn. 16 will have:

$$(f_{LO} - f_r) - \Delta f \leq (2f_x - f_t) - f_{LO} \leq (f_{LO} - f_r) + \Delta f \tag{17}$$

$$(f_{LO} - f_r) - \Delta f \leq (2f_t - f_x) - f_{LO} \leq (f_{LO} - f_r) + \Delta f \tag{18}$$

Thus, if frequency f_x of external radio source fulfills the Eqn. 17 or Eqn. 18 the desired signal at the receiver could be masked by intermodulation interference. The above concept is presented through flowchart in Fig. 17 (Cakaj, et. al. 2008). Input parameters in Fig. 17 are: f_x is frequency of any radio source in front of low noise amplifier of the satellite receiving system, f_t uplink transmit frequency, f_r is downlink receiving frequency and B is downlink receiver's bandwidth.

The level of respective signal should be compared with the level of desired signal at IF input. For comparison of these levels it is sufficient the relationship in between the relative values. Usually this is checked by measurement with spectrum analyzer at IF check point (refer to Fig. 12). The criteria for amplitudes comparison between the desired and interference signal depends on the Earth's station size and dedication. The criteria, between downlink carrier level and interference signal level ranges from 20 dB to 30dB (http://www.satsign.net/interfer.html). This is mathematically expressed by Eqn. 19, as:

$$S_{(IF)}(\text{dB}) - N_{in(IF)}(\text{dB}) \geq (20 \div 30)\text{dB} \tag{19}$$

here $S_{(IF)}$ is desired signal power and $N_{in(IF)}$ intermodulation interference signal power at IF input. These two power levels can be calculated or measured in order to conclude about the receiver's disturbance as considered in flow chart in Fig. 17.

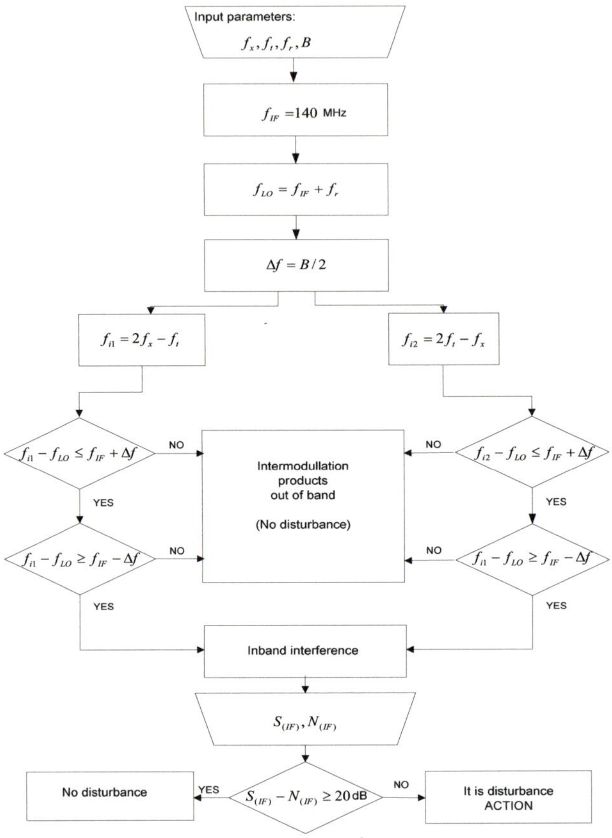

Fig. 17. Intermodulation interference modelling flowchart

Considering above flowchart it is structured intermodulation interference calculator presented in Fig. 18 (Cakaj, et. al., 2008).

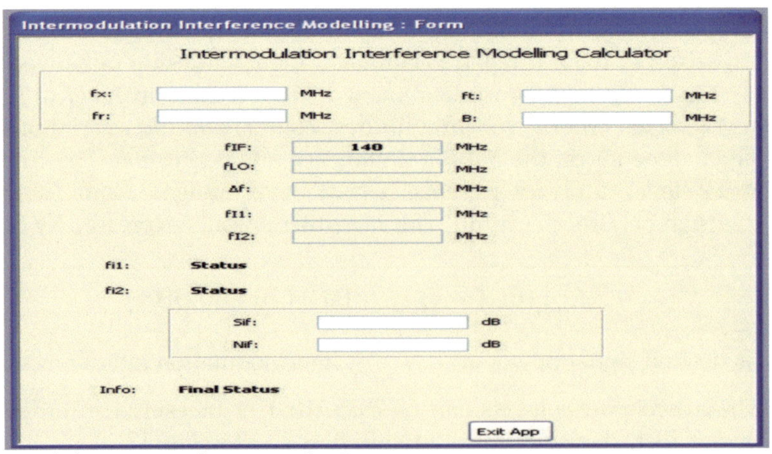

Fig. 18. Intermodulation interference calculator

Usually, only one of the treated components falls within a passband and cause the disturbance. So, if intermodulation components are out off band, then under **Status** (see Fig. 18) for f_{in}, $n = 1,2$ will show up this text: "*Intermodulation products out of band (no distrurbance)*", and no further analyses are needed. In case when one of components falls within a band, then under **Status** for f_{in}, $n = 1,2$ will show up this text: "*In band interference*" and further analyses related to the amplitude level are needed. If amplitude of interference is under limited level at **Final Status** will show up text as, "*No disturbance*", and if the amplitude of interference level is above planned limit shows up the text: "*It is disturbance (Action)*". Based on the modelling concept, the intermodulation interference calculator is introduced. Applying this calculator, for the particular discussed case of the satellite ground station system with uplink transmit frequency $f_t = 2055$ MHz, downlink transmit frequency of $f_r = 2232$ MHz and bandwidth of $B = 100$ KHz, the intermodulation interference disturbs receiving system if in front of low noise amplifier is present signal of frequency $f_x = 1598$ MHz or $f_x = 2283.5$ MHz.

6. Conclusion

The performance of the ground station could be disturbed by intermodulation interference because of permanent presence of uplink signal. The reason behind intermodulation interference is eventual nonlinearity of low noise amplifier's transfer characteristic. Generally, if spurious signals generated as intermodulation products behind low noise amplifier fall within a passband of a receiver and the signal level is of sufficient amplitude, it can degrade the performance of the receiver. So, the receiver's operation will be disturbed. A methodology for analyzing the impact of intermodulation interference on reception performance has been described. These analyses are of high importance on the final decision of the ground station design. The introduced "intermodulation interference calculator" based on modeling concept could be applied on uplink signal frequency selection in order to avoid the interference. This methodology is applicable for MEO (Medium Earth Orbiting) systems, also.

7. References

Anritsu, (2000). Intermodulation Distortion (IMD) Measurements, Microwave Measurements Division, Morgan Hill, CA 95037-2809, United States, Sept, 2000.

Cakaj, Sh., Keim, W. and Malaric, K. (2005). Intermodulation by uplink signal at Low Earth Orbitng ground station. A paper, *Proc. IEEE 18th International Conference on Applied Electromagnetics and Communications - ICECom*, pp. 193-196, Dubrovnik, Croatia, September, 2005.

Cakaj, Sh., Keim, W. and Malaric, K. (2007). Communication duration with low Earth orbiting satellites, *Proceedings of IEEE & IASTED, 4th International Conference on Antennas, Radar and Wave Propagation,* pp. 85-88, Montreal, Canada, May- June 2007.

Cakaj, Sh. & Malaric, K. (2007). Rigorous analysis on performance of LEO satellite ground station in urban environment, *International Journal of Satellite Communications and Networking,* Vol. 25 (6), pp. 619-643, UK, November/December 2007.

Cakaj, Sh., Malaric, K. and Scholtz, A.L. (2008). Modelling of interference caused by uplink signal for Low Earth Orbiting satellite grounds, *IASTED, International Conference on Applied Simulation, and Modelling ASM 2008*, pp.187-191, Corfu, Greece, June, 2008.

Cakaj, Sh. (2008). Analysis of parameter influence on performance of LEO scientific satellite ground stations in urban areas, PhD thesis, pg. 175, Zagreb, Croatia, Jan. 2008.

Carroll, K.A., Zee, R.E., and Matthews J. (1998). The MOST Microsatellite mission: Canada's first space telescope, 12th Annual USU/AIAA Conference on small satellites, Logan Utah, 1998.

Difonzo, D.F. (2000). *Satellite and Aerospace*, The Electrical engineering handbook, chapter 74 Ed. Richard C Dorf, Boca Raton: CRC Press LLC, 2000.

Elbert, B. (2000) *Ground segment and Earth station handbook*, Artech House Inc, Norwood, 2000.

Essex, E.A., Webb, P.A., Horvath, I., McKinnon, C., Shilo, N. M., and Tate, B.S. (2007), Monitoring the ionosphere/plasmasphere with Low Earth Orbit satellites: The Australian microsatellite FedSat, Cooperative Research Center for Satellite Systems, Department of Physics, La Trobe University, Bundoora, Australia 2007.

Grillmayer, G., Lengowski, M., Walz, S., Roeser, H.P., Huber, F. and Wegmann, T. (2004). Flying laptop - microsatelite of the University of Stuttgart for Earth observation and technology demonstation, *55th Astronautical Congress*, IAC-04- IAA.4.1.P.08, Vancouver, Canada, October 2004.

Keim, W., Kudielka. V. and Scholtz. A.L. (2004). A scientific satellite ground station for an urban environment, *Proceedings of IASTED, International Conference on Communication Systems and Networks*, pp. 280-284, Marbella, Spain, September, 2004.

Keim, W. and Scholtz, A.L.(2006). Performance and reliability evaluation of the S-band, at Vienna satellite ground station, Talk, *IASTED, International Conference on Communication System and Networks*, Palma de Mallorca, Spain, 5 pages, 2006.

Landis, J.S. and Mulldolland, J.E. (1993). *Low cost satellite ground control facility design*, IEEE, Aerospace & Electronic systems, 2 (6), pp. 35-49, US, 1993.

Oberright, J.E. (2004). *Satellite artificial*, World Book Online Reference Center, Inc, 2004.

Maral, G. and Bousquet, M. (2002). *Satellite communication systems*, John Willey & sons, Ltd, Chichester, UK, 2002.

Parrington, A. J. Lt. Col. (1991). Toward a rational space - transportation architecture, *Airpower Journal*, USAF, winter 1991.

Richharia, M. (1999). *Satellite communications systems*, McGraw Hill, New York, 1999.

Roddy, D. (2006) *Satellite communcations*, McGraw Hill, New York, 2006.

Zaim A. H., Perros, H.G. and Rouskas, G. (2002). Performance analysis of LEO satellite networks, Department of computer science, North Carolina University, Raleigh, NC, Networking 2002, LNSC 2345, pp. 790-801, USA, 2002.

Zee R. E., and Stibrany, P. (2002). The MOST Microsatellite: A low -cost enabling technology for future space science and techology missions, *Canadian Aeronautics and Space Journal*, Vol. 48(1), pp. 1-11, Canada, March 2002.

6

Inverse Synthetic Aperture Radar Simulators as Software-defined Countermeasure Systems: Security by Obfuscation and Deception for Electronic & Computer Networks Warfare

Theodoros G. Kostis
Dept. of Information & Communication Systems Engineering,
University of the Aegean
HELLAS

1. Introduction

In the eighth episode of season five of the 1962 series of "Mission: Impossible" head operative Peter Graves inflates a life-sized plastic decoy detailing himself so to confuse in order to escape his opposing counterparts. It comes as no surprise that this episode is distinctively titled "Decoy". A decoy is a person, device or event of at least lesser and of preferable minimal value that serves purposes of security by distraction and obfuscation. This function is performed by introducing one or many replicas of a person, device or event in order to conceal the valuable original asset from the adversary interest groups that are actively seeking the friendly beneficiary with malevolent intent.

In our case the valuable asset is a military naval vessel or fleet that requires protection from airborne threats of enhanced electromagnetic nature or advanced radar surveillance and tracking sensor technologies. This work promotes the thesis that the current state of affairs in the field of modern air defence at sea demands distraction and obfuscation solutions based on software defined radar systems. Specifically the generation of the concept of coherent deception that is used to oppose high range resolution radar systems is argued to be more straightforward when performed by software-defined radar systems based on simulator sub-systems than by using dedicated to particular countermeasures hardware platforms of electronic protection for two main reasons. First with a simulator system it is easier to adjust the false target properties to the actual target properties so the adversary will not be able to distinguish the real target thus providing initial targeting hindrances. And then the convenience of adding reality enhancement effects, like the various noise and glint elements found in an actual returned high range resolution radar signal, thus increasing the confidence of the adversary regarding the validity of the contact. Therefore with a simulator system it is easier to adapt to sensor technology limitations and to incorporate the laws of physics in the countermeasure design always keeping in mind that the ultimate goal is to deceive the radar operator and radar system loop with emphasis on the human element. The executive summary of this project is shown in Figure 1 in a visual form.

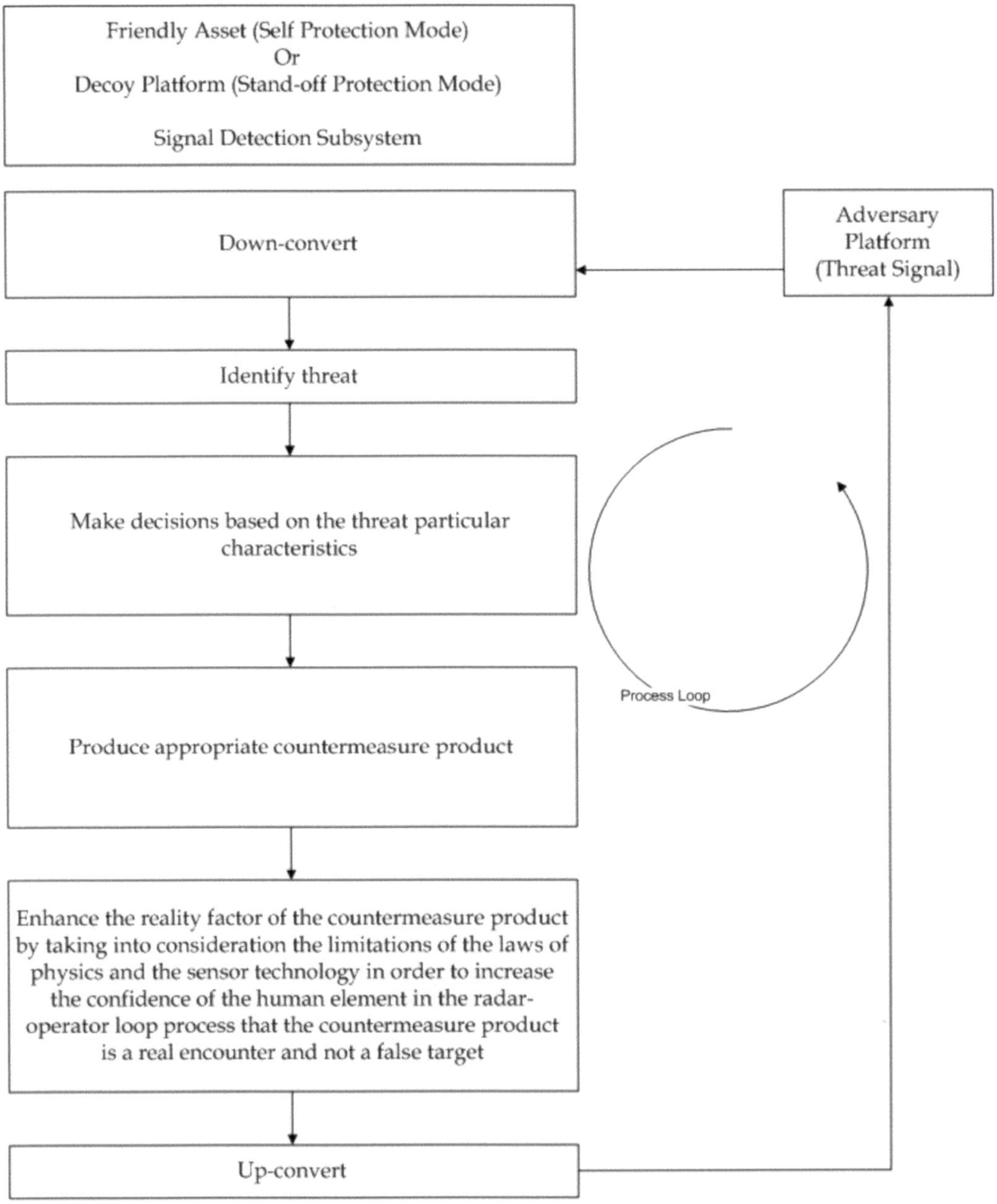

Fig. 1. Visual executive summary of the project.

In this chapter we will create a virtual environment that is considered to accept as inputs the just-in-time characteristics of a threat signal, pass them through a transfer function which is a simulator system and then produce false target images that are realistic because they abide by the current sensor technology limitations and the prevalent laws of physics.

In section 2 we argue that since coherent countermeasures are different from conventional naval countermeasures the concept of air defence at sea when high range resolution miniaturised sensors are involved needs to be reinvented. Here the literature review is presented for ISAR simulators and coherent countermeasures because our contribution is the amalgamation of these two fields. In section 3 we apply the concepts of conceptual modelling to the field of coherent countermeasures. In section 4 we present our implementation procedure, in the forms of the computing methodology, the algorithm design and the final simulator implementation. The results of this work can be found in section 5. Here the simulator is proven to be able to produce ISAR images affected by higher reflectivity on lower coordinates and angular glint effects which is a common case with extended military targets. Also we argue that the computing methodology can be reused in the domain of computer networks warfare by presenting the dual problem space decomposition for the case of a computer network jammer device. We also discuss the project success factor by ascertaining the ability of the current effort to be able to implement a simulator prototype of the initial conceptual model. Finally in section 6 concluding remarks are given and we also make a recommendation for future work by suggesting that the simulator should be recoded with the use of concepts from the field of parallel programming in order to increase its execution speed.

2. Coherent Countermeasures for Air Defence at Sea & ISAR Simulators

Distance is an integral factor in countermeasure activities. When the decoy signal is produced on-board the friendly asset it is called self-protection and when it is produced off-board it is called stand-off protection [Hill, 1988]. The large volume and weight of the countermeasure technology up to the 1990's demanded solutions of self-protection. Stand-off protection was usually performed either by friendly platforms that were far away from the threat signal or chaff systems, that is low value passive elements that would attract the threat away from its target because they exhibited greater radar cross section than the protected platform. For the above reasons conventional radar countermeasure techniques fell into two major categories: angle deception and range deception. In the first case an example is Inverse Gain Jamming. With this method the jamming function is performed by transmitting replicas of the adversary signal back to the hostile sensor. A strong replica when the illuminating signal is weak and vice versa either evens out the phases or over compensates the sensor producing either way the deception effect. With the second method an example is Range Gate Pull-Off (RGPO). The hostile radar concentrates on the target by placing a range gate of a few hundred meters around the target. Because it no longer looks for other signals it is termed that the radar has locked on the target. The RGPO method breaks the lock by making the hostile radar lose this gate thus producing the deception effect. Both methods work for conventional radar systems and will not deceive a high resolution sensor [Wiegand, 1991]. Both above countermeasure methods are applied to conventional radar tracking systems, like the monopulse method. But they are not efficient when the target is viewed by a high range resolution system in stand-off mode or when the missile platform is equipped with a miniaturized high range resolution sensor (ISAR mode). Therefore the problem of air defence at sea needs to be re-invented for there is a need for direct ISAR countermeasures that would oppose a miniaturized high range resolution radar sensor.

2.1 Review of the State of the Art

We will perform a literature review on conventional ISAR simulators and then on coherent deception techniques in order to be able to draw comparisons and build the foundations of our work.

2.1.1 ISAR Simulators

Earlier studies by [Shillington et al, 1991] have described a technique used to simulate ISAR images of a ship model while under angular motions such as yaw, pitch and roll. [Porter et al 1994] have presented the theoretical analysis of SAR techniques as can be applied to ISAR imaging of ship targets. Emphasis is given in the exploitation of information resulting from the point spread function. Also foundations are laid towards the study of interference effects (glint). [Haywood et al, 1994] have introduced the ISARLAB software package which is a comprehensive set of functions that emulate the particular functions of an ISAR system. And [Emir et al, 1997] have developed a simulation program which can generate ISAR images of ships. The method is based on the localization of dominant scatterers and has applications in evaluating the performance of automatic ship classifiers.
Recent studies by [Wong et al, 2006] have clearly presented the mathematical basis of the Inverse Synthetic Aperture process. [Ling et al, 2006] have investigated the acquisition of top or side view ISAR images with the proper cross range scaling. The technique is based on the measurement of slopes of the two main feature lines of the ship, which are the center line and the stern line. This process has the advantage of using only the acquired image to complete its tasks. [Lord et al, 2006] have investigated methods to obtain three dimensional radar cross section (RCS) images using the ISAR concept. Results are provided towards the degradations effect of specular multipath effects on the final image. [Rice et al, 2006] have described a method of ISAR image classification based on a comparison of Range-Doppler imagery to existing three dimensional ship reference models. This technique uses a sequence of ISAR images in order to estimate the dominant ship motion. In all above indicative work there is no mention of the computing force that provides the motion of the radar and target platforms.
Our work makes an attempt to fill in the details of an ISAR simulation analysis in a virtual reality environment which is supported by a software defined radar system.

2.1.2 Coherent Deception Techniques

Using a simulator in the context of a software defined radar system falls under the coherent deception electronic attack technique. In this manner multiple targets can be generated which must have features nearly identical to the real ship target. And in order to ensure correct geometry and realistic false target velocities there is a need to take into account an estimation of the range, velocity and heading of the threat signal, as stated in [Baldwinson, 2008]. From [Yuan] it is concluded that is is beneficial to implement the false target signal entirely algorithmically. The purpose of the research is to obscure the real target into a cloud of other plausible yet false targets as stated by [Rui]. The analysis in [Xiaohan] states that the fake target mask, which are mainly coordinates and backscatter intensities, are stored in advance and that the Doppler's slope is important in the deception imaging process because it helps the threat signal to focus on the false target. We address this point in our simulations. Further false target geometry explanations can be found in example in [Rongbing, 2007] where a geometry and signal model is presented. For an ASIC (application specific integrated circuit) approach [Fouts et al 2005] have implemented the first documented hardware-based complete false target generator system. Nevertheless the exact contents of the look-up table that synthesizes the target are not fully discussed.

3. Conceptual Modelling for Coherent Countermeasures

We need to establish the fact that an ISAR simulator can be used as a software-defined radar system in order to perform coherent countermeasure activities. For that reason we have implemented an ISAR simulator which addresses the reflectivity solution of an extended naval target as seen by an airborne high range resolution sensor [Kostis et al, 2005; Kostis et al, 2006; Kostis et al, 2007; Kostis, 2008]. We found that the design could easily be extended to accommodate an added value which is a glint effects generator [Kostis EUSAR, 2008; Kostis et al, PCI2007]. For ISAR countermeasures purposes we argue that by injecting glint effects in the digital signal processing process the simulator can now produce more realistic results [Kostis, 2008]. This added value is necessary in order to add realistic effects to the false target as stated by [Neri, 2007]. For this value added process there are two methods of creating angular glint, Poynting vector and phase gradient. The first method is discussed in [Chen] where glint is calculated by the deviation of the Poynting vector and the heading vector. The second method is discussed in [Ming] where and RCS (radar cross section) based compensation method is presented. For our purposes we have used the approaches found in [Schleher] and [Shirman] where they base the glint estimation on the transversal component of the interconnecting vector between the two interfering sources.

From our work stems the research question of how useful, economic and straightforward it would be for this ISAR simulator to support a software defined radar system in order to perform electronic warfare functions. In this section we present the conceptual modelling steps of the simulator. And in the next section we present the results that bear the proof that this software defined system is capable to produce functions of security by obfuscation.

We are considering the case that the threats are equipped with high resolution microwave (radar) sensors that are capable of resolving the ship target in slant, cross and even height ranges while always tracking their most prominent points. Relevant effective soft-kill methods, which means deceive rather than destroy, is the capture of the threat signal in digital radio frequency memory, its down-conversion, its injection with false target reflectivity data by digital signal processing means, its up-conversion and final re-transmission to the threat sensor [Neri, 2007].

Our major contribution is at the provision of an Interferometric Inverse Synthetic Aperture Radar simulator which can generate realistic false target effects by adding glint noise to the false target reflectivity solution. The threat signal always tries to compensate for this noise as it is an inherent characteristic of an extended target.

3.1 Application Domain Definition

The task of Application Domain Definition is given to the SMEs that have authoritative information about the actual situational context. Usually at this point in time the SMEs will hold several meetings with the SEs and discuss the theoretical and practical milestones that have to be observed during the course of the project. Usually at this stage the SEs will have only superficial knowledge about the subject matter. On the other hand SEs that can perform the task of SMEs are valuable for any particular situation. We now explain the operational abilities of High Range Resolution radar systems by presenting a short relevant theoretical background. The main theoretical aspects for ISAR imaging are in order of logical progression: SAR imaging, spotlight mode of SAR imaging leading to ISAR imaging.

A SAR system has an antenna aperture which is synthesised by the combination of relatable parts rather than the real dimensions of its physical antenna. The SAR imaging principle is based on two foundations:

- Coherence.
- Sampling. The digitisation of continuous processes. The synthetic array is made up in a radar digital signal processor.

The major advantage of SAR systems is much better slant and cross range resolutions. A numerical example will be utilised to illustrate all the above in mathematical terms. Starting with a conventional 10GHz radar with an antenna aperture of 3 meters looking down to a target 10 Km away, the cross range resolution is :

$$\Delta x = \frac{\lambda}{d} R = \frac{0.03}{3} 10000 = 100m \tag{1}$$

This azimuth resolution is very low because a single resolution cell is illuminated at any one time. For example two ships less than 100 meters apart at the same range would appear as only one echo. Thus they cannot be resolved by the radar of Figure 2.

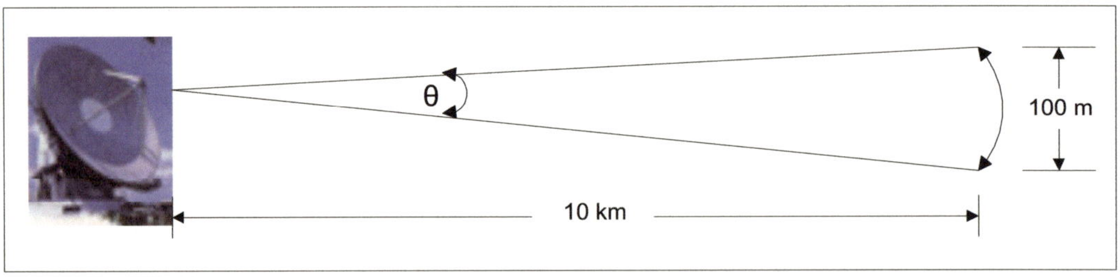

Fig. 2. Conventional Radar Angular Resolution or Real Aperture Radar (RAR).

Now assuming stationary targets and employing an airborne SAR system at the same frequency and range the azimuth resolution $\Delta\chi$ can be brought from 100 meters down to 3 meters, as shown in Figure 3.

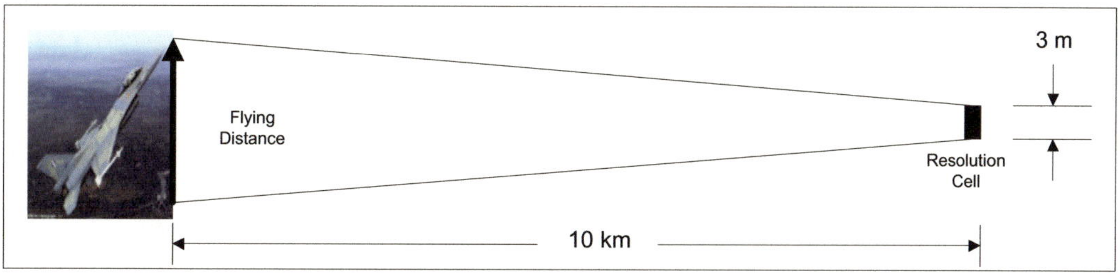

Fig. 3. Synthetic Aperture Radar (SAR).

The fly time should equal the distance of :

$$\Delta x = 3m = \frac{\lambda}{d} R \Rightarrow R = \frac{3d}{\lambda} = \frac{3*3}{0.03} = 300m \tag{2}$$

Therefore when the airborne synthetic aperture system flies for 300 meters around or across the target the azimuth resolution becomes much finer at only 3 meters long.

When the radar beam is focused on one point in space the concept is call Spotlight Synthetic Aperture Radar, as shown in Figure 4.

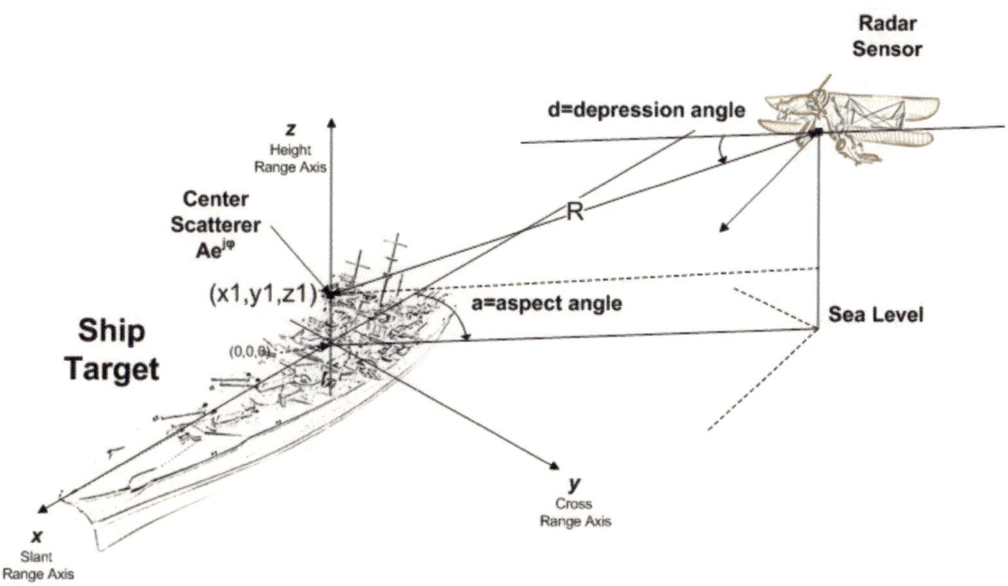

Fig. 4. Spotlight Synthetic Aperture Radar.

Spotlight SAR is the dual of the Inverse Synthetic Aperture Radar concept that will be used to image the naval target. The duality is that in Spotlight SAR the radar is moving where the target remains still. In ISAR imaging the radar is still where the target provides the motion that synthesizes the extended antenna aperture that leads to the higher resolution image.

In order to create false targets an introductory procedure is shown in Figure 5 [Kostis et al, IOP MST 2009].

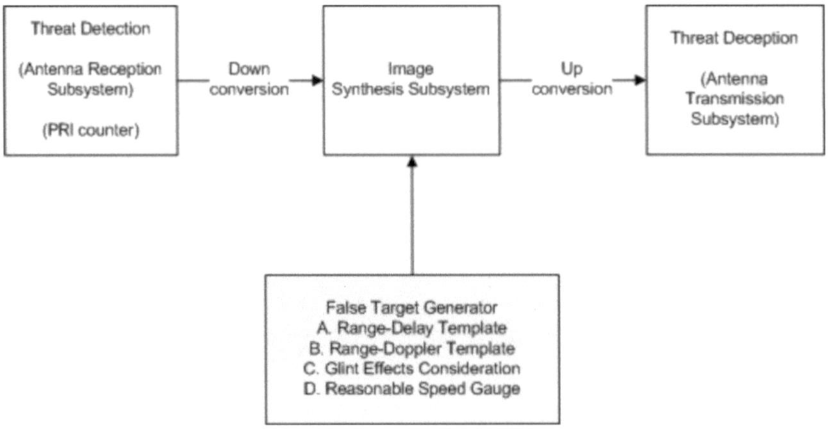

Fig. 5. The position of the False Target Generator Subsystem

Care must be given to the False Target Generator subsystem. Its outcome must resemble a signal that has all the necessary characteristics of an inverse scattering coming from a true target. For example the signal must contain mild or severe elements of angular glint noise. In other words the reality factor is decided by the ability of the false target generator subsystem.

3.2 Problem Space Decomposition

The entities and processes that must be represented for the successful accomplishment of the simulation are defined. For this project the list of entities as shown in Table 1.

	Simulation	Reality
1	Target cartesian coordinates plus inherent amplitude & phase	Target physical properties & electromagnetic signature
2	Radar slant range and cross range cartesian coordinates with respect to the center of the target	Most prominent appears to be the middle of the ship for this project. But it could be in the stern or the bow of the ship.
3	Sea-level distance from radar to target	FM height finder radar (altimeter) on airborne platform
4	Radar operational parameters	ISAR system particulars
5	Aspect angle from radar to target	Change of aspect angle from radar to target provides the resolution acquisition process

6	Glint Effects	Physical Phenomenon
7	Pace Engine	Target movement due to forces of nature
8	ISAR processor details	Range-Doppler processing
9	ISAR system output	Slant Range Profile and ISAR Image of target

Table 1. Entities

Now we can draw the necessary associations between the entities and come up with the corresponding processes, as shown in Table 2. Again as above the comparison between the reality and the simulation is strongly taken into account.

	Simulation	Reality
A	Provide information to the Pace Engine of target Cartesian coordinates to the pace engine	Physical presence and movement of target
B	Provide information to the Pace Engine of radar two-dimensional (slant ranger and cross range) coordinates	Physical presence and movement of radar
C	Provide information to the Pace Engine of radar's third (height range) dimensional coordinates	Measurement - captures reality with a sensor
D	Provide information to the ISAR Processor about the radar's operational parameters	Instrumentation – operational information
E	Aspect angle variation	Caused by changes in target/radar location
F	Glint Effects Injection	Digital Signal processing Conditioning (Masking)
G	From Pace Engine to rotated points database	Caused by changes in time
H	From Pace Engine Database to ISAR Processor	Recording Process – processes history of target in computer memory
I	From points database to ISAR processor	Computer process – Range-Doppler Processing - translates reality to computer memory

Table 2. Processes

3.3 Entity Abstraction Degree

The representational abstraction of the involved entities is finalized in this step. The level of accuracy, precision, resolution and fidelity of the entities and processes is determined. The main element that can have various levels of detail is the target's initial reflectivity solution at an aspect angle of forty-five degrees. First the extended naval target is modelled as an isotropic or directive point scatterers model, as shown in Figure 6 [Kostis et al, IJSSST 2009].

Bismarck Reflectance Map

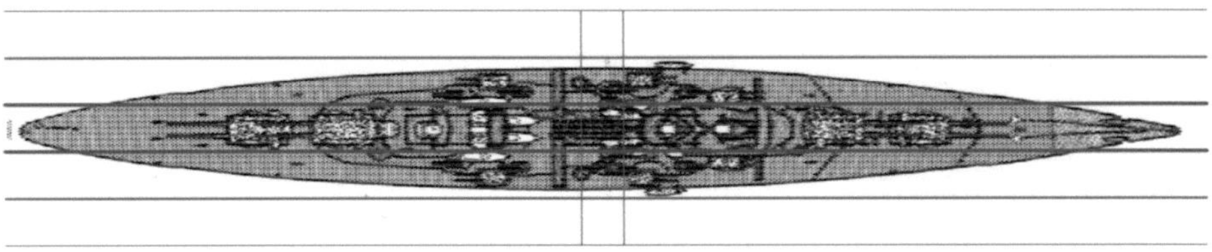

141 2 0.01 180	136 2 0.01 270	131 2 0.01 270	126 2 0.01 45	121 2 0.01 90	116 2 0.01 45	111 2 0.01 0	106 2 0.01 0	101 2 0.01 0	096 2 0.01 0	091 2 0.01 0	086 2 0.01 0	081 2 0.01 0	076 2 0.01 45	071 2 0.01 90	066 2 0.01 180	061 2 0.01 0	056 2 0.01 90	051 2 0.01 45	046 2 0.01 0	041 2 0.01 90	036 2 0.01 45	031 2 0.01 270	026 2 0.01 180	021 2 0.01 0	016 2 0.01 0	011 2 0.01 45	006 2 0.01 90	001 2 0.01 45
142 2 0.01 0	137 2 0.01 0	132 2 0.01 0	127 14 0.05 0	122 14 0.05 0	117 14 0.1 0	112 14 0.15 0	107 14 0.2 0	102 14 0.2 0	097 15 0.4 0	092 16 0.6 0	087 16 0.8 90	082 18 0.40 0	077 19 0.8 0	072 17 0.8 0	067 16 0.8 90	062 17 0.8 0	057 16 0.55 90	052 14 0.6 45	047 14 0.35 315	042 14 0.3 0	037 14 0.3 0	032 14 0.25 270	027 14 0.2 180	022 14 0.15 0	017 14 0.05 90	012 2 0.01 45	007 2 0.01 180	002 2 0.01 45
143 14 0.05 45	138 14 0.15 45	133 14 0.15 45	128 14 0.2 45	123 15 0.2 45	118 20 0.5 45	113 18 0.6 45	108 20 0.2 45	103 22 0.6 45	098 24 0.7 45	093 26 0.5 45	088 27 1 45	083 44 0.3 180	078 14 0.15 45	073 30 1 90	068 49 0.8 270	063 44 0.8 180	058 44 0.75 0	053 23 0.75 0	048 22 0.6 0	043 22 0.35 45	038 20 0.3 45	033 18 0.6 0	028 14 0.2 0	023 15 0.2 315	018 14 0.2 0	013 14 0.2 0	008 14 0.15 0	003 14 0.1 45
144 2 0.01 0	139 2 0.01 0	134 2 0.01 0	129 14 0.05 315	124 14 0.05 0	119 14 0.1 0	114 14 0.15 0	109 14 0.2 0	104 14 0.2 315	099 15 0.4 0	094 16 0.6 0	089 16 0.8 90	084 18 0.4 0	079 19 0.8 0	074 17 0.8 0	069 16 0.8 90	064 17 0.8 0	059 16 0.55 90	054 14 0.6 45	049 14 0.35 0	044 14 0.3 0	039 14 0.3 0	034 14 0.25 0	029 14 0.2 270	024 14 0.15 0	019 14 0.05 0	014 2 0.01 315	009 2 0.01 0	004 2 0.01 0
145 2 0.01 0	140 2 0.01 0	135 2 0.01 0	130 2 0.01 0	125 2 0.01 0	120 2 0.01 0	115 2 0.01 0	110 2 0.01 0	105 2 0.01 270	100 2 0.01 0	095 2 0.01 0	090 2 0.01 0	085 2 0.01 0	080 2 0.01 0	075 2 0.01 0	070 2 0.01 0	065 2 0.01 315	060 2 0.01 0	055 2 0.01 0	050 2 0.01 315	045 2 0.01 0	040 2 0.01 0	035 2 0.01 0	030 2 0.01 0	025 2 0.01 315	020 2 0.01 0	015 2 0.01 0	010 2 0.01 0	005 2 0.01 0

LEGEND

145 Cell Number
0 Height
1 Reflectivity Amplitude
0 Refletivity Initial Phase

Fig. 6. Single Layer Model

Then the false target is synthesised by taking the reflectivity grouping of multiple layers across the ship superstructure. An example is shown in Figure 7, where another layer is included in the calculations.

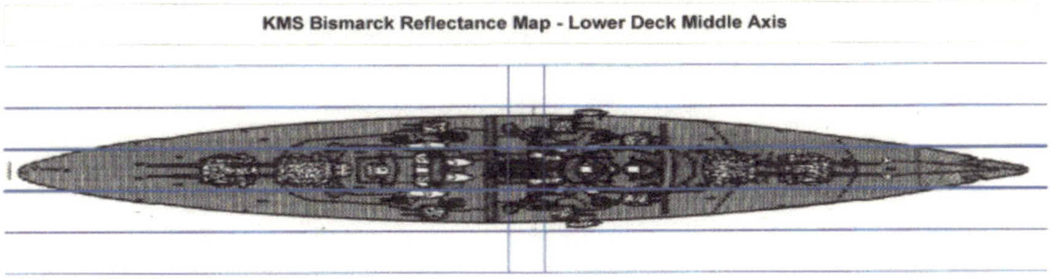

143 1 5 45	138 14 15 45	133 14 15 45	128 14 20 45	123 15 20 135	118 20 50 45	113 18 60 45	108 20 20 45	103 22 60 135	098 24 70 45	093 26 50 45	088 27 100 45	083 44 10 180	078 14 10 45	073 30 10 90	068 49 10 270	063 44 10 180	058 44 75 0	053 23 75 45	048 22 60 0	043 22 35 45	038 20 30 45	033 18 60 0	028 14 20 0	023 15 20 315	018 14 20 0	013 14 20 0	008 14 15 0	003 1 10 45	5/5
						155 20 0			154 60 270			153 10 90	152 40 135	151 20 0	150 40 0	149 80 180		148 50 0		147 80 90		146 40 0							4/5
												161 20 0	160 40 270	159 20 0	158 80 0	157 80 90		156 20 0											3/5
												167 20 0	166 20 0	165 10 0	164 20 315	163 30 90		162 20 0											2/5
													172 80 0	171 20 0	170 25 90	169 60 45		168 20 0											1/5

LEGEND
145 Cell Number
1 Height
1 Reflectivity Amplitude
0 Reflectivity Initial Phase

Fig. 7. Middle layer reflectivity generation.

Now the inverse scattering modelling is affected by the pace engine. The Pace engine is the computing moving force that proceeds the points on the ship in time to new locations from their initial values depending on the motion of the ship. The movement is performed by an affine transformations module that provides roll, yaw, pitch and translations functions. All time processions actions are placed into the context of a three-dimensional environment, which is depicted in Figure 8.

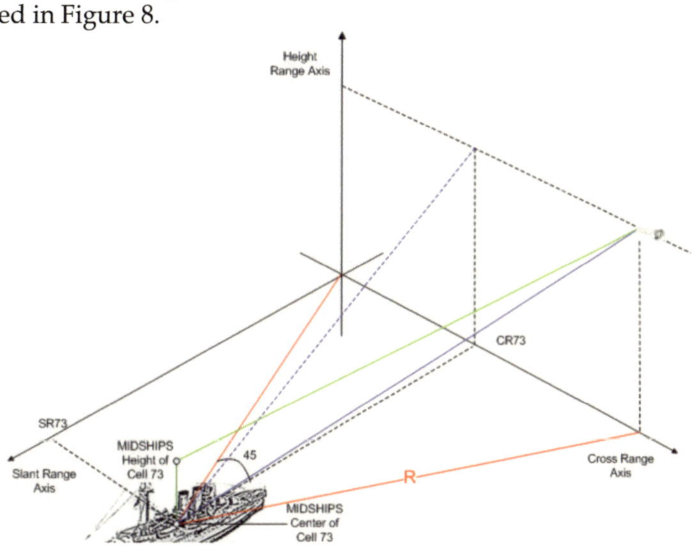

Fig. 8. Synthetic Environment Modelling

And the graphical representation of the inverse scattering is shown in Figure 9.

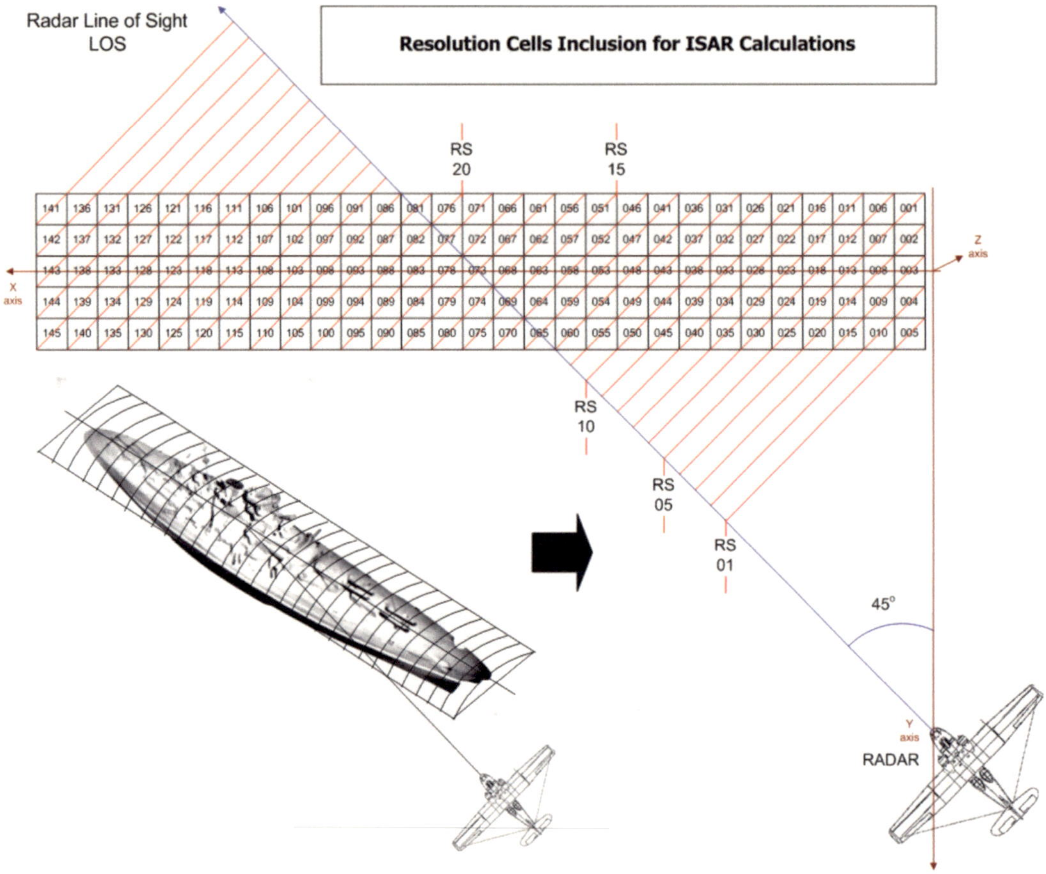

Fig. 9. Theoretical implementation (Polar Format Approximation)

3.4 Entity Relationship Identification

The relationships among the entities are identified in this design phase. It is ensured that all constraints and boundary conditions are properly imposed by the simulation context. All operational and functional requirements are taken into consideration, as shown in Figure 10.

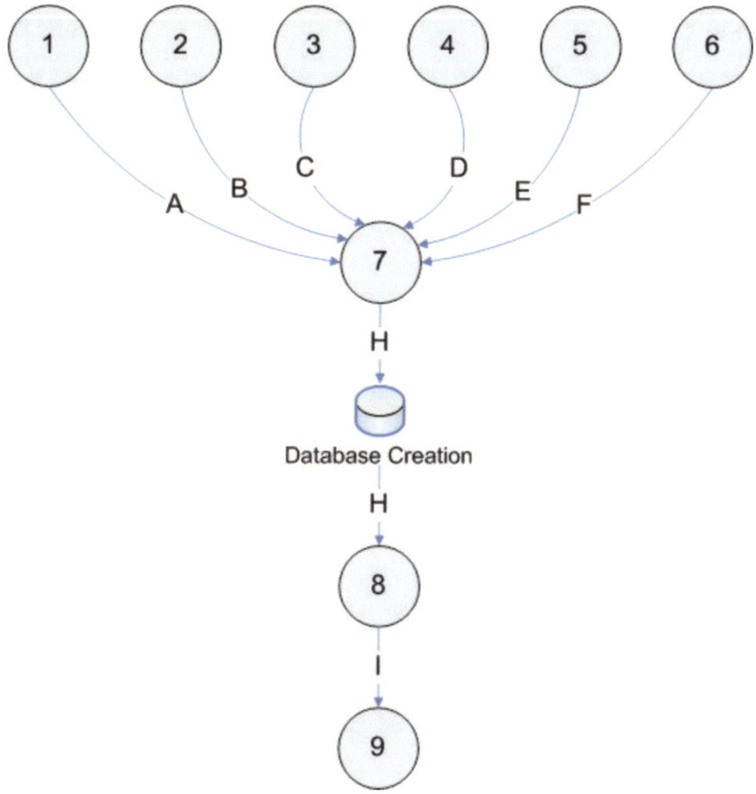

Fig. 10. Entity Relationship (E-R) identification

4. Implementation Procedure

The implementation procedure follows the rules of a complex system. In other words many individual components or transfer functions of the simulator when combined give a unique property or emergence to the output. Also the current implementation is process oriented. Every point on the target is passed through all transfer functions of the simulator in order to produce its corresponding output. The emergence of the system becomes obvious when all the points are put together in a graph. Each individual point cannot tell its tale. All of the points produce top view images or side view images of the target. This decision depends on the building blocks of the simulator.

4.1 Computing Methodology

The set of methods that define the processes and the order of this project is to be achieved is shown in Figure 11.

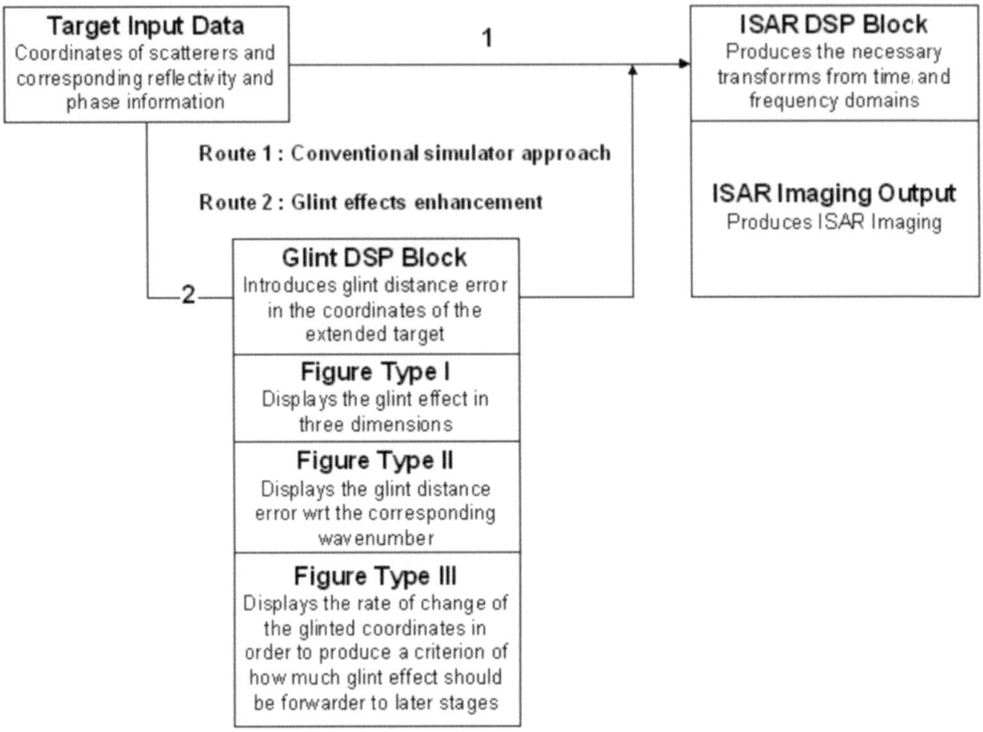

Fig. 11. Computing Methodology

4.2 Simulator Implementation

The simulator software implementation followed the process oriented technique as shown in Figure 12.

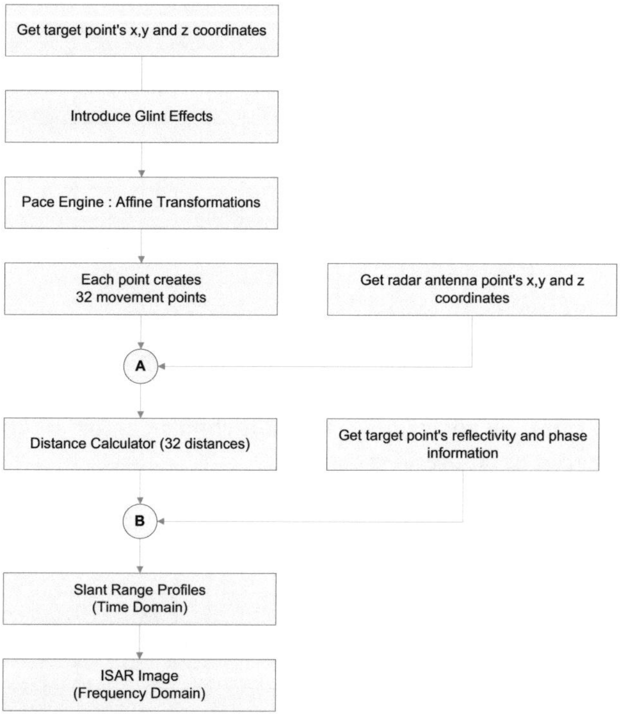

Fig. 12. Simulator Implementation of the FB-14 modular software system

The conceptual design and software implementation steps are now complete. The process resulted in the creation of the FB-14 software defined radar system. The system design is highly modular. That means that the context of the software defined radar system can be easily verified, validated, reused and extended. We then move on to assess the results obtained from our efforts.

5. Simulation Results

The results correspond to ISAR images expected to be obtained by the range Doppler method. These results were formally presented at the International Journal of Systems, Science & Technology. There is a value added function that adds glint effects to the output in order to increase the validity of the output which was presented at the Measurement, Science & Technology Journal of the Institute of Physics.. The third stage of this project was presented at NATO SET-136 Specialist's Meeting on Software Defined Radar.

5.1 Single Layer & Multi-Layer Model Results

Invoking the single layer model which involves only the top points of the superstructure, the output of Figure 13 is created.

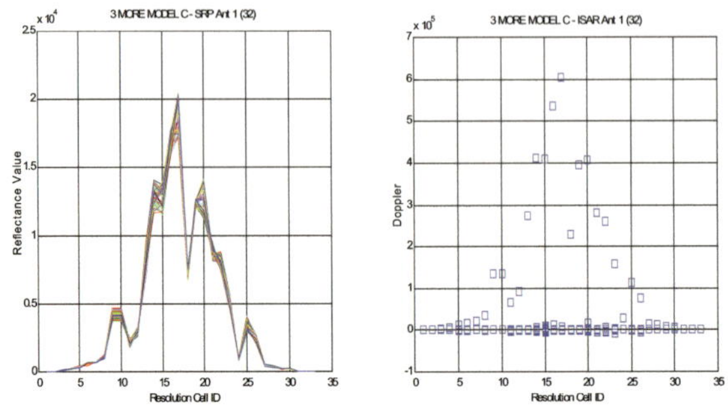

Fig. 13. Single Layer Slant Range Profile and corresponding ISAR image

Next by invoking the multiple layer model which involves the top and middle points of the superstructure, the output of Figure 14 is created.

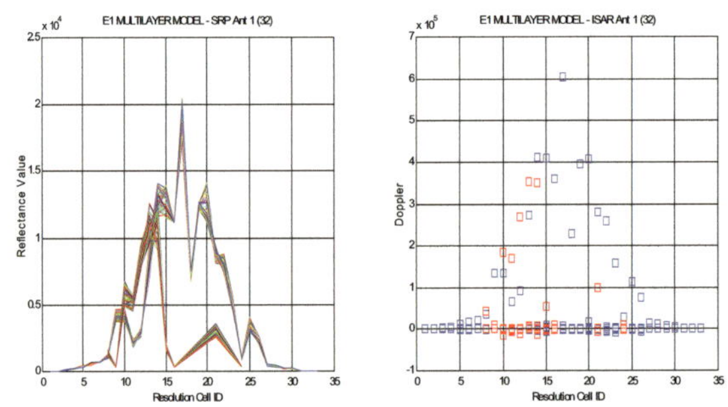

Fig. 14. Multiple Layer Slant Range Profile and corresponding ISAR image

5.2 ISAR Reflectivity Results & Issues for Military Targets

Military targets are different from civilian targets in the fact that there are many high reflectivity centers of reflectivity on lower coordinates. These high reflectivity values distort the ISAR image accordingly and killed ISAR operators look for these distortions in order to classify or even identify a radar contact. Our simulator can produce such effects as shown in Figure 15. Outputs of two antennas situated on a baseline of one meter away from each other are shown in order to demonstrate how different the image can be even when the antennas are very close to each other.

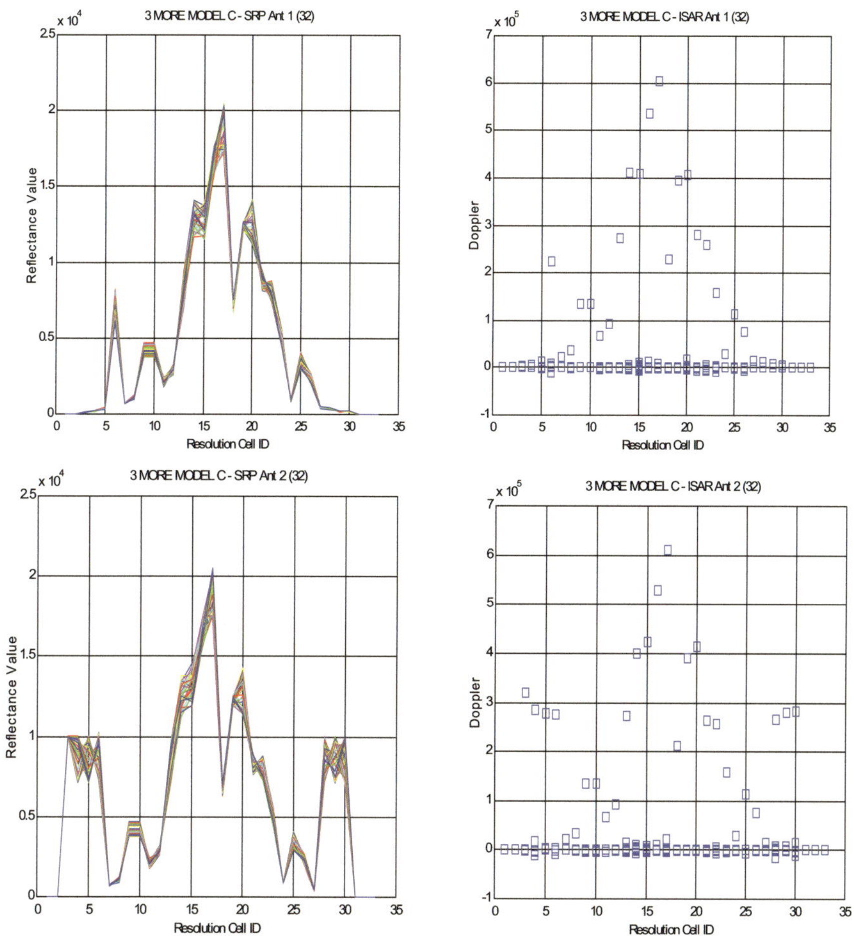

Fig. 15. ISAR Shortcomings Effect using the Single Layer Model.

5.3 Angular Glint Results & Issues for Military Targets

In order to increase the validity of the simulator output to the adversary radar-operator system the phenomenon of angular glint is introduced.

The first result is inspired by [Skolnik, 2001] and demonstrates the glint effect in a three dimensional synthetic environment with respect to the real target points. We call this component Glint Effect in 3D at the target and is shown in Figure 15(a).

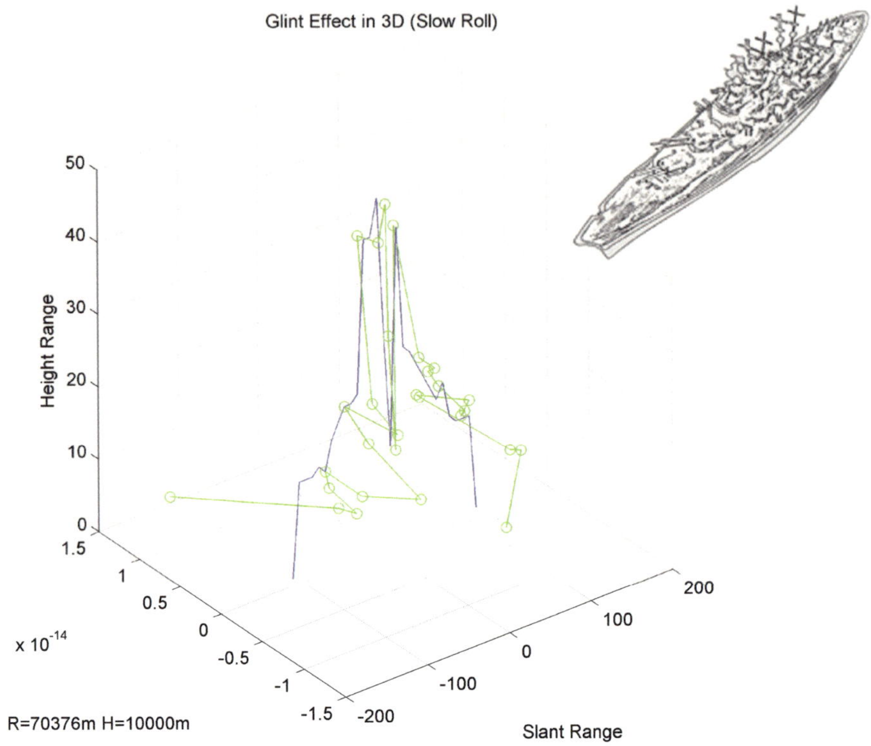

Fig. 16.

This is the glint mask that is applied to the false target. In order to better visualise this stage which corresponds to the input of the project a three dimensional type of graph is selected because the distortion of the original points can be better seen in this configuration.

The second module is inspired by [Barton, pp. 101-103] and depicts the glint effect in as seen from above the target by the radar. The Glint Effect in 2D is shown in Figure 15(b).

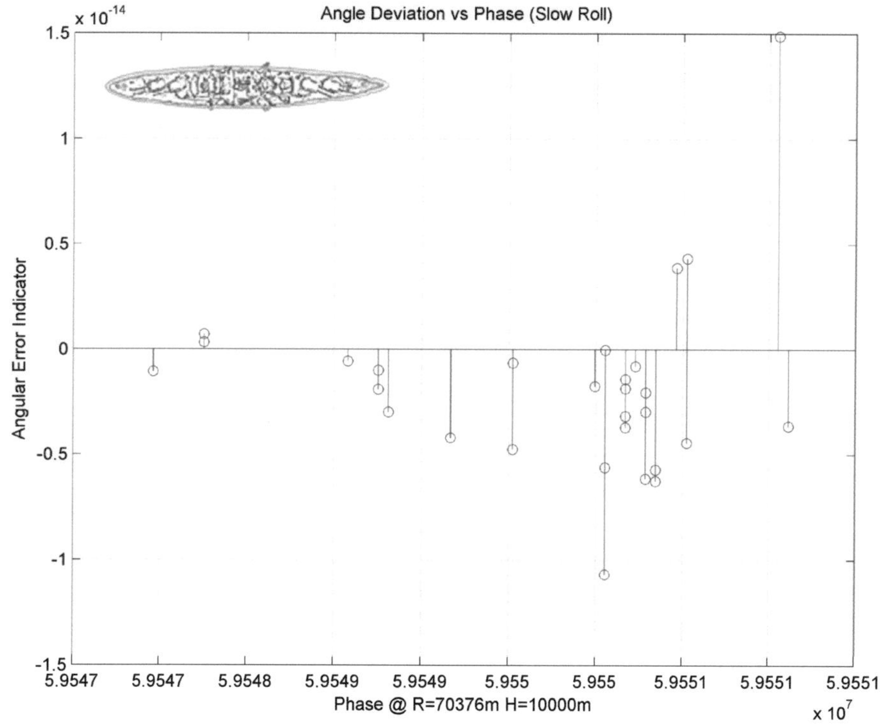

Fig. 17.

This is the glint results as it is received by the threat signal. In order to better visualise this stage which corresponds to the output of the project a two dimensional type of graph is selected, because the wavenumber distortion can be better seen in this configuration.

We use the final module to investigate the effect that the angular error has on the velocity vector back at the received threat signal. Using this method we try to measure the factor of realism of our glint formula. This result is shown in Figure 18.

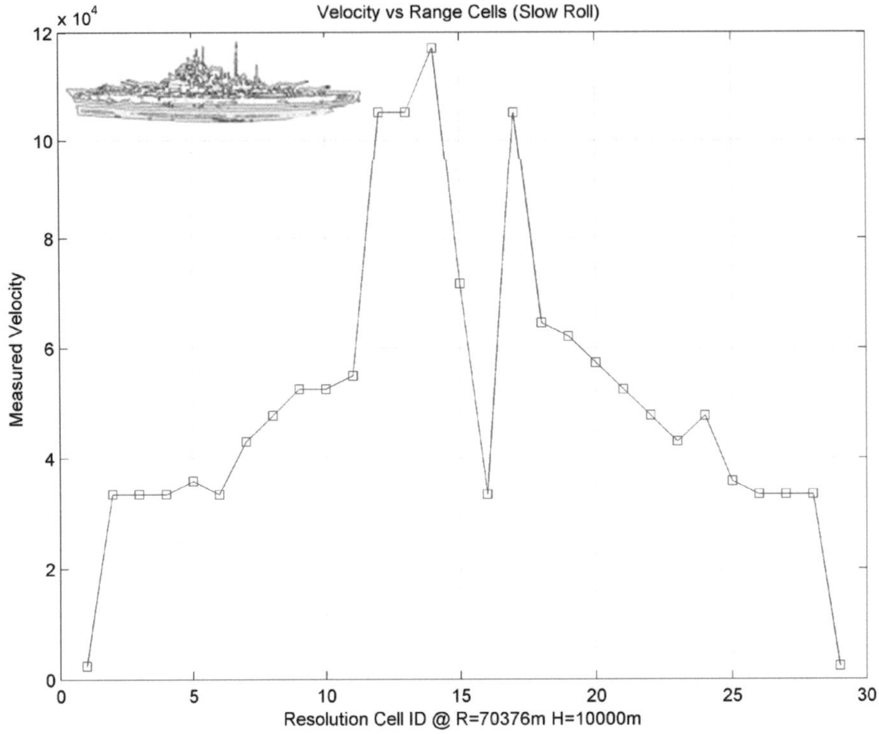

Fig. 18. Starting Point - Range @ 38nmi (70.376 Km) / Height @ 32808ft (10000m)

This is a graph that can be created because the target performs a pure roll motion which in high resolution imaging results in a side-view of the target. The threat system can perform such tests after storing the history of the received signal in order to ascertain its validity either as a side-view or as a top view image. According to this data mining process the threat system could output a decision of how the target is oriented. In this case the verdict would be that the target is mostly performing a roll and is a naval target of great proportions.

5.4 Domain Reusability: Computer Networks Security

Up to now we have devised a computing methodology in order to create false target entities. Also an effort is made so that these entities possess qualities that resemble the real situation as close as possible. By looking at the steps of the application domain definition and problem space decomposition for the electronic warfare case we found that the same computing methodology can be used for the computer networks warfare case. Generally the community of interest (COI) for this project is military training and network-centric operations and warfare [Balci et al, 2007, p.176]. For example the application domain definition for the computer networks case is shown in Figure 19, which is identical in principle to the previous study for the electronic warfare case.

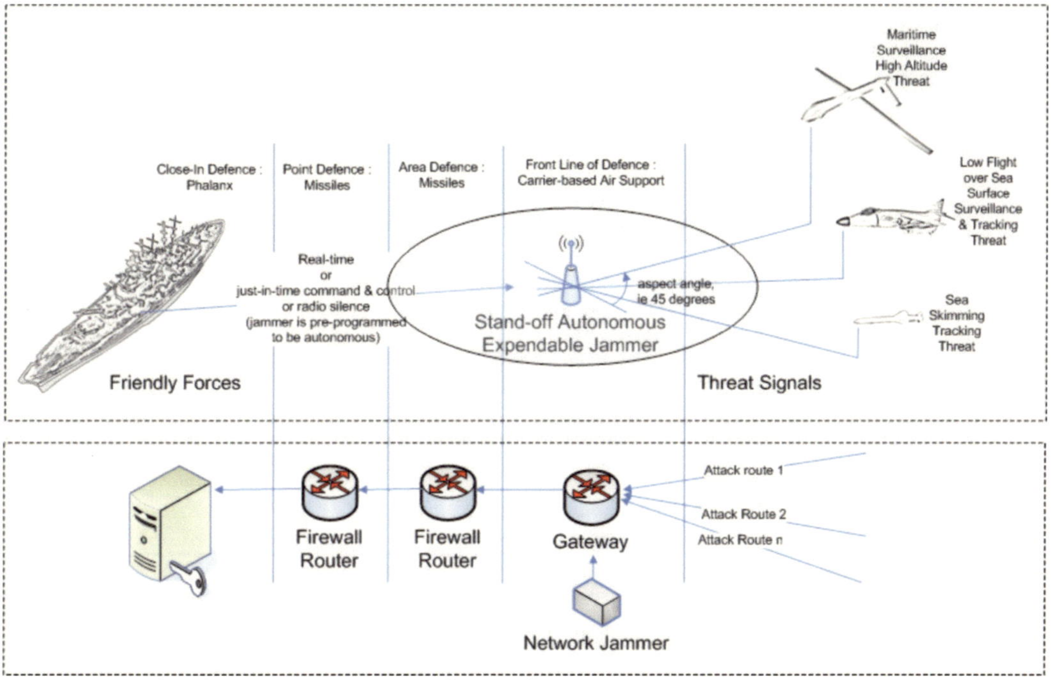

Fig. 19. ADD for the Computer Networks Warfare case.

A brief comparison with the electronic warfare case brings the contents of Table 3 for the entities and Table 4 for the processes for the computer networks warfare case.

	CNW Simulation Entity	CNW Entity Attributes	EW Simulation Entity	EW Entity Attributes
A	Open ports emulation	Server hardware and software characteristics and functionalities	Target Cartesian coordinates plus inherent amplitude & phase as point scatterers input to a simulator system	Target physical properties & electromagnetic signature
B	Computer entity emulation - Operating System attribute	Ping times from black hat to white hat computer – main point of existence	Radar slant range and cross range cartesian coordinates with respect to the center of the target Sea-level distance from radar to target	Most prominent appears to be the middle of the ship for this project. But it could be in the stern or the bow of the ship. FM height finder radar (altimeter) on airborne platform

C	Physical routes of computer attack via a variety of networks and platforms	B. Extra net/server characteristics that helps the hacker to recognize target.	Type of vessel	Superstructure characteristics Geometry of worldspace
D	Port scanning & mapping abilities Information gathering Open ports OS Version Service Packs	Probing target computer Hacker's pre-attack actions Information gathering for the specific target Possible vulnerabilities	Radar operational parameters	ISAR systems particulars
E	Reality factors that affect the black hat professional's opinion about the validity of the target	Hacker: ANALYSIS of the information gathering results Decision about the validity of a probe	Glint representation details	Physical phenomenon impossible to disregard
F	Data properties through time	Packet and traffic inspection	Pace Engine	Target movement due to forces of nature Change of aspect angle from radar to target provides the resolution acquisition process
G	Specialized Applications - Database Server Processing	SQL Input - SQL Injection	ISAR processor details	Range-Doppler processing
H	Special Network Node Properties	Data Traffic	ISAR system output	Slant Range Profile and ISAR Image of the target

Table 3. Entities for the Computer Networks Warfare Case

	Simulation	Reality		
1	Close environment - server hidden	Net/Server properties	Provide information to the Pace Engine of target Cartesian coordinates to the pace engine	Physical presence and movement of target
2	Motivation profit and/or spy/destroy	Hacker's motivation	Provide information to the Pace Engine of radar two-dimensional (slant ranger and cross range) coordinates	Physical presence and movement of radar
3	pro-Hacker public/private tools	Hacker's knowledge/Tools	Provide information to the Pace Engine of radar's third (height range) dimensional coordinates	Measurement - captures reality with a sensor
4	Complex network environment	Possible Net/Server architecture/characteristics	Provide information to the ISAR Processor about the radar's operational parameters	Instrumentation - operational information
5	Many servers (fussiness)	Possible Net/Server architecture/characteristics including normal the net's/server's fussiness and attitudes.	Aspect angle variation	Caused by changes in target/radar location

6	Time Alterations of target characteristics	Target may alter characteristics due (service packs, admin observations, service requirements, new machines (for network)	Glint Effects Injection	Digital Signal processing Conditioning (Masking)
7	What the black hat professional sees - the output of the multiple false host generator	Information gathering concluded for the specific target	From Pace Engine to rotated points database	Caused by changes in time
8	Time Alterations of target characteristics	Target may alter characteristics due (service packs, admin observations, service requirements, new machines (for network)	From Pace Engine Database to ISAR Processor	Recording Process - processes history of target in computer memory

Table 4. Processes for the Computer Networks Warfare Case

5.5 Current Deficiencies: Computational Complexity Issues & Future Work

This research approach formulated a prototype in order to establish the credibility of the effort. Actual implementations call for parallel processing elements in order to speed up the processing of the false target generation. The complete computing methodology is very easy to translate to a parallel algorithm version and this will be shown in future works. It is noteworthy to mention that the Fast Fourier Transform algorithm that this project is using in order to create the final stage (frequency domain representation) can use the advantages of parallel processing.

For future research we propose improvements in the software engineering side with the introduction of the concepts of parallel processing and additions to the reality output of the project like sea clutter effects. The main issue in the synthesis of coherent countermeasures is the high speed that is required in order to complete all the numerical transactions. Therefore the domain of parallel programming fits nicely in this situation. We can propose an embedded system with many processors that help the synthesis process to be completed in the shortest time possible. Also added-value aspects of this world can be incorporated in the future like sea clutter effects. Sea is a rich environment that needs to be convincingly replicated in open seas and litortal environments.

6. Discussion

[Salt, 2008] has published a very interesting paper detailing pitfalls in the realisation, usage and expectations of simulation system implementations in general. Let us discuss how this implementation stands to the test of the seven habits of highly defective simulation projects.

- Trifle Worship. The overall design of the model has a satisfactory amount of detail. The balance between precision and accuracy yields an output that is satisfactory.

- Belief in Answers. The main aim of the simulation is to prove that ISAR images can be generated. Other secondary answers from this work, like signal-to-noise ration studies are possible but not relevant to the primary purpose. Therefore the modellers have understood the purpose of the system under investigation.

- Connectionism. There are no different models connected to each other. There is only one model that is constructed in a highly modular manner.

- The Black Box Mistake. Substantial work has been done in order to conduct white box testing. Verification and validation tests have been widely published in conferences and research journals. These tests are conducted in part and in whole of the simulation model.

- Methodolatry. Methods and processes are observed in all aspects of the implementation of the simulator. We don't claim that it is a fixed drill for conducting the domain reusability entities and processes section. Nevertheless following an established method provides a solid head start towards venturing into the implementation of similar, parallel and yet interestingly diverse fields of electronic warfare.

- The Dead Fish Fallacy. The design of the simulator is highly modular. This attribute provides the implemented model with great potential for reusability and extendibility options. Therefore the dynamic complexity of the project has received the attention required. For example the diagramming method depicts in different instances the entity-relationship class diagrams and the executable representations of the code.

- The Jehovah Problem. The differences between the model and the reality it represents have been duly noted. The functional decomposition of the simulator implementation is available. Nevertheless the valuable part of this work is the behaviour of the system to different inputs and not its inner functions. The model provides behaviour, not an answer. It tries to simulate the inverse scattering of a high range resolution radar system in order to infect the adversary radar operator with its behaviour. The degree of this infection is important because over a threshold it makes the adversary human element to want to investigate the area of the incoming signal. Because its behavioural aspects appear worthwhile and tempting to be investigated.

7. Conclusions

Software-defined radar concepts and techniques can be used in an effective and adaptable manner in order to provide deception countermeasures against coherent radar systems by utilizing a simulator base. The main contribution of this work is the derivation of a computing methodology which can be applied for both electronic warfare and computer networks warfare fields. And the main purpose of this work is to provide security functions through obfuscation of the real asset in an environment of other false entities thus further proving deception services by luring the hostile parties to engage false entities or in any way avoid the real asset. It is worthwhile to point out that the design tools of coherent countermeasures, being dynamically pictorial in nature, are no different than a painting or a movie feature. As is art forgery, the more the resemblance to the real prototype the higher the chances a buyer will be persuaded to invest in the false copy. Because the buyer will be infected, as Tolstoy so vividly explained, with the artistic persuasion of the false masterpiece. In a final note, the act of implementing coherent countermeasures using a simulator base is an integral part of the amazing field of Art.

8. References

Abrash M., 1997, Graphics Programming Black Book, Coriolis Group, ISBN 1-576-10174-6.

Balci O., Ormsby W. F., 2007, Conceptual Modelling for Designing Large-Scale Simulations, Journal of Simulation, pp. 175-186, Operational Research Society Ltd, 1747-7778/07.

Baldwinson J., Antipov. I., A Modelling and Simulation Tool for the Prediction of Electronic Attack Effectiveness, Electronic Warfare & Radar Division, Defence Science and Technology Organisation, Bld. 205L, West Avenue, Edinburgh, SA, 5111, Australia.

Barton D. K. (2005), Radar System Analysis and Modeling, ISBN 1-58053-681-6, pp. 101-104, Artech House, 2005.

Boccara N., 1985, Modelling complex systems, Springer Verlag, ISBN 9780387158853.

Carrara W. G., Goodman R. S., Majewski R. M., 1995, Spotlight Synthetic Aperture Radar, Artech House, ISBN 0-89006-728-7.

Chant C. (2001), Air War in the Falklands 1982, Osprey Publishing, ISBN 1841762938.

Chen J., Yang F., Zhang K., Xu J. (2008), Angular Glint Modelling and Simulation for Complex Targets, In ICMMT 2008 Proceedings.

Crisp D J., The State-of-the-Art in Ship Detection in Synthetic Aperture Radar Imagery, *In DSTO-RR-0272,* Intelligence, Surveillance and Reconnaissance Division, Information Sciences Laboratory, Department of Defence, Australian Government.

Doerry A. W., 2008, Ship Dynamics for Maritime ISAR Imaging, SAND2008-1020, Sandia National Laboratories.

Emir E., Topuz E., 1997, Simulation of ISAR images of ships for localization of dominant scatterers, In Radar 97 (Conf. Publ. No. 449) 14-16 Oct 1997 Page(s):273 – 275.

Fouts D. J., Kendrick R. Macklin, Daniel P. Zulaica (2005). Electronic Warfare Digital Signal Processing on COTS Computer Systems with Reconfigurable Architectures, *In the Journal of Aerospace Computing*, Information & Communication, Vol. 2, October 2005

Hajduch G., Le Gaillec J.M., Garello R., Airborne High Resolution ISAR Imaging of ship targets at sea, IEEE Transactions on Aerospace and Electronic Systems, 2004, 40, (1), pp. 378-384.

Haywood, B., Anderson, W.C., Morris, J.T., Kyprianou, R. (1997). Generation of point scatterer models for simulating ISAR images of ships, *In Radar 97*, (Conf. Publ. No. 449), Issue 14-16, Oct 1997 Page(s):700 - 704.

Haywood B., Kyprianou R., Zyweck A., 1994, ISARLAB: a radar signal processing tool, In IEEE International Conference on Acoustics, Speech & Signal processing, Vol. 5.

Hill J. R. (1988). Air Defence at Sea, Ian Allan Ltd, Shepperton, Surrey, ISBN 0-7110-1742-5, 1988.

Jane's Military Review (2005). Tactical UAV's : Redefining and refining the breed, 10 August 2005.

Kleb B., 2007, Toward Scientific Numerical Modeling, NATO RTO AVT-147 Symposium on Computational Uncertainty in Military Vehicle Design, Athens, Greece.

Kostis T.G., Baker C.J., Griffiths H.D. (2005), Interferometric Inverse Synthetic Aperture Radar, Proceedings of the London Communications Symposium 2005, London, England, pp. 1-4.

Kostis T. G., Baker C.J., Griffiths H.D. (2006). An Interferometric ISAR System Model for Automatic Target Identification, *In EUSAR 2006*, VDE, Dresden, Germany.

Kostis T. G., Katsikas S.K., 2007, Three-Dimensional Multiple Layer Extended Target Modeling for ISAR Studies in Target Identification, Panhellenic Conference on Informatics, Patras, Greece.

Kostis T. G. (2008). Simulator Implementation of an Inverse Synthetic Aperture Radar System for an Extended Naval Target in a Three Dimensional Synthetic Environment, *In the Tenth International Conference on Computer Modeling and Simulation (UKSIM 2008)*, pp.366-371, Cambridge, England.

Kostis T. G. (2008). Glint Effects Simulation for an Extended Naval Target using an Interferometric-ISAR System Model, *In European Synthetic Aperture Radar Conference (EUSAR 2008)*, Friedrichschafen, Germany.

Kostis T. G., Galanis K. G., Katsikas S. K. (2008). Simulator Implementation of an IF-ISAR System for Studies in Target Glint, *In Panhellenic Conference on Informatics*, pp.140-144, Samos, Greece.

Kostis T. G. (2008). Proof of Concept for the Extensibility Attribute of an ISAR Simulator for Studies in Target Glint, *In IST 2008 Workshop*, Chania, Greece.

Kostis T. G., Katsikas S. K. 2008, Inverse Synthetic Aperture Radar Simulator Implementation for an Extended Naval Target for Electronic Warfare Applications, submitted to International Journal of Simulation: Systems, Science and Technology (http://ducati.doc.ntu.ac.uk/uksim/Journal.htm) and currently under review.

Kostis T. G., Galanis K. G., Katsikas S. K. 2008, Angular Glint Effects Generation for False Target Image Enhanced Masking in Transponder Decoys: Conceptual Modelling and Proof of Concept for a Naval Extended Target under Advanced Airborne Threats, submitted to the Institute of Physics Measurement Science & Technology and currently under review.

Le Chevalier F. (2002). Principles of Radar and Sonar Signal Processing, Artech House, ISBN 1-58053-338-8.

Li C., Zhu D. (2008). The Detection of Deception Jamming against SAR based on Dual-Aperture Antenna Cross-Track Interferometry, IEEXplore.

Li J., Ling H., Chen V. (2003). An Algorithm to Detect the Rresence of 3D Target Motion from ISAR Data, *In Multidimensional Systems and Signal Processing*, 14, 223-240, Kluwer Academic Publishers.

Lane P. C. R. and Gobet F., 2008, A Methodology for Developing Computational Implementations of Scientific Theories, EUROSIM / UKSIM08, Cambridge, England, 2008.

Ling W., Daiyin Z., Zhaoda Z., 2008, Image-based scaling for ship top view ISAR images, Journal of Electronics (China) Publisher Science Press, co-published with Springer-Verlag GmbH ISSN0217-9822 (Print) 1993-0615 (Online) Issue, Volume 25, Number 1 / January, 2008 DOI10.1007/s11767-006-0071-z Pages 76-83

Lord R. T., Willie N., Gaffar M. Y. A., 2006, Investigation of 3-D RCS Image Formation of Ships Using ISAR., In European Synthetic Aperture Radar Conference, (EUSAR 2006).

Lynch D., 2004, Introduction to RF Stealth, Sci-tech Publishing, ISBN 9781891121210.

Neri F. 2007, Introduction to Electronic Defence Systems, Artech House, Chapter 5-6, ISBN 9781580531795.

Neugebauer E., Steinkamp D. (2007). Representation, *In NATO Modeling and Simulation Group*, RTO MSG-067 Lecture Series, pp. 2-1~2-4, Athens, Greece.

Ming J., Analyses and Compensation for Radar Target Angular Glint, 6th International Symposium on Antennas, Propagation and EM Theory, 2003, Proceedings, 2003.

OTA-BP-ISS-136, 1994, U.S. Congress, Office of technology Assessment, Virtual Reality and Technologies for Combat Simulation - Background Paper.

Pastina D., Spina C., 2008, Slope-based frame selection and scaling techniques for ship ISAR imaging, IET Signal Processing, 2, (3), pp.265-276.

Porter, N.J. Tough, R.J.A., 1994, Processing schemes for hybrid SAR/ISAR imagery of ships, In IEE Colloquium on Radar and Microwave Imaging, Nov 1994 Page(s):5/1 - 5/5.

Rice F., Cooke T., Gibbins D., 2006, Model based ISAR ship classification, Elsevier, Digital Signal Processing, Volume 16, Issue 5, September 2006, Pages 628-637, DASP 2005.

Rihaczek A. W.; Hershkowitz S. J. (2000). *Theory & Practice of Radar Target Identification*, Artech House, ISBN 1-58053-081-8, Massachusetts.

Rongbing G., YuLing L. Zhenghong Y. (2007), Primary Exploration on ISAR Image Deception Jamming, IEEEXplore.

Rui C, Ming-liang XLL, Research on Jamming Effect Evaluation Method of ISAR, IEEEXplore.

Salt J. D. (2008). The Seven Habits of Highly Defectrive Simulation Projects, Operational Society ltd, 1747-7778/08.

Schleher C.D. (1999). Electronic Warfare in the information Age, Artech House, ISBN 0-89006-526-8.

Siouris G. M. (2003). Missile Guidance and Control Systems, Springer-Verlag, ISBN 0-387-00726-1, 2003.

Shillington, K.R., Jahans, P.A. Buller, E.H. Tunaley, J.K.E., 1991, An ISAR simulator for ships, In Antennas and Propagation Society International Symposium, 1991, Page(s):1032 - 1035 vol.2.

Shirman Y. D. (2002). Computer Simulation of Aerial Target Radar Scattering, Recognition, Detection and Tracking, ISBN 1-58053-172-5, Artech House, pp. 223-231, 2002.

Skolnik M. I (2001). Introduction to Radar Systems, McGraw Hill, ISBN 0-07-290980-3, pp. 229-232, Sec. 4.4, Fig. 4.15, 2001.

Stavropoulos D. B. (2008). The End of Dainitz's Wolves, Journal of Military History, Issue 143, pp.20-35, in Hellenic, ISSN 1109-0510, July 2008.

Stavropoulos D. B. (2008). San Carlos Bay, 21st May 1982: A Long Day for the British Navy in the Falklands Conflict, Journal of Military History, Issue 148, pp.66-81, in Hellenic, ISSN 1109-0510, July 2008.

Stimson G. (1998). Introduction to Airborne Radar, Sci-Tech Publishing ISBN 1-891121-01-4.

Schleher D. C., 1986, Electronic Warfare in the Information Age, Artech House, ISBN 0-89006-526-8.

Seybold, J. S.; Bishop, S. J., 1996, Three-dimensional ISAR imaging using a conventional high-range resolution radar, In Proceedings of the 1996 IEEE National Radar Conference, Issue ,Page(s):309 - 314, DOI 10.1109/NRC.1996.510699

Smith R., Knight S., "Applying Electronic Warfare Solutions to Network Security" in Canadian Military Journal, 2005, pp. 49–58.

Van Dongen M., Kos J., (1995), The Analysis of Ship Air Defence: The Simulation Model SEAROADS, *In Naval Research Logistics*, Vol. 42, pp. 291-309, John Wiley & Sons.

Wiegand R. J. (1991). Radar Electronic Countermeasures System Design, pp.12, Artech House, ISBN 0-89006-381-8, 1991.

Wong S. K., Riseborough E. and Duff G., 2006, An Analysis of ISAR Image Distortion based on the Phase Modulation Effect, In EURASIP Journal on Applied Signal Processing, Vol. 2006, pp. 1-16.

Xiaohan L., Jianguo W. (2008). Analysis of Deception Jamming to ISAR Image System, IEEEXplore.

Yuan L. I., Xue-mei L. U. O., Gao-huan L. V. (2008). The Study of Multi-False Targets Synthesizing Technology against Chirp ISAR, In ICMMT 2008 Proceedings.

7

Distance evaluation between vehicle trajectories and risk indicator

Abdourahmane KOITA and Dimitri DAUCHER
LEPSIS/LCPC (Laboratoire Central des Ponts et Chaussées)
58, Boulevard Lefebvre 75015 Paris, France

1. Introduction

This study, dealing with the vehicle trajectories modeling, is a subject of a scientific research in our *Laboratory*, within the framework of a research program on road safety. For many years, road accidents have been the focus of attention of the authorities and vehicle manufacturers. The accidents due to the vehicle loss control have very serious consequences in human terms (WHO, 2004).
In the literature, the first research works on the vehicle loss control risk consisted in defining a critical failure speed in a bend or a speed profile to be respected according to the road geometrical characteristics and the vehicle dynamic state (Lauffenburger, 2003). Other works in progress consist of using a dynamic vehicle model, to carry out an analysis of sensitivity in order to determine the most influential parameters on the answer of this model.
In addition, the LCPC (Laboratoire Central des Ponts et Chaussées) launched a research operation MTT (Métrologie des Trajectoires et du Trafic) and the research projects SARI/RADARR and DIVAS. Within this framework, several observatories of vehicle's trajectories (edge of way or instrumented vehicle) in bend were developed then deployed in order to analyze the trajectory stability and to understand how it would be possible to detect a failing trajectory.

In this study, we developed a new method to evaluate risk of trajectory failure by using experimental data measurements. The method consists of defining a metric (or distance) able to compare trajectories each other in order to evaluate the handling loss risk. Then we determined the limit states (or the critical sections) which govern the intersection between Vehicle, Infrastructure and Driver (V/I/D) in the safety trajectory space. Indeed the very complex systems (with several configurations variables) and a strongly constrained environment can cause failure modeling of many algorithms, due to their complexity.
However the probabilistic trajectories modeling are used in order to estimate the risk indicator. It consists in considering some parameters as random variables in order to take into account the risks induced to the infrastructure, the vehicle, the behavior of the driver and the environment (weather or traffic). Lastly, we will calculate the probability of going beyond of the threshold applied to the distance.

The results can also be used on the one hand: to find the characteristics of the infrastructure which will be modified in order to minimize the lane crossing risk, and in addition: to warn the driver by detecting the failure trajectory. The originality of this method is not only the use of a particular norm (taking into account the vehicle position, velocity and acceleration) to compare trajectories between them, but also the use of reliability analysis of the vehicle trajectories.

In this chapter, after the introduction, in the first part, we define vehicle's trajectory as a vectorial stochastic process. In the second part, a functional filter (Mahalanobis distance and Euclidean distance) judiciously chosen are used to project on IR the set of the observed trajectories in order to get a stationary scalar process. In Third part, we will use a statistic analysis on our scalar process in order to characterize and to identify it. Then, one identifies the whole of the parameters intervening in each limit state by using the constraints applied to the vehicle. Lastly, we will use reliability analysis method to build a risk indicator. The approach consists of drawing lots configurations at random by probability laws and to connect between them to generate an ideal trajectory. We will calculate their probability function. Then with the already defined safety margin, we make the comparison of the probability obtained in that admitted preliminary. The safety margin which bounds the failure domain to the safety domain is determined by the limit state function. The risk of lane crossing is quantified by the risk indicator (reliability) estimate.

2. Vehicle trajectory definition

2.1 Deterministic function

The vehicle trajectory, during an amount of time $T = [0, \tau]$ is the resultant of an interaction between vehicle, infrastructure and driver. It can be defined by the knowledge of the following deterministic function:

$$\begin{aligned}&\Phi : \mathrm{T} \rightarrow \mathrm{IR}^6 \\ &\mathrm{t} \mapsto \Phi(\mathrm{t}) = \left(\mathrm{x(t)}, \mathrm{y(t)}, \frac{\partial \mathrm{x}}{\partial \mathrm{t}}(t), \frac{\partial y}{\partial \mathrm{t}}(t), \frac{\partial^2 \mathrm{x}}{\partial \mathrm{t}^2}(t), \frac{\partial^2 y}{\partial \mathrm{t}^2}(t) \right)\end{aligned} \tag{1}$$

Where the parameters of function $\Phi(t)$ represented the vehicle longitudinal position, the lateral position, the longitudinal velocity, the lateral velocity , the longitudinal acceleration and the lateral acceleration. The sample $\{x_k, k \in K_N\}$ is considered as a discretized trajectory of a two-dimensional second order mean-square continuous, at times $\{t_k, k \in K_N\}$.
However, the behavior of the dynamical system to investigate is fundamentally nonlinear. It expresses the dynamics of a system whose mechanical behaviour and connections are very complex. Consequently, it is necessary to take into account various levels of uncertainty (uncertainty of measurements, risks on control,...). For example, the same driver circulating with the same vehicle on the same road under the same conditions will not twice reproduce the same trajectory within the meaning of (1). Obviously, it's very important and necessary to take into account this random part.

2.2 Vectorial stochastic process

It is thus more judicious to model the trajectories of a triptych V-I-D (Vehicle, Infrastructure, Driver), by realizations of a vectorial stochastic process (Koita et al., 2008) in the following form:

$$\tilde{U} : \mathrm{T}\times\Omega \rightarrow \mathrm{IR}^6$$
$$(\mathrm{t},\omega) \mapsto \tilde{U}(\mathrm{t},\omega) = \left(\mathrm{x}(\mathrm{t},\omega), \mathrm{y}(\mathrm{t},\omega), \frac{\partial \mathrm{x}}{\partial \mathrm{t}}(t,\omega), \frac{\partial y}{\partial \mathrm{t}}(t,\omega), \frac{\partial^2 \mathrm{x}}{\partial \mathrm{t}^2}(t,\omega), \frac{\partial^2 y}{\partial \mathrm{t}^2}(t,\omega) \right) \quad (2)$$

where Ω is the realizations space.

As soon as the driver changes, the experimental trajectories collected are discrete realizations of different stochastic processes. From this definition, we use a database of trajectories. This database is made up of L realizations of experimental trajectories resulting from the same vectorial stochastic process noted U of the form :

$$U : \mathrm{T}\times\Omega \rightarrow \mathrm{IR}^6$$
$$(\mathrm{t},\omega) \mapsto U(\mathrm{t},\omega) = \left(\mathrm{x}(\mathrm{t},\omega), \mathrm{y}(\mathrm{t},\omega), \frac{\partial \mathrm{x}}{\partial \mathrm{t}}(t,\omega), \frac{\partial y}{\partial \mathrm{t}}(t,\omega), \frac{\partial^2 \mathrm{x}}{\partial \mathrm{t}^2}(t,\omega), \frac{\partial^2 y}{\partial \mathrm{t}^2}(t,\omega) \right) \quad (3)$$

The reader will find in (Koita, 2008) more complete information on the experimental observations and especially methodology used to say that the trajectories considered result from the same stochastic process. To illustrate our remarks on the trajectories observed, the figure (1) represent a realization of the process.

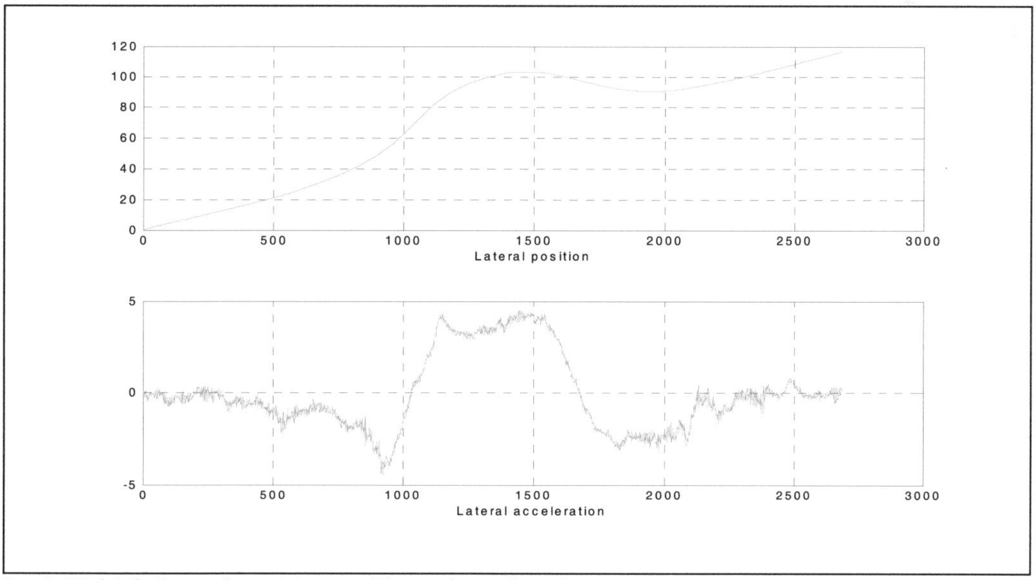

Fig. 1. Vehicle lateral position and lateral acceleration

The trajectories of the studied process represent a behavior of control identified on a given turn. The final goal of this study being to analyze the risk of failed trajectory, therefore we choose to work on the behavior of control of fast trajectories. The drivers having realized these trajectories were considered in a normal stress state at the time of the experimentation.

From this definition of the vehicle trajectory, a particular trajectory was defined with the aim of comparing later, all the observed trajectories to this particular trajectory. This particular trajectory will be regarded as reference trajectory for all the study.

2.3 Reference Trajectory

There exists in the literature several work concerning the reference trajectory for example (Lauffenburger et al, 2000) predict the reference trajectory by the splines method according to the road reference frame and a behavioral model of the driver. The reference trajectory considered in this study is the average function of the whole of the trajectories.

$$\begin{aligned} m_U &: \mathrm{IR} \rightarrow \mathrm{Mat}_{\mathrm{IR}}(6,1) \\ (\mathrm{t}) &\mapsto m_U(\mathrm{t}) = \overline{U}(t) = \frac{1}{L}\sum_{l=1}^{L} \mathrm{U(t)} \end{aligned} \tag{4}$$

This choice is justified on the one hand, in the data measurements where we note that most of the drivers roll while following the road center and on the other hand, the distance which we will use later in this study to compare trajectories between them. It is a distance which estimates the difference between a variable and its median value. The average trajectory can be also justified as trajectory of reference because not only it grants more weight in the majority of the observed trajectories having similar values but also it remains sensitive to all the trajectories observed of the turn in particular to the extreme trajectories. What is useful and necessary to take account of all the information delivered by the turn and received by the drivers (perception of the road).

After having defined the vehicle trajectory like vectorial stochastic process, no one needs a statistical analysis of this process. But before that, the other studies on the same database showed the partial stationary of a parameter or several parameters at the same time but never a complete stationarity of all the parameters of the trajectory at the same time. The same studies showed that none stationarity of this process comes at the same time from the none stationarity of its moments (the average μ, the standard deviation σ, etc).

From now, we will make a projection of this vectorial process on a functional filter. The goal of this projection is not only to work on a scalar process easy to analyze but especially to obtain a stationary scalar process. The important role of the stationarity of the process is the interval of prediction of the failure of the trajectory is different compared to an evolutionary process.

3. Distance evaluation between trajectories

We noted through the first observations on the measurements data, that the trajectory parameters are not stationary throughout the turn, because as soon as the driver changes, the experimental trajectories collected are discrete realizations of a different process. To conclude, it is obviously necessary to be placed within a framework where one lays out of observations of the same process of sufficient number. The goal of this section will be to transform our vectorial process U in scalar process making a projection without losing the information contained in the system interaction (V/I/D).

Starting from this sample (or class) of trajectories having similar statistical properties, it will be advisable to analyze statistically the scalar process $D_i = g(U)$ where i={E,M}. This implies the use of a suitable topological distance, the choice was made on the Mahalanobis distance D_M (Xinrong, 2001) and the Euclidean distance D_E (Lanequel, 1992), with standard variables.

This approach of modeling consists of considering the distance like a realization during the time of a process. One regards the trajectory parameters as random in order to taking into account of the risks relating to the infrastructure, vehicle, driver and environment (weather or traffic).

3.1 Euclidean distance (norm)

It is a distance in the Euclidean metric space whose characteristic is to grant the same weight to all the components of the vector or the matrix. It is defined by the following equation:

$$D_E = d(U, \bar{U}) = \sqrt{(U - \bar{U})(U - \bar{U})^T} \tag{5}$$

This distance obtained is a scalar and its major disadvantage is to not taken into account of the correlation between components (in our case, the trajectory parameters). The projection of a vectorial process U(t) give a scalar process $D_E(t)$ defined by:

$$\begin{aligned} D_E &: \Omega \times \mathrm{T} \rightarrow \mathrm{IR} \\ (\mathrm{t},\omega) &\mapsto D_E(\mathrm{t},\omega) = \sqrt{\left(U(t,\omega) - \bar{U}(t)\right)\left(U(t,\omega) - \bar{U}(t)\right)^T} \end{aligned} \tag{6}$$

3.2 Mahalanobis distance

In statistics, the Mahalanobis distance is a measurement of distance introduced by P.C Mahalanobis in 1936. It is based on the correlation between variables by which various models can be identified and analyzed. This distance is associated with particular metric called Mahalanobis metric. It is a distance to the probabilistic direction between a measurement and a Gaussian probability law. Therefore, it is usable when one can approximate the distribution of the data by a normal law. One made tests of adequacy to show that the distribution of the observations data follow a normal law.

The characteristic of this distance is to estimate the deviation between a reference trajectory and an observed trajectory even if the components of the trajectory don't have the same magnitude. It grants a less important weight to the most disturbed components. It is also a method of dissimilarity measurement between two random vectors of same sample.
In practice, we suppose that one has *L* observations of the process U(t) in the discretizations $0 = t_0 < t_1 < \ldots < t_{M-1} = T$ of the interval *[0, T]*.

In these conditions, one can define the Mahalanobis distance between vector $\overline{U}$ of the reference observations and vector U of the discrete observations of the mth trajectory by:

$$D_M = d(U, \overline{U}) = \sqrt{\left[(U - \overline{U})^T \Sigma^{-1} (U - \overline{U})\right]} \tag{7}$$

Where Σ is a variance-covariance matrix of the random vector $(U, \overline{U})$.
The projection of a vectorial process U(t) give a scalar process $D_M(t)$ defined by :

$$\begin{gathered} D_M : \Omega \times T \rightarrow IR \\ (t, \omega) \rightarrow D_M = \sqrt{\left[(U(t,\omega) - \overline{U}(t))^T \Sigma^{-1} (U(t,\omega) - \overline{U}(t))\right]} \end{gathered} \tag{8}$$

3.3 Application

To illustrate our remarks at the distances between trajectories, the figure (2) shows an example of distance calculation with the methods (Mahalanobis and Euclidean). These two distances represent the deviation between reference trajectory (or average) and the observed trajectories.

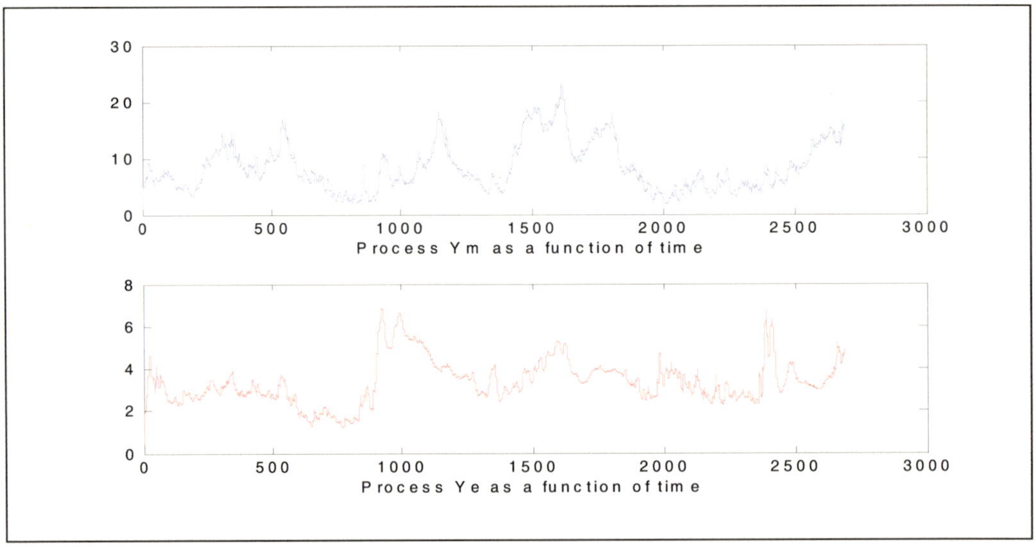

Fig. 2. Distance between trajectories

We can notice the existence of similarity zones between the scalar processes $D_M(t)$ and $D_E(t)$ in the figure (2) but also great differences exist sometimes. This first result explains that the correlation between the parameters can play a very important role. Therefore, a significant difference between both methods exists. We note that the Euclidean distance D_E is less sensitive to the parameters variations than the Mahalanobis distance D_M.

The figure (3) represents the temporal mean and standard deviation of the processes $D_E(\omega,t)$ and $D_M(\omega,t)$. In blue, we have the Mahalanobis distance and in red the Euclidean distance.

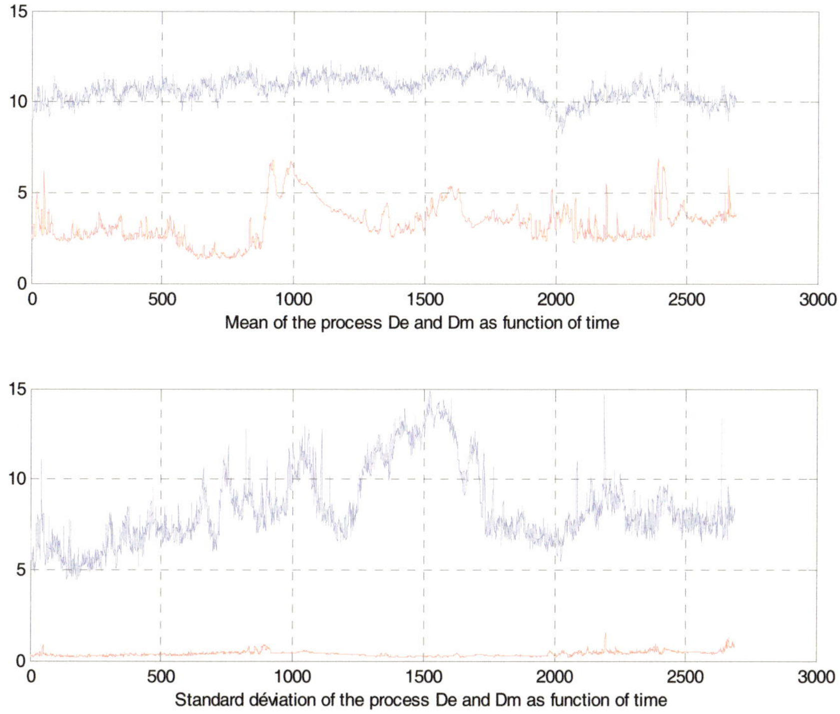

Fig. 3. Mean and Standard deviation of scalar processes

The figure (3) shows that these functions vary according to time and present a difference between them. We also notice that the processes are positive by construction because being distances thus they are not centered.

In order to obtain a centered scalar process, we have done a new transformation on the processes $D_M(t)$ and $D_E(t)$. We obtained the centered scalar processes $Y_m(t) = D_M(w,t) - m_{Dm}(t)$ and $Y_e(t) = D_E(w,t) - m_{De}(t)$. Where $m_{Dm}(t)$ and $m_{De}(t)$ are the average distance of the processes $D_M(w,t)$ and $D_E(w,t)$. The next step consists of doing a statistic analysis of these scalar processes.

4. Scalar process analysis

In this part, at first we will check the stationarity assumptions of scalar processes $Y_M(t)$ and $Y_E(t)$. Then, in the second section, we will describe the characterization of these processes. Afterwards, a third section will make it possible to identify the law of these processes. Lastly, a fourth section we will identify the law of maximum processes.

4.1 Stationary and ergodicity analysis

That is to say a function Y(t) with ($t \in R_+$) : Y(t) is a function or a random process, for each time t_1 fixed, $Y(t_1)$ is a random variable. The process Y(t) is entirely characterized (in probability) if one knows the probability density function (pdf) united multivariate of all finite collection (vector). (Bouleau, 1994)

$$Y_E=\{Y(t_1), Y(t_2),\ldots.. Y(t_i),\ldots.. Y(t_M)\} \text{ and } Y_M=\{Y(t_1), Y(t_2),\ldots.. Y(t_i),\ldots.. Y(t_M)\} \quad (9)$$

For all t_i and finite M.

After having defined a stochastic process, it is necessary to check the assumptions of stationarity and ergodicity of the scalar process Y(t). A random process is stationary by definition, if its moments are invariants by translation of time. We checked this assumption of two-order stationarity on our observations data by calculating the mean, the variance and the auto covariance function of the process Y(t). (Kree, 1983). By construction, the average and the variance are respectively equal to zero and the unit because the process was standardizes.

$$m_Y \equiv IE(Y(\omega,t)) = 0 = \text{constante } (\forall t) \text{ and } Var(Y(\omega,t)) = \sigma^2_Y = 1 = \text{constante } (\forall t) \quad (10)$$

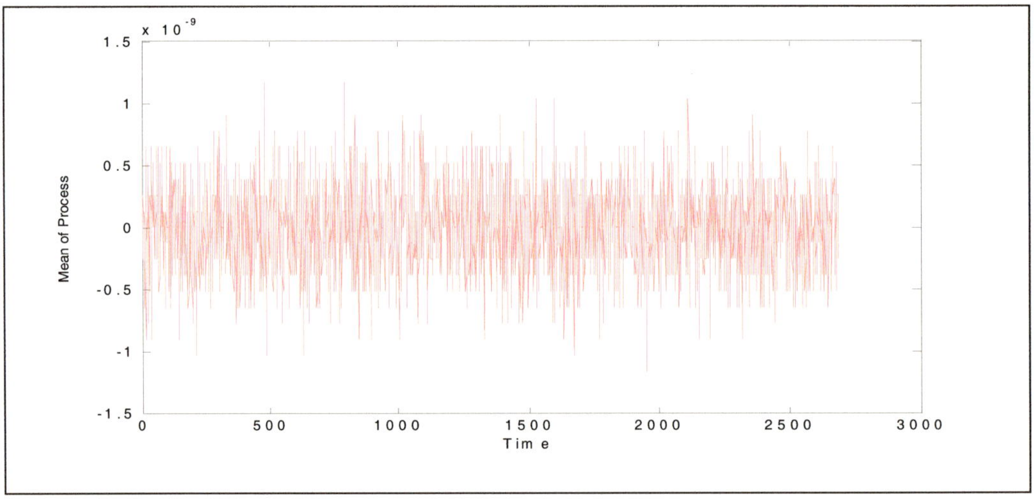

Fig. 4. Mean of the centered scalar process as a function of time (ms).

The auto-covariance function $C_Y(t_1,t_2)$, is the function of two variables t1 and t2 given by :

$$\begin{aligned}
&C_Y : R\times R \rightarrow R \\
&(t_1,t_2) \rightarrow C_Y(t_1,t_2) = Cov(Y(t),Y(t+\delta)) = C_{YY}(t_{i+1}-t_i) = C_{YY}(\delta) \\
&\delta = t_{i+1} - t_i
\end{aligned} \quad (11)$$

The figure (5) represents the auto-covariance function of processes D_E et D_M

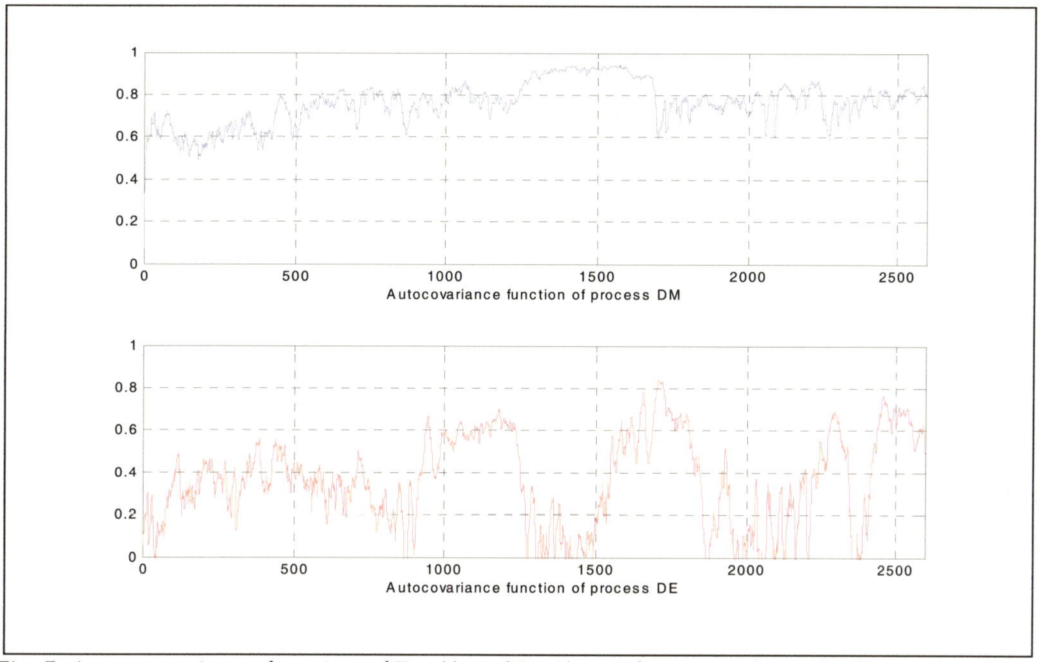

Fig. 5. Auto-covariance function of Dm(t) and De(t) as a function of time (ms).

We have just shown that the average, the standard deviation and the auto-covariance function do not depend on time. Thus, the processes $Y_M(t)$ and $Y_E(t)$ are stationary with order 2. After having checked the assumption of stationarity of the process, it is interesting to check the assumption of the process ergodicity. A process is ergodic, if the equivalence between the overall average (mean) and the space average on an infinite interval is verified:

$$m_Y \equiv E\left(Y(\omega,t)\right) \Leftrightarrow m_Y = \lim_{T \to \infty} \frac{1}{T}\int_0^T Y(s)ds = \text{constante} \tag{12}$$

By checking the assumption on our observations data, we note that it is checked. After having checked these assumptions, we use also a statistical test of stationarity (Xiao, 2007),

4.2 Scalar process characterization

To characterize processes Y_M and Y_E, we will estimate the power spectral density, the probability density and the function of distribution (Soize, 2000).

Power Spectral Density function Estimate

The objective of this section consists in considering the Power Spectral Density of the process Y(t) in order to be able to generate trajectories resulting from the same process. In referent in the preceding section of this study, it was checked that the process Y(t) is stationary at second-order. A transformation was made on the scalar process of kind have a new centered process. The PSD is obtained by using this following formula:

$$\hat{S}_{L,T}(\omega) = \frac{1}{2\pi}\frac{1}{L}\sum_{l=1}^{L}\left|\hat{X}^{l}(\omega)\right|^{2}$$
$$\hat{X}^{l}(\omega) = \int_{0}^{T} W_T(t) X^{l}(t) e^{-i\omega t}\, dt \tag{13}$$

Where W_T is a temporal window (Hamming model). For $l=1....L$, where L is the number of trajectories in the class. The figure (6) shows estimated Power Spectral Density of Y_m and Y_e. We have obtained negative PSD because we have used log function to make a zoom on the figures.

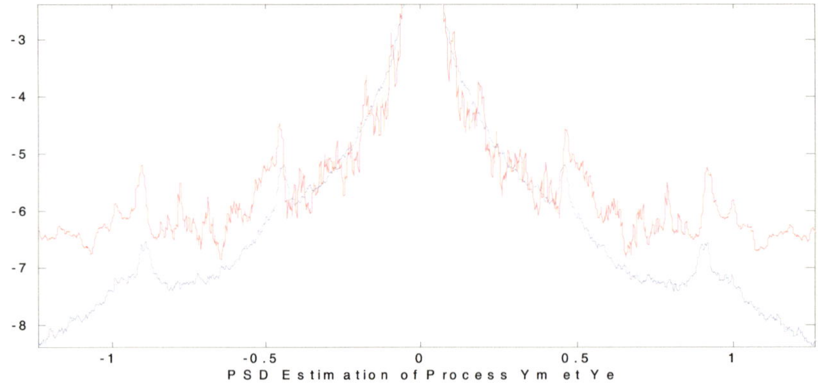

Fig. 6. Power Spectral Density estimates of the process Y_e and Y_m.

The red and blue curves correspond respectively to the PSD of the processes Y_m and Y_e.

Probability Density function Estimate

As previously, to characterize the processes $Y_m(t)$ and $Y_e(t)$ in a complete way, it is necessary to estimate its probability density P_Y and its distribution function F_Y. Estimated P_Y and F_Y are then defined by the following relations:

$$\left\{\begin{aligned} \hat{P}_X^M(x) &= \sum_{j\in J_M} \frac{N_j}{\delta N} 1\mathrm{I}_{D_j}(x);\ x \in \overline{X} \\ \hat{F}_X^M(x) &= \sum_{j\in J_M} \frac{\sum_{k=1}^{j} N_j}{N} 1\mathrm{I}_{D_J}(x);\ x \in \overline{X} \end{aligned}\right\} \tag{14}$$

Where $1\mathrm{I}_{D_j}$ is a indicator function of D_j

The two curves in the figure (7) represent the probability density function of the processes $Y_m(t)$ and Ye(t). The probability density of the process $Y_m(t)$ tends towards a Gamma law whereas the process $Y_e(t)$ tends towards a Gaussian law.

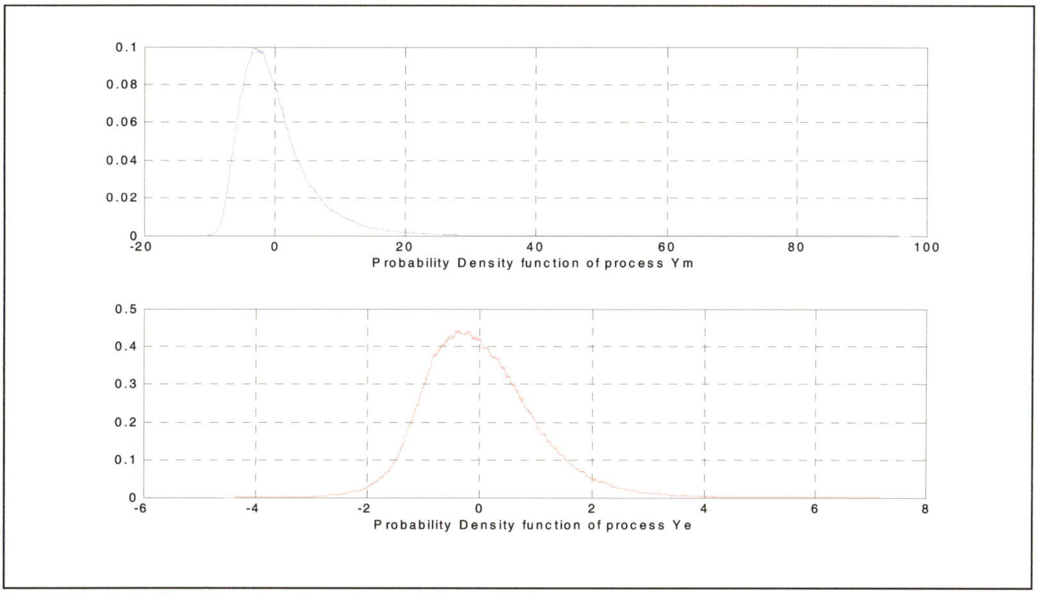

Fig. 7. Probability Density function of Y_m and Y_e.

Distribution function Estimate

The two curves in the figure (8) represent the distribution function of the processes Y_m and Y_e. We note a big difference between them as in the probability density.

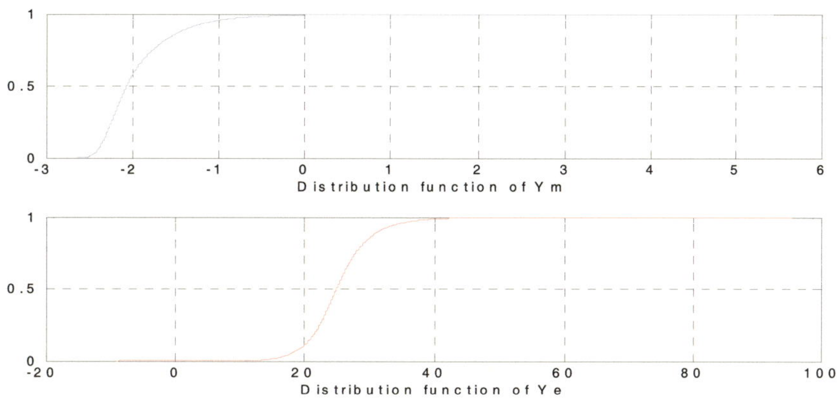

Fig. 8. Distribution function of processes Y_m and Y_e.

After the characterization of process $Y_E(t)$ and $Y_M(t)$, the next section will consist to identify the scalar process $Y_E(t)$ and $Y_M(t)$.

4.3 Scalar process identification

We initially calculated the kurtosis (K) and skewness (S) coefficients to have an idea of the classical probability laws to use for the approximation of the processes $Y_E(t)$ and $Y_M(t)$ laws.

Kurtosis coefficient

The kurtosis coefficient is a statistic which measures the degree of probability of the extreme events. More, it is large, more the tails of distribution are thick compared to those of the normal law, i.e. more of the extreme events can potentially occur. This coefficient noted K is calculated by:

$$K = \frac{\mu_X^4}{\sigma_X^4} - 3 \quad \text{where} \quad \mu_X^4 = \frac{\sum X_E^4}{N} \tag{15}$$

Skewness coefficient

The skewness coefficient measures the degree of asymmetry of the distribution. For a perfectly symmetrical distribution (for example, a normal law), the coefficient of asymmetry S= 0. If the coefficient S>0, the distribution is asymmetrical on the left: there is a strong probability that an event is with the top of the average that in lower part (the modal value is with the top of the average). If, the distribution is asymmetrical on the right: there is a weaker probability than an event is with the top of the average than in lower part (the modal value is with the lower part of the average). This coefficient noted S is calculated by the following equations:

$$K = \frac{\mu_X^3}{\sigma_X^3} \quad \text{where} \quad \mu_X^4 = \frac{\sum X_E^4}{N} \tag{16}$$

	Kurtosis	Skewness
Process Y_M	8.6970	2.5454
Process Y_E	3.84	1.5286

Table 1. Kurtosis and skewness coefficient of processes Y_E and Y_M

While referring on the one hand, visually on the figure (7) and on the other hand, by looking at the kurtosis and the skewness coefficients, we note that the laws of our processes can be approximated by classical laws (Bouleau, 1986). The use of the comparison criterions (Lelu, 2002) made it possible to choose the best approximations for the two laws characterized previously. The normal law was selected for the Euclidean distance and the Gumbel law for the Mahalanobis distance. The figure (9) represents the target law of probability of scalar processes $Y_M(t)$ and $Y_E(t)$ as well as the law of probability of the approximations of these processes.

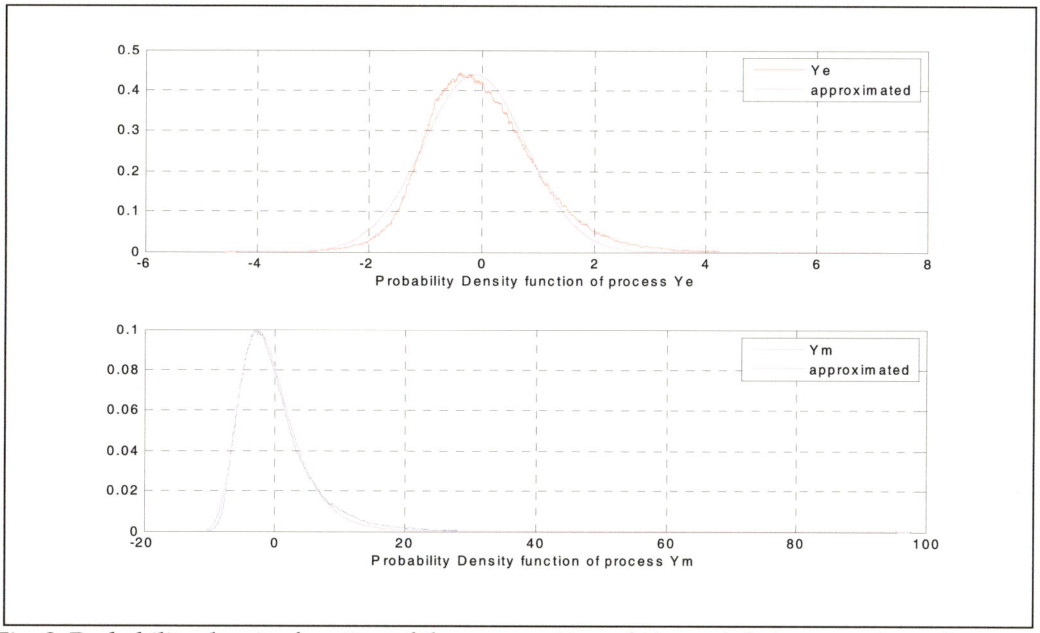

Fig. 9. Probability density function of the process Ye and Ym and their approximated

The figure (9) shows a better approximation for our laws especially for the Gumbel law. The theoretical laws obtained enable us to simulate distances between trajectories for the studied bend. These simulated distances will have the same statistical properties as the sample of distances which was used to build the model of distances. The figure (10) represents an example of distance obtained with the measured trajectories and another obtained by simulation of process $Y_E(t)$. The red curve corresponds to that obtained by the data of measurements and the blue one corresponds to that simulated.

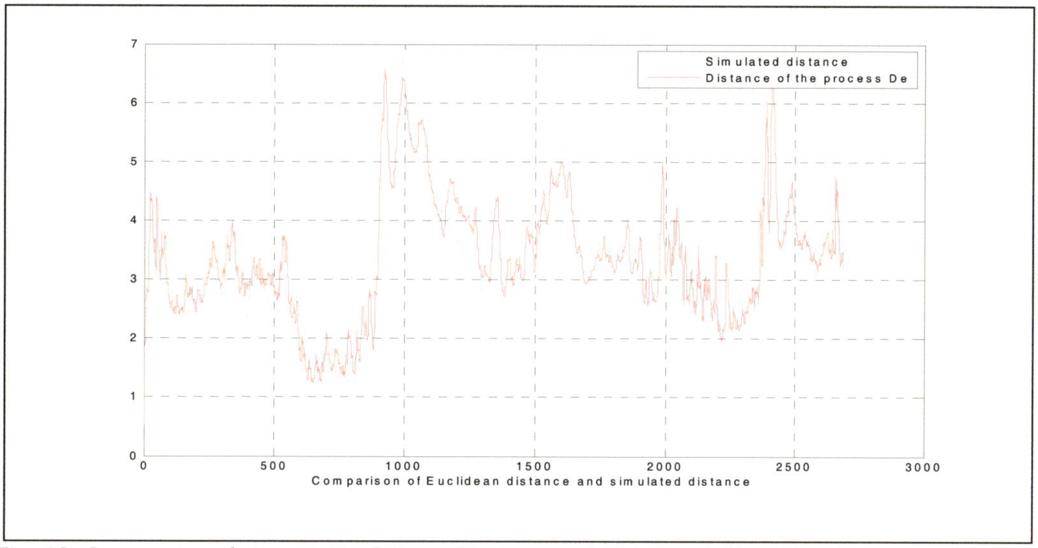

Fig. 10. Comparison between Euclidean distance and simulated distance

We can conclude that the model based on distances implemented is validated. The next section will be to identify the law of the maximum of processes $Y_E(t)$ and $Y_M(t)$.

4.4 Identification of process maximum law

In the section (1) of this part, we showed that scalar processes $Y_M(t,w)$ and $Y_E(t,w)$ respectively follow the law of Gumbel and the normal law. To estimate trajectory probability of failure, we will identify the law of maximum of the scalar processes $Y_E(t)$ and $Y_M(t)$. The purpose of the maximum law identification is to eliminate any temporal aspect along the bend.
According to the stability principle, if the law of an initial process is of type I, II or III, corresponding to a law of maximum, then the law of maximum is of the same type. The extreme law of type I (Gumbel) has as an asymptotic law of the maximum(Jacob, 1993). This law is represented by the following formula:

$$\begin{cases} F_n(x) = \exp\left[-e^{-(\alpha_n(x-u_n))}\right] \\ f_n(x) = \alpha_n e^{-(\alpha_n(x-u_n))} \exp\left[-e^{-(\alpha_n(x-u_n))}\right] \end{cases} \quad (17)$$

Where u_n is a location parameter, representing the mode (or the most probable value) of U_n and the characteristic value of X. $u_n\alpha_n$ measures the dispersion of this variable while α_n is the maximum intensity of X. The figure (11) represents the estimate of the law of the maximum of process Ye (T) and its approximation.

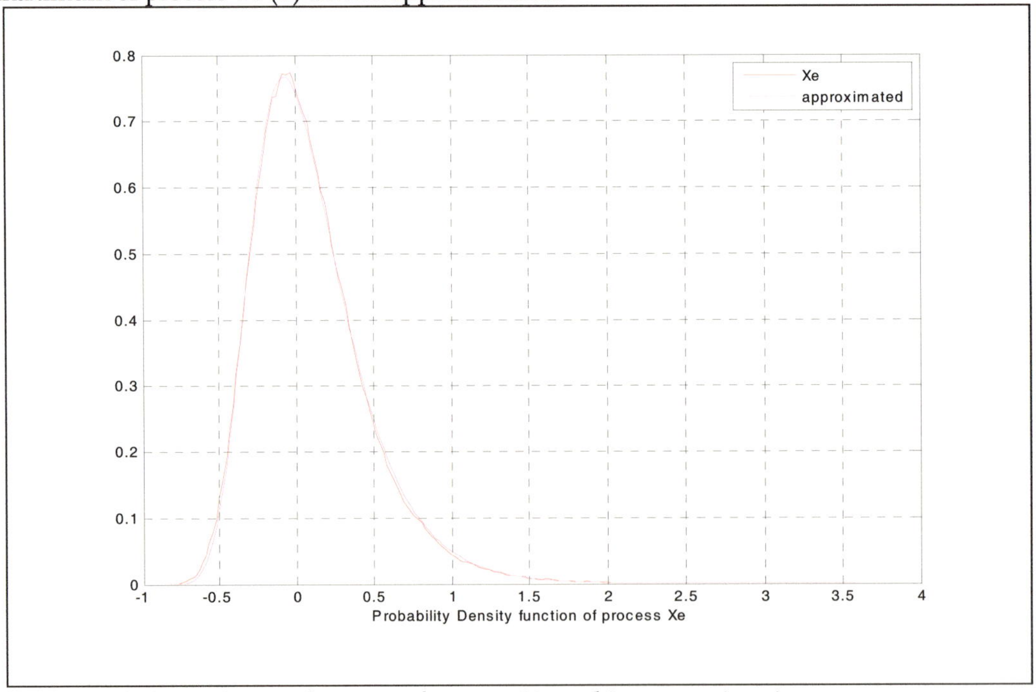

Fig. 11. Probability density function of process Xe and its approximation

We can conclude that the law of maximum of a Gaussian process is a law of Gumbel. For these laws of maximum, to estimate the trajectory probability of failure, it is necessary to define the trajectories limit states. The next step will be to determine these limit states.

5. Trajectory stability criteria

The final aim of this study is to estimate the trajectory probability of failure knowing its variation compared to the reference trajectory. For that, it is necessary to define the safety field of the trajectory. In this part, we will determine the trajectory criteria of stability. Then we will speak about the limit states of the trajectories. Finally we will calculate the threshold distance $D_{threshold}$ not to be exceeded to remain in safety.

5.1 Trajectories stability criterion

Security criteria

Safety criteria in longitudinal control can be treated as a problem to assure a minimal distance between vehicles. In this study, we will insist on the criterion of comfort.

Comfort criteria

Passenger comfort in public ground transportation is determined by the changes in motion felt in all directions, as well as by the other environmental effects. Typically, acceleration magnitude is taken as a comfort metric. Consequently, the jerk, i.e. the acceleration's derivate better reflects a human comfort criterion. As its name suggests, jerk is important when evaluating the destructive effect of a motion on a mechanism or the discomfort caused to passengers. The movement of delicate instruments needs to be kept within specified limits of jerk as well as acceleration to avoid damage.

In (Zakowska,2008) comfort due to motion changes in a vehicle's longitudinal direction has been treated; When designing a train and elevators, engineers will typically be required to keep the jerk less than (2 m/s^3) for passengers comfort. However, the bounded longitudinal jerk in this study is less than (3 m/s^3).

The main theoretical assumption is: a subject driving on a self-explaining road assumes a correct and safe trajectory and the local lateral accelerations depend only on the road curvature geometry. If the driver corrects the vehicle's trajectory more than what road curvature imposes, the road is not self-explaining and, consequently, it can be unsafe. If the local transversal accelerations do not depend only on the actual road curvature, they are biased by driver's corrections of trajectory. The local variability of lateral acceleration shows clearly the corrections of trajectory that the driver assumes and this could be so labeled as a discomfort index. These repeated local oscillations represent a violation of the driver expectancy. Authors have used formula (18) to estimate pathologic discomfort:

$$PD = \int_{s=0}^{s=L} \left| a_t(s) \right| ds \approx \sum_{j=0}^{N} \left| \left(\frac{\partial^2 y}{\partial t^2} \right)_j - \frac{\partial x / \partial t}{\rho_j} \right| \tag{18}$$

By applying this criterion to the representative sample of trajectories observed on the same studied turn, we obtained after standardization, PD ranging between (0.15 and 1). However, the bounded pathologic discomfort in this study is less than (0.75). All the trajectories which do not respect these two criteria are regarded as unstable.

5.2 Trajectories limit state

Constraints obtained through the preceding criteria give practical limits of variations for the vehicle kinematics parameters in security and comfort conditions. This subset D_S is made up of the trajectories which respect the comfort criterion.

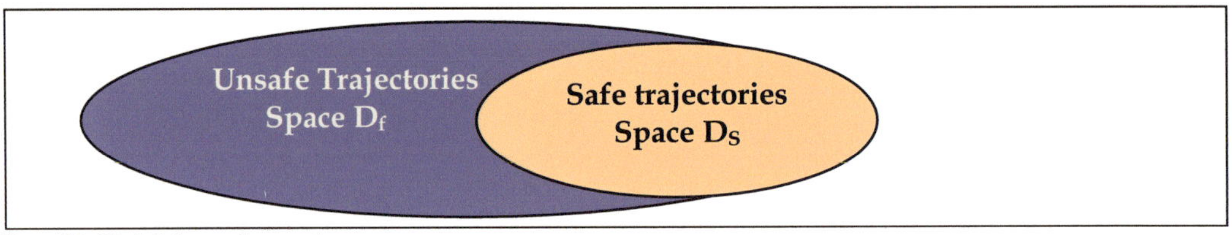

Fig. 12. Vehicle trajectories space

However, the bounded trajectory parameters are less than: {transversal position (2m), longitudinal speed (22m/s), lateral speed (9m/s), longitudinal acceleration (3m/s²) and lateral acceleration (4 m/s²)}.

5.3 Threshold Distance

The distances calculated starting from the observed trajectories lie between (0, 15). In this study, we choose a threshold distance equal to (10) beyond which the trajectory is unstable. This assumption is checked through the limit states previously definite. The figure (13) represents the delimitation zone of the safe distances and that of the unsafe distances. The two zones are separated by the distance threshold. This distance threshold will be used in the next step to estimate the trajectory probability of failure.

The last step of this study will consist to apply the analysis reliability of civil engineer.

6. Reliability analysis of trajectories

In this part of the chapter, we propose tools of the probabilistic reliability theory to assess safety indices of trajectories. The method consists to treat firstly the function of limit state and the transformation of the physical space variables towards the space of the normalized variables. Then, the reliability indice will be calculated. Lastly, as any analysis reliability engineer, one will evaluate the probability of failure (PF) associated with the selected limit state. We recall that the stationnarity assumption takes all its sense in this part to predict a failing trajectory.

We point out that the maximum of the process $Y_E(t)$ or $Y_M(t)$ is represented by:

$$Y(\omega) = \text{Sup}_{t\in[0,T]} \left| d(U(t,\omega), \overline{U}(t)) \right| \tag{19}$$

Y(ω) is a regular random variable for which one has a good approximation of his law. Let G : IR → IR ; x → G(x) = y – d where d is an element of IR+ and G is the limit state function.

We choose to define the safety and the failure events by :
$E_s = \{\omega \in \Omega \text{ such } G(X(\omega)) < 0\}$ and $E_f = \{\omega \in \Omega \text{ such } G(X(\omega)) \geq 0\}$
And the safety domain and the unsafe domain by :
$D_s = \{x \in IR \text{ such } G(x) < 0\}$ and $D_f = \{x \in IR \text{ such } G(x) \geq 0\}$
It acts, once known the probability density P_Y of the random variable X and after having defined the events E_s and E_f, it is necessary to calculate the probabilities $P(E_s)$ and $P(E_f)$.
We obtain :

$$P_f = P(E_f) = \int_{D_f} p_Y(y)dy \quad \text{and } P(E_s) = 1-P(E_f) \tag{20}$$

This is why, one interests only in the estimate of P_f
We based then on a classical result of the probabilities calculation which says that under certain conditions (that we will suppose satisfied here), one can always build a regular transformation T such as if X is a Gaussian v.a. standard with values in IR, then one with the equality in law Z= T (X). The safety and the failure events are written by:

$E_s = \{\omega \in \Omega \text{ such } \Gamma(Z(\omega)) < 0\}$ and $E_f = \{\omega \in \Omega \text{ such } \Gamma(Z(\omega)) \geq 0\}$, where $\Gamma = GoT^{-1}$
The images per T of the safety and failure fields are written as for them:
$\Delta_S = T(D_s) = \{x \in IR \text{ such } \Gamma(x)) < 0\}$ and $\Delta_f = T(D_f) = \{y \in IR \text{ such } \Gamma(y)) < 0\}$
One has then:

$$P_f = \int_{IR} 1_{\Delta_f}(x) p_X(x)dx \quad \text{where} \quad p_X(x) = \frac{e^{-x^2/2}}{\sqrt{2\pi}} \tag{21}$$

The law of Y being known it is possible to obtain an approximation of PF either by using a method of the Monte Carlo type or by using methods of approximation (FORM and SORM methods) (Lemaire, 2005). For that we must initially define the index of Hasofer-Lind:
$\beta_{HL} = d(O, \Delta_f)$ where O is origin point of IR. To get β_{HL} consists to solve the following problem:

$$\begin{cases} \text{Find } y^* \in IR \text{ such that } : \\ \|y^*\| = \underset{y \in \Delta_f}{Min} \|y\| \end{cases} \tag{22}$$

FORM method

Elle consiste à effectuer une approximation du 1er ordre de Δ_f au voisinage de y*

$$P_f \text{ est approchée par } P_f^L = \Phi(-\beta_{HL}) \quad \text{avec } \beta_{HL} = \frac{\Gamma(y^*) - \langle \nabla\Gamma(y^*), y^* \rangle}{\|\nabla\Gamma(y^*)\|}$$

and Φ is the distribution function of Gaussian law in IR.

SORM Method

It consists in carrying out a second order approximation of Δ_f in au voisinage de y*
We can use for example the following approximation (due à Breitung):

$$P_f^L \approx \Phi(-\beta_{HL}) \left| \sum_{i=1}^{d-1} (1 - \beta_{HL} \chi_i(y^*)) \right|^{-1/2}$$

avec $\chi_i(y^*)$, $i = 1,\dots,d-1$ les courbures principales de Γ_Q au design point y^*

7. Conclusion

The goal of this chapter was to estimate the trajectory probability of failure by using metric (or distance) between the trajectories starting from data of experimental measurements.

Initially, after having defined the trajectory of the vehicle and its properties, we considered a sample of trajectories resulting from the same stochastic process vectorial. The trajectories of the process are the solutions of a stochastic differential equation controlled by the system of control. Then, we projected the dated measurements of this process on IR in order to bring back to have scalar problem. This step passes by the use of judiciously selected functional (one based on the use of the Euclidean distance, the other based on the use of the Mahalanobis distance).

Afterwards, we considered the process (scalar) of deviations with the average distance of the sample. It is this process which we sought to characterize. An statistical analysis was carried out on this scalar process with an aim of studying the stationnarity. The stationnarity assumption was not rejected for these processes.

Then, to identify the model of distance between trajectories, on the one hand, we characterized each process by estimating the probability law, the function of distribution and the power spectral density. In addition, we identified the laws of probability of each process by a reasonable approximation. The validation of this approximation was made by using the integral criterion.

Then, after having identified the law of maximum of the two preceding laws and by using of the safety and comfort criteria of the trajectory, we estimated the probability of failure.

Finally, we present simulation results of the proposed methods. The validation is carried out by means of experimental measures.

8. References

Bouleau, N., 2002, «*Probabilités de l'ingénieur. Variables aléatoires et simulation*», Hermann, 383 pages. ISBN : 2-7056-6430-4

Bouleau, N., 1988, «*Processus stochastiques et applications*», Hermann, ISBN : 2-7056-1420-20
Jacob, B., 1993, «*Approximation de la loi des valeurs extrêmes*», Cours de genie civil, Ecole Nationale des Ponts et Chaussées, France
Arai, T. & Kragic, D. (1999). Name of paper, In: *Name of Book in Italics,* Name(s) of Editor(s), (Ed.), page numbers (first-last), Publisher, ISBN, Place of publication
Lauffenburger, J. Ph.; Basset, M.; Coch, F. and Gissinger, G. L., «*Driver-aid system using Path planning for lateral vehicle control*», 2003, Control Engineering Practice, volume 11/2, Février, pp. 215-229.
Koita, A. and Daucher, D., 2008, «*Protocole expérimental : recueil de données de mesures de trajectoires en virage*» , rapport interne LCPC.
Koita, A. and Daucher, D., 2009, «*Stochastic Analysis of Vehicle Trajectories in Bend: toward a risk indicator construction*», ICOSSAR 2009, International Conference on Structural Safety and Reliability, September 13-17, Osaka, Japan.
Kanayama, Y. and Hartman, B., 1997, «*Smooth local path planning for autonomous vehicles*», Int. Robotics Research, Vol. 16 No. 3, pp. 263.84
Kree, P. and Soize, C. 1983. «*Mathematics of random phenomena*», Dordrecht
Lelu, A., 2002, «*Comparaison de trois mesures de similarité utilisées en documentation automatique et analyse textuelle*» JADT., coord. IRISA, St. Malo, 13-15 Mars 2002
Lanequel, L. 1992. *Euclidean distance matrix analysis of the muzzle region in Adapis.* ISSN 0764 - 4450, vol 314. N 12, pp 1387-1393.
Lauffenberger, J. P. 2002. *Contribution à la surveillance temps réel du système, conducteur - vehicule-environnement, élaboration d'un système d'aide à la conduite.* Université Haute Alsace, Mulhouse. PHD Thesis
Lemaire, M., 2005, «*Fiabilité des structures, Couplage Mécano-.abiliste statique*», Hermes, 2005, ISBN 2-7462-1057-6
Pugachev, V., 1982, «*Théorie des probabilités et statistique mathématique*», Moscou, Edition MIR,
Soize, C., 1993, «*Méthodes mathématiques en analyse du signal*», MASSON, 1993
Takahashi, A.; Hongo, T. and Ninomiya, Y. «*Local Path Planning and Motion Control for AGV in Positionning*», Proc. IROS, pp 392-395, Tsukuba, Japan
World Mortality Database. «*WHO Mortality statistics. World Health Organization*», 2004.
Xiao J., P. Borgnat, P. Flandrin, 2007: "*Testing stationarity with time-frequency surrogates,*" XVth European Signal Proc. Conf. EUSIPCO-07, Poznan
Xinrong Z. Huili, Z and Yongxin, Y. 2001. «*Mahalanobis distance image segmentation based on two-dimensional histogram.* SPIE Journal proceedings, ISBN 0-8194-4278-X
Zakowska, L.; Benedetto, A.; Calvi, A and D'Amico, F., 2009, «*The Effect of curve Characteristics on driving behavior: a driving simulator study*», TRB 88 th Annual Meeting (January 11-15, 2009) USA

8

Optimization problems for controlled mechanical systems: Bridging the gap between theory and application

M. Chyba[a], T. Haberkorn[b], R.N. Smith[c]
[a] *University of Hawaii, Honolulu, HI 96822 USA*
Mathematics, College of Natural Sciences
[b]*Université d'Orléans, 45067 Orléans Cedex 2, France*
Laboratoire MAPMO
[c] *University of Southern California, Los Angeles, CA 90089, USA*
Robotic Embedded Systems Laboratory, Department of Computer Science

1. Introduction

Mechanical control systems have become a part of our everyday life. Systems such as automobiles, robot manipulators, mobile robots, satellites, buildings with active vibration controllers and air conditioning systems, make life easier and safer, as well as help us explore the world we live in and exploit it's available resources. In this chapter, we examine a specific example of a mechanical control system; the Autonomous Underwater Vehicle (AUV). Our contribution to the advancement of AUV research is in the area of guidance and control. We present innovative techniques to design and implement control strategies that consider the optimization of time and/or energy consumption.

Recent advances in robotics, control theory, portable energy sources and automation increase our ability to create more intelligent robots, and allows us to conduct more explorations by use of autonomous vehicles. This facilitates access to higher risk areas, longer time underwater, and more efficient exploration as compared to human occupied vehicles. The use of underwater vehicles is expanding in every area of ocean science. Such vehicles are used by oceanographers, archaeologists, geologists, ocean engineers, and many others. These vehicles are designed to be agile, versatile and robust, and thus, their usage has gone from novelty to necessity for any ocean expedition.

Formally, AUVs are characterized by a Lagrangian of the form kinetic energy minus potential energy. This is commonly referred to as the class of *simple* mechanical control systems, see (Lewis & Murray, 1997) and (Bullo & Lewis, 2004). Theoretically, an AUV is represented by a complex, non-linear, dynamic system of equations to model and control. Practically speaking, providing solutions to the motion planning problem, which considers the optimization of some cost function, will result in a more robust control scheme for the vehicle, and therefore increase its autonomy. Thus, an AUV poses an interesting research problem from both theoretical and practical viewpoints, and it is an excellent platform to generate advances in both areas simultaneously.

An interesting practical problem in the study of autonomous vehicles in general, is energy consumption. Since an AUV must carry its own power source throughout the entire duration of a mission, it is critical to consider the energy demands that certain control strategies or planned trajectories require. Hence, the theory behind a solution to the motion planning problem for AUVs must consider energy consumption to ensure that the solution is practically implementable. For example, in (Chyba et al., 2009a) the authors design control strategies that reduce the number of times the actuators are required to change direction. Such a strategy keeps the actuators operating in a steady-state, which reduces error in thrust application. Implementation results of these strategies onto a test-bed vehicle are presented, and match well with theoretical predictions. In addition, energy consumption for the presented strategies was kept near the computed minimum value.

Another practical concern for AUV implementation is under-actuation. Some vehicles are designed to operate in an under-actuated condition, while others fully-actuated vessels need to be prepared to deal with actuator failure(s) resulting from any number of mechanical issues. In an effort to conserve energy, it may be beneficial to operate an AUV in an under-actuated, but fully-controllable condition. Additionally, early consideration of under-actuated path planning results may assist in vehicle design to implement effective redundancy onto a vehicle. Such consideration at the design stage could also aide in the construction of a fully-controllable but under-actuated vehicle for more cost-effective applications. One approach to control strategy design for under-actuated vehicles is by use of kinematic reductions as done in (Smith, 2008) and (Smith et al., 2009a). Here, the authors designed control strategies for under-actuated AUVs and present the results of their implementation onto a test-bed vehicle. In these papers, the equations of motion for an AUV are derived in the framework of differential geometry. There are many advantages to describing a controlled mechanical system in this way (c.f., (Bullo & Lewis, 2004) and (Lewis, 2007)), thus it is the point of view that we adopt in the present chapter.

Based upon previous results presented in (Chyba et al., 2009a), (Smith, 2008) and (Smith et al., 2009a), we propose a control strategy design method that accounts for the two essential features necessary in the guidance and control of AUVs; namely minimizing energy consumption and incorporating under-actuation. The reader should keep in mind throughout this article, that bridging the gap between theory and application is our main goal. Hence, we are motivated to design control strategies that can be implemented onto a real vehicle, and not ones that can only be implemented in numerical simulations. For our specific AUV application, we need to design control strategies that are piecewise constant with respect to time, and that only require a small number of direction changes of the actuators. In this chapter, we neglect external uncertainties and disturbances, such as currents, as our experiments are conducted in the controlled environment of a swimming pool. Research is ongoing to merge the presented control strategies with existing adaptive control systems to account for external disturbances.

We remark that guidance and control of AUVs is not the only practical application dealing with cost optimization that requires the type of control structure we consider. In particular, research has shown that an ideal radiation delivery strategy for cancer treatment is to administer a period of intense treatment followed by period of rest. Continuous drug administration is possible, but at this time requires long hospital stays, and is thus not practical. Research is ongoing to develop methods and materials for specialized drug delivery ((Ledzewicz & Schättler, 2009)). Another example of a system utilizing a piecewise constant control structure while minimizing energy consumption is a home heating and cooling system. It is impractical and inefficient for the system to continuously adjust the input air temperature to a home. This would require the system to remain powered on all the time. Instead, as has been established in many other optimal control problems, the optimal strategy has a *bang-bang* structure. This bang-bang structure is easy to implement in practice, however, optimal solutions may contain chattering, a large number of discontinuities (i.e., instantaneous changes in the control), which cannot be implemented on a physical system. To remedy this issue, we present the STP algorithm. This control strategy design algorithm provides an implementable solution to the optimization problem, while also keeping the optimization criteria close to optimal.

2. Modeling

In this chapter, we identify a simple control mechanical system with a second-order forced affine connection control system (FACCS) on a differentiable, configuration manifold, $Q = \mathbb{R}^3 \times SO(3) \cong SE(3)$. Our motivation is to exploit inherent geometric properties and symmetries of the mechanical system to provide solutions to the motion planning problem.

2.1 Mechanical Control Systems

An FACCS is a 5-tuple $(Q, \nabla, F, \mathcal{Y}, U)$, where Q is the configuration manifold for the system, ∇ is an affine connection defined on Q, F represents the external forces, $\mathcal{Y}$ is a set of vector fields defined on Q and $U \subset \mathbb{R}^m$. We refer to the set $\mathcal{Y}$ as the set of input control vector fields. If we assume $\mathcal{Y}$ to be given by $\sum_{i=1}^{m} \sigma_i F_i$, the equations of motion take the form:

$$\nabla_{\gamma'}\gamma' = \mathbb{G}^{\#}(F(\gamma'(t))) + \sum_{i=1}^{m} \mathbb{G}^{\#} F_i(\gamma(t))\sigma_i(t), \tag{1}$$

where $\mathbb{G}^{\#}$ is the inverse of the kinematic energy metric $\mathbb{G}$ and ∇ is the Levi-Civita connection associated to $\mathbb{G}$. The control $\sigma(.)$ is a measurable bounded function that takes its values in U.

There is a vast amount of literature devoted to the study of mechanical control systems, the references listed here are only those that are directly related to our work.

2.1.1 Underwater Vehicles

The control strategies presented in the following sections were designed with the intention to implement them onto a test-bed AUV. Here, we do not present the experimental results from these implementations, however we refer the interested reader to (Smith, 2008) for results of the implementation of the kinematic control strategies given in the simulation section onto a test-bed AUV.

A very detailed description of the equations of motion for a submerged rigid body can be found in (Smith et al., 2009a). In this chapter we just briefly recall these results to introduce the model. The equations of motion for a general simple mechanical control system (rigid body) submerged in a real fluid subjected to external forces can be written as:

$$\nabla_{\gamma'}\gamma' = \mathbb{G}^{\#}(P(\gamma(t))) + \mathbb{G}^{\#}(F(\gamma'(t))) + \sum_{i=1}^{6} \mathbb{I}_i^{-1}(\gamma(t))\sigma_i(t), \tag{2}$$

where $\mathbb{G}^{\#}(P(\gamma(t)))$ represents the potential or restoring forces and moments arising from gravity and the vehicle's buoyancy, and $\mathbb{G}^{\#}(F(\gamma'(t)))$ represents the dissipative drag forces and moments. The input control vector fields $\mathbb{I}_i^{-1}$ are given by $\mathbb{I}_i^{-1} = \mathbb{G}^{\#}\pi_i = \mathbb{G}^{ij}X_j$, where $X_1, ..., X_6$ is the standard left-invariant basis for SE(3), $\pi_1, ..., \pi_6$ is its dual basis and $\mathbb{G}^{ij}$ is the i,j-entry of the kinetic energy matrix $\mathbb{G}^{\#}$. These input vector fields are also expressed as the ith column of the matrix $\mathbb{I}^{-1} = \begin{pmatrix} M^{-1} & 0 \\ 0 & J^{-1} \end{pmatrix}$, where M and J represents the mass and inertia matrix (including added mass and the added mass moments of inertia). Finally, the $\sigma_i(t)$ are the controls. In this formulation we assume that we have six input controls that act upon each of the six degrees-of-freedom (6DOF); we assume three forces acting at the center of gravity along the body-fixed axes and three pure torques about these three body-fixed axes.

These equations, written as a first order control system on TQ, take the form

$$\begin{aligned} Y'(t) &= S(Y(t)) + \text{vlft}(\mathbb{G}^{\#}P(\gamma(t)))(Y(t)) + \text{vlft}(\mathbb{G}^{\#}F(\gamma'(t))) \\ &+ \sum_{i=1}^{m} \text{vlft}\, \mathbb{I}_i^{-1}(\gamma(t))\sigma_i(t), \end{aligned} \tag{3}$$

which is equivalent to:

$$\dot{\boldsymbol{b}} = R\boldsymbol{\nu}, \tag{4}$$

$$\dot{R} = R\hat{\boldsymbol{\Omega}}, \tag{5}$$

$$M\dot{\boldsymbol{\nu}} = -\boldsymbol{\Omega} \times M\boldsymbol{\nu} + D_{\boldsymbol{\nu}}(\boldsymbol{\nu})\boldsymbol{\nu} - g(\boldsymbol{b}) + \boldsymbol{\sigma}_{\nu}, \tag{6}$$

$$J\dot{\boldsymbol{\Omega}} = -\boldsymbol{\Omega} \times J\boldsymbol{\Omega} - \boldsymbol{\nu} \times M\boldsymbol{\nu} + D_{\Omega}(\boldsymbol{\Omega})\boldsymbol{\Omega} - g(\boldsymbol{\eta}_2) + \boldsymbol{\sigma}_{\Omega}. \tag{7}$$

Here, $(b, R) \in \text{SE}(3)$, $b = (b_1, b_2, b_3)^t \in \mathbb{R}^3$ denotes the position vector of the body, and $R \in \text{SO}(3)$ is a rotation matrix describing the orientation of the body. The operator $\hat{\ } : \mathbb{R}^3 \to \mathfrak{so}(3)$ is defined by $\hat{y}z = y \times z$. The vectors $\nu = (\nu_1, \nu_2, \nu_3)^t$ and $\Omega = (\Omega_1, \Omega_2, \Omega_3)^t$ denote the translational and angular velocities, respectively in the body-fixed frame. The drag forces and moments are accounted for in $D_{\boldsymbol{\nu}}(\boldsymbol{\nu})$ and $D_{\Omega}(\boldsymbol{\Omega})$, respectively. Finally, $\boldsymbol{\eta}_2 = (\phi, \theta, \psi)^t$, $g(\boldsymbol{b})$ and $g(\boldsymbol{\eta}_2)$ represent the restoring forces and moments, respectively and $\boldsymbol{\sigma}_{\nu} = (\sigma_1, \sigma_2, \sigma_3)^t$ and $\boldsymbol{\sigma}_{\Omega} = (\sigma_4, \sigma_5, \sigma_6)^t$ account for the external control forces acting on the submerged rigid body.

Since the end goal of our control strategy design is practical implementation, we include a description of the physical parameters assumed for the test-bed vehicle upon which our calculations are based. We assume that the vehicle has three planes of symmetry and take the center of the body-fixed reference frame to be located at the center of gravity C_G. The main hull of the vehicle is assumed to be a sphere, with eight actuators positioned around the equator. These thrusters are evenly distributed around the sphere with four oriented vertically and four oriented horizontally. Additionally, we assume that the center of buoyancy (C_B) is located relatively close to C_G, with respect to the diameter of the spherical hull. Numerical values used for modeling the physical and hydrodynamic parameters of the test-bed vehicle are presented in Table 1. These values were derived from estimations and experiments performed on the actual vehicle. Viscous drag is modeled by use of a diagonal matrix containing nonlinear terms with respect to velocity. A more detailed description of the actual

Mass	123.8 kg	$B = \rho g \mathcal{V}$	1215.8 N	C_B	$(0, 0, -7)$ mm
Diameter	0.64 m	$W = mg$	1214.5 N	C_G	$(0, 0, 0)$ mm
$M_f^{\nu_1}$	70 kg	$M_f^{\nu_2}$	70 kg	$M_f^{\nu_3}$	70 kg
I_{xx}	5.46kg m^2	I_{yy}	5.29kg m^2	I_{zz}	5.72kg m^2
$J_f^{\Omega_1}$	0kg m^2	$J_f^{\Omega_2}$	0kg m^2	$J_f^{\Omega_3}$	0kg m^2

Table 1. Main dimensions and hydrodynamic parameters.

test-bed vehicle used for implementation experiments can be found in (Chyba et al., 2009a) and (Smith, 2008). Depending upon the control strategy design method, different estimations to calculate the dissipative drag coefficients were used. The kinematic motion method estimated the drag coefficient as a function of the velocity by use of the standard formula from hydrodynamics $D = \frac{1}{2}\rho C_D \nu|\nu|$. The drag coefficient was then chosen to correspond to the average velocity of the motion. The computation of the optimal trajectories employs the STP algorithm, which encounters difficulties when presented with a non-differentiable term ($|\nu|$). Thus, for this trajectory design method we estimate the coefficient as a linear plus a cubic function of velocity. As previously mentioned, both estimations are based upon full-scale model tests performed on the actual test-bed vehicle used in the implementation experiments.

As previously noted, the test-bed vehicle has eight thrusters that do not act directly at C_G. The transformation between the 6DOF controls and the controls for the eight thrusters is realized via a linear matrix. Following (Chyba et al., 2009a), the relation is given by $\sigma = TCM\gamma$ where:

$$TCM = \begin{pmatrix} -e_1 & 0 & e_1 & 0 & e_1 & 0 & -e_1 & 0 \\ e_1 & 0 & e_1 & 0 & -e_1 & 0 & -e_1 & 0 \\ 0 & -1 & 0 & -1 & 0 & -1 & 0 & -1 \\ 0 & -e_3 & 0 & -e_3 & 0 & e_3 & 0 & e_3 \\ 0 & e_3 & 0 & -e_3 & 0 & -e_3 & 0 & e_3 \\ e_2 & 0 & -e_2 & 0 & e_2 & 0 & -e_2 & 0 \end{pmatrix} \quad (8)$$

$e_1 = \sqrt{2}/2, e_2 = 0.4816, e_3 = -0.2699$. In this chapter, we will refer to the control applied to the actual thrusters as the 8-dimensional (8-D) control. The thrusters are powered independently, hence the domain of control is a box in the 8-D space of the real control. We assume that all the thrusters are bounded similarly by:

$$\gamma_i \in [\gamma^{\min}, \gamma^{\max}] = [-11.7331, 9.7993]\ N.$$

3. Optimization

3.1 Statement of the Problem

Control theory deals with systems that can be governed. As a consequence, it is very natural to ask for the most efficient control strategy for a given criterion. In the supplementary chapters of (Bullo & Lewis, 2004) and in (Coombs, 2000), the authors investigate mechanical control theory and produce a version of the maximum principle for affine connection control systems. We will not discuss this approach here. Here we will state the problem, define the criterion to be minimized and introduce some terminology. This is sufficient for the purpose of this chapter. In the sequel of the chapter, a configuration at rest is a state of the system such that the velocity variables are zero.

The problem is as follows: "Given a mechanical control system and a set of initial and final configurations at rest, we would like to find a control strategy that steers the system from the initial configuration to the final configuration while minimizing a prescribed criterion." Notice that in what follows, we assume the existence of an optimal control strategy and we focus on designing such a strategy. From a mathematical point of view, a criterion is defined on a time interval $[0, T]$ by:

$$C(T,u) = \int_0^T l(t,\chi(t),\sigma(t))dt + g(T,\chi(t)), \tag{9}$$

where l is a function that is continuously differentiable with respect to its variables and g is a continuous function. The main objective of this research is to design control strategies for an AUV that are efficient in terms of their energy consumption and time duration. The energy consumption criterion is largely dependent upon the considered mechanical system, in this chapter the criterion we use is based on our test-bed vehicle, see (Chyba et al., 2009a). The vehicle is powered solely by on-board batteries, hence its autonomous abilities are directly related to the life-span of this power supply. As seen above, the vehicle is controlled by eight external thrusters. These thrusters draw power from a bank of 20 batteries. All other on-board electronics such as the computer and sensors run on a separate bank of four batteries which supply enough power for the vehicle to operate nearly indefinitely when compared to the life-span of the thruster batteries. Thus, minimizing energy consumption for a given trajectory directly corresponds to minimizing the amount of current pulled by the thrusters. We can write the consumption criterion of the eight thrusters as:

$$C(\gamma) = \int_0^T \sum_{i=1}^{8} Amps(\gamma_i(t))dt, \tag{10}$$

where the final time T is chosen based upon how much emphasis we opt to put on the time-efficiency of the trajectory. Let $T_{\min}$ be the minimum time to connect two terminal configurations at rest, we define c_T as:

$$T = c_T \cdot T_{\min},\ c_T \geq 1. \tag{11}$$

Note that the way we consider the problem, for $c_T = 1$ the solution of the minimum time and minimum consumption problems are the same. In (Chyba et al., 2009a), the authors examine the evolution of energy consumption as a function of c_T. It was found that there exists an optimal c_T that produces the best energy consumption for the vehicle, this value depends on the final configuration and on the parameters of the vehicle. The function Amps was determined experimentally on the test-bed vehicle, we found:

$$Amps(\gamma_i) = \begin{cases} -0.4433\gamma_i & = & \alpha_-\gamma_i & ,\text{if } \gamma_i \leq 0 \\ 0.2561\gamma_i & = & \alpha_+\gamma_i & ,\text{if } \gamma_i > 0 \end{cases}, \tag{12}$$

where $Amps(\gamma_i)$ (A) is the current pulled when the thrust γ_i (N) is applied by the thruster.

3.2 Maximum Principle and Terminology

The maximum principle is one of the most fundamental tools of optimal control and provides necessary conditions for a trajectory to be optimal. We refer the reader to (Pontryagin et al., 1962) for the original text that introduced the maximum principle. See (Bonnard & Chyba, 2003), (Agrachev & Sachkov, 2004) for more modern and geometric versions and (Sussmann, 2000) for a more general version.

Let us introduce $\chi = (\eta, \nu, \Omega)$, and consider the optimal control problem of finding a path that steers our AUV from an initial configuration χ_0 to a final configuration χ_T, while minimizing an integral criterion of the form $\int_0^T l(\chi(t), \gamma(t))dt$, where $\gamma(t)$ is the 8-D control. For instance, for the time minimization problem, we have $l(\chi, \gamma) = 1$ and for the energy consumption minimization problem, we have $l(\chi, \gamma) = \sum_{i=1}^{8} Amps(\gamma_i)$ and $T = c_T T_{min}$, $c_T \geq 1$.

We will not explicitly state the maximum principle here, as it is not directly used in our numerical simulations. However, based on this principle we will introduce some terminology to describe different types of controls (see also (Sussmann, 1991)). The terminology is related to the 8-D control $\gamma = (\gamma_1, ..., \gamma_8)^t$ introduced in Section 2, but it should be noted that this can be generalized to any other thruster configurations. A bang-bang control $\gamma_i : [0, T] \to [\gamma^{\min}, \gamma^{\max}]$ is a control that only assumes the values $\gamma^{\min}$ or $\gamma^{\max}$ for almost every $t \in [0, T]$. If in addition, γ_i is actually a.e. constant on $[0, T]$, then we will call it a bang control. A switching time (or simply just a switching) of γ_i is a time $t \in [0, T]$ such that γ_i is not bang on any interval of the form $(t - \delta; t + \delta) \in [0, T], \delta > 0$. A control with finitely many switchings is called regular bang-bang. It is clear that a regular bang-bang control is a control composed of a finite number of concatenated bang arcs. For our purposes, we include the following additional definition. A piecewise constant (PWC) control γ_i that takes its values in the set $\Gamma_i = \{(\gamma^{\max}, \gamma^{\max}), (\gamma^{\max}, \gamma^{\min}), (\gamma^{\min}, \gamma^{\max}), (\gamma^{\min}, \gamma^{\min})\}$ is said to be a Γ_i-valued PWC control. Note that for this chapter all Γ_i are identical but it is a straightforward generalization to assume unique bounds on each individual thruster. One can then define a Γ-valued control to be bang (resp. bang-bang, regular bang-bang, Γ-valued PWC) if each of its two components is bang (resp. bang-bang, regular bang-bang, Γ_i-valued PWC). Notice that a regular bang-bang control is a Γ-valued PWC control, except that the converse is not necessary true. Another type of control, called singular, plays a major role in optimal control strategy. The definition of singular controls is related to the maximum principle and the switching functions. We do not discuss the details of a singular control here because our STP algorithm is only concerned with PWC controls, as singular controls are continuously evolving, and hence very difficult to implement on a real vehicle.

3.3 Numerical Algorithm

In (Chyba et al., 2009b) the authors conduct an analysis of the singular extremals, however it is clear that an optimal synthesis is out of reach because of the complexity of the problem. For this reason, we turn to numerical methods.

We distinguish two types of numerical methods in optimal control, namely indirect methods and direct methods. The indirect methods based on the maximum principle use shooting techniques to numerically solve a boundary value problem, see for instance (Cesari, 1983). Direct methods, on the other hand, transform the problem into a finite dimensional optimization problem. Each method has its advantages and disadvantages. Direct methods offer less precision than indirect methods, however they are much more robust and not very sensitive to the initialization condition, contrary to indirect methods. Moreover, to apply an indirect method, we must know the structure of the optimal control in advance (such as the number of switchings, for instance). As it was shown in (Chyba et al., 2009a) the optimal control strategies for our problem are very complex and we cannot extract such information *a priori*. For these reasons we use a direct method to carry out our computations.

As mentioned, direct methods are a rewriting of the optimal control problem as a finite dimensional optimization problem. There are many ways to rewrite an optimal control problem. Here we reparameterize the time domain $[0, T]$ as $[0, 1]$, and choose a discretization $0 = t_0 < t_1 < \cdots < t_N = 1$ of $[0,1]$. Then, we write the discretized optimal control problem with unknowns T, $\chi^i = \chi(t_i)$, $i = 1, \cdots, N$ and γ^i, $i = 0, \cdots, N-1$. The result is a large-scale, nonlinear optimization problem whose nonlinear constraints are the discretized dynamics (for an Euler scheme) of the form $\chi^{i+1} = \chi^i + T(t_{i+1} - t_i)\dot{\chi}^i(\chi^i, \gamma^i), i = 0, \cdots, N-1$ and $\chi^N = \chi^T$. We call this the non-linear problem. Methods to solve nonlinear optimization problems are well developed. We choose to use the interior point method IpOpt (Waechter & Biegler, 2006), together with the modeling language AMPL (Fourer et al., 1993). For our direct method, we use Heun's fixed-step integration scheme.

From previous results (Chyba et al., 2009a), it is clear that the optimal control strategies are not suitable for implementation onto a test-bed vehicle (we include them in our study for the purpose of comparison). Their unsuitability is due to their complexity and the large number of actuator changes required during the implementation. The motivation to introduce the switching time parametrization (STP) algorithm was to produce efficient trajectories that are implementable on an autonomous underwater vehicle. At first, the considered cost to be minimized was time. In (Chyba et al., 2009a), the STP algorithm was used to produce efficient trajectories which optimized a combination of time and energy consumption. In the next section, we recall the important features of the STP algorithm, a detailed description can be found in the original article cited above.

3.3.1 Switching Time Parametrization Algorithm

The STP algorithm is based on the use of a direct method. The main idea is to impose the structure of the control strategy and compute trajectories having this structure that are optimal with respect to the given cost. More precisely, we fix the number of switching times along the trajectory, preferably to a small number, then we numerically determine the optimal trajectory from these candidates. Critical for the convergence of the algorithm is to introduce the values of the constant thrust arcs as parameters of the optimization problem. This new optimization problem is called $(STPP)_p$ (Switching Time Parameterization Problem) where p refers to the number of switching times. The unknowns are the time durations of the constant thrust arcs, and the values of the constant thrust arcs. Notice that our construction produces PWC control strategies, but they are not necessarily bang-bang. The new optimization problem, $(STPP)_p$, takes the following form:

$$(STPP)_p \left\{ \begin{array}{lcl} \min\limits_{z \in \mathcal{D}} t_{p+1}, & & \\ t_0 & = & 0, \\ t_{i+1} & = & t_i + \xi_i \ , \ i = 1, \cdots, p, \\ \chi^{i+1} & = & \chi^i + \int_{t_i}^{t_{i+1}} \dot{\chi}(t, \gamma^i) dt, \\ \chi^{p+1} & = & \chi^T, \\ z & = & (\xi_1, \cdots, \xi_{p+1}, \gamma^1, \cdots, \gamma^{p+1}), \\ \mathcal{D} & = & \mathbb{R}_+^{(p+1)} \times \mathcal{U}^{p+1}, \end{array} \right. \tag{13}$$

where ξ_i, $i = 1, \cdots, p+1$ are the time arc-lengths and $\gamma^i \in \mathcal{U}$, $i = 1, \cdots, p+1$ are the values of the constant thrust arcs.

To integrate the dynamic system of $(STPP)_p$ we use *DOP853*, a high order adaptive step integrator, (Hairer et al., 2003). The possibility of using a high-precision integrator for the STP-control strategies is facilitated by the fact that we drastically reduced the number of unknowns, with respect to the nonlinear problem. This results in a considerable savings in computational time with the use of our STP algorithm.

Finally, since the STP algorithm is directed towards the implementation of the control strategy onto a test-bed AUV, we add a linear junction between the constant thrust arcs to avoid instantaneous switching of the physical actuators. This linear junction has a time duration of $\delta t = 0.9\ s$ (30 refresh periods of our test-bed vehicle's CPU).

4. Simulations

As mentioned in the introduction, under-actuation plays a central part in the guidance and control of AUVs. For the following under-actuated scenario, we may assume that the AUV malfunctions for one reason or another; battery failure, an actuator quits or electronics short out. Depending on the number and arrangement of the actuators, in the event that one or more actuators stop working or is turned off, the vehicle can lose direct control in one or more degrees-of-freedom (DOF). Once we do not have direct control on all six DOF, we consider the vehicle to be under-actuated. In this scenario, the vehicle may not be able to realize any given configuration, making the motion planning problem even more difficult.

From the description of the assumed test-bed vehicle presented in section 2.1.1, we note that there are two different orientations of the thrusters. We shall call a thruster oriented such that the output force is parallel to the (body-frame) b_3-axis a *vertical* thruster, and a thruster oriented such that the output force is perpendicular to the (body-frame) b_3-axis a *horizontal* thruster. In this section we consider the center of gravity to be $7mm$ below the center of buoyancy. This choice is motivated by experimental work that was conducted on the real vehicle, see (Chyba et al., 2008, 2009a), (Smith, 2008) and (Smith et al., 2009b). Based on these assumptions of the locations of C_G and the center of buoyancy, we may assume that a vertical thruster contributes only to heave, roll and pitch controls, while a horizontal thruster contributes only to surge, sway and yaw controls. Thus, our assumed fully-actuated submersible controls heave, roll and pitch with one set thrusters we will call V. While surge, sway, and yaw are controlled with another set of thrusters called H. Suppose for the under-actuated scenario that we lose the ability to control either H or V. Losing control of the thruster set V would limit the motion of the vehicle to a plane. However, losing H would not affect the kinematic controllability of the vehicle; these results are proven in (Smith, 2008) and (Smith et al., 2009a).

This section is divided into three parts. First we apply the STP algorithm to the energy consumption cost and design implementable trajectories for the presented under-actuated scenario. Secondly, from previous work, we recall control strategies for the identical under-actuated scenario designed by the use of kinematic motions. We conclude with a comparison of both control strategies.

4.1 Mission Scenario 1

Based on the controllability results mentioned previously, we assume that we only have direct control of the vertically-oriented thrusters. We first demonstrate that the vehicle can realize motion in a direction that is not directly controllable. Suppose that we would like our vehicle to realize a pure surge displacement. From our previous assumptions, we have no control of the horizontally-oriented thrusters, thus we do not have the use of the input control vector field $\mathbb{I}_1^{-1}$. We only have direct control upon roll, pitch and heave (i.e., $\{\mathbb{I}_3^{-1}, \mathbb{I}_4^{-1}, \mathbb{I}_5^{-1}\}$). Is it possible to reach $\eta_{final} = (a, 0, 0, 0, 0, 0)$, for $a \in \mathbb{R}$, in this proposed under-actuated condition? From Proposition 4.1 of (Smith, 2008), we can compute that the vehicle is kinematically controllable, and hence, the answer to the question is yes; any configuration is reachable from any other via kinematic motions. This fact is also proven in (Smith et al., 2009a), however, a simple calculation shows that $\text{Lie}^{\infty}(\mathbb{I}_3^{-1}, \mathbb{I}_4^{-1}, \mathbb{I}_5^{-1}) = TQ$. Let us choose $a = 1.25$ m. Since we have direct control of the pure heave motion, and we assume a positively buoyant vehicle, it is clear that reaching the configuration $\eta_{final} = (1.25, 0, b, 0, 0, 0)$, for $b \in \mathbb{R}^+$, will prove that the vehicle can realize the prescribed surge displacement. We choose $\eta_{final} = (1.25, 0, 2.165, 0, 0, 0)$ as the goal configuration for this mission. Below we present two methods to accomplish this displacement.

4.1.1 STP motions

In this section, we present a complete study for trajectories ending at the final configuration η_{final} chosen above. First, we compute the minimum time and minimum energy consumption trajectories, without imposing any implementation restriction. Then, we apply the STP algorithm to the same final configuration and compare our results to the optimal ones.

Assuming failure of all the horizontal thrusters, the minimum time control strategy to steer the AUV from the origin to η_{final} can be seen in Figure 1. Notice that we represent the control in the 6DOF rather than in 8 dimensions to emphasize the fact that our approach is valid for other thrusters configurations. The minimum time is approximately $t_{\min}^{1,vert} \approx 11.249011\ s$ with a corresponding energy consumption of $C_{t_{\min}^{1,vert}} \approx 199.476331\ A.s.$ As it can be seen in Figure 1, the computed trajectory consists of a large pitch angle followed by significant thrust in the heave direction of the body-fixed frame. We remark that the minimum time for the same initial and final configurations, but in the fully actuated case, is $t_{\min}^1 \approx 7.535102\ s$ with a corresponding energy consumption of $C_{t_{\min}^1} \approx 235.141099\ A.s.$ Thus, losing the use of the horizontal actuators, the time optimal trajectory is 49% longer but we use 15% less energy.

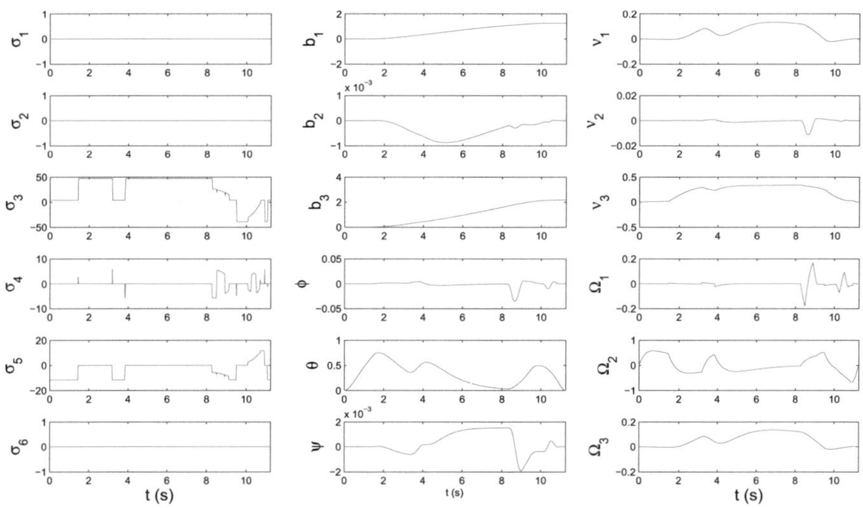

Fig. 1. *Minimum time solution for η_{final} and failure of the horizontal thrusters.*

Figure 2 shows the solution to the minimum energy consumption problem in the under-actuated situation with a final time of $t_f = 16.6$ *s*, which correspond to $c_T = t_f/t_{\min}^{1,vert} \approx 1.47$. The minimum energy consumption control strategy consumes $C_{\min}^{1,vert} \approx 93.389150$ *A.s*, which

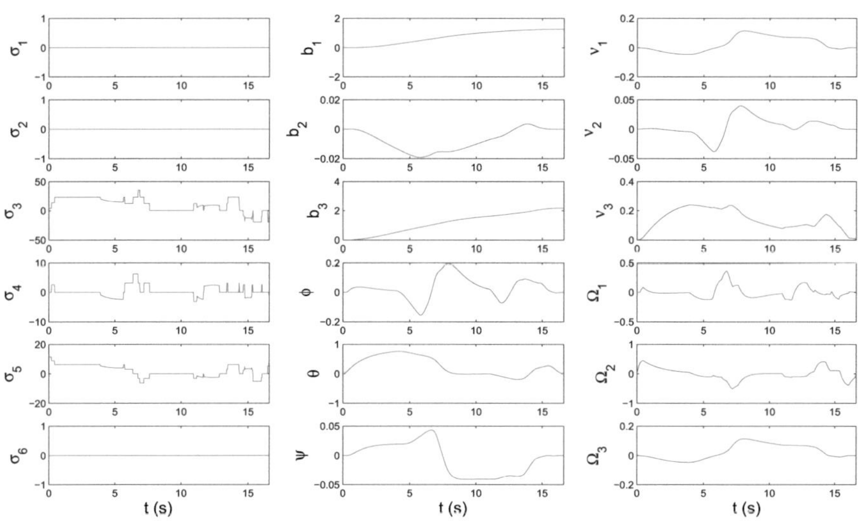

Fig. 2. *Minimum consumption solution for η_{final}, $t_f = 16.6$ s and failure of horizontal thrusters.*

represents a gain of slightly more than 53% when compared to the under-actuated time minimum trajectory. A larger reduction in energy consumption could be realized if we were to allow more time. Our choice of the final time here is dictated by our desire to compare our results to those calculated by use of kinematic motions. In the fully actuated case, the minimum energy consumption is given by $C^1_{\text{min}} \approx 69.746188\ A.s$. This represents about 3.37 times less energy than is consumed during the fully-actuated time minimum trajectory. The fact that the gain is more significant in the fully-actuated case is that this situation corresponds to a c_T coefficient of $t_f/t^1_{\text{min}} \approx 2.2$, which is closer to the optimal c_T corresponding to this mission.

Application of our STP algorithm to the under-actuated time minimum problem, we obtain the results shown in Table 2. We remark that it is quite surprising to see the existence

#switch	t_{min} (s)	Cons. (A.s)	switching times (s)
2	16.002832	148.895085	(11.4449, 13.3028)
3	15.634220	148.640740	(8.5415, 11.0682, 12.9342)
4	≈ 15.620850	147.826597	(6.8255, 8.6255, 11.1208, 12.9208)
5	≈ 15.606090	157.978504	(4.3083, 6.8127, 8.6477, 11.1053, 12.9057)

Table 2. *STP minimum time for horizontal thruster failure.*

of an admissible STP control strategy with only 2 switching times. To reach a final time close to the optimal time, we need to increase the number of switching times. The STP trajectory with two switching times is about 40% slower than the time minimal trajectory. Notice that the trajectories with an approximation sign in front of the minimum time are strategies for which the STP method did not converge to a solution satisfying the first order necessary condition, but nevertheless, provided and admissible strategy.

The STP algorithm applied to the under-actuated scenario for the minimization of energy consumption with a final time of 16.6*s* is given in Table 3. We notice a gain of 7% in the

#switch	Consumption (A.s)	switching times (s.)
2	150.253134	(11.7619, 13.9000)
3	137.254314	(7.3433, 12.1000, 13.9000)
4	126.330384	(7.5304, 10.3000, 12.1000, 13.9000)

Table 3. *STP minimum consumption for horizontal thruster failure and* $t_f = 16.6$ s.

case of three switching times and a gain of about 15% in the case of 4 switching times. The controls and the trajectory are respresented on Figure 6 below for the two switching times strategy.

4.1.2 Kinematic motions

This section recalls the results from (Smith, 2008) and (Smith et al., 2009a) on control strategies obtained through the use of kinematic motions. We refer the reader to these references for more theoretical details on the control strategies depicted below and to (Bullo & Lewis, 2004) for a general treatise on kinematic reductions for mechanical control systems.

One way to reach the desired configuration is to pitch the vehicle an angle α and hold this pitch angle while applying a body-pure heave (i.e., apply a control along the z-axis of the body-fixed reference frame) until the vehicle realizes the 1.25 m surge displacement. The value of α depends upon the final configuration. For this experiment, we must take $\alpha = 30°$, which corresponds to $b = 2.165$ m. A general depiction of this motion is presented in Figure 3.

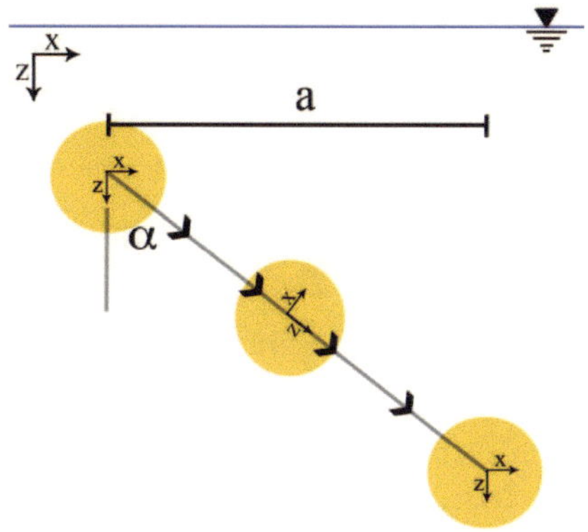

Fig. 3. *A generalization of the intended trajectory designed with kinematic motions.*

With $\eta_{final} = (1.25, 0, 2.165, 0, 0, 0)$, we present two separate control strategy designs for this mission. Given that the set of input control vector fields is $\mathcal{I}_3^{-1} = \{\mathbb{I}_3^{-1}, \mathbb{I}_4^{-1}, \mathbb{I}_5^{-1}\}$, the decoupling vector fields for this system are the constant multiples and linear combinations of the set $\mathcal{D} = \{X_3 = (0,0,1,0,0,0), X_4 = (0,0,0,1,0,0), X_5 = (0,0,0,0,1,0)\}$, see (Smith et al., 2009a).

The basic idea of this motion is to point the bottom of the AUV at η_{final} by following the integral curves of X_4 (pitch motion), then follow the integral curves of X_3 (body-pure heave motion) to realize the displacement. At the end of the body-pure heave motion, the vehicle will be in the configuration $(1.25, 0, 2.165, 0, 30°, 0)$. We can undo the pitch motion by following the integral curves of $-X_4$, however, in practice, the righting moments take care of this angular displacement without having to apply any control forces; thus saving energy. It is important to notice that for the mathematical model using the righting moments to bring back the vehicle into a zero pitch angle takes a very large time because the coordinate θ actually oscillates around the zero. So it is a very efficient option for the experimental aspect of the project as the vehicle is asked to reach the final configuration within a prescribed tolerance and not exactly.

If we want to realize a surge displacement greater than 1.25 m, we may concatenate the following designed trajectory with one using the negative of the prescribed roll angle and body-pure heave control to create a V-shaped motion, as depicted in Figure 4. This would realize a 2.5 m displacement. Concatenating more V-shaped motions will allow for greater surge displacements.
On the other hand, we could successively implement the trajectory given here followed by a pure heave motion of 2.165 m. This would create a sawtooth-type trajectory as shown in Figure 5.
The distance of 1.25 m is arbitrarily chosen and depends upon the pitch angle prescribed as well as the length of the body-pure heave motion. Altering each of these, we can also create

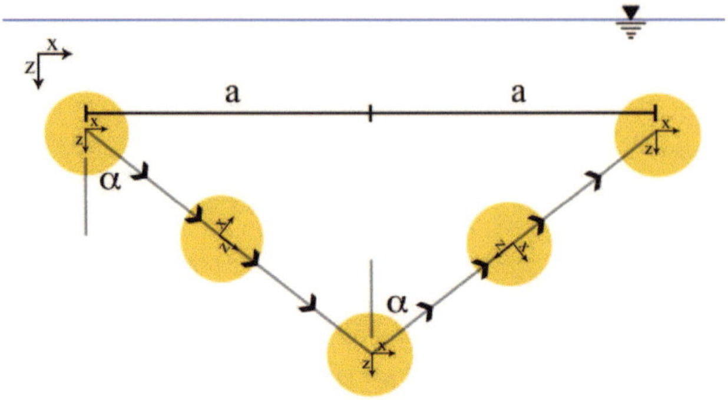

Fig. 4. *Concatenation of the presented kinematic motion trajectory to create a V-shaped motion.*

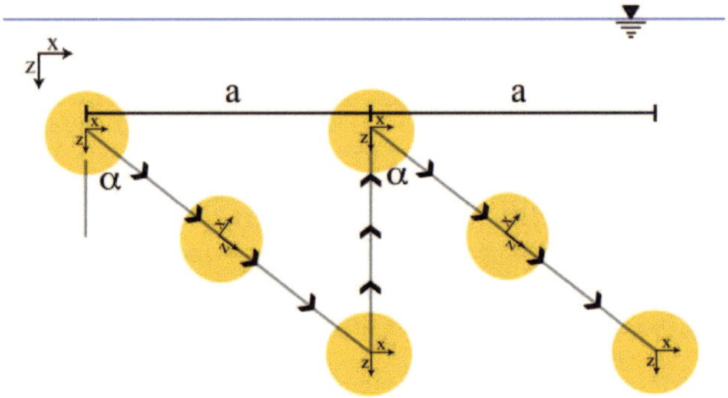

Fig. 5. *Successive concatenation of the presented trajectory with pure heave motions to create a sawtooth-shaped motion.*

different surge displacements.

The six-dimensional under-actuated control strategy for the kinematic motion is given at Table 4 (the times represent the junction times of the PWC strategy).

Time (s)	Applied Thrust (6-dim.) (N)
0	(0,0,0,0,0,0)
0.9	(0,0,1.126,0,4.2553,0)
5.9	(0,0,1.126,0,4.2553,0)
6.8	(0,0,31.166,0,4.2553,0)
12.373	(0,0,31.166,0,4.2553,0)
13.273	(0,0,-23.431,0,4.2553,0)
15.7	(0,0,-23.431,0,4.2553,0)
16.6	(0,0,0,0,0,0)

Table 4. Discretized control structure using kinematic motions.

This control strategy has two swicthing times and the energy consumed for the above trajectory is 138.458 A.s. This control strategy has been calculated in several steps. First differential geometric techniques are used to generate a continuous control as a function of time. But as discussed earlier, input for the test-bed vehicle requires a PWC control structure over discretized time intervals with in addition linear junctions to link the constant arcs. Hence the second step of the process is to adapt the continuous control into a PWC control. This is done by ensuring that the work required to perform the desired motion is equivalent for both the continuous and PWC control, see (Smith, 2008) for more details. The last step is to simply connect the constant arcs via linear junctions of 0.9 seconds.

4.1.3 Comparison

The control strategy based on decoupling vector fields was calculated by applying inverse kinematics to the concatenation of kinematic motions available to the under-actuated vehicle. During the trajectory design phase of this process, one is allowed to arbitrarily parameterize the time necessary to traverse the chosen path. In the presented example, the parameterization was chosen so that the test-bed vehicle could perform the given motion at a normal operational velocity. Such a choice of parameterization did not take into account any time or energy consumption optimization. However, the ability to reparameterize the duration of the kinematic motion does give rise to the question of whether or not this type of trajectory design can be made time or energy optimal.

Our intent here is to compare the STP control strategies to the one derived from the kinematic motion. But the comparison is not completely straightforward. Indeed, we have to keep in mind that the discretized control given in Table 4 is an adaptation of the continuous control strategies calculated as a concatenation of integral curves of kinematic reduction of rank one. The procedure to compute the PWC control and the addition of the linear junction were introduced for the purpose of implementation on our test-bed vehicle. A consequence is that we obtained a control easily implementable but that as the disadvantage to not exactly reached the desired configuration. It is also very important to remember that in the design of the kinematic discretized control we use the fact that in practice the vehicle will bring back the pitch angle to zero on its own which is once again unrealistic from the mathematical model point of view. On the other extreme the STP trajectories are designed to reach exactly the final configuration and hence are more constrained. No consideration on the experimental aspect is taken into account while computing that controls. Notice that comparison of the STP trajectories with the continuous control obtained via kinematic reduction would not make sense because for the continuous motion the bounds of the control are not taken into account. It is only during the second step of the procedure when computing the PWC adaptation that we design a control satisfying the constraint of the domain of control.

In Figure 6 we represent the following three control strategies and their corresponding trajectories. The solid line represents the STP strategy, the dashed line is the discretized kinematic motion strategy and in dotted line is the minimum consumption strategy. All three strategies are defined on the same time interval $[0, 16.6]$. A first remark concern the type of control involved in these three strategies. From the maximum principle, we know that the minimum consumption control strategy is a concatenation of bang and singular arcs for the 8 dimensional control (here we represent the 6DOF control). This strategy a large number of switching times and hence is not implementable on a test-bed vehicle. The STP and

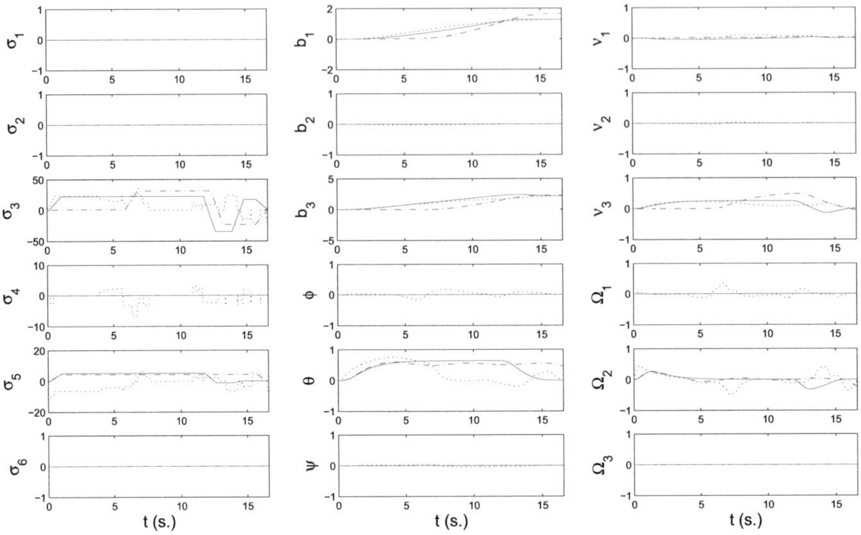

Fig. 6. *Minimum consumption (dotted), STPP with 2 switching times (plain) and discretized kinematic motion (dashed).*

discretized kinematic control strategies are obtained from PWC controls with the addition of linear junction to avoid instantaneous actuator changes. Notice that the switching times are differently distributed along the trajectory. However, if we look at the trajectories themselves they are quite comparable. The major difference can be seen in the θ variable where the discretized kinematic motion does not end-up at zero. This is due to the fact that, in practice, the righting moment will compensate for this error. The energy consumption for these three strategies is respectively 93.39, 153.47 and 138.46. It is surprising that the STP control strategy consumes more energy than the discretized kinematic motion. This is explained by our first observation that they do not reach the exact same final configuration and mostly because in the discretized kinematic motion, the righting moment is used during the experimentation to bring θ back to zero. To fully compare these strategies, future work will consist in experimental testing to extract the energy consumption the test-bed vehicle used during the experiment (and not the energy consumption corresponding to the simulation on the mathematical model) for both strategies and compare the results.

4.2 Mission Scenario 2

For the second mission we would like to realize a pure surge motion. Here we consider a 2.5 m pure surge while maintaining a constant depth, hence we have $\eta_f = (2.5, 0, 0, 0, 0, 0)$.

4.2.1 STP motions

In the fully actuated case the minimum time is approximatively $t^2_{\min} \approx 8.564220\ s$, while the corresponding consumption is $C_{t^2_{\min}} \approx 269.422890\ A.s.$ The trajectory consists in a very large pitch angle in order to maximize the thrust available to travel along the b_1 direction. In the case of the failure of the horizontal thrusters the minimum time is approximatively $t^2_{\min} \approx 16.794176\ s$, while the corresponding consumption is $C_{t^{2,vert}_{\min}} \approx 255.853619\ A.s.$

Notice that the duration is almost double without the vertical thrusters but that the energy consumption is almost identical.

The solution of the minimum consumption problem with failure of the horizontal thrusters is given on Figure 7 for $t_f = 17.7\ s$. The minimum consumption is $C^{2,vert}_{\min} \approx 157.115555\ A.s$

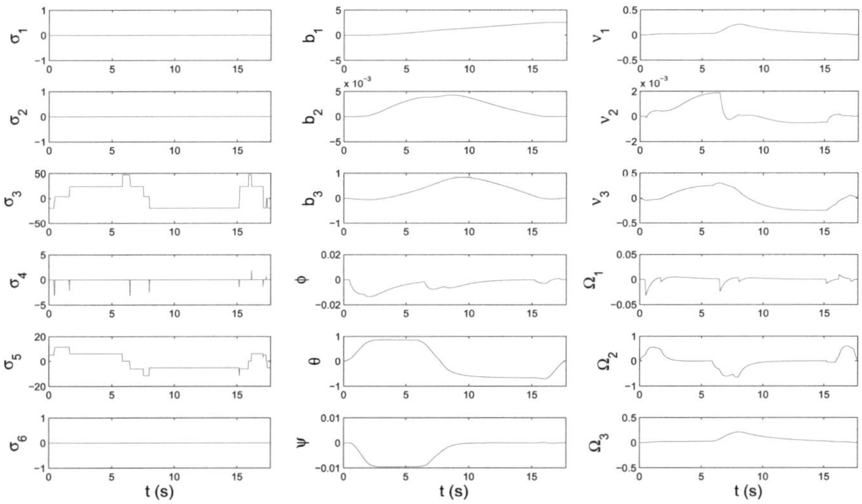

Fig. 7. *Minimum consumption solution in the under-actuated case.*

which represents a gain of 38.6%. This apparent small gain in consumption becomes much more significant when coupled with the fact that the prescribed final time is extremely close to the minimum time; we have $c_t = 1.05$. Once again the final time was chosen with respect to the kinematic motion that will be described below. In the fully actuated case (presented in Figure 8), we have $c_T = 2.07$ and the minimum consumption is $C^2_{\min} \approx 54.769702\ A.s$, which represents a gain of almost 80%.

Table 5 gives the values obtained when applying the STP algorithm for the energy consumption minimum problem to the fully actuated case with a final time of $17.7s$. The STP control

$\#switch$	Consumption (A.s)	switching times (s)
1	79.544612	13.6427
2	$\approx$ 68.489915	(8.8584, 14.9966)
3		No better than 2 switchings
4	$\approx$ 61.851409	(3.2792, 8.2950, 11.4516, 14.9999)

Table 5. *STPP minimum consumption .*

strategy with one switching in the fully actuated case represents about 70% less consumption of energy with respect to the minimum time solution and about 45% more consumption of energy with respect to the minimum consumption solution. The STP control strategy for one switching time as well as its corresponding trajectory are represented in Figure 8.

4.2.2 Kinematic motions

The six-dimensional discretized control strategy is given in Table 6. This motion was param-

Time (s)	Applied Thrust (6-dim.) (N)
0	(0,0,0,0,0,0)
0.9	(12.128,0,1.3,0,0,0)
12.49	(12.128,0,1.3,0,0,0)
13.39	(-7.35,0,1.3,0,0,0)
16.8	(-7.35,0,1.3,0,0,0)
17.7	(0,0,0,0,0,0)

Table 6. Discretized control strategy.

eterized to last for 17.7 s, and consumed a total of 99.167 A.s of energy. Note that for this control strategy, we use the horizontally-oriented thrusters to realize the surge motion, while utilizing the vertically-oriented thrusters to counteract the positive buoyancy of the vehicle to maintain a constant depth. Thus, we must be fully-actuated to implement this control strategy. We can compare this to a 33.2 s duration for the V-shaped concatenated motion, which would consume 276.916 A.s of energy. This is near twice the time and three times the energy consumption. If we assume that we use the vehicle's positive buoyancy to achieve the pure heave motion in the sawtooth trajectory, thus expending no energy along that portion, we have an overall time greater than 33.2 s and an energy consumption of 276.916 A.s.

4.2.3 Comparison

We begin with the initial remark that in the under-actuated scenario, one may initially think that the use of less actuators results in expending less energy. Here, we show that this is not the case. For the under-actuated kinematic motion presented, the energy used to maintain the list angle α requires the available actuators to expend excessive of energy for the duration of the mission. There are many ways to design a trajectory by the use of kinematic motions, and here we only present one. It would be interesting to explore the energy consumption minimization problem for kinematic motions that have the same final configuration and duration. In conclusion, in the event of an actuator failure or other malfunction, the under-actuated kinematic motion would definitely get the vehicle back home, however this motion would not be the best choice to conserve battery life while on deployment.

In Figure 8 the following three control strategies can be seen: the minimum consumption (dotted), the STP with one switching time (solid) and the discretized kinematic motion (dashed). All these are calculated for a fully actuated vehicle.
We can see that the STP and kinematic motion are very similar in terms of control strategy and trajectory. However, the STP trajectory uses almost 20% less energy than the kinematic motion. The control strategy that minimizes the energy consumption differs much more dramatically from the other ones, in particular it shows a very large number of switching times and concatenations between bang and singular arcs. The trajectory differs only for the roll angle and the angular velocity Ω_3. The main advantage regarding the STP trajectory in this

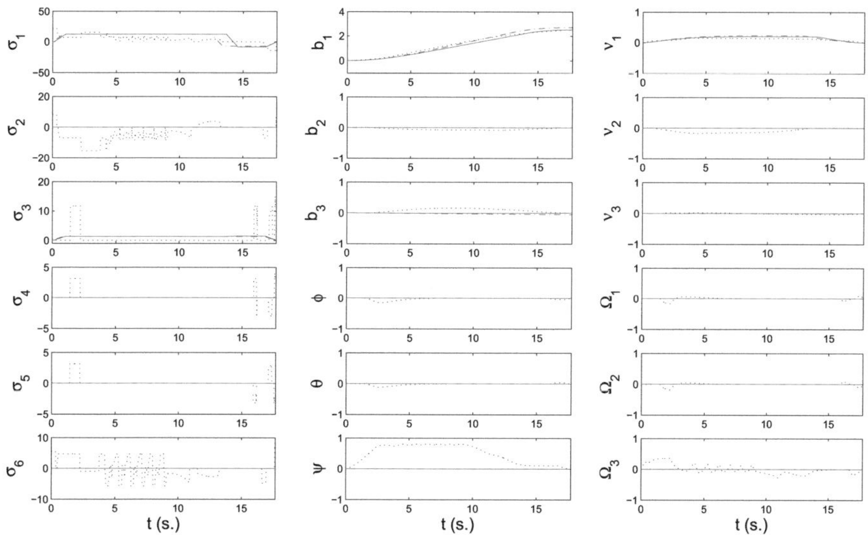

Fig. 8. *Minimum consumption (dotted), STPP with 1 switching time (solid) and discretized kinematic motion (dashed) for Mission 2.*

mission scenario concerns the under-actuated case. The discretized PWC kinematic motion, as presented here, would produce an extremely unefficient control strategy in terms of energy consumption while the STP algorithm would provide a much better solution (not presented in this paper).

5. Acknowledgments

The authors would like to thank the National Science Foundation for their support. The research presented in this paper is supported by NSF Grants DMS-030641 and DMS-0608583.

6. References

Agrachev A.A.; Sachkov Y.L. (2004) Control Theory from the Geometric Viewpoint. *Spriunger-Veralg, Series: Encyclopaedia of Mathematical Sciences*, Vol. 87, Control Theory and Optimization, 412 pages.

Bonnard B.; Chyba M. (2003) Singular Trajectories and their Role in Control Theory. *Springer-Verlag, Series: Mathematics and Applications*, Vol 40, 357 pages.

Bullo F.; Lewis, A. D. (2004), Geometric Control of Mechanical Systems, *Springer-Verlag, New York-Heidelberg-Berlin*, Number 49 in Texts in Applied Mathematics, 726 pages.

Cesari L. (1983) Optimization Theory and Applications. Problems with Ordinary Differential Equations. *Springer-Verlag*, New York, 542 pages.

Chyba M.; Haberkorn T.; Smith R.N.; Choi S.K. (2008) Design and implementation of time efficient trajectories for an underwater vehicle. *Ocean Engineering*, 35/1, pp. 63-76.

Chyba M.; Haberkorn T.; Singh S.B.; Smith R.N.; Choi S.K. (2009a) Increasing Underwater Vehicle Autonomy by Reducing Energy Consumption. *Ocean Engineering, Special Issue on Autonomous Underwater Vehicles*, Vol 36/1, pp. 62-73.

Chyba M.; Haberkorn T.; Smith R.N.; Wilkens G.R (2009b) A Geometric Analysis of Trajectory Design for Underwater Vehicles. *Discrete and Continuous Dynamical Systems-B*, Volume: 11, Number: 2.

Coombs T.A. (2000) Time-optimal control of two simple mechanical systems with three degrees of freedom and two inputs. *MSc Thesis*, Queen's University.

Fourer R.; Gay D.M.; Kernighan B.W. (1993) AMPL: A Modeling Language for Mathematical Programming. *Duxbury Press*, Brooks-Cole Publishing Company.

Fossen T.I. (1994) Guidance and Control of Ocean Vehicles, *John Wiley & Sons.*

Ledzewicz U; Schättler H. (2009) On The Optimality Of Singular Controls For A Class of Mathematical Models For Tumor Anti-Angiogenesis. *Discrete and Continuous Dynamical Systems Series B*, Vol 11, Number 3, pp. 691-715.

Lewis A.; Murray R. (1997) Configuration Controllability of Simple Mechanical Control Systems. *SIAM Journal on Control and Optimization archive*, Vol 35/3, pp. 766 - 790.

Lewis A. (2007) Is it Worth Learning Differential Geometric Methods for Modelling and Control of Mechanical Systems? *Robotica*, 25(6), pp. 765-777.

Pontryagin L.S.; Boltyanski B.; Gamkrelidze R.; Michtchenko E. (1962) The Mathematical Theory of Optimal Processes. *Interscience*. New York.

Smith R.N. (2008) Geometric Control Theory and its Application to Underwater Vehicles. *PhD Dissertation*, University of Hawai'i at Manoa.

Smith R.N.; Chyba M.; Wilkens G.R.; Catone C. (2009a) A geometrical approach to the motion planning problem for a submerged rigid body. *International Journal of Control.* Volume 82, Issue 9, pp. 1641 - 1656.

Sussmann H.J.; Tang G. (1991) Shortest paths for the Reeds-Shepp car: a worked out example of the use of geometric techniques in nonlinear optimal control. *Rutgers Center for Systems and Control (Sycon) Report 91-10.*

Sussmann H.J. (2000) New Theories of set-valued Differentials and new versions of the Maximum Principle of Optimal Control Theory. *Published in the book Nonlinear Control in the Year 2000, A. Isidori, F. Lamnabhi-Lagarrigue and W. Respondek Eds.; Springer-Verlag*, pp. 487-526.

Waechter A.; Biegler L.T. (2006) On the Implementation of an Interior-Point Filter-Line Search Algorithm for Large-Scale Nonlinear Programming. *Research Report RC 23149*, IBM T.J. Watson Research Center, Yorktown, New York.

9

Modelling and Simulation of the Shape Optimization Problems

Pawel Skruch and Wojciech Mitkowski
AGH University of Science and Technology, Department of Automatics
Poland

1. Introduction

Optimum shape design is an interesting and important field both mathematically and for industrial applications. Uniqueness, stability and existence of solution are important theoretical issues for scientists. Practical implementation issues are critical for realization for engineers and designers. As examples of industrial applications we can consider weight reduction in car engine, aircraft structures, electromagnetically optimum shapes, such as in stealth airplanes. There is also a great interest in shape optimization for fluid flow systems. The engineers and designers are interested in reducing the drag force on the wing of a plane or on a vehicle, or in reducing the viscous dissipation in hydraulic valves, pipes and tanks. The computation of optimal profiles that minimize the aerodynamic drag, the viscous energy which is dissipated in the fluid, the volume and weight of building structures plays nowadays a very important role.

In this paper, we investigate a methodology for the shape optimization problem. The problem consists in finding a shape (in two or three dimensions), which is optimal in a certain sense and satisfies certain requirements. In other words, we would like to find a bounded set D, which minimizes a functional $J(D)$ and satisfies constraints $B(D)=0$. The problem typically involves the solution of a system of nonlinear partial differential equations, which depend on parameters that define a geometrical domain. The solution is usually obtained numerically, by using iterative methods, for example by the finite element method (Strang & Fix, 1973). The continuum description of the geometrical domain is discretized with different meshing strategies. Some of them are fixed grid strategies (Xie & Steven, 1993; Li et al., 1999; Garcia & Gonzales, 2004), design element concepts (Imam, 1982), adaptive mesh strategies (Belegundu & Rajan, 1988) and remeshing strategies. The shape optimization problems are discussed by many scientists, and to mention only a few we note the works (Belegundu & Chandrupatla, 1999; Atanackovic, 2001; Delfour & Zolesio, 2001; Mohammadi & Pironneau, 2001; Skruch, 2001; Allaire, 2002; Bendsøe & Sigmund, 2003; Haslinger & Mäkinen, 2003; Allaire et al., 2004).

In recent years, some attempts have been made to use optimal control theory for the shape optimization problems (Szefer & Mikulski, 1978, 1984; Mitkowski & Skruch, 2001; Skruch, 2001; Laskowski, 2006; Skruch & Mitkowski, 2009). In this paper, we continue investigations of this topic and we show that the method based on the Pontryagin maximum principle

(Pontryagin et. al., 1962; Boltyanskii, 1971; Mitkowski, 1991) can be used for solving the formulated task of optimization. Of course, a general solution and proof are very often impossible. Therefore the main focus in this paper will be put on numerical solutions and simulations. The computer program has been designed in the MATLAB/Simulink environment. It uses an iterative method, that is, we start with an initial guess for a shape, and then gradually evolve it, until it falls into the optimum shape. Using the program we show how to find optimum shapes for different types of beam design. The approach can be also successfully applied to shape optimization of many mechanical systems.

The paper is organized as follows. In section 2 we formulate the problem. General solution of the problem is presented in section 3. To illustrate our approach, we consider a single span beam with rectangular cross-section (section 4), I cross-section (section 5) and a clamped beam with rectangular cross-section (section 6). We also show how to implement numerical solution of the problem (sections 4.2, 5.2 and 6.2). Numerical simulation results are presented in sections 4.3, 5.3 and 6.3. The study of the existence of local minimum for the optimization problem is given in section 4.4.

The following notation is used throughout this chapter:

$\|\cdot\|_\infty$	norm in the space $\mathrm{L}^\infty(T,X)$
γ	volume mass density of the beam material
b	width of the beam's cross-section
E	Young's modulus
h	height of the beam's cross-section
I	moment of inertia
l	length of the beam
$\mathrm{L}^\infty(T,X)$	Banach space with the norm $\|f\|_\infty = \operatorname*{ess\,sup}_{t\in T}\|f(t)\|$, $f:T\to X$
$\mathrm{PC}(T,X)$	space of piecewise continuous functions $f:T\to X$
R	set of real numbers
R^n	real n – dimensional vector space over R
$\mathrm{W}^{1,\infty}(T,X)$	Banach space with the norm $\|f\|_{1,\infty} = \max\left(\|f\|_\infty, \left\|\frac{\mathrm{d}f}{\mathrm{d}t}\right\|_\infty\right)$
w^{T}	transpose of the vector w

2. Formulation of the problem

Consider a physical system of which the statics can be described by the following equation

$$\frac{\mathrm{d}\boldsymbol{x}(\xi)}{\mathrm{d}\xi} = \boldsymbol{f}(\boldsymbol{x}(\xi),\boldsymbol{u}(\xi),\xi), \tag{1}$$

where $\boldsymbol{x}\in \mathrm{W}^{1,\infty}([\xi_0,\xi_1],\mathrm{R}^n)$, $\xi_0,\xi_1\in\mathrm{R}$, $\xi_0<\xi_1$, $\xi\in[\xi_0,\xi_1]$, $\boldsymbol{u}\in U_{\mathrm{ad}}$, U_{ad} stands for the set of admissible controls

$$U_{\mathrm{ad}} = \{\boldsymbol{u}\in \mathrm{PC}([\xi_0,\xi_1],\mathrm{R}^m)\subset \mathrm{L}^\infty([\xi_0,\xi_1],\mathrm{R}^m) : \boldsymbol{u}(\xi)\in U\}, \tag{2}$$

$$U = \{ \boldsymbol{v} \in \mathrm{R}^m : \boldsymbol{u}_{\min} \le \boldsymbol{v} \le \boldsymbol{u}_{\max}, \boldsymbol{u}_{\min} < \boldsymbol{u}_{\max} \},\ \boldsymbol{u}_{\min}, \boldsymbol{u}_{\max} \in \mathrm{R}^m, \tag{3}$$

$\boldsymbol{f} : \mathrm{R}^n \times \mathrm{R}^m \times \mathrm{R} \to \mathrm{R}^n$ is a vector function that is continuous with respect to each variable and whose partial derivative $\nabla_{\boldsymbol{\theta}} \boldsymbol{f}(\boldsymbol{\theta}, \boldsymbol{\eta}, \tau)$ exists and is continuous for all $(\boldsymbol{\theta}, \boldsymbol{\eta}, \tau) \in \mathrm{R}^n \times \mathrm{R}^m \times \mathrm{R}$. Geometrical and strength constraints are imposed on the system in the form of equalities and weak inequalities

$$I_i(\boldsymbol{x}, \boldsymbol{u}, \xi_0, \xi_1) = \int_{\xi_0}^{\xi_1} G_i(\boldsymbol{x}(\xi), \boldsymbol{u}(\xi), \xi) \mathrm{d}\xi + \gamma_i(\xi_0, \boldsymbol{x}(\xi_0), \xi_1, \boldsymbol{x}(\xi_1)) \le 0, \quad i = 1,2,\ldots,p, \tag{4}$$

$$E_j(\boldsymbol{x}, \boldsymbol{u}, \xi_0, \xi_1) = \int_{\xi_0}^{\xi_1} B_j(\boldsymbol{x}(\xi), \boldsymbol{u}(\xi), \xi) \mathrm{d}\xi + \beta_j(\xi_0, \boldsymbol{x}(\xi_0), \xi_1, \boldsymbol{x}(\xi_1)) = 0, \quad j = 1,2,\ldots,q, \tag{5}$$

where $G_i : \mathrm{R}^n \times \mathrm{R}^m \times \mathrm{R} \to \mathrm{R}^n$, $\gamma_i : \mathrm{R} \times \mathrm{R}^n \times \mathrm{R} \times \mathrm{R}^n \to \mathrm{R}$, $B_j : \mathrm{R}^n \times \mathrm{R}^m \times \mathrm{R} \to \mathrm{R}^n$, $\beta_j : \mathrm{R} \times \mathrm{R}^n \times \mathrm{R} \times \mathrm{R}^n \to \mathrm{R}$, $i = 1,2,\ldots,p$, $j = 1,2,\ldots,q$. Existence of the constraints (3), (4) and (5) should secure the solutions the proper physical meaning. We assume that the functions G_i, B_j, γ_i, β_j are continuous with respect to each variable, the partial derivatives $\nabla_{\boldsymbol{\theta}} G_i(\boldsymbol{\theta}, \boldsymbol{\eta}, \tau)$, $\nabla_{\boldsymbol{\theta}} B_j(\boldsymbol{\theta}, \boldsymbol{\eta}, \tau)$ exist and are continuous for all $(\boldsymbol{\theta}, \boldsymbol{\eta}, \tau) \in \mathrm{R}^n \times \mathrm{R}^m \times \mathrm{R}$, moreover, the partial derivatives $\nabla_{\tau_k} \gamma_i(\tau_0, \boldsymbol{\theta}_0, \tau_1, \boldsymbol{\theta}_1)$, $\nabla_{\boldsymbol{\theta}_k} \gamma_i(\tau_0, \boldsymbol{\theta}_0, \tau_1, \boldsymbol{\theta}_1)$, $\nabla_{\tau_k} \beta_j(\tau_0, \boldsymbol{\theta}_0, \tau_1, \boldsymbol{\theta}_1)$, $\nabla_{\boldsymbol{\theta}_k} \beta_j(\tau_0, \boldsymbol{\theta}_0, \tau_1, \boldsymbol{\theta}_1)$, $k = 0,1$ exist and are continuous for all $(\tau_0, \boldsymbol{\theta}_0, \tau_1, \boldsymbol{\theta}_1) \in \mathrm{R} \times \mathrm{R}^n \times \mathrm{R} \times \mathrm{R}^n$. The shape optimization problem involves the constrained minimization of a cost function. In our case the cost function will be formulated as

$$J_0(\boldsymbol{x}, \boldsymbol{u}, \xi_0, \xi_1) = \int_{\xi_0}^{\xi_1} G_0(\boldsymbol{x}(\xi), \boldsymbol{u}(\xi), \xi) \mathrm{d}\xi + \gamma_0(\xi_0, \boldsymbol{x}(\xi_0), \xi_1, \boldsymbol{x}(\xi_1)). \tag{6}$$

Here, the functions G_0 and γ_0 are from the same class as G_i and γ_i, $i = 1,2,\ldots,p$. The cost function may represent any design requirement of the physical system such as displacement of a chosen point, surface or volume of an element, etc..

The problem is to determine the quadruple $(\boldsymbol{x}, \boldsymbol{u}, \xi_0, \xi_1) \in \mathrm{W}^{1,\infty}([\xi_0, \xi_1], \mathrm{R}^n) \times U_{\mathrm{ad}} \times \mathrm{R} \times \mathrm{R}$ which satisfies the equation (1), constrains (4), (5) and minimizes the cost function (6).

3. General solution of the problem

These types of problems as presented shortly in section 2 can be solved using one of the variants of the Pontryagin maximum principle (Ioffe & Tikhomirov, 1979; Alekseev et al., 1987; Hartl et al., 1995; Bania, 2008). In this approach the key role plays the Hamiltonian $H_0 : \mathrm{R}^n \times \mathrm{R}^n \times \mathrm{R}^m \times \mathrm{R} \times \mathrm{R} \times \mathrm{R}^p \times \mathrm{R}^q \to \mathrm{R}$ defined as

$$H_0(\boldsymbol{\psi},\boldsymbol{x},\boldsymbol{u},\xi,\lambda_0,\boldsymbol{\lambda},\boldsymbol{\mu})=\boldsymbol{\psi}^{\mathrm{T}}\boldsymbol{f}(\boldsymbol{x},\boldsymbol{u},\xi)-\sum_{i=0}^{p}\lambda_i G_i(\boldsymbol{x},\boldsymbol{u},\xi)-\sum_{j=1}^{q}\mu_j B_j(\boldsymbol{x},\boldsymbol{u},\xi), \tag{7}$$

where the function $\boldsymbol{\psi}\in \mathrm{W}^{1,\infty}([\xi_0,\xi_1],\mathrm{R}^n)$, $\lambda_0\in\mathrm{R}$, $\boldsymbol{\lambda}=[\lambda_1,\lambda_2,\ldots,\lambda_p]^{\mathrm{T}}\in\mathrm{R}^p$, $\boldsymbol{\mu}=[\mu_1,\mu_2,\ldots,\mu_q]^{\mathrm{T}}\in\mathrm{R}^q$. The number λ_0 and the vectors $\boldsymbol{\lambda}$, $\boldsymbol{\mu}$ are called Lagrange multipliers.

Suppose a quadruple $(\boldsymbol{x}^*,\boldsymbol{u}^*,\xi_0^*,\xi_1^*)$ gives the local minimum in the problem described above. Then according to Pontryagin maximum principle, there exist the Lagrange multipliers $\lambda_0^*\geq 0$, $\boldsymbol{\lambda}^*\geq 0$, $\boldsymbol{\mu}^*$ and the function $\boldsymbol{\psi}^*$ that satisfy the following:

(a) adjoint equations

$$\frac{\mathrm{d}\boldsymbol{\psi}^*(\xi)}{\mathrm{d}\xi}=-\nabla_x H_0(\boldsymbol{\psi}^*(\xi),\boldsymbol{x}^*(\xi),\boldsymbol{u}^*(\xi),\xi,\lambda_0^*,\boldsymbol{\lambda}^*,\boldsymbol{\mu}^*), \tag{8}$$

(b) state equations

$$\frac{\mathrm{d}\boldsymbol{x}^*(\xi)}{\mathrm{d}\xi}=\boldsymbol{f}(\boldsymbol{x}^*(\xi),\boldsymbol{u}^*(\xi),\xi), \tag{9}$$

(c) maximum condition

$$H_0(\boldsymbol{\psi}^*(\xi),\boldsymbol{x}^*(\xi),\boldsymbol{u}^*(\xi),\xi,\lambda_0^*,\boldsymbol{\lambda}^*,\boldsymbol{\mu}^*)\geq H_0(\boldsymbol{\psi}^*(\xi),\boldsymbol{x}^*(\xi),\boldsymbol{v},\xi,\lambda_0^*,\boldsymbol{\lambda}^*,\boldsymbol{\mu}^*),\ \ \boldsymbol{v}\in U, \tag{10}$$

(d) nontriviality conditions

$$\lambda_0^*+|\boldsymbol{\lambda}^*|+|\boldsymbol{\mu}^*|+\|\boldsymbol{\psi}^*\|_\infty>0, \tag{11}$$

(e) complementary conditions

$$\lambda_i^* I_i(\boldsymbol{x}^*,\boldsymbol{u}^*,\xi_0^*,\xi_1^*)=0,\ \ i=1,2,\ldots,p, \tag{12}$$

(f) continuity of the function $H_0(\boldsymbol{\psi}^*(\xi),\boldsymbol{x}^*(\xi),\boldsymbol{u}^*(\xi),\xi,\lambda_0^*,\boldsymbol{\lambda}^*,\boldsymbol{\mu}^*)$ for $\xi\in[\xi_0^*,\xi_1^*]$,

(g) transversality conditions

$$\boldsymbol{\psi}^*(\xi_0^*)=\nabla_{\theta_0}\varphi(\xi_0^*,\boldsymbol{x}^*(\xi_0^*),\xi_1^*,\boldsymbol{x}^*(\xi_1^*),\lambda_0^*,\boldsymbol{\lambda}^*,\boldsymbol{\mu}^*), \tag{13}$$

$$\boldsymbol{\psi}^*(\xi_1^*)=-\nabla_{\theta_1}\varphi(\xi_0^*,\boldsymbol{x}^*(\xi_0^*),\xi_1^*,\boldsymbol{x}^*(\xi_1^*),\lambda_0^*,\boldsymbol{\lambda}^*,\boldsymbol{\mu}^*), \tag{14}$$

$$H_0(\boldsymbol{\psi}^*(\xi_0^*),\boldsymbol{x}^*(\xi_0^*),\boldsymbol{u}^*(\xi_0^*),\xi_0^*,\lambda_0^*,\boldsymbol{\lambda}^*,\boldsymbol{\mu}^*)=-\nabla_{\tau_0}\varphi(\xi_0^*,\boldsymbol{x}^*(\xi_0^*),\xi_1^*,\boldsymbol{x}^*(\xi_1^*),\lambda_0^*,\boldsymbol{\lambda}^*,\boldsymbol{\mu}^*), \tag{15}$$

$$H_0(\boldsymbol{\psi}^*(\xi_1^*),\boldsymbol{x}^*(\xi_1^*),\boldsymbol{u}^*(\xi_1^*),\xi_1^*,\lambda_0^*,\boldsymbol{\lambda}^*,\boldsymbol{\mu}^*)=\nabla_{\tau_1}\varphi(\xi_0^*,\boldsymbol{x}^*(\xi_0^*),\xi_1^*,\boldsymbol{x}^*(\xi_1^*),\lambda_0^*,\boldsymbol{\lambda}^*,\boldsymbol{\mu}^*), \tag{16}$$

where $\varphi:\mathrm{R}\times\mathrm{R}^n\times\mathrm{R}\times\mathrm{R}^n\times\mathrm{R}\times\mathrm{R}^p\times\mathrm{R}^q\to\mathrm{R}$ is defined as follows

$$\varphi(\tau_0,\boldsymbol{\theta}_0,\tau_1,\boldsymbol{\theta}_1,\lambda_0,\boldsymbol{\lambda},\boldsymbol{\mu})=\sum_{i=0}^{p}\lambda_i\gamma_i(\tau_0,\boldsymbol{\theta}_0,\tau_1,\boldsymbol{\theta}_1)+\sum_{j=1}^{q}\mu_j\beta_j(\tau_0,\boldsymbol{\theta}_0,\tau_1,\boldsymbol{\theta}_1). \tag{17}$$

The maximum principle has been and remains an important and effective tool in the many areas in which optimal control plays a role. There have been many advances of this principle in the last fifty years that extended its applicability. It should be underlined that the theorem gives only necessary conditions of optimality. Existence of solutions needs separate studies.

4. Optimal design of a single span beam with rectangular cross-section

4.1 Equation of a physical system

Beams are used to support and strengthen structures ranging from silos to bridges to towering skyscrapers. In this section we explore the shape optimization problem associated with the static deformation of beams. The strategy is to mathematically describe the quantities that affect the deformation of a beam, and to relate these quantities through differential equations that describe the bending of a beam. Then using the method based on the Pontryagin maximum principle, we show how to choose the beam's cross-section in order to assure minimum deflection at the end point of a beam.

Consider a single span beam with rectangular cross-section working under self-weight (fig. 1). The statics of the beam can be described using the following equation

$$\frac{d^2}{d\xi^2}\left[EI(\xi)\frac{d^2y(\xi)}{d\xi^2}\right]=-u(\xi), \tag{18}$$

where $\xi\in[0,l]$, $u(\xi)=\gamma bh(\xi)$, $y(\xi)$ represents vertical displacement of the beam along the interval $[0,l]$, l stands for the length of the beam, b is the width of the beam's cross-section, h is the height of the cross-section, E is the Young's module, $I(\xi)$ is the moment of inertia of the cross-section, γ is the volume mass density of the beam material.

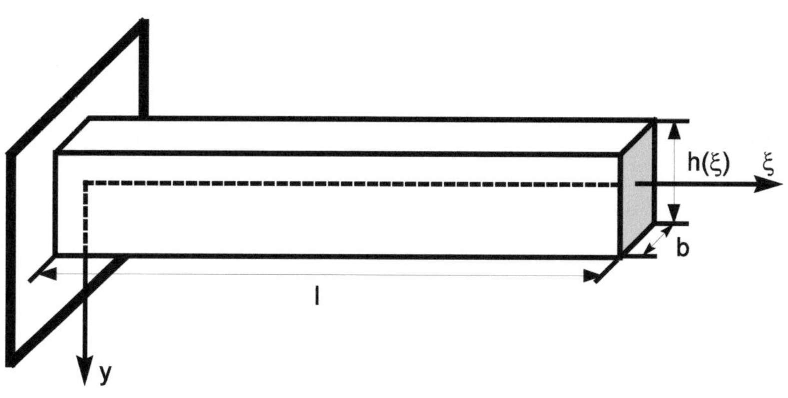

Fig. 1. Single span beam under self-weight

For state notation of the equation (18) we introduce the vector

$$\boldsymbol{x}(\xi) = [x_1(\xi) \quad x_2(\xi) \quad x_3(\xi) \quad x_4(\xi)]^{\mathrm{T}}, \tag{19}$$

where

$$\begin{cases} x_1(\xi) = y(\xi), \\ x_2(\xi) = \dfrac{\mathrm{d}y(\xi)}{\mathrm{d}\xi}, \\ x_3(\xi) = EI(\xi)\dfrac{\mathrm{d}^2 y(\xi)}{\mathrm{d}\xi^2}, \\ x_4(\xi) = \dfrac{\mathrm{d}}{\mathrm{d}\xi}\left[EI(\xi)\dfrac{\mathrm{d}^2 y(\xi)}{\mathrm{d}\xi^2}\right], \end{cases} \tag{20}$$

$$I(\xi) = \frac{bu(\xi)^3}{12}, \tag{21}$$

and additionally we define the vector

$$\boldsymbol{f}(\boldsymbol{x}(\xi), u(\xi)) = \begin{bmatrix} x_2(\xi) \\ \dfrac{12 x_3(\xi)}{Ebu(\xi)^3} \\ x_4(\xi) \\ -u(\xi) \end{bmatrix}. \tag{22}$$

Then our system can be written shortly in the classical form

$$\frac{\mathrm{d}\boldsymbol{x}(\xi)}{\mathrm{d}\xi} = \boldsymbol{f}(\boldsymbol{x}(\xi), \boldsymbol{u}(\xi)), \tag{23}$$

with the boundary conditions

$$x_1(0) = x_2(0) = x_3(l) = x_4(l) = 0. \tag{24}$$

The boundary condition $x_1(0) = 0$ says that the base of the beam (at the wall) does not experience any deflection. We also assume that the beam at the wall is horizontal, so that the derivative of the deflection function is zero at that point, i.e. $x_2(0) = 0$. The boundary condition $x_3(l) = 0$ models the assumption that there is no bending moment at the free end of the cantilever. The boundary condition $x_4(l) = 0$ models the assumption that there is no shearing force acting at the free end of the beam (see also Laskowski, 2006). It should be noted that the values $x_3(0)$, $x_4(0)$, $x_1(l)$ and $x_2(l)$ are unknown. Side conditions concerning strength constraints and geometry are imposed on the dimensions of the cross-section, so that

$$U_{\mathrm{ad}} = \{u \in \mathrm{PC}([0,l], \mathrm{R}) : u(\xi) \in U\}, \tag{25}$$

$$U = \{v \in \mathrm{R} : H_1 \le v \le H_2, H_1 < H_2\},\ H_1, H_2 \in \mathrm{R}. \tag{26}$$

The deflection at the end point of the beam is the optimality criterion

$$J(u) = x_1(l). \tag{27}$$

The cost function (27) can be also expressed in the following form

$$J(u) = x_1(l) = \int_0^l x_2(\xi)\mathrm{d}\xi. \tag{28}$$

We want to determine such $u \in U_{\mathrm{ad}}$, which minimizes the functional (28) and satisfies the state equations (23) with the boundary conditions (24).
In order to solve the formulated problem, we use the Pontryagin maximum principle. Therefore we introduce the Hamiltonian

$$H_0(\boldsymbol{\psi}, \boldsymbol{x}, u, \lambda_0) = \psi_1 x_2 + \psi_2 \frac{12x_3}{Ebu^3} + \psi_3 x_4 - \psi_4 u - \lambda_0 x_2, \tag{29}$$

where the variable $\lambda_0 \geq 0$ and the function $\boldsymbol{\psi}(\xi) = [\psi_1(\xi) \quad \psi_2(\xi) \quad \psi_3(\xi) \quad \psi_4(\xi)]^{\mathrm{T}}$ satisfies the equation

$$\frac{\mathrm{d}\boldsymbol{\psi}(\xi)}{\mathrm{d}\xi} = -\nabla_x H_0(\boldsymbol{\psi}(\xi), \boldsymbol{x}(\xi), u(\xi), \lambda_0), \tag{30}$$

it is

$$\frac{\mathrm{d}\boldsymbol{\psi}(\xi)}{\mathrm{d}\xi} = \begin{bmatrix} 0 \\ -\lambda_0 - \psi_1(\xi) \\ -\psi_2(\xi)\dfrac{12}{Ebu(\xi)^3} \\ -\psi_3(\xi) \end{bmatrix}. \tag{31}$$

The transversality conditions lead to the following boundary values

$$\psi_3(0) = 0, \quad \psi_4(0) = 0, \tag{32}$$

$$\psi_1(l) = 0, \quad \psi_2(l) = 0. \tag{33}$$

According to the Pontryagin maximum principle for the optimal control u^* there is

$$H_0(\boldsymbol{\psi}^*, \boldsymbol{x}^*, \boldsymbol{u}^*, \lambda_0^*) = \max_{v \in U} H_0(\boldsymbol{\psi}^*, \boldsymbol{x}^*, v, \lambda_0^*). \tag{34}$$

The optimal control u^* can be obtained from the condition $\partial H_0 / \partial u = 0$ with the help of the system of the adjoint equations (31) and the boundary conditions (32), (33).
We assume that $\lambda_0 = 1$. Then from (31) we can obtain

$$\psi_1(\xi) = 0, \quad \psi_2(\xi) = l - \xi. \tag{35}$$

Invoking the condition $\partial H_0 / \partial u = 0$ we have the equation

$$u(\xi)=\sqrt[4]{(\xi-l)\frac{36x_3(\xi)}{Eb\psi_4(\xi)}}\,, \tag{36}$$

from which we shall obtain the optimal control u^*. In the formulated optimization problem the constraints (26) cause that not the whole space is an admissible region. Because

$$\lim_{\xi\to 0_+}\sqrt[4]{(\xi-l)\frac{36x_3(\xi)}{Eb\psi_4(\xi)}}=+\infty\,, \tag{37}$$

$$\lim_{\xi\to l_-}\sqrt[4]{(\xi-l)\frac{36x_3(\xi)}{Eb\psi_4(\xi)}}=0\,, \tag{38}$$

then the optimal solution has the final form

$$u^*(\xi)=\begin{cases} H_2, & \text{for } \xi\in[0,\xi_a] \\ \sqrt[4]{(\xi-l)\dfrac{36x_3(\xi)}{Eb\psi_4(\xi)}}, & \text{for } \xi\in(\xi_a,\xi_b] \\ H_1, & \text{for } \xi\in(\xi_b,l] \end{cases} \tag{39}$$

The optimal control (39) has a purely formal character because we do not know the functions $x_3(\xi)$, $\psi_4(\xi)$ and the ranges $[0,\xi_a]$, $(\xi_a,\xi_b]$, $(\xi_b,l]$ in which the individual relations (39) hold. These unknowns can be found in a numerical way.

4.2 Solution method

To find effectively the optimal control $u^*(\xi)$, it is necessary to solve the system which consists of nonlinear ordinary differential equations of the first-order with the boundary conditions defined at initial and end points. The solution of this system is possible only in a numerical way. The following algorithm has been implemented in the MATLAB/Simulink environment. The algorithm for numerical solution of the shape optimization problem for the single span beam with rectangular cross-section uses simple shooting method (see for example Keller, 1971; Roberts & Shipman, 1972; Matauek, 1973; Lastman, 1974). Interesting results regarding solution methods of boundary value problems can be found in (Mufti et al., 1969; Miele et al., 1972; Meyer, 1973; Laporte & Le Tallec, 2003).

- **Assumptions**
  The system (19), (22), (23), (24) has a solution and the optimal control exists.
- **Step 1**
  For arbitrarily chosen values $x_3(0)$ and $x_4(0)$ solve the problem in the interval $[0,\xi_a]$ using the model created in Simulink. In this model time works as geometrical variable ξ. Then find ξ_a such that $u^*(\xi_a)=H_2$ using the equation (36).
- **Step 2**
  Based on the results from the previous step determine the end conditions $\boldsymbol{x}(\xi_a)$. They will be used as initial conditions in the next step.

- **Step 3**
  Find ξ_{b} such that $u^*(\xi_{\mathrm{b}}) = H_1$ using the equation (36).
- **Step 4**
  Solve the problem in the interval $(\xi_{\mathrm{a}}, \xi_{\mathrm{b}}]$ using the model created in Simulink and determine the end conditions $\boldsymbol{x}(\xi_{\mathrm{b}})$. These values will be used as initial conditions in the next step.
- **Step 5**
  Solve the problem in the interval $(\xi_{\mathrm{b}}, l]$ using the model created in Simulink.
- **Step 6**
  Calculate the norm $|x_3(l)| + |x_4(l)|$ and compare it with 0. First approximation for the optimal control $u^*(\xi)$ can be obtained from (39).
- **Step 7**
  Based on the norm $|x_3(l)| + |x_4(l)|$ recalculate the points $x_3(0)$ and $x_4(0)$ using the Nelder-Mead simplex (direct search) method (fmins function included in MATLAB).
- **Step 8**
  The steps 1-8 are repeated many times until $|x_3(l)| + |x_4(l)| < \varepsilon$.

The algorithm uses the MATLAB/Simulink environment to represent and solve the system (see fig. 2). State variable formulation allows the use of a wide variety of fixed step and variable step integration algorithms from Simulink. Simulation results can be displayed on Simulink scopes while the simulation is running or sent to workspace or disk file. The user can access a variety of MATLAB functions for processing and plotting of waveforms stored in the MATLAB workspace. It should be noted that time step integration methods are used to solve the mechanical system. In other words, one-dimensional computational domain related to beam's geometry is represented by time domain.

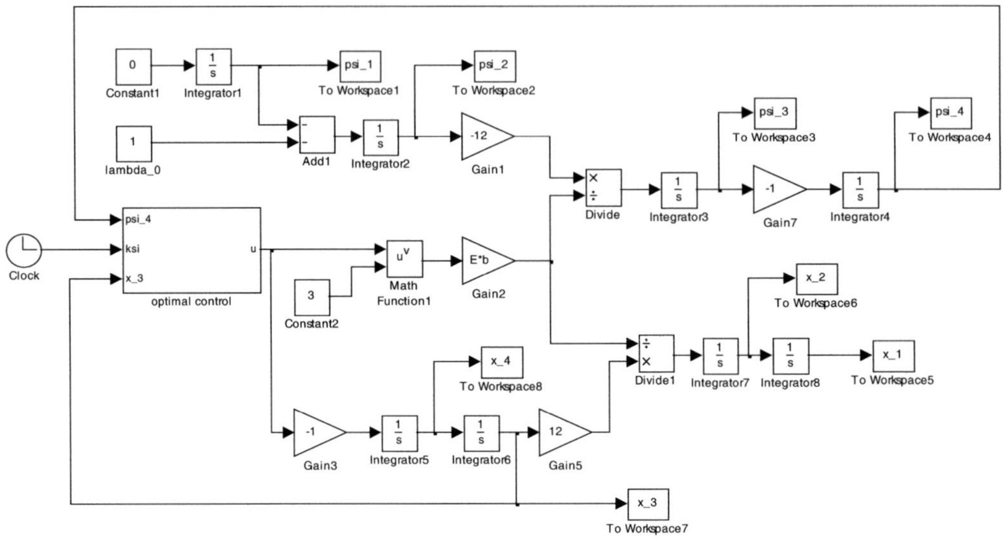

Fig. 2. Model of the system in Simulink environment

4.3 Numerical simulation results

Simulation effects are shown in figs. 3-8. Fig. 3 presents the optimal height $h(\xi)$ of the cross-section. Fig. 4 presents the optimal shape of the beam. Figs. 5 and 6 illustrate the state variables $x_1(\xi)$, $x_2(\xi)$, $x_3(\xi)$ and $x_4(\xi)$ along the interval $[0,l]$. Figs. 7 and 8 show the set of adjoint functions ψ_i, $i=1,2,3,4$. Calculations were made for the following data: $l=2.0$ [m], $b=0.1$ [m], $H_1=0.1$ [m], $H_2=0.2$ [m], $E=2.1\cdot 10^{11}$ [N/m^2], $\gamma=76500$ [N/m^3].

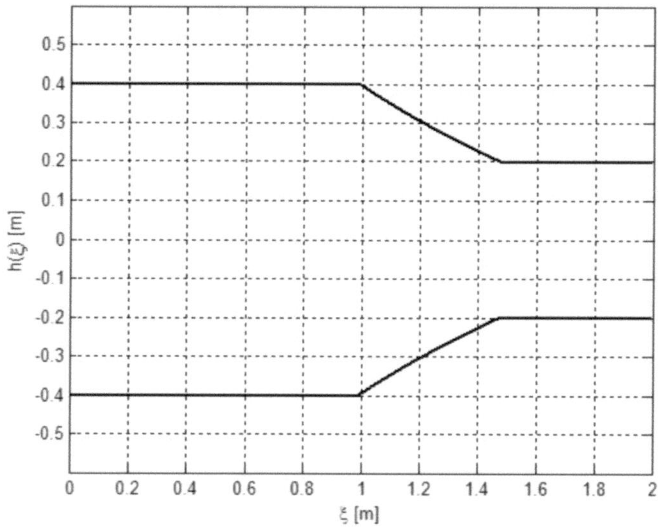

Fig. 3. The height of the cross-section, $\xi_a = 0.99$ [m], $\xi_b = 1.47$ [m]

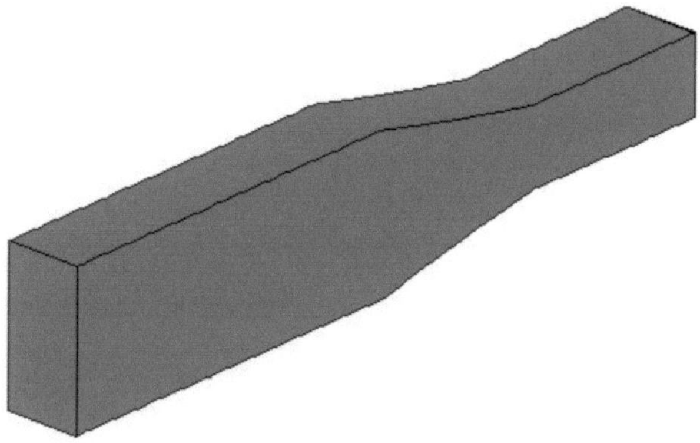

Fig. 4. Optimal shape of the beam

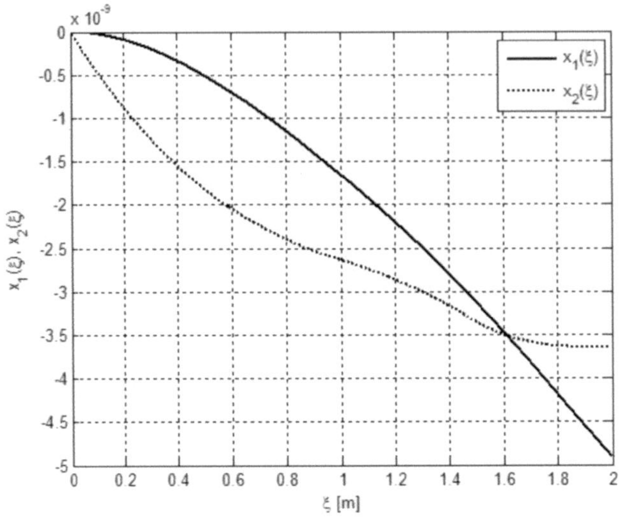

Fig. 5. The state variables $x_1(\xi)$, $x_2(\xi)$

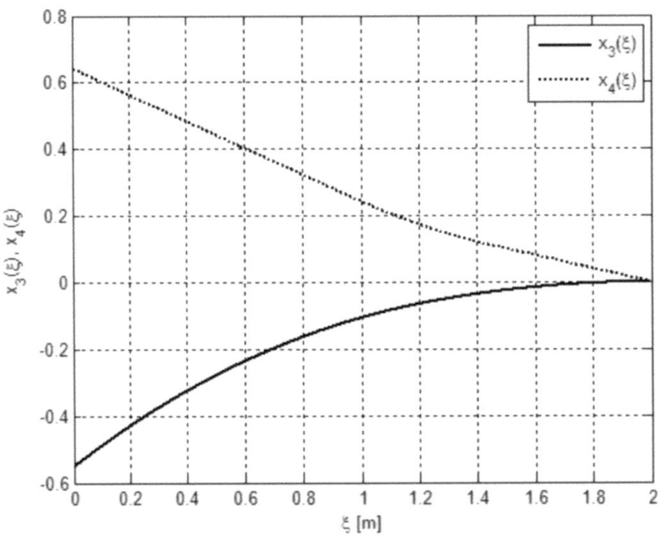

Fig. 6. The state variables $x_3(\xi)$, $x_4(\xi)$

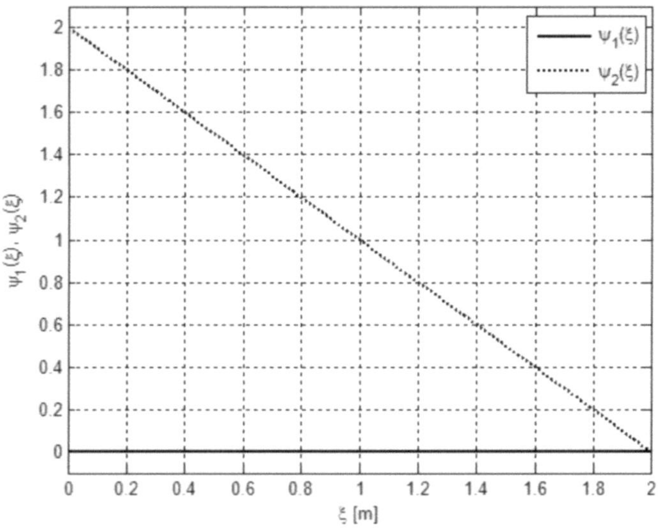

Fig. 7. The adjoint functions $\psi_1(\xi)$, $\psi_2(\xi)$

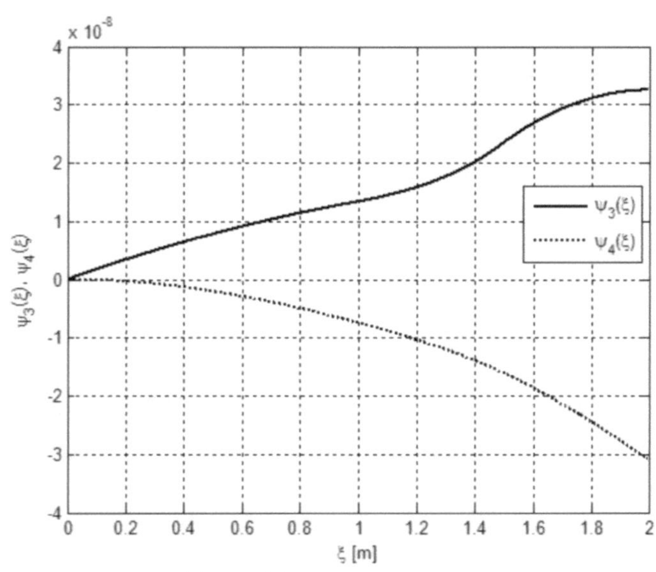

Fig. 8. The adjoint functions $\psi_3(\xi)$, $\psi_4(\xi)$

4.4 Study of the existence of local minimum

The Pontryagin maximum principle gives a necessary condition for an optimum. It does not assure that the solution of the problem really exists and is unique. A general proof of existence, uniqueness and stability is usually impossible. This needs an extensive study and will not be provided in this paper. However, these issues are important from theoretical point of view. Some attempts have been made by (Skruch, 2001; Skruch & Mitkowski, 2008) how to handle this numerically. In some neighbourhood of the candidate for optimal shape K0 (see fig. 9) we choose other shapes K1, K2, K3 and K4. These shapes are described by the following equations:

$$K1:\ y(\xi) = -0.7576\xi + 0.9606, \tag{40}$$

$$K2:\ y(\xi) = 0.5628\xi^{-1} - 0.3606, \tag{41}$$

$$K3:\ y(\xi) = 0.2398\xi^{-2} - 0.0379, \tag{42}$$

$$K4:\ y(\xi) = 0.1252\xi^{-3} + 0.0664. \tag{43}$$

Then for every shape we need to calculate the cost function J that is the deflection at the end point of the beam. Fig. 10 presents results of this calculation; for the shapes in the neighbourhood of the candidate for optimal shape K0 we obtain worse values of the cost function J.

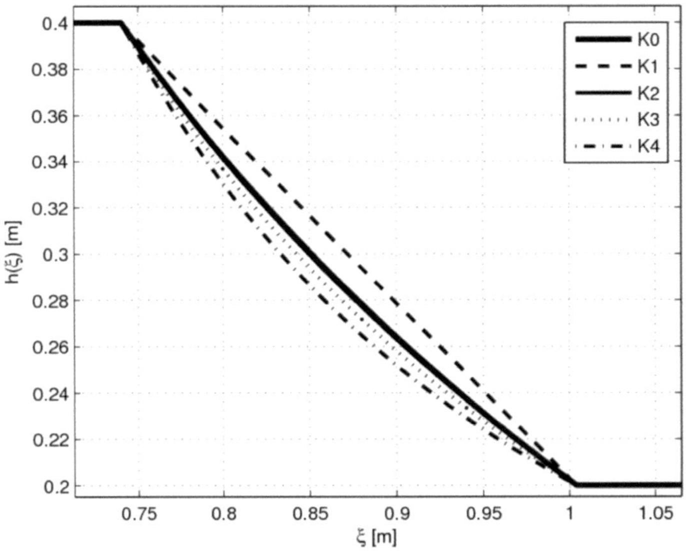

Fig. 9. The candidate for optimal shape K0 and the shapes in neighbourhood K1, K2, K3 and K4

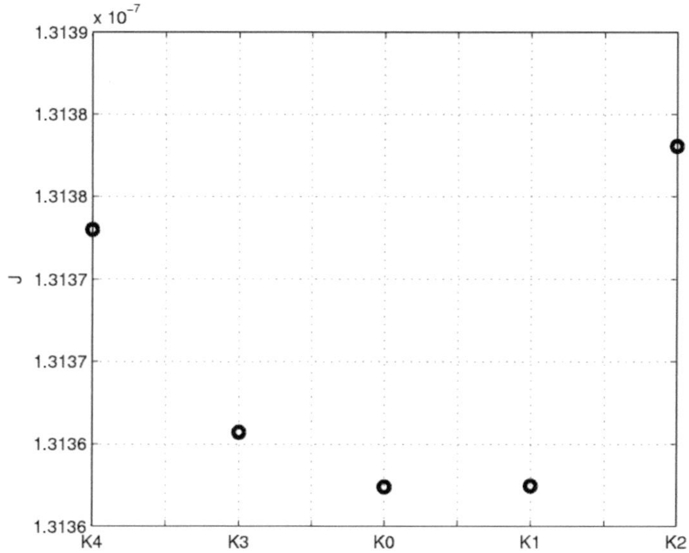

Fig. 10. The cost function J in the neighbourhood of the candidate for optimal control K0

Other neighbourhood of the candidate for optimal shape is presented in fig. 11. The candidate for optimal shape is depicted using bold line. The neighbourhood contains shapes in the form of straight lines with different points ξ_a and ξ_b (thin lines). Then for every shape we calculated the deflection of the beam at the end point. The results of these calculations are shown in fig. 12. For the shapes in the neighbourhood we obtain worse values of the cost function J than for the shape K0 .

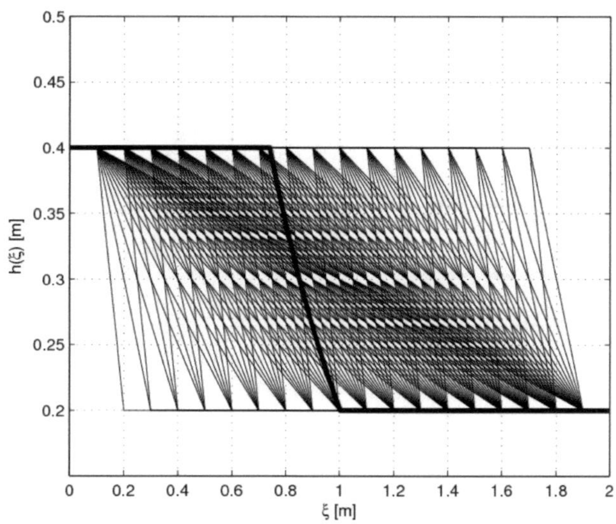

Fig. 11. The neighbourhood of the candidate for optimal shape

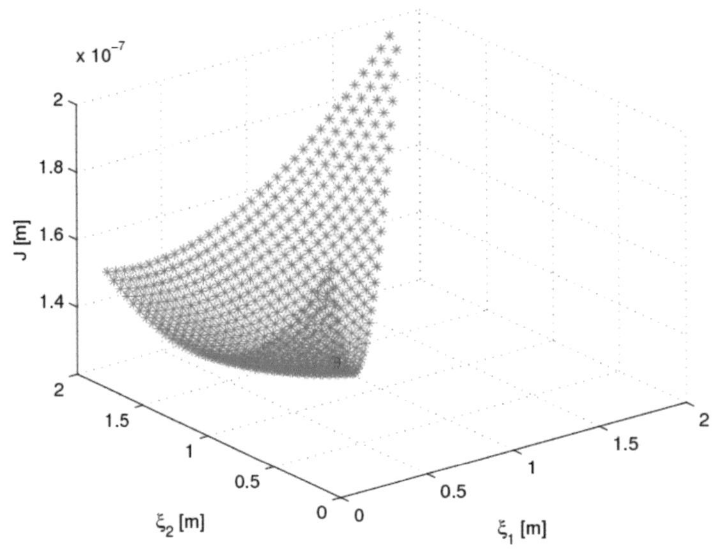

Fig. 12. The cost function J in the neighbourhood of the candidate for optimal shape

5. Optimal design of a single span beam with I cross-section

5.1 Equation of a physical system

The methodology presented in section 3 can be used for solving other types of shape optimization problems. Also the algorithm presented in section 4 can be easily adapted to other types of problems.

Consider for example a single span beam with I cross-section working under self-weight (fig. 13).

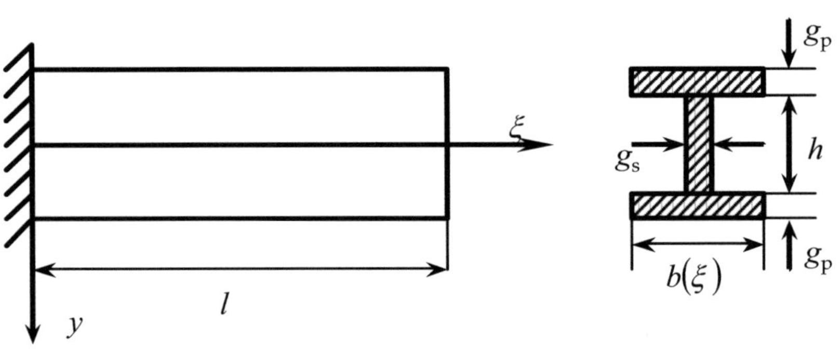

Fig. 13. Single span beam with I cross-section

The statics of the beam can be described using the following equation

$$\frac{\mathrm{d}\boldsymbol{x}(\xi)}{\mathrm{d}\xi} = \boldsymbol{f}(\boldsymbol{x}(\xi), u(\xi)), \tag{44}$$

where $\boldsymbol{x}(\xi)=[x_1(\xi) \;\; x_2(\xi) \;\; x_3(\xi) \;\; x_4(\xi)]^{\mathrm{T}}$, $u(\xi)=\gamma b(\xi)h$, $\xi\in[0,l]$, and

$$\boldsymbol{f}(\boldsymbol{x}(\xi),u(\xi))=\begin{bmatrix} x_2(\xi) \\ \dfrac{x_3(\xi)}{a+cu(\xi)} \\ x_4(\xi) \\ -u(\xi) \end{bmatrix}, \tag{45}$$

$$a=E\frac{g_s h^3}{12}, \quad c=2Eg_p\left(\frac{h}{2}+\frac{g_p}{2}\right)^2. \tag{46}$$

Here $x_1(\xi)$ represents vertical displacement of the beam along the interval $[0,l]$, $x_2(\xi)$ indicates the slope of the beam at ξ, $x_3(\xi)$ can measure in physical terms the bending moment of the beam at ξ, $x_4(\xi)$ can measure the shearing force on the beam at ξ, l stands for the length of the beam, $b(\xi)$ is the width of the beam's cross-section, h is the height of the cross-section, E is the Young's module, γ is the volume mass density of the beam material. The static beam equation is fourth-order (it has a fourth derivative) and the mechanism for supporting the beam gives rise to four boundary conditions

$$x_1(0)=x_2(0)=x_3(l)=x_4(l)=0. \tag{47}$$

For the control variable u we introduce geometrical and strength constraints that define a set of admissible controls

$$U_{\mathrm{ad}}=\{u\in \mathrm{PC}([0,l],\mathrm{R}) : u(\xi)\in U\}, \tag{48}$$

$$U=\{v\in\mathrm{R} : H_1\le v\le H_2, H_1<H_2\},\; H_1,H_2\in\mathrm{R}. \tag{49}$$

The cost function denotes the deflection at the end point of the beam and it is defined by the functional

$$J(u)=x_1(l). \tag{50}$$

We want to determine $u\in U$ which minimizes the functional (50) and satisfies the state equation (44) with the boundary conditions (47).

5.2 Solution method

In order to solve the formulated problem we can use the Pontryagin maximum principle and follow the method presented in sections 3 and 4. The Hamiltonian constructed for this case together with the system of adjoint equations lead to the conditions which determine the candidate for the optimal control. The constraints appearing in this problem are identical as in the problem from section 4, therefore the complete analysis for the optimal control is very similar.

5.3 Numerical simulation results

The numerical solution of the formulated problem has been carried out using the program designed in MATLAB/Simulink environment. Fig. 14 presents optimal design of the single span beam with I cross-section. Calculations were made for the following data: $l = 2.0$ [m], $h = 0.2$ [m], $H_1 = 0.2$ [m], $H_2 = 0.4$ [m], $E = 2.1 \cdot 10^{11}$ [N/m^2], $\gamma = 76500$ [N/m^3], $g_p = 0.002$ [m], $g_s = 0.0013$ [m].

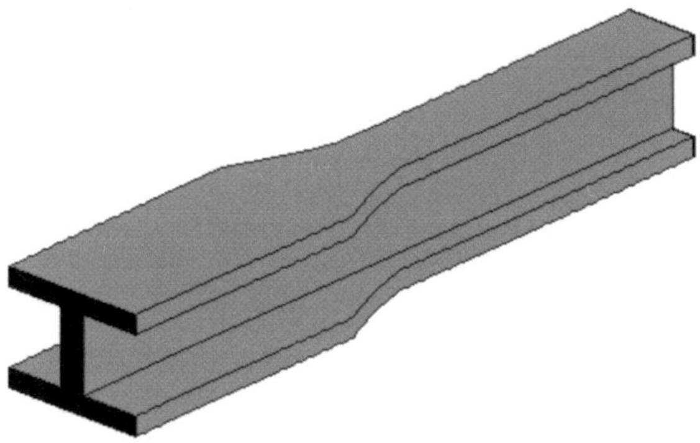

Fig. 14. Optimal shape of the beam with I cross-section

6. Optimal design of a clamped beam with rectangular cross-section

6.1 Equation of a physical system

Consider a clamped beam with rectangular cross-section (fig. 15).

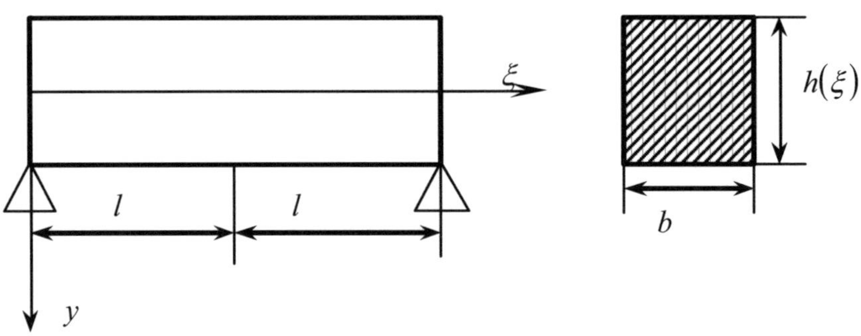

Fig. 15. Clamped beam with rectangular cross-section

The state equation describing statics of the beam has the form

$$\frac{d\boldsymbol{x}(\xi)}{d\xi} = \boldsymbol{f}(\boldsymbol{x}(\xi), u(\xi)), \tag{51}$$

where $\boldsymbol{x}(\xi) = [x_1(\xi) \quad x_2(\xi) \quad x_3(\xi) \quad x_4(\xi)]^T$, $u(\xi) = \gamma b h(\xi)$, $\xi \in [0, l]$, and

$$\boldsymbol{f}(\boldsymbol{x}(\xi), u(\xi)) = \begin{bmatrix} x_2(\xi) \\ \dfrac{12 x_3(\xi)}{E b u(\xi)^3} \\ x_4(\xi) \\ -u(\xi) \end{bmatrix}. \tag{52}$$

All parameters have the same meaning as for the single span beam with rectangular cross-section working under self weight. The beam cannot experience deflection neither at the left-hand nor at right-hand support, therefore $x_1(0) = 0$ and $x_1(2l) = 0$. The beam does not experience also any torque what means that $x_3(0) = 0$ and $x_3(2l) = 0$. The boundary conditions can be rewritten equivalently to the form

$$x_1(0) = x_2(l) = x_3(0) = x_4(l) = 0. \tag{53}$$

Strength constraints and geometry are imposed on the dimensions of the cross-section defining the set of admissible controls

$$U_{\text{ad}} = \{u \in \text{PC}([0, l], \text{R}) : u(\xi) \in U\}, \tag{54}$$

$$U = \{v \in \text{R} : H_1 \le v \le H_2, H_1 < H_2\}, \; H_1, H_2 \in \text{R}. \tag{55}$$

The deflection at the middle point of the beam can be the optimality criterion

$$J(u) = x_1(l). \tag{56}$$

We want to determine $u \in U$ which minimizes the functional (56) and satisfies the state equation (51) with the boundary conditions (53).

6.2 Solution method

In order to solve the formulated problem we can use the Pontryagin maximum principle and follow the method presented in sections 3 and 4.

6.3 Numerical simulation results

Fig. 16 presents optimal shape of the clamped beam with rectangular cross-section. Calculations were made for the following data: $l = 2.0$ [m], $b = 0.05$ [m], $H_1 = 0.25$ [m], $H_2 = 0.5$ [m], $E = 2.1 \cdot 10^{11}$ [N/m^2], $\gamma = 22000$ [N/m^3].

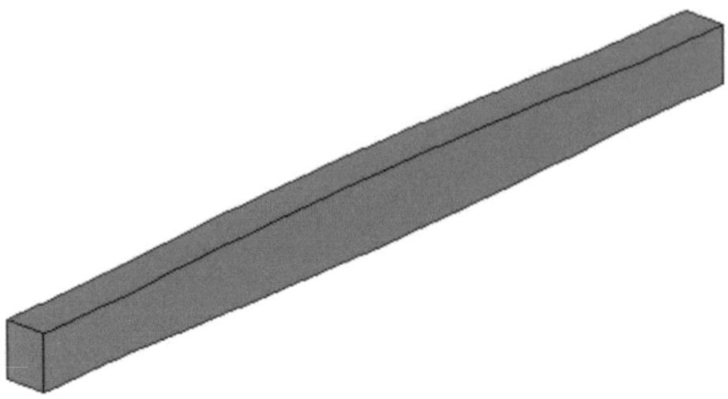

Fig. 16. Optimal shape of the clamped beam

7. Conclusions

We have investigated a shape optimization problem. As it has been shown the problem is not always trivial and the general proof can be very difficult. By using effective Pontryagin's method of optimization, the numerical algorithm has been designed and implemented. The simulation results show the effectiveness of the proposed method.

8. Acknowledgment

This work was supported by Ministry of Science and Higher Education in Poland in the years 2008-2011 as a research project No N N514 414034.

9. References

Alekseev, V.M.; Tikhomirov, V.M. & Fomin, S.V. (1987). *Optimal Control*, Consultants Bureau, New York

Allaire, G. (2002). *Shape Optimization by the Homogenization Method*, Springer, Berlin, Heidelberg, New York

Allaire, G.; Jouve, F. & Toader, A.M. (2004). Structural optimization using sensitivity analysis and a level-set method, *J. Comput. Phys.*, Vol. 194, No. 1, pp. 363-393

Atanackovic, T.M. (2001). On the optimal shape of a rotating rod. *J. Appl. Mech.*, Vol. 68, No. 6, pp. 860-864

Bania, P. (2008). *Optimization Algorithms in Nonlinear Model Predictive Control*, Ph.D. thesis, AGH University of Science and Technology, Faculty of Electrical Engineering, Automatics, Computer Science and Electronics, Cracow, Poland

Belegundu, A.D. & Rajan, S.D. (1988). A shape optimization approach based on natural design variables and shape functions. *Comput. Methods Appl. Mech. Eng.*, Vol. 66, No. 1, pp. 87-106

Belegundu, A.D. & Chandrupatla, T.R. (1999). *Optimization Concepts and Applications in Engineering*, Prentice Hall, New Jersey

Bendsøe, M.P. & Sigmund, O. (2003). *Topology Optimization: Theory, Methods and Applications*, Springer, Berlin, Heidelberg

Boltyanskii, V.G. (1971). *Mathematical Methods of Optimal Control*, Holt, Rinehart & Winston, New York

Delfour, M.C. & Zolesio, J.-P. (2001). *Shapes and Geometries – Analysis, Differential Calculus, and Optimization*, Society for Industrial and Applied Mathematics, Philadelphia

Garcia, M.J. & Gonzales, C.A. (2004). Shape optimization of continuum structures via evolution strategies and fixed grid finite element analysis. *Struct. Multidiscip. Optim.*, Vol. 26, No. 1-2, pp. 92-98

Haslinger, J. & Mäkinen, R. (2003). *Introduction to Shape Optimization: Theory, Approximation, and Computation*, Society for Industrial and Applied Mathematics, Philadelphia

Hartl, R.F.; Suresh, P.S. & Vickson, R.G. (1995). A survey of the maximum principles for optimal control problems with state constraints. *SIAM Rev.*, Vol. 37, No. 2, pp. 181-218

Imam, M.H. (1982). Three-dimensional shape optimization, *Int. J. Numer. Methods Eng.*, Vol. 18, No. 5, pp. 661-673

Ioffe, A.D. & Tikhomirov, V.M. (1979). *Theory of Extremal Problems*, North-Holland, Amsterdam

Keller, H.B. (1971). Shooting and embedding for two-point boundary value problems, *J. Math. Anal. Appl.*, Vol. 36, No. 3, pp. 598-610

Laporte, E. & Le Tallec, P. (2003). *Numerical Methods in Sensitivity Analysis and Shape Optimization*, Modeling and Simulation in Science, Engineering and Technology, Birkhäuser, Boston

Laskowski, H. (2006). *Optimal Modelling of Steel-Concrete Combined Girders in View of the Control Theory*, Ph.D. thesis, Cracow University of Technology, Faculty of Civil Engineering, Cracow, Poland

Lastman, G.J. (1974). Obtaining starting values for the shooting method solution of a class of two-point boundary value problems, *J. Optim. Theory Appl.*, Vol. 14, No. 3, pp. 263-270

Li, Q.; Steven, G.P.; Querin, O.M. & Xie, Y.M. (1999). Evolutionary shape optimization for stress minimization. *Mech. Res. Commun.*, Vol. 26, No. 6, pp. 657-664

Pontryagin, L.S.; Boltyanskii, V.G.; Gamkrelidze, R.V. & Mishchenko, E.F. (1962). *The Mathematical Theory of Optimal Processes*, John Willey, New York

Matauek, M.R. (1973). Direct shooting method for the solution of boundary-value problems, *J. Optim. Theory Appl.*, Vol. 12, No. 2, pp. 152-172

Meyer, G.H. (1973). *Initial Value Methods for Boundary Value Problems*, Academic Press, New York

Miele, A; Naqvi, S.; Levy, A.V. & Iyer, R.R. (1972). *Numerical Solution of Nonlinear Equations and Nonlinear Two-Point Boundary-Value Problems*, Advances in Control Systems, Vol. 8, Edited by C.T. Leondes, Academic Press, New York

Mitkowski, W. (1991). *Stabilization of Dynamic Systems*, WNT, Warsaw

Mitkowski, W. & Skruch, P. (2001). Optimization of beams shape, *Proceedings of the conference AUTOMATION 2001*, pp. 356-363, Warsaw, 28-30 March 2001, Poland

Mohammadi, B. & Pironneau, O. (2001). *Applied Shape Optimization for Fluids*, Oxford University Press, Oxford

Mufti, I.H.; Chow, C.K. & Stock, F.T. (1969). Solution of ill-conditioned linear two-point boundary value problems by the Riccati transformation, *SIAM Rev.*, Vol. 11, No. 4, pp. 616-619

Roberts, S.M. & Shipman, J.S. (1972). *Two-Point Boundary Value Problems: Shooting Methods*, American Elsevier Publishing Company, New York

Skruch, P. (2001). *Shape Optimization*, Master thesis, AGH University of Science and Technology, Faculty of Electrical Engineering, Automatics, Computer Science and Electronics, Cracow, Poland

Skruch, P. & Mitkowski, W. (2009). Optimum design of shapes using the Pontryagin principle of maximum. *Automatyka* (accepted for publication)

Strang, G. & Fix, G.J. (1973). *An Analysis of the Finite Element Method*, Prentice-Hall, Englewood Cliffs, New York

Szefer, G. & Mikulski, L. (1978). Optimization of beams with the use of the Pontryagin extremum principle. *Archives of Civil Engineering*, Vol. XXIV, No. 3, pp. 337-345

Szefer, G. & Mikulski, L. (1984). Optimal design of elastic arches with I cross-section. *Eng. Trans.*, Vol. 32, No. 4, pp. 467-480

Xie, Y.M. & Steven, G.P. (1993). A simple evolutionary procedure for structural optimization, *Comput. Struct.*, Vol. 49, No. 5, pp. 885-896

10

Simulation of the Impact of the Plough Body Parameters, Soil Properties and Working Modes on the Ploughing Resistance

Arvids Vilde and Adolfs Rucins
Latvia University of Agriculture
Latvia

1. Introduction

Ploughing is one of the most power-consuming and expensive processes in agricultural production. It is known from our previous investigation (Vilde, 1999) that the draft resistance of ploughs and energy requirement for ploughing depend on the plough body parameters and on such soil properties as its hardness, density, friction and adhesion. These properties and the tillage quality depend mainly on mechanical composition and humidity of the soil.

However, there were no sufficient analytical correlations that would enable to determine the impact of the plough body parameters on the draft resistance of the share-mouldboard surface and the plough body, as a whole, as well as on the ploughing quality and expenses depending on the body parameters, on the humidity and composition of soil.

In literature there is difference of opinions on the impact of plough body working width on its specific draft resistance. F. P. Ciganov in this dissertation had written that decreasing of the body width decreases specific draft resistance of ploughing (Ciganov, 1969). W. R. Gill and G. E. Vanden Berg have opposite views. Their data show that "specific draft generally tended to decrease as size of cut increased" (Gill & Vanden Berg, 1967, p. 262). In the Kverneland plough prospect has written that by increasing the furrow width from 35 cm to 45 cm (14" to 18") the consumption of diesel fuel is reduced by as much as 18% and working capacity will be increased by up to 30% (Rucins & Vilde, 2005b).

The purpose of the investigations was to study the factors that determine the quality and energy requirement of ploughing, the impact of body parameters, working modes and speed, as well as soil properties on it and to find technical solutions to improve the ploughing efficiency.

2. Materials and Methods

On the basis of the survey a hypothesis has been advanced that the draft resistance of soil tillage machines, as well as ploughs depends on two types of effective forces: the forces related to physical and mechanical properties of soil (its mechanical strength) which manifest themselves as the penetration resistance of operating parts, soil deformation resistance and adhesion; and the forces caused by the mass of the soil moving along the lifting surface (gravity and inertia forces). Therefore both the relationships of the material resistance and theoretical mechanics have been applied for an analytical estimation of the draft resistance of operating parts, as well as their component elements.

The objects of the research are the forces acting on the plough body and its draft resistance depending on the body design parameters, as well as the physical and mechanical properties of soil and the mode of operation. On the basis of the previous investigations (Vilde, 1999) a computer algorithm has been worked out (Rucins & Vilde, 2005a) for the simulation of the forces exerted by soil upon the operating (lifting and supporting) surfaces of the plough body, and the draft resistance caused by these forces (Fig. 1).

Mathematical methods and computer algorithms worked out for the simulation of soil tillage processes allow calculating the forces acting upon the machine operating parts and their optimal design (including the plough body) for qualitative soil tillage with minimum energy consumption.

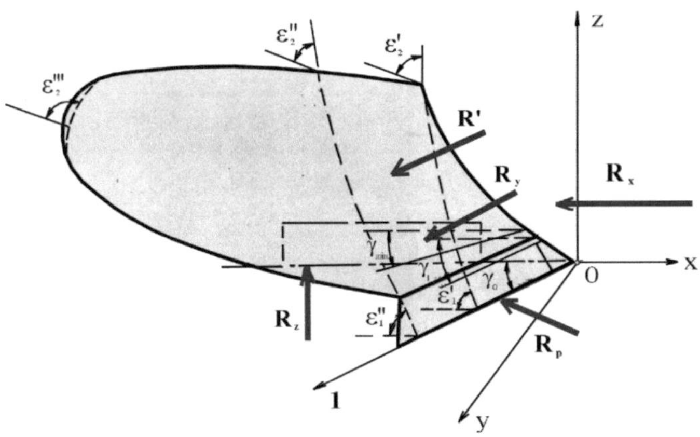

Fig. 1. Scheme of the plough body, its parameters and acting forces.

According to our previous investigations (Vilde 1999) the draft resistance R_x of the plough body is determined by the share of the cutting resistance R_{Px}, the resistance caused by the gravity (weight) R_{Gx} of the soil slice lifted, by the inertia forces R_{Jx}, by soil adhesion R_{Ax} and by weight R_{Qx} of the plough body itself (including a part of the weight of the plough).

$$R_X = \Sigma R_{ix} = R_{Px} + R_{Gx} + R_{Jx} + R_{Ax} + R_{Qx} \quad (1)$$

The vertical reaction R_z and the lateral reaction R_y of the operating part are defined by corresponding partial reactions:

$$R_Z = \Sigma R_{iz} \; ; \qquad R_y = \Sigma R_{iy} \quad (2; 3)$$

The total draft resistance R_x of the operating part is composed of the resistance of the working surface R'_x and the resistance of the supporting (lower and lateral) surfaces R''_x:

$$R_x = R'_x + R''_x = \Sigma R'_{ix} + f_0 (\Sigma R_{iz} + \Sigma R_{iy} + p_{Axy} S_{xy} + p_{Axz} S_{xz}) \quad (4)$$

where: f_0 is the coefficient of the soil friction along the working and supporting surfaces of the plough body; p_{Axy} and p_{Axz} – the specific adhesion force applied, respectively, to the lower and the lateral supporting surfaces of the body; S_{xy} and S_{xz} - the surface area, respectively, of the lower and the lateral supporting surfaces of the body.

The friction resistance F_x is a constituent part of these reactions and their components (Rucins et al. 2003), and, by analogy, we can write that

$$F'_x = \Sigma F'_{ix} = F'_{Px} + F'_{Gx} + F'_{Jx} + F'_{Ax} + F'_{Qx} = R'_x - R'_{xo} \quad (5)$$

$$F''_x = f_0 (R_z + R_y + p_{Axy} S_{xy} + p_{Axz} S_{xz}) = R''_x \quad (6)$$

$$F_x = F'_x + F''_x \quad (7)$$

The friction resistance of the share-mouldboard surface is defined as the difference between the total resistance (general value of the partial resistance) and resistance R_{xo} in operation without friction (f_0= 0).

$$F_{ix} = R_{ix} - R_{ixo}; \qquad F_x = R_x - R_{xo} \quad (8; 9)$$

Ratio λ_F of the friction resistance in the partial and total resistance (reaction) is determined from their correlations:

$$\lambda_{Fix} = F_{ix} R_{ix}^{-1}; \qquad \lambda_{Fx} = F_x R_x^{-1} \quad (10; 11)$$

Ratio λ_R of the supporting reactions in the partial and total draft resistance is determined from correlation:

$$\lambda_{Rx} = R_i R_{ix}^{-1} \quad (12)$$

2.1. Cutting resistance R'_{Px} is proportional to soil hardness ρ_0 and the share edge surface area ω:

$$R'_{Px} = k_p \rho_0 \omega = k_p \rho_0 ib \quad (13)$$

where k_p is the coefficient involving the impact of the shape of the frontal surface of the ploughshare edge; i and b - the thickness and width of the edge.

It is evident from formula (5) that the friction of soil along the edge does not influence the cutting resistance of the edge.

At a sharp ploughshare (the rear bevel is absent):

$$R_{Pz} = 0 \quad (14)$$

At a blunt (threadbare) ploughshare having rear bevel the vertical reaction R_{Pz} on the hard soils can reach the summary value of vertical reactions, this summary value arising from

other forces acting on the share-mouldboard surface (soil gravity and inertia) and the weight of the body Q.
At an inclined ploughshare a lateral reaction R_{Py} arises, its value being affected by the friction reaction.

$$R_{Py} = k_p \rho_0 \, ib \, ctg(\gamma_0 + \varphi_0) \quad (15)$$

where γ_0 is the inclination angle of the edge towards the direction of movement (the wall of the furrow); φ_0 - the angle of friction.
When friction is absent, $f_0 = 0$, $\varphi_0 = 0$ and

$$R_{Pyo} = k_p \rho_0 \, ib \, ctg \, \gamma \quad (16)$$

Friction of soil along the ploughshare edge reduces the lateral pressure of the ploughshare (the pressure of the plough body against the wall of the furrow).
The resistance of the supporting surface

$$R''_{Px} = k_p \rho_0 \, ib \, f_0 \, ctg(\gamma_0 + \varphi_0) = F''_{Px} \quad (17)$$

The total cutting resistance

$$R_{Px} = k_P \rho_0 \, ib\left[1 + f_0 \, ctg(\gamma_0 + \varphi_0)\right] \quad (18)$$

The lateral cutting resistance of the knife is determined by formulae, similar to those for the cutting resistance from below. Consequently, similar to the above formulae will also be the formulae defining the impact of friction on the total resistance of the knife.

2.2 Forces caused by the weight of the lifting soil strip:

$$\begin{aligned} R'_{Gx} \approx\ & q\delta g k_y r \sin^{-1}\gamma \{ [(\sin\gamma \cos\varepsilon_1 + \cos^2\gamma \sin^{-1}\gamma) e^{f_0 \sin\gamma(\varepsilon_2 - \varepsilon_1)} - \\ & -(\sin\gamma \cos\varepsilon_2 + \cos^2\gamma \sin^{-1}\gamma)]\cos\varepsilon_1 + (\cos\varepsilon_1 e^{f_0 \sin\gamma(\varepsilon_2 - \varepsilon_1)} - \cos\varepsilon_2) * \\ & * (\cos\varepsilon_1 - f_0 \sin\varepsilon_1 \sin\gamma)^{-1} \sin\varepsilon_1 \left[\sin\varepsilon_1 \sin\gamma + f_0(\sin^2\gamma \cos\varepsilon_1 + \cos^2\gamma)\right] \} \end{aligned} \quad (19)$$

$$R_{G_z} \approx q\delta g r \sin^{-1}\gamma \, (\varepsilon_2 - \varepsilon_1) \quad (20)$$

$$R_{Gy} \approx q\delta g r \sin^{-1}\gamma (\varepsilon_2 - \varepsilon_1)(\varepsilon_1 + 0.52) \, ctg\gamma \quad (21)$$

$$R''_{Gx} = f_0 (R_{Gz} + R_{Gy}) = F''_{Gx} \quad (22)$$

2.3. Forces caused by the soil inertia:

$$R'_{Jx} = q\,\delta v^2 k_y^{-1} \sin\gamma \{ (\sin\gamma \cos\varepsilon_1 + \cos^2\gamma \sin^{-1}\gamma) e^{f_0 \sin\gamma(\varepsilon_2-\varepsilon_1)} - $$
$$-(\sin\gamma\cos\varepsilon_2 + \cos^2\gamma \sin^{-1}\gamma) + (\cos\varepsilon_1 - f_0 \sin\varepsilon_1 \sin\gamma)^{-1} e^{f_0 \sin\gamma(\varepsilon_2-\varepsilon_1)} *$$
$$* \sin\varepsilon_1 \left[\sin\varepsilon_1 \sin\gamma + f_0 (\sin^2\gamma \cos\varepsilon_1 + \cos^2\gamma)\right] \} \tag{23}$$

$$R_{Jz} = q\,\delta\, v^2 k_y^{-1} \sin\gamma \sin\varepsilon_2\, e^{f_0 \sin\gamma\,(\varepsilon_2-\varepsilon_1)} \tag{24}$$

$$R_{Jy} \approx q\,\delta\, v^2 k_y^{-1} \sin\gamma \cos\gamma\,(1-\cos\varepsilon_2) \tag{25}$$

$$R''_{Jz} = f_0 (R_{Jz} + R_{Jy}) = F''_{Jx} \tag{26}$$

2.4. Forces caused by soil adhesion:

$$R'_{Ax} = p_A\, b r \sin^{-1}\gamma\,(e^{f_0 \sin\gamma\,(\varepsilon_2-\varepsilon_1)} - 1)\{ \sin\gamma \cos\varepsilon_1 + \cos^2\gamma \sin^{-1}\gamma +$$
$$+ (\cos\varepsilon_1 - f_0 \sin\varepsilon_1 \sin\gamma)^{-1} \sin\varepsilon_1 \left[\sin\varepsilon_1 \sin\gamma + f_0 (\sin^2\gamma \cos\varepsilon_1 + \cos^2\gamma)\right] \} \tag{27}$$

$$R_{Az} = 0 \tag{28}$$

$$R_{Ay} = 0 \tag{29}$$

$$R''_{Ax} = f_0\,(p_{Axy} S_{xy} + p_{Axz} S_{xz}) = F''_{Ax} \tag{30}$$

where: q - the cross section area of the strip to be lifted; δ - the density of soil; k_y - the soil compaction coefficient in front of the operating part; f_0 - the soil friction coefficient against the surface of the operating element; v - the speed of the movement of the plough body; p_A - the specific force of soil adhesion to the operating surface; b - the surface width of the soil strip; ε_1 and ε_2 are correspondingly the initial and the final angles of the lifting (share - mouldboard) surface; γ - the inclination angle of the horizontal generatrix towards the direction of movement (the wall of the furrow); g - acceleration caused by gravity (g = 9.81).

2.5. The draft resistance caused by the ploughs weight Q:

$$R''_{Qx} = Qf_0 \tag{31}$$

The soil friction coefficient and the specific force of soil adhesion are not constant values. Their values decrease with the increase in speed (Vilde, 2001, 2003). This is considered in calculations.

The resistance of the supporting surfaces of the plough body depends on the values of the reacting forces. Yet their value is dependent, in many respects, on the manner of unification and perfection of the hydraulically mounted implements of the tractor. The vertical reaction of the plough with modern tractors having power regulation is transferred to the body of the tractor, and it affects the plough resistance to a considerably lesser degree (Rucins & Vilde; Rucins et al., 2006).

The obtained correlations (1)–(31) allow determination of the forces acting on the plough body and its draft resistance depending on the body parameters, as well as evaluation of their impact on the ploughing efficiency: energy and the fuel consumption and the quality of work. These parameters are: the initial and the final angles of the lifting (share - mouldboard) surface ε_1 and ε_2 ; the inclination angle of the horizontal generatrix towards the direction of movement (the wall of the furrow) γ_i (see Fig. 1) and regularity (law-governed nature) of its variation; the thickness of the share edge i; the radius r of the lifting (share - mouldboard) surface and the area of the lifting and supporting surfaces $2\pi r(\varepsilon_2 - \varepsilon_1)b$, S_{xy} and S_{xz}.

Soil hardness ρ_0 is characterising the resistance to the penetration of the flat round steel tip having a cross-section area of 1 cm^2 depends on its mechanical composition and humidity. As a result of the research it is found out that soil hardness of natural structure, depending on its granulometric composition and humidity, and containing the organic matter from 1.4 to 1.9% of its total mass, as determined by Yu.Yu. Revyakin's hardness gage is subject to the following relationship (Vilde, 2003):

$$\rho_0 = \delta_0 (b'' + d'' m) e^{-l'' W^n} \tag{32}$$

where ρ_0 - soil hardness characterising the resistance to the penetration of the flat round steel tip having a cross-section area of 1 cm^2, N m^{-2}; δ_0 - soil (dried) density, kg m^{-3}; m - the contents of physical clay (particles of the size <0.01 mm, %); W - absolute soil humidity, %; b'', d'' and l'' - coefficients; n - exponent; e =2.718... For the investigation of soil the coefficients and the exponent entered into formula (32) have the following values: b'' = 1100; d'' = 200; l'' = 4.10^{-3} and n = 2.

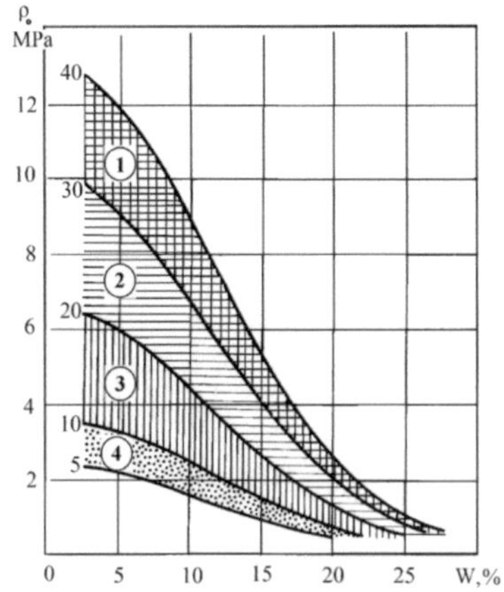

Fig. 2. Dependence of the hardness of soils having different mechanical composition on their humidity: 1 – medium loam; 2 – light loam; 3 – loamy sand; 4 – adhesive sand. The numbers at the soil hardness curves stand for the percentage of the physical clay in the soil. Soil hardness is determined by Yu.Yu. Revyakin's hardness gage having a flat tip with a cross-section area 1 cm^2.

Hardness variations of soils having different mechanical composition that depends on their humidity calculated according to formula (1) is graphically presented in Figure 2.
The graph allows to trace the change of soil hardness of a certain mechanical composition depending on its humidity, and to fix the hardness range of the represented soil types - adhesive sand, loamy soil, light and medium loam.
Soil density δ is dependent on the strata density (the mass of a volume unit of the dried soil) δ_0 and soil humidity W:

$$\delta = \delta_0 (1 + W) \tag{33}$$

Observations indicate that the density of mineral soils may vary in a very wide range: from 700 kg m^{-3} for dry, loose (freshly ploughed) soil to 2200 kg m^{-3} for wet, compact soil, but generally it varies from 1200 to 1800 kg m^{-3}. The resistance of the operating parts of the soil tillage machines varies in proportion to soil density (Vilde, 2001, 2003).
As a rule, all the sources provide sliding resistance coefficients of soil. In order to clarify the nature of the sliding resistance for soil on the working surfaces of the tillage machines, Deryagin's binomial sliding (slipping) resistance formula (Deryagin, 1963) is used as more adequate (Vilde, 2001, 2003):

$$f = f_0 (1 + p_A p^{-1}) \tag{34}$$

where f - the resistance coefficient of soil sliding along a surface; f_0 - the friction coefficient of soil along a surface; p - the specific pressure of the layer (soil) upon the surface; p_A - the specific soil adhesion force to the surface.
In order to determine the coefficient of friction and the specific adhesion depending on sliding speed, the soil sliding resistance is assessed at a speed to 5 m s^{-1} and at several different values of the specific pressure between the sliding surfaces. On the basis of these data, by the method of least squares, is determined the coefficients of friction and specific adhesion force, after that dependencies were deduced between them and the mechanical composition, and humidity of soil (Vilde et al., 2007):

$$f_0 = (a + e^{-[b_1(b_2 - m)]^2}) e^{-b_3 W^2} + (c + dm) e^{-[(k + lm)(t + zm - W)]^2} \tag{35}$$

where a; b_1, b_2, b_3, c, d, k, l, t, z - the indices depending on the type of soil, the material and the condition of the surface of the object along which the soil slides; e = 2.718; W – absolute humidity of soil, %; m – the content of physical clay in soil (the particle size <0.01 mm).
Variations in the specific adhesion force p_A of soil correspond to the relation of the type:

$$p_A = (a' + b'p) + (c' + d'm) e^{-\left[(k' + l'm)(t' + z'm - W)\right]^2} \tag{36}$$

where p_A - the specific pressure of the layer (soil) upon the surface; a ', b' , c ', d' , k' , l' , t' , z'- the indices depending on the type of soil, the material and the condition of the surface along which the soil slides.
As an example, the values of these indices for the polished steel surfaces are:
a = - 0.43; b_1 = 0.007; b_2 = 130; b_3 = 0.1; c = 0.32; d = 0.002; k = 0.05; l = 0.0005; t = 10; z = 0.14;
a′ = 0.2; b′ = 1...2.5; c′ = 0.1; d′ = 0.003; k′ = 0.1; l′= 10^{-4}; t′=15; z′ = 0.2.

The numerical values of the indices in Formulae (35) and (36) for mineral soils and some steel surfaces are determined for a residual soil (ground), the sliding velocity and temperature being close to 0.
Variations of the friction coefficient and the specific force of soil adhesion to steel depending on the humidity and mechanical composition of soil are presented in Figures 3 and 4.

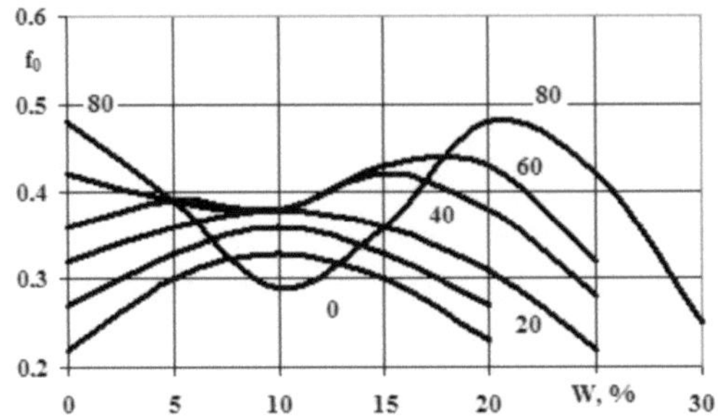

Fig. 3. Variations of the friction coefficient of soils having different mechanical composition along steel depending on the humidity of the soil. The numbers on the curves stand for percentage content of physical clay (particles of the size less than 0.01 mm) in soil.

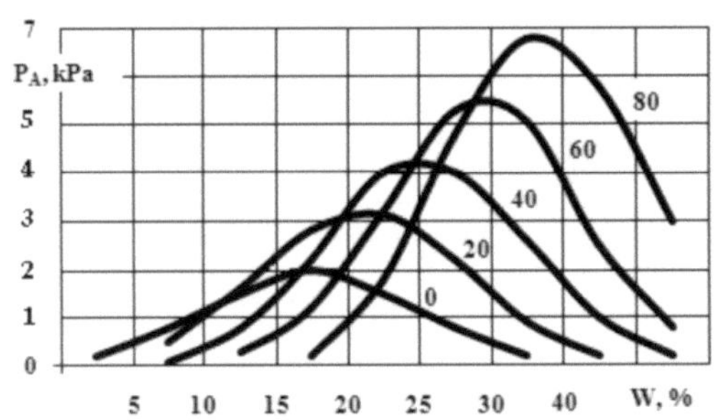

Fig. 4. Variations of the specific adhesion force of soils having different mechanical composition along steel depending on the humidity of soil at the pressure of 100 kPa. The numbers on the curves stand for percentage content of physical clay (particles of the size less than 0.01 mm) in soil.

Further, as it was mentioned above, the soil sliding resistance along steel depends on the sliding speed, the structure of soil, the humus content and the surface temperature. The effect of these parameters may be considered by respective coefficients. In view of this we can write:

$$f_0' = f_0 k_v k_{st} k_h k_t \tag{37}$$

$$p_A' = p_A k_v' k_{st}' k_h' k_t' \tag{38}$$

where f'_0 and p'_A - the coefficients of sliding resistance and specific adhesion force of soil to steel at a certain speed of sliding, structure, humus content in soil, and temperature; f_0 and p_A - the coefficients of sliding resistance and specific adhesion force to steel of residual soil not containing humus at a temperature, close to 0 °C; k_v and k_v' - the coefficients of velocity; k_{st} and k'_{st} - the coefficients of the soil structurality; k_h and k'_h - the coefficients of the humus content; k_t and k'_t - the temperature coefficients.

There are decoded some of these coefficients. For example, the coefficients of velocity k_v and k'_v are (Vilde, 2003):

$$k_v = k_{vmrg}\left[1 + a(1 + bv^n)^{-1}\right] \tag{39}$$

$$k_v' = k_{vmrg}'\left[1 + a'(1 + b'v^{n'})^{-1}\right] \tag{40}$$

where k_{vmrg} and k'_{vmrg} - the marginal value of the velocity coefficient; v - the speed of sliding, m s^{-1}; a, a' and b, b' - indices; n and n' - exponents of indices.

It is highly probable that the marginal value of the velocity coefficient depends on the mechanical composition and humidity of soil yet the data to prove this are presently absent.

The parameters entering Formulae (39) and (40) that are calculated on the basis of experimental data by M.I. Bredun have the following values for wet soil with distinctly pronounced adhesion: k_{vmrg}= 0.66; $k_v'_{mrg}$ = 0.2; a = 0.52; a'= 4; b = 0.50; b'= 1; n = 2; n'= 2. (Bredun, 1964).

Variations of the coefficients indicating the influence of the speed of sliding for the given type of soil are shown in Figure 5.

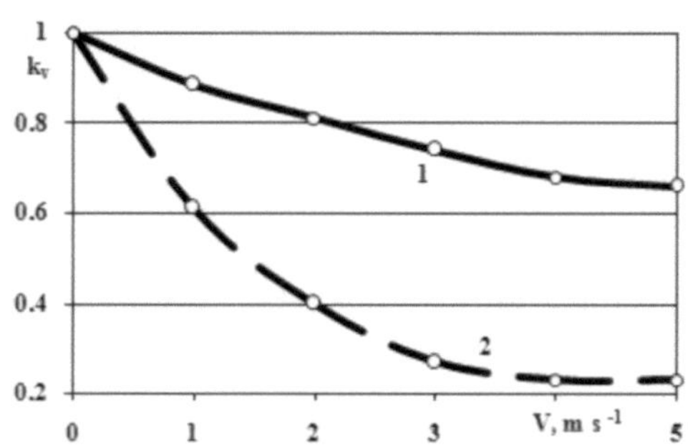

Fig. 5. Variations of the coefficients indicating the influence of the speed of sliding upon the coefficient of friction and specific adhesion for wet soil. 1 – variations of coefficient k_v; 2 – variations of coefficient k'_v.

There is insufficient amount of data for deriving mathematical dependencies characterising the influence of temperature upon the friction coefficient of soil along steel. When temperature rises the specific adhesion force of soil to steel decreases forming a parabolic curve that on the basis of the data provided by H.G. Riek (Riek & Vorkal, 1965) described by the following relation:

$$p_A = p_{A_0}(1 - 10^{-4}t^{-2}) \tag{41}$$

where p_{A_0} - the specific adhesion force to steel at a temperature, close to 0°C; t - the temperature of adhesive surfaces, °C.

There are no data either to deduce dependencies of the influence between the structure and the humus content upon the soil sliding resistance along steel. According to the data by H.G. Riek, if for a wet residual (paste-like) soil the coefficient of structurality k'_{st} is accepted as being 1, for a structured soil it will be 0.75...0.80.

The optimum humidity of soil at which the draft resistance will be minimal is determined by equating the first derivative its function to zero:

$$dR_x(dW)^{-1} = 0 \tag{42}$$

Because of the complexity of this equation in its full view, partial decisions can be used, and the optimum humidity of soil can be determined from the variables of the partial resistance depending on the humidity of soil, its mechanical structure, and the speed of work of the plough.

3. Results

The materials of the calculations carried out using the correlations indicated above present the values and regularity of the changes in the forces acting on the share-mouldboard and the supporting surfaces, the draft resistance of the share-mouldboard and the supporting surfaces, as well as the total resistance of the plough body and its components under working conditions depending on the body parameters, soil properties and the working speed. Possibilities to reduce the tillage energy requirement have been clarified.

3.1 Simulation of the Impact of the Plough Body Parameters on the Ploughing Resistance

The presented work discusses, as an example, the theoretical research results of the forces acting on the plough body and the specific draft resistance at various angles γ of the horizontal generatrices and at various values of initial lifting angle ε_1 of the plough body (at the angle between the horizontal generatrix of the operating surface and the vertical longitudinal plane γ=40°) depending on the speed of operation, as well as at various its working width when ploughing loamy soils that predominate in Latvia. The calculations were carried out with the computer according to the foregoing formulaes.

As an example, the following values of the basic factors were taken into consideration, which affect the resistance of the share-mouldboard surface and the plough body.

Parameters of the plough body:

Thickness of the share blade and knife	$i = 0.004$ m
Working width of the share	$b_s = 0.35$ m
The initial angle of the lifting strip of soil	$\varepsilon_1 = 20°\text{-}40°$
The final angle of the lifting strip of soil	$\varepsilon_2 = 100°$
The angle between the horizontal generatrix of the operating surface and the vertical longitudinal plane	$\gamma = 15°\ldots90°$
The radius of the curvature of the lifting surface	$r = 0.5$ m
The area of the lower supporting surface	$S_{xy} = 0.0157$ m^2

The area of the lateral supporting surface $S_{xz} = 0.068\ m^2$
The weight on the plough body $Q = 200\ kg$
Physical and mechanical properties of soil:
The hardness of soil $\rho = 4.1\ MPa$
The density of soil $\delta = 1600\ kg\ m^{-3}$
The coefficient of soil friction against the surface of the operating element $f_0 = 0.4$
The adhesion force $p_{A0} = 2.5\ kPa$
The mode and status of work:
The body working width 0.30...0.50 m
The ploughing depth $a = 0.20\ m$
The cross section area of the lifted soil strip $q = 0.06...1.00\ m^2$
The soil compaction coefficient in front of the operating part $k_y = 1.1$
The working speed $v = 1...5\ m\ s^{-1}$

The inclination angle γ of the horizontal generatrix of the real share-mouldboard surfaces of plough bodies lies between 26°...50°. Steeper surfaces (γ > 50°) refer to the slanting blades of bulldozers.

The calculation results of the draft resistance of the lifting surface, of supporting surfaces and of plough body in total depending on the inclination angle γ of the horizontal generatrix and speed v (ε_1 = 30°) are presented in Fig. 6 – 8, those values depending on initial lifting angle – in Fig. 9 – 11.

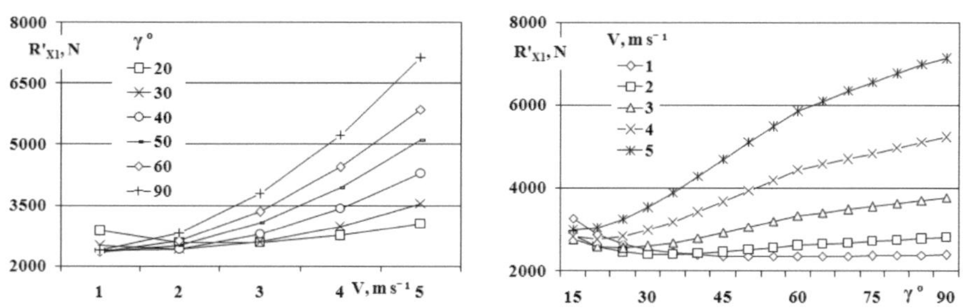

Fig. 6. Total draft resistance of the share-mouldboard surface caused by soil gravity, inertia forces, adhesion and share cutting resistance depending on speed v and the inclination angle γ of the horizontal generatrix.

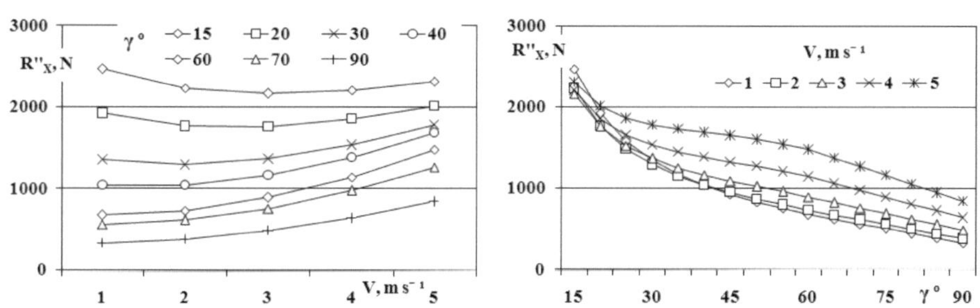

Fig. 7. Total draft resistance of the supporting surfaces depending on speed v and the inclination angle γ of the horizontal generatrix.

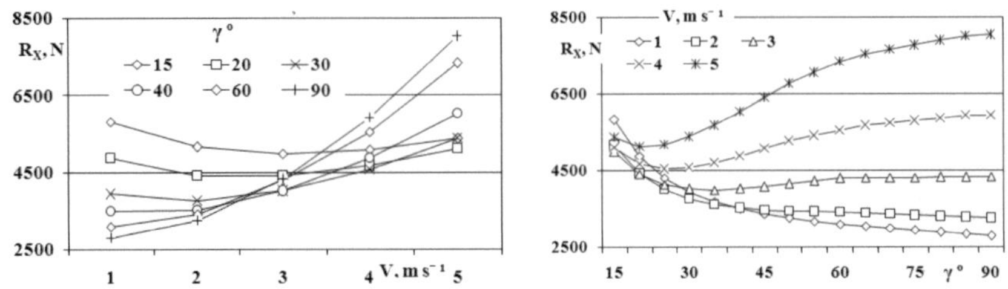

Fig. 8. Total draft resistance of the plough body depending on speed v and the inclination angle γ of the horizontal generatrix.

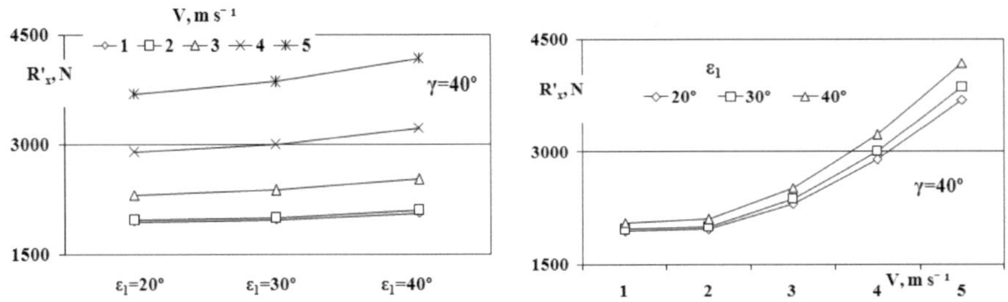

Fig. 9. Total draft resistance of the lifting surface caused by soil gravity, inertia forces and adhesion depending on the initial lifting angle ε_1 and speed v.

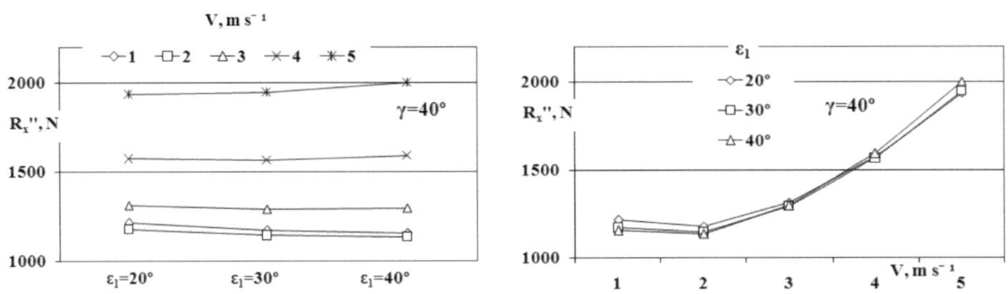

Fig. 10. Summary draft resistance of the plough body supporting surfaces depending on the initial lifting angle ε_1 of the soil strip and speed v.

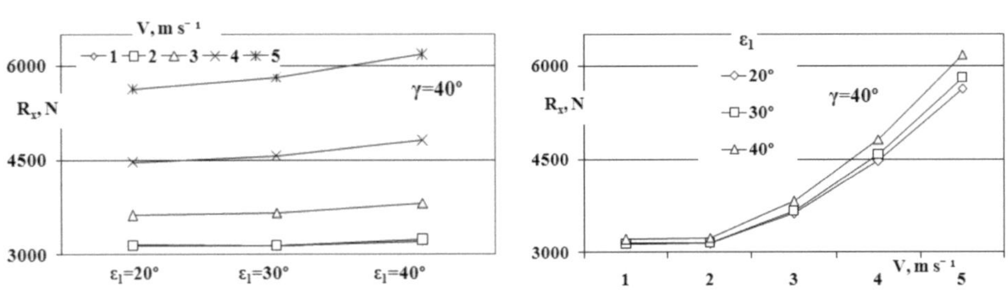

Fig. 11. Total draft resistance of the plough body depending on the initial lifting angle ε_1 of the soil strip and speed v.

Further the presented work discusses too, as an example, the research results of the forces acting on the plough body and the specific draft resistance of the plough body at various its working width when ploughing loamy soils that predominate in Latvia.
The calculation results of the specific draft resistance of the plough body and its components are presented in Fig. 12 –15 and Table 1.

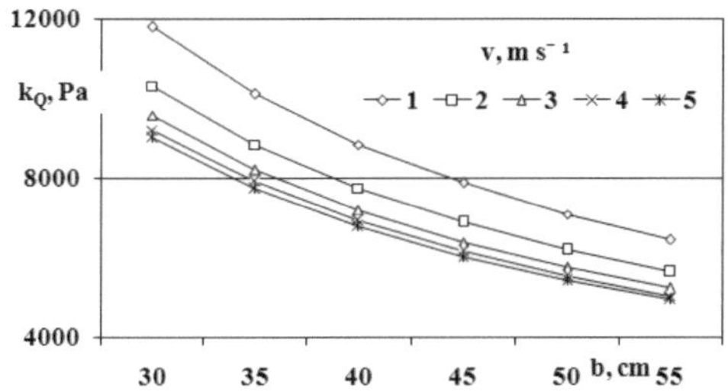

Fig. 12. The specific draft resistance k_Q of the plough body caused by its weight Q depending on the body working width b at various speeds v.

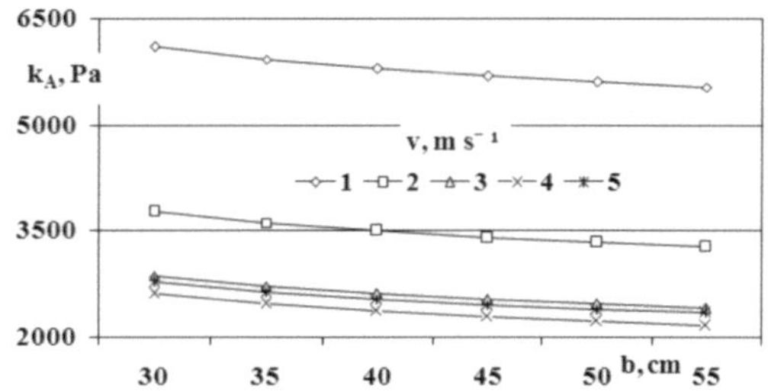

Fig. 13. The specific draft resistance k_A of the plough body caused by soil adhesion depending on the body working width b at various speed v.

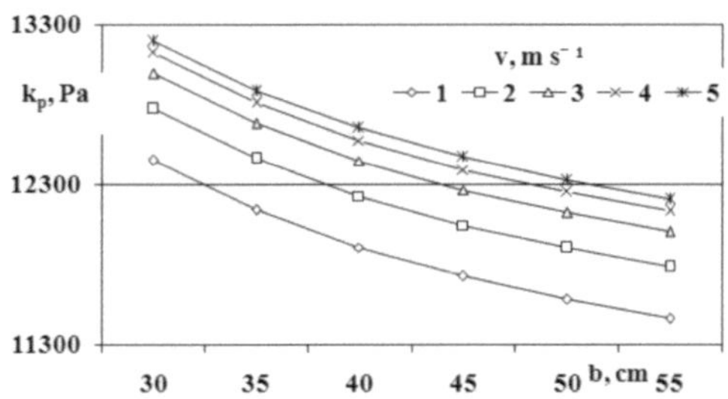

Fig. 14. The specific draft resistance of the plough body k_P caused by cutting resistance R_{Px} depending on the body working width b at various speed v.

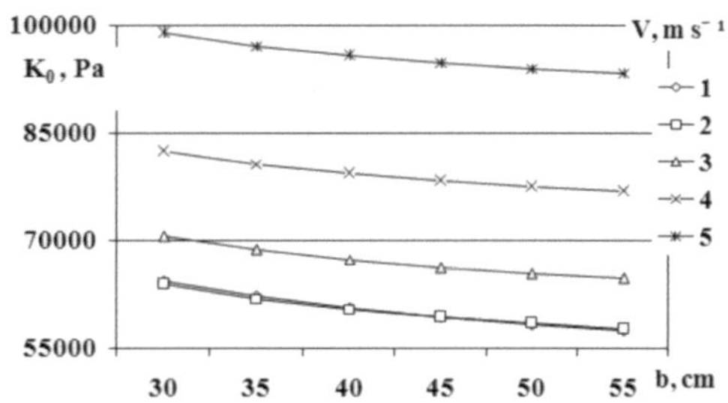

Fig. 15. Total specific draft resistance of the plough body K_0 depending on the body working width b by various speed v.

v, m s^{-1}	1	2	3	4	5
k_G, Pa	31616	28575	27100	26390	26013
k_J, Pa	2311	8386	17933	31080	47897
k_G+k_J, Pa	33928	36962	45034	57471	73911

Table 1. Specific draft resistance caused by soil weight k_G and inertia forces k_J.

Experimental studies are carried out on the "Kverneland Vary Width" plough, having bodies working width from 30 cm to 50 cm. Results are shown in graph (Figure 16).
The graph (Fig. 16.) shows how the specific draft resistance and energy consumption in ploughing depends on the working width of each body. Increasing it the energy capacity and specific fuel consumption in ploughing decreases by 10-16%. The greater is the

ploughing depth, the greater is the effect due to the increased working width of the body. This phenomenon is caused by more high soil hardness and density of deeper soil layers.

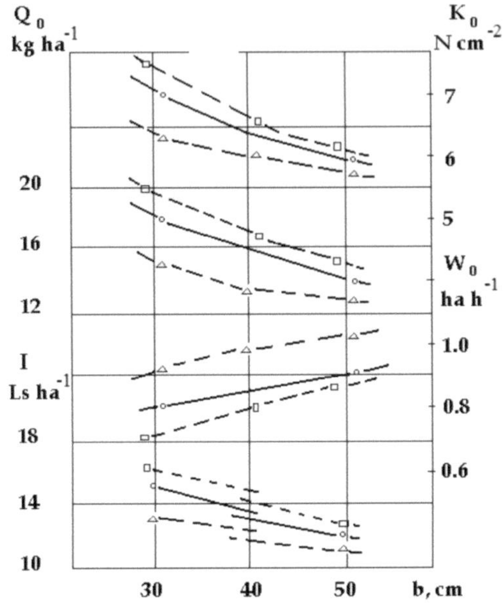

Fig. 16. Variations of energetic and economic characteristics of the Kverneland AB-85 plough with semihelicoidal bodies No 8 depending on the body width in ploughing grassland on a loamy soil at the speed 8.7-9 km h^{-1}: b - the body width, cm; K_0 - the specific draft resistance, N cm^{-2}; Q_0 - the specific fuel consumption, kg ha^{-1}; W_0 - the direct labour productivity, ha h^{-1}; I - ploughing costs Ls ha^{-1} (1 Ls = 1.42 EUR).- -□ - - the ploughing depth of 24 cm; ---o--- the ploughing depth of 22 cm; -- Δ-- the ploughing depth of 19 cm.

In loamy soil increase in the working width of the bodies at the ploughing depth of 18…19 cm decreases the specific fuel consumption by 2…3 kg ha^{-1} but at the depth of 24 cm by 4…5 kg ha^{-1}. Correspondingly, there is a rise in labour efficiency, and the ploughing costs fall by 2…4 Ls ha^{-1}. (2.84…5.68 EUR ha^{-1}). Therefore, when ploughs are used that have a possibility to vary the working width, it is recommended to work at the maximum width and, if necessary (insufficient power of the tractor), to reduced the number of bodies.
Thus, for example, in the aggregate with the MTZ-82 tractor it is more purposeful to work with the Kverneland AB-85 two-body plough with the working width of each body 50 cm (the total width 1 m) than with three bodies having the width of 33 cm each and the same working width.
The obtained materials show that by increasing the initial lifting angle ε_1 (inclination angle of share toward furrow bottom) the draft resistance increases. For economical ploughing the initial lifting angle of the soil slice (the angle between share and furrow bottom) must have a minimal value - 24°…30°. The smallest inclination angle is not desirable because by wear out of the share there is a possibility at the blunt (threadbare) ploughshare to obtain a rear bevel which can hinder the plough body from going into soil. This phenomenon is observed with the Kverneland plough bodies No. 8 having a 20° inclination angle of their outer part.

More complicated is the impact of the inclination angle γ of the horizontal generatrix. Depending on the working speed the change of its value can impact the value of the draft resistance positively or negatively, that is, to decrease or increase the draft resistance. When the inclination (angle γ) of the generatrix is increased, the resistances, because of the soil weight and adhesion, fall but the resistance due to the inertia forces increases, particularly when operating at higher speeds. The decrease of the first ones can be explained by the fact that its length decreases at a steeper share-mouldboard surface, and, because of this, there is a decrease in the mass of soil sliding along it. Decreasing the area of its surface leads to a lower resistance due to soil adhesion. As a result, the total draft resistance of the share-mouldboard surface shows a marked minimum, which, at a greater operating speed, moves towards lower inclination values of the horizontal generatrix. Thus, if the speed increases, the optimum inclination value of the horizontal generatrix for the minimum draft resistance decreases. In loamy soils, at the initial lifting angle ε_1 =30°, when the operating speed is 1…3 m s^{-1}, its optimum value for the share-mouldboard surface on its initial part is correspondingly 40°…25°, for the plough body, as a whole, they can be 65°…33° (if working in a floating mode). When the vertical reaction of the plough (or part of it) with modern tractors having power regulation is transferred to the body of the tractor, the optimal inclination value of the horizontal generatrix obtains medium indices – approximately 50°…30°. At contemporary ploughing speeds 2…2.5 m s^{-1} (7…9 km h^{-1}) the optimal inclination of the horizontal generatrix on the initial part of the share-mouldboard surface is 38°…34°. To ensure sufficient turning of the slice, the angle of the top generatrix must not be less than 48° (Rucins & Vilde, 2006).

If radius r of the mouldboard increases, the draft resistance of the body increases, which is connected with increased partial resistance caused by the weight and adhesion of the soil. For general- purpose ploughs its value varies within the range of 0.5 m.

The working width of the body influences its draft resistance too. If the working width of the body is increased from 30 cm to 50 cm (at constant frontal width of the share), the specific consumption of energy, fuel and the ploughing costs decrease (in loamy soil by 10…16%) but labour efficiency correspondingly increases (Rucins & Vilde, 2005b).

The cutting resistance is proportional to the thickness of the share edge. To obtain a low value of the cutting resistance, its value must be minimal – 2…3 mm. In the ploughing process the share wears out and the thickness of its edge increases to 5 mm, and more. This causes increased draft resistance, especially in hard (dry loamy) soils. Therefore self-sharpening shares are better which do not lose their sharpness in ploughing process.

The conducted investigations show that those ploughs generally meet the requirements mentioned above which have bodies with gently sloping semi-helicoidal or helicoidal share-mouldboard surfaces, such as, the Kverneland plough body No. 8.

There may be cases (at quite a flat share-mouldboard surface) when the draft resistance in wet loamy soils does not increase but even decreases whereas its speed increases (within the range of 1…2 m s^{-1}). Such a phenomenon may occur when the decrease in resistance, due to the lower friction coefficient and specific soil adhesion, proceeds more intensely than the growth in the resistance caused by the soil inertia forces within the given range of speeds.

In such a way, the deduced analytical correlations and the developed computer algorithm enable simulation of the soil coercion forces upon the share-mouldboard surface of the plough body, taking into consideration its draft resistance, as well as determination of the optimum parameters at minimum resistance.

3.2 Simulation Impact of Soil Friction on the Ploughing Resistance

As an example, the calculation results of the impact of the soil friction coefficient f_0 upon the draft resistance of the plough body share-mouldboard (lifting) surface, as well as reacting forces on the supporting surfaces, the draft resistance and the total draft resistance of the entire plough body at the inclination angle $\varepsilon_1 = 30°$ of the share (initial soil slice lifting angle), at the inclination angle $\gamma = 30°...50°$ of the horizontal generatrix and at various speeds v are presented in the following graphs.

The draft resistance of the lifting (share-mouldboard) surface is presented in Fig. 17, the draft resistances of the supporting surfaces - in Figs. 18 and 19, and the total draft resistance of the plough body – in Fig. 19.

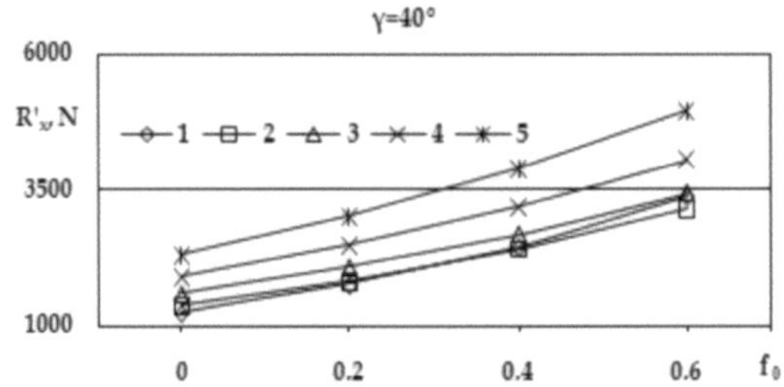

Fig. 17. Impact of the soil friction coefficient f_0 upon the total draft resistance of the plough body share-mouldboard surface caused by the soil gravity, the inertia forces, adhesion and soil cutting resistance at the inclination angle of the horizontal generatrix: $\gamma = 40°$.

From the graphs (Fig. 17) it follows that at the soil friction coefficient $f_0 = 0.3...0.4$ and at the speed $v=2...3$ m s^{-1}, presently predominating-in ploughing, the draft resistance caused by friction takes 36…42% of the total draft resistance of the share-mouldboard surface.

The graph (Fig. 18 a) shows that at the values of the friction coefficient $f_0 = 0.3...0.4$ the lateral reaction caused by the soil cutting decreases on 36…55 %.

It follows from the graphs below (Fig. 18 b) that the increase in speed increases the draft resistance of the supporting surfaces caused by soil friction. The value of the inclination angle of the horizontal genetratrix γ at the interval $\gamma = 35°...45°$ has only a little influence on the draft resistance of the supporting surfaces.

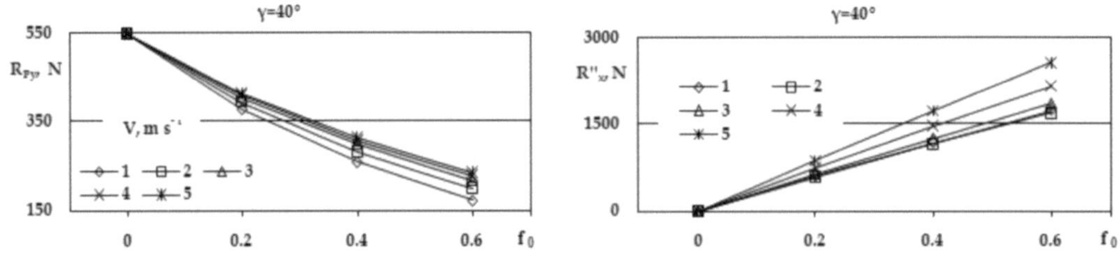

Fig. 18. a - Impact of the soil friction coefficient f_0 upon the lateral reaction caused by the soil cutting with the plough share at the inclination angle of the cutting edge $\gamma_0 = 40°$. b - impact of the soil friction coefficient f_0 upon the draft resistance of the supporting surfaces of the plough body at the inclination of the horizontal generatrix $\gamma = 40°$.

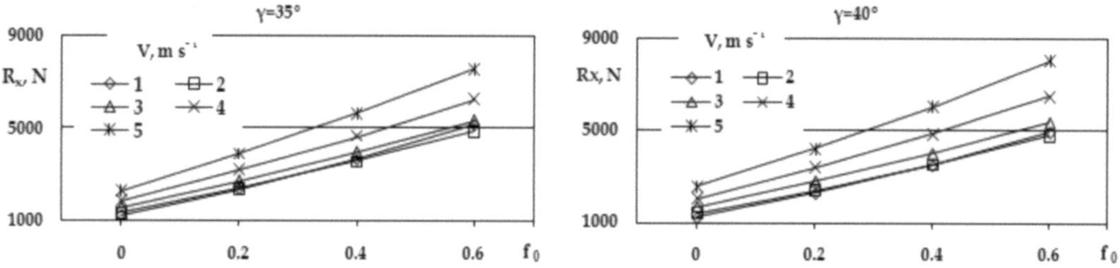

a b

Fig. 19. Impact of the soil friction coefficient f_0 upon the total draft resistance of the plough body at the inclination angle of the horizontal generatrix: a - γ =35°; b - γ = 40°.

It follows from the graphs above (Fig. 19) that at the values of the friction coefficient f_0 = 0.3...0.4 the draft resistance caused by the soil friction takes 46…62 % of the total draft resistance of the plough body. It follows that the total draft resistance is approximately proportional to the friction coefficient. Increasing the speed decreases the share (ratio λ_F) of the friction resistance in the total draft resistance of the plough body. This phenomenon can be explained by the decreasing value of the friction coefficient when the speed is increasing (Vilde et al., 2007).

From the graphs (Fig. 19) it is evident too that at the values of the friction coefficient f_0 = 0.3...0.4 increasing the inclination angle of the horizontal genetratrix γ in the interval γ = 35°…40° increases the draft resistance of the plough body. This phenomenon is in agreement with the previous conclusions that the optimal values for the inclination angle of the horizontal genetratrix γ on the initial part of the share-mouldboard surface are 34…38° (Rucins & Vilde, 2007).

It follows from formulas (19)-(27) too, that increasing the initial lifting angle ε_1 increases the draft resistance of the share-mouldboard surface, including the resistance of the soil friction (Rucins at al., 2007), but increasing the working width of the body decreases the specific draft resistance of ploughing (Rucins & Vilde, 2005b). It was established from them that the optimal values of the initial lifting angle are ε_1 = 28°...32° and the optimal working width of the plough body – b = 45...50 cm.

From the presented example it is evident that the draft resistance of the supporting surfaces is considerable. It can reach 25…30 % of the total plough body draft resistance, or 36…44 % of its share-mouldboard draft resistance.

Therefore it is very important for the reduction of the energy consumption of ploughing to reduce the draft resistance of the supporting surfaces. It may be obtained by using a contemporary hang-up device with the tractors, for example, power regulation allowing the transfer of the vertical reactions of the plough to the body of the tractor (Vilde et al., 2004). It may decrease the draft resistance of the ploughs to 6…10%.

3.3 Simulation Impact of Soil Humidity on the Ploughing Resistance

The methods and equations given above allow studying the regularities of the ploughing draft resistance depending on the humidity of soil, its mechanical composition, the plough body parameters, and its working speed. As an example, comparative studies for simulation the impact of the soil humidity on the ploughing resistance have been made with ploughs having semi-helicoidal bodies with the main parameters given before. Further there is

showed results of simulation impact of the soil humidity on the ploughing resistance for the body with working width 0.45 m.
The indices of some soil properties used in the calculations are given in Table 2.

Type of soil	Content of physical clay m, %	Humidity w, %	Density δ, кg m^{-3}	Coefficient of friction f_0	Specific force of adhesion p_A, Pa	Hardness ρ_0, MPa
Loamy sand	10	5	1260	0.34	600	3.4
		10	1320	0.36	1600	2.5
		15	1380	0.33	2500	1.6
		20	1440	0.27	2300	0.8
Clay	40	5	1575	0.40	200	12.0
		10	1650	0.38	800	8.9
		15	1725	0.41	2200	5.2
		20	1800	0.37	4000	2.8
		25	1875	0.27	4000	1.2
Clay dark chestnut (temno-kashtanovaya) (Mogilnij, 1957)	63	5	1520	0.64	0	11.0
		10	1595	0.45	200	9.0
		15	1670	0.30	1100	6.5
		20	1740	0.30	3150	4.3
		25	1810	0.42	5400	2.0
		30	1875	0.62	5100	1.0

Table 2. The indices of some soil properties used in calculations

The draft resistance of the plough body and its elements depending on the soil humidity at various working speeds and soil types is shown by the following graphs (Fig. 20).
The graphs above show that variations in the soil humidity have lesser impact on the plough body resistance on the light sandy-loam soils, but a considerable impact – on the clay soils. The clay soils show minima of the resistance at humidity - 18…25%. Such a change of the ploughing resistance depending on the soil humidity is obtained also in the investigations by other researchers, for example, P. U. Bahtin, I. P. Mogilnij a.o. (Bahtin, 1960, pp. 250-259; Mogilnij, 1957, pp. 473-479).
The correlations obtained allow assessment of the ploughing resistance depending on the soil humidity, mechanical composition and the working speed of the plough, determination of the optimal soil humidity range when the tillage capacity is the lowest. Humidity most of all impacts the soil hardness and cutting resistance which considerably dominates in the summary resistance of the plough body. An increase in the soil humidity leads to a decrease in the ploughing resistance that is more remarkable on the clay soils.

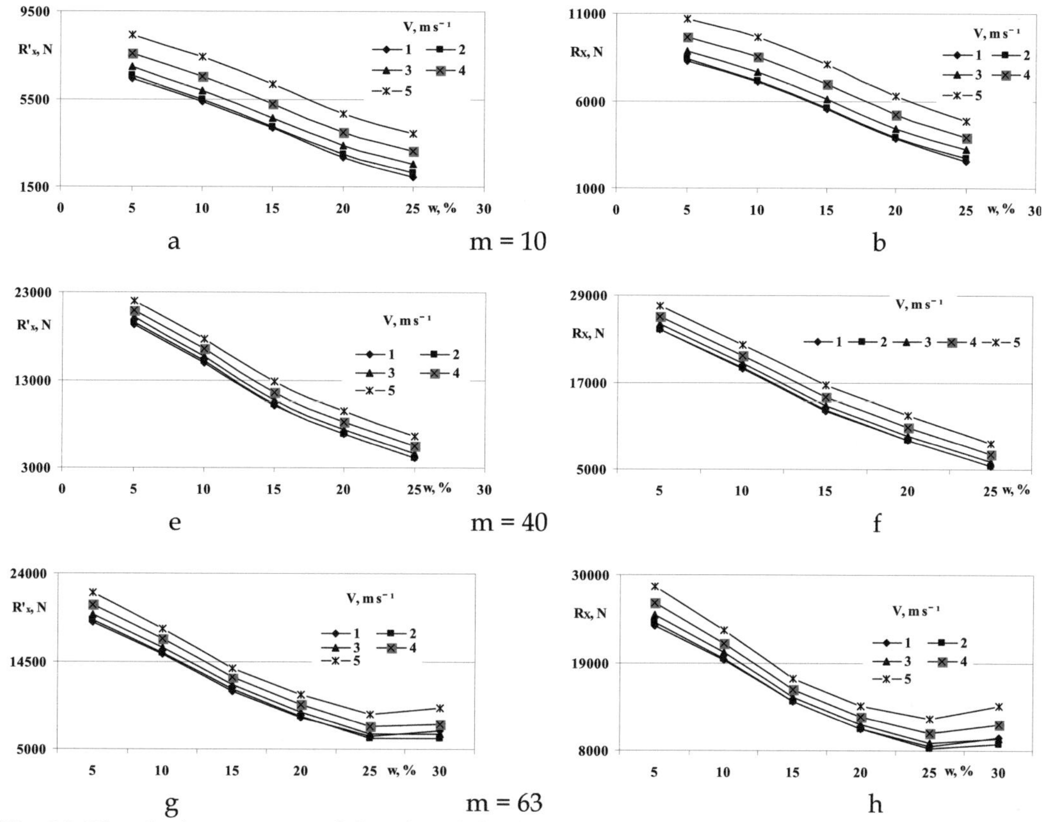

Fig. 20. The draft resistance of the plough body depending on the soil humidity of some soil types and speeds at γ = 40°: a, c, e, – the resistance of the share-mouldboard surface; b, d, f, – the total draft resistance.

4. Discussion

The research material presented by other authors (Vagin, 1965, 1967; Zelenin, 1968; Sineokov & Panov, 1977; Gill & Vanden Berg, 1967) includes analytical correlations for the determination of separate components of draft resistance (caused by the forces of gravity, inertia, soil deformation) fit for simple two-sided and three-sided wedges. However, there are no analytical dependencies for the determination of the draft resistance of curved and complicated wedges (share-mouldboard surfaces). Publications in the theory of share-mouldboard surfaces and determination of the resistance to soil sliding along them (Gyachev, 1961; Goryachkin, 1968; Donner & Nichols, 1934; Gill & Vanden Berg, 1967) are chiefly of general theoretical character and are little significance for practical calculations and clarification of optimum parameters of operating parts. Even the most outstanding scientists in the field of soil tillage machines recognise that "at the present stage of the plough theory the forces of soil resistance arising due to the impact of soil upon the plough bodies cannot be determined through calculations" (Sineokov & Panov,1977, p. 137).

The draft resistance of the operating parts with curved operating surfaces is determined exclusively in an experimental way. In order to clarify the design and adjustment parameters of the operating parts, their physical modelling (simulation) and comparative studies are carried out under various conditions, which is connected with great losses of labour, finances and time; however, not always the best solutions among those compared are optimum ones. Introduction of powerful tractors and subsequent increasing the working speeds need further improvement of the design of soil tillage machines and optimisation of their parameters in accordance with the new conditions and requirements of work. Yet this is hampered by the absence of a reliable theoretical basis, which leads to a delay in the development of the designs of operating parts of soil tillage machines and their disagreement with contemporary requirements.

In the sources provided by other authors there are no materials about the application of the simulation methods in order to study the impact of the plough body parameters, as well as the soil friction properties on the draft resistance of the plough bodies. In order to obtain a better design of the plough body, a series of different bodies were built and tested (Larsen, 1968; Burchenko et al., 1976; Burchenko, 2001; Nikiforov & Ivanov, 1973). Yet it is bound with a great loss of resources, labour and time, so the best solution of the compared variants may not always be the optimum ones.

The materials of our investigations carried out by using the correlations indicated above present the values and regularity of the changes in the forces, the soil friction, acting on the share-mouldboard and the supporting surfaces, the draft resistance of the share-mouldboard and the supporting surfaces, as well as the total resistance of the plough body and its components under the working conditions depending on the body parameters, the soil friction coefficient and the working speed. In such a way it is possible to discover the draft resistance structure of the body, to assess the ratio of each element in the total resistance, to search and find possibilities how to reduce the tillage energy requirement.

On this background special attention should be centred on methods of theoretical estimation of the technological impact upon soil and the draft resistance of the operating parts of the machine as a function of their design parameters under particular conditions of work even if these methods are merely approximate. They enable more profoundly substantiated calculation of machine designs and finding optimum parameters of the operating parts that would ensure qualitative soil tillage with minimum losses of energy resulting in higher yields of the cultivated crops, reduced losses of labour and financial means, i.e., higher efficiency of agricultural production.

To succeed in solving the fixed tasks a new complex approach was needed in order to conduct investigations which consists in the review of a design and parameters of operating parts and machines in close connection with the technological process performed by them, natural and production conditions, modes of work and energetic resources. On the basis of observations we carried out theoretical research applying the relationships of theoretical mechanics (the d'Alembert principle, the Eulerian theorem) to reveal the correlations and mathematical dependencies among phenomena, material destruction, analytical geometry and mathematical analysis. After that the agreement between the calculated and experimental data was proved under laboratory and field conditions. Such an approach allowed working out general propositions concerning the course of the technological process of soil tillage. The methods of mechanics and mathematics applied for its description allowed to state the impact of forces of soil upon the operating parts and their elements, to substantiate rational solution of their design, optimise their parameters, as well as the principal parameters of soil tillage machines and aggregates.

Representation of the total draft resistance of the working part as the sum of partial resistances (resistance to the penetration of the edge into soil, resistance to its deformation, gravity and inertia forces, forces of friction) can also be found in the works by other researchers (Vagin, 1965, 1967; Sineokov & Panov, 1977). However, in contrast to them, there is a different approach in our paper to the division of the total resistance into components (a separate treatment is given to the resistance caused by soil adhesion, attention is paid to the force acting from the adjacent zone of the operating surface, the forces of friction are discussed together with the forces that cause the previous ones, there is considered the impact of other components upon the resistance to soil adhesion). This ensured a possibility to analyse more profoundly and thoroughly the change of each component of the working parts parameters and operating conditions, to determine their influence on the variations in the total resistance and clarify the ways and prospects of their minimisation.

Such a methodical approach allowed deduce generalised analytical correlations that characterise the impact of forces of soil upon the operating parts of soil tillage machines and their elements, to reveal the essence of processes going on in soil tillage, to state the principal factors which influence the resistance of the operating parts. The obtained analytical dependencies of the draft resistance of the wedge and the operating parts are confirmed by experimental data. They do not contradict the well-known relationships and data provided by other researchers, yet in a number of cases they treat in a different way the phenomena that occur during soil tillage and their impact on draft resistance.

So, for instance, in comparison with the Goryachkin rational formula of draft force, the expressions of draft resistance deduced by the author of this paper are more complete since they allow to determine the draft resistance of the machine (plough body) depending on their design and adjustment parameters, physical and mechanical properties of soil, the speed of movement and working conditions. V.P. Goryachkin held the view that the value of the second term in his formula which is proportional to the area of the cross section of the lifted slice of soil is dependent on the resistance to soil deformation but the impact of soil gravity upon the draft resistance of the plough is insignificant and can be ignored (Goryachkin, 1968).

In contrast to this, we found out that the value of the second term depends mainly on the weight of the lifted slice of soil which is actually proportional to the area of its cross section but the resistance caused by soil deformation, especially in soft soils, is insignificant and can be neglected.

Our studies and the obtained expressions of the specific draft resistance confirm V.V.Katsygin's suggestion proposed by analogy with hydrodynamics about the technological pressure of the strip of soil (Katsygin, 1964) although for its definition he presents dependencies of quite different character. According to our studies, the value of the first component of the technological pressure - static pressure - depends on the weight of the slice (column) of soil which is supported by the operating surface of the working part (plough body), and the pressure from the side of soil during the penetration of it in soil. The value of the second component - the dynamic pressure - is defined by the changing amount of motion (kinetic energy) of the slice of soil along the operating surface.

Consequently, the technological pressure of the slice of soil both by the essence of the phenomenon and the form and contents of expressions for their definition is similar to analogous expressions known in hydrodynamics.
The most rational one is such a design of operating parts that ensures qualitative realisation of the technological process with minimum losses of energy, i.e., having minimum specific resistance. It may be related to a unit of the area of the cross section of the of soil slice - K_0, or to a unit of the working width of the machine – K_1 (Vilde, 1999).
In an expanded form the specific resistance written in accordance with the Goryachkin formula of the draft force (Goryachkin, 1968):

$$R_x = f_0 Q + kaB + \varepsilon aBv^2 \tag{43}$$

may be presented by the expression

$$K_0 = R_{Qx} q^{-1} + (R_{Px} + R_{Gx} + R_{Dx} + R_{Ax}) q^{-1} + R_{Jx} q^{-1} \tag{44}$$

$$K_0 = k_Q + k + \varepsilon v^2 \tag{45}$$

where k and ε are resistance coefficients determined in the Goryachkin formula (43) only in an experimental way but in formulaes (44) and (45) offered by us – through theoretical calculations; k_Q - the component of specific resistance caused by the proper weight of the machine; B - the working width of the machine; a - the depth of soil cultivation.
The sum of the last two terms in formula (45) defines the technological pressure p_0 of the strip mentioned by V.V. Katsygin (Katsygin 1977):

$$p_0 = k + \varepsilon v^2 \tag{46}$$

In the last expression k is static pressure and εv^2 the dynamic pressure of the soil slice.
Formulas (1) to (45) offered by us allow to determine through calculation the total resistance of a soil tilling machine or an operating part, as well as its components. They allow also calculating the specific resistance and coefficients of its components k_Q, k and ε:
In a general way

$$k = (R_{Px} + R_{Gx} + R_{Dx} + R_{Ax}) q^{-1} \tag{47}$$

$$k_Q = R_{Qx} q^{-1} \tag{48}$$

$$\varepsilon = R_{Jx} q^{-1} v^{-2} \tag{49}$$

The representation of draft resistance in the form of three components obstructs their experimental determination. Therefore we have proposed a two-term formula of draft resistance according to which the total draft resistance of the machine is defined as a static resistance that does not directly depend on the working speed, and a dynamic resistance the value of which is related to the working speed. In this case the specific draft resistance is presented by the expression.

$$K_0 = k' + \varepsilon v^2 \tag{50}$$

where k′ - the coefficient of static resistance; ε – the coefficient of dynamic resistance.

$$k' = k_Q + k \tag{51}$$

In a similar way the specific resistance related to a unit of the working width is expressed:

$$K_1 = R_x B^{-1} \tag{52}$$

$$K_1 = k'_1 + \varepsilon_1 v^2 \tag{53}$$

where k'_1 - the static resistance of the machine related to a unit of the working width; ε_1 - the coefficient of the dynamic resistance of the machine related to a unit of the working width.
The propositions worked out, the presented methods and research materials allow a new, scientific approach to the development of more rational designs of soil tillage machines, to the improvement of the existing designs and methods of their application.
On the basis of this theoretical research methodology is worked out how at experimental tests to determinate energetic characteristics of the soil tillage machines including ploughs obtaining their coefficients of static and dynamic resistance for compare their (Vilde, 1998).
The existing data allow to draw only some of the relationships linking the frictional properties of soil (the sliding friction coefficient and the specific adhesion force) with individual parameters of its physical condition (mechanical composition and humidity) and the conditions of the sliding process (the speed of sliding and the surface temperature). In order to specify the numerical values of the coefficients and exponents entering the relationships deduced and to arrive at more generalised regularities, it is necessary to carry out a series of complex studies of the frictional properties of various soils under different conditions. A principal diagram has been worked out for such studies in the Baltic region.
Such an all-round investigation of the frictional properties of soil is a highly labour-consuming process. Thus, in order to search out the sliding resistance of mineral soils along steel under various conditions, it is necessary to take more than one million of measurements (Vilde, 1973). Therefore the selective method should be widely used to minimise labour input, and mechanised equipment applied to determine the sliding resistance of soil on the material studied.

5. Conclusions

1. The deduced analytical correlations and the developed computer algorithm enable simulation of the soil coercion forces upon the operating surfaces of the plough body, determination of its specific draft resistance depending on the body design, the working parameters and soil properties and motivation of the optimal values of parameters.
2. Presentation of the draft resistance of the plough body as the sum of its components – the cutting resistance of the soil slice, the resistance caused by its weight, the soil inertia forces and adhesion - allows analysis of the forces acting upon the share-mouldboard surface, finding out the character of their changes depending on speed and the parameters of the surface, and assessment of their ratio in the total resistance.
3. The main parameters affecting the ploughing efficiency are: the initial and the final angles of the lifting (share-mouldboard) surface; the inclination angle of the horizontal generatrix

towards the direction of the movement and the regularity of its variation; the thickness of the share edge; the radius of the lifting surface and the area of the lifting and supporting surfaces.
4. Increase in the inclination of the horizontal generatrix leads to a decrease in the draft resistance caused by the weight and adhesion of soil but it increases the resistance caused by inertia forces, particularly, when the speed increases. The inclination of the generatrix (the edge of the share) does not affect the cutting resistance of the soil slice.
5. In loamy soils, when the speed grows from 1 to 3 m s^{-1}, the optimum value of the inclination angle between the horizontal generatrix of the share-mouldboard surface and the wall of the furrow decreases from 65°…40° to 33°…25° . At the ploughing speed 2…2.5 m s^{-1} it is 38°…34°.
6. To ensure sufficient turning of the slice, the angle of the top generatrix must not be less than 48°.
7. Increasing the working width of the body from 30 cm to 50 cm (at a constant frontal width of the share), the specific consumption of energy, fuel and the ploughing costs decrease (in loamy soil by 10…16%) but the labour efficiency correspondingly increases.
8. The impact of the soil-metal friction upon the draft resistance of the plough body is significant. It may reach 50…60% of total draft resistance including the resistances of the supporting surfaces (25…30%). Therefore measures will be taken to diminution it, for example, using antifriction materials (Teflon or others).
9. The draft resistance of the supporting surfaces is considerable. It can reach 25…30% of the total plough body draft resistance, or 42…54% of its share-mouldboard draft resistance.
10. The correlations obtained allow assessment of the ploughing resistance depending on the soil humidity, mechanical composition and the working speed of the plough, determination of the optimal soil humidity range when the tillage capacity is the lowest. Humidity most of all impacts the soil hardness and cutting resistance which considerably dominates in the summary resistance of the plough body. An increase in the soil humidity leads to a decrease in the ploughing resistance that is more remarkable on the clay soils. The optimum humidity of sticky clay soils when ploughing at a speed 2…2.5m s^{-1} is 18…25%.
11. The optimal values of the main parameters of the bottoms for contemporary ploughs, working at the speeds of 2...2.5 m s^{-1} are: the inclination angle of share towards the furrow bottom – 28°…32°; the inclination angle of the horizontal generatrix towards the furrow wall on the initial part of the share-mouldboard surface – 34°…38°, on the top - not less than 48°; the working width of the bottom – 45…50 cm.
12. The use of bodies having optimal parameters allows obtaining a good ploughing quality, reduction of the draft resistance by 12…20% and a corresponding rise in the efficiency, saving fuel and financial means for ploughing.

6. References

Donner, R.D & Nichols, M.L. (1934). Dynamics of Soil Flow Mouldboard Surfaces Related to Scouring. *Agricultural Engineering,* vol. 15, No.1, pp. 9-12.
Gill, W.R. & Vanden Berg, G.E. (1967). *Soil Dynamics in Tillage and Traction.* Agriculture Handbook No. 316. Washington. 511 p.

Larsen, L.W. Lovely, W.G. & Bockup C.W. (1968). Predicting draught forces using model mouldboard ploughs in agricultural soils. In: *Trans. American Society of Agricultural Engineers*, 11, pp. 665-668.

Riek, H.G. & Vorkal, W. (1965). Experimentelle Untersuchungen iiber die Adhäsion zwischen Boden und festen Werkstoffen. *Landtechnische Forschung*, Jg. 15, H. 5, S. 157-162.

Rucins, A. & Vilde, A. (2004). Mathematical modelling of the operation of plough bodies to determine their draft resistance and optimum parameters. In: TEKA *Commission of Motorization and Power Industry in Agriculture*, Volume IV. Polish Academy of Sciences Branch in Lublin. Lublin, Poland, pp. 177–184.

Rucins, A.; Vilde A. & Tanas, W. (2006). Forces acting on a plough body. In: TEKA *Commission of Motorization and Power Industry in Agriculture*, Volume VI. Polish Academy of Sciences Branch in Lublin. Lublin, Poland, pp. 135-145.

Rucins, A. & Vilde, A. (2006). Impact of the Plough Body Parameters on the Soil Tillage Efficiency. *Proceedings 5th International Scientific Conference. Engineering for Rural Development.* Latvia University of Agriculture, Faculty of Engineering, Jelgava, Latvia, pp. 42 - 47.

Rucins, A. & Vilde, A. (2005a). Modelling forces acting on the plough body. In: *Simulation in Wider Europe*. 19th European Conference on modelling and Simulation ECMS 2005 June 1-4, Riga, Latvia, pp. 414-419.

Rucins, A. & Vilde, A. (2005b). Impact of the working width of the plough body on the tillage efficiency. In: *Research for rural development 2005. International scientific conference proceedings.* Jelgava, 19-22 May, 2005. Jelgava, Latvia, pp. 36-42.

Rucins, A.; Vilde, A. & Nowak, J. (2007). Impact of the share inclination angle on the ploughing resistance. In: TEKA *Commission of Motorization and Power Industry in Agriculture*, Volume VII. Polish Academy of Sciences Branch in Lublin, Lublin, Poland, pp. 199–209.

Rucins, A.; Vilde, A. (2003). Impact of soil-metal friction on the draft resistance of ploughs. *Research for rural development 2003. International scientific conference proceedings* Jelgava, Latvia 21-24 May, 2003. Jelgava, Latvia University of agriculture, pp. 61-63.

Vilde, A.; Rucins, A. & Sevostjanovs, G. (2007) Impact of Speed on the Soil Sliding Resistance. In: *International Conference 'Technical and Technological Progress in Agriculture'*, No 12, 20–21 September 2007. Raudondvaris, Lithuania, pp. 34–38.

Vilde, A. (2004). Mechanical and mathematical foundations for modelling the dynamics of soil tillage machine operating parts. In: TEKA *Commission of Motorization and Power Industry in Agriculture*, Volume IV. Polish Academy of Sciences Branch in Lublin. Lublin, Poland, pp.228–236.

Vilde, A. (2003). The impact of soil moisture and composition on its properties and energy consumption of tillage. In: TEKA *Commission of Motorization and Power Industry in Agriculture*, Volume III. Polish Academy of Sciences Branch in Lublin. Lublin, Poland, pp. 249–255.

Vilde, A. (1999). Dynamics of the soil tillage machine operating parts and their elements. In: *Proceedings of the Latvia University of Agriculture*, Vol.1 (295). Jelgava, Latvia, pp. 36-44.

Vilde, A. (1998). Energetical estimation of soil tillage machines by testing. Theoretical motivation and methods. *Proceedings of the Latvia University of Agriculture. B – Technical sciences,* Nr. 13 (290), Jelgava, Latvia, pp. 39- 54.

Бредун, М. И. (1969). К вопросу исследования фрикционно-адгезионных свойств почвы. *Труды ВИМ,* т. 36, Москва, с. 103-121.

Бурченко, П.Н.; Иванов, А.Н.; Кашаев, Б.А.; Кирюхин, В.Г. & Мильцев, А.И. (1976). Результаты исследования рабочих органов скоростных плугов. В кн.: *Повышение рабочих скоростей машинно-тракторных агрегатов.* Москва: Колос, с. 215-218.

Бурченко, П.Н. (2001). К теории развертывающейся лемешно-отвальной поверхности корпуса плуга. В кн.: *Машинные технологии и техника для производства зерновых, масличных и зернобобовых культу. Сборник научных докладов,* том 3, часть 1. Москва: ВИМ, с. 38-51.

Вагин, А. Т. (1965). К вопросу взаимодействия клина с почвой. Обоснование основных параметров агрегатов для послойного внесения удобрений в почву В кн.: *Вопросы сельскохозяйственной механики.* Минск: Урожай, т.15, с. 4-152.

Вагин, А. Т. (1967). К вопросу обоснования параметров рабочих органов для основной обработки почв. - В кн.: *Вопросы сельскохозяйственной механики.* Минск: Урожай, т.16, с. 57-98.

Вилде, А.А. (1976). К вопросу резания грунта клином. В кн.: *Механизация и электрификация сельского хозяйства.* Рига: Звайгзне, вып. 2 (9), с. 115-129.

Вилде, А.А. (1973). О рациональности конструкции рабочих органов почвообрабатывающих орудий для работы на повышенных скоростях. В кн.: *Повышение рабочих скоростей машинно-тракторных агрегатов.* Москва: Колос, с. 367-374.

Вилде, А.А. (1983). К определению сопротивления отделению пласта от почвенного массива. В кн.: *Механизация и электрификация сельского хозяйства.* Рига: Авотс, вып. 8 (15), с. 184-203.

Вилде, А.А. (1973). Исследование закономерностей сопротивления скольжению почвы по стали. В кн.: *Труды ЛатвНИИМЭХ,* т. IV. Рига: Звайгзне, с. 183-195.

Дерягин, Б. В. (1963). *Что такое трение.* М., 1963, 230 стр.

Гячев, Л.В. (1961). *Теория лемешно-отвальной поверхности.* Зерноград. 317 с.

Горячкин, В.П. (1968). *Собрание сочинений.* 2-е изд. Москва: Колос, т.2. – 456 с.

Кацыгин, В.В. (1954). Основы теории выбора оптимальных параметров мобильных сельскохозяйственных машин и орудий. В кн.: *Вопросы сельскохозяйственной механики.* Минск: Урожай, т.13, с. 5-147.

Могильный, И. П. (1957). Влияние влажности на удельное сопротивление и трение металлов корпуса плуга о почву. *Научные труды Украинской СХА,* т. IX, Киев, с. 473-479.

Никифоров, П.Э. & Иванов, А.Н. (1973). Исследование рабочих органов плугов для работы со скоростями 10-15 км/ч. В кн.: *Повышение рабочих скоростей тракторов и сельскохозяйственных машин.* Москва: ЦИНТИАМ, с. 197-203.

Синеоков, Г.Н. & Панов, Н.И. (1977). *Теория и расчет почвообрабатывающих машин.* Москва: Машиностроение. 328 с.

Зеленин, А.Н. (1968). *Основы разрушения грунтов механическими способами.* Москва: Машиностроение. 376 с.

11

Modelling the interoperability and the use of control equipment in an electrical substation

Gregorio Romero, Jesús Félez, Mª Luisa Martínez and Joaquín Maroto
Universidad Politécnica de Madrid
Spain

1. Introduction

Simulators can be defined as information systems which reliably reproduce specific phenomena and they are mainly used in training, although their field of application has grown to include manufacturing and medicine among others.

In electrical engineering, simulation is an indispensable tool when working with complex systems due to the fact that it enables engineers to understand how systems work without actually needing to see them. They can learn how they work in different circumstances and optimize their design with considerably less cost in terms of time and money than if they had to carry out tests on a physical system. By using computer simulation, not only can an electrical system be designed, but it can also be optimized and its behaviour examined in depth more quickly and cheaply than by using prototypes, tests or analytical studies. Therefore, by being able to see the responses produced as the different parameters are varied, a much deeper understanding of the system under study is reached.

In order to properly simulate a virtual world, technologies such as realistic graphics and dynamic simulation with real-time calculations must be used. Peripherals must be used for the system to interact with the user and the immersion comes as a result of stimuli to sight, hearing and touch. A critical factor is the possibility to solve the equations in real-time; that is, there should be no delay compared to the normal environment's response. There is an important amount of effort being directed towards these objectives.

This paragraphs deals with the development of an operation simulator for training and the fundamental objective is to develop a simulator for electrical substations. It will present the methodology to model, simulate and optimize the interoperability and the use of control equipment in electrical an substation to train operators by means of a virtual reality environment.

This chapter is organized as follows. In Section 2, the objectives to develop in the successive pages are obtained and are analyzed the state-of-the-art concerning simulation of the electrical domain too, all of which allows writing the technical basis necessary to describe an application with the technical characteristics here presented. In Section 3, each of the substation components is reproduced in three dimensions and the laws of behaviour associated with it are implemented by using the Bond Graph technique to complete the functionality of the substation. It enables systems belonging to the different areas of physics to be modelled in a way that is both intuitive and close to reality. Firstly, this part of the chapter develops the simulation models of different elements that characterise an electrical substation in isolation, such as sources, loads, switches and transformer. Later they are put together to model the full system and finally the system thus developed is compared with the one developed in a specific electrical simulation program working with different manoeuvres to validate it. Section 4 built the previous modules into a larger and more complex computer system composed of the actual substation control system, the Geographical Information System, which defines the topology of the network, and the functional system which simulates the electrical behaviour of the substation. One of the advantages of doing this is that the final application can automatically update in the virtual environment any changes to the substation's design and it allows access from this environment to information on every component. In Section 5, the visuals, the communications manager and the behaviour modules of the substation are implemented by using distributed interactive simulation in a hardware configuration and it has the same interface as that used in the control system of the real substation. In this way, the system developed can be integrated into a replica of the complete power supply network control system emulating a real substation, it being able to fully interact with the global system, and allow totally real situations to be simulated. Section 6 gives conclusions of this chapter.

2. Objectives

An electrical substation (fig. 1) is a subsidiary station of an electricity generation, transmission and distribution system where voltage is transformed from high to low or the reverse using transformers. Electric power may flow through several substations between generating plant and consumer, and may be changed in voltage in several steps.

Fig. 1. Real electrical substation

The operations at electrical substations, especially when performed manually or during maintenance, can be considered high-risk activities for the people performing them. Therefore, the use of simulators for training can be particularly beneficial.

In order to properly simulate a virtual world, technologies such as realistic graphics and dynamic simulation with real-time calculations must be used (Vince, 1995). Peripherals must be used for the system to interact with the user and the immersion comes as a result of stimuli to sight, hearing and touch (Miller et al., 1998). It is possible, therefore, to produce immersion in the system by providing visual, tactile and acoustic feedback to the user. One of the most common applications of virtual reality lies in simulator development.
Simulators can be defined as information systems which reliably reproduce specific phenomena (Houghton, 1989), (Farrington et al., 1994). The first simulators were mainly used in training (Bayarri et al., 1996), although their field of application grew to include manufacturing (Singh et al., 1996) and medicine (Schroer et al., 1996) among others.
An additional issue, also related to computing performance, is dynamic simulation. The idea is to reproduce the actual physical behaviour by applying the equations governing the simulated system (Weghorst, 1998). A critical factor is the possibility to solve the equations in real-time, that is, there should be no delay compared to the normal environment's response. There is an important amount of effort being directed to these objectives (García de Jalón & Bayo, 1993).
The fundamental objective is to develop a simulator for operations at electrical substations.

2.1 Features

Such as appear in the previous lines, the fundamental objective is to develop an operation simulator for training at electrical substations. Aimed at giving the simulator the highest possible degree of realism, it must be equipped with the following features:

- To be able to closely represent an electrical substation. This implies designing 3D geometrical models of all the elements which make up the substation.
- To be interactive. Communication between the Information System and the users must adopt as real a form as possible. Interactivity is obtained by the system responding through the peripherals to user-initiated events.
- To be immersive. For the user to feel he or she is inside the virtual environment, visual and acoustic feedback must be provided through the hardware (helmet with tracking system and sound), with the objects of the environment presented in 3D stereoscopic display.
- The system must replicate, as closely as possible, the actual functioning of the installation. To obtain it, the functioning logic of the installation must be coded into the system, so that objects react to user input with the appropriate movement and behavior. Furthermore, all objects must strictly adhere to the physical laws governing their behavior; in this case, the laws of movement affecting simultaneously 3D objects and the physical principles of electricity which, logically, define the behaviour of an electrical substation.
- To be integrated into a network, so that it becomes a multi-user system where multiple users can simultaneously input into the same virtual environment, following defined behavioural rules.

These objectives must be attained by interconnecting the different hardware and software elements. The following sections describe how these elements work and their relationship.

3. Modelling of installations

3.1 Three-dimensional geometrical models

Simultaneously to the development of the software application, the 3D geometrical models needed by the VR application can be constructed (fig. 2). These models are based on existing drawings, on paper or in digital format, and on actual pictures. The geometric models need to be optimized to a high level of realism by optimizing the mesh size, using LOD (Level Of Detail) objects, and applying textures.

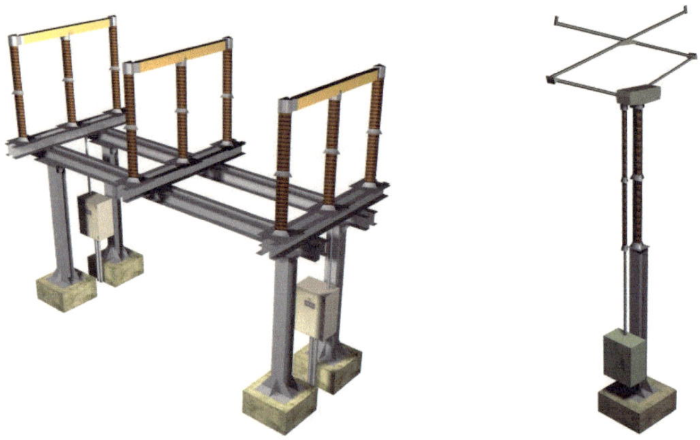

(a) (b)

Fig. 2. Electric 3D models. (a) Thriphasic disconnector. (b) Monophase pantograph.

The models can be constructed using commercial 3D software, so that the system imports popular or standard commercial formats such as *AutoCAD*, *3Dstudio*, *Proengineer*, *Multigen*, *IGES*, *DXF*, or *VRML*. This will make maintenance by the technical department of the company where the application will be installed much easier.

Fig. 3. 3D Geometry and textures of the full electrical substation´s model.

When the 3D models of the different components need to be inserted to make the full 3D model of the substation (fig. 3), it´s necessary the insertion of repeated elements as blocks, so that identical geometrical models (i.e., high voltage towers) need not be duplicated. This means a reduction in the resources necessary to store the substation, in download time from the network, and in processing power to render the substation in real time. Excessive detail in the geometrical modelling means an increase in the time needed to render it, so that it can become impossible to offer real time experiencing. The rendering must be optimized by applying textures to the 3D model. This greatly simplifies the rendering without losing realism (fig. 3).

3.2 Laws of electrical behavior

When it comes to analyzing a three-phase electrical circuit, which is what we are dealing with, it may be assumed that the three phases are balanced and therefore behave similarly.

For this reason, when simulating an electrical substation, it is possible to work with the single-line circuit of one of the phases where the line and the different elements to be taken into account can be more easily analyzed.

Figure 4 shows a typical single-line substation circuit diagram where two active input positions can be seen (lines 'L1' and 'L2') and two output positions (lines 'L3' and 'L4'). Additionally, there is one input and two output positions in reserve.

This diagram shows how the two input positions are connected to a common busbar and the two output positions terminate in another busbar, also common to both of them. This leads to the different input or output branches being placed in parallel and the power transformer being situated between both parts.

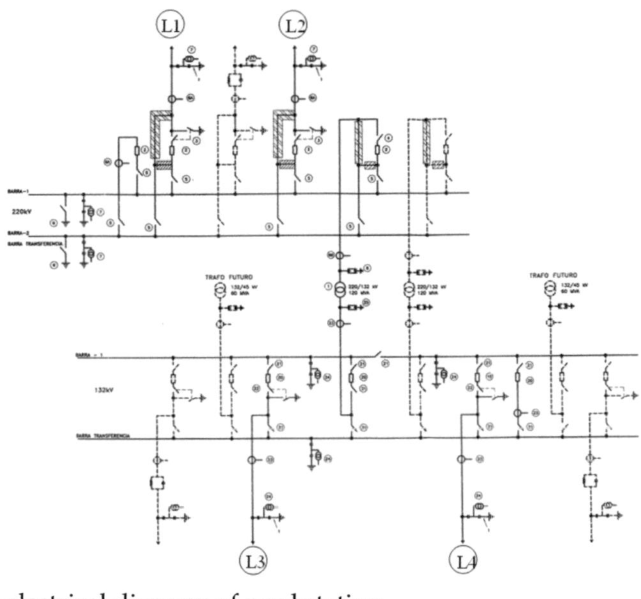

Fig. 4. Single-line electrical diagram of a substation

There is a wide range of commercial brands on the market offering products for electrical domain simulation (*SPICE, LabVIEW PSCAD, Dymola, Simulink, Simplorer,...*). These are powerful tools, but require the engineer to have a perfect knowledge of the electrical field.

An alternative methodology to can simulate an electrical substation is the Bond Graph technique. The Bond Graph technique enables systems belonging to the different areas of physics to be modelled in a way that is both intuitive and close to reality (Karnopp et al., 1990). It is a perfect technique for representing elements belonging to the area dealt with in this paper and it´s possible apply it in any program that permit the simulation of models based in this technique (Romero et al., 2008); in addition, no extraordinary knowledge of this technique and electric field are required to understand the process. There is a series of elements that are needed for this type of facility to operate, which are described below.

3.2.1. Switches

In an electrical system actions need to be carried out to vary its layout or topology. Certain manoeuvres are simply necessary to connect or disconnect loads, others to interrupt the passage of current in the event of failure and others to earth some part of the system (Poyraz et al., 1999).

An automatic switch can establish, support, and interrupt currents under normal circuit conditions, as well as establish, support for a determined period of time and interrupt currents under abnormal specified circuit conditions, such as a short-circuit. In a Bond-Graph, a resistance port placed in series (fig. 5) can be modelled with the rest of the circuit to which the values have to be introduced as a conditioned parameter. If the switch is closed, the resistance value will be zero, while if it is open the value is very high, preventing the passage of flow or current.

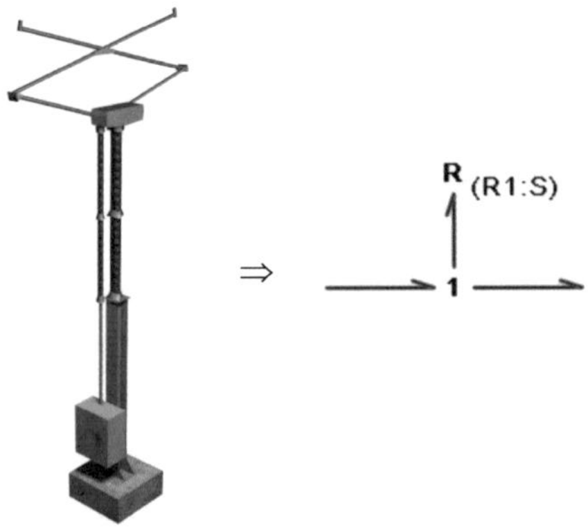

Fig. 5. Modelling a switch by using the Bond-Graph technique.

To open or close a switch, the resistance value can either be based on a function that evolves over time or set to the value that other circuit parameters acquire. In this latter case, relays can be generated to open the switch if a current level is exceeded in some element. Likewise, but making its operation conditional on normal circuit conditions or on abnormal conditions for a determined period of time, a contactor can be modelled. This type of apparatus can support and interrupt currents under normal circuit conditions, including specified in-service overload conditions temporarily, as well as support specified abnormal circuit conditions for a determined period of time, such as short-circuits. This is the case with voltage and intensity transformers that are at the beginning of the 'L1' and 'L2' input positions and at the end of the 'L3' and 'L4' output positions.

3.2.2 Loads

Regarding load modelling, it must be borne in mind that in an electrical node, the current is divided by the cables connected to it, the voltage at all points of the contact being equal. This

behaviour is obtained in a Bond Graph with type '0' nodes, where the (current) is equal to the sum of the output flows and the effort of the bonds it joins is the same, while with type '1' nodes the input current is equal to the output current less what is lost in the element, such as happens with elements in series.
In three-phase systems (Bose, 2005), the loads can be connected either in a triangle or a star, and this in turn, to earth or insulated. In an insulated three-phase star load the resistance and inductance of each phase will be joined by a type '1' node, since the Bond Graph elements are in series, and subsequently the bonds of each of the three phases will be joined by a type '0' node, of common potential representing the neutral of the star. If the neutral is rigidly earthed, the bonds joining it will need to be set to zero potential. This can be achieved with a zero level effort source joined to the '0' node representing the neutral, as shown in figure 6.

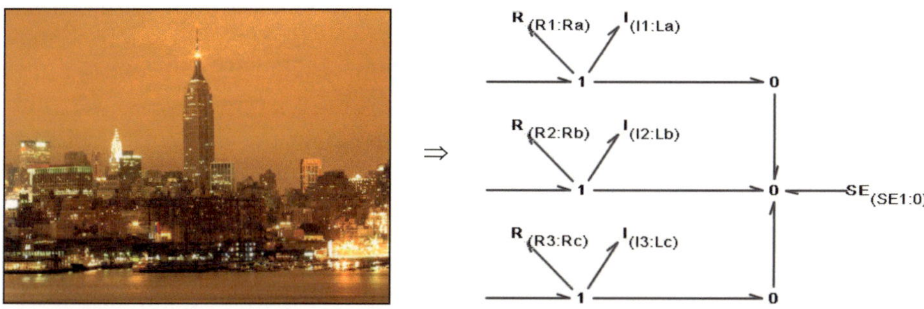

Fig. 6. Model of a three-phase load in a star with rigid neutral to earth in Bond Graph.

3.2.3 Sources

As with the loads, the effort sources (voltage) represented by the Bond Graph technique are ideal sources and generate a potential difference across the terminals that is constant and independent of the load. Unlike ideal sources the potential difference produced by real sources is dependent on the load to which they are connected. A real voltage source may be considered an ideal voltage source, 'U', in series with a resistance 'R', denominated internal resistance. In order to obtain real sources in a Bond-Graph, a resistance port needs to be added to act as an internal resistance using a node '1', so that it will be in series.

Fig. 7. Model of a three-phase voltage source with neutral to earth in Bond Graph.

By joining the single-phase effort forces in an appropriate star or triangular layout, three-phase systems can be attained. In the case under study, three-phase, star voltage sources can be obtained by connecting the different effort sources in type '1' nodes, and subsequently, all of them in a type '0' node and a zero value effort force that simulates the earth (fig. 7).

3.2.4 Transformer

The transformer comprises two primary and secondary coils and enables the electric power to be transformed, with specific magnitudes of voltage and intensity, into other usually different voltages. The electromagnetic part of a transformer comprises a magnetic nucleus and windings. The windings around the nucleus form the primary and secondary coils, with 'N1' and 'N2' number of turns respectively. When an alternating current is applied to the primary, an alternating current flows through it, which, in turn, produces an alternating flow in the nucleus whose direction is determined by Ampere's law applied to this coil.
Due to the periodical variation of this flow induced electromagnetic forces are created in the coils and this leads to a voltage in the terminals of the secondary coil whose ratio to the primary is 'r' -transformation ratio -, and which value is the relation between 'N1' and 'N2'.
As commented in previous paragraphs, this suggests using the transformer element in a Bond Graph to model an electrical transformer where the output flow is equal to the input flow multiplied by the ratio of the transformer 'r', and the output effort is the input effort divided by the ratio, the same as happens with intensities and voltages in an ideal transformer. However, real transformers have losses and therefore, the resistance of the coils and the dispersion flows need to be taken into account. This must be done with the 'R1' and 'R2' resistances, for the primary and secondary coils, and with the 'X1' and 'X2' reactance. An approximate equivalent circuit (fig. 8) is usually worked with, which is obtained by grouping the impedances in series; in this way, the resistances and reactances of the short-circuit ('Xcc' and 'Rcc') can be obtained easily.

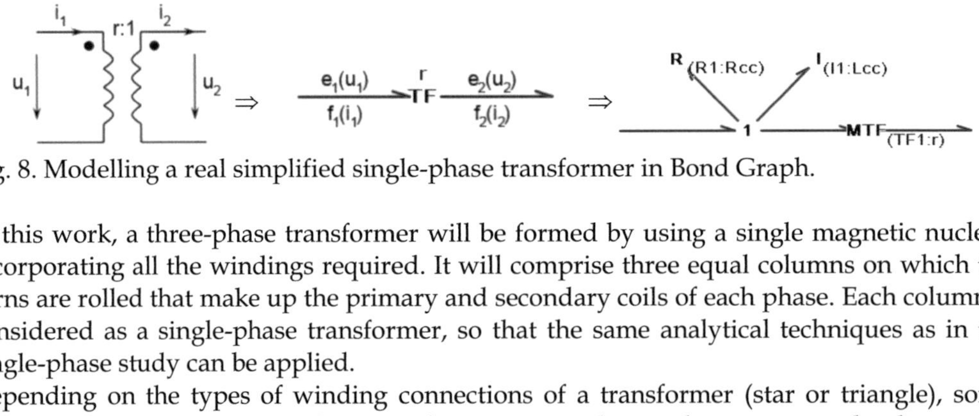

Fig. 8. Modelling a real simplified single-phase transformer in Bond Graph.

In this work, a three-phase transformer will be formed by using a single magnetic nucleus incorporating all the windings required. It will comprise three equal columns on which the turns are rolled that make up the primary and secondary coils of each phase. Each column is considered as a single-phase transformer, so that the same analytical techniques as in the single-phase study can be applied.
Depending on the types of winding connections of a transformer (star or triangle), some phase differences may appear between the primary and secondary compound voltages and the concept of phase-lag index appears. In our substation, a transformer with 'Yy' configuration has the primary and secondary connected in a star; in this type of connection, the phase-lag between the primary and the secondary is 0°, and therefore, can be modelled using three single-phase transformers with no parallel branch, since the effort outputs will be the effort inputs divided by the ratio of the 'TF' element. Since this value is a scalar, there will be no phase-lag between them, the same as with the flows.

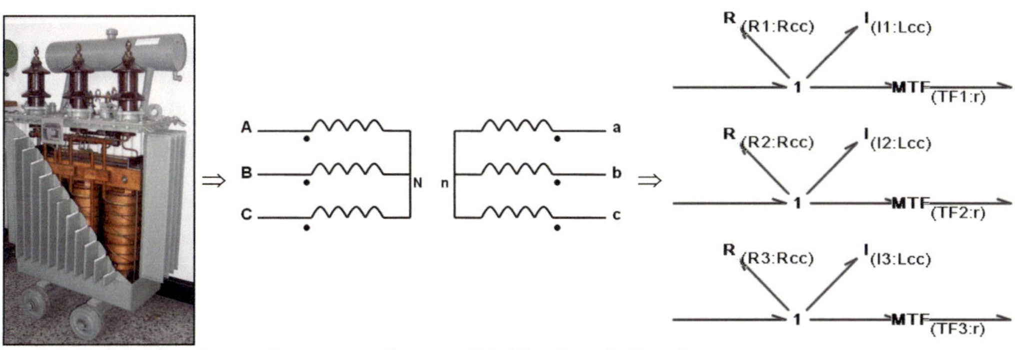

Fig. 9. Model of a three-phase transformer 'Yy' by Bond Graph.

3.3 Full electrical substation´s model

In order to proceed to the electrical substation simulation, it is necessary to draw a simplified three-phase diagram showing the different elements dealt with in the preceding paragraphs. The different Bond Graph models analyzed will have to be substituted in order to generate a valid simulation model like the presented in figure 10.

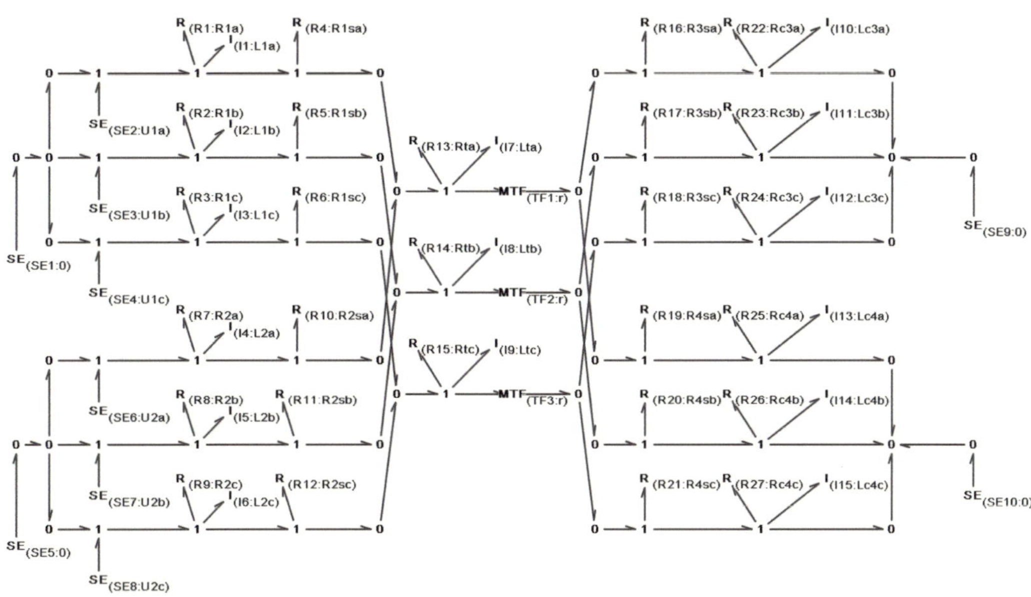

Fig. 10. Model of an electrical substation in a Bond Graph.

A typical configuration of a substation will contain a source and a load at each of the input positions, corresponding to some power stations, and a load in the output positions equal to the demand of a city, as can be seen in figures 10 and 11. A usual occurrence to simulate in this type of installation is a temporary interruption of the service at any of the input or output positions; for this reason, a series of switches must be also added corresponding to the cut-offs.

3.4 Opening and closing maneuvers

To be sure of the configuration of a typical substation it has been developed an example of electrical substation. In this sample, some apparent powers of 4 GVA and 5 GVA have been taken into account in the input positions respectively, and of 60 MVA and 90 MVA in the output positions; in the equations (1) to (4) the equivalent impedances and resistances has been obtained.

$$Z_{cc_1} = \frac{(220\ kV)^2}{4\ GVA} = 12{,}1\ \Omega \Rightarrow L_{cc_1} = 38{,}515\ mH\ (with\ R_{cc_1} = 0{,}2\ \Omega) \tag{1}$$

$$Z_{cc_2} = \frac{(220\ kV)^2}{5\ GVA} = 9{,}68\ \Omega \Rightarrow L_{cc_2} = 30{,}812\ mH\ (with\ R_{cc_1} = 0{,}2\ \Omega) \tag{2}$$

$$Z_{c_3} = \frac{(132\ kV)^2}{60\ MVA} = 290{,}4\ \Omega \Rightarrow L_{c_3} = 402{,}921\ mH, R_{c_3} = 261{,}36\ \Omega \tag{3}$$

$$Z_{c_4} = \frac{(132\ kV)^2}{90\ MVA} = 193{,}6\ \Omega \Rightarrow L_{c_4} = 268{,}611\ mH, R_{c_4} = 174{,}24\ \Omega \tag{4}$$

To see how one position affects another, 4 seconds will be simulated bearing in mind that the line 'L1' switches are open between t=0.3 sec. and t=1 sec., and those of the 'L2' line between t=2.3 sec. and t=3 sec., while the remainder will be closed at all times. In order to validate this, the same exercise has been done with *PSCAD ©* elements too.

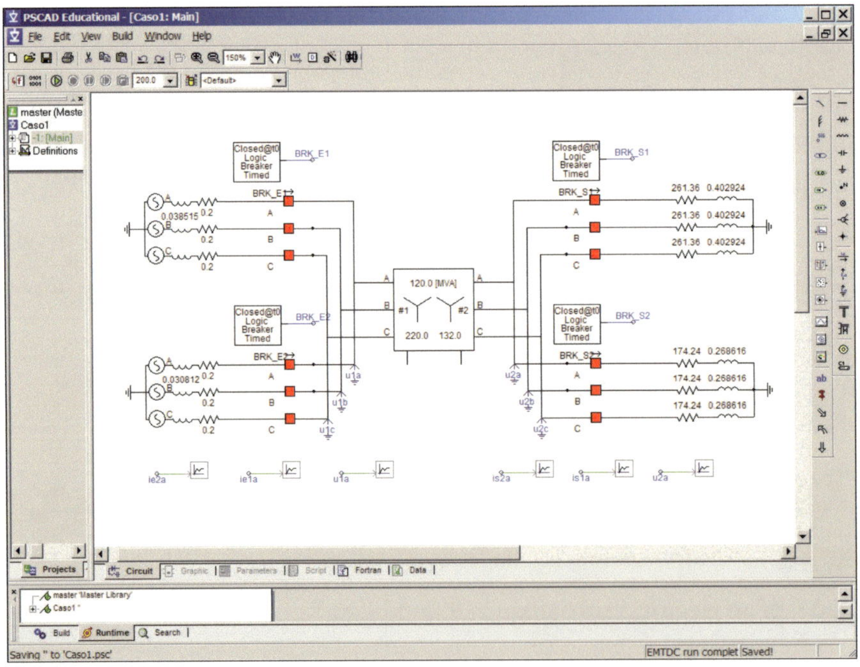

Fig. 11. Scheme of an electrical substation drawn in *PSCAD ©* software.

In figure 12 the results show the intensity [A] vs time [seconds] flowing through a single phase in each of the positions 'L1', 'L2', 'L3' and 'L4'; they are equal to those performed with the Bond Graph model developed in figure 10 and obtained by using the dynamic simulation module of the developed simulator.

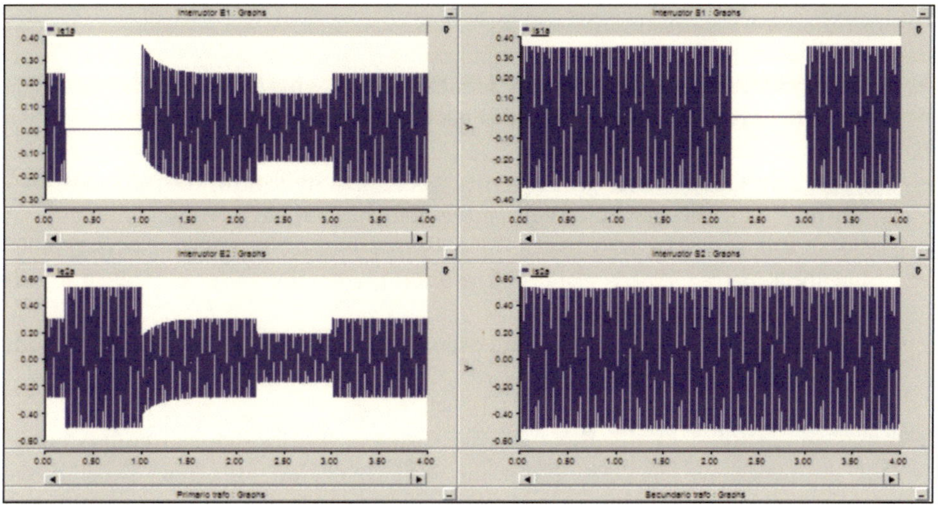

Fig. 12. Electric simulation results (Intensity [A] vs time [sec.]).

In this simulation the currents required for the 'L3' and 'L4' positions are 0.39 A and 0.55 A respectively when the four switches are closed. Regarding the supply from the power stations in the 'L1' and 'L2' positions, 0.24 A and 0.32 A are supplied respectively, whose sum after applying the transformation ratio is the total current required of 0.94 A. On the other hand, when the 'L1' position switch is opened, all the current must be supplied by the power station in position 'L2'. When it is closed again, in the transitory process it can be seen that the current in position 'L2' is the difference between that demanded by the load and that supplied by the power station in the other position.

Regarding the opening of the switch in position 'L3', it can be seen how the current demanded drops to 0.55 A.

Thus, the model developed for the simulation of an electrical substation using the Bond Graph technique may be considered as valid.

4. Implementation of the project

4.1 Additional applications

The relationship between the different modules of the simulator must be done in the Installations Database (BDI), which must be designed to maintain and look-up graphical and textual information on the installations and elements of the power supply and telecommunications networks.

The information stored in the BDI must be organized on different levels (planning, study, development, operation) together with cartographic information.

The basic functionality of the BDI is as follows:

- Queries: queries against graphical and textual information in the database.
- Maintenance: maintenance of the information in the database.
- Map editing: generation of hard copy and on-screen maps.
- Network analysis: queries based on the topological connections of the network.
- Information exchange: import/export information to/from other systems or official bodies.

The BDI must include the following data:

a. Textual data:

- Every element must be uniquely identified through a code.
- Identification and technical data of each installation.

b. Graphical data:

- Cartographic database: Rural (communications, hydrographic information, limits, altitude, etc.) and urban (streets, sidewalks, blocks, etc.) maps.
- Detail maps: precise location of the network over a cartographic background.
- Location maps: larger scale representation of the network's location over a cartographic background.
- Schematic drawings: schematic drawings of manoeuvres at substations and transformation centres.

The information included in the BDI affords, through the topological connections of its Geografical Informations System (GIS), a full overview of the substations and transformation centres, their internal and external connections and their operational logic (fig. 13).

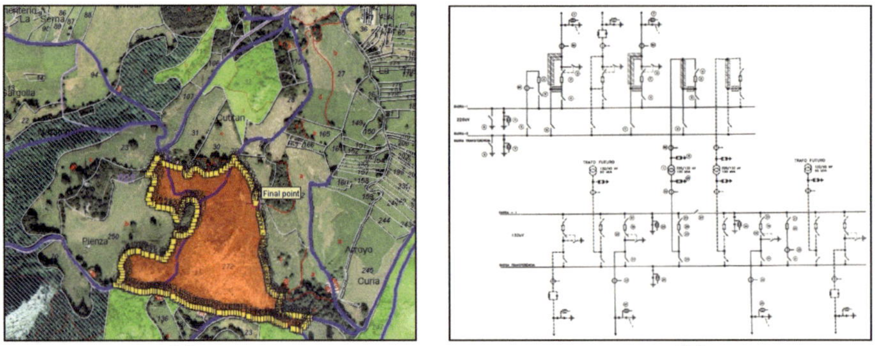

(a) (b)

Fig. 13. (a) Geographical database. (b) Schematic drawings of electrical systems

4.2 Technical basis of the application

To arrive at the functionality indicated in the section 2, several software tools will be used. The core of the application will consist of C/C++ code, which accesses the 'OpenSceneGraph' graphical libraries APIs (Yuan et al., 2007).

The realist aspect of the application allows the user to work with a physical mechanism within a virtual reality environment; that is, to interact with it through devices such as a mouse, stereoscopic glasses, HMDs or gloves.

The 3D geometrical models can be imported by the virtual reality application, which applies to each object properties such as interference and object collision detection, pre-set trajectories and tasks. In order to increase the realism of the whole, colours, transparencies, labels, and lights have been added to the geometries.

Fig. 14. Action sequence on the substation's elements.

Once the geometrical and operational data have been loaded, the virtual environment of the substation can be manipulated. Figure 14 shows the controls of one of the pantographs of the substation. When the button on the pantograph's control console is pressed, it moves from open (horizontal position) to closed (vertical position) or from closed to open.

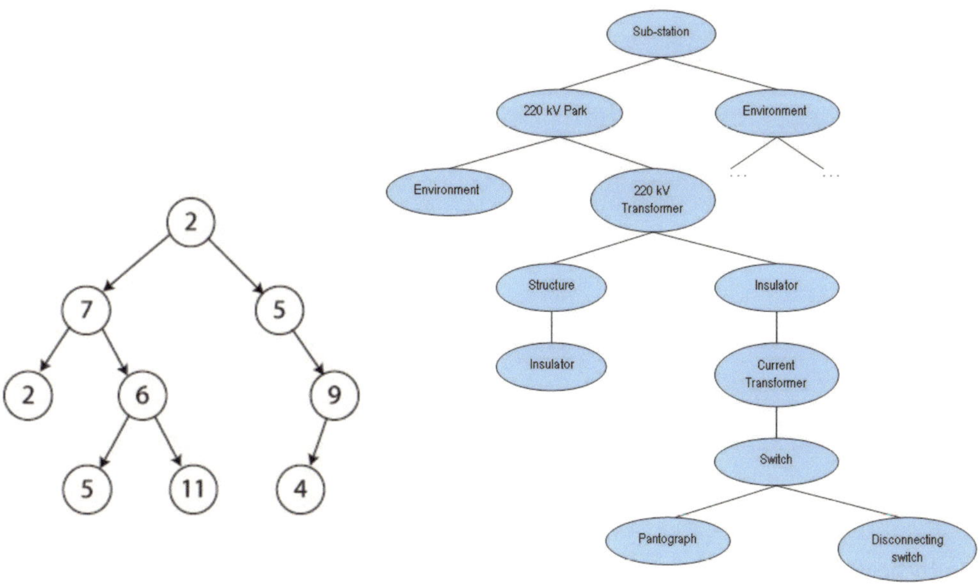

(a) (b)

Fig. 15. (a) Scene graph philosophy. (b) Scene graph structure of an electrical substation.

In order to view the movement of the mechanisms in real time, a scene graph with hierarchical object structure (fig. 15.a) must be created. The nodes, that is, the elements which include information on geometry, position or light, are the elements which make up the scene graph; these elements contain the geometrical, position and light information respectively. The nodes are sorted by hierarchy, which means that they are linked vertically and present a tree-like structure. Figure 15.b shows a section of the scene graph corresponding to a sample substation.

Depending on the element with which we interact, several different actions must be performed on the virtual substation. The substation is composed of static physical elements, such as transformers, control elements such as consoles, and assemblies with movement such as pantographs or switches.

- The most general action, which can be applied to every element, is navigation. This consists of interactively changing the viewpoint through the mouse. This is done through what in virtual reality terminology is known as a 'motion link' between the computer's input device and the camera's viewpoint. As the input sensor (the mouse, in this case) moves, the viewpoint of the scene changes interactively.
- Operation of mechanisms. There is also a module which performs the kinematic calculations corresponding to show the positions of the parts which make up a mechanism, such as the pantograph in figure 16.a, so that the moment the system drivers are operated (degrees of freedom) the model will produce a movement following preset kinematic constraints. In order to define the mechanism's kinematic behaviour, the system drivers (system input), as well as the kinematic joints making up the system's movement constraints, must be configured. The corresponding scene graph is shown in figure 16.a:

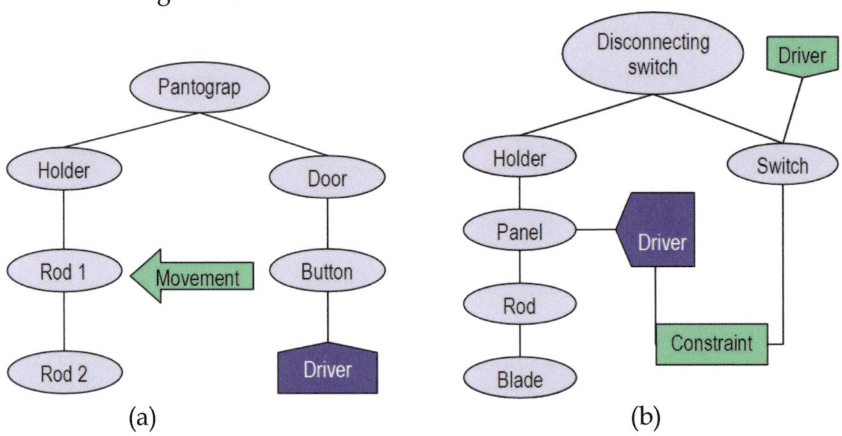

Fig. 16. Scene graph. (a) Manoeuvring of the pantograph. (b) Manoeuvre constraints.

- The third type of action is modifying the electrical state: connected, disconnected, grounded, etc. This type of action may or may not be accompanied by a concrete physical movement, but must always be registered and taken into account. In the virtual environment it is indicated by a change in colour, for instance. In most cases, electrical manoeuvres of this type are subject to operational constraints; i.e., you cannot ground a live element. These constraints are also shown in the scene graph, as in figure 16.b.

4.3 Integration of BDI and VR

When the Installations Database (BDI) and the virtual reality application (VR) are integrated, it allows transparent access to information in both systems and, depending on the level of difficulty, integration can be approached differently:

- LEVEL 1 - Queries

The following types of queries are allowed:

- Queries, from the VR application, of textual data corresponding to the modeled elements. A 3D element is selected and the Database Query Application invoked with the identification code of the selected element. A screen is then displayed allowing standard operations of this application (navigating through the hierarchy of installations, locating the element, generating reports, etc.).
- Accessing the virtual model of a substation: a substation is displayed using the corresponding textual data contained in the BDI.
- Locating an element from the BDI: from the BDI, an element can be physically located within the substation.

- LEVEL II - Symbology / Behaviour

This level allows the user to define, based on specific textual attributes, the symbology and/or dynamic behaviour of substation elements:

- Model: differentiate elements based on model or material.
- State: changing the appearance of an element, based on its state (open, closed).
- Voltage: same as above, following a live/without voltage criteria.

5. Distributed Interactive Simulation

The last phase consists in implementing this system within a Distributed Interactive Simulation (DIS) environment. The objective is to develop a virtual reality system which meets the specifications of the previous phases, i.e., integration in BDI, realistic behaviour laws, and which allows several users simultaneous access to the same installation from different workstations.

This application is based on Object/Property/Event architecture, and offers the following functionality:

- Standard storage, manipulation and retrieval of objects from a shared database.
- Creation of properties (such as the position of an object) that allow for easy storage of user-defined data (for instance, movement coordinates when an object is moved).
- Triggering of reactions to property changes. A property change is known as an event.
- Property sharing, enabling multi-user simulations.
- The final objective of this phase has been the development of a client/server architecture which allows multi-user, simultaneous generation of interactive graphic simulations.

The software developed is made up of a set of interconnected applications. This solution presents greater scalability if a single application is used that simultaneously takes charge of the substation graphic display and the simulation of its logic and behaviour.

This scalability allows the implementation of a multiuser environment. Moreover, it gives independence in respect of the power of the computer where the program is being run, since processing can be distributed among different computers.

This section describes the methodology implemented, which allows for the interconnection of new behaviour modules and the presence of several visuals, thus allowing simultaneous real-time interaction among various users. A distributed environment has been generated made up of the following applications:

5.1 Visuals

These are based on OpenSceneGraph and it gives great flexibility to the developed software, since it allows for a future migration towards operating systems that are different from Windows.

It must include its own programming language (macro language), which enables simple and efficient virtual environments to be generated along with their editing. This language not only allows objects to be inserted, but also contains a set of instructions that enables elements to be inserted, such as atmospheric effects, animated characters, etc... Thanks to this functionality, the user can generate a plain text file, which, together with the 3D geometries, allows any virtual scenario to be reproduced. It allows the loading of geometries generated by graphic design programs and has the capacity to reproduce large scale scenarios with the help of a dynamic load module.

5.2 Communications manager

This allows the state of the actuators to be sent from the behaviour modules to the visuals, as well as the position and orientation of all the elements in the simulation. It also allows the states of the sensors to be sent from the visuals to the behaviour modules.

Its main functions are to interconnect all the applications that form part of the simulation and to manage all the communication flows. Its main feature is to allow the automatic configuration of all the communications from a set of parameters supplied by the user of the software developed. These parameters will define both the policy and the features of these communications. It is based on 'CORBA' (Diaz et al., 2007), which means that applications generated with different programming languages can be integrated.

The following problems have had to be resolved while developing the application:

- Access to variables. A variable cannot be both modified and read at the same moment in time by two threads that are trying to access it simultaneously. Error detection and management. The application must detect errors associated with communications and rectify those capable of rectification.
- Thread management. The communications manager must simultaneously manage data transmission to the display units together with their receipt by the simulators..

Since we are dealing with an application through which all the communications pass, its code is highly optimized. Any loss of performance in the application will affect all the other applications it communicates with, transferring this low performance situation to them. Optimization has been carried out by a meticulous use of dynamic and fixed matrix lists, by minimizing the number of operations present in the algorithms, and selecting and compacting any areas that need to be blocked in order to avoid their simultaneous use by more than one thread.

The Communications Manager is based on a protocol that allows communications to be simply configured, it being possible to set their UDP or TCP type. However, as a general rule, one should tend towards UDP data transmissions whenever possible, since this type takes up fewer resources. The Communications Manager has been implemented with CORBA technology. The CORBA components are objects that display services through interfaces that are described in a standard language called IDL (Interface Definition Language), with a similar syntax to that of Java and C++. An IDL definition is then converted, using a language-dependent tool, into one or more files, from which the customer and server, respectively, are coded. In the software developed, an IDL has been defined aimed at being implemented in simulators without the need to modify the different modules comprising the distributed architecture. Therefore, the programmer only has to develop the simulator or set of simulators making up this distributed environment.

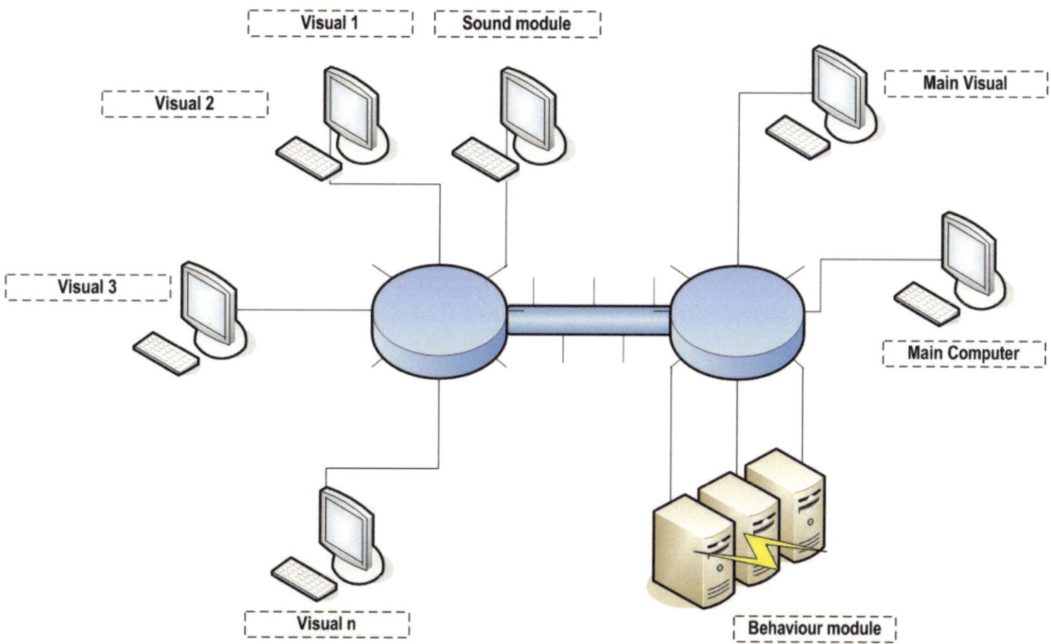

Fig. 17. General architecture of the system.

Moreover, with the help of the interface, the user need only worry about simulating the behaviours, leaving aside managing communications, detecting errors associated with such management, and developing a distributed architecture. The communications manager takes control of all communications by sending the necessary information to each module at an appropriate rate. To this end, each module carries out the following functions:

1. Starting up: the Communications manager assigns a single identifier to each module.
2. Synchronizing: The module clocks and the Manager become synchronized. To obtain good synchronization a maximum error must be set in accordance with a sequence in which it send the information from each of the objects controlled every 'n' milliseconds.

Figure 17 shows the general architecture of the developed system.

5.3 Behavior modules

A visual without a behaviour module allows a scenario to be reproduced at a particular instant. However, if it is wished to reflect the evolution of the environment according to time, and therefore represent the different states that the elements gradually acquire in that environment, a module entrusted to calculate this evolution is needed.

In the developed simulator, the logic associated with behaviour has been introduced by means of a module that allows the interpretation of a set of files containing the behaviour of the elements, coded in a language with syntax the same as a PLC. Thus, a programmable automaton language interpreter for inserting basic behaviour has been developed.

The programmable automation functions in such a way that the outputs depend on the instantaneous value of the inputs. However, the evolution of logic functions of automatism require a specific calculation time. In order to ensure that the input values are not changed during this evaluation, synchronous processing modes are used that only take account of the inputs, and update the outputs in specific instants of time. Their functioning can be summed up as follows:

1. Start of cycle.

   Storage of input values at a particular instant. Running the program; during the entire process, the value of the inputs that is stored remains constant. Simultaneous updating of outputs.
2. End of cycle.
3. Repetition of the process.

The behaviour module, therefore, works as an automaton emulator in such a way that with some particular inputs some outputs are generated that are reflected in the environment. In order to generate the variables making up the emulator's outputs, the figure of the sensor has been created inside the visuals, which takes charge of reading the value of a particular property at the start of each automaton cycle.

The actuators have been created in the same way so that the environment can be acted on. These are elements that act on a particular property with the ability to change its value. Both the actuators (behaviour module outputs) and the sensors (behaviour module inputs) are treated as binary-type variables, that is, their possible values are '0' or '1'. Described below are the sensors implemented, their main features and scope of use.

Types of sensors implemented:

- State: This controls whether a visual element is activated or not. It thus allows the user not only to know if a geometry is visible or not, but also if a light is 'on' or 'off', if a fog-type node is active, etc.
- Position: This informs if a node is in a position near the sensor. This check is made by means of ranging. Linear position: This detects if a node intersects with the imaginary segment, which, setting out from a point 'P' at the centre of a node, has the direction of a vector '(x,y,z)'. The size of the segment is a user-specified parameter. The most typical example of one would be a photoelectric cell.
- Switch: This behaves like a push-button, that is, it lets current pass only and exclusively during a cycle. At that instant its value is true and then passes to false during the remaining instants even though the button continues to be pressed.
- Button: While the button remains pressed, it lets the current pass taking the true value, passing to false value when the pressing finishes. Movement: This checks the different properties of a movement.

Types of actuators implemented:

- Node visibility control: this lets a node be activated or deactivated, thereby allowing the geometries to be visible or not. If it is a light-type, it switches it 'on' or 'off', and if a fog-type, it can make it act or not. Variation in the properties of a movement.
- Determining the state of a sound.
- Acting on a Switch element: this allows the child of a switch to be selected each time that it takes the true value or rotate among the various children.

With the help of these sensors and actuators, all the actions needed to manage an electrical substation can be generated, opening or closing phases, operating switches, etc...

6. Conclusions

An application designed for training electrical substation operators by using a virtual reality application has been set out in this chapter.

The application allows full viewing of any of the substations in the power supply network, allowing navigation into the virtual world and interaction with the elements. Each of the substation components has been reproduced in the simulation model, including the behavior laws associated with it, so the complete functionality of the substation can be simulated. It may be said that the Bond Graph technique is a simple and effective mathematical modelling technique that lets the model be understood without losing the physical sense of each of its components, no matter how complex it may be. Its methodology unified for different physical domains enables the electrical part to be joined to other parts of the systems that appear in engineering, such as, mechanics or hydraulics, it being unnecessary to change the simulation environment or computer application when machines need to be joined to mechanical shafts, pumps or turbines,...

The virtual reality application has been implemented in such a way that the system developed can be integrated into a replica of the complete power supply network control system emulating a real substation, it being able to fully interact with the global system and allow totally real situations to be simulated.

There is no doubt that being able to simulate expensive installations with virtual models which afford the same functionality is an extremely interesting possibility. This virtual reality application is a tool aimed at this interest.

In this complex issue, important technologies and methodologies, such as virtual reality, dynamic simulation, databases, GIS, computer networking, all join together to offer a real time solution.

7. References

Bayarri, S., Fernandez, M. & Perez, M. (1996). "Virtual reality for driving simulation", *Communications of the ACM*, Vol. 39, Iss. 5, pp. 72 - 76, ISSN 0001-0782, New York, United States.

Bose, A. (2005). "Three-Phase Alternating Current Systems". *The Electrical Engineering Handbook*, Elsevier Science & Technology, pp. 709-711, ISBN 0-12-170960-4.

Diaz, M, Garrido, D, & Troya, JM. (2007). "Development of distributed real-time simulators based on CORBA". *Simulation Modelling Practice and Theory*, vol. 15, Iss. 6, pp. 716 - 733, Elsevier B.V., ISSN 1569-190x.

Farrington, P. A., Schroer, B. J., Swain, J. J. & Feng, Y. (1994). "Simulators as a tool for rapid manufacturing simulation", *Proceedings of the 26th Conference on Winter Simulation*, pp. 994 - 1000, ISBN 0-7803-2109-X, Orlando, Florida, United States.

García de Jalón, J. & Bayo, E. (1993). "*Kinematic and Dynamic Simulation of Multibody Systems*". Springer-Verlag, ISBN 0-387-94096-0, New York, United States.

Houghton, P. D. (1989). "SMAS: an expert system for configuring a research flight simulator", *Proceedings of the 2nd International Conference on Industrial and Engineering Applications of Artificial Intelligence and Expert Systems*, Vol. 2 , pp. 601 - 609, ISBN 0-89791-320-5, Tullahoma, Tennessee, United States.

Karnopp, D.C., Margolis, D.L. & Rosenberg, R.C. (1990). "*System Dynamics: a Unified Approach*". 2nd edition, Wiley Interscience, ISBN 0471621714, New York, United States.

Miller, M. S., Clawson, D. M., Sebrechts, M. M., & Knott, B. A. (1998). "Interface design for inducing and assessing immersion in virtual reality", *Proceedings of the CHI 98 Conference Summary on Human Factors in Computing Systems*, pp. 343 - 344, ISBN 1-58113-028-7, Los Angeles, California, United States.

Poyraz, M., Demir, Y., Gülten, A. & Köksal, M. (1999). "Analysis of switched systems using the Bond Graph methods". *Journal of the Franklin Institute*, Vol. 336, Iss. 3, pp. 379 - 386, Elsevier, ISSN 0016-0032, Oxford, England.

Romero, G., Félez, J., Maroto, J. & Mera, J.M. (2008). "Simulation of an electrical substation using the Bond Graph technique". *Proceedings of 10th International Conference on Modelling and Simulation*, pp. 584 - 589, ISBN 0-7695-3114-8, Cambridge, England.

Schroer, B. J., Farrington, P. A., Swain, J. J. & Utley, D. R. (1996). "A generic simulator for modeling manufacturing modules", *Proceedings of the 28th Conference on Winter Simulation* , pp. 1155 - 1160, ISBN 0-7803-3383-7, Coronado, California, United States.

Singh, G, Feiner, S. K. & Thalmann, D. (1996). "Virtual reality: software and technology" *Communications of the ACM*, Vol. 39, Iss. 5, pp. 35 - 36, ISSN 0001-0782, New York, United States.

Vince, J. (1995). "Virtual Reality Systems". Addisson Wesley, ISBN 0-201-87687-6.

Weghorst, S. (1998). "Virtual reality applications in health care", *Proceedings of the CHI 98 Conference Summary on Human Factors in Computing Systems*, pp. 375, ISBN 1-58113-028-7, Los Angeles, California, United States.

Yuan, P, Wang, SJ, Zhang, JW, & Liu, HG. (2007). "Virtual reality platform based on open sourced graphics toolkit OpenSceneGraph". *Proceedings of the 10th International Conference on Computer-Aided Design and Computer Graphics*, pp. 361-364, ISBN 978-1-4244-1578-6, Beijing, China.

Wikipedia website, http://www.wikipedia.org

12

Study about controlling and optimizing the power quality in case of nonlinear power loads

Panoiu Manuela and Panoiu Caius
Polytechnical University of Timişoara
România

1. Introduction

An electrical arc furnace EAF transforms the electrical power into thermal power by melting in electric arc furnace the raw materials and wastes. During the arc furnace operation, the random property of arc melting process and the control system are the main reasons of the electrical and thermal dynamics. That will cause serious power quality problems to the supply system, (Andrews et al., 1996), (Wu et al., 2002), (Panoiu et al., 2006), (Panoiu et al., 2007 b). Therefore, the installed power reaches up to 1 MW/t. The AC arc furnace has a non-linear current-voltage characteristic. Therefore it acts as a source of disturbance in the network in which it is supplied. It emits both harmonics and interharmonics and generates voltage unbalances, voltage dips and voltage fluctuations.
However, one of the most substantial disadvantages of arc furnace is caused by the reactive power due to the non-linearity of the electric arc. The significant values of the reactive power cause important losses of active power, therefore the efficiency are affected (Panoiu, 2001), (Panoiu & Panoiu 2007), (Panoiu et al., 2007 c) and (Panoiu et al., 2007 d).
In scope of improving the efficiency of the entire installation it is necessary to use a complex installation for reactive power compensation, harmonics currents filter and load balancing. In order to design such complex installation it is necessary to perform a simulation of the electric arc furnace installation. This simulation is based on the electric arc modelling using PSCAD-EMTDC simulation program. The proposed solution is based on some measurements made at a steel factory in Romania, where there is in function a 100 MVA UHP EAF.

2. Measurements on 30 kV line voltage supply

The measurements were made at a 3-phase power supply installation of a 3-phase EAF of 100 t, where is not connected reactive power compensation installation, neither the filters for the harmonic currents or the load balancing device. It is been used a computer with a data acquisition board. All measurements were made on low and medium line voltage supply. In scope of determining the voltages and currents form variations and spectral characteristics of them and also the form variations of quality energy indicators, the measurements were made during the whole duration of process.

The waveforms of the currents and voltages on the low line voltage supply are detailed presented in (Panoiu, 2001) and (Panoiu et al., 2006).
Because our interest is referring to 30 kV line voltage supply, in this chapter are presented the measurements results on this line.
In figure 1 is presented the waveform of the voltage and current in melting phase and in figure 2 the waveform in the phase of stable burning of the electric arc.

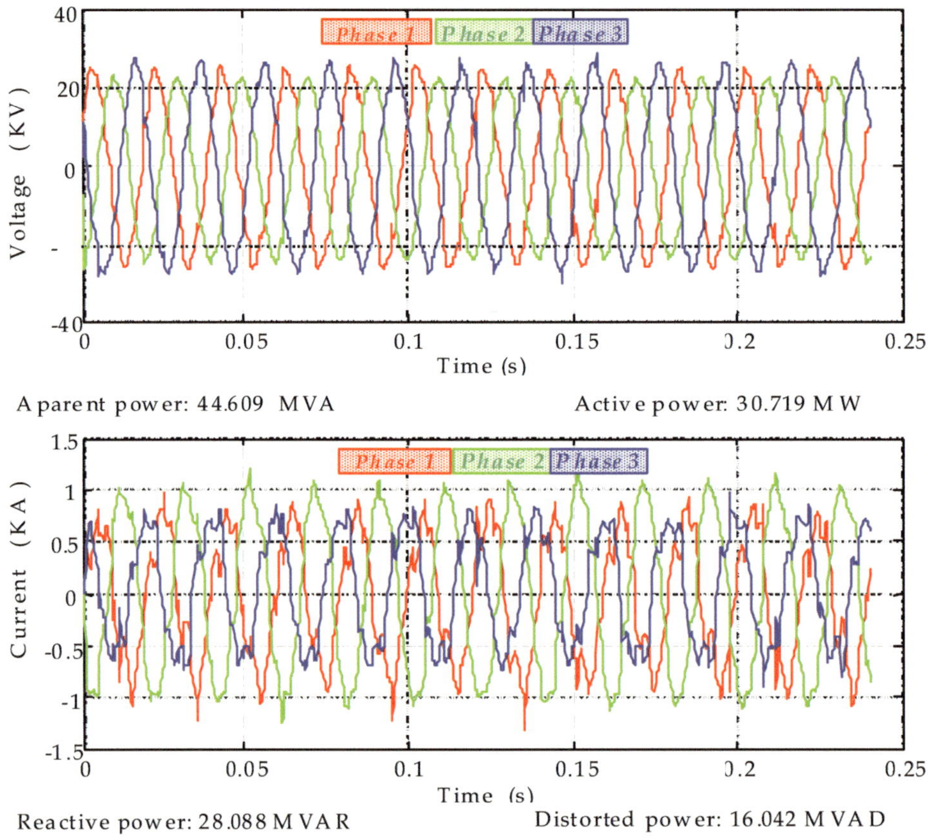

Fig. 1. The voltages and currents time variation on 30 kV line voltage supply in melting phase after 12 minutes from the start of charges.

It can be observed that in the melting phase the voltages and currents are strong distorted. Also, it can be noticed that because the amplitudes of the currents and voltages on the 3 phases are unequal, the load is strongly unbalanced. In the phase of the electric arc stable burning, that appears towards the final of the heat making, especially during the stable burning and reduction (deoxidation) processes, is found that the distortions that appear in the currents and voltages wave forms are more reduced.
The spectral characteristics of the current and voltage, presented in figures 3 and 4, were obtained by using a Matlab program to process the data acquired and using the Fast Fourier Transform. The graphical representations are made from 0 Hz to 1000 Hz, which correspond to a 20th maximum harmonic order.

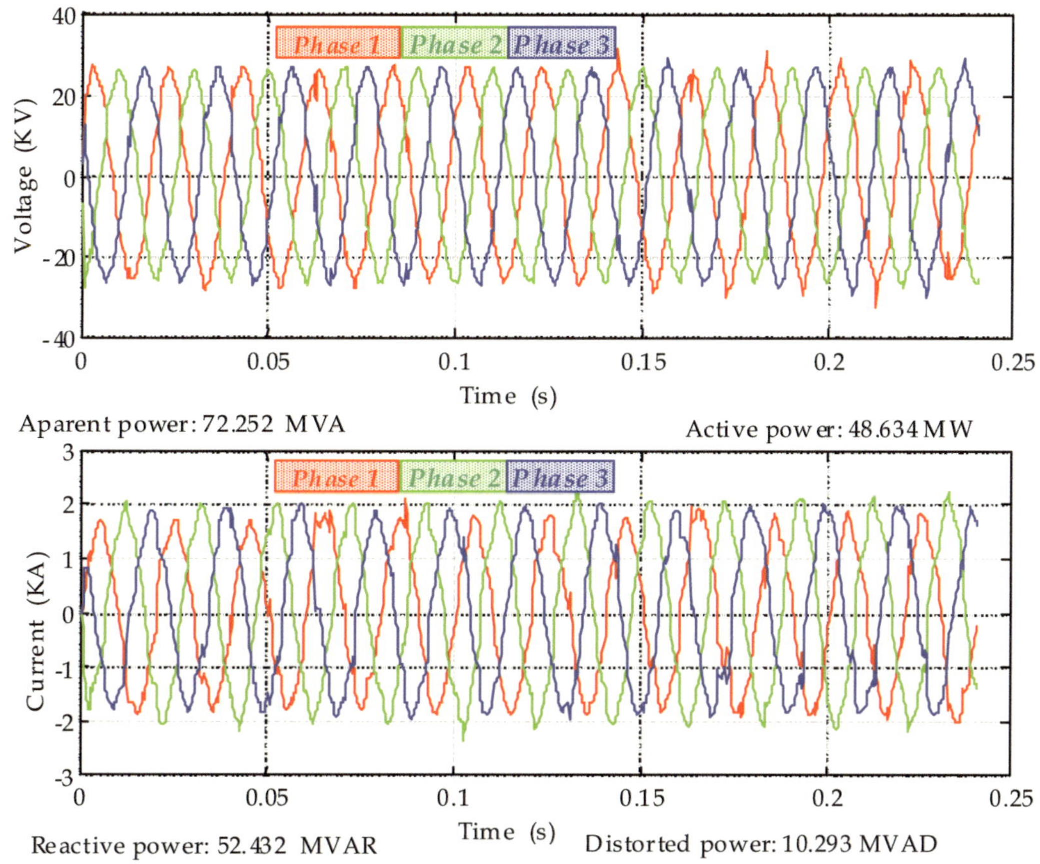

Fig. 2. The voltages and currents time variation on 30 kV line voltage supply in melting phase after 2 hours and 13 minutes from the start of charges.

As regards the voltage on the low voltage line, in the melting phase one can notice the presence of harmonics of 5th, 7th, 11th and 13th order, but also the components of other frequencies than the harmonics (inter-harmonics), while in the oxidation phase is found practically only the presence of the fundamental. This proves that in the melting phase the voltage waveform are much more distorted that in the stable burning phase. In the currents case, is found that in the melting phase is predominant the fundamental frequency component, the other harmonics and inter-harmonics having amplitudes roughly equal, which demonstrates that, in this phase, the current wave is strongly distorted.

In figure 5 is presented the variation of the active and reactive powers on the entire melting process duration. It can be observed that the maximum value is approximately 55 - 60 MW for active power and 50 MVAR for reactive power. These values are used in designing of the reactive power compensation installation and currents harmonic filters.

From the presented above, resulted that, regardless the technological phase, the currents and voltages from the low voltage line are distorted on the entire heat-making duration. Also the unbalanced character of the load it is significant.

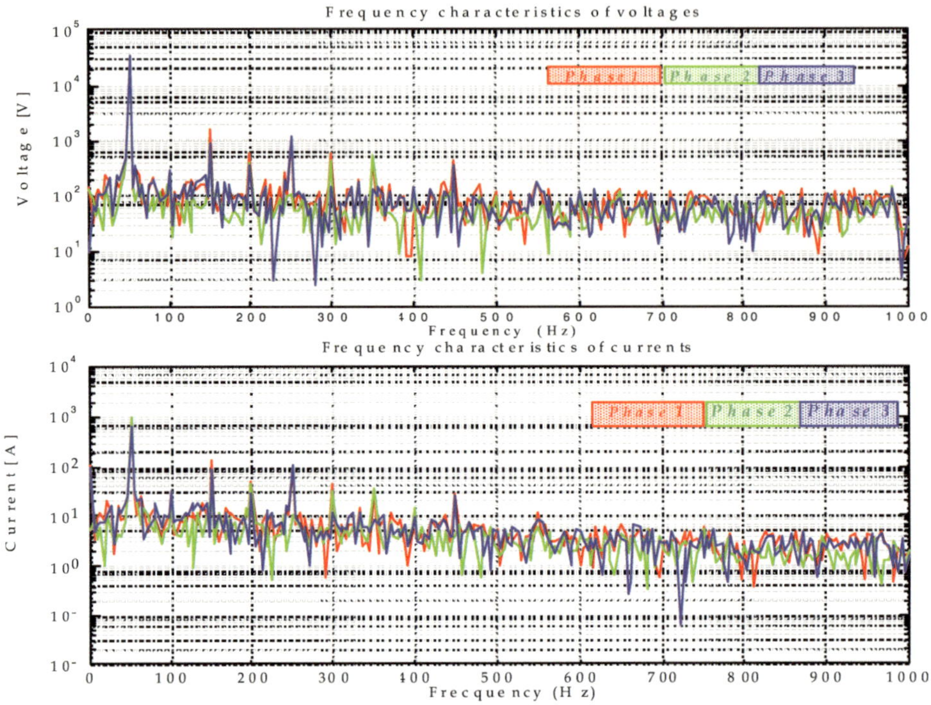

Fig. 3. The frequency characteristics for voltages and currents on 30 kV line voltage supply in melting phase after 12 minutes from the start of melting.

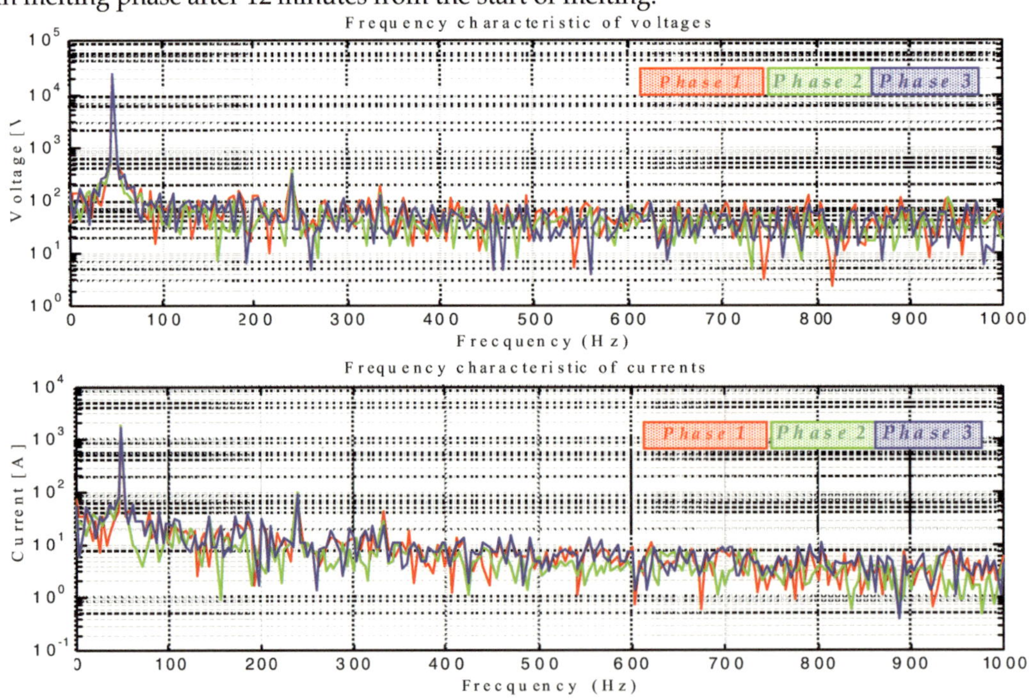

Fig. 4. The frequency characteristics of voltages and currents on 30 kV line voltage supply in melting phase after 2 hours and 13 minutes from the start of melting.

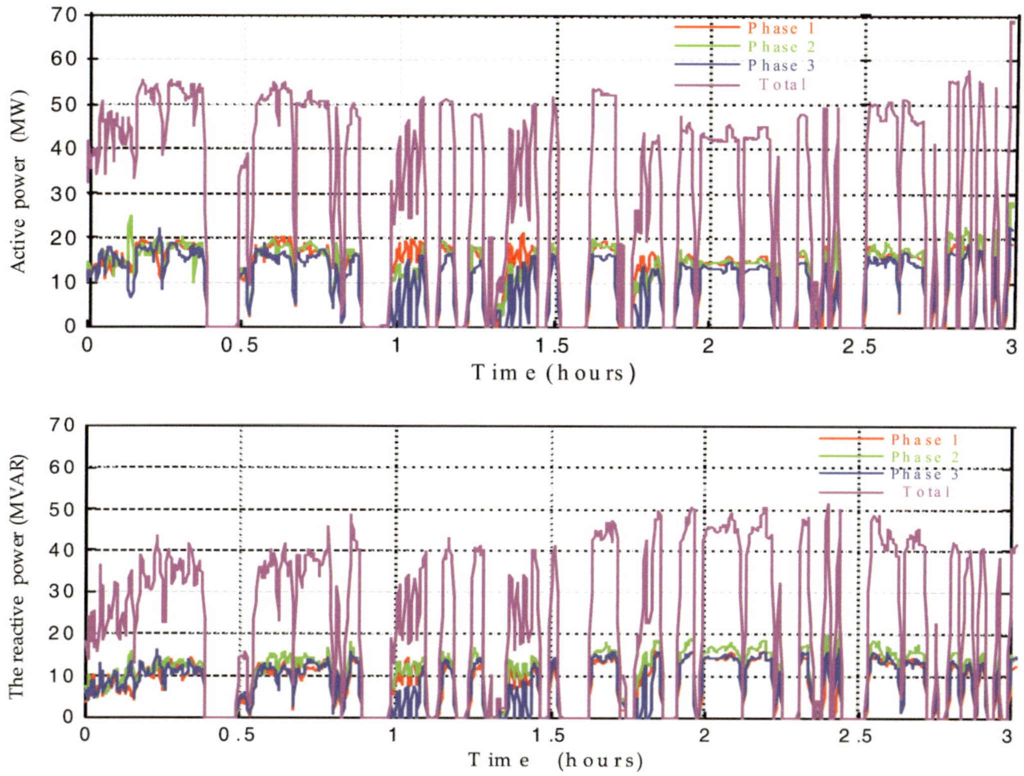

Fig. 5. The variation of the active and reactive powers on the entire melting charge duration.

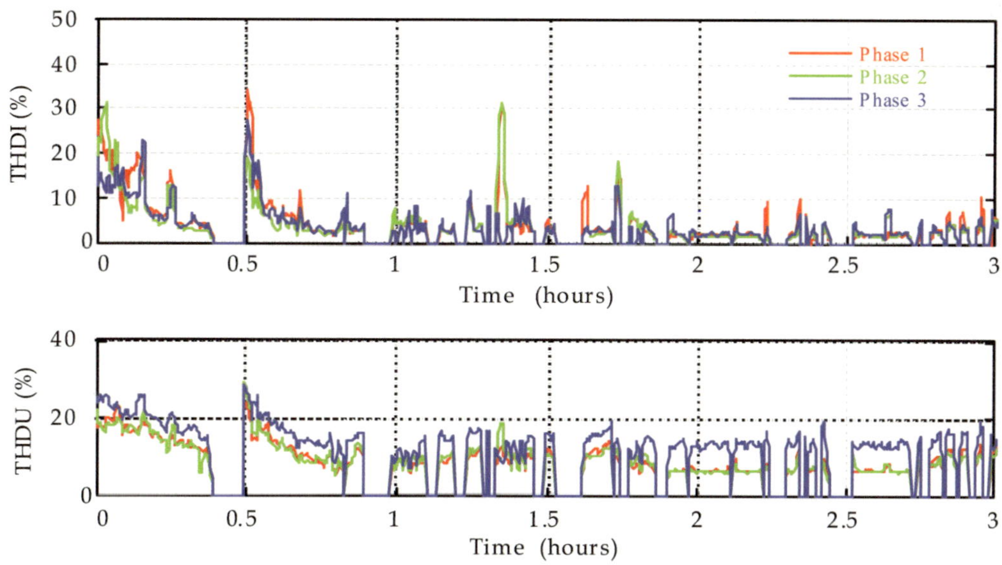

Fig. 6. The variation of the total harmonic distortion of the current and voltage on the entire melting charge duration

In figure 6 is presented the variation form of the total harmonic distortion for the current and voltage waveforms.
There were obtained values between 5 - 25% for total harmonic distortion voltage, respectively 5 - 35%, higher in the melting phase, for the total harmonic distortion current. Comparing these values with the international standards where the value of the permitted total harmonic distortion on the low voltage line is 8% results that these exceed the international standards.

3. Simulation of the electrical installation functioning of the electric arc furnace

3.1. Models of the electric arc

In (Montanari et al., 1994), (Tang et al., 1997), (Panoiu, 2001), (Boulet et al., 2003), (Cano & Tacca, 2005), (Panoiu & Panoiu, 2006) and (Panoiu & Panoiu, 2007) were presented some models for the electric arc. Studying these models, in this chapter was chosen the model based on the empirical relation between the arc current, arc voltage and arc length. This model, given in (Montanari et al., 1994), (Tang et al., 1997), (Panoiu & Panoiu, 2006) and (Panoiu & Panoiu, 2007), considers the characteristic current-voltage described by relation

$$U_A = U_{th} + \frac{C}{D + I_A} \tag{1}$$

In this relation U_A and I_A are the arc voltage and arc current, and Ud are the threshold voltage. The C and D constants determine the difference between the current increasing part and current decreasing part of the current–voltage characteristic (C_a, D_a irrespective C_b, D_b). The typical values are: U_d = 200 V, C_a = 190000 W, C_b = 39000 W, D_a = D_b = 5000 A (Montanari et al., 1994) and (Tang et al., 1997). Because the real values of the model parameters depend on the voltage arc variations, the dynamic arc voltage–current characteristic must be an arc length function, given by relation (2) in which U_{A0} represent the value of the arc voltage for a reference arc length l_0 and k is the ratio between the threshold voltage value for arc length l, $U_{th}(l)$ and the threshold voltage value for arc length l_0, $U_{th}(l_0)$.

$$U_A = k \cdot U_{A0}(I_A) \tag{2}$$

The dynamic model for electric arc presumes that the relation between the threshold voltage value and the arc length can be expressed by:

$$U_{th} = A + Bl \tag{3}$$

In (3) A is a constant equal with the sum of cathode and anodic threshold voltages ($A \cong 40V$) and B represent the threshold voltage on the unit length, having usual values of 10 V/cm. The dependency of k by the electric arc length is given by:

$$k(l) = \frac{A + B \cdot l}{A + B \cdot l_0} \tag{4}$$

The PSCAD-EMTDC electrical scheme of the EAF is presented in figure 7.

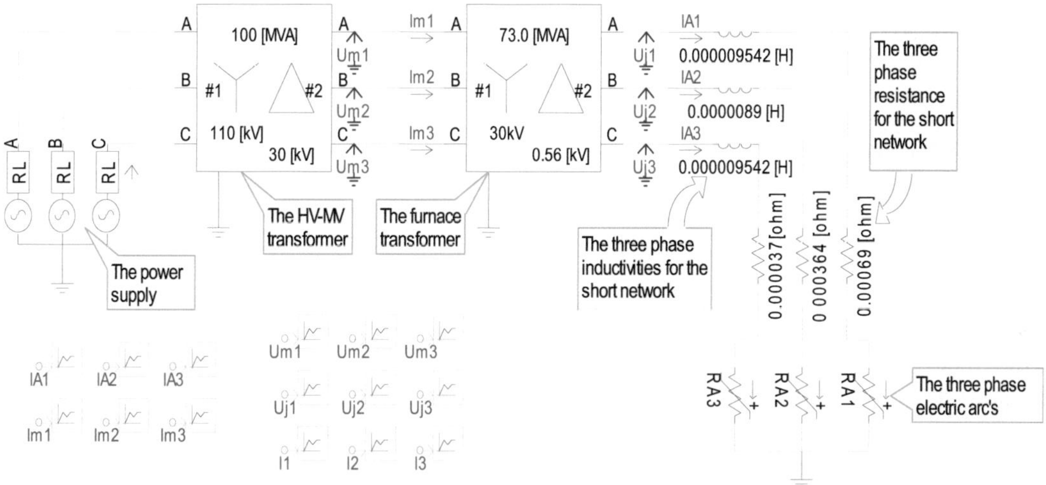

Fig. 7. The simulation circuit for the electrical installation of the EAF.

The parameters of the electrical installation of the EAF were measured on the actual installation at a steel factory. The relation (5) and (6) present the values of the short network parameters. The resistances on each phase are:

$$\begin{aligned} R_{r1} &= 0.6908\,\mathrm{m\Omega}, \\ R_{r2} &= 0.3640\,\mathrm{m\Omega}, \\ R_{r3} &= 0.0372\,\mathrm{m\Omega}, \end{aligned} \tag{5}$$

The total inductivities on each phase are:

$$\begin{aligned} L_{r1} &= L_{r3} = 9.5422\,\mu\mathrm{H} \\ L_{r2} &= 8.9416\,\mu\mathrm{H} \end{aligned} \tag{6}$$

Because the impedances of medium voltage supplying line are small compared with the ones from the low voltage line, these were included in the EAF transformer parameters. The values of the main parameters of the EAF transformer are 73 MVA, 30KV/0,6KV, Δ/Y connections.

3.2. The reactive power compensation, harmonics filters and load balancing installation design

To determine the values of the elements of the harmonic filters and reactive power compensation installation it was used the measurement results performed on the installation of the 100 tones electric arc furnace, presented in figure 5.

Starting from these results and taking into consideration the desired power factor of $\cos\Phi = 0.95$, the total reactive power which must be compensated is given by relation (7).

$$Q_{total} = 84.2 \text{ MVAR} \tag{7}$$

The total reactive power which must be compensated is composed by two parts. The first part is the fixed reactive power which is chosen taking into consideration the figure 5 and it is given by relation (8).

$$Q_{const} = 25.8 \text{ MVAR} \tag{8}$$

The fixed reactive power is composed by the reactive power which is obtained on fundamental frequency due to harmonic filters and a reactive power due to the fixed battery. Taking into account the measurements on the 30 kV supplying line feed, the nominal currents for the filters design are $I_n^5 = 100\text{A}$, $I_n^7 = 50\text{A}$, $I_n^{11} = 25\text{A}$ and $I_n^{13} = 25\text{A}$. These values have been determined from measured data using FFT (Fast Fourier Transform). To determine the values of the filters capacitors it is necessary to know the values of the kth order harmonics currents, because, following the standards, a capacitor with a certain nominal voltage U_{n50}, corresponding to the fundamental with the frequency of 50 Hz and a certain nominal current I_{n50} can function in a long time distorted regime characterized by $U_{ef} = 1.1 \cdot U_{n50}$ and $I_{ef} = 1.3 \cdot I_{n50}$, which mean a overloading by 43%. For this reason it is important to determine the nominal value for the k – harmonic. The harmonic filters were designed using these values and were obtained the component values from figure 8. The reactive power from harmonic filters is given by relation (9) and the reactive power from fixed battery is given from relation (10).

$$Q_F = Q_F^5 + Q_F^7 + Q_F^{11} + Q_F^{13} = 12.53 \text{ MVAR} \tag{9}$$

$$Q_{fixed\ battery} = 13.27 \text{ MVAR} \tag{10}$$

In conclusion the constant reactive pover is composed from four parts due to the harmonic filters and one part due to the fixed battery, as in relation (11).

$$\begin{aligned} Q_F^5 &= 6.785 \text{ MVAR}, \\ Q_F^7 &= 2.494 \text{ MVAR}, \\ Q_F^{11} &= 1.628 \text{ MVAR}, \\ Q_F^{13} &= 1.624 \text{ MVAR}, \\ Q_{fixed\ battery} &= 13.27 \text{ MVAR}. \end{aligned} \tag{11}$$

Knowing the maximum value of the reactive power during the whole charge and the reactive power of the harmonic filters, it can be determined the variable reactive power needed to be compensated. From the condition that the voltage variation to be less then 0.4% result that the number of steps of the fixed reactive power compensation installation is 14. From the value of the variable reactive power, relation (12), result the value of a step reactive power from relation (13).

$$Q_{var} = 58.4 \text{ MVAR} \tag{12}$$

$$\Delta Q_{step} = 4.17 \text{ MVAR} \tag{13}$$

In figure 9 is presented the PSCAD-EMTDC simulation scheme for the electrical installation of the EAF with all improvement power quality installations.

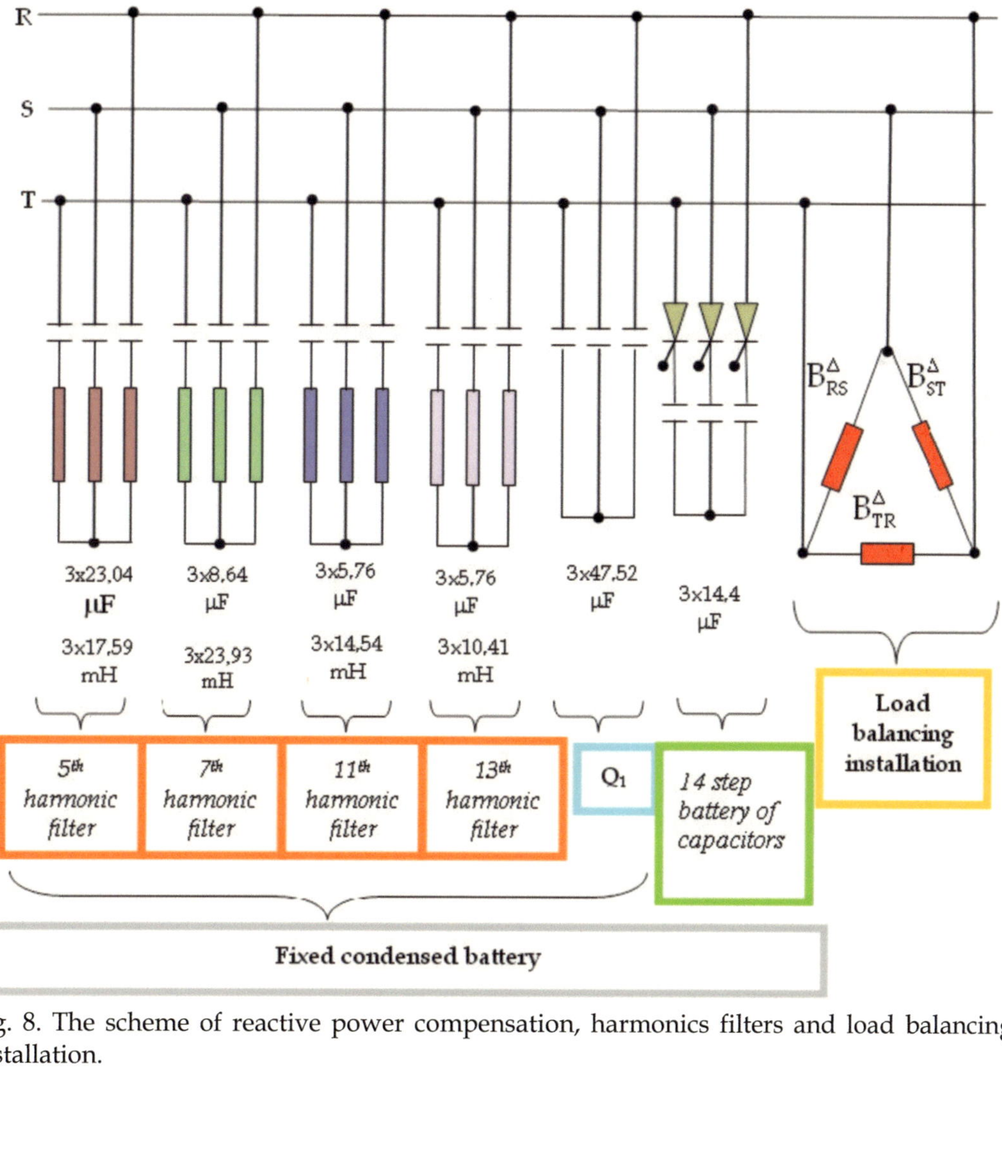

Fig. 8. The scheme of reactive power compensation, harmonics filters and load balancing installation.

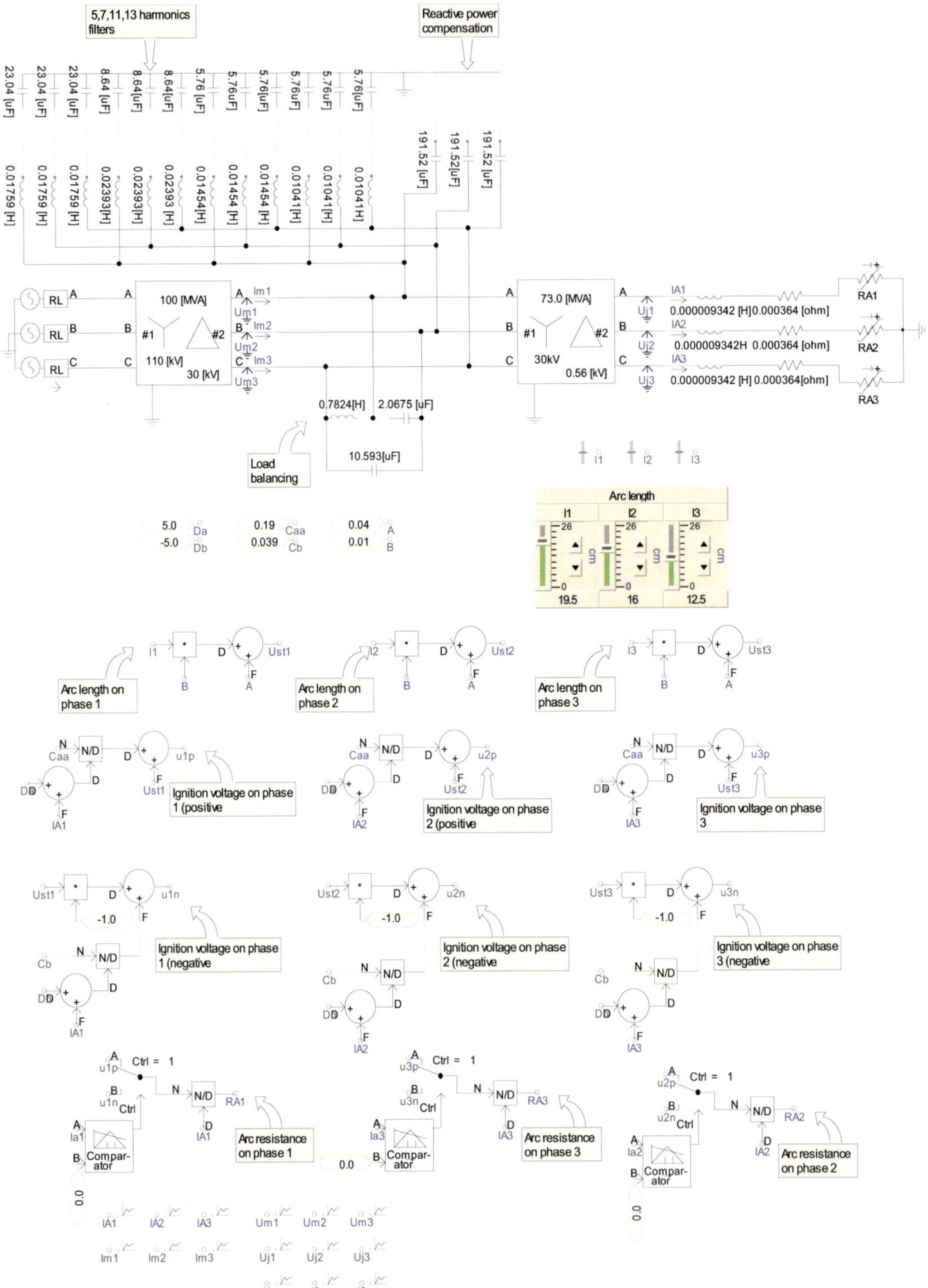

Fig. 9. The PSCAD-EMTDC simulation scheme for the electrical installation of the EAF.

4. Simulation results for the UHP EAF

For simulation it was use an electric arc model which is detailed presented in (Panoiu & Panoiu 2007), (Panoiu et al., 2007 a) and (Panoiu et al., 2007 d). In order to obtain conclusions about the effects of reactive power compensation, current harmonics filters and load balancing, simulations were made in five different cases, presented in the next sections.

4.1. Simulation results without improving the functioning regime

Because the EAF power supply is made through a 3-phase network with 3 conductors, the homopolar currents that appear have small values, thus they can be neglected. In these conditions, the expression for power factor is given by relation (14) (Buta et al., 1996), (Ionescu & Pop, 1998) and (Buta & Pană, 2000):

$$k_p = \frac{\cos\phi_1^+}{\sqrt{1 + k_{ni1}^2 \cdot \left(1 + \sum_{k=2}^{\infty}\left(\gamma_{I_k}^-\right)^2\right) + \sum_{k=2}^{\infty}\left(\gamma_{I_k}^+\right)^2}} \tag{14}$$

From the analysis of the expression for power factor it found that this emphasizes both the non-symmetric regime, by the asymmetry coefficient k_{ni1}, and the non-sinusoidal one, by the level of the harmonic currents of direct and reverse sequence for the harmonics of rank higher than one, γ_{Ik}^- and γ_{Ik}^+ .

As regards the effect of the three elements, meaning the circulation of the reactive power on the fundamental, the unbalance of the currents, respectively their non-sinusoidal upon the loss increasing in the network, this one is different. If it is considered the loss reduction by applying of the three optimization actions as being

$$\frac{\Delta P}{\Delta P_{min}} = \frac{1 + k_{ni1}^2 \cdot \left(1 + \sum_{k=2}^{\infty}\left(\gamma_{I_k}^-\right)^2\right) + \sum_{k=2}^{\infty}\left(\gamma_{I_k}^+\right)^2}{\cos^2\phi_1^+}, \tag{15}$$

it can be established the sensitivity of the loss reduction by each of the reminded actions, calculating the partial derivatives. Thus can be calculated:

- the sensitivity of the loss reduction with load balancing on the fundamental,

$$\frac{\partial\left(\Delta P / \Delta P_{min}\right)}{\partial k_{ni1}} = 2 \cdot k_{ni1} \cdot \frac{1 + \sum_{k=2}^{\infty}\left(\gamma_{I_k}^-\right)^2}{\cos^2\phi_1^+} \tag{16}$$

- the sensitivity reffering to harmonics atenuation

$$\frac{\partial\left(\Delta P / \Delta P_{min}\right)}{\partial \gamma_{Ik}^-} = \frac{2 \cdot k_{ni1}^2 \cdot \gamma_{Ik}^-}{\cos^2\phi_1^+} \tag{17}$$

respectively

$$\frac{\partial\left(\Delta P / \Delta P_{min}\right)}{\partial \gamma_{Ik}^{+}} = \frac{2 \cdot \gamma_{Ik}^{+}}{\cos^{2} \phi_{1}^{+}} \tag{18}$$

- the sensitivity against the improvement of the power factor on fundamental:

$$\frac{\partial\left(\Delta P / \Delta P_{min}\right)}{\partial \cos \phi_{1}^{+}} = -\frac{2}{\cos^{3} \phi_{1}^{+}}\left[1 + k_{ni1}^{2} \cdot \left(1 + \sum_{k=2}^{\infty}\left(\gamma_{I_k}^{-}\right)^{2}\right) + \sum_{k=2}^{\infty}\left(\gamma_{I_k}^{+}\right)^{2}\right] \tag{19}$$

Studying the usual values of the quantity that are part of the relations (16) - (19), it results that the optimization actions efficiency in power loss reductions is given, in the importance order, by the reactive power compensation for improving the power factor, reducing the harmonics currents and load balancing. In table 1 are presented the results obtained by simulations in conditions where not performed any optimization action.
The presented data were determined by simulation using PSCAD-EMTDC, where the unbalanced regime was obtained for unequal values of the electric arc length (Panoiu et al., 2007 a). The results were obtained based on the data obtained by simulations, using Matlab program.

	The fundamental	*5th harmonic*	*7th harmonic*	*11th harmonic*	*13th harmonic*
$\underline{I}_R$	-458.16-1324.82 j	-18.02+46.25 j	6.89+26.80 j	-9.58-3.44 j	-8.19+2.20 j
I_R	1401.81	49.64	27.67	10.17	8.48
$\underline{I}_S$	-876.95+1248.53 j	-27.63-16.91 j	6.80-24.86 j	0.83-3.00 j	7.07-1.39 j
I_S	1525.73	32.39	25.77	3.11	7.21
$\underline{I}_T$	1335.10+76.29 j	45.65-29.34 j	-13.69-1.94 j	8.75+6.43 j	1.11-0.81 j
I_T	1337.28	54.27	13.82	10.86	1.38
$\underline{I}^{+}$	-567.17-1300.31 j	-12.53+1.93 j	10.07+19.39 j	-1.99-3.97 j	-3.92+2.85 j
I^{+}	1418.62	12.68	21.85	4.44	4.84
$\underline{I}^{-}$	109.48-23.63 j	-5.54+44.34 j	-3.20+7.59 j	-7.55+0.58 j	-4.32-0.59 j
I^{-}	112.00	44.68	8.24	7.57	4.36
$\underline{I}^{0}$	(-1+7 j)4e-013	(-4.5-5 j)e-013	(2.5-4 j)e-013	(-8-1.8 j)e-013	(-3.5-2 j)e-013
I^{0}	7.41e-013	6.7328e-013	4.58e-013	8.11e-013	4.07e-013
k_{ni} [%]	7.90	352.32	37.70	170.58	90.11
k_{nu}[%]	0.05	368.09	37.50	191.39	85.77
γ_{IkR}	0.98815	0.03499	0.01950	0.00717	0.00598
γ_{IkS}	1.07550	0.02283	0.01817	0.00219	0.00508
γ_{IkT}	0.94266	0.03825	0.00974	0.00765	0.00097
γ_{UkR}	1.00036	0.00092	0.00062	0.00026	0.00024
γ_{UkS}	0.99946	0.00061	0.00056	0.00010	0.00020
γ_{UkT}	1.00017	0.00100	0.00031	0.00028	0.00004

Table 1. Simulations results without reactive power compensation, load balancing and harmonics filtering.

Analyzing the presented results is found that:

- the power supply system is unbalanced, fact which results from the values of the asymmetry coefficients of currents and voltages (much higher for harmonics) and due to the high value of the reverse sequence component of the current, both for fundamental, 112 A, and for harmonics. It must be noticed that the 5th harmonic has the effective value of the reverse sequence current of 44.68 A.
- the EAF is an important harmonics generator in the power supply line, which results from the high values of direct sequence currents, respectively reverse sequence of the harmonics of rank 5, 7, 11 and 13. Also is found an important unbalance of the harmonic currents, especially for the 5th harmonic.
- the values of the homopolar currents obtained following simulations are very small, fact which justifies the previously made approximations.

In figure 10 are represented the phasors of currents and voltages, as well as of their components of direct and reverse sequence.

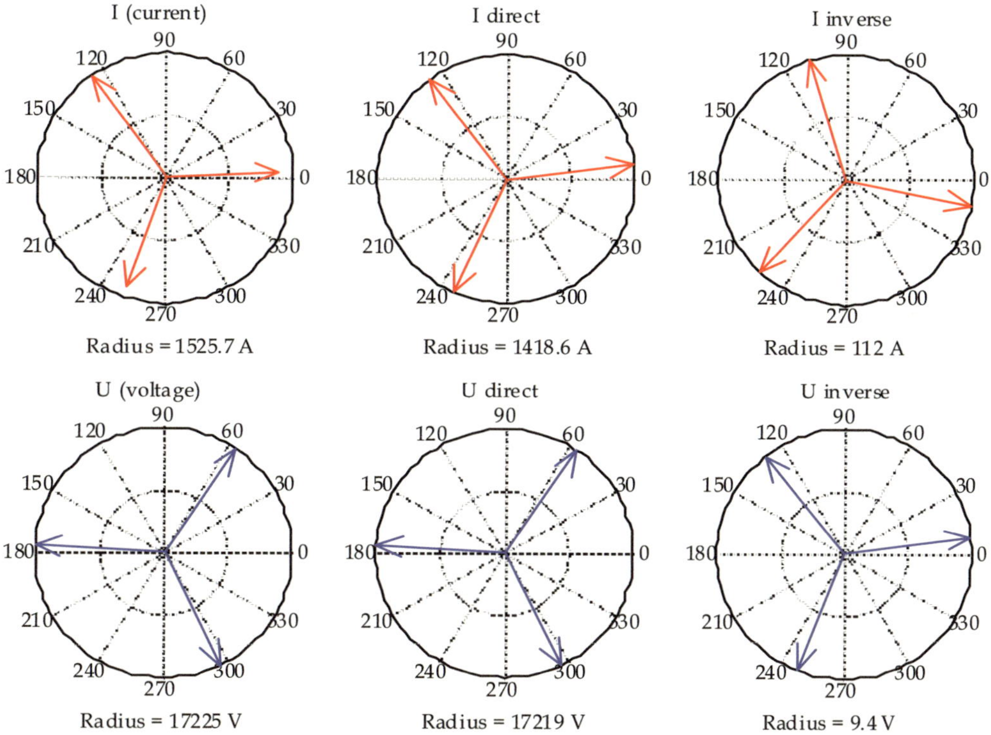

Fig. 10. Current and voltage phasors without any quality energy improvement action

4.2. Simulation results with reactive power compensation

In this situation is not taken into account the presence of the unbalanced and non-sinusoidal regime, for the improvement of the power factor being made a symmetrical transversal capacitive compensation. The values of the compensation currents, the same on each phase, are determined from the cancelling condition of the reactive component of the direct sequence current corresponding to the fundamental, which leads to $\cos\phi_1^{+c} = 1$, i.e.

$$I_m\left(\underline{I}_1^{+c}\right)=0 \tag{20}$$

The Y compensator designing is made starting from the currents and voltages values, from table 1, resulted following simulation of electrical installation operation for which was not performed any optimization action. These values are

$$\begin{aligned} \underline{I}_R &= -458.2-1342.8\,j\ A \\ \underline{I}_S &= -876.9+1248.5\,j\ A \\ \underline{I}_T &= 1335.1+76.3\,j\ A \end{aligned}\ ,\qquad \begin{aligned} \underline{U}_R &= 7598-15459\,j\ V \\ \underline{U}_S &= -17172+143.5\,j\ V \\ \underline{U}_T &= 9574.1+4315\,j\ V \end{aligned} \tag{21}$$

Based on these results the currents and voltages direct sequence components (Buta et al., 1996) and (Buta & Pană, 2000) are given by:

$$\begin{aligned} \underline{I}^+ &= -567.16-1300.3\,j = 1418.6\cdot e^{-j\,113.56^\circ} \\ \underline{U}^+ &= 7601.5-15450.7\,j = 17219\cdot e^{-j\,63.80^\circ} \end{aligned} \tag{22}$$

The value of the capacity, necessary for compensation, results from the cancelling condition of the reactive component for direct current, is given by relation:

$$C^Y=\frac{I^+\cdot\sin\left(\underline{I}^+,\underline{U}^+\right)}{\omega U^+}=200.18\ \mu F. \tag{23}$$

The simulations performed on the step most closely to the value given by (23), for the compensation installation previously calculated, $C_1^Y=205.92\ \mu F$, have shown that on this step is not succeeding a total cancelling of the reactive component for direct current, the phase difference being $\Delta\phi_1=-1.4422^\circ$.

Making simulations on the previous step, $C_2^Y=191.52\ \mu F$, it was found that the phase difference increased to the value $\Delta\phi_2=3.4229^\circ$, with inductive character. Even if further to an iterative process was found that the optimal value for capacity, for which is obtained a null phase difference, is $C_{optim}^Y=201.7\ \mu F$, close to the value given by the relation (23), the results of the compensation action, presented in table 2, are the ones obtained at the operation on the optimal step of the compensation installation, where $C_1^Y=205.92\ \mu F$.

In case of reactive power compensation, it should not intervene upon the reverse component of the current on fundamental, but, in return, the direct sequence component is reduced from I_1^+ to $I_1^{+c}=I_1^+\cdot\cos\phi_1^+=\mathrm{Re}\left(\underline{I}_1^+\right)$, I_1^+ respectively $\cos\phi_1^+$ being the direct current, respectively the power factor on fundamental. In accordance, the asymmetry coefficient on fundamental, after compensation, becomes

$$k_{ni1} = \frac{I_1^-}{I_1^+ \cdot \cos\phi_1^+} \qquad (24)$$

It can be observed that the asymmetry coefficient on fundamental is increasing the smaller is the power factor before compensation. In case of reactive power compensation the non-symmetry regime is emphasizing.

	The fundamental	*5th harmonic*	*7th harmonic*	*11th harmonic*	*13th harmonic*
$\underline{I}_R$	537.55-842.88 j	-15.01+51.92 j	13.06+28.78 j	-12.11-0.02 j	-7.79+7.00 j
I_R	999.70	54.04	31.61	12.11	10.47
$\underline{I}_S$	-955.84+147.55 j	-31.90-15.42 j	2.71-29.00 j	-0.58-3.79 j	6.93-5.35 j
I_S	967.16	35.43	29.13	3.83	8.76
$\underline{I}_T$	418.29+695.33 j	46.91-36.50 j	-15.77+0.22 j	12.69+3.81 j	0.86-1.65 j
I_T	811.45	59.44	15.77	13.25	1.86
$\underline{I}^+$	427.36-817.82 j	-13.45+3.34 j	15.04+19.79 j	-3.85-3.80 j	-2.80+5.31 j
I^+	922.75	13.86	24.86	5.41	6.00
$\underline{I}^-$	109.57-24.91 j	-1.53+48.75 j	-2.01+8.95 j	-8.32+3.84 j	-4.96+1.69 j
I^-	112.37	48.78	9.17	9.16	5.24
$\underline{I}^0$	(2.7-2.4 j)e-013	(-6.5-5 j)e-013	(-1-1.5 j)e-013	(3.7-7 j)e-013	(7.5-7 j)e-013
I^0	3.6e-013	8.1e-013	1.9e-013	7.7e-013	1.009e-012
k_{ni} [%]	12.18	351.98	36.89	169.49	87.34
k_{nu}[%]	0.05	350.09	36.97	166.46	87.96
γ_{IkR}	1.08340	0.05857	0.03425	0.01312	0.01135
γ_{IkS}	1.04813	0.03839	0.03157	0.00415	0.00949
γ_{IkT}	0.87939	0.06441	0.01709	0.01436	0.00202
γ_{UkR}	1.00037	0.00100	0.00068	0.00030	0.00027
γ_{UkS}	0.99947	0.00065	0.00063	0.00010	0.00023
γ_{UkT}	1.00016	0.00109	0.00034	0.00033	0.00004

Table 2. Simulations results using only reactive power compensation.

In figure 11 there were represented the phasors of the fundamental currents and voltages, as well as of the direct and reverse sequence components. Is found that, on one side, the current and voltage phasors for the direct sequence are in phase, but also a decreasing of the value of current combined with the increase of the value of voltage.

4.3. Simulation results with load balancing

In this situation it does intervene upon the load balancing without aiming the improvement of the power factor or harmonics decrease. Compensation is non-symmetrical and is possible by means of a circuit in Δ connection, which contains only susceptances, connected in parallel with the mains, in the section where the balancing is desired. This method consists in the computing of element for the load balancing installation using the current and voltage values obtained after the best compensation of the reactive power, the balancing installation being in this case a compensator in Δ conection that can compensate totally the reactive power difference.

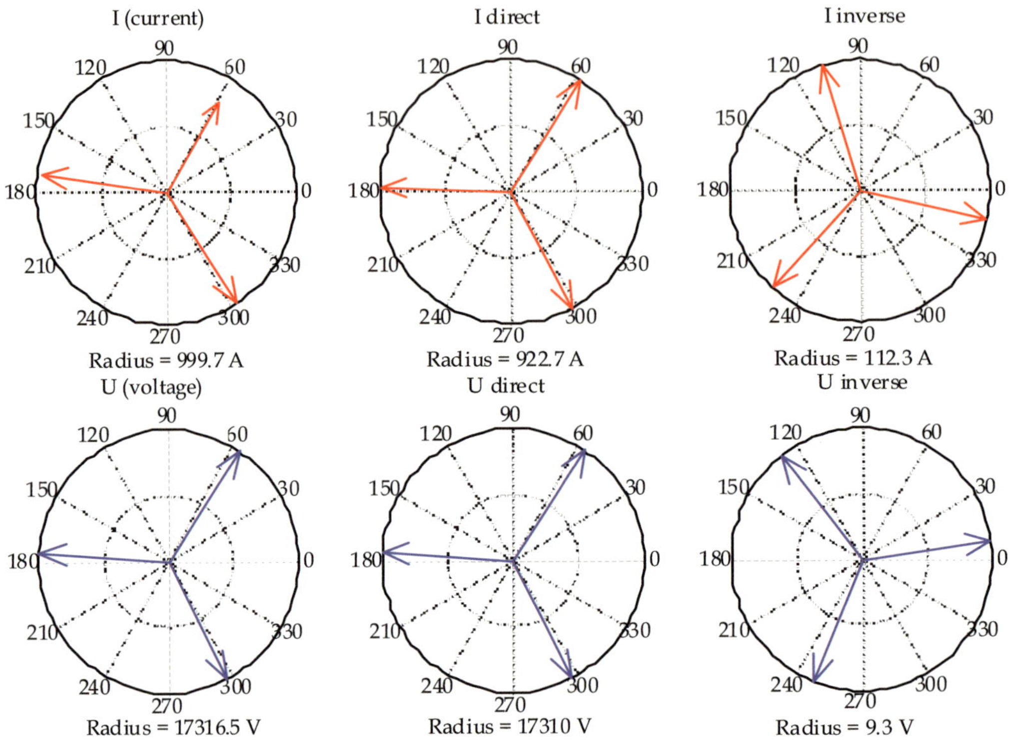

Fig. 11. Current and voltage phasors using only reactive power compensation

The advantages of the proposed method consist in:

- reactive power compensator assembly – balancing installation which has the same performances as a reactive power total compensator together with a balancing installation which does not consume reactive power;
- the load balancing installation, even if it consumes reactive power, has so small values of elements that the thyristors from the structure will not be overloaded. In these conditions it can be achieved also a continuous tunning of the compensators reactive power.

The computing of the balancing installation starts from determination of the currents and voltages values in case of the best reactive power compensation, using the optimal value of the a compensation capacity $C_{optim}^{Y} = 201.7\ \mu F$. These values were obtained based on the data resulted following simulation, being given by the relations

$$\begin{aligned}
\underline{I}_R^S &= 516.93 - 852.41\, j\ A \\
\underline{I}_S^S &= 952.32 + 167.66\, jA \\
\underline{I}_T^S &= 435.39 + 684.74\, j\ A \\
\underline{U}_R^S &= 7624.4 - 15547\, j\ V \\
\underline{U}_S^S &= -17260 + 1163.9\, j\ V \\
\underline{U}_T^S &= 9635.6 + 4381\, j\ V
\end{aligned} \tag{25}$$

Based on (25) it can be computed the load admittances in Y connection

$$
\begin{aligned}
\underline{Y}_R^S &= G_R\text{-}jB_R = 0.057343 + 0.005128\,j = 0.057572 \cdot e^{j\,5.1102^\circ} \\
\underline{Y}_S^S &= G_S\text{-}jB_S = 0.055577 - 0.005966\,j = 0.055896 \cdot e^{-j\,6.1270^\circ} \\
\underline{Y}_T^S &= G_T\text{-}jB_T = 0.046861 + 0.001123\,j = 0.046875 \cdot e^{j\,1.3728^\circ}
\end{aligned}
\tag{26}
$$

It is found the presence of an unbalance regarding the modules of the three admittances, while their phases are very small, fact which shows that it was achieved a correct compensation. Based on the load admittances values in Y connection, it can be determined the load admittances values in Δ connection according to the relations provided in (Buta & Pană, 2000).

$$
\begin{aligned}
G_{RS}^S &= \frac{1}{6}\left[(G_R + G_S) + \frac{1}{\sqrt{3}}(B_S - B_R)\right] = 0.01988773 \\
B_{RS}^S &= \frac{1}{6}\left[(B_R + B_S) + \frac{1}{\sqrt{3}}(G_R - G_S)\right] = 0.00030963 \\
G_{TR}^S &= \frac{1}{3}\left[G_R + \frac{1}{\sqrt{3}}(B_R - B_S)\right] = 0.01697944 \\
B_{TR}^S &= \frac{1}{3}\left[B_R + \frac{1}{\sqrt{3}}(G_S - G_R)\right] = -0.00204928 \\
G_{ST}^S &= \frac{1}{3}\left[G_S + \frac{1}{\sqrt{3}}(B_R - B_S)\right] = 0.01639071 \\
B_{ST}^S &= \frac{1}{3}\left[B_S + \frac{1}{\sqrt{3}}(G_S - G_R)\right] = 0.00164883
\end{aligned}
\tag{27}
$$

Designing of the compensator in Δ connection is made based on the cancelling conditions of the reverse sequence current, according to the relation (24) and also cancelling the reactive power absorbed from the mains. This leads to the equations system

$$
\begin{aligned}
&-G_{RS} + 2G_{ST} - G_{TR} + \sqrt{3}(B_{TR} - B_{RS}) = 0 \\
&\sqrt{3}(G_{TR} - G_{RS}) + B_{RS} - 2B_{ST} + B_{TR} = 0 \\
&G_{RS} - G_{TR} - \sqrt{3}(B_{RS} + B_{TR}) = 0
\end{aligned}
\tag{28}
$$

In (28) was used the notations from (29), where the exponent ^{S} define the load elements and the exponent $^\Delta$ defines the compensator elements. Solving the equations system (28) and considering as unknown the compensator susceptances there were obtained the values from (30).

$$
\begin{aligned}
&G_{RS} = G_{RS}^S, && G_{ST} = G_{ST}^S, && G_{TR} = G_{TR}^S, \\
&B_{RS} = B_{RS}^S + B_{RS}^\Delta && B_{ST} = B_{ST}^S + B_{ST}^\Delta && B_{TR} = B_{TR}^S + B_{TR}^\Delta
\end{aligned}
\tag{29}
$$

$$B_{RS}^{\Delta} = -B_{RS}^{S} + \frac{1}{\sqrt{3}}\left(G_{ST}^{S} - G_{TR}^{S}\right) = -0.00064953$$
$$B_{ST}^{\Delta} = -B_{ST}^{S} + \frac{1}{\sqrt{3}}\left(G_{TR}^{S} - G_{SR}^{S}\right) = -0.00332793 \quad (30)$$
$$B_{TR}^{\Delta} = -B_{TR}^{S} + \frac{1}{\sqrt{3}}\left(G_{RS}^{S} - G_{ST}^{S}\right) = 0.00406828$$

In this case the compensator in Δ connection has the elements

$$C_{RS} = 2.0675 \ \mu F$$
$$C_{ST} = 10.5931 \ \mu F \quad (31)$$
$$L_{TR} = 0.7824 \ H$$

With these values, following the performed simulations, it was obtained the results presented in table 3.

	The fundamental	*5th harmonic*	*7th harmonic*	*11th harmonic*	*13th harmonic*
$\underline{I}_R$	-567.81-1300.14 j	-17.94+46.50 j	6.93+26.98 j	-9.60-3.30 j	-8.21+2.37 j
I_R	1418.72	49.84	27.86	10.15	8.55
$\underline{I}_S$	-844.92+1143.65 j	-27.99-16.50 j	6.61-25.54 j	0.37-2.89 j	7.21-1.92 j
I_S	1421.91	32.49	26.38	2.92	7.46
$\underline{I}_T$	1412.73+156.49 j	45.93-30.01 j	-13.54-1.44 j	9.23+6.19 j	1.00-0.45 j
I_T	1421.37	54.86	13.62	11.11	1.10
$\underline{I}^+$	-568.51-1301.39 j	-12.81+1.80 j	10.41+19.33 j	-2.11-4.22 j	-3.68+2.95 j
I^+	1420.15	12.93	21.95	4.72	4.71
$\underline{I}^-$	1.15+1.43 j	-5.22+44.54 j	-3.53+7.67 j	-7.44+0.85 j	-4.56-0.65 j
I^-	1.83	44.85	8.44	7.49	4.60
$\underline{I}^0$	(2.2-1.2 j)e-013	(-4.7-6 j)e-013	(9+9.1 j)e-013	(7.3+3 j)e-013	(6.4+4.4 j)e-014
I^0	2.5e-013	7.6e-013	1.3e-012	7.9e-013	6.4e-013
k_{ni} [%]	0.13	346.75	38.45	158.66	97.65
k_{nu}[%]	0.00	371.23	39.34	193.33	96.09
γ_{IkR}	0.99900	0.03510	0.01962	0.00715	0.00602
γ_{IkS}	1.00124	0.02288	0.01858	0.00205	0.00525
γ_{IkT}	1.00086	0.03863	0.00959	0.00782	0.00077
γ_{UkR}	1.00001	0.00092	0.00062	0.00026	0.00024
γ_{UkS}	0.99998	0.00062	0.00057	0.00010	0.00020
γ_{UkT}	1.00000	0.00101	0.00029	0.00028	0.00003

Table 3. Simulation results using only load balancing.

Analyzing the obtained results it can conclude the following:

- the reverse sequence currents value is very small, fact which demonstrates that it was achieved a good load balancing;
- as regards the currents on the three phases, is found a very good symmetry on the fundamental of the currents of the three phases;

• the asymmetry factor is much reduced compared with the version where there was not action for power quality improvement, presented in table 1;

In figure 12 are represented the currents and voltages phasors as well as of direct and reverse sequence components.

As in case of reactive power compensation, it was a matter of finding some values of the load balancing installation for which should be obtained a value as smaller of the current's reverse sequence component. Following an iterative process, it was found that the optimal values of the balancing installation are given from relation (32), for which was obtained an effective value of the reverse sequence current of $I^{-} = 0.8752\text{A}$, smaller than the one presented in table 3.

$$\begin{aligned} C_{RS,optim} &= 2.10 \ \mu F \\ C_{ST,optim} &= 10.60 \ \mu F \\ L_{TR,optim} &= 0.79 \ H \end{aligned} \tag{32}$$

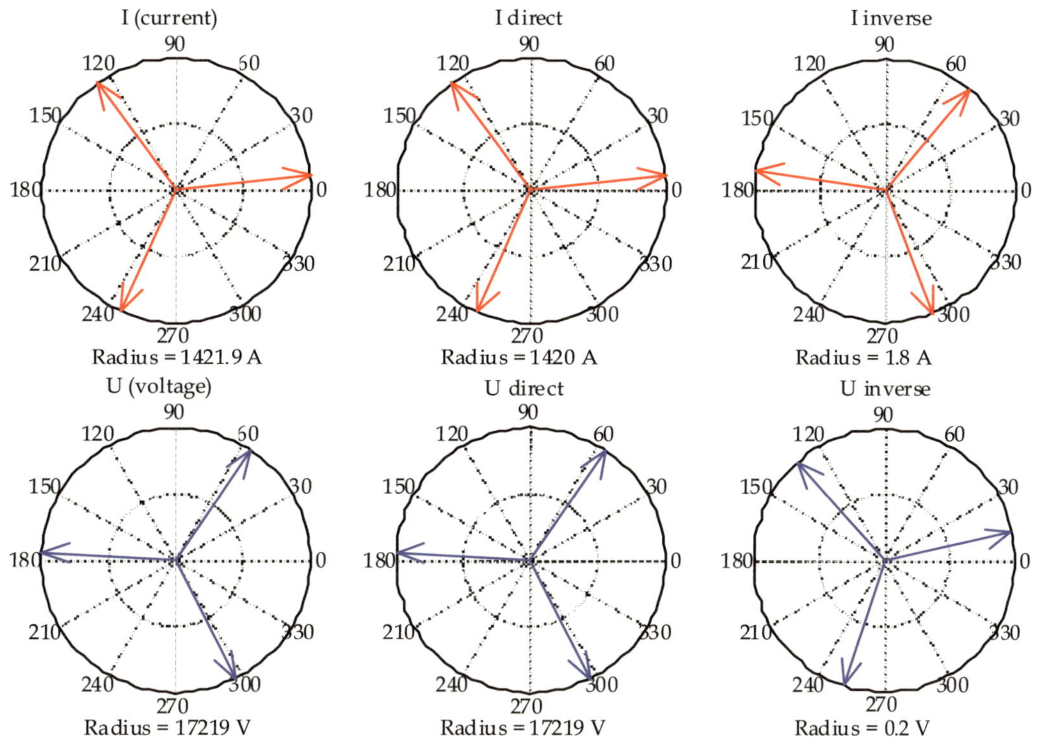

Fig. 12. Current and voltage phasors using only load balancing

4.4. Simulation results with currents harmonics filtering

The filtration of current harmonics is achieved using filters of pass-band type of rank I (Chiuță & Conecini, 1989). Taking into account that normally the main harmonics of the current and voltage are the ones of rank 5, 7, 11 and 13, the analysis of the filters influence was made using the values determined for these filters.

It is known that the dimensioning of resonant circuits can be made based on two criteria, (Chiuță & Conecini, 1989), (Buta & Pană, 2000):

- for circuits in with filtration has the main role;
- for double scope circuits, compensation – filtration.

In case of the filters designed resulted that the calculated filters delivers reactive power on fundamental, see relation (11), in such way that in case of a consumer with inductive character is expected to contribute also to the improvement of the power factor of the consumer-filter unit.

Following the performed simulations using simultaneously the 4 harmonic filters, there were obtained the results presented in table 4, based on which is found as follows:

- the harmonic currents values are strongly diminished, both for the direct sequence component and also for the inverse sequence one;
- because the capacitors disposal on the three phases are identical, it results a compensation of the direct sequence component of the load current.

From this reason results a decrease of their effective values and an emphasizing of the non-symmetry of currents, fact which results also from the values of the non-symmetry coefficients on fundamental.

	The fundamental	*5th harmonic*	*7th harmonic*	*11th harmonic*	*13th harmonic*
$\underline{I}_R$	-167.25-1225.60 j	3.29+6.77 j	5.99+5.25 j	-3.09+0.09 j	-1.93+1.11 j
I_R	1236.96	7.53	7.96	3.09	2.22
$\underline{I}_S$	-947.08+947.05 j	-3.57+1.40 j	-2.35-7.21 j	-0.12-1.05 j	1.84-0.94 j
I_S	1339.35	3.84	7.59	1.05	2.07
$\underline{I}_T$	1114.33+278.56 j	0.28-8.17 j	-3.64+1.97 j	3.21+0.96 j	0.09-0.16 j
I_T	1148.62	8.18	4.14	3.35	0.18
$\underline{I}^{+}$	-276.93-1207.51 j	-1.84+1.05 j	5.57+2.90 j	-1.06-0.95 j	-0.82+1.01 j
I^{+}	1238.86	2.11	6.28	1.43	1.30
$\underline{I}^{-}$	109.48-17.23 j	5.14+4.65 j	0.45+2.32 j	-2.09+0.96 j	-1.11+0.07 j
I^{-}	110.83	6.93	2.36	2.30	1.11
$\underline{I}^{0}$	(-6-1.7 j)e-013	(-5.4-1.2 j)e-013	(1-3.3 j)e-013	(-7.3-1.2 j)e-013	(3-4.2 j)e-013
I^{0}	6.2e-013	5.6e-013	3.5e-013	7.4e-013	5.2e-013
k_{ni} [%]	8.95	327.85	37.67	161.36	85.80
k_{nu}[%]	0.11	1129.99	43.48	608.33	59.92
γ_{IkR}	0.99847	0.00608	0.00643	0.00250	0.00179
γ_{IkS}	1.08111	0.00310	0.00612	0.00085	0.00167
γ_{IkT}	0.92716	0.00660	0.00334	0.00270	0.00015
γ_{UkR}	1.00075	0.00034	0.00048	0.00025	0.00026
γ_{UkS}	0.99894	0.00021	0.00038	0.00019	0.00020
γ_{UkT}	1.00031	0.00026	0.00024	0.00021	0.00010

Table 4. Simulation results using only current harmonics filtering.

In figure 13 are presented the phasors of the fundamental frequency currents and voltages, as well as of their direct and inverse sequence components.

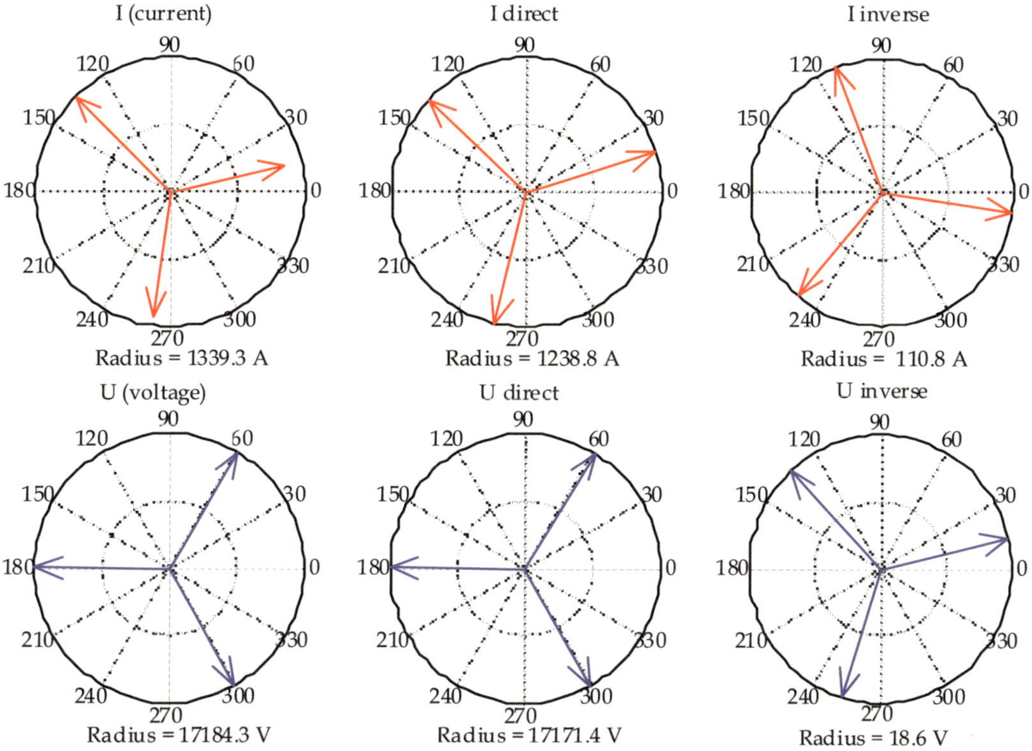

Fig. 13. Current and voltage phasors using only current harmonics filtering

4.5. Simulation results with reactive power compensation, load balancing and current harmonics filtering

From the previous presented is resulting that the performing of one single optimization action from the three ones is not fully advantageous. Thus, usually is eliminated the cause for which was applied the respective measure, while the other perturbation are emphasizing or does not modify. Neither the simultaneous approach of each two of the three aspects doesn't solve totally the problem because, usually, the elimination of two forms the perturbations leads to emphasize of the third.

The most favourable situation, that leads to optimization of the main operation regime, up to the one very close to the ideal one, is obtained obviously, by acting for the simultaneous solving of the three problems (Buta & Pană, 2000). This can be achieved by using of two compensators, one in Y connection and the other one in Δ connection. The first one is mandatory when is desired the filtration of the current harmonics and the second one for balancing. Each of them can fulfil also the compensation function of the reactive power on fundamental frequency. To be noticed, therefore, two designing possibilities of the two compensators, such as:

- Compensator Y fulfils both the filtration and compensation function of the reactive power on fundamental, up to the required level, and compensator Δ fulfils only the load balancing function. Compensation of the reactive power on fundamental will be achieved by the three-phase units of filter, designing of their component capacities being made in such way that the sum of the reactive powers on the direct sequence component for the fundamental frequency to be exactly the reactive power necessary for compensation. This compensation solution is efficient in case of its application in grid sections with small load variations.

- Compensator Y is consisted from filtration units, symmetrically dimensioned, from the condition that the installed capacitive reactive power to be minimum, the Δ compensator having the function that, besides balancing, achieves also the rest of reactive power compensation on the direct sequence component for the fundamental frequency up to the desired level, aiming the improvement of the power factor or voltage adjustment. Due to the possibilities of achieving the Δ compensator with variable susceptances, this compensation solution presents a significantly higher flexibility and efficiency.

From theoretical viewpoint, the two designing methods are absolutely similar. Having in view the fact that the calculated installation is part of the first category, the performed analysis was achieved only for the first case. The results obtained in the case where it does intervene in all the three directions are presented in table 5.

	The fundamental	*5th harmonic*	*7th harmonic*	*11th harmonic*	*13th harmonic*
$\underline{I}_R$	476.56-789.50 j	4.15+6.64 j	6.94+4.57 j	-3.25+0.90 j	-1.70+1.85 j
I_R	922.18	7.83	8.31	3.38	2.51
$\underline{I}_S$	-922.28-19.46 j	-4.70+1.81 j	-3.42-6.83 j	-0.35-0.93 j	1.58-1.43 j
I_S	922.49	5.04	7.64	0.99	2.13
$\underline{I}_T$	445.72+808.96 j	0.55-8.45 j	-3.52+2.26 j	3.61+0.03 j	0.12-0.42 j
I_T	923.62	8.46	4.18	3.61	0.43
$\underline{I}^+$	477.69-789.42 j	-0.91+2.00 j	6.07+2.32 j	-1.32-0.74 j	-0.53+1.31 j
I^+	922.70	2.20	6.50	1.51	1.41
$\underline{I}^-$	-0.55-0.09 j	4.70+4.64 j	0.77+2.36 j	-1.89+1.57 j	-1.17+0.54 j
I^-	0.55	6.60	2.48	2.45	1.29
$\underline{I}^0$	(-4+6.2 j)e-013	(-2.7+8 j)e-014	(1.4+3 j)e-013	(-2.9+3 j)e-013	(2.7-0.5 j)e-013
I^0	7.48873e-013	2.8905e-013	3.55604e-013	4.23877e-013	2.7628e-013
k_{ni} [%]	0.06	300.76	38.17	162.29	91.53
k_{nu}[%]	0.00	296.36	37.83	159.13	90.89
γ_{IkR}	0.99944	0.00848	0.00901	0.00366	0.00272
γ_{IkS}	0.99977	0.00546	0.00828	0.00107	0.00231
γ_{IkT}	1.00099	0.00917	0.00453	0.00391	0.00047
γ_{UkR}	0.99999	0.00031	0.00042	0.00024	0.00020
γ_{UkS}	1.00001	0.00020	0.00039	0.00007	0.00017
γ_{UkT}	1.00000	0.00034	0.00022	0.00026	0.00003

Table 5. Simulation results using reactive power compensation, load balancing and current harmonics filtering.

Both from table 5 and from the graphical representation of the current and voltage phasors from figure 14 is note the following:

- It was achieved a good reactive power compensation, that results because the phase difference between the direct sequence phasors of the current and voltage for fundamental frequency is very small, these being practically in phase;

- the small value of the reverse sequence components for current and voltage shows that it was achieved a good balancing also. This process can be improved in case when the balancing installation elements are calculated as in paragraph 4.3, but as input values are considered the current and voltage values obtained following the reactive power compensation action;
- the small values of the harmonic currents presented in table 5 show that it was achieved a good filtration also;
- in generally, the quality of the electric power in the node in which was intervened is much improved.

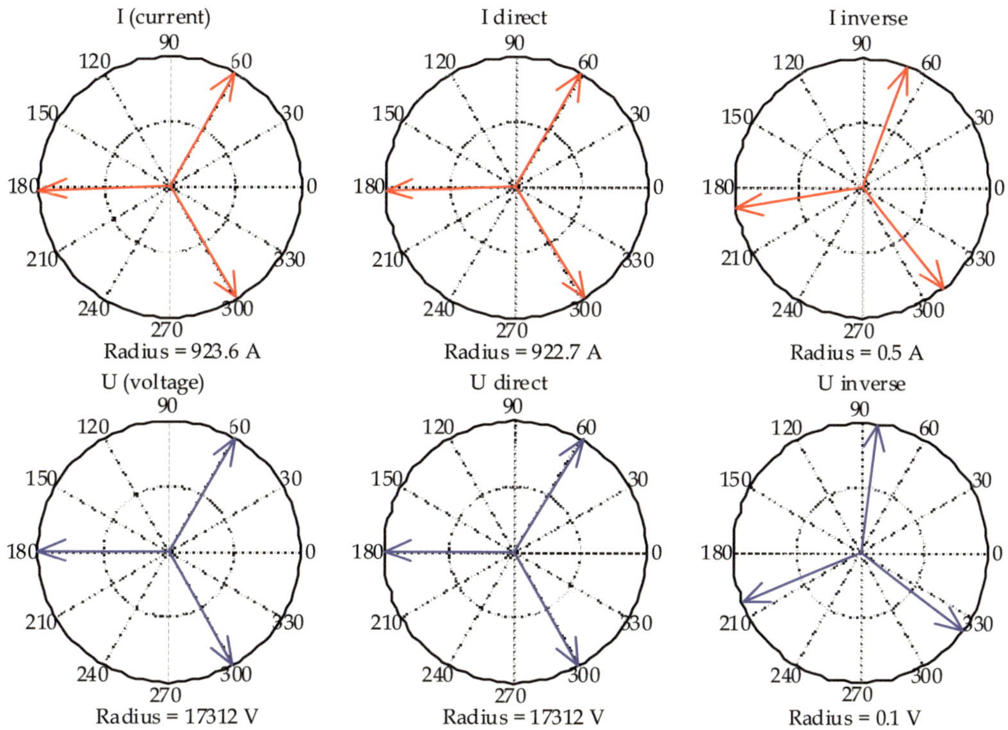

Fig. 14. Current and voltage phasors using reactive power compensation, load balancing and current harmonics filtering

5. Conclusions

From the earlier presented simulations for the 5 cases presented were resulted conclusions referring to the obtained effects in increasing of the power quality in the node in which is acting. The most important indicators are presented in table 6.
Based on these results it can be concluded:

- in the situation in which is acting in only one action of increasing of power quality, the action has effects on reactive power circulation, on currents non-symmetry and non-sinusoidal regime. These effects are synthesized in table 7.

- In situation in which is acting in all three directions is obtaining the best improvement of the power quality in the node in which is acting.

		Without any action	*Only reactive power compensation*	*Only load balance*	*Only currents filtering*	*All three actions*
Y	C	–	205,92 μF	–	–	162,72 μF
	L	–	–	–	–	–
Δ	C_{RS}	–	–	2,0675 μF	–	2,0675 μF
	C_{ST}	–	–	10,5931 μF	–	10,5931 μF
	L_{TR}	–	–	0,7824 H	–	0,7824 H
	U [V]	17219,4	17310,2	17219,2	17171,4	17312,2
	U_1 [V]	17219,4	17310,2	17219,2	17171,4	17312,1
	U_k [V]	20,0996	22,1964	20,2206	25,4385	38,5512
	I [A]	1425,16	932,313	1422,1	1244,61	923,842
	I_1 [A]	1423,76	929,741	1420,67	1244,09	922,762
	I_k [A]	63,17	69,199	63,7738	36,075	44,6559
	$\underline{I}^+$ [A]	-567,17-1300,31 j	427,36-817,82 j	-568,51-1301,39 j	-276,93-1207,5 j	477,69-789,42 j
	I^+ [A]	1418,62	922,75	1420,15	1238,86	922,70
	$\underline{I}^-$ [A]	109,48-23,63 j	109,57-24,91 j	1,15+1,43 j	109,48-17,23 j	-0,55-0,09 j
	I^- [A]	112,00	112,37	1,83	110,83	0,55
	k_{ni}[%]	7,90	12,18	0,13	8,95	0,06
	k_{nu}[%]	0,05	0,05	0,00	0,11	0,00
	k_{ps}	0,645947	0,999684	0,645573	0,737698	0,99957
	k_{pn}	-7,236e-006	-9,967e-006	-1,784e-008	-1,317e-005	-1,127e-009
	k_{pd}	-9,481e-005	-0,000177896	-9,539e-005	-2,494e-005	-7,145e-005
	k_p	0,645845	0,999496	0,645478	0,73766	0,999499
	S[MVA]	73,621	48,416	73,462	64,115	47,981
	S_1[MVA]	73,549	48,282	73,388	64,088	47,925
	S_k[MVA]	3,264	3,594	3,296	1,861	2,322
	P[MW]	47,359	47,904	47,365	47,107	47,904
	Q[MVAR]	55,966	-1,185	56,052	43,068	-1,390
	D[MVAD]	6,708	6,919	3,379	6,072	2,342
	σ	1,25E-04	3,01e-009	6,27e-010	1,49e-009	1,02e-009
	Thdi	4,443	7,472	4,489	2,905	2,839
	Thdu	3,17	3,28	3,17	1,48	2,22
	Thdpi	11,117	18,966	11,255	6,625	5,891
	Thdpu	13,18	13,51	13,20	6,05	7,91

Table 6. Electrical installation simulation results depending on action of quality energy improvement.

Efect on: → *Action:* ↓	***Reactive power circulation***	***Unbalancing currents***	***Non sinusoidal regime***
Reactive power compensation	Eliminating	Accentuating	Accentuating
Load balancing	Not eliminating	Eliminating	Accentuating
Harmonic currents filtering	Reducing	Accentuating	Eliminating

Table 7. Sinthesis of actions interdependency reffering to reactive power compensation, harmonic currents filtering and load balancing.

6. References

Andrews, D.; Bishop, M.T.; Witte, J.F. (1996). *Harmonic measurements, analysis and power factor correction in a modern steel manufacturing facility*, IEEE Transactions on Industry Applications, vol. 32, no. 3, May-June, pp. 617-624.

Boulet, B.; Lalli, G.; Agersch, M. (2003). *Modeling and Control of an Electric Arc Furnace*, Proceedings of the American Control Conference, Denver, Colorado, pp. 3060-3064.

Buta, A.; Pană, A.; Ivaşcu, C. (1997). *Reactive power compensation criteria in unbalanced electrical networks*, Energetica, vol. 45, pp. 289-294.

Buta, A.; Pană, A. (2000). *Simetrization of distribution electrical networks*, Technical Printing House, Timişoara.

Cano, P.E.A.; Tacca, H.E. (2005). *Arc Furnace Modeling in ATP-EMTP*, The 6th International Conference on Power Systems Transients (IPST), 19-23 June, Montreal, Canada.

Chiuţă, I.; Conecini, I. (1989). *The compensation of the distorted functioning regime*, Technical Printing House, Bucureşti.

IEEE Standard 519-1992, "*IEEE Recommended Practices and Requirements for Harmonic Control in Electrical Power Systems*," New York, 1992.

Ionescu, T.; Pop, O. (1998). *The power delivery engineering systems*, Technical Printing House, Bucureşti.

Montanari, G.C.; Loggini, M.; Cavallini, A.; Pitti, L.; Zaminelli, D. (1994). *Arc-Furnace model for the Study of Flicker Compensation in Electrical Networks*, IEEE Transactions on Power Delivery, vol. 9, no. 4, pp. 2026-2036.

Panoiu, M. (2001). *Some processes simulation based on three phase electric arc furnace modeling*, Ph.D. Thesis, Politechnical University of Timisoara, Romania.

Panoiu, M.; Panoiu, C. (2006). *Modeling and simulating the AC electric arc using PSCAD EMTDC*, Proceedings of the 5th WSEAS International Conference on System Science and Simulation in Engineering, Tenerife, Spain, 16-18 December.

Panoiu, M.; Panoiu, C.; Sora, I. (2006). *Experimental Research Concerning the Electromagnetic Pollution Generated by the 3-Phase Electric Arc Furnaces in the Electric Power Supply Networks*, Acta Electrotehnica, no. 2, vol 47, pp. 102-112.

Panoiu, M.; Panoiu, C. (2007). *Simulation Results for Modeling the AC Electric Arc as Nonlinear Element using PSCAD EMTDC*, WSEAS Transaction on Circuits and Systems, vol. 6, Jan, pp. 149-156.

Panoiu, M.; Panoiu, C.; Sora I. (2007). *Modeling Of Three Phase Electric Arc Furnaces*, Acta Electrotehnica, vol. 48, no. 2, pp. 124-132.

Panoiu, M.; Panoiu, C.; Sora, I.; Osaci, M. (2007). *Simulations Results on the Reactive Power Compensation Process on Electric Arc Furnace Using PSCAD-EMTDC*, International Journal of Modelling, Identification and Control, vol. 2, no. 3, , pp. 250-257.

Panoiu, M.; Panoiu; C.; Sora, I.; Osaci, M. (2007). *Using a Model Based on Linearization of the Current – Voltage Characteristic for Electric Arc Simulation*, Proceedings of the 16th IASTED International Conference on Applied Simulation and Modelling ~ASM 2007~ , Palma de Mallorca, Spain, August 29 – 31, pp. 99-103, ISBN 978-0-88986-687-4, Acta Press Printing House.

Panoiu, M.; Panoiu, C.; Sora, I.; Osaci, M. (2007). *About the possibility of power controlling in the Three-Phase Electric Arc Furnaces using PSCAD EMTDC simulation program*, Advances in Electrical and Computer Engineering , vol. 7, number 1 (27), ISSN 1582-7445, pp. 38-43.

Panoiu, M.; Panoiu, C.; Sora, I.; Osaci, M.; Muscalagiu, I. (2007). *Modeling, Simulating and Experimental Validation of the AC Electric Arc in the Circuit of Three-Phase Electric Furnaces*, EUROSIM 2007 Congress, Ljubljana, Slovenia, Book of Abstract, pp. 241, CD-Proceedings, 10 pg., ISBN 3-901608-32-x, CD-Proceedings, ISBN 987-33-901608-32-2.

Tang, L.; Kolluri, S.; Mark, F. Mc-Granaghan. (1997). *Voltage Flicker Prediction for two simultaneously operated Arc Furnaces*, IEEE Transactions on Power Delivery, vol. 12, no. 2.

Wu, C. J.; Huang, C. P.; Fu T. H.; Zhao, T. C.; Kuo, H. S. (2002). *Power factor definitions and effect on revenue of electric arc furnace load*, International Conference on Power System Technology Proceedings, vol. 1, pp. 93-97.

13

Using adaptive filters in controlling of electrical resistance furnace temperature based on a real time identification method

Panoiu Caius and Panoiu Manuela
Polytechnical University of Timişoara
România

1. Introduction

The slow processes are characterized by approximate models, having time constants greater than 10 seconds and very often containing time delay. To choose the controller there are some criteria which are verified in practice, taking into consideration the process characteristics and the imposed performance.
The heating process of an electrical resistance furnace is a slow process and is very difficult to control it because the parameters values of the system of the electrical resistance furnace cannot be compute with accuracy. These values are adequate for designing the controller of the heating process.
Because the parameters of the system can be modified in the heating process, it is required to compute them in real time. In order to solve this problem, for the identification of the system it can be used an adaptive filter (Alexander, 1986). The adaptive filter coefficients values are changing on every iteration, having as consequence that the parameters of the system can be also computed also on every iteration. The temperature control system is conditioned by the convergence of the adaptive algorithm. One of the convergence criterions for an adaptive filter is the initial value of the parameters of the filter so, for this reason, the initial values were computed using an on-line method. The process parameters values can be computed from the adaptive filter coefficients (Oppenheim & Schafer, 1986).
Knowing the process parameters values, it can be computed the controller parameters values, taking into consideration the criteria of tuning controllers.
An experimentally determination leads to the conclusion: if the values of the samples are distorted by the additive noises, it has to be used a smoother filter.

2. The parameters process identification methods

2.1. The on-line identification method of slow process parameters with time constant and delayed time

In some applications, such as heating process of electrical resistance furnace, the output signal is delayed comparative to the input signal by a time constant, as in relation

$$y(t) = x(t-\tau) \quad , \tau > 0 \quad , \tag{1}$$

where τ is a delayed time constant or time propagation constant.
The transfer function of such a process is

$$H_{\tau}(s) = e^{-\tau s} . \tag{2}$$

In (Dumitrache et al., 1993) it is shown that the model of the electrical resistance furnace is a model with a time constant and a delayed time defined by the relation:

$$H(s) = \frac{K \cdot e^{-\tau s}}{1 + Ts} , \tag{3}$$

where T, $\tau > 0$.
In (3) K is the amplification coefficient, τ is the delayed time and T is the time constant.
The on-line identification method, that is presented in (Panoiu et al., 2008 c), consists in applying of an input signal to a system whom balanced state is described by the (X_0, Y_0) point. The relation (4) describes this input signal.

$$x(t) = \begin{cases} X_1 & 0 \le t \le T_0 \\ X_0 & t > T_0 \end{cases} . \tag{4}$$

The input signals form is presented in figure 1.

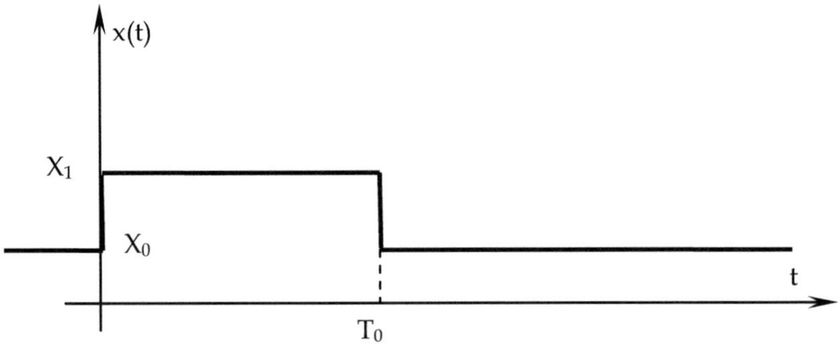

Fig. 1. The input signal form.

Applying this kind of input signal instead of the step signal presents two advantages. The first advantage consists in the fact that it can be observed if the Y output can be stabilized in the same stationary Y_0 point, or not. If the Y_0 value can't be reached, we conclude that or the process is no stationary, which can conduct to a better approach of the model, or a perturbation appeared during the experiment, so the experiment must be resumed. The second advantage consists in the fact that the differences $x(t) - X_0$ and $y(t) - Y_0$ are null after a time interval that is larger than process stabilization time interval, so the integrals

$$I_{XK} = \int_0^{\infty} (-t)^K \left[x(t) - X_0\right] \cdot dt \tag{5}$$

$$I_{YK} = \int_0^{\infty} (-t)^K \left[y(t) - Y_0\right] \cdot dt, \tag{6}$$

where $K = 0,\ 1,\ \ldots,$ will be finite.

Taking into consideration that the chosen model depends by N parameters, the identification process consists in evaluation of H(s) function and the first N-1 derivatives in origin. The result is an N equation system with N variables. The solution of this equation system is the N system parameters.

The N-1 derivatives can be determined in recursive way, by the relation:

$$Y(s) = H(s) \cdot X(s), \tag{7}$$

from which result

$$Y(0) = H(0) \cdot X(0), \tag{8}$$

and by successive derivations it can be obtained the general relation for the kth order derivative in origin

$$H^{(K)}(0) = \frac{Y^{(K)}(0) - \sum_{i=1}^{K} C_K^i H^{(K-i)}(0) \cdot X^{(i)}(0)}{X(0)} \tag{9}$$

where

$$Y^{(K)}(0) = \int_0^{\infty} (-t)^K \left[y(t) - Y_0\right] \cdot dt, \tag{10}$$

$$X^{(K)}(0) = \int_0^{\infty} (-t)^K \left[x(t) - X_0\right] \cdot dt, \tag{11}$$

with K= 0, 1, . . ., N-1.

The integrals that are obtained from (10) and (11) can be computed on a finite domain, $0 \le t \le T_i$ where T_i represents the limits of integration. Using (9) it was computed successive for the model given by the relation (3):

$$\begin{aligned}
&H(0) = K \\
&H'(0) = -K \cdot (T + \tau) \\
&H''(0) = K \cdot \left[(T + \tau)^2 + T^2 \right]
\end{aligned} \quad , \tag{12}$$

These relations permit the evaluation of the model parameters.

$$\begin{aligned}
&K = H(0) \\
&T = \sqrt{\frac{H''(0)}{H(0)} - \left(\frac{H'(0)}{H(0)} \right)^2} \quad , \\
&\tau = -\frac{H'(0)}{H(0)} - T \ .
\end{aligned} \tag{13}$$

The performances of this method were determined by choosing a system which has the system function as in equation (3). The values of the parameters model were chosen as in (14), and the values of the test signal parameters were chosen as in (15). The units of all time constants are seconds.

$$T = 7, \ K = 5, \ \tau = 4 \quad , \tag{14}$$

$$T_0 = 50, \ T_i = 100, \ T_e = 0.1 \ . \tag{15}$$

The influence of the parameters model values was studied by taking different values for one of them and keeping constant the other two. The results are presented in tables 1, 2 and 3. From table 1 it can be observe that amplification coefficient has no influence on computed values, comparative to influence of time constant and delay time, presented in tables 2 and 3. These influences increase as duration of time constant and delay time are increasing referring to test impulse duration and time integration.

In conclusion this identification method has the disadvantage that if the test impulse duration and time integration are not correlated with the real values of the parameters model, the measurements are wrong. The reducing of errors can be obtained by increasing the test impulse duration and time integration.

2.2. Adaptive method of process parameters identification

One of the problems that appear in processes whose model has a time constant and a delayed time, defined by the relation (3) is that of obtaining a transfer function through a dimensionally finite system, which actually means to approximate by a rational function the $e^{-\tau s}$ function (Panoiu et al., 2008 b), (Panoiu et al., 2008 d). The transfer function which approximate $H_\tau(s)$ from relations (2) and (3), is note by $H_{\tau a}(s)$, as in relation (16).

k	k_c	$\varepsilon_{k_c}(\%)$	T_c	$\varepsilon_{T_c}(\%)$	τ_c	$\varepsilon_{\tau_c}(\%)$
1	0,9998	0,0200	6,9324	0,9657	4,0039	0,0975
2	1,9996	0,0200	6,9324	0,9657	4,0039	0,0975
3	2,9994	0,0200	6,9324	0,9657	4,0039	0,0975
4	3,9992	0,0200	6,9324	0,9657	4,0039	0,0975
5	4,9990	0,0200	6,9324	0,9657	4,0039	0,0975
6	5,9988	0,0200	6,9324	0,9657	4,0039	0,0975
7	6,9986	0,0200	6,9324	0,9657	4,0039	0,0975
8	7,9984	0,0200	6,9324	0,9657	4,0039	0,0975
9	8,9982	0,0200	6,9324	0,9657	4,0039	0,0975
10	9,9980	0,0200	6,9324	0,9657	4,0039	0,0975

Table 1. The influence of amplification coefficient on computed values of parameters process with (T=7, τ =4).

T	k_c	$\varepsilon_{k_c}(\%)$	T_c	$\varepsilon_{T_c}(\%)$	τ_c	$\varepsilon_{\tau_c}(\%)$
1	5,0000	0,0000	0,9996	0,0400	3,9512	1,2200
3	5,0000	0,0000	2,9999	0,0033	3,9504	1,2400
5	4,9999	0,0020	4,9951	0,0980	3,9544	1,1400
7	4,9990	0,0200	6,9324	0,9657	4,0039	0,0975
9	4,9946	0,1080	8,7054	3,2733	4,1682	4,2050
11	4,9835	0,3300	10,2409	6,9009	4,4733	11,8325
13	4,9632	0,7360	11,5243	11,3515	4,8985	22,4625
15	4,9329	1,3420	12,5771	16,1527	5,4058	35,1450
17	4,8927	2,1460	13,4338	20,9776	5,9585	48,9625
19	4,8438	3,1240	14,1302	25,6305	6,5284	63,2100

Table 2. The influence of time constant on computed values of parameters process, with (k=5, τ =4).

τ	k_c	$\varepsilon_{k_c}(\%)$	T_c	$\varepsilon_{T_c}(\%)$	τ_c	$\varepsilon_{\tau_c}(\%)$
1	4,9994	0,0120	6,9520	0,6857	0,9887	1,1300
2	4,9993	0,0140	6,9462	0,7686	1,9932	0,3400
4	4,9990	0,0200	6,9324	0,9657	4,0039	0,0975
6	4,9987	0,0260	6,9151	1,2129	6,0171	0,2850
8	4,9983	0,0340	6,8936	1,5200	8,0334	0,4175
10	4,9977	0,0460	6,8669	1,9014	10,0534	0,5340
12	4,9970	0,0600	6,8337	2,3757	12,0779	0,6492
14	4,9959	0,0820	6,7926	2,9629	14,1079	0,7707
16	4,9946	0,1080	6,7418	3,6886	16,1445	0,9031
18	4,9928	0,1440	6,6791	4,5843	18,1890	1,0500

Table 3. The influence of delayed time on computed values of parameters process, with (T=7, k=5).

$$H_{\tau a}(s)=\frac{1+c_1\cdot s+c_2\cdot s^2+\cdots+c_n\cdot s^n}{1+d_1\cdot s+d_2\cdot s^2+\cdots+d_n\cdot s^n},\ d_n\neq 0 \tag{16}$$

The coefficients of the transfer function $H_{\tau a}(s)$ can be determined by equalizing the decomposed function $H_{\tau a}(s)$ around the origin with the decomposed function $H_{\tau}(s)$ around the origin. Such an approximation is known as Padé approximation of rank (n + k), where n represent the degree of the polynomial at the denominator and k the degree of the polynomial at the nominator of the $H_{\tau a}(s)$. In (Dumitrache et al., 1993) are present the usual Padé approximation of rank (2 + 0), (2 + 1), (1 + 1) and (2 + 2).

$$\begin{aligned}&H_{\tau a1}(s)=\frac{1}{1+\tau s+\frac{\tau^2}{2}\cdot s^2},\quad H_{\tau a2}(s)=\frac{1-\frac{1}{3}\tau s}{1+\frac{2}{3}\tau s+\frac{\tau^2}{2}s^2},\\&H_{\tau a3}(s)=\frac{1-\frac{\tau}{2}s}{1+\frac{\tau}{2}s},\quad H_{\tau a4}(s)=\frac{1-\frac{\tau}{2}s+\frac{\tau^2}{12}\cdot s^2}{1+\frac{\tau}{2}s+\frac{\tau^2}{12}\cdot s^2}\end{aligned} \tag{17}$$

The system function of the discrete system is obtained by using one of the Padé approximations of the function $e^{-\tau s}$ and is given by relation (18).

$$H_a(s)=\frac{K}{1+s\cdot T}\cdot H_{\tau a}(s) \tag{18}$$

The system function of the discrete system is obtained by using an equivalence method for the analog filter with a numeric one. The two methods that we are studied are:
1. The approximation of differential equation by finite difference method, in which the system function is obtained from relation (19)

$$H(z)=H_a(s)\Big|_{s=\frac{1}{T_e}\cdot\left(1-z^{-1}\right)} \tag{19}$$

2. The bilinear transform method, in which the system function is obtained from relation (20)

$$H(z)=H_a(s)\Big|_{s=\frac{2}{T_e}\cdot\frac{1-z^{-1}}{1+z^{-1}}} \tag{20}$$

Irrespective of Padé approximation, the general expression of the system function can be written as:

$$H(z)=\frac{b_0+b_1\cdot z+b_2\cdot z^2+b_3\cdot z^3}{1+a_1\cdot z+a_2\cdot z^2+a_3\cdot z^3} \tag{21}$$

It was determined the coefficients of the system function in the case of using both methods of equivalence and all the 4 Padé approximations. In case if is used the first approximation the coefficients value are presented in table 4.

$s=\frac{1}{T_e}\left(1-z^{-1}\right)$	$H_{\tau_1}(s)$ Pade' (1+1)	$H_{\tau_2}(s)$ Pade' (2+0)	$H_{\tau_3}(s)$ Pade' (2+1)	$H_{\tau_4}(s)$ Pade' (2+2)
b_0	$-\frac{kT_e(\tau-2T_e)}{(T+T_e)(\tau+2T_e)}$	$\frac{2kT_e^3}{(T+T_e)\left(2T_e^2+2\tau T_e+\tau^2\right)}$	$\frac{2kT_e^2(3T_e-\tau)}{(T+T_e)\left(6T_e^2+4\tau T_e+3\tau^2\right)}$	$\frac{kT_e\left(12T_e^2-6\tau T_e+\tau^2\right)}{(T_e+T)\left(12T_e^2+6\tau T_e+\tau^2\right)}$
b_1	$\frac{k\tau T_e}{(T_e+T)(2T_e+\tau)}$	0	$\frac{2k\tau T_e^2}{(T+T_e)\left(6T_e^2+4\tau T_e+3\tau^2\right)}$	$\frac{kT_e\left(6\tau T_e-2\tau^2\right)}{(T_e+T)\left(12T_e^2+6\tau T_e+\tau^2\right)}$
b_2	0	0	0	$\frac{kT_e\tau^2}{(T_e+T)\left(12T_e^2+6\tau T_e+\tau^2\right)}$
a_1	$-\frac{2\tau T+2T_eT+T_e\tau}{(T_e+T)(2T_e+\tau)}$	$-\frac{2T(T_e+\tau)^2+4\tau T_e^2}{(T_e+T)\left(2T_e^2+2\tau T_e+\tau^2\right)}$	$-\left(\frac{4\tau T_e+6\tau^2}{6T_e^2+4\tau T_e+3\tau^2}+\frac{T}{T_e+T}\right)$	$-\left(\frac{T}{T_e+T}+\frac{6\tau T_e+2\tau^2}{12T_e^2+6\tau T_e+\tau^2}\right)$
a_2	$\frac{\tau T}{(T_e+T)(\tau+2T_e)}$	$\frac{\tau\left(2T_e^2+3\tau T_e+\tau^2\right)}{(T_e+\tau)\left(2T_e^2+2\tau T_e+\tau^2\right)}$	$\frac{3\tau^2(T_e+T)+T\left(4\tau T_e+6\tau^2\right)}{(T_e+T)\left(6T_e^2+4\tau T_e+3\tau^2\right)}$	$\frac{T\left(6\tau T_e+2\tau^2\right)+\tau^2(T_e+T)}{(T_e+T)\left(12T_e^2+6\tau T_e+\tau^2\right)}$
a_3	0	$-\frac{T\tau^2}{(T_e+T)\left(2T_e^2+2\tau T_e+\tau^2\right)}$	$\frac{-3\tau^2T}{(T+T_e)\left(6T_e^2+4\tau T_e+3\tau^2\right)}$	$-\frac{\tau^2T}{(T_e+T)\left(12T_e^2+6\tau T_e+\tau^2\right)}$

Table 4. The coefficients values of the numerical system function obtained by using approximation of differential equation by finite difference method.

In case if is used the second approximation the coefficients value are presented in table 5.
It was study the filter behaviour for all the four Padé approximations, for different system parameter values and the conclusion is that for assurance convergence of the adaptive filter coefficients to the real values is necessary to use a greater value for sampling period as the number of poles is greater (Panoiu et al., 1996). From tables 4 and 5 it can be observed that the only approximation that gave the system function with only 2 poles is the Padé approximation (1+1), this approximation being used in the following actions.
In tables 6 and 7 are presented the relations which offer the system parameters values starting from the numerical filter coefficients. There are presented also the situations in which are not found such kind of relations.
In conclusion, this method of determining the system parameters value has the advantage that if the system parameters value is changing during the process, the adaptive filter can permit to determine the instantaneous parameters value.

$s=\frac{2}{T_e}\left(\frac{1-z^{-1}}{1+z^{-1}}\right)$	$H_{\tau_1}(s)$ Pade' (1+1)	$H_{\tau_2}(s)$ Pade' (2+0)	$H_{\tau_3}(s)$ Pade' (2+1)	$H_{\tau_4}(s)$ Pade' (2+2)
b_0	$\frac{kT_e(T_e-\tau)}{(T_e+2T)(T_e+\tau)}$	$\frac{kT_e^3}{(T_e+2T)\left[(T_e+\tau)^2+\tau^2\right]}$	$\frac{kT_e^2(3T_e-2\tau)}{(T_e+2T)(3T_e^2+4\tau T_e+6\tau^2)}$	$\frac{kT_e(3T_e^2-3\tau T_e+\tau^2)}{(T_e+2T)(3T_e^2+3\tau T_e+\tau^2)}$
b_1	$\frac{2kT_e^2}{(T_e+2T)(T_e+\tau)}$	$\frac{3kT_e^3}{(T_e+2T)\left[(T_e+\tau)^2+\tau^2\right]}$	$\frac{kT_e^2(9T_e-2\tau)}{(T_e+2T)(3T_e^2+4\tau T_e+6\tau^2)}$	$\frac{kT_e(9T_e^2-3\tau T_e-\tau^2)}{(T_e+2T)(3T_e^2+3\tau T_e+\tau^2)}$
b_2	$\frac{kT_e}{T_e+2T}$	$\frac{3kT_e^3}{(T_e+2T)\left[(T_e+\tau)^2+\tau^2\right]}$	$\frac{kT_e^2(9T_e+2\tau)}{(T_e+2T)(3T_e^2+4\tau T_e+6\tau^2)}$	$\frac{kT_e(9T_e^2+3\tau T_e-\tau^2)}{(T_e+2T)(3T_e^2+3\tau T_e+\tau^2)}$
b_3	0	$\frac{kT_e^3}{(T_e+2T)\left[(T_e+\tau)^2+\tau^2\right]}$	$\frac{kT_e^2(3T_e+2\tau)}{(T_e+2T)(3T_e^2+4\tau T_e+6\tau^2)}$	$\frac{kT_e}{T_e+2T}$
a_1	$\frac{2(T_e^2-2T\tau)}{(T_e+2T)(T_e+\tau)}$	$\frac{T_e-2T}{T_e+2T}+\frac{2(T_e^2-2\tau^2)}{(T_e+\tau)^2+\tau^2}$	$\frac{T_e-2T}{T_e+2T}+\frac{6(T_e^2-2\tau^2)}{(3T_e^2+4\tau T_e+6\tau^2)}$	$\frac{T_e-2T}{T_e+2T}+\frac{2(3T_e^2-\tau^2)}{3T_e^2+3\tau T_e+\tau^2}$
a_2	$\frac{(T_e-2T)(T_e-\tau)}{(T_e+2T)(T_e+\tau)}$	$\frac{T_e-2T}{T_e+2T}\cdot\frac{2(T_e^2-2\tau^2)}{(T_e+\tau)^2+\tau^2}+\frac{(T_e-\tau)^2+\tau^2}{(T_e+\tau)^2+\tau^2}$	$\frac{6(T_e-2T)(T_e^2-2\tau^2)}{(T_e+2T)(3T_e^2+4\tau T_e+6\tau^2)}+\frac{(T_e-2\tau)^2+2(T_e^2+\tau^2)}{(3T_e^2+4\tau T_e+6\tau^2)}$	$\frac{2(T_e-2T)(3T_e^2-\tau^2)}{(T_e+2T)(3T_e^2+3\tau T_e+\tau^2)}+\frac{3T_e^2-3\tau T_e+\tau^2}{3T_e^2+3\tau T_e+\tau^2}$
a_3	0	$\frac{(T_e-2T)\left[(T_e-\tau)^2+\tau^2\right]}{(T_e+2T)\left[(T_e+\tau)^2+\tau^2\right]}$	$\frac{(T_e-2T)(3T_e^2-4\tau T_e+6\tau^2)}{(T_e+2T)(3T_e^2+4\tau T_e+6\tau^2)}$	$\frac{2(T_e-2T)(3T_e^2-3\tau T_e+\tau^2)}{(T_e+2T)(3T_e^2+3\tau T_e+\tau^2)}$

Table 5. The coefficients values of the numerical system function obtained by using bilinear transform method.

$s=\frac{1}{T_e}(1-z^{-1})$	τ	T	k
$H_{\tau_1}(s)$ Pade' (1+1)	$\frac{2T_e}{\frac{b_0}{b_1}+1}$	$\frac{T_e}{-\frac{a_1}{a_2}-2-\frac{2T_e}{\tau}}$	$\frac{b_1}{a_2}\cdot\frac{T}{T_e}$
$H_{\tau_2}(s)$ Pade' (2+0)	-	-	-
$H_{\tau_3}(s)$ Pade' (2+1)	$\frac{3T_e}{\frac{b_0}{b_1}+1}$	$\frac{-T_e}{1-\frac{3\tau^2}{(6T_e^2+4\tau T_e+3\tau^2)\cdot a_3}}$	$-\frac{3}{2}\cdot\frac{b_1}{a_3}\cdot\frac{T}{T_e^2}\cdot\tau$
$H_{\tau_4}(s)$ Pade' (2+2)	$\frac{3T_e}{\frac{1}{2}\frac{b_1}{b_2}+1}$	$\frac{-T_e}{\frac{\tau^2}{(12T_e^2+6\tau T_e+\tau^2)\cdot a_3}+1}$	$\frac{b_0(T_e+T)(12T_e^2+6\tau T_e+\tau^2)}{T_e(12T_e^2-6\tau T_e+\tau^2)}$

Table 6. The relations between system parameters value and numerical coefficients value obtained by using approximation of differential equation by finite difference method.

$s=\frac{2}{T_e}\left(\frac{1-z^{-1}}{1+z^{-1}}\right)$	τ	T	k
$H_{\tau_1}(s)$ Pade' (1+1)	$\left(1-\frac{2b_0}{b_1}\right)T_e$	$\frac{T_r}{2}\cdot\frac{2a_2T_e-a_1T_e+a_1\tau}{2a_2\tau-a_1T_e+a_1\tau}$	$\frac{2b_0\left(T_e^2-2T\tau\right)}{a_1T_e\left(T_e-\tau\right)}$
$H_{\tau_2}(s)$ Pade' (2+0)	-	-	-
$H_{\tau_3}(s)$ Pade' (2+1)	$\frac{3}{2}T_e\frac{\frac{b_1}{b_0}-3}{\frac{b_1}{b}-1}$	$\frac{T_e}{2}\cdot\frac{1-a_1+\frac{6\left(T_e^2-2\tau^2\right)}{\left(T_e+2\tau\right)^2+2\left(T_e^2+\tau^2\right)}}{1+a_1-\frac{6\left(T_e^2-2\tau^2\right)}{\left(T_e+2\tau\right)^2+2\left(T_e^2+\tau^2\right)}}$	$\frac{b_0\left(T_e+2T\right)\left[\left(T_e+2\tau\right)^2+2\left(T_e^2+\tau^2\right)\right]}{T_e^2\left(3T_e-2\tau\right)}$
$H_{\tau_4}(s)$ Pade' (2+2)	-	$\frac{T_e}{2}\cdot\frac{b_0-b_1a_3}{b_0+b_1a_3}$	$b_3\frac{T_e+2T}{T_e}$

Table 7. The relations between system parameters value and numerical coefficients value by using bilinear transform method.

3. Study of characteristics of the IIR-OSLMS filters

Since the values of the parameters of the system model can be finding by knowing the values of the adaptive filter, it was had to choose the optimal identification algorithm with respect to the convergence rate, as well as to stability. It was also had to choose the form of implementation, direct or lattice, as well as the method of equivalence for the analogical filter with a numeric one (Regalia, 1992), (Myuma, 2003), (Punchalard, 2006).

Towards, there were tested 3 identification algorithms: the gradient algorithm, the Steiglitz Mc-Bride algorithm and the SHARF one, each of them being implemented both in direct and lattice form, by using one of the two methods of equate for the analogical filter with a numerical filter. For this, the authors identified the parameters of the unknown system with the transfer function and tested the algorithms in identical conditions. The value chose for the simulated system were: $\tau = 4$ seconds, K=5 and sampling period T_e=2 seconds. The tests were made considering that the unknown system is a fixed filter, with the coefficients obtained based on relations presented in tables 4 and 5.

The three identification algorithms implemented in two equivalence method are presented in hypothesis of using the (1+1) Padé approximation. The tested structures were filter implementation in direct form and filter implementation in lattice form (Regalia, 1991).

3.1. Gradient algorithm

In figure 2 is presented the structure of an adaptive filter based on gradient algorithm. The implementation can be done in direct form and in lattice form (Haykin, 1991).

a) Gradient algorithm in direct form of implementation is described by the equation (22).

$$\begin{pmatrix}\mathbf{a}(n+1)\\ \mathbf{b}(n+1)\end{pmatrix}=\begin{pmatrix}\mathbf{a}(n)\\ \mathbf{b}(n)\end{pmatrix}+\mu\cdot\begin{pmatrix}-\mathbf{Y}_A(n)\\ \mathbf{X}_A(n)\end{pmatrix}\cdot e(n) \tag{22}$$

In (22) μ is the adaptation coefficient, e(n) is the output error, **a** and **b** are the matrix coefficients of nominator and denominator (Chen & Gibson, 1992), (Miao et al., 1994). In figure 3 is represented the coefficients form variations for direct form of implementation.

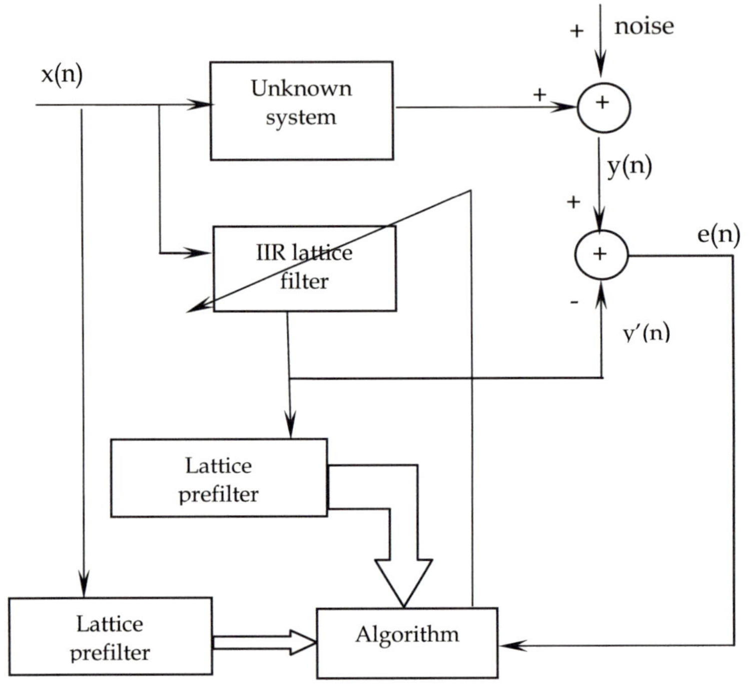

Fig. 2. Implementation of adaptive filter based on gradient algorithm.

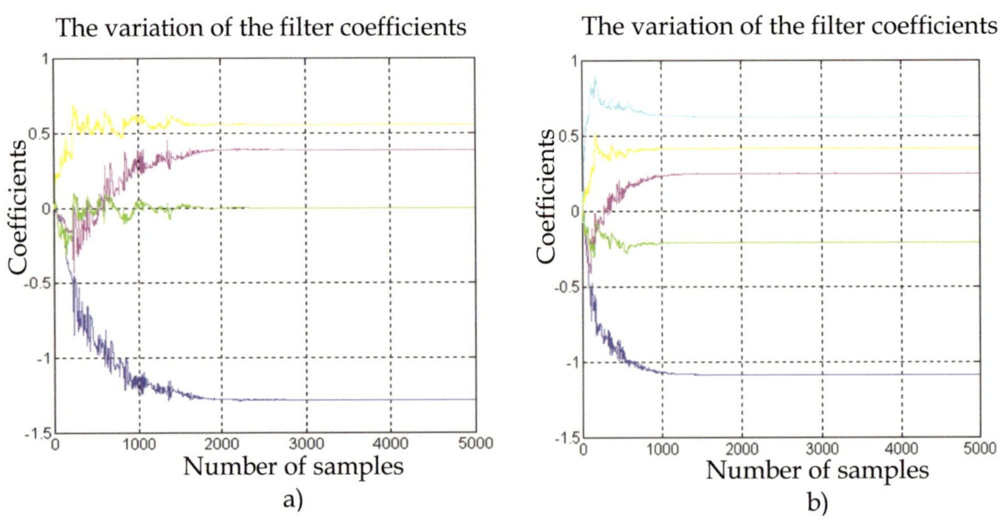

Fig. 3. The variation of adaptive filter coefficients using (1+1) Padé approximation, gradient algorithm implemented in direct form ($\alpha = 0.2$; $T_e = 2s$): a) using approximation of differential equation by finite difference method; b) using bilinear transform method.

b) Gradient algorithm in lattice form of implementation is described by the equation (23).

$$\begin{pmatrix} \mathbf{k}(n+1) \\ \mathbf{b}(n+1) \end{pmatrix} = \begin{pmatrix} \mathbf{k}(n) \\ \mathbf{b}(n) \end{pmatrix} + \mu \cdot \begin{pmatrix} -\mathbf{U}_A(n) \\ \mathbf{X}_A(n) \end{pmatrix} \cdot e(n) \tag{23}$$

In (23) **k** and **b** are the matrix coefficients of lattice implementation structure. In figure 4 is represented the coefficients form variations for lattice form of implementation.

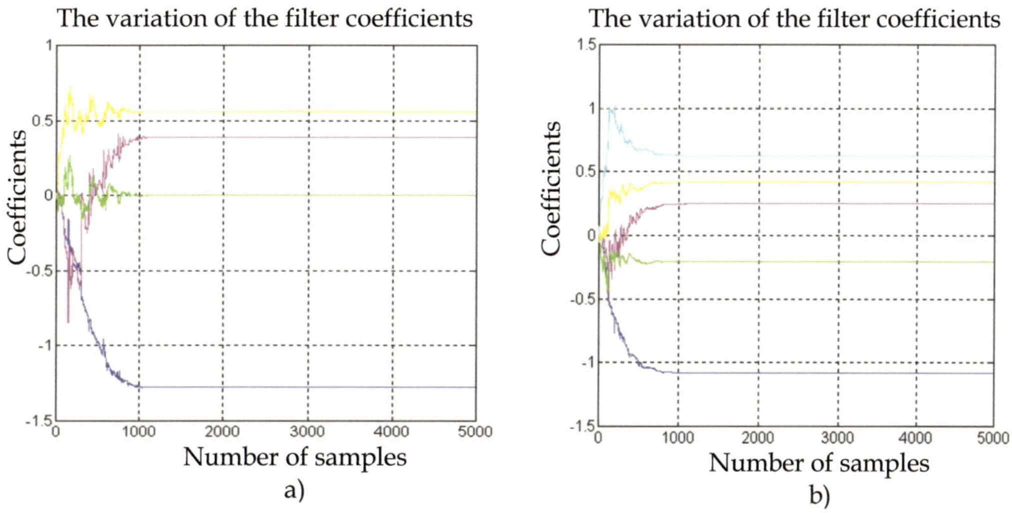

Fig. 4. The variation of adaptive filter coefficients using (1+1) Padé approximation, gradient algorithm implemented in lattice form ($\alpha = 0.2$; $T_e = 2s$): a) using approximation of differential equation by finite difference method; b) using bilinear transform method.

3.2. Steiglitz-McBride algorithm

In figure 5 is presented the structure of an adaptive filter based on Steiglitz-McBride algorithm. The implementation can be done also in direct form and in lattice form.

a) Steiglitz-McBride algorithm in direct form of implementation is described by the equation (24). In figure 6 is represented the coefficients form variations for direct form of implementation.

$$\begin{pmatrix} \mathbf{a}(n+1) \\ \mathbf{b}(n+1) \end{pmatrix} = \begin{pmatrix} \mathbf{a}(n) \\ \mathbf{b}(n) \end{pmatrix} + \mu \cdot \begin{pmatrix} -\mathbf{D}_A(n) \\ \mathbf{X}_A(n) \end{pmatrix} \cdot e(n) \tag{24}$$

b) Steiglitz-McBride algorithm in lattice form of implementation is described by the equation (25). In figure 7 is represented the coefficients form variations for lattice form of implementation.

$$\begin{pmatrix} \mathbf{k}(n+1) \\ \mathbf{b}(n+1) \end{pmatrix} = \begin{pmatrix} \mathbf{k}(n) \\ \mathbf{b}(n) \end{pmatrix} + \mu \cdot \begin{pmatrix} -\mathbf{U}_A(n) \\ \mathbf{X}_A(n) \end{pmatrix} \cdot e(n) \tag{25}$$

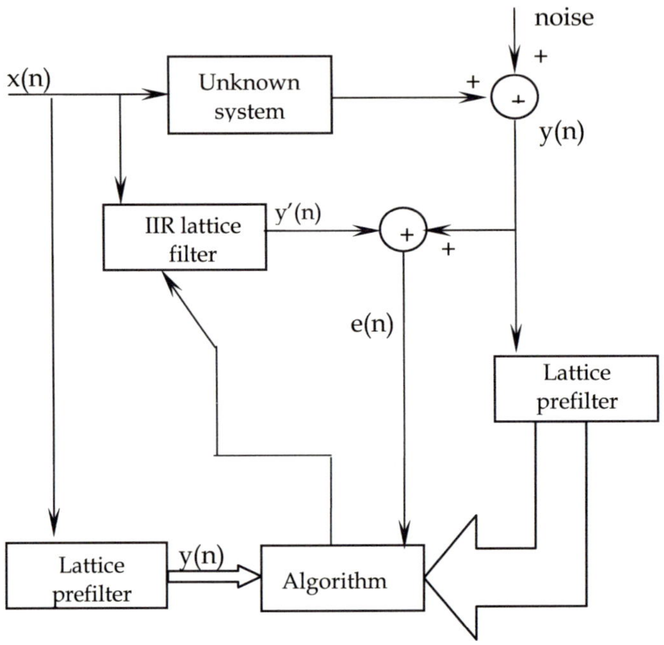

Fig. 5. Implementation of adaptive filter based on Steiglitz-McBride algorithm.

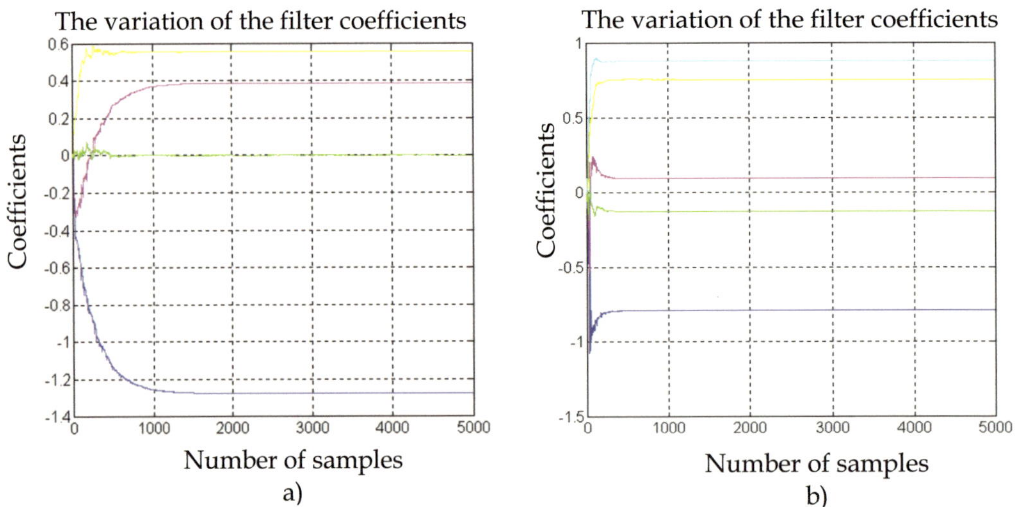

Fig. 6. The variation of adaptive filter coefficients using (1+1) Padé approximation, Steiglitz-McBride algorithm implemented in direct form ($\alpha = 0.2$; T_e = 2s): a) using approximation of differential equation by finite difference method; b) using bilinear transform method.

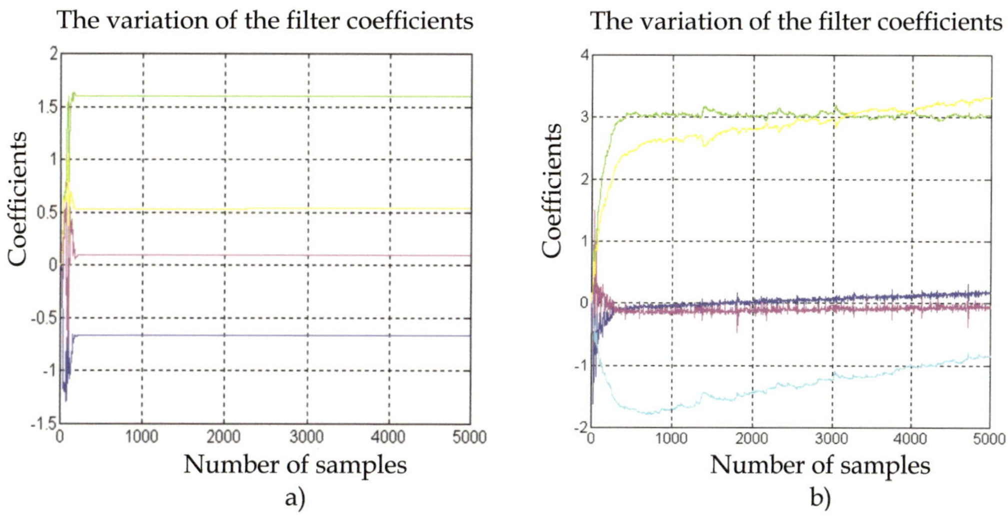

Fig. 7. The variation of adaptive filter coefficients using (1+1) Padé approximation, Steiglitz-McBride algorithm implemented in lattice form ($\alpha = 0.2$; T_e = 2s): a) using approximation of differential equation by finite difference method; b) using bilinear transform method.

3.3. SHARF algorithm

In figure 8 is presented the structure of an adaptive filter based on SHARF algorithm. The implementation can be done also in direct form and in lattice form.

a) SHARF algorithm in direct form of implementation is described by the equation (26). In figure 9 is represented the coefficients form variations for direct form of implementation.

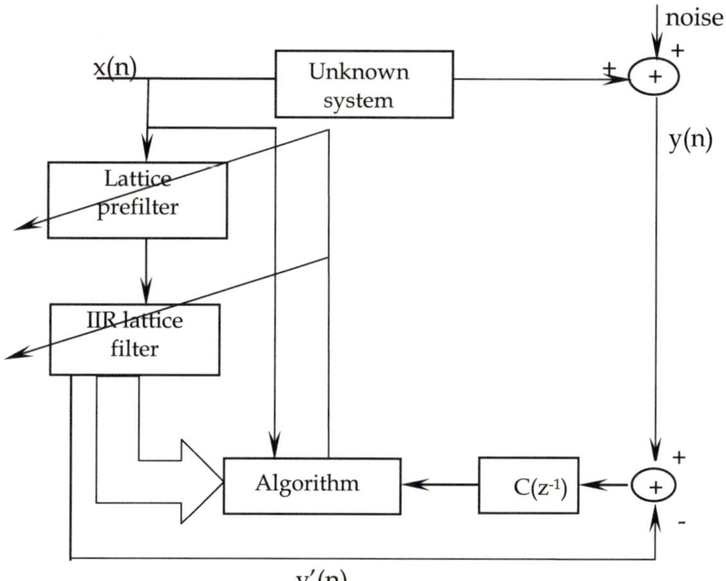

Fig. 8. Implementation of adaptive filter based on SHARF algorithm.

$$\begin{pmatrix} \mathbf{a}(n+1) \\ \mathbf{b}(n+1) \end{pmatrix} = \begin{pmatrix} \mathbf{a}(n) \\ \mathbf{b}(n) \end{pmatrix} + \mu \cdot \begin{pmatrix} -\mathbf{y}(n) \\ \mathbf{x}(n) \end{pmatrix} \cdot c(n) \tag{26}$$

where

$$c(n) = e(n) - 0.6 \cdot e(n-1) \tag{27}$$

b) SHARF algorithm in lattice form of implementation is described by the equation (28), where c(n) is the same as in (27). In figure 10 is represented the coefficients form variations for lattice form of implementation.

$$\begin{pmatrix} \mathbf{k}(n+1) \\ \mathbf{b}(n+1) \end{pmatrix} = \begin{pmatrix} \mathbf{k}(n) \\ \mathbf{b}(n) \end{pmatrix} + \mu \cdot \begin{pmatrix} -\mathbf{u}(n) \\ \mathbf{x}(n) \end{pmatrix} \cdot c(n). \tag{28}$$

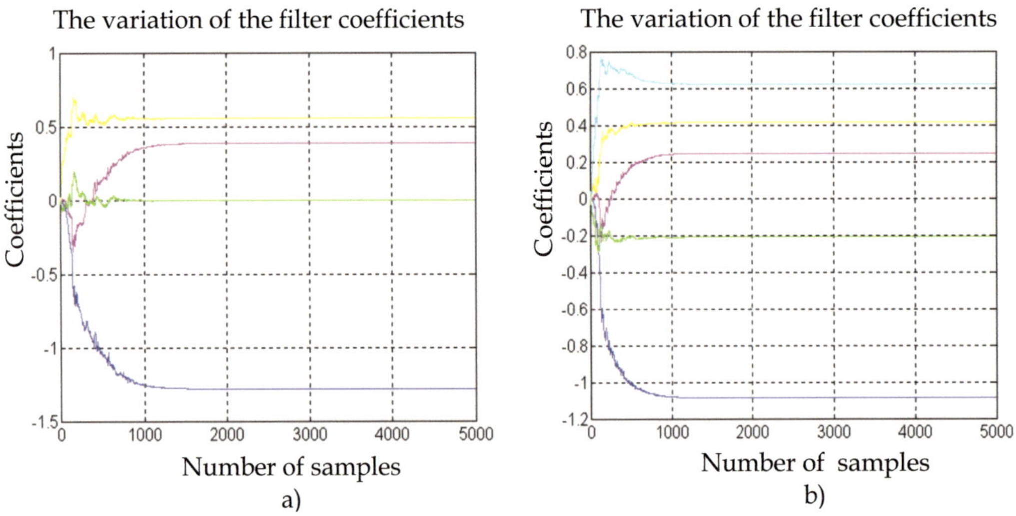

Fig. 9. The variation of adaptive filter coefficients using (1+1) Padé approximation, SHARF algorithm implemented in direct form ($\alpha = 0.2$; T_e = 2s): a) using approximation of differential equation by finite difference method; b) using bilinear transform method.

The results of the tests presume to identify the heating process of the furnace, lead us to the conclusion that the Padé (1+1) approximation allows the easiest determination once the coefficients of the numeric adaptive filter are known (Pomsathit, 2006).
We also determined experimentally that the most efficient algorithm of identification is the SHARF algorithm, implemented in its lattice form, the equivalence of the analogous filter with a numeric one being done by the method of the approximation of the differential equation with finite differences.

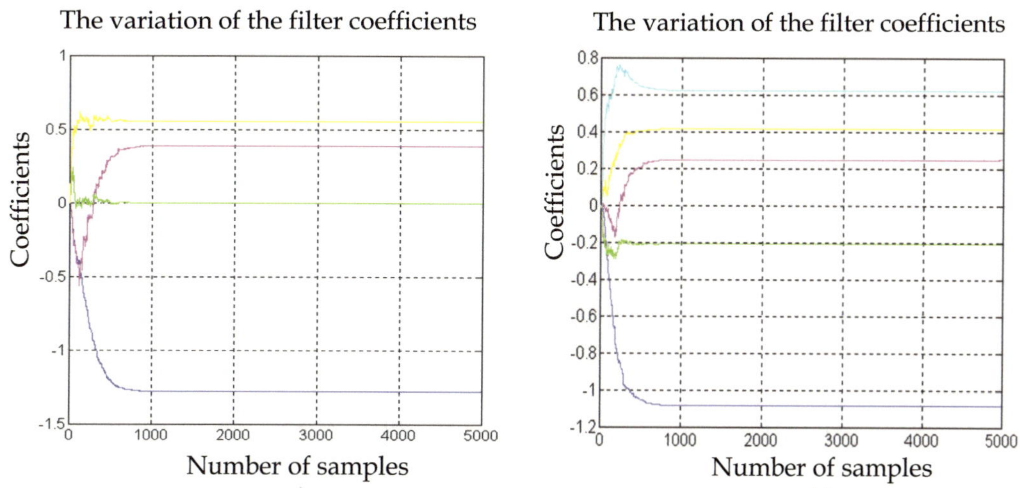

a) b)

Fig. 10. The variation of adaptive filter coefficients using (1+1) Padé approximation, SHARF algorithm implemented in lattice form ($\alpha = 0.2$; T_e = 2s): a) using approximation of differential equation by finite difference method; b) using bilinear transform method.

4. Adaptive controllers

4.1. The used criteria in tuning controllers

The process of temperature control can be accomplished by choosing the type of controller according to particular criteria. Choosing and tuning the controllers for cool time processes represents one of the most difficult problems in the practice of automatic control both because of the difficulties in precisely determining the cool time characterizing the process, and due to the adverse influence of the cool time on the transitory behaviour of an automatic controlling system. The criteria that can be used for the tuning of cool time controlers are:

- Criteria based on the method of stability limit;
- Criteria based in the results of identification;
- Experimental criteria considering the functioning process.

Since the temperature adaptive controlling method is based on the identification of process parameters, are presented four criteria based on the results of identifying the process parameters, criteria which are used for slow process (Dumitrache et al., 1993).

a) The Ziegler - Nichols relations

- for P – controllers

$$K_{R\ opt} = \frac{T}{K \cdot \tau}; \tag{29}$$

- for PI – controllers

$$K_{R\ opt} = \frac{0.9T}{K \cdot \tau}, \quad T_{i\ opt} = 3.3\tau \tag{30}$$

b) The Oppelt relations:
- for P – controllers

$$K_{R\ opt} = \frac{T}{K \cdot \tau} \tag{31}$$

- for PI – controllers

$$K_{R\ opt} = \frac{0.8T}{K \cdot \tau}, \quad T_{i\ opt} = 3\tau \tag{32}$$

c) The Kopelovitch relations

Controller type	Aperiodic answer with minimal duration	Oscillatory answer at $\sigma = 20\%$
P	$K_{R\ opt} = \frac{0.3 \cdot T}{K \cdot \tau}$	$K_{R\ opt} = \frac{0.7 \cdot T}{K \cdot \tau}$
PI	$K_{R\ opt} = \frac{0.6 \cdot T}{K \cdot \tau}$ $T_{i\ opt} = 0.8\,\tau + 0.5\,T$	$K_{R\ opt} = \frac{0.7 \cdot T}{K \cdot \tau}$ $T_{i\ opt} = \tau + 0.3\,T$

Table 8. The values of tuning parameters, according to Kopelovitch.

d) The Chien, Hrones, Roswich relations

Controller type	Aperiodic answer with minimal duration	Oscillatory answer at $\sigma = 20\%$ with minimal duration
P	$K_{R\ opt} = \frac{0.3 \cdot T}{K \cdot \tau}$	$K_{R\ opt} = \frac{0.7 \cdot T}{K \cdot \tau}$
PI	$K_{R\ opt} = \frac{0.35 \cdot T}{K \cdot \tau}$ $T_{i\ opt} = 1.2\,\tau$	$K_{R\ opt} = \frac{0.6 \cdot T}{K \cdot \tau}$ $T_{i\ opt} = \tau$

Table 9. The optimal values of the tuning parameters for a step variation of the input.

Controller type	Aperiodic answer with minimal duration	Oscillatory answer at $\sigma = 20\%$ with minimal duration
P	$K_{R\ opt} = \frac{0.3 \cdot T}{K \cdot \tau}$	$K_{R\ opt} = \frac{0.7 \cdot T}{K \cdot \tau}$
PI	$K_{R\ opt} = \frac{0.6 \cdot T}{K \cdot \tau}$ $T_{i\ opt} = 4\,\tau$	$K_{R\ opt} = \frac{0.7 \cdot T}{K \cdot \tau}$ $T_{i\ opt} = 2.3\,\tau$

Table 10. The optimal values of the tuning parameters for a noise variation of the input.

4.2. Implementation of adaptive controllers

As it was presented in the previous paragraph, the P or PI controllers are advisable to be chosen for time constant and time delay process. The system functions of analogical system can be obtained starting from relation between the output controller signals due to his input signal.

In case of using the P controllers, the output equation is given by relation (33) and the analogical system function is given by relation (34).

$$y_R(t) = K_R \cdot x(t), \tag{33}$$

$$H_R(s) = K_R \tag{34}$$

In case of using the PI controllers, the output equation is given by relation (35) and the analogical system function is given by relation (36).

$$y_R(t) = K_R \cdot x(t) + \frac{K_R}{T_i}\int_0^t x(\tau)d\tau, \tag{35}$$

$$H_R(s) = \frac{K_R}{T_i} \cdot \frac{1 + sT_i}{s} \tag{36}$$

Starting from the adaptive filter coefficients at n^{th} iteration it can be computed the process parameters, T, τ and K. Depending on the chosen adaptive controller and also on the used criteria in tuning controller it can be determined the values of controller parameters, based on the process parameters. In this manner it can be obtained the transfer function of the controller.

The system function of the numerical system can be obtained with one of the two equivalence method. Irrespective of the equivalence method of the analog filter with the numeric one and the type of controller, the general relation for determining the output magnitude of the numeric controller is:

$$y(n) = b_0 \cdot x(n) + b_1 \cdot x(n-1) + a_1 \cdot y(n-1) \tag{37}$$

Depending of the kind of controller and of used equivocation method, in table 11 are presented the coefficients relations on equation (37), as functions on parameters controller and sampling period.

4.3. Noise cancellation

It was experimentally determined that during the temperature measurement process appear impulse noises with high amplitude due to functioning of the voltage controller rectifier.

Equivalence method	Controller	b_0	b_1	a_1
Approximation of differential equation by finite difference method	P	K_R	0	0
	PI	$K_R\left(1+\frac{T_e}{T_i}\right)$	$-K_R$	1
Bilinear transform method	P	K_R	0	0
	PI	$\frac{K_R}{2T_i}(T_e+2T_i)$	$\frac{K_R}{2T_i}(T_e-2T_i)$	1

Table 11. The coefficients value of numerical controller.

The temperature control process inside the electric resistance furnace presumes to know exactly the instantaneous temperature value that means elimination necessity of the high amplitude and short duration impulse influence (Panoiu & Panoiu, 2007).
To study the possibility of noise cancellation it was applied a test impulse and the temperature values were measured. The impulse duration was 20 minute, the test duration was 40 minutes and sampling period was 0.2 seconds. The results are presented in figure 11.

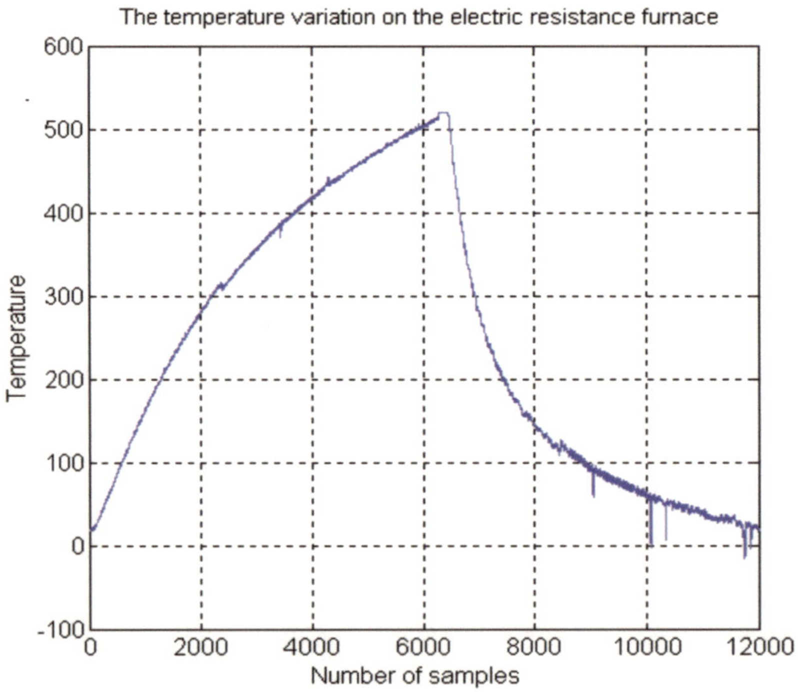

Fig. 11. The variation of the measured temperature.

Taking this fact into consideration, in temperature measurement process was used a MLMS filter with window length of 75 samples. For this filter it was experimentally determined that the temperature can be adjusted on-line and it can be realised an optimal noise rejection. In figure 12 is presented the temperature variation form using MLMS filter.

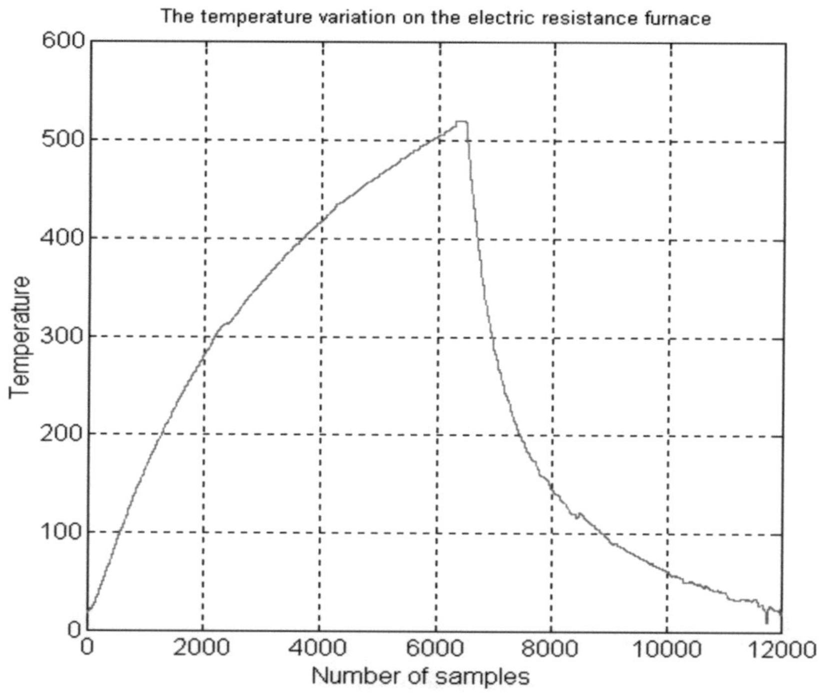

Fig. 12. The variation of the measured temperature after noise cancellation.

4.4. The measurement of the electric resistance furnace parameters using the on-line identification method

Until this point is presented the situation of using an adaptive filter in order to identify the parameters of the slow processes. In this case, using another method, i.e. on-line identification method, is necessary to determine the approximated values of the system parameters. Using these values the initial values of the adaptive filter coefficients will be determined (Panoiu & Panoiu, 2005), (Panoiu et al., 2008 a).

The parameters of the model of the electric resistance furnace heating were determined using the on-line identification method. The experiment consists in applying during the impulse test on the resistance terminals the highest rectifier voltage that produces the furnace heating. During this interval the temperature increases inside the furnace. After this impulse test, the supplying voltage is disconnected and the temperature decrease. The impulse test was 20 minutes duration, the integration period was 40 minutes and sampling period was 0.2 seconds. In order to determine the parameters of the furnace heating model, were made 10 measurements with null initial conditions. The measurements results are presented in table 12.

Taking into consideration the results presented in table 12, the initial values of parameters of the furnace heating model were chose: K=440, $T = 275$ seconds and $\tau = 66$ seconds.

Because the SHARF algorithm present reduced variations of the adaptive filter coefficients, irrespective of the implementation form or of the equivocation method, between an analogical filter with a numeric filter, this algorithm was used in the process of adaptive identification of the parameters of the furnace heating model.

Number of measurement	K_{meas}	T_{meas} (seconds)	τ $_{meas}$ (seconds)
1	442,60	274,22	66,21
2	438,56	272,21	64,87
3	450,88	280,34	65,38
4	443,24	275,33	66,86
5	436,22	271,00	67,12
6	445,78	278,22	66,43
7	436,50	270,29	63,26
8	447,87	279,24	65,96
9	440,26	275,34	67,28
10	438,22	273,37	66,32

Table 12. The parameters of the furnace heating model.

Because the lattice form of implementation present a convergence speed greater than the direct form of implementation, it was used the lattice form of implementation of the adaptive filter (Voltz & Kozin, 1992).
Because the number of the adaptive filter coefficients using Padé approximation (1+1) is more reduced in case of approximation of differential equation by finite difference method then in case of bilinear transform method, the first method was used.
With the initial chosen values of the parameters of the furnace heating model, it was tested the convergence of the adaptive filter coefficients using some of the sampling period values. Experimentally was concluded that the optimal sampling period is 30 seconds, as necessary time interval between two consecutive adjustments of the power discharged by the electric resistance. In figure 13 is presented the variation form of the adaptive filter coefficients using SHARF algorithm, implementing the adaptive filter in lattice form and using the approximation of differential equation by finite difference method.

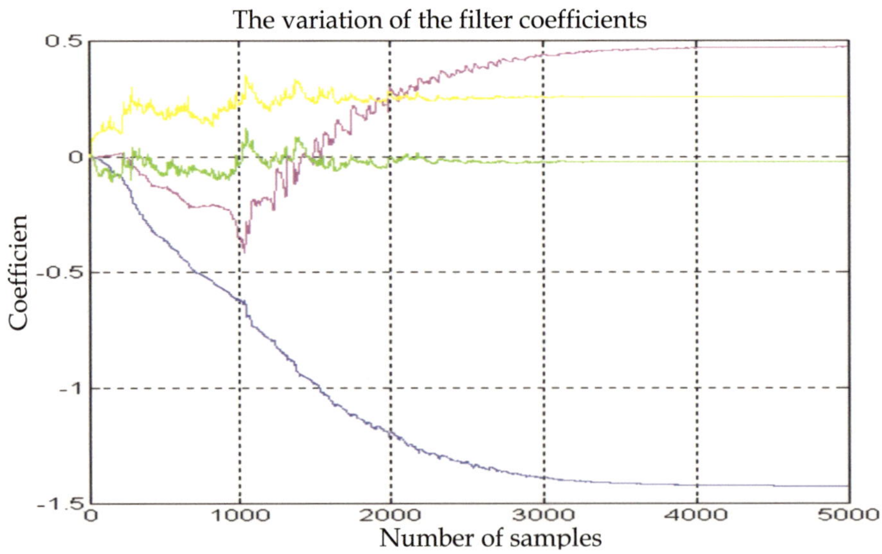

Fig. 13. The variation of adaptive filter coefficients.

5. The adaptive temperature control system

5.1. The structure of the adaptive temperature control system

The implemented adaptive temperature control system has the structure given in figure 14, including the following elements:

- the electric resistance of furnace, representing the system whose output, temperature, is controlled by the modification of the power dissipated over its electric resistance;
- the voltage controller rectifier (VCR) whose role is to allow the controlling of the output voltage value, according to the level of the input DC voltage;
- the temperature transducer (T), used for obtaining a voltage proportional to the temperature. We used a chromel-alumel temperature transducer with the maximum measurable temperature of 1200°C and a maximum output voltage of 48 mV;
- the voltage amplifier (A) used to increase the output voltage of the temperature transducer, in view of obtaining an output voltage of 20 V, corresponding to the range of measurements allowed by the system in use;
- one computer;
- the data acquisition board ADA3100 used both in the output voltage digital to analogous conversion of the amplifier and in the output voltage digital to analogous conversion meant to act upon the voltage-controlled converter. This data acquisition board has the following characteristics:
    - 8 analogical input channels that can be used differential or single ended;
    - 2 analogical output channels;
    - 8 digital input lines and 8 numeric output lines;
    - input voltage domain: $\pm 5V$, $\pm 10V$ or $0\text{-}10\ V$, selectable by program;
    - output voltage domain: $\pm 5V$, $\pm 10V$, $0-5V$ or $0\text{-}10\ V$, selectable by program;
    - possibility to choose the input signal amplification of 1, 2, 4, 8, 16 or adjustable before the analogous to digital conversion.

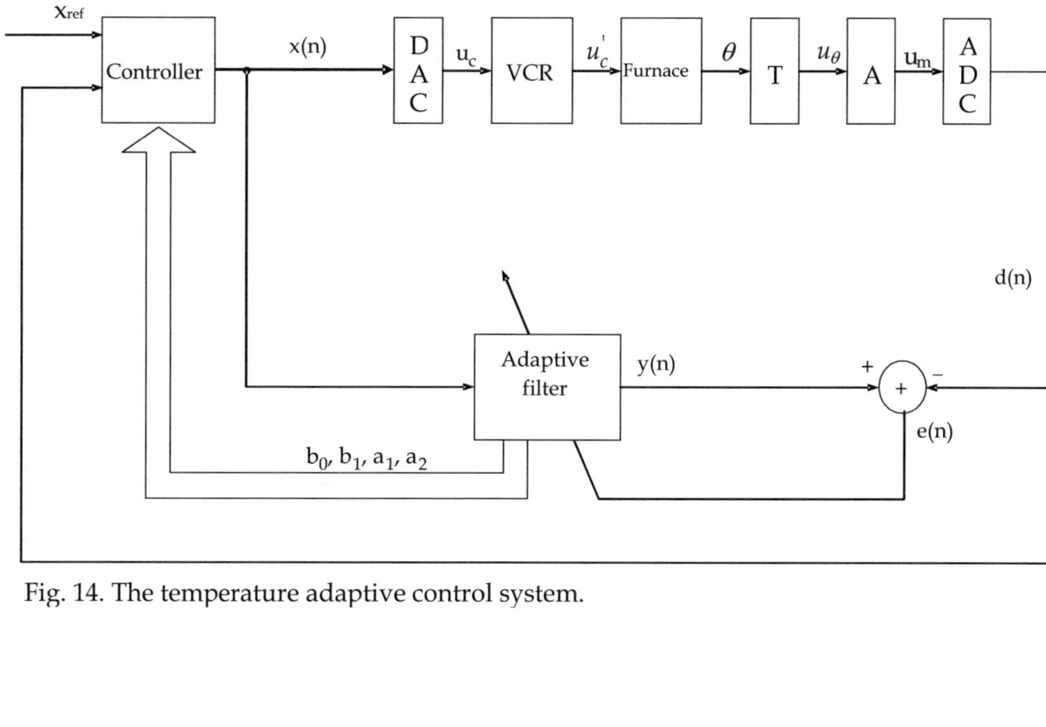

Fig. 14. The temperature adaptive control system.

5.2. Experimentally results

Experiments were realised using the adaptive control system presented in figure 14. All criteria of tuning controllers were tested in the same condition. These are referring to the imposed temperature which is desired to obtain. In all experiments this temperature is 200°C.

In figures 15 is presented the temperature variation obtained by using Ziegler-Nichols relation with P and PI controller.

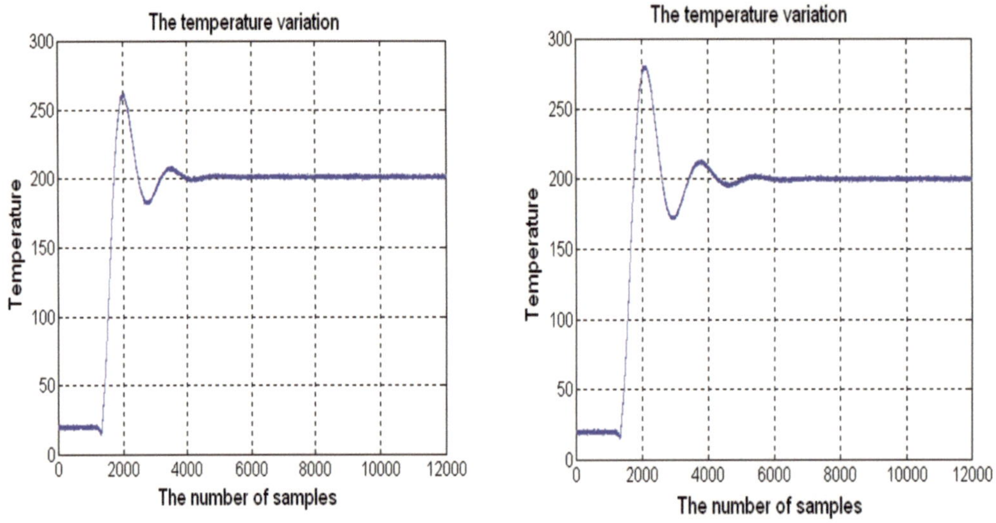

a) for P controller b) for PI controller

Fig. 15. The temperature variation using Ziegler-Nichols relations.

In figure 16 is presented the temperature variation obtained by using Oppelt relation with P and PI controller.

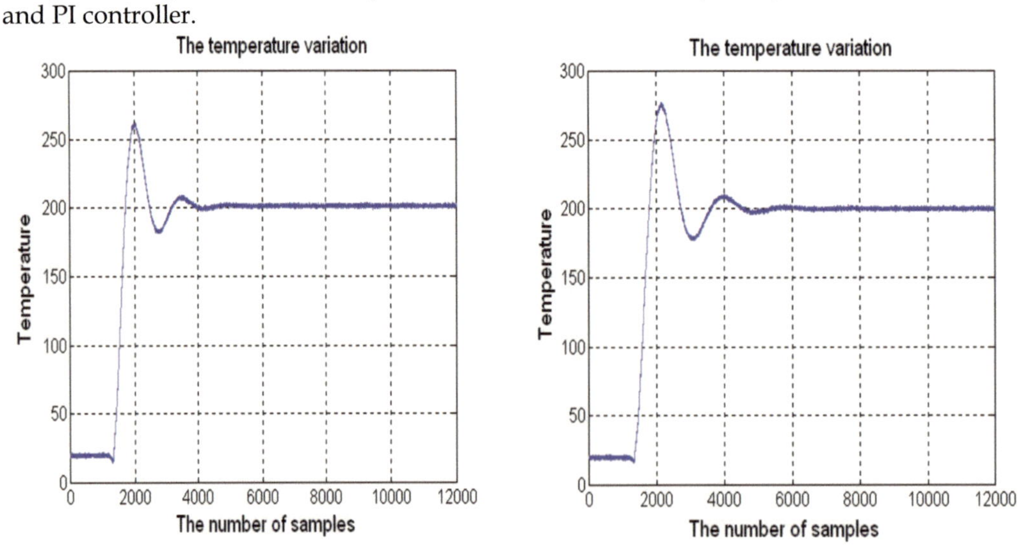

a) for P controller b) for PI controller

Fig. 16. The temperature variation using Oppels relations.

In figure 17 is presented the temperature variation obtained by using Kopelovici relations for aperiodic answer with minimal duration.

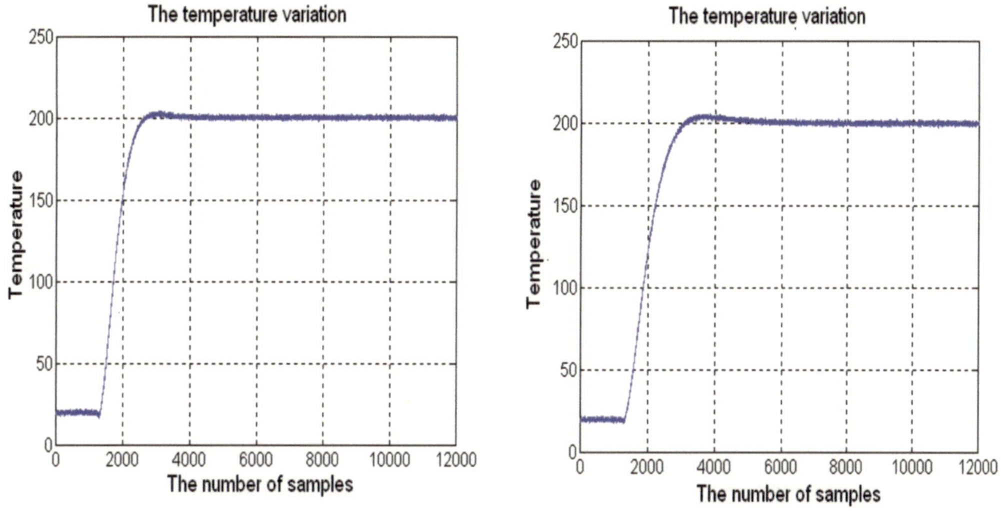

a) for P controller b) for PI controller

Fig. 17. The temperature variation obtained by using Kopelovici relations for aperiodic answer with minimal duration.

In figure 18 is presented the temperature variation obtained by using Kopelovici relations for oscillatory answer at $\sigma = 20\%$ with minimal duration.

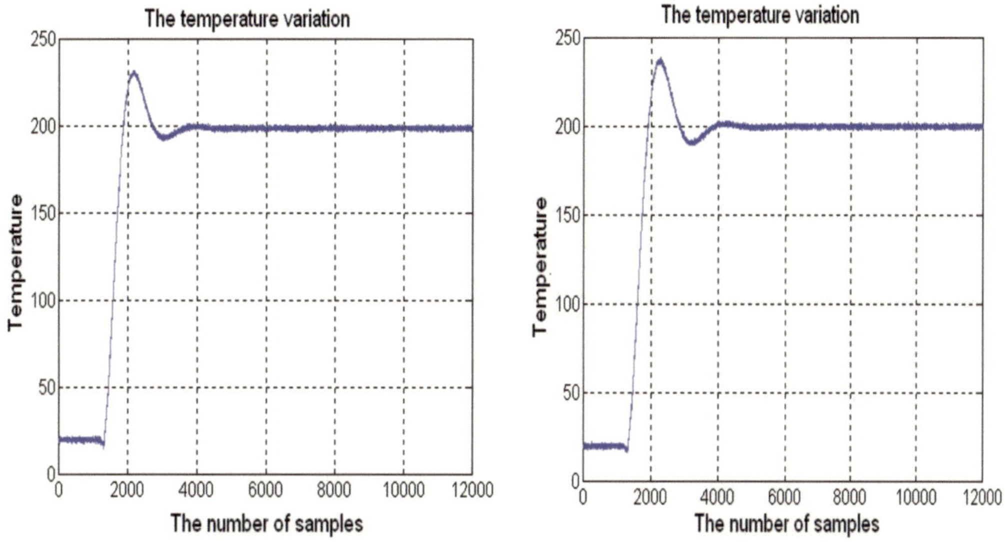

a) for P controller b) for PI controller

Fig. 18. The temperature variation obtained by using Kopelovici relations for oscillatory answer at $\sigma = 20\%$ with minimal duration.

In figure 19 is presented the temperature variation obtained by using Chien, Hrones, and Reswich relations for oscillatory answer at $\sigma = 20\%$ with minimal duration.

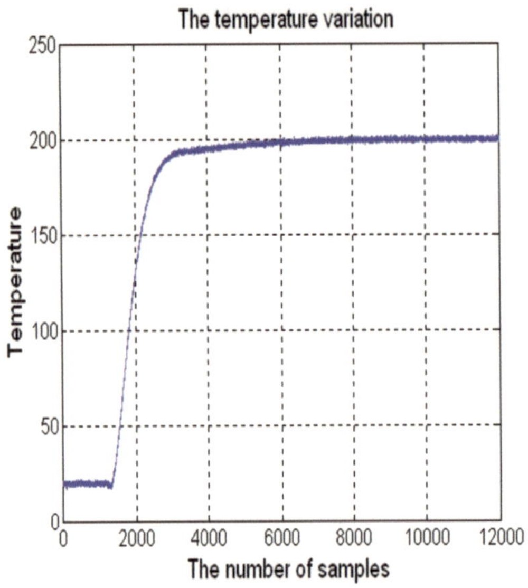

a) for P controller

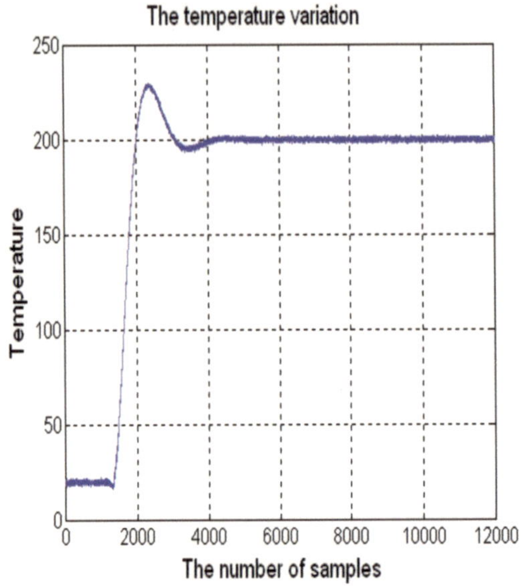

b) for PI controller

Fig. 19. The temperature variation obtained by using Chien, Hrones and Reswich relations for oscillatory answer at $\sigma = 20\%$ with minimal duration.

6. Conclusions

The online identification method has two disadvantages. The first of them consists in the fact that if the test impulse duration and the integration duration are not chosen in correlation with the real values of the process parameters the measured values of the process parameters present high errors. The second disadvantage consists in the fact that for measuring the values of the process parameters the system must be taken out from its steady state and the measured values are considered constant until the next measurement is performed.

The transfer function of the system can be obtained by using a Padé approximation of the transfer function associated to a delayed time process. The system function of the numerical system is obtained by using an equivocation method of the analogical filter with a numerical filter. Two equivalence methods of the analogical filter with a numerical filter were analysed: the approximation of differential equation by finite difference method and the bilinear transform method.

Based on equivalence methods it were determined the computing relations of the filter coefficients knowing the values of the process parameters as well the mutual relations of determining the values of the process parameters knowing the values of the adaptive filter coefficients for the 4 Padé approximations that are treated in the technical literature.

It was studied 3 identification algorithms, implemented in direct form and also in lattice form. The conclusion is that irrespective of the algorithm type, the lattice implementation form presents a convergence speed higher than the direct implementation form. Also, the

SHARF algorithm has the smallest oscillation of the coefficients values, irrespective of the implementation form. Based on the accomplished study, it was used in identification process of the parameters of the furnace heating the SHARF algorithm, implemented in lattice form and using the method of the integral approximation using the rectangle method.
The next step consist in experimentally demonstration that in order the adaptive filter to be availed in identification of the slow processes parameters, is necessary to determine with approximation the values of the system parameters, based on a previous measurement, using another method. Using these values, it has to be determined the initial values set of the adaptive filter coefficients.
In the final part are presented the experimental conclusions that are obtained in the temperature controlling process using the criteria based on the identification results in choosing the controllers parameters.
The experimental results obtained in the process of temperature control, using the criteria based on the results of identification in choosing the controller parameters, confirm the fact that the using of the adaptive method of furnace temperature control presents some advantages, such as:
First advantage consist in the fact that the measurements of the parameters of the electric resistance furnace heating process consists in their calculation after each correction interval of the power given by the electric resistance, knowing the updated values of the adaptive filter coefficients. In this way, it is no longer necessary to take the system out of its steady state, as it is the case with the on-line identification method.
The second advantage consists in that since we practically know at each moment the parameters of the furnace heating process, the values of the numeric controller parameters are chosen in each interval of power control according to the values of the process parameters.
Finally, the performances obtained by this method allow a better control of the temperature, in the sense of reducing the time to reaching the preset temperature value in the case of applying a step signal to the standard input of the controller. Moreover, after the preset temperature value is reached, the oscillations around it are smaller than in the case of using a constant-parameter controller.

7. References

Alexander, S.Th. (1986). *Adaptive Signal Processing*, Springer Verlag, New York Inc.

Chen, S. W.; Gibson, J. S. (1992). *A New Unwindowed Lattice Filter for RLS Estimation,* IEEE Transactions on Signal Processing, vol 40, No. 9, September, pp. 2158-2165.

Dumitrache,I.; Dumitru, S.; Mihu, I.; Munteanu, F.; Muscă, Gh.; Calcev, C. (1993). *Electronical Automatisation*, E.D.P.Bucureşti.

Haykin, S. (1991). *Adaptive Filter Theory*, Prentice Hall, Englewood Cliffs, New Jersey.

Miao, K. X.; Fan, H.; Doroslovacki, M. (1994). *Cascade Lattice IIR Adaptive Filters*, IEEE Transactions on Signal Processing, vol. 42, No.4, April, pp. 721-742.

Myuma, A.; Nishimura, S.; Hinamoto, T. (2003). *Improved mse analysis of a gradient algorithm for an adaptive IIR notch filter*, Proceedings of the 46th IEEE International Midwest Symposium on Circuits & Systems, vol. 1-3, pp. 764-767.

Oppenheim, A. V.; Schafer, R. W. (1986). Digital Signal Processing, Prentice Hall, Inc., Englewood Cliffs, New Jersey.

Panoiu, C.; Panoiu, M.; Negruț, D. (1996). *Implementation of Adaptive Transversals Filters using Variable Step Size Adaptive Algorithm*, Automatic Control and Testing Conference A96-Theta 10-Cluj.

Panoiu, C.; Panoiu, M. (2005). *The temperature adaptive control algorithm*, MicroCAD, International Scientific Conference, 10-11 March , Section I Automation and Telecommunication, pp. 37-42, Miskolc, Hungaria.

Panoiu, C.; Panoiu, M. (2007). *MALMS- a New OSLMS Filter*, Proceedings of the 4th IASTED International Conference Signal Processing, Pattern Recognition, and Applications, Innsbruck, Austria, pp. 94-98.

Panoiu, C.; Toma, L.; Panoiu, M.; Rob R. (2008). *Properties of IIR-OSLMS Adaptive Filters*, Proceedings of the 27th IASTED International Conference on Modelling, Identification and Control, ISBN 978-0-88986-711-6, 11-13 February, Innsbruck, Austria, pp. 460 - 465.

Panoiu, C.; Panoiu, M.; Toma, L.; Rob R. (2008). *A Real-Time Identification Method of Slow Process Parameters Using Adaptive IIR-OSLMS Filters*. WSEAS TRANSACTIONS on SYSTEMS, Issue 10, Volume 7, October, pp. 1143-1154, ISSN: 1109-2777.

Panoiu, C.; Panoiu, M.; Toma, L. (2008). *Temperature adaptive control based on modeling the heating process of an electric resistance furnace*, Proceedings of the 16th IASTED International Conference on Applied Simulation and Modelling, pp. 277 - 282, Corfu, Greece.

Panoiu, C.; Panoiu, M.; Toma, L.; Rob R. (2008). *A real-time Identification Method of a slow Process Parameters Using an Adaptive Algorithm*, Proceedings of the 8th WSEAS International Conference on Systems Theory and Scientific Computation, Rodos, Grecia, 20-22 august, pp. 148-153.

Pomsathit, A.; Wattanaluk, P.; Sangaroon, O. et al, (2006). *Variable step-size algorithm for lattice form structure adaptive IIR notch filter*, International Conference On Communications, Circuits And Systems Proceedings, vol. 1-4 pp. 332-335.

Punchalard, R.; Loetwassana, W.; Koseeyaporn, S. (2006). *Performance analysis of the equation error adaptive IIR notch filter with constrained poles and zeros*, International Symposium On Communications And Information Technologies, vol. 1-3, pp. 1142-1145.

Regalia, P. A. (1991). *An Improved Lattice - Based Adaptive IIR Notch Filter*, IEEE Transactions on Signal Processing, vol. 39, No. 9, September, pp. 2124-2128.

Regalia, P. A. (1992). *Stable and Efficient Lattice Algorithms for Adaptive IIR Filtering*, IEEE Transactions on Signal Processing, vol. 40, No. 2, February, pp. 375-388.

Voltz, P. J.; Kozin, F. (1992). *Almost-Sure Convergence of the Continuous-Time LMS Algorithm*, IEEE Transactions on Signal Processing, vol. 40, No. 2 February, pp. 395-401.

14

Simulation of On-Board Supercapacitor Energy Storage System for Tatra T3A Type Tramcars

Leonards Latkovskis, Viesturs Brazis and Linards Grigans
Institute of Physical Energetics
Riga Technical University
Latvia

1. Introduction

The most efficient and low emission kind of public transport is a rail transport. Tram based light rail transit has been chosen by city government as the main urban transportation solution in Riga. However, the running trams in Riga have been produced in 1976-1987 (type T3 with a rheostat accelerator) and 1988-1990 (type T3M with a thyristor drive).

In Eastern Europe and even in old EU countries for many decades old trams with DC traction drive have still been in use for the reasons that the exploitation resource of mechanical parts of rolling stocks in the rail electric transport is mostly 30-50 years and that the cost of a new tramcar is approximately 1-2.5 million Euros, which makes it difficult for many transport operator companies to renew the old fleet before its complete physical wear. Therefore, the reconstruction of tramcars has been made to prolong their exploitation period by 10-20 years, with replacing the traction equipment by newer and more energy-efficient one, providing regenerative braking that allows 20-40% of the consumed energy to be returned (Rankis, I. & Brazis, V., 2000). Although the best energy saving and improvement of tramcar performance could be achieved by replacing a DC drive with an asynchronous one, the rise in the cost of the electrical part seldom pays off in the 10, maximum 20 post-reconstruction years. This forces to restrict the renovation to replacement of rheostat and thyristor control systems by transistor ones, with old DC traction motors left (Joller, J., 1998).

A large reconstruction of 191 T3 type tramcars to T3A took place in the Riga city from the 1998 to 2002. The renewed tramcars obtained regenerative braking capability and can provide reduction of the energy consumption up to 40%.

However, the regenerative braking energy is not completely used in typical existing traction drive system because none of the substations is equipped with a reversible rectifier. The real energy saving strongly depends on other trams connected to the same section of overhead line. If a number of trams are connected to the DC overhead, part of the regenerative braking energy could be distributed to other trams when they are operated in traction mode, but in the case of several tram simultaneous breaking the energy could not be utilized and is wasted in braking rheostat. It is often impossible for the tramcars to instantly consume regenerative energy at low traffic density in off-peak hours and on easily loaded lines, since in the overhead supplying zone of a single traction substation at one tram's braking other

trams infrequently can simultaneously utilise the energy in the traction mode (Barrero, R. et al, 2008 A) or even are not located in this net supplying zone.
Using methodology described in (Latkovskis, L. & Grigans, L., 2008 A) the wasted energy for two substations feeding approximately 3 km long distances of overhead line of tram lines № 6 and № 11 has been estimated (Latkovskis, L. & Grigans, L., 2008 B). It yields 147MWh and 125MWh per year correspondingly. Taking into account that there are 34 substations in Riga, the total wasted energy is estimated by order of 3GWh per year.
There are three basic solutions for saving the untapped braking energy:

- modification of substations by replacing old rectifiers with reversible ones;
- installation of stationary energy storages at substations or near the optimal connection points of the overhead power supply line;
- installation of onboard energy storage devices on the electric vehicles.

Equipment of substations with reversible rectifiers has several drawbacks:

- the necessity to modify substations, including replacement of power transformers or installation of additional ones;
- simple reversible thyristor rectifiers have a low power factor and distorted line current, while transistor rectifiers with a sinusoidal current waveform are rather complicated and expensive;
- none of substation reversible rectifier types are able to shave peak energy consumption, on the contrary, they increase the power system voltage fluctuations with opposite regenerated energy flow;

To obtain the useful utilization of regenerative energy and reduce overall energy consumption, braking energy should be temporarily saved in energy storage system (ESS) until the correspondent power consumer is connected to the overhead line. Only energy storage system could join the regenerative energy storage task with peak power reduction and overhead voltage stabilization. The ESS could be installed stationary in substation, weak spots of network or onboard on vehicle.
In difference from heavy rail transport with predictable acceleration and deceleration areas mostly near stations, curves, hills, switches etc., the city traffic conditions with low speeds, frequent acceleration and sudden braking is characterised by dissipated starting and braking zones along transport network. The energy transfer from a tramcar to the other vehicle or substation at a distance from several hundred meters up to few kilometres is coupled with considerable energy losses, which decreases the power saving up to 10% (Rankis, I. & Brazis, V., 2000). Therefore the most effective way of the regenerative energy using without transfer losses is installation the onboard ESS.
The modern trams have increased dynamical properties and average speed, which leads the highest current constraints on overhead line and introduce large voltage drops in the traction mode (Destraz, B. et al, 2007). The starting power peaks represent a problem of availability of enough power feeding network, otherwise large voltage drops occur, which significantly reduce tram dynamic performance parameters. Overhead resistance increases with distance from substation, which causes permanent undervoltage far from substation and eliminates the stationary ESS effect to voltage stabilising. Only onboard ESS provides direct stored energy applying to the place of consuming, which improve dynamic behaviour of the vehicle by else having the same acceleration in weaker network or higher acceleration in well feed overhead lines. Onboard ESS allows increasing the number of trams without

need of building new expensive substations, which is important in the case if traffic increasing is necessary periodically for limited time.

Important advantage of onboard ESS is autonomous traction feature and full regenerative braking energy storage possibility, restricted by storage capacity only. The braking energy transfer to onboard ESS is independent from overhead availability, which is especially important in Riga due to specific Tatra T3A type tramcar power circuit drawbacks and overhead network construction. The Riga overhead network has a lot of tram and trolleybus crossings and disconnections with neutral parts, where energy transfer is impossible. Also the regenerative braking is not allowed on automated rail and overhead wire frogs, because the travel direction is switched by high or low tram load. Future planned tram tunnels and introduction of shared tram and trolleybus operation on public transport lines increases the demands for tram autonomous traction possibility with limited speed and distance to ensure fast vehicle removing from intersections, tunnels and other places, where it disturbs other traffic.

One of the most perspective energy storage devices is a large capacity supercapacitor battery which is chosen for tram ESS. In comparison with chemical accumulator batteries and rotating fly-wheels the supercapacitors have better charge and discharge dynamic characteristics despite the smaller total energy capacity. The supercapacitor advantages are also independence of parameters on the environment temperature, smaller weight, lower cost and dimensions than other types of energy storage system type.

Therefore the most attention is paid to the maximum storage of regenerative energy, applying as simple as possible technical solutions, which would allow the least rise in the cost of traction equipment without decreasing the tramcar operation safety. Such storage is achieved using a single-stage pulse converter without intermediate DC conversions (Latkovskis, L. & Bražis, V. 2007). Due to lack of speed sensor and difficult access to traction and braking signal outputs of the tram T3A, the control system of ESS is developed independent of the tram controller. In difference from ESS with speed sensor (Barrero, R.; et al., 2008 A), which must be recommended for brand new vehicles, the proposed solution with independent ESS converter control system could be easily connected to existing tram without reengineering traction circuit and tram control system hardware and software. In such system are two independent PWM unlinked clock signal for tram DC converter and ESS current controller. As the ESS is connected to the filter capacitor of tram DC converter therefore interference of DC converter and ESS current controller has been investigated in both synchronous and asynchronous operation modes of the both converters.

The ESS straightforward constant current charging has compatibility problems with line parameters (Sejin N.; et al., 2008). Supercapacitor charging with a constant power requires incorporation of the ESS control system into vehicle traction drive and modifying the last (Szenasy, I., 2008). The charging algorithm with constant filter capacitor voltage is chosen for providing the automatic whole braking energy saving without significant modification of the existing tram power circuit.

The PSIM and Matlab/Simulink simulation is performed for tramcar starting and braking processes in different situations with and without another tram connected to the overhead line and for autonomous traction mode.

The DC PWM tram converter is represented in two versions - as a continuous and a pulsed current source. By applying the pulsed current PSIM model the interference between ESS and DC PWM tram converter is investigated.

2. Power circuit of ESS and T3A tramcar traction drive

While connecting supercapacitor energy storage system to the existing T3A tramcar power scheme it is necessary to take into account that it must provide:

- two-way voltage boost/buck energy interchange between the T3A power circuit and the supercapacitor,
- smoothed charge/discharge current of the supercapacitor,
- smoothed and radio-frequency filtered line current,
- controllable initial charge of the supercapacitor,
- protection of the supercapacitor against overcurrents caused by overhead short circuits.

A simple solution of ESS power stage may be achieved connecting it to the tram filter capacitor (Latkovskis, L. & Bražis, V., 2007) at supercapacitor's voltage always being lower than the filter capacitor's voltage V_{Cf} (Rufer, A., 2003), (Barrero, R.; et al., 2008 B). A simplified circuit diagram of the energy storage system and its connection to the T3A tramcar power circuit is shown in Fig.1.

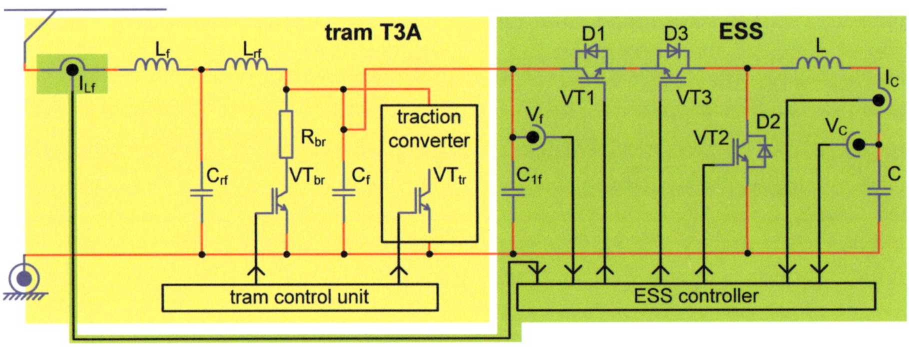

Fig. 1. A simplified circuit diagram of ESS and its connection to the T3A tramcar power circuit

The ESS consists of supercapacitor *C* and bidirectional DC/DC power converter. IGBT *VT1* and diode *D2* works as a voltage buck converter in the supercapacitor *C* charging mode, but *VT2* and *D1*, at switched on *VT3*, as a voltage boost converter in the supercapacitor *C* discharging mode. IGBT *VT3* is necessary for protection of the supercapacitor *C* in the cases, when a short circuit or undervoltage occurs in the overhead line or tram traction converter. To prevent overcurrents and uncontrolled discharge of supercapacitor, *VT3* is switched off when ESS input voltage is lower than supercapacitor voltage.

The ESS is connected to the tram's filter capacitor C_f =5100μF which is therefore also used as a basic element for the buck/boost converter of ESS. Capacitor C_{1f} only compensates inductances of the connecting cables and must be placed as close as possible to the elements *VT1, VT2, VT3* and *C*; its capacitance is considerably lower than that of C_f. Such a connection allows to exploit tram's radio-frequency filter L_{rf}, C_{rf} and input choke L_f for smoothing pulsed currents flowing from ESS to the overhead line.

The ESS is developed as an entirely autonomous device having no links to the tram control unit. Two current and two voltage sensors are used for ESS control purposes. Three of them

are placed inside of ESS and only tram input current sensor should be installed in the tram power circuit.
Fig. 2 shows the simplified four-axle tram T3A traction drive circuit with a DC chopper and DC traction motors in running, a) and braking, b) modes of operation.

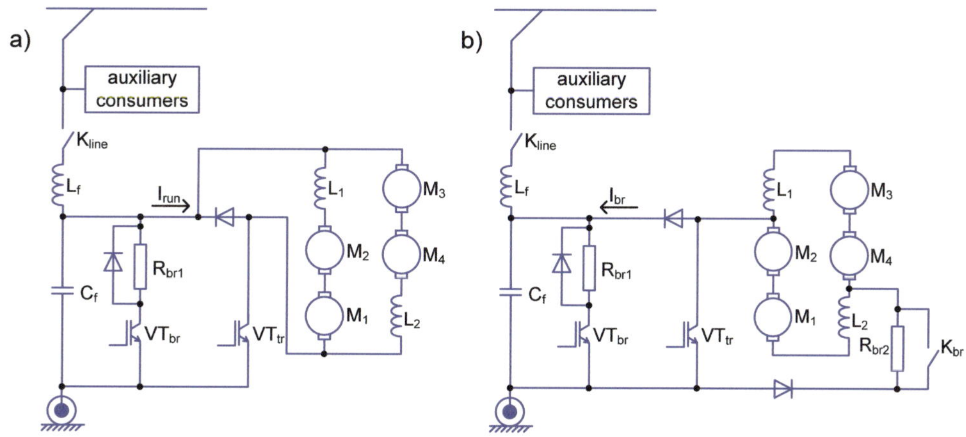

Fig. 2. A simplified circuit diagram of the tram T3A traction drive: a) in running mode, b) in braking mode.

IGBT VT_{tr} is a main switch for both buck (Fig. 2, a) and boost (Fig. 2, b) configurations of DC chopper. IGBT VT_{br} operates in a case when there are no consumers for the braking current I_{br}. Then voltage of capacitor C_f begins to rise and the tram control system works as the voltage stabilizer with a 780V setting. The energy is dissipated in the brake rheostat R_{br1}. This is the untapped energy which must be saved in ESS and then returned back when tram accelerates. When tram is braking at a high speed, the counter EMF of motors exceeds the supply voltage. To make the braking process controllable, an additional braking rheostat R_{br2} is included into the power circuit, which is short-circuited by contactor K_{br} when the speed falls below 30 km/h. The portion of braking energy dissipated in R_{br2} may be considered as a technological and for this type of drive cannot be saved in ESS.
The pulse currents of the DC chopper are closed through the capacitor C_f, whereas the overhead line current is smoothed by the choke L_f. Both transistors VT_{tr} and VT_{br} are steered by pulse width modulators with constant switching frequency 1000Hz.

3. Model of the tram traction drive with on-board ESS

The PSIM model of the T3A tram traction drive with installed on-board ESS is shown in Fig.3. The voltage source *V1* and diode *D1* represent the feeding substation and *R1* is an equivalent resistance of the connecting cables and overhead line. The current source *I2* simulates another tram connected to the same overhead line. The DC chopper of the tram is represented in two versions - as a continuous and a pulsed current source. In Fig. 3 the continuous current source *I1* is used. The positive direction of currents *I1* and *I2* shown in Fig. 3 corresponds to the running mode and negative - to the braking mode of operation of the both trams. The filter capacitor's voltage limiter (VT_{br} and R_{br1} in Fig. 2) is substituted with voltage source *V2*=780V and diode *D2*.

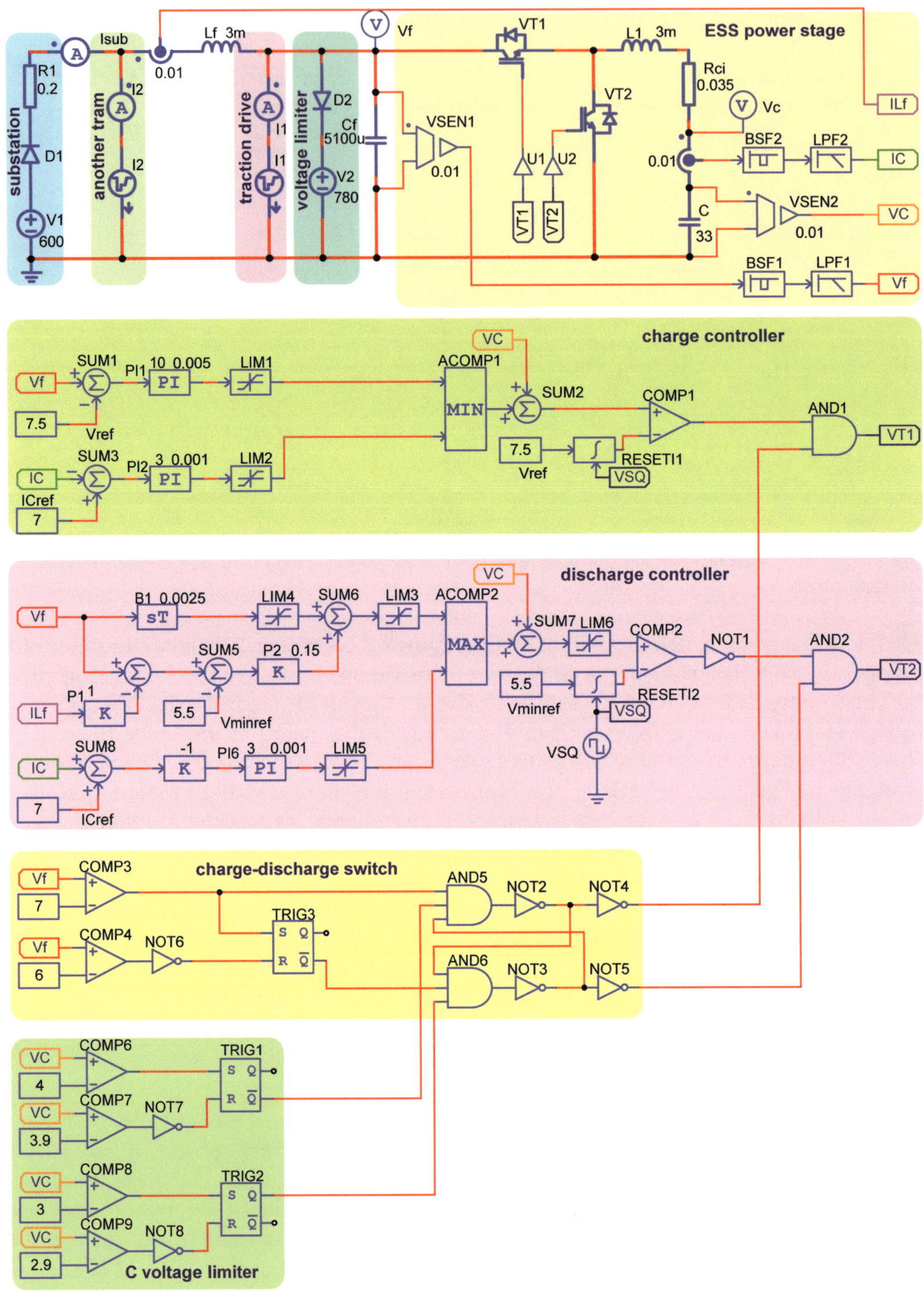

Fig. 3. PSIM model of an onboard ESS installed on the tram T3A

ESS power stage contains IGBTs *VT1* and *VT2*, choke *L1* and supercapacitor *C*. Since IGBT VT3 (see Fig. 1) is used only for protection purposes, it is eliminated from the PSIM model. The equivalent series resistance R_{Ci} of supercapacitor *C* is calculated for parallel connection of two modules containing 160 or 180 series-connected single capacitors *Maxwell* 3000F, 2.7V each, adding a 0.1mΩ connection resistance to the 0.29 mΩ internal resistance of a single capacitor.

Fig. 4 shows the pulsed current source model of the DC chopper while Fig. 5 explains principle of its operation. IGBTs VT_r and VT_b commutate current sources I_{DC1} and I_{DC2} to the output line forming positive or negative pulses of chopper current I_{ch} with a 500A amplitude. Pulse width is proportional to the steering voltage V_I which is compared with sawtooth voltage V_{saw} and its inverse value by comparators A1 and A2 respectively. V_{saw} has 1000Hz frequency and 5V amplitude.

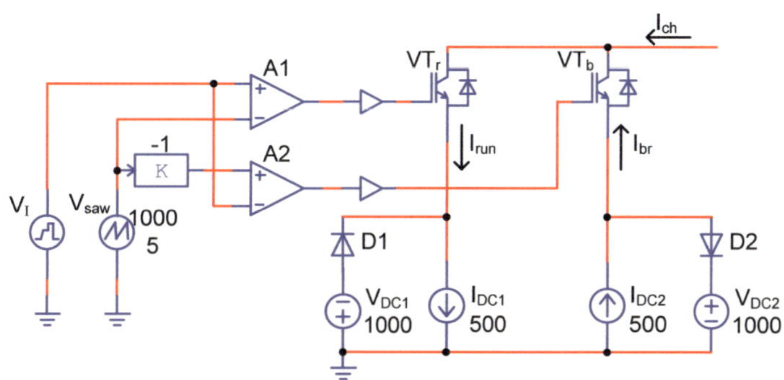

Fig. 4. PSIM model of the pulsed current source

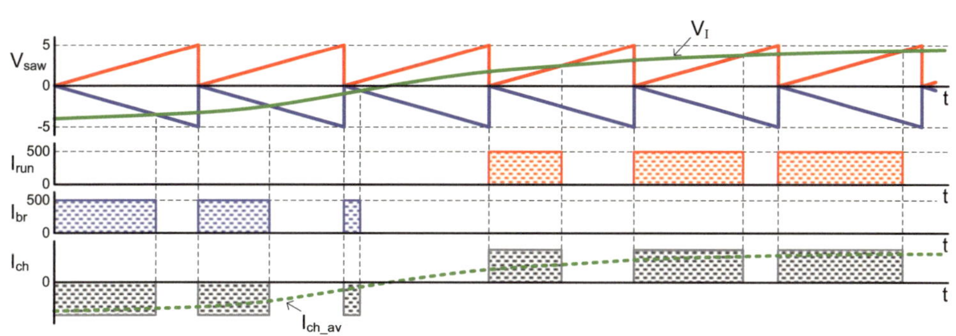

Fig. 5. Diagrams of the pulsed current source model

At positive values of the voltage V_I transistor VT_r operates and I_{ch}=I_{run}. At negative V_I operates VT_b and I_{ch}=-I_{br}. The average value of current pulses I_{ch_av} is proportional to V_I with scale 1V=100A. Voltage sources V_{DC1} and V_{DC2} and diodes *D1* and *D2* eliminate overvoltages when IGBTs are off.

The pulsed current source model noticeably increase simulation time that is why it is used only when interference between the tram DC chopper and ESS converter is investigated (see section 7).

4. ESS control system

Control system of ESS (see Fig. 3) contains supercapacitor charge controller, discharge controller, charge-discharge mode switch and supercapacitor voltage limiter.

The main task of the ESS controller is to store all tramcar braking energy not allowing its dissipation in a braking rheostat. To store the energy a capacitor must be discharged to the voltage V_{Cmin} at the beginning of braking. As the braking energy depends on the tramcar speed, the processes of charging and discharging the supercapacitor may be controlled in compliance with the tramcar's real speed. Unfortunately, such a control principle could not be provided in T3A tramcars due to the lack of a speed sensor.

Two voltages and two currents are measured for ESS control purposes: filter capacitor voltage V_f, supercapacitor voltage V_C, supercapacitor current I_C and tram input filter current I_{Lf}. Since filter capacitor voltage V_f and supercapacitor current I_C have 1000Hz ripple with significant amplitude, the measured signals are filtered by using 1000Hz band-stop filters *BSF1*, *BSF2* and low-pass filters *LPF1*, *LPF2* with cut-off frequency 800Hz.

4.1 Charge controller

A simplified equivalent circuit diagram of ESS in tram braking mode i.e. supercapacitor charge mode is shown on Fig. 6.

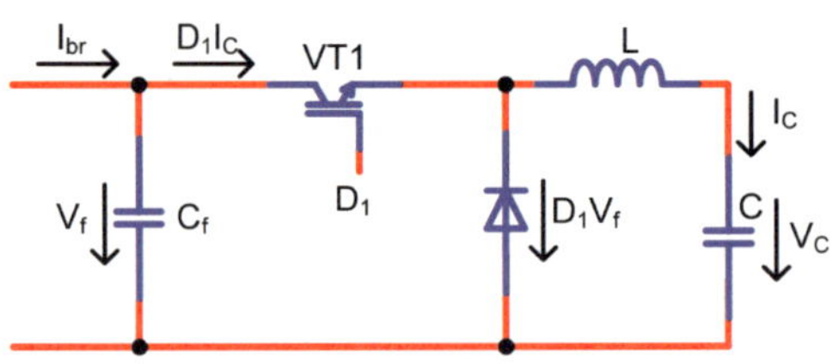

Fig. 6. A simplified circuit diagram of ESS in charge mode

For simplicity all circuit elements are suggested to be ideal and energy dissipative resistances are ignored. Voltages V_f, D_1V_f and currents I_C, D_1I_C are the average values with averaging interval being equal to the switching period of VT1, where D_1 is a duty ratio.

All braking energy will be saved in ESS if

$$D_1I_C=I_{br} \tag{1}$$

Then capacitor C_f current is zero and voltage V_f is constant. Therefore, if the control system maintains the filter capacitor's voltage V_f constant, the controller automatically provides such a duty factor D_1 that Eq. (1) is valid. The setting for the filter capacitor's voltage V_{ref} must be selected slightly lower than 780 V. However, a second control loop is needed for the supercapacitor's current to limit it to an allowable level in the emergency cases when the braking power exceeds the rated value.

Assuming supercapacitor C as a voltage V_C source, the Fig. 4 circuit equations are

$$V_f(s)=\frac{1}{sC_f}(I_{br}(s)-D_1I_C(s))\ ; \tag{2}$$

$$I_C(s) = \frac{1}{sL}(D_1 V_f(s) - V_C) \tag{3}$$

Solving (2) and (3) for $V_f(s)$ and $I_C(s)$ yields

$$V_f(s) = \frac{sLI_{br}(s) + D_1 V_C}{s^2 LC_f + D_1^2} \tag{4}$$

$$I_C(s) = \frac{D_1 I_{br}(s) - sC_f V_C}{s^2 LC_f + D_1^2} \tag{5}$$

Equation (4) is an open-loop transfer function for the filter capacitor voltage V_f. Note that it depends nonlinearly on the control variable D_1. The open-loop system is stable and the steady-state voltage, obtained from (4) at s=0, $V_f\big|_{t=\infty} = V_C / D_1$, and steady state current obtained from (5) at s=0 $I_C\big|_{t=\infty} = I_{br} / D_1$. Hence, by choosing $D_1=D_{10}=V_C/V_{ref}$ feedforward may be introduced. It provides steady-state voltage $V_f=V_{ref}$ and facilitates performance of the feedback loop. The latter can be implemented by adding a small deviation d_1 to the duty ratio: $D_1=D_{10}+d_1$. The circuit diagram and operating principle of a pulse width modulator (PWM) with feedforward and feedback is shown in Fig. 7.

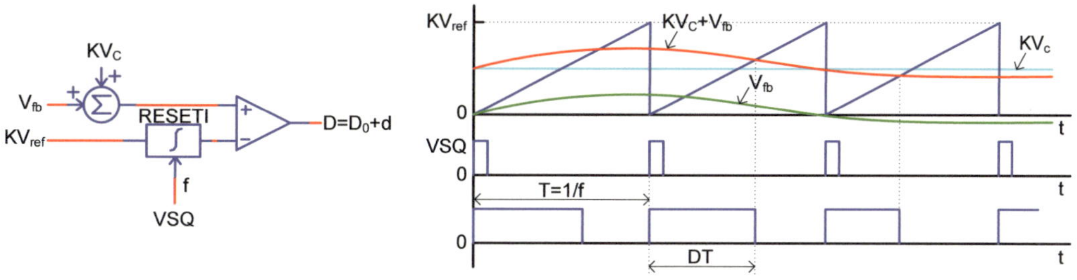

Fig. 7. A pulse width modulator with feedforward and feedback

Resetable integrator *RESETI* generates sawtooth voltage with switching period $T=1/f$ and amplitude KV_{ref}, where K is a gain of the voltage sensors. The pulse duty ratio at the comparator output $D=V_C/V_{ref}+V_{fb}/KV_{ref}=D_0+d$. Feedback voltage V_{fb} is bipolar and increase in V_{fb} causes increase in the duty ratio D and, as it results from (4), decrease in the filter capacitor voltage V_f. Such a PWM is used in both charge and discharge controllers.

The voltage control loop of the charge controller (see Fig. 3) consists of summator *SUM1*, proportional-integral (PI) controller *PI1* and voltage limiter *LIM1*. Reference voltage is set to V_{ref}=750V.

Supercapacitor current feedback is necessary for current limiting at allowable value which is set to I_{Cref}=700A. When current limiting takes place, all braking energy cannot be stored in ESS because $I_{br}>D_1 I_C$ and Eq. (1) is not valid. Voltage V_f raises up to value V_{fmax}=780V set by voltage limiter. Part of braking energy is dissipated in the braking rheostat (in voltage source V2 in Fig. 3). In this case transfer function for $I_C(s)$ is obtained from (3) substituting $V_f(s)=V_{fmax}$:

$$I_C(s) = \frac{1}{sL}(D_1 V_{f\max} - V_C) \tag{6}$$

The transfer function (6) is linear regarding to the control variable D_1 but an open-loop system is unstable.

Current control loop of the charge controller (see Fig. 3) consists of summator *SUM2*, PI controller *PI2* and voltage limiter *LIM2*. The feedback voltage applied to the pulse width modulator is the lesser of two control loop signals chosen by analogue comparator *ACOMP1*. In the voltage control mode $I_C<I_{Cref}$, the output signal of *LIM2* has the upper value and current control loop is disconnected. Similarly, in the current control mode $V_f>V_{ref}$, the output signal of *LIM1* has the upper value and the voltage control loop is disconnected.

4.2 Discharge controller

The equivalent circuit diagram of ESS in tram drive mode i.e. supercapacitor discharge mode is shown in Fig. 8. The I_{run} is an averaged current of the traction drive chopper in tram running mode.

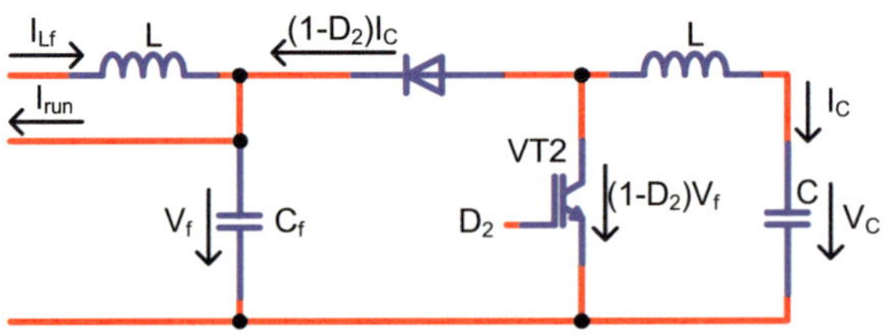

Fig. 8. A simplified circuit diagram of ESS in discharge mode

Suffering the same assumptions as in the previous section the circuit equations are

$$V_f(s) = \frac{1}{sC_f}((1-D_2)I_C(s) + I_{Lf}(s) - I_{run}(s)) \tag{7}$$

$$I_C(s) = \frac{1}{sL}(V_C - (1-D_2)V_f(s)) \tag{8}$$

Solving (7) and (8) for $V_f(s)$ yields

$$V_f(s) = \frac{(1-D_2)V_C + sLI_{Lf}(s) - sLI_{run}(s)}{s^2LC_f + (1-D_2)^2} \tag{9}$$

Equation (9) is very similar to (4) with $(1\text{-}D_2)$ instead of D_1. As $(1\text{-}D)$ is an inverted D, the same PWM may be used for discharge controller by adding logic inverter to the modulator output.

Supercapacitor current control loop is similar to that of the charge controller. The difference is in an opposite sign of the supercapacitor current and added analogue inverter.

Voltage control loop differs significantly from the charge controller because in the discharge mode ESS should have declivous VA characteristic. It is achieved with use of proportional (P) controller *P2* instead of PI controller and by adding input current I_{Lf} to the voltage feedback signal. Differentiator *B1* improves dynamic characteristics and stability of the voltage feedback loop. Since duty ratio *(1-D)* decreases and voltage V_f increases with increase in the feedback voltage V_{fb}, the greater voltage of both control loops, chosen by analogue comparator *ACOMP2,* is applied to the PWM. Voltage reference for discharge mode is set V_{minref}=550V.

4.3 Charge-discharge switch

Charge-discharge mode switch is a very important part of the controller which vastly influences stable operation of ESS. The lack of running-braking mode signal due to autonomous conception of ESS complicates switch design, because information about tram drive mode should be extracted from the available measurements of currents and voltages. The objectives for choice of the proper charge-discharge switch solution are as follows:

- simultaneous setting of the both modes is not permissible,
- the circuit L_f, C_f, *L1* and *C* (Fig. 3) has a low damping factor and fast switching from one mode to other can cause rising oscillations in it,
- a neutral position - no mode is set, is permissible and is a good choice for achieving stable operation of the system,
- current I_{Lf} cannot help to determine tram drive mode and only filter voltage V_f should be used for it.

The charge-discharge switch is realized with two voltage comparators *COMP3, COMP4,* RS trigger *TRIG3* and a trigger build on the elements *AND5, AND6, NOT2…NOT5.* It's performance is illustrated in Fig. 9.

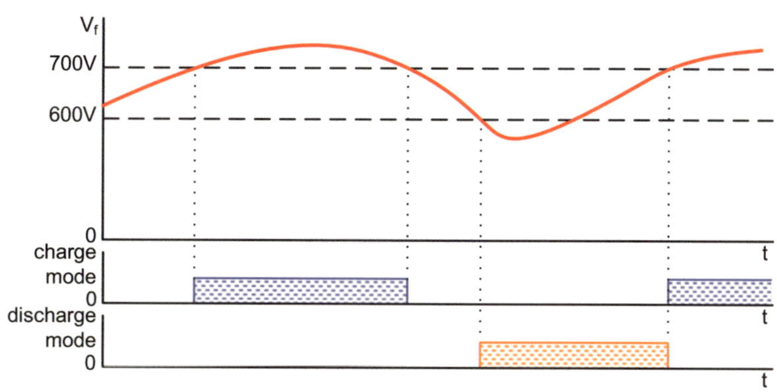

Fig. 9. Diagrams of charge-discharge mode signals

The charge mode is allowed when V_{Cf} >700V, but the discharge mode is set when voltage falls down to 600V level.

4.4 Supercapacitor voltage limiter

The maximum permissible voltage of supercapacitor V_{Cmax}=2.5*N*V has been chosen, where *N* is a number of series connected 2.7V 3000F capacitors. The minimum supercapacitor voltage V_{Cmin}=0.5V_{Cmax} has been commonly used e. g. (Barrero, R. et al, 2008 A) and is recommended by manufacturers of supercapacitors. Then 75% of its energy capacity is used at the power capability varying from $V_{Cmin}I_{Cref}$=0.5P_{max} to P_{max}. However, as it is discussed in (Latkovskis,

L. & Bražis, V., 2007), the braking power has its maximum at the beginning of tram braking when ESS has its minimum power capability. That is why more narrow voltage range has been chosen - $V_{Cmin} \approx 0.67 V_{Cmax}$. It yields 55% of the supercapacitor energy capacity to be utilized at power capability $0.67 P_{max}$ at the beginning of tram braking.
Supercapacitor voltage limiter consists of four voltage comparators *COMP6…COMP9*, two logic inverters *NOT7, NOT8* and two RS triggers *TRIG1, TRIG2*. Fig. 10 illustrates its operating principle.

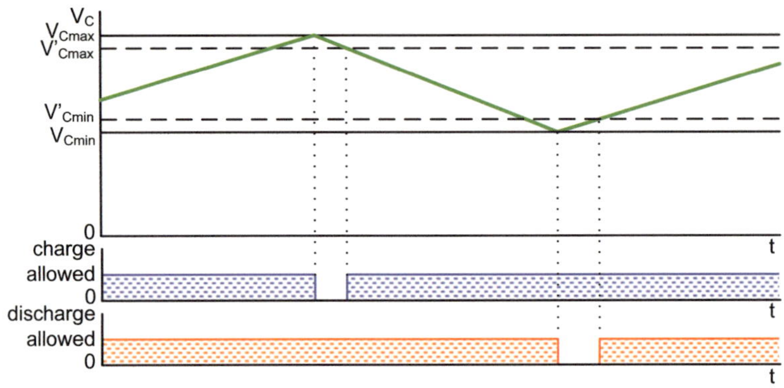

Fig. 10. Signal diagrams of supercapacitor voltage limiter

The charge mode is disabled when voltage reaches V_{Cmax}. It is permit again when voltage falls down to the level V'_{Cmax}. The discharge is disabled when supercapacitor voltage falls down to V_{Cmin}, and permit again when voltage rises up to V'_{Cmin}.
The resulting parameters of the supercapacitor bank and chosen voltage limiter settings for two parallel and *N* series connected single capacitors are shown in the Table 1.

N	C, F	R_{Ci}, mΩ	V_{Cmax}, V	V'_{Cmax}, V	V_{Cmin}, V	V'_{Cmin}, V	E, kJ
160	37.5	31.2	400	385	270	285	1633
180	33.3	35.1	450	430	300	320	1873

Table 1. Parameters of the supercapacitor bank and the voltage limiter settings

5. Optimization of the control system parameters

The first aim of the PSIM simulation was establishment of an optimal structure of the ESS control system and optimization of its feedback loop parameters to achieve stable operation and transient processes without overshoots and oscillations.
The filters *BSF1, BSF2, LPF1* and *LPF2* have been included in outputs of the voltage and current sensors, because presence of an AC component in the feedback signal causes nonlinearity of PWM and can be a reason of unstable operation of ESS. Second order band-stop filters *BSF1* and *BSF2* with 1000Hz central frequency eliminate the first harmonic of the ripple and low-pass filters *LPF1* and *LPF2* attenuate high order harmonics. Cut-off frequency 800Hz for *LPF1* and *LPF2* has been chosen as an optimal. At lower cut-off frequencies feedback performance worsens due to increased signal delay.

Parameters of PI controllers are optimized by frequentative simulation of ESS at different modes of operation using PSIM "parameter sweep" option. At chosen gain of the PI controller the time constant is varied. Then value of the time constant giving the best transient process is chosen and gain is varied. After some iteration the best combination of the gain and the time constant is found. The optimal values of control system parameters are shown in Fig. 3.

6. Simulation of ESS operation modes

The PSIM/Simulink simulation is performed for tramcar starting and braking processes in different situations with and without another tram connected to the overhead line. The typical load conditions in one overhead section are:

- single tram operation - only one tram is placed in overhead feeder section at low traffic density, no energy consumers and sources are available on DC line.
- two trams independent running - regenerative energy could be fully or partially used depending on both tram operation mode conditions,
- autonomous running in the case of net voltage unavailability.

If only one tram is running in overhead feeder section, then ESS supercapacitor capacity must be enough for storing the amount of one braking cycle energy. The braking energy could not be transferred to trams, which are supplied from other overhead sections and needs peak energy shaving. Such load situation is typical for Riga with city's radial tram lines system in suburban areas and single-track lines with exchange stops (lines 5 and 10), where no multiple tram driving at time is allowed in either direction.

The increase in number of simultaneously recuperating trams (more than 4-6) and presence of non-recuperating vehicles decreases the untapped regenerative energy (Latkovskis, L. & Grigans, L., 2008 B), therefore it is expected, that most difficult ESS working conditions would be if few trams are operated on two-track lines separated from other traffic outside city centre. Common situation on separated track is that the starting and braking is performed mostly at stops, when distance and consequently energy losses between two trams at the same stop are negligible, therefore the two tramcar energy exchange situation is chosen for simulation, where the braking and starting modes of both trams could been randomly shifted each from other. The model supposes, that tramcar with supercapacitor is working together in one feeder section with conventional T3A tram without any ESS. At low traffic density when single car trams are used, the conventional tram could start with its maximum traction current and brake with maximum braking current, which causes significant ESS voltage fluctuations. In the case, that double-car trams are used instead of single car, the power and current values doubles, but the shape of the characteristics remains the same if both coupled tramcars in each train-set have properly equal adjusted synchronised control systems.

The property of ESS to operate without overhead line voltage allows autonomous tram traction and braking. The autonomous traction is necessary for limited distances to restore interrupted traffic, e.g. in case of overhead damage, therefore the reduced performance of tram traction characteristics is allowed. The autonomous braking could eliminate regenerative energy losses, when tram passes overhead "dead" spots and switches.

For the simulation of ESS operation each tram is substituted with piecewise current source, which allows to change the number of tramcars by adding more sources without slowing the modelling speed. The traction DC converter of the tram with ESS is substituted by continuous current source *I1* (see Fig. 3), conventional tram - with continuous current source *I2*. The current *I1* shape is taken from 51s long factory test measurements of maximum loaded tram with maximum acceleration and deceleration at speed 55km/h and braking current peak 480A. The tramcar traction DC buck converter provides acceleration from beginning of starting to 6s, and two stage field weakening from 6s to 39s, then follows regenerative braking from 39s to 51s, with additional resistance bypassing at 45s.

a)

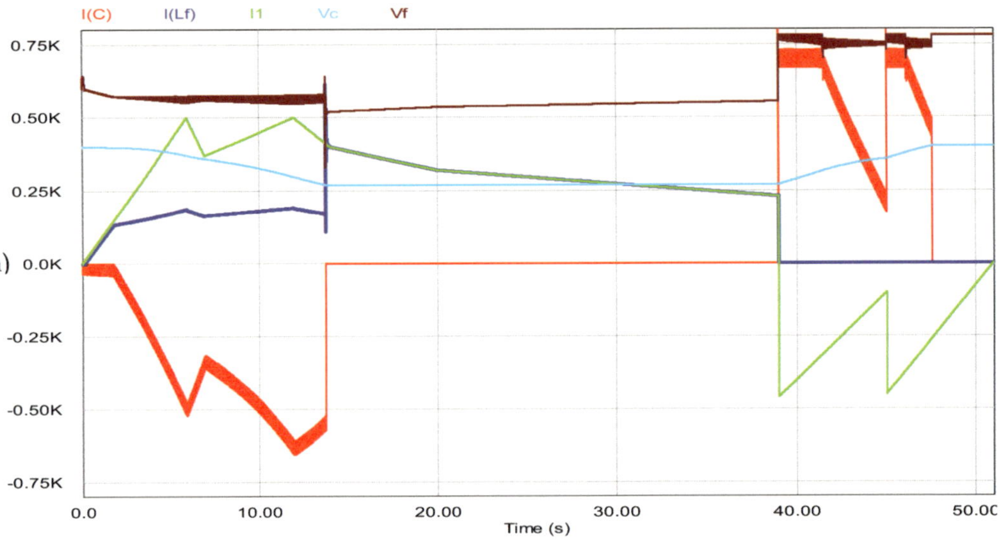

b)

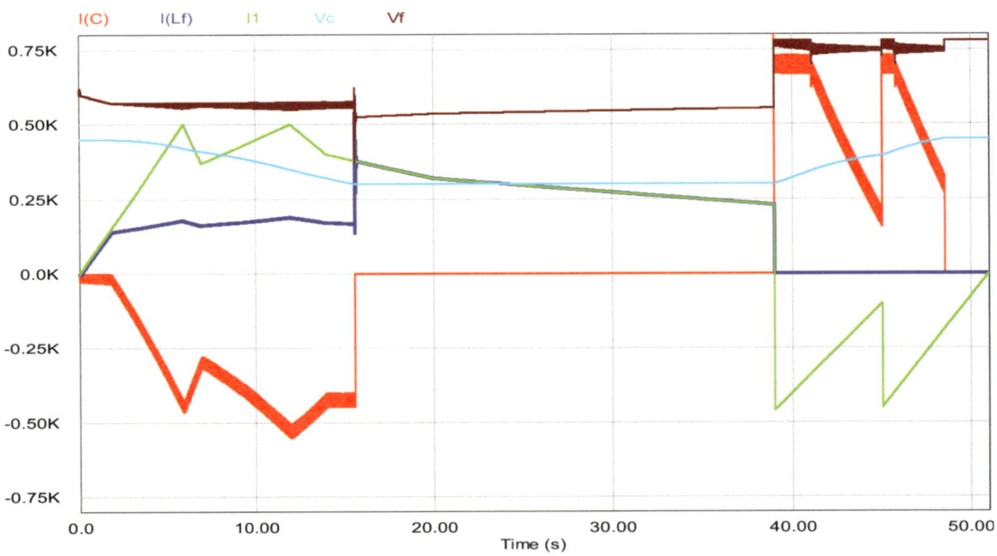

Fig. 11. PSIM simulation results of single tram for two values of supercapacitor capacitance: 37.5F (a) and 33.3F (b)

In the case of single tram operation current source *I2* value is set to zero. For research of two tram operation the current source *I2* diagram is shifted in time towards the first tram diagram, while the current shape is the same. In the autonomous mode of operation tram with ESS is disconnected from overhead line and other trams by setting the current source *I2* and the voltage source *V1* to zero.

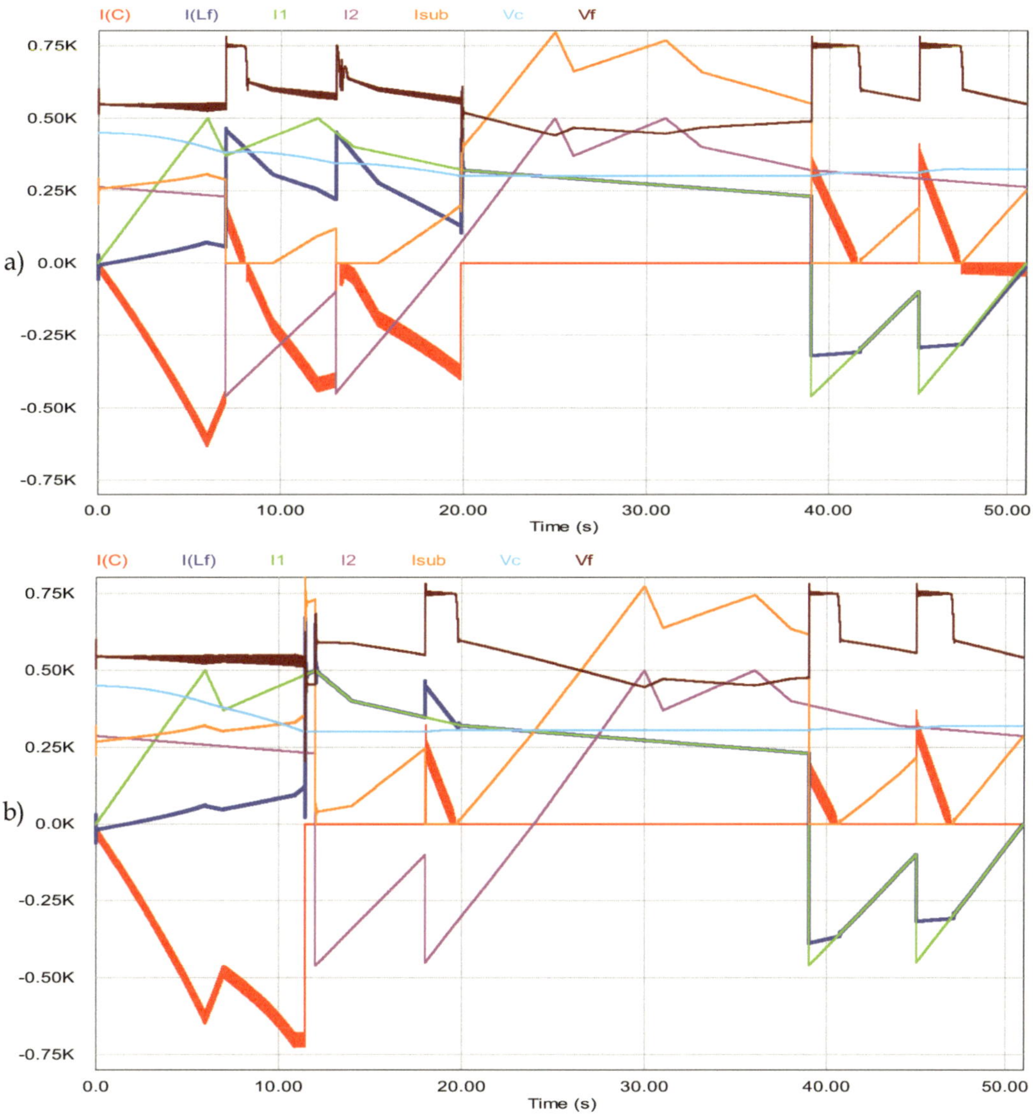

Fig. 12. PSIM simulation results of two tram operation at various tram starting time shift

The results of PSIM simulation for single tram with two variants of ESS supercapacitor capacitance 37.5F and 33.3F is shown in Fig. 11,a,b. Capacitance 33.3F has higher energy capacity and absorbs more energy due to the higher maximum and minimum voltage settings (see Table 1.), which allows to store more energy at the beginning of braking.

Therefore it ensures shorter time of current limiting, when regenerative energy partially is dissipated in braking rheostat. The power peak shaving time (the time of supercapacitor discharge to the minimum allowed voltage) with 33.3F supercapacitor is extended to 15.59s in comparison with 13.72s for 37.5F ESS capacitance. The total time of the current limiting at 700A level is 4s for 37.5F ESS and 3s for 33.3F ESS. The capacitance 33.3F is chosen for further simulations.

In the case of two trams independent running no current restriction is observed when one tramcar brakes (Fig. 12.). The excessive regenerative energy is transferred to ESS from both trams. The shift between starting moments of the both trams strongly influences the regenerative energy transferring. If the second tram begins braking at the moment of the first tram field weakening (Fig. 12., a.), this causes the ESS charging with surplus energy in time interval 7s...8s. Due to peak shaving the substation maximal current is significantly reduced to 306A and even in time intervals 7s...9.6s and 12s...15.4s $I_{sub}=0$. The ESS converter switching between charging and discharging modes passes without unstable oscillations. Fig. 12, b shows the case when another tram brakes at second stage of field weakening of the first tram. It causes shorter supercapacitor discharge time (12s) because both trams operate in the traction mode for longer time.
Simulation results of tram autonomous operation are shown in Fig. 13. Due to the restricted ESS capacity the autonomous traction with maximum traction current is possible up to first 9s, when supercapacitor voltage drops close to the lower limit and filter capacitor voltage decreases to 500V. It corresponds to vehicle speed approximately 27km/h.

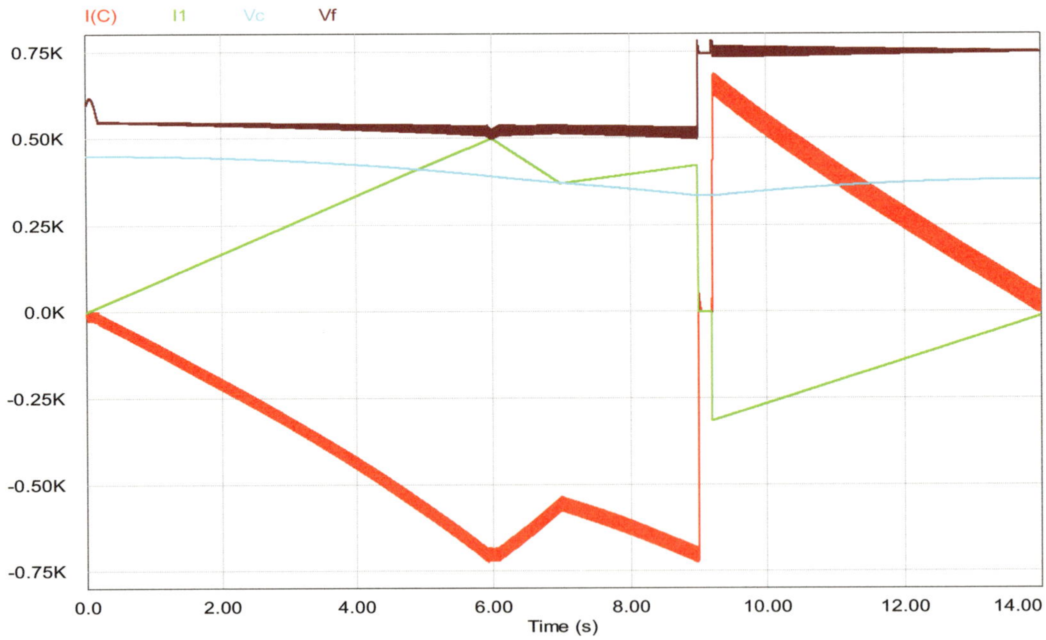

Fig. 13. PSIM simulation of tram autonomous operation

Because the prolonged traction with field weakening due to limited ESS power is impossible, it's recommended to restrict the autonomous traction with DC motor full field connection only (up to 6s acceleration time with speed 20-25km/h). The 0.2s long switching from traction to braking mode is stable and not significantly different from simplified instant mode switching.
Overhead voltage failure at different stages of tram movement also has been simulated. Fig. 14 shows a case when overhead voltage failure happened at 42s, when tram was braking at full speed. One can ensure that it didn't cause abnormal operation of tram equipment.

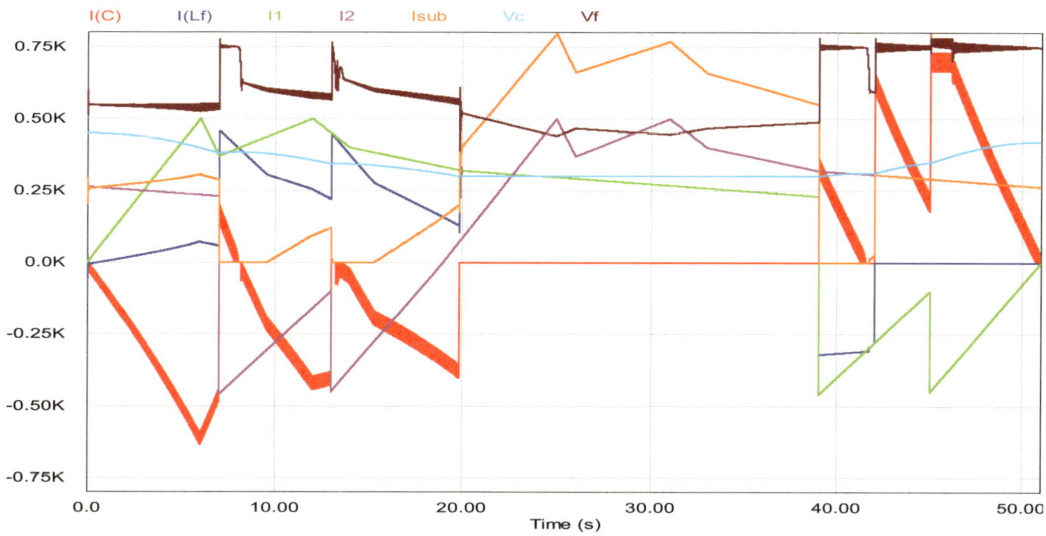

Fig. 14. Simulation of overhead voltage failure at tram braking (42s)

The ESS cannot store all regenerative braking energy if tramcar maximum traction and braking currents are taken from the factory tram test methodology, but in real traffic conditions the maximum acceleration and deceleration values are not widely observed. Fig. 15 shows the 300s long drive test simulation with currents *I1* and *I2* recorded on tram T3A running in line Nr 6. ESS accumulates all braking energy even when two trams are braking simultaneously (275-285s).

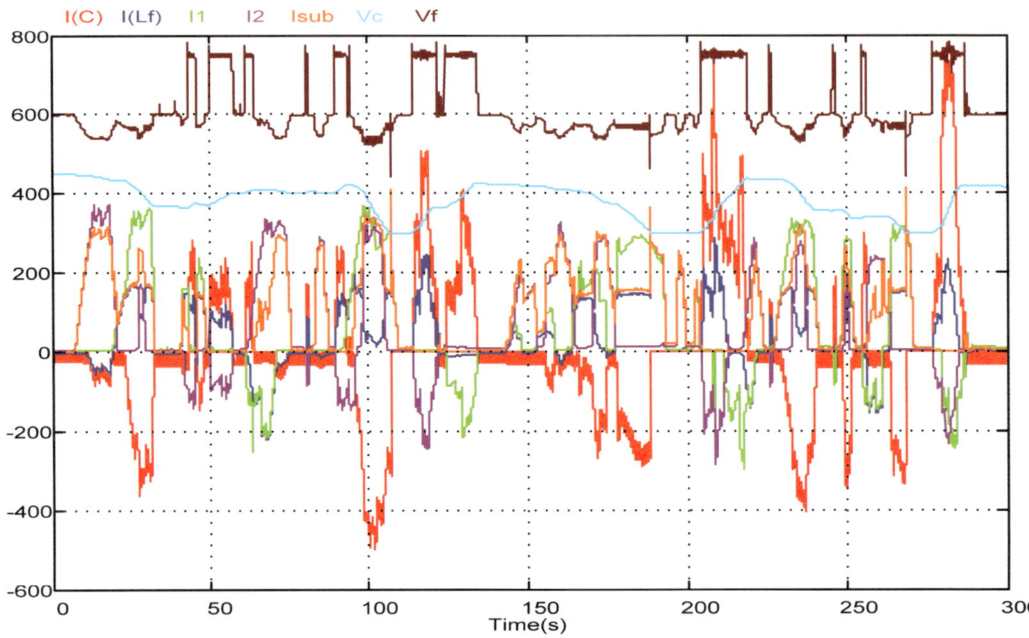

Fig. 15. PSIM/Matlab simulation of tram operation in real traffic driving conditions

7. Interaction between ESS and traction converter

By applying a pulsed current PSIM model of DC PWM tram converter the control system's stability is investigated in both synchronous and asynchronous operation modes of the tram DC converter and ESS current controller. In the section 6 for faster and simplest simulation the tram power scheme was substituted by linear current supply. In the real situation tram DC converter generates current pulses with 1000Hz frequency with almost constant amplitude and variable pulse width. Filter capacitor C_f is common for both converters. Due to its relatively small capacitance (5100μF) current pulses causes considerable capacitor voltage ripple which can affect performance of the energy storage device. The aim of PSIM simulation is:

- to investigate how the interference between two converters affects performance of the voltage control loop,
- to optimize parameters of PID control loops,
- to ascertain whether the action of both converters should be synchronized or not.

In synchronous operation mode the tram DC converter and ESS switching frequency is set 1000Hz. The asynchronous operation is tested in two modes with small and great difference in converter frequencies, where the tram DC converter frequency is set correspondingly 1001Hz and 1005Hz. The ESS converter frequency always remains 1000 Hz.

Because the autonomous traction could be provided with limited speed, the correct comparison of converter operation modes at various tram load conditions could be made only with acceleration at full DC motor field up to 25km/h (6s starting time) and braking from this speed. Such restriction also helps to reduce simulation time.

Fig. 16 demonstrates the interaction between ESS and single tramcar traction converter in synchronous mode of operation.

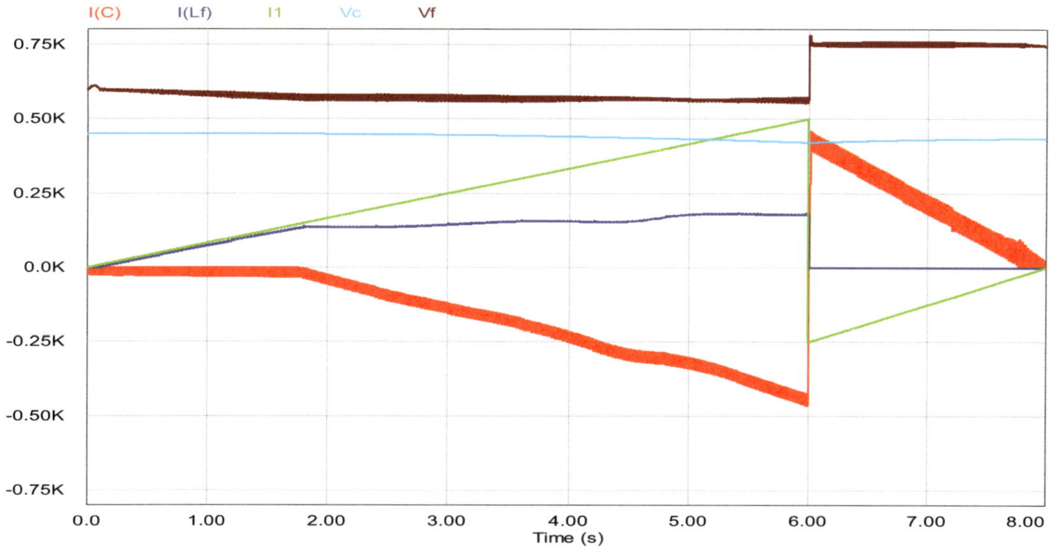

Fig. 16. Interaction between ESS and traction converter in synchronous operation mode

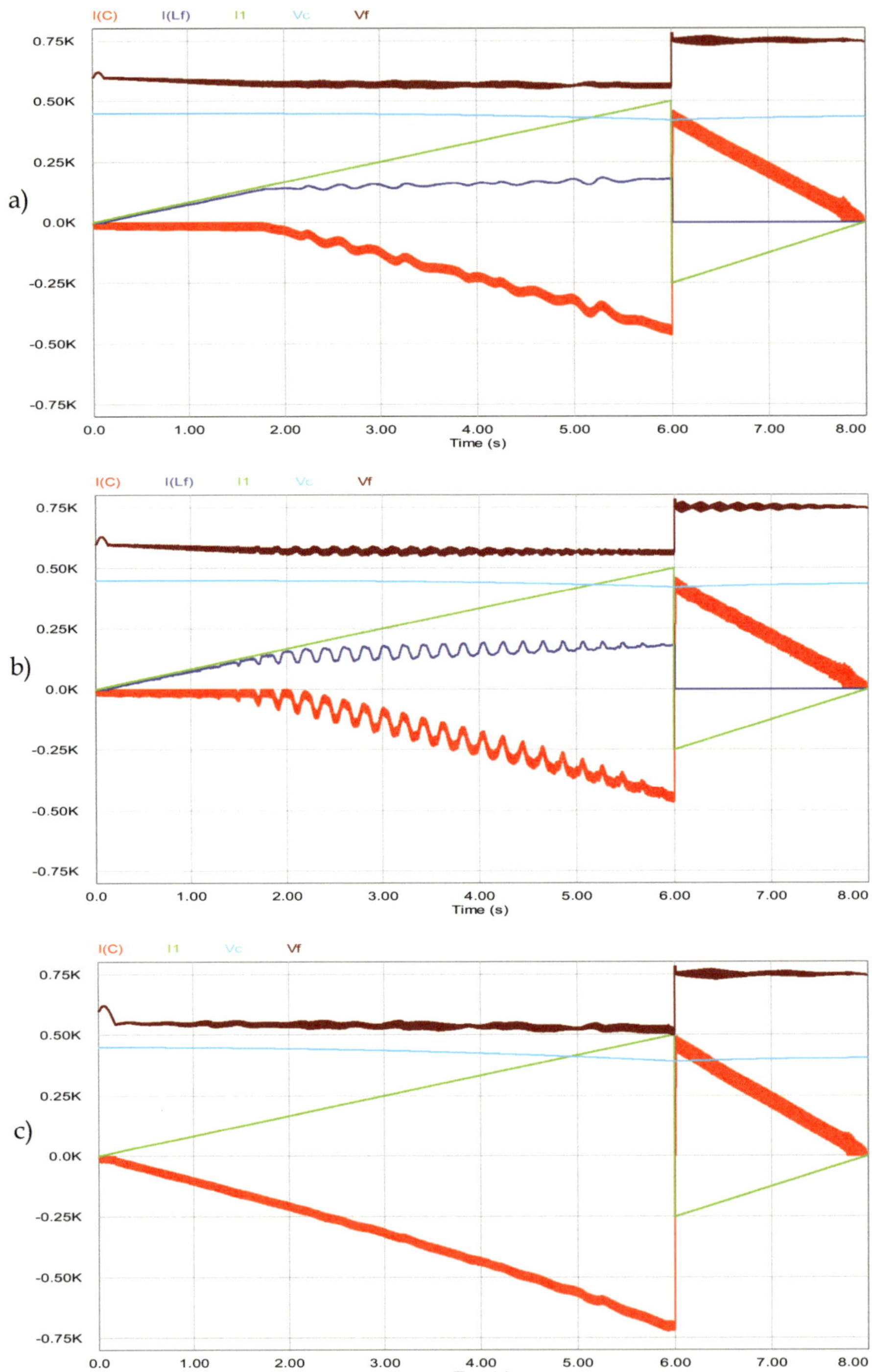

Fig. 17. Asynchronous operation mode with 1Hz (a) and 5Hz (b) difference in both converter switching frequencies, and autonomous traction mode (c) with 1Hz difference

The same situation in asynchronous operation mode with 1Hz (a) and 5Hz (b) difference in switching frequencies of the both converters is shown in Fig. 17. Fig. 17,c demonstrates autonomous traction with 1Hz difference in converter switching frequencies. The width of curves for the voltage V_f and current I_C in Fig. 17 is equal to their ripple amplitudes.

Analysing obtained results of pulsed current source simulation and comparing them to that of simulation with continuous DC current source the following conclusions has been made:

- no significant difference in currents and voltages between the case with continuous DC current and pulse current source is observed,
- the final charge of the supercapacitor is the same in all cases; efficiency factor of the energy storing ≈0.96 has been achieved,
- observed voltage V_f ripple amplitude oscillations is a result of interference between two pulsed current sources with different frequencies 1001Hz and 1000Hz and is not caused by control systems instability,
- although the voltage ripple in the voltage PID control loop is significant, it does not cause malfunction of the control system in the both synchronous and asynchronous operation modes of the traction and the energy storage converters.

One can observe that the mode of operation (synchronous or asynchronous) does not affect considerably process of the supercapacitor charging if difference in frequencies does not exceed 1Hz. At 5Hz difference supercapacitor and line current ripples become significant.

Fig. 18 shows waveforms of the chopper current $I1_{pulse}$, switch current $I_{(VT1)}$, supercapacitor discharging current I_C and filter capacitor voltage V_f in an asynchronous mode of operation with 1Hz difference in the switching frequencies of the both converters and expanded scale of time.

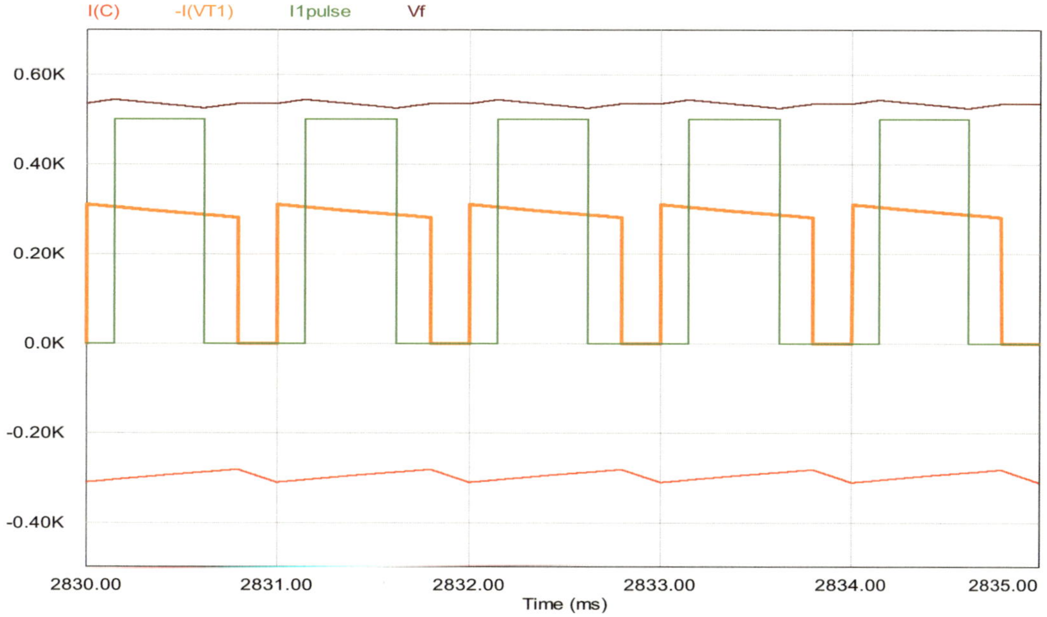

Fig. 18. Voltage and current diagrams in an asynchronous operation mode of ESS and traction converter

One can ensure that the voltage V_f and current I_C ripples are caused by the switched-mode operation of the power converters and are not a result of instable operation of the energy storage device control system. The precision of tram control system quartz clock signal ensures less than 1Hz difference between both converter working frequencies; however low frequency oscillations with frequency up to 5Hz could occur due to the control system adjusting restrictions.

8. Conclusion

1. Simulation results show stability of ESS control system in all operation modes, and ESS ability to utilize braking energy of the tram with high efficiency.
2. Installation of a supercapacitor in a T3A tramcar allows storing efficiently all the energy returned during the braking time independently of other overhead-connected consumers.
3. The complete braking energy storage is provided if in the ESS controller the filter capacitor voltage feedback is introduced. To limit the supercapacitor current to an allowable level a current control loop is needed as well.
4. The difference between synchronous and asynchronous mode of converters operation is insignificant if difference in switching frequencies of the tram DC chopper and ESS converter does not exceed 1Hz. Such accuracy can be easy achieved by using quartz oscillators; therefore the synchronization of both converter switching frequencies is not necessary.
5. Although ESS and tram traction converter control systems are independent, this causes drawbacks - complicated operation algorithms of the ESS control system that reduce its stability margin.
6. For better recognition of tram driving modes and oscillation dampening the control system must be upgraded with speed sensor. When ESS is developed for brand-new tramcar, the ESS and traction converter control systems must be synchronised. Tram control system commands must be sent to ESS controller.
7. The future research could be done for the ESS and tram control system integration in automatic traffic control and signalisation system, which allows to collect and predict information about braking energy amount and even manage optimal multiple tram traffic.

9. References

Barrero, R.; Tackoen, X.; Van Mierlo, J. (2008 A). Analysis and configuration of supercapacitor based energy storage system on-board light rail vehicles. *Proceedings of the 13th International Power Electronics and Motion Control Conference EPE-PEMC 2008*, Poznan, 1-3 September 2008, pp. 1535-1540.

Barrero, R.; Tackoen, X.; Van Mierlo, J. (2008 B). Improving energy efficiency in public transport: Stationary supercapacitor based Energy Storage Systems for a metro network *Vehicle Power and Propulsion Conference, VPPC '08.* IEEEDate: 3-5 Sept. 2008, Pages: 1 – 8

Destraz, B.; Barrade, P.; Rufer, A.; Klohr, M. (2007) Study and simulation of the energy balance of an urban transportation network. *European Conference on Power Electronics and Applications, EPE 2007,* 2-5 Sept. 2007, Pages: 1 - 10 Digital Object Identifier 10.1109/EPE.2007.4417349

Joller, J. (1998). Research of trams traction drives. Baltic Electrical Engineering Review 1 7, Vilnius, pp. 17–20.

Latkovskis, L.; Bražis, V. (2007). Application of supercapacitors for storage of regenerative energy in T3A tramcars. *Latvian Journal of Physics and Technical Sciences, Riga,* N5, pp. 23-33, ISSN 0868-8257.

Latkovskis, L.; Bražis, V. (2008). Simulation of the Regenerative Energy Storage with Supercapacitors in Tatra T3A Type Trams. *Proceedings of the Tenth International Conference on Computer Modeling and Simulation (UKSIM 2008),* Cambridge, UK, 1-3 April 2008, pp. 398-403.

Latkovskis, L.; Grigans, L. (2008 A). A Method for Estimation of the Untapped Regenerative Braking Energy in Urban Electric Transport. *CD-ROM of Conference of Young Scientists on Energy Issues CYSENI 2008,* Kaunas, May 2008, pp. IV-41 - IV-48.

Latkovskis, L.; Grigans, L. (2008 B). Estimation of the Untapped Regenerative Braking Energy in Urban Electric Transportation Network. *Proceedings of the 13th International Power Electronics and Motion Control Conference EPE-PEMC 2008,* Poznan, 1-3 September 2008, pp. 2089-2093.

Rankis, I.; Brazis, V. (2000). Simulation of tramcar's energy balance. *2nd Intern. Conf. "Simulation, Gaming, Training and Business Process Reengineering in Operations",* Riga, pp. 160–163.

Rufer, A. (2003). Power-Electronic Interface for a Supercapacitor-Based Energy-Storage Substation in DC-Transportation Networks. *EPE Conference proceedings* Toulouse, pp. D1–D8.

Szenasy, I. (2008). Improvement the energy storage with ultracapacitor in metro railcar by modeling and simulation. *Vehicle Power and Propulsion Conference, VPPC '08.* IEEEDate: 3-5 Sept. 2008, Pages: 1 - 5.

Sejin, N.; Jaeho, Ch.; Hyung-Cheol, K.; Eun-Kyu, L. (2008). PSiM based electric modeling of supercapacitors for line voltage regulation of electric train system. *Power and Energy Conference, PECon 2008.* IEEE 2nd International Date: 1-3 Dec. 2008, Pages: 855 - 859.

Modelling and Simulating Chip Design Processes

Amir Hassine
Institute of Microelectronic Systems, Leibniz Universität Hannover
Germany

1. Introduction

When the semiconductor industry emerged from anonymity in the 1960's, almost no one expected it to gain such a tremendous importance in human kind's life. 1981 Bill Gates, although he today denies to have said it, stated that "640K – program memory – ought to be enough for anybody". Indeed, no other industry than the semiconductor industry has experienced such a growth: The Semiconductor Industry Association[1] reports about an average annual growth rate of over 16% from 1975 to 2000. It is even said to be the most productive industry in the world today (Goodall et al., 2006). Continuous improvements in EDA[2] tools, reusability and technologies have made it possible to design complex functionalities and integrate hundreds of millions of transistors on a single chip.

None the less, figures reveal another - less pleasant – fact: managerial expertise in the chip design industry seems to lag behind technical expertise and progress. The ITRS[3] reported several times about a lingering and increasing design productivity gap: the number of available transistors growing faster than the ability to meaningfully design them.

Managers are nowadays faced with many challenges concerning design projects: They have to exchange resources, restructure the process, train designers etc. However, trial and error of several alternatives is not practicable due to narrow time to market windows and severe budget restrictions. In absence of simulative possibilities, decisions do not rely on evaluating the alternatives regarding their productivity and costs, but on estimations and gut feelings and are mostly biased. For planning decisions, it is therefore necessary to provide tools that support decision makers in evaluating different solutions in an objective and transparent manner.

Due to the rapid progress in the semiconductor industry, the wide range of available tools and resources and the immense competition as well as time and budget pressures, the

---

[1] Semiconductor Industry Association, *www.sia-online.org*

[2] Electronic Design Automation

[3] International Technology Roadmap for Semiconductors, *http://public.itrs.net*

necessity to investigate modelling and simulation design systems has emerged as a prevalent issue. The lack of tools to predict required resources and process runs is the principal reason for late project cancellations and delays. Just as worrying as the long-term growth slow down to 8-10%, so are the estimated $ 2 to $ 4 billion losses yearly due to project cancellations and aborts (Numetrics, 2006). Moreover, 85% of IC[4] projects miss their targeted schedules (Collett, 2004).

With simulative approaches, decision makers would be able to compare several process arrangements regarding their productivity and costs and choose the appropriate one instead of relying on estimations and gut feelings.

In this chapter a model and a simulator are presented to address the missing tools in the field of modelling and simulating chip design processes (CDPs). The model regards resources and design artefacts within a CDP in a generic manner. Thus, it is also applicable to any other engineering or production process.

2. State of the art

Triggered by the design gap, several contributions focussed on defining and measuring productivity (Hassine & Barke, 2005) (Numetrics, 2000) as well as establishing business and technical KPIs[5] (Leppelt et al., 2006). Infrastructures for data collection (Fenstermaker et al. 2000) and analysis methods (Kahng & Mantik, 2001) have therefore been elaborated and partially marketed. However, formalization and simulation of design systems have barely been addressed.

The prediction of the productivity of chip design processes still relies on simple estimations. It is in best cases based on the outcome of previous comparable projects. However, each chip design process is admittedly unique and thus the estimations often lead to grave deviations from plans and budgets.

Apart from (Matzke & Strube, 2006) (Ermolayevet al., 2006) and (Sohnius et al., 2007) few efforts have investigated modelling and simulating chip design processes in a granular way. The approach presented aims at modelling design processes in general and is based on multi-agent systems (MAS). The latter use the approach of collaborating agents (software programs) to solve a given problem. Thereby the agents stand for the elements of the original to be modelled and are endowed with behaviors, preferences, the ability to act with the environment, etc. The approach sets the emphasis on modelling human resources by means of agents. The latter are endowed with different abilities in carrying out activities, play different roles (manager, designer, etc.), negotiate with each other, build up teams and cooperate to execute tasks assigned to them.

The added value yielded by the agents is measured by so-called Units of Welfare (UoW) but are not specified deeply in detail. Furthermore, the simulation does not aim at optimizing the productivity of the whole process but at minimizing the total process duration. Above

---

[4] Integrated Circuit

[5] Key Performance Indicators

all and because of ethical, acceptance and feasibility reasons the approach is very likely to face strong resistance by industrials.

3. The RS Model

Within chip design processes - seen as a sequence of activities - design artefacts (DAs) are transformed into different states and/or are verified regarding their compliance to the constraints set. Each activity includes several resources and its duration as well as the quality of its outputs depend on the resources allocated, e.g. designer's experience, and on the DA properties, e.g. complexity. On this note, the Request Service (RS) model models resources as providers of services. The latter are requested by the activities to process DAs.

A series of attributes describes the resources, services and DAs in a quantitative and qualitative way. Calculation models specify activities' duration and outcome.

A petri-net-like notation is adopted to graphically represent the CDP elements in the RS model. Since the goal is a computer aided simulation, the scenarios to be modelled and simulated have to be expressed in a machine-readable manner. Ontologies are used to formally represent the CDP domain because they offer an easy way to separate the generic knowledge about CDPs from specific process instances to be simulated. Furthermore, it allows for splitting up the model from implemented simulators using it.

In order to better comprehend the RS model, the following section illustrates basic knowledge about Petri nets and ontologies.

3.1. Prerequisites

3.1.1 Petri nets

Petri nets have been developed by Carl Adam Petri in the 60s and represent in their original form a time-independent and purely causal concept for modelling discrete systems. A Petri net is constituted of:

- Transitions (rectangles): active elements in a system, e.g. actions or events
- Places (outlined circles): passive elements, e.g. states or conditions
- Edges relating transitions and places.

Places contain tokens (black filled circles). The latter represent dynamic elements being transported and transformed, e.g. information. When a transition fires, tokens are removed from pre-located places (respectively to the activity) and transformed/transported to a post-located one. The number of transported tokens is specified by the edge weight (Fig. 1).

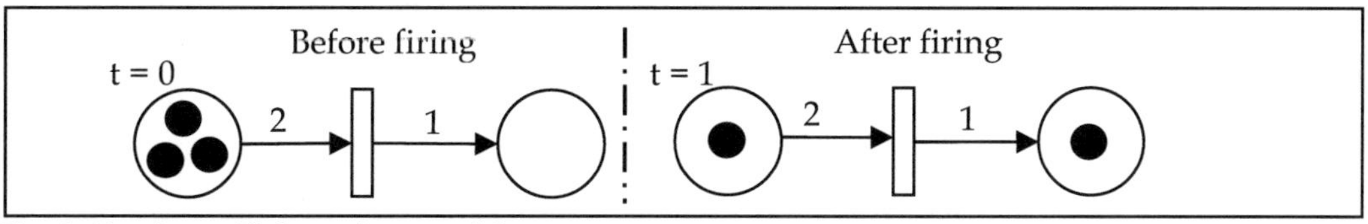

Fig. 1. Petri net: Firing of a transition

The so-called - low-level - Petri nets are highly formal and thus mathematically analysable. However marks contained in such nets are not distinguishable and transitions fire as soon as marks are available in pre-located places. Over time, several extensions have been added to the original Petri nets and new variations -- High-level and timed Petri nets - arose. The main new features are:

- Tokens are distinguishable through attributes/colours/values. Furthermore they may be tested and evaluated by guards in the transitions.
- Temporal behaviour can be assigned to any Petri net element. Transitions may for example fire after a defined or stochastic period, marks' transportation may be retarted by the edges, etc.

In spite of the various extensions, even simple processes are still sometimes hard to model. Particularly significant scenarios for this work, where marks should be shared by several transitions simultaneously (Conflict, Fig. 2) and scenarios where marks are transported or transformed in factions (Fig. 3) are not representable with Petri nets.

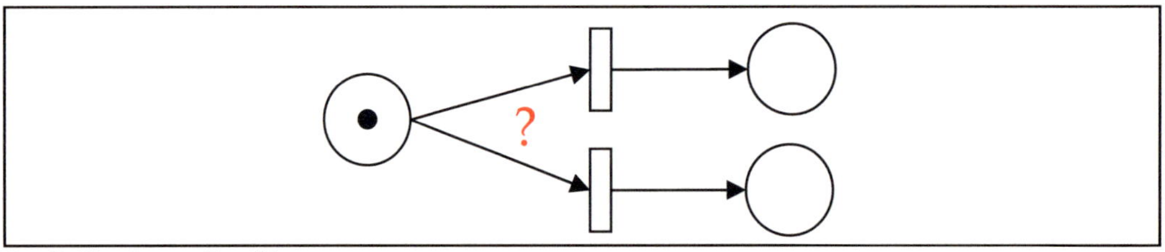

Fig. 2. Petri net: Conflict

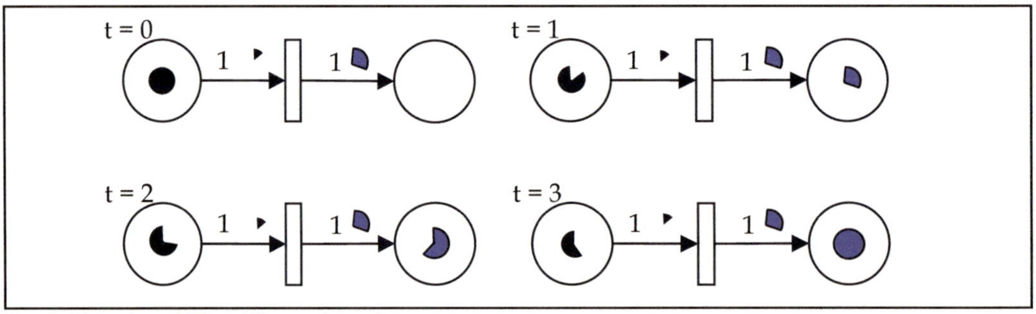

Fig. 3. Fractional Handling of marks

3.1.2 Ontologies

Ontology is a formal representation of knowledge within a specific domain. It not only specifies the syntax and the terminology used, but also and particularly it specifies the semantic binding of the concepts. Several languages are available to author ontologies. We opted for the OWL[6], a XML-derivative endorsed by the World Wide Web Consortium[7].

---

[6] Web Ontology Language, www.w3.org/TR/owl-features

[7] W3C, www.w3.org.

For illustration purposes, assume the following scenario to be modelled: A designer (actor) is a resource and may execute at most one activity at the same time. In contrast, an activity may be executed by several designers simultaneously, but at least by one. Finally, activities and actors are specified by names. In the following, a UML[8]-like notation is adopted to illustrate ontologies graphically.

The T-Box (Terminological Box) specifies the generic knowledge. It defines the concepts, e.g. Resource, Activity, DA, etc., their attributes and the relations and restrictions between the concepts. The A-Box (Assertions Box) contains concrete instances of the concepts, attributes and relations defined in the T-Box and hence, describe a concrete process to design a concrete DA using concrete resources/services. The semantic specified in the T-Box is assertive for the A-Box and defines how individuals are related to each other.

As shown in Fig. 4 and Fig. 5, the concepts (called Classes in OWL) to be modelled are Actor, Resource and Activity. To model a specific occurrence of the modelled scenario, e.g. Actors A_1 executing Activity Act_1, instances of the corresponding concept (Individuals) have to be created. The attributes (Datatype Properties) specify the concepts and accordingly their instances.

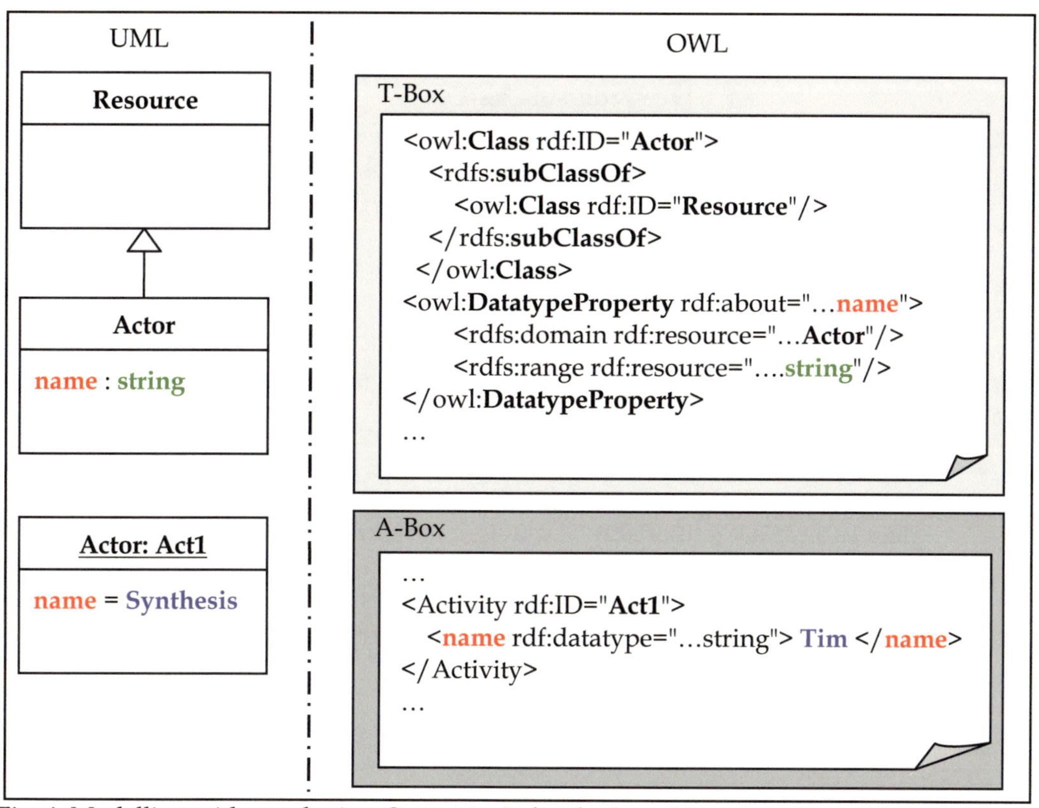

Fig. 4. Modelling with ontologies: Concepts, Individuals and Datatype Properties

[8] Unified Modelling Language, *www.uml.org*

Relations (Object Properties) describe the semantic between the concepts. By means of cardinalities, relations may be refined and constrained (Fig. 5).

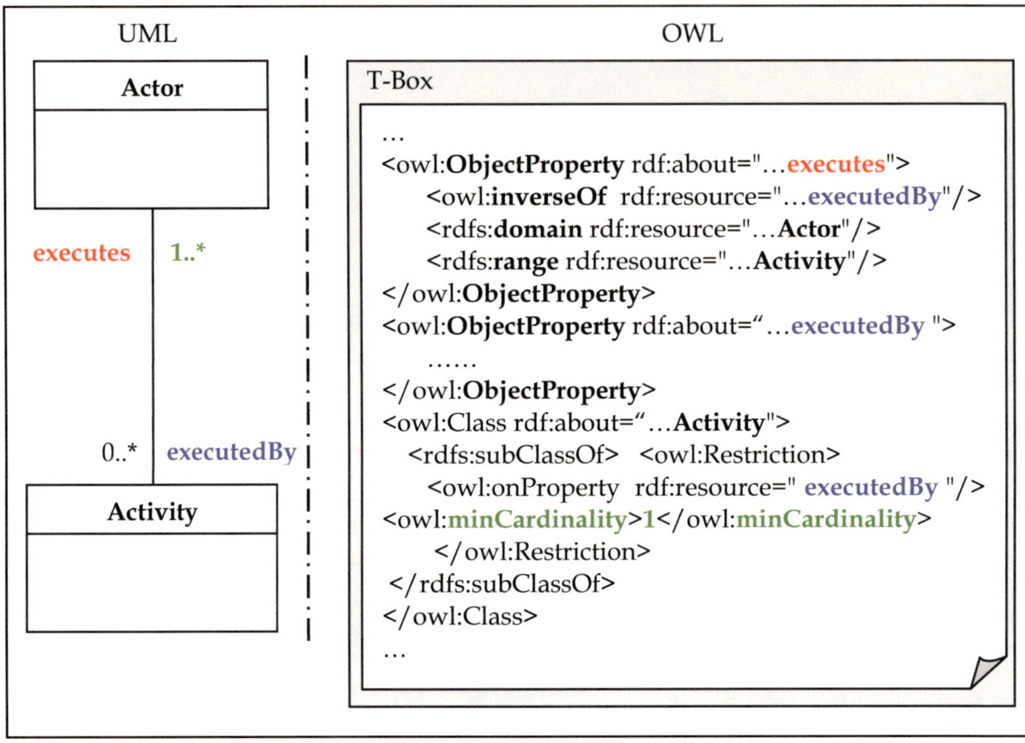

Fig. 5. Modelling with ontologies: Object Properties and Cardinalities

3.2. Modelling resources

A resource is modelled as provider of services. A service is requested and used or consumed by an activity. Services have the following attributes:

- *workpower*: denotes the quality and/or quantity of the service offered. This may be a single value as it is the case of the RAM offered by a computer or a mapping of values to targets, e.g the ability of a designer to carry out activities.
- *availability*: of the service in h/day.
- *intensity*: to which the service is portioned. Services may be delivered at the amount requested (~), e.g. RAM, or at a fixed amount (=) independently from the request, e.g. the automation level to which a tool automates activities.
- *repartition*: describes how services are shared in case of concurrent requests. Services may be not shareable and delivered to the first requesting (FCFS, First Come First Served), e.g. RAM allocation, or may be split equally ($\forall$ =) or weighted according to the requests (%).

Furthermore, a cost model is assigned to each service expressing the costs per *workpower* and time unit entailed through using the service.

In some cases, services are not - literally - consumed but affect the way how activities are executed. Thus, assigning costs for example to the automation level of a tool or setting limits to the availability of such services is a counterintuitive way to address the accessibility to the resource itself and the costs generated. To avoid doing so, every resource offers the special service "Access". This service can be restricted in its availability and shareability (*workpower*). Costs caused by non-consumable resources can then be modelled by assigning costs to the corresponding Access service. The services described above cling to each service of a resource and may have different values within the same resource.

Fig. 6 and Fig. 7 depict the T-Box of the resource ontology and a corresponding tool A-Box.

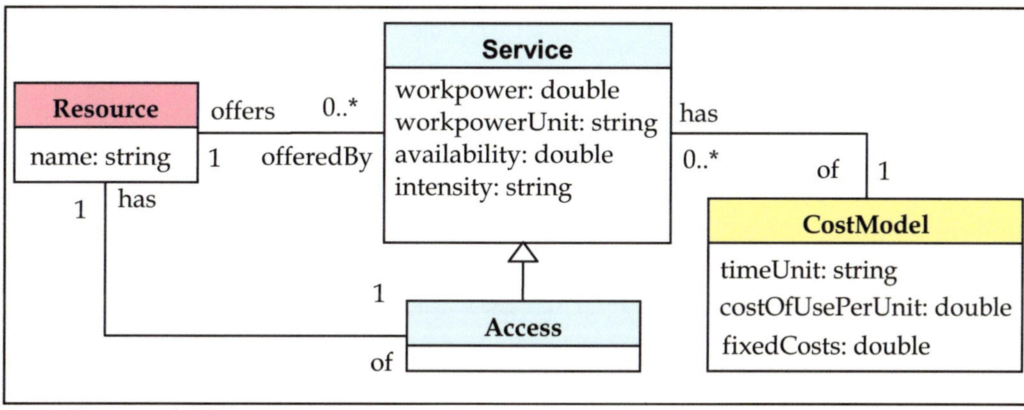

Fig. 6. Resource's T-Box

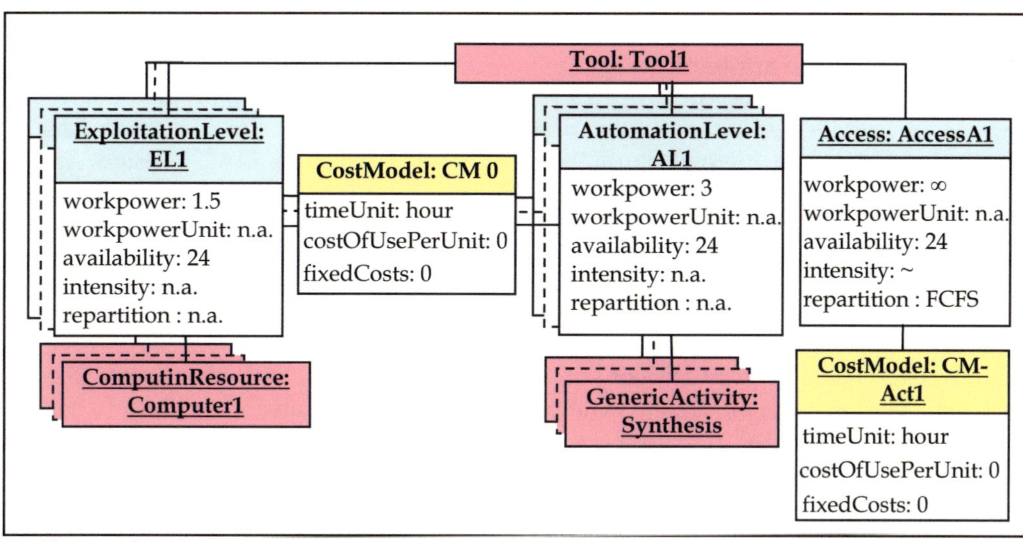

Fig. 7. A tool A-Box

A tool offers the service automating design activities to a certain extent (*AutomationLevel*) and the possibility to use a computing resource (*ExploitationLevel*). The latter allows for example for recognizing overdesigned computing resource as is the case for instance when a tool without multiprocessor capability runs on a multi-processor computer. Costs are generally not incurred by the tool itself but by the licenses. Similarly, simultaneous tool usages are also typically limited by the licenses.

For graphical representation purposes a Petri net-like notation is adopted (Fig. 8): Places represent resources and tokens residing in them stand for the different resource's services. The services' attributes are appended to the tokens (brackets). In case of several similar services with different values, services may be summarized in a table.

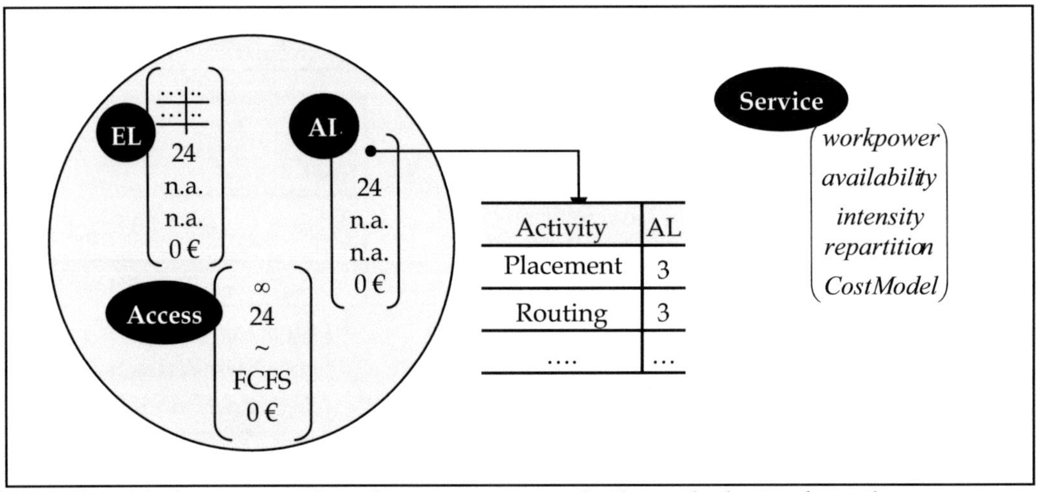

Fig. 8. Graphical representation of resources, exemplarily on the basis of a tool resource

3.3. Modelling design artefacts

In addition to the resources, the properties of the DAs and states being processed affect the duration of activities and the quality of their outcome to a decisive extend. DAs are described through two hierarchies of indicators and parameters: DAC (Design Artefact Complexity) addresses the technical characteristics of the DA whereas the DAQ (Design Artefact Quality) addresses its qualitative aspects. Both are applicable for the DA as a whole and are transitive for its states. They are typically approximated at the beginning of a design process and become more and more accurate as the process progresses. A Detailed description is given in (Leppelt et al., 2006).

The different states the DA undergoes within a CDP are specified through a format (e.g. text document, Verilog, DEF, GDSII, etc.) and a hierarchy of quality attributes (QA). In contrast to the DAC and DAQ, QA are state specific and not predefined. They may be adjusted to the user's needs to include parameters that are not defined in the DAC/DAQ.

Design artefacts are graphically represented similar to resources (Fig. 9, showing a cut-out of DAC and DAQ hierarchies). A place now stands for a design artefact and the tokens stand for the different DA states. The states' attributes (Format and the QA hierarchy) are appended to the tokens. Fig. 10 shows the design artefact's ontology.

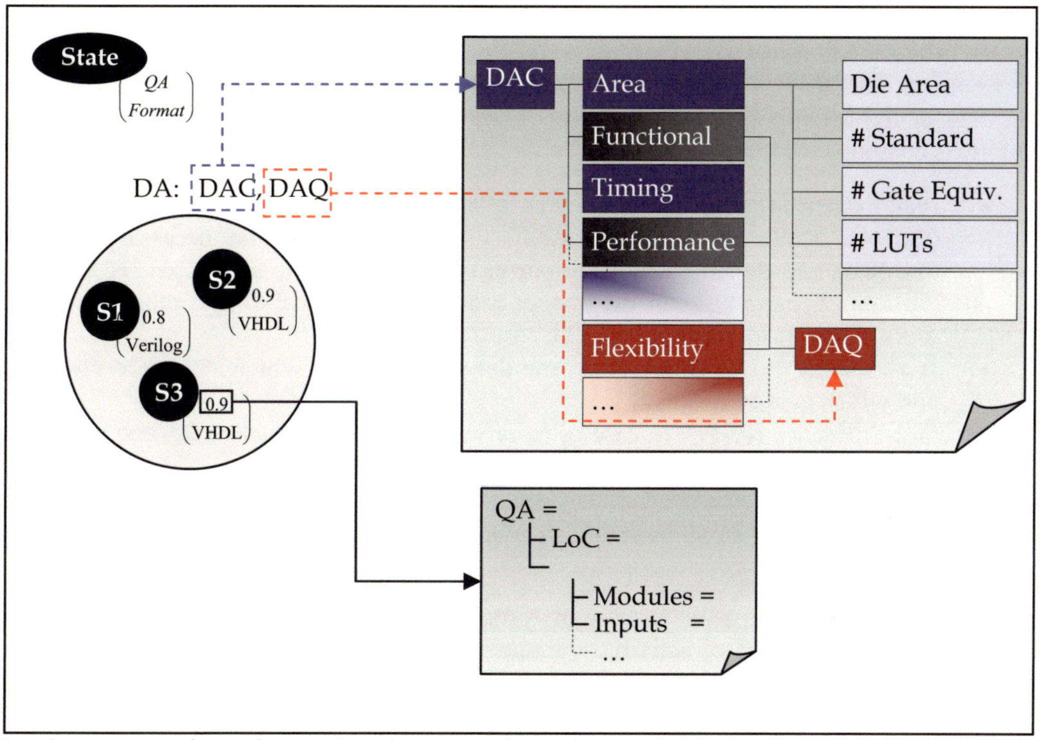

Fig. 9. A cut-out from the DAC and DAQ and graphical representation of design artefacts.

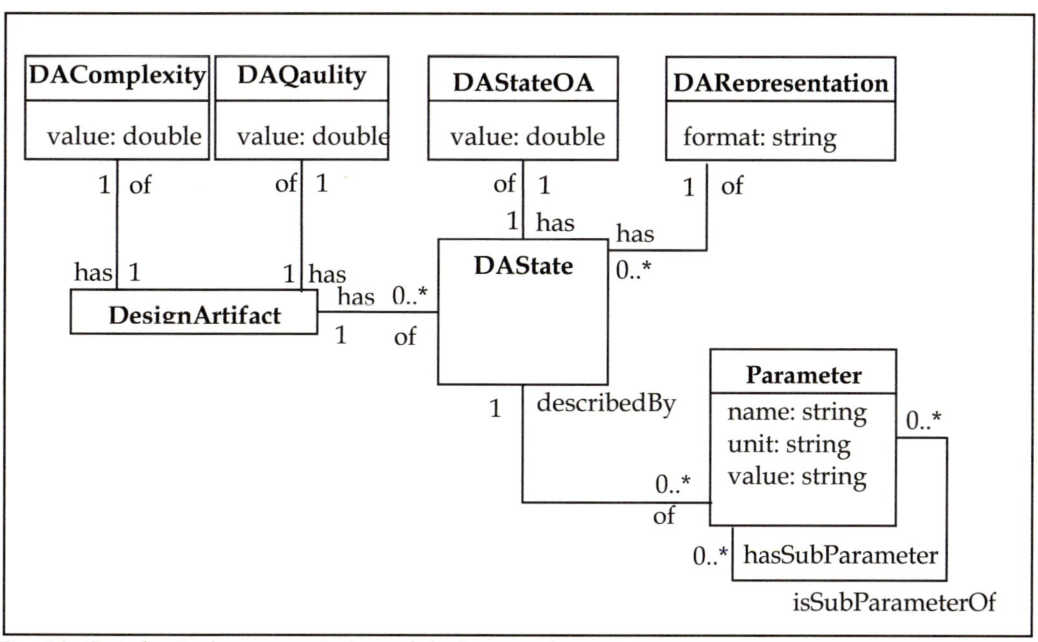

Fig. 10. Ontological representation of design artefacts

3.4. Modelling activities

Design artefacts are transformed within activities into different states. The services granted by resources and the properties of the DAs and states being transformed determine the duration of the activity and the quality of its output. The transformation behavior of an activity is composed of three parts:

- *Pre-Production (Pr-Pr)*: Before an activity starts, the input states have to be available (reqDA). Minimum amounts/qualities of services may be necessary to start (minReq) and dependent on the current case, more or less services are required (optReq). For example, in the case of a larger or a critical design more RAM or a more experienced designer may be required.
- *Production (Pr)*: Determines the time the activity takes, which states are produced and which quality results.
- *Post-Production (Ps-Pr)*: In case of insufficient outcome's quality, iterations may be initiated.

Activities are represented by transitions (rectangles) consisting of three blocks as described above (Fig. 11).

Beside the elements of a chip design process, i.e. resources, activities and DAs, transformation behaviours of activities - requests and calculation functions for activities' duration and quality dependent on resources/services and input DAs/states - must be formalized.

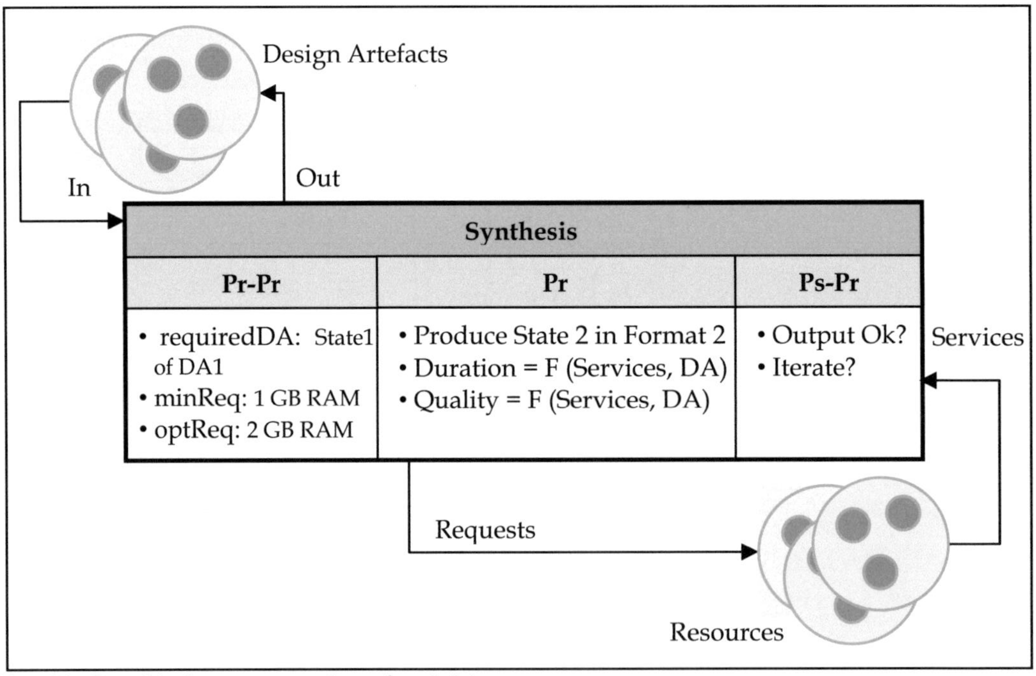

Fig. 11. Graphical representation of activities

It is very likely that such calculation models will often have to be revised, improved and adjusted. Therefore, they have to be expressed in a flexible way allowing for later changes without having to change the code of an implemented simulator. The simulator offers an interface to read in calculation models expressed in a specific developed notation – Prefix-Selector-Point (PSP) – from XML files. The developed notation generated from a context-free grammar PSP_G.

PSP_G is a 4-tuple (T, N, S, P) where

- Terminals T = {. , (,) , [,] , ` , ' , value, instance, indicator, parameter} ∪ O ∪ R ∪ S ∪ A where
  O = {+, -, x , &, | , , /, >=, <=, =, . . . }: Operators
  R = {Quality, QA, Complexity, . . . }: Reserved words
  S = {Access, RAM, AbilitWrtTool, . . . }: Services
  A = {workpower, availability, . . . }: Attributes
- Non-terminals N = {OPERATOR, SERVICE, ATTRIBUTE, RESOURCE, COMPUTER, ACTOR, LICENSE, TOOL, SUPPORT, DALIBRARY, GA, DA, DASTATE, INDICATOR, PARAMETER, DAC, DAQ, STATEQA, OPTCRIT, FORMULA, OPERAND}
- Start symbol S = Formula
- Productions P={
  OPERATOR ::= + | - | x |&| / | ...,
  SERVICE ::= Access|RAM| AutomationLevel | . . . ,
  ATTRIBUTE ::= workpower | availability | . . . ,
  RESOURCE ::= COMPUTER | ACTOR | LICENSE | TOOL | SUPPORT DALIBRARY,
  COMPUTER ::= instance,
  ACTOR ::= instance,
  LICENSE ::= instance,
  TOOL ::= instance,
  SUPPORT ::= instance,
  DALIBRARY ::= instance,
  GA ::= instance,
  DA ::= instance,
  DASTATE ::= instance,
  INDICATOR ::= indicator,
  PARAMETER ::= Parameter.Parameter | parameter,
  DAC ::= DA.Quality | DA.Quality.INDICATOR | DA.Quality.INDICATOR.PARAMETER,
  DAQ ::= DA.Complexity | DA.Complexity.INDICATOR | DA.Complexity.INDICATOR.PARAMETER,
  STATEQA ::= DA.DAState.QA | DA.DAState.QA.PARAMETER,
  OPTCRIT ::= Quality | Speed | Cost,
  FORMULA ::= (OPERATOR, OPERAND, OPERAND) | REQDA,
  OPERAND ::= value | FORMULA | OPERAND,OPERAND | RESOURCE.SERVICE.ATTRIBUTE |

RESOURCE.SERVICE[instance] | DA.DAC | DA.DAQ |
DA.STATEQA | Optimization.OPTCRIT,
REQDA ::= DA.DAState | DA.DAState,DA.DAState,
}

The terminals *indicator* and *parameter* are to be substituted through indicator and parameter names defined in the DAC, DAQ and QA. *instance* is to be substituted through names of concrete concept instances and *value* $\in \Re$. Calculation models and request rules are generated by applying the production rules of the PSG_G and substituting the corresponding variables. The sentences derived from the PSP_G typically have the form (operator, operand, operand) where operand may represent a point separated address.

To illustrate, assume for example that in order to start, an activity requires that the assigned computer $Comp_C$ offers at least 1 GB free RAM and that the assigned License Lic_L is adequate for using tool $Tool_T$ (*minReq*). In the following, the derivation of the corresponding phrase in the PSP notation is described. The highlighted words are non-terminals to be substituted in the next step by applying a PSP_G production rule:

minReq: Formula ⇒ (**Operator**, Operand, Operand)
⇒ (&, **Operand**, Operand)
⇒ (&, **Formula**, Operand)
⇒ (&, (**Operator**, Operand, Operand), Operand)
⇒ (&, (>=, **Operand**, Operand), Operand)
⇒ (&, (>=, **Resource.Service.Attribute**, Operand), Operand)
⇒ (&, (>=, instance.RAM.workpower, **Operand**), Operand)
⇒ …
⇒ (&, (>=, instance.RAM.workpower, value), **Operand**)
⇒ (&, (>=, instance.RAM.workpower, value), **Formula**)
⇒ …
⇒ (&, (>=, instance.RAM.Workpower, value),
(=, instance.AllowsUsing[instance], value)
)

Replacing the terminals *instance* and *value* through instances' names and figures results in the concrete condition to start the activity in question:
(&, (>=, $Comp_C$.RAM.Workpower, 1), (=, Lic_L.AllowsUsing[$Tool_T$], 1))

To allow generic formulas, the PSP notation is extended to permit the use of generic entries like [Tool] instead of the instance name $Tool_T$. The assignment of a concrete tool is thus done by the simulator itself based on the process entered.

4. The RS Simulator

Adrenalin is a simulator implemented in Java based on the RS model. It offers different views for data entry, a simulation and a charts view for simulation results. The data entry is guided through the semantic specified in the ontologies and thus guarantees a semantically correct entry. Activities' behavioural models are read in from an auxiliary XML file.

Simulation results are also logged allowing for a transparent backtracking of simulation runs. Fig. 12 illustrates the setup of the simulator.

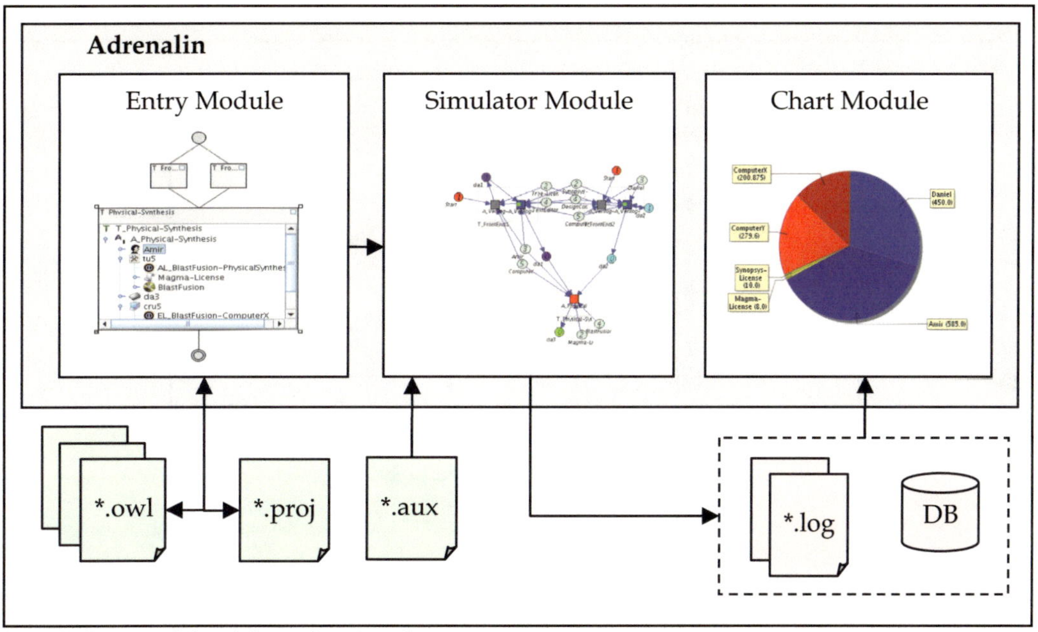

Fig. 12. Setup of the Adrenalin simulator

The simulator allows users to answer the most urgent questions about process duration and costs and to compare alternatives to recognize potential bottlenecks and identify critical factors such as deadline over-run, resource overload or wastage:

1. How much time would the process take?
2. How much would it cost?
3. Which quality would be reached?
4. Which resources arrangement is appropriate to handle a given design complexity?
5. Which design complexity is manageable with a given resources arrangement?

In the present implementation, the resources allocation to activities is considered as given. The simulation can then deliver answers to the first three questions. The other questions can be addressed by manually adjusting the process, re-allocating resource and re-simulation.

Fig. 13 depicts a basic simulation step. Each step is made up of four phases:

- Check phase: Activities check availability of needed input DA states (*Pr-Pr*).
- Request phase: Activities send out their requests.
- Grant phase: If *minReqs* are satisfiable, resources grant activities as much as possible from the requested services (*optReqs*) taking into account their services properties, e.g. shareability.

- Produce phase: Activities produce a portion of their output (*Pr*). After the whole production finishes (*Ps-Pr*) and dependent on the achieved quality, activities decide about initiating iterations or writing out corresponding DA states.

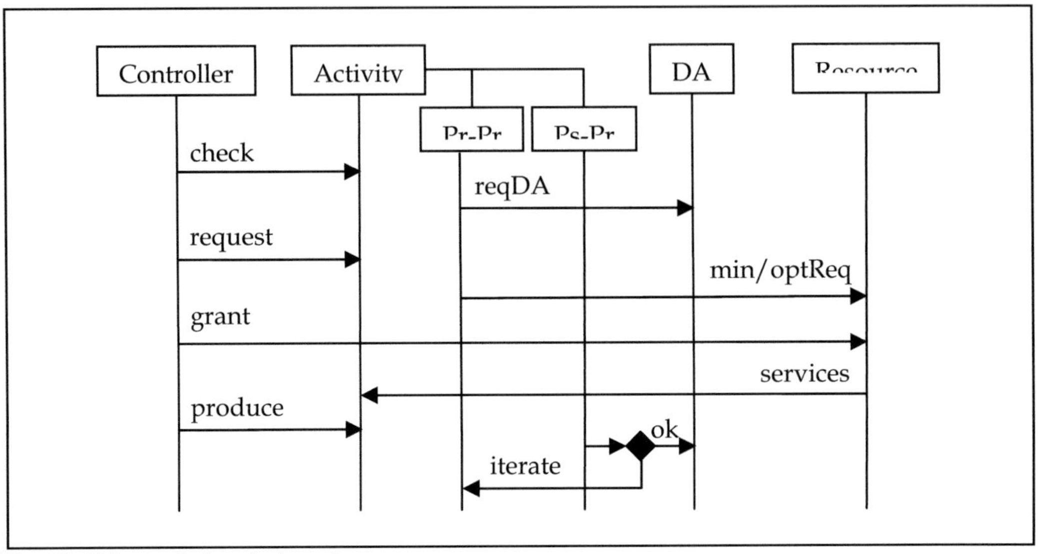

Fig. 13. Principal simulation steps

5. Calibration and results

Calibration of the simulator, e.g. calculation models for activities' duration and quality, is a continuous and recursive process. To illustrate, three data sets have been investigated and integrated into the simulator by means of the PSP notation to determine behaviour of some activities.

Set_1 is composed of five digital designs used by an industry partner to configure new tools or tool versions: A scalable design in four different sizes ranging from 200 to 1,600 kGates and a 42 kGates sized design. Duration, memory usage and normalized CPU factors (CPUF) are available. Set_2 consists of data for logical synthesis of 31 industrial digital designs that have been or are intended to be produced. The design codes contain up to 70,000 lines. Set_3 is composed of nine free downloadable[9] non-synthesized verilog codes of digital designs with lines of code (LoC) ranging between 2,300 and 94,000 lines.

From each set, some designs were not used in the investigation. Untried designs served as a benchmark to evaluate the accuracy of the determined metrics. The statistical computing language R[10] has been used to determine metrics to predict

- memory usage and duration of some physical synthesis activities dependent on design size and CPUF (Set_1) and

[9] Opencores, www.opencores.org.
[10] The R Project for Statistical Computing, www.r-project.org.

- logical synthesis' duration and the number of nets generated thereby dependent on code's design attributes and the CPUs of the computing resources used (Set_2 and Set_3).

The metrics determined for Set_1 show very accurate prediction of activity duration and memory usages. However four of the five investigated designs represent a scalable design and thus, the metrics are primarily relevant for comparable designs. Set_2 and Set $_3$ which contain more heterogeneous data also produce accurate predictions especially for longer activities and more complex designs (Fig. 14).

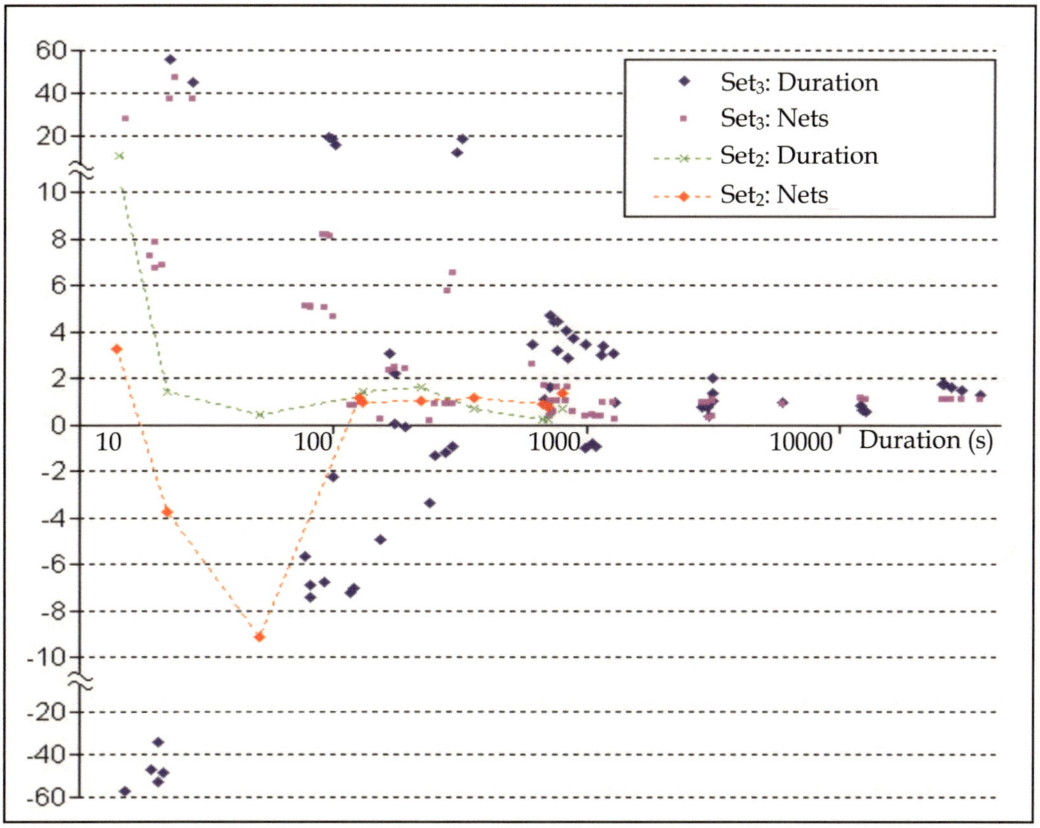

Fig. 14. Ratio of predicted to real values for Set_2 and Set_3

6. Conclusion

This work addresses the lack of approaches to model and simulate chip design processes. In cooperation with leading semiconductor industries, a simple though expressive model to represent design processes has been developed. The model is endowed with the formalism necessary to allow for computer aided simulation. Adrenalin, the simulator based on the RS model, gives users the possibility to try several process alternatives and compare them to each other in a simulative and thus cheap and fast way.

Generating calculation models is a continuous and recursive process. The interface offered by Adrenalin to read in calculation models from XML files and the formalized PSP notation allow for later adjustment without editing the simulator code.

The exemplary investigation of some industrial data has produced accurate results in estimating activity durations and thus attests to the predictability and ability to simulate chip design processes.

Future work will continue to generate further calculation models using more data for calibration and combining further input variables to substantiate the metrics. Furthermore, the focus will be set on automating re-arrangements of planned processes in order to determine controllable complexity and needed resources in case of given resources and complexity respectively.

7. References

Goodall, A.; Fandel, D., Alan, A.; Landler, P. & Huff, H. R. (1998). Long-term Productivity Mechanisms of the Semiconductor Industry, *Proceedings of American Electrochemical Society Semiconductor Silicon*, pp. 125–143

Hassine, A. & Barke, E., (2005). Measure Your Design Value to Improve It, *Proceedings of IEEE International Engineering Management Conference*, pp. 668–672

Collett, R. (2004). Benchmarking IC Development Capability - Why?, *Fabless Forum*, Vol. 11

Numetrics (2006), IC Product Lifecycle Management and Portfolio Optimization - Critical Elements of an Enterprise Solution, *White Paper, Numetrics Management Systems Inc.*

Numetrics (2000). Measuring IC and ASIC Design Productivity, *White Paper, Numetrics Management Systems Inc.*

Leppelt, P., Hassine, A. & Barke, E. (2006). An Approach to Make Semiconductor Design Projects Comparable, *Proceedings of Asia Pacific Industrial Engineering Management Systems Conference*, pp. 2067–2074

Fenstermaker, S.; George, D.; Kahng, A.,Mantik, S. & Thielges, B. (2000). METRICS: A System Architecture for Design Process Optimization, *Proceedings of IEEE Design Automation Conference*, pp. 705–710

Kahng, A. & Mantik, S. (2001). A System for Automatic Recording and Prediction of Design Quality Metrics, *Proceedings of International Symposium on Quality Electronic Design*, pp. 81–86

Sohnius, R.; Ermolayev, V.; Jentzsch, E. & Matzke, W.-E. (2007). An Approach for Assessing Design Systems: Design System Simulation and Analysis for Performance Assessment, *Proceedings of International Conference on Enterprise Information Systems*, pp. 231-236

Matzke, W.-E. & Strube, G. (2006). A Management Tool for the Performance Management of Distributed (global) Dynamic Engineering Design Processes, Proceedings of IEEE International Engineering Management Conference, pp. 146-151

Ermolayev, V.; Jentzsch, E.; Karsayev, O.; Keberle, N.; Matzke, W.-E.; Samoylov, V.; & Sohnius, R. (2006). An Agent-Oriented Model of a Dynamic Engineering Design Process, In: *Agent-Oriented Information Systems III*, Vol. 3529/2006, pp. 168-183, Springer Berlin/Heidelberg

16

Advanced Numerical Methods for non-Premixed Flames

Annarita Viggiano
Department of Environmental Engineering and Physics
University of Basilicata
Italy

1. Introduction

Engine designers are under increasing pressure to reduce emissions and pollutants. Multidimensional models, as well as advanced experimental techniques, provide fundamental knowledge to meet regulations in terms of efficiency and emissions.
Recently, considerable efforts have been addressed to develop advanced numerical techniques and comprehensive theoretical models, in order to study the dynamic of flames under the operating conditions typical of internal combustion engines, aircraft engines, gas turbine combustors, etc. (Bilger *et al.*, 2005; Hilbert *et al.*, 2004). Dealing with high Reynolds number reactive flows, invaluable knowledge can be achieved by using accurate numerical methodologies, such as Large-Eddy Simulation (LES) (Pitsch, 2006) and Direct Numerical Simulation (DNS) (Moin & Mahesh, 1998). The frontier research in this field concerns the coupling of such techniques with proper combustion models, in order to study engineering combustion devices fueled by conventional hydrocarbons, hydrogen and renewable bio-based fuels.
In this work, a DNS methodology, coupled with detailed kinetic mechanisms for fuel oxidation, is described. This technique is implemented in an in-house developed CFD software package for the analysis of multicomponent free shear flows (Magi, 2004). Such a tool solves the Navier-Stokes equations for reacting flows by using a detailed description of thermal and transport properties and an accurate modelling of chemical source terms. A high order compact finite difference scheme is adopted for the solution of the partial differential equations (Lele, 1989; 1992). Although the computational code is able to perform both LES and DNS analysis, the latter is used in this work. MPI libraries are employed to fully parallelize the code, thus allowing to execute the computations on high performance parallel machines.
In this contribution, the software package is used to simulate the reacting mixing layer between two streams of air and fuel with different velocity, even though the same methodology has been used to simulate other interesting phenomena for the study of combustion systems, such as the autoignition of fuel in starting transient jets (Viggiano & Magi, 2004; Viggiano, 2009). The role of some physical parameters, such as the mixture fraction, the scalar dissipation rate and the initial conditions, in terms of temperature and velocity, has been explored. The localization of the ignition spots and the ignition delay time have been investigated and the results have been compared with those of several experimental and numerical works in the literature (Mastorakos *et al.*, 1997; Mastorakos, 2009; Sreedhara & Lakshmisha, 2000). Besides,

the importance of using a detailed reaction mechanism for a better understanding of the phenomena has been addressed (Viggiano, 2009). The most important findings are summarized in this contribution. Some works in the literature are referred to for further reading.
This chapter is organized as follows. First of all, the mathematical model and the numerical method are given. Then, the computational setup is described. Finally, the results are discussed and the conclusions are summarized.

2. The mathematical model

2.1 The governing equations

The flow field is computed by solving the mass, momentum and energy conservation equations for a compressible, multicomponent mixture of thermally perfect gases. Although the software package solves these equations both in three-dimensional and in two-dimensional configuration, the latter is used in this work. Hence, the governing equations read

$$\frac{\partial \mathbf{W}}{\partial t} + \frac{\partial(\mathbf{F}_{\mathrm{E}} - \mathbf{F}_{\mathrm{V}})}{\partial x} + \frac{\partial(\mathbf{G}_{\mathrm{E}} - \mathbf{G}_{\mathrm{V}})}{\partial y} + \mathbf{S} = 0, \tag{1}$$

where $\mathbf{W}$ is the unknown vector, the symbols $\mathbf{F}$ and $\mathbf{G}$ stand for the fluxes along x and y directions, respectively, the subscripts E and V relate to the convective and diffusive terms, respectively, while $\mathbf{S}$ stands for the source term.
The unknown vector is defined as

$$\mathbf{W} = [\rho_i, \rho u, \rho v, \rho E]^T, \tag{2}$$

where ρ_i is the density of the i-*th* chemical species, ρ is the mixture density computed as

$$\rho = \sum_{i=1}^{N_s} \rho_i, \tag{3}$$

where N_s is the total number of the chemical species, u and v are the Cartesian components of the velocity vector $\mathbf{u}$ and E is the total specific energy, given by

$$E = \sum_{i=1}^{N_s} Y_i e_i + \frac{u^2 + v^2}{2}. \tag{4}$$

In Eq. 4 Y_i and e_i are the mass fraction and the internal specific energy of the i-*th* chemical species, respectively.
The convective fluxes are given by

$$\mathbf{F}_{\mathrm{E}} = \left[\rho_i u, \rho u^2 + p, \rho u v, \rho u H\right]^T \tag{5}$$

$$\mathbf{G}_{\mathrm{E}} = \left[\rho_i v, \rho u v, \rho v^2 + p, \rho v H\right]^T, \tag{6}$$

where p is the pressure and H is the total specific enthalpy, equal to

$$H = E + \frac{p}{\rho}. \tag{7}$$

The diffusive terms are

$$(\mathbf{F}_{\mathrm{V}}, \mathbf{G}_{\mathrm{V}}) = \left[-\rho_i \mathbf{u_i}, \underline{\underline{\tau}}, \mathbf{u} \cdot \underline{\underline{\tau}} - \mathbf{q}\right]^T, \tag{8}$$

with

$$\rho_i \mathbf{u_i} = -\rho D_i \nabla Y_i \tag{9}$$

$$\underline{\underline{\tau}} = \mu \left[\nabla \mathbf{u} + (\nabla \mathbf{u})^T \right] - \frac{2}{3} \mu \nabla \cdot \mathbf{u} \mathbf{I} \tag{10}$$

$$\mathbf{q} = -\lambda_t \nabla T + \sum_{i=1}^{N_s} h_i \rho_i \mathbf{u_i}, \tag{11}$$

where D_i and h_i are the diffusion coefficient and the static enthalpy of the i-*th* chemical species, respectively, μ is the molecular viscosity, λ_t is the thermal conductivity and T is the temperature. Equation 9, that models the diffusion of the generic chemical compound into the mixture, is a generalization of Fick's law for binary mixtures.
The source term reads

$$\mathbf{S} = \left[-\dot{W}_i, 0, 0, 0 \right]^T, \tag{12}$$

where $\dot{W}_i$ is the partial density change rate of the i-*th* chemical species due to chemical reactions. By considering a q-*th* generic reaction in the form

$$\sum_{i=1}^{N_s} \nu_{iq}^{'} C_i \leftrightarrow \sum_{i=1}^{N_s} \nu_{iq}^{''} C_i \quad q = 1, ..., N_R, \tag{13}$$

where, for each chemical species i, $\nu^{'}$ and $\nu^{''}$ are the forward and reverse stoichiometric coefficients, respectively, the symbol C stands for the generic chemical species and N_R is the total number of reactions, $\dot{W}_i$ is given by (Glassman, 1996; Kuo, 2005)

$$\dot{W}_i = M_i \sum_{q=1}^{N_R} \left(\nu_{iq}^{''} - \nu_{iq}^{'} \right) \left(k_{fq} \prod_{l=1}^{N_s} [X_l]^{\delta_{lq}^{'}} - k_{rq} \prod_{l=1}^{N_s} [X_l]^{\delta_{lq}^{''}} \right), \tag{14}$$

where M_i is the molecular weight of the i-*th* chemical species, k_{fq} and k_{rq} are the forward and reverse rate constants of the q-*th* reaction, $[X_l]$ is the molar concentration of the l-*th* chemical species, while $\delta^{'}$ and $\delta^{''}$ are the reaction orders in the forward and reverse direction, respectively. By using the Arrhenius expression, the forward and reverse rate constants for the q-*th* reaction are written as

$$k_q = A_q T^{\beta_q} \exp \left(\frac{-E_{aq}}{RT} \right), \tag{15}$$

where A_q is the pre-exponential factor, β_q is the temperature exponent, E_{aq} is the activation energy and R is the universal gas constant.
The pressure is computed by means of the equation of state

$$p = T \sum_{i=1}^{N_s} \rho_i R_i, \tag{16}$$

where R_i is the gas constant for the i-*th* chemical species.

2.2 The transport and thermodynamic properties

The transport properties of the multicomponent mixture are computed by using Wilke's law (Coffee & Heimerl, 1981; Hirschfelder *et al.*, 1964). The viscosity and the thermal conductivity of the mixture are given by

$$\mu = \sum_{i=1}^{Ns} \frac{\mu_i}{1 + \sum_{j \neq i} \phi_{ij} \frac{X_j}{X_i}} \tag{17}$$

$$\lambda_t = \sum_{i=1}^{Ns} \frac{\lambda_{ti}}{1 + 1.065 \sum_{j \neq i} \phi_{ij} \frac{X_j}{X_i}} \tag{18}$$

where μ_i, λ_{ti} and X_i are the viscosity, the thermal conductivity and the mole fraction of the i-*th* chemical species, respectively, while ϕ_{ij} is given by

$$\phi_{ij} = \frac{1}{8^{\frac{1}{2}}} \left(1 + \frac{M_i}{M_j}\right)^{-\frac{1}{2}} \left[1 + \left(\frac{\mu_i M_j}{\mu_j M_i}\right)^{\frac{1}{2}} \left(\frac{M_i}{M_j}\right)^{\frac{1}{4}}\right]^2. \tag{19}$$

The diffusion coefficient of the i-*th* chemical species in the mixture is given by

$$D_i = \frac{1 - X_i}{\sum_{j \neq i} \frac{X_j}{D_{ij}}}, \tag{20}$$

where D_{ij} is the binary diffusion coefficient.
The properties of the pure species, i.e. μ_i, λ_{ti} and D_{ij}, are computed according to the classic kinetic theory (Hirschfelder *et al.*, 1964).
In the computation of the thermodynamic properties, the gas is assumed to be thermally perfect, hence enthalpy and internal energy only depend on temperature. Following Gordon & McBride (1971), the specific heat at constant pressure for the i-*th* chemical species is given by a polynomial temperature curve fit

$$c_{pi} = \left(a_i + b_i T + c_i T^2 + d_i T^3 + e_i T^4\right) R_i, \tag{21}$$

where R_i is the gas constant for the i-*th* chemical species. As

$$dh_i = c_{pi} dT, \tag{22}$$

the enthalpy is given by

$$h_i = \left(a_i T + \frac{b_i}{2} T^2 + \frac{c_i}{3} T^3 + \frac{d_i}{4} T^4 + \frac{e_i}{5} T^5 + f_i\right) R_i. \tag{23}$$

The polynomial coefficients are given by Gordon & McBride (1971). Two sets of seven polynomial coefficients are used; the first one reproduces the thermodynamic properties for the high range of temperatures ($1000 - 5000$ K), whereas the second set is relative to the low range of temperatures ($300 - 1000$ K). Finally, the thermodynamic properties of the mixture are computed as

$$c_p = \sum_{i=1}^{N_S} c_{pi} Y_i \tag{24}$$

$$h = \sum_{i=1}^{N_S} h_i Y_i. \tag{25}$$

3. The numerical method

3.1 The spatial discretization

The governing equations are discretized by using a compact finite difference scheme, which is a generalization of the classical Padé scheme (Abraham & Magi, 1997; Lele, 1992; Poinsot & Lele, 1992). In each computational grid point, (i, j), the first (second) derivative of a generic variable f is written as a function of the values of f and its first (second) derivatives in the neighbouring grid points. This technique is an attempt to reproduce, by means of a finite difference scheme, the features of spectral techniques. Indeed, such a scheme has a formal accuracy comparable, in a wide range of wavenumbers, to that of spectral approaches.
For a uniform mesh with mesh size h, the first and second derivative expressions along direction i are

$$\begin{aligned}\beta f'_{i-2}+\alpha f'_{i-1}+f'_i+\alpha f'_{i+1}+\beta f'_{i+2} &= \\ a\frac{f_{i+1}-f_{i-1}}{2h}+b\frac{f_{i+2}-f_{i-2}}{4h}&+c\frac{f_{i+3}-f_{i-3}}{6h}\end{aligned} \tag{26}$$

$$\begin{aligned}\beta f''_{i-2}+\alpha f''_{i-1}+f''_i+\alpha f''_{i+1}+\beta f''_{i+2} &= \\ a\frac{f_{i+1}-2f_i+f_{i-1}}{h^2}+b\frac{f_{i+2}-2f_i+f_{i-2}}{4h^2}&+c\frac{f_{i+3}-2f_i+f_{i-3}}{9h^2},\end{aligned} \tag{27}$$

where the subscript j is removed for the sake of clarity. By using the Taylor series expansion and imposing the scheme to be sixth order accurate, the following relations between the coefficients are obtained

first derivative

$$\begin{aligned}a+b+c &= 1+2\alpha+2\beta \\ a+2^2b+3^2c &= 2\frac{3!}{2!}\left(\alpha+2^2\beta\right) \\ a+2^4b+3^4c &= 2\frac{5!}{4!}\left(\alpha+2^4\beta\right)\end{aligned} \tag{28}$$

second derivative

$$\begin{aligned}a+b+c &= 1+2\alpha+2\beta \\ a+2^2b+3^2c &= \frac{4!}{2!}\left(\alpha+2^2\beta\right) \\ a+2^4b+3^4c &= \frac{6!}{4!}\left(\alpha+2^4\beta\right).\end{aligned} \tag{29}$$

With the above relations, Eqs. 26 and 27 become families of two parameters schemes. For three-diagonal schemes ($\beta = 0$) and right hand size stencil equal to 5 ($c = 0$), the following values of the coefficients are obtained

first derivative

$$\alpha=\frac{1}{3},\beta=0,a=\frac{14}{9},b=\frac{1}{9},c=0 \tag{30}$$

second derivative

$$\alpha=\frac{2}{11},\beta=0,a=\frac{12}{11},b=\frac{3}{11},c=0. \tag{31}$$

In the computational nodes near the boundaries Eqs. 26 and 27 still apply with the following values of the coefficients (classical Padé scheme with fourth order accuracy)

first derivative

$$\alpha = \frac{1}{4}, \beta = 0, a = \frac{3}{2}, b = 0, c = 0 \tag{32}$$

second derivative

$$\alpha = \frac{1}{10}, \beta = 0, a = \frac{6}{5}, b = 0, c = 0. \tag{33}$$

In the boundary nodes $i = 1$ and $i = N + 1$, one side relations are used

$$f_1^{'} + \alpha f_2^{'} = \frac{1}{h}\left(af_1 + bf_2 + cf_3 + df_4\right), \tag{34}$$

$$f_{N+1}^{'} + \alpha f_N^{'} = \frac{1}{h}\left(-af_1 - bf_2 - cf_3 - df_4\right), \tag{35}$$

$$f_1^{''} + \alpha f_2^{''} = \frac{1}{h^2}\left(af_1 + bf_2 + cf_3 + df_4 + ef_5\right), \tag{36}$$

$$f_{N+1}^{''} + \alpha f_N^{''} = \frac{1}{h^2}\left(af_1 + bf_2 + cf_3 + df_4 + ef_5\right). \tag{37}$$

In order to obtain a third order accuracy, the following values of the coefficients are employed

first derivative

$$\alpha = 2, a = -\frac{5}{2}, b = 2, c = \frac{1}{2}, d = 0 \tag{38}$$

second derivative

$$\alpha = 11, a = 13, b = -27, c = 15, d = -1, e = 0. \tag{39}$$

As the scheme has a very low numerical dissipation, the high wavenumber instabilities are not damped. This is especially true in reactive multicomponent mixture. Hence, in the simulation of the reacting mixing layer, filtering techniques are used (Lele, 1992). The general filtering scheme along i direction is

$$\alpha\tilde{f}_{i-1} + \tilde{f}_i + \alpha\tilde{f}_{i+1} = af_i + \frac{d}{2}\left(f_{i+3} + f_{i-3}\right) + \frac{c}{2}\left(f_{i+2} + f_{i-2}\right) + \frac{b}{2}\left(f_{i+1} + f_{i-1}\right), \tag{40}$$

where $\tilde{f}_i$ is the filtered value. By imposing the scheme to be sixth order accurate, the Taylor series expansion gives the following relations for the coefficients

$$\begin{aligned} a &= \frac{1}{16}\left(11 + 10\alpha\right), \; b = \frac{1}{32}\left(15 + 34\alpha\right), \\ c &= \frac{1}{16}\left(-3 + 6\alpha\right), \; d = \frac{1}{32}\left(1 - 2\alpha\right). \end{aligned} \tag{41}$$

Hence, a one-parameter schemes family is obtained where α value determines the amount of waves to be filtered. In this work, α is imposed equal to 0.435, as this value ensures that the undesired instabilities are damped.

3.2 The temporal discretization

Equation 1 is advanced in time by using an explicit compact storage fourth order Runge-Kutta (RK) scheme (Gill, 1951) regarding the convective and diffusive terms, while the source term is solved in an implicit fashion. Hence, by writing Eq. 1 in the following compact form

$$\frac{\partial \mathbf{W}}{\partial t} = f(\mathbf{W}), \tag{42}$$

the RK scheme computes the $\mathbf{W}$ value at the new time step, $\mathbf{W}^{n+1}$, from the value at the old time step, $\mathbf{W}^n$, through 4 stages. In each stage, the computation of f is performed by using an implicit method for the source term, as described by Viggiano (2009).

4. The computational setup

The simulations of the reacting mixing layer are performed by using a rectangular computational domain. The streamwise dimension of the domain is equal to 1.5 cm, while the transverse one is chosen in order to avoid that the perturbation due to mixing reach the boundaries. Hence, by assuming a presumed value of the spreading rate of the mixing layer, based upon experimental studies in the literature, a ratio between the streamwise and transverse dimensions is fixed and the latter is computed from the former. Therefore, the transverse dimension is 0.4 cm in this computational case.

The domain is discretized by using a uniform mesh with cells of 40 μm. The aspect ratio of the cells is equal to 1, as the high gradients in all directions due to combustion require spatial accuracy in the stream direction as well as in the transverse one.

The order of magnitude of the computational time step, Δt, is $\mathcal{O}(10^{-5}\text{ ms})$ to satisfy numerical stability for explicit schemes. If the highest temperature in the domain exceeds 1300 K, the Δt is reduced to $\mathcal{O}(10^{-6}\text{ ms})$ in order to deal with the strong stiffness of the equations at high temperatures.

As the boundary conditions are concerned, the Navier-Stokes Characteristic Boundary Conditions (NSCBC) (Poinsot & Lele, 1992), extended to multicomponent flows (Abraham & Magi, 1997), are used. It was shown that these conditions give good results in the simulation of high Reynolds number flows as well as of high viscous flows (Poinsot & Lele, 1992). In the simulations presented in the following section, a subsonic inflow condition is imposed on the inlet boundary, while partially non-reflecting conditions are used on the remaining boundaries. The inlet mean velocities of n-heptane and air streams are imposed equal to 10 m/s and 3.82 m/s, respectively.

As the initial conditions are concerned, the mixing layer between two streams of air and fuel with different mean streamwise velocity is considered. The two layers velocities merge by means of a hyperbolic tangent profile. Near the splitter plate, a disturbance (Michalke, 1964) is superimposed on the flow field. The amplitude of the disturbance, v', is expressed by means of an exponential function, thus limiting the instability to the neighbourhood of the splitter plate

$$v' = 1.2\mathrm{e}^{-\frac{\left(x-\frac{L}{2}\right)^2}{2\left(\frac{\vartheta_i}{3}\right)^2}} \left[\sin\left(2\pi\frac{t}{P}\right) + \sin\left(\pi\frac{t}{P}\right) + \sin\left(\frac{2}{3}\pi\frac{t}{P}\right)\right], \tag{43}$$

where x is the transverse coordinate, L is the transverse dimension of the domain, ϑ_i is the initial momentum thickness, assumed equal to 0.0003 m, and P is the period of the fundamental harmonic, equal to $2 \cdot 10^{-1}$ ms. The hyperbolic tangent profile is also used to set the initial

density field. The initial value of pressure is equal to 40.5 bar and the initial temperature is 1000 K in the entire domain.
n-Heptane is chosen as model fuel and the 4-step mechanism, described by Muller *et al.* (1992), is used to model the autoignition. This mechanism was derived starting from a 1011 elementary reactions mechanism involving 171 chemical species. By using steady state assumptions for some intermediate species, a mechanism of 16 global reactions is obtained, that is controlled by the original elementary kinetic rates. Finally, the 16 reactions were reduced to the following 4 global steps

$$\begin{aligned} F &\overset{1}{\Longrightarrow} X \\ X + 11O_2 &\overset{2}{\Longrightarrow} P \\ F + 2O_2 &\overset{3}{\Longleftrightarrow} I \\ I + 9O_2 &\overset{4}{\Longrightarrow} P \end{aligned} \tag{44}$$

where F is the fuel, X stands for $3C_2H_4 + CH_3 + H$, I for $HO_2C_7H_{13}O + H_2O$ and P is the product resulting from the reactions, i.e. $7CO_2 + 8H_2O$. The reactions above are not the elementary ones, so an adjusted kinetic model is needed.
The 4-step mechanism is an attempt to describe, with a very small number of reactions, the chain branching at low temperature as well as the decomposition and subsequent oxidation of hydrocarbons at high temperature. The global reaction 3 is representative of the chain propagation process. The reaction 4 describes the chain branching and the subsequent oxidation to the final products. The activation energy of the reverse reaction $3b$ is higher than the forward one, $3f$. This ensures that at low temperature the reaction $3f$ is faster than $3b$. At high temperature, the backward reaction becomes dominant, thus leading to the transition from the first stage of ignition to the second one. The reaction 1 becomes important and leads to the decomposition of the fuel into the C_2H_4 and CH_3 hydrocarbons and H radicals. Finally, the reaction 2 describes the oxidation to the reaction products.
The simulations of the mixing layer are performed by using the following procedure. A non-reacting mixing layer between two streams of air and fuel is initially developed up to 1.8 ms from the start of computation. This time is sufficient in order to obtain a fully-developed mixing layer. Then, the time is reset to zero and chemical reactions are numerically switched on. In such a way, t_{ig} gives the chemical delay, that is comparable with the delay time obtained in a zero-dimensional configuration, if the initial composition and temperature of the mixed reactants are the same as in the two-dimensional case.
The ignition delay time is defined as the time when the following condition is satisfied (Viggiano & Magi, 2004)

$$\frac{dT}{dt} = 6 \cdot 10^6 \frac{K}{s}. \tag{45}$$

In two-dimensional simulations, Eq. 45 is used with T equal to the maximum value of temperature in the domain, $T_{\max}$.

5. Results

Figure 1 shows the temperature and density field of the developed mixing layer at $t = 1.8$ ms. As a consequence of the initial perturbation at the splitter plate, vortices are formed. While the mixing layer grows in the streamwise direction, the stream of fuel sweeps away the surrounding air and the contours at constant density are wrinkled. The overall effect is the air

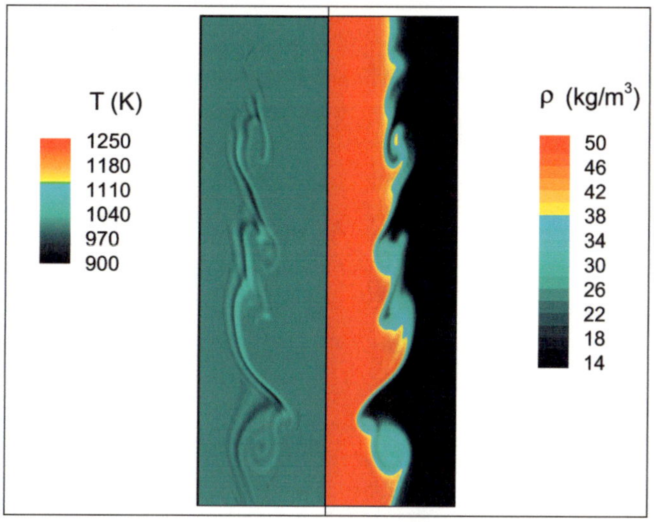

Fig. 1. Temperature and density field in a developed mixing layer.

entrainment in the fuel stream. As a consequence of the high strain rate in the mixing region, temperature locally increases, reaching the maximum value of 1070 K in the domain.

The ignition phenomenon is analysed by starting from the flow configuration shown in Fig. 1. Figure 2 shows the results in terms of contour lines at constant temperature (on the left) and fuel mass fraction (on the right) at three times. The time is computed from the numerical activation of the chemical reactions. In the frames, the white line corresponds to the isoline of stoichiometric mixture fraction ($Z = 0.062$). The figure shows that the temperature increases in some zones on the rich side of the mixture, close to the stoichiometric conditions. In these ignition spots, temperature increases slowly, at first, and then more rapidly.

As the localization of ignition spots is concerned, Fig. 2 shows that the most reactive zones correspond to regions where the temperature was higher at the start of the computation when chemistry was switched on. In this case, temperature is a key factor for the ignition to occur. This is in agreement with the results in the literature (Muller *et al.*, 1992; Viggiano & Magi, 2004) concerning the dependence of the ignition delay time on temperature in zero-dimensional configuration. The 4-step mechanism does not capture the NTC and t_{ig} is always reduced by increasing the temperature.

Besides, by analysing the contour lines at constant fuel mass fraction in the same figure, the ignition spots are found where a suitable rate between air and fuel occurs. This second condition is satisfied in the wrinkled interface between the two streams and in some small regions in the fuel stream, where air entrainment is more effective.

In Fig. 3 the values of mixture fraction characterizing the high temperature reactive zones are picked out by plotting the temperature versus mixture fraction in each computational grid point for several times. In this work, the mixture fraction, Z, is computed as the ratio between the mass of hydrogen and carbon and the total mass of the mixture. The increase of temperature is spread over a wide range of mixture fraction values, $0.18 < Z < 0.24$, up to $t = 0.08$ ms. Then, the combustion is shifted towards richer mixture.

The ignition delay time is equal to 0.11 ms.

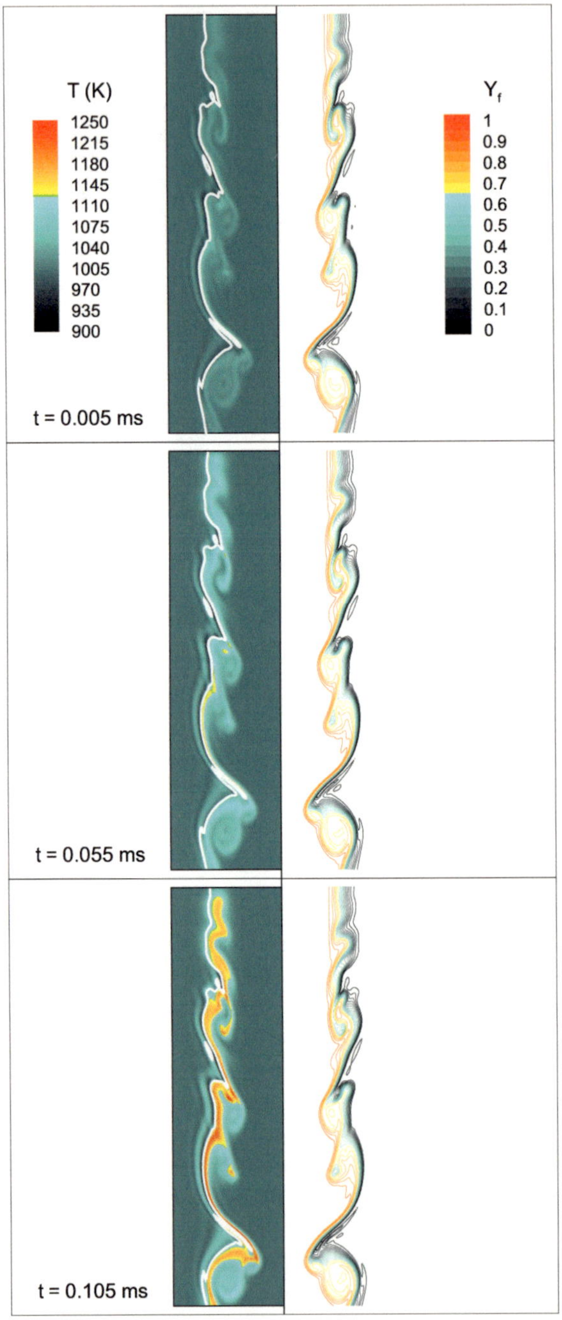

Fig. 2. Autoignition in a developed mixing layer: contours at constant temperature and fuel mass fraction at different times. The stoichiometric conditions are shown with a white line.

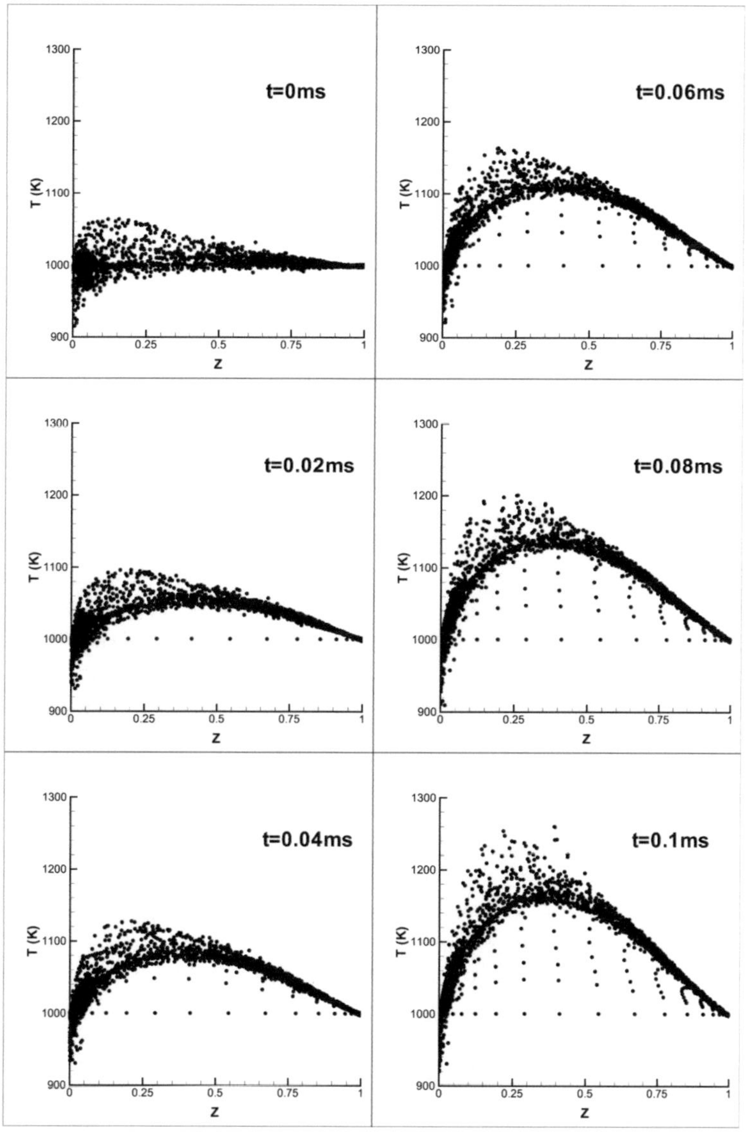

Fig. 3. Autoignition in a developed mixing layer: scatter plots of temperature versus mixture fraction.

Therefore, zero-dimensional simulations are performed in order to make a comparison with the results of the two-dimensional code. The initial conditions of the zero-dimensional computations are set equal to the most reactive conditions in the two-dimensional developed mixing layer, thus $T = 1070$ K and $0.18 < Z < 0.24$. The t_{ig} varies from 0.1 ms for $Z = 0.18$ to 0.07 ms for $Z = 0.24$. These results are in good agreement with the two-dimensional ones. The small differences are likely due to a non uniform value of Z in the ignition regions for the two-dimensional case.

6. Conclusions and further reading

A DNS methodology, coupled with accurate numerical schemes and proper combustion models, for the analysis of non-premixed reacting flows is presented. This numerical approach allows a comprehensive simulation of the physical process, as, by using proper computational grids, it accurately captures both the fluid dynamics and the chemistry scales of the phenomena.

In this work, the proposed methodology is used for the simulation of the ignition in a mixing layer, developed between two streams of air and *n*-heptane in a high pressure environment, thus assessing the potentiality of the software package. The results, in terms of ignition delay time and most reactive mixture fraction, are consistent with the thermochemistry of the problem, as confirmed by zero-dimensional computations. Besides, the role of temperature and of mixture fraction in determining the evolution of ignition is shown.

The same methodology was used by Viggiano & Magi (2004) for the study of ignition in a transient jet. The localization of the ignition spots was investigated and the effect of some physical parameters, such as the initial temperature of fuel and air and the velocity of the jet, was shown. The reader is referred to that work for further details.

Besides, the role of chemical kinetic mechanisms and of fluid dynamics on the ignition in transient jets was further explored by Viggiano (2009), by implementing more detailed mechanisms for the oxidation of *n*-heptane in the same software package. The employment of a detailed kinetic mechanism is fundamental if the initial temperature of the reactants is equal or higher than about 800 K. For lower temperature values, the fluid dynamics is determining in the localization of ignition spots and even a global mechanism, such as the 4-step one, could give reliable results.

7. References

Abraham, J. & Magi, V. (1997). Exploring Velocity Ratio and Density Ratio Effects in a Mixing Layer Using DNS. *International Journal of Computational Fluid Dynamics*, 8, 147-151.

Bilger, R.W.; Pope, S.B.; Bray, K.N.C. & Driscoll, J.F. (2005). Paradigms in turbulent combustion. *Proceedings of the Combustion Institute*, 30, 21-42.

Coffee, T.P. & Heimerl, J.M. (1981). Transport Algorithms for Premixed Laminar, Steady-State Flames. *Combustion and Flame*, 43, 273-289.

Gill, S. (1951). A Process for the Step-by-Step Integration of Differential Equations in an Automatic Computing Machine. *Proc. Cambridge Phil. Soc.*, 47, 96-108.

Glassman, I. (1996). *Combustion*, Academic Press, 3rd edition, ISBN: 978-0122858529.

Gordon, S. & McBride, B.J. (1971). Computer Program for Calculation of Complex Chemical Equilibrium Compositions, Rocket Performance, Incident and Reflected Shocks and Chapman-Jouguet Detonations. NASA report SP-273.

Hilbert, R.; Tap, F.; El-Rabii, H. & Thévenin, D. (2004). Impact of detailed chemistry and transport models on turbulent combustion simulations. *Progress in Energy and Combustion Science*, 30, 61-117.

Hirschfelder, J.O.; Curtiss, C.F. & Byron Bird, R. (1964). *The Molecular Theory of Gases and Liquids*, John Wiley & Sons, ISBN: 978-0471400653.

Kuo, K. (2005). *Principles of Combustion*, Wiley-Interscience, 2nd edition, ISBN: 978-0471046899.

Lele, S.K. (1989). Direct Numerical Simulation of Compressible Free Shear Flows, *AIAA Paper 89-0374*.

Lele, S.K. (1992). Compact Finite Difference Schemes with Spectral Like Resolution. *Journal of Computational Physics*, 103, 16-42.
Magi, V. (2004). Private Communications.
Mastorakos, E.; Baritaud, T.A. & Poinsot, T.J. (1997). Numerical Simulations of Autoignition in Turbulent Mixing Flows. *Combustion and Flame*, 109, 198-223.
Mastorakos, E. (2009). Ignition of turbulent non-premixed flames. *Progress in Energy and Combustion Science*, 35, 57-97.
Michalke, A. (1964). On the Inviscid Instability of the Hyperbolic Tangent Velocity Profile *Journal of Fluid Mechanics*, 19, 543-556.
Moin, P. & Mahesh, K. (1998). Direct Numerical Simulation: A Tool in Turbulence Research. *Annual Review of Fluid Mechanics*, 30, 539-578.
Muller, U.C., Peters, N. & Liñán, A. (1992). Global Kinetics for N-Heptane Ignition at High Pressure. *Proceedings of the Combustion Institute*, 24, 777-784.
Pitsch, H. (2006). Large-Eddy Simulation of Turbulent Combustion. *Annual Review of Fluid Mechanics*, 38, 453-482.
Poinsot, T.J. & Lele, S.K. (1992). Boundary Conditions for Direct Simulations of Compressible Viscous Flows. *Journal of Computational Physics*, 101, 104-129.
Sreedhara, S. & Lakshmisha, K.N. (2000). Direct Numerical Simulation of Autoignition in a Non-Premixed, Turbulent Medium. *Proceedings of the Combustion Institute*, 28, 25-34.
Viggiano, A. & Magi, V. (2004). A 2-D Investigation of the *n*-Heptane Autoignition by means of Direct Numerical Simulation. *Combustion and Flame*, 137, 432-443.
Viggiano, A. (2009). Exploring the Effect of Fluid Dynamics and Kinetic Mechanisms on *n*-Heptane Autoignition in Transient Jets. *Combustion and Flame*, doi:10.1016/j.combustflame.2009.10.004.

Optimization of Full ECF Bleaching Sequences Using Novel Models

Sandeep Jain and Gérard Mortha
Grenoble INP – PAGORA, International School of Paper, Print Media and Biomaterials
France

1. Introduction

Elemental Chlorine Free (ECF) bleaching continues to dominate the world bleached chemical pulp market. In 2005, ECF production reached over 70 million tons, and more than 20 million tons of new production is expected by 2010 to meet the world's growing demand, totalling nearly 90% of world market share. The choice of bleaching technology is a result of many considerations like investment costs, operating costs, the discharge into environment, health and safety and product quality of bleached pulp. Today research emphasis is oriented towards process optimization with the purpose of saving high cost chemicals such as chlorine dioxide, improving environmental aspects by reducing water consumption, AOX (adsorbable organic halide) and COD (chemical oxygen demand) in the effluents, and achieving better control of bleach plant. However, even though major improvements in bleaching technology have been made, with the tougher environmental regulations, increasing chemical costs and tighter customer demand, there is a need for accurate and robust process optimization and control of bleach plant. Modelling bleaching process provides an efficient way to predict important bleaching results and tendencies which would be of considerable use in bleach plant optimization as well as in process control.

From a historical perspective, most bleach optimization studies in the past focused on oxygen delignification (O), chlorine or chlorine dioxide substitution (C, (CD) or (DC)) and subsequent brightening with chlorine dioxide (e.g., D_1 and D_2) and hypochlorite (Reeve, 1989a-b, 1996b-c; Berry, 1996; Van Lierop et al., 1986a-b; Berry & Fleming, 1986; Anderson, 1991). The goal was to obtain a final brightness with these stages that afforded the lowest chemical cost and minimum environmental impact, yet providing a strong, high quality pulp. Unfortunately, only a handful of published studies have re-examined bleach optimization since the conversion to Elemental Chlorine Free (ECF) bleaching (Hart & Connell, 2003; Fletcher et al., 2000; McDonough et al., 1997, 1996; Basta et al., 1992). This is particularly true when one considers the variables in the first extraction stage (E) of bleach sequence, since this stage is often taken for granted as an integrated extension of the previous stage (Brogdon et al., 2003, 2004a-c). Mackinnon (1987) developed a FORTRAN simulation program for the first chlorination and second alkaline extraction stages. Kinetic expressions of the chlorination and oxidative extraction were derived to match experimental data and the simulation was used to compare operation strategies. Bialkowsky (1990) used first-order plus dead-time transfer functions to represent the dynamics of bleaching systems. The model was used to review control engineering principles and how bleach plant process variability can be minimized. Ulinder (1992) used the Simon's IDEAS simulation package to model the oxygen bleaching stage. The model was used to test an advanced kappa number control scheme. Mortha et al. (2001) used Excel-VBA simulator to predict the variations of kappa number, pH, brightness and chlorine dioxide consumption at each step of a multistage DEDED bleaching sequence.

More sophisticated models which describe multi-stage ECF bleaching process were developed recently (Jain et al., 2007, 2008a-b, 2009). The main focus of this study was to develop a computer-based simulator for the simulations of multistage ECF bleaching sequences and to demonstrate its multi-purpose applications, such as a tool for prediction, decision, diagnosis, process regulation, process optimization or education. The simulator was based on the new and improved kinetic, stoichiometric and COD predictive models for all chlorine dioxide and extraction stages developed during this research. The simulator built under Visual Studio 2005 software (Microsoft Co.) predicts the variations of kappa number, pH, brightness, bleaching chemicals consumption and effluent load at each step of a multistage ECF bleaching sequence. The accuracy of simulator models was tested for a vast range of literature and experimental data. The steady-state models developed are directly applicable to the elemental chlorine free bleaching of unbleached as well as oxygen delignified softwood and hardwood kraft pulps.

This chapter discusses and presents the applications of this simulator in form of case studies by addressing several major optimization issues of ECF bleaching like the optimal splitting of the ClO_2 charge between the different D stages, the impact of extraction stage pH, the use of H_2O_2 and O_2 in first extraction stages (EO, EP, EOP), the optimum end pH or amount of NaOH to be added for a target final pH in D_1 or D_2 stages, the effect of stock kappa number of an unbleached pulp on ClO_2 gain etc. Other optimization issues like effect of process parameters and important tendencies in each chlorine dioxide and extraction stages will also be demonstrated, both for softwood and hardwood. The results manifested can be effectively used by mill personnel for pollution abatement and process optimization assessments, either when planning new lab studies or when designing new bleach plants or modifying an existing bleach plant.

2. The ECF Bleaching Simulator

The simulator for ECF sequence was developed using object oriented Visual Studio 2005 software platform. The interface is developed in Visual Basic while the simulations are carried out in Visual C++ environment. The model is composed of individual modules that represent each bleaching stage. The different stages that can be simulated are:

- D_o: first chlorine dioxide stage
- E_o: first alkaline extraction stage
- EO_o: first alkaline extraction stage reinforced with oxygen
- EP_o: first alkaline extraction stage reinforced with hydrogen peroxide
- EOP_o: first alkaline extraction stage reinforced with oxygen and hydrogen peroxide
- D_1: second chlorine dioxide stage
- E_1D_2: second extraction stage and third chlorine dioxide stage

Figure 1 demonstrates the general organization of the simulator. The simulator starts with a welcome screen. The user has the option of choosing the working language, either French or English, in order to proceed to next step which is the selection of a sequence. The different stages are listed and the user has to make a logical sequence (in the progressive format $D_oE_oD_1E_1D_2$) by selecting each stage in the sequence one by one. The next step involves data entering for each stage. Once the user has completed the data entering for each stage, a verification screen comes to confirm if the user has entered all data and is sure to proceed further to the start of simulation. At the end of simulation, the results in the form of Crystal reports for each stage are displayed one by one. Once the user has seen all reports, the next step is the display of a screen which asks user either to use database or to exit or to go back to the sequence selecting screen for a new simulation. At each step, there is inbuilt error handling and, also, there is possibility of consulting the "Help" menu.

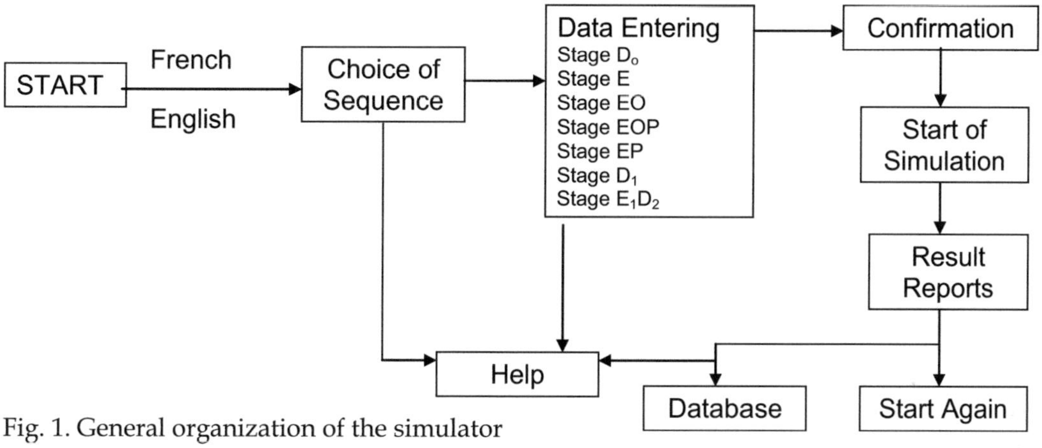

Fig. 1. General organization of the simulator

3. Framework of bleaching models used

The multistage ECF bleaching sequence simulator is based on a set of combined kinetic, stoichiometric and COD equations, which were developed during the course of this research (Jain et al., 2007, 2008a-b, 2009). There exists, for each stage, a relationship between the entering pulp properties, the conditions prevailing within the stage, and the properties of the pulp leaving it. In principle, this relationship is described by a set of mathematical models, the output of which might serve as one of the necessary inputs to a similar set of models of the following stage. A collection of such sets of models, one for each stage of the sequence, constitutes a predictive model of the entire sequence.

4. Experimental conditions for case studies

The general conditions used during the discussion of case studies are summarized in table 1. Certain conditions, which vary from these standard conditions for different cases discussed, will be specified during the discussion.

	D_o	E/EO/EP/EOP	D_1	E_1	D_2
Wood species+	SW/HW	SW/HW	SW/HW	SW/HW	SW/HW
Kappa number	25, 30 (SW) 15, 20 (HW)	-	-	-	-
ClO_2,% on total ClO_2	65%	-	23.23%	-	11.67%
Temperature, °C	50	70	70	70	70
H_2O_2, kg/t	0	0-2	0	0	0
pH	-	12	-	12	-
Consistency, %	10	10	10	10	10
Time, min.	60	60	120	60	150
Pressure O_2 bar	-	5	-	-	-

+SW: softwood, HW: hardwood

Table 1. Standard conditions used for discussed case studies

5. Results and Discussion

5.1 Optimizing the charge of ClO_2 in an ECF sequence

One of the most interesting applications of the simulator is to optimize the splitting of the ClO_2 charge between the different D stages. The expected benefit may be to lower the total ClO_2 charge to reach a final brightness or to optimize brightness for a given ClO_2 charge. In the following part, we design as "TCM" the total chlorine multiple, defined as the factor to multiply the kappa number to obtain the total ClO_2 charge, expressed in % Cl on pulp, applied for D(EO)DED or DEDED type sequence for softwood or hardwood Kraft pulps.

Figure 2 shows the effect of varying the TCM on the final brightness, in the case of a softwood Kraft pulp of kappa number 25. The amount of ClO_2 applied in D_o was chosen at three levels: 35%-50%-65%, based on the total ClO_2 applied during the sequence. Three tendencies are shown: first, a better brightness can be obtained by lowering the ClO_2 charge applied in the D_o stage, second, the brightness gain obtained by increasing the TCM starts to lower as TCM value increases whatever the ClO_2 charge applied in D_o and third, there is a limit upto which charge in D_o stage can be lowered and an optimum is achieved which can vary for different values of TCM used. Further, when a higher TCM value is used, the amount of ClO_2 required in D_o is higher to reach optimum final brightness as compared to the cases with lower value of TCM. For example, in figure 2, at TCM values higher than 0.3, the optimum amount of ClO_2 applied in D_o was about 50% based on the total ClO_2 applied during the sequence, where as, at TCM values lower than 0.3, the optimum amount of ClO_2 applied in D_o was 35% based on the total ClO_2 applied during the sequence. Similar observations were made for the case of a hardwood Kraft pulp as illustrated in figures 3-5. However, as compared to softwoods, a lower ClO_2 percentage (based on the total ClO_2 applied during the sequence) is required to be applied in the D_o stage to reach the optimum brightness. This might be attributed to the fact that the amount of lignin present in hardwoods is low as compared to that in softwoods leading to low delignification requirements in D_o stage and better brightness gain possibility in subsequent D stages.

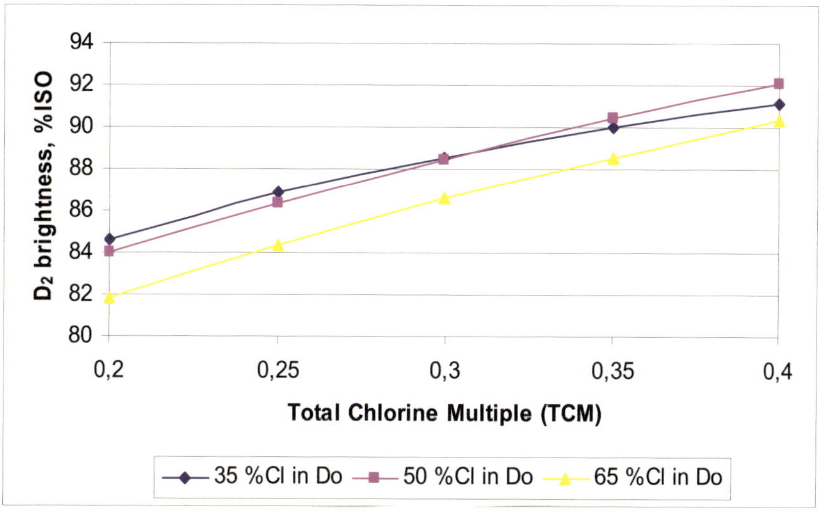

Fig. 2. D(EO)DED sequence optimization; effect of varying Total Chlorine Multiple (TCM) on the final brightness, at varying charge of ClO_2 applied in D_o. ClO_2 charge ratio $D_1/(D_1+D_2)$ = 66.7%, softwood Kraft pulp of kappa number 25

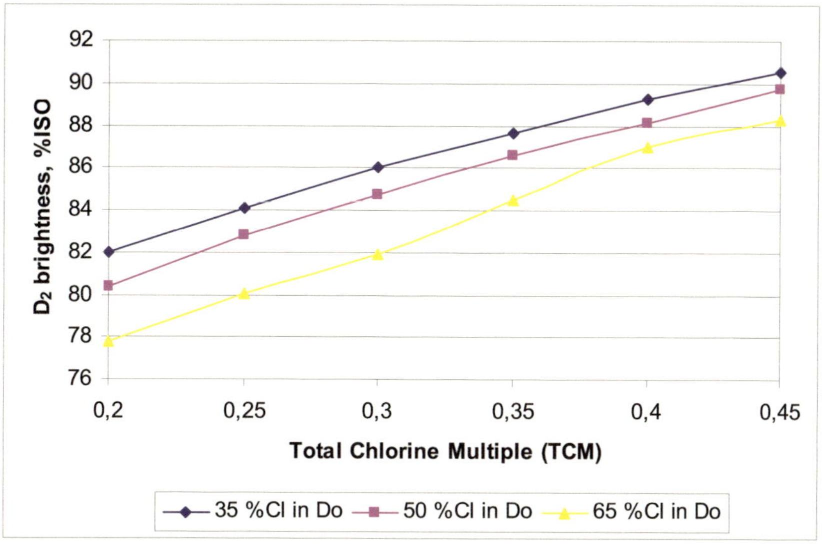

Fig. 3. D(EO)DED sequence optimization; effect of varying Total Chlorine Multiple (TCM) on the final brightness, at varying charge of ClO_2 applied in D_o. ClO_2 charge ratio $D_1/(D_1+D_2)$ = 66.7%, hardwood Kraft pulp of kappa number 15

It is equally interesting to note that the above tendencies do not change with the facts whether a lower final brightness is targeted or a higher initial kappa number is used. This is clear while comparing three cases of hardwood Kraft pulps, first, with a lower kappa number of 15 subjected to D(EO)DED sequence for higher target brightness and, second, with a lower kappa number of 15 subjected to DEDED sequence (without oxygen reinforcement in first alkali extraction stage) for lower target brightness and, third, with a higher kappa number of 20 subjected to DEDED sequence (without oxygen reinforcement in first alkali extraction stage) for lower target brightness.

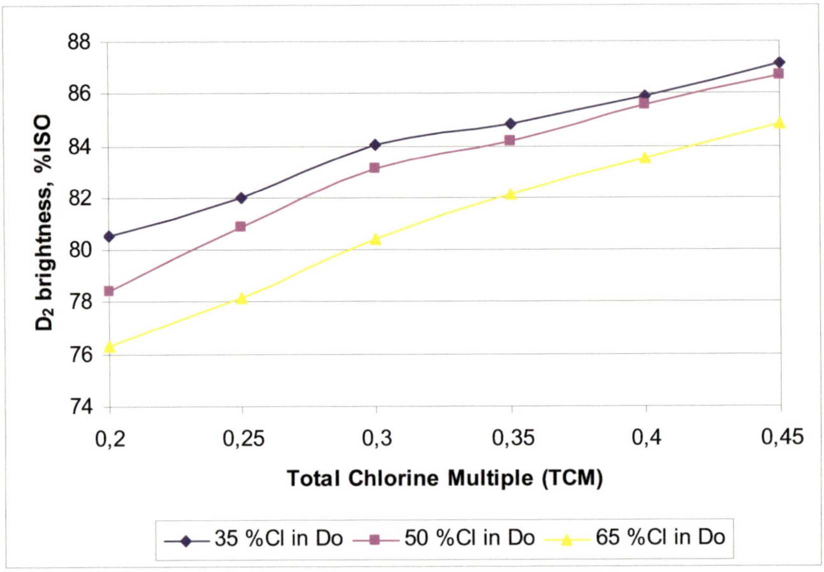

Fig. 4. DEDED sequence optimization; effect of varying Total Chlorine Multiple (TCM) on the final brightness, at varying charge of ClO_2 applied in D_o. ClO_2 charge ratio $D_1/(D_1+D_2)$ = 66.7%, hardwood Kraft pulp of kappa number 15

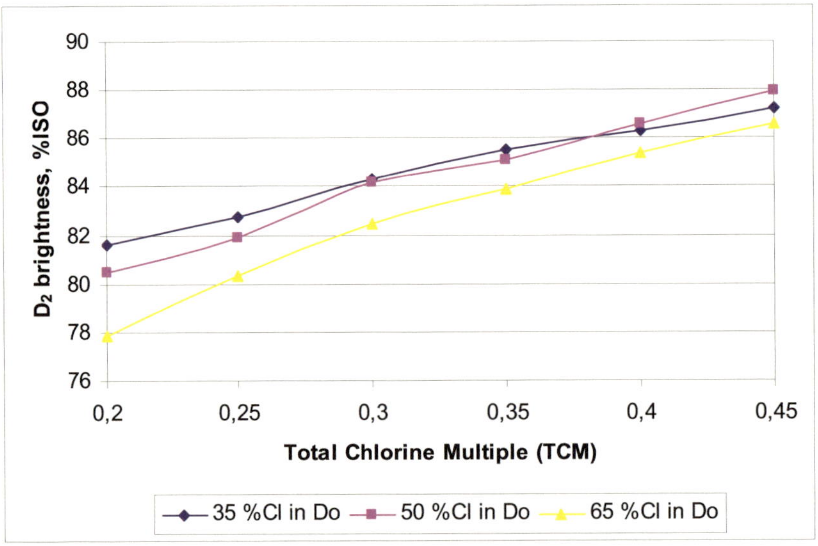

Fig. 5. DEDED sequence optimization; effect of varying Total Chlorine Multiple (TCM) on the final brightness, at varying charge of ClO_2 applied in D_o. ClO_2 charge ratio $D_1/(D_1+D_2)$ = 66.7%, hardwood Kraft pulp of kappa number 20

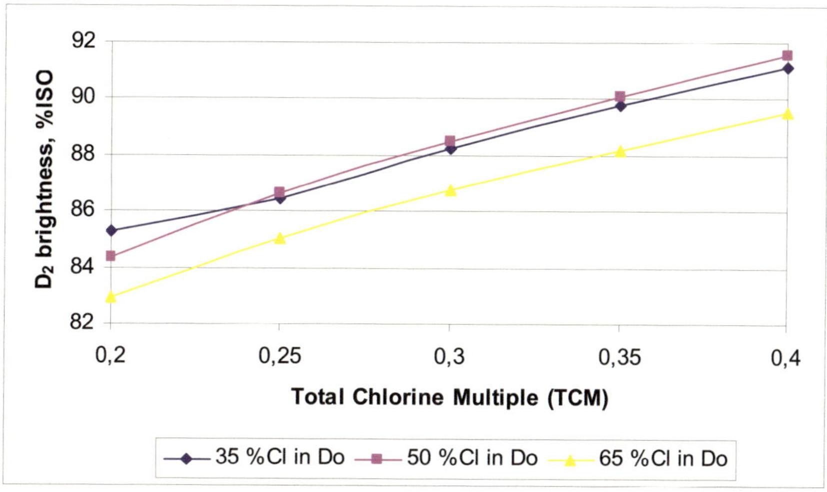

Fig. 6. D(EO)DED sequence optimization; effect of varying Total Chlorine Multiple (TCM) on the final brightness, at varying charge of ClO_2 applied in D_o. ClO_2 charge ratio $D_1/(D_1+D_2)$ = 50%, softwood Kraft pulp of kappa number 25

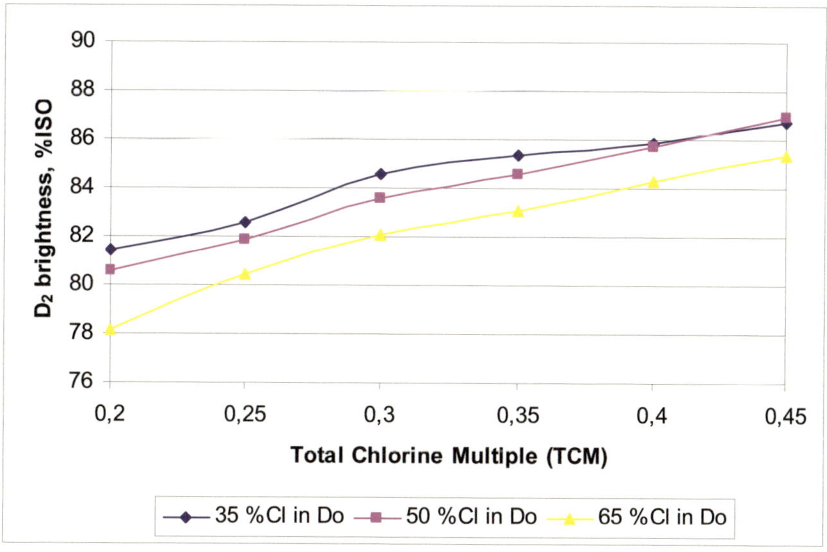

Fig. 7. DEDED sequence optimization; effect of varying Total Chlorine Multiple (TCM) on the final brightness, at varying charge of ClO_2 applied in D_o. ClO_2 charge ratio $D_1/(D_1+D_2)$ = 50%, hardwood Kraft pulp of kappa number 15

The above results were obtained by applying a ratio of 2/3 of ClO_2 charge in D_1, based on the total charge (D_1+ D_2). One can see in figure 6 that, for softwood Kraft pulp, reducing the ratio to 50% results in a slightly increased final brightness at low values of TCM and a slightly decreased final brightness at high values of TCM when compared to figure 2. However, this does not change the above described tendencies. Further, there is a shift observed in the TCM value limit for the optimum value of ClO_2 charge in D_o when compared to figure 2. At TCM values higher than 0.24, the optimum amount of ClO_2 applied in D_o was about 50% based on the total ClO_2 applied during the sequence, whereas, at TCM values lower than 0.24, the optimum amount of ClO_2 applied in D_o was 35% based on the total ClO_2 applied during the sequence. This means that the optimum amount of ClO_2 applied in D_o, based on the total ClO_2 applied during the sequence, depends on both the TCM value as well as the ratio of ClO_2 charge in D_1, based on the total charge (D_1+ D_2). Similar observations were made for the case of a hardwood Kraft pulp as illustrated in figure 7.

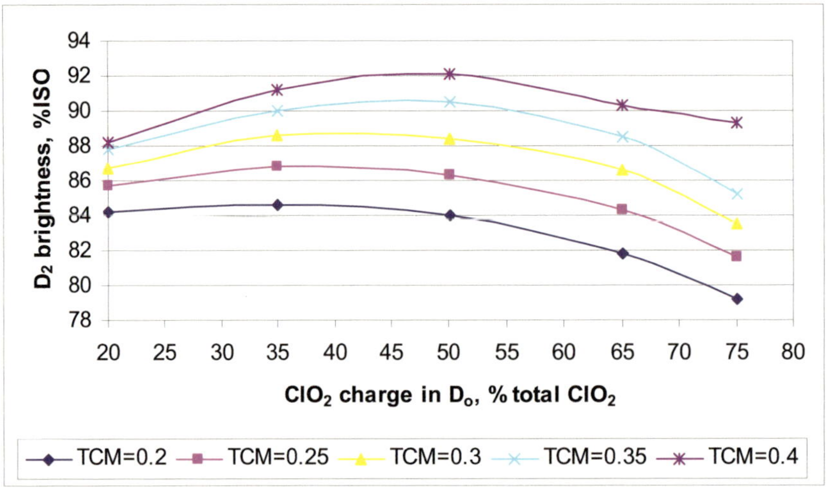

Fig. 8. D(EO)DED sequence optimization; effect of varying Total Chlorine Multiple (TCM) on the final brightness, at varying charge of ClO_2 applied in D_o. ClO_2 charge ratio $D_1/(D_1+D_2)$ = 66.7%, softwood Kraft pulp of kappa number 25

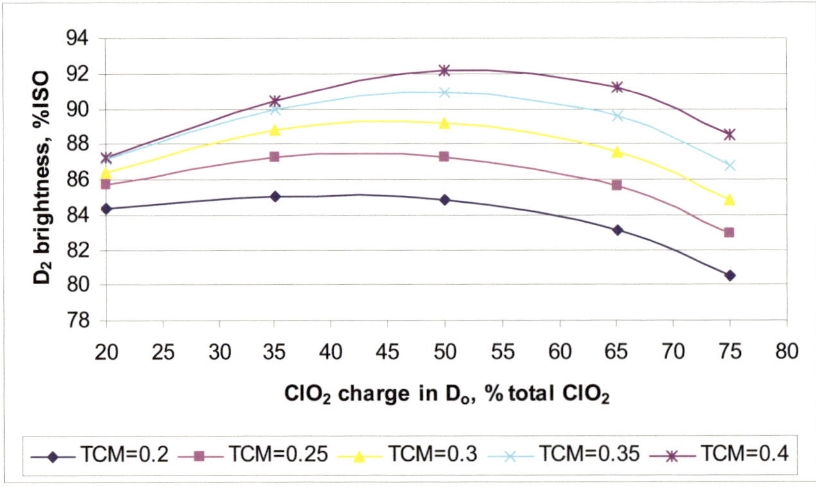

Fig. 9. D(EO)DED sequence optimization; effect of varying Total Chlorine Multiple (TCM) on the final brightness, at varying charge of ClO_2 applied in D_o. ClO_2 charge ratio $D_1/(D_1+D_2)$ = 66.7%, softwood Kraft pulp of kappa number 30

It is shown in figures 8 and 9 that for the case of softwood Kraft pulps the best ClO_2 percentage to apply in D_o should be searched between 33% and 55% (based on the total sequence ClO_2 charge), but this also depends on the kappa number of the unbleached pulp. It can also be seen that at low values of TCM optimum brightness is lower as compared to high values of TCM which results in higher values of optimum brightness. Further, a shift on the optimum amount of ClO_2 applied in D_o, based on the total ClO_2 applied during the sequence, for optimum brightness is observed. As value of TCM increases, the amount of ClO_2 applied in D_o should be increased to reach optimum brightness. This trend is even clearer at initial kappa number of 30 as illustrated in figure 9.

Similar observations were made for the case of a hardwood Kraft pulp as illustrated in figure 10. However, for the case of hardwood kraft pulps the best ClO_2 percentage to apply in D_o should be searched at quite low value ranging 20% to 45% (based on the total sequence ClO_2 charge). This can again be attributed to the fact that the amount of lignin present in hardwoods is low as compared to that in softwoods leading to low delignification requirements in D_o stage and better brightness gain possibility in subsequent D stages. Applying a ClO_2 charge ratio $D_1/(D_1+D_2)$ of 66.7% was chosen for representation as it is close to an optimum value for increasing final brightness.

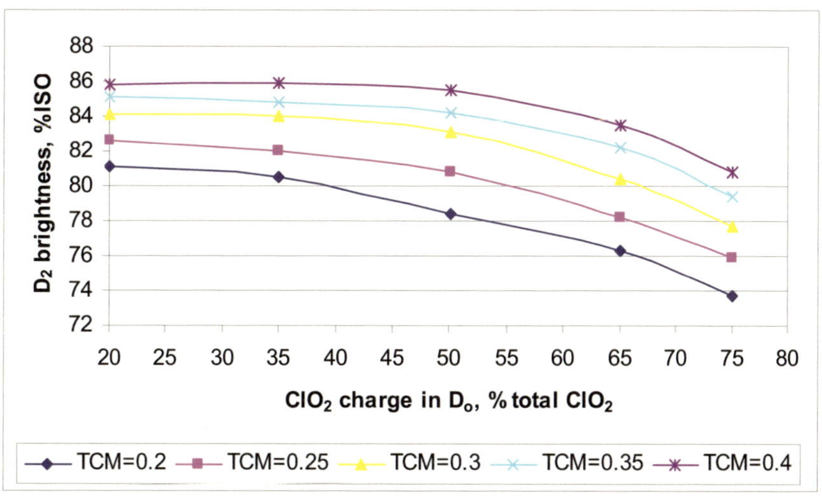

Fig. 10. DEDED sequence optimization; effect of varying Total Chlorine Multiple (TCM) on the final brightness, at varying charge of ClO_2 applied in D_o. ClO_2 charge ratio $D_1/(D_1+D_2)$ = 66.7%, hardwood Kraft pulp of kappa number 15

It is shown in figures 11 and 12 that although the curves for D_2 stage are pretty flat, the best ClO_2 ratio to apply in D_1 should be searched between 50% and 70% for softwoods and between 40% and 60% for hardwoods (based on the total ClO_2 charge (D_1+ D_2)), but this also depends on the kappa number of the unbleached pulp. Applying 35%, 50% and 64% of the total ClO_2 charge in D_o were chosen for representation. Like in the optimal ClO_2 charge split between D_o and subsequent stages, it can be observed again that in hardwood pulps better brightness gain can be obtained by using higher ClO_2 charge in subsequent D stage (while splitting ClO_2 between D_1 and D_2) which again is contrary for softwood pulps.

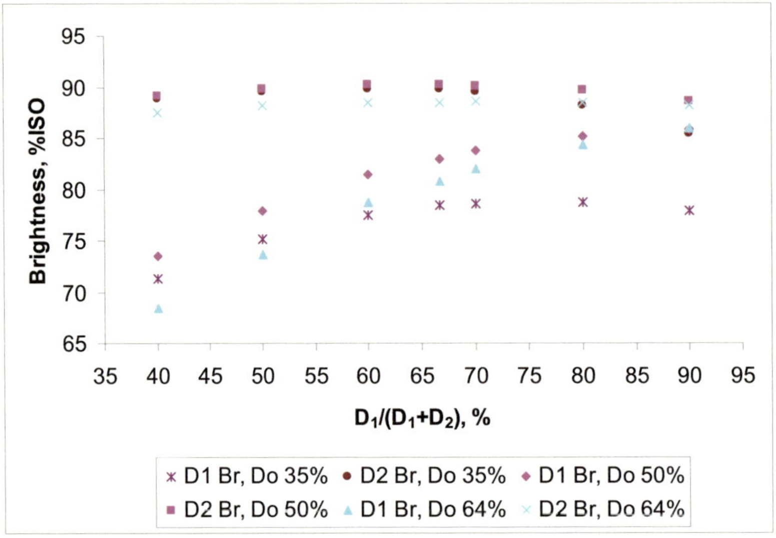

Fig. 11. D(EO)DED sequence optimization; effect of varying the ClO_2 charge ratio between D_1 and D_2 on the final brightness, at varying charge of ClO_2 applied in D_o stage. TCM = 0.343, softwood Kraft pulp of kappa number 25

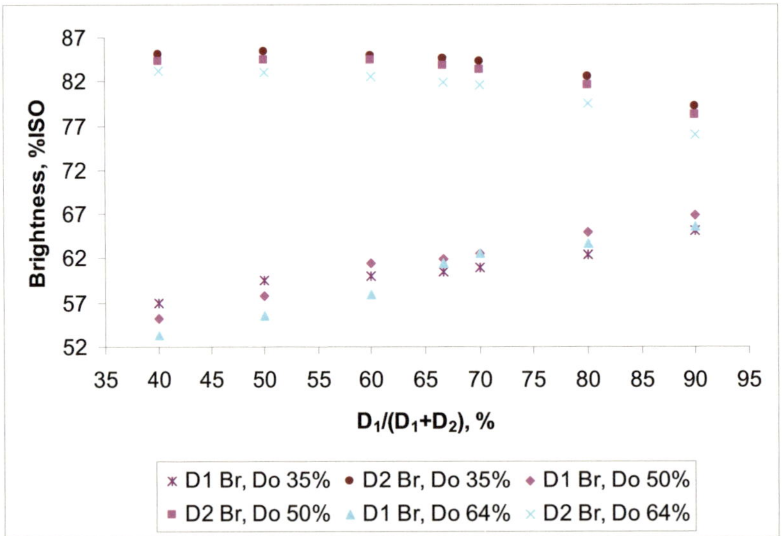

Fig. 12. DEDED sequence optimization; effect of varying the ClO_2 charge ratio between D_1 and D_2 on the final brightness, at varying charge of ClO_2 applied in D_o stage. TCM = 0.343, hardwood Kraft pulp of kappa number 15

A mill approach can also be to optimize the kappa number after D_o(EO) or D_oE stage to reach the highest final brightness. This is illustrated in figures 13-16 for softwood and hardwood Kraft pulp. In figures 13 and 14, for softwood Kraft pulp with kappa numbers of 25 and 30, the different curves represent varying TCM values. As expected, the optimal kappa number after D_o(EO) depends on the TCM value. At low TCM, the kappa number after D_o(EO) should be kept rather high, which means a decrease of the ClO_2 charge to apply in D_o to keep a sufficient amount of ClO_2 for D_1 and D_2. Whereas at high TCM, the optimum kappa number after D_o(EO) is found at higher percentages of ClO_2 in D_o, based on the total ClO_2 charge applied.

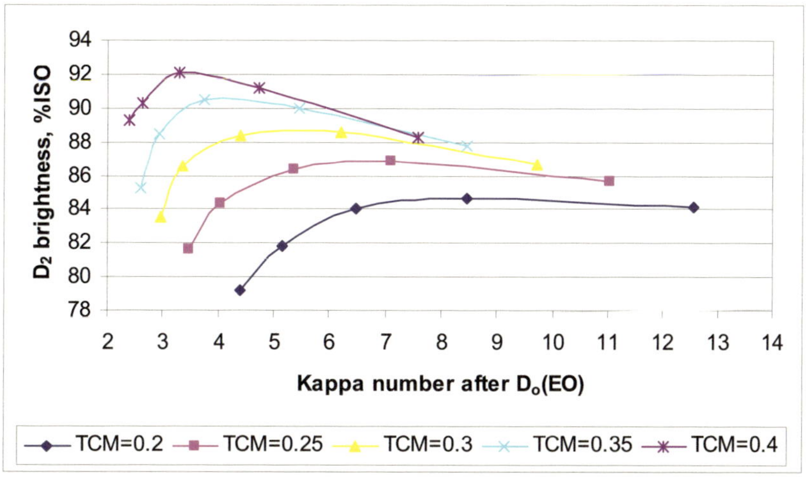

Fig. 13. D(EO)DED sequence optimization; search of an optimal value of kappa number after D_o(EO), at varying TCM. ClO_2 charge ration $D_1/(D_1+D_2) = 66.7$, softwood Kraft pulp of kappa number 25

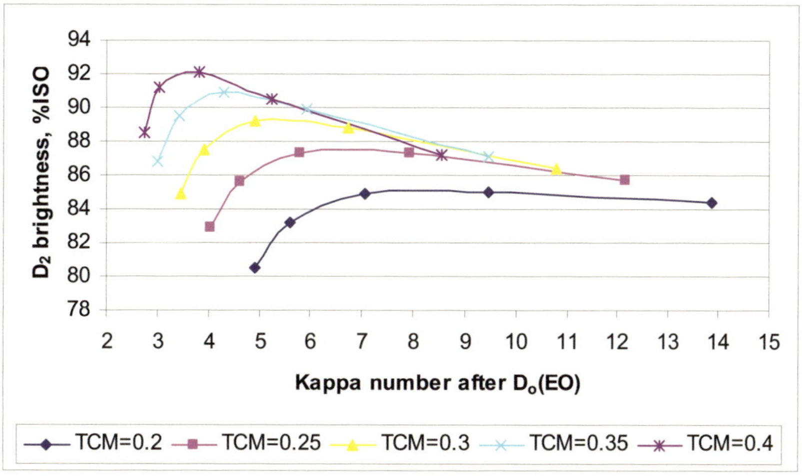

Fig. 14. D(EO)DED sequence optimization; search of an optimal value of kappa number after D_o(EO), at varying TCM. ClO_2 charge ration $D_1/(D_1+D_2) = 66.7$, softwood Kraft pulp of kappa number 30

Similar observations were made for the case of a hardwood Kraft pulp as illustrated in figure 15. In figure 16, it is shown that searching an optimal kappa number after D_o(EO) at constant TCM values depends also on the kappa number of the unbleached pulp. It is shown that the optimal kappa after D_o(EO) is increased with an increase of the unbleached pulp kappa number. Also, it is clear that the lower the unbleached pulp kappa number is, the higher the TCM value should be.

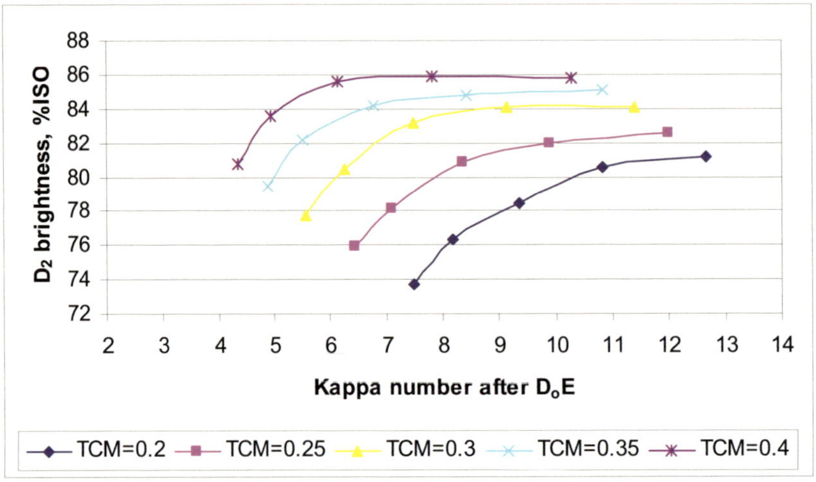

Fig. 15. DEDED sequence optimization; search of an optimal value of kappa number after D_oE, at varying TCM. ClO_2 charge ration $D_1/(D_1+D_2)$ = 66.7, hardwood Kraft pulp of kappa number 15

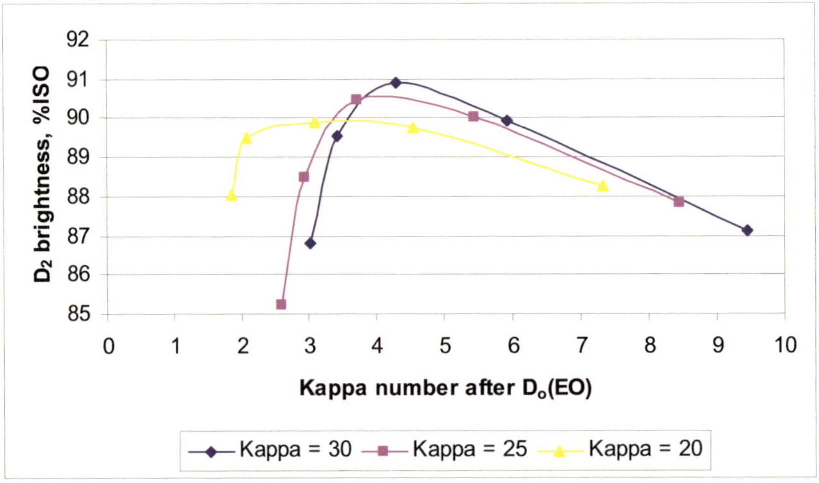

Fig. 16. D(EO)DED sequence optimization; search of an optimal value of kappa number after D_o(EO), for softwood pulps with different unbleached kappa numbers. ClO_2 charge ration $D_1/(D_1+D_2)$ = 66.7. Constant TCM value of 0.35

The conclusion of this study is that the simulator can provide a valuable help for the search of optimized ClO_2 charges to apply in the different stages of an ECF bleaching sequence. The best choices depend on the kappa number of unbleached pulp and on the total ClO_2 charge applied. In all cases studied, the model predicted that the ClO_2 charge in D_o should not be over 55-60% of the total charge, and that the charge in D_1 should be in the range 50-70% of the charge applied for D_1+D_2.

5.2 Optimum pH in first alkali extraction (E_o) stage

Typically extraction stages are not in the focus of optimization activities. They are operated in mills as a part of the process that needs little attention because not much can be gained or lost if conditions are changed. A wide range of conditions is thought to be suitable and applied on industrial scale: Temperature between 70°C and 85°C, residence time between as little as 20 minutes and up to 1.5 hours, a pH between 10 and 12.5. The addition of smaller or higher amounts of oxygen and/or hydrogen peroxide is made sometimes with rather poor evaluation of their effectiveness. Once a stage is in operation, changes are not considered because no impact of any significance is expected.

There is no visible impact of a higher extraction stage temperature on kappa number and brightness within the range of 75°C to 95°C. Results stay identical. Decreasing the retention time from 1.5 h to just 0.5 h similarly had no real impact. Changes are within 0.1 to 0.2 kappa units (Suess & Filho, 2005). However, impact of a higher extraction stage pH can be significant. Despite of a high input of chlorine dioxide, the amount of organic material dissolving is higher in the subsequent E_o stage than in the D_o stage itself. Consequently, the effect achieved in the E_o stage is rather important for the following final bleaching process. As stated above, the amount of potentially extractable material depends on the input of chlorine dioxide in the previous stage. The more oxidation is taking place in the D_o stage, the more oxidized lignin can be solubilized in the E_o stage. Nearly two thirds of the total COD result from the E_o stage.

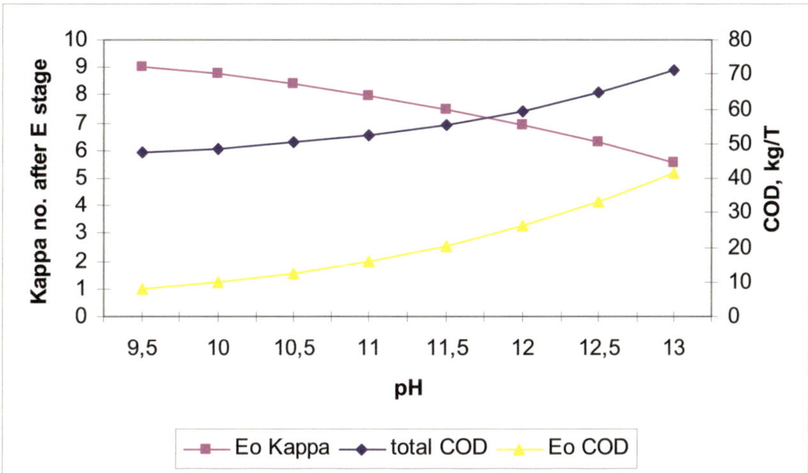

Fig. 17. Effect of E_o stage pH on kappa number and COD released. Conditions as in table 1

Following chlorine dioxide delignification the impact of E stage pH on kappa number and final bleaching are analyzed. A Kraft pulp with an initial kappa number of 25 was used in the study involving the simulation of a conventional ECF bleaching sequence $D_oE_oD_1E_1D_2$ with a total chlorine multiple (TCM) of 0.343 and standard process conditions (table 1). The percentage of total ClO_2 in D_o stage was taken as 64% and two third of rest of ClO_2 was used in D_1 stage. Figure 17 illustrates the final kappa number and COD released in E_o stage at different values of pH used during E_o stage. It can be seen that when the pH is increased the reduction in kappa number is much less as compared to the corresponding increase in COD released. For example, as the pH is increased from 11.5 to 12.5, the kappa number is decreased from 7.49 to 6.27 (a gain of 1.22 units, i.e., 16.3% gain) while the COD released increases from a value of 20.35 kg/t to 33.12 kg/T (an increase of 12.77 kg/t, i.e., 63% increase). Similarly, as shown in figure 18, as the pH is increased from 11.5 to 12.5, the final brightness after D_2 stage is increased from 84.62 %ISO to 85.5 %ISO (a gain of 0.88 units, i.e. about 1% gain) while the total sequence COD released increases from a value of 55.46 kg/t to 64.69 kg/t (an increase of 9.23 kg/t, i.e., about 17% increase). The corresponding resistant COD also increases. Hence, it is clear that higher pH in E_o stage should be evited and a pH between 11 and 12 should be searched for the optimum gain.

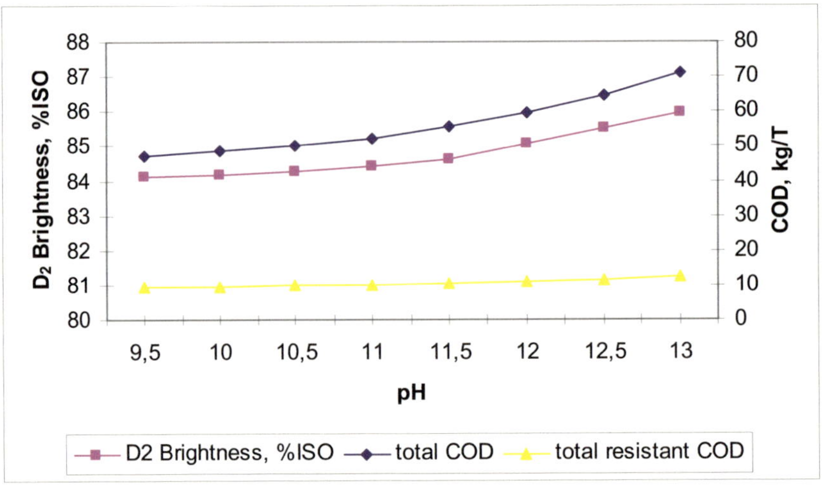

Fig. 18. Effect of E_o stage pH on final sequence brightness and total COD/resistant COD released. Conditions as in table 1

5.3 Gain by addition of O_2 and H_2O_2 in first extraction stages (EO, EP, EOP)

Earlier studies prior to the wide spread adoption of ECF bleaching examined the oxidative reinforced extraction processes with C, (CD) and (DC) delignified Kraft pulps. These studies showed that the addition of oxygen to extraction enhances delignification and occurs within the first few minutes when sufficient oxygen pressure [~0.21 MPa (~30 psig)] is applied (Berry, 1996; Van Lierop et al., 1989a-b, 1986a-b; Berry & Fleming, 1986). Due to these attributes, the (EO) gained wide acceptance as an integral part of Kraft pulp bleach sequences due to its low capital costs to implement and its ability to reduce chemical bleaching cost. Likewise, the use of peroxide in oxidative reinforced extraction ((EP) and (EOP)) is known afford similar enhancements in delignification and brightening capacity (Berry, 1996; Anderson, 1991; Reeve, 1989a-b, 1996c; Basta et al., 1992; Brogdon et al., 2004). Although the cost of peroxide in the past often limited its use in the first extraction stage (Reeve, 1996a), today the costs are more economically attractive to use in optimizing current ECF bleaching processes.

The addition of hydrogen peroxide or oxygen in ECF bleaching sequence $D_oE_oD_1E_1D_2$ aims at a chlorine dioxide demand optimization and an increase of the production. The simulator can provide valuable help to apply such a strategy. This is demonstrated by a scenario for an unbleached softwood Kraft pulp of kappa number of 25 with TCM value of 0.42 in order to search the replacement ratio of kg ClO_2/kg H_2O_2 by optimizing charge in last two chlorine dioxide stages of the sequence through addition of H_2O_2. Table 2 illustrates several final options. As can be seen in table 2, an addition of 1 kg/t H_2O_2 in first extraction stage at optimized ClO_2 charge split between D_1 and D_2 stages resulted in same final D_2 brightness of about 87 %ISO but at reduced total ClO_2 charge and reduced COD generated which is a significant gain. A replacement ratio of 0.66 kg ClO_2/kg H_2O_2 is achieved to reach same target brightness of about 87 %ISO which, depending on pulp and bleaching conditions, can be much higher than this value. Further, at higher charges of H_2O_2, the final brightness of pulp can be improved significantly without necessarily increasing the COD discharge.

ClO_2 in D_o (% Cl)	ClO_2 in D_1 (% Cl)	ClO_2 in D_2 (% Cl)	H_2O_2 in EP (kg/t)	D_2 Brightness (%ISO)	Total COD (kg/t)
6.72	2.52	1.26	0.00	86.97	59.5
6.72	2.52	1.26	0.25	87.13	46
6.72	2.52	1.26	1.00	87.85	50.4
6.72	2.22	1.11	1.00	86.96	50.4
6.72	2.22	1.11	2.00	89.28	55

Table 2. Comparison of several options when H_2O_2 is applied in first extraction stage. Conditions as in table 1

Table 3 demonstrates another example of useful addition of hydrogen peroxide or oxygen in ECF bleaching sequence by comparing three sequences: DEDED, D(EO)DED with application of O_2 in first extraction stage and D(EP)DED with application of H_2O_2 in first extraction stage. It is again evident that significant gain in ClO_2 charge can be achieved by application of O_2 and H_2O_2 to reach same brightness of 89.2 %ISO. However, while comparing the cases of O_2 and H_2O_2 separately, it can be seen that applying O_2 results in higher ClO_2 gain, but at the same time, it results in higher amount of COD and AOX formation for the entire sequence. The very good benefit brought by addition of hydrogen peroxide in first extraction stage, with the net improvement of D_2 stage brightness and rather no effect in COD discharge, a result generally known in mills, confirms further the good predictability of the simulator.

Sequence	Brightness % ISO	COD kg/t	Resistant COD, kg/t	Total ClO_2 charge, %	ClO_2 gain, %	AOX gain, %
DEDED	89.2	57.7	10.2	4.2	-	-
D(EP)DED	89.3	52.4	9.6	3.7	12.6	6.9
D(EO)DED	89.2	72.4	11.3	3.4	19.8	13.8

Table 3. Comparison of sequences when of O_2 or H_2O_2 is applied in first extraction stage. Conditions as in table 1

5.4 Optimum pH in first and second ClO_2 (D_1 and D_2) stages

When chlorine dioxide reacts with pulp, organic and hydrochloric acids are formed and the pH decreases. The rate of pH decrease is extremely high with most of the change occurring in the first 10 minutes of reactions (Wartiovaara, 1982). Sodium hydroxide is added to the pulp before addition of chlorine dioxide to increase the starting and final pH. Earlier studies showed that maximum brightness was achieved over a broad range of pH. However, in these studies, buffer solutions were used so that the pH was constant. A more appropriate simulation of the falling pH during a chlorine dioxide bleaching stage showed the optimal end pH to be in the range 3.5 to 4 (Rapson et al., 1979). Chlorate formation decreases and chlorite formation increases with increasing pH. Although chlorite reacts with pulp when the pH is low (<4), it has been clearly shown that, as the pH increases above 4, its reactivity with pulp drops very rapidly. At a pH greater than 5, chlorite is stable and therefore its potential for bleaching is not realised. Only a small amount of sodium hydroxide is required to achieve a particular end pH. There is, therefore, significant danger in deviating from optimum end pH when improper amounts of NaOH are added or an improper end pH is chosen.

The simulator can provide valuable help to apply such a strategy. For instance, it is shown on the graph of figure 19 that the optimum pH for the D_1 stage is around 3 while that for the D_2 stage is around 4 to achieve maximum gain in brightness when the initial brightness of 55 %ISO and 75 %ISO are used in D_1 and D_2 stages, respectively. It should be noted that this optimum end pH values might vary depending on the type of pulp, initial brightness levels and process conditions used during these stages. The simulator can thus be a handful tool when such variations are taken into account while searching for optimum pH values during these stages.

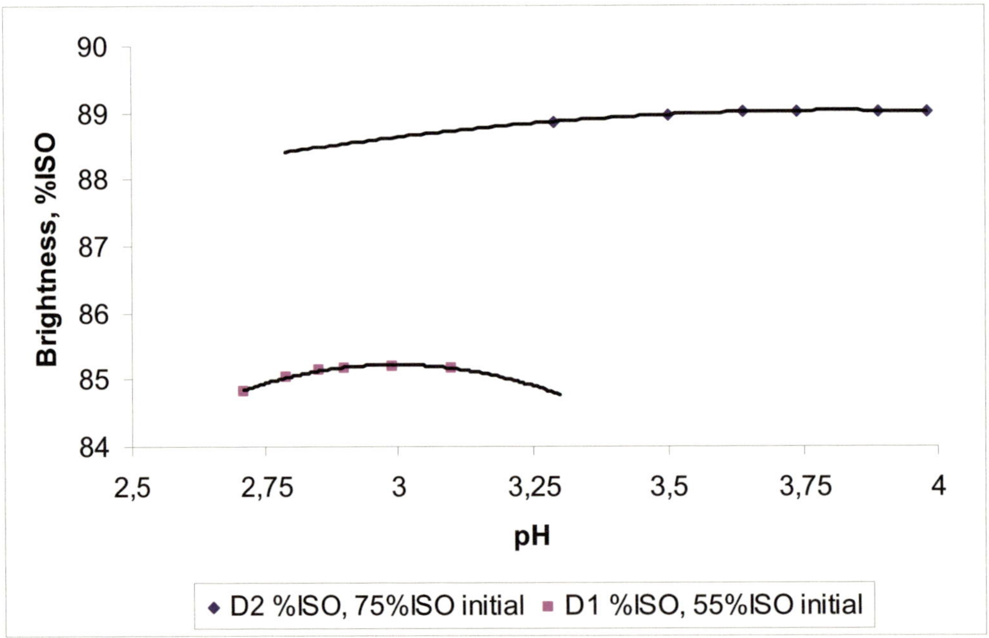

Fig. 19. Optimum pH in D_1 and D_2 stages (softwood Kraft pulp of kappa number 25)

For example in figure 20, it is illustrated that the value of optimum pH changes as initial brightness entering D_1 stage or the ClO_2 charge applied changes. Four cases are discussed for a softwood Kraft pulp of initial kappa number 25 subjected to D(EO)DED bleaching sequence. In the cases with low brightness entering D_1 stage, higher optimum pH values are required as compared to the cases with high brightness entering D_1 stage. Further, as the ClO_2 charge applied increases the required optimum pH values decreases. These observations can be explained by the fact that low entering brightness to D_1 stage corresponds to higher entering kappa number in D_1 stage which means that the pulp is still reactive and maximum oxidation power of ClO_2 can be used in D_1 stage by producing less ClO_2^- and ClO_3^- at high pH and also consuming all ClO_2^- at this pH value. For high entering brightness, i.e., lower entering kappa number in D_1 stage, the pulp reactivity is significantly lower, and thus, a correspondingly lower optimum pH values can be used. Also, as the ClO_2 charge applied increases, the use of maximum oxidation power of ClO_2 is slightly reduced due to higher concentration of ClO_2. Moreover, at higher pH, extraction of lignin degradation products is favoured which is required for the pulp with higher entering kappa number in D_1 stage.

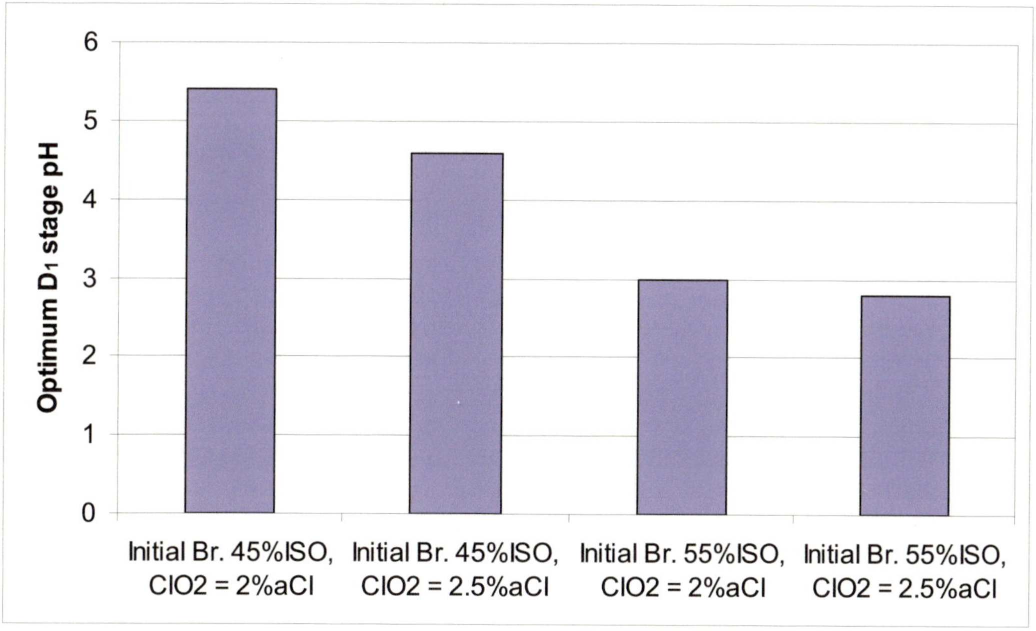

Fig. 20. Optimum pH in D_1 stage at varying initial brightness and ClO_2 charges (softwood Kraft pulp of kappa number 25)

Figure 21 illustrates the final brightness values at different ClO_2 charges for an initial brightness of 55 %ISO and 75 %ISO used in D_1 and D_2 stages, respectively, for the cases when the pH is non-adjusted and the pH is at its optimum value. It can be seen that at low ClO_2 charges, optimum pH is very close to non-adjusted pH and thus the gain from optimizing pH is negligible. On the other hand, at higher ClO_2 charges the gain in brightness at optimum pH can be upto 1 %ISO when compared to non-optimized pH. This can be particularly useful at the end of bleaching for the D_2 stage where a gain of 1 unit of brightness is a significant gain.

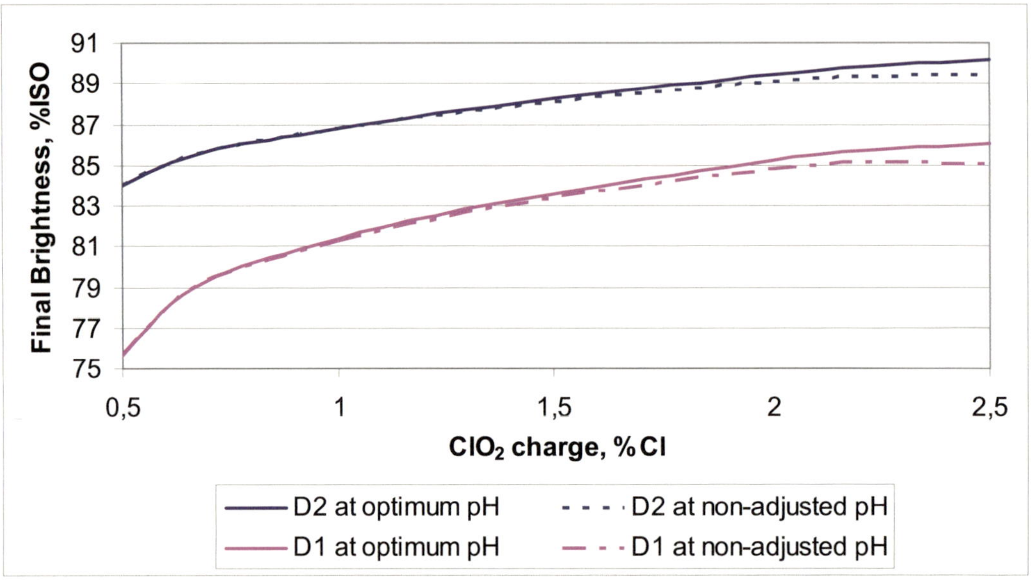

Fig. 21. Gain in brightness at optimum pH in D_1 and D_2 stages (softwood Kraft pulp of kappa number 25)

5.5 ClO_2 gain by reducing the kappa number of the unbleached pulp

Higher kappa number before bleaching would mean higher consumption of bleaching chemicals and an increase in the COD and AOX discharges in bleaching effluent prior to effluent treatment. However, a higher yield is obtained at higher kappa number after cooking. The benefits of optimizing the cooking kappa number as a means of increasing pulp yield has been identified (Lindblad & Lindstrom, 1984, Gullichsen et al., 1999), further investigated (Bjorklund et al., 2002, 2003) and attempted on the commercial scale (Hart & Connell, 2003). Johansson et al. (2005) found that an increase in kappa numbers from 26 to 30 after cooking and from 11 to 13 after being O_2 prebleached allowed an increase in pulp production by 3 ± 1% and reduction in wood consumption by approximately 2.5% However, there was an increase in bleaching costs and increase in COD in the effluents.

Decreasing the kappa number of the stock is an interesting strategy to reduce reactant consumptions and costs during bleaching, provided the yield and quality of the pulp can be preserved. The simulator can provide valuable help to apply such a strategy. For instance, it is shown on the graph of figure 22 which value of TCM should be applied for a softwood pulp when reducing the kappa number from 30 to 25. Two scenarios are presented: the first when a conventional ClO_2 charge is applied in D_o (two thirds of the total charge), and the second when the ClO_2 charge in D_o was optimized for each value of TCM.

In the first case, the simulator predicts an increase of the TCM when decreasing the kappa number to reach the same brightness; for instance, bleaching a softwood pulp of kappa number 30 to 90 %ISO would require a TCM value of 0.36, whereas a pulp of kappa number 25 would require a 0.39 value; this corresponds to a saving of 0.4% ClO_2 on pulp. In the case of an optimized bleaching sequence, the TCM value to apply to reach the same level of brightness can be much reduced (around 0.325 for initial kappa 30 and 0.34 for initial kappa 25). Thus, the ClO_2 saving would be 0.48% ClO_2 on pulp. Therefore, the simulator predicts that it should be possible to optimize cost saving at each change of the stock kappa number. This is an important result to consider for industrial applications.

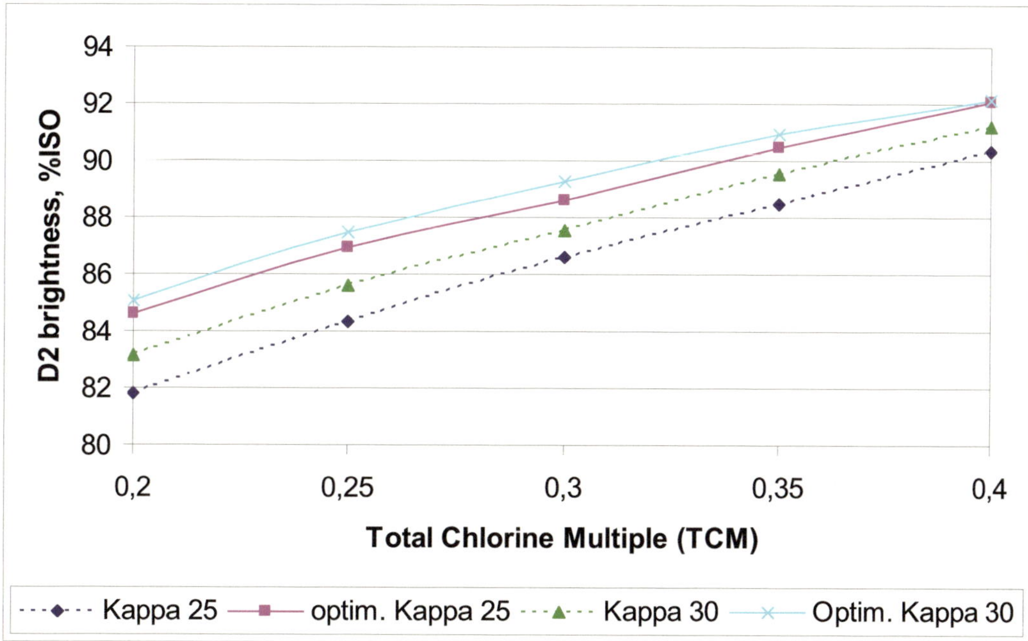

Fig. 22. Predicting ClO_2 charges when stock kappa number is varied for optimal bleaching (optimal charge in D_o at each TCM), conventional bleaching (65% ClO_2 in D_o), (softwood Kraft pulp)

5.6 Comparison of effects of process conditions in different stages

Another useful application of the simulator is demonstrated by comparing the effects of different process conditions on the final bleaching results like brightness and effluent load. According to the specific requirements and possibilities, the choice of necessary process change can be effectuated. To study this, a scenario was taken with a base ECF bleaching sequence of $D_oE_oD_1E_1D_2$ operating at initial kappa number of 25 for softwood Kraft pulp and initial kappa number of 15 for hardwood Kraft pulp and TCM of 0.343. The amount of ClO_2 applied in D_o was chosen at 64%, based on the total ClO_2 applied during the sequence and a ratio of 2/3 of ClO_2 charge in D_1 was applied, based on the total charge (D_1+D_2). The other conditions are shown in table 4. Several cases were considered: increase of temperature in D_o stage, increase of temperature and pH in E_o stage, increase of temperature and time in D_1 and D_2 stages, decrease of ClO_2 applied in D_o stage based on total ClO_2 applied during the sequence and the addition of H_2O_2 in first extraction stage.

	D_o	E_o	D_1	E_1	D_2
ClO_2, % on total	64%	-	24%	-	12%
Temperature, °C	50	60	70	70	70
NaOH,%	-	1%	-	2%	-
pH	-	11	-	12	-
Consistency, %	10	10	10	10	10
Time, min.	60	60	120	60	150

Table 4. Conditions used in comparison of effects of process conditions in different stages

Figure 23 (for softwood) compares the results obtained for each of these cases. It can be seen that for softwood Kraft pulp, an increase in temperature of D_o stage from 50°C to 60°C did not affect significantly the final bleaching results. The final D_2 stage brightness was increased slightly from 84.27 %ISO for base case with D_o stage temperature 50°C to 84.4 %ISO for an increase in D_o stage temperature to 60°C. The total COD (resp., resistant COD) formed in whole sequence was decreased slightly from 50.66 kg/t (resp., 9.81 kg/t) for base case with D_o stage temperature 50°C to 49.28 kg/t (resp., 9.43 kg/t) for an increase in D_o stage temperature to 60°C. Hence, there is no significant gain observed by increasing D_o stage temperature. However, at high temperatures (80-90°C), the gains can be significant. Moreover, it should be noted that the time at which ClO_2 is totally consumed during D_o stage is short which further justifies applying rather low temperatures during this stage.

The next two cases shown in figure 23 are an increase in temperature or an increase in pH of E_o stage from a value of 60°C and 11 to 70°C and 12, respectively. An increase in temperature or pH of E_o stage did not affect significantly the final D_2 stage brightness which increased slightly from 84.27 %ISO for base case with E_o stage temperature 60°C and pH 11 to 84.4 %ISO for an increase in E_o stage temperature to 70°C and to 84.61 %ISO for an increase in E_o stage pH to 12. However, the COD released was significantly increased. The total COD (resp., resistant COD) formed in whole sequence was increased substantially from 50.66 kg/t (resp., 9.81 kg/t) for base case with E_o stage temperature 60°C and pH 11 to 52.39 kg/t (resp., 9.97 kg/t) for an increase in E_o stage temperature to 70°C and 56.68 kg/t (resp., 10.53 kg/t) for an increase in E_o stage pH to 12. This means that conditions in E_o stage should be as mild as possible.

The next cases taken are increase in temperature or an increase in retention time of D_1 stage from a value of 70°C and 120 min. to 80°C and 180 min., respectively. It can be seen that a slightly higher final brightness is obtained for both cases; however, the total COD is unaffected. An increase in temperature or time of D_1 stage increased slightly the final D_2 stage brightness from 84.27 %ISO for base case with D_1 stage temperature 70°C and 120 min. to 85.2 %ISO for an increase in D_1 stage temperature to 80°C and to 85.09 %ISO for an increase in D_1 stage time to 180 min. The total COD (resp., resistant COD) formed in whole sequence remains unaffected at 50.66 kg/t (resp., 9.81 kg/t). Similarly, an increase in temperature or an increase in retention time of D_2 stage from the values of 70°C and 150 min. to 80°C and 180 min., respectively, was studied. It can be seen that these changes did not affect significantly the final bleaching results, a slight increase in final brightness and no significant change in COD released.

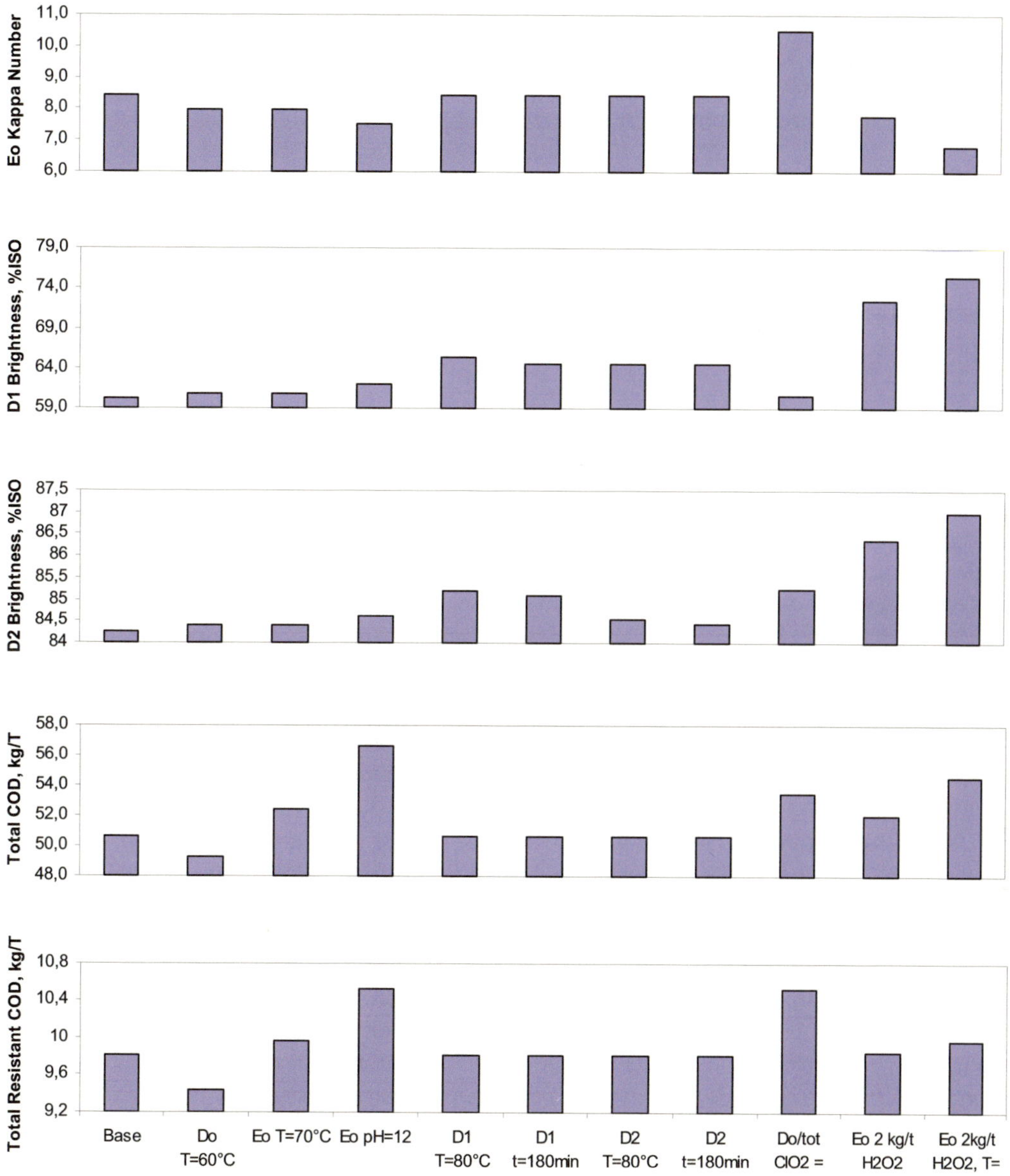

Fig. 23. Comparison of effects of change in process conditions in different stages, softwood Kraft pulp of kappa number 25

In earlier sections we observed that decreasing the percentage of total sequence ClO_2 in D_o stage can give final brightness gain. However, this comes at price of a slight increase in COD released as shown in next case in figure 23. The final D_2 stage brightness was increased slightly from 84.27 %ISO for the base case having D_o stage charge at 64% of total ClO_2 to 85.25 %ISO for a decrease in D_o stage charge to 50% of total ClO_2. The total COD (resp., resistant COD) formed in whole sequence was increased from 50.66 kg/t (resp., 9.81 kg/t) for base case having D_o stage charge at 64% of total ClO_2 to 53.5 kg/t (resp., 10.52 kg/t) for a decrease in D_o stage charge to 50% of total ClO_2.

Finally, the effect of reinforcing E_o stage with H_2O_2 was studied. Two scenarios were taken: first, 2 kg/t of H_2O_2 was applied in E_o stage and second, the E_o stage temperature was increased to 70°C in addition to 2 kg/t H_2O_2 applied. Interestingly, best results are obtained by reinforcing E_o stage with H_2O_2. As can be seen in figure 23, an addition of 2 kg/t H_2O_2 at base temperature of 60°C increased the final D_2 brightness from 84.27 %ISO (base case) to 86.67%ISO which is a significant gain. However, total COD (resp., resistant COD) formed in whole sequence was slightly increased with addition of H_2O_2 from 50.66 kg/t (resp., 9.81 kg/t) for base case to 51.99 kg/t (resp., 9.84 kg/t). An increase of temperature in EP stage from 60°C to 70°C substantially improved the results. The final D_2 brightness was increased from 84.27 %ISO (base case) to 87%ISO which is again a significant gain. However, total COD (resp., resistant COD) formed in whole sequence was increased with addition of H_2O_2 from 50.66 kg/t (resp., 9.81 kg/t) for base case to 54.52 kg/t (resp., 9.97 kg/t). Interestingly, even though the total COD increased with addition of H_2O_2, the value of resistant COD was not significantly affected. This is obvious as the addition of H_2O_2 degrades slightly the cellulose, thereby, increasing the COD value. However, this extra COD coming from cellulose is biodegradable and thus, the values of resistant COD are not much affected.

6. Conclusions

A novel computer-based simulator for the simulations of multistage ECF bleaching sequences was developed. The simulator predicts the variations of kappa number, pH, brightness, bleaching chemical consumption and COD formed at each step of a multistage ECF bleaching sequence. The simulator was based on the new and improved kinetic, stoichiometric and COD predictive models for all chlorine dioxide and extraction stages, developed during the course of research. The steady-state models are directly applicable to the elemental chlorine free bleaching of softwood and hardwood, in general, and with adjustment of its parameters, to the bleaching of pulp made from specific wood species. Multi-purpose applications for this simulator, such as a tool for prediction, decision, diagnosis, process regulation, process optimization or education, were demonstrated through several optimization issues like the optimal splitting of the ClO_2 charge between the different ClO_2 stages (D_o, D_1 and D_2), the impact of extraction stage pH, the use of H_2O_2 and O_2 in first extraction stages (EO, EP, EOP), the optimum end pH or amount of NaOH to be added for a target final pH in D_1 or D_2 stages, the effect of stock kappa number of an unbleached pulp on ClO_2 gain etc. Finally, another useful application of the simulator was established by comparing the effects of different process conditions on the final bleaching results like brightness and effluent load. Several cases were considered for both softwood and hardwood: temperature change in D_o stage, temperature and pH change in E_o stage, temperature and time change in D_1 and D_2 stages, amount of ClO_2 applied in D stages and the addition of H_2O_2 in first extraction stage. The simulator proved to be a useful tool in comparing such effects for eventual process modification and improvement. The results manifested can be effectively used by mill personnel for pollution abatement and process optimization assessments, either when planning new lab studies or when designing new bleach plants or modifying an existing bleach plant.

7. References

Anderson, J.R. (1991). Hydrogen Peroxide Use for Improved Environmental Performance, In: *Bleach Plant Operations Seminar*, TAPPI Press, Atlanta, pp. 149

Basta, J.; Andersson, L.; Blom, C.; Forsström, A.; Wäne, G. & Johansson, N.G. (1992). New and Improved Possibilities in D100 Bleaching, *TAPPI Pulping Conference*, TAPPI Press, Atlanta, pp. 547

Berry, R. & Fleming, B. (1986). Using Oxygen-Alkali Extraction to Simplify the Chlorination Stage, *Journal of Pulp Paper Science*, 12(5), pp. J152

Berry, R. (1996). Oxidative Alkaline Extraction, In: *Pulp Bleaching: Principles and Practice.* C.W. Dence & D.W. Reeve, Eds., TAPPI Press, Atlanta

Bialkowski, W.L. (1990). Bleach Plant process Control, *In: Bleach Plant Operations*, TAPPI Seminar Notes, pp. 189

Bjorklund, M.; Germgard, U.; Jour, P. & Forsstrom, A. (2002). AOX formation in ECF bleaching at different kappa numbers - influence of oxygen delignification and hexenuronic acid content, *Tappi Journal*, 1(7), pp. 20-24

Bjorklund, M.; Germgard, U.; Jour, P. & Forsstrom, A. (2003). TCF & ECF bleaching effluent COD at varying kappa numbers after cooking, *Appita Journal*, 56(3), pp. 200-205

Brogdon, B.; Mancosky, D. & Lucia, L. (2003). New Insights into Lignin Modification During Chorine Dioxide Bleaching Sequences (III): Modifications in (EO) vs. E Stages, *12th Int. Symp. on Wood and Pulping Chem.*, Madison, WI., June 9-12, Vol. 1, pp. 57

Brogdon, B., Mancosky, D. & Lucia, L. (2004a). New Insights into Lignin Modification During Chorine Dioxide Bleaching Sequences (I): Chlorine Dioxide Delignification, *J. Wood Chem. Technol.*, 24(3)

Brogdon, B.; Mancosky, D. & Lucia, L. (2004b). New Insights into Lignin Modification During Chorine Dioxide Bleaching Sequences (II): Modifications in Extraction (E) and Chlorine Dioxide Bleaching (D_1), *J. Wood Chem. Technol.*, 24(3)

Brogdon, B.; Mancosky, D. & Lucia, L. (2004c). New Insights into Lignin Modification During Chorine Dioxide Bleaching Sequences (VI): Modifications in (EP) and (EOP) Stages, and its Impact on D_1 Stages, *TAPPI Fall Conf.*, TAPPI Press, Atlanta

Fletcher, D. E.; Connell, J.D. & Pearson, J. (2000). Optimization of Bleach Plant Chemical Efficiency, *International Pulp Bleaching Conference*, PAPTEC, Montreal, PQ Canada

Gullichsen, J.; Isotalo, I. & Poukka, O. (1999). Optimal delignification degrees of cooking and oxygen/alkali stage in production of ECF bleached softwood kraft, *Pap.Puu*, 81(4), pp. 316

Hart,P. & Connell, D. (2003). The effect of digester Kappa on the bleachability and yield of EMCC softwood pulp", *TAPPI Fall technical conference*, Chicago, USA, 26-30 Oct., Session 41, pp. 11

Jain, S. & Mortha G. (2007). Multistage ECF bleaching sequence simulator, *PAGORA Days*, Grenoble, 16-18 October

Jain S.; Mortha G. & Calais C. (2008a). New and Improved Models for All Stages in Full ECF Bleaching Sequences of Softwoods and Hardwoods, *10th International Conference on Computer Modeling and Simulation (uksim 08)*, IEEE Press, April, pp. 272-277

Jain S.; Mortha G. & Calais C. (2008b). New Predictive Models for COD from All Stages in Full ECF Bleaching Sequences", *10th International Conference on Computer Modeling and Simulation (uksim 08)*, IEEE Press, April, pp. 278-283

Jain S. (2009). Modelling unit operations in the paper pulp production fiberline: Kraft cooking and ECF bleaching sequence, PhD Thesis, Grenoble INP, France

Johansson, B.; Aggarwal, P.; Bjornwall, T.H.; Basta, J. & Forsstrom, A. (2005). High cooking Kappa number for increased pulp production and better pulp quality, *International Pulp Bleaching Conference*, Stockholm, June 14-16, pp. 81

Lindblad, P. & Lindstrom, L. (1984). Optimated oxygen bleaching of sulphate pulp:Kappa number decides the results, *Svensk Papperstidning*, 87(13), pp. 12-15

Mackinnon, J. (1987). Dynamic Simulation of the First Two Stages of a Kraft Softwood Bleach Process, Master's Thesis, McGill Univ.

McDonough, T. (1996). Brightness Development in the Final ClO_2 Stages of an ECF Kraft Pulp Bleaching Sequence: Modeling and Effects of Pulping Conditions, *TAPPI Pulping Conf.*, TAPPI Press, Atlanta, pp. 201

McDonough, T.; Rawat, N. & Turner, M. (1997). ECF Bleachability of Softwood Kraft Pulps Made with Different Effective Alkali Charges, *51st APPITA Annl. Gen. Conf.*, pp. 255

Mortha, G., Lachenal, D. & Chirat, C. (2001). Modeling multistage chlorine dioxide bleaching", *11th International symposium on wood and pulping chemistry*, Nice, France11-14 June, III, pp. 447-451

Rapson, W.H. & Strumila, G.B. (1979). In: *The Bleaching of Pulp* (R.P. Singh Ed.), Tappi Press, Atlanta, pp. 133

Reeve, D.W. (1989a). Brightening Process Variables, In: *Pulp and Paper Manufacturing: Vol. 5. Alkaline Pulping*, M.J. Kocureck, Ser. Ed., 3rd Ed., The Joint Textbook Committee of the Paper Industry, Atlanta

Reeve, D.W. (1989b). Bleaching Chemistry, In: *Pulp and Paper Manufacturing: Vol. 5. Alkaline Pulping*, M.J. Kocureck, Ser. Ed., 3rd Ed., The Joint Textbook Committee of the Paper Industry, Atlanta

Reeve, D.W. (1996a). Introduction to Principles and Practice of Pulp Bleaching, In: *Pulp Bleaching: Principles and Practice*, C.W. Dence & D.W. Reeve, 3rd Eds., Tappi, Atlanta

Reeve, D.W. (1996b). Chlorine Dioxide in Delignification, In: *Pulp Bleaching: Principles and Practice*, C.W. Dence and D.W. Reeve, 3rd Eds., TAPPI Press, Atlanta

Reeve, D.W. (1996c). Chlorine Dioxide in Bleaching Stages, In: *Pulp Bleaching: Principles and Practice,* C.W. Dence and D.W. Reeve, 3rd Eds.; TAPPI Press, Atlanta

Suess, H. U. & Filho, C.L. (2005). ECF Bleaching of Hardwood Pulp: How much effect can be achieved in the E stage, *38th ABTCP annual conference*, São Paulo

Ulinder, J.D. (1992). Fixed Time Zone Methodology for Plug Flow Simulation as Applied to an Oxygen Delignification Reactor, *Proc. Of Control Systems*, Canada, pp. 181

Van Lierop, B.; Liebergott, N.; Teodorescu, G. & Kubes, G. (1989a). Extraction, Part I: Reaction Variables, In: *Bleach Plant Operations Seminar*, TAPPI Press, Atlanta, pp. 45

Van Lierop, B. & Liebergott, N. (1989b). Extraction, Part II: Oxidative Extraction, In: *Bleach Plant Operations Seminar*, TAPPI Press, Atlanta, pp. 52

Van Lierop, B.; Liebergott, N. & Kubes, G. (1986a). Pressure in an Oxidative Extraction Stage of a Bleach Sequence, *Tappi J.*, 69(5), pp. 75

Van Lierop, B.; Liebergott, N.; Teodorescu, G. & Kubes, G. (1986b). Using Oxygen in the First Extraction Stage of a Bleach Sequence, *J. Pulp Paper Sci.*, 12(5), pp. J133

Wartiovaara, I. (1982). The influence of pH on the D_1 stage of a D/CED_1 bleaching sequence, *Paperi ja Puu – paper och Tra*, N°9, pp. 534-545

18

A Lattice Gas Approach to the Mexico City Wind Field Estimation Problem

Alejandro Salcido and Ana Teresa Celada Murillo
Instituto de Investigaciones Eléctricas, División de Energías Alternas
México

1. Introduction

Although in 1992 the United Nations Environment Programme and the World Health Organization included Mexico City among the megacities with the worst air pollution problems (UNEP & WHO, 1992), the environmental actions carried out by the local governments of the Mexico City Metropolitan Area (MCMA) in the following fifteen years, particularly in the period 2000-2006, produced very important reductions in the emissions of air pollutants. Emission reductions around 86% in sulphur dioxide (SO_2), 60% in carbon monoxide (CO), 30% in nitrogen oxides (NO_x), 50% in PM_{10} (particulate matter < 10 μm in diameter), and 40% in volatile organic compounds (VOC), were reported for the years 1990-2006 in the official emission inventory (SMA-GDF, 2008). Nevertheless, nowadays, close to 1.8 megatons of CO, 187 kilotons of NOx, 6 kilotons of SO_2, 21 kilotons of PM_{10}, and 512 kilotons of VOC are still being produced in the MCMA and released to its ambient atmosphere every year (SMA-GDF, 2008). The critical air pollutants in MCMA are ozone (O_3), PM_{10} and $PM_{2.5}$ with concentrations above their daily and annual US air quality standards (Bravo & Torres, 2002). Ozone, however, is by far the most important air pollutant because of the frequency of occurrence of high levels, persistence, and spatial distribution (Bravo & Torres, 2002; Bonner et al., 1998; Osornio-Vargas et al., 2006).

Besides the emissions, however, other very important factors, such as the geographical setting, the topography, the meteorology, and the properties of the urban surface, and their possible interactions, must be taken into account in the analyses to understand properly the complexity and gravity of the MCMA air pollution problem. The MCMA is situated inside a subtropical basin (19.0-20.0 °N, 98.5-99.5 °W) which extends over an area of 60 x 60 km^2, approximately, and has an average altitude of 2240 m. As it is shown in Figure 1, the MCMA is surrounded by high mountains on three sides: west, south and east. To the west and south are the *Sierra Las Cruces* and the *Sierra Ajusco-Chichinautzin* (which its highest point is the peak *Cruz del Marques* in the volcano *Ajusco*, with an altitude of 3937 m). To the east, starting with the *Sierra Santa Catarina*, there is a north-south barrier consisting of three peaks, with the volcanoes *Iztaccihuatl* and *Popocatepetl* reaching elevations of 5222 and 5465 meters above sea level (masl), respectively. At the southeast corner of the MCMA basin the terrain falls, creating a low-lying gap through the mountains. To the north, the basin extends into the Mexican plateau and the arid interior of the country, with the *Sierra de Guadalupe* creating a small 800 m barrier above the basin floor. Its climate, otherwise, is usually classified into two seasons: the rainy season from May to October, and the dry season from November to April. This classification stems from the two main meteorological patterns on the synoptic scale: dry westerly winds with anticyclonic conditions from November until April, and moist flows from the East due to the weaker trade winds along the other six months. Very often, however, the meteorology at the MCMA is more complex than this simple classification. Important interactions of the basin with the Mexican plateau and the lower coastal areas may occur. Moreover, due to the MCMA location, large-scale pressure gradients are generally weak, and a very strong solar radiation is registered there throughout the year. In 2001, the MCMA global solar radiation ranged 150-300 W/m^2 in average, with maximum values from 800 to 1100 W/m^2; and wind speeds from 2 to 3 m/s were observed at urban sites, and from 3 to 4 m/s in suburban areas, in average (Salcido et al, 2003a). These conditions, combined with the surrounding mountains, are ideal for the development of thermally driven winds, including upslope, downslope, and heat island winds.

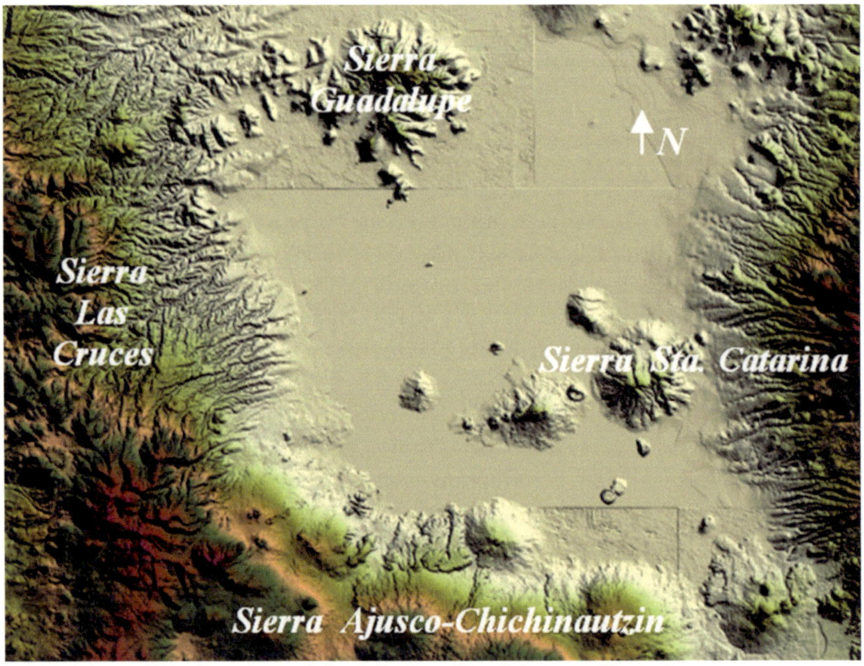

Fig. 1. Main topographic features of the Mexico City Metropolitan Area

The knowledge of the wind circulation events and their possible organization in patterns constitute an important issue to understand how the emissions of air pollutants may be dispersed in an urban settlement and how its air pollution may be exported towards the neighboring sites. Although the MCMA is surrounded by high mountains and it may lead to the trapping of air pollution up to for several days, it is also frequent that the mixing height may reach values higher than 2600 m above ground level (Salcido et al, 2003b), and these conditions favor exportation of air pollution from the MCMA to its surroundings (Castro & Salcido, 2006). On another hand, because the changes in the urban design and the spatial distribution of the built can affect the surface wind circulation in the cities, the short and long term evolution of the urban wind patterns are relevant also for urban bioclimatic studies. Nowadays, this is also a particularly important issue in relation with the MCMA air pollution problem because in the last seven years the urban morphology was changed significantly by the construction of a second traffic floor above the Periferico freeway (a primary via which surrounds the city from north to south) and by an explosive growing of the number of the skyscrapers and other big buildings in the city. These all are wind field applications that belong to the meso-γ scale or turbulence scale meteorology problems.

The theoretical basis of meteorology is in the Navier –Stokes equations, which constitute a system of coupled and non-linear partial differential equations. For small velocities, these equations can be linearised and solved without much difficulty, analytically if the solid boundaries involved are simple, and numerically otherwise. However, when air flow velocities are large, instabilities may appear and exact analytical methods can no longer be used. Even numerical methods are difficult to use, chiefly because scales of different sizes must be taken into account, which forces grids either to be very small or variable.

In practice, a lot of powerful computer simulation tools for diagnostic and prognostic purposes, ordinarily known as meteorological models, have been developed (and still are being developed) to find out the wind fields and other meteorological variables for a variety of applications. A diagnostic model simply provides an estimate of a steady state condition because it contains no time-tendency terms, includes little physics in its calculations and provides meteorological fields derived by appropriate interpolation and extrapolation of available data. A prognostic model, instead, does incorporate meteorology physics and can be used to forecast the space-time evolution of the system by numerical integration of time-dependent differential equations. However, the numerical solutions depend strongly on boundary conditions and initial values; so that special care must be taken to correctly initialise all meteorological variables in the computational domain and to correctly define the time-varying physics at the boundaries. Two excellent prognostic meteorological models are the PSU/NCAR mesoscale model (known as MM5) and the Weather Research and Forecasting (WRF) model. These two models are complex and heavy numerical simulation instruments adequate only for mesoscale meteorology problems (MM5, 2003).

A quite different strategy to simulate fluid behaviour has been developed in the last two decades using the cellular automata techniques introduced by John von Neumann and Stanislaw Ulam in the early 1950s (von Neumann, 1966). Fully discrete models obeying cellular automata rules have been developed for the microscopic motion of the particles of a gas, such that the coarse-grained behaviour (in the thermodynamic limit) lies in the same universality class as the fluid flow phenomenon. This class of dynamical systems, known as lattice gas models, consist of a regular lattice, each site of which can have a finite number of states representing the directions of motion of the gas particles, and evolves in discrete time steps obeying a set of homogeneous local rules which define the system dynamics. These rules must be defined in such a way that the physical laws of conservation of mass, momentum and energy are fulfilled during the propagation and collisions of the gas particles (Boghosian, 1999). Typically, only the nearest neighbours are involved in the updating of any lattice site.

The first attempt along these lines was undertaken by Leo P. Kadanoff and Jack Swift in 1968 (Kadanoff & Swift, 1968). The Kadanoff-Swift model exhibits many features of real fluids, such as sound-wave propagation, and long-time tails in velocity autocorrelation functions. As the authors noted, however, it does not faithfully reproduce the correct motion of a viscous fluid (Boghosian, 1999). The next advance in the lattice modelling of fluids came in the mid 1970's, when J. Hardy, O. de Pazzis and Y. Pomeau introduced a new lattice model (the HPP model, named for its authors) with a number of innovations that warrant discussion here (Hardy et al, 1973; Hardy et al., 1976). Like the Kadanoff-Swift model, the HPP model gives rise to anisotropic hydrodynamic equations that are not invariant under a global spatial rotation. At the time, this was not considered a problem, since the real purpose of these models was to study the statistical physics of fluids, and both models could do this well. Traditional computational fluid dynamicists, however, were not inclined to take notice of this as a serious numerical method unless and until a way was found to remove the unphysical anisotropy (Boghosian, 1999). Thirteen years passed from the introduction of the HPP model to the solution of the anisotropy problem in 1986 by Uriel Frisch, Brosl Hasslacher and Yves Pomeau (Frish et al, 1986), and simultaneously by Stephen Wolfram (Wolfram, 1986). Frisch, Hasslacher and Pomeau demonstrated that it is possible to simulate the Navier-Stokes equations of fluid flows by using a cellular automaton of gas particles on a hexagonal lattice, with extremely simple translation and collision rules governing the movement of the particles. In the FHP model, named after the authors of the first reference given above, all the particles have unit mass and move with the same speed hopping from site to site in a hexagonal two-dimensional lattice. The dynamics of this system involves a set of collision rules such that momentum and particle number are conserved (kinetic energy is trivially conserved). From a strict theoretical point of view, it is not clear at the present time if the lattice gas collective equations are equivalent to the Navier-Stokes equations, or if they include them as a particular case. However, there has been a growing interest in studying the viscous fluid flow using lattice gas models due to its great facility to handle complex boundary and initial conditions, and also because the computer simulations have shown that lattice gases behave like normal fluids under some restricted conditions (Hasslacher, 1987; Salcido & Rechtman, 1991, 1993; Rechtman & Salcido, 1996; Salcido, 1993, 1994). The FHP model, in particular, is now considered as an efficient way to simulate viscous flows at moderate Mach numbers in situations involving complex boundaries. However, it is unable to represent thermal or diffusional effects since all particles have the same speed and are of the same nature (Chen et al., 1989). Maybe the simplest lattice gas with thermal properties is a nine-velocities model defined on a square two-dimensional lattice where particles may be at rest or travelling to their nearest or next nearest neighbours (Chen et al., 1989; Rechtman et al., 1990, 1992; Salcido & Rechtman, 1991, 1993; Rechtman & Salcido, 1996).

One of the first attempts to use a lattice gas as an alternative approach in air pollution modelling applications can be found in the work by A. Salcido (Salcido, 1993, 1994; Salcido et al., 1993). There, it is shown how the lattice gas rules, in spite of their relative simplicity, are sufficient to simulate, at least qualitatively, some complex processes affecting unsteady dispersion, including momentum exchange with the surrounding atmosphere and deposition. More recent attempts are found in the work by A. Sciarretta and R. Cipollone (Sciarretta & Cipollone, 2001, 2002; Sciarretta 2006), where a comprehensive stochastic lattice gas model, which provides also reliable quantitative predictions, is presented.

In this work we describe and apply a two-dimensional (2D) lattice gas approach to estimate the MCMA surface wind field from the hourly meteorological data registered at the stations of the official atmospheric monitoring network. This approach is based on the simplest lattice gas with thermal properties. It is a square lattice gas model with interactions up to

second nearest neighbours that conserve the number of particles, momentum and kinetic energy. Within this framework, the best wind field estimate is given by the steady state lattice gas flow which is consistent with the wind velocity values imposed to a number of control lattice sites representing the positions of the meteorological stations, and with a number of forbidden lattice sites that represent the solid boundaries defined by the MCMA topography. The application to the MCMA study case was carried out for the meteorological conditions which prevailed there during the 1994 summertime. As a first step, a model wind direction state, which reflects in a discrete and simplified way the main features of the complex spatial structure of the surface wind circulation events, is used to obtain the density of states of wind direction of the MCMA, as well as a qualitative and quantitative identification of the main wind circulation patterns for daytime and nighttime hours of the dry and rainy seasons of 1994. This first analysis phase helped us to select the particular (but important) daytime and nighttime MCMA wind circulation events which we considered as study cases for the lattice gas simulation of the respective wind fields. The computer simulations were carried out using wind velocity data obtained during a four-site micrometeorological campaign we carried out in Mexico City during the 1994 summertime. The results were compared against the wind data registered by the stations of the official atmospheric monitoring network of Mexico City. A previous description of these results was reported by A. Salcido, A. T. Celada and T. Castro in 2008 (Salcido et al., 2008).
The rest of this chapter is organized as follows: Section 2 is dedicated to describe the basis of the nine-velocity lattice gas model, its equilibrium theory, and some of the simulations we have carried out to test the hydrodynamic behavior of this model. In Section 3, the lattice gas approach we are proposing for the wind field estimation problem is detailed. In Section 4, the characterization of the MCMA wind circulation events that prevailed there in 1994 is presented in terms of the density of states of wind direction and the main wind circulation patterns that can be identified by means of parameters such as the mean wind direction, the vorticity and the divergence of the MCMA wind direction states. In Section 5, it is described and discussed the application of the lattice gas model in estimating the MCMA wind field for some particular wind circulation events which occurred at both daytime and nighttime hours of the 1994 summertime, as well as the comparison of the simulation results against wind velocity data registered at the stations of the official atmospheric network of Mexico City. Finally, it is included a section devoted to conclusions and suggestions for future work.

2. The Nine-Velocity Lattice Gas Model

We will consider a cellular automaton defined on a square 2D lattice containing N_X times N_Y sites. The state at any lattice site **r** indicates the presence or absence of particles travelling in nine allowed directions defined by the vectors:

$$\mathbf{e}_\alpha = \begin{cases} 0 & \alpha = 0 \\ \cos((\alpha-1)\frac{\pi}{4})\mathbf{u}_1 + \sin((\alpha-1)\frac{\pi}{4})\mathbf{u}_2 & \alpha = 1,\ldots,8 \end{cases} \tag{1}$$

where $\mathbf{u}_1$ and $\mathbf{u}_2$ are unit vectors along the positive directions of X and Y axes, respectively. The time step and the lattice step along the axes are both defined as unit. The allowed particle speeds c_α and kinetic energies ε_α (assuming particles of unit mass) are defined by

$$c_\alpha = \begin{cases} 0 & \alpha = 0 \\ 1 & \alpha = 1,3,5,7 \\ \sqrt{2} & \alpha = 2,4,6,8 \end{cases} \tag{2}$$

$$\varepsilon_\alpha = \frac{c_\alpha^2}{2} = \begin{cases} 0 & \alpha = 0 \\ \frac{1}{2} & \alpha = 1,3,5,7 \\ 1 & \alpha = 2,4,6,8 \end{cases} \tag{3}$$

This means that the model only takes into account particle interactions to the nearest and the next nearest neighbours. An exclusion principle is obeyed by the lattice gas particles in the sense that at any site **r** and at any time t there can be no more than one particle moving in each of the allowed directions $\mathbf{e}_\alpha$. This exclusion principle has deep consequences on the collective (or macroscopic) behaviour of the model.
The state $S(\mathbf{r},t)$ at any lattice site **r** at any time t is given by a set of nine Boolean fields, $S_\alpha(\mathbf{r},t)$. Each one of these field variables takes the value 1 (0) in the presence (absence) of a particle traveling in direction α at site **r** and time t. The time evolution of the model is defined by a set of, at least, three homogeneous local operators, **T**, **C** and **B**, that represent the translation of particles, the collision between particles, and the collision of particles against fixed obstacles or solid boundaries, respectively. Formally, this can be expressed as

$$S(\mathbf{r},t+1) = \mathbf{B} \circ \mathbf{C} \circ \mathbf{T}\left(\left\{ S(\mathbf{r}',t) \,\middle|\, \mathbf{r}' \in V_r \right\}\right) \tag{4}$$

where V_r denotes the neighborhood of site **r** that contains the site itself, and its nearest and next nearest neighbors. As it is illustrated in Figure 2, the translation operator **T** explores all the sites in the neighborhood and moves the particles pointing towards the central site to it. These particles form the input state for the collision operator **C** and the output is some other state that has the same number of particles, momentum and energy. The nontrivial collisions of two and three particles are shown schematically in Figure 3 where an open circle indicates a particle at rest and each entry represents all its possible rotations. For each entry, any state may be chosen as the input of the collision and the remaining states are the possible outputs. Although Figure 3 shows only the nontrivial two and three particle collisions, the evolution of the automaton takes into account all particle collisions that can occur involving up to 9 particles. The translation and collision operators define the lattice gas microdynamics and are applied synchronously to all the sites of the lattice. The obstacle operator takes into account boundary conditions and the presence of obstacles. A particle that collides with an obstacle may invert its direction (to simulate, on the collective level, a no-slip condition) or may be reflected (to simulate now a slip condition). Other operators can be introduced to simulate effects due to heating or gravitational forcing (Rechtman et al., 1990; Salcido & Rechtman, 1991). The heating operator, for example, attempts to simulate a heat exchange between the system and its surroundings in such a way that the average energy of the system assumes a given value. A simple implementation of the heating operator is as follows. After the action of the translation, collision and obstacle operators a

small percentage of sites is chosen at random, the average energy is calculated and compared with a given energy control value. If the average energy takes a value greater (smaller) than the control energy, a new state is assigned to each of the chosen sites that has the same number of particles but smaller (greater) energy.
In spite of the simplicity of the rules that define the microdynamics of this model, the computer simulations show that at the collective level it behaves very similar to a real gas under certain conditions, but also can have a non classical behavior under other conditions.
In the next two subsections, we present first the equilibrium theory of the 9-velocity lattice gas model and later some few computer simulations we carried out to test its hydrodynamic behavior, both qualitatively and quantitatively.

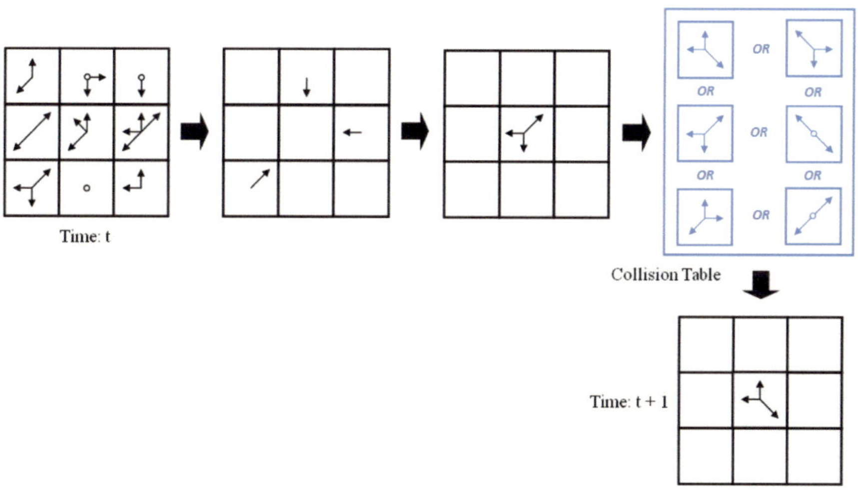

Fig. 2. The propagation and collision of the lattice gas particles.

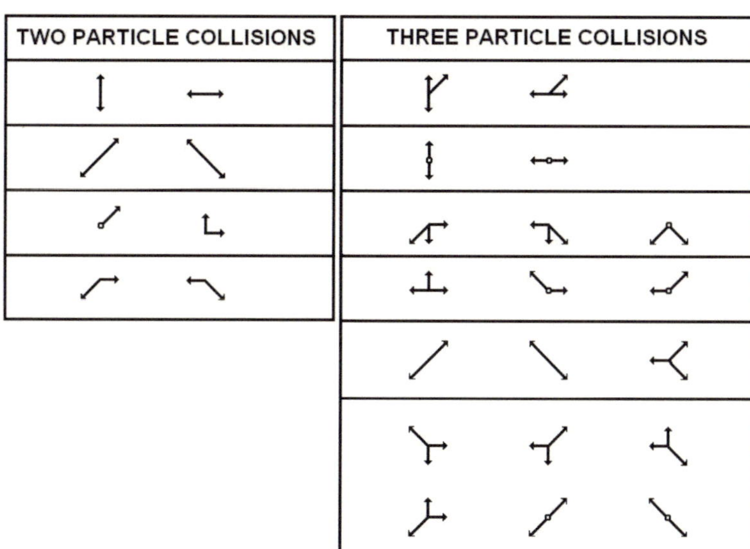

Fig. 3. Collisions involving two and three particles.

2.1 Equilibrium Properties

Let n, e and n_α denote the average number of particles per site, the average energy per site, and the average number of particles per site moving in direction $\mathbf{e}_\alpha$ at site $\mathbf{r}$ and at time t, respectively. Then

$$n = \sum_\alpha n_\alpha \tag{5}$$

$$e = \sum_\alpha n_\alpha \varepsilon_\alpha \tag{6}$$

Due to the exclusion principle there are a lower bound ($e_{\min}$) and an upper bound ($e_{\max}$) on the energy per site e which depend on the average number of particles per site n as follows:

$$e_{\min} = \begin{cases} 0 & 0 \le n < 1 \\ \dfrac{n-1}{2} & 1 \le n < 5 \\ n-3 & 5 \le n \le 9 \end{cases} \tag{7}$$

$$e_{\max} = \begin{cases} n & 0 \le n < 4 \\ \dfrac{n+4}{2} & 4 \le n < 8 \\ 6 & 8 \le n \le 9 \end{cases} \tag{8}$$

The graphs of these functions are shown in Figure 4. The area between the two curves represents the set of the allowed states (n, e) of the model.

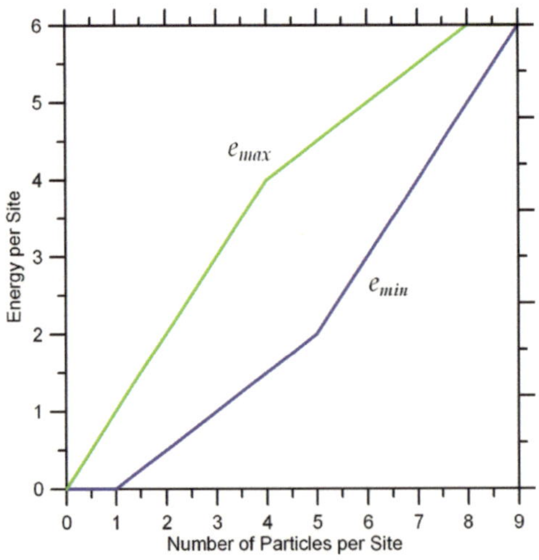

Fig. 4. Minimum and maximum allowed energies.

Now, following the microcanonical equilibrium statistical mechanics, the equilibrium thermodynamic properties can be obtained from the distribution densities $\tilde{n}_\alpha$ that maximize the entropy per site of the system (Salcido & Rechman, 1991)

$$s = -k\sum_{\alpha}\left[n_\alpha \ln n_\alpha + (1-n_\alpha)\ln(1-n_\alpha)\right] \tag{9}$$

under the constraints imposed by the equations (5) and (6). In this equation k is the Boltzmann constant, which hereafter will be considered equal to 1, for simplicity. By employing the method of undetermined Lagrange multipliers, the distribution densities $\tilde{n}_\alpha$ of the equilibrium states are obtained:

$$\tilde{n}_\alpha = \frac{1}{1+e^{(a+b\varepsilon_\alpha)}} \tag{10}$$

where a and b are the Lagrange multipliers. Now, to get some insight about the physical meaning of the Lagrange multipliers a and b, we note that, using equations (10), the entropy can be written as

$$s = an + be - \sum_{\alpha}\ln(1-\tilde{n}_\alpha) \tag{11}$$

Then, a formal comparison of this equation with the well known Euler equation of thermodynamics for a gas of particles,

$$s = -\frac{\mu}{T}n + \frac{1}{T}e + \frac{P}{T} \tag{12}$$

suggests the following thermodynamic-like interpretation:

$$\begin{aligned} a &= -\frac{\mu}{T} \\ b &= \frac{1}{T} \\ \frac{P}{T} &= -\sum_{\alpha}\ln(1-\tilde{n}_\alpha) \end{aligned} \tag{13}$$

In the Euler equation (12), s is the entropy per unit volume, n is the density of the number of particles, T is the temperature, μ is the chemical potential, e is the internal energy per unit volume, and P is the pressure.

Strictly speaking, the first two equations (13) just define the new parameters T and μ in terms of the Lagrange multipliers a and b, and the last one defines P. However, the use of these properties, which we will call temperature (T), chemical potential (μ), and pressure (P)

of the lattice gas, opens a useful framework for the physical analysis and interpretation of lattice gas behavior. In terms of the temperature and chemical potential, the distribution densities $\tilde{n}_\alpha$ of the equilibrium states can be expressed as

$$\tilde{n}_\alpha = \frac{1}{1+e^{(\varepsilon_\alpha - \mu)/T}} \tag{14}$$

So, at equilibrium the lattice gas particles will organize themselves among the possible velocities according to a Fermi-Dirac distribution. This is a consequence of the exclusion principle that must be obeyed by the lattice gas particles. Under equilibrium conditions, as it is implied also by equation (14), the same number of particles moves along each diagonal direction and also along the vertical and horizontal ones:

$$\tilde{n}_1 = \tilde{n}_3 = \tilde{n}_5 = \tilde{n}_7 \qquad \tilde{n}_2 = \tilde{n}_4 = \tilde{n}_6 = \tilde{n}_8 \tag{15}$$

These theoretical results agree with the computer simulations we performed to test the equilibrium properties of the model. We started with a 200 x 100 sites lattice and particles tossed at random in position and direction of motion keeping the average number of particles per site n fixed. With a heating operator, the lattice gas was cooled or heated for 500 time steps to fix its energy to a given control value and then left to equilibrate for another 500 time steps. Finally the experimental distributions densities were computed. In Figure 5, the plots for the theoretical equilibrium distribution densities $\tilde{n}_0$, $\tilde{n}_1$, and $\tilde{n}_2$, including the corresponding simulation results, are presented for $n = 1$ and $n = 3$. This figure shows also that a population inversion takes place in the high energy limit.

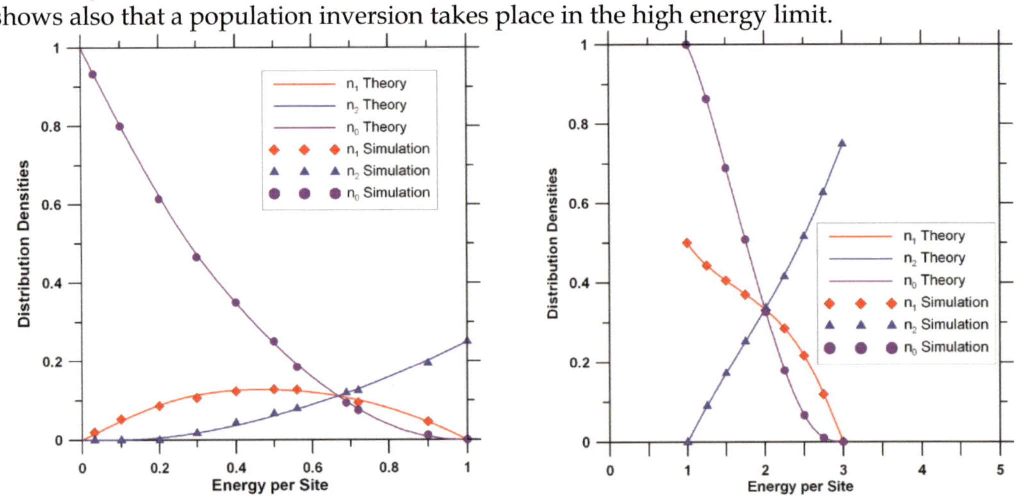

$n = 1$ $n = 3$

Fig. 5. Comparison of the theoretical and experimental (simulated) equilibrium distribution densities for average numbers of particles $n = 1$ ($e_{min} = 0$ and $e_{max} = 1$) and $n = 3$ ($e_{min} = 1$ and $e_{max} = 3$).

In figures 6, the plots for the entropy per site (Fig. 6a), the temperature (Fig. 6b), the pressure (Fig. 6c), and the chemical potential (Fig. 6d), as functions of the energy per site *e*, for a number of particles per site *n* = *1*, are presented.

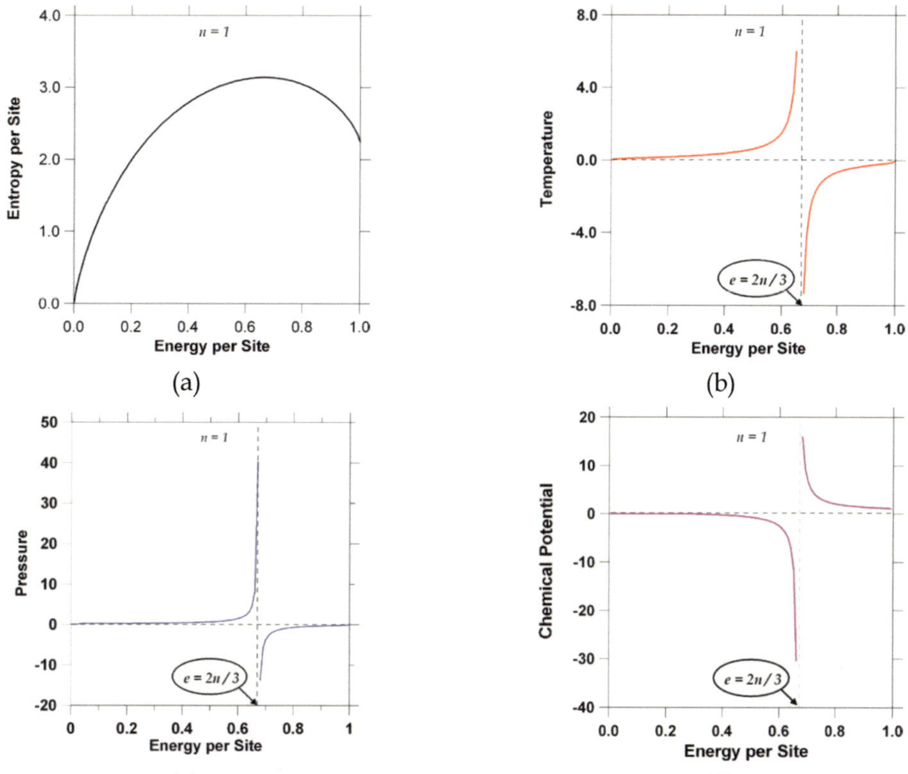

Fig. 6. (a) entropy per site, (b) temperature, (c) pressure, and (d) chemical potential, them all plotted as functions of the energy per site, for *n* = *1*.

This figures show that the thermodynamic properties of the lattice gas models have non-classical behaviors. Temperature and pressure, in particular, can assume positive and negative values with an infinite discontinuity at the energy *e* = *(2/3)n*. This is a consequence of the exclusion principle and of the finite nature of the energy spectrum in these systems. However, it is worth to mention that, in spite of this non classical behavior, for small values of *n* (that is, in the low density limit) the relation between pressure and temperature can be written as the state equation of an ideal gas:

$$P = -T\sum_{\alpha} \ln(1-n_{\alpha}) \xrightarrow[n\to 0]{} P = nT \tag{16}$$

This result is an indication that, under restricted conditions, the lattice gas may be useful as a model of a classical gas. Other equilibrium thermodynamic properties, such as the specific heat and compressibility, can also be computed from the equilibrium distribution densities.

2.2 Qualitative Hydrodynamic Behavior of the 9-Velocity Lattice Gas

Here we present the results of three different computer simulations we carried out to test the hydrodynamic behavior of the 9-velocity lattice gas model at a qualitative level. The first two simulations show that the model gas behaves as expected in flows past fixed obstacles, and the last one tests the model ability to simulate wave phenomena.

Simulation of flows past fixed obstacles. Figures 7 show the sequences of velocity field sketches obtained from the simulation of the flow past a solid bar (left) and a wedge (right), respectively. A lattice with 300 x 200 sites was used. No gravity neither heating effects were considered. We imposed a flow by initially putting particles at random in the upwards directions ($\mathbf{e}_0$, $\mathbf{e}_1$, and $\mathbf{e}_2$) with an average number of particles per site n = 2.7. Particles leaving the top row were introduced in the bottom row randomly but moving upwards. The obstacle operator was defined in the other vertical sides of the lattice and on the obstacle boundary in order to simulate a no-slip condition at the collective level. Both sequences correspond to 2000 time steps of the automaton evolution. Each velocity field was constructed from the experimental distribution functions defined as averages over cells containing 7x7 lattice sites. The left hand sequence shows two vortexes opposite to each other growing past a horizontal bar as time proceeds, such as it is expected for this flow for Reynolds numbers within a certain range. Note also the fluid velocity goes to zero on solid boundaries. In the sequence of the flow past the wedge, it is interesting to observe how the presence of solid wall at right side of the channel forces the development of an adjacent vortex although no obstacle is located there. It would not occur if the system could extend infinitely in the horizontal direction.

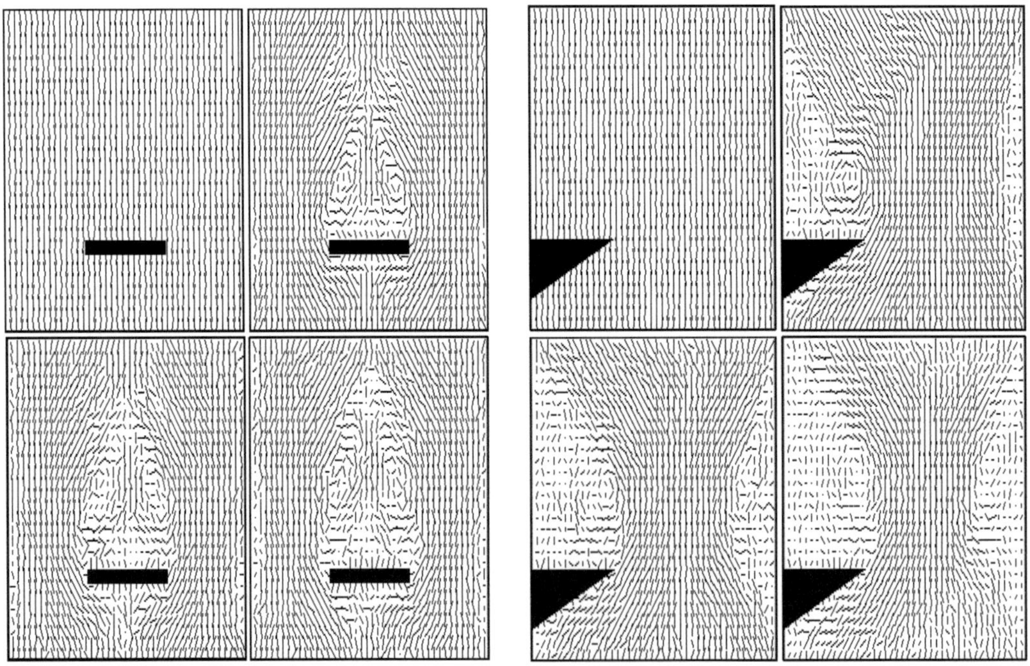

Fig. 7. Lattice gas simulation of the flow past a horizontal bar (left) and a wedge (right), along a vertical channel. No gravity neither heating effects were included.

Simulation of wave phenomena. Figure 8 shows a sequence of the development of a density wave in a closed square box starting from an initial condition where the gas density is uniform everywhere with exception of a centred empty circular hole. A 200 x 200 sites lattice with periodic boundary conditions was used for the computer simulations and no gravity neither heating effects were considered. The gas particles were tossed at random in position and direction of motion keeping an average number of particles per site $n = 2$. Then all the particles located inside a centered circle of given radius were deleted to simulate an empty hole (that is, an initial density perturbation), and the system was allowed to evolve during a number of time steps that was large enough to record the density wave patterns of a full period, at least. As it can be observed, the sequence of density patterns resembles very strongly the wave phenomena which take place in a real gas system.

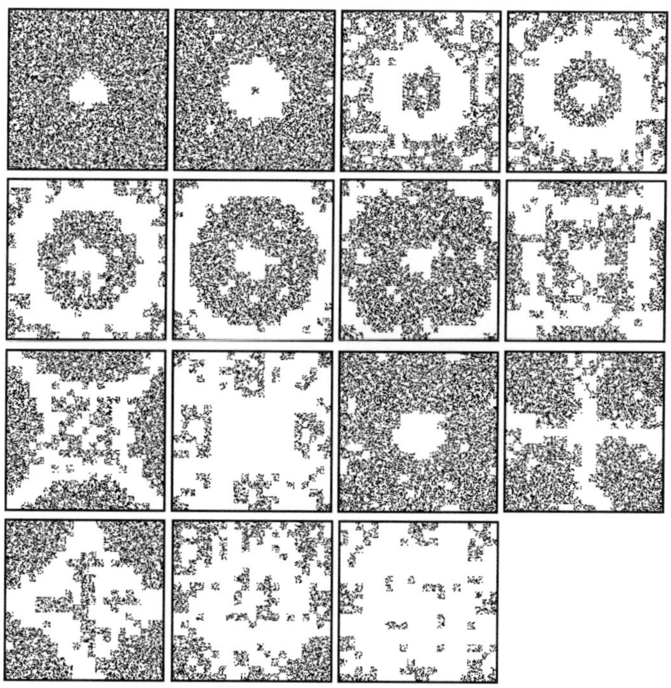

Fig. 8. Lattice gas simulation of a density wave. Initial state: uniform gas with a centred hole (empty) contained in a square box.

2.3 Simulation of Viscous Flows

We have performed two different computer simulations to carry out a simple comparison the 9-velocity lattice gas behaviour against the solutions of the Navier-Stokes equations for the well known Poiseuille and Couette plane flows.

Poiseuille Flow. The steady state flow between two stationary parallel plates driven by an imposed pressure gradient is known as the plane Poiseuille flow. The first simulation we have performed deals with a flow situation more complex than the Poiseuille flow: the relaxation from uniform to equilibrium of the flow between two stationary parallel plates. We used a square lattice with side length $L = 207$ lattice sites. The model gas was contained between two straight line boundaries at $Y = 0$ (bottom lattice side) and $Y = 207$ (top lattice side). The initial distribution densities were calculated assuming a horizontal flow with uniform velocity $U = 0.15$, an average number of particles per site $n = 2.5$, and an average temperature $T = 10$ (all the magnitudes expressed in the lattice gas units). The obstacle operator **B** was implemented for the top and bottom sides of the lattice in order to simulate a flow along a 2D channel with stationary rigid walls. Periodic boundary conditions were imposed on the other two lattice sides, such that no pressure gradient was present along the channel and the evolution of the system was influenced only by the rigid boundaries. The transversal average velocity profiles are shown in Figure 9. Here we can observe, in agreement with the solution of the Navier-Stokes equations for the plane Poiseuille flow, how a parabolic velocity profile decreases with time, indicating dissipation of momentum and energy due to the collisions of the particles each other and with the solid boundaries.

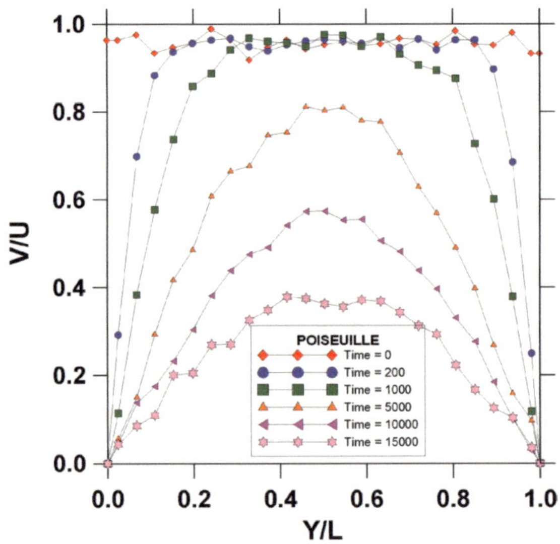

Fig. 9. A non-steady Poiseuille flow. Relaxation from uniform to rest of a 2D flow between two stationary parallel plates.

Couette Flow. The steady state flow between two parallel plates in relative motion is known as the plane Couette flow (see Figure 10 (left)). We performed a lattice gas simulation of the development of a plane Couette flow in two dimensions. A square lattice with side length $L = 207$ lattice sites was considered. The initial distribution densities were calculated by assuming that the gas is initially at rest with an average number of particles per site $n = 2.5$ and an average temperature $T = 10$ (in the lattice gas units). The model gas was contained between two straight line boundaries at $Y = 0$ (top lattice side) and $Y = 207$ (bottom lattice side). The obstacle operator **B** was implemented for the bottom side of the lattice in order to simulate a stationary rigid wall. A uniform in average horizontal velocity, $U = 0.15$ (in the lattice gas units), was imposed at the first five top rows of lattice sites to simulate a moving plate. Periodic boundary conditions were imposed on the left and right sides of the lattice (this way, the pressure gradient is zero and that the only forcing on the fluid is forcing due to the moving plate). Ten computer simulations, 15,000 time-steps each, were done with the same initial and boundary conditions. The vertical profiles of average velocity were obtained for time-steps $t = 0, 200, 1000, 5000$ and 15000. These profiles are shown in Figure 10. It can be observed in this figure how, due to the viscosity of the lattice gas, the relative velocity between the top and bottom boundaries gradually forces the movement of the model gas (initially at rest) with a clear tendency towards a linear profile. The viscosity makes the fluid stick to the boundary which is why a shear develops within the interior of the fluid. The time evolution of the simulated velocity profile and its asymptotical form are in agreement with the solution of the Navier-Stokes equations for the development from rest to the steady state of the laminar viscous flow between two parallel rigid plates in uniform relative motion (Batchelor, 1967).

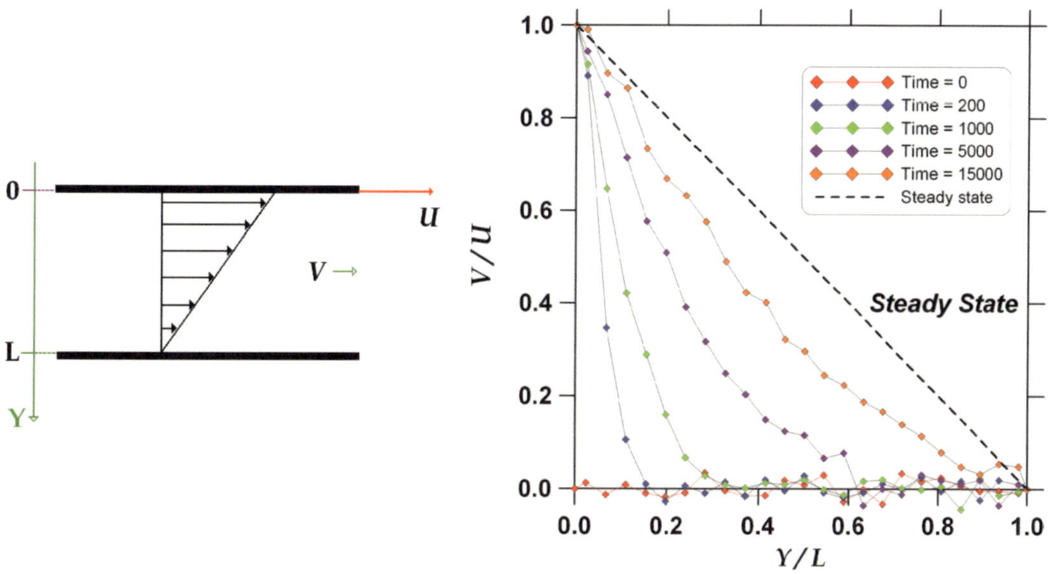

Fig. 10. Simulation of the Couette flow. Development from rest to the steady state.

3. Lattice Gas Simulation of Wind Fields

One of the main attractive features of the fluid flow simulation with lattice gas models is its ability to handle complex initial and boundary conditions. This is one of the reasons why we considered convenient to investigate the lattice gas possibilities as an alternative approach for solving the problems (both diagnosis and prognosis) of the wind fields prevailing in topographically complex terrains.

A simple meteorological outline of the wind field diagnosis problem is as follows: At the stations of an atmospheric monitoring network, the meteorological variables of pressure, temperature, and wind speed and wind direction are measured at a number of sites spatially distributed over a topographically complex and relatively large region. So, for any given time, the meteorological data registered at the network stations are to be used offline to estimate the wind velocity at any given point within the spatial domain of interest.

Within the framework of the computational fluid dynamics, the approach to the problem is focused on solving numerically the set of balance differential equations to find out the steady state of the system that complies the constraints imposed by the boundary (complex topography) and time asymptotic (measured values) conditions. Otherwise, in the lattice gas

approach to the wind field estimation problem, the available data of pressure, temperature and wind velocity are used to compute the steady state distribution functions, $n_\alpha(\mathbf{r}_i)$, for a given number of control lattice sites $\mathbf{r}_i$. The topographic data, on another hand, are used to define some special domains of lattice sites which are to be forbidden to the particles of the model gas; these particular domains are defined in order to represent the fixed obstacles in the computer simulations, and the obstacle operator will affect the particles arriving to their boundaries. Once the system has been prepared, it is allowed to evolve during a given number of time steps. The number of time steps that the system requires to reach a steady state depends on the size of the lattice and on the number of control points it comprises.
Under equilibrium conditions, the values of the distribution functions at the control points can be computed using the equilibrium formalism of the section 2.1 after an appropriate scaling procedure to express the meteorological data in the lattice gas units. Out of equilibrium, the same approach can be used by assuming local equilibrium conditions and using a constrained perturbation technique in order to satisfy the desired local velocity conditions for a given number of particles per site n. So,

$$n_\alpha = \tilde{n}_\alpha + \delta n_\alpha \,, \quad \sum_\alpha \delta n_\alpha = 0 \,, \quad \mathbf{v}(\mathbf{r},t) = \frac{1}{n}\sum_\alpha c_\alpha \mathbf{e}_\alpha \delta n_\alpha \tag{17}$$

The outputs of the computer simulations are average distribution functions computed over cells of 9 x 9 lattice sites. While the simulation goes on, the average distribution densities, denoted as $f_\alpha(\mathbf{x}, t)$, can be computed as frequently as it is desired for each cell position $\mathbf{x}$, and they are used to calculate the wind velocity $\mathbf{v}(\mathbf{x}, t)$ as follows:

$$\mathbf{v}(\mathbf{x},t) = \frac{1}{f}\sum_\alpha c_\alpha \mathbf{e}_\alpha f_\alpha(\mathbf{x},t), \quad f(\mathbf{x},t) = \sum_\alpha f_\alpha(\mathbf{x},t) \tag{18}$$

Before considering a real and practical study case, a few computer simulations were carried out to test the lattice gas capabilities in modelling of situations of turbulent flow similar to those ones which prevail in the atmospheric surface layer. Our main concern was to find out the ability of the model to reproduce the well known quasi-logarithmic wind velocity profile

$$u(y) = \frac{u_*}{\kappa}\left[\ln\left(\frac{y}{y_0}\right) - \Psi_M\left(\frac{y}{L}\right)\right] \tag{19}$$

where u is the mean wind velocity, u_* is the friction velocity, κ is the von Karman constant, y is the height over the earth surface, y_0 is the roughness length, L is the Monin-Obukhov length, and Ψ_M is a universal function which takes into account corrections to the logarithmic profile due to the atmospheric stability conditions (Garrat, 1992).
The computer simulations were performed with a lattice that comprised 207 x 207 sites. Periodic boundary conditions were imposed on the left and right sides of the lattice. The bottom side ($y = 0$) was filled with small obstacle towers whose heights were chosen randomly to simulate a roughness length equal to 5 % of the lattice side length ($y_0 \sim 10.35$).

The lattice gas was assumed initially at rest on the average, with a number of particles per site $n = 2.5$, and a temperature $T = 10$. In the top lattice side ($y = 207$) it was imposed a fixed horizontal velocity U using the first five lattice rows as control points. Ten computer simulations, *35000* time steps each one, were made for $U = 0.1, 0.3, 0.5, 0.7$ and 0.9 with the same initial and boundary conditions. In Figure 11 there are shown the mean wind velocity profiles obtained for $U = 0.3$ and times $t = 0, 1000, 5000, 10000, 20000, 25000, 30000$ and *35000*. In this figure we note that the system reached the steady state flow conditions (continuous straight line), that the steady state velocity profile is linear such as it is predicted by the Navier-Stokes equations in the laminar case (Batchelor, 1967), and that, because the roughness of the bottom lattice side, the wind velocity became zero near (but not at) the surface ($V/U \sim 0$ at $Y/L \sim 0.058$).

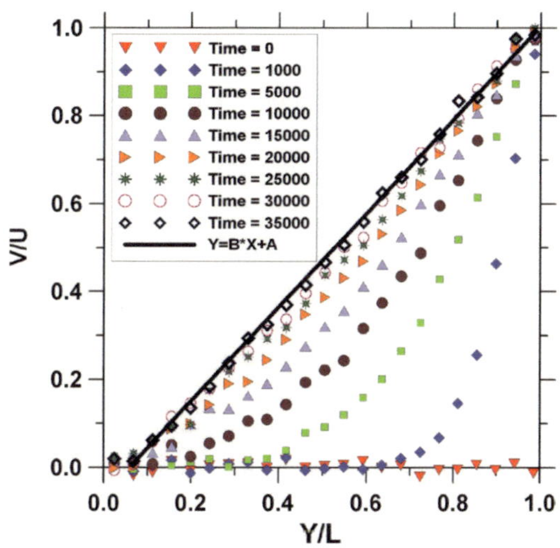

Fig. 11. Lattice gas simulation of the Couette flow development from rest to the steady state, when a no null roughness length is associated to the bottom stationary plate.

In figure 12 there are shown the wind velocity profiles for $t = 35000$ and $U = 0.1, 0.3, 0.5, 0.7$ and 0.9, and it can be observed that the velocity profile deviates from the linear case as U increases. This is what really happens on the transition of the flow from a laminar state to a turbulent one. For $U = 0.9$ the velocity profile is, in fact, quasi-logarithmic. In this figure, the solid curve corresponds to the equation (19) with $u_*/k = 0.3$ and Ψ_M given by

$$\Psi_M = a(y - y_0)\ln\left(\frac{y+1}{b(y-1)}\right) \tag{20}$$

where $y_0 = 10.5$, $a = 0.2$ and $b = 1.016$. Although the 9-velocity lattice gas model may have a clearly non-classical behaviour at energies higher than $2n/3$, the results of the various simulations that we have performed show that it can be useful for some meteorological applications, such as the wind field estimation problem, if it is handled carefully. The ranges of values of the density and the energy which are safe for a particular practical application might be identified previously.

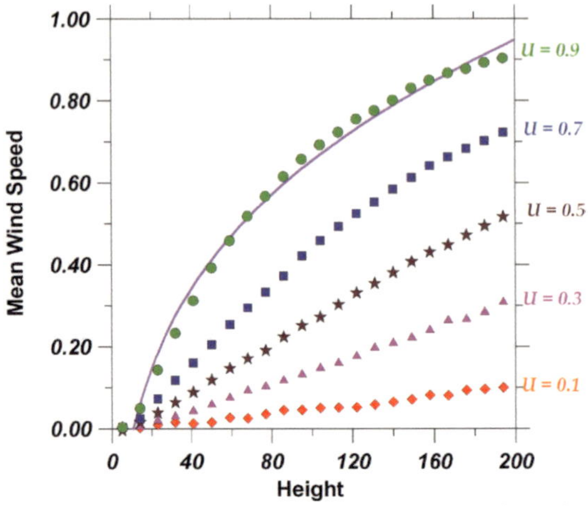

Fig. 12. Lattice gas simulation of the transition of the Couette flow from a laminar state to a turbulent one.

4. The Main Wind Circulation Events at Mexico City in 1994

In this section, the wind circulation events which occurred in the Mexico City Metropolitan Area throughout the year 1994 are identified, described, and organized. For the purposes of the present work, the main goal of this task is to have good enough criteria to identify and select, among the 8760 wind circulation possibilities (in an hourly base), the most important scenarios for the computer simulations. A very recent description of the methodology we have applied to select our simulation scenarios was reported briefly by M. S. Jimenez, A. T. Celada and A. Salcido in 2008 (Jimenez et al, 2008), and more precisely by A. T. Celada and A. Salcido in 2009 (Celada & Salcido, 2009).

4.1 Meteorology Databases

In 1994, with the economical support of the Mexico City government, under the initiative COPERA, personnel of the Instituto de Investigaciones Eléctricas (IIE) carried out, from June to September, the first experimental campaign of micrometeorological measurements in surface, simultaneously in 4 sites of the Mexico City Metropolitan Area (Salcido et al, 1994). For this purpose, the MCMA was geographically divided in the quadrants North-East (NE), North-West (NW), South-East (SE), and South-West (SW), taking the Zócalo of Mexico City as origin. One micrometeorological station was installed at each quadrant. In Figure 13, there are shown the relative positions of the micrometeorological stations installed by the IIE in the MCMA. Each station was equipped with an ultrasonic 3D anemometer-thermometer, and conventional sensors for temperature, pressure, relative humidity, and solar radiation. The 3D wind velocity components were measured with a 10 Hz sampling rate by the ultrasonic anemometer, and the other variables were measured at 1Hz. Averages over 10 minute periods were computed for all variables.
On another hand, since 1984, it is operating an automatic atmospheric monitoring network (RAMA, for its name in Spanish) in Mexico City and its surroundings, financed by the local governments. In 1994, the RAMA comprised 32 stations, 10 of which with the ability to measure meteorology (wind speed, wind direction, temperature, and relative humidity),

providing public reports of the hourly average values. In the RAMA database, the 1-hour averages are identified by the number of the hour of the day. The RAMA historical database is now available on the internet site http://www.sma.df.gob.mx/simat/home_base.php. In Figure 14, the seven meteorological stations of the RAMA with the best performance in 1994 are shown. In Table 1, we reported the numbers of hours, month by month, for which the seven selected RAMA stations were operating simultaneously with a 100% performance.

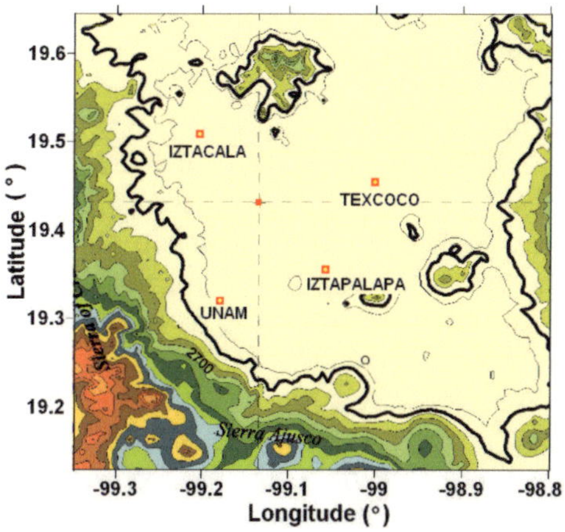

Station Name	MCMA Quadrant	UTM (Zone 14)	
		Easting	Northing
Texcoco	NE	499.562	2151.650
Iztacala	NW	480.094	2158.647
UNAM	SW	481.587	2136.731
Iztapalapa	SE	492.298	2140.504
Zócalo	Origin	486.011	2148.699

Fig. 13. Relative positions of the four stations that the IIE installed in the MCMA to perform a micrometeorological campaign from June to September in 1994. In the table, the positions are expressed in UTM coordinates (in Km).

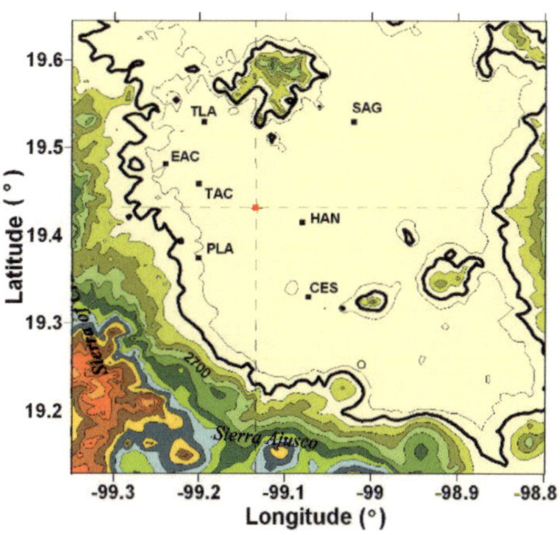

ID	Station Name	MCMA Quadrant	UTM (Zone 14)	
			Easting	Northing
SAG	San Agustin	NE	496.794	2159.651
TLA	Tlanepantla	NW	478.521	2159.233
EAC	ENEPAcatlan	NW	474.580	2154.443
TAC	Tacuba	NW	478.774	2151.088
PLA	Plateros	SW	480.249	2139.878
HAN	Hangares	SE	491.251	2147.420
CES	Cerro de la Estrella	SE	492.909	2137.308

Fig. 14. Relative positions of the seven meteorological stations of the RAMA with the best performance in 1994. In the table, the positions are expressed in UTM coordinates (in Km). The official IDs and the quadrants to which they belong are also reported.

Month	JAN	FEB	MAR	APR	MAY	JUN	JUL	AUG	SEP	OCT	NOV	DEC
Hours	411	125	357	402	316	292	377	304	492	306	383	249

Table 1. Monthly distribution of the hours for which the selected RAMA stations were operating simultaneously with a 100% performance.

Although the field campaign carried out by the IIE took place within the period of the summer rainy season of 1994, the existence of two independent sources of meteorology data (IIE and RAMA) for the same period did open, for the first time, an opportunity particularly interesting for the purposes of the characterization and modelling of the Mexico City winds. One of the databases can be used as input for the models, and the other one may be useful for the comparison purposes.

4.2 The Wind Direction States Representation Model

By considering the MCMA divided in quadrants, such as it was done in the previous subsection, a very simple description of its wind circulation events can be carried out. At a given time, we define the *wind direction state* of the MCMA as the set of the four wind direction sectors (N≡0, NE≡1, E≡2, SE≡3, S≡4, SW≡5, W≡6 or NW≡7) that correspond to the wind direction average values at the MCMA quadrants, which are computed from the wind speed and wind direction values registered by the RAMA stations located inside each quadrant. So, at any given time, the wind direction state at the MCMA may be expressed as a 4-digits octal number ranging from 0000 to 7777 (from 0 to 4095, in base 10). It is a mapping of the infinite possibilities of the wind circulation events at the MCMA (each expressed by an spatial distribution of the wind velocity) into the 4096 possible wind direction states. The highest order digit represents the sector of the mean wind direction at the quadrant NE, and the next digits represent, in decreasing order, the sectors of the mean wind directions at the quadrants NW, SW, and SE, respectively. So, the octal number 1070 (decimal 568) represents the wind direction state with North-easterly wind at the NE quadrant, Northerly wind at the NW quadrant, North-westerly wind at the SW quadrant, and Northerly wind at the SE quadrant, as it is shown in Figure 15.

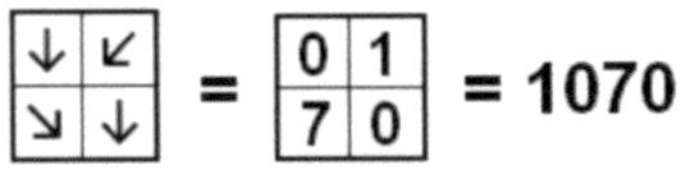

Fig. 15. Octal representation of a MCMA wind direction state. It has winds from NE, N, NW and N, at the NE, NW, SW and SE quadrants, respectively.

The frequency distribution of the wind direction states (normalized to 1 or, equivalently, to 100) constitutes a convenient way to distinguish which of them can be observed at the study area under different conditions, and also for conveying their probabilities of occurrence. It will be referred as the *density of states of wind direction*. On another hand, the 4096 wind direction states can be organized in groups by taking into account the following three characteristics of any wind direction state:

- θ: the wind direction sector of the average value of the four mean wind directions of the quadrants (it has 9 possible values: Ø, N, NE, E, SE, S, SW, W, NW)‡;
- ω: the sign of the vorticity of the state (3 possibilities: anticyclonic = -1, null vorticity = 0, and cyclonic = 1); and
- γ: the sign of the divergence of the state (3 possibilities: convergent winds = -1, null divergence = 0, and divergent winds = 1).

‡ The symbol Ø is used to indicate that the wind directions at the quadrants are opposite in pairs, and their average is not defined. The state 1054 (octal) is an example.

The concept of wind direction state, with its three associated attributes, (θ, ω, γ), may be understood as a meso-β scale representation model of the wind circulation events. Refined versions of this simple representation model may be implemented. Within the framework of this representation, the state illustrated in the Figure 15 belongs to the group of the North-Cyclonic-Convergent states, denoted by the triad (θ,ω,γ) = (N, 1, -1). There are 81 (θ,ω,γ)–groups in which the 4096 wind direction states can be organized in response to the particular wind driving forces (such as, the topography and the meteorological conditions) which prevail at the MCMA. So, the mechanisms which drive the winds at the MCMA constitute the main influence factors to the population of its (θ, ω, γ)–groups.

4.3 The 1994 Mexico City Wind Direction States

From the RAMA 1994 database, we found that the seven stations selected for our study were operating simultaneously with 100% performance only during 4014 of the 8760 possible hours, which were distributed throughout the year as described in Table 1. Among these events, only 985 wind direction states were different each other. In Figure 16, the distribution of frequencies of the wind direction states normalized to 100 (i.e. the density of states of wind direction) is shown for the 4014 hours.

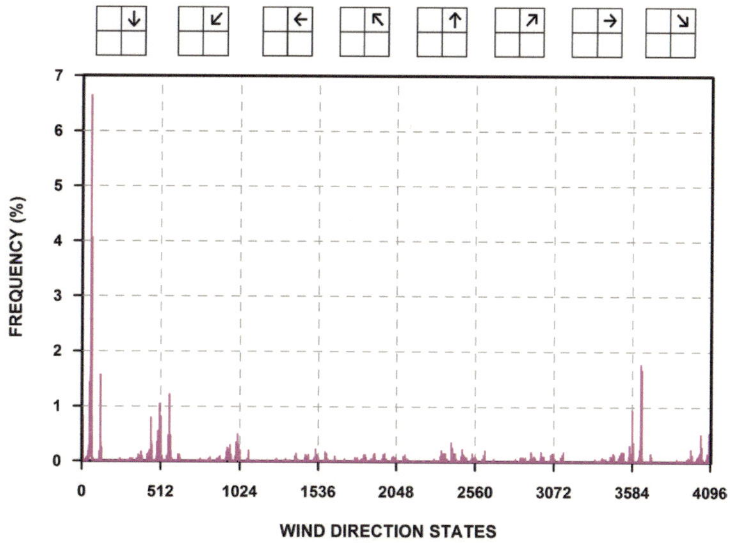

Fig. 16. The density of states of wind direction of the MCMA for the 1994 year. Here, the states are expressed in the decimal base (0 … 4095). The plot contains information of 4014 hours of the total 8760 possible hours.

The plot in this figure shows eight packets of 512 states each, ordered according to the wind direction sector at the quadrant NE. This quadrant is particularly important because its North side is the main opening of the MCMA to the wind flows, as it was shown in Figure 1. The states from 0 to 1023 and from 3584 to 4095 represent wind events with a Northerly, North-easterly or North-westerly flow component at the NE quadrant, while the states from 1536 to 3071 represent wind events with a Southerly, South-westerly or South-easterly flow component at the same quadrant. The wind direction states with the highest frequencies did belong, in order of population, to the packets 0-511, 3584-4095, and 512-1023, whose states showed, respectively, a Northerly, North-westerly or North-easterly flow component at the NE quadrant. The individual states with the highest frequencies, in decreasing order, were 56, 63, 0, 57, 3640, 55, 3647, 120, 48, 568, 1 and 504 (see Figure 16). These observations are in agreement with the information reported by Secretaria del Medio Ambiente of Mexico City about the predominant Northerly/North-easterly winds at MCMA (SMA-GDF, 2006). Moreover, wind flows from these directions were also described by Doran and collaborators in 1998 (Doran et al., 1998) and by Doran and Zhong in 2000 (Doran & Zhong, 2000) as Northerly and/or North-easterly winds from the Mexican Plateau. Table 2 contains a representation of the wind direction states with the highest frequencies and the respective (θ,ω,γ)–group each belongs to.

STATE (Decimal)		FREQ (%)	GROUP (θ, ω, γ)	STATE (Decimal)		FREQ (%)	GROUP (θ, ω, γ)	STATE (Decimal)		FREQ (%)	GROUP (θ, ω, γ)
56	↓ ↓ ↘ ↓	6.65	(N, 1, -1)	3640	↓ ↘ ↘ ↓	1.77	(NW, 0, 0)	48	↓ ↓ → ↓	1.44	(N, 0, -1)
63	↓ ↓ ↘ ↘	4.06	(NW, 1, -1)	55	↓ ↓ → ↘	1.72	(NW, 1, -1)	568	↓ ↙ ↘ ↓	1.22	(N, 1, -1)
0	↓ ↓ ↓ ↓	3.71	(N, 0, 0)	3647	↓ ↘ ↘ ↘	1.67	(NW, 1, 1)	1	↓ ↓ ↓ ↙	1.15	(N, -1, -1)
57	↓ ↓ ↘ ↙	1.77	(N, 0, -1)	120	↙ ↓ ↘ ↓	1.57	(N, 1, 0)	504	↘ ↓ ↘ ↓	1.05	(NW, -1, -1)

Table 2. The wind direction states of the MCMA which had the highest frequencies in 1994.

Because of the obvious differences between the wind driving forces which prevail during diurnal and nocturnal conditions, the daytime occurrence frequencies of the wind direction states differ from those of nighttime situations. To study these differences, we organized the 1994 wind direction states in 6-hour packets: Night (hours 1-6), Morning (hours 7-12), Afternoon (hours 13-18), and Evening (hours 19-24). In Figure 17, the occurrences of the states with the highest frequencies at the density of states are presented for the annual case, and also for the night, morning, afternoon, and evening 6-hour packets. In this figure we observed that, in 1994, the behaviour of the state 56, the state with the highest annual frequency, shows an occurrence frequency that grows as one moves from night hours (1-6 packet) to the evening hours (19-24 packet). Otherwise, for the state 63, that one with the second highest annual frequency, its occurrence frequency decreases as one moves from the night to the afternoon 6-hour packets, and then it grows, recovering at the evening packet the value it had at the night packet. Finally, the behaviour of the state 0, which got the third highest annual frequency, is opposite to that of the state 63: it occurrence grows from the night to the afternoon packets, and then it decreases at the evening hours. The behaviour of these particular MCMA wind direction states seems to follow the 24 hours periodicity of the sunlight. Other states, like the state 120, seem to be insensible to this periodicity. It is worth of mention that our previous observations show that, in spite of its simplicity, our meso-β scale representation model is able to reflect the main features of the wind circulation events that prevail in the MCMA, or at least some of them. It must be underlined, however, that the results of this state model will be sensible to the number and the spatial distribution of the stations at the quadrants, particularly for small or poor distributed meteorological networks.

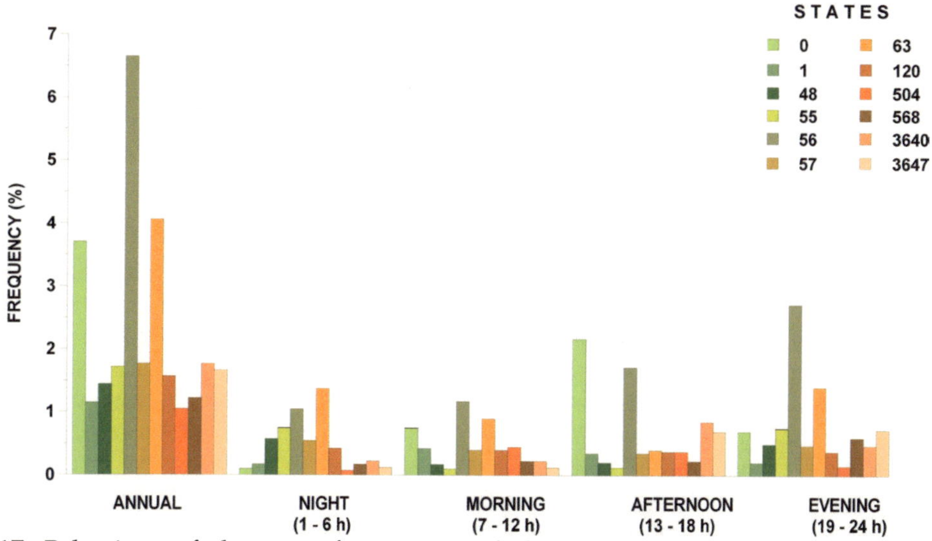

Fig. 17. Behaviour of the most frequent wind direction states of the MCMA in 1994. Comparison of the annual frequency distribution with the corresponding to the night, morning, afternoon, and evening 6-hour packets.

In addition, we organized the 1994 MCMA wind direction states in (θ, ω, γ)–groups; their population percentages are shown in Figure 18. In this figure, it can be observed that the most populated groups in 1994 were the North-Cyclonic-Convergent (N, 1, -1) with the highest population, the Northwest-Cyclonic-Convergent (NW, 1, -1) with the second highest population, and the Northwest-Anticyclonic-Convergent (NW, -1, -1) in third place. The (θ, ω, γ)–groups with the smaller populations were those with θ = E, Ø and SE, almost independently of the other attributes (ω and γ).

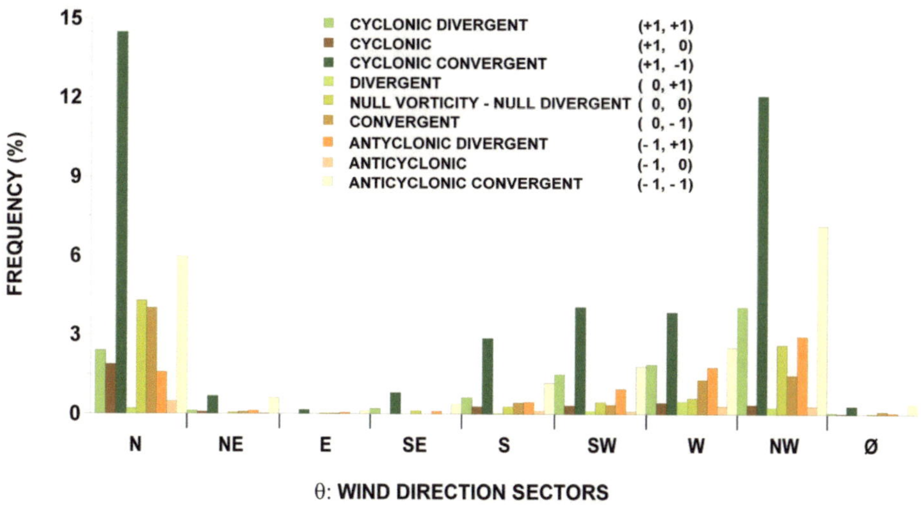

Fig. 18. Frequency distribution (or population) of the (θ, ω, γ)–groups for the year 1994.

5. Lattice Gas Simulation of Mexico City Wind Fields

In this section, it is described and discussed the application of the 9-velocity lattice gas model in estimating the MCMA wind field for some particular wind circulation events which occurred at both daytime and nighttime hours of the 1994 summertime. The comparison of the simulation results against wind velocity data registered at the stations of the official atmospheric network (RAMA) of Mexico City, are also presented.

5.1 Selection of the Mexico City Wind Scenarios

In Section 4, we have seen that from the wind circulation events which occurred in the Mexico City Metropolitan throughout the year 1994, those ones with a Northerly, Northeasterly or Northwesterly wind at the NE quadrant were found with the highest frequencies. Following this observation, for the purpose of applying the 9-velocity lattice gas model to simulate the Mexico City Metropolitan Area wind field, we chose as simulation scenarios the wind events which prevailed at the 9:00 (morning), 15:00 (afternoon) and 21:00 (evening) hours (LST) of the days July 31 and August 26, 1994. The wind direction states of the chosen wind scenarios were computed, separately, with the data of the RAMA stations and the data of the IIE campaign; both results are reported in Table 3. Here we can observe that the wind direction states of the six chose scenarios belong to the first two packets of the density of states (Figure 16). It is interesting to observe in Table 3 that, although very similar (particularly for the morning and afternoon wind scenarios), the wind directions states obtained with the IIE database differ from those found with the RAMA data. The main reason for these differences is that, whilst the RAMA database was prepared with data of a total of seven stations, the IIE database was obtained with data of only one station at each quadrant of the MCMA. Moreover, at the quadrants, the station positions of the IIE network did not coincide with positions of RAMA stations.

For each one of the wind scenarios chosen for computer simulation, the input database for the wind field lattice gas model was prepared (such as it was outlined in Section 3) from the data of pressure, temperature and wind velocity taken from the four meteorological stations of the IIE network. The data of the RAMA network were kept as information of reference for the comparison purposes of the study. Once scaled to fix the lattice gas units, the meteorological data of the IIE stations were used to find the perturbations of the local equilibrium distribution densities congruent with the velocity control values at the lattice sites that represent the positions of the stations.

5.2 Simulations and Results

The simulation spatial domain, a rectangular region of the MCMA with side length of 70 Km in the west-east direction and 60 Km in the north-south direction, was represented by a lattice containing 396 x 324 sites. The boundary conditions at the free lattice sides were imposed by assuming that the values of pressure, temperature and wind velocity were there equal to the corresponding average values over the four control sites. In all the other lattice sites, the lattice gas was assumed, on the average, as initially at rest and under conditions of thermodynamic equilibrium. For each wind scenario, the lattice gas model was run five times, 5000 time steps each. The simulated wind velocity distribution for each scenario was computed from the distribution densities obtained as a direct output of the computer simulation.

Date: 1994/07/31						
	RAMA STATIONS			IIE STATIONS		
LOCAL TIME	STATE (Decimal)		GROUP (θ, ω, γ)	STATE (Decimal)		GROUP (θ, ω, γ)
09:00	**448**	↘ ↓ ↓ ↓	**(N, -1, -1)**	**0**	↓ ↓ ↓ ↓	**(N, 0, 0)**
15:00	**64**	↙ ↓ ↓ ↓	**(N, 1, 1)**	**1**	↓ ↓ ↓ ↙	**(N, -1, -1)**
21:00	**318**	↑ ↓ ↘ →	**(W, 1, 1)**	**10**	↓ ↓ ↙ ←	**(NE, -1, -1)**

Date: 1994/08/26						
	RAMA STATIONS			IIE STATIONS		
LOCAL TIME	STATE (Decimal)		GROUP (θ, ω, γ)	STATE (Decimal)		GROUP (θ, ω, γ)
09:00	**57**	↓ ↓ ↘ ↙	**(N, 0, -1)**	**1**	↓ ↓ ↓ ↙	**(N, -1, -1)**
15:00	**64**	↙ ↓ ↓ ↓	**(N, 1, 1)**	**0**	↓ ↓ ↓ ↓	**(N, 0, 0)**
21:00	**553**	↓ ↙ ↗ ↙	**(N, -1, - 1)**	**556**	↓ ↙ ↗ ↑	**(Ø, +1, -1)**

Table 3. The MCMA wind direction states which prevailed the days (July 31 and August 26, 1994) selected for the lattice gas simulation of the Mexico City wind field.

A comparison between the wind direction states produced by the lattice gas simulations of the chosen wind scenarios, and the wind direction states obtained from the data of the RAMA stations, are shown in Table 4. In this table, in general, it is observed a quite good qualitative agreement between both sets of wind direction states, excepting those for the 21:00 h scenario of the first day. However, as we will see later, the stations Tlanepantla and Tacuba of the RAMA network did not report the wind data that day.

Date: 1994/07/31				
	RAMA STATIONS		**LATTICE GAS SIMULATION**	
LOCAL TIME	STATE (Decimal)	GROUP (θ, ω, γ)	STATE (Decimal)	GROUP (θ, ω, γ)
09:00	**448** ↘ ↓ ↓ ↓	**(N, -1, -1)**	**904** → ↙ ↙ ↓	**(N, -1, 0)**
15:00	**64** ↙ ↓ ↓ ↓	**(N, 1, 1)**	**960** ↘ ↙ ↓ ↓	**(N, 0, -1)**
21:00	**318** ↑ ↓ ↘ →	**(W, 1, 1)**	**721** ↖ ↙ ← ↙	**(E, -1, 1)**

Date: 1994/08/26				
	RAMA STATIONS		**LATTICE GAS SIMULATION**	
LOCAL TIME	STATE (Decimal)	GROUP (θ, ω, γ)	STATE (Decimal)	GROUP (θ, ω, γ)
09:00	**57** ↓ ↓ ↘ ↙	**(N, 0, -1)**	**448** ↘ ↓ ↓ ↓	**(N, -1, -1)**
15:00	**64** ↙ ↓ ↓ ↓	**(N, 1, 1)**	**960** ↘ ↙ ↓ ↓	**(N, 0, -1)**
21:00	**553** ↓ ↙ ↗ ↙	**(N, -1, - 1)**	**960** ↘ ↙ ↓ ↓	**(N, 0, -1)**

Table 4. Comparison of the MCMA wind direction states obtained from data of the RAMA stations (left) and from the lattice gas simulations (right) for the chosen wind scenarios.

In Figures 19 and 20, sketches of the wind fields estimated for the MCMA are shown. Quantitative results of the wind velocities estimated with the lattice gas model at the sites of the stations of the RAMA network are reported in Table 5. These tables include also the wind velocity data registered at the RAMA stations for the chosen wind scenarios. Of course, it is not surprising that for the four control stations it was found a fair agreement between the measured wind velocity values and those estimated with the lattice gas model. In fact, the lattice sites which were representing these stations in the computer simulations were updated with the velocity control values each time step.

Date: 1994/07/31	09:00				15:00				21:00			
	Measured		Estimated		Measured		Estimated		Measured		Estimated	
Station	WSP (m/s)	WDR (°N)	WSP (m/s)	WDR (°N)	WSP (m/s)	WDR (°N)	WSP (m/s)	WDR (°N)	WSP (m/s)	WDR (°N)	WSP (m/s)	WDR (°N)
IZTACALA	1.00	353	0.95	355	2.50	354	2. 53	354	1.24	356	1.30	356
TEXCOCO	1.92	351	1.97	350	2.51	339	2.55	340	1.35	355	1.36	355
UNAM	0.97	5	1.00	3	1.33	8	1.34	8	0.45	25	0.49	24
IZTAPALAPA	0.71	4	0.78	0	2.23	47	2.30	47	1.79	71	1.83	70
TLANEPANTLA	----	----	1.55	313	----	----	4.13	318	----	----	4.13	318
SN. AGUSTIN	1.70	339	2.88	30	2.59	347	4.40	25	2.55	6	2.34	33
ACATLAN	1.21	300	0.88	305	3.53	32	2.19	334	3.40	200	1.52	170
TACUBA	----	----	0.38	297	----	----	2.16	326	----	----	1.23	153
HANGARES	1.70	324	2.53	24	4.10	15	3.30	14	2.41	216	2.00	40
C. ESTRELLA	1.21	2	1.08	338	2.28	26	1.79	348	1.88	341	0.43	9
PLATEROS	1.16	352	0.97	21	2.37	352	1.24	31	2.41	311	1.00	45

Date: 1994/08/26	09:00				15:00				21:00			
	Measured		Estimated		Measured		Estimated		Measured		Estimated	
Station	WSP (m/s)	WDR (°N)	WSP (m/s)	WDR (°N)	WSP (m/s)	WDR (°N)	WSP (m/s)	WDR (°N)	WSP (m/s)	WDR (°N)	WSP (m/s)	WDR (°N)
IZTACALA	2.11	2	2.13	1	3.92	0	3.85	0	1.92	9	1.97	7
TEXCOCO	2.73	14	2.79	13	5.12	351	5.19	351	3.83	54	3.92	53
UNAM	1.64	1	1.75	2	2.03	351	2.01	353	1.19	208	1.23	207
IZTAPALAPA	1.63	53	1.68	52	4.29	6	4.41	6	1.89	193	1.95	193
TLANEPANTLA	2.59	17	2.96	323	4.87	30	5.11	324	2.91	20	2.02	320
SN. AGUSTIN	2.50	16	2.67	18	4.91	343	6.14	24	3.17	25	2.50	12
ACATLAN	2.19	41	2.03	334	3.84	72	2.67	340	2.95	49	1.27	324
TACUBA	2.41	359	1.70	308	3.62	343	2.69	311	2.91	321	1.07	315
HANGARES	2.82	46	1.82	21	6.69	9	4.68	22	3.13	44	1.36	35
C. ESTRELLA	----	----	1.81	345	----	----	3.18	347	----	----	0.89	314
PLATEROS	1.56	329	1.35	351	2.37	353	2.20	12	1.52	243	0.46	25

Table 5. Comparison of the values of wind speed and wind direction measured at the RAMA stations and estimated with the lattice gas model.

Although the comparison with the velocity values measured at the RAMA stations is not direct neither trivial because many of them were strongly influenced by the big obstacles in the surroundings, the velocity values estimated with the lattice gas model at the sites of the RAMA stations show a reasonable agreement with the available experimental data. In fact, on the average, the wind velocity values estimated with the model differ from the experimental ones in a 30 per cent, very roughly. However, a more carefully inspection evidences situations where the agreement is quite good, as it is the case for the ACATLAN station at 9:00 h of the first day, or the SAN AGUSTIN station also at 9:00 h of the second day, or at the PLATEROS station at 15:00 h also the second day. In general, the worst estimations occurred near to the solid boundaries, and we think this is due to the strong boundary conditions we have imposed there (particles arriving to solid boundaries are strictly constrained to invert its direction of motion). Of course, it is necessary to explore the effects of some other possibilities of boundary conditions at the solid obstacles at large spatial scales.

On another hand, it must be underlined that the simulations we carried out were two dimensional; this means, in particular, that the presence of the urban buildings has be neglected completely, and that the conservation of the number of particles in the microdynamics of the model may lead to lateral flows under wind forcing conditions that, in reality, could be driving vertical flows. It may be the case when the wind direction states belong to highly convergent or divergent winds, such as those thermally produced by the heat island effect, or in combination with the particular topographic features of the MCMA that define a closed region.

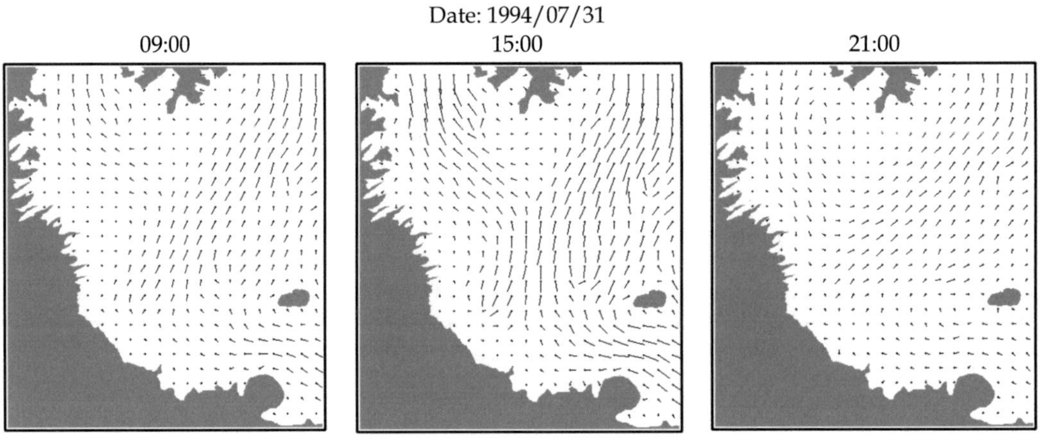

Fig. 19. The MCMA wind fields estimated with the 9-velocity lattice gas model. The velocity vectors are represented by needles, each extending from the centre (dot) of a cell that comprises 9x9 lattice sites. Date: July 31, 1994.

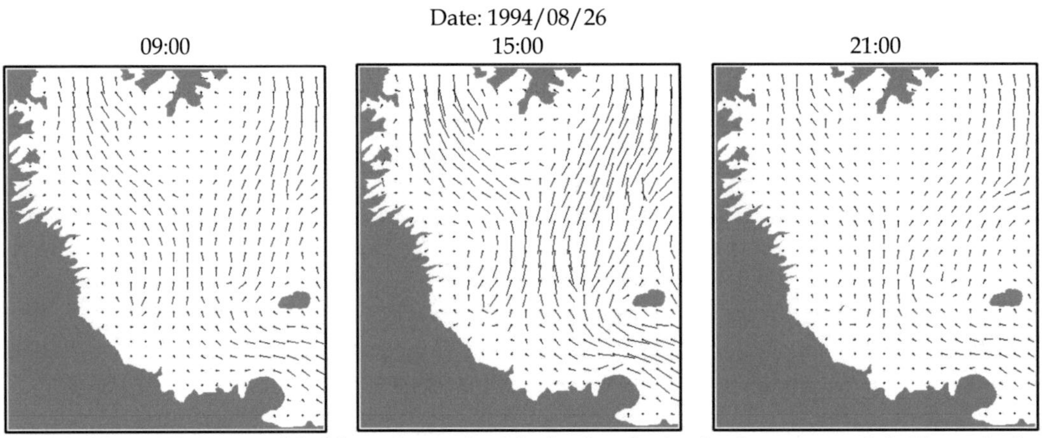

Fig. 20. The MCMA wind fields estimated with the 9-velocity lattice gas model. The velocity vectors are represented by needles, each extending from the centre (dot) of a cell that comprises 9x9 lattice sites. Date: August 26, 1994.

6. Conclusion

In this chapter we have presented an application of the 9-velocity lattice gas model as an alternative and innovative approach to the wind field estimation problem in two dimensions. The computer simulations performed to test the model showed off that it is capable to reproduce steady and non steady laminar and turbulent well known flow situations. In particular, it was able to reproduce the typical surface layer quasi-logarithmic wind profile. This wind field model, however, is still in an experimental phase, but, as an important part of its validation and calibration, we have applied it to estimate the wind field of the Mexico City Metropolitan Area for daytime and nighttime conditions of the 1994 summertime, specifically for the hours 9:00, 15:00 and 21:00 (LST) of the days July 31 and August 26. The results we have obtained through the computer simulations for this study case, as well as for the preliminary test simulations, have shown a reasonable agreement (both qualitative and quantitative) between the measured and estimated velocity values, and it suggests strongly that the model could be, in fact, a very useful tool for a wide variety of practical fluid flow applications.

There exist, however, some important features of the 9-velocity lattice gas model that one must keep in mind in developing practical applications with it. The equilibrium behaviour of the model is not the classical one that an ordinary fluid presents. The entropy as function of energy has a maximum value for any given number of particles per site, and this behaviour is reflected in the dependence on energy of the temperature and pressure, which may assume not only positive values, but also negative ones. However, as the number of particles per site goes to zero (i.e. in the limit of low densities), the behaviour of the model seems to be closer to the classical one. On other hand, it is very important to extend the model to three dimensions in order to consider some of the important and frequent wind scenarios that prevail at Mexico City and its surroundings (for example, the thermally driven and upslope and downslope winds). From the technical point of view, it is not a difficult task, but the development of very fast codes will be important to keep reasonable the duration of the model runs.

7. References

Batchelor, G. K. (1967). *An Introduction to Fluid Dynamics*. Cambridge University Press, ISBN-13: 978-0521663960, ISBN-10: 0521663962, Cambridge.

Bonner, J. C.; Rice, A. B.; Lindroos, P. M.; O'Brien, P. O.; Dreher, K. L.; Rosas, I.; Alfaro-Moreno, E. & Osornio-Vargas, A. R. (1998). Induction of the lung myofibroblast PDGF receptor system by urban ambient particles from Mexico City. *Am. J. Respir. Cell. Molec. Biol.*, 19, 4, (October 1998) 672–680, ISSN: 1044-1549.

Bravo, H. A. & Torres, R. J. (2002). Air Pollution levels and trends in the Mexico City metropolitan area, In: *Urban Air Pollution and Forests: Resources at Risk in the Mexico City Air Basin,* M. Fenn, L. Bauer, and T. Hernández, (Eds.), 121–159, Springer-Verlag, ISBN:978-0-387-95337-3, New York.

Boghosian, B. M. (1999). Lattice Gases and Cellular Automata. *Future Generation Computer Systems*, 16, 2, (December 1999) 171-185(15). ISSN: 0167-739X.

Castro, T. & Salcido, A. (2006). Influencia de la Contaminación Atmosférica de la Zona Metropolitana de la Ciudad de México en Tres Sitios Perimetrales, In: *Contaminación Atmosférica V*, Leopoldo Garcia-Colin Scherer, Juan Ruben Varela Ham (Eds.), 119-144, El Colegio Nacional, ISBN: 970-640-303-5, Mexico.

Celada, A. T. & Salcido, A. (2009). The Mexico City 2006 Wind Direction States, *Proceedings of the 20th IASTED International Conference on Modelling and Simulation (MS 2009)*, pp. 51-58, ISBN: 978-0-88986-799-4, Banff, Alberta, Canada, July 2009, Acta Press, Anaheim, Calgary, Zurich.

Chen, S.; Lee, M.; Zhao, K. H. & Doolen, G. D. (1989). A Lattice Gas Model with Temperature, *Physica D: Nonlinear Phenomena*, 37, 1-3, (July 1989) 42-59, ISSN: 0167-2789.

Chopard, B. & Droz, M. (1998). *Cellular Automata Modeling of Physical Systems*, CambridgeUniversity Press, ISBN-13: 9780521673457, Cambridge.

d´Humieres, D.; Lallemand, P. & Frish, U. (1986). Lattice Gas Models for 3D Hydrodynamics, *Europhys. Lett.*, 2, 4, (August 1986) 291-297, ISSN: 0295-5075.

Doran J. C.; Abbott S.; Archuleta J.; Bian X.; Chow J.; Coulter R. L.; Wekker S. F. J.; Edgerton S.; Elliott S.; Fernandez A.; Fast J. D.; Hubbe J.M.; King C.; Langley D.; Leach J.; Lee J.T.; Martin T.J.; Martinez D.; Martinez J.L.; Mercado G.; Mora V.; Mulhearn M.; Pena J.L.; Petty R.; Porch W.; Russell C.; Salas R.; Shannon J.D.; Shaw W.J.; Sosa G.; Tellier L.; Templeman B.; Watson J.G.; White R.; Whiteman C. & Wolfe, D. (1998). The IMADA-AVER boundary layer experiment in the Mexico City Area. *Bulletin of the American Meteorological Society*, 79, 11, (November 1998) 2497-2508, ISSN:1520-0477.

Doran J. C. & Zhong S. (2000). Thermally Driven Gap Winds into the Mexico City Basin, *Journal of Applied Meteorology*, 39, 8, (October 2000) 1330-1340, ISSN:08948763.

Frish, U.; Hasslacher, B. & Pomeau, Y. (1986). Lattice-Gas Automata for the Navier-Stokes Equation, *Phys. Rev. Lett.*, 56, 14, (April 1986) 1505-1508, ISSN: 1079-7114.

Garrat, J. R. (1992). *The Atmospheric Boundary Layer*, Cambridge University Press, ISBN:0-521-38052-9, Cambridge.

Hardy, J.; de Pazzis, O. & Pomeau, Y. (1976). Molecular Dynamics of a Classical Lattice Gas: Transport Properties and Time Correlation Functions, *Phys. Rev. A*, 13, 5, (May 1976) 1949-1961, ISSN: 1050-2947.

Hardy, J.; Pomeau, Y. & de Pazzis, O. (1973). Time Evolution of a Two-Dimensional Model System. I. Invariant States and Time Correlation Functions, *J. Math. Phys.* 14, 12, (December 1973) 1746-1759, ISSN: 0022-2488.

Hasslacher, B. (1987). Discrete Fluids, *Los Alamos Science*, 15, *Special Issue*, (1987) 175-217.

Jimenez, M. S.; Celada, A. T. & Salcido, A. (2008). The density of states of wind direction of the Mexico City Metropolitan Area: Year 2001, *Proceedings of the IASTED International Symposium on Environmental Modelling and Simulation (EMS 2008)*, pp. 301-307, ISBN: 978-0-88986-777-2, Orlando, USA, November 2008, Acta Press, Anaheim, Calgary, Zurich.

Kadanoff, L. P. & Swift, J. (1968). Transport Coefficients near the Critical Point: A Master-Equation Approach, *Phys. Rev.* 165, 1 (1968) 310-322, ISSN: 0031-899X.

MM5. (2003). MM5 Community Model. http://www.mmm.ucar.edu/mm5/mm5-home.html.

Osornio-Vargas, A. R.; Bonner, J. C.; Alfaro-Moreno, E.; Martinez, L.; Garcia-Cuellar, C.; Ponce-de-Leon-Rosales, S.; Miranda, J. & Rosas, I. (2003). Proinflammatory and cytotoxic effects of Mexico City air pollution particulate matter in vitro are dependent on particle size and composition. *Environ. Health Perspect.*, 111, 10, (August 2003) 1289–1293, ISSN: 0091-6765.

Rechtman, R.; Salcido, A. & Bagnoli, F. (1990). Thermomechanical Effects in a Nine-Velocities Two-Dimensional Lattice Gas Automaton, In: *Lectures on Thermodynamics and Statistical Mechanics*, M. López de Haro and C. Varea (Eds), 182-200, World Scientific., ISBN 981-02-0243-1, Singapore.

Rechtman, R.; Salcido, A. & Bagnoli, F. (1992). Some Near-Equilibrium Properties of a Nine-Velocities Lattice Gas Automaton for Two-Dimensional Hydrodynamics, In: *Complex Dynamics*, R. Livi, J-P. Nadal and N. Packard (Eds), 133-139, Nova Science Publishers Inc., ISBN: 1560720182, New York.

Rechtman, R. & Salcido, A. (1996). Lattice Gas Self Diffusion in Random Porous Media, *Fields Institute Communications,* 6 (1996) 217-225, ISSN: 1069-5265.

Rothman, D. & Zaleski, S. (1997). *Lattice-Gas Cellular Automata, Simple Models of Complex Hydrodynamics*, Cambridge University Press, ISBN: 0-521-55-201-X, Cambridge.

Salcido, A. & Rechtman, R. (1991). Equilibrium properties of a cellular automaton for thermofluid dynamics. In: *Nonlinear Phenomena in Fluids, Solids and Other Complex Systems,* P. Cordero and B. Nachtergaele (Eds), 217-229, Elsevier, ISBN: 0444887911, ISBN-13: 9780444887917, Amsterdam.

Salcido, A. & Rechtman, R. (1993). Lattice Gas Simulations of Flows Through Two-Dimensional Porous Media, *Proceedings of the International Symposium on Heat and Mass Transfer in Energy Systems and Environmental Effects*, pp. 222-226, Cancun, Mexico, August 1993, International Centre for Heat and Mass Transfer, Cancun.

Salcido, A. (1993). Lattice Gas Model for Transport and Dispersion Phenomena of Air Pollutants, In: *Transactions on Ecology and the Environment Vol. 1*, P. Zannetti, C.A. Brebbia, J.E. Garcia Gardea and G. Ayala Milian (Eds.), 173-181, WIT Press, ISSN: 1743-3541, Southamptom.

Salcido, A.; Merino, R. & Saldaña, R. (1993). Lattice Gas Model for Wind Fields over Complex Terrains. *Proceedings of the International Symposium on Heat and Mass Transfer in Energy Systems and Environmental Effects*, pp. 526-531, Cancun, Mexico, August 1993, International Centre for Heat and Mass Transfer, Cancun.

Salcido, A. (1994). First Evaluations of a Lattice Gas Approach to Air Pollution Modelling. In: *Transactions on Ecology and the Environment Vol. 3*, J. M. Baldasano, C. A. Brebbia, H. Power and P. Zannetti (Eds.), 141-150, WIT Press, ISSN 1743-3541, Southamptom.

Salcido, A.; Rodas, A.; Saldaña, R.; Miranda, U.; Sozzi, R. & Fraternali, D. (1994). Estudio de la Micrometeorología del Valle de México (Segunda Fase). Instituto de Investigaciones Eléctricas. Final Technical Report: IIE/15/0032/1 02/F (1994). Mexico.

Salcido, A; Celada, A. T.; Villegas, R.; Salas, H.; Sozzi, R. & Georgiadis, T. (2003a). A micrometeorological database for the Mexico City Metropolitan Area., *Il Nuovo Cimento*, 26C, 3, (May/June 2003) 317-355, ISSN: 11241896.

Salcido, A.; Sozzi, R. & Castro, T. (2003b). A Least Squares Variational Approach to the Convective Mixing Height Estimation Problem. *Environmental Modelling & Software,* 18, 10, (December 2003) 951-957, ISSN: 13648152.

Salcido, A.; Celada-Murillo, A. T. & Castro, T. (2008). Lattice Gas Simulation of Wind Fields in the Mexico City Metropolitan Area, *Proceedings of the 19th IASTED International Conference on Modelling and Simulation (MS 2008)*, pp. 95-100, ISBN: 9780889867413, Quebec, Canada, May 2008, Acta Press, Anaheim, Calgary, Zurich.

Sciarretta, A. & Cipollone, R. (2001). A lattice gas model for the evaluation of transport and diffusion parameters of stack emissions in air. In: *Air Pollution IX*, G. Latini and C. A. Brebbia (Eds), WIT Press, ISBN: 1853128775, Southampton.

Sciarretta, A. & Cipollone, R. (2002). On the evaluation of pollutant gas dispersion around complex sources by means of a lattice gas model. In: *Air Pollution X*, C. A. Brebbia and J. Martin-Duque (Eds), pp. 33-42, WIT Press, ISBN: 185312916X, Southampton.

Sciarretta, A. (2006). A lattice gas model with temperature and buoyancy effects to predict the concentration of pollutant gas released by power plants and traffic sources, *Mathematical and Computer Modelling of Dynamical Systems*, 12, 4, (August 2006) 313-327, ISSN: 1387-3954.

SMA-GDF. (2006). *Informe Climatológico Ambiental del Valle de México 2006*. Secretaria del Medio Ambiente del Gobierno del Distrito Federal. México.

SMA-GDF. (2008). *Inventario de Emisiones de Contaminantes Criterio de la Zona Metropolitana del Valle de México 2006*. Secretaría del Medio Ambiente. Gobierno del Distrito Federal. México.

Toffoli, T. (1984). Cellular automata as an alternative to (rather than an approximation of) differential equations in modeling physics, *Physica D*, 10, 1, (January 1984) 117-127, ISSN: 0167-2789.

UNEP (United Nations Environment Programme) & WHO (World Health Organization). (1992). *Urban Air Pollution in Megacities of the World*, Blackwell Publishers, Oxford.

Von Neumann, J. (1966). The *Theory of Self-Reproducing Automata*, University of Illinois Press, ISBN: 0598377980, Urbana.

Wolfram, S. (1986). Cellular Automaton Fluids I. Basic Theory, *J. Stat. Phys.* 45, 3-4, (November 1986) 471-526, ISSN: 00224715.

Zannetti, P. (1990). *Air Pollution Modelling. Theories, Computational Methods and Available Software*, Computational Mechanics Publications, ISBN: 0442308051, Southampton, Boston, New York.

19

A CFD Study of Passive Solar Shading

[1]Baxevanou C.A.*, [1]Fidaros D.K., [2]Tzachanis A.D.
[1]*Centre for Research and Technology-Thessaly, Institute of Technology and Management of Agricultural Eco-systems, Technology Park of Thessaly, 1st Industrial Area of Volos, 38500 Volos, Greece, cbaxe@cereteth.gr, dfeid@cereteth.gr*
[2]*Technological Educational Institute (TEI) of Larissa, Dept. of Mechanical Engineering, 41110 Larissa, Greece, tzach@teilar.gr*

Abstract

In the present study is investigated numerically the flow and transport phenomena in a test cell with its south side partially shaded by trailing plants and the cover shaded by a shelter. The two dimensional unsteady transport equations for the velocities, turbulence, energy and spectral intensity of radiation are solved numerically by a finite volume numerical model. The turbulent nature of the flow is simulated by the well known two equation k-ω high Re model while the incident radiation is used the Discrete Ordinates (DO) model and two wavelength bands are considered for the solar and thermal radiation. The model efficiently renders the buoyancy effects inside the cell, the cooling capacity of the plants, the heat transfer phenomena of solar radiation and heat conduction through the cell walls. The thermophysical and spectral optical properties of the involved materials were taken into account and not only the shading effect of trailing plant. The model was validated successfully via comparison with measured data that correspond in one day of August in Central Greece. A parametric study was carried out for other 4 months (May, June, July and September). The results are given in terms of fields of flow, radiation and temperature inside the test cell and in the space between this and the shading devices (shelter and trailing plants). Daily variations of average temperatures, solar radiation, air flow velocities and cooling load reduction are also given. The cooling load reduction ranges between 34 kWh/month per wall meter in September, and 63 kWh/month per wall meter in July, even without taking into account the temperature reduction due to the plants transpiration. The developed model can be used for the evaluation of various plants performance as passive solar shading configurations.

Notation

a	porous permeability [m^2]
C_2	inertial resistance factor [1/m]
C_p	specific heat capacity [J/(kg K)]
d	thickness [m]
e	specific energy (per unit mass) [J/Kg]

f_b	buoyancy force [Nt/m³]
f_d	diffuse fraction of incident radiation [-]
h	sensible enthalpy [J/Kg], convective heat transfer coefficient [W/m²K]
G	normal solar irradiation [W/m²]
$\overline{H_b}$	monthly average daily beam irradiation [Wh/m²]
$\overline{H_d}$	monthly average daily diffuse radiation [Wh/m²]
$\overline{H_{tot}}$	the monthly average daily radiation [Wh/m²]
I	radiation intensity [W/m²]
I_v	radiation intensity normal to vertical plane [W/m²]
I_h	radiation intensity normal to horizontal plane [W/m²]
I_λ	radiation intensity for wavelength λ [W/(m² src)]
$I_{b\lambda}$	black body intensity given by the Planck function [W/m²]
k	turbulent kinetic energy [J/Kg], Thermal conductivity [W/mK]
k_{eff}	effective conductivity [W/mK]
k_t	turbulent thermal conductivity [W/mK]
L	latitude [deg]
n	refractive index of medium b [-], number of the day of a year [-]
NT	total daily duration of sunlight [h]
Nu	nusselt number [-] (Nu=convection/conduction) $Nu = hL/K$
P	pressure [Pa]
r_i	reflectivity of medium I [-]
$\vec{r}$	position vector [-]
R_b	the ratio of beam irradiation on the plane to that on a horizontal plane [-]
S_h	radiation source term [J]
$\vec{s}$	radiation direction vector [-]
t	time [s]
time	time since sunrise [sec]
t_s	sunrise time [h]
T	temperature [K]
Ta	ambient temperature [K]
T_0	operating reference temperature [K]
U_i	average velocity in i-direction [m/s]
x_i	component in i-direction [m]

Greek Letters

α	absorptivity [-]
α_λ	spectral absorption coefficient [1/m] – or extinction coefficient
β	Thermal expansion coefficient [1/K], the surface slope [deg]
γ	the surface azimuth angle [deg]
δ	declination [deg]
ε	turbulent dissipation rate [J/(Kg s)], emissivity [-]
θ_a	angle between the normal to the surface and the incident radiation [deg]
θ_b	angle between the normal to the surface and the refracted radiation [deg]
θ_z	solar zenith angle [deg]

λ	wavelength [m^{-1}]
μ	viscosity [Pa sec]
μ_t	turbulent viscosity [Pa sec]
ρ	density [kg/m^3]
ρ_0	constant flow density [kg/m^3]
σ_s	scattering coefficient [1/m]
$(\tau_{ij})_{eff}$	effective stress tensor [Nt/m^2]
τ_i	transmissivity of medium i [-]
Φ	phase function [-]
ω	specific dissipation rate [s^{-1}] , hour angle [deg]
ω_s	sunrise hour angle [deg]
Ω'	solid angle [deg]

1. Introduction

The placing of plants in the vicinity of the south walls of a building as solar protection system is an old and well-known technique in traditional architecture and a basic parameter in bioclimatic design, especially for countries with a climate characterized by long hot days in the summers. Plants offer the potential of solar control in buildings as well as of passive cooling. Deciduous plants can reduce excessive solar heat gains during the summer allowing the solar light to reach the building's interior during the summer. This way they contribute in reduction of air conditioning devices usage during the periods of peak power demand (Achard, P. & Gicquel, R., 1986; Goulding, J. R. et al., 1993). It has been proved that by adding one tree the cooling energy savings can vary in the range of 12-24%. Three trees per house could reduce the cooling load from 17% to 57% (Akbari, H. et al., 1997; Raeissi, S. & Taheri, M., 1999). Plants can achieve this reduction operating in two ways: a) operating as natural shading and b) reducing the air temperature through transpiration. Plants not only improve the building's energy performance during summer but they also affect appearance of them as they can be incorporated in the architectural design offering an acceptable and aesthetical result (Carter, C. & De Villiers, J., 1987; Goulding, J. R. et al., 1992).

In the present study a numerical model is developed in order to study the transport phenomena in a test cell with its south façade partially shaded by trailing deciduous plant called *Parthenocissus quinquefoliant*. It is taken into account the plants' shading effect taking account their optical properties and their ability of heating storage but not the transpiration. The numerical model will be validated against existed measurements. Then a parametric numerical study will allow the systematic quantification of the energy gains which could establish a new way of thinking for passive cooling design.

2. Literature review

Until now the majority of studies about plants as passive solar devices, concerned the experimental investigation of the energy saving and alteration of the building internal microclimate offered by the plants' shadow.

According to measurements in two houses (Akbari, H., Kurn, D. M. et al., 1997) the cooling energy saving yielded by trees appearance can reach levels up to 30% corresponding to daily savings of 3.6 to 4.8 kWh/d. Experimental investigation of shading with trees, positioned around buildings - especially on the southern side (Papadakis, G. et al., 2001) have also been performed. The results have shown that trees constitute an excellent passive cooling system, being able to reduce the peak solar heat gain from 600 W/m^2 to 180 W/m^2, even with measured temperatures in the sunlit and in the shaded area of about 42°C and 33°C respectively.

Another group of studies developed analytical models which usually have been incorporated in software. In the paper (Tzachanis, A. D. & Sdravopoulou, C., 2002) the periodic steady heat gain in buildings is simulated with a dynamic model. In the work (Liu, Y. & Harris, D. J., 2008) an energy software package, the ESP-r, was used in order to study the effect of trees sited in the north of a house, in the heating-energy consumption.

Recently numerical methods are used for the study of heat transfer mainly in solar chimneys (Gan, G., 2006; Miyazaki, T. et al., 2006) used in the south facades. Numerical methods are more widely used for study of the microclimate developed in urban street canyons (Erell, E. & T. Williamson, 2006; Ali-Toudert, F. & Mayer, H., 2007).

As far it concerns numerical studies for the use of plants as passive solar systems there are some hybrid approaches like the one presented in (Mochida, A. et al., 2006) where a CFD model is used for the study of convective and radiative heat transports phenomena around buildings and the program 'TRNSYS' for the heat load calculations inside them.

In the numerical study (Baxevanou, C. A. et al., 2008) the test cell of present study was investigated considering the plants only as a shading device without taking into account exact optical and thermal properties and the temporal heat storage. Nevertheless this preliminary work was the starting point for the numerical model presented here.

3. Physical problem

In the present study the flow and transport phenomena inside and around a test cell with its south side shaded by trailing plant is investigated numerically. The physical model is an experimental setup of a cubic shaped test cell having a volume of approximately 30m^3 build at the TEI of Larissa, Greece (Tzachanis, A. D., 2008). This set-up gives the possibility to carry out experiments "in situ" with the instrumentation and the data acquisition system being placed inside the cell and is presented in Fig.1. Its south face is shaded by trailing plant called *Parthenocissus quinquefoliant*. The test cell walls are fabricated by a 5 cm sandwich material consisting of a 4.8 cm polyurethane layer with steel claddings. The whole construction was placed on a steel frame with wheels enabling easily the orientation change of the cell. Over the ceiling there is an inclined shelter of the same material that allows the cell cooling by convection from the air circulating between the ceiling and the shelter.

Fig. 1. A front view of the passive solar system

3.1 Geometry

In the following Fig.2 the geometry of a test cell cross-section is presented.

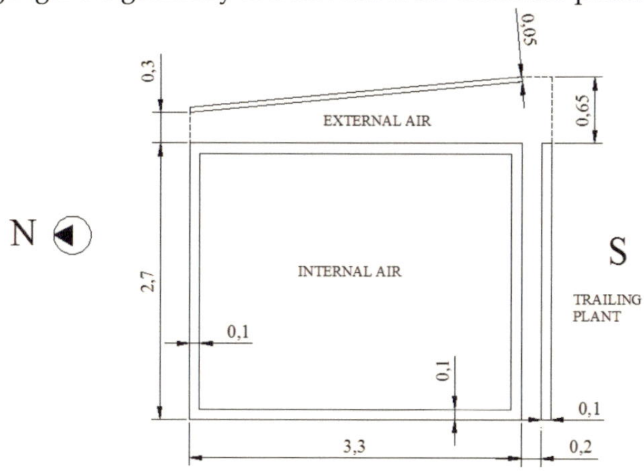

Fig. 2. Cross-section geometry

3.2 Properties

In the following tables the thermophysical and spectral optical properties of the involved materials are given. As it is said the walls are sandwich of polyurethane and steel cladding painted white. In this simulation is considered as a homogenous material with the effective properties given in the following Table 1. The plants' optical properties correspond to tomato crop according to (Zhang, Y. et al., 1997) and they are radiation wave length depended. They are given for two spectral bands, the first is considered as solar band and corresponds to wavelength λ=0-1.1 μm and the second is considered as thermal band and corresponds to wavelength λ=1.1–100 μm. The trailing plants are modelled as porous medium where the 40% of the total volume is air. The air is considered to contain enough vapors to present noticeable absorptivity (Modest, M. F., 2003).

Property	Air	Plant		Walls
		λ=0-1.1	λ=1.1-100	
Density, ρ [Kg/m³]	1.225	700		807
Specific Heat Capacity, Cp, [J/KgK]	1006.43	2310		465
Conductivity, k [W/m]	0.0242	0.173		0.0255
Viscosity, μ [Pasec]	1.789×10^{-5}	-		-
Thermal expansion coefficient, β [1/K]	0.00343	-		-
Absorptivity, α	0.19	0.71	0.95	0.85
Refractive index, n	1	2.69	1.22	24.62
Emissivity, ε	0.05	0.59		0.45
Transmissivity, τ	0.81	0.08	0	0

Table 1. Material properties

4. Mathematical model

In this work we study the flow and the transport phenomena developed in the air inside the test cell, the air between the test cell and the shading devices (shelter and trailing plants) and the solid materials involved (test cell walls, shelter and trailing plants). The flow is assumed to be 2D, incompressible, unsteady and turbulent since those phenomena are studied along the symmetry cross-section in the North-South plane as shown in Fig.2. This simplification is adopted in this study in order to save computational effort although the aspect ratio of the sides is rather small. The flow and transport phenomena for air flow and heat and radiation transfer are described by the Navier-Stokes equations (Ferziger, J. H. & Perić, M., 2002).

4.1 Transport equations

The time-averaged Navier-Stokes equations, for the mass and momentum transport are given as follow (Launder, B. E. & Spalding, D. B., 1974):

Continuity equation

$$\frac{\partial U_i}{\partial x_i} = 0 \tag{1}$$

Momentum conservation

$$\rho\left(\frac{\partial U_i}{\partial t} + U_j \frac{\partial U_i}{x_j}\right) = -\frac{\partial P}{\partial x_j} + \frac{\partial}{\partial x_j}\left[(\mu + \mu_t)\frac{\partial U_i}{\partial x_j}\right] + f_b + S_i \tag{2}$$

Where, U_i the time averaged i-direction velocity, ρ the density, P the pressure, μ the viscosity, μ_t the turbulent viscosity, f_b the buoyancy force, t the time and S_i source term expressing the pressure drop across the plants which are considered to be porous medium.

4.2. Boussinesq approximation

The density variation is calculated according to the Boussinesq model in order to take into account the natural convection effects. The use of Boussinesq model offers faster convergence, than considering the density variable in all equations. In this model the density is a constant value in all solved equations except from the buoyancy term calculation in the momentum equation:

$$f_b = (\rho - \rho_0) g \approx -\rho_0 \beta (T - T_0) g \tag{3}$$

This way the ρ is eliminated from the buoyancy term using the Boussinesq approximation:

$$\rho = \rho_0 (1 - \beta \Delta T) \tag{4}$$

Where β is the thermal expansion coefficient, T the temperature, ρ_o and T_o the corresponding reference values for density and temperature and g the gravity acceleration.

4.3 Porous media Treatment

The trailing plants, which are a shading device, are simulated as porous media adding a momentum source term S_i to the Navier-Stokes fluid flow equation. This term express the pressure drop caused in the flow by their presence and it is composed by a viscous loss term known as Darcy law and an inertial loss term, according to the following:

$$S_i = -\left(\frac{\mu}{\alpha} u_i + C_2 \rho u_i^2 \right) \tag{5}$$

where, a is the porous permeability and C_2 the inertial resistance factor.

4.4 Energy Treatment

Energy Conservation is described by the following equation

$$\rho \left(\frac{\partial h}{\partial t} + U_i \frac{\partial h}{\partial x_i} \right) = k_{eff} \frac{\partial}{\partial x_i} \left(\frac{\partial T}{\partial x_i} \right) + S_h \tag{6}$$

Where ε is specific energy (per unit mass), k_{eff} the effective conductivity, $(\tau_{ij})_{eff}$ the effective stress tensor and S_h source term which add the radiation contribution to the energy conservation equation. Auxiliary relationships for the calculations of quantities appeared in energy equation are presented here. Specifically relationships are given for the calculation of effective and turbulent conductivity as well as for the energy and enthalpy.

Effective Conductivity

$$k_{eff} = \gamma k_{feff} + (1 - \gamma) k_s \tag{7}$$

Where γ is the porosity, when γ=1 there is only fluid, k_{feff} the fluid effective conductivity and k_s the solid conductivity. The fluid effective thermal conductivity is given by

$$k_{feff} = k_f + k_t \tag{8}$$

Where k_f is the fluid conductivity and k_t the turbulent conductivity given by

Turbulent Conductivity

$$k_t = \frac{C_p \mu_t}{\Pr_t} \tag{9}$$

Where, C_p is the specific heat capacity and Pr_t the turbulent Prandtl number while the enthalpy h is given by the equation

$$h = \int_{T_0}^{T} C_p dT \tag{10}$$

The calculation of the energy equation source term is important because incorporates the effect of radiation in the energy balance and it is taken from the solution of the radiative transport equation. When the velocity takes null value, as it happens in solid materials, the above equation is decreased in the equation of conductivity for heat transfer.

$$\rho \frac{\partial T}{\partial t} + k_s \frac{\partial^2 T}{\partial x_i^2} + S_h = 0 \tag{11}$$

4.5. Turbulent model

The flow in both internal and external air is turbulent. The effect of turbulence is implemented via the high Re k-ω model of Wilcox [21](Wilcox, D. C., 1998).
Turbulent kinetic energy, k, transport equation is given by

$$\rho \frac{\partial k}{\partial t} + \rho U_j \frac{\partial k}{\partial x_j} = \tau_{ij} \frac{\partial U_i}{\partial x_j} - \beta^* \rho k \omega + \frac{\partial}{\partial x_j}\left[\left(\mu + \mu_\tau \sigma^*\right)\frac{\partial k}{\partial x_j}\right] \tag{12}$$

Where, ω is the specific dissipation rate, for which the transport equation is

$$\rho \frac{\partial \omega}{\partial t} + \rho U_j \frac{\partial \omega}{\partial x_j} = \alpha \frac{\omega}{k} \tau_{ij} \frac{\partial U_i}{\partial x_j} - \beta \rho \omega^2 + \frac{\partial}{\partial x_j}\left[\left(\mu + \mu_\tau \sigma\right)\frac{\partial \omega}{\partial x_j}\right] \tag{13}$$

with $\omega = \frac{\varepsilon}{\beta^* k}$, $\mu_\tau = \frac{k\rho}{\omega}$, α=5/9, β=3/40, β*=9/100, σ=1/2 and σ*=1/2, where ε is the turbulence dissipation rate.

4.6. Radiation model

In order to simulate the effect of solar incident radiation on the trailing plants, the shelter and the test cell walls, the Discrete Ordinates (DO) model is used. In this model it is assumed that radiation energy is 'convected' through the medium at its own speed simultaneously in all directions. The DO model allows the solution of radiation at semi-transparent walls. It can be used to non-gray radiation using a gray-band model. So it is adequate for use with participating media with a spectral absorption coefficient α_λ that varies in a stepwise fashion across spectral bands. The DO radiation model solves the Radiative Transfer Equation (RTE) for a finite number of discrete solid angles, each associated with a vector direction $\vec{s}$ fixed in the global Cartesian system (x,y,z). It transforms the RTE equation into a transport equation for radiation intensity in the spatial coordinates (x,y,z). The DO model solves for as many transport equations as there are directions $\vec{s}$ (Raithby, G. D. & Chui, E. H., 1990; Chui, E. H. & Raithby, G. D., 1993). The RTE for spectral intensity $I_\lambda(\vec{r},\vec{s})$ turns to

$$\nabla\left(I_\lambda(\vec{r},\vec{s})\vec{s}\right) + \left(a_\lambda + \sigma_s\right) I_\lambda(\vec{r},\vec{s}) = a_\lambda n^2 I_{b\lambda}(\vec{r}) + \frac{\sigma_s}{4\pi}\int_0^{4\pi} I_\lambda(\vec{r},\vec{s}')\Phi(\vec{s}\cdot\vec{s})d\Omega \tag{14}$$

In this equation the refractive index, the scattering coefficient and phase function are assumed independent of wavelength. The phase function Φ, is considered isotropic. The angular space 4π at any spatial location is discritized into $N_\theta x N_\varphi$ solid angles of extent ω_i, called control angles. The angles θ and φ are the polar and azimuthal angles, and are measured with respect to the global Cartesian system (x,y,z). In our case a 3x3 pixilation is used. Although in this equation the refraction index is taken constant, in the calculation of black body emission as well as in the calculation of boundary conditions imposed by semi-transparent walls the band length depended values of refractive index are used. This angular discretization provides us with a moderate computational cost but it may introduce discretization errors at boundaries when the solid angles are bisected by them (Raithby, G. D., 1999). Solving a problem with a fine angular discretization is very CPU-intensive. The RTE equation is integrated over each wavelength. Then the total intensity $I(\vec{r},\vec{s})$ in each direction $\vec{s}$ at position $\vec{r}$ is computed using

$$I(\vec{r},\vec{s}) = \sum_{\kappa} I_{\lambda_\kappa}(\vec{r},\vec{s})\Delta\lambda_\kappa \tag{15}$$

Where, the summation is over the wavelength bands. The RTE equation is coupled with the energy equation through a volumetric source term given by the following equation (Kim, S. H. & Huh, K. Y., 2000):

$$S_h = -\frac{\partial q_{r_i}}{\partial x_i} = a_\lambda\left(4\pi I_{b\lambda}(\vec{r}) - \int_{4\pi} I(\vec{r},\vec{s})d\Omega\right) \tag{16}$$

The spectral absorption coefficient, α_λ is computed from the absortpivity, α, according to the media thickness, d:

$$\alpha_\lambda = \frac{1}{d}\ln\left(\frac{1}{1-\alpha}\right) \tag{17}$$

5. Numerical model

The problem is simulated through 2D transport equations for mass, momentum, turbulence, energy and spectral radiation. Those transport equations (1, 2, 6, 12, 13 and 14) are solved numerically using the finite volume method.

5.1 Grid geometry

For the simulation is used a structured collocated grid consisted of 18864 cells as shown in the following Fig.3. The internal air field is consisted of 12400 cells. The external air field is consisted of 3744 cells. The plants are considered porous media consisted of 432 cells. The transport equations are also solved inside the solid walls which are discretized to 4 series and inside the shelter which is discretized to 3 series of cells resulting to 2288 cells in total.

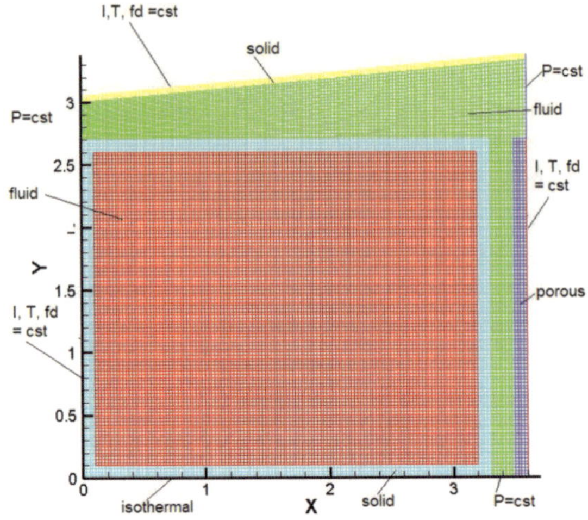

Fig. 3. Grid and Boundary conditions

5.2 Boundary conditions

The floor was assumed as a constant temperature wall, opaque which emits diffusively at an emissivity of ε = 0.92/0.72 depended on the wavelength band. For all the examined cases the floor temperature is set to T=293 K which is a simplifying approach.

In the North wall a mixed heat transfer boundary condition (combination of radiation and convection) is applied at the external boundary of the solid region. As far it concerns the radiation it is considered semi-transparent material where all the incident radiation is diffusive. A semi-transparent boundary condition implies that the incident radiation is reflected or transmitted by the surface. For that, the absorption coefficient of the adjacent solid zone is taken high enough to ensure that the whole transmitted radiation will be absorbed. This way the whole wall becomes opaque and the incident radiation is either reflected from the surface either absorbed, increasing the wall temperature. The heat transfer coefficient is taken h=7.1 W/mK.

The same boundary condition is imposed at the external surface of the shelter, where the heat transfer coefficient is set h=20 W/mK, and at the external south surface of the plants, where the heat transfer coefficient is set h=7.1 W/mK too. In the plants external surface the wall non-slip condition is substituted by a zero shear stress boundary condition. In this case the absorption coefficient of the adjacent porous material does not absorb all the transmitted incident radiation, but only a part of it.

All the internal walls are considered to be semi-transparent surfaces where the solid and fluid zones are coupled. This way the values of the variables are transferred from the one medium to the other. The trailing plants are considered as porous media with viscous resistance coefficient $\left(\frac{1}{a}\right) = 27380\,[m^{-2}]$, where a is the permeability and inertial resistance coefficient C_2= 1.534 [m^{-1}]. The porous material is coupled with the external boundary surface and the adjacent fluid. The equations of energy and radiations are also solved in all the solid and porous areas of the computational field. The flow both in the internal and the external fields is considered turbulent since the Ra number for the internal flow is 1.5×10^{10} and the Re number for the external flow is more than 1.9×10^{4}.

All the openings from where external air can enter or leave the computational field (right down opening between test cell and plants, right up opening between shelter and plants and left up opening between test cell and shelter) are considered as boundaries with constant pressure equal with atmospheric. The flow direction is determined by the whole field behavior as it is developed due to temperatures and the arising buoyancy forces. The air temperature in openings is set equal to the external air temperature.
When radiation reflected and transmitted from a specular semi-transparent surface, as it happens partly in our case, its direction is altered. The reflected radiation is given by

$$I_{W,a}(\vec{s}_r) = r_a(\vec{s}) I_{W,a}(\vec{s}) + \tau_b(\vec{s}') I_{W,b}(\vec{s}_b) \tag{18}$$

Where, $I_{W,a}$ radiation intensity in the medium a, which is the air in our case, $I_{W,b}$ radiation intensity in the medium b, which is the solid, $\vec{s}$, direction of the incident radiation (from a to b), $\vec{s}_r$ direction of the reflected radiation, $\vec{s}'$, direction of the radiation incident to the surface from the solid side (from b to a), r_a, the interface air reflectivity and τ_b, the interface solid transmissivity. The radiation transmitted from the semi-transparent wall towards the solid is given by

$$I_{W,b}(\vec{s}_t) = r_b(\vec{s}') I_{W,b}(\vec{s}) + \tau_a(\vec{s}') I_{W,a}(\vec{s}_b) \tag{19}$$

Where, $\vec{s}$ is the direction of the refracted radiation inside the solid, r_b, the interface solid reflectivity and τ_a, the interface air transmissivity. The radiation directions are given by

$$\vec{s}' = \vec{s}_t - 2(\vec{s}\cdot\vec{n})\vec{n} \tag{20}$$

Where, $\vec{n}$ is the normal to boundary unit vector, and

$$\vec{s}_r' = \vec{s} - 2(\vec{s}\cdot\vec{n})\vec{n} \tag{21}$$

The interfaces' reflectivities and transmissivities are given by

$$r_a(\vec{s}) = \frac{1}{2}\left(\frac{n_a\cos\theta_b - n_b\cos\theta_a}{n_a\cos\theta_b + n_b\cos\theta_a}\right)^2 + \frac{1}{2}\left(\frac{n_a\cos\theta_a - n_b\cos\theta_b}{n_a\cos\theta_a + n_b\cos\theta_b}\right)^2 \tag{22}$$

$$\tau_b(\vec{s}') = 1 - r_a(\vec{s}) \tag{23}$$

finally $r_b = r_a$ and $\tau_a = \tau_b$.
Where, n_a is the air refractive index, n_b the solid refractive index, θ_a the angle between the normal to the surface and the incident radiation direction $\vec{s}$ and θ_b, the angle between the normal to the surface and the refracted radiation direction inside the solid $\vec{s}_t$. It is obvious that in the case of unsteady calculations, those parameters should be calculated in every time step in each surface since the angle of incident radiation varies through the whole day.

$$\theta_b = \arcsin\left(\frac{n_a}{n_b}\sin\theta_a\right) \tag{24}$$

It should be noted that the above holds for $n_a < n_b$. The angle θ_a is given by (Duffie, J. A. & Beckman, W. A., 1991)

$$\cos\theta_a = (A - B)\sin\delta + \left[C\sin\omega + (D + E)\cos\omega\right]\cos\delta \tag{25}$$

$A = \sin\phi\cos\beta$, $B = \cos\phi\sin\beta\cos\gamma$, $C = \sin\beta\sin\gamma$, $D = \cos\phi\cos\beta$, $E = \sin\phi\sin\beta\cos\gamma$
Where, φ is the latitude (φ= 39° 38 in our case), δ is the declination, β is the surface slope, γ is the surface azimuth angle and ω is the hour angle. For the vertical south wall of plants it is

taken β=90° and γ=0°. For the shelter external surface it is taken β=5° and γ=180°. The angles δ and ω are given by

$$\delta = 23.45 \sin\left(\frac{360(284+n)}{365}\right) \tag{26}$$

$$\omega = \left[(t_s + t) - 12\right]15 \tag{27}$$

Where, n is the day of the year, t_s and is the sunrise time.

5.3 Numerical details

The SIMPLEC (Patankar, S. V., 1980) algorithm is used for pressure-velocity coupling, yielding an elliptic differential equation in order to formulate the mass conservation equation. The discretisation of the convective terms in the Reynolds averaged transport equations is materialized by the QUICK scheme for the momentum equations, a second order upwind scheme (SOU) for the turbulence and radiation transport equations and by a third order MUSCL for the energy conservation equation. For the diffusive terms a central difference scheme is adopted. The convergence criterion was set to 10^{-4} for the continuity, momentum and turbulence equations while for energy the criterion was 10^{-8} and for radiation 10^{-6}. For the radiation model two wavelength bands are considered corresponding to solar spectrum (λ=0 -1.1 μm) and to thermal band (λ=1.1 – 100 μm).

6. Reference case

In order to validate the numerical model our study began with the simulation of a summer day for which experimental data about incident solar radiation, ambient temperature and temperatures developed inside the test cell infrastructure exists. For the validation it was chosen the simulation of 22nd of August of 2006 (Tzachanis A.D., 2008).

6.1 Experimental configuration

The experiments, used for validation, were carried out at the South-orientated façade of the test cell during a hot summer period (July to September) in Larissa, a Greek city with a climate characterized by long hot days in the summer. The measured data are presented in paper (Tzachanis, A.D, 2008). With a set of pyranometers with and with out shading rings were measured the diffuse irradiation, the beam irradiation and the global irradiation in a horizontal plane, as well as the global irradiation and the ground reflected irradiation in a vertical plane. The temperatures were also measured in the ambient, sunlit wall, shadowed wall and in the gap between the plants and the south wall by NiCr thermocouples.

6.2 Numerical configuration

The daily variations of incident irradiations and ambient temperature were approached with polynomials, in order to be used as boundary conditions in the simulation. The corresponding polynomials are given following

For the irradiation in vertical plane

$$I_v = -6.7 - 7.48x10^{-3} time + 6.21x10^{-6} time^2 - 2.38x10^{-10} time^3 + 2.33x10^{-15} time^4 \tag{28}$$

For the irradiation in horizontal plane

$$I_h = -1.74 + 6.28x10^{-3}time + 4.57x10^{-6}time^2 - 1.83x10^{-10}time^3 + 1.79x10^{-15}time^4 \quad (29)$$

For the ambient temperature

$$T_{amb} = 2.13 - 5.87x10^{-4}time + 2.29x10^{-7}time^2 - 1.72x10^{-11}time^3 + 5.97x10^{-16}time^4 - 1x10^{-20}time^5 + 6.43x10^{-26}time^6 \quad (30)$$

Where, *time* is the time since sunrise in secs. In both plane the percentage of diffuse irradiation f_d was 30%. Since there are not experimental measurements, it was supposed that the north wall received the half irradiation than the plants' vertical surface and that all of this irradiation was diffusive, f_d=1. In the 22nd of August in Larissa (φ=39.38°, L=22.25°) the solar sunrise time is 6h 39′ 36″. Our simulation will begin from 6h 00′ 00″ in the morning giving the opportunity to the flow field to reach a steady state condition, before the boundary conditions begin to alternate. The whole period of simulation is the total solar day from 6 h 00′ 00″ up to 19h 20′ 00″, a few minutes after the sunset. The time step is dτ=1 sec. The simulation results are saved every 60 secs.

6.3 Model validation

The numerical model was validated against the experimental measurements. Three temperatures were compared. The temperature developed in the gap between the plants and the shaded south wall, the temperature developed on the shaded south wall and the temperature developed on the sunlit surface. As simulated temperatures are considered the average temperatures: a) on a line across the gap in the elevation of 1.35 m for the gap temperature, b) on the surface of the south wall, for the shaded wall temperature, and c) in the surface on the sunlit shelter for the sunlit temperature. In the following figures 4, 5 and 6 the measured and simulated temperatures temporal profiles are given. The simulated temperatures are also compared with the temperatures calculated by steady-state simulations realized for the hours 8:00, 10:00, 12:00, 14:00, 16:00 and 18:00.

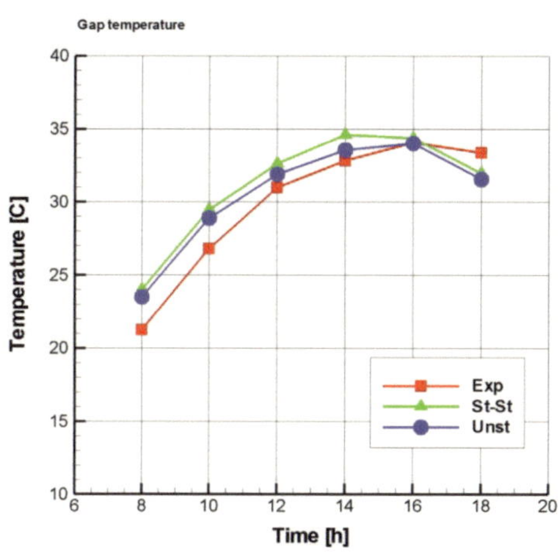

Fig. 4. Temporal profile of gap temperature

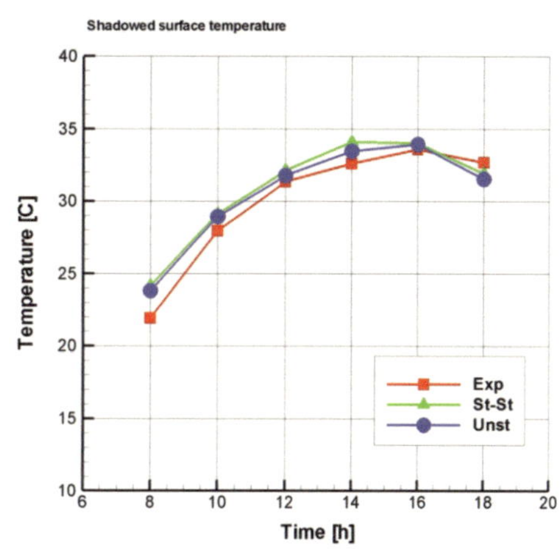

Fig. 5. Temporal profile of shadowed surface temperature

As far it concerns the gap and shaded surface temperatures we observe a fairly good approach with the unsteady simulation giving better results from the steady-state simulation since it takes into account the phenomenon of thermal storage. The average deviation of unsteady simulation to the measured temperatures is of the order of 10%. Almost all the day the real temperatures are lower than the predicted. This is due to the fact that transpiration and the subsequent temperature decrease is not incorporated in the proposed model.

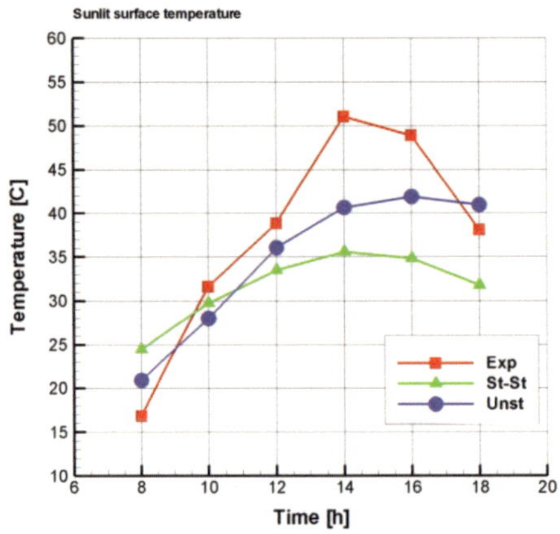

Fig. 6. Sunlit surface temporal temperature profile

As far it concerns the sunlit surface temperature profile we observe significantly more important improvement of temperature predictions passing from steady-state to unsteady radiation, in the order of 30% but the predicted values are still away from the measured especially for the hours between 14:00 and 16:00. As it has been pointed in the boundary conditions section a mixed boundary condition, taking account both convection and radiation, has been implemented to the shelter outer surface. Since the field around the shelter outer surface is not solved in this simulation a constant convection coefficient was adopted during all the day. It is likely at the afternoon hours the external wind speed to be enough low, so as to it led to a convection coefficient much lower than assumed. This could explain the deviation between measured and simulated temperatures during those hours.
In general the comparison is considered successful and the model is considered to simulate with fairly accuracy the transport phenomena takes part in the studied field. In following figures the most important flow and heat parameters in 6 characteristic hours are given in terms of iso-contours, streamlines and profiles. In fig.7 the temperature iso-contours inside the test cell are given for the hours 8:00, 10:00, 12:00, 14:00, 16:00 and 18:00.

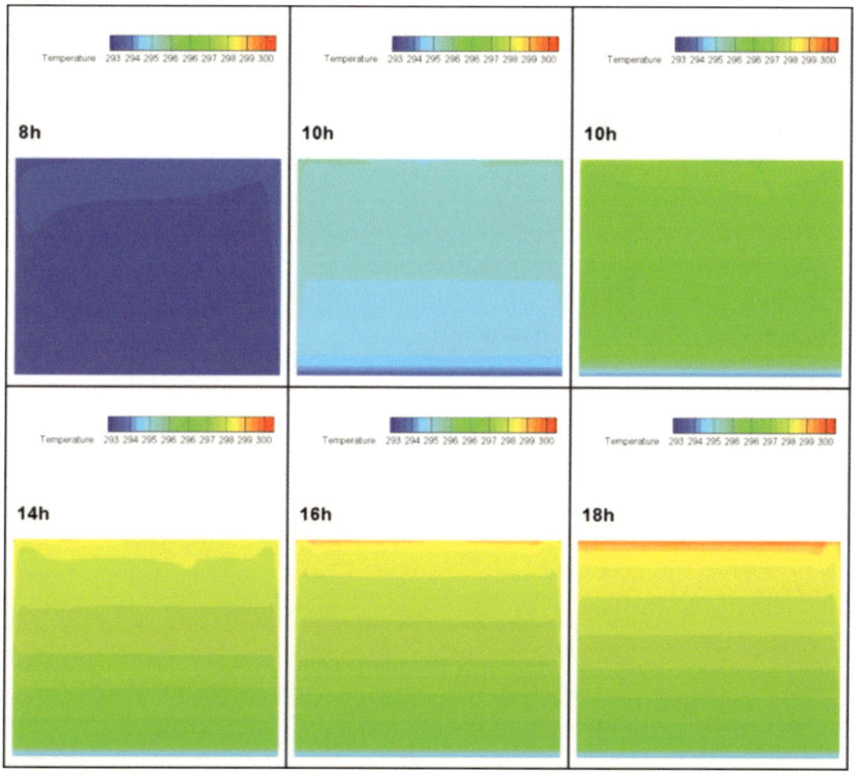

Fig. 7. Temperature iso-contours

During the day the temperature does not exceed the 27 °C, with the higher temperatures appearing at 18:00 h in the afternoon in the top of the cell. Although the north wall receives only diffusive radiation with the half intensity than the south the plants existence provide enough shadow to keep the south wall temperature low enough to cancel the appearance of any temperature gradient. The temperature in the floor remains 20 °C because it was selected to adopt the particular simplifying admission of isothermal boundary condition. In Fig.8 the temperature iso-contours around the test cell and between the cell and the shading devices are presented. In the external studied field the temperature can be as high as 36 °C, due to increased external air temperature and the heating through conduction, convection and irradiation. The higher temperature is observed in the 16:00 in the afternoon.

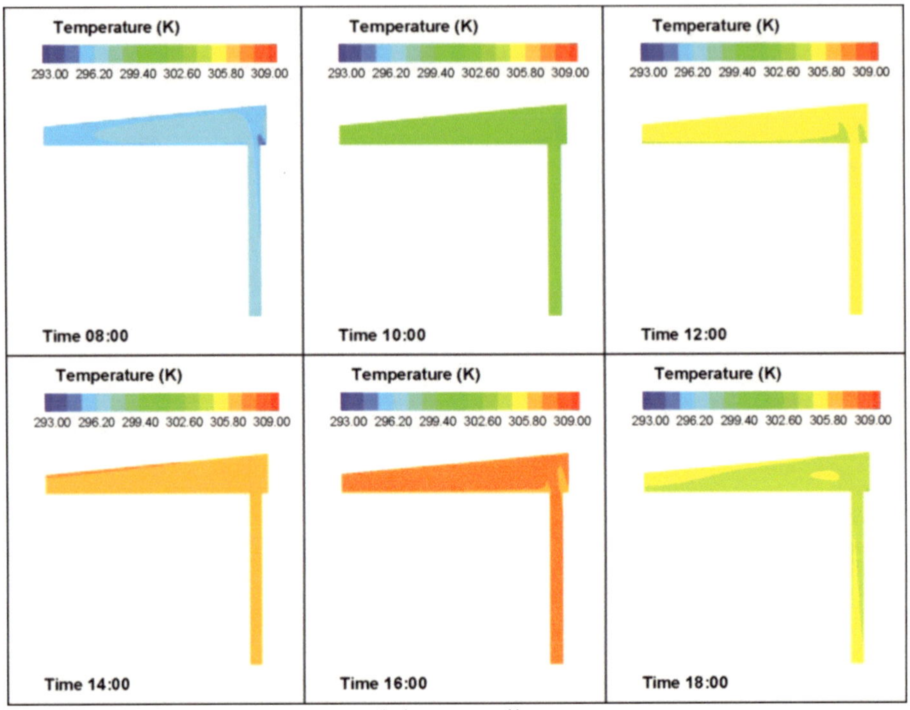

Fig. 8. Temperature iso-contours around the test cell

Finally in the figures 9 and 10 the temperature profiles along the x and y symmetry axes of the test cell are presented. The luck of any horizontal temperature gradient is verified. In the horizontal symmetry axis the temperature increase until 14:00 and then remains almost constant. The same behavior is observed along the vertical axis where the higher gradient appears during the afternoon.

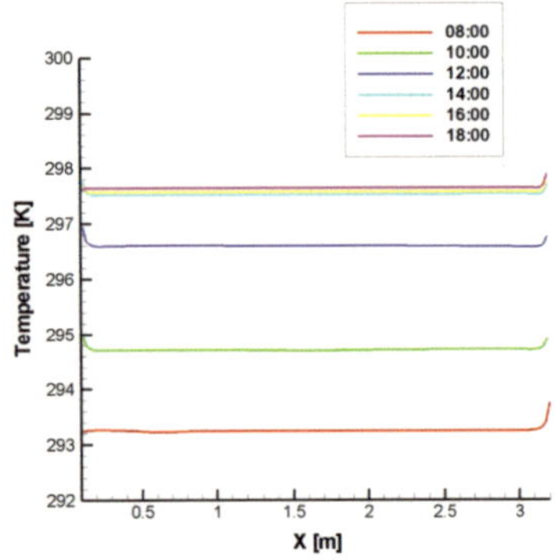

Fig. 9. Horizontal symmetry axis temperature profile

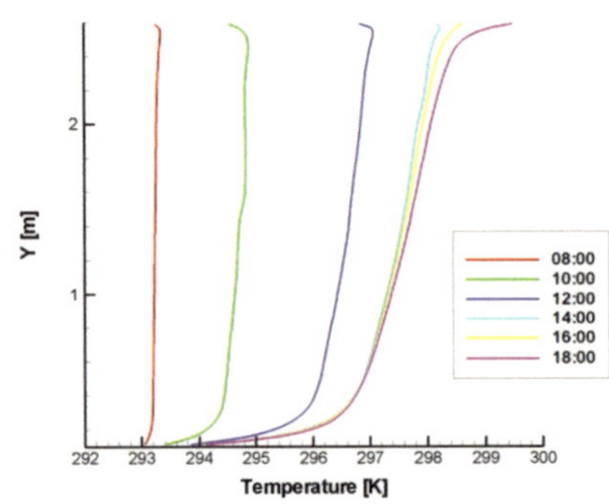

Fig. 10. Vertical symmetry axis temperature profile

In the figures 11 and 12 the streamlines and the isobaric contours are presented for the internal and the external field and the same hours.

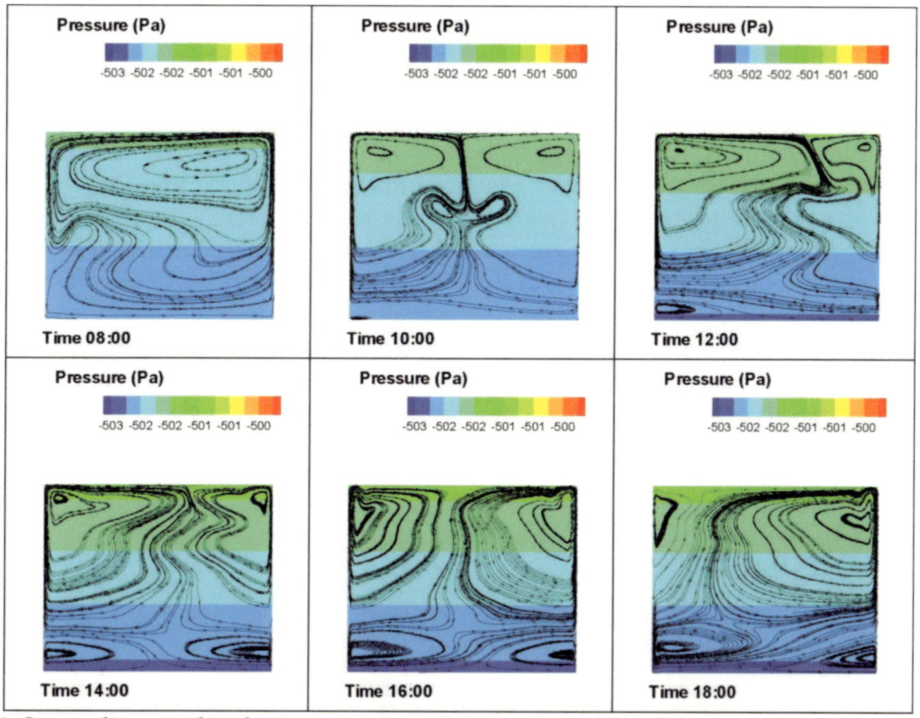

Fig. 11. Streamlines and isobaric contours inside the test cell

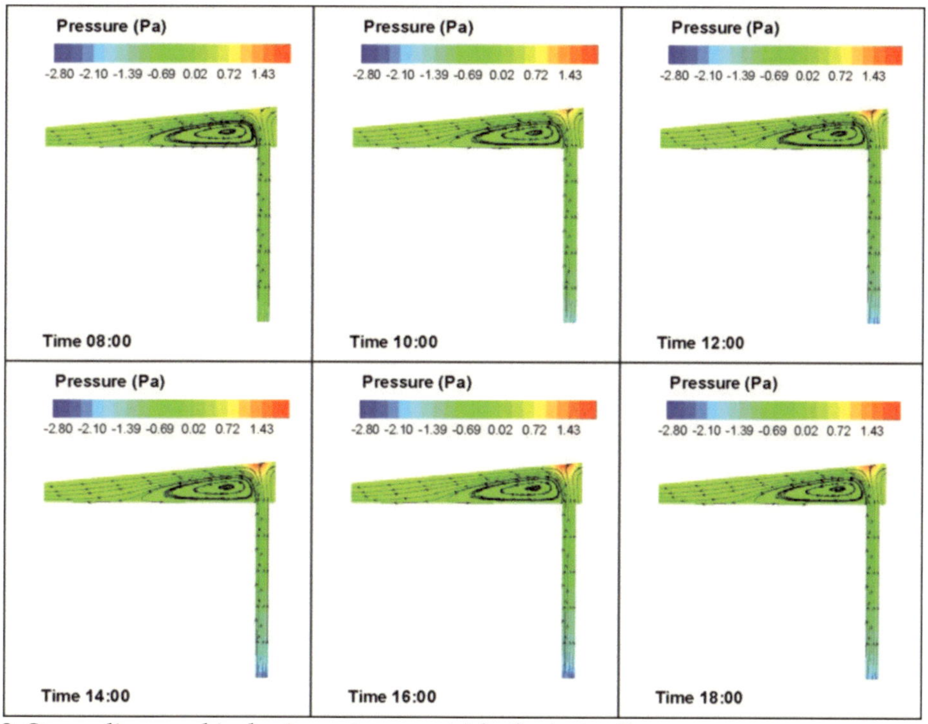

Fig. 12. Streamlines and isobaric contours outside the test cell

In both internal and external field the only driving force is the buoyancy. At the beginning of the day a unique big recirculation appears in the top left corner covering the whole internal field. Very soon it breaks in two recirculations sited in the top left and the top right corners, in the most heated areas of external walls. Other two smaller recirculations appears in the middle of the cell at 10:00, almost disappears at 12:00 and finally are established in the left and right bottom corners were they remains until the end of the day. From morning to the afternoon the left recirculation increases at the expense of the right one and then it decreases again as the ambient temperature, and consequently the north wall temperature, decreases. At the end of the day the right top recirculation is becoming dominant again. The external field flow pattern, between the test cell and the shading devices, remain almost unaltered as far it concerns the form. A solar chimney is developed between the plants and the south wall enforcing the external air to enter from the bottom and leave from the top openings, in the left between the test cell and the shelter and in the right between the shelter and the plants. The flow is separated in the cell left corner and reattached in the middle of the cell top forming and big recirculation. In the following figures 13, 14, 15 and 16 the u and v velocity components are given along the x and y symmetry axes inside the test cell.

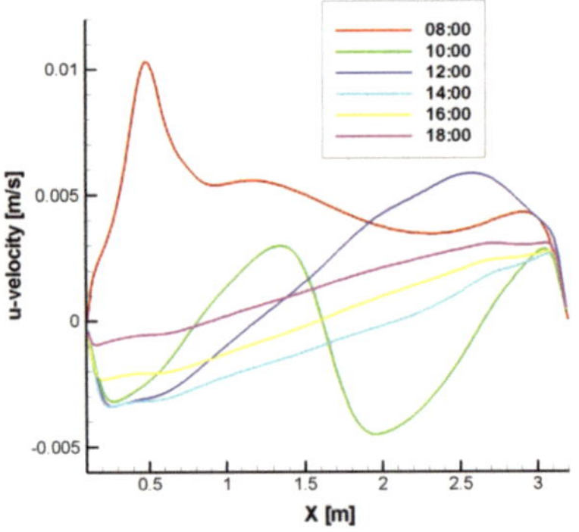

Fig. 13. u-velocity along x-symmetry axes

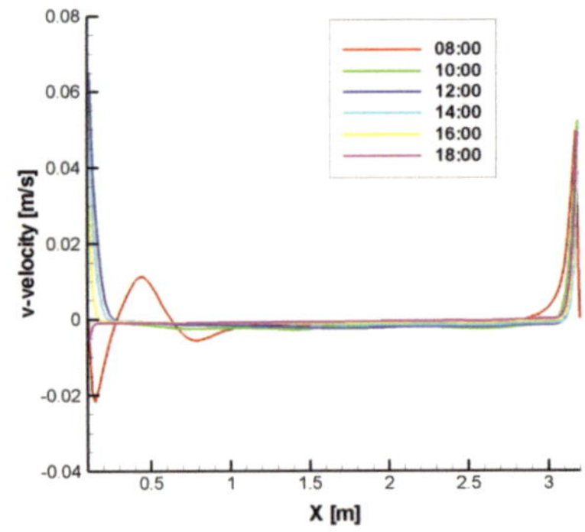

Fig. 14. v-velocity along x-symmetry axes

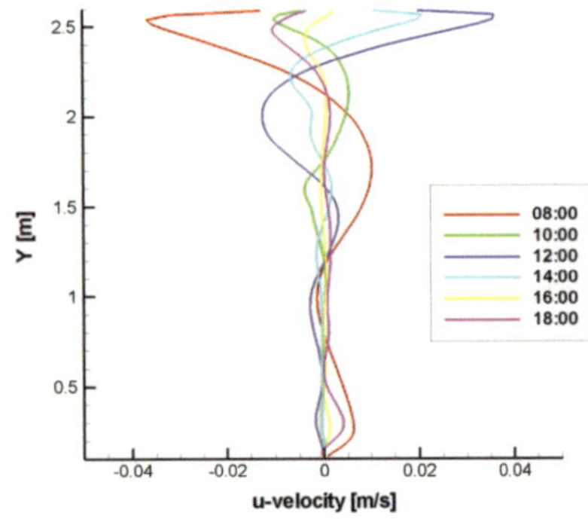

Fig. 15. u-velocity along y-symmetry axes

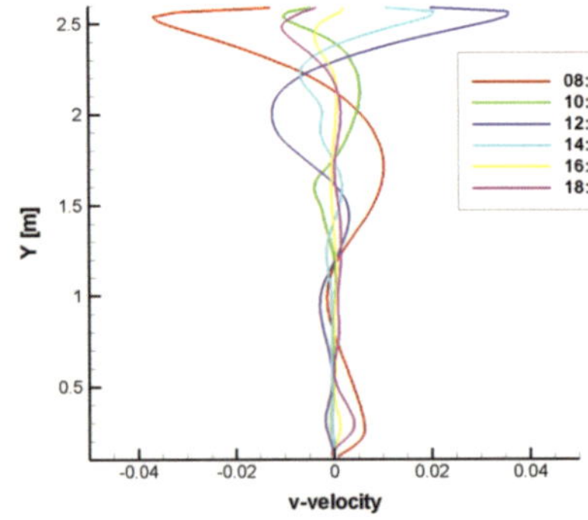

Fig. 16. v-velocity along y-symmetry axes

In all the cases velocities remains very low and don't exceed 0.08 m/s. Boundary layers seem to be well modeled. The v-velocity in horizontal axis remains almost zero except the areas close to the solid boundaries and almost time independent. In the vertical axis the most extreme behavior are observed for the hours 8:00 and 12:00, when the internal field is altered until it reaches the almost steady afternoon condition. The same holds for the u component of velocity along the vertical axis. Along the horizontal axis u velocity component seems to undergo more severe alterations from morning to noon and it stabilizes during the afternoon.

In the figure 17 the iso-contours of the solar band incident radiation is presented. Plants prevent quite efficiently the entrance of solar radiation decreasing it up to 50%. The direct result is the reduction of the south wall temperature and consequently of the cooling loads. Finally in the figure 18 the Nusselt number profile in the shelter inner surface is given.

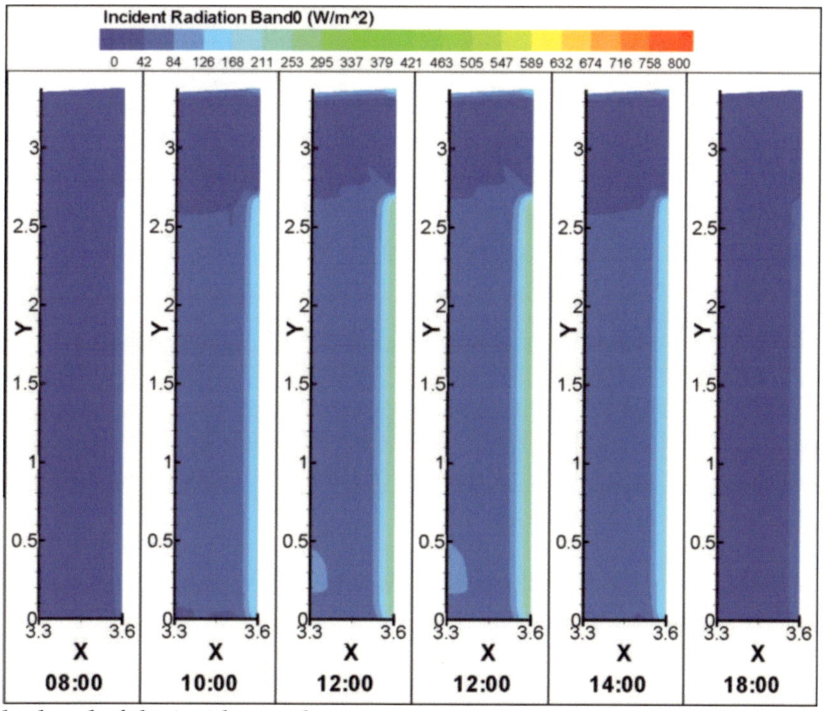

Fig. 17. Solar band of the incident radiation iso-contours

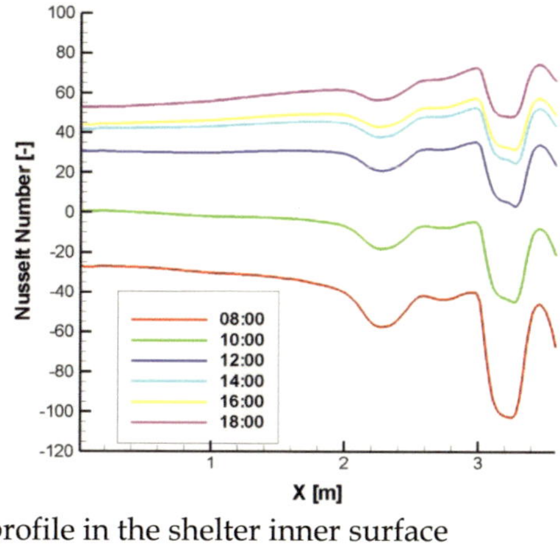

Fig. 18. Nusselt nuber profile in the shelter inner surface

In the site where the big recirculation appears a sudden drop of Nusselt number value occurs. Such a behavior would be impossible to be predicted with the usual semi-empirical analytical calculating tools based on the geometry and Re and Pr numbers. This figure reveals the CFD contribution in the common engineering problems since it allows the formulation a deep and accurate image of the real transport phenomena and a more precise estimation of the cooling loads and the gains arising from passive solar shading devices

7. Parametric study

The validated model was used for a parametric study in order to estimate the alteration of test cell mirco-climate due to the presence of plants during the whole summer. Four more characteristics days from May to September were simulated. Since there are not measured climatic data for those days, meteorological data available by CRES (Centre from Renewable Energy Sources of Greece) were used. In the Table 2 the monthly average daily radiation $\overline{H_{tot}}$ and the monthly average daily diffuse radiation $\overline{H_d}$ in horizontal plane are given. The 22nd day of each month is chosen as representative. In the same table the monthly average fraction of diffusive radiation $\overline{f_d}$ is given, along with the number of the day of the year, n.

Day	n [-]	$\overline{H_{tot}}$ [kWh/m²-d]	$\overline{H_d}$ [kWh/m²-d]	$\overline{f_d}$
22 May	142	6.66	1.97	0.30
22 June	173	7.13	2.00	0.28
22 July	203	7.74	1.82	0.24
22 September	265	4.94	1.44	0.29

Table 2. Radiation data for parametric study

From the above data it is calculated the monthly daily average beam irradiation in horizontal plane, $\overline{H_b}$ by the relation:

$$\overline{H_b} = \overline{H_{tot}} - \overline{H_d} \tag{31}$$

Taking into account the total duration of sunlight, NT, and assuming a sinusoidal variation we can calculate the beam normal irradiation $G_{b,nt}(\beta=0)$ [kW/m²] at any time of the day.

$$G_{b,nt}\left(\beta=0\right) = G_{b,n\max}\left(\beta=0\right)\sin\left[\frac{\pi \cdot time}{NT}\right] \tag{32}$$

Where, $G_{b,nmax}(\beta=0)$ is the maximum value of beam normal irradiation, in kW/m², given by

$$G_{b,n\max}\left(\beta=0\right) = \overline{H_b}\frac{\pi}{2NT} \tag{33}$$

The total number of sunlight hours, NT is calculated by

$$NT = \frac{2\omega_s}{15} \tag{34}$$

Where, ω_s, the sunrise hour angle given by

$$\omega_s = a\cos\left[-\tan\phi\tan\delta\right] \tag{35}$$

The total irradiation normal to the surface of sunlit test cell surfaces, $G_{tot,nt}(\beta)$ is given by

$$G_{tot,nt}\left(\beta\right) = \frac{G_{b,nt}\left(\beta\right)}{\overline{f_d}} \tag{36}$$

Where, $G_{b,nt}(\beta)$ the beam irradiation normal to the surface with inclination angle β given by

$$G_{b,nt}(\beta) = R_b G_{b,nt}(\beta{=}0) \tag{37}$$

In this relationship R_b is the ratio of beam irradiation on the plane to that on a horizontal surface at any time given by

$$R_b = \frac{\cos\theta_a}{\cos\theta_z} \tag{38}$$

Where, θ_z, is the zenith angle calculated by

$$\cos\theta_z = \sin j \sin\delta + \cos j \cos\omega \cos\delta \tag{39}$$

The irradiation in the plants surface is calculated with $\beta=90^o$ and $\gamma=0^o$, while the irradiation in the shelter with $\beta=5^o$ and $\gamma=180^o$. The irradiation on the north wall is taken half the irradiation on the plants and it is considered purely diffusive.

As far it concerns temperature it was assumed that it follows sinusoidal variation during the day under a rule of thumb

$$T(t) = a\sin(t) + b \tag{40}$$

$$t = \frac{time \cdot \pi}{NT} \text{ [hr]} \tag{41}$$

Where a and b are coefficients calculated from the minimum and maximum temperatures. The minimum and maximum temperatures have been retrieved from NASA meteorological site and are given in the table 3.

Table 3. Temperature for parametric study

Day	Minimum T [°C]	Maximum T [°C]	NT [h]	a [-]	b [-]
22 May	10.8	25.7	14.36	14.9	10.8
22 June	15.0	30.9	14.78	15.9	15.0
22 July	17.6	33.0	14.36	15.4	17.6
22 September	14.1	28.7	11.95	14.6	14.1

All the simulations covered the whole periods of sunlight. The time step used was dτ= 2sec.

8. Results

In the figures 19 (a-e) the daily variation of characteristic average temperatures are given for the months May, June, July, August and September. Specifically in each figure are given the ambient temperature, the average room temperature, the average temperature in the gap between the south wall and the plants, the average temperature of the shaded south wall and the average temperature of the sunlit surface. The gap average temperature is the one taken in a line from the south wall to the porous plants at the elevation of 1.35 m. The picture is completed with fig. 19.f, the daily variation of ambient temperature imposed as external boundary condition for the five months. In all the cases the gap and the shaded surface temperatures are almost equal to the ambient temperature as it is imposed by the convection of the air stream entering the computational field from the bottom opening. The room temperature remains low enough and the sunlit temperature becomes far higher than the ambient one due to the solar radiation and the temporal heat storage. The highest ambient temperatures are found in July and August. In the figures 20 (a-e) the corresponding daily variations of average solar band radiation in the porous plants and in the gap are given, with the external solar band incident radiation in horizontal surface given in fig. 20.f. In months close to the summer solstice very small amounts of solar band radiation are allowed to pass from the porous plants due to the incident angle and the optical properties. It should be noted that for the months May, June, July and September the percentage of ground reflected radiation and its direction was not taken into account.

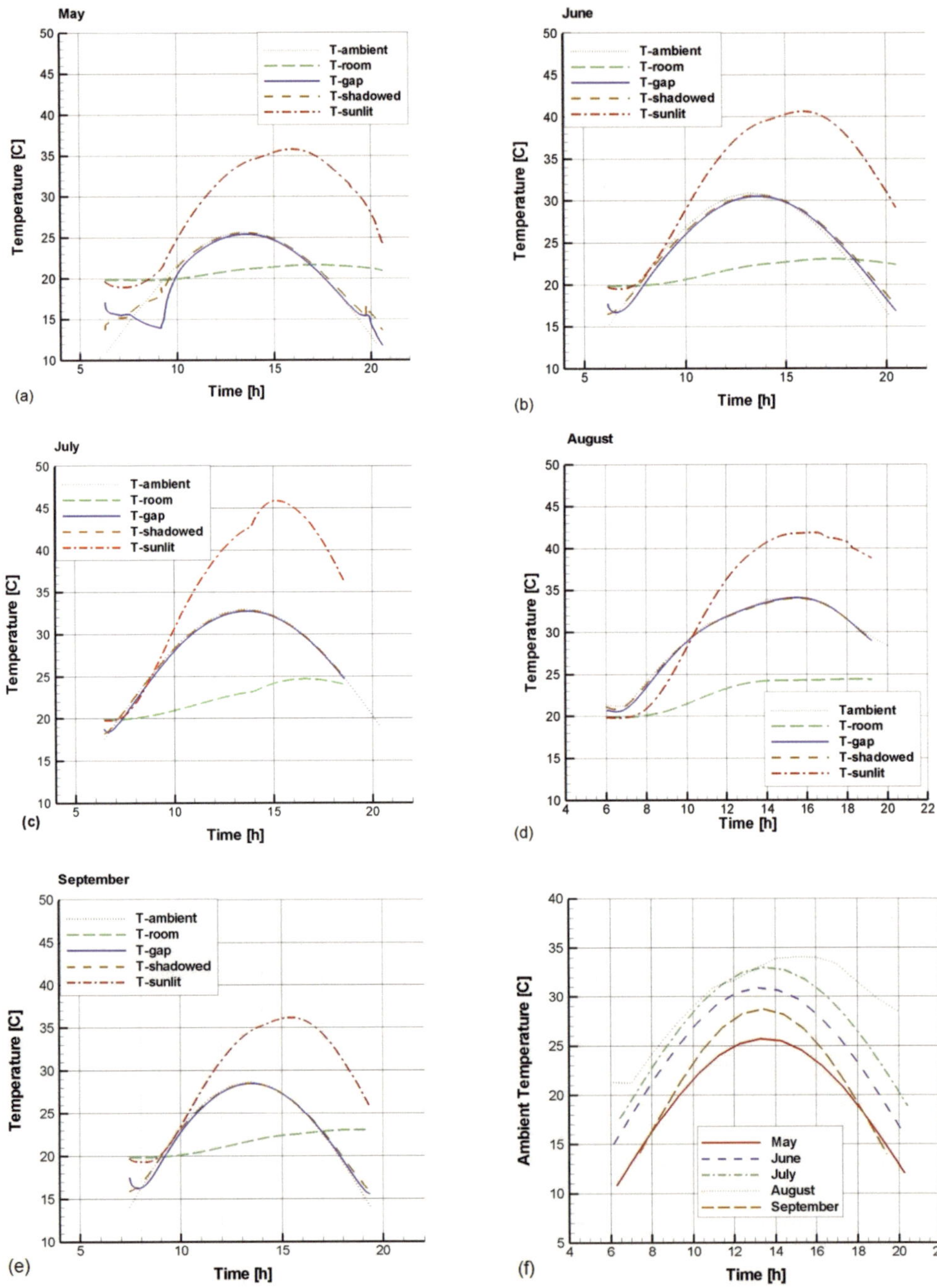

Fig. 19. Daily variation of average temperatures (a-e) and of ambient temperature (f)

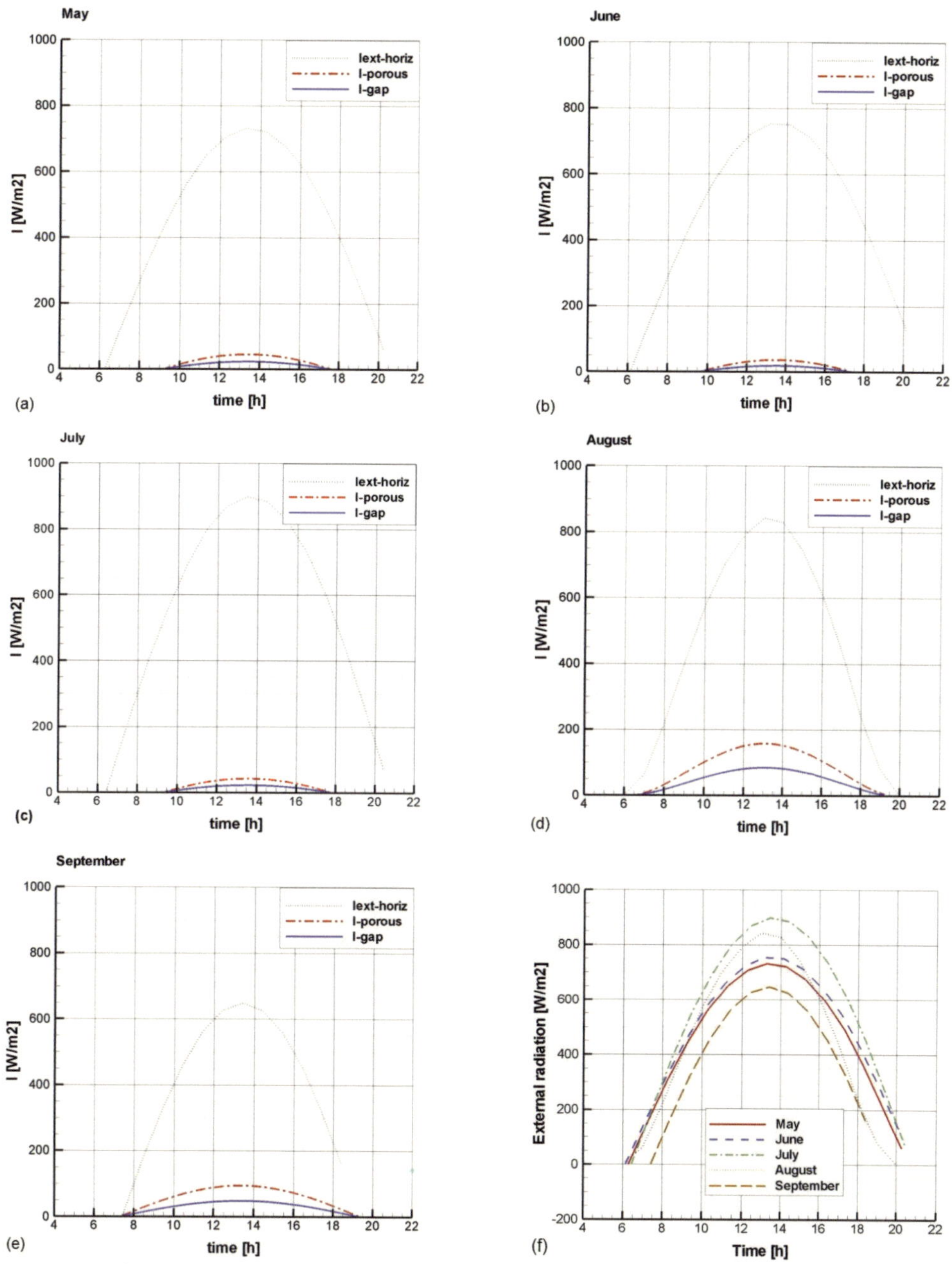

Fig. 20. Daily variation of average solar band radiation (a-e) and of external radiation incident on horizontal surface

In the figures 21 and 22, the daily variation of the average velocity magnitudes inside the room and in the gap between the plants and the south wall are given. The temperatures inside the room are very low as it was expected. They begin from relatively high values in the morning and the decrease stabilising for the rest of the day to very low values. This behaviour is common to all months and agrees with the daily alteration of streamlines studied for August in Figure 11. In the gap it is observed that the higher the normal radiation in the plants external surface the higher the velocities in the created solar chimney.

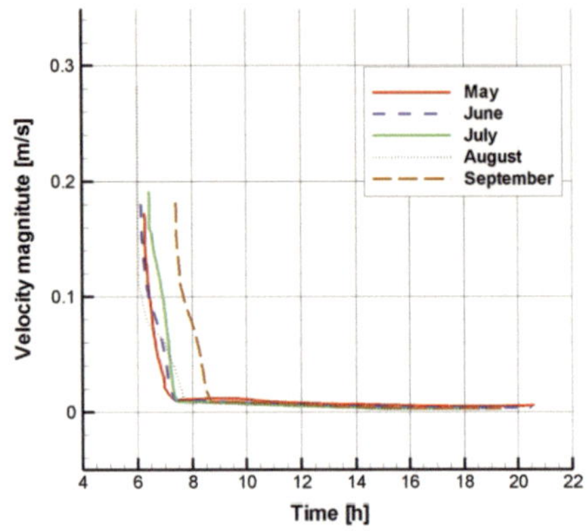

Fig. 21. Daily variation of room average velocities magnitude

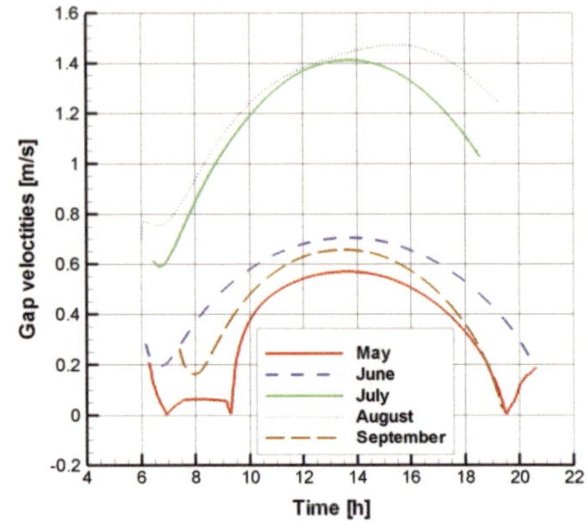

Fig. 22. Daily variation of gap average velocities magnitude

The basic goal of the plants use as passive solar shading devices is to decrease the cooling loads during the summer. Without the presence of the plants the south wall would have the sunlit surface temperature and energy should be consumed in order to remove the heat gain. This energy corresponds to the cooling load reduction achieved by the trailing pants presence. In the next figures 24 and 25 the daily variation of cooling load reduction and degree hours for the five examined months are presented. The degree hours (DH) and the cooling load reduction (CL) are calculated according to the following formulas

$$DH = (Tsunlit - Tshaded) * time \text{ [dh]} \tag{42}$$

$$CL = DH * area * surface\ heat\ transfer\ coefficient \text{ [Wh/m]} \tag{43}$$

Where the area is the south wall area per meter (*area* = 2.7 m^2/m) and the *heat transfer coefficient* has been extracted from simulation results for the south wall surface.

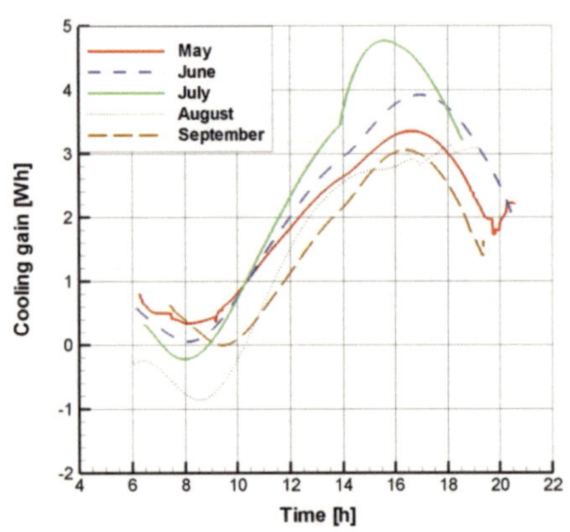

Fig. 23. Daily variation of cooling load reduction

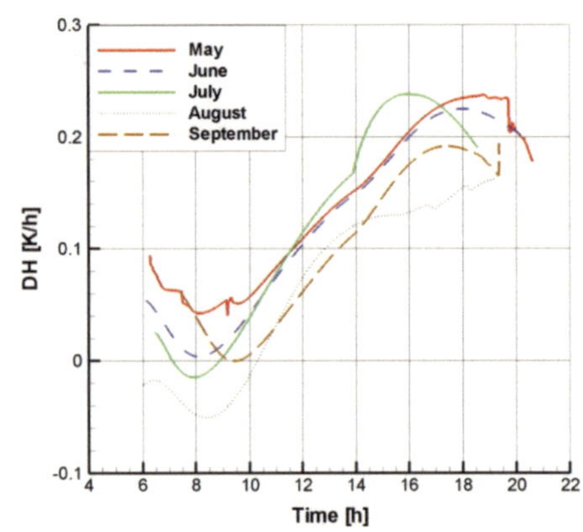

Fig. 24 Daily variation of degree hours

Integrating the cooling load reduction in the whole day time period the total daily energy saves can be calculated. In the Table 3 the energy saves per wall meter are summarized for the five examined months. August results agree with the energy saves calculated by experimentally measured data in (Tzachanis, A. D. 2008).

a/a	Month	Daily energy save [Wh/m]	Monthly energy save [kWh/m]
1	May	1651	51.81
2	June	1850	55.50
3	July	2038	63.18
4	August	1098	34.04
5	September	1127	33.81
		TOTAL	238.34

Table 3. Energy saving achieved by the trailing plants presence

9. Discussion

In the present work a CFD model was developed using a finite volume method for the simulation of flow and transport phenomena occurring in a test cell partially shaded by trailing plants and a shelter. The model was validated against obtained experimental measurements. It slightly overestimates the temperatures developed in the gap between the test cell south wall and the plant as well as the temperatures in the shaded south wall because it does not take into account the temperature reduction through transpiration. As far it concerns the temperature of sunlit surface a discrepancy is observed during some noon hours probably due to consideration of constant heat transfer coefficient as a boundary condition in the shelter external surface. Nevertheless the differences are small enough to consider the simulation successful and the model able to predict the developed flow, radiation and temperature patterns.

Inside the room the temperature during the whole day remains quite low due to thick insulation and the presence of the shading plants. The later is verified by the absence of horizontal temperature gradient although the north wall receives the half radiation of the south sunlit plants surface, which is also totally diffusive. The flow pattern inside the room alternates intensively during the first morning hours and it is stabilized in the afternoon hours. Between the test cell and the shading devices (trailing plants and shelter) a solar chimney is developed resulting in temperatures close to the ambient ones. In the whole computational field the only driving force is the thermal buoyancy. The time of maximum temperature is shifted towards the afternoon due to temporal heat storage phenomenon. The incident solar radiation is significantly reduced by the plants which are considered porous material with homogenous thermophysical and optical properties especially close the summer solstice when the incident angle increases.

The contribution of using CFD techniques for study of similar problems is revealed from the Nusselt number profile on the shelter inner surface, indicatively given in the figure 18, which would be impossible to be predicted with analytical semi-empirical tools.

The parametric study allows the calculation of cooling load reduction, offered by the presence of plants in the south wall vicinity, during the whole period of high ambient temperatures of the year. It shows considerable reduction of cooling loads which could lead to important energy save during a period with high power demand. The quantification of this energy save was the basic object of the simulation realised in this work.

10. Conclusion – Suggestion

The placing of plants near the south walls offer important reduction in buildings cooling loads, as it is known from traditional architecture and bioclimatic design principles. In the present work their effect was simulated using Computational Fluid Dynamic (CFD) techniques allowing the quantification of energy saving during the hot summer period. The developed model is considered successful since it compares well with existing experimental measurements.

Nevertheless the model can be improved further. One important step is the introduction of the mechanism of temperature reduction due to the plants transpiration that could allow better estimation of temperatures fields. Another step could be the 3D simulation that would allow more accurate calculation of the expected energy saving.

A better approach of the boundary condition imposed on the test cell ground would give a more realistic estimation of the flow and temperature pattern developed inside the test cell, allowing the extraction of conclusion about the comfort conditions there.

One important parameter is the value of the thermophysical and spectral optical properties of the involved materials. Especially as far it concerns the plant it would be very useful to measure accurately the optical properties and use them in a more appropriate wavelength band discretization. The model can be used for the evaluation of different plants performance and it can allow the design of effective passive solar shading systems.

11. References

Achard, P. & Gicquel, R. (1986). *European Passive Solar Handbook:Basic principles and concepts for passive solar architecture,* Commission of the European Communities, Directorate-General XII for Science, Research and Development (Brussels)

Akbari, H., Kurn, D. M., Bretz, S. E. & Hanford, J. W. (1997). Peak power and cooling energy savings of shade trees, *Energy and Buildings,* 25(2), *pp.* 139-148

Ali-Toudert, F. & Mayer, H. (2007). Effects of asymmetry, galleries, overhanging facades and vegetation on thermal comfort in urban street canyons, *Solar Energy,* 81(6), *pp.* 742-754

Baxevanou, C. A., Fidaros, D. K. & Tzachanis, A. D. (2008). *Plant's shading effect in a test cell - A CFD study*. Applied Simulation and Modelling, Corfu, Greece, Acta Press.

Carter, C. & De Villiers, J. (1987). *Principles of passive solar building design: with microcomputer programs,* 0080336361, New York.

Chui, E. H. & Raithby, G. D. (1993). Computation of radiant heat transfer on a nonorthogonal mesh using the finite-volume method, *Numerical Heat Transfer, Part B: Fundamentals,* 23(3), *pp.* 269-288

Duffie, J. A. & Beckman, W. A. (1991). *Solar engineering of thermal processes,* Wiley, 0471510564, New Jersey.

Erell, E. & T. Williamson (2006). Simulating air temperature in an urban street canyon in all weather conditions using measured data at a reference meteorological station, *International Journal of Climatology,* 26(12), *pp.* 1671-1694

Ferziger, J. H. & Perić, M. (2002). *Computational Methods for Fluid Dynamics,* Springer, 3540420746, Berlin.

Gan, G. (2006). Simulation of buoyancy-induced flow in open cavities for natural ventilation, *Energy and Buildings,* 38(5), *pp.* 410-420

Goulding, J. R., Lewis, J. O. & Steemers, T. C. (1992). *Energy Conscious Design: A Primer for European Architects,* BT Batsford Ltd., London.

Goulding, J. R., Lewis, J. O. & Steemers, T. C. (1993). *Energy In Architecture The European Passive Solar Handbook,* Batsford for the Commission of the European Communities, 0713469188

Kim, S. H. & Huh, K. Y. (2000). A new angular discretization scheme of the finite volume method for 3-D radiative heat transfer in absorbing, emitting and anisotropically scattering media, *International Journal of Heat and Mass Transfer,* 43(7), *pp.* 1233-1242

Launder, B. E. & Spalding, D. B. (1974). The numerical computation of turbulent flows, *Computer Methods in Applied Mechanics and Engineering,* 3(2), *pp.* 269-289

Liu, Y. & Harris, D. J. (2008). Effects of shelterbelt trees on reducing heating-energy consumption of office buildings in Scotland, *Applied Energy,* 85(2-3), *pp.* 115-127

Miyazaki, T., Akisawa, A. & Kashiwagi, T. (2006). The effects of solar chimneys on thermal load mitigation of office buildings under the Japanese climate, *Renewable Energy,* 31(7), *pp.* 987-1010

Mochida, A., Yoshino, H., Miyauchi, S. & Mitamura, T. (2006). Total analysis of cooling effects of cross-ventilation affected by microclimate around a building, *Solar Energy,* 80(4), *pp.* 371-382

Modest, M. F. (2003). *Radiative Heat Transfer,* Academic Press, 0125031637.

Papadakis, G., Tsamis, P. & Kyritsis, S. (2001). An experimental investigation of the effect of shading with plants for solar control of buildings, *Energy and Buildings,* 33(8), *pp.* 831-836

Patankar, S. V. (1980). *Numerical heat transfer and fluid flow,* Taylor & Francis, 0891165223, Hemisphere.

Raeissi, S. & Taheri, M. (1999). Energy saving by proper tree plantation, *Building and Environment,* 34(5), *pp.* 565-570

Raithby, G. D. (1999). Discussion of the finite-volume method for radiation, and its application using 3D unstructured meshes, *Numerical Heat Transfer, Part B: Fundamentals,* 35(4), *pp.* 389-405

Raithby, G. D. & Chui, E. H. (1990). Finite-volume method for predicting a radiant heat transfer in enclosures with participating media, *Journal of Heat Transfer,* 112(2), *pp.* 415-423

Tzachanis, A. D. (2008). The contribution of natural shading with climbing plants to the energy balance of a building, *Geotechnical Scientific Topics of GOETEE,* In press*pp.*

Tzachanis, A. D. & Sdravopoulou, C. (2002). *Simulation on the periodic steady heat gain in buildings.* 2nd IASTED International Conference on Power & Enrgy Systems (Euro PES), Crete, Greece.

Wilcox, D. C. (1998). *Turbulence Modeling for CFD,* DCW Industries, 0963605151, California.

Zhang, Y., Mahrer, Y. & Margolin, M. (1997). Predicting the microclimate inside a greenhouse: an application of a one-dimensional numerical model in an unheated greenhouse, *Agricultural and Forest Meteorology,* 86(3-4), *pp.* 291-297

20

Improvement of Production Lines using a Stochastic Approach

Cecilia Zanni-Merk and Philippe Bouché
LGECO - INSA de Strasbourg
24 Bd de la Victoire, 67084 Strasbourg, France
{cecilia.zanni-merk, philippe.bouche}@insa-strasbourg.fr

1. Introduction

The search for productivity sources makes the improvement of the contemporary production systems necessary. The production actors are, in a systematic and permanent way, engaged in three stages: the audit, the diagnosis and the search for solutions to improve their production systems.

For the audit of production systems, different Internet and Intranet technologies allow measuring and storing the state of the different production resources in real time.

From these data and during the stage of analysis of production flows, the production personnel and the staff in charge must be able to find and formalize the problems inducing a faulty operation of the manufacturing system. Solutions must be imagined in order to increase the productivity at a given cost.

Nowadays, the stages of diagnosis and solution search are primarily instrumented by little formalized expert knowledge. This lack of formalism generates heavy development costs, does not guarantee reproducibility and does not support the necessary knowledge capitalization for the improvement of the production system within the same company. To solve these problems, a solution consists in formalizing the necessary knowledge to set and solve the problems related to that lack of productivity from the data collected during the audit stage. This formalization has to give birth to software tools for assisting the involved actors in a permanent and proactive way.

Several works have been carried out on the performance evaluation of unreliable production lines (Tempelbeier & Burger, 2001; Van Bracht, 1995; Xie, 1993). However, research on the simultaneous consideration of maintenance policies, production planning and quality improvement from an industrial point of view has still to be done.

Confronted with these industrial problems, there are two research lines. On the one hand, there is a great number of scientific works on the detailed modelling of production resources and activities. On the other hand, a much less developed research line is interested in the modelling of problem solving in production systems design. From these two categories, our research group is interested in the understanding and modelling of the field experts reasoning during the stages of production flow analysis and solution searching. We are also interested in automating this reasoning in order to bring proactive software assistance.

With this goal in mind, we will study the different behaviours of the production line that would lead to a lack of productivity, according to three axes:

- The production axis, by indicating the losses that are incurred by problems in the production planning (ergonomy of a workstation, lack of training of an operator, etc.),
- The quality axis, by indicating in which measure the quality problems affect the productivity,
- The maintenance axis, by taking into account the losses due to maintenance operations.

We will also be interested by the study of "cause-effect" relationships among these behaviours: is the lack of training of the operator causing quality problems encountered later?

This article presents, therefore, our approach for performance analysis and improvement of production flows in the three dimensional space we have just described. The approach is based on statistical and probabilistic methods and is a new case of application of the stochastic approach (Le Goc et al., 2006).

Section 2 presents the industrial context and describes the project. Section 3 presents the data graphical representation before setting the definition of phenomena in Section 4. Section 5 effectively presents the stochastic approach. Section 6 presents an application of the method on a real industrial case. Identification of breakdown models will be the base to propose action plans, presented in Section 7. Section 8 gives a quantification of the losses incurred by the occurrences of these anomalous events in the line. Section 8 states our conclusions and perspectives of future work.

2. The industrial context

As we have presented in previous communications (Zanni et al., 2007; Bouché & Zanni, 2008a; Zanni & Bouché, 2008b), our group is interested in the development of a software tool for allowing the decision makers in companies to have an analysis of their production line flows. This analysis will consist in a general and by-workstation productivity evaluation, the main objective being the maximization of this productivity in terms of the number of good produced parts in a given time window.

This diagnosis will be followed by an action plan for the improvement of the line, according to three criteria (quality, maintenance and yield) and a valorisation of the losses that could have been avoided if the action plan was executed. The general idea is to maximize the productivity by improving the production cycle time and by reducing the workstations breakdowns / outages and the number of rejected parts.

We are using a data acquisition system that, after having placed sensors in strategic places (Fig. 1) of the production line, allows the measuring of different indicators.

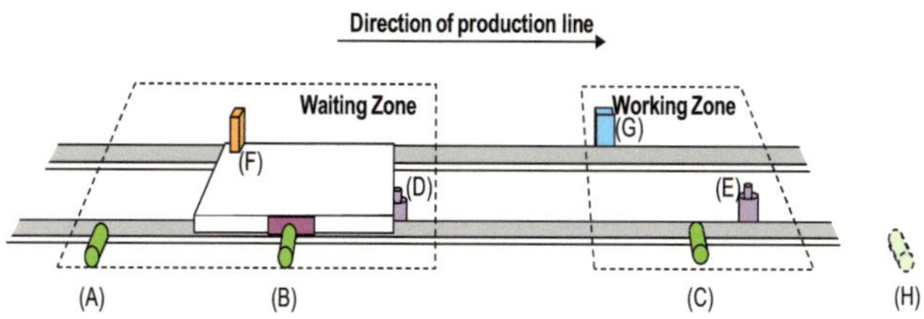

Fig. 1. Location of sensors in a workstation

During the production stage, we are able to detect if the part is good or bad (and, eventually, the associated fault code) and the times of (Fig. 2):

- The arrival of the part to the workstation (Sensor B),
- The beginning of processing of the part in the workstation (Sensor C),
- The end of processing of the part in the workstation (this fact is detected automatically for an automatic workstation or with an action on a sensor for a manual workstation),
- The exit of the part from the workstation (Sensor H).

They aim at defining a set of durations linked with the different stages of the work on the piece on the workstation (Fig. 2).

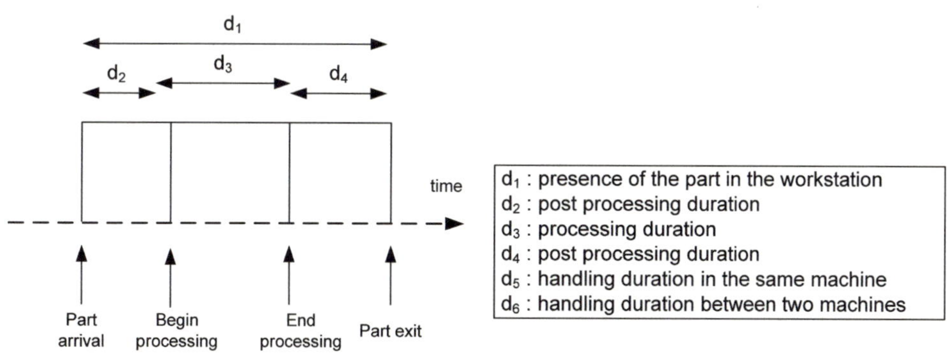

Fig. 2. Indicators to be measured during production

It is important to note that the only durations including effective working on a piece (d_1 and d_3) are durations with a value added.

The other durations are considered without a value added because they correspond to waiting, handling, or other *non productive* activities.

In the case of the failure of a workstation, the indicators we measure are (Fig. 3):

- The failure beginning time,
- The failure end time,
- The identification code of the failure.

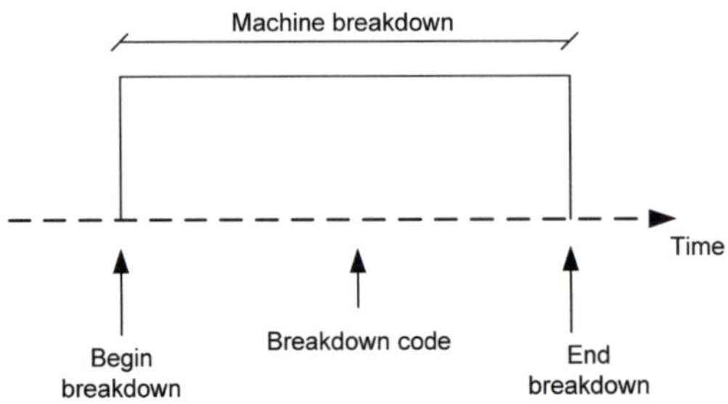

Fig. 3. Indicators to be measured during the breakdown station

The data acquisition system will also provide other necessary information, in particular, the control parameters of the workstations, i.e. some workstation characteristics that will be specific for each process plan. It will also provide maintenance data, information on production modifications, and other relevant information.

We study production lines such as the one described in Fig. 4:

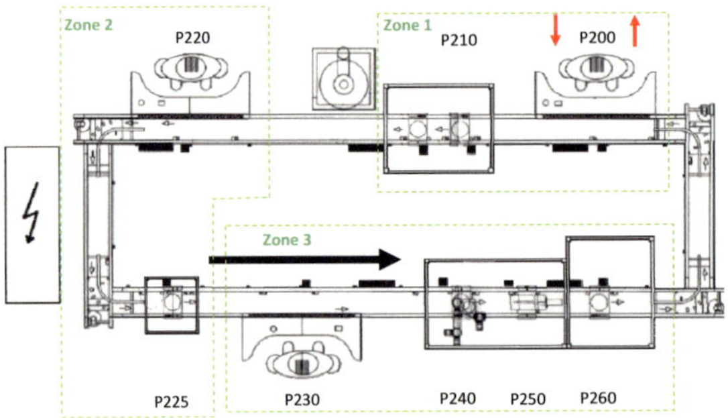

Fig. 4. Example of a production line

This is a closed loop, where there is a set of workstations, which can be automatic or manual. In Fig. 4, workstation P200, for example, is the point where pieces are injected in the line and where they go out. In addition, a finite set of pallets turns around the loop. This fact allows the transportation of the pieces from a workstation to the next one.

This organisation makes necessary to take into account a last set of parameters, which are:

- The instance of the production plan,
- The working team.

To take these parameters into account, data are separated by production type and/or by working team; the idea is to guarantee that time periods for analysis are uniform.

3. Data graphical representation

These data can be analyzed with frequencies and sequential methods.

In first place, we proceed to a Poisson analysis. A Poisson process is a process of enumeration, which describes the evolution of a quantity in time (Fig. 5). In our study, it will be a question of tracing the evolution in time of durations d_1, d_2... In the case of a perfect process, the Poisson curve is a line characterized by its slope λ (we will also speak about the speed of the Poisson process).

$$\lambda = \frac{\textit{number of parts}}{\textit{time}} \tag{1}$$

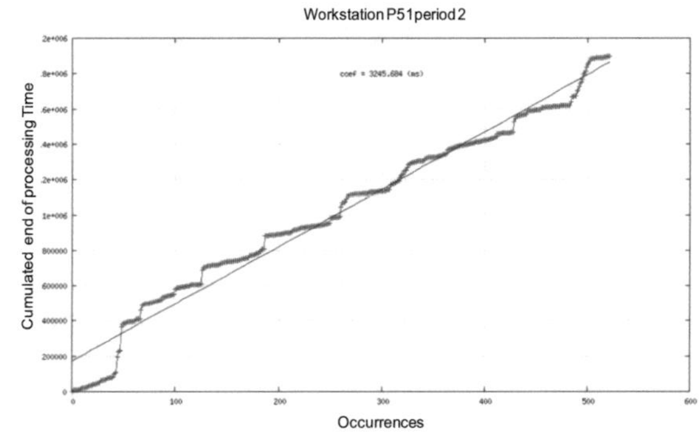

Fig. 5. Poisson process of evacuation times of a workstation

In real processes, we will observe various slopes, which will make possible, for example, to determine the moments when the production is faster, if there are intervals of drift in the workstation, and to define ranges where the behaviour of the station requires a more thorough analysis.
In second place, we can study the evolution of the working time with a model inspired in control charts, which are used in Statistical Process Control (Ishikawa, 1982). We trace the different durations of the tasks according to time (Fig. 6).

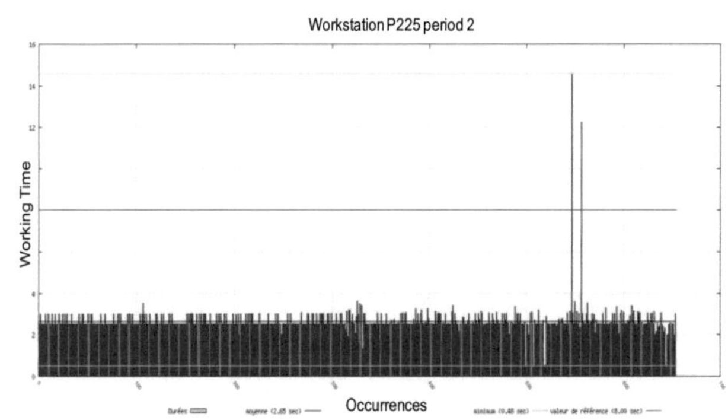

Fig. 6. "Control chart" of processing times of a workstation

That will make possible the study of possible drifts of the workstation to check if the process is under control; to identify the workstations where improvements could be made; or to identify changes of rate/rhythm or perturbations.
Finally, we can analyse properties of the distribution of durations (Fig. 7). We trace the frequency of the durations to study the setting under statistical laws of the station to consider.
From these curves, a certain number of analyses may be carried out, such as the analysis of dispersions, of aberrant values, or others.
Other graphical representation, such as synthesis representations, could be imagined. Nevertheless, the three types of presented representations are, for us, the base of the

analysis. This is a first method to have a better view of reality, and to identify specific zones of bad behaviour or specific phenomena. It corresponds to the more specific level of abstraction. To make better studies, we need to build meta-data, which will be associated to specific events or behaviours of the production. These behaviours cannot be directly deduced from data.
A set of transformations has to be applied to data to obtain the expression of certain behaviour under the form of a "phenomenon". The next section will define what we call a phenomenon before showing how we can compute phenomena from data.

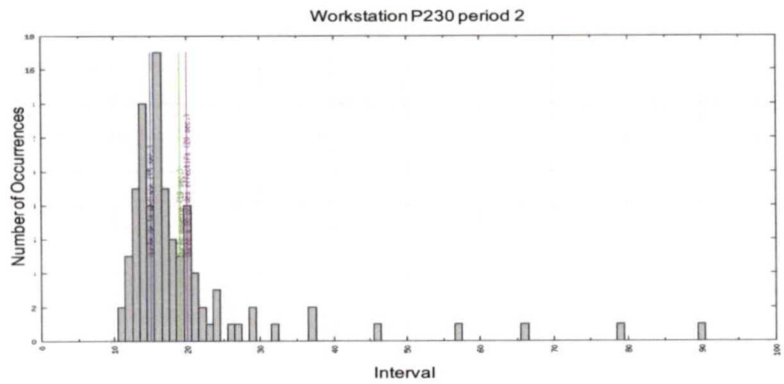

Fig. 7. Distribution of the processing times of a workstation

4. Phenomena

Phenomena are the expression of particular behaviours. They are described by a set of attributes, and at least (Le Goc, 2004b):

- A name,
- A characterization of the localisation in the production line,
- Two dates:
  - A begin date,
  - An end date.

4.1 Definition of Phenomena

While studying durations, we consider three parameters at the base of the Statistical Process Control principles (Ishikawa, 1982):

- The stability of the evolution of the duration to verify if the behaviour is stable or not (Fig. 8),

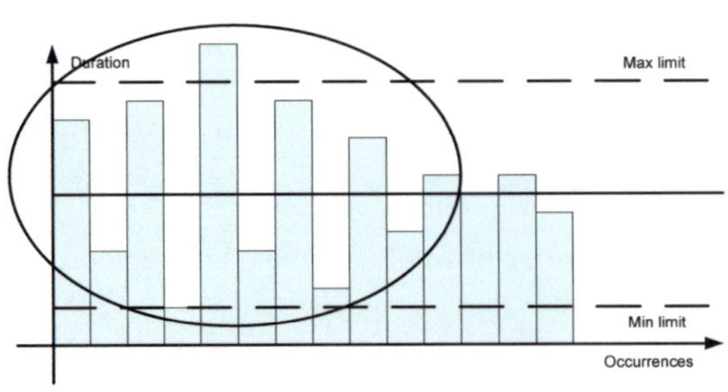

Fig. 8. Instability

- The drift of the evolution of the duration to check if the behaviour is constant or if there are positive or negative drifts (Fig. 9),

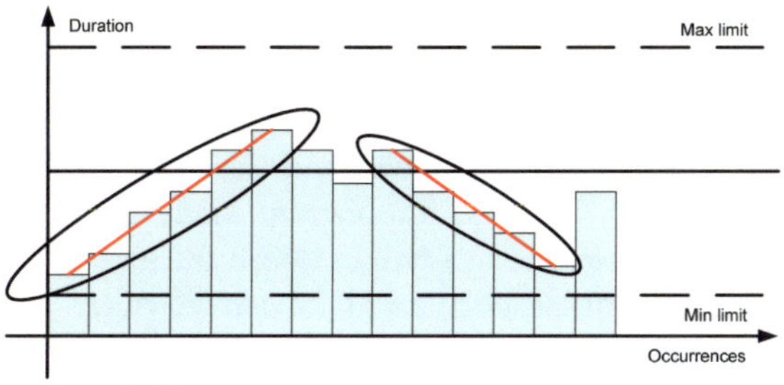

Fig. 9. Positive and Negative Drift

- The analysis of the values of the duration to verify if they are out of bounds (Fig. 10).

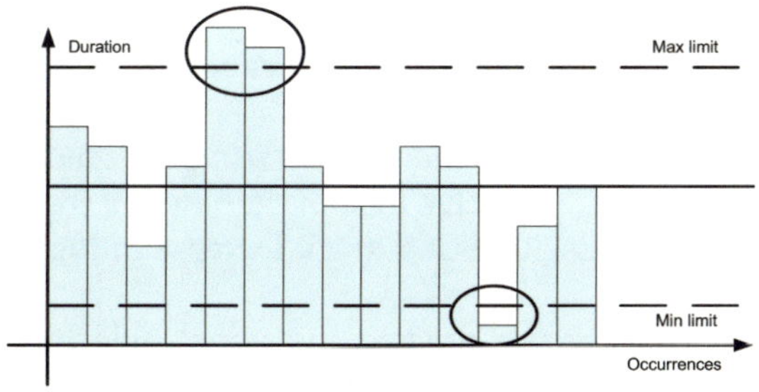

Fig. 10. Out of bounds values

These three characteristics are worth being studied on durations that are with a value added that is to say, if they are the result of an activity (human or made by a robot), such as d_3, the processing duration.

If the duration is with a value added, like in an automatic handling, the only point of interest will be to study the drift of the evolution of the duration.

Now we have six durations:

- d_1: the presence of the part in the machine,
- d_2: the pre-processing duration,
- d_3: the processing duration,
- d_4: the post-processing duration,
- d_5: the handling duration in the same workstation,
- d_6: the handling duration between two workstations.

As d_1 is the sum of d_2, d_3 and d_4, we will not make studies on this duration.

As d_2, d_4, d_5 and d_6 are durations without a value added, we will only study the drift on these durations.

In addition, to finish, we will carry out all the studies on d_3, the only duration with a value added.

Apart from these "duration linked" phenomena and that are related with the "production" axis of our space of study, we must also consider a set of phenomena related the "quality" and "maintenance" axes.

Regarding the "quality" axis, there are no studies on durations. There is only a discrete event characteristic of the behaviour that indicates that a piece is bad at a control workstation.

Other specific behaviours share the same characteristic as the last one, that is, the fact that there is only a discrete event of the behaviour: the start and the end of the production

Finally, we have phenomena related to the "maintenance" axis. We are able to detect the period of time when the workstation is stopped and the fault code that produced this stop. Studies on this duration (and its subcomponents, such as the time to wait for the maintenance team to arrive or the time interval between the arrival of the maintenance team and the effective restart of the workstation) might be carried out.

4.2 Phenomena related to the Production Axis

The following subsection gives a complete description of the phenomena we have retained with their characterization from an industrial point of view.

4.2.1 The Stock_Saturation phenomenon

It can be deduced from data of post-processing durations (d_4) and is characterized by an increase of the slope of those cumulated durations.

More precisely, on the Poisson curves, a *Stock_Saturation* phenomenon will be an increase of the speed of the process and thus a positive drift of the slope of the curve. On control charts, this phenomenon will be the translation of a quick increase in the execution times of a task in time (Fig. 11).

When there is a stock saturation, the workstation is not able to make the piece exit the working zone; this is why we detect this phenomenon by an increase of the speed of the post-processing duration.

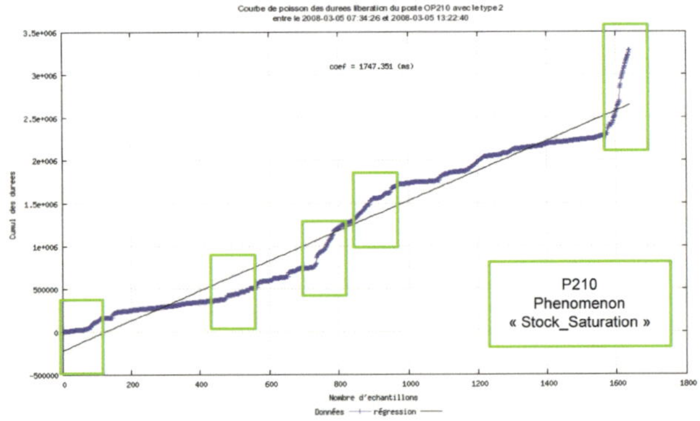

Fig. 11. Example of the *Stock_Saturation* phenomenon

4.2.2 The Workstation_Drift phenomenon

It is the expression of a drift of the production time on a workstation. We can observe it in the Poisson curves or the control charts with the study of the processing duration (d_3).

More precisely, on the Poisson curves, a *Workstation_Drift* phenomenon will be an increase or a decrease of the speed of the process and thus a positive or negative drift of the slope of

the curve. On control charts, this phenomenon will be the translation of a regular increase or decrease in the execution times of a task in time.
We will use two phenomena to differentiate if the drift is positive or negative (Fig. 12):

- *Positive_Worstation_Drift*
- *Negative_Workstation_Drift*

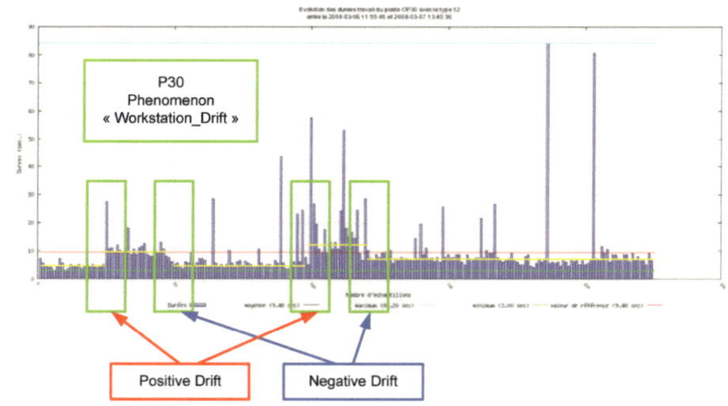

Fig. 12. Example of the *Drift* Phenomena

4.2.3 The Workstation_Instability phenomenon

It can be deduced from the working duration on a workstation (d_3).
The objective is to verify if the behaviour is stable or if there is any instability in the work.
It will be characterized by a great variability of durations on the control charts (Fig. 13).
In fact, SPC establishes that *two consecutive measurements that deviate from each other more than twice the value of the standard deviation indicate instability* (second rule of Shewart (Shewart, 1939)). In our case, this rule can be only applied to aberrant values.
Therefore, to detect this phenomenon, we identify, firstly, the couples of successive values in the current sample, which deviate from each other more than twice the standard deviation.
If this number of couples is, at least, 10 % of the size of the sample, we say we are in presence of a *Workstation_Instability* phenomenon

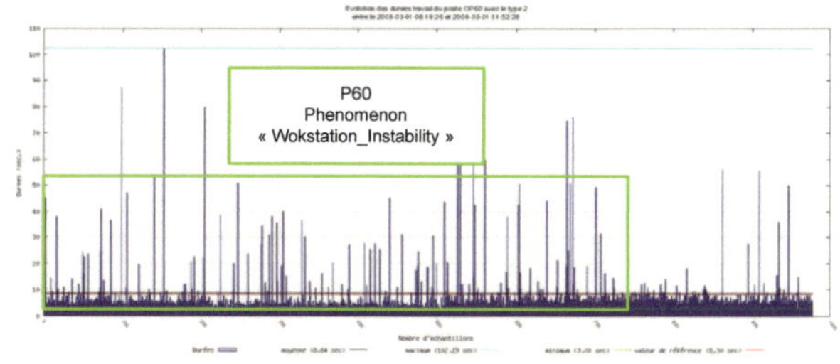

Fig. 13. Example of the *Workstation_Instability* phenomenon

4.2.4 The Out_Of_Bounds_Time phenomenon

It can be deduced from the working duration on a workstation (d_3).
The objective is to analyze this duration to identify if there are values out of limit. If values are bigger than the maximum limit, the speed of the workstation is too slow; we will have a *Slow_Working_Period* phenomenon. If values are under the minimum limit, the speed of the

workstation is too fast (which could be the cause of workstation failure or of the production of bad pieces), we will have a *Fast_Working_Period* phenomenon (Fig. 14).

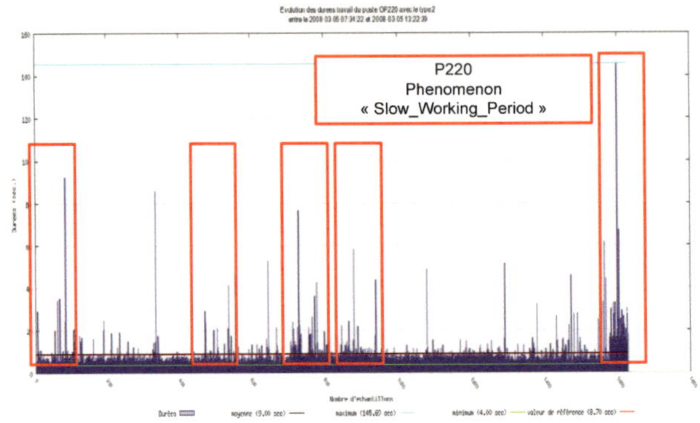

Fig. 14. Example of the *Slow_Working_Period* phenomenon

4.2.5 The Lack_Of_Components phenomenon

It can be deduced from data of pre-processing durations (d_2). It will be characterized by an increase of the slope of the cumulated pre-processing duration.

More precisely, on the Poisson curves, a *Lack_Of_Components* phenomenon will be an increase of the speed of the process and thus a positive drift of the slope of the curve. On control charts, this phenomenon will be the translation of a quick increase in the execution times of a certain task in time.

The lack of components makes impossible that the workstation begins its work; this is why we detect this phenomenon by an increase of speed of the pre-processing duration.

4.2.6 The Handling_Speed phenomenon

It can be deduced from data of handling durations in the same workstation (d_5). It will be characterized by an increase or a decrease of the slope of those cumulated durations.

This leads to the definition of two phenomena:

- *Slow_Handling_Speed*
- *Fast_Handling_Speed*

It is important to consider the case where the handling speed is too fast, because even if it is not a direct cause of productivity losses, it could cause saturation on workstations or other problems in the production line.

4.2.7 The Lack_Of_Stock phenomenon

It can be deduced from data of handling durations between two workstations (d_6). It will be characterized by an increase of the slope of those cumulated durations.

The lack of stock makes impossible that the workstation begins its work because there are no pieces in transit between two workstations; this is why we detect this phenomenon by an increase of speed of the handling duration between those two workstations.

4.2.8 Completeness of this set of phenomena

This set of phenomena has been defined in collaboration with experts of production, and in function of the goal of the analyses. The list we have retained is complete according to the explanations in section 4.1 (Fig. 15):

Studies on durations			
	Stability of the evolution of the duration	Drift of the evolution of the duration	Analysis of values of the duration
d_1			
d_2		Lack_Of_Components	
d_3	Workstation_Instability	Workstation_Positive_Drift	Slow_Working_Period
		Workstation_Negative_Drift	Fast_Working_Period
d_4		Stock_Saturation	
d_5		Slow_Handling_Speed	
		Fast_Handling_Speed	
d_6		Lack_Of_Stock	

Fig. 15. List of phenomena on durations

4.3 Phenomena related to the Quality Axis

The main element that we must consider for the quality axis is the production of bad pieces. In this case, we will not really have a phenomenon but just a discrete event (which is a kind of phenomenon where the end date is the same as the begin date).

Therefore, we will characterise the production of bad pieces by a *Bad_Piece* phenomenon with, at least, the following information:

- Date of detection,
- Fault code (if available),
- Localisation of the detection place.

4.4 Phenomena related to the Maintenance Axis

These phenomena are not deduced from durations, we obtain them directly from the data acquisition system.

We have a measure of the gravity of the failure on four levels:

- *Type 1 - Energy cut-off (air, electricity…) and immediate halt of the workstation cycles:* In general, this type of failure announces an emergency stop (light barrier crossed through, emergency stop button triggered…). Everything must be stopped in the position in which it is (for example, if a hydraulic or pneumatic actuator moves by its own weight without energy, there will be blockers to lock the actuator movements).
  To continue working with the workstation it is required:
  - To correct the problem (to give off the immaterial barriers, to rearm the emergency stop keys …) ,
  - To switch on energy on the workstation (electric, pneumatic…),

  - To acknowledge the failures appeared in the PLC (programmable logic controller),
  - To reset the workstation (with the initial settings of all the components),
  - To set on "start" the PLC cycle.
- *Type 2- Dead halt of the PLC cycles and immobilization of movements:* The cycles are stopped, but energies are not cut.
  In this scenario, movements are just blocked, but energy flows are not cut. In general, this type of failure is reported when a sensor is faulty. For example, the movement of an actuator arrives to its end without having triggered the corresponding sensor (for example, the end of movement sensor is out of order). The PLC will indicate a type 2 failure indicating the defective component.
  At our industrial partner's, when a workstation has a type 2 failure, all the pieces in progress are declared as bad, and therefore, cannot be re-injected in the line for further processing.
  To continue working with the workstation it is required:
  - To correct the problem (often we will have to switch to manual mode to release actuators of the workstation),
  - To acknowledge the failures appeared in the PLC,
  - To reset the workstation (if necessary),
  - To set on "start" the PLC cycle.
- *Type 3 – Message*: This type of failure has just for informational purposes. The workstation cycles are not stopped and energy flows are not cut.
  For example, a grease barrel reaches its low-level limit; a type 3 message will indicate this fact. If it is not replaced and it is empty, a type 2 failure will be declared with the consequent workstation stop.
  In addition, this type of message is used to indicate to the operator what he has to do with the product in front of him. These kinds of failures are acknowledged automatically.
- *Type 4 - A particular definition of our industrial partner and only in a few of his production lines:* This failure is the same as a Type 2 one, but the product can be taken again for further work after resumption of the cycle.

Therefore, we have defined four phenomena for each workstation:

- *Failure_Level_1*
- *Failure_Level_2*
- *Failure_Level_3*
- *Failure_Level_4*

They will be characterized by the gravity and their start and end dates.

4.5 How to build phenomena from data

After having established all phenomena and their description, we will see two examples of the algorithms we use to build phenomena.

For example, if we consider the *Workstation_Drift* phenomenon, it is the expression of a drift of the production time on a workstation. We can observe it in the Poisson curves or the control charts with the study of the processing duration (d_3) (Fig. 16).

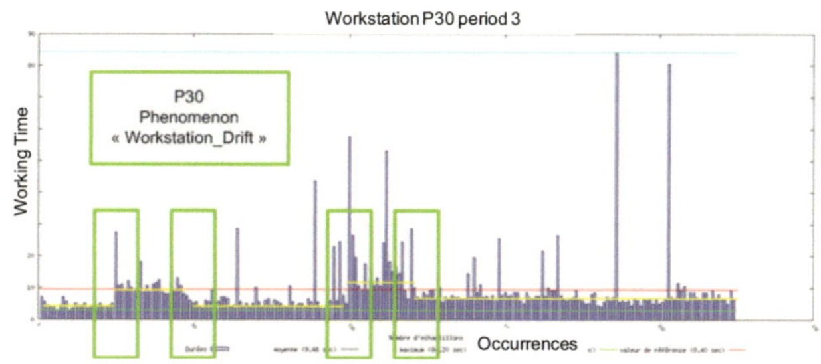

Fig. 16. Visual observation of the *Workstation_Drift* phenomenon

To compute occurrences of this phenomenon, we will calculate the slopes of the Poisson processes that are associated with this workstation during the considered time window. If we observe several slopes, named successively λ_1, λ_2... λ_n and that these slopes are decreasing, then we can diagnose a *Workstation_Drift* phenomenon.

$$\begin{aligned}&\forall \lambda_i, i \in [1,n], \text{IF } \lambda_i > \lambda_{i+1} \\ &\text{THEN } \textit{Workstation\_Drift}\end{aligned} \tag{2}$$

In the same way, the processing durations on a workstation can be directly used to diagnose a *Workstation_Drift* phenomenon. It will be characterized by an increase of the average of durations.

$$\begin{aligned}&\forall d_i, i \in [1,n], \text{IF Average}(d_1, ..., d_k) < \text{Average}(d_{k+1}, ..., d_n) \\ &\text{THEN } \textit{Worstation\_Drift}\end{aligned} \tag{3}$$

Let us consider the data in Fig. 17:

occurrence	date	added up durations	slope	lambdas
1084	19/09/2007 19:01	18759881		
			97771,96	0,00010233
1388	19/09/2007 20:00	21730557		
			12599,15	0,00007937
1611	19/09/2007 20:53	14540168		

Fig. 17. Data of workstation P200 of the production line

The slopes values on this manual workstation lead us to say that we are in presence of a *Workstation_Drift* phenomenon from 20h00 to 20h53.

The idea is to calculate the slopes on a temporal horizon that is coherent with the production line speed and the considered workstation and to compare the slopes regularly. The algorithm to build occurrences of this phenomenon is depicted in Fig. 18:

```
Constant : h time windows characterized by two dates d1 (begin) et d2 (end)
Constant : p tolerance
Variables : λ1 past slope, λ2 curent slope
Boolean : C Boolean uses to know if we are in Workstation drift period (1) or not (0)

Data :     NbOc (di) Number of pieces treated at time di
                DC (di) Cumulated period of work at time di

Temporal loop on h
        Compute λ2 = (NbOc(d2) – NbOc (d1))/(DC(d2)-DC(d1))
        Compare λ1 et λ2
        IF the difference is upper than p
            THEN IF  C = 0
              THEN     Init occurrence of phenomenon Workstation_Drift
                       Begin date phenomenon = d1
                       C=1
        IF difference is lower than p
              THEN IF C = 1
                       THEN     Stop occurrence of phenomenon Worstation_Drift
                                End date phenomenon = d1
                                C=0
        Make change the time, actualize d1 et d2
        Change value λ1 with value λ2
```

Fig. 18. Algorithm for identifying the *Workstation_Drift* phenomenon

Considering Fig. 16, the application of this algorithm will give us four occurrences of the *Workstation_Drift* phenomenon.

To have another example, let us consider the *Stock_Saturation* phenomenon. It can be deduced from data of post processing durations (d_4). It will be characterized by an increase of the slope of the cumulated post processing duration. Fig. 19 shows an example of a time window for workstation P210 where we can observe five occurrences of this phenomenon.

It is important to remark that now we have to consider five occurrences of the *Stock_Saturation* phenomenon rather than all the data on the same time window. We make, also, the assumption that, if no phenomenon is detected, the behaviour of the production line is correct.

Therefore, because phenomena are meta-knowledge, we are able to build a sequence of phenomena, which contains more information than the original data but "lighter" than the original set.

The construction of phenomena is, then, a kind of a discrete event abstraction (Le Goc, 2004a).

Post analysis may be performed on the phenomena sequence, by application of the stochastic approach to identify the correlations that can exist among phenomena. Next subsection will show the bases of the stochastic approach and the way we can use it to obtain fault models. These models will serve in the last step of our development to build action plans.

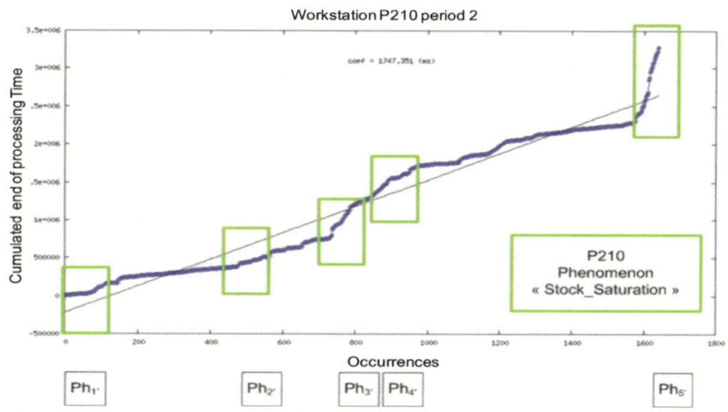

Fig. 19. Example of the *Stock_Saturation* phenomenon

5. The Stochastic Approach

A sequence $\omega=\{o_k\}_{k=0,\ldots,m-1}$ is an ordered set of m occurrences $o_k \equiv (t_k, x, i)$ of discrete events $e_k \equiv (x, i)$, where:

- $x \in X$ is the name of a discrete variable,
- $i \in I_x \subseteq \aleph$ is a discrete value of x, and
- $t_k \in \Gamma=\{t_i\}$, $t_i \in \Re$ is the time of the assignation of the discrete value i to the variable x so that: $o_k \equiv (t_k, x, i) \Leftrightarrow x(t_k) = i$.

We have a continuous clock structure. Occurrences may happen at different times, but not necessary at regular intervals (that is to say, $t_{k-2}-t_{k-1} \neq t_{k-1}-t_k$):

$$\begin{aligned}&\forall t_k \in \Re, \forall i \in \aleph, \exists t_{k-1} < t_k, \\ &x(t_{k-1}) \neq i \wedge x(t_k) = i \Rightarrow o_k \equiv (t_k, x, i)\end{aligned} \tag{4}$$

A couple (o_k, o_n) of two successive occurrences of discrete events related to a variable x describes the modification of the values of the variable x over the interval $[t_k, t_n[$:

$$\begin{aligned}&\forall o_k \equiv (t_k, x, i), o_n \equiv (t_n, x, j), \\ &(o_k, o_n) \Rightarrow \forall t \in [t_k, t_n[, x(t) = i \wedge x(t_n) = j\end{aligned} \tag{5}$$

As a consequence, a sequence $\omega=\{o_k\}$ of discrete event occurrences $o_k \equiv (t_k, x, i)$ concerning variable x describes the temporal evolution of a discrete function $x(t)$ defined on $\aleph$.

$$\begin{aligned}&R(C^i, C^o, [\tau^-, \tau^+]) \Leftrightarrow \exists o_n, o_k \in \omega, \\ &(o_n :: C^o) \wedge (o_k :: C^i) \wedge (d(o_n) - d(o_k) \in [\tau^-, \tau^+]) \\ &where\ \forall o_k \equiv (t_k, x, i) \in \omega, d(o_k) = t_k\end{aligned} \tag{6}$$

A discrete event class is a set $C^i=\{e_i\}$ of discrete events $e_i \equiv (x, i)$. The notation "$e_i::C^i$" (resp. "$o_k::C^i$" or "C^i_k") denotes that the discrete event e_i (resp. the occurrence $o_k \equiv C^i_k$) belongs to the class C^i. A timed binary relation R $(C^i, C^o, [\tau^-, \tau^+])$ describes an oriented relation between two discrete event classes that is timed constrained. "$[\tau^-,\tau^+]$" is the time interval for observing an occurrence of the output class C^o after the occurrence of the input class C^i (equation 3).

5.1 Abstract Chronicle Model

In this context, an abstract chronicle model is a set of binary relations with timed constraints between classes of discrete events. Such a model is called an "ELP" model (ELP is the acronym of Event Language of Processing, (Le Goc et al., 2006)). For example, the ELP model $M_{123}=\{R_{12}(C^1, C^2, [\tau_{12}^-, \tau_{12}^+]), R_{23}(C^2, C^3, [\tau_{23}^-, \tau_{23}^+])\}$ of Fig. 20 is made of two binary relations between three discrete event classes. A sequence ω satisfies the M_{123} ELP model when:

$$\begin{aligned}&\exists o_k, o_n, o_m \in \omega, (o_k :: C^1) \wedge (o_n :: C^2) \wedge (o_m :: C^3)\\&\wedge (d(o_n) - d(o_k) \in [\tau_{12}^-, \tau_{12}^+]) \wedge (d(o_m) - d(o_n) \in [\tau_{23}^-, \tau_{23}^+])\end{aligned} \tag{7}$$

ELP models can be used to predict the occurrences of discrete event classes (like C^3 in the ELP model M_{123}) in an unknown sequence ω'.

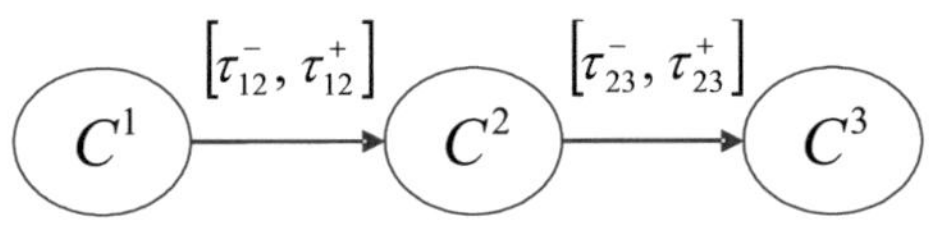

Fig. 20. ELP representation of the M_{123} model

To this aim, rules of the equation 5 form can be used in a diagnosis task. When such a rule predicts an occurrence of a discrete event class with a minimal confidence, the corresponding ELP model is called a "signature" (Le Goc et al., 2006).

$$\begin{aligned}&\forall \omega', \forall o_k, o_n \in \omega',\\&(o_k :: C^1) \wedge (o_n :: C^2) \wedge (d(o_n) - d(o_k) \in [\tau_{12}^-, \tau_{12}^+])\\&\Rightarrow \exists o_m \in \omega', (o_m :: C^3) \wedge (d(o_m) - d(o_n) \in [\tau_{23}^-, \tau_{23}^+])\end{aligned} \tag{8}$$

To measure the confidence of such rules, we define the anticipating ratio of an abstract chronicle model as the number of sub sequences of a sequence ω that matches the complete abstract chronicle model, divided by the number of the sub sequences that matches the abstract chronicle model but without the final binary relation (the class C^3 in Fig. 20). An abstract chronicle model is a signature when its anticipating ratio is equal to or greater than 50%.

5.2 The Stochastic Representation

When the discrete event classes are independent and the distribution of the inter-occurrence times of a discrete event class complies with a Poisson law of the form $f(t)=1-e^{-\lambda t}$[1], the couple

---

[1] λ is the average number of occurrences in a unit of time and is called the Poisson rate (Cassandras & Lafortune, 2001).

made by the process and its monitoring Knowledge Based System (KBS) can be considered as a stochastic discrete event generator (Le Goc et al., 2006).
Consequently, a sequence of discrete event classes provided by such a generator can be represented under the dual form of a homogeneous Markov chain and its associated superposition of Poisson processes. A chronicle model is then connected with a specific path in the state space of the Markov chain, and the timed relations will be provided by the corresponding superposition of Poisson processes.
To represent a sequence $\omega=(C^i{}_k)_{k\in K=\{0,\ldots,m\}}$ as a Markov chain $X=(X(t_k);\ k\in K)$, the set of discrete event classes $C^{\omega}=\{C^i\}_{i=0\ldots n-1}$ in ω is assimilated to with the state space $Q=\{i\}_{i=0\ldots n-1}$ of X. A binary sub sequence $\omega'=(C^i{}_{k-1},\ C^j{}_k)$ of ω corresponds then to a state transition in X: $X(d(C^i{}_{k-1}))=i\rightarrow X(d(C^j{}_k))=j$, where d is the function providing the time of a class occurrence. A simple depth-first backward search algorithm (i.e. from an output class to the input classes) is used to generate the tree of the most probable paths that lead to an output class (Le Goc et al., 2006).
This tree and the matrix of transition probabilities are a first representation of the sequence of alarms. This result is interesting because, whatever the length of the sequence of alarms, it is entirely contained in a finite matrix. The tree of sequential relations can then be used to produce a functional model[2] of the couple (process, KBS) or to find signatures of the form of the equation 5.
To constitute a timed binary relation of the form $R(C^i, C^j, [\tau^-, \tau^+])$, the timed constraint $[\tau^-, \tau^+]$ is simply added to the sequential relation $R_s(C^i, C^o)$. Such a timed constraint is related with the average delay $D_{i\text{-}j}=E[d(C^j{}_k)-d(C^i{}_{k-1})]$ between two successive occurrences $o_{k-1}::C^i$ and $o_k::C^j$ in a specific $\omega_s^{i\text{-}j}$ sequence that contains only the occurrences of the two classes C^i and C^j of the sequence ω_s. The average delay D_{ij} between the occurrences of two classes C^i and C^j of ω is evaluated from two types of Poisson processes:

- A Poisson process $(N_{i\text{-}j}(t\text{-}t_{min});\ t\in T)$ that counts the number of sub sequences $\omega'=(C^i{}_{k-1},\ C^j{}_k)$ in each $\omega_s^{i\text{-}j}$,
- A compound Poisson process $(N^D{}_{i\text{-}j}(t\text{-}t_{min});\ t\in T)$ associated to each Poisson process $(N_{i\text{-}j}(t\text{-}t_{min});\ t\in T)$.

The average delay D_{ij} is then given by (Le Goc et al., 2006):

$$D_{ij} = E\left[d\left(C_k^j\right) - d\left(C_{k-1}^i\right)\right] = \frac{1}{\lambda_{i-j}} = \frac{N_{i-j}^D\left(t_{\max} - t_{\min}\right)}{N_{i-j}\left(t_{\max} - t_{\min}\right)} \tag{9}$$

In our applications, the timed constraints are often intervals of the form $[0, 2/\lambda_{i\text{-}j}]$, which takes into account 60% of the occurrences[3].
These data structures and the associated algorithms have been implemented in a Java platform with a set of tools to help experts analysing sequences of phenomena. There are two algorithms linked with the stochastic approach: The BJT4T algorithm (Backward Jump with Timed constraints for Trees) and the BJT4S algorithm (Backward Jump with Timed constraints for Signatures) (Bouché et al., 2008b).

---

[2] A functional model is the description of all variables of the system and relations which can exist among these variables.
[3] See (Le Goc et al., 2006) to a more detailed explanation of this choice of timed constraints.

The role of the BJT4T algorithm is to compute the set of the most probable timed binary relations $R(C^i, C^j, [\tau^-, \tau^+])$ in a set Ω of sequences ω_i that leads to a specific discrete event class C^j. The BJT4S algorithm evaluates the anticipating ratio of each branch of the tree: the signatures are the branches of the tree having an anticipating ratio greater that an arbitrary threshold (we have made the choice to use 50%, see (Bouché et al., 2008b)).

6. Example: Identification of fault models on real data

In the following of this chapter, we will use data of a company that provides automotive parts (such as door locks). More precisely, we will show data from one production line of this company, even if we have all data on long periods, we will only use data on one week for this example.
In first place, we obtain the phenomena log (Fig. 21).

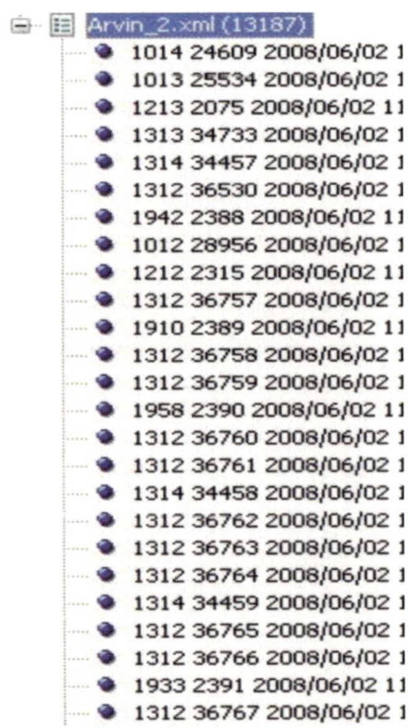

Fig. 21. Example of a log of a production line

Afterwards, we may carry out probabilistic studies, in order to identify if there exist correlations among phenomena and the temporal constraints on these correlations. The first step of the stochastic approach is, then, to build the transition matrix from the log of phenomena (Fig. 22).
The transition matrix is a counting matrix; we make the sum of transitions that we can observe from two phenomena in the log of phenomena. On the matrix of Fig. 22, the number 4 on the first row means that in the log of phenomena we have observed four transitions from a phenomenon 1012 to a phenomenon 1014.

	1012	1013	1014	1112	1113	1114	1212	1213	1214	1312	1313	1314	1901
1012	0	0	4	0	0	0	0	0	0	15	0	3	0
1013	9	5	60	0	14	11	4	2	1	87	16	26	0
1014	8	64	3	0	15	5	4	3	0	68	22	4	0
1112	0	0	0	0	0	0	0	0	0	3	0	3	0
1113	2	14	23	0	0	20	1	1	0	69	26	9	0
1114	0	7	1112,1014		56	0	0	2	0	36	15	8	0
1212	0	1	3	0	1	0	0	0	0	10	1	3	0
1213	3	2	7	0	3	0	1	0	1	7	4	6	0
1214	0	2	0	0	0	1	0	3	0	1	2	0	0
1312	9	82	54	5	56	32	8	7	4	851	99	43	0
1313	8	27	22	0	14	9	3	3	0	131	74	16	0
1314	7	21	8	0	12	1	5	4	0	64	13	4	0
1901	0	0	0	0	0	0	0	0	0	0	1	0	0
1904	0	0	0	0	0	0	0	0	0	0	0	1	0
1905	0	1	1	0	0	0	0	0	0	2	0	0	0
1906	0	1	0	0	0	0	0	0	0	0	0	0	0
1907	0	8	5	0	9	0	0	0	0	6	3	5	0
1909	0	0	1	0	0	0	0	0	0	1	0	0	0

Fig. 22. The transition matrix

As we have explained in section 0, the next step is the use of a representation under the dual form of a Markov chain model and a superposition of Poisson processes (Fig. 23). The transition matrix is used to compute the Markov matrix where we will have the probabilities of transition among phenomena. The transition matrix will also be used to determine, then, the time constraints among phenomena in the superposition of Poisson processes.

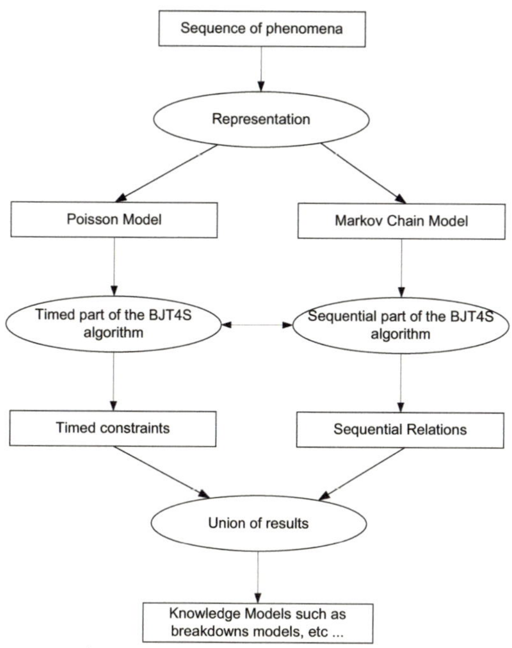

Fig. 23. The Stochastic Approach

The objective is to produce *behavioural models of breakdowns*. These models may be used to perform real time diagnosis, but also to define action plans and corrections on the production line. Fault models will probably reveal implicit links among the workstations of the considered line.

The application of the stochastic approach corresponds to the generic level of analysis of our project. The stochastic approach produces behavioural models that, according to our experience, are realistic indeed and can be used to make prediction or diagnosis.
Fig. 24 shows an example of correlation between two phenomena detected on workstations P210 and P220 (see the production line in Fig. 4).
We detect the *Slow_Working_Period* phenomenon on workstation P220 and the *Stock_Saturation* phenomenon on workstation P210. It is easy to see that, if there is an important working time on workstation P220, the line will be slowed down and a consequence is the saturation of stock that can be observed on workstation P210.
Therefore, to improve performance of the line in this context, the problem will not be to eliminate the *Stock_Saturation* phenomenon but to improve the working time on workstation P220. With a single action, we can act on two phenomena.

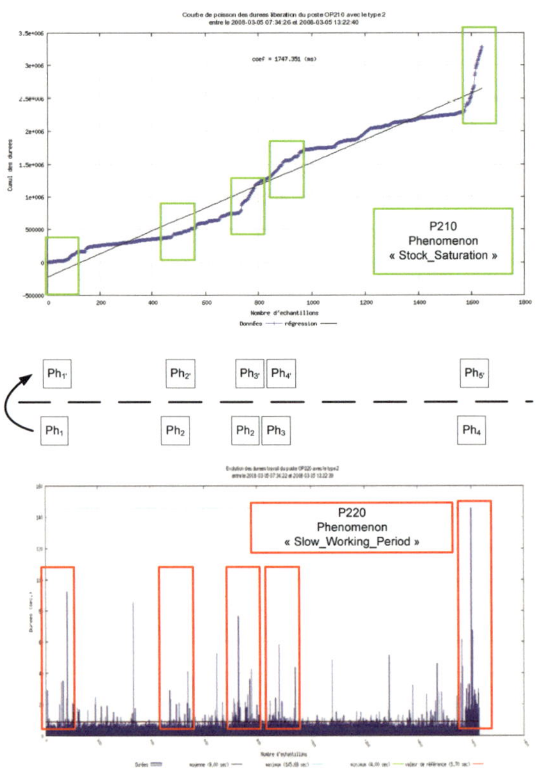

Fig. 24. Example of a correlation between two phenomena

While taking into account all the observations from the other workstations we realise that this binary relation can be generalized to all the production line to produce a global binary relation between two phenomena (Fig. 25):

Fig. 25. Example of a binary relation between two phenomena

On our data, the stochastic approach permits to build the following tree of sequential relations (Fig. 26). The base of the tree (it is an arbitrary choice) is the phenomenon 1953, which corresponds to a *Failure_Level_2* phenomenon on workstation P140.

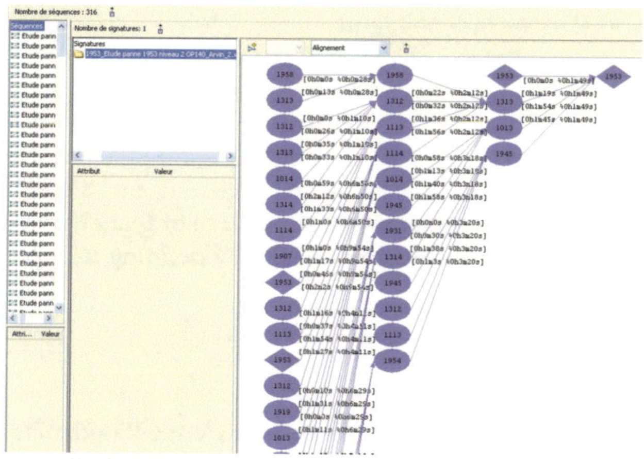

Fig. 26. Tree of sequential relations

From this tree, the BJT4S algorithm extracts the 1953 class signature in Fig. 27. A signature is the branch of the tree, which has an anticipating ratio greater than 50%.

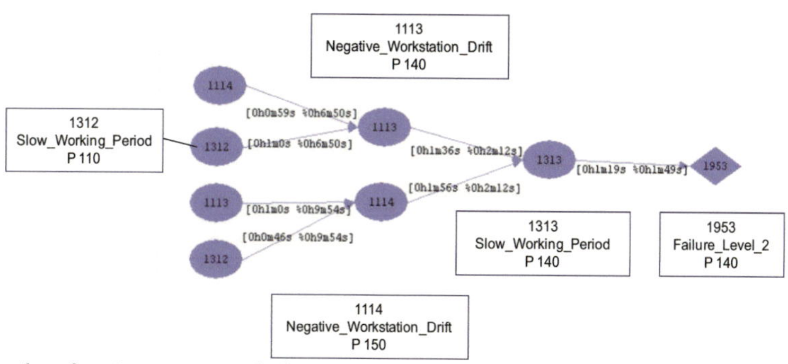

Fig. 27. Example of a signature or behavioural model

To explain how this model has to be read, let us consider the branch 1312 ⇒ 1113 ⇒ 1313 ⇒ 1953 in Fig. 27. This means that:

If we observe the occurrence of a *Slow_Working_Period* phenomenon on workstation P110

Followed by an occurrence of a *Negative_Workstation_Drift* phenomenon on Workstation P140 in the time interval [0s, 1m],

Followed by an occurrence of a *Slow_Working_Period* phenomenon on workstation P140 in the time interval [0s, 1m36s],

Then *there is a strong probability* to observe an occurrence of a *Failure_Level_2* phenomenon on workstation P140 in the time interval [0s, 1m19s].

The idea is, therefore, to use such a rule in a diagnosis task to make impossible the occurrence of such a succession of phenomena that leads to a severe failure. In this way, it is

possible to improve the performance of the production line, by preventing the occurrence of a serious phenomenon.
It is important to note that, by these means, we can identify relations among phenomena on different workstations. Therefore, we propose a global method of analysis that is not limited to the study of all workstations independently.
These models will be the base of the proposal of action plans to improve the performance of the production line in study. They can also be used on-line with a real time supervision system. In fact, the goal will be to observe phenomena on line, and to compare them with the knowledge base of fault models. If we detect the beginning of a model, we can generate an alarm to warn the operator on the risk of the occurrence of a total breakdown. In this way, corrective actions can be done before the occurrence of that eventual total breakdown.
Fault models can also be used to make new studies, by defining new phenomena with high abstraction levels.

7. Action plans

This project fits into the heuristic approach to knowledge-based diagnosis (Zanni et al., 2006). The basic assumption of this approach is that diagnosis is a heuristic process. It implies that experts rely on associational knowledge of the form *observations* → *faults*, that knowledge derives from experience with the device under consideration (a production system in our case) and that it can be elicited from domain experts.
The systems built under this approach can reach a high level of performance and may be very efficient in their reasoning.
However, what has to be done when we have identified a fault or an unsatisfactory state?
The goal of the supervisor of the production line is, precisely, to make the unsatisfactory state(s) disappear: an action is required when the state of the process is not satisfactory, and otherwise nothing has to be done.
Therefore, when required, the supervisor must decide and propose an action on the process.
An action is a modification of at least one of the input variables of the process. The causal relations between the variables will transform and propagate a modification of an input variable on the internal variables and ultimately on the output variables (Le Goc, 2004a).
To control the behaviour of a process, the relations linking causes to effects must be known. The natural form of the expert knowledge is the "if-then" rule. Conceptually, the simpler form of such a relation is:

If the process is in the state X and
If the action U is executed (10)
Then the process produces the output Y

In this rule, the process output Y is the effect of applying a modification U. This relation depends on the process state X. The causal relation can be modelled, then, as a ternary predicate in first order logic of the form (Le Goc, 2004b) $C(Y, X, U)$.
In our case, the state X is the set of indicators measured by the data acquisition system and, particularly, the control parameters of the workstations.
Modifications of the set-up parameters of the workstations (whose set represents the action U) will produce changes in the state X that will be reflected as an output Y.

Our objective is to control the process behaviour.
To express this fact, it is necessary to reformulate the previous rules, by the introduction of a new term, the goal *G* of the supervisor (Le Goc, 2004a).

If the goal G is to obtain the output Y and
If the process is in the state X (11)
Then the action U must be carried out

Formally, the causal relation is now a 4-arity predicate *I(Y, U, X, G)* such that:

$$I(Y, U, X, G) \Longleftrightarrow C(Y, X, U) \wedge Equal(Y, G) \tag{12}$$

The pieces of knowledge *I (Y, U, X, G)* are the ones that we have elicited in the knowledge acquisition stage for the generic analysis. We have worked with experts on the development of an ontology of actions, with the associated phenomena. Fig. 28 shows a part of this ontology:

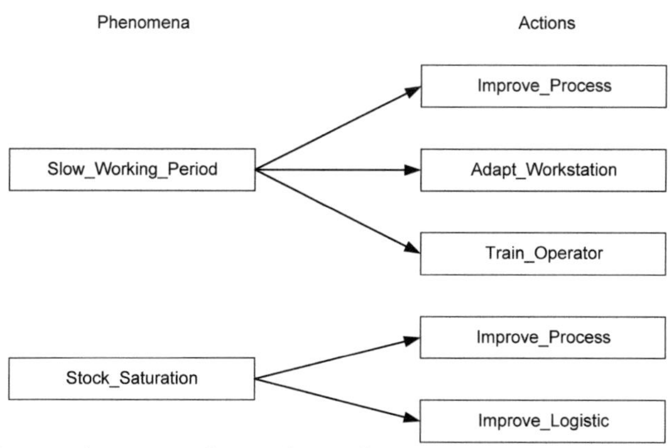

Fig. 28. A part of the ontology on relationships phenomena - actions

In this way, if we consider the model of a breakdown on Fig. 25, to improve the production line, we must act on the *Slow_Working_Period* phenomenon. Therefore, we will propose to improve the process, to adapt the workstation, or to train the operator.
The ontological study has been carried out by considering different sources. In particular, diverse ontologies on production systems or enterprise ontologies have been studied. Our main sources have been the MASON ontology (Lemaignan et al., 2006) and the one on Unified Assembly System Design developed by the University of Nottingham, the Royal Institute of Technology (Sweden) and the New University of Lisbon (Lohse et al., 2005)
Others ontologies we have considered are the TOVE (Fox, 1992; Fox & Grüninger, 1998) and the ENTREPRISE (Ushchold et al, 1998) ontologies.

8. Losses

To conclude, we remind that all this work has been done with the goal of improving the performance of the production lines. In fact, for our industrial partner *to improve performance of his production line* means *to produce more good pieces in a certain time window*.
Therefore, we can estimate the losses incurred (due to non-quality or to fault/breakdowns) in a given time period (Zanni & Bouché, 2008b).
Losses due to non-quality can be evaluated by the number of bad pieces produced per hour.

$$\begin{aligned} L_{quality} &= \textit{Total quantity of produced bad pieces / production time} \\ L_{quality} &= \textit{Number of bad pieces / hour} \end{aligned} \tag{13}$$

Losses due to production factors can be evaluated by the difference between the theoretical number of pieces that the line can produce (according to the specifications of the line) and the effective number of good pieces produced.

$$\begin{aligned} L_{production} &= \textit{(Theoretical number of pieces – Number of effectively} \\ &\quad \textit{produced pieces) / production time} \\ L_{production} &= \textit{Number of non produced pieces / hour} \end{aligned} \tag{14}$$

We need to consider, also, the losses produced by maintenance problems. These losses may be evaluated as the total time of breakdown multiplied by the work pace of the line divided by the total production time. In this way, we have the number of non-produced pieces during breakdowns.

$$\begin{aligned} L_{maintenance} &= \textit{Breakdown periods * work pace of the production line /} \\ &\quad \textit{production time} \\ L_{maintenance} &= \textit{Number of non produced pieces during break / hour} \end{aligned} \tag{15}$$

If we make the addition, we obtain a global estimation of losses:

$$\begin{aligned} Losses &= L_{quality} + L_{production} + L_{maintenance} \\ Losses &= \textit{Number of bad pieces / hour +} \\ &\quad \textit{Number of non produced pieces / hour + Number of pieces non} \\ &\quad \textit{produced during breakdowns / hour} \end{aligned} \tag{16}$$

The amount of these losses may be very important; on one of the lines we study, we have estimated losses in *185 pieces / hour*. This line should produce *450 pieces / hour*, that is, the losses represent more than 40%.
Estimation of losses will permit us to evaluate the pertinence of the proposed action plans. With this aim, we will implement a simulator of the production line, on which we can test them.

9. Conclusions

We have presented a global method based on a knowledge-based approach for the development of a software tool for modelling and analysis of production flows.

To the best of these authors understanding, the reasoning on the number of produced parts and the recommendations according to the three criteria, quality, maintenance and production, have not been fully addressed yet. In addition, the generic vs. specific analysis (global vs. by-workstation) approach will make the tool flexible and available for use by the production staff on site (not necessarily at ease with other possible performance indicators) and decision makers.

The method we propose is based on data processing and data mining techniques. Different kinds of techniques are used: graphic representation of the production, identification of specific behaviours to identify phenomena, and research of correlations among them on the production line. Most of these techniques are based on statistical and probabilistic analyses. To carry on high-level analyses, a stochastic approach is used to identify fault models.

Fault models can finally be used to propose action plans, which can be studied by simulation before implementation.

Therefore, the following steps of our project include the development of a simulator. We will use it to compute the effects of the action plan. The principle will be to build new sequences of data with the specifications of the action plan and to introduce them into real data to compute the effects. If a proposition of an action has no effect, it is not necessary to implement it. Furthermore, if the implementation of that action does not produce significant improvements (according to the decision maker) in the quantity of good pieces that were produced, a non-application of the action might be envisaged.

Our future works also include the possibility of exploring a new generation of expert system using multi-agents techniques for on-line analysis and diagnosis production chains.

The idea is to introduce, for each workstation in the line, an autonomous agent capable of monitoring its operation. To do this, it will generate the characteristic of the workstation behaviour, from statistics and probabilistic computations. Therefore, each workstation will be able to make its own diagnosis, based on its own behavioural models, but it will also be able to have a global view of the behaviour of the whole line through exchanges with the rest of the agents.

This communication among the agents will permit them to act together for the optimization of the operation of the line or to produce high-level alarms to prevent the occurrence of major failures.

10. References

Bouché, P. & C. Zanni. (2008a). A Stochastic Approach for Performance Analysis of Production Flows. *In ICEIS 2008, 10th International Conference on Enterprise Information Systems*, Barcelona, Spain.

Bouché, P.; Le Goc, M. & Coinu, J. (2008b). A global model of sequences of discrete event class occurrences. *In ICEIS 2008, 10th International Conference on Enterprise Information Systems*, Barcelona, Spain.

Cassandras, C.G. & Lafortune, S. (2001). *Introduction to dicrete event systems*. Kluwer Academic Publishers.

Fox, M.S. (1992). The TOVE Project: A Common-sense Model of the Enterprise, Industrial and Engineering Applications of Artificial Intelligence and Expert Systems, Belli, F. and Radermacher, F.J. (Eds.), *Lecture Notes in Artificial Intelligence* # 604, Berlin: Springer-Verlag, pp. 25-34.

Fox, M.S. & Grüninger, M. (1998). Enterprise Modeling, *AI Magazine*, AAAI Press, Fall 1998, pp. 109-121.

Ishikawa, K. (1982). *Guide to Quality Control*. Unipub / Quality Resources.

Le Goc, M. (2004a). SACHEM, a Real Time Intelligent Diagnosis System based on the Discrete Event Paradigm. *Simulation*. The Society for Modeling and Simulation International Ed., vol. 80, n° 11, pp. 591-617.

Le Goc, M. (2004b). The discrete event concept as a paradigm for the perception based diagnosis of SACHEM. *Journal of Intelligent Systems* 8(3/4), 239–290.

Le Goc, M.; Bouché, P. & Giambiasi, N. (2006). Temporal Abstraction of Timed Alarm Sequences for Diagnosis. *In: the proceedings of COGIS'06, COGnitive systems with Interactive Sensors*, Paris, France.

Lemaignan, S.; Siadat, A.; Dantan, J.-Y. & Semenenko, A. (2006). MASON: A Proposal For An Ontology Of Manufacturing Domain. *Distributed Intelligent Systems: Collective Intelligence and Its Applications, 2006. DIS 2006*. IEEE Workshop on , vol., no., pp. 195-200, 15-16.

Lohse, N.; Valtchanov, G.; Ratchev, S.; Onori, M. & Barata, J.A. (2005). Towards a Unified Assembly System Design Ontology using Protégé. *In: 8th Intl. Protégé Conference*, Madrid, Spain.

Shewhart, W.A. (1939). *Statistical Method from the Viewpoint of Quality Control*. The Graduate School, U.S. Department of Agriculture, Washington, 1939.

Tempelbeier, H. & Burger M. (2001). Performance evaluation of unbalanced flow lines with general distributed processing times, failures and imperfect production. *IEE Transactions* 33(4), 419–446.

Uschold, M.; King, M.; Moralee, S. & Zorgios, Y. (1998). The Enterprise Ontology. *The Knowledge Engineering Review*, 13, pp 31-89

Van Bracht, E. (1995). Performance analysis of a serial production line with machine breakdowns. *In: IEEE symposium on emerging technologies and factories automation*. Paris, France.

Xie, X. (1993). Performance analysis of a transfer line with unreliable machines and finite buffers. *IEE Transactions* 25(1), 99–108.

Zanni, C.; Le Goc, M. & Frydman, C. (2006). A conceptual framework for the analysis, classification and choice of knowledge-based diagnosis systems. *International Journal of Knowlegde-Based & Intelligent Engineering Systems* 10(2), 113–138.

Zanni, C.; Barth, M. & Drouard, L. (2007). A Knowledge-Based Tool for Performance Analysis of Production Flows. *IFAC MCPL 2007 – The 4th International Federation of Automatic Control Conference on Management and Control of Production and Logistics*, Sibiu, Rumania.

Zanni, C. & Bouché, P. (2008a). A Global Method for Modelling and Performance Analysis of Production Flows. *In EUROSIM/UKSIM 2008 10th International Conference on Computer Modelling and Simulation*, p740-745, Emmanuel College, Cambridge, England.

Zanni, C. & Bouché, P. (2008b). A Stochastic Approach to Improve Performance of Production Lines. *In EMSS 2008 20th European Modeling and Simulation Symposium (Simulation in Industry)*, Campora San Giovanni, Amantea (CS), Italy.

21

Modelling and Simulation of an Automated Warehouse for the Comparison of Storage Strategies

Valentina Colla and Gianluca Nastasi
Scuola Superiore Sant'Anna
Pisa, Italy

1. Introduction

Among the different kinds of plants that can be simulated, warehouses are surely one of the most common, because of the need of an easy and fast retrieve of the different items to dispatch, independently on the system adopted for their storage. In particular, the progress of industrial automation has promoted the widespread adoption of automated warehouses in a great number of industries of different types. The great advantages that such systems can bring in term of productivity, safety, quality and competitiveness are able to justify their high costs. However the efficiency of any warehouse (automated or not) is determined by factors such as layout, conveyors type, typologies of the products to be stored, shapes of the packages, and storage strategies. Nevertheless, it could happen, after a warehouse had been set up, that some conditions change: production cycles may vary, new product typologies can be introduced, new production lines can be added, etc. so that an intervention on the warehouse in order to keep the desired efficiency becomes necessary. In these circumstances, warehouse layout, product packages and conveyors type are very often constraints, while storage strategies can be relatively easily modifiable. A scrupulous modelling and simulation phase of the warehouse and the eventual automated material handling system could provide a valuable test bench for designing, testing and comparing of new storage polices.

Throughout the chapter a theoretical discussion on the modelling and representation of a warehouse will be provided. An overview of "discrete-event simulation" and its derivate "trace-driven simulation" will be presented: their features will be described as well as two different ways (longitudinal and transversal analyses) to model the problem in order to employ these techniques in an effective manner. A typical automated warehouse will be used as example by characterizing it through events and entities. Besides, the usage of data coming from actual information systems as simulation inputs will be discussed.

Some Key Performance Indicators (KPIs) useful in the evaluation of the efficiency of a warehouse will be defined and used to derive objective functions that need to be optimized in order to improve storage strategies and warehouse performances. As a practical case study, the modelling and the simulation with the trace-driven technique of an existing

automated warehouse for the storage of steel products will be presented. A software system able to simulate the warehouse behaviour will be presented and discussed with the help of the Unified Modelling Language (UML) (Arlow&Neustadt, 2005), which will be used to describe the identified entities, and their relationships. The features of the simulator will be presented as well as its design and some hints on its development in C++.
The modular structure of the software and of its end-user interface will also be analysed in deep details, in order to illustrate how such kind of tools can be used for improving the warehouse management through the development, implementation and test of different storage strategies.
Finally some indications on the storage strategies optimization will be provided and some results will be analyzed by means of the comparison of defined KPIs.

2. The problem

Automated warehouses are complex systems. They often have several constraints due to their layout (single or multi level), the type of material handling system (conveyors, bridge cranes, automated guided vehicle systems, forklift trucks, etc.), the shapes and properties of packages (stacking or not stacking), storage and order picking polices (static or dynamic allocation, first-in first-out, etc.). The optimization of their performances requires the formulation of a model. Previously mentioned elements cannot be easily translated into mathematical terms, thus making difficult the application of traditional operational research techniques (e.g. the simplex algorithm). The risk is in the simplifications that such techniques would require to obtain a usable model (Jones et al., 2002). Moreover, the required optimization is often multi-objective, whose aim is to provide a number of possible solutions that represents different trade-offs between different goals. A better way to cope with this problem consists in describing the model by means of a programming language, that is, in other words, to develop a simulator.
By means of a simulation program it is possible to replicate in a controlled environment the behaviour of a real system in different conditions. More in general, a simulation is an auxiliary tool that allows both analysis and synthesis of dynamic systems, which allows to measure the performances of existing systems for different structural features as well as to assess at design-time the behaviours of the system for different operative conditions.
The importance of simulation is highlighted by the following tasks it can accomplish:

- Study and analysis of interactions between single components of complex systems;
- Impact assessment of potential changes to an existing system;
- Design-time evaluation on the performances of a system for different operative conditions;
- Performance analysis of an existing system;
- Generation of an artificial history of a system;
- Parameters optimization;
- Analysis of possible bottlenecks;
- Capacity planning;
- Assessment of performances of different systems in the same conditions;
- Analysis of system behaviour in rare and risky conditions;
- Estimation of not-measurable variables and quantities;
- Exploration and assessment on new management policies.

In this optic, a general purpose programming language (e.g. C/C++, Java) allows describing the model with the necessary degree of detail. Some tools already exist that can make easier the duty of building a simulator, such as GUI-based software and framework libraries. Nonetheless they have some limitations, as will be explained in the next section, that do not allow a complete customization and an exploitation of most advanced optimization techniques.

3. Approaches to the simulation of a warehouse: existing tools

Warehouse design or re-design often require the use of a simulator for different reasons:

- provide a proof of concept;
- test warehouses performances with different throughput;
- optimize the layout;
- optimize storage strategies;
- answer "what if" questions.

The problem is common and, over the years, different tools have been developed in order to help designers and users. Existing tools can be divided in three main categories: GUI-based simulation software, framework libraries and specialized programming languages. In the following sections these solutions will be briefly illustrated and some available tool will be cited.

3.1 GUI-based simulation software

This kind of software is internally very complex and they have very high costs. They allow building simulators visually, relatively quickly and with a minimal effort by using graphical elements and libraries of entities, without the need to write code. Most of these tools consist of two components: a build environment, which allows the definition of the physical and the logical model of the plant by means of component libraries and CAD tools, and an engine, which interprets these models and actually simulates them. Advanced tools (e.g. AutoMod™ or Siemens Tecnomatix™) can also visualize the simulation in a 3D environment (LeBaron&Jacobsen, 2007).
One of the key features of the GUI-based simulation software that makes them so quick and easy to use, i.e. the component library, is also one of their limitations. Actually not all warehouses employ standard elements and the implementation of new modules in these environments are not straightforward.
Besides, the investments necessary to buy this kind of software can be hardly justified when there is the need to simulate only one plant. In facts, the targets of these systems are more likely to be warehouse designers and builders or very large companies.
Another limitation is represented by the difficult integration of custom advanced optimization techniques, like those that will be presented after in this chapter.

3.2 Framework libraries

The aim of this kind of solutions is to help programmers developing custom simulators by providing a set of standard objects, methods and functions, which may be used to build a simulation engine. There exist several libraries for almost all known general purpose

programming languages (especially Java), both freeware and commercial, and most of them are based on "Discrete-Event Simulation" (DES) principles.
Unfortunately, the majority of these tools is oriented to networks simulation (e.g. OMNeT++ and Ns2) (Varga, 2001) and cannot be adapted to the simulation of warehouses in a simple way (if the license allows it). Moreover, with the existing framework libraries it is difficult to exploit historical data obtained from warehouses information systems in order to drive the simulation by means of known inputs, therefore the development of a "Trace-Driven Simulation" (TDS) is not possible or it requires too much effort.

3.3 Specialized programming languages

First specialized programming languages oriented to simulation were developed during '50s and '60s in the context of manufacturing companies in order to speed up the realization of simulation models, which were, until that time, made in Fortran, Assembler or even manually.
Most popular and used languages were GPSS (Gordon 1962) and SIMSCRIPT (Markowitz 1963) and SIMULA (Dahl&Nygaard 1966). These languages and their evolutions are nowadays encapsulated in advanced build environment, like those presented in Sec. 3.1.
If on the one side the specialization of this kind of languages helps by simplifying the modelling of the problem thank to a targeted set of constructs and instructions, on the other side they impose some restrictions and boundaries, as in the case of framework libraries.

4. Warehouse modelling

As highlighted in previous sections, using existing tools could be of great help, although in some cases the development of a custom simulator becomes necessary.
In literature three main simulation paradigms do exist (Borshchev&Filippov, 2004): System Dynamics (SD), Discrete-Event Simulation (DES), and Agent Based (AB). The first one is the less recent and it is based on the concepts of stocks (e.g. of material, money) and continuous flows between them; it aggregates single entities and events, concentrating on polices and strategies. DES is a well-known and widely adopted paradigm, also by commercial software. In DES entities are passive and respond to predetermined events, which are organized in an ordered queue. AB is, vice versa, a relatively new paradigm, used mainly in academic researches, mainly suitable for social and biological studies; it is based on active and autonomous entities that define in a bottom-up way the global system behaviour by means of their interactions.
The choice of which model to adopt in the simulation of an automated warehouse naturally falls on DES: in fact such a system is actually a collection of entities (e.g. production lines, conveyors, cranes) that respond to fixed events (e.g. production orders, picking messages).
In this section an overview of DES and its derivates will be presented as well as two different ways (longitudinal and transversal analyses) to model the problem in order to apply these techniques in an effective manner.

4.1 Discrete-Event Simulation

To better understand what DES is, let's introduce some definitions (Banks et al., 2004):

- *clock*: variable representing the simulation time;

- *system state*: collection of variables that contains all necessary information needed to describe the system itself, especially those that shall be analyzed;
- *event*: instantaneous happening that changes the system state; an event is defined as *conditioned* or *dependant* if it always occurs together with another event, *primary* or *independent* vice versa;
- *pending events queue*: ordered list of events for which the occurrence time is known;
- *entity*: system component that requires an explicit representation of its own model;
- *attributes*: properties that describe a certain entity;
- *entity set*: temporary or permanent collection of entities organized by a certain logic;
- *activity*: time interval of specified amount during which determined actions are carried out by a single entity or by an entity set;
- *delay*: time interval of unspecified duration.

In DES the system evolves according to the program shown in Fig. 1. At the beginning the system, the events queue and the clock are initialized: an initial state for the system and all its entities is assigned, the queue is filled with programmed events and the clock is reset. Subsequently, as long as the events queue is not empty, the simulation enters in its main loop where the nearest event is scheduled by updating the clock to the event time. The event is than signalled to the system that propagates it to all its entities. Entities affected by the event carry out defined actions, which, in turn, have two side effects: the system state changes and new events could be triggered and pushed into the events queue. When there are no more events, or a stop condition is met, the simulation breaks the loop and a report of the observed system state variables should be returned in order to be analyzed.

```
system.init();
events_queue.init();
clock.reset();
while( !events_queue.empty() )
{
    event = events_queue.next();
    clock = event.time();
    system.signal(event);
    system.update_status();
    events_queue.update();
}
system.report();
```

Fig. 1. Discrete-Event Simulation main loop

4.2 Model characterization

The most critical phase in DES modelling is, without any doubt, the identification of entities, activities and events that characterize the system and its evolution.

Two methods will be here reviewed: *longitudinal* (or *by process*) and *transversal* analyses. Both methods are based on the distinction between *resident* (e.g. production lines) and *transient* (e.g. semi-worked products) entities (Bratley et al., 1987).

Adopting the first form of analysis means representing the system dynamics - i.e. the sequence of events - as flows of transient entities. For example, let us consider a production system in which material is handled from one equipment to another along a certain transformation process. Thus, using longitudinal analyses, semi-worked items correspond to transient entities, which are affected by a sequence (a list of events) of transformations

(activities) carried out by various equipments, i.e. resident entities are here seen as resources (of work). At the end of each activity, the attributes of transient entities establish the system state and they can trigger new events (e.g. alarms).
Vice versa, the adoption of transversal analysis implies the description of the system dynamics in term of cycles of resident entities. Let us apply this method to our example: each machine carries out a cyclic sequence (events list) of operations (activities), during which a new resource is transformed in a semi-worked product. At the end of each cycle, attributes of resident entities establish future events and they modify the state of transient entities.
Nevertheless, it is always convenient to apply both analyses in order to spot every event or entity and then to simplify the model by eliminating superfluous and redundant elements.

4.3 Simulation initialization

In order to start a simulation, an initialized pending events queue is necessary. The initialization can be done in various ways:

- *random initialization* can be used when no prior knowledge of events timing is assumed;
- *stochastic initialization,* on the contrary, can be employed when an *a priori* characterization of events statistics is provided (e.g. frequency, distribution);
- *trace initialization* is applied when historical or log data regarding events can be obtained from, for example, an information system (e.g. production orders, malfunctions).

When the last type of initialization is used, the simulation takes the name of *Trace Driven Simulation,* which is a well-known technique especially in the field of computer architecture evaluation (e.g. cache, memory) (Fu&Patel, 1994), but that can easily be extended to other traceable systems, like warehouses, for example.
On the one hand, this kind of simulation provides some key advantages by using "real" data:

- simulation credibility;
- easy and straightforward model validation;
- direct and impartial comparison between simulated results and measurements on the real system.

On the other hand, this method can be applied only when the system to simulate, or a similar system, already exists and data logs are available.

5. Key Performance Indicators

In order to assess, compare and improve the performances of a warehouse and employed storage strategies, it is convenient to define a set of Key Performance Indicators (KPIs) (Chan, 2003). Such KPIs can be used as system state variables or even as objective functions of an optimization system linked to the simulator.
Generally KPIs should be customized on the particular warehouse system in exam so as to adapt them to its peculiarities and to emphasize any desired aspects.

In this section some general KPIs will be presented together with some more specialized indicators, suitable for warehouses organized in aisles with dynamic compartment allocation and products stored in stacks (see Sec. 7).

5.1 Throughput

Throughput the measure of the number of items that enter or exit during a time unit (hour, shift, day)

$$T_{in} = I_{in} / \Delta t \tag{1}$$

$$T_{out} = I_{out} / \Delta t \tag{2}$$

where T is the throughput, I is the number of inbound (in) or outbound (out) items.

5.2 Average Stock

It expresses the average quantity of products stored in the warehouse during a certain amount of time.

$$\overline{S} = \frac{\sum_{i=1}^{N} S(i)}{N} \tag{3}$$

where N is the number of observed days, S(i) is the stock measured the i-th day, which can be expressed as number of products or total weight (it depends on the typology of material).

5.3 Receptivity

It is a measure of the quantity of items a warehouse can host. For warehouses that use static allocation, receptivity is rather simple to calculate; otherwise it's assumed to be approximately equal to the maximum quantity of items that has been recorded or during the simulation or by the information system.

5.4 Receptivity Saturation Coefficient

It express how much the warehouse has been exploited in a certain period of time

$$RSC = \overline{S} / R \tag{4}$$

where $\overline{S}$ is the average stock in the observed period and R is receptivity.

5.5 Handling potentiality

In Automatic Storage and Retrieval Systems (AS/RSs) it measures the average number of handled items as

$$HP = \frac{\sum_{i=1}^{N} I_{in}(i) + I_{out}(i)}{N} \tag{5}$$

where I_{in} and I_{out} are, namely, the number of inbound and outbound items in the i-th time interval and N is the total number of considered time intervals.

5.6 Fragmentation

It is a measure of space breakup, useful for warehouses with dynamic compartments allocation. It is defined as

$$F(i) = 1 - \frac{NS_0}{NS(i)} \tag{6}$$

where NS_0 is the number of empty spaces present at time t=0 (e.g. in a warehouse organized in n aisles NS_0=n) and NS(i) is the number of empty spaces in the i-th observed time interval.

6. Programming tips

In this section some hints regarding the implementation of a warehouse simulator will be illustrated, with particular emphasis on object-oriented programming, reusable design patterns, data structures, and maintenance. The reference programming language is C++, but the concept hereafter exposed can be simply extended to other high level programming languages.

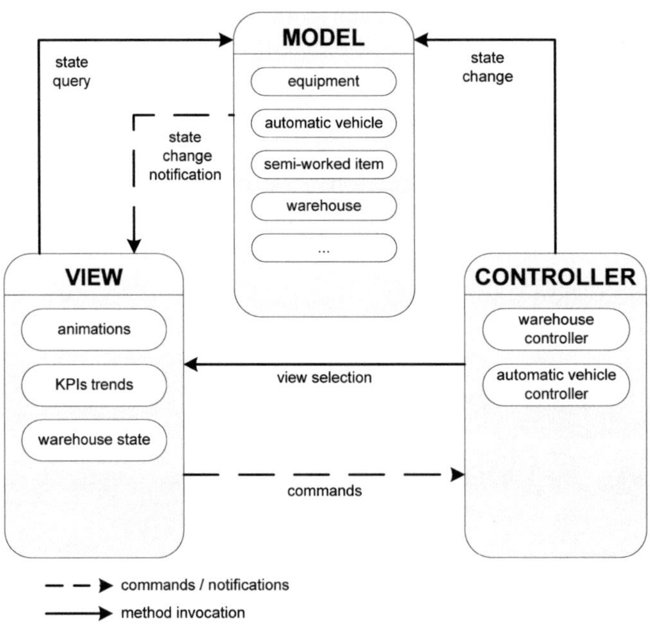

Fig. 2. Example of Model-View-Controller design pattern

6.1 Model-View-Controller

In interactive simulations, the Graphic User Interface (GUI) offers a direct visualization of the dynamic behavior of the modelled system and it provides to the analyst a way to directly interact with the simulation that he is executing. Typically the software modules dedicated to visualization and user-interaction are integrated in the module responsible of the model simulation. Nevertheless such integration makes hard the design and especially the maintenance of complex simulators and it imposes unnecessary constraints to GUIs development (Krasner&Pope, 1988). In order to obtain more robust and easier to maintain simulators, the software should be designed following the *Model-View-Controller* (MVC) design pattern: *models* are represented by identified entities, *controllers* implement models logic and are responsible for state transitions, while *views* manage GUIs and user interactions by routing commands to *controllers* (Fig. 2). The MVC design pattern has been employed with success in several complex simulation applications (Narayanan et al., 1997). The net separation of duties simplifies modeling and programming, it makes the system more robust and it eases debugging and maintenance of the application.
Models, views and controllers should be mapped on separated classes: even if this technique probably produces a higher number of classes, some of them are very simple, especially models, so that however the complexity decreases and the code become more linear.

6.2 Strategy design pattern

Strategy is a behavioral design pattern (Gamma et al., 1994) that allows a high degree of modularity in the implementation of different strategies and polices (e.g. storage, picking, ordering strategies) by delineating a family of algorithms through the definition of a common interface and by making them easily interchangeable. By means of this design pattern it is possible to choose which polices to employ at run-time and, besides, it makes very easy the addition of new strategies, also after the software is already developed. In Fig. 3 the UML diagram of the classes is shown: classes that implements concrete strategies (*ConcreteStrategyA* and *ConcreteStrategyB*) are derived from the abstract base class *AbstractStrategy*, which declares an abstract method *algorithm()*. The *Context* class has a pointer to the abstract base class, to which the address of a particular instance of one of the concrete derived classes is assigned on the base of the strategy that has to be applied.

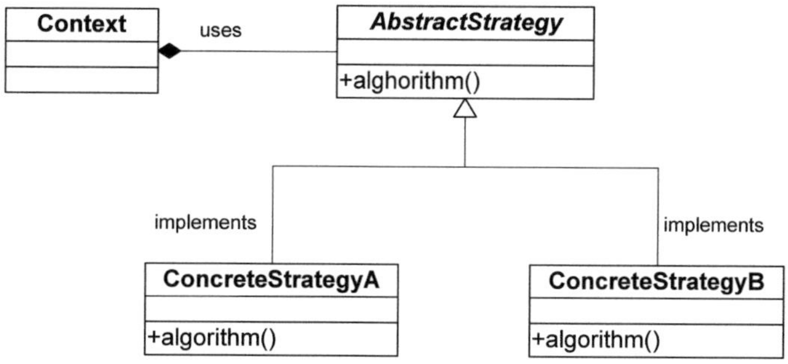

Fig. 3. UML class diagram of a typical Strategy pattern.

For example, let us consider a warehouse with three different allocation strategies (StrategyA, StrategyB and StrategyC), where each of these polices tends to optimize a

different KPI. The inputs for the three algorithms are the same: the item to be placed and the state of the warehouse. A common interface can therefore be defined by means of an abstract class *AllocationStrategy* that declares an abstract virtual method *allocate(item i, warehouse w)*. This method is therefore mandatorily implemented by subclasses, which will encapsulate the different strategies.
When, for example, it is necessary to allocate an item by means of *StrategyA*, an object of this type is instantiated and its address assigned to the pointer owned by *WharehouseController*. When it will call the *allocate* method, the invocation will be translated, thank to the polymorphism rules, in an invocation of the allocation method of the concrete class *StrategyA*.
By applying this scheme it is therefore possible to realize different families of strategies (allocation, reordering, picking) each one containing several possible strategies able to optimize different KPIs or that employ different optimization techniques.

6.3 Visualization and animations

Sometimes it could be convenient to visualize interactively the evolution of the simulation: charts showing trends of main KPIs, diagrams representing allocated compartments and animations of the material handling system could be very helpful for both the researcher and the final user.
While charts are relatively simple to implement thank to the great number of both freely and commercially available modules, custom animations or diagrams could be more tricky to develop. GDI+, DirectX and OpenGL are only few of the technologies that can be used to realize such elements: the first one is helpful for bi-dimensional diagrams and animation, while the other two are employed mainly for coding 3D environments.
Although all these technologies are well documented, the design of data structures that models such animation remains the most difficult step to accomplish. Unfortunately there are not general data structures that can be employed out-of-the-box, but they should be designed and customized around the particular problem.
However, for the sake of example, let us consider a material handling system composed by automated vehicles linked to rail tracks. Each vehicle is autonomous and it is able to respond to mission messages (e.g. pick an item, store an item). Such system could be modelled by means of a graph: rail tracks can be represented by weighted arches, where weights are proportional to trunks length and nodes represent tracks intersections. Vehicles are autonomous entities, thus coded by means of instances of vehicle classes. The position of a vehicle is determined by the arch to which it is linked and by the amount of covered space on that arch. At each clock event, vehicles move forward by a certain amount of space, proportional to their speed. Each vehicle instance checks if the track portion it has to cover is free in order to prevent collision and railroad switches are driven so as to respect precedence and priorities.

7. A case study

In this section a warehouse simulation case study will be presented. The actual plant will be illustrated as well as the storage strategies optimization problem that makes necessary the development of a simulator. A description of the simulation software will be then provided by means of UML diagrams and screenshots.

7.1 The plant

The analyzed plant (Fig. 4) produces steel tubes of different qualities, lengths and shapes, which are stored and sold in packs of the same typology. The plant is composed by an area where tubes are manufactured by means of four production lines (profilers) which are able to lengthwise solder steel strips and to produce tubes with different shapes. These lines are connected by means of an automated material handling system to a storage area where final products are stored until customers order them: this system is composed by 43 peculiar automated cranes, called trolleys, which can move by means of a rail tracks suspended to the plant ceiling. The trolleys are equipped with electromagnets capable to capture one pack of tubes, they are capable of self-governing movements thanks to an on-board Programmable Logic Controller (PLC) and they can also communicate with each other and with the warehouse main PLC by means of radio-frequency transceivers. The task of the main PLC is to assign missions to trolleys which can be of three types:

- pack retrieval at the end of one of the production line, transportation to the storage area and subsequent stacking;
- pack retrieval in the storage area for dispatching;
- pack reordering inside the storage area.

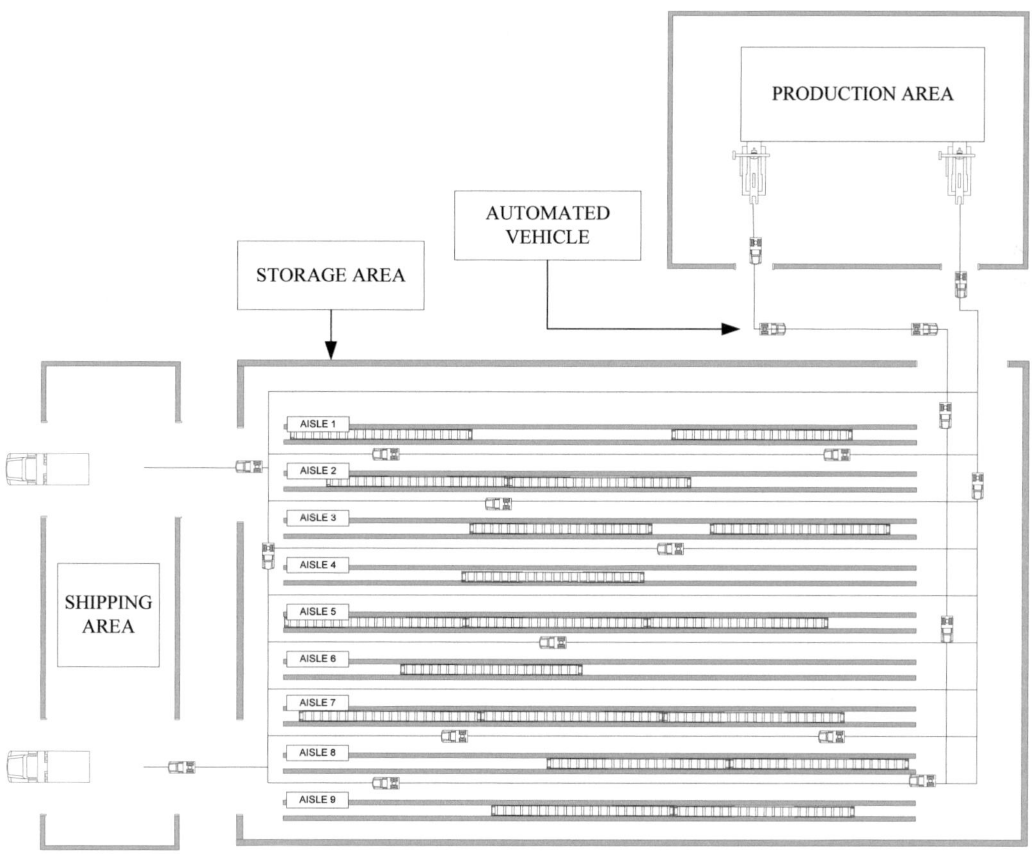

Fig. 4. Plant layout.

The warehouse is connected to the information system of the company, thanks to which it receives production and dispatching orders, by thus minimizing the human intervention. The storage area is divided in 9 aisles that are 90 meters in length, where tubes are stored in dynamically allocated compartments, each one composed by the same typology of product (there can be more than 1000 different typologies). Each compartment is in turn composed by one or more stacks of packs, where the number of stacks is calculated in order to ensure a steady structure and is a function of the number and section dimensions of packs to store (each typology has default pack sizes). Compartments take up the entire width of an aisle and are placed with a predetermined slope with respect to the aisle itself due to the motor position on the trolleys and to the path of the rails. Furthermore, three big pillars (called physical poles) are placed in each aisle to prevent accidental falls of all the stacks.

7.2 Storage strategies

As previously described, the allocation subsystem is entirely automated: when a production order is received by the central mainframe, the latter sends an allocation order to the warehouse management system, which in turn pre-allocates and configures an adequate compartment. If a compartment suitable for a peculiar typology of tubes is already available, the system exploits it, otherwise a new compartment is allocated: the stack composition and compartment occupation are calculated and a suitable free space is picked out. The algorithm looks for available empty spaces in the aisles, which are coded by their starting position and width, and chooses the first empty space that allows to insert a new compartment. If it is not possible to insert that stacks configuration, a new stacks configuration will be calculated, by decrementing the compartment by one stack at time. This subsystem is based on heuristic rules which tend to optimize free linear space and favour distribution of packs along different aisles in order to have a sort of redundancy that enhances insertion and drawing parallelism, by also limiting conveyors traffic problems. In the reordering subsystem, up to now three different strategies are implemented:

- *FIFO reordering*: In order to prevent tubes oxidation, formerly produced packs that belong to almost empty compartments are put over new ones. Handlings for FIFO reordering are carried out by considering:
  - the number of packs in the considered compartment;
  - the compartment ageing;
  - the number of activation of the FIFO reordering in a day.
- *Stacks reordering*: this kind of reordering consists in compacting compartments containing few packs, so that they can be rearranged in a compartment with fewer and higher stacks. Stacks reordering are carried out by considering:
  - the maximum number of packs to reorder;
  - the maximum number of activations of the stacks reordering per day.

  When there are some stacks which satisfy these two conditions, a new compartment is created with a more compact configuration.
- *Space reordering*: the goal is to defragment free spaces in order to obtain bigger free spaces instead of many small ones. This strategy is carried out by considering:
  - the number of movable packs;
  - the size of adjacent empty spaces.

7.3 The problem

The illustrated strategies actually employed in this plant are based on heuristics and do not allow a full exploitation of the available storage space so that it became necessary a precise study with the aim of improving warehouse performances. Simulation is a basic step toward performances optimization of the automated warehouse because direct trials on the real system are obviously not possible and a simulator allows a comparison of the results of different storage strategies in terms of KPIs values and trends.
Although some general warehouse simulation tools already exist, as depicted in Sec. 3, the peculiarity of the considered system and the will to employ advanced optimization techniques imposed the design of a specific simulator.

7.4 Entities and events identification

By applying both analysis methods presented in Sec 4.2, the model can be characterized by means of the identification of entities, events and activities. As the longitudinal analysis is concerned, tube packs can be identified as the transient entities, characterized by quality, length, and shape (properties) and by activities like production, handling, storage and dispatching. Each activity begins with an event generated or by the information system (e.g. production order, dispatching) or by the end of a previous activity (e.g. the handling of a pack starts after the end of its production). Vice versa, by using the transversal analysis, three different types of resident entities can be identified in profilers, automated cranes and warehouse management system. Each of these entities is in fact characterized by cycles of activities - the same listed before -, which in turn operate on the transient entities (tube packs). The initialization of the event queue is done on the basis of data extracted from the plant information system (trace driven simulation - see Sec. 4.3), which contain the details about production and dispatching orders (date, time, typology).

7.5 Design and implementation

In the design of the simulator the techniques presented in Sec. 6 are employed. In particular, the MVC design pattern fits very well with DES entities decomposition. Each entity in facts can be mapped on a model, i.e. on a class in which members represent properties and internal state of the entity and methods represent activities. Some controllers should be also defined: a warehouse controller, responsible of the management of storage space which implements storage strategies and logics, a vehicle controller, responsible of managing vehicles missions and rail switches and a simulation engine, which owns the pending events queue and the simulation clock. Finally, several types of views can be added as needed, allowing an interactive visualization of the simulation evolution: for example a view that summarize the plant state (orders in production, quantity of stored products, allocation state) as illustrated by the screenshot in Fig. 5, a view showing KPIs trends by means of charts or a view showing the automated vehicles system animation. In Fig. 6 an UML diagram of the classes that compose the simulator is shown.

7.6 Strategies optimization and comparison

As described above, the main aim of the simulator is to provide a benchmark through which optimization, testing and comparison of new storage strategies can be done. As a first step towards the optimization, the current storage strategies were reviewed and modified in order to be more rigorous by including strict objective functions. This work, discussed in (Colla et al., 2008), allowed a clean improvement of all KPIs, by providing an increment of the total amount of storable products.

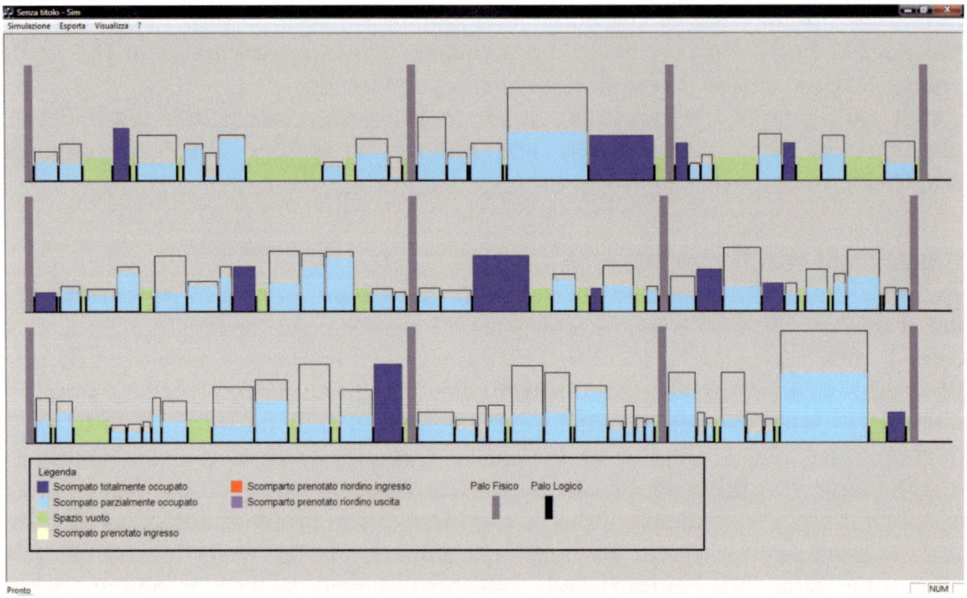

Fig. 5. Screenshot representing the allocation state of three aisle

More advanced techniques based on genetic algorithm are still under development.
The results of each simulation can be then exported as spreadsheets containing KPIs values sampled at a predefined frequency in order to allow easy comparisons, statistic evaluations and data analyses.

8. Conclusion

A typical warehouse simulation problem has been presented in Sec 2. In Sec. 3 existing free and commercially available tools for warehouse simulation have been described, presenting pros and cons of their adoption. Sec. 4 is devoted to the illustration of Discrete-Event Simulation and its derivates, providing modelling and analysis methods. In Sec. 5 typical Key Performance Indicators are derived. Some hints and tips are provided in Sec. 6, which may help in the development and programming of simulator software. Finally, in Sec. 7 a case study of the implementation of a simulator of a real warehouse for storage strategies comparison is described.

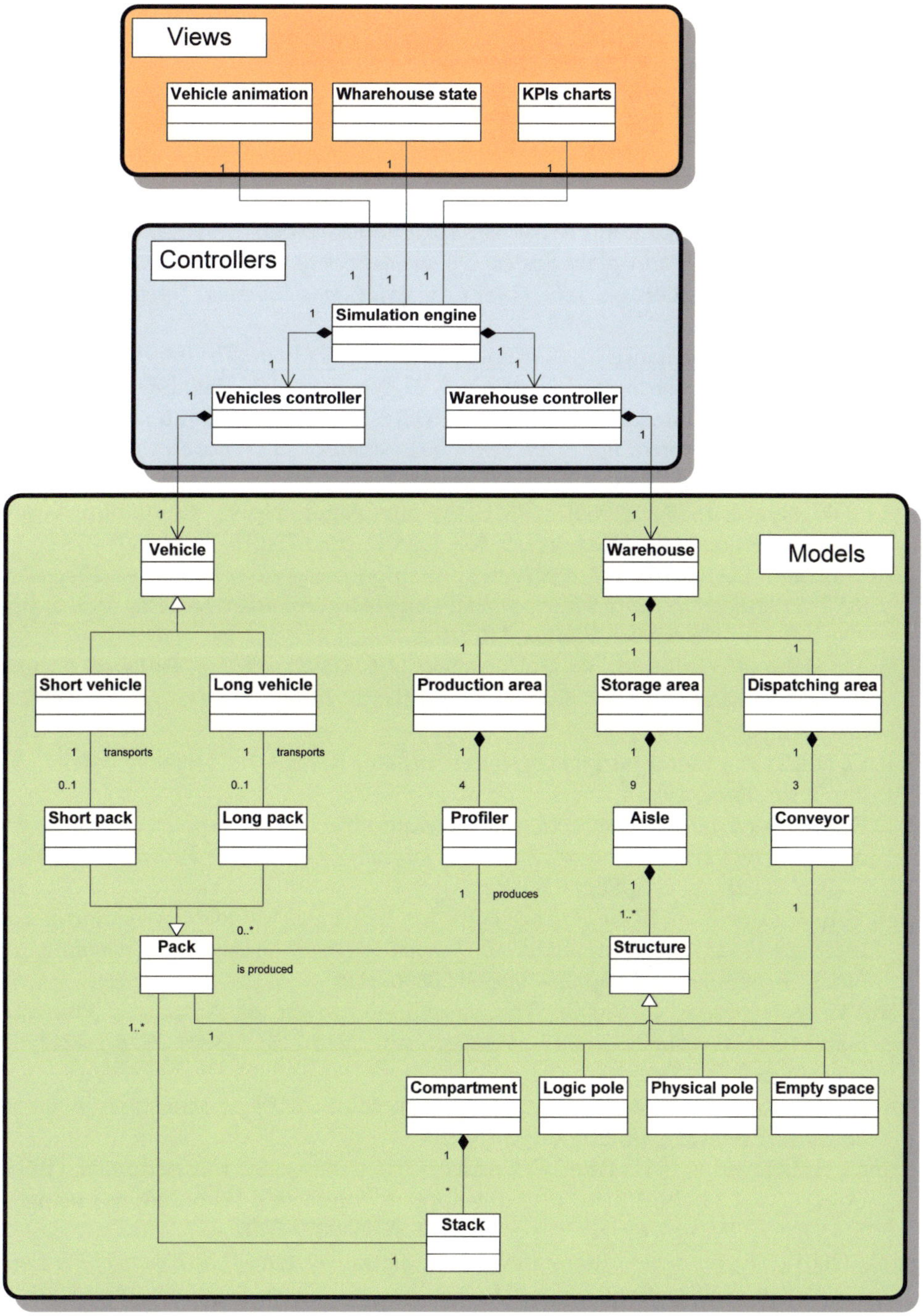

Fig. 6. UML diagram of the classes illustrating MVC design pattern decomposition.

9. References

Arlow, J. & Neustadt, I. (2005). *UML 2 and the Unified Process: Practical Object-Oriented Analysis and Design*, Addison-Wesley, ISBN 978-0321321275

Banks, J.; Carson, J.; Nelson, B.L. & Nicol, D. (2004). *Discrete-Event Simulation*, Prentice Hall, ISBN 978-0131446793

Borshchev, A. & Filippov, A. (2004). From System Dynamics and Discrete Event to Practical Agent Based Modeling: Reasons, Techniques, Tools. *Proceedings of the 22nd International Conference of the System Dynamics Society*, July 2004, Oxford, England

Bratley, P; Fox, B.L. & Schrage, L.E. (1987). *A guide to simulation*, Springer, ISBN 978-0387964676

Chan, F.T.S. (2003). Performance measurement in a supply chain. *The International Journal of Advanced Manufacturing Technology*, Vol. 21, No. 7, pp. 534–548, ISSN 1433-3015

Colla, V.; Nastasi, G.; Matarese, N. & Ucci, A. (2008) Simulation of an automated warehouse for steel tubes, *Proceedings of the Tenth International Conference on Computer Modeling and Simulation*, pp.150-155, ISBN 0-7695-3114-8

Dahl, O. & Nygaard, K. (1966). SIMULA, an Algol based simulation language. *Communications of the ACM*, Vol. 9, No. 9, 1966, pp. 671-678, ISSN 0001-0782

Fu, J.W.C. & Patel, J.H. (1994). Trace driven simulation using sampled traces, *Proceedings of the Twenty-Seventh Hawaii International Conference on System Sciences*, Vol. 1, pp 211-220, ISBN 0-8186-5090-7, Wailea, HI, USA

Gamma E.; Helm, R.; Johnson, R. & Vlissides, J.M. (1994). *Design Patterns: Elements of Reusable Object-Oriented Software*, Addison-Wesley Professional, ISBN 978-0201633610

Gordon, G. (1962). A general purpose system simulator (GPSS). *IBM Systems Journal*, Vol. 1, No. 1, pp. 18-32, 1962

Jones, D.F.; Mirrazavi, S.K. & Tamiz, M. (2002). Multi-objective meta-heuristics: an overview of the current state-of-the-art. *European Journal of Operational Research*, Vol. 137, No. 1, (Feb. 2002), pp. 1-9, ISSN 0377-2217

Krasner, G.E. & Pope S.T. (1988). A Cookbook for Using the Model-View-Controller User-Interface Paradigm in Smalltalk-80, *Journal of Object-Oriented Programming*, Vol. 1, No. 3, September 1988, pp. 26-49, ISSN 0896-8438

LeBaron, T. & Jacobsen, C. (2007). The simulation power of Automod, *Proceeding of Simulation Conference, 2007 Winter*, pp. 210-218, ISBN 978-1-4244-1306-5, Washington DC, Dec. 2007

Markowitz, H.; Karr, H.W. & Hausner, B. (1963). *SIMSCRIPT: a simulation programming language*. Prentice Hall, Englewood Cliffs

Narayanan, S.; Schneider, N.L.; Patel, C; Carrico T.M.; DiPasquale, J. & Reddy, N. (1997). An object-based architecture for developing interactive simulations using java. *SIMULATION*, Vol. 69, No. 3, pp. 153-171, ISSN 0037-5497

Varga, A. (2001). The omnet++ discrete event simulation system. *Proceedings of the European Simulation Multiconference*, pp. 319- 324, Prague, Czech Republic, June 2001, SCS - European Publishing House

22

Swarm Intelligence for Optimization in the Urban Water Industry

Joaquín Izquierdo, Idel Montalvo, Rafael Pérez-García & Carlos D. Alonso
Centro Multidisciplinar de Modelación de Fluidos
Universidad Politécnica de Valencia
Camino de Vera, s/n, 46022, Valencia
Spain

1. Introduction

Many engineering design problems can be cast as optimization problems. The urban water industry is no exception. Design is necessary to implement new configurations, improve existing systems, continue satisfying consumer needs, and to expand to meet new conditions. In this context, we consider the design of new Water Distribution Systems (WDS), and Wastewater Systems (WWS); as well as the rehabilitation and enlargement of existing systems. Taking into account the uncertainty of much of the data on problems in existing configurations, it is frequently necessary to solve difficult inverse problems where optimization techniques are of paramount importance. The calibration, identification, and detection of leaks in a WDS, which are truly important problems in the water industry, can be addressed as optimization problems. Due to increasing urban development, optimisation represents a permanent source of challenge for the management of many resources, especially water. The challenge of planning, designing, and managing urban water systems is increasingly difficult because various systems are needed, and new systems are constantly being developed; while existing systems need enlargement and rehabilitation. Furthermore, there is a great deal of concern regarding the search for mechanisms of sustainable water supply at a reasonable cost.

In this chapter, Particle Swarm Optimization (PSO), a well-established evolutionary optimization technique, is applied to problems in the urban water industry. Originally designed to deal with continuous variables, the PSO variant considered in this chapter overcomes three typical weaknesses in this optimization technique. Firstly, it is adapted to consider mixed discrete-continuous optimization as the problems we consider involve the use of both continuous and discrete variables. Secondly, one of the main drawbacks associated with PSO, namely, the difficulty in maintaining good levels of population diversity, and balanced local and global searches, is overcome. This formulation finds optimum, or near-optimum, solutions much more efficiently; and with considerably less computational effort, because it introduces a richer population diversity. Requiring fewer generations is a major advantage in real water distribution or wastewater systems, where cost and time constraints prohibit repeated runs of an algorithm and hydraulic evaluations. Finally, the cumbersome aspect, common to all metaheuristics, of choosing the right parameter values is tackled through self-adaptive and dynamic parameter control. The variant herein proposed is applied to: (i) designing a WDS; (ii) designing wastewater networks; and (iii) calibrating and identifying leaks in a WDS. These are only three among the huge pool of optimization problems that can be addressed by the proposed PSO variant. This technique has also provided excellent convergence characteristics, and good final solutions when applied to different real-world problems.

2. Antecedents

Optimization in water systems is considerably more difficult than simulation of these systems. Typically, optimization is a constrained nonlinear search problem involving both continuous and discrete variables. Thus, the problem is a mixed continuous and discrete constrained nonlinear optimization problem that is often highly dimensional. There may be many local optima in the search space; and there is no single optimization model, or search algorithm, for solving the problem without compromising solution accuracy, computational efficiency, and problem completeness.

Classical methods of optimization involve the use of gradients, or higher-order derivatives of the fitness function. However, they are not well suited for many real-world problems because they cannot process inaccurate, noisy, discrete, and complex data. Therefore, robust methods of optimization are often required to generate suitable results.

During the last decade, many researchers in the water field have shifted direction, leaving aside traditional optimization techniques based on linear and nonlinear programming, and embarking on the implementation of evolutionary algorithms: Genetic Algorithms (Savic & Walters, 1997; Wu & Simpson, 2001; Matías, 2003; Wu & Walski, 2005); Ant Colony Optimization (Maier et al., 2003; Zecchin et al., 2005); Simulated Annealing (Cunha & Sousa, 1999); Shuffled Complex Evolution (Liong & Atiquzzaman, 2004); and Harmony Search (Geem, 2006), among others.

Particle Swarm Optimization (PSO) is one of the evolutionary algorithms that has shown great potential and good perspectives for the solution of various optimization problems (Dong et al., 2005; Herrera et al., 2009; Janson et al., 2008; Jin et al., 2007; Izquierdo et al., 2008a; Izquierdo et al., 2008b; Liao et al., 2007; Montalvo et al., 2008b; Pan et al., 2007). The PSO algorithm was developed by (Kennedy & Eberhart, 1995) and is a multi-agent optimization system inspired by the social behaviour of a group of migrating birds trying to reach an unknown destination. The aim of this chapter is to show that this algorithm, with several modifications, can be used to find solutions for several optimization problems in urban water systems. PSO is similar to other evolutionary techniques in that it does not guarantee the global optimum; and may prematurely converge to local optima, especially in complex multi-modal search problems. Nevertheless, PSO can be easily implemented, and is computationally inexpensive, since memory and CPU speed requirements are low.

The structure of the chapter is as follows. We first briefly describe three kinds of important problems in the water industry, namely, the design of WDS, the design of WWS, and the calibration and identification of leaks in a WDS. Secondly, we present a mixed continuous-discrete variant of PSO endowed with an enriched diversity feature, which greatly improves the performance of conventional PSO. This variant can also avoid the cumbersome task of parameter selection because it uses a self-adapting technique managed by the algorithm itself. Finally, we show the results of specific applications to selected case-studies, some of which are well-known benchmark problems in the literature. In the case of the design of WDSs, a real-world water distribution network is also considered, which shows the ability of the presented technique to solve real-world problems.

3. The addressed problems

In this section, different problems in the water industry are considered, namely, the design of WDSs and WWSs, and the calibration and identification of leaks in a WDS. These problems have already been addressed using various optimization techniques by other authors (Mariles & Nava, 2007; Botrous et al., 2000; Martínez, 2007; Zecchin et al., 2006), among others.

3.1 The design of a WDS

The optimal design of a WDS consists in determining the values of all the involved variables in such a way that the investment and maintenance costs of the system are minimal, subject to a number of constraints (Izquierdo et al., 2004). A general strategy for solving the optimal design problem of a WDS involves the balancing of several factors: finding the lowest costs for layout and sizing using new components; reusing or substituting existing components; creating a working system configuration that fulfils all water demands; adhering to the design constraints; and guaranteeing a certain degree of reliability for the system (Goulter & Coals, 1986; Goulter & Bouchart, 1990).

The benchmark cases we initially consider have been used traditionally in the literature, and are standard examples used to demonstrate the application of a wide range of tests and analyses. The fitness function that has been traditionally used takes only pipeline costs into account. Nevertheless, a generalization to broader classes of fitness functions is straightforward, as shown below. Hence, in order to facilitate comparisons with the results obtained by other authors for these benchmark cases, we start by using the following fitness function to estimate the costs:

$$F(D) = \sum_{i=1}^{P} C(D_i) \cdot L_i \,. \tag{1}$$

P is the number of pipes in the network, $D = (D_i)$ is the vector of pipe diameters (which is P-dimensional and its components belong to a discrete set of commercially available diameters), $C(D_i)$ is the unit cost per unit length of diameter D_i , and L_i is the length of the i-th pipe. It should be noted that $C(\cdot)$ is a nonlinear function of diameter.

To restrict ourselves to the same rules used in the literature to deal with the benchmark problems, only three kinds of constraints are considered here: continuity equations and energy equations (strongly nonlinear) enforced in the hydraulic model; and lack of satisfaction of minimum pressures at demand nodes. Accordingly, the total cost of the network is considered as the sum of the network cost (1), and a penalty cost. This total cost is defined as

$$F = \sum_{i=1}^{P} C(D_i) \cdot L_i + \sum_{j=1}^{K} p_j \cdot v_j \ . \qquad (2)$$

K is the number of constraints, $v_j = (P_{\min} - P_j) \cdot H(P_{\min} - P_j)$, where H(·) is the Heaviside step function, is the j-th constraint violation; and p_j represents the penalty parameter corresponding to constraint j with a large value to ensure that infeasible solutions have a cost greater than any feasible solution.

In addition, the distribution of flowrates through the network, and the piezometric head values, must satisfy the classical equations of continuity and energy enforced in the hydraulic model. The complete set of equations may be written, by using block matrix notation (Izquierdo et al., 2004), as

$$\begin{pmatrix} A_{11}(q) & A_{12} \\ A_{12}^{t} & 0 \end{pmatrix} \begin{pmatrix} q \\ H \end{pmatrix} = \begin{pmatrix} -A_{10} H_f \\ Q \end{pmatrix}, \qquad (3)$$

where A_{12} is the so-called connectivity matrix that describes the way demand nodes are connected through the lines. Its size is $P \times N_p$ with N_p being the number of demand nodes and P the number of lines; q is the vector of the flowrates through the lines; H the vector of unknown heads at demand nodes; A_{10} is an $P \times N_f$ matrix, with N_f being the number of fixed head nodes with known head H_f ; and Q is the N_p-dimensional vector of demands. Finally, $A_{11}(q)$ is an $P \times P$ diagonal matrix. System (3) is a nonlinear problem, whose solution is the state vector $x = (q,H)^t$ of the system. Continuity and energy equations are enforced by the use of EPANET2 (Rossman, 2000), which is the benchmark hydraulic analysis tool used worldwide.

The first case considered is the New York Tunnel water supply network (see Fig. 1, left), which has been examined several times in the literature (Savic & Walters, 1997; Matías, 2003; Maier et al., 2003). A complete detailed description can be seen in (Dandy et al., 1996). The system has a fixed head reservoir, 21 tunnels, and 19 nodes. The objective of the New York Tunnel (NYT) problem is to determine the most economically effective design for adding to the existing system of tunnels forming the primary water distribution system for the city of New York. Because of age and increased demands, the existing gravity flow tunnels were found to be inadequate to meet the pressure requirements for the projected consumption level. The construction of additional gravity flow tunnels parallel to the existing tunnels was considered. All 21 tunnels are considered for duplication. There are 15 available discrete diameters, and one extra possible decision, which is the 'do nothing' option. The second considered case is the Hanoi pipe network (Fig. 1, right), also studied extensively by various researchers (Savic & Walters, 1997; Matías, 2003; Zecchin et al., 2005; Cunha & Sousa, 1999; Zecchin, 2003). The complete setting can be found in (Wu & Simpson, 2001). This network consists of a single fixed head source at an elevation of 100m, 34 pipes, and 31 demand nodes organized in three loops and two ramified branches. The objective is to specify the diameters (from a set of six commercially available diameters) for the 34 pipes, so that the total cost of the network is minimal, and the pressure at each node of consumption is at least 30m.

The problems faced in the optimal design of WDSs are considerable. Furthermore, this simple variant for the design of a WDS is NP-hard. The NYT system, with 21 pipes, and 15 potential commercial pipe diameters, has 16^{21} possible pipe diameter combinations (including the null option) that constitute the search space of the problem. The Hanoi problem, with 34 pipes and 6 potential pipe diameters, has 6^{34} possible pipe diameter combinations. These modest networks would require a considerable amount of time for an exhaustive search algorithm to navigate the entire search space of almost $2{\cdot}10^{25}$ and $2.87{\cdot}10^{26}$ potential solutions, respectively.

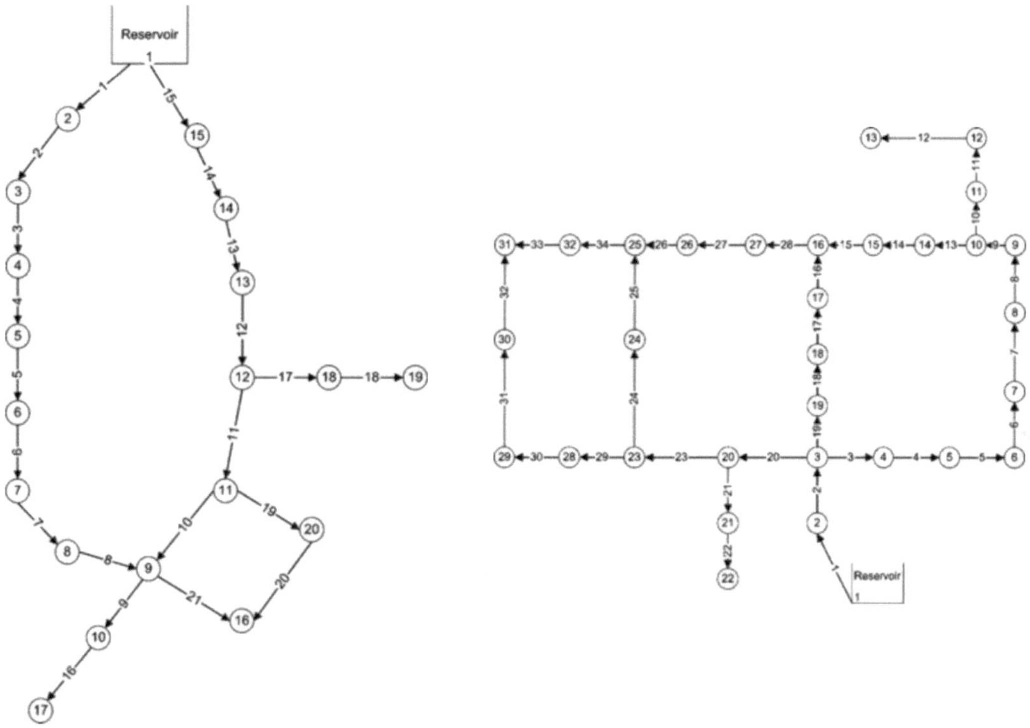

Fig. 1. NYT (left) and Hanoi (right) water distribution networks

In the case of real-world problems, design must consider other aspects, in particular, reliability. The term reliability refers to the ability of the network to provide consumers with adequate and high quality supply, under normal and abnormal conditions. Both hydraulic and mechanical reliability are considered. The former refers to uncertainty resulting mainly from nodal demand and pipe roughness. The latter usually refers to failures of system components, such as pipe breakage. However, there is no universal agreement about the best measure of reliability, redundancy, or resilience; nor what are acceptable levels for these concepts (see, for example, (Savic, 2005)). In this chapter, we considered a proposal recently raised in (Martínez, 2007), since it enforces a certain level of reliability on a system by considering costs incurred by a lack of supply satisfaction. Interestingly, in all the cases we have analyzed, the system improvement obtained by considering these costs in the fitness function implies only a moderate increase in the initial investment costs. Of course, other proposals can be found in the literature.

Following (Martínez, 2007) reliability is added from an economic point of view, by considering the costs of the water not delivered due to problems in the system. As a result, the fitness function adds this additional cost:

$$F(D)=\sum_{i=1}^{L} c_i(D_i)L_i+\sum_{j=1}^{N} \mathrm{H}(H_{\min}-H_i)\cdot p\cdot(H_{\min}-H_i)+\sum_{i=1}^{L} w_i\cdot L_i\cdot D_i^{-u}. \quad (4)$$

Here, w_i is a coefficient associated with each pipe, in the form $a\cdot t_f\cdot(c_f+c_a\cdot V_f)$; $a\cdot L\cdot D^{-u}$ gives the number of expected failures per year of one pipe, as a function of diameter, D_i, and length, L_i, (a and u are known constants); t_f is the average number of days required to repair the pipe; c_f is the average daily repair cost; c_a is the average cost of the water supplied to affected consumers, in monetary units per unit volume; and $V_f=86400\cdot Q_{\text{break}}$ is the daily volume of water that should be supplied to the affected consumer due to the loss of water of Q_{break} in cubic meters per second.

The scenarios considered here follow the approach of 'breaking', in turn, all the pipes of a specific design to check if all the constraints are fulfilled by the design. If the test is negative, the design is suitably penalized. In this way, designs develop increasing reliability. To undergo these tests, the system must be analyzed for any of the specific 'breakages'.

In the case study we present here - which corresponds to a real-world network - (see Fig. 2) the minimum pressure allowed is 15m, and the available commercial diameters are given in Table 1.

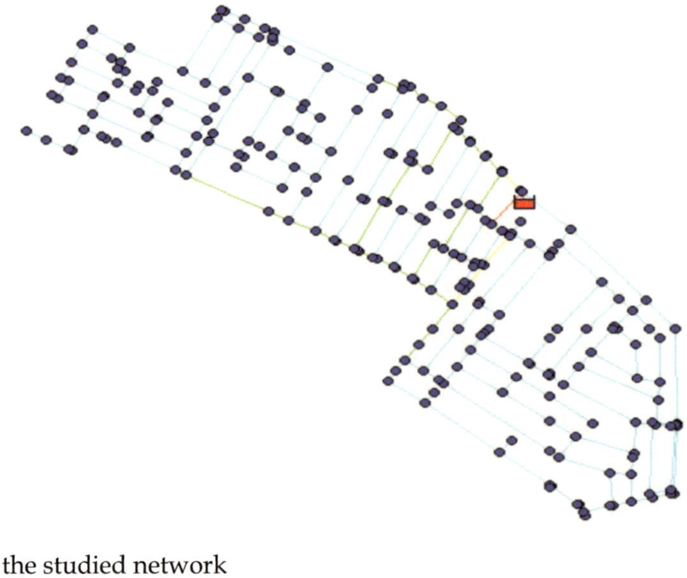

Fig. 2. Layout of the studied network

This table also includes the Hazen-Williams coefficient, C, used in the hydraulic model, and the unit cost of the available and variously sized pipes.

This network, which is fed by a tank, has 294 lines amounting to 18.337km of pipes, and 240 nodes consuming 81.53l/s in total. The dimensionality of this problem, which is of moderate size, is immense.

Diameter (mm)	$C_{H\text{-}W}$	Cost ($units)
100	140	117.14
150	140	145.16
200	140	191.42
250	140	241.09
300	140	333.16

Table 1. Commercially available diameters for the case-study in Fig. 2

3.2 The design of WWS

The design of wastewater collection networks involves the simultaneous use of continuous and discrete variables. For the sake of simplicity and comparison, let us consider a network with no special elements, such as pumps, drops, tanks, and other sewer system elements. The decision variables will then be pipe diameters and slopes. While slopes are clearly continuous variables, diameters must be treated as discrete, since they have to adjust to the range of commercial pipes that are available for the design. The PSO version we present in Section 4 is able to deal simultaneously with both continuous and discrete variables. To evaluate the proposed algorithm, a small water collection system has been designed - using both continuous and discrete variables. The network is shown in Fig. 3.

Peak flows, in litres per second, at the inlets of the network are associated with the nodes, numbered 1 to 7. A more general treatment of this problem should consider sets of hydrographs at system inlet points, rather than fixed pipe design flows. As we intend to use dynamic programming for comparison purposes, we only consider steady state behaviour. Nevertheless, various distributions of input flows, enabling more realistic designs that are compatible with different loads, may be straightforwardly considered by the PSO-based technique. In Fig. 3, the line lengths and ground elevation of the nodes are given.

The design constraints consider the ratio of flow depth for the diameter of any pipe to be lower than 80%, and the velocity not to exceed 4m/s. In addition, all the pipes must be buried at least one metre deep. The fitness function accounts for the costs of the pipes and excavation works. Finally, as in any hydraulic problem, continuity and energy equations complete the set of constraints (see Izquierdo et al., 2004). Non-linearity is associated to the energy equations, all the other constraints and fitness function being linear.

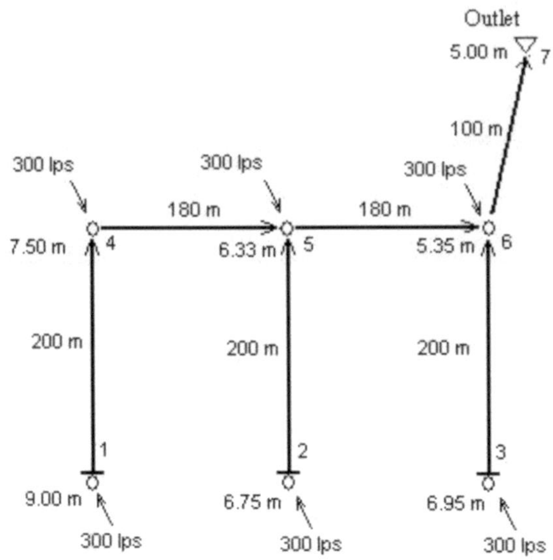

Fig. 3. A sample network

The total cost of the network is considered as the sum of the network cost and a penalty cost, defined as

$$F = \sum_{i=1}^{\#pipes} C_i \cdot L_i + \sum_{i=1}^{\#pipes} Ex_i + \sum_{j=1}^{\#constr} p_j \sum_{i=1}^{\#pipes} v_{ij}^2 \,, \tag{5}$$

where C_i = diameter cost, L_i = length, and Ex_i = excavation costs for pipe i; v_{ij} is the j-th constraint violation at pipe i, and p_j represents the penalty parameter corresponding to constraint j with a large value – to ensure that infeasible solutions have a cost greater than any feasible solution.

3.3 Calibration of a WDS and leak identification

Computational modelling of WDS has become important for WDS authorities. Nevertheless, hydraulic models can only offer a very accurate description of processes provided there is no missing, or uncertain, data; and provided that initial and/or boundary conditions and the forcing terms are precisely defined. In real-life applications, it is a very difficult task to create precise conditions for models. To be useful, any WDS hydraulic model should first be calibrated. Calibration is the process by which a certain number of model parameters are adjusted until the model closely mimics the behaviour of the real system. For WDSs, pipe roughness and leaks are the classes of parameters where uncertainty concentrates. For new pipes, roughness is assessed directly by lab tests. However, for an already existing WDS, the old manual methods used formerly (and even currently) are inaccurate. Much better results can be achieved if calibration of the analyzed WDS model is formulated via optimization problems using a fitness function that tries to reconcile the difference between the measured pressures and the predicted pressures that the hydraulic simulation computer model yields with assumed system parameters. This is a typical example of so-called inverse analysis.

To obtain good values for the system losses, roughness coefficients and flowrates through the pipes must be known with accuracy. Nevertheless, flowrates cannot be accurately assessed if there are any leaks in the system. Leak identification is a difficult problem that can often only be assessed globally through lumped audits performed in certain zones of the network, or in its entirety. There are a number of proposals in the literature for detecting and identifying anomalies and topological errors (see, for example, (Izquierdo et al., 2007), and quotes therein); yet, this state estimation process still represents an important challenge facing water supply managers. For the state estimation process, use is made of the mathematical model of the network. The nonlinear relations among flowrates and heads describing the system balances are confronted by the specific measurements taken using telemetry and other systems. These measurements are compared with the corresponding measurements provided by the model. Discrepancies are then minimized, so enabling roughness coefficients and leak magnitudes to become the variables of the fitness function. The complexity of water systems only enables a few real-time measurements to be made, which only incompletely represent the network state. Obviously, the larger the number of real measurements, the better the accuracy with which roughness coefficients and leaks are obtained. Discrepancies between measured and theoretical (given by the model) pressure heads are then minimized using the fitness function below:

$$F = \sum_{j=1}^{n} p_j \cdot \left| H_j^{\mathrm{m}} - H_j^{\mathrm{c}} \right|, \tag{6}$$

where n is the number of demand junctions where measurements are available, and p_j is the penalty for the discrepancy between H_j^{m}, which is the measured piezometric head at node j, and H_j^{c}, which is the calculated piezometric head at node j. The penalty factor is taken as a large number if $\left| H_j^{\mathrm{m}} - H_j^{\mathrm{c}} \right|$ is larger than a tolerance threshold allowed for node j, and zero otherwise.

By minimizing (6), the problem variables should approach the values of their corresponding real parameters.

4. PSO and the considered variant

All evolutionary algorithms share two prominent features. Firstly, they are population-based. A certain number of individuals, grouped as a population, are used to explore the solution space and find the optimum in the system. In PSO, each bird of the flock is a potential solution and is referred to as a particle. Secondly, there is communication and information exchange among individuals in the test population. In this framework, the birds, besides having individual intelligence, also develop some social behaviour and coordinate their movement towards a destination (Kennedy & Eberhart, 1995). Initially, the process starts from a swarm of M particles, X_i, moving within the search space, $S \subset R^d$, where d is the number of variables involved, each representing a potential solution of the problem

$$\text{Find } \min_{X \in S} F(X) \text{, subject to appropriate constraints,}$$

where F is the fitness function associated with the problem, which we consider to be a minimization problem without loss of generality. The optimal solution is then searched for by iteration. The performance of each particle is measured using this fitness function, according to the problem in hand.

In each cycle of the iteration, t, the i-th particle is associated with the following: (i) its current position, $X_i = (x_{i1} \ldots x_{id})$; (ii) its best position, $Y_i = (y_{i1} \ldots y_{id}) = \text{argmin}(F(X_i(t)), F(X_i(t\text{-}1)))$, reached in previous cycles; and (iii) its flight velocity $V_i = (v_{i1} \ldots v_{id})$, which makes it evolve. The bird which is in the best position, $Y^* = \text{argmin}\{F(X_i(t), i = 1,\ldots, M\}$, is identified for every t.

4.1 Manipulation of particles

In each generation, the velocity of each particle is updated – based on its best encountered position, the best position encountered by any particle, and a number of parameters:

$$V_i \leftarrow \omega V_i + c_1\, rand(\,)\, (Y_i - X_i) + c_2\, rand(\,)\, (Y^* - X_i). \tag{7}$$

In each dimension, particle velocities are clamped to minimum and maximum velocities, which are user-defined parameters,

$$V_{\min} \leq V_{ij} \leq V_{\max}, \tag{8}$$

in order to control excessive roaming by particles outside the search space. These very important parameters are problem-dependent. They determine the resolution with which regions between the present position and the target (best so far) positions are searched. If velocities are too great, particles might fly through good solutions. If they are too slow, on the other hand, particles may not explore sufficiently beyond locally good regions – becoming easily trapped in local optima and unable to move far enough to reach a better position in the problem space. Usually, $V_{\min}$ is taken as $-V_{\max}$.

The position of each particle is also updated every generation. This is performed by adding the velocity vector to the position vector,

$$X_i \leftarrow X_i + V_i. \tag{9}$$

The parameters in (7) are as follows: c_1 and c_2 are two positive acceleration constants, called the cognitive and social parameters, respectively; *rand*( ) represents a function that creates random numbers between 0 and 1 (two independent random numbers enter Equation (7)); ω is a factor of inertia suggested by (Shi & Eberhart, 1998) that controls the impact of the velocity history on the new velocity.

Expression (7) is used to calculate the i-th particle's new velocity, a determination that takes into consideration three main terms: the particle's previous velocity, the distance of the particle's current position from its own best position, and the distance of the particle's current position from the swarm's best experience (position of the best particle). Thus, each particle or potential solution moves to a new position according to expression (9).

The previously described algorithm can be considered as the standard PSO algorithm, which is applicable to continuous systems and cannot be used for discrete problems. Various approaches have been put forward to tackle discrete problems with PSO (Al-Kazemi & Mohan, 2002; Rastegar et al., 2004; Liao et al., 2007; Shi et al., 2007). The approach we propose for discrete variables plainly involves the use of the integer part of the discrete velocity components. This way, the new velocity of discrete components will be an integer and, as a consequence, the new updated positions will share this characteristic since the initial population, in its turn, must also have been generated using only integer numbers. According to this simple idea, expression (7) will be replaced by

$$V_i \leftarrow fix(\omega V_i + c_1\, rand(\,)\, (Y_i - X_i) + c_2\, rand(\,)\, (Y^* - X_i)), \tag{10}$$

for discrete variables, where $fix(\cdot)$ is a function that takes the integer part of its argument. However, it should be taken into account that the new velocity discrete values must be controlled by suitable bounds as in (8). There is, however, a singular aspect regarding velocity bounds that must be taken into consideration so that the algorithm can treat both continuous and discrete variables in a balanced way. In (Izquierdo et al., 2008a), it was found that using different velocity limits for discrete and continuous variables produces better results.

4.2 Manipulation of parameters

The role of the inertia, ω, in (7) and (10) is considered critical for the convergence behaviour of the PSO algorithm. Although inertia was constant in the early stages of the algorithm, currently it is allowed to vary from one cycle to the next. As it facilitates the balancing of global and local searches, it has been suggested that ω could be allowed to adaptively decrease linearly with time - usually in a way that initially emphasizes global search and then, with each cycle of the iteration, increasingly prioritizes local searches (Shi & Eberhart, 1999). A significant improvement in the performance of PSO, with decreasing inertia weight across the generations, is achieved by using (Jin et al., 2007)

$$\omega = 0.5 + \frac{1}{2(\ln(t)+1)}. \tag{11}$$

However, in the variant we propose, the acceleration coefficients and clamping velocity are neither set to a constant value, as in standard PSO, nor set as a time-varying function, as in adaptive PSO variants (Arumugam & Rao, 2008). Instead, they are incorporated into the optimization problem (Montalvo et al., 2009). Each particle is allowed to self-adaptively set its own parameters by using the same process used by PSO - and given by expressions (7) or (10), and (9). To this end, these three parameters are considered as three new variables that are incorporated into position vectors X_i. In general, if d is the dimension of the problem, and p is the number of self-adapting parameters, the new position vector for particle i will be:

$$X_i = (x_{i1}, \ldots, x_{id}, x_{id+1}, \ldots, x_{id+p}). \tag{12}$$

Obviously, these new variables do not enter the fitness function, but rather they are manipulated by using the same mixed individual-social learning paradigm used in PSO.

Also, V_i and Y_i, which give the velocity and thus-far best position for particle i, increase their dimension, correspondingly.

By using expressions (7) or (10), and (9), each particle is additionally endowed with the ability to adjust its parameters by taking into account the parameters it had at its best position in the past; as well as the parameters of the leader, which facilitated this best-particle's move to its privileged position. As a consequence, particles use their cognition of individual thinking and social cooperation to improve their positions; as well as improving the way they improve their position by accommodating themselves to the best-known conditions, namely, their conditions and their leader's conditions when they achieved the thus-far best position.

4.3 Enriched diversity

PSO's main drawback is the difficulty in maintaining acceptable levels of population diversity while balancing local and global searches; as a result, suboptimal solutions are prematurely obtained (Dong et al., 2005). Some evolutionary techniques maintain population diversity by using some more or less sophisticated operators or parameters. Several other mechanisms for forcing diversity in PSO can be found in the literature (Angeline, 1998; Løvbjerg et al., 2001; Parsopoulos et al., 2001a; Parsopoulos et al., 2001b; Zhang & Xie, 2003). In general, the random character that is typical of evolutionary algorithms adds a degree of diversity to the manipulated populations. Nevertheless, in PSO those random components are unable to add sufficient diversity. As shown in (Montalvo et al., 2008b) frequent collisions of birds in the search space, especially with the leader, can be detected. This caused the effective size of the population to fall and the algorithm's effectiveness to be consequently impaired. The study in (Izquierdo et al., 2009a) introduces a PSO derivative in which a few of the best birds are selected to check collisions, and colliding birds are randomly re-generated if collision occurs. This random re-generation of the many birds that tend to collide with the best birds has been shown to avoid premature convergence as it prevents clone populations from dominating the search. The inclusion of this procedure into PSO greatly increases diversity; as well as improving convergence characteristics and the quality of the final solutions.

4.4 The algorithm

The modified algorithm can be given by the following pseudo-code, with t as the iteration number.

- $t = 0$
- Generate a random population of M particles: $\{X_i(t)\}_{i=1}^{M}$, according to (12)
- Evaluate the fitness of the particles (only the first d variables enter the fitness function)
- Record the local best locations $\{Y_i(t)\}_{i=1}^{M}$; the values of the corresponding parameters are also recorded
- Record the global best location, $Y^*(t)$, and the list of the m best particles to check collisions (including their corresponding parameters)
- While (not termination-condition) perform the following:

- Determine the inertia parameter $\omega(t)$, according to (11)
- Begin cycle from 1 to number of particles M
  - Start
    - Calculate new velocity, $V_i(t+1)$, for particle i according to (7), and take its integer part (for discrete optimization) for the first d variables, according to (10)
    - Update position, $X_i(t+1)$, of particle i according to (9)
    - Calculate fitness function for particle i
    - If particle i has better fitness value than the fitness value of the best particle in history, then set particle i as the new best particle in history, and update the list of the m best particles
    - If particle i is not currently one of the m best particles but coincides with one of the selected m best particles, then re-generate particle i randomly (including its parameters)
  - End
- $t = t + 1$

• Show the solution given by the best particle

Different termination conditions, such as the number of fitness function evaluations, maximum run time, convergence in the fitness or search space, may be stated (Shi et al., 2007). For most of the cases considered here, the termination condition stops the process if, after a pre-fixed number of iterations, no improvement in the solution had been obtained.

The performance of the approach introduced herein can be observed in the next section - using the results obtained for the problems presented in Section 3.

5. Application of the PSO considered variant to the addressed problems

5.1 Design of WDSs

In (Izquierdo et al., 2009a) it is shown that, for the NYT and Hanoi networks, a small representative sample of the algorithm's runs can be used to consistently achieve near optimal results at a much reduced computational cost, which is of paramount importance from a practical point of view. By using the obtained results, the probability of a single run obtaining a solution differing by less than a certain percentage from the best-known solution was obtained. These probabilities have been plotted in Figure 4. It can be observed that for both studied problems, for example, one single run of our algorithm gives a solution that is less expensive than 5.5% of the best-known solutions with a probability of 86%. Additionally, there is an almost complete guarantee that in only one single run of the algorithm, a solution will be obtained with a cost under 1.1 times the best-known solution cost.

The best solution found by the used PSO variant is shown in Table 2 for the New York system, and in Table 3 for the Hanoi system; together with other best solutions found in the literature.

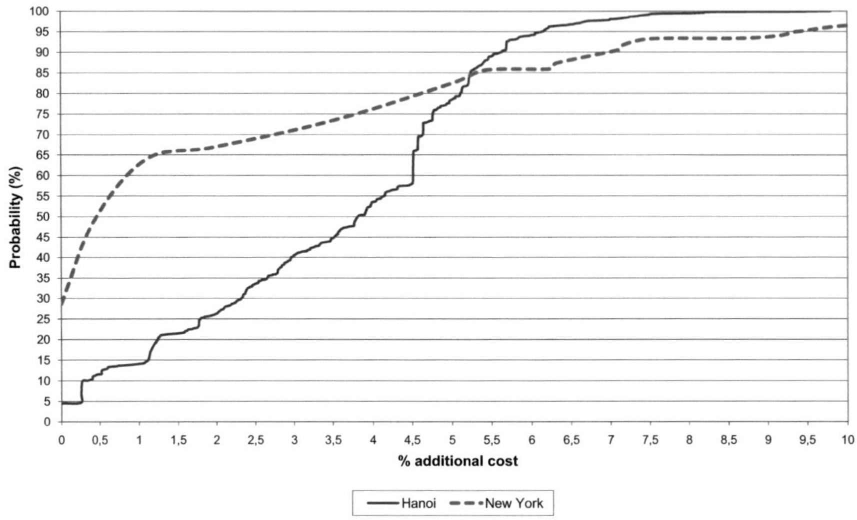

Fig. 4. Probability of first-run good solution

Method	GA	GA	ACO	GA	PSO	PSO
Ref.	(Matías, 2003)	(Zecchin, 2003)	(Maier et al. 2003)	(Savic & Walters, 1997)	(Montalvo et al., 2008a)	(Montalvo et al., 2009)
Cost	38.64	38.8	38.64	40.42	38.64	38.64

Table 2. Optimal design cost (×10^6) for the NYT network

Method	GA	GA	GA	ACO	PSO	PSO
Ref.	(Matías, 2003)	(Wu & Simpson, 2001)	(Savic & Walters, 1997)	(Zecchin et al., 2005)	(Montalvo et al., 2008a)	(Montalvo et al., 2009)
Cost	6.093	6.182	6.195	6.367	6.133	6.081

Table 3. Optimal design cost (×10^6) for the Hanoi network

Parameter V_{max} was set to 50% of maximum variable range, and the stopping condition to 200 iterations. The number of used particles was 100.

The real-world problem in Figure 2 is solved (Izquierdo et al., 2009b) by using the two fitness functions defined in (4) and (2), with and without reliability considerations, respectively. A colour code has been used to aid an understanding of the results. With reference to the pipes: the blue, green, yellow, and red colours represent 100, 150, 200, and 250mm pipes, respectively. Regarding nodes: dark blue represents pressure above 15m;

light blue, between 14 and 15m; green, between 12 and 14m; yellow, between 10 and 12m; and, finally, nodes with a pressure under 10m are represented in red.

This network, which is fed by a tank, has 294 lines amounting to 18.337km of pipes and 240 nodes consuming 81.531/s in total. Figure 3 (left) presents the solution obtained by using (4), which includes reliability. This solution is a mere 3.65% more expensive than the solution obtained using (2), with no reliability consideration. The diameters for this last case can be observed in Figure 3 (right). Table 4 presents a comparison of the initial investment costs for both solutions.

Diameter (mm)	Without reliability		With reliability	
	Length (m)	Cost ($units)	Length (m)	Cost ($units)
100	17 731.10	2 077 021.41	15 822.31	1 853 425.63
150	606.39	88 023.28	2077.69	301 597.04
200	0.00	0.00	328.79	62 937.56
250	0.00	0.00	108.70	26 206.24
300	0.00	0.00	0.00	0.00
Total cost ($units)	2 165 044.69		2 244 166.47	

Table 4. Comparison between costs for both solutions

Fig. 3. Network design and state: (left) with reliability no matter what pipe is out of service; (right) without reliability with the marked pipe out of service

The effect of closing the pipe indicated by the arrow can be observed in Figure 3 (right) for the solution without reliability. It shows the considerable impact produced by a closed pipe: almost half of the nodes (those not in dark blue) do not have the minimum required pressure of 15m. Figure 4 (left) shows that this does not happen for the more reliable design obtained by using (4) since, no matter which pipe is out of service, all the nodes are in dark blue.

5.2 The design of WWS

Flow behaviour through the pipes can be modelled by any of the codes to analyze sewer systems available in the market. In this particular case, we have used the EPA-SWMM package (Rossman, 2005). Even though any part of the analysis provided by this package may be used within the evolutionary algorithm, in the case of this paper only steady state formulation (for peak flows) will be performed for comparison purposes. In effect, given the low dimensionality of the network under study, good results can be obtained using dynamic programming. We use these results as a reference to compare with the results given by PSO, since dynamic programming is theoretically capable of finding the global optimum solution with the only limitation of the discretization used for continuous variables (pipe slopes in our case).

In this case, parameter V_{max} was set to 50% of maximum variable range for diameters, and 20% of variable range for slopes (continuous variables); and the stopping condition was set at 800 iterations.

Sixty executions were performed for the problem at hand. In only one of the sixty cases was the algorithm unable to find a feasible solution. In the other 98.3% of cases, different feasible solutions were found. The average cost for these best solutions is 221.29×€10^3. The best solution is 203.055×€10^3. Also, the same network was designed by using dynamic programming, giving a cost of 206.7×€10^3. Therefore, PSO has found a better solution than the solution provided by dynamic programming, since a discretization of 0.2m for the excavation depth has been used with this last technique. However, an additional experiment using dynamic programming with a finer discretization of 0.1m was also performed, and the obtained result was 204.0×€10^3. Of course, this value is lower than the value obtained with the coarser discretization, but it still does not improve upon the best solution obtained with PSO. Thus, this algorithm shows itself able to go beyond the limits of very fine dynamic programming discretizations.

5.3 Calibration of WDSs and leak identification

The proposed procedure has been applied to the Hanoi network, already considered in section 3.1. The network topology uses the design data given in (Wu & Simpson, 2001) regarding the length of the pipes and the demand at the junctions. As stated by (Wu & Simpson, 2001), pipe diameters were unknown, since it was a design problem. Here, we have assigned design values to the diameters of the pipes. Also a roughness coefficient of 130 (C of Hazen-Williams) has been assigned to all the pipes. Additionally, five new demand nodes have been considered in order to mimic the system leaks. By using EPANET2 (Rossman, 2000), the network was analyzed and the computed head values at the junctions were stored. These pressure heads, together with the assigned Hazen-Williams coefficient and the localization and magnitude of the leaks, synthetically represent the real (measured) values of the network.

To assess the performance of the algorithm, roughness coefficients were allowed to vary between 80 and 140, and leak exponents between 0 and 1.5 for the original network with identification of leaking pipes.

The algorithm was run 100 times, and always the difference between measured and calculated pressure heads was smaller than 0.15mca.

Parameter V_{max} was set to 7% of maximum variable range. The execution stopped if no improvement was obtained after 200 iterations, or if the fitness function reached a value of 0. A population of 300 particles was used.

6. Conclusion

Optimization problems in the field of urban hydraulics are complex by nature and difficult to solve using conventional optimization techniques. In particular, for large WDSs and WWSs, the optimization process for construction and maintenance requires considerable resources every year. Also, growing concern has arisen over water loss in existing WDSs, as they often contain many aging elements, and so the calibration of friction and leakage is of paramount importance in urban water systems. These problems can involve both continuous and discrete variables. PSO is an evolutionary optimization algorithm that can be adapted to deal with both types of variables.

In this work, PSO has been applied to three different problems and good solutions have been found in all the considered case-studies. The ability to deal with both continuous and discrete variables, as well as a feature that increases the diversity of the population of birds, has been considered. This feature makes the algorithm converge with less iteration, thus saving time, which is of paramount importance in real problems related to water systems. Finally, the laborious aspect that pervades all metaheuristics regarding how to perform appropriate parameter adjustments has been overcome by using a self-adaptive parameter control, which renders PSO parameters subject to evolution. Additionally, this formulation obviates the tedious pre-processing task of parameter fine-tuning.

The first problem is the design of WDSs. The performance of the considered PSO variant has been illustrated by application to two well-known benchmark networks, and the results have been compared with those obtained using other evolutionary algorithms. Comparison of the results shows that this formulation finds optimum, or near-optimum, solutions much more efficiently, and with considerably less computational effort. It is noteworthy that for the Hanoi system, the average cost of the 100 performed runs was 6.297 million dollars, only 3.56% higher than the best-known solution. In the case of the New York system, the result is 39.738 million dollars or 2.91% higher than the best-known solution. The average number of generations needed to obtain the best solution for the Hanoi system is 700, with 105 being the minimum number of generations to obtain the best solution. For the New York system, these figures are 230 generations for the best solutions, and 16 for the minimum number of generations to obtain the best solution.

We also have tackled the robust design of such a WDS. The solution cannot ignore the evaluation of aspects related to different scenarios and certain failure conditions. By considering only the initial investment costs, cheaper designs will be produced; but these designs will suffer serious difficulties coping with abnormal situations. We have shown, through one real-world case study, that more reliable designs do not necessarily involve immoderate increases in investment. Interestingly, the same case study shows, nonetheless, much better performances for reliable designs when failure events are represented by pipes being out of service. The concept of reliability used here takes into account the economic impact of the water not delivered due to this type of failure during the life of the network.

In the problem of the design of wastewater systems, PSO performance was compared with an exact method, namely dynamic programming. PSO found a better solution than that provided by dynamic programming when a discretization of 0.2m for the excavation depth was used. However, after refining this discretization to 0.1m, PSO still outperforms dynamic programming. Therefore, PSO is able to go further beyond the limits of very fine dynamic programming discretizations, and interestingly, avoids becoming trapped in the dimensionality curse.

This algorithm has also shown good performance when applied to the problem of calibration and leak identification in a WDS. Pressure differences were lower than 0.15m in all the 100 algorithm executions for the considered case-study – after having found suitable values for pipe roughness and leak magnitudes. New studies should be performed with reduced redundancy in the number of measured parameters. The same approach should be also applied to other networks, since this is a problem that has received little attention in the literature.

The main advantages of the method are that it does not require sophisticated operators, nor parameters: and is thus simpler than other evolutionary techniques. This method does not need initial feasible particles, nor do the re-generated particles need to be feasible; and finally, it is robust in handling diverse fitness functions and various constraints. Furthermore, having fewer generations is a major advantage in real water distribution systems, where cost and time constraints prohibit repeated runs of an algorithm and hydraulic evaluations. From the studied benchmark problems, it can be inferred that obtaining 'good' solutions with the proposed algorithm is straightforward, since there is no need for *a priori* parametric study. This algorithm is also relatively inexpensive as the computational cost increased only slightly because of the relatively small increase in the dimensionality of the search space. Therefore, the algorithm is desirable when the goal is to quickly obtain good solutions that are not necessarily very close to the optimum.

Optimization has been carried out using a variant of PSO, devised by the authors, that considers both discrete and continuous variables. This variant has increased population diversity and self-adaptively manages its parameters. This optimization tool is very useful since other terms (load or service conditions, rehabilitation costs, life-long costs, other reliability measurements, and so on) can be added to the fitness function without rendering the problem more conceptually complex. In addition, this tool can be easily combined with hydraulic network simulation modules, so allowing great versatility in the analysis of candidate solutions.

Finally, the abilities of these particles to decide, as a group, how to move inside the search space, and change their behaviour during the search processes, as well as finding very good solutions in a relatively short period of time, constitutes an open-door environment that could be perfectly exploited to address multi-objective formulations regarding optimization problems in different fields. If one of these capabilities is missing, the PSO algorithm would not be so useful as an optimization tool; and it is precisely the assembly of these capabilities that makes the PSO algorithm a powerful multi-agent system for solving problems in the water industry.

7. References

Al-Kazemi, B. & Mohan, C.K. (2002). Multi-phase discrete particle swarm optimization, *JCIS*, pp. 622–625.

Angeline, P.J. (1998). Using selection to improve particle swarm optimization, *Proceedings of the IEEE Congress on Evolutionary Computation*, pp. 84–89, Anchorage, Alaska, USA.

Arumugam, M.S. & Rao, M.V.C. (2008). On the improved performances of the particle swarm optimization algorithms with adaptive parameters, cross-over operators and root mean square (RMS) variants for computing optimal control of a class of hybrid systems. *Appl. Soft Comput.*, 8(1): 324-336.

Botrous, A.; El-Hattab, I. & Dahab, M. (2000). Design of wastewater collection networks using dynamic programming optimization technique, *Proceedings of the ASCE Nat. Conf. on Environmental and pipeline Engineering*, pp. 503-512, Kansas City, MO, United States, American Society of Civil Engineers.

Cunha, M.C. & Sousa, J. (1999). Water distribution network design optimization: simulated annealing approach, *Journal of Water Resources Planning and Management*, 125 (4), 214–221.

Dandy, G.C.; Simpson, A.R. & Murphy, L.J. (1996). An improved genetic algorithm for pipe network optimization, *Water Resources Research*, 32(2), 449-458.

Dong, Y., Tang, B.X.J. & Wang, D. (2005). An application of swarm optimization to nonlinear programming, *Computers & Mathematics with Applications* 49 (11-12), pp. 1655–1668.

Geem, Z.W. (2006). Optimal cost design of water distribution networks using harmony search, *Engineering Optimization*, 38 (3), pp. 259–280.

Goulter, I.C. & Coals, A.V. (1986). Quantitative approaches to reliability assessment in pipe networks, *Journal of Transportation Engineering*, 112 (3), 287–301.

Goulter, I.C. & Bouchart, F. (1990). Reliability-constrained pipe network model, *Journal of Hydraulic Engineering*, 116 (2), 211–229.

Herrera, M.; Izquierdo, J.; Montalvo, I.; García-Armengol, J. & Roig, J.V. (2009). Identification of surgical practice patterns using evolutionary cluster analysis, *Mathematical and Computer Modelling*, doi: 10.1016/j.mcm.2008.12.026.

Izquierdo, J.; Pérez, R. & Iglesias, P.L. (2004). Mathematical models and methods in the water industry, *Mathematical and Computer Modelling*, 39 (11-12), 1353–1374.

Izquierdo, J.; López, P.A.; Martínez, F.J. & Pérez, R. (2007). Fault detection in water supply systems using hybrid (theory and data-driven) modelling, *Mathematical and Computer Modelling*, 46, 3-4, 341-350.

Izquierdo, J.; Montalvo, I.; Pérez, R. & Fuertes, V.S. (2008a). Design optimization of wastewater collection networks by PSO, *Computer & Mathematics with Applications*, 56(3), 777–784.

Izquierdo, J.; Minciardi, R.; Montalvo, I.; Robba, M. & Tavera, M. (2008b). Particle Swarm Optimization for the biomass supply chain strategic planning, *Proceedings of 4th Biennal Meeting, iEMSs 2008: International Congress on Environmental Modelling and Software*, pp. 1272-1280, Barcelona, Spain.

Izquierdo, J.; Montalvo, I.; Herrera, M. & Pérez, R. (2009a). A derivative of Particle Swarm Optimization with enriched diversity, submitted to Computational Optimization and Applications.

Izquierdo, J.; Montalvo, I.; Pérez, R. & Herrera, M. (2009b). Robust Design of Water Supply Systems through Evolutionary Optimization. *POSTA09. Third Multidisciplinary Symposium on Positive Systems: Theory and Applications*, accepted, Valencia, Spain.

Janson, S.; Merkle, D. & Middendorf, M. (2008). Molecular docking with multi-objective Particle Swarm Optimization, *Applied Soft Computing* 8, 666–675.

Jin, Y.X.; Cheng, H.Z.; Yan, J.I. & Zhang, L. (2007). New discrete method for particle swarm optimization and its application in transmission network expansion planning, *Electric Power Systems Research*, 77(3-4), 227-233.

Kennedy, J. & Eberhart, R.C. (1995). Particle swarm optimization, *Proceedings of the IEEE International Conf. on Neural Networks*, pp. 1942-1948, Piscataway, NJ, USA.

Liao, C.J.; Tseng, C.T. & Luarn, P. (2007). A discrete version of particle swarm optimization for flowshop scheduling problems, *Comput. Oper. Res.*, 34 (10), 3099–3111.

Liong, S.Y. & Atiquzzaman, M. (2004). Optimal design of water distribution network using shuffled complex evolution, *Journal of the Institution of Engineers*, Singapore 44 (1), 93–107.

Løvbjerg, M.; Rasmussen, T.K. & Krink, T. (2001). Hybrid particle swarm optimiser with breeding and subpopulations, *Proceedings of the Genetic and Evolutionary Computation Conf.*

Maier, H.R.; Simpson, A.R.; Zecchin, A.C.; Foong, W.K.; Phang, K.Y.; Seah, H.Y. & Tan, C.L. (2003). Ant colony optimization for design of water distribution systems, *Journal of Water Resources Planning and Management*, 129 (3), pp. 200–209.

Mariles, Ó.A.F. & Nava, A.P. (2007). Calibración del factor de fricción y localización de fugas en una red de tuberías de agua potable, *Proceedings of the VII SEREA - Seminario Iberoamericano sobre Planificación, Proyecto y Operación de Sistemas de Abastecimiento de Agua*, Morelia, México.

Martínez, J.B. (2007). Quantifying the economy of water supply looped networks. *Journal of Hydraulic Engineering*, ASCE, 133(1): 88-97.

Matías, A.S. (2003). Diseño de redes de distribución de agua contemplando la fiabilidad, mediante algoritmos genéticos, *PhD thesis*, Universidad Politécnica de Valencia, Valencia, Spain.

Montalvo, I.; Izquierdo, J.; Pérez, R. & Tung, M.M. (2008a). Particle Swarm Optimization applied to the design of water supply systems, *Computer & Mathematics with Applications*, 56(3), 769–776.

Montalvo, I.; Izquierdo, J.; Pérez, R. & Iglesias, P.L. (2008b). A diversity-enriched variant of discrete PSO applied to the design of Water Distribution Networks, *Engineering Optimization*, 40(7), 655–668.

Montalvo, I.; Izquierdo, J.; Pérez, R. & Herrera, M. (2009) Improved performance of PSO with self-adaptive parameters for computing the optimal design of Water Supply Systems, submitted to Computer-Aided Design.

Pan, Q.K.; Tasgetiren, F. & Liang, Y.C. (2008). A discrete particle swarm optimization algorithm for the no-wait flowshop scheduling problem, *Computers and Operations Research*, 35(9), 2807-2839.

Parsopoulos, K.E.; Plagianakos, V.P.; Magoulas, G.D. & Vrahatis, M.N. (2001a). Stretching technique for obtaining global minimizers through particle swarm optimization, *Proceedings of the Workshop on Particle Swarm Optimization*, Indianapolis, IN, USA.

Parsopoulos, K.E.; Plagianakos, V.P.; Magoulas, G.D. & Vrahatis, M.N. (2001b). Improving particle swarm optimizer by function stretching, in: *Advances in Convex Analysis and Global Optimization*, Nonconvex Optimization and Applications series, pp. 445–457, Kluwer Academic Publishers, The Netherlands.

Rastegar, R.; Meybodi, M.R. & Badie, K. (2004). A new discrete binary particle swarm optimization based on learning automata, *Proceedings of the 2004 International Conference on Machine Learning and Applications*.

Rossman, L. (2005). *Storm Water Management Model user's manual (version 5.0)*. U.S. Environmental Protection Agency, Cincinnati, USA.

Rossman, L.A. (2000). *EPANET, users manual*, U.S. Environmental Protection Agency, Cincinnati, USA.

Savic, D.A. & Walters, G.A. (1997). Genetic algorithms for least cost design of water distribution networks, *Journal of Water Resources Planning and Management*, 123 (2), 67–77.

Savic, D.A. (2005). Coping with risk and uncertainty in urban water infrastructure rehabilitation planning, *Acqua e città - i convegno nazionale di idraulica urbana*, S'Agnello (NA), pp. 28-30.

Shi, X.H.; Liang, Y.C.; Lee, H.P.; Lu, C. & Wang, Q.X. (2007). Particle swarm optimization-based algorithms for tsp and generalized tsp, *Inf. Process. Lett.*, 103 (5), pp. 169–176.

Shi, Y. & Eberhart, R.C. (1998). A modified particle swarm optimizer, *Proceedings of the IEEE Congress on Evolutionary Computation*, pp. 69-73, Piscataway, NJ, USA.

Shi, Y & Eberhart, R.C. (1999). Empirical study of particle swarm optimization. *Proceedings of the IEEE Congress on Evolutionary Computation*. Washington, DC, USA.

Wu, Z.Y. & Simpson, A.R. (2001). Competent genetic-evolutionary optimization of water distribution systems, *Journal of Computing in Civil Engineering*, 15 (2), 89–101.

Wu, Z.Y. & Walski, T. (2005). Self-adaptive penalty cost for optimal design of water distribution systems, *Journal of Water Resources Planning and Management*, 131 (3), 181–192.

Zecchin, A. (2003). Max-min ant system applied to water distribution system optimisation, in: *MODSIM 2003: International Congress on Modelling and Simulation*.

Zecchin, A.C.; Simpson, A.R.; Maier, H.R. & Nixon, J.B. (2005). Parametric study for an ant algorithm applied to water distribution system optimization, *IEEE Trans. Evolutionary Computation*, 9 (2), 175–191.

Zecchin, A.C.; Simpson, A.R.; Mayer, H.R.; Leonard, M.; Roberts, A.J. & Berrisford, M.J. (2006). Application of two ant colony optimisation algorithms to water distribution system optimisation, *Mathematical and Computer Modelling*, 44(5-6), pp. 451-468.

Zhang, W.J. & Xie, X.F. (2003). DEPSO: hybrid particle swarm with differential evolution operator, in: *IEEE International Conf. on Systems, Man and Cybernetics*, 2003, vol. 4, pp. 3816–3821.

23

Modelling and Simulating Large Scale Vehicular Networks for Smart Context-aware Telematic Applications

Ansar-Ul-Haque Yasar, Davy Preuveneers and Yolande Berbers
Department of Computer Science, Katholieke Universiteit Leuven
Belgium

1. Introduction

Developing context-aware telematic applications for vehicles equipped with smart embedded computing devices and communication capabilities with the ability to provide the right information at the right time and place has always been a challenge for researchers. We can address this issue by providing the developers a way to model application specific abstractions for context-aware communication and to test various algorithms and communication protocols in a simulated environment. In this chapter we present certain requirements for modelling telematic application specific abstractions and a framework for simulating context-aware information mediation in large scale vehicular networks. We have used this framework to analyze the requirements by simulating plain broadcasting and our relevance backpropagation algorithms to compare context dissemination in large scale vehicular networks using OMNET++. Initial experiments show that taking the context of vehicles into account significantly improves the bandwidth, availability and context signal-to-noise ratio.

Intelligent telematic application development is a research area that has gained a lot of attention from the research community. In application areas include emergency message transmission, collision avoidance, congestion monitoring and intelligent parking space location. According to the European Transport Whitepaper (EC, 2001) in the year 2000 around 40,000 people lost their lives in the EU by road traffic accidents and 1.7 million were injured costing around EUR 160 billion. Mostly the cause of such incidents is directly related to human error with a very small number of technical or system failures. Such issues can be handled by making intelligent use of information provided by the embedded electronic devices inside vehicles such as GPS or PDAs which will assist drivers but also the information provided by other vehicles or stationary beacons next to the roads. For example, in Figure 1, the bus on the right-hand corner of the figure is interested in going to the right. But it was informed by the vehicles already there about road traffic congestion on that part of the road. Similarly, the same information about this traffic congestion is also being disseminated to the static nodes like parking meters so that parking on a congested road can be avoided and road signs so that the traffic flow can be redirected. In this example, it is clear that the information about the traffic congestion on a path should not be sent to every vehicle and static node but only to those vehicles and static nodes which are interested in such information. It implies that we have to model application specific abstractions by taking the context of the vehicles into account in order to optimize the message flow and reduce communication overhead. As a result a critical aspect in the development of such intelligent applications is *getting the right information at the right time and place* (Yasar et al., 2008).

Context is any relevant information that can be used to characterise the situation of entities and an entity is a person, place, or object that is considered relevant to the interaction between a user and an application, including the user and applications themselves (Abowd et al., 1999). A system is *context-aware* if it uses context to provide relevant information and/or services to the user, where relevancy depends on the user's task (Abowd et al., 1999). Context-aware dynamic settings in intelligent transportation and traffic management systems employ sensor network technologies to create new opportunities for co-operation and exchange of context information between nodes. Traditionally, ad hoc networks have been commonly in use as communication medium between mobile devices and/or a server at the backend (Riva et al., 2007). In order to establish intelligent transportation using the relevant context information flow between vehicles and other static nodes like a parking meter, traffic light or any other road sign we need to model abstractions for context-aware communication and analyze different algorithms and communication protocols incorporating the requirements over certain networks in a simulated environment.

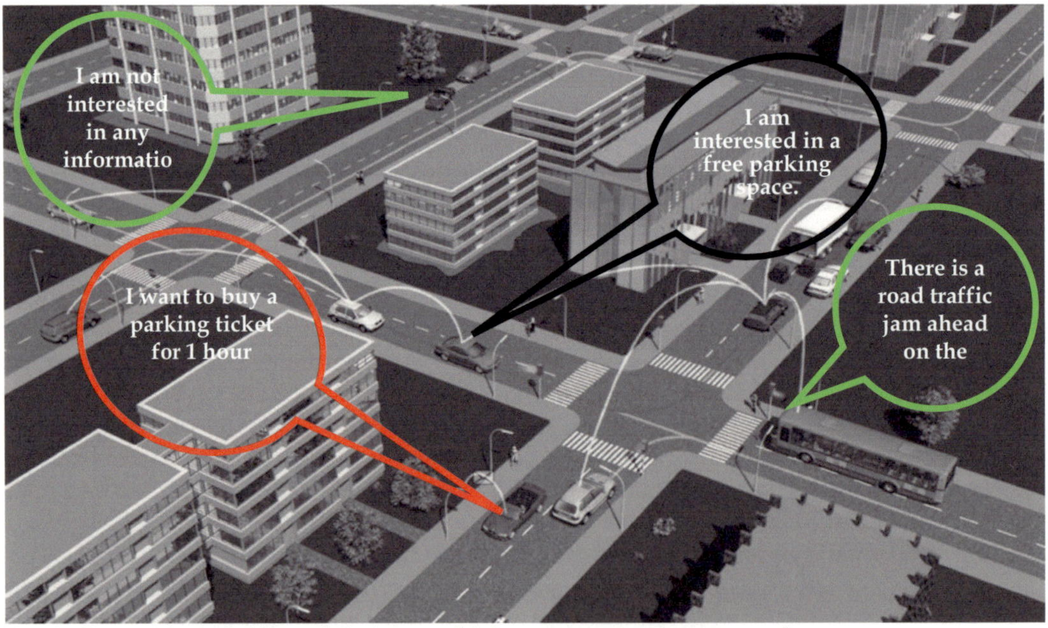

Fig. 1. City wide scalable mobile inter-vehicle communication network.

In this chapter, we will discuss both how we model context-aware telematic application specific abstractions for large scale vehicular networks and how we simulate interactions between moving vehicles and static nodes using broadcasting and our relevance backpropagation algorithms over Bluetooth and WiFi networks. Using our large scale vehicular network framework with context-driven adaptive communication protocols, we can not only model abstractions and investigate the impact of different communication routing schemes but also measure various quality of service parameters in vehicular mobility awareness for different traffic scenarios and versatile telematic application requirements using OMNET++ (Preuveneers et al., 2008) as shown in lower two layers in Figure 2. This figure illustrates our layered vision for smart telematic applications running on top of our middleware. Our relevance backpropagation algorithm resides in the middleware and models abstractions for telematic applications by filtering and routing of information in between the applications. We use simulate the large scale vehicular network using OMNET++ for relevant context information dissemination at the lowest layer.

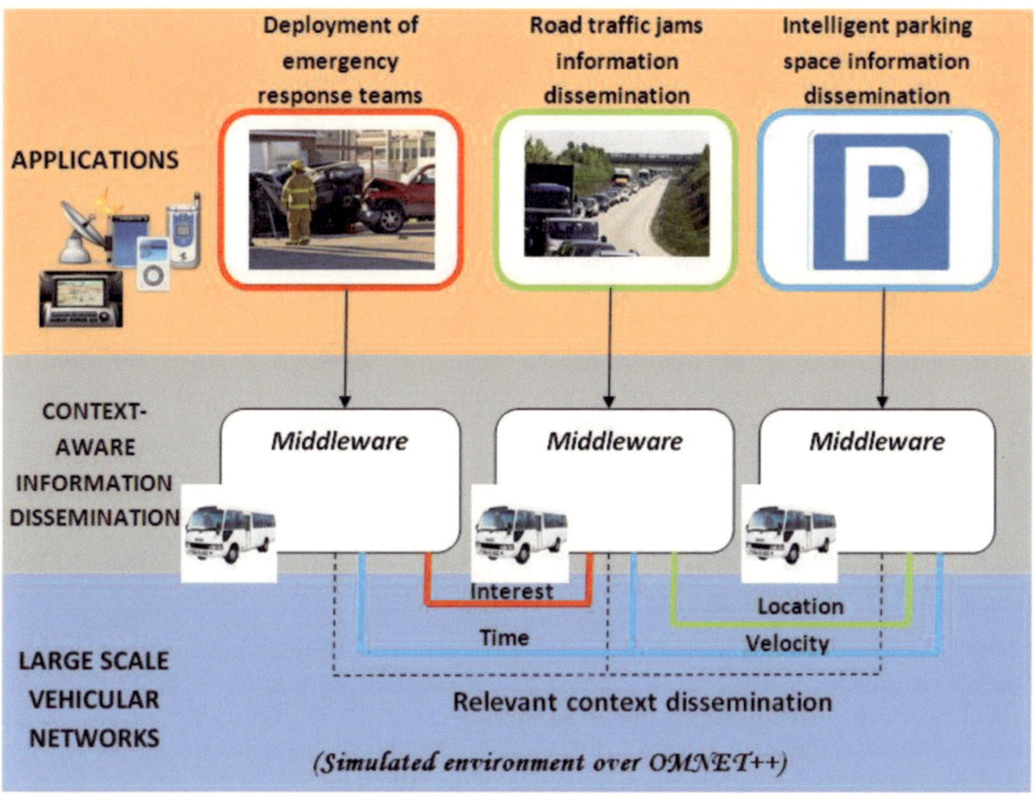

Fig. 2. Context-aware information dissemination in large scale vehicular networks.

We will describe the application specific modelling abstractions, certain set of requirements for context-aware information dissemination in a vehicle network and the design of our large scale vehicle network simulation framework in section 2 and 3 respectively. By means of simulated experimentation, we will illustrate the advantages and disadvantages of different communication schemes for a given telematic application in section 4. Moreover in section 4, we will provide insight on how telematic application developers can leverage from the simulation framework to analyze the behaviour of their applications in a simulated realistic vehicular network setting. In section 5 we discuss some of the related work. We end this chapter with our conclusions and research ideas about future work in section 6.

2. Large scale vehicular networks

The vehicle manufacturers worldwide are producing vehicles in a rapidly growing amount. They are equipped with highly efficient, reliable and cheap embedded computing devices due to the increased demand for smart vehicles to ensure a safe and pleasurable driving experience. With these technological advancements in vehicles, more and more mobile social vehicular networks will come into practice exchanging bulks of information. One of the key concerns for telematic applications in such networks is scalability. In this section we will define scalability, list some motivating scenarios and mention requirements for modelling and simulating various aspects of such networks.

2.1 Defining scalability

The expression '*Scalability*' has often been a vital but a complex facet to address. In terms of context-aware communication the '*Scalability*' can refer, but not limited, to the following properties;

- Large **number of participants** e.g. 100,000 vehicles in a metropolitan city like Brussels, London or Amsterdam.

- Large **number of interactions in terms of message passing between the participants** e.g. mobile social networking information exchanged between 50,000 passengers at an international airport.

- Large **area of interaction** e.g. playing geo-caching within a country or a continent.

- Longer **time span** e.g. maintaining context information about 10,000 vehicles inside a smaller city over a time span of one year to predict traffic congestions on a road.

For vehicular networks, in particular, we refer to it by covering both the aspects of the large number of vehicles and the large number of messages being passed. In order to further extend and explain the concept we present two scenarios in section 2.2 related to the deployment of emergency response teams and emergency messages dissemination and intelligent parking space information transmission to vehicles.

We deal with a large scale vehicle network in the scenarios involving different kinds of mobile and sensor networks like IEEE's 802.11x, Evolution-Data Optimized (EVDO) Rev X and Bluetooth. As it is very likely that there are other embedded devices like cellular phones, laptops, GPS etc, communicating over other kind of networks like GSM and satellite network are also present along with the vehicle's on board embedded computer can also be used for better and optimized performance.

2.2 Motivating scenarios

In this section we describe two motivating scenarios enabling the development of a middleware supporting scalable context-aware inter-vehicle communication. These scenarios are related to the deployment of emergency response teams and emergency messages dissemination and intelligent parking space information transmission to vehicles.

2.2.1 Deployment of emergency response teams and emergency message dissemination to vehicles in a traffic incident

Deployment of Emergency Response Teams to a traffic incident has always been a crucial point with authorities. Traditionally in case of an incident information is sent to the concerned authorities about the type, location and time of incident over the cellular or wired telephone networks and there might be a road traffic jam at the same place. The problem with the current system is that vehicles are often informed too late and the message itself is usually broadcasted to all the vehicles, also to those that are not in the neighbourhood of the accident. Let us consider a scenario where an accident occurs between two vehicles travelling from Leuven to Brussels on the highway E40 causing a traffic jam. A vehicle owner on the same side of the road informs the emergency response teams using his cellular phone after the incident has occurred. The emergency response teams arrive on the location after 10mins to rescue the victims and to put up a sign informing about the incident 500m away to inform the upcoming cars so that they can change their routes to avoid a traffic jam. But within this time frame quite a large number of vehicles are blocked on the road due to the accident which might take time to clear up.

In this scenario the 'large-scale' is mainly in terms of the number of participants and the messages passed between the participants. The types of interactions in this scenario can either be in the form of a query or a message, for example:

1. What is the location of the accident?
2. Which response team is the nearest?
3. Which network is suitable to send information?
4. Send emergency signal to all the vehicles traveling towards the accident.

The participants in a vehicular network will have such interactions in an ad hoc manner covering a large area.

2.2.2 Intelligent parking space information dissemination to vehicles in a metropolitan city

Nowadays, most of the new vehicles have an embedded Global Positioning System (GPS) device to assist the drivers while driving from one location to another. Let us take a typical case of Brussels city during the rush hours when there are thousands of vehicles on the roads. Brussels is one of the most popular cities in Europe and a tourist attraction as well. Several of these vehicles are in search for a parking space near their destination. The parking spaces are badly managed and are not intelligently used for providing parking information to the vehicles. Even the installed GPS is of no use in this situation. Traditionally the parking information is displayed on electronic boards within the city for different parking spots. In some cases when a particular vehicle finds a vacant parking space and reaches that parking space it is usually occupied by another vehicle as the information about free parking space was either too old or the information changed on the electronic board as soon as the vehicle passed by it. So in most of the cases either the vehicles park too far away from their destinations or waste a huge amount of time in search for a nearby parking space. In another case if someone wants to park in Brussels city near the central station on a Sunday at 6.30pm with a maximum parking charge of 1 EUR / hour but the nearest parking space in that location has limited timings on weekends between 6am till 6pm and higher parking fee of 1.50 EUR / hour. Such constraints can be taken into account in vehicular networks as well in order to make context-aware intelligent decisions.

In this scenario the 'large-scale' is mainly only in terms of the messages passed between the participants. Different types of interactions in this scenario either in the form of a query or a message are listed as under:

1. Is there a free parking spot within 500m?
2. How much is the parking fee?
3. What are the timings?
4. Inform other cars interested in a parking spot about a free space.

The participants in such a scenario will have such meaningful interactions in an ad hoc manner spreading the relevant information intelligently.

2.3 Requirements for modelling and simulating context-aware communication in large scale vehicular networks

In order to provide a context-aware scalable solution in terms of a modelling and simulation framework we have to identify a set of requirements supporting such communication. We will first briefly summarize the basic requirements (Yasar et al., 2008) for modelling large scale vehicular networks which are, but not limited to, mentioned as under:

R1: Location and direction-aware delivery of messages
It is always desirable to know the exact location of an incident for context-aware applications e.g.in scenarios 2.2.1 in case of an accident on the road the authorities should be notified about the exact location to react fast. Similarly, a context-aware application should be able to sense, manipulate and disseminate context information about direction and velocity of vehicles in the network to predict certain situations like traffic congestions or traffic accidents in specific regions.

R2: Temporal relevance
It is the desired behaviour of a context-aware application dealing with timeliness of information and routing efficiency. In a context-aware application on time arrival of information has always been a challenge using an efficient route. For example, if a road maintenance work is underway on 20th Apr 2009 between 10am and 5pm at Naamsestraat, Brusselsstraat and Lei in Leuven city so the information about traffic congestion or road condition is only valid on this specific date and time.

It is required that that only the relevant context information arrives at a particular node on the right time and place. Temporal relevance involves efficient filtering of irrelevant information at intermediate nodes for optimal routing and faster delivery of context information. For example, in scenarios 2.2.2 the information about free parking space at a certain location in Brussels should arrive on time to all the vehicles interested in parking information and the stationary nodes like sign boards. The vehicles and the stationary nodes can then further disseminate the information if considered relevant for their neighbouring nodes.

It is enviable to test and analyze several algorithms and protocols taking into account the defined requirements. This imposes a new requirement for our simulated framework in a large scale vehicular network. We will now briefly summarize them as follows;

R3: Analyze throughput, communication overhead and delivery efficiency
It is quite important to be able to quantify how much data that is being transmitted over the network is actually used by network peers both in total and on average for any given communication protocol scheme on an application basis. The quantification will guide the researchers to properly analyze, improve and compare various algorithms and protocols based on the parameters like throughput, communication overhead and routing efficiency.

The main goal is to use the requirements listed above and compare different algorithms and communication protocols for context-aware large scale inter-vehicle communication. Later in the chapter we will discuss and illustrate comparisons between several algorithms and communication protocols taking into account these requirements.

3. Modelling and simulating context-aware large scale vehicular networks

In this section we will discuss modelling criteria for context-aware large scale vehicular networks and types of available communication networks with regard to the type of network and dissemination technique in use. We later also talk about some of the available solutions for context-aware communication and the reasons for not using in vehicular networks along with our algorithm supporting all requirements.

3.1 Modelling context-aware large scale vehicular networks

In order to model application specific abstractions for context-aware large scale vehicular networks we need to know about;

- number of nodes in the network
- available communication links
- number of producer and consumer nodes
- context information being disseminated

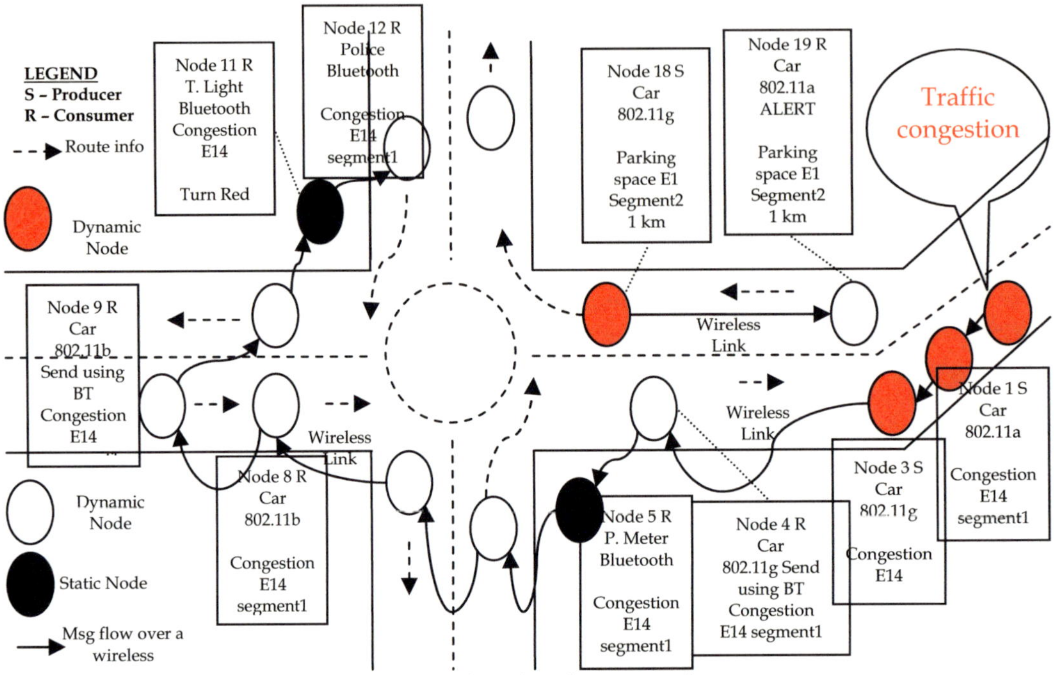

Fig. 3. Modelling context-aware large scale vehicular networks.

The model in Figure 3 shows several nodes in the network each with independent communication capabilities using various kinds of wireless networks. The red nodes and the white nodes are dynamic mobile nodes like vehicles in the network. Whereas, the black nodes are the static nodes like traffic lights, parking meters or road traffic sign. The red colour depicts that the node is an information producer which could either be either static or dynamic. The dotted arrows show the direction in which a node is travelling and the full arrows show an active communication link between two or more nodes using any kind of network mentioned in Table 1. Both arrows can have a different orientation for a single node. The boxes represent the context information the nodes are interested in which has been sent by a producer like the node's identification, preferred network, network in use may be due to receiver's limitation and the message. For example, in Figure 3, nodes will be only interested in information about the communication link to use and the throughput of the communication link being used but not the frequency information to perform computations about the fast and efficient available route.

- **Types of communication networks**

There are various kinds of wireless networks available for providing us with communication support. None of the available wireless networks are built specifically to serve the inter-vehicular communication needs. Researchers (Mahajan et al., 2007) working in this domain constantly test these available wireless networks like IEEE's 802.11x, Evolution-Data Optimized (EVDO) Rev X and Bluetooth to use for inter-vehicle communication.

Standard / Characteristics	IEEE 802.11x a.k.a WiFi			EVDO Rev X		Bluetooth	
	802.11b	*802.11g*	*802.11a*	*Rev A*	*Rev B*	*Ver. 1.2*	*ÈDR 2.0*

Throughput / Data Rate	11Mbps	54Mbps	54Mbps	3.1Mbps	9.3Mbps	1Mbps	3Mbps
Operational Frequency	2.4Ghz	2.4Ghz	5Ghz	CDMA 2000	CDMA 2000	2.4Ghz	2.4Ghz
Max. Range (outdoor)	200 - 250 meters	200 - 400 meters	50 - 150 meters	5 - 8 kms	5 – 8 kms	10 meters	100 meters
Modulation Scheme	CCK	OFDM	OFDM	16QAM	64QAM	GFSK	DQPSK
Spectrum Type	U.L.B.	U.L.B.	U.L.B.	L.B.	L.B.	U.L.B.	U.L.B.

Table 1. Characteristics of various wireless networks for inter-vehicular communication.

<u>Legend</u>:

- CCK – Complementary code keying
- CDMA - Code division multiple access
- OFDM – Orthogonal frequency-division multiplexing
- QAM – Quadrature amplitude modulation
- GFSK – Gaussian Frequency-Shift Keying
- DQPSK – Differential Quadrature Phase Shift Keying
- U.L.B. – Unlicensed band
- L.B. – Licensed band

In Table 1, we have listed several characteristics of some of the possible candidates like IEEE's 802.11x, the 3G EVDO flavours and Bluetooth network for inter-vehicle communication. EVDO Rev X has some potential advantages over WiFi such as the fact that signals can travel on same cell sites as cell phones, no limited coverage and seamless connectivity. The throughput / data rate characteristic mentioned in the Table 1 is hypothetical and the practical value may vary based on the operational environment. The values for the spatial coverage or maximum range are also for outdoor environments as these networks will be embedded inside vehicles. In our simulated experimentation over OMNET++ we make use of IEEE 802.11 and Bluetooth networks.

3.2 Simulating context-aware large scale inter-vehicle communication

The simulated environment enable the research community to test and analyze various kinds of algorithms and protocols over large scale networks like vehicular networks due to its efficient and accurate computation capabilities, low cost and no risk to human life. Simulators can be very efficiently used to create a close to real controlled environment to analyze the required things.

We incorporated the modelling requirements mentioned in section 2.3 along with our relevance backpropagation algorithm for reasoning and routing of contextual information, into our simulated environment over OMNET++ network simulator. We performed several experiments to test these requirements over two popular and most widely used networks namely WiFi and Bluetooth for wireless communication between various kinds of nodes. The details about our experimentation over a simulated environment are described in section 4.

3.2.1 Methods for information dissemination

In this section we discuss an important aspect of exchanging messages between the nodes and the context providers in a large scale vehicle network. Context information is either disseminated proactively using broadcast also known as the ***push model*** or ***on-demand*** also known as the pull model in applications for such a large scale network (Bokareva et al., 2004). We focus on the ***push model*** which has a potential of bootstrapping a large scale vehicular network (Bokareva et al., 2004). The aim of the data push model is to exchange context information among a set of moving vehicles on regular intervals. The pull model can also be implemented using the same techniques as used in the push model (Bokareva et al., 2004) (Ye et al., 2002). Two main techniques used by (Bokareva et al., 2004) to exchange contextual information are described below.

3.2.1.1 Flooding technique for communication

In the **flooding** technique also known as the plain **broadcasting** technique the context information received by a vehicle is stored locally and then the same information is forwarded using a re-broadcast to others. In a large scale, dynamic and mobile vehicle network flooding may overload the network especially in the case of high traffic volumes thus violating some of the requirements mentioned earlier in section 3.3. This technique is very useful in the case where the network under consideration is relatively small because efficiently routing the context information to specific nodes is more expensive in terms of network bandwidth and throughput.

3.2.1.2 Dissemination technique for communication

Dissemination is another generic technique which intelligently broadcasts the context information only to the interested nodes. In the case of a large scale vehicle network each time a vehicle receives the context information broadcasted by a context provider it re-broadcasts the context information only to the interested neighbours. The information about the interest of the neighbours is determined by themselves. The dissemination technique reduces the amounts of context information and does not overload the network, which makes it a scalable solution for transmission of context information over large scale networks. Some types of this kind of dissemination are discussed below:

- **Directed diffusion:** It is the data-centric communication technique widely used for wireless sensor networks. The vehicles request the context information by periodically broadcasting an interest for the required data. Each node will create a link with other nodes or a context provider from which it receives the context information of interest. The link also specifies the data rate and the direction towards which the context information should be sent. Once the link is created between the nodes and the context provider, the context provider will start sending information of interest to the nodes probably along multiple paths. As soon as the node wants to receive the context information, it will select a specific neighbour from which it will receive the information later on, thus defining a directed broadcast of the context information over a large scale network.

- **Two-Tier data dissemination:** It is a decentralized architecture where a grid structure is used to divide the network into cells. The context providers located at the boundary of the cell need to forward the context information to other cells. The context information is flooded within a cell. One tier is the cell at the nodes current location and the other one at the cell's boundary. The query is first propagated over the network to create a path between the node and the context provider and then the same path is used for the propagation of the context information. This technique involves a lot of intelligent routing mechanisms and information storage overhead creating complexities in the libraries for large scale networks application development.

- **Gradient broadcast:** This technique makes use of a cost variable during the transmission of context information. Initially the context providers set the cost to reach a node at infinity. The information is then broadcasted over multiple paths in the network where each of the intermediate context provider or a node calculates the cost of receiving the message (Bokareva et al., 2004). At the end each of the context providers or nodes would have calculated the cost for it to send the context information to a particular node. The cost data is later on used to optimally transmit the context information over the network with a minimal cost. This is highly efficient for transmission of context information over a large scale vehicle network but at the same time it creates overhead for each node to calculate the cost information. This could be an issue given the limited processing capabilities of nodes in large scale vehicle networks.

3.3 Adaptive context mediation in large scale vehicular networks

The network plays a vital role in a large scale environment to process and deliver information from one node to another. We list certain network specific requirements in detail for modelling and simulating adaptive context mediation in large scale vehicle networks. In our analysis (Yasar et al., 2008) we discovered three major requirements;

- **Throughput:** Throughput is an important factor for information propagation over a large scale dynamic mobile network. It measures the amount of relevant context information being sent over the network by the context provider and compares that with the amount that the context information received by the node that subscribed to that information.

- **Bandwidth:** In large scale and dynamic mobile networks bandwidth usage for context-awareness has always been a matter of concern. Therefore, the context information should be passed between the context provider and the nodes in an efficient manner.

- **Time to Live (TTL):** Some of the applications make use of the TTL to decide about the relevance of context information for a particular node in the network. If the TTL has expired the information is considered to be no more relevant to be transmitted over the network. TTL also participates in limiting the use of network bandwidth.

3.4 Relevance backpropagation algorithm

Current peer-to-peer communication protocols like Gossip, Pastry and Chord (Williamson et al., 2006) are inappropriate for scalable context-aware information dissemination as the relevancy of information cannot be determined at intermediate nodes during interaction between several nodes and also no routing algorithm takes relevance of context into account.

Algorithm 1. Relevance Backpropagation (input: fromPeer, contextMessage)

```
(messageRelevant, messageUnused, messageForwarded) = (false, false, false)
while (BeaconNewNode)
if (InFilterReceived(contextMessage.ID)) then
   BackpropagateMessage(fromPeer, DUPLICATE, contextMessage.ID)
else
   AddFilterReceived(fromPeer, context.Message.ID)
if (InFilterRelevant(contextMessage)) then
   messageRelevant = true
   BackpropagateMessage(fromPeer, RELEVANT, contextMessage.ID)
   if (InFilterUnsed(contextMessage)) then
   messageUnused = true
   LabelMessage(contextMessage, UNUSED)
else
   LabelMessage(contextMessage, IRRELEVANT)
if (contextMessage.hopsLeft > 0) then
   contextMessage.hopsLeft = contextMessage.hopsLeft - 1
   for each Peer p in ForwardFilter (adjacentPeers, contextMessage.ID) do
      messageForwarded = true
      ForwardMessage (p, contextMessage)
if (not messageForwarded) then
   if (not messageRelevant) then
      BackpropagateMessage(fromPeer, IRRELEVANT, contextMessage.ID)
   else if (messageUnused) then
        BackpropagateMessage(fromPeer, UNUSED, contextMessage.ID)
end while
RecalibrateNetwork( )
```

In order to solve these issues with the current available solutions we have extended the earlier work by (Preuveneers & Berbers, 2007) on the *relevance backpropagation algorithm* by integrating the requirements for large scale context-aware communication mentioned in section 3.1. The characteristics of the algorithm are as under:

i. The context information is initially plain broadcasted to the adjacent nodes unless maximum number of hops is reached. Each node forwards the information to its immediate neighbours and waits for the feedback backpropagated to it.

ii. Intermediate nodes will decide based on feedback backpropagated by the neighbouring nodes to reduce the number of peers to forward the information to. The feedback which is backpropagated contains information about the relevance of the context information received earlier as shown in Algorithm 1 lines 4, 9, 22 and 24.

iii. Each forwarding node reduces the hop counter, adds its identification and marks the message relevancy tag if the information is relevant for its purpose as shown in Algorithm 1 lines 7, 8 and 16.

iv. The feedback technique is based on context information like *position, velocity, direction, time-to-live, interest* etc that decides whether the data that was received is relevant or not and also help determine the information relevancy on the intermediate nodes. This way the irrelevant context information can filtered out at an intermediate node.

v. The feedback to the source node is backpropagated if the context information is *relevant, irrelevant, unused or duplicate* information is received as shown in Algorithm 1 lines 4, 9, 22 and 24. This will reduce the information dissemination only to the interested nodes.

vi. A vehicular network is highly dynamic in nature and application dependent. As the context information can be provided by the application itself the routing of the information is adapted accordingly and perhaps different for various applications.

vii. All the nodes in the network send out a beacon upon arrival in the network. So the network re-calibrates itself if a new node sends an arrival beacon or an old node no longer transmits the feedback after a certain period of time as shown in Algorithm 1 line 2 and 26.

viii. In this mechanism the goal is to efficiently filter and intelligently route the relevant information as close to the source as possible in a dynamic network. The routing information also directly proportional to the relevancy of information.

The conditions under which a node backpropagates a feedback are:

- **Relevant context:** The context information received by a node is either relevant for its own purpose or by one of its adjacent peers.

- **Irrelevant context:** The context information received by a node cannot be used for its own purpose and maximum number of hops has reached or it has no neighbouring nodes for which the context information might be relevant.

- **Unused context:** The context information received by a node is either not used or used infrequently. In this case the node will generate a message asking the transmitting peer to increase the transmission delay.

- **Duplicate context:** The context information received by a node has already been sent it by another node in the neighbourhood. In this case the node will ask the transmitting peer to stop sending this duplicate information in the future.

This algorithm is a best-effort algorithm which adapts itself according to the network configuration. The algorithm becomes intelligent with feedback information propagated in the network.

4. Evaluation of different protocols and algorithms

In this section we will discuss our simulated experimentations and the results obtained. In our scenario 2.2.1 and scenario 2.2.2 the solution we propose is to make use of the adaptive context mediation in large scale vehicle network. This can be achieved by using our relevance backpropagation mechanism in both the scenarios. In scenario 2.2.1 the context information will only be sent out to the vehicles moving towards the incident alerting them about an incident over a large scale network of vehicles. Similarly in scenario 2.2.2 the context information regarding the free parking space will also be disseminated only to the vehicles within a region of 2 km and moving towards the direction of the free parking space by making use of the relevance backpropagation to achieve adaptive context mediation in large scale vehicular networks.

4.1 Experimentation test bed

We use OMNET++ ver. 4.0, a real time discrete network simulator, to test our relevance backpropagation algorithm over a large scale vehicular network using real datasets. The OMNET++ simulator was setup over UBuntu ver. 8.10 (a flavour of linux) installed over a considerably powerful Dell desktop machine with 2.0 Ghz Core 2 Duo processor and 2 GB of memory.

We have used real time data from a multi-user distributed car simulator collected earlier by the authors (Yasar et al., 2008). The parameters we have taken into account are for each node to perform simulated experiments with OMNET++. We make use of these parameters and compute various factors to differentiate between the various algorithms and protocols used for communication in a large scale vehicular network.

(i) Time
(ii) Velocity
(iii) Direction
(iv) x and y coordinates
(v) Number of sent packets
(vi) Number of received packets
(vii) Number of forwarded packets
(viii) Time-to-live (TTL)

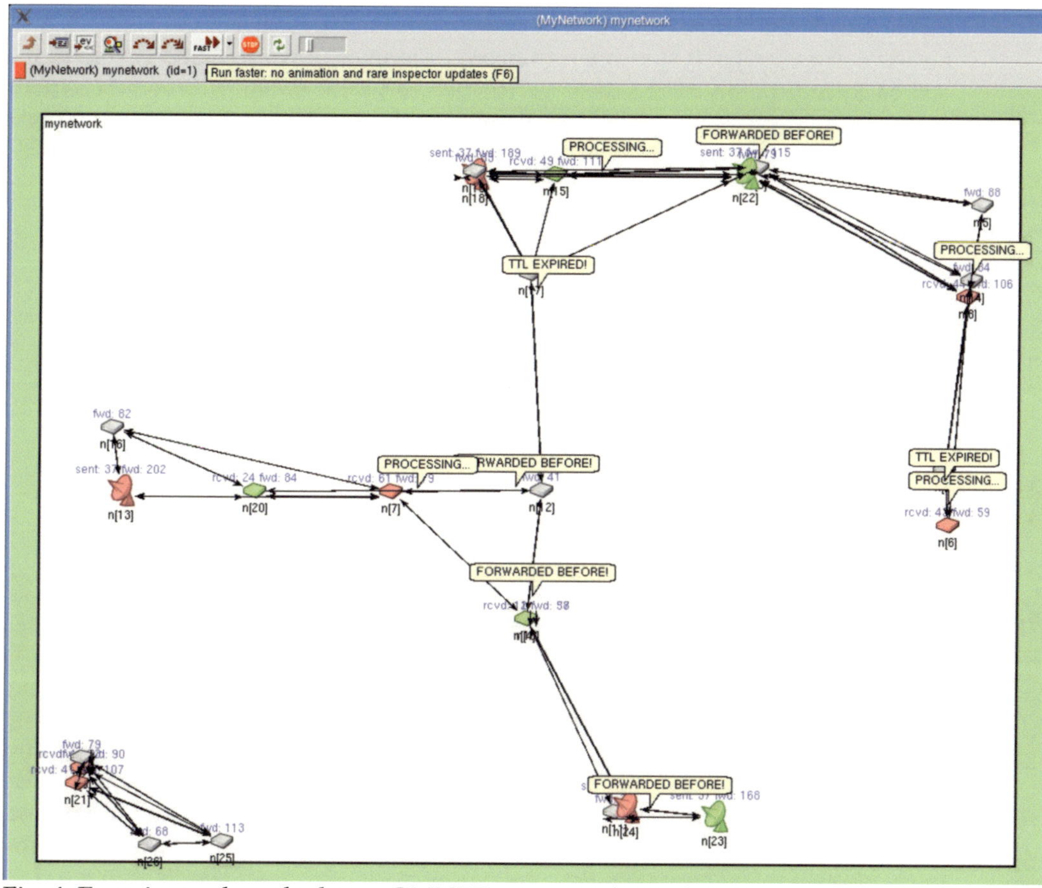

Fig. 4. Experimental test-bed over OMNET++ to simulate vehicular networks.

In our experiments, we let nodes move around like cars and let connections appear and disappear according to the range to other nodes. Some nodes acted as context provides whereas other nodes acted as context receivers. All nodes forward the information to their peers as long as the maximum TTL has not been reached and all context constraints are met. Figure 4 shows a visualization of the experiment with 27 nodes. There are green, red and gray nodes in the network where the colour depicts the information interest. The antennas are information producers whereas the other nodes are information consumers. We carried out 4 experiments with plain broadcasting and with our relevance backpropagation mechanism over WiFi and Bluetooth network configurations and simulated for a period of 1 hour of context dissemination each. The results for these experiments are explained more in detail below.

4.2 Discussion of Results

In the experiment using the flooding mechanism the context information was broadcasted in the network to every node. In our experiments with the relevance backpropagation algorithm only relevant context information was sent out to the interested nodes in the network.

- ***Bandwidth*** is the sum of all the sent and forwarded messages in the network and measure in megabits. It shows a significant difference in bandwidth utilization for our backpropagation mechanism up to 45% and 90% under wifi and Bluetooth networks respectively as shown in Figure 5. The results shown here have been rescaled on the x-axis and have no specific units.

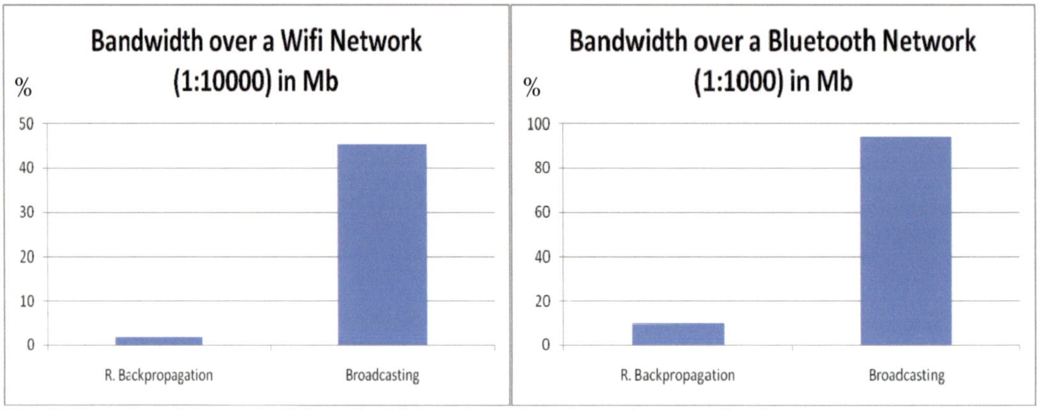

Fig. 5. Simulated (rescaled) bandwidth using plain broadcast and relevance backpropagation over WiFi and Bluetooth networks.

- ***Signal-to-Noise ratio (SNR) of the context information*** is calculated by dividing the total amount of received packets by the sum of total packets sent and forwarded by each node. It is also significantly about 25% higher in the relevance backpropagation mechanism compared to plain broadcasting over WiFi and Bluetooth networks. It illustrates that nodes get more relevant information (i.e. the nodes receive less information they are not interested in) as shown in Figure 6. The results shown here have been rescaled on the x-axis and have no specific units.

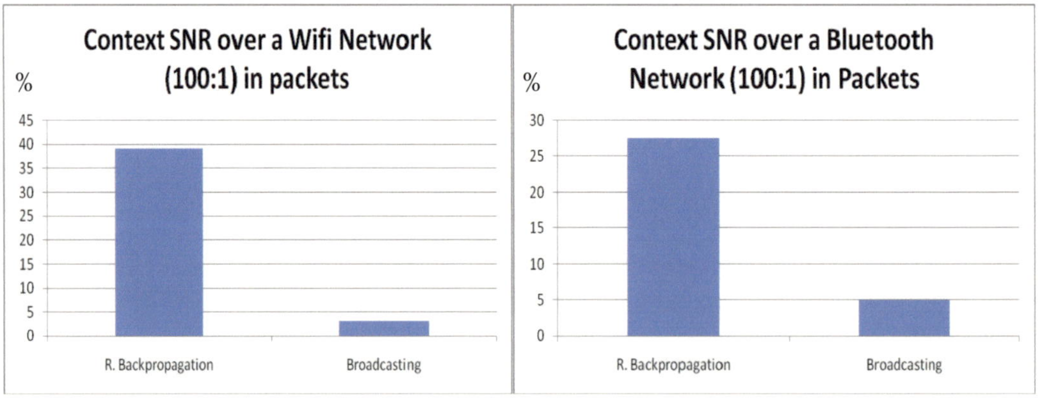

Fig. 6. Simulated (rescaled) CSNR using plain broadcast and relevance backpropagation over WiFi and Bluetooth networks.

- ***Throughput*** of the network is the ratio of the total amount of the information requested by the subscribers by the total amount of the information sent over the network by the context providers. The 15-20% lower throughput can be explained by the fact that messages are only routed where they are relevant, in some cases broadcasting may deliver messages that our approach does not. However this difference does not outweigh the bandwidth utilization as shown in Figure 7. The results shown here have been rescaled on the x-axis and have no specific units.

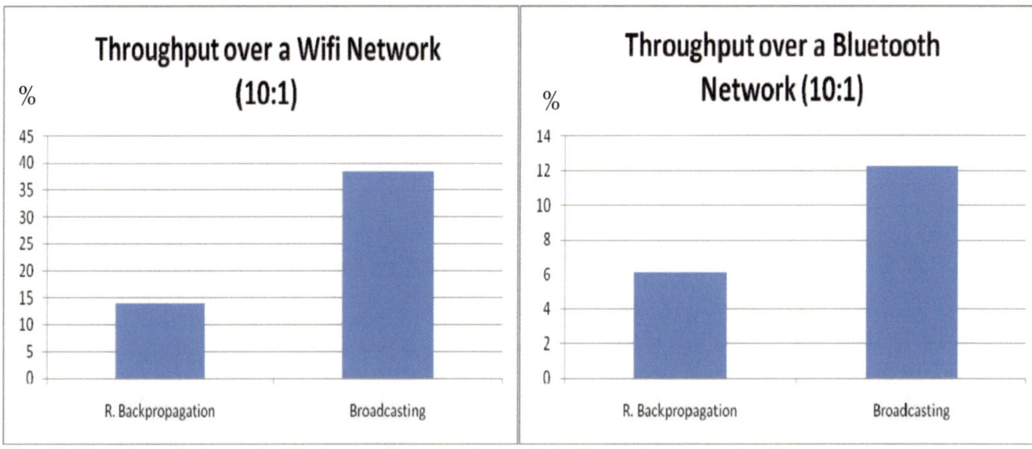

Fig. 7. Simulated (rescaled) throughput using plain broadcast and relevance backpropagation over WiFi and Bluetooth networks.

- ***Timeliness*** is the ratio of the number of messages dropped because the TTL was expired versus the number of messages forwarded by each of the node in the network. In relevance backpropagation the timeliness of the information is slightly higher than in plain broadcasting about 2% using WiFi and Bluetooth networks as shown in Figure 8. The results shown here have been rescaled on the x-axis and have no specific units.

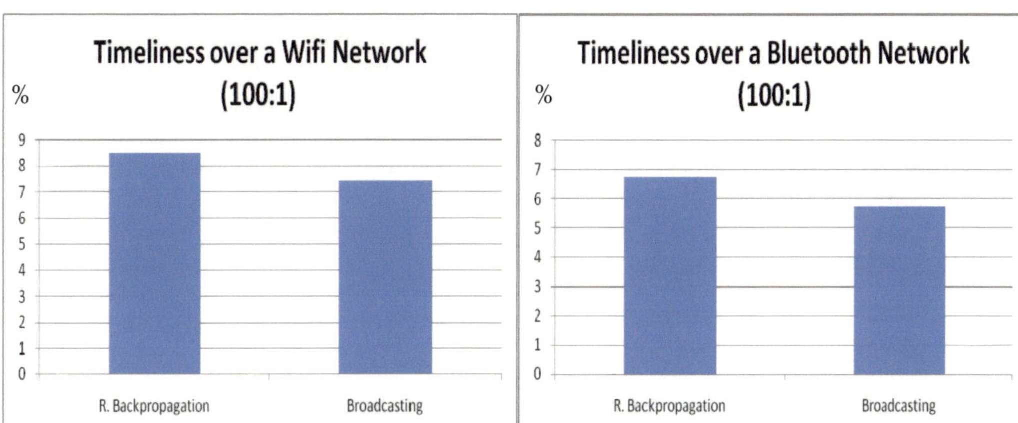

Fig. 8. Simulated (rescaled) timeliness using plain broadcast and relevance backpropagation over WiFi and Bluetooth networks.

- The ***availability*** parameter is the ratio of the sum of all the forwarded messages versus the number of messages that were received again and already forwarded previously. The availability of the context information is about 2% higher in the simulation results when using our relevance backpropagation mechanism in directed diffusion over a large scale network using WiFi and Bluetooth networks as shown in Figure 9. The results shown here have been rescaled on the x-axis and have no specific units.

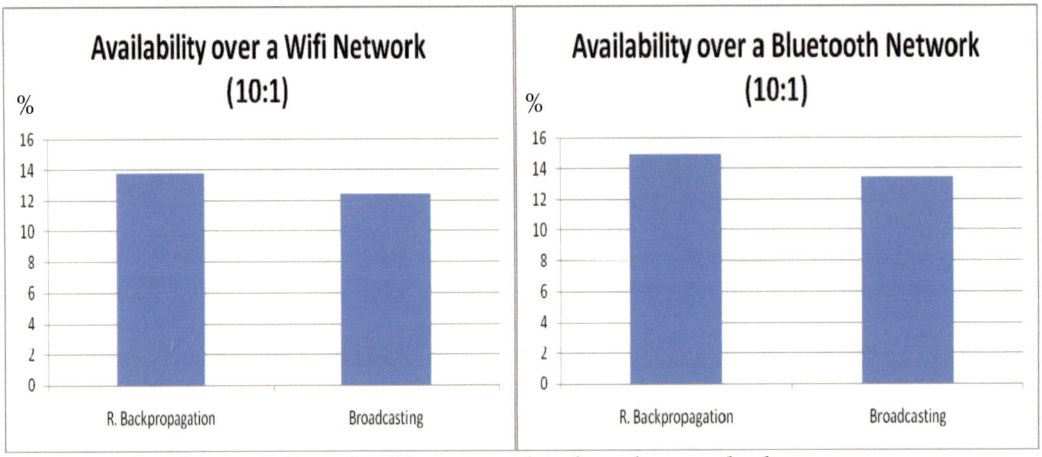

Fig. 9. Simulated (rescaled) availability using plain broadcast and relevance backpropagation over WiFi and Bluetooth networks.

Reduced bandwidth usage is an achievement in the area of network communications. One might argue that in the current modern era of technology and communication the world has enough bandwidth available for use. But with the growing demand for high speed communication this resource which we enjoy today will be scarce in the near future.

Using the current set of requirements into our relevance backpropagation algorithm, a best effort algorithm, we see a significantly reduced bandwidth requirement in a context-aware large scale vehicular network. In our research work we do not investigate the complete set of requirements for context-aware smart telematic applications into our algorithm over OMNET++ and on real vehicles so the results may vary accordingly. For example, we do not take the context of priority of information into account for urgent message delivery to the nodes in a vehicular network so we also do not know the effects on such constraints on the results in a simulated environment.

5. Related work

In (Nadeem et al., 2006), the authors present a formal model of data dissemination in Vehicle Ad-Hoc networks (VANETs). They measure how the performance of data dissemination is affected by bi-directional lane mobility. Three models of data dissemination are explained and simple broadcasting technique is found to be sufficiently enough in their simulated experiments. In our research, we deal with the directional dissemination of context information.

The authors present an idea about the WiFi-based connectivity and communication between base stations and moving vehicles in (Mahajan et al., 2007). Vehicles mobility cause gray periods of poor connectivity which according to the authors are caused by variability in the urban radio environment combined with the vehicle traversing areas of poor coverage. We envision that for large scale vehicle network the use of simple WiFi based communication will be impractical.

In (Celik et al., 2006), the authors address the issue of optimal data dissemination broadcasts to a network of wireless cells in a large mobile network. They propose that there should be a mix of a single broadcast for the entire network along with an individual broadcast for each of the wireless cells. The authors found a significant improvement in the performance of the network using their simulation results. Our approach uses the idea of disseminating the context information only within the area of spatial coverage.

The importance of caching context information has also been addressed in (Anandarajah et al., 2006). As disconnections between nodes in large scale networks may occur due to nodes mobility, the authors discuss smart caching algorithms that improve the traditional methods for distributed systems by using various kinds of meta-data. In our research, relevance backpropagation algorithm handles the dynamic nature of a mobile network without creating a communication overhead.

A comparative performance comparison between three data dissemination protocols (i) Directed Diffusion, (ii) Two-Tier Data Dissemination and (iii) Gradient Broadcast for wireless sensor networks is discussed by the authors (Bokareva et al., 2004). In our research, we found that two-tier dissemination and gradient broadcasting over a large scale network are not cost efficient in terms of implementation complexity and processing overhead. So we make use of a combination of directional diffusion and gradient broadcast of context information in a better manner by using spatial coverage and information relevance feedback acting as a cost function in gradient broadcast so that the context information can only be directed to a specific region with minimal cost and effort.

6. Conclusion and Future work

In this chapter, we describe certain requirements to model context-aware application specific abstractions in large scale vehicular networks and simulate interactions between moving vehicles and static nodes using broadcasting and our relevance backpropagation algorithms to evaluate context-aware telematics applications over Bluetooth and WiFi networks. Using our large scale vehicular network framework with context-driven adaptive communication protocols over OMNET++, we can not only model abstractions and investigate the impact of different communication routing schemes but also measure various quality of service parameters in vehicular mobility awareness for different traffic scenarios and versatile telematic application requirements.

The simulation results show that by using our relevance backpropagation mechanism significant reduction in bandwidth utilization up to 45% and 90% under WiFi and Bluetooth networks respectively. Similarly, timeliness and availability of context information also improves by 2% in both the networks. SNR of context information is also improved about 25% with a very minor overhead of about 15-20% in throughput under both network types.

We are planning to investigate the network and context properties to get a broader view of the communication mechanisms used earlier for our simulated experiments. We also plan to model requirements for simulating 3G networks like EVDO using our relevance backpropagation algorithm over OMNET++. We intend to further look into the *on-demand* communication technique and compare the results with our current push-model for communication.

In the future we also plan to investigate the same network parameters by inter-connecting a real embedded smart device like a PDA, GPS or an embedded vehicular computer with the simulation environment to analyze the behaviour of the real smart devices. Later on this will enable us to see how our relevance backpropagation mechanism can be improved over other large scale networks with real applications.

7. References

Abowd, G.D.; Dey, A.K.; Brown, P.J.; Davies, N.; Smith, M. & Steggles, P. (1999). Towards a better understanding of context and context-awareness. *Proceedings of the 1st international symposium on Handheld and Ubiquitous Computing*, pages 304-307, Springer-Verlag, London, UK.

Anandarajah, M.; Indulska, J.; & Robinson, R. (2006). Caching context information in pervasive systems. *Proceedings of the 3rd international Middleware Doctoral Symposium*. MDS '06, vol. 185, ACM, Melbourne.

Bokareva, T.; Bulusu, N. & Jha, S. (2004). A performance comparison of data dissemination protocols for wireless sensor networks. *Proceedings of IEEE Globecom Wireless Ad Hoc and Sensor Networks Workshop*, IEEE, Dallas.

Celik, A.; Holliday, J. & Hurst, Z. (2006). Data Dissemination to a Large Mobile Network: Simulation of Broadcast Clouds. *Proceedings of the 7th international Conference on Mobile Data Management*, IEEE Computer Society, Washington, DC.

European Commission (2001). European transport whitepaper. URL: http://ec.europa.eu/transport/white_paper/documents/index_en.htm, last access on 13/04/2009.

Mahajan, R.; Zahorjan, J. & Zill, B. (2007). Understanding wifi-based connectivity from moving vehicles. *Proceedings of the 7th ACM SIGCOMM Conference on internet* Measurement.ACM, New York.

Nadeem, T.; Shankar, P.; & Iftode, L. (2006). A comparative study of data dissemination models for vanets. *Proceedings of 3rd International conference on Mobile and Ubiquitous systems,* IEEE, San Jose.

Preuveneers, D. & Berbers, Y. (2007). Architectural backpropagation support for managing ambiguous context in smart environments. *Proceedings of C. Stephanidis, editor, HCI, volume 4555 of Lecture Notes in Computer Science*, pages 178-187, Springer, Berlin.

Preuveneers, D.; Yasar, A. & Berbers, Y. (2008). Architectural styles for opportunistic mobile communication: Requirements and design patterns, *Proceedings of Mobility conference*, ISBN: 978-1-60558-089-0, ACM, Taiwan.

Riva, O.; Nadeem, T.; Borcea, C. & Iftode, L. (2007). Context-Aware Migratory Services in Ad Hoc Networks. *IEEE Transactions on Mobile Computing* 6, 12 Dec. 2007.

Williamson, G.; Stevenson, G.; Neely, S.; Coyle, L.; & Nixon, P. (2006). Scalable information dissemination for pervasive systems: implementation and evaluation. *Proceedings of the 4th international Workshop on Middleware For Pervasive and Ad-Hoc Computing (MPAC 2006)*, ACM, Melbourne.

Yasar, A.; Preuveneers, D. & Berbers, Y. (2008). Adaptive context mediation in dynamic and large scale vehicular networks using relevance backpropagation, *Proceedings of Mobility conference*, ISBN: 978-1-60558-089-0, ACM, Taiwan.

Ye, F.; Luo, H.; Cheng, J.; Lu, S.; & Zhang, L. (2002). A two-tier data dissemination model for large-scale wireless sensor networks. *Proceedings of the 8th Annual international Conference on Mobile Computing and Networking*. MobiCom '02. ACM, New York.

24

Using Modelling and Simulation to Evaluate Network Services in Maritime Networks

David Kidston
Communications Research Centre
Canada

1. Introduction

Maritime networks are composed of a number of mobile and static nodes that have some intermittent wireless connections, as is typical of mobile ad-hoc networks (MANETs), but also have steady (satellite) links and are continuously powered, as is typical of fixed wired networks. Combined, these characteristics provide unique operational challenges not conducive to the use of existing MANET or fixed network techniques. Since maritime units operate in a low bandwidth environment, the efficiency of network services is critical. The lack of power constraints and slower mobility require a less dynamic solution than that required for MANETs. The problem we deal with in this chapter is how to manage the Quality of Service (QoS) achieved by application traffic while optimising the use of semi-reliable and limited-capacity links. This is a traffic engineering (TE) problem.

As part of a research effort to provide enhanced communications capabilities in a maritime network, we proposed and then investigated a number of network services using the OPNET discrete event simulation (DES) tool. The modelling of this type of network provided some unique challenges. The combination of link types has not been previously described in the literature and existing link models had to be customised for their unique low bandwidth characteristics. Similarly, routing in this kind of mobile environment has not been studied. Finally, there has been limited work on modelling the traffic characteristics of maritime networks.

We begin this chapter with a description of the network, mobility, and traffic models developed to simulate the maritime environment. This is followed by a description of four network services that were designed to aid in network management and provide improved QoS in maritime networks. The first service is a traffic monitoring service that matches the amount of traffic it produces with its knowledge of the current load of the network. Second, a traffic prioritisation service uses weighted fair queuing (WFQ) to prioritize traffic in the maritime environment based on dynamically assigned priorities. Third, an adaptive routing service uses multi-path labelled switching (MPLS) to divert traffic from overloaded links. Fourth, we describe our resource reservation service (RRS), a distributed admission control protocol designed to provide some guarantees of end-to-end bandwidth for critical traffic in the maritime environment. The RRS includes a number of features specifically tailored for maritime networks including multi-route probing, aggregated pre-emption, and improved

robustness. In our simulations, these services were found to provide network awareness and significantly improve the timeliness of prioritised flows.
This chapter continues with a description of the results of our simulations, which we gathered based on a process based on five criteria developed to provide improved credibility. The chapter ends with a review of the limited related work in this area followed by a number of conclusions and a discussion of possible future work in this area.

2. Maritime Networks

We based our models of a maritime network on a naval task fleet deployment. In such deployments, a relatively small number of nodes (ships) are dispatched as a group. This is commonly between 2 and 5 nodes (AUSCANZUKUS, 1999). In addition, one or more shore stations provide most server-based application services and act as a satellite switching centre. This environment may also be applicable to a commercial enterprise such as a shipping company or emergency operations at sea such as coast guard duties, though these alternatives have not been investigated. A typical maritime network is shown in Figure 1.

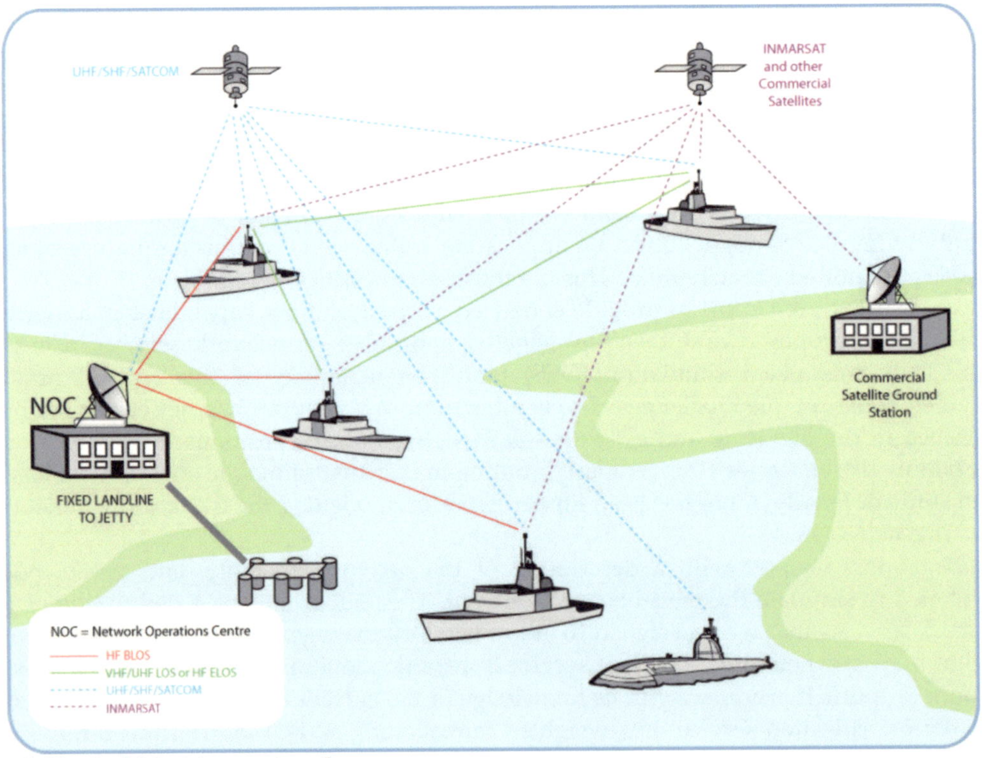

Fig. 1. Typical Maritime network

Maritime networks thus consists of a Network Operation Centre (NOC) which acts as a land based relay for all satellite communication, a limited number of mobile nodes (ships or potentially maritime land/air units), and the bearers that connect them. A commercial satellite ground station may also be included. The features of maritime networks critical to our network model are expanded upon in the following subsections.

2.1 Communication Bearers

A maritime network is composed of a variety of strategic and tactical communications links. The communications bearers available to transfer information within the network include: commercial satellite (e.g. INMARSAT B), ship-to-shore satellite networks (e.g. SHF SATCOM), High Frequency (HF) extended and beyond line-of-sight (HF ELOS/BLOS) and UHF/VHF line-of-sight (UHF/VHF LOS). A sample of the communications types and capabilities from (AUSCANZUKUS, 2003) are given below in Table 1.

Link Type	Rate	Use
UHF/VHF LOS Radio	Shared 64 kbps	Main data bearer for ship-to-ship communication. Used over short distances (20-50 Nm)
HF BLOS Radio	4.8-9.6 kbps	Email, chat, low data rate apps. HF Sky wave (2000-3000 Nm)
HF ELOS Radio	4.8-9.6 kbps	Email, chat, low data rate apps. HF Surface wave (200-300 Nm)
INMARSAT B Satellite	64 kbps	Main satellite connection for most ships - point to point data bearer
SHF Satellite	Up to 512 kbps	High capacity satellite - point to point data bearer.
25Khz UHF Satellite	Up to 48 kbps	Low bandwidth satellite with limited IP capability (Email, chat, low data rate apps)
5Khz UHF Satellite	Up to 9.6 kbps	Low bandwidth satellite (Email, chat)

Table 1. Communications Subnet Matrix

Mobile maritime nodes (ships) most commonly communicate using a combination of two modes. First, they may communicate back to their strategic network operation centre (NOC) using satellite communications (e.g. INMARSAT, SHF SATCOM). Satellite communications can also be relayed at the NOC to provide indirect ship-to-ship communications. Satellite communications provide high bandwidth but high delay and high cost communications. Second, ships communicate directly with other ships via limited range radio (e.g. UHF/VHF LOS). Recently UHF/VHF relay technology has improved to the point that LOS radio systems may form mobile ad-hoc networks (MANETs) (Jorgensen et al. 2005). These networks provide low cost, low bandwidth and low delay communications over a limited distance.

2.2 Routing Capabilities

Naval maritime networks are now IP-based (AUSCANZUKUS, 2003). By default, the network topology is driven by the routing protocols used to achieve connectivity (e.g. OSPF). Each network is typically divided into separate Autonomous Systems (AS). In maritime networks an AS is a collection of mobile nodes and shore station nodes connected by a collection of backbone subnets. The shore-stations may be gateways to a third party backbone WAN (e.g. Internet Service Provider) or to another military WAN.

Routing in this environment currently relies on OSPF within an AS with the link cost metric set to increase with decreasing bandwidth (Holliday, 2005). This means that the link with the highest bandwidth is used to the exclusion of any other links that may be available. Due to its high bandwidth, SATCOM will be used predominantly. When low-bandwidth LOS links are the only links available, they are often overloaded with high bandwidth traffic. Between autonomous systems, BGP4 is used, though we are currently assuming a single autonomous system (thus a single OSPF area).

As mentioned in Section 2.1, technology has been developed to allow maritime nodes to form a MANET from their available LOS bearers. Combining the dynamic high link-error rate MANET with the high bandwidth but high delay satellite links creates a need to look at mobility and application QoS requirements in terms of routing in this environment. This work provides some insight into the impact of using OSPF in this environment as opposed to a MANET specific routing protocol.

2.3 Traffic Characterisation

The optimisation goal of traffic engineering (TE) is to support conflicting information exchange requirements while making the most efficient use of the currently available communication capabilities. Previous anecdotal evidence has suggested typical application types in this environment are text messaging, email, video, imagery, web, targeting, intelligence, collaborative planning, and voice. In order to understand the traffic characteristics of this type of network and what impact TE schemes may have, an accurate traffic model is critical. Figure 2 provides a more complete description of the traffic as seen during a Canadian naval exercise (Sibbald, 2004).

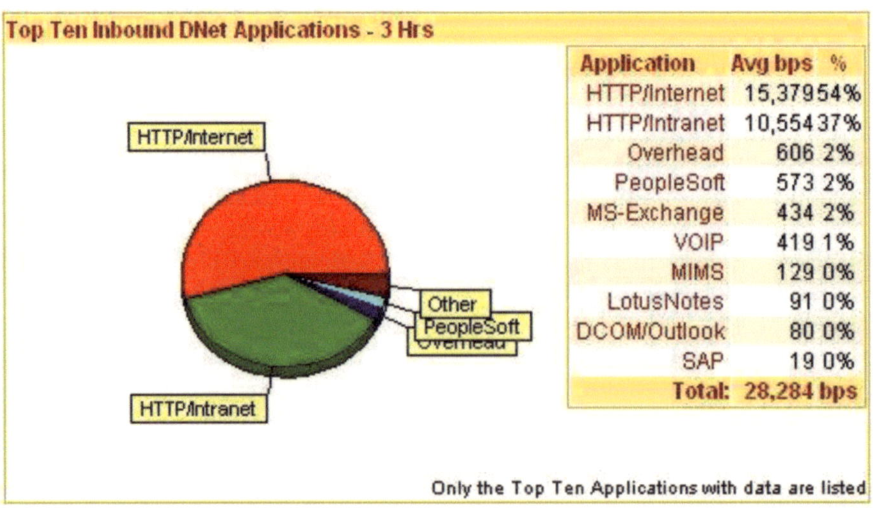

Fig. 2. Traffic Breakdown for a Naval Exercise

This chart divides the inbound traffic to a maritime node by application type. Internet and defence-based intranet web traffic took up a strong majority (91%) of the bandwidth. The remaining traffic was split between network overhead (i.e. routing), personnel and logistics management (PeopleSoft, MIMS, LotusNotes, SAP), email/collaboration (MS-Exchange, Outlook), and voice calls (VOIP). We will be using this mix in our traffic models described in Section 3.3.

Application/Network	Max Avg bps in/out	Peak bps in/out	Type	Priority
MCOIN (command and control)	24 / 35 K	45 / 80 K	Op	6
VOIP	5 / 16 K	50 / 140 K	Op	6
RSVP (network overhead)	continuous	.08 K	Net	5
OSPF (network overhead)	continuous	.26 K	Net	5
IGMP (network overhead)	continuous	.05 K	Net	5
TFTP (server to server)	0.3 / 0.6 K	22 / 30 K	Net	5
MS-Exchange (email)	30 / 48 K	60 / 130 K	Adm	4
Lotus Notes (Domino Replication)	0.2 / 0.5 K	18 / 38 K	Adm	4
DCOM (Outlook)	1 / 4.6 K	30 / 92 K	Adm	4
SAP (server to server)	0.7 / 1.2 K	28 / 64 K	Adm	3
Supply Program (MIMS/CFSSU)	0.1 / 1 K	3 / 10 K	Adm	3
Pay System (CCPS)	0.6 / 0.9 K	8 / 15 K	Adm	3
Pers Admin System (PeopleSoft)	2 / 4 K	6 / 30 K	Adm	3
Intranet (web)	6 / 8 K	60 / 100 K	adm	3
PC Anywhere (NM tool)	1.2 / 2.4 K	21 / 82 K	Net	2
Internet (web)	37 / 48 K	60 / 150 K	Rec	2
WindowsMedia (music/video)	7 / 15 K	35 / 120 K	Rec	2
MPEG Video (recreational)	2 / 34 K	30 / 64 K	Rec	2

Table 2. Application Bandwidth Requirements

During the same naval exercise, Table 2 was developed to specify fleet and ship data traffic usage and priorities. The maximum average and peak usage requirements for each of a variety of different types of applications as they are used in the navy are also provided. The traffic types shown are operational (Op), network overhead (Net), administrative (Adm), and recreational (Rec). One application that may not be obvious is Maritime Command Operational Information Network (MCOIN), which is the Canadian Navy's shore-based Command, Control, and Information System. The priorities listed provide an idea of the importance attached to the information being carried, and informs the network operator of how different traffic classes can be constructed to give preferential treatment within the network. Though the traffic mix and traffic priorities may vary over time it provides a reasonable description of the traffic that can be found in maritime networks, and more importantly the relative perceived priority of various traffic types. The priority information was used in the development of the traffic prioritisation service described in Section 4.2.

When multiple traffic types converge onto a single network, there is a requirement to ensure that time-sensitive (prioritised) information is delivered before less urgent traffic. Therefore, TE and communications management techniques must be applied to ensure that the priorities for information delivery are met. Our network services are described in Section 4.

3. Maritime Network Model

Based on this description of the maritime environment, a network model was developed using the OPNET discrete event simulation (DES) tool. In order to acess the operation of the network services, several areas of the model had to be investigated. First, to determine the effect of network size, two network sizes were chosen based on maritime deployments; a small network, consisting of a NOC and a single four ship task force, and one larger network, consisting of a NOC and two four ship task forces. Second, the mobility of the two networks sizes was investigated. Finally, a maritime traffic model was developed.

3.1 Network Topology

Two network topologies were used in the simulations. The small network consists of five nodes and the large network has nine nodes as shown in Figures 3 and 4 respectively.

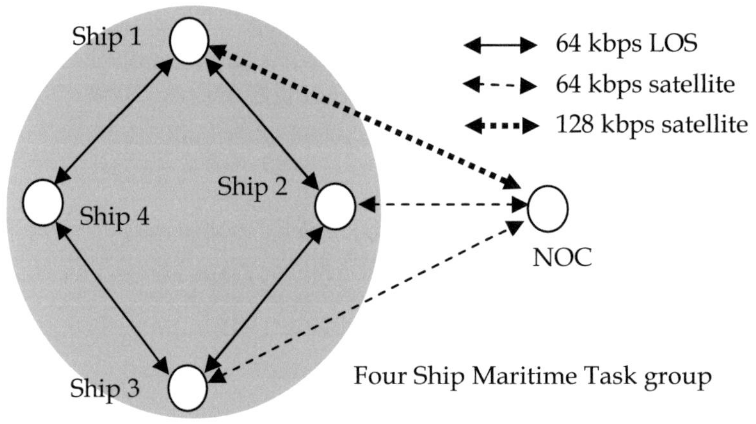

Fig. 3. Small Network

The connectivity of the small network model showing all the wireless links is shown in Figure 3. The link types are as follows. Ships 1-3 have satellite communications to the NOC (indirectly via satellite) with ship 2 and ship 3 using a 64kbps link while ship 1 has a 128kbps link. Each ship also has two 64 kbps radio links which form a ring. This implies that Ship 4 is only connected via LOS links from Ship 1 and Ship 3. The small configuration was designed based on the description of a single naval task force (AUSCANZUKUS, 2003).

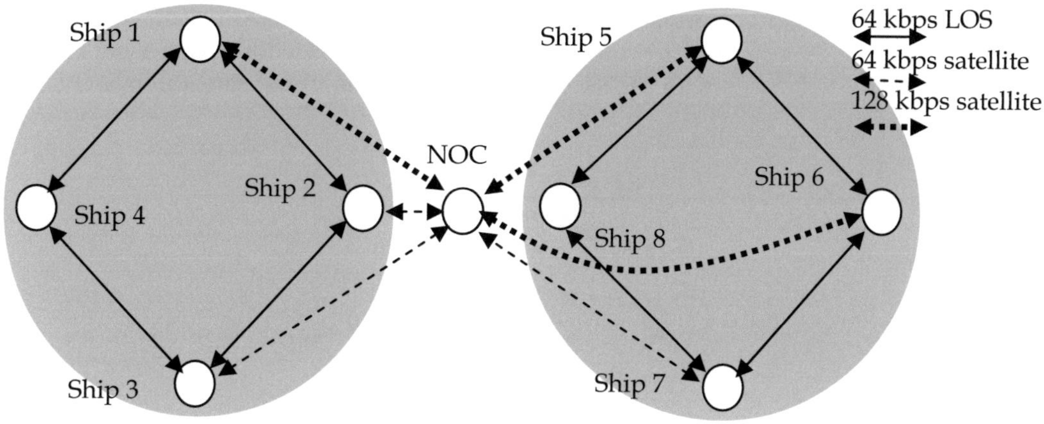

Fig. 4. Large Network

The configuration of the large network model is shown in Figure 4. In this network Ships 1-3 and 5-7 have satellite links to the NOC with Ships 2, 3, and 7 at 64 kbps and Ships 1, 5 and 6 at 128 kbps. The line of site (LOS) links has been configured similarly for both four ship tasks groups. The large network configuration provides the opportunity to investigate more complex interactions between two task groups initially at some distance from each other. The mobility model described in Section 3.3 has the two task groups travel within LOS range of each other causing new connectivity and interference/bandwidth sharing.

In order to realise this network in OPNET, the base Cisco 7204 model was used for simulating the routing capability of the NOC. Ships use a custom built node model that includes capabilities for both point-to-point and wireless 802.11 links.

The point-to-point link model was used for satellite links as this most closely follows the leased bandwidth operation of satellite communications. The 802.11 link model was used for the LOS wireless links because it provides a wireless MAC that can simulate features such as fading and interference. The 802.11 model was modified to operate at the 64kbps LOS bandwidth rate and simulations indicate an operational throughput of approximately 42 kbps. One drawback of this approach is that while 802.11 uses CDMA, maritime LOS is most often TDMA. More work is required to validate our assumption that this difference is not significant at low banwidth.

3.2 Mobility Model

The base geographical configuration of a task force is shown in Figure 5. With a LOS range of 18 Nautical Miles (Nm) and satellite capability for 3 ships the static topology on the small network shown in Figure 3 is achieved. The large network is composed of two task groups similarly configured but initially outside of LOS communication range of each other.

Maritime mobility is modeled here as a combination of two parts. Intra-task group mobility is based on the Nomadic Community model (Sanchez & Manzoni, 2005). Using this model the individual nodes of each task group move randomly within 3 Nm of their "base" position (as shown in Figure 5) causing links to fail when they exceed 18 Nm and recover when they are at most 18 Nm apart. Based on the nominal 30 nm/hour speed of maritime nodes, analysis suggests that LOS links in this model have a mean time between failures (MTBF) of about 5.5 hours and a mean time to recovery (MTTR) of 12.5 minutes. Note that since the NOC is connected to mobile nodes by satellite, such links are available at all times to the nodes at which such links are operational. Since modern satellite systems can achieve MTBF rates of > 5,000 hours with MTTR of < 1.0 hour, the failure of satellite links has not been modeled.

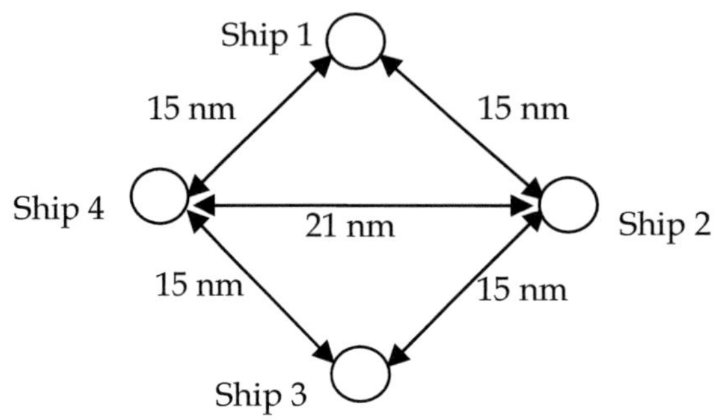

Fig. 5. Task force geometric configuration

To give an idea of the impact of this type of mobility considers ship 4 which does not have a satellite link to the NOC. The preferred gateway to NOC of ship 4 in the network was analysed. In this model, ship 4 is connected via LOS links only. The preferred gateway is ship 1 96.2% of the time, ship 3 3.7% of the time, and ship 4 is disconnected from the network 0.1 % of the time. Note that since ship 1 has a higher speed satellite link, it is therefore preferred over ship 3.

The second part of maritime mobility is inter-task group mobility, which applies only to the large network. In this model, the two task groups begin 18 Nm away from each other (at the closest point) at a random angle (from 0° to 360°). The first task group then approaches the other steadily at 30 knots (Nm/hour) on a set heading evenly distributed from this angle -45° to +45° with 0° being directly towards the centre of the other task group. In combination with intra-task group mobility, there will be link failures and recoveries based on the 18 Nm range of the LOS links. This mobility model is outlined graphically in Figure 6.

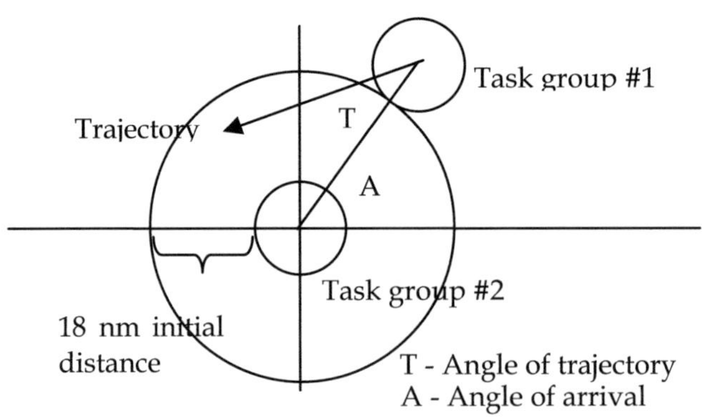

Fig. 6. Inter-task group mobility

For the results described here, a single set of angles was used to simplify the simulations. The angle of arrival was set to 45° and the angle of trajectory was likewise set to -30° giving a trajectory similar to that shown in Figure 6. To give an idea of the impact of this aspect of the model, we discuss here the connectivity of ships 4 and 8. During the simulation, ship 4 is within range of ships 6 and 7 for an average of 66 minutes over the 130 minute run. Similarly, ship 8 comes within range of ship 1 for an average of 45 minutes during the simulation run. Note that though ships 4 and 8 do not have satellite communications, during the inter-task group mobility they come within range of ships in the other task group with high speed satellite (ships 1 and 6) and will thus prefer them over low speed satellite within their group. A 130 minute simulation time was chosen since it is also the time during which ships from one task group are within LOS range of each other

3.3 Traffic Model

Two different traffic loads were developed; nominal and heavy, with traffic distributions as given below. The resulting bandwidth, base OPNET traffic type, and application priority are given in Table 3.

Application	Avg bandwidth (kbps) nominal	Avg bandwidth (kbps) high	Type	Priority
Mcoin	.27 +/- .04 in .18 +/- .03 out	2.95 +/- .09 in 2.18 +/- .09 out	ftp	4
Voice Call	1.82 +/- .17 in 1.84 +/- .19 out	1.79 +/- .15 in 1.88 +/- .17 out	G. 729A	<=4
Over-head	.57 +/- .02 in .56 +/- .01 out	.56 +/- .02 in .57 +/- .01 out	ftp	3
Admin	.77 +/- .05 in .53 +/- .03 out	1.85 +/- .08 in 1.31 +/- .04 out	data-base	2
Intranet	10.57 +/- .41 in .65 +/- .02 out	11.93 +/- .53 in 0.83 +/- .05 out	http	1
Email	.45 +/- .06 in .39 +/- .05 out	1.06 +/- .09 in .81 +/- .08 out	smtp	1
Internet	14.97 +/- .56 in .97 +/- .05 out	22.07 +/- .60 in 2.71 +/- .06 out	http	0
Music/ Video	.30 +/- .03 in .13 +/- .05 out	.65 +/- .06 in .23 +/- .06 out	ftp	0

Table 3. Simulated Baseline Traffic

The nominal traffic models have been designed as closely as possible to the background traffic in maritime networks described in Figure 2 and Table 2. The traffic types in Table 2 have been simplified, with Overhead as an amalgamation of RSVP, OSPF, IGMP, and TFTP. Similarly, the Admin class encompasses Lotus Notes, DCOM, SAP, Supply Program, Pay system, and Personnel Admin System.

Based on the application, a corresponding OPNET traffic type was chosen and configured with an appropriate load. The bandwidth measurements shown in Table 3 were taken in

OPNET with all traffic (except voice) passing simultaneously across a 64kbps LOS link. This measurement was used to provide nominal traffic upon which our network services interacted. The voice call was measured separately over the same link. All bandwidths assume a normal distribution from 20 measurements with the given mean and a 95% two-way confidence interval. All measurements in this chapter are reported in the same way. The priority given in Table 3 corresponds to the priority given in Table 2 and is used to determine weightings in the traffic prioritisation service.

Traffic has been modeled based on pre-existing OPNET types as noted in the table. Also included is the priority of the application taken from Table 2. The high load traffic described above assumes increased traffic at times of high activity within the maritime network.

The high load traffic described above assumes increased traffic at times of high activity within the maritime network. Traffic has been modeled based on pre-existing OPNET types as noted in the table. The priority given in Table 3 corresponds to the priority from the network exercise in Table 2. QoS marking and associated WFQ weights are given in the TPS Section 4.2 below.

In both network topologies, traffic servers are on the NOC. This affects all traffic except for network overhead and voice calls. Overhead traffic is evenly spread between all nodes (including nodes in the other task group for the large network). Voice traffic is point to point and used only as noted for particular measurements.

4. Network Service Models

4.1 Traffic Monitoring Service

A Traffic Monitoring Service (TMS) was designed to measure the incoming and outgoing traffic of a node and distribute this information in summary form to all interested (subscribed) nodes in the maritime network. Currently, there is little if any logging of network traffic in maritime networks, and such monitoring is a critical need in order to provide the NOC staff with an up-to-date view of the operational state of the network. This is commonly termed the Network Common Operational Picture (NetCOP), of which this service would provide a part.

The TMS provides traffic information at a policy defined basis. Three "levels of detail" are supported; base, enhanced, and detailed. These levels provide increasingly detailed reports on the current traffic situation in the network but require increasing levels of bandwidth consumption and longer delays. The level of detail active at a particular time is tailored to the locally perceived load of the network. It is expected that base-level detail can be sent regularly without impacting network operations. Enhanced and detailed information can be sent intermittently or periodically at a very low rate. Timers and retransmissions of the summary data are used for fault tolerance.

In **base mode**, each node provides a summary of the aggregate traffic going in and out of that node (as total bandwidth or a percentage per traffic type). In **enhanced mode**, the service provides detail on the various priority levels and the current load at each level (tied to TPS service). More bandwidth is required to broadcast/multicast to all peer nodes in network. In **detailed mode**, traffic is further subdivided into individual long term flows and includes information such as delay, jitter and packet loss ratios (if available from protocols such as RTP). This is again node/link centered. Significant bandwidth is required to broadcast/multicast this information to all peer nodes in the network.

In order to model this service, three custom application types were created in OPNET, one for each level of detail. Loadings based on common SNMP style communications implied by the type of detail required were configured at each level. The impact of the different levels of traffic on the network and the delay and bandwidth requirements of each could then be studied. In Sections 5.2 and 5.3 we discuss the delay of the service and use the changes in the services delay to illustrate the utility of the traffic prioritisation and adaptive routing services described below. We also discuss the utility of switching between different levels of detail based on the current load on the underlying network.

4.2 Traffic Prioritisation Service

The Traffic Prioritisation Service (TPS) provides a mechanism to rank traffic by importance and prioritise resource allocation accordingly. It associates traffic to different classes of service that have relative priority between each another, and thus supports different forwarding requirements. Effectively, the service provides end-to-end (network-wide as opposed to a point-to-point) preferential treatment for certain applications. This allows relative traffic priority to be maintained from source to destination, including over the relay points. This preferential treatment is commonly known as DiffServ or soft QoS.

There are currently six classes of service: priority 0 (Best Effort), priority 1 (Background), priority 2 (Standard), priority 3 (Excellent Effort), priority 4 (Streaming), and priority 5 (Reserved). Weighted Fair Queuing (WFQ) was used, with WRED in the priority 0 (Best Effort) class. Resource allocations are given in Table 4 below.

Priority	Class Name	Weight	Notes
0	Best Effort	6	Recreational traffic
1	Background	6	Low priority applications
2	Standard	8	Operational applications
3	Excellent Effort	12	Routing and Management traffic
4	Streaming	18	Multimedia applications
5	Reserved	50	Up to 50% of bandwidth can be reserved for RSS flows.

Table 4. WFQ weightings for QoS used in measurements

In WFQ the relative weights correspond to the relative percentage of bandwidth that is assigned to each class of traffic. Since the weights assigned were engineered to add to 100, the assigned weight is the percentage of available bandwidth for each class if the link is fully loaded. Note that this means that if, for example, only one flow is in the standard class and there are three flows in the excellent effort class, the standard class flow will get at most 8% of the available bandwidth while each excellent effort flow will get an average of 4%. Thus bandwidth is assigned per class and not per flow. One of the most useful aspects of this scheme is what happens when one class is not fully saturated. Any bandwidth not used by a certain class is divided between the remaining classes, again in weighted order. Thus the reserved class (an additional priority class added to enable the RRS service described below) gains 50% of the bandwidth allocation not used by the other classes.

This service was one of the simplest to model in OPNET as it simply requires the application of existing QoS features. One of the interesting issues with OPNET was applying DiffServ to wireless models as this requires some understanding of the operational bandwidth in order for the described weightings to be allocated correctly to the link. Since the bandwidth available on the link changes depending on environmental conditions and the number of other nodes transmitting on the same frequency, calculating the operational bandwidth requires extensive knowledge of the current state of the network. The model used here assumes a nominal bandwidth of 42 kbps over a two-user 64 kbps LOS link.

4.3 Adaptive Routing Service

Since maritime nodes may have multiple WAN links of varying capacity, it may be useful for applications to use only a subset of the available links. This may be for reasons of delay sensitivity (e.g. for VOIP calls) or because of the bandwidth capabilities and error/failure rate of the link (e.g. for ftp communications).

The Adaptive Routing Service (ARS) provides an alternative routing method for matching a traffic class to WAN resources. Essentially, it indicates what types of traffic must/should travel over a certain type of bearer. It makes use of resource availability (i.e. does the bearer possess sufficient bandwidth to meet the requirements of that traffic class) and resource suitability knowledge (i.e. will the bearer meet the QoS requirements of that traffic class).

The benefits of such routing flexibility are significant. Besides ensuring that traffic of a given class will flow over a bearer that supports it, ARS offers a solution to the well-known load balancing problem. Traffic from the same source and destination can be directed to travel over different routes. Since the path selected is also based on the traffic type instead of simply the route cost (shortest path), ARS provides a better distribution of traffic across the WAN links and thus better utilisation of available network bandwidth.

The ARS was modelled through the use of MPLS tunnels. An overlay on the network was created specifically for VOIP calls. VOIP calls were then routed over the least loaded links. In an actual implementation, multiple MPLS overlays could be created to avoid links that cannot support the QoS requirements of the application flow.

4.4 Resource Reservation Service

The RRS has been designed with a number of features to deal with the specific requirements of maritime environments. This includes probing multiple routes in parallel for load balancing and an increased acceptance rate, a priority and pre-emption scheme to favour the most critical flows, fault tolerance mechanisms to deal with mobility and link errors, and dynamic reconfiguration of its parameters to meet changes in operational requirements.

The RSS consists of four phases. In the first phase, global link information is used to generate multiple routes between the source of the requesting flow and the destination. The second phase of the algorithm probes the potential routes separately to determine if sufficient resources are available (which increases the acceptance rate). In the third phase, an acceptable path is selected and committed (which promotes load balancing), potentially pre-empting lower priority flows (which prioritises the most critical flows). Finally, in the fourth phase, the reservation is maintained until the traffic flow is terminated by the user, the reservation lifetime ends, the reservation is ended manually, or the network can no longer support its requirements. Mobility is handled by assuming the network is stable for the period of call setup, and network maintenance handles topology changes while the reservation is active as described below. A detailed functional description of this service is given in (Kidston et al., 2007)

4.4.1 Reservation Protocol Models

In order to evaluate the impact of the specialised features of the RRS in maritime networks, our simulations compare it with both RSVP, a standard reservation protocol for fixed networks, and INSIGNIA, a reservation protocol proposed for MANETs. There are significant differences in the operation of the three reservation protocols simulated. The largest difference is that RRS includes multi-routing and pre-emption. In RRS, each reservation is made with up to 3 parallel probes to exercise the partially disjoint multi-routing aspect of the protocol. The priority mechanism of the service was also exercised by assigning each new reservation one of three priority levels (low, medium, and high) with equal probability. Requests of lower priority may be pre-empted (dropped) in order to admit a higher-priority flow. High-priority flows are not pre-empted, and may only be blocked from being accepted by other high priority flows. Pre-empted flows are called admitted (they were initially accepted), but unsuccessful (they terminated before their scheduled end time). If a request is not initially admitted, it is also unsuccessful. No additional attempts are made to establish a reservation.

In order to implement the RRS, some OPNET models had to be modified and new ones created. Our approach was to use the existing IP networking models and simply add RRS packet processing capability on top, so RRS messages could be processed and forwarded as required. First, a significant change was required to the OSPF model in the ship's routers. In order to capture changes in network topology and determine the type and nominal bandwidth of the link from the OSPF cost, a software tap was added to the existing OPNET model. This tap forwards all link state database (LSDB) changes to the local RRS model, which maintains its own internal representation of the network connectivity. Two additions were made to the network node models for simulating RRS. The first was a simple process for generating reservations that submits new request interrupts at a configurable rate to the RRS process. The second was the RRS process itself, which includes all the logic previously described for forwarding packets and reserving resources.

The RSVP model was based on the description in (Braden et al, 1997). The main differences from the RRS model is the lack of multi-routing (only the default route is probed), pre-emption (no prioritisation method is included in RSVP), and fault tolerant features (timers and retransmissions of RRS packets).

The implementation of the INSIGNIA (Lee et al., 2001) model was also derived from the RRS model, though in this case significant changes were required. Since INSIGNIA reserves resources per hop, resources are reserved right away if available, otherwise no resources are reserved further in the route and a report is sent from the destination that the request was not successful. If resources are reserved all the way to the destination, success is reported.

4.4.2 Reservation Request Models

In order to assess the operation of the reservation protocols, two variables were investigated. First, the impact of the **source** of requests was investigated with two different models. Second, in order to determine the effect of network **loading**, two network reservation request arrival rates were chosen.

For all protocols, the total time a reservation remained active was based on an exponential distribution with mean of 270 seconds. Reservations are for 8 kbps, with a maximum of 50% of each link's bandwidth available for reservations. These values were chosen to simulate voice connections.

The source of reservations arriving in the network was varied to investigate the impact of the multi-routing aspect of the RRS. Reservations may either originate uniformly from all nodes in the network (uniform model), or originate only from a single node (single source model). In the uniform model, the request generation process was activated on all nodes, while in the single source model the request generation process was activated only on a single node chosen randomly at the beginning of each simulation.
Considering the effect of different request source models, four reservation inter-arrival rates were used to simulate reservation saturation (nominal loading) and reservation overload (high loading). The inter-arrival time for reservations using the uniform model were exponentially distributed and centered on 60 seconds for nominal request load and 30 seconds for high load. These rates were chosen to saturate and overload the network with reservations respectively. For the single source model, the inter-arrival time was set to 30 seconds for nominal load and 15 seconds for high load for the same reasons. Note that since the request loads are not the same for uniform and single source request models, the results of these two source models should not be directly compared.

5. Results

5.1 Methodology (Credibility)

Wireless network simulations research has come under increasing scrutiny of late. Recent publications have raised questions about the credibility of past simulation work and have suggested different methods by which this can be resolved. For example in (Andel & Yasinsac, 2006) the lack of credible results in mobile ad-hoc network (MANET) simulations are blamed on a number of systemic problems. Without documenting all settings and data sets, simulations are not repeatable. Without addressing the sources of randomness and the data collection techniques, simulations cannot be statistically valid. Without comparing results with a real-world implementation, simulations cannot be empirically validated. Finally, without identifying the scenario, the traffic will not be complete (i.e. unrealistic). Similarly, in (Kurkowski et al, 2005) the authors studied a collection of 114 peer-reviewed MANET simulation papers presented at the MobiHoc symposium between 2000 and 2005. They found that 85 percent of the papers were not rigorous because they did not specify all parameters used in their simulations. For example, 30 percent of the papers did not identify the simulation environment used. Others did not include parameters such as transmission range, number of simulation runs, traffic type or mobility model. They focused on the need for unbiased and statistically valid methods.
As an exercise we decided to investigate what it would take to make our own simulation results properly credible. For this work we have combined the issues into a single list and attempted to apply these five principles to our own simulations. In order for simulation research to be credible it must be:

- **Repeatable**, where experiments describe all configuration settings;
- **Rigorous**, where the model settings varied, and how much they are varied, exercise the feature under investigation
- **Complete**, where the model is not oversimplified (avoiding ambiguous or incorrect conclusions)
- **Statistically Valid**, where the method of analysis is described and follows mathematical principles;

* **Empirically Valid**, where simulations are compared against a real world example.

To provide **repeatability**, the following settings were used in all simulations except where specifically noted. OPNET version 11.0 PL1 was used with the node and link models as noted below. Additional models were created or existing models were modified in some cases in order to model the RRS. Runs of 130 minutes were used for all measurements. Statistics gathering began after 270 seconds. This value was chosen because it is approximately three times the amount of time required for routing to converge and applications to reach steady state. The OSPF routing protocol was used with a hello interval of 10s, dead interval of 40s, delay of 1s, and retransmission interval of 5s.

In order to provide **rigorous** and **complete** results the following approach has been taken. The main metrics of interest in the work relate to the acceptance and pre-emption rate engendered by RRS and how those rates are affected by various request loads and source distributions. The simulation setup described below provides the complete set of network level configurations that were changed to provide minimal but sufficient variability to exercise the RRS as described here. The variability in the application performance can thus be fully ascribed to the changes in request configuration and the RRS itself.

To ensure the results described here are **statistically valid**, the following approach was taken. Twenty runs were made for the simulations to have tight error bounds. Statistics are averaged over each run. All results are quoted with a 95% confidence interval, which gives values within the specified range 19 times out of 20. The mean is calculated by summing the result of each run and dividing by the number of results. The standard deviation is calculated as the square root of the variance of this mean. From this the standard error is calculated as the standard deviation over the square root of the number of results. Finally, the two way 95% confidence interval is calculated as an (+/-) offset of the mean with a value 2.093 times the standard error for 20 measurements.

For **empirical validity**, the simulations were previously compared with an existing prototype that implements RRS in a wired test-bed (Kidston & Kunz, 2008). In that paper, we showed the RRS simulation results matched the operation of a prototype.

5.2 TMS Simulation results:

Based on the topology, mobility and background traffic described in Section 3, the delay of injecting Traffic Monitoring Service (TMS) traffic into the network was measured as shown in Table 5 and Table 6.

	Nom Load delay (s)	High Load delay (s)
Base Mode	3.8 +/- 0.5	6.9 +/- 0.7
Enhanced Mode	13.2 +/- 0.9	23.6 +/- 1.2
Detailed Mode	27.8 +/- 2.2	55.7 +/- 2.5

Table 5. TMS Delay in seconds, Small Network

	Nom Load delay (s)	High Load delay (s)
Base Mode	4.3 +/- 0.3	7.2 +/- 0.6
Enhanced Mode	15.6 +/- 0.9	28.2 +/- 2.2
Detailed Mode	35.2 +/- 1.8	61.5 +/- 3.2

Table 6. TMS Delay in seconds, Large Network

As can be seen, the effect of increased load is readily apparent in maritime networks, with the TMS delay almost doubling from nominal to heavy background traffic. For both the small and large network the base mode delay during nominal load is approximately four seconds, which for a non critical network service is most likely acceptable. However the enhanced and detailed modes have a much longer delay. This may be acceptable if the information is not being used interactively.

In order to investigate the impact of adding adaptability to this process, the service was modified to switch between detail modes to limit the maximum delay while delivering the most information possible. The following graph (Figure 7) shows the effect of adaptability on the operation of the TMS. Note that in this graph the TPS service described in Section 5.3 was also active.

In this simulation the TMS is attempting to ensure that the response time is at most 30s by reducing the detail mode to base if the response time exceeds 60s and to enhanced if it exceeds 30s. Similarly it will increase the monitoring to enhanced if it is less than 3s and currently at base and to detailed if it is less than 3s and currently at enhanced. In Figure 7 the small network begins with no background traffic. At 20 minutes, heavy background traffic is added. Nominal background traffic began at forty minutes. The figure shows clearly the switch from detailed mode after a 90+ second delay after 20 minutes and to enhanced mode after a 2 second delay after 40 minutes. Different policies of when and what should cause the switch between detail modes could also be implemented. This result shows that the causes and results of such changes can be modelled and compared in OPNET.

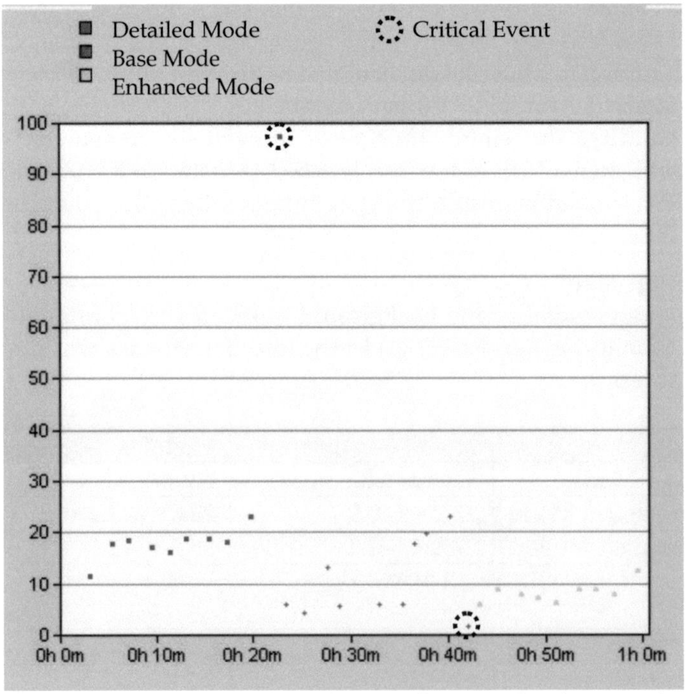

Fig. 7. Traffic monitoring adaptability example - small network - dynamic load

5.3 TPS Simulation results

The TPS service described in Section 4.2 was enabled and the TMS simulations rerun with the following results.

(with QoS)	Nom Load delay (s)	High Load delay(s)
Base Mode	2.3 +/- 0.3	4.6 +/- 0.5
Enhanced Mode	10.4 +/- 1.3	15.0 +/- 1.4
Detailed Mode	22.2 +/- 2.1	37.2 +/- 2.5

Table 7. TMS Delay in seconds, Small Network with TPS

(with QoS)	Nom Load delay (s)	High Load delay(s)
Base Mode	3.4 +/- 0.3	5.7 +/- 0.7
Enhanced Mode	12.3 +/- 1.1	20.3 +/- 2.3
Detailed Mode	26.8 +/- 2.0	45.2+/- 3.2

Table 8. TMS Delay in seconds, Large Network with TPS

Table 7 and Table 8, when compared with Table 5 and Table 6 respectively, show a significant improvement in the TMS delay. This confirms that DiffServ-style QoS can reduce the delay of prioritized flows in this environment. Further studies in OPNET could be completed to determine the impact of alternative WFQ weightings and alternate operational bandwidth assignments to the LOS links.

In another test to gauge the effect of TPS on different types of traffic, the delay of a voice call between the NOC and ship 4 in the small network was measured with and without TPS enabled. The default route for such traffic is to relay through ship 1. At low load one call was made with priority 4 and the delay measured was .67 +/- .12 seconds without TPS and .13 +/- .01 with. At high load, two identical calls were made; one at priority 2 and the other at priority 4. Without TPS, the end to end packet delay was the same for both calls at 1.4 +/- 0.3 seconds. With TPS, the high-priority call had a delay of 0.7 +/- 0.2 seconds while the low-priority flow's delay was 1.4 +/- 0.4 seconds. Since an acceptable voice delay is approximately 500ms TPS enables a single acceptable voice call at nominal load, but at high load two voice calls are not possible even with TPS. Note however that since background traffic uses the default route via Ship 1, the other LOS link via Ship 3 is currently unloaded.

5.4 ARS Simulation results

In order to improve utilization of the network, an MPLS overlay was introduced to allow traffic travelling from the NOC to Ship 4 to take different routes depending on the application type and priority. In this case high priority voice traffic was to travel via Ship 3 while all other traffic will travel over the default route via Ship 1. When this was done, the load on the Ship 1 to Ship 4 LOS link was reduced from an average utilization of 90.5% to 10.8% while the loads on the alternate LOS link from ship 3 to ship 4 was increased from almost nothing to 10-16%. The large reduction in average bandwidth on the default route is partly caused by a reduction in TCP based retransmissions.

With the combination of TPS and ARS, the impact on the delay of voice packets is significant. The high-priority voice call taking the alternate lightly loaded route via Ship 3 has a delay of 0.19 +/- 0.03 seconds while the lower priority voice call with the default route has a delay of 0.43 +/- 0.10 seconds. This arrangement using the combination of ARS and TPS made the high priority flow of acceptable and the low priority flow at least marginal.

5.5 RRS Simulation results

This section describes the RRS results. Results for RSVP and INSIGNIA are included for comparison. First, the acceptance rates of RRS and RSVP are compared in several parts. Next, the different nature of maintaining reservations in INSIGNIA leads to an alternative comparison. Finally some conclusions on the performance of RRS are given.

5.5.1 RRS vs. RSVP, Static Network Model

Our evaluation begins with the acceptance rates in RRS and RSVP in a static network (no mobility). Table 9 provides the percentage (%) of the requests that were able to reserve resources from source to destination at the time of the request. A margin of error is given at the 95% confidence interval.

Network	Load	Source	RRS	RSVP
Small	Nominal	Uniform	93.1 +/- 0.6	78.1 +/- 1.0
		Single	91.2 +/- 0.7	64.9 +/- 1.2
	High	Uniform	75.3 +/- 1.0	57.3 +/- 0.7
		Single	67.6 +/- 1.1	40.2 +/- 0.8
Large	Nominal	Uniform	88.8 +/- 0.5	67.8 +/- 0.8
		Single	88.4 +/- 1.1	58.4 +/- 1.5
	High	Uniform	68.6 +/- 0.7	48.6 +/- 0.5
		Single	65.2 +/- 1.0	37.3 +/- 0.7

Table 9. Acceptance Rates, Static Network

The most immediate conclusion that can be drawn from Table 9 is that RRS provides superior acceptance rates to RSVP in all scenarios. An improvement of 19-41% over RSVP is achieved when the source of requests is uniformly distributed, and an improvement of 41-75% with a unique source of reservations. However, the reservation success rate, defined as a reservation which gains end-to-end resources from the beginning to the end of its request, should also be considered. In this case the reservations lost to pre-emption in RRS reported in Table 12 must be included. Since these protocols use the same two-phase commit strategy for reserving resources, the improvement by RRS can be attributed primarily to two factors: the use of pre-emption to admit higher priority flows; and the use of multi-routing to route around congested links. These effects are discussed in more detail in Section 5.5.3.

5.5.2 Effect of Mobility on RRS and RSVP

The acceptance rates of RRS and RSVP were also simulated using the mobile network model, with results shown in Table 10.

A comparison of Table 9 and Table 10 shows that the mean acceptance rates of the mobile network are generally lower than in the static case, i.e. within or below the 95% confidence interval of each other in all but two cases. In the large network at nominal load, the single source model of RRS has a mean in the mobile case 3.3% above the mean of the static network while at high load RRS similarly has a mean 1.3% above the mean of the static network using the single source reservation model. This would suggest that mobility has a small negative effect on raw acceptance rate in the small network, with a more variable effect in the large network.

Network	Load	Source	RRS	RSVP
Small	Nominal	Uniform	91.6 +/- 0.7	77.0 +/- 0.9
		Single	90.5 +/- 1.0	63.5 +/- 1.7
	High	Uniform	74.1 +/- 0.8	56.5 +/- 0.9
		Single	67.2 +/- 1.4	40.1 +/- 0.7
Large	Nominal	Uniform	88.1 +/- 1.1	64.7 +/- 1.0
		Single	91.7 +/- 1.1	57.5 +/- 1.3
	High	Uniform	67.5 +/- 0.5	48.3 +/- 0.6
		Single	66.5 +/- 1.4	37.7 +/- 1.0

Table 10. Acceptance Rates, Mobile Network

The effect of link failures on active reservations is related in Table 11 with the given percentage of accepted flows having lost their resources at some point along their route.

Network	Load	Source	RRS	RSVP
Small	Nominal	Uniform	2.0 +/- 0.6	1.7 +/- 0.6
		Single	1.5 +/- 0.7	1.7 +/- 0.8
	High	Uniform	1.3 +/- 0.6	1.6 +/- 0.5
		Single	1.0 +/- 0.3	1.0 +/- 0.7
Large	Nominal	Uniform	4.3 +/- 0.3	4.3 +/- 0.3
		Single	4.8 +/- 0.9	4.2 +/- 0.9
	High	Uniform	3.6 +/- 0.3	3.8 +/- 0.4
		Single	3.7 +/- 0.9	4.4 +/- 0.8

Table 11. Reservation Failure Rates (due to mobility)

The direct comparison of Table 10 does not take into account the reservations later lost to the link failures associated with mobility. Mobility can cause existing successful reservations to be lost when links fail, thus increasing the number of subsequent reservations admitted as shown in Table 11.

The mean failure rates for RRS and RSVP can be seen to fall within the 95% confidence interval of each other in all cases. This is as expected, since they are based on the same underlying mobility model and a similar reservation release mechanism. Reservation recovery mechanisms were not included in the RRS and RSVP model. Considering the relatively low number of failed flows relative to the number of accepted flows, it is unlikely that such features are worth the additional overhead in this low bandwidth environment.

Considering the link failure rate, the total number of successful reservations can be calculated to determine the effect of mobility on RRS and RSVP individually. A successful reservation is defined as a reservation that maintains their resources end-to-end without loss due to a link failure or pre-emption. In this section we look only at link failures. In RRS, the effect of mobility (failure rate) with the single source reservation model has very little effect, with only 1.2-2.3% fewer successful reservations with mobility when compared to the static case. The effect is slightly larger in the uniform source model with 2.9-5.1% fewer successful reservations overall. RSVP shows a similar trend, though with a slightly larger effect. Compared with the static model, 1.2-5.7% fewer reservations were successful in the mobile network for single sourced reservations, while the uniform model had 3.0-8.7% fewer with mobility. The difference between single source and uniform models is explained by the fact that the uniform model saturates the links more evenly, while the single source model suffers from bottlenecks around the reservation source. This leads to more reservations on average being lost for a particular link failure in the uniform model. From this we conclude that there is a slight (single digit percent) negative effect from mobility on reservation success, with uniform reservations experiencing approximately double the effect found using the single source request generation model. In order to properly compare RRS and RSVP using the idea of successful reservations, we look in the following section at the other cause of reservation failures, pre-emption.

5.5.3 Effect of Pre-Emption

By investigating the effect of pre-emption rates in RRS, we gain a better understanding of the difference in reservation success between RRS and RSVP. The percentage of accepted flows which lost their resources due to pre-emption is given in Table 12.

Network	Load	Source	RRS (static)	RRS (mobile)
Small	Nominal	Uniform	8.3 +/- 0.5	8.2 +/- 0.7
		Single	15.0 +/- 1.1	15.8 +/- 1.3
	High	Uniform	21.7 +/- 0.7	21.0 +/- 1.2
		Single	35.8 +/- 0.9	35.7 +/- 1.2
Large	Nominal	Uniform	8.9 +/- 0.5	8.7 +/- 0.4
		Single	18.1 +/- 1.1	17.1 +/- 1.0
	High	Uniform	19.2 +/- 0.5	18.9 +/- 0.5
		Single	34.4 +/- 0.8	34.2 +/- 1.0

Table 12. Pre-emption Rates (RRS only)

From this table we can see that pre-emption is significantly impacting existing RRS flows, particularly in the high load scenarios. In the maritime environment, this level of loss may be acceptable considering that no high-priority flows are affected, only low priority and to a lesser extent medium priority flows. This ensures the acceptance of high-priority reservations, except in extreme cases, where they may be blocked by other high-priority reservations. This is unlikely to occur in even the high-load models simulated here given the relatively low pre-emption rates and an even distribution of requests between the three priority classes.

Comparing the static and mobile network model results, the pre-emption rates are within the 95% confidence interval of each other in both the static and mobile scenarios. This is to be expected, since with similar reservation rates in both mobile and static case, the mix of reservations in the network is similar. With similar network priorities and similar number of reservations, the pre-emption rate should also be similar. Though within error bounds, a slightly higher pre-emption rate in the static case can be seen. Since there are slightly more reservations made in this case, additional pre-emption can be expected.

In order to quantify the effect of priority on acceptance and pre-emption rates in RRS, we investigated the large static network scenario with uniform high traffic. Priority was found to have a significant impact on acceptance rate, with high priority traffic having an acceptance rate of 87.9 +/- 0.7 percent while medium and low-priority flows had an acceptance rate of 64.7 +/- 0.9 and 49.7 +/- 0.9 percent respectively, for an acceptance rate of 68.6 +/- 0.7 percent overall. Similarly, while high-priority flows were not pre-empted, medium-priority flows had a pre-emption rate of 25.4 +/- 0.7 percent and low-priority flows had a pre-emption rate of 42.8 +/- 1.6 percent, for a pre-emption rate of 19.2 +/- 0.5 percent overall. This shows that priority has a significant impact on both acceptance and pre-emption rates, with high-priority flows gaining service similar to RSVP (i.e. no pre-emptions) but with an improvement of 80.9 percent in mean acceptance rate over RSVP for the large static network scenario with high traffic.

The amount of pre-emption measured, especially at high load, gives rise to the question of whether RRS is in fact an improvement on RSVP in terms of successful reservations. Simple subtraction of the pre-emption rate from acceptance rate is however not appropriate, as reservations must have achieved their resources for at least some period of time in order to be pre-empted. Based on the percentage of accepted flows that were not pre-empted (or lost due to link failures) the reservation success (completion) rate improvement of RRS over RSVP can be measured. Analysis shows there is a large difference in mean improvement rates in high vs. nominal load scenarios. At high load, an improvement of only 3-8% more successful reservations over RSVP can be achieved in the small network and 14-17% in the large network, regardless of mobility or traffic source model. At nominal load, a greater improvement is possible, in the small network 9% and 20% for uniform and single source models respectively. In the large network at nominal load there are some mobility effects. The static network gains 19% and 24% for uniform and single source models respectively, and the large mobile network RRS reservations gain 24% and 31% for uniform and single source models respectively. This shows that at nominal load the multi-routing effect is especially effective for single sourced requests while at high load there is little difference between the two request models.

It should be noted that though RRS does pre-empt low-priority flows, these flows gain some advantage from the use of reserved resources for the period of time before they are pre-empted. Investigating the effect of priority level on resource hold times (reservation success) we again looked at the large static scenario with uniform high traffic. In this scenario we found that high-priority flows were not pre-empted (as expected), but both medium and low-priority flows which were accepted had on average a significant period in which they did gain their required resources. Medium-priority flows that were eventually pre-empted kept their reserved resources for 65.2 +/- 4.2 percent of their allocated time period on average. Similarly, low-priority flows maintained their reserved resources for 36.6 +/- 2.7 percent of their allocated time. Thus, though pre-empted flows do not gain full advantage of reserved resources throughout their lifetime, RRS does provide them with significant periods of advantage based on their priority.

5.5.4 RRS vs. INSIGNIA

In order to compare RRS with INSIGNIA, it is important to remember that in INSIGNIA flows are granted resources per-hop for as far along their current route as they are available instead of end-to-end. This means that if a link does not have resources, later links in the flow will not reserve resources. The unfortunate consequence seen in these simulations is that resources are kept by flows on the first part of their path, and yet flows still fail to achieve end-to-end reservations. As shown in Figure 8, this reduces the total number of successful end-to-end reservations in the network because resources are wasted on non-viable reservations.

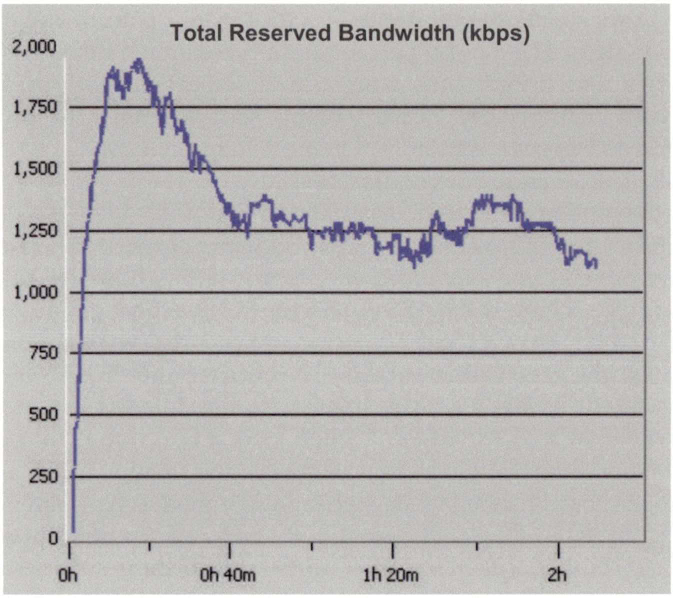

Fig. 8. Example of Network-Wide Reserved Bandwidth in INSIGNIA

Figure 8 shows the total amount of reserved bandwidth on all links in the network at a particular time in one simulation run of the large network with no mobility, nominal request load, and with the uniform reservation arrival model. It shows that at the beginning of the simulation, from about 5 minutes to 25 minutes, a large number of reservations are successful and the total amount of end-to-end reserved bandwidth in the network peaks around 1800 - 1900 kbps (out of a theoretical maximum of 2176 kbps "reservable"). After this, the total amount of reserved bandwidth decreases until a steady state is achieved at about 40 minutes. From this point on, successful reservations hold approximately 1250 kbps of network bandwidth. The remaining reservable bandwidth at this point is tied up by reservations which do not have end-to-end resources but are still holding resources on the beginning of their route, blocking other reservations from getting sufficient resources to be successful themselves.

In Table 13 and Table 14 below, the acceptance rate given is the percentage of new flows which gain resources on all links in their route on the first try. Upgrades are the percentage of flows which at some point did not have end-to-end resources then gain such resources. Downgrades are the percentage of accepted or upgraded flows which at some point had end-to-end resources and then lose the resources on any link. Since there is no pre-emption in INSIGNIA this can only happen because of mobility.

Network	Load	Source	Acceptance	Upgrade
Small	Nominal	Uniform	20.8 +/- 1.2	16.3 +/- 1.1
		Single	14.4 +/- 0.6	17.7 +/- 1.0
	High	Uniform	6.7 +/- 0.3	14.8 +/- 0.6
		Single	6.6 +/- 0.7	10.1 +/- 0.7
Large	Nominal	Uniform	22.7 +/- 0.9	6.9 +/- 0.5
		Single	47.5 +/- 2.1	5.3 +/- 0.8
	High	Uniform	9.7 +/- 0.4	8.7 +/- 0.4
		Single	27.9 +/- 0.8	4.7 +/- 0.5

Table 13. INSIGNIA Results (Static Network)

Network	Load	Source	Acceptance	Upgrade	Downgrade
Small	Nominal	Uniform	18.1 +/- 0.9	18.5 +/- 0.9	4.9 +/- 1.0
		Single	14.6 +/- 1.7	20.6 +/- 1.8	5.1 +/- 2.3
	High	Uniform	6.2 +/- 0.3	14.7 +/- 0.7	3.5 +/- 1.2
		Single	7.1 +/- 0.6	12.2 +/- 1.4	4.3 +/- 1.6
Large	Nominal	Uniform	19.7 +/- 0.8	10.4 +/- 0.6	8.8 +/- 1.1
		Single	45.1 +/- 1.6	11.5 +/- 1.6	4.4 +/- 1.2
	High	Uniform	8.5 +/- 0.3	9.3 +/- 0.5	11.3 +/- 1.1
		Single	27.3 +/- 1.0	9.7 +/- 0.8	7.5 +/- 0.8

Table 14. INSIGNIA Results (Mobile Network)

Considering the results of these two tables, it can be seen that INSIGNIA performs very poorly in the maritime environment with low acceptance rates (most below 30%). These results would not be acceptable in a maritime environment, especially considering the lack of priority mechanisms for critical flows.

Comparing these two tables to determine the effect of mobility, it can be seen that the static network model provides a slightly higher initial acceptance rate, which is to be expected when links may be down due to mobility when new requests arrive. Comparison of the acceptance rates show the static results are within 13 percent of the mobile results in all cases respectively. Conversely, upgrades are higher in the mobile network. This is due to the fact that when links become available due to mobility there is a greater chance for existing reservations to gain end-to-end resources using the newly available link. When both upgrades and downgrades are taken into account, the static and mobile results for partially successful reservations are similar and within +/- 17%. Partially successful reservations are defined as reservations which achieve end-to-end reservations at some point in their lifetime. Interestingly, the uniform source distribution resulted in 7-17% more partially successful reservation in the static network model (compared to the mobile model) while the single source distribution resulted in 2-10% less. Because fewer links become fully subscribed in the single source distribution due to the bottleneck around the source, it does not suffer as many lost reservations when a link fails as, on average, there are fewer reservations in the network. Uniformly distributed requests are conversely more sensitive to link outages since all links are more likely to have a high number of reservations.

5.5.5 Conclusions of RRS Results

Looking at our results in terms of the operational requirements for maritime networks, the overall RRS acceptance rate of 91-93% on average for nominal loadings regardless of mobility is acceptable. In the critical high load case, the RRS acceptance rate of 67-75% on average may seem low but it should be noted that the pre-emption mechanism used in RRS ensures that high-priority flows are accepted at the cost of lower-priority flows losing their resources. For example, in the heavily loaded static network with uniform requests, 87.9% of high priority traffic was accepted on average, while low-priority traffic was accepted only 49.7% of the time on average.

To evaluate the effectiveness of RRS in a maritime environment with dynamic topology, it was compared with the archetypical fixed network reservation protocol RSVP and a MANET reservation protocol INSIGNIA. With mean acceptance rates of 64-78% on average at nominal load and 40-57% at high load it is unlikely that RSVP would be acceptable in this environment. INSIGNIA's performance was even worse with mean acceptance rates of 14-21% at nominal load and 6-7% at high load. In a raw comparison of acceptance rates, RRS is 19-76% better than RSVP and 86-1095% better than INSIGNIA.

From these results, it can be seen that the multi-routing and pre-emption features of RRS provide a higher acceptance rate compared with RSVP with similar loss rates during link failures. This improved acceptance rate does however come at the cost of pre-empted lower priority flows. In order to determine the impact of pre-emption, RRS and RSVP were compared in terms of successful reservations which maintain their resources end-to-end throughout their lifetime. It was found that RRS still outperformed RSVP by 3-8% at high load and 9-20% at nominal load. These numbers highlight that probing multiple routes makes a significant difference only when the network is not already saturated with requests.

Another interesting conclusion from these simulations is that the mobility models simulated have only a marginal negative effect on both acceptance rates and reservation success. Comparing the results for the different mobility models, the acceptance rates for RRS and RSVP with mobility are within or slightly below the 95% confidence interval of the static model in most cases.

6. Related Work

There has been, to the best of our knowledge, no network modelling work on maritime networks. However, there has been some recent work on improving networking in this area, for instance in applying static DiffServ QoS to maritime networks (Barsaleau & Tummala, 2004). This paper showed that throughput and delay guarantees were hard to achieve in this environment, but queuing and dropping mechanisms, if properly tuned, could provide limited service differentiation. This work does not consider the dynamic nature of the maritime environment, where the importance attached to different classes or even flows of information vary with time. The use of modelling in this environment would greatly aid investigations in the type of tuning required in different circumstances before incurring the expense of deployment on operational platforms.

The Resource Reservation Protocol (RSVP) (Braden et al, 1997) is a well known standard that reserves resources for unicast or multicast flows along the default path(s) from sender to receiver(s). RSVP delivers quality-of-service (QoS) requests to all nodes along the path(s) of the flows and establishes and maintains "soft" state related to the requested service. This provides support for dynamic reservation membership and automatic adaptation to routing changes. During reservation setup, RSVP transports traffic and policy control parameters that provide direction to nodes as to whether the flow should be admitted. From the point of view of maritime networks, while RSVP does provide a basic end-to-end service, it uses the default route (which is quickly saturated), does not support prioritisation (a requirement), and assumes network reliability (lacks fault tolerance mechanisms). These issues were addressed in the RRS design.

The adaptation of existing fixed-network-based QoS mechanisms into a MANET environment has been investigated from many different angles, all of them distributed. INSIGNIA (Lee et al, 2001) is an IntServ-based in-band signalling system for providing QoS reservation services on top of existing MANET routing protocols. The INSIGNIA framework supports distributed resource reservation, restoration, and end-to-end adaptation irrespective of the underlying routing protocol. Reservations are accomplished through the use of a specialized IP option field added to all packets. When a packet arrives at a node, a reservation is made on the outgoing link as long as the reservation was successful so far on its route and there are sufficient resources on the local link. End-to-end adaptation to available bandwidth is possible through the use of user-supplied policies that inform applications as to the available bandwidth reported by the protocol. As was seen in the simulations, this single phase commit strategy fails in congested networks.

7. Conclusions and Future Work

In this chapter we have described a network model of maritime networks and, using modelling and simulation, investigated the impact of several network services designed to provide traffic engineering. In order to add credibility to our results we followed a process to ensure it would be: repeatable, by including all parameter settings; rigorous, where the variables investigated are well described and correctly exercise the simulated model; complete, in that the model is sufficiently detailed; statistically valid, in that the mathematical analysis is sufficient and correct; and empirically valid, such that the results of the simulation match well with a real world example.

Four network services were described. The traffic monitoring service (TMS) provides details on the traffic generated, received and passing through the local node. Three levels of detail are possible, and the amount of information sent to interested parties, most often simply the network operation centre, can be tuned so that the status information is delayed by a maximum amount. Simulations showed that in both small (four ship) and larger (eight ship) networks, the data could be updated at least every 30 seconds by switching to lower levels of detail when the intervening network was loaded.

The second type of service was the traffic prioritisation service (TPS). By assigning applications to different DiffServ classes, the delay of more important application traffic could be reduced. Simulations showed that the TMS delay could be significantly reduced when assigned a high priority. It also showed that in a small network voice calls that had unacceptable delay without TPS could be made acceptable with TPS.

The third network service, the adaptive routing service (ARS), uses MPLS to divert traffic from links that cannot meet the QoS requirements of the application. Simulations showed that alternate routes could be used to make voice calls with unacceptable delay characteristics acceptable. This shows that altering the relationship between queuing resources and applications can achieve a desired service level for some traffic.

The fourth network service, the resource reservation service (RRS), uses distributed two phase admission control for guaranteed end-to-end bandwidth reservations. This service includes several novel features designed specifically for maritime networks including multi-path probing and bi-directional reservations. The value of multi-path probing is demonstrated by simulation giving RRS an acceptance rate 19-76% better than RSVP and 86-1095% better than INSIGNIA, two alternative reservation protocols.

Our main conclusion is that, though non-trivial, it is possible and valuable to create a maritime network model using OPNET. Such models can be used for testing the impact of new network applications and services as well as tuning existing services. It also showed that altering routing can lead to more optimal use of link b/w resources, and can also lead to better QoS for critical traffic. The combination of TPS and ARS provided improved delay, but there can still be problems for critical application flows in times of high usage, congestion, and low connectivity from mobility. For this case RRS provides a high probability resource reservation service (RRS).

Several simplifying assumptions were made in this work including the use of 802.11 models instead of true VHF LOS models. Further work is required to see if this was a valid replacement.

There remain many possible avenues to further this work on evaluating network services for the maritime environment. Other scenarios could be investigated with more ships, and different mobility models. There is also quite some scope to further investigate the impact of different configurations on the operation of the various network services, especially RRS, as many parameters from the number of probes to the pre-emption strategy can be changed.

8. Acknowledgement

This work was supported by Defence R&D Canada (DRDC).

9. References

Andel, T.R & Yasinsac, A., On the Credibility of MANET Simulations, *IEEE Computer Magazine*, Vol. 39, No. 7, (Jul. 2006): 48-54, ISSN: 0018-9162.

Anh, G-S. et al. (2002) Supporting Service Differentiation for Real-Time and Best Effort Traffic in Stateless Wireless Ad Hoc Networks (SWAN), *IEEE Transactions on Mobile Computing*, Vol. 1, No. 3, (Jul.-Sep. 2002): 192 - 207, ISSN: 1536-1233

AUSCANZUKUS (1999) Multi-National Naval Task Group (MNTG) Final Report, *Naval C4 JWID Publication JWID99-R*, Washington, DC, Sep 1999.

AUSCANZUKUS (2003) Maritime Tactical Wide Area Networking (MTWAN), *Publication ACP 200*, Washington, DC, Jul 2003

Barsaleau D. & Tummala, M. (2004) Testing of DiffServ Performance over a U.S. Navy Satellite Communication Network, *Proceedings of MILCOM 2004*, pp. 528 – 534, ISBN: 0-7803-8847-X, Monterey, CA, Oct. – Nov 2004.

Braden, R. et al., "Resource ReSerVation Protocol (RSVP) -- Version 1 Functional Specification", IETF RFC 2205, Sep. 1997.

Holliday, P. (2005). "Techniques for Efficient Network Layer Failover in Maritime Tactical Wide Area Networks (MTWAN), *Proceedings of MILCOM 2005*, pp. 52 - 55, Vol. 1, ISBN: 0-7803-9393-7, Atlantic City, NJ, Oct. 2005.

Jorgenson, M., Reichelt, C., & Johnson, T. (2005). Operation of the Dynamic TDMA Subnet Relay System with HF Bearers, *Proceedings of MILCOM 2005*, pp. 338 - 343, Vol. 1, ISBN: 0-7803-9393-7, Atlantic City, NJ, Oct. 2005.

Kidston, D. & Labbé, I. (2006). A Service Oriented Framework for Policy-Based Management of Maritime Mobile Networks, *Proceedings of MILCOM 2006*, pp. 1-7, ISBN: 1-4244-0617-X, Washington, D.C., Oct. 2006.

Kidston, D. et al (2007) A Policy-Based Resource Reservation Service for Maritime Tactical Networks, *Proceedings of MMNS*, pp. 149-160, ISBN: 978-3-540-75868-6 San José, California, Oct-Nov. 2007.

Kidston, D. & Kunz T. (2008) Towards Network Simulations Credibility: Lessons from Applying Five Key Principles, *Proceedings of MILCOM 2008*, pp. 1-6, ISBN: 978-1-4244-2676-8, San Diego, CA, Nov. 2008.

Kurkowski, S., Camp, T., & Colagrosso, M, MANET Simulation Studies: The Incredibles, *Mobile Computing and Communication Review*, Vol. 9, No. 4, (Oct. 2005): 50-61, ISSN:1559-1662.

Lee, S-B., Ahn, G-S., & Campbell, A. (2001) Improving UDP and TCP Performance in Mobile Ad Hoc Networks with INSIGNIA, *IEEE Communications Magazine*, Vol. 39, No. 6 (Jun. 2001): 156-165, ISSN: 0163-6804.

Sanchez, M. & Manzoni, P. (2001) ANEJOS: A Java-based simulator for ad-hoc networks, *Future Generation Computer Systems Magazine*, Vol. 17, No. 5. (March 2001): 573 - 583, ISSN: 0167-739X.

Sibbald, LCdr. (2004) MARPAC PacketShaper Trial Hot Wash-Up, *MARPAC HQ Presentation N60*, Washington, DC, Nov 2004.

25

Modelling, Simulating and Autonomous Planning for Urban Search and Rescue

Vaccaro, J. and Guest, C.
University of California San Diego
United States of America

1. Introduction

This chapter presents a search and rescue simulation for a partially flooded city. The simulation makes use of novel approaches in the areas of modeling, simulation, and optimization. The model for the city is derived from Compact Terrain DataBase data. The section on modeling shows how this data can be preprocessed to make it suitable for simulation applications. Particular attention is given to preparing the data so that the resulting simulations can be run quickly and efficiently. The optimization section presents a hierarchical multi-agent planning and execution algorithm. The algorithm generates plans for multiple sorties of multiple agents. It then monitors the execution of each plan to provide on-the-fly improvements dictated by environmental uncertainties.

Parts of the flooded city remain above the water, but even some of these have become isolated because of flooded roads. City residents in these isolated portions must be rescued by boat or helicopter. In other portions of the city, one or more floors of buildings remain above the waterline, and the same options for rescue exist. In portions of the city that are above the waterline and remain connected to the mainland, there are still residents that require rescue. They may be too sick, injured, or frightened to evacuate themselves. These residents can be rescued with busses or helicopters. The simulation includes blockage of roads by high water and fallen trees at random locations. Helicopters can also be used for rapid reconnaissance to determine which portions of the city are accessible by road, and where to direct survey, supply, and rescue operations. They can also be used to deliver vital supplies rapidly to residents that cannot immediately be rescued.

2. Modelling

The environment modeled in this application is a small city that has been partially flooded. The city includes geological features such as rivers and frontage on a lake, as well as man-made features such as roads and buildings. All of this information is encoded in a general purpose format known as Compact Terrain DataBase (CTDB). CTDB is widely used for military and other applications.

CTDB represents three primary area types in urban terrain: natural terrain, developed terrain, and Multi-Elevation Structures (MES) (Witte, 2005). Natural terrain consists of soil type (modeled as triangles with vertices in three spatial coordinates), water (two-dimensional polygons), trees (points specified in two-dimensions), and canopies (two-dimensional polygons). Developed terrain includes roads, railroads, and canals, which are all defined as two-dimensional linear shapes. MES data includes buildings, monuments, and walls, which are defined as two-dimensional polygons with height. More detailed descriptions of the data format are given in the approach section.

For all CTDB data, urban terrain is gridded into square blocks (e.g., 256 by 256 meter squares) that divide many two-dimensional, and three-dimensional shapes into separate parts. This presents a problem for reconstructing the data into simulation objects, for example, treating buildings as a single object, and for keeping roads, rivers, and lakes properly connected. Since the simulation data is not intended for human use, but for computer processing, the visual aspects are less important than the object information. Creating simulation objects requires fusing fragmented shapes. Fusing shapes to create objects is done by drawing and filling them, which is described in detail below. Once objects are created, they form the basis for determining movement waypoints and connectivity.

The objective of preprocessing is to combine, segment, and repartition CTDB data into a compact format for simulation, while retaining the freedom of movement and connectivity of the original data. The freedom of movement is retained by creating waypoints at strategic locations, and connectivity is retained by connecting the waypoints in a manner that reflects their relationship in a traversable sense. For example, a road waypoint connected to a road waypoint signifies a traversable road, or a sky waypoint connected to a building top signifies a helicopter drop or rescue path. Using only waypoints and connectivity does not give the look and feel of a real life simulation for human use, but it does make all planning options available to computer algorithms.

The simulation uses agents of multiple types: busses, boats, and helicopters. For each type of agent, there is a corresponding set of waypoints. Agents of specific types are restricted to a particular set of waypoints, and paths. Planning of agent paths is simplified by clustering waypoints that are indistinguishably close together. This reduced set of waypoints is then preprocessed to determine shortest paths between all pairs of waypoints. Experiments have shown that reducing waypoint sets is important for efficiently computing the shortest paths for each waypoint type (Chandy & Mistra, 1982).

In this model, where each action choice has a pre-calculated shortest path, many options can be contemplated in successionto create a plan of action. This enables planning for many agents within an environment of multiple waypoint types.

This approach to modeling a high performance gaming environment to simulate S&R planning operations incorporates several desirable features: (1) a compact and computable data representation, (2) very fast simulation, (3) environment observation models, and (4) multi-agent planning. The following sections address each of these features in detail.

2.1 Feature One: Compact and Computable

A compact and computable environment representation is formulated through recomposing the CTDB into a network form, using waypoints and connections. CTDB data represents a virtual 3D world that human planners can navigate through with high visual acuity. For computer simulation purposes, there is no need to have a fully continuous and uniform representation; a tractable abstract representation is sufficient. Waypoints and connections provide a sufficient representation. Though the concept is simple, the challenge is developing a useful model that takes into account many different possible environmental features. For the example S&R application, only roads, rivers, buildings, open water and land areas, and terrain elevation are considered.

Roads and rivers are relatively simple to recompose, because they are given in CTDB as 2D linear segments with a width. Every curve requires many segments, while straight portions may be only one segment. Waypoints are created at both ends of each segment and are shared with all connecting segments. Connections between waypoints are simply the segments themselves. This approach works in most cases, but it is important to make sure that all segment intersections are included, because many times they are not represented explicitly. In such cases an additional waypoint is inserted at the intersection.

Rivers are a special case because they can be traveled by boat, but their banks can also be traveled by foot or may be flooded. Riverbank waypoints are generated in most cases by creating waypoints paralleling the river at a distance of half its width on both sides of the river. This does not work in the case of river intersections. These intersections are completed by adding a waypoint at the closest point between intersecting river segments that is beyond both rivers' widths.

Building waypoints and connections are implemented in three regions: interior, nearby exterior, and access points to the building. Given that many buildings are not single CTDB objects, but a combination of 3D volumes, merging is required. This is done by projecting all overlapping or connected volumes to the x-y plane (the ground) and then filling all internal pixels to determine the total footprint of the building object. Figure 1 illustrates this process.

To start, one building volume is chosen, and any other building sharing vertices with the chosen volume is selected. As they are added, selected buildings are eliminated from the list of unprocessed buildings. This is iterated until there are no more shared vertices. Next, the largest distance among all pairs of vertices of all the building volumes selected is computed, and a square image canvas with edge length twice that distance is generated to ensure that the object is filled correctly. The canvas grid is initially filled with all zeros. Next, each building volume is drawn and filled on the canvas with the value one. For example, filling each shape is performed by selecting the center-point and painting the object. If filling the object changes more than half the grid points on the canvas, then painting the location is outside the building object and undone and a new point to paint from is selected. Next, all interior building vertices are filtered out by keeping only those volume vertices that neighbor an outer pixel of value zero. Figure 1 shows the image of building volumes, where the single interior vertex is labeled as a 'triangle' and the exterior vertices are labeled as 'stars' and 'squares'. All 'triangle' coordinates are assumed as interior points and removed.

Remaining vertices are now reconnected such that they follow the outer wall. This is done by cycling through all connecting vertex pairs from all volumes, and keeping those pairs that have both vertices on the exterior. For illustrative purposes, Figure 1 shows all the vertex pairs by placing a 'diamond' on either side of the center connections. Those walls with a diamond outside of the wall are kept. The heavier shaded walls in Figure 1 represent the kept walls.

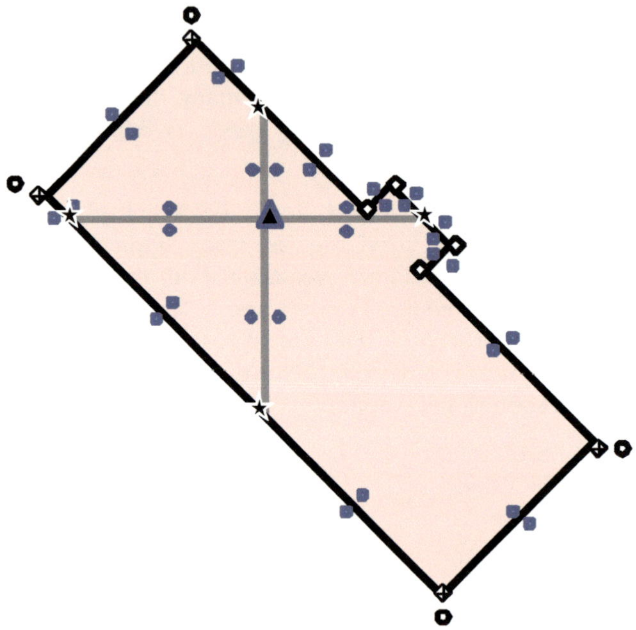

Fig. 1. Merging building volumes into one object

There are still some vertices that are in the middle of walls that can be eliminated without changing the outline of the building. Now that the complete perimeter of the building is known, the 'middle of wall' vertices can be eliminated by taking out all vertices where the walls on either side are colinear. 'Middle of wall' vertices are represented as 'stars' in Figure 1 and are eliminated.

There is now a building object with at least three connecting vertices, but often times more (i.e., in Figure 1 the 'hollow diamond' symbols represent a sufficient set of perimeter vertices). This process is continued from the first step until all building volumes are used.

For simplicity, only four exterior waypoints are defined near each building, unless only three vertices define the entire building object. These nearby waypoints are chosen by projecting the outermost perimeter vertices an additional two meters away from the building center.

The outermost vertices (corners) are chosen as follows: the first corner is the furthest from the center of mass of all filled points on the canvas, the second corner is furthest from the first corner selected, the third corner is furthest from the first and second corners in combined distance, and the fourth corner is farthest from the combined first, second and third corners. In Figure 1, the chosen corners are those with an 'x' in the 'square'. The nearby exterior building waypoints generated from these extreme corners are shown as 'circles' in

Figure 1. The connections among these waypoints are constructed such that they do not cross (i.e., minimal spanned distance). When buildings are very near one another, outside waypoints from multiple buildings are clustered if they are less than three meters apart. In other words, these nearby waypoints from multiple buildings are combined as one, while retaining their previous connectivity to other waypoints.

In CTDB, buildings often come with floor plans, but for this S&R application, we assume only two interior waypoints per floor, and two on the rooftop. One waypoint represents a location observable from the outside, while the other represents a hidden location. The pair of waypoints on each floor are connected. Connection between floors, exiting the building, and going to the roof are accessed only through the hidden waypoints. Both the hidden and observable waypoints are placed near the center of each floor, because observability is considered equal in all directions.

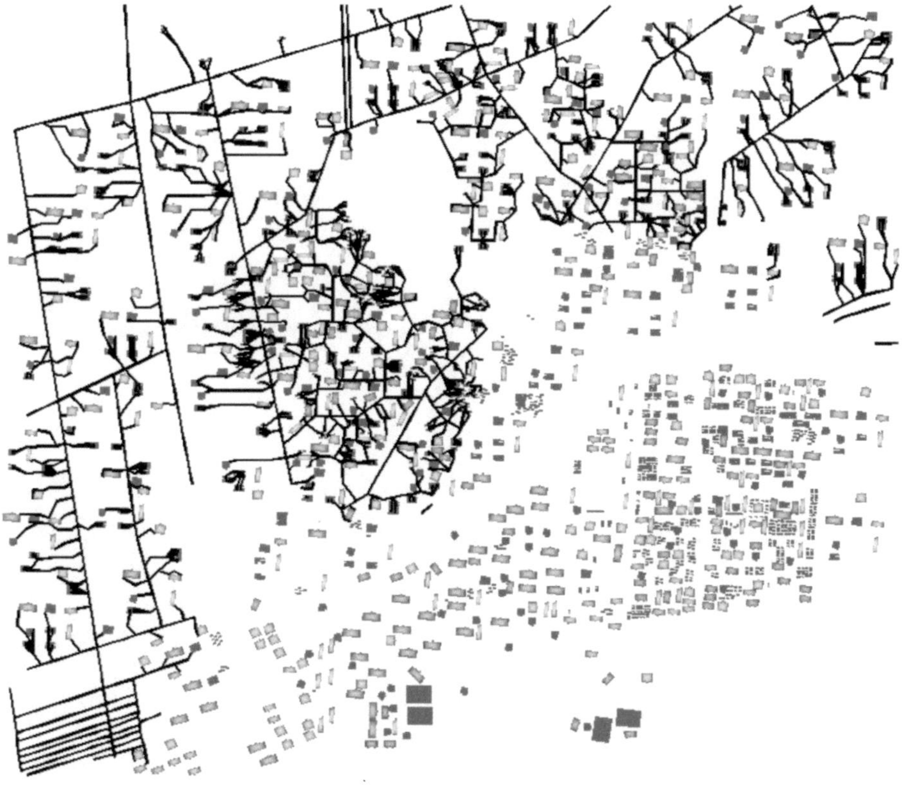

Fig. 2. City roads under maximum flood conditions

Building exit connections provide access to the nearest road for S&R evacuation purposes. These connections are found by considering each building exterior waypoint and determining the road nearest to it. Then the shortest of these lengths is selected as the road acces for that building. Buildings that share the same road waypoint are clustered together and considered as a single bus or boat stop. The stops are used in planning evacuations for each clustered set of buildings.

Open land and water area waypoints are necessary for regions where there are no roads or buildings. For simplicity, a hexagonal grid of waypoints with 75 meters edge length is projected on the 2D image of roads, water bodies, and buildings to provide a complimentary set of waypoints. All such waypoints within fifteen meters of an existing waypoint, on a road, in a water body, or within a building are removed. All other projected waypoints are kept as open area waypoints.

Connections between waypoints are implemented to complete the model. All waypoints, excluding building interior waypoints are connected using Delaunay triangles (Isenburg et al., 2006). Next, all Delaunay connections are projected onto the same 2D image used above. All connections that cross over roads, rivers or buildings are rejected and the remaining connections are kept. All connections discussed earlier (roads, rivers, buildings, etc.) are added to this connection model, and redundant connections are removed. This completes the surface model connectivity. Figure 2 illustrates a diagram of usable road connections during a flood at its highest level.

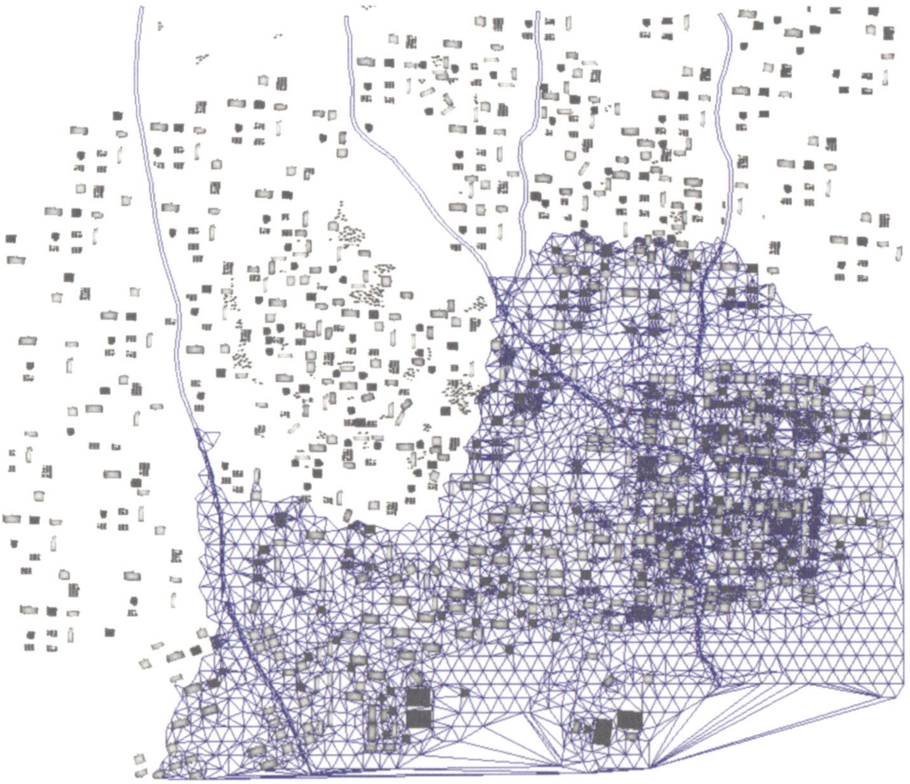

Fig. 3. City water routes under maximum flood conditions

Terrain elevation is also required in the model, because water level determines whether surface waypoints can be traveled by land or by water. In the example application, boats, busses and helicopters are used. Boats can traverse all waypoints below the waterline and busses can travel only road connections above waterline. Connections to and from buildings are adapted to the lowest floor not underwater. Figure 3 illustrates the boat movement model during a flood at its highest level.

Helicopter paths require an air movement model. For simplicity, a sky waypoint is placed above each building at a constant elevation slightly above the tallest building height. Connections are made between each sky waypoint and to the building rooftop observable waypoint. In addition, a hexagonal grid of sky waypoints with 100 meters edge length is added wherever the added waypoint is not within fifteen meters of an existing sky waypoint. All sky waypoints are connected with one another via Delaunay triangles, but this time all connections are kept. A helicopter base is added at the most strategic (i.e., as deemed by an expert) open area waypoint and connected to the nearest sky waypoint. Figure 4 illustrates the helicopter movement model with all the sky-waypoints and connections, which allows any building to be visited.

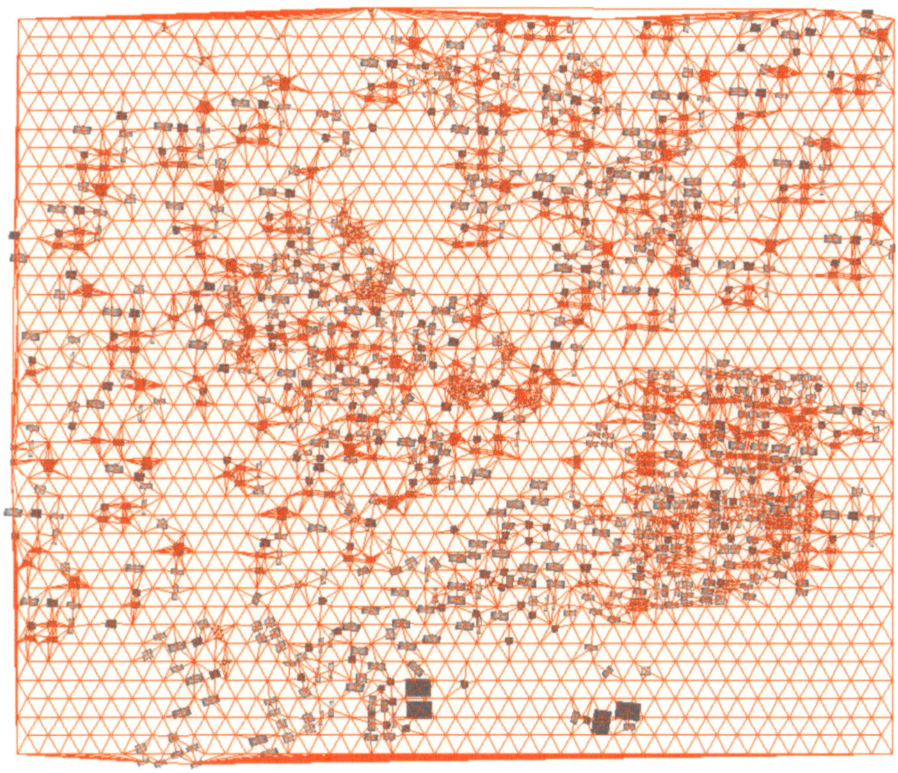

Fig. 4. City helicopter routes under any conditions

2.2 Feature Two: Very Fast Planning Simulation

Very fast planning simulation is enabled by pre-computing all shortest paths for all pairs of waypoints for boats, busses, and helicopters. Boat and bus paths can also be computed for different water levels, but for the example application only one water level was used. For simplicity, the positions of boat and bus stops are the same, whether they are above or below the waterline. Each vehicle also requires a base where rescued residents are dropped off, so boat bases are put at the highest point of each river, a bus base is placed at the highest road waypoint. A helicopter base is placed at another strategic location. Figure 5 illustrates the bases and elevation terrain under normal conditions. The busses assume all routes are open as shown in this figure, but learn to adapt their planning based on the true available routes shown in Figure 2.

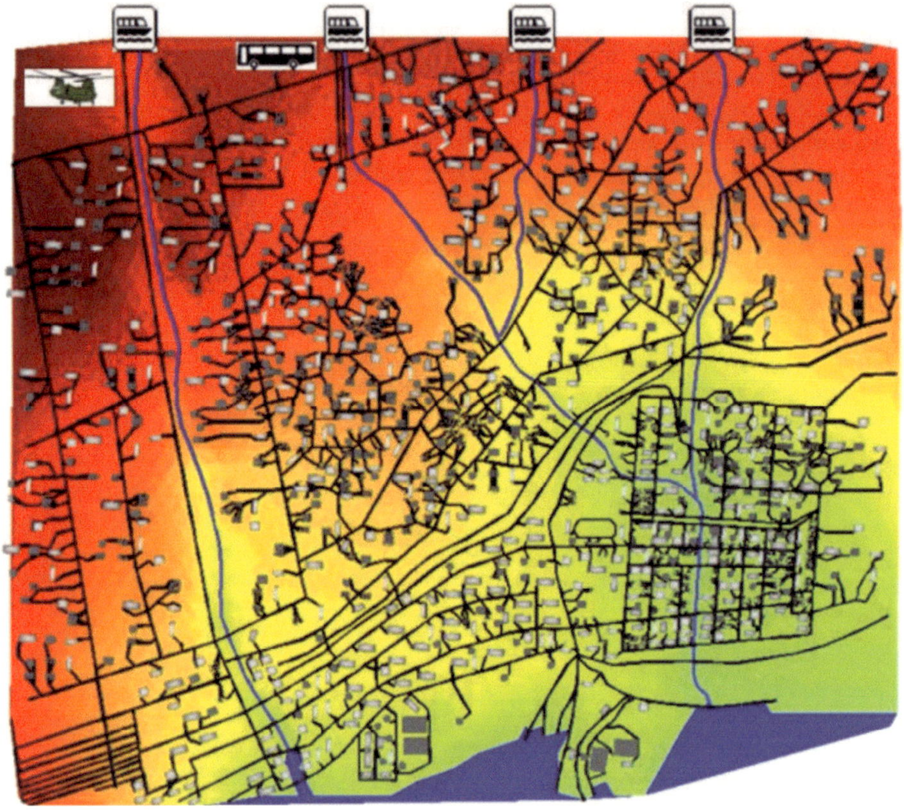

Fig. 5. City with bases under normal conditions

Preprocessing for shortest paths is done for all road waypoints for busses, all water waypoints for boats, and all sky waypoints for helicopters (Chandy & Mistra, 1982). This produces two matrices for each domain: a path matrix which indicates every waypoint one must traverse to go from any waypoint to another; and a distance matrix that indicates the distance between every pair of waypoints. The number of matrix lookups for a trip is the number of waypoints traversed on a path between the starting and ending waypoints. To begin, using the *path matrix*, cross reference the starting waypoint number as a row with the ending waypoint number as a column. This first lookup tells which waypoint to traverse first. In the same location in the *distance matrix*, the entry gives the distance traveled to the first waypoint. Next, lookup this new waypoint number in the path matrix as a row with the corresponding destination number as a column again, and iterate this procedure until the path matrix entry matches the destination.

In addition to preprocessing for the shortest paths, line-of-sight for helicopters is also preprocessed. Line-of-sight for boats and busses is not used, because they rely heavily on sensing road access and building content by direct use of waypoints (can be considered as tactile sensing). Helicopters, on the other hand are not in direct contact with roads, water, or buildings, thus, they require a line-of-sight mapping. For simplicity, line-of-sight can only observe waypoints that are in close proximity (less than 50 meters on the surface plane), and is restricted as the speed of the helicopter increases. Flying over roads and water, a helicopter can determine whether the surface is available for boats or busses. Flying over buildings, a helicopter passing slowly enough, can determine that individuals are in the buildings, provided they are at the buildings' observable points. The probability of spotting people is inversely proportional to the helicopter speed. The probability of spotting someone within the 50 meter range is one minus three-halves the current speed divided by the top speed of a helicopter. The top speed of every helicopter is given as 200 kilometers per hour.

2.3 Feature Three: Environment Observation Models

Model observations include road conditions, waterway conditions, and the number of people in a building. Road observations determine which roads are open to bus travel. Water observations determine which waterways are open for boat travel. Buildings observations include people of four types: injured, unsupplied, supplied, and dead.

At the start of the simulation, there are 20,000 stranded people in buildings, and for simplicity, they do not move unless rescued. All people are randomly placed as follows: first, a floor location is chosen and one to ten individuals are placed in that location, with an average of 5.5. Both selection processes are random using a uniform distribution. This two step process continues until all 20,000 people are allocated.

At the start of the simulation, the people are divided into three categories: supplied, unsupplied, and injured. There are no dead people at the start of the simulation. The simulation assumes that half of the locations are supplied and half are not. Also, 5% of the locations have an injured individual. Thus, there are about 10,000 supplied and 10,000 unsupplied individuals on average, and about 180 injured individuals (20000/5.5 x 0.05). The times for survival of unsupplied and injured individuals are selected from the following probability density functions. For unsupplied, a natural lognormal distribution is used, with the mean (m) = 3.9 (exp(3.9) = 50 hours) and the standard deviation (sd) = 0.11, providing a range of 30 to 72 hours. For injured, a normal distribution is used, with the m = 16 (hours) and sd = 7, providing a range 1 to 36 hours. Values calculated as less than zero hours for injured individuals are reset to one hour, thus giving the injured at least some minimal lifespan. Injured and unsupplied people are on a time clock and die if not reached in time.

There are two sets of values for each observation type. One is the actual state, and the other is known state. The known state values are initialized to assumed values. The road model assumes all roads are open, and the water model assumes all low lying areas are flooded and traversable by boat. The building model assumes the person quantities are unknown for every floor of every building until observed. Using the same procedure described above, buildings not yet searched are randomly populated with people that are missing (those not accounted for from the 20,000).

Time Constraints /Delays	*Boats*	*Busses*	*Rescue Copters*	*Survey Copters*
Floor Search	300 sec	200 sec	600 sec	n/a
Building Evacuation	40 sec/ person	20 sec/ person	120 sec/ person	n/a
Road Blocks	n/a	600 sec	n/a	n/a
Backtrack	n/a	60 sec	n/a	n/a
Bad Plan	n/a	10 sec/ plan	n/a	n/a
Drop Off People	300 sec	300 sec	300 sec	300 sec
Drop Off Supplies	n/a	n/a	300 sec	300 sec
Turn Around	n/a	30 sec	n/a	n/a
Building Submerged	120 sec	n/a	120 sec	n/a
On Base No Orders	1200 sec	1200 sec	1200 sec	1200 sec
Off Base No Orders	120 sec	120 sec	120 sec	120 sec
Reinitialize Plan	600 sec	600 sec	600 sec	600 sec

Table 1. Time Costs and Delays

The known model learns real model information by tactile and visual sensing. Tactile sensing of travel routes is accomplished by boats and busses by visiting waypoints. As boats and busses follow connections, they discover whether they are open. Surface travel routes are also viewed by helicopters. Helicopters flying over surface waypoints can see if they are water or land, and slower helicopters can see more distant waypoints (range is 100 meters in the surface plane). For this application, survey helicopters travel much slower and have a better probability of seeing waypoint conditions below than do high-speed rescue helicopters. The probability of seeing roads is the same as spotting people as described above.

Agent or Vehicle Actuators	*Boats*	*Busses*	*Rescue Copters*	*Survey Helicopters*
Purpose	Search Bldgs; Rescue People	Search Bldgs; Rescue People	Search Bldgs; Rescue People; Drop Supply	Survey Road and Water Access; Spot People; Drop Supplies
Travel speed	40 km/hr	50 km/hr	100 km/hr	45 km/hr
Move	Water	Road	Sky	Sky
Range	4 hrs	8 hrs	1.5 hrs	1.5 hrs
Capacity	8 people	50 people	10 people	n/a
Supplies	n/a	n/a	1 Drop	12 Drops

Table 2. Agent or Vehicle Actuators

Tactile and visual sensing is also implemented for observing people. People are assumed to not travel without the aid of a rescue vehicle. Visual sensing is done only by helicopters. People can be spotted, but their type cannot be identified, such as injured, unsupplied, etc.

Tactile observations are done by searching buildings. Boats, busses, or rescue helicopters search a building on the first visit. They identify the occupancy of each building floor, and as many people as possible will be evacuated. Search times within buildings, and other time costs are shown in Table 1. Rescue capacities and other possible actions for each vehicle type are identified in Table 2. In summary, values with incomplete initial information include blocks in roads and water, and building contents.

2.4 Feature Four: Multi-Agent Planning

For S&R operations, multiple agents can travel by roads, waterways, and air to survey surface routes, spot, supply, or rescue people in buildings. Each agent has a purpose, a travel speed, a set of movement waypoints, a refueling range, a passenger capacity, and can possibly drop supplies. These parameter values are shown in Table 2. Each vehicle is an agent, and each agent type: boats, busses, and survey and rescue helicopters have different options, depending on their current state and observed models (building content and movement paths). More specifically, the options available depend on the accumulation of observations for movement and building content, and the current agent's state in regards to its location, fuel capacity, supplies available, and open passenger seating. Otherwise the vehicle is planned to return to base. A set of actions is selected as either a stop location or specific building, depending on the vehicle. Boats and busses must first locate a stop, and then choose to go to the building with that stop area. Helicopters choose buildings directly. A plan is formed when enough actions are chosen in succession for each agent until that agent must return to base. The total number of vehicles used in the simulation is arbitrarily set to twenty. Through the optimization process, planners learn how many of each vehicle type to requisition within the overall limit of twenty.

Available actions depend on the vehicle type and state of the vehicle. Boats and busses can choose any boat or bus stop as a destination, respectively. Boat and bus stops can serve multiple buildings. Plans for agents also need to select which buildings at each stop to visit. It is assumed that a boat or bus does not leave a stop until they are full of passengers, or all buildings at that stop have been searched. Helicopters are categorized as rescue or survey type. Rescue helicopters can choose any single building for search and rescue, and they drop a single supply package when they search the first building that has people. Survey helicopters survey roads, and spot or supply people within buildings. All vehicles return to base when their fuel time is spent, when the vehicle is full of passengers, or in the case of the survey helicopters, their supplies have run out, (see Table 2).

As agent actions are taken, the environment responds with time penalties, which are determined by travel speed shown in Table 2, and other time delays as shown in Table 1. Plans are made based on known observation values described in the previous section. Each vehicle's plan is considered complete when a return to base is included in the plan. Planning beyond one round trip for a vehicle has proven fruitless, because the real model values differ greatly from assumed values for long-term plans.

3. Example

There are four main features described above that went into implementing the S&R model. The best way to show the impact of considering these features is through example results.

Each feature is exemplified below by showing results that pertain to that feature. Results are based on playing out sixty games using a planner that picks random actions for each plan. If an agent plan encounters conditions that prevent its completion, a random, feasible, extension to the plan is provided. The planning section of this chapter addresses planners that learn to make effective, more focused choices.

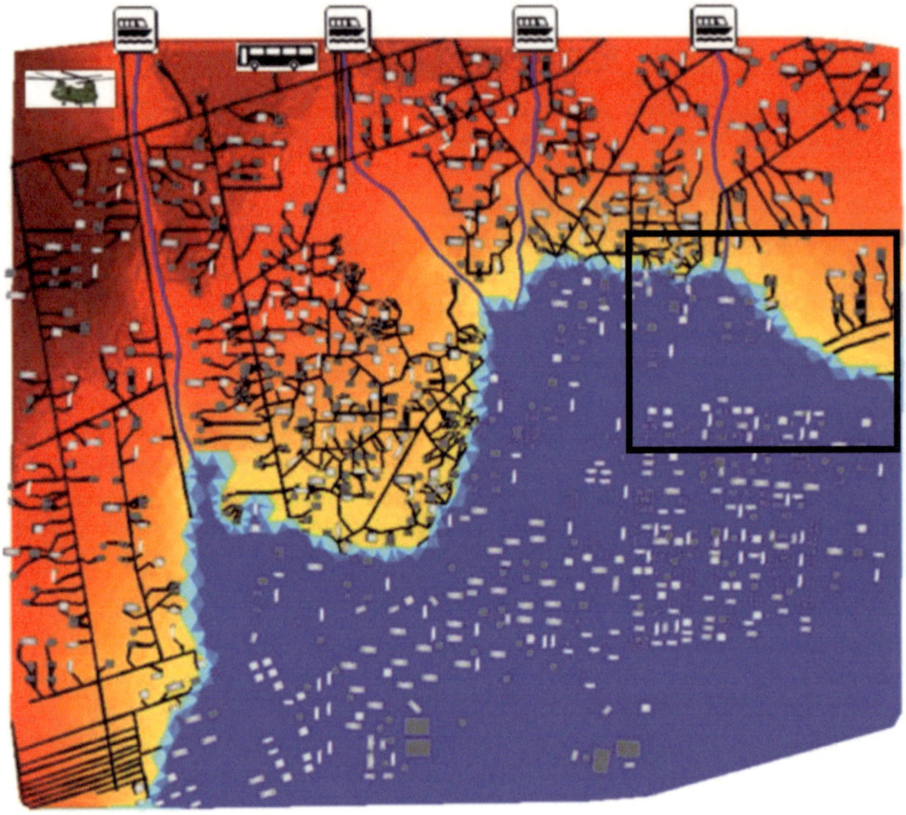

Fig. 6. City simulation example map

3.1 Feature One: Compact and Computable

To better understand the order of magnitude of this S&R problem, Figure 6 shows a top-down picture of the terrain model used. The city is approximately 4 km x 5 km. Normally, processing and computation is done over the terrain mapped in Figure 6, instead of the waypoints and connections derived from the CTDB data and illustrated in Figures 2, 3 and 4. Using waypoints and connections reduces the complexity of the space substantially by eliminating the waste of computing over every cubic meter of ground and space, and instead, computing action paths based on connected waypoint types. Within these 20 square km, there are 20,000 stranded people, twenty agents of various types, an initially unknown water level, road blocks, building locations where people require rescue, and bases to drop off people. Specifically, there are 3649 buildings with over 12,000 floor locations, 2135 bus stops, over 900 boat stops, four upstream boat bases, and a bus and helicopter base. There are over 31,000 total waypoints for this application, instead of millions of cubic meters to compute on.

A cross-sectional view is shown in Figure 7. This view shows all waypoints and connections for a small grid section of the city, shown by the small square section outlined in Figure 6. Sky waypoints are shown on top and building connections, roads and waterways are shown below.

3.2 Feature Two: Very Fast Simulation

Due to the shortest path lookup tables described in Section 1.2, single actions for a plan are not waypoint to waypoint, but from origin to destination. This feature allows for very fast simulation speeds. The computation times are results from software developed in Matlab® particularly for this simulation, and are performed on a MacBook Pro running Matlab in a Microsoft Windows XP BootCamp environment. Complete S&R operations were run in an average of 7.66 minutes computer time, corresponding to 5525 minutes on average of real-world simulation time. That is a speed up of over a 700 times.

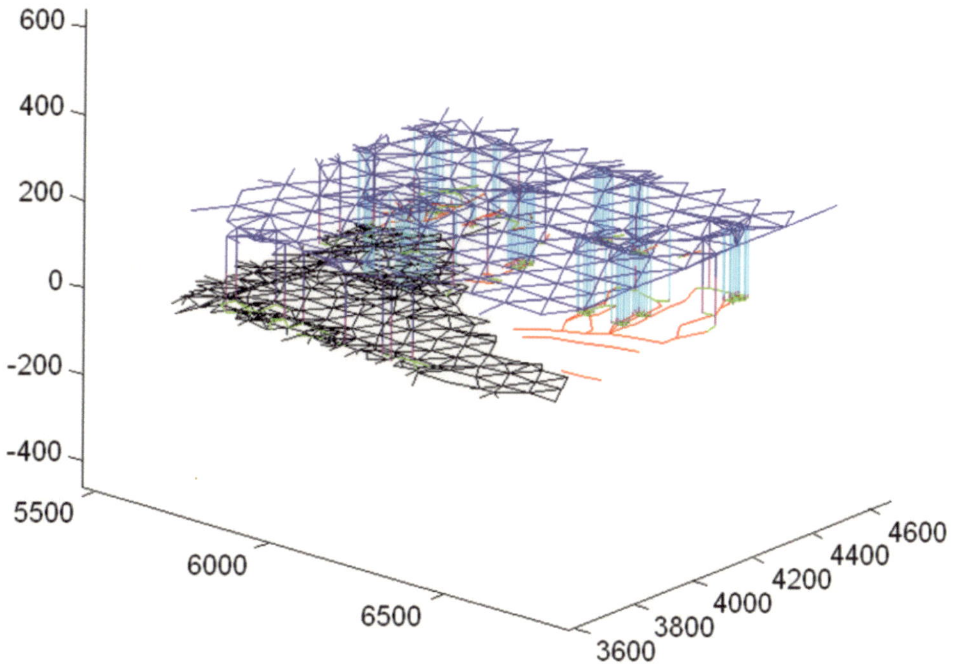

Fig. 7. Waypoint Connectivity

3.3 Feature Three: Environment Observation Models

Over the course of one example game, Figure 8 shows the changes in the observation models. The figure shows the accumulation of route information via both land and water, and the proportion of buildings searched and cleared, and people rescued over time.

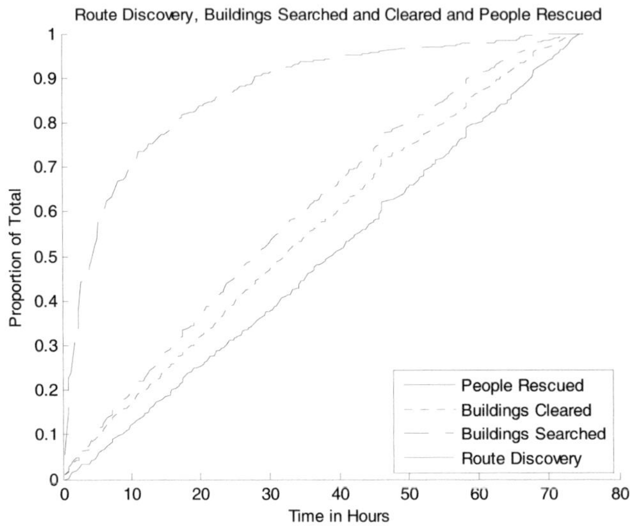

Fig. 8. Observation Models

3.4 Feature Four: Multi-Agent Planning

Over the course of sixty example games, there were twenty agents used in each game of various types. Over the course of an entire game, agents had plans of average length equal to about sixteen thousand visited waypoints. That is over nineteen million traversed waypoints for each of the twenty vehicles in sixty games.

4. Planning

The preceding sections of this chapter examined modeling a flooded city for a search and rescue operation. This section examines the development of an automated planner that directs the operation effectively and efficiently. Much as a human planner, the automated planner discussed here improves its performance through practicing many simulated search and rescue operations. To explore a variety of planning parameters, multiple automated planners compete against one another in tournaments. Characteristics shared by successful planners in one tournament are passed on to a new generation of planners in the next tournament.

4.1 Problem Domain

The search and rescue (S&R) problem is representative of a class of problems that has been difficult for automated planning systems. These problems share the following characteristics:

- Partially observable; the state of the environment is only partially known.
- Very large state-space representations ($> 10^{100}$)

- Finite but large set of available actions (> 10^3)
- Known state transitions (possibly stochastic)
- Finite set of measurable features
- A finite set of goals

Planning problems for large partially observable complex environments highlight three challenges in particular: (1) balancing exploration of the environment for new information against exploitation of obtained information to directly achieve goals; (2) determining where to assign credit in choosing actions, especially for long action sequences; and (3) providing a scalable framework, where the speed of the simulation is minimally affected by the number of agents or actions available.

In a partially observable environment, balancing exploration and exploitation is very important to the success of a complex mission. Several approaches have been tried. Reinforcement learning systems use temporal difference to consider action strings of length greater than one, but fail to deliver on plans that take a large number of steps and where the state-action pairs exceed 10^{20} combinations (Levinson et al., 1991), (Tesauro, 2002), (LaValle, 2006). Learning classifier systems focus on longer string plans, but usually use discrete rule sets and have not been tested on problems of the size presented here (over 10^{100} states) (Velagic, 2006). In the application presented, planning lengths are long, dozens of actions per iteration, and thousands over the course of one complete simulation. Also, uncertainty in the initial state is large, thus the search for a better planner requires generalization over the state space instead of formulating specific state-action pair rewards.

The credit assignment problem is also important in planning for large partially observable environments. Planning has three phases: generating, executing, and evaluating plans. How to merge these three aspects into the planning cycle will be described in detail. The form of the solution is important in answering many questions related to assigning credit: How often should the planner re-plan? How often should the model be updated before re-planning? How will the different types of agents cooperate? What features of the environment are important factors in developing a good plan?

4.2 Approach

The approach for developing an effective automated planner has five tiers, from the inner cycle of dynamic planning, executing, and evaluating plans for planners and agents, through the highest level of adapting planners' strategies using tournament play of multiple games. Figure 9 illustrates this ADP&E implementation framework.

The core cycle (1) is concerned with agent action and environment response., Individual agent action sequences are planned, executed, and evaluated in the model environment, over many cycles, and for all agents in the correct time sequence. At the second level, agents execute a given plan. Third, the planner is the conceiver and conductor of a plan. A planner has a set of parameters that determine its choice of planned actions, and how often to re-plan those actions. Fourth, a game is a theatre where action sequences can be executed in the real model environment. The final goal state must be achievable, because human intervention is prohibited in this framework and a game only completes when the final goal is achieved. Fifth, tournaments of games are arranged, so that planner parameter settings can improve over the course of many tournaments. Through evaluating each planner's progress, and modifying the best planner's parameters, planners can improve their effectiveness.

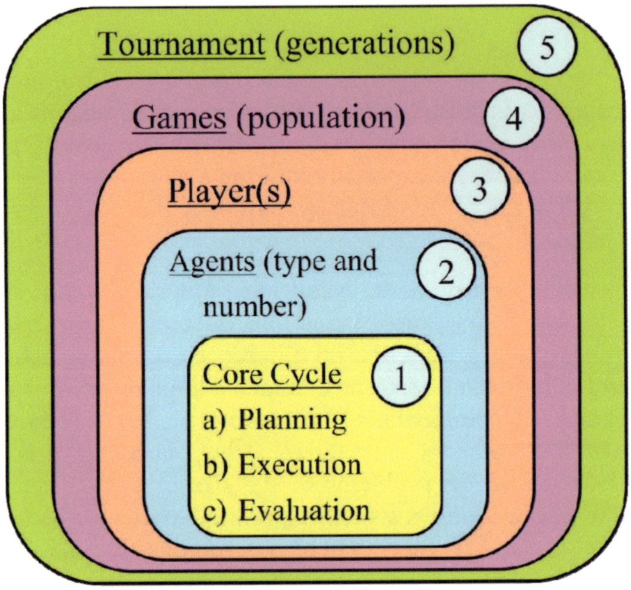

Fig. 9. ADP&E Implementation Framework

All five tiers are interdependent in the time domain. In a typical computing environment, the core cycle builds plans and performs action-response simulations within milliseconds of computation time. Agent operations of many planned actions are performed within seconds. A planner completes many necessary operations to an endgame within minutes. A game set for one tournament generation takes hours. A completed tournament, where planners' parameters converge on a successful strategy takes several days. The computation times are results from software developed in Matlab® for this paper and are provided to indicate relative scales.

4.2.1 Tier One: Core Cycle

At the heart of this approach is the core planning cycle. Figure 10 illustrates this cycle. The core cycle has three components: (1) *plan-generator* (PG); (2) *plan-executor* (PX); and (3) *plan-evaluator* (PV). The plan-generator strings together individual actions to form plans for all agents. The plan-executor executes the planned actions in time order for a period that completes a single task for one of the agents. A task is considered as a search and rescue operation for a single building.. The plan-evaluator evaluates how well the remaining plan will execute given new information acquired as a result of the partially executed plan.

The three core-cycle components share three internal objects. These three objects are *plans*, *models*, and *expectations*. Plans are generated by PG, executed by PX and evaluated by PV repeatedly until a simulation is complete. Models are used in PG to predict future states, are used in PE to observe the real environment states, and are used in PV to observe whether expectations have been met. The models used in PG and PV are virtual-state models, which initially contain only part of the information in the real-state model used in PX. The real-state model is where a plan is executed. Virtual-state models do not include many real state values until observed. Expectations measure how well a plan achieves a desired goal. Expectations are predicted in PG and compared to actual progress in PV. Each agent has an expectation for its plan. If, during execution, expectations are met to a prescribed degree, a plan is retained; otherwise a plan is reformulated in PG. The motivation to retain a plan is a tradeoff of planning-time verses the risk associated with continuing the current plan. This tradeoff parameter is called risk aversion and is part of the planner that will be discussed in detail later.

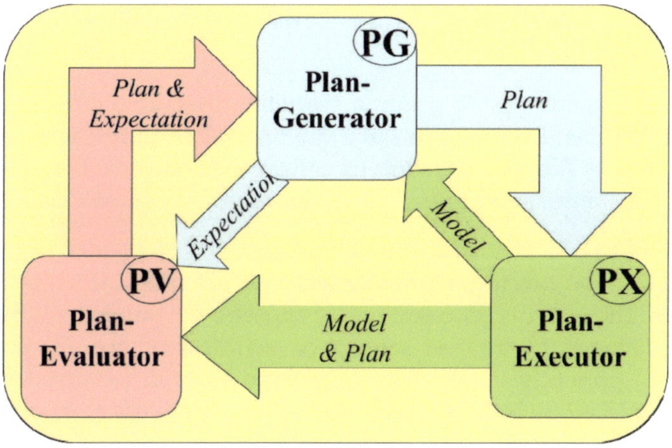

Fig. 10. Planning Core Cycle

4.2.2 Tier Two: Agents

Agents are the instruments of the plans. Agents possess various actuators and sensors. For the S&R problem, the agents are the vehicles used in the model environment. Tables 2 and 3 illustrate all the agent categories and their associated characteristics. Table 1 shows the agents' temporal parameters. Each agent has an individual plan, a timestamp, a location, a fuel level, a passenger list, a speed, and a remaining time constraint.

4.2.3 Tier Three: Planners

The planner has a set of control parameters that affect generating, executing, and evaluating plans. Each action within a plan is chosen according to the planner's characteristics. The planner's characteristics are defined by parameters used in four areas: (1) model update time, (2) risk aversion for re-planning, (3) numbers of each agent type given limited resources, and (4) the nine decision features described in this section.

For partially-observable environments, the model update parameter is paramount. It determines how frequently the virtual-state model is updated to more closely resemble the true real-state model of the environment. The information in these updates comes from the sensor input of the agents. This refresh enables the planner better to predict results of future actions. For this application, the model update parameter was not adapted but set to a relatively small time increment. Specifically, every time a vehicle returned to base, all agents were required to report all of their newly acquired sensor data (about 20 minutes real-world time). This assumption was necessary, because results showed that not updating the virtual model frequently enough caused worse results than randomly searching with continual updates.

Another important planner parameter is risk aversion, r, (0 <= r <= 1). Risk aversion trades time required to plan against the desire to re-plan. This competition is based on whether a plan is meeting expectations as evaluated in PV. When the risk aversion parameter is high, the tendency is to re-plan often, when risk aversion is low, the tendency is to stick to the current plan and thereby avoid the time for re-planning. Specifically, if the risk aversion parameter is set to one, then expectations must be met completely or the planner will re-plan. If the risk aversion parameter is set to zero, then the planner will not re-plan unless the agent no longer has a plan.

The numbers of each agent type to use in a partially observable problem is unknown and therefore made adaptable. Experiments have shown that an unrestricted number of agents leads to minimal loss of life and therefore trivializes the problem. Therefore, as in the real-world, resources are limited, and in this particular case, only twenty agents of all types are allowed.

Observable factors in the execution environment that are relevant to the planning process are called features. The nine decision features to choose a destination are: (1) action distance, (2) nearest base distance, (3) nearest same type vehicle distance, (4) people present, (5) injured present, (6) presently unsupplied, (7) people spotted, (8) preceived survival time, and (9) previously visited by boat or bus. These features were used because they are quickly calculable from the environment for each possible action and seem relevant to choosing actions. At each time step an agent has thousands of potential actions (3649 buildings) to choose from, and plans may have action sequence lengths in the dozens. This makes a tree search method impractical. Nor does one want to restrict an agent to follow a deterministic rule set based on any specific feature or combination of features, because that would severely limit the search space of all possible plans. Therefore, a new method was developed that does not restrict the search space. It combines a Monte Carlo (MC) method of choosing actions and weighted Beta distributions (WBDs) (Vaccaro & Guest, 2008) for representing decision preferences.

For our purposes, MC represents taking a random choice from many possibilities, and the WBDs represent the density functions of actions from which to make those choices. Each WBD required for each feature and agent type has three parameters: w, α, and β. The probability mass function of the WBD is as follows:

$$f\left(x; w, \alpha, \beta\right) = w \frac{\Gamma\left(\alpha+\beta\right)}{\Gamma\left(\alpha\right)\Gamma\left(\beta\right)} x\left(1-x\right)^{\beta-1} \tag{1}$$

where α is the alpha parameter, β is the beta parameter, w is the weight parameter, x is a vector of feature values corresponding to all possible actions, and Γ is the Gamma function (Nadarajah & Kotz, 2007).

MC implements taking a random choice from many possibilities and the WBDs represent the probability density functions of choosing particular actions from among those choices. The WBD for each feature and agent type has three required parameters. Boats and busses use only the first eight of the nine decision features listed above, while both helicopter types use all nine features. Thus, there are 34 WBDs required, and thus, 102 WBD parameters for this S&R problem. The three WBD parameters are weight, alpha and beta; all initial values are randomly chosen. For each agent, each weight is greater than or equal to zero and all weights sum to one. The alpha and beta parameters are restricted to be greater than zero and give a variety of possible distributions, as shown in the results section. The reason WBDs are used is that they do not restrict the search space if the initial parameters are correctly set. For instance, if all WBDs have alpha and beta parameters set to {1, 1}, then the probability of selecting any action is equally likely at every time step, independent of the weightings.

The process of using MC and WBD together is as follows. First, for each agent under consideration, a mass function is calculated for each feature type for all possible actions (equation above without weight w). The mass function is a vector of length equal to the number of possible actions and each mass represents its particular influence in action selection. Before w can be applied, each mass function is normalized to sum to one, to represent a probability mass function. Next, each mass function is multiplied by the corresponding weight (w) assigned to that agent and feature. Finally, all resulting mass functions corresponding to each agent are summed. These new mass functions, which holds the accumulated influence of all features for each agent, is normalized and expressed as a distributed mass function (0, 1) to form a reference lookup table for each action. At this point the selection process begins. First, a random number is chosen from a uniform density (0, 1), and this random variable chooses the action by looking up the corresponding action linked to that number in the distributed mass function table. Note that, the greater a feature's weight, the greater its influence, and the BD settings focus on influential feature values.

In summary, a planner has a risk aversion parameter and four parameters that represent the numbers of each vehicle type. Since the boat and bus agents use eight of the nine decision features, there are 24 WBD parameters (8 weights, and 16 alpha and beta) for both boat and bus type vehicles. Since helicopters use all nine features, there are 27 WBD parameters (9 weights, and 18 alpha and beta) for both survey and rescue helicopter vehicles. Thus, the total parameters for a planner number 107 = 1 + 4 + 24 + 24 + 27 + 27.

4.2.4 Tier Four: Games

The fourth tier in this implementation framework is games. For this S&R application, a game is the complete evacuation of the city. The game level is where results are accumulated to determine the effectiveness of a planner. Results include the planner parameters described above, and how many residents died in the S&R operation.

4.2.5 Tier Five: Tournaments

The fifth tier is tournament play. The tournament tier compares the accumulated results from all planners in a generation. For the S&R application, each generation is a sixty game tournament with twenty planners competing. Each simulation run uses a different randomly initialized environment. Each planner plays three games to determine its effectiveness in generalizing for partially observable environments. The score for each planner is the maximum number of dead residents for all three games. Obviously, a low score is better. Improving the planners' capabilities is adapted using a genetic algorithm. The genetic algorithm follows these rules:

The top 4 performing planners return for next generation

Next 4, mutate decision feature weights {34 parameters in all}, vehicle number {4} and risk aversion {1}

Next 4, mutate the BD parameters {68 parameters}

Next 4, crossover decision feature weights {34 parameters}, vehicle number {4} and risk {1}

Next 4, crossover the BD parameters {68 parameters}

The weights, risk aversion, and vehicle number are mutated differently. Each weight is adjusted by adding a random variable selected from a normal distribution with mean zero and standard deviation 0.2. The weight is adjusted not to be negative or exceed one. The weights are then renormalized to sum to one.

Each risk aversion parameter has a 50% probability of being changed. If selected to change, it is adjusted using a normal distribution with mean zero and standard deviation 0.05; not to be negative or exceed one. Each number of vehicle type parameter is also adjusted with a 50% probability. Each vehicle type has the probability of incrementing or decrementing the number by one, provided the number is greater than zero and the numbers of all vehicle types sum to twenty.

Mutation of the BD parameters is a special case, because the values must only be greater than zero. Thus, a log normal density function is used to pick the adjustment in the alpha and beta parameters. The mean of the density function chosen is 2 over the generation number and the standard deviation is the square root of the mean. This lognormal density produces an adjustment in the BD parameters to be very large at first and decrease with each subsequent generation. Experimental results have shown this to be prudent in providing enough variability in the BD densities.

For all crossovers, a planner is picked based on how well it did with respect to other planners. Planners with better than average performance are put in a pool with probability of selection proportional to their score above the average. Each selected planner is combined with each top planner using crossover. The new planners are initially a copy of each selected top planner. Crossover is performed by cycling through each parameter and giving a 50% chance of acquiring a parameter from the randomly chosen planner paired with the top planner.

The genetic algorithm runs for many tournament generations until the planners' parameters show some degree of convergence, or when the capability of the planners seems to show little progress in improvement.

5. Simulation Example

The process of developing an effective planner is better understood by describing the example implemented for this application. Note that in Table 1 helicopters hovering over buildings take far longer to search buildings than busses or boats, and busses are by far the quickest. Busses evacuate the buildings the quickest per person, because they do not have to deal with water or hovering in midair. Busses are the only vehicle that experience problems with road blocks and have additional time penalties associated with making plans to travel on unknown roads. Only helicopters drop off supplies.

Agent or Vehicle Sensors	*Boats*	*Busses*	*Rescue Helicopters*	*Survey Helicopters*
Route Access via Trial	YES	YES	n/a	n/a
Route Access via Sight	NO	NO	LIMITED	YES
Survivors via Search	YES	YES	YES	NO
Survivors via Search	NO	NO	LIMITED	YES

Table 3. Agent or Vehicle Sensors

Decision features one, two and three are measurements of distance. These decision features have a continuous range of values (i.e., zero to 6500 meters). Note that "Action Distance" is for a particular leg of the trip, and "Nearest Vehicle Distance" pertains only to same type vehicles.

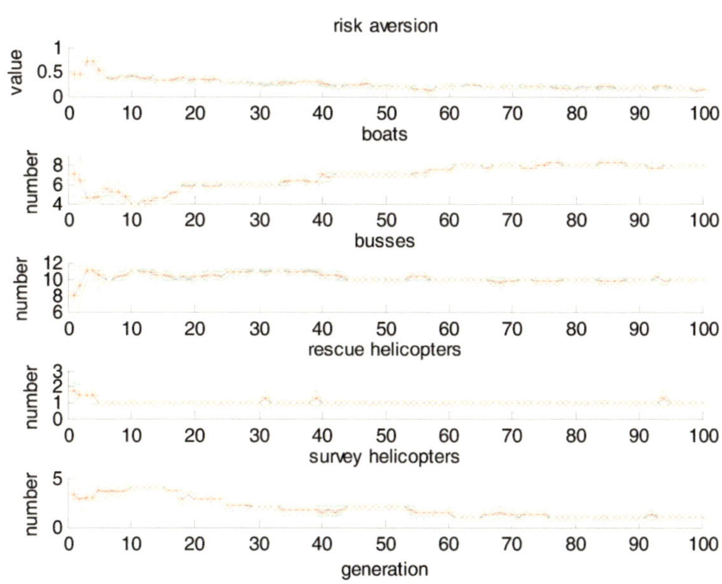

Fig. 11. Risk Aversion and Number of Vehicle Types

Since many stops and buildings are initially unsearched and have varying numbers of people left behind in a building once searched, decision features four, five, and six are multi-valued. For unsearched buildings, a value of negative one is used and for searched buildings the range of values used is distributed as $\log_{10}(PLB+1)$, where PLB is the number of people left behind. For feature seven, all stops and building locations are assigned zero unless people are spotted. For instance, if a helicopter spots a person at a building, then the value assigned to that building is one. However, for stops it is different. For a stop, the fraction of buildings in which people have been spotted at that stop is used instead. For feature eight, survival time is the projected amount of time available for unsupplied or injured people before they die. An estimated time is given for all stops and buildings, then, as people are discovered, their projected lifespan time is used to update the feature. It is presumed that all unsupplied and injured people will die within 75 hours. Thus 75 hours is assumed for all unsearched locations. This feature value will change with time. People not retrieved in time will have a negative lifespan and will be dead if their building was previously searched, and presumed dead for an unsearched building. Buildings where supplies are dropped add 48 hours to the life span for unsupplied people in those buildings. Injured people must be rescued to survive, because supplies do not extend their lifetime.

Feature nine, is a simple binary value. If a boat or bus has searched a building, then the value is one, otherwise the feature value is zero.

All feature values are normalized to be between zero and one. For decision features one, two and three, the largest diagonal distance across the city is used to normalize the decision features (6500 meters). All other feature values are normalized by subtracting the minimum and dividing by the range. For example, for feature eight, all values are kept between -100 and 100, thus, 100 is added and the result is divided by 200.

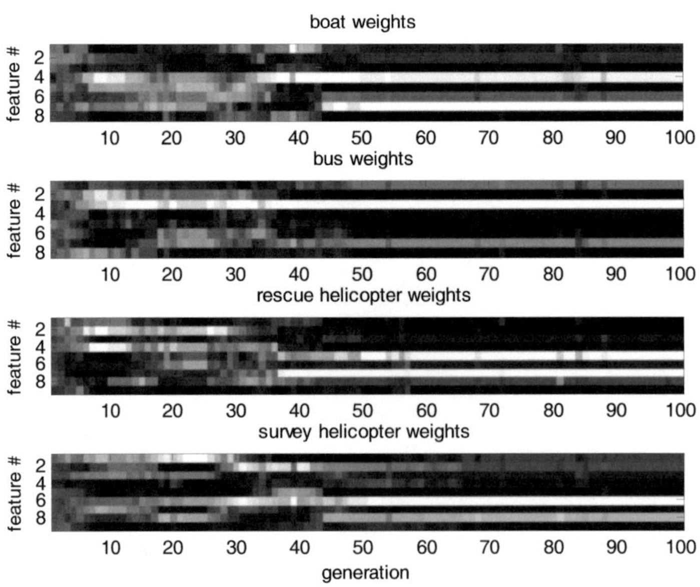

Fig. 12. Decision Feature Weights

The number of vehicles of each type is not predetermined, but the total is limited to twenty vehicles, with a minimum of one vehicle of each type to ensure that the game will run to completion. A game run completes with the evacuation of all buildings.

6. Results

The results are in five areas: (1) risk aversion, (2) number of vehicle types, (3) decision feature weights, (4) decision feature beta density functions, and (5) resulting evacuation progress in saving lives. All results are for 40 generations of tournament play.

The risk aversion parameter is used to trade off time to plan against failure of the current plan to meet expectations. Time to plan is fixed at ten minutes of simulated time per plan per agent. Expectations are based on a point system where an agent is given three points per injured person rescued, two points per unsupplied person, one point per supplied person, and zero points per dead person rescued. The evolution of the risk aversion parameter is shown in the top graph of Figure 11. The final converged value is around 0.25, thus, if a plan achieved just 25% of its expected points, replanning was not triggered. In another experiment, a 20 minute penalty for replanning produced a zero risk aversion level, meaning the time to plan was too costly to ever re-plan unless there was no way to proceed with the current plan.

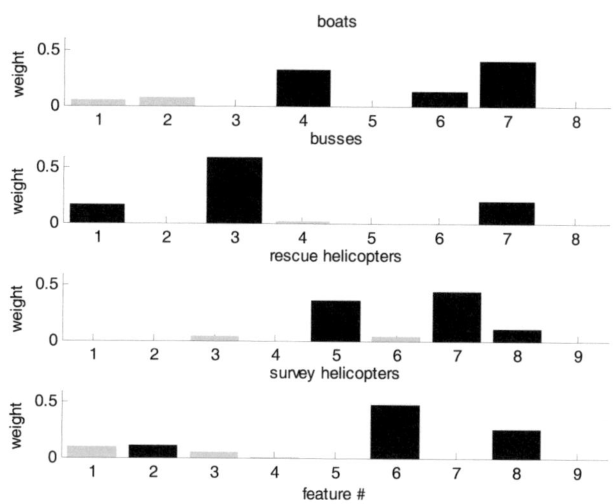

Fig. 13. Final Decision Feature Weights

The numbers of vehicle type are shown in the four lower graphs of Figure 11. In later generations, boats number around seven, busses around ten, rescue helicopters around one, and survey helicopters around two.

The decision feature weights are shown in Figures 12 and 13. Figure 12 presents the change in weights over tournament generations. Note that in all image figures (12, 14, 15, 16, and 17), that lighter shades indicate higher values. Figure 13 illustrates the final weights observed in generation forty. The three black bars indicate the three largest weights. Also, that the feature numbers on the left of Figure 12, and on the bottom of Figure 13 are the same as displayed in Figure 11.

The decision feature beta density functions shown in Figures 14, 15, 16, 17 and 18 correspond to the black bars in Figure 6. This points out the decision features that exhibited the highest influence. Figures 14 through 17 shows the density functions across all forty generations, while Figure 18 shows the final density functions. Note that sometimes the shading goes dark in Figures 14 through 17. This indicates that the weight was low for that generation (Figure 12) and had little influence. Figure 18 provides a good summary of influential features. Each graph directly corresponds to a black bar in Figure 13.

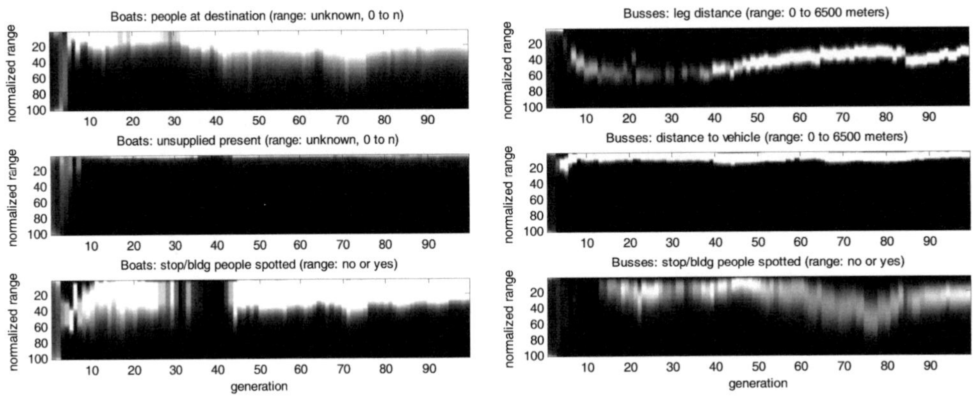

Fig. 14 and 15. Boat Features Weighted Beta Densities and Bus Features Weighted Beta Densities

The feature densities for boats are in the top row of graphs of Figure 18. The first graph indicates that since boats are slow, they tend to take tasks nearby. The second graph indicates that boats are also faster at searching buildings than helicopters, so they are sent to buildings that need searching. The third graph indicates that it is better for a boat to go to a building that has enough supply time, and therefore fewer dead.

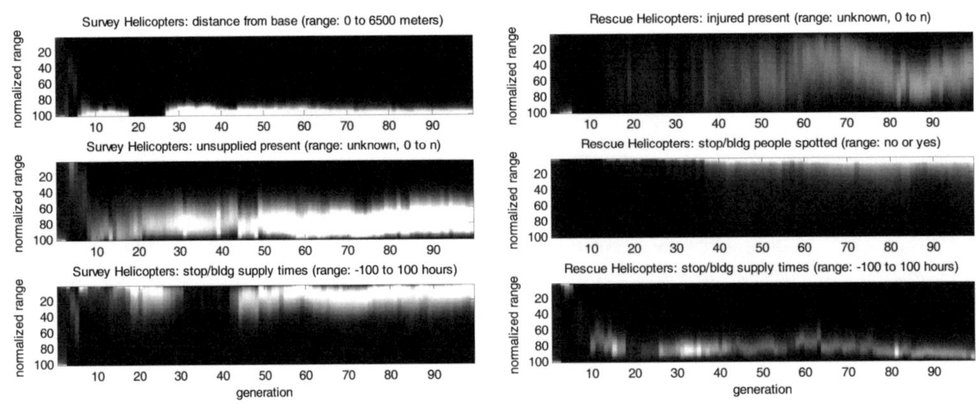

Fig. 16 and 17. Rescue Copter Features Weighted Beta Densities and Survey Copter Features Weighted Beta Densities

The feature densities for busses are in the second row of graphs in Figure 18. The first graph strongly indicates a need to choose actions near other busses. Since busses encounter road blocks due to trees and water, staying near other busses increases the chances of finding an open path. The second and third graphs in row two indicate a slight additional preference to go where few people are injured and where people have not been spotted.

The feature densities for rescue helicopters are in the third row of graphs in Figure 18. The three graphs indicate a preference to go to buildings where people are injured, where no one has been spotted, and where people still have supply time remaining.

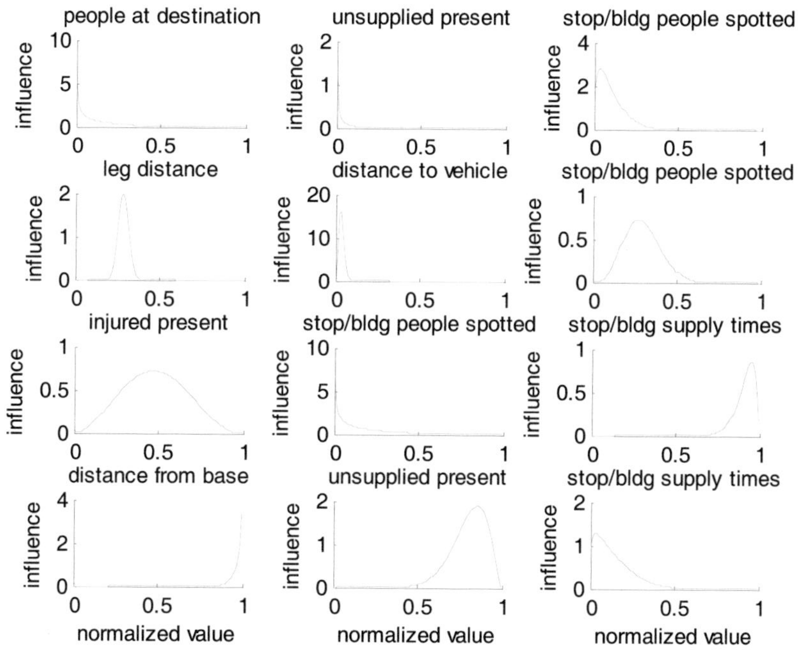

Fig. 18. Largest Feature Weighted Beta Densities

The feature densities for survey helicopters are in the final row of graphs of Figure 18. The three graphs indicate a preference to go far from the base, to go where people are not injured, and to go where people require supplies. Since the busses cannot go far from the base due to water levels, it makes a lot of sense for helicopters to supply people far from the base first.

The evacuation progress of the top performering planners is shown in Figure 19. Evacuation progress improves drastically over the first few generations and then slowly after that.

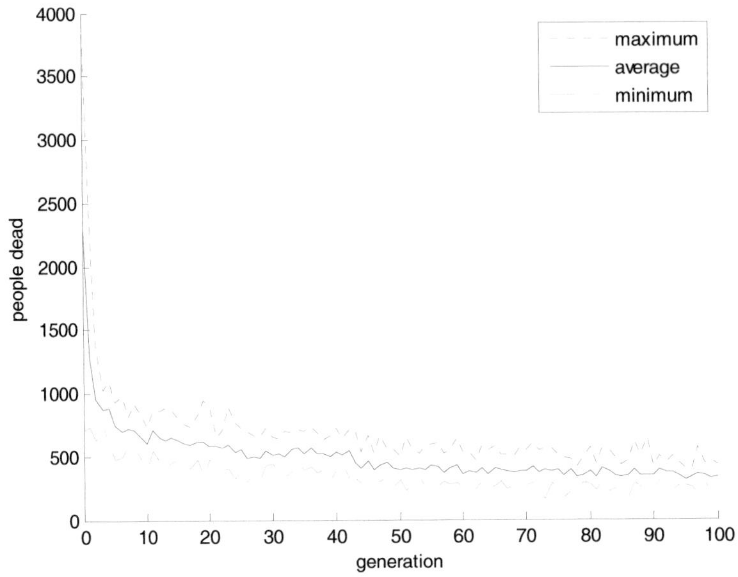

Fig. 19. Evacuation Progress of Top Four Performers

7. Conclusions

The chapter presented a three main advances: (1) a modeling approach for generating an urban terrain model from a Compact Terrain DataBase (CTDB) for computer-simulation of a search and rescue (S&R) operation, (2) a implementation strategy for integrating the model into an autonomous dynamic planning and execution (ADP&E) framework for gaming simulations, and (3) an evolutionary strategy for using simulation results to improve the ability of the planner. This approach is not considered an optimal strategy given that the approach has only been applied to a partially observable S&R operation described here. Many advances can be made to improve the generalization of this approach to more problems with multiple planners.

8. References

Witte, T.; *A survey of 3-D urban mapping and visualization capabilities from an army perspective*, Proceedings of the ISPRS Joint Conference, V. XXXVI, March, 2005.

Chandy, K. M., Mistra J.; *Distributed computation on graphs: shortest path algorithms*, Communications of the ACM, V. 25, No. 11, November, 1982, pp. 833-837.

Isenburg, M., Liu, Y., Shewchuk, J., & Snoeyink, J.; *Streaming computation of Delaunay triangulations*, ACM Transactions on Graphics 25(3), July 2006, pp. 1049-1056.

Levinson, R., Hsu, F. H., Schaeffe, J., Marsland, T. A., & Wilkins, D. E.; *The role of chess in artificial-intelligence research*, ICCA Journal, V. 14, N. 3, 1991, pp. 153-161.

Tesauro, G.; *Programming backgammon using self-teaching neural nets*, Artificial Intelligence, V. 134, 2002, pp. 181-199.

LaValle, S. M.; *Planning Algorithms*, Book: Cambridge University Press, 2006.

Velagic, J., Lacevic, B., Osmic, N.; *Efficient Path Planning Algorithm for Mobile Robot Navigation with a Local Minima Problem Solving*, International Conference on Industrial Technology, December, 2006, pp. 2325-2330.

Vaccaro, J., Guest, C.; *Automated Dynamic Planning and Execution for a Partially Observable Game Model: Tsunami City Search and Rescue*, World Congress on Computational Intelligence (WCCI'08), June 2008.

Nadarajah, S., Kotz, S.; *Multitude of beta distributions with applications*, Statistics: A Journal of Theoretical and Applied Statistics, Volume 41, Issue 2 April 2007, Pages 153-179.

APPLICATIONS OF SOFT COMPUTIONG IN ENGINEERING PROBLEMS

Hitoshi Furuta, Koichiro Nakatsu and Hiroshi Hattori
Department of Informatics, Kansai University, Takatsuki, Osaka 569-1095, Japan
furuta@res.kutc.kansai-u.ac.jp, inside2@sc.kutc.kansai-u.ac.jp, hattori@sc.kutc.kansai-u.ac.jp

Keywords: Artificial Intelligence, Adaboost, Damage Detection, Fuzzy Logic, Genetic Algorithm, GMDH, Life-Cycle Cost, Maintenance Program, Restoration Scheduling.

1. Introduction

Recently, great attention has been paid to soft computing technology, because of its applicability and easiness of computation in engineering problems. This chapter introduces several applications of the soft computing in various real engineering problems. First, a new optimal restoration scheduling method is described, which was developed for damaged road networks by using Genetic Algorithm (GA). The method can propose an early restoration plan for lifeline systems after earthquake disasters. Here, two issues are focused on, the first of which is such an allocation problem that which groups will restore which disaster places, and the second is such a scheduling problem what order is the best for the restoration. In order to solve the two problems simultaneously, GA is applied, because it has been proven to be very powerful in solving combinatorial problems. However, road networks after earthquake disasters have an uncertain environment, that is, the actual restoring process should be performed by considering various uncertainties simultaneously. Therefore, GA Considering Uncertainty (GACU) was developed to treat various uncertainties involved.
Next, an optimal maintenance planning of bridge structures using multi-objective genetic algorithm is described, which can provide several practical scheduling candidates that the bridge owner can select by considering the situation and constraints.
A structural health monitoring system is introduced, which can treat the changes of systems and environments. By adapting to the environment, it is not necessary to prepare any previous knowledge and examination for the underlying structures and environment. In other words, it is not necessary to use a precise modelling and analysis method before conducting the health monitoring. In the system, both Adaboost and GMDH (Group Method of Data Handling) are used for the learning and compared by paying attention to the accuracy of prediction.

In order to establish a rational maintenance program for structures, it is necessary to collect enough data about the material and structural characteristics and to evaluate the structural damage in a quantitative manner. However, it is difficult to avoid the subjectivity of inspectors when visual data are used for the evaluation of damage or deterioration. The method can evaluate the damage condition of existing structures by using the visual information given by digital photos. It is based upon such new technologies as image processing, photo-grammetry, pattern recognition, and artificial intelligence.

2. Optimal Restoration Scheduling of Damaged Road Networks Using Genetic Algorithm

The purpose of this research is to propose an early restoration for lifeline systems after earthquake disasters. Here, two issues are focused on, the first of which is such an allocation problem that which groups will restore which disaster places, and the second is such a scheduling problem what order is the best for the restoration. In order to solve the two problems simultaneously, Genetic Algorithm (GA) is applied, because it has been proven to be very powerful in solving combinatorial problems. However, road networks after earthquake disasters have an uncertain environment, that is, the actual restoring process should be performed by considering various uncertainties simultaneously. GA Considering Uncertainty (GACU) can treat various uncertainties involved, but it is difficult to obtain the schedule which has robustness. In this study, an attempt is made to develop a decision support system of the optimal restoration scheduling by using the improved GACU.

2.1 Genetic Algorithm Considering Uncertainty

Here, it is assumed that a road network is damaged, in which multiple portions are suffered from damage so that it cannot function well. The objective of this study is the realization of quick restoration of the lifeline system. It is intended to determine the optimal allocation of restoring teams and optimal scheduling of restoring process. Then, the following conditions should be taken into account [1] [2]:

1. The optimal allocation of restoring team, optimal scheduling of restoring process, and optimal selection of restoring method must be determined simultaneously.
2. A portion of the road network is suffered from several kinds of damage that have a hierarchical relation in time.

As an example of restoration, a road network is considered, which has 164 nodes as shown in Figure 1. This model corresponds to an area damaged by the 1995 Kobe earthquake. For this road network, the following restoration works are necessary to recover the function:

1. work (A): work to clear the interrupted things : 38 sites (1 - 38)
2. work (B) : work to restore the roads : 50 sites (1 - 50)

Then, the limitation and restriction of each work should be considered, for instance, work (B) should be done after work (A). Work (B) consists of the following three works; work to repair the roads, work to reinforce the roads and work to rebuild the roads. The waiting places of restoring teams for work (A) and work (B) are shown by the number A (1-8) and B (1-8), respectively.

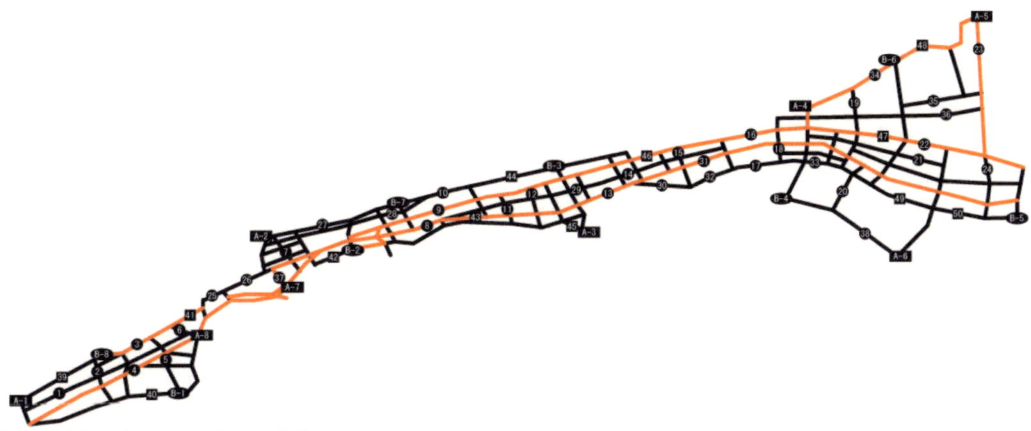

Fig. 1. Road network model

2.2 Restoration Scheduling

Weighting factors are prescribed for the links with damage, which are denoted by w_i (i=1~n_L). n_L is the total number of damaged links. Then, the restoring rate after q days, R^q, is expressed as follows:

$$R^q = \frac{\sum_{i \in J^q} w_i \times l_i}{\sum_{i \in J^0} w_i \times l_i} \tag{1}$$

where l_i is the distance of the i–th link, J^0 is the set of damaged links, J^q is the number of restored links until q days after the disaster, and w_i is the weighting factor of the i-th link. Then, the objective function can be calculated by using the restoring day and the restoring rate.

Restoring times are calculated for each restoring work, and the minimum days necessary for each work is given as

$$d = h / t_1 \tag{2}$$

where h is the restoration time required to complete the restoration work. In this research, the restoration time is calculated by using the restoration rate for each work and the capability value. The relation between the restoration rate for each work and the capability of the teams are shown in Figure 2. The restoration rate is given as follows:

a) Small damage: In the small damage, there is no difference in capability between each team. The restoration will be completed during a fixed time. Here, 4 hours are assumed.

$$h = h_t \tag{3}$$

b) Moderate damage: In the moderate damage, there is some difference in capability between every teams, however, every teams can restore the damage.

$$h = D / A \tag{4}$$

where D is the amount of damage and A is the capability of the team, that is, the restoring amount per an hour.

c) Large damage: In the large damage, only some teams can restore, because other teams have no restoring equipment and facility necessary for the large damage.

$$h = \infty (A < A_c) \qquad (5)$$
$$h = D / A (A \geq A_c)$$

The working hours per day of a restoration team is calculated by Equation 6, where t_m is the moving time to a site given by Equation 7. The shortest distance from the waiting place of the restoration team to the site is expressed as L (km), and the moving speed of the team is set to be v (km/h). h_c is the preparation time that is necessary for every works.

$$t_1 = t_0 - 2t_m - h_c \qquad (6)$$

$$t_m = L / v \qquad (7)$$

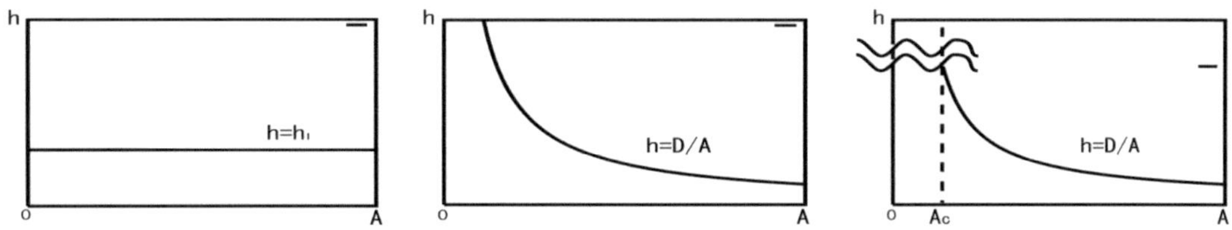

a) Small damage b) Moderate damage c) Large damage

Fig. 2. Relations between restoration rate for each work and capability of teams

2.3 Influence of Uncertainty

At a devastated area after an earthquake disaster, the circumstances are changing with aftershock, fire and bad weather. The devastated area may have another damaged and the circumstances may not be constant. This is due to the uncertainty of a damage which occurs from the followings:

1. **Delay:** Delay induces the increase of restoring days of a work. The delay of the work influences the whole restoring schedule.
2. **Impossibility to restore:** Impossibility to restore is the situation that a team without sufficient restoring equipment and facility is assigned to large damage work. Such a team cannot restore the large damage work. Impossibility of work to restore causes failure of restoring schedule.

2.4 Genetic Algorithm Considering Uncertainty

In order to obtain the restoration schedule which has robustness to the uncertainty of damage, it is necessary to implement sampling many times. In GA considering uncertainty (GACU) [3], objective function is defined as the expected value of $F'(x)$ to consider the search process as the sampling.

$$F'(x) = F(x) \ \textit{with Uncertainty} \tag{8}$$

F(x) contains a variable element, that is, uncertainty, so that *F′(x)* is changing according to the uncertainty. It is assumed that the number of sampling is age of individual. This sampling is performed by considering the evolution mechanism of inheritance, that is, gene of parents is resembled to that of children. The procedure of GACU is given as follows:

STEP 1. Generation of initial population
STEP 2. Selection of parents
STEP 3. Crossover and mutation: generation of new individuals
STEP 4. Evaluation: evaluation of new individuals and re-evaluation and adding age of alive individuals
STEP 5. Natural selection

STEP 2 to 5 are repeated until the convergence is achieved

2.5 Uncertainty of Optimal Restoration Schedule

When a restoration team arrives at the disaster site, the disaster circumstances may be different from those predicted, because devastated situations are constantly changing by the aftershock, fire disaster and bad weather, which are likely to make damage worse. Such a change of devastated area affects the scheduling process, because it takes more days than those scheduled, and furthermore it may be impossible to restore unless the restoration teams have enough ability. Therefore, in this paper, the amount of damage and the delay will be treated as uncertain factors and the restoration scheduling problem is formulated as an optimization problem with uncertainties. The influences of delay are shown in Figure 3.

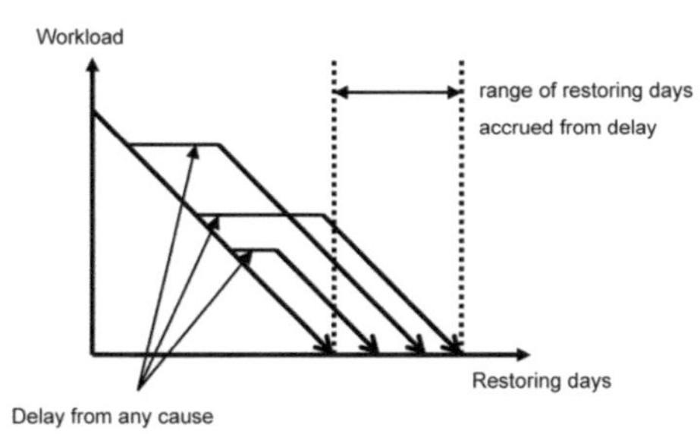

Fig. 3. The influences of delay

2.6 Application of Genetic Algorithm Considering Uncertainty

GACU is applied to obtain the optimal robust restoration schedule. Table 1 presents the parameters of GACU used here. The optimal robust schedule is presented in Figures 4 and 5. The effects of increasing the damage examined by 1000 simulations are shown in Table 2. Table 3 presents the effects of the delay examined by 1000 simulations. It is seen that teams without restoring equipment are not assigned to large damage works and medium damage works which are changeable to large damage and waiting time is properly assured to avoid the effects of delay. In addition, most of larger damage works are assigned to restoration team with high ability. The schedule is not only robust but also optimum for the early restoring. In this paper, assuming that a road network has an uncertain damage, it is intended to obtain the optimal restoring schedule considering uncertainty. From the results obtained, it is concluded that the proposed method using GACU is useful for obtaining the optimal restoring schedule with robustness to uncertainty of damage.

Population	Probability of Crossover	Probability of Mutation	Generation
500	0.6	0.005	2000

Table 1. Parameters of GACU

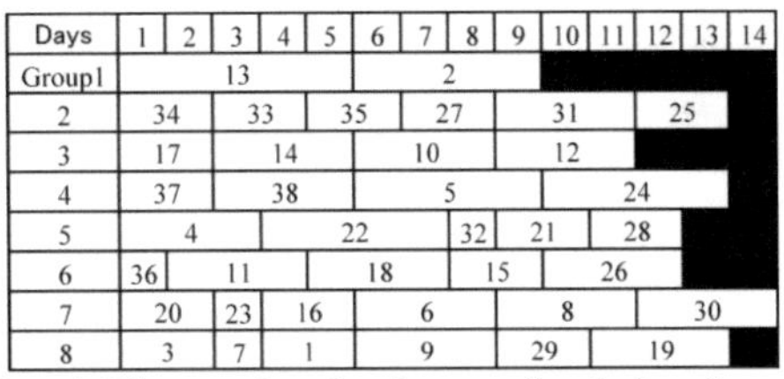

Fig. 4. The optimal robust schedule of Work (A)

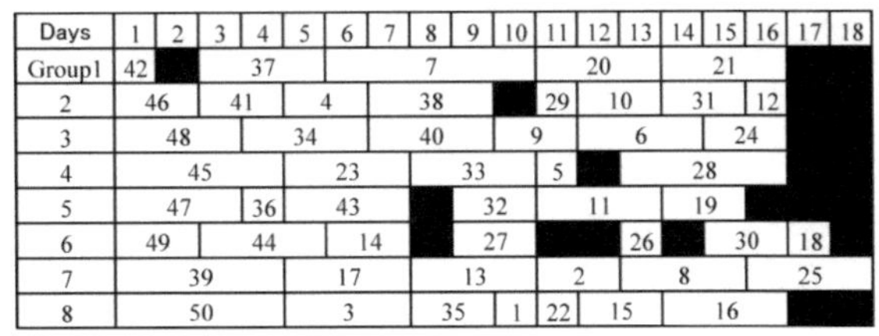

Fig. 5. The optimal robust schedule of Work (B)

Probability changed	Average of evaluation	Impossible to restore
5%	6.87	0/1000
10%	7.00	0/1000
20%	7.27	0/1000

Table 2. Effects of increasing the damage examined by 1000 simulations

Probability changed	Evaluation	SimpleGA	GACU
5%	Evaluation(Ave)	7.52	7.88
	Evaluation(Max)	8.80	7.97
	Evaluation(Min)	7.11	7.18
	Standard deviation	0.52	0.47
10%	Evaluation(Ave)	9.12	7.91
	Evaluation(Max)	17.22	8.31
	Evaluation(Min)	7.11	7.18
	Standard deviation	2.12	0.57
20%	Evaluation(Ave)	15.04	8.01
	Evaluation(Max)	17.56	8.41
	Evaluation(Min)	14.35	7.20
	Standard deviation	3.22	1.29

Table 3. Effects of the delay examined by 1000 simulation

3. Optimal Maintenance Planning of Bridge Structures Using Multi-Objective Genetic Algorithm

In order to establish a rational maintenance program, it is necessary to develop a cost-effective decision-support system that can provide us with a practical and economical plan

[4]. Although low-cost maintenance plans are desirable for bridge owner, it is necessary to consider various constraints when choosing an appropriate actual maintenance program. For example, the minimization of maintenance cost requires to prescribe the target safety level and the expected service life time. The predetermination of requirements may lose the variety of possible maintenance plans. Namely, it may be possible to find out a better solution that can largely extend the service life if the safety level can be sensitively decreased even with the same amount of maintenance cost.

3.1 Concrete Bridge Model

A group of ten concrete highway bridges are considered in this study. Maintenance management planning for ten consecutive piers and floor slabs (composite structure of steel girders and reinforced concrete (RC) slabs) is considered here [5]. Each bridge has the same structure and is composed of six main structural components: upper part of pier, lower part of pier, shoe, girder, bearing section of floor slab, and central section of floor slab.
Environmental conditions can significantly affect the degree of deterioration of the structures and may vary from location to location according to geographical characteristics such as wind direction, amount of splash, etc. To take the environmental conditions into account, the deterioration type and year from completion of each bridge are summarized in Table 4.

Bridge number	Years from completion	Deterioration type
B01	2	neutralization of concrete
B02	2	neutralization of concrete
B03	0	chloride attack (slight)
B04	0	chloride attack (medium)
B05	0	chloride attack (severe)
B06	0	chloride attack (medium)
B07	0	chloride attack (severe)
B08	1	chloride attack (medium)
B09	1	chloride attack (slight)
B10	1	chloride attack (slight)

Table 4. Years from completion and type of deterioration caused by environmental conditions

3.2 Maintenance Strategies and Life-Cycle Cost

In order to prevent deterioration in structural performance, several options such as repair, restoring, and reconstruction are considered. Since the effects may differ even under the same conditions, average results are adopted here. Maintenance methods applicable to RC slab may vary according to the environmental conditions and are determined considering several assumptions [6].
Life-Cycle Cost (LCC) is defined as the total maintenance cost for the entire bridge group during its life. This is obtained by the summation of the annual maintenance costs through the service life of all the bridges. The future costs are discounted to their present values. However, the discount rate is assumed to be zero in this study. Other costs, such as indirect

construction costs, general costs, and administrative costs, etc., are calculated in accordance with Cost Estimation Standards for Civil Construction [7]. The direct construction costs consist of material and labor costs and the cost of scaffold. For calculating the construction costs, the following assumptions are taken into account:

1. The cost of scaffold can be reduced by sharing. For example, scaffold can be shared for repairing the bearing and the bearing section of RC slab, consequently reducing the scaffolding cost.
2. Indirect construction costs, such as general administrative costs, can be saved by implementing several repairs in the same year. The ratio of indirect to maintenance costs decreases as the direct costs increase. The value of LCC is reduced when multiple components are repaired simultaneously.

3.3 Multi-Objective Genetic Algorithm (MOGA)

Genetic Algorithm (GA) is an evolutionary computing technique, in which candidates of solutions are mapped into GA space by encoding. The following steps are employed to obtain the optimal solutions [8]: a) initialization, b) crossover, c) mutation, d) natural selection, and e) reproduction. Individuals, which are solution candidates, are initially generated at random. Then, steps b, c, d, and e are repeatedly implemented until the termination condition is fulfilled. Each individual has a fitness value to the environment. The environment corresponds to the problem space and the fitness value corresponds to the evaluation value of objective function. Each individual has two aspects: Gene Type (GTYPE) expressing the chromosome or DNA and Phenomenon Type (PTYPE) expressing the solution. GA operations are applied to GTYPE and generate new children from parents (individuals) by effective searches in the problem space, and extend the search space by mutation to enhance the possibility of individuals other than the neighbour of the solution. GA operations that generate useful children from their parents are performed by crossover operation of chromosome or genes (GTYPE) without using special knowledge and intelligence. This characteristic is considered as one of the reasons of the successful applications of GA.

3.4 Application of MOGA to Maintenance Planning

It is desirable to determine an appropriate life-cycle maintenance plan by comparing several solutions for various conditions [6]. A new decision support system is developed here from the viewpoint of multi-objective optimization, in order to provide various solutions needed for the decision-making.

In this study, LCC, safety level and service life are used as objective functions. LCC is minimized, safety level is maximized, and service life is maximized. There are trade-off relations among the three objective functions. For example, LCC increases when service life is extended, and safety level and service life decrease due to the reduction of LCC. Then, multi-objective optimization can provide a set of Pareto solutions that cannot improve an objective function without making other objective functions worse.

Then, objective functions are defined as follows:

$$\textit{Objective function 1} \ : \ C_{total} = \Sigma LCC_i \rightarrow min \quad (9)$$

where LCC_i = LCC for bridge i

$$\textit{Objective function 2} \ : \ Y_{total} = \Sigma \ Y_i \rightarrow max \quad (10)$$

Constraints : $Y_i > Y_{required}$

where Y_i = Service life of bridge i , $Y_{required}$ = Required service life

$$\textit{Objective function 3} \ : \ P_{total} = \Sigma \ P_i \rightarrow max \quad (11)$$

Constraints : $P_i > P_{target}$

where P_{target} = Target safety level

The above objective functions have trade-off relations to each other. Namely, the maximization of safety level or maximization of service life cannot be realized without increasing LCC. On the other hand, the minimization of LCC can be possible only if the service life and/or the safety level decreases.

3.5 Numerical Example

In the implementation of MOGA, the GA parameters considered are as follows: number of individuals = 2000, crossover rate = 0.60, mutation rate = 0.05 and number of generations = 5000. Figures 6 to 9 present the results obtained by MOGA. Each figure shows the comparison of the results of the 1st generation (iteration number) and the 5000th generation. In Figure 6, the solutions at the 1st generation spread over the design space. This means that the initial solutions can be generated uniformly. After the 5000th generation, the solutions tend to converge to a surface, which finally forms the Pareto set as the envelope of all solutions. The number of solutions at the 5000th generation is much larger than that at the 1st generation. This indicates that MOGA could obtain various optimal solutions with different LCC values, safety levels, and service lives. From Figure 6, it is seen that MOGA can find out good solutions, all of which evolve for all the objective functions, and the final solutions are sparse and have discontinuity. In other words, the surfaces associated with the trade-off relations are not smooth. This implies that an appropriate long term maintenance plan cannot be created by the repetition of the short term plans.

In Figure 7, the vertical axis represents safety level, whereas the horizontal axis represents LCC. Although at the 1st generation, the solutions may have a rather linear relation between safety level and LCC, the relation shows non-linearity through the convergence process. This implies that the safety level may be significantly increased if the LCC can be slightly increased, when the service life is fixed. Figure 8 presents the relation between LCC and service life. Since LCC and service life have a rather perfect positive linear correlation, it can be said that the service life can be extended if LCC can be increased. On the other hand, there is no distinct relation between safety level and service life, as shown in Figure 9. It should be noted that the safety level may not be raised even if the service life is shorten, under a constant LCC. Namely, the relation between safety level and service life is so unclear that the extension of service life should be done with careful examination.

Finally, it is confirmed that the proposed method using MOGA can provide many near-optimal maintenance plans with various reasonable LCC values, safety levels and service lives.

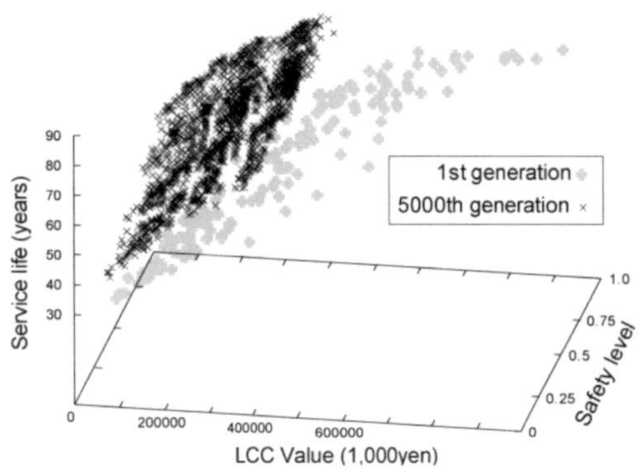

Fig. 6. Pareto solutions obtained by MOGA

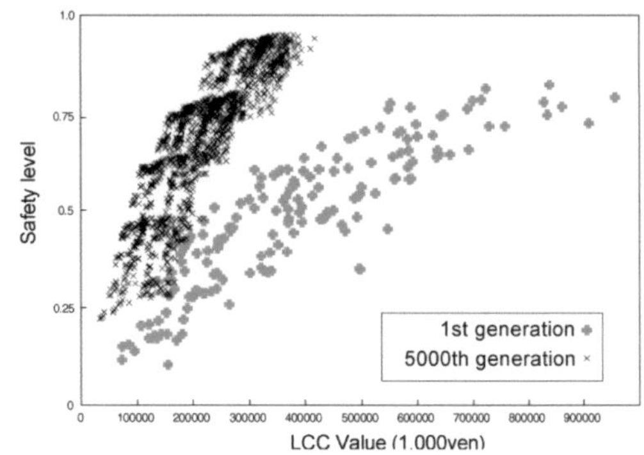

Fig. 7. Relation between LCC and safety level

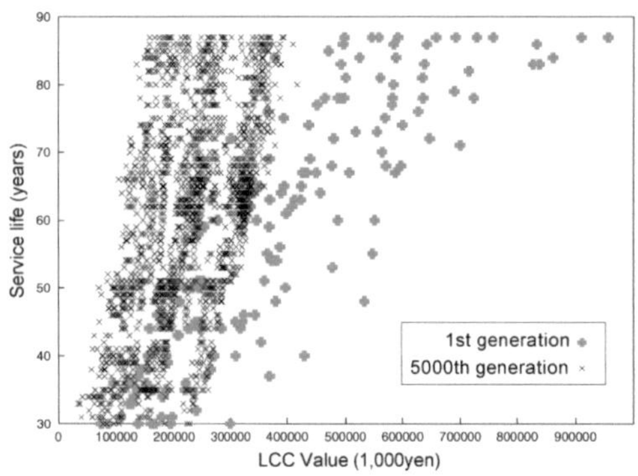

Fig. 8. Relation between LCC and service life

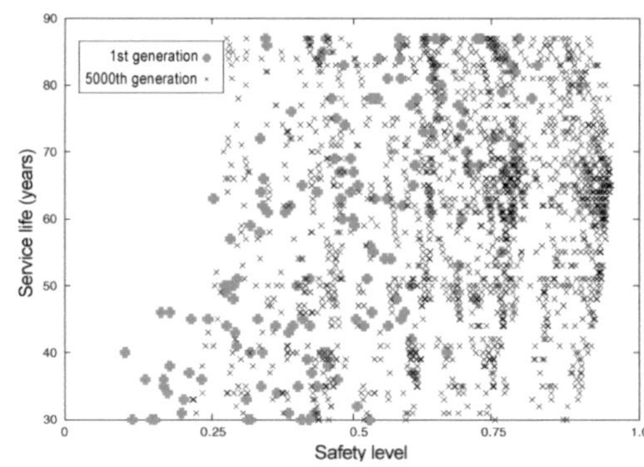

Fig. 9. Relation between safety level and service life

4. Health Monitoring System Using Learning System

Recently, many researches have been made on health monitoring of existing structures such as buildings, bridge and other civil structures. Many structures are becoming superannuated and deteriorated. Furthermore, in Japan, natural disasters like typhoon and earthquake have occurred frequently so that the damage assessment of existing structures is very important. In order to evaluate the damage state of structures health monitoring technology is quite promising to provide useful information. In the health monitoring, there are still some problems in modelling, analysis and experimental examination for practical use.

An attempt was made to develop a structural health monitoring system that can adapt to the structural systems and environments, by introducing the learning ability. By introducing the learning ability, it is not necessary to prepare any previous knowledge and examination for the underlying structures and environment. In other words, it is not necessary to use the precise modelling and analysis method before conducting the health monitoring.

4.1 AdaBoost

Boosting method uses such two learning algorithm with high precision (Strong learning algorithms) and learning algorithm with low precision (Weak learning algorithm). AdaBoost is one of the Boosting methods. AdaBoost is used for pattern recognition problems frequently.

The AdaBoost creates several learning hypotheses by using given weak learning algorithms at a round cycle. At the round cycle, re-sampling of learning data are performed by using the given probability distribution. At the next round, probability is updated to choose data that make errors at the round. By repeating this process, it is possible to obtain plural hypothesis that have different characteristics. The strong algorithm gives unification by combining each weak learning algorithm with weights. Figure 10 shows the concept of AdaBoost.

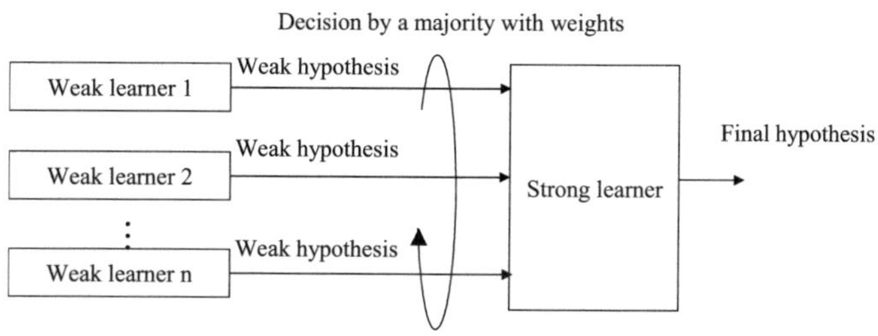

Fig. 10. Conception of AdaBoost

AdaBoost executes the recognition by combining plural weak learning algorithms like Figure 10, where no restriction exists on each weak learning algorithm. For even equal number of input and output data, it allows to use all different algorithms. By using a soft computing method like neural network for the weak learning algorithm, it is possible to obtain the same advantage.

The AdaBoost can obtain the high quality and versatile hypothesis by few teaching data. It also has such merits that algorithm is easy and the number of parameters adjusted is few.

4.1.1 Procedure of Adaboost

Adaboost can apply to the pattern recognition problem with multiple classifications. In this case, the 2-value with -1 and 1 is treated. Adaboost is repeated t (t=1, 2, 3, …, T) times. Procedure of Adaboost is shown below.

Step 1: Obtain the learning data

Give the teaching data (x_1, y_1), ..., (x_n, y_n).

Step 2: Initialize the probability distribution

Initialize the probability distribution using the next equation. In this equation, $D_t(i)$ is the probability distribution of teaching data i at round t.

$$D_t(i) = 1 / m \tag{12}$$

Step 3: Steps 4 to 6 as a round and repeat T times

Step 4: Obtain weak hypothesis h_t

By learning setting times of weak learning algorithm, obtain weak hypothesis. The learning data is chosen by probability based $D_t(i)$. Then, precision of weak hypothesis is calculated by the next equation using probability of error using D_t.

$$\varepsilon_t = P_{ri-Di}[h_t(x_i) \neq y_i] = \sum_{i:h_t(x_i) \neq y_i} D_t(i) \tag{13}$$

Step 5: Decide the importance of weak hypothesis

Decide the importance of weak hypothesis used the majority decision with the weight by the next equation.

$$\alpha_t = \frac{1}{2} \ln\left(\frac{1-\varepsilon_t}{\varepsilon_t}\right) \tag{14}$$

Step 6: Update probability distribution

Update probability distribution of teaching data by the recognition result when using weak hypothesis h_t. Probability of teaching data producing the error recognition by h_t is increased, and learning is concentrated to the difficult teaching data. Equation to update of the probability distribution is as follows:

$$D_{t+1}(i) = \frac{D_t(i)}{Z_t} \times \begin{cases} e^{-at} (h_t(x_i) = y_i) \\ e^{at} (h_t(x_i) \neq y_i) \end{cases}$$

$$= \frac{D_t(i) e^{-\alpha_t y_i h_t(x_i)}}{Z_t} \tag{15}$$

In this equation, Z_t is the factor to normalize the probability distribution.

Step 7: Obtain final hypothesis

Final hypothesis H_t is obtained by the majority decision with weighs of weak hypotheses. The equation to obtain the H_t is .

$$H(x) = \mathrm{sgn}\left(\sum_{t=1}^{T} \alpha_t h_t(x)\right) \tag{16}$$

4.2 Vibration Analysis

In this section, vibration analysis is done by numerical simulation. At the numerical simulation, deterioration of objective structure and the vibration characteristics of structural change are assumed. Vibration at intact situation and deteriorated situation are compared using a multiple freedom structure. Through the numerical simulation, it is concluded that the method can find the deterioration of structure by analyzing vibration response.

4.2.1 Vibration

Vibration of structure can be defined by the next equation.

$$M \cdot u''(t) + C \cdot u'(t) + K \cdot u(t) = 0 \tag{17}$$

In the equation, u(t) is the displacement of structure at time t, M is mass, C is damping ratio and K is stiffness. Equation 17 has no external force, and therefore it is called free vibration. However, usually external force exists.

$$M \cdot u''(t) + C \cdot u'(t) + K \cdot u(t) = p(t) \tag{18}$$

where p(t) is external force.

4.2.2 Wind force

In this research, wind is used for the external force. Wind force is calculated by wind velocity as follows:

$$F = \frac{1}{2} C\rho A V^2 \sin^2 \alpha \tag{19}$$

where C is wind coefficient, ρ is air density, A is effective area and α is effect angle. Those values used in this research are shown in Table 5.

air density	0.125 ($kgf \cdot sec^2/m^4$)
Coefficient	2
effect angle	90 (°)
effect area	200 (m^2)

Table. 5 Parameters

4.2.3 Method of vibration analysis

Runge-Kutta method is used to solve the differential equations for the numerical simulation. The following simultaneous equations are solved.

$$\begin{cases} P = u'(t) \\ P' = -(C \cdot P + K \cdot u(t) + P(t)) / M \end{cases} \tag{20}$$

4.2.4 Model of structure

A three-degree-of-freedom structure is employed for the object model. Therefore, Equation 18 is extended to a matrix form.

$$[M] \cdot \{u''(t)\} + [C] \cdot \{u'(t)\} + [K] \cdot \{u(t)\} = \{p(t)\} \tag{21}$$

In this equation, [M], [C] and [K] are the matrices of mass, damping and stiffness. The matrices of three-degree-freedom structure used in this research are shown as follows:

$$M = \begin{bmatrix} m_1 & 0 & 0 \\ 0 & m_2 & 0 \\ 0 & 0 & m_3 \end{bmatrix} \tag{22}$$

$$C = \begin{bmatrix} c_1 + c_2 & -c_2 & 0 \\ -c_2 & c_2 + c_3 & -c_3 \\ 0 & -c_3 & c_3 \end{bmatrix} \tag{23}$$

$$K = \begin{bmatrix} k_1 + k_2 & -k_2 & 0 \\ -k_2 & k_2 + k_3 & -k_3 \\ 0 & -k_3 & k_3 \end{bmatrix} \tag{24}$$

where m_i, k_i and c_i are mass, damping factor and stiffness of each story.

4.2.5 Pilot study

In this section, numeric simulation is done using sine curve for the external force. In the numerical simulation, the intact situation and deteriorated situation at each story are compared. The deterioration is assumed to reduce 10% of stiffness at every 10000 steps. Figure 11 to Figure 13 show the difference of displacement for the intact situation and the situation that deterioration occur at each story. Figure 12 shows the difference of displacement for the intact situation and the situation that deterioration occurs at the first story.

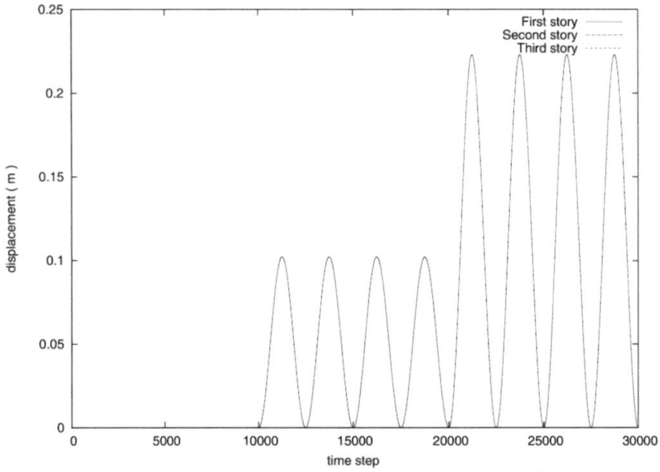

Fig. 11. Difference of displacement (Case of degradation accrual first story)

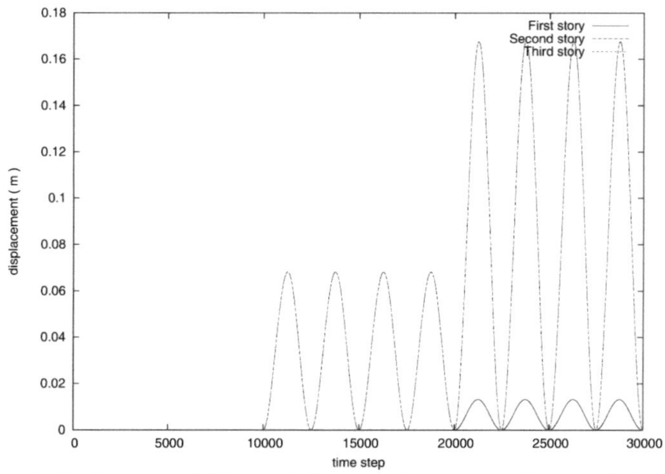

Fig. 12. Difference of displacement (Case of degradation accrual second story)

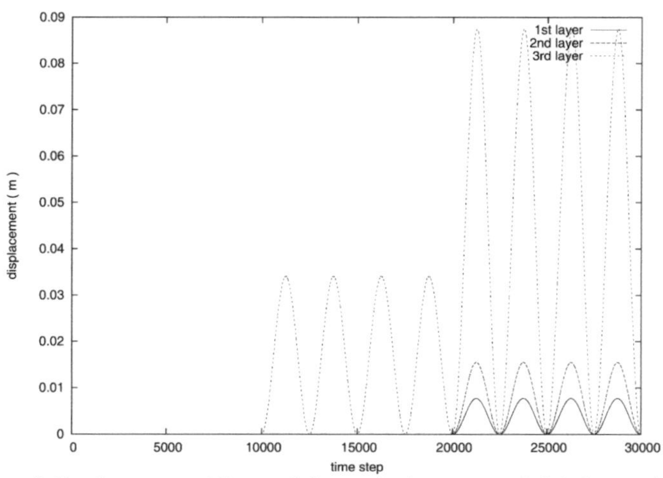

Fig. 13. Difference of displacement (Case of degradation accrual third story)

From Figure 11 to Figure 13, the behavior of structure changes by position, even the same size deterioration. Whereas the differences of response of each story is the same when the first story has deterioration, the difference of response of the first story is smaller than other stories and second story's one and third story's one are the same, when the second story has deterioration. Also, the difference of response of the third story is bigger than other stories and the first story and those of the second story is the same, when the second story has deterioration. Then, it is confirmed that it is possible to identify the difference of intact structure and the structure with damage at the i-th story. Herewith, it is possible to identify the position of deterioration by comparing the difference of response.

4.3 Proposed System

Structure of the proposed system is shown in Figure 14.

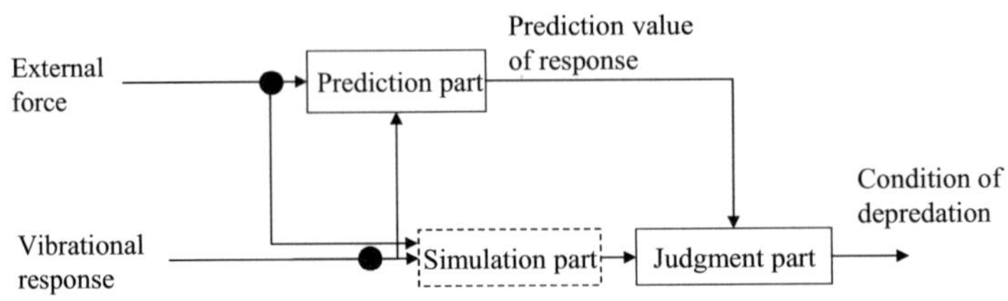

Fig. 14. Structure of proposed system

The proposed system is composed of a prediction part that learns the vibration response and predicts the next response, judgment part that detects the deterioration by analyzing the vibration response, and simulation part that analyze a vibration. Inputs to the proposed system are external force and vibration response, that is, displacement and velocity of structures. Outputs from the proposed system are the probability of deterioration and the position of deterioration.

In this research, GMDH is used for the prediction part, so that versatile rules are obtained and calculation time can be reduced. At the judgment part, fuzzy reasoning is used to detect the deterioration by comparing the prediction value and the observed value. Input data for fuzzy reasoning are prediction errors and prediction error rates. Fuzzy rule using in this research is shown in Table 6.

Input value		Output value
Error	Error ratio	Possibility of degradation
Zero	Zero	Zero
	Small	Zero
	Medium	Zero
	Big	Small
Small	Zero	Small
	Small	Small
	Medium	Medium
	Big	Medium
Medium	Zero	Medium
	Small	Medium
	Medium	Medium
	Big	Big
Big	Zero	Medium
	Small	Medium
	Medium	Medium
	Big	Big

Table 6. Fuzzy rules

By using fuzzy reasoning, calculation time can be shorten. Position of deterioration is identified by comparing prediction errors of each story. In this research, comparing the difference of prediction error of story, the story with the biggest difference is defined as the deterioration position.

4.4 Observations

In this section, numerical examination is done using sine curve and actual wind velocity. The proposed system learned those vibration responses in advance. Figure 15 shows the difference of prediction value and observed value when external force is sine curve.

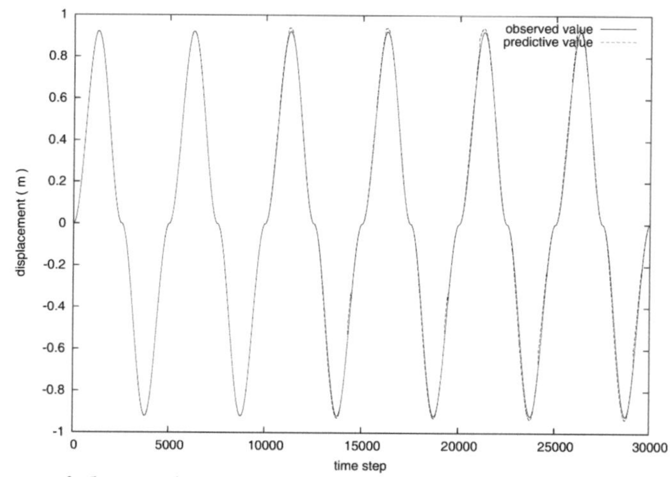

Fig. 15. Comparison of observed value and predictive value without deterioration

From Figure 15, it can be confirmed that the proposed system can identify the vibratinal characteristic by learning and predicting the vibration response. Figure 16 shows the transition of error of prediction value when the second story has deterioration.

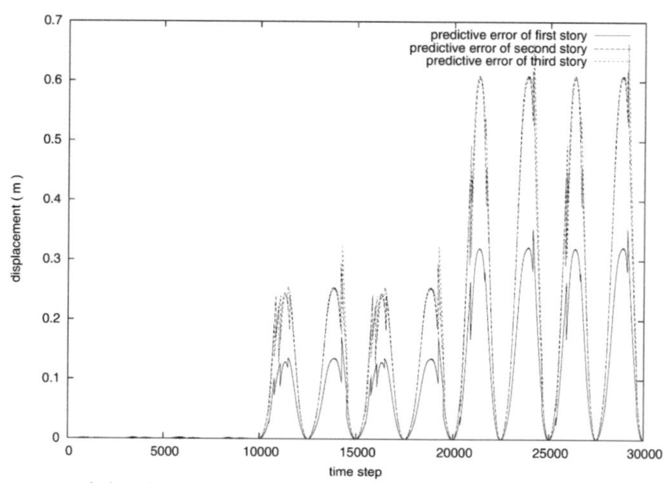

Fig. 16. Prediction error of displacement

From Figure 16, the proposed system predicts the change of stiffness and which story is deteriorated by every 10000 steps. When structural characteristic changes, the prediction error is increased. When the first story or the third story has deterioration, similar result is obtained. Figure 17 shows the output of the proposed system.

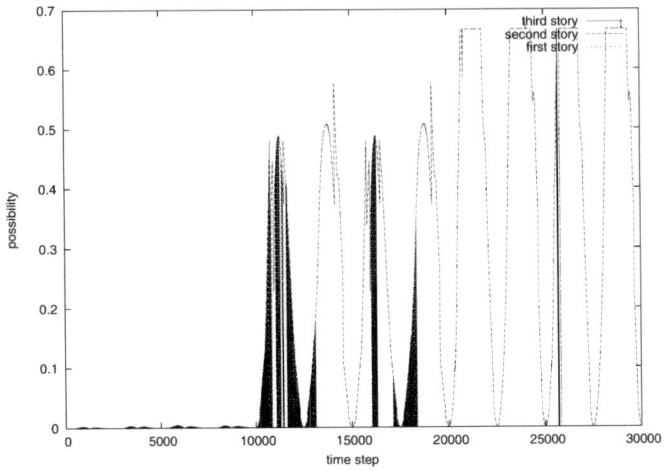

Fig. 17. Result of the proposed system

From Figure 17, the first step to 10000th step, the proposed system shows the intact state; it has no deterioration, but over 10000th step, possibility of deterioration of the second story is increased. The proposed system can identify the deterioration at real time.

Figure 18 shows the difference of prediction value and observed value when the external force is wind velocity.

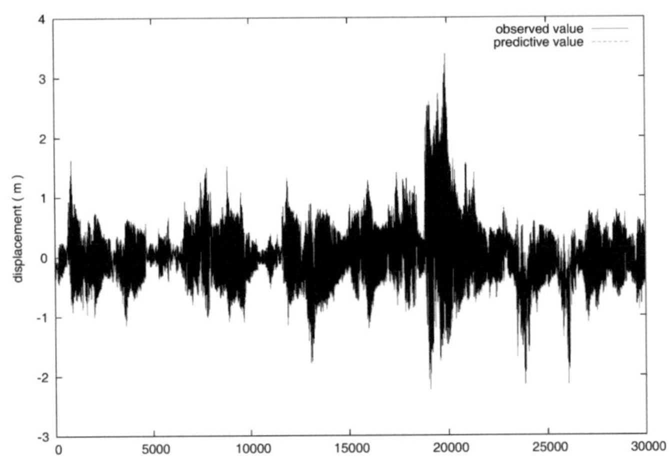

Fig. 18. Comparison of observed value and predictive value without deterioration

From Figure 18, it is confirmed that the proposed system can identify the vibrational characteristic by learning and predicting the vibration response. Figure 20 shows the transition of error of prediction value when the third story has deterioration.

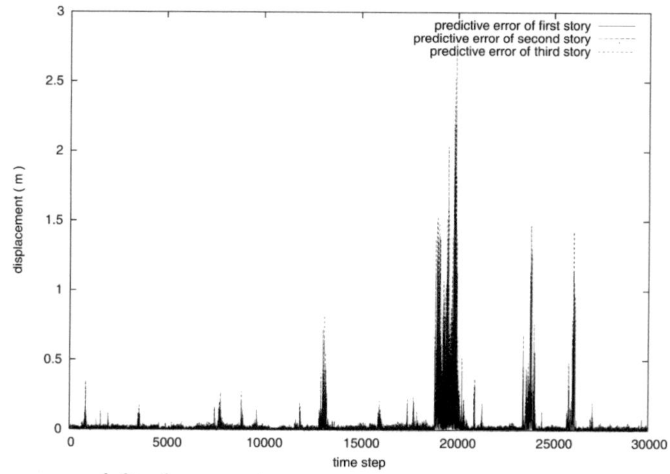

Fig. 19. Prediction error of displacement

At the simulation, stiffness is deteriorated 10% at every 10000 step. From Figure 19, the prediction error is increased by deterioration occurs. Figure 19 shows the output of the proposed system.

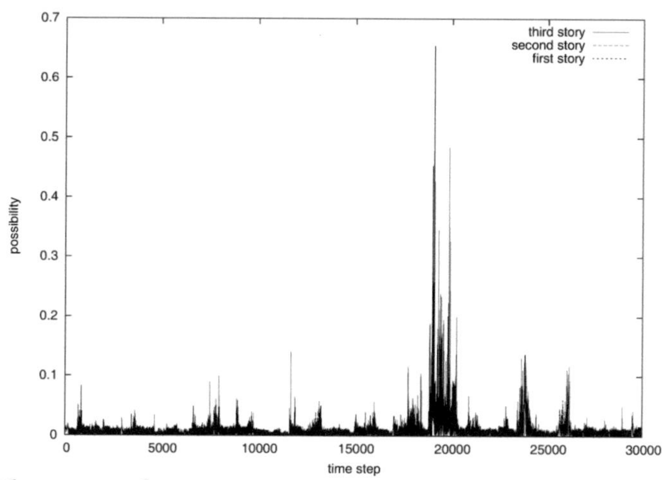

Fig. 20. Result of the proposed system

From Figure 20, up to the 10000th step, although deterioration possibility is shown, it is judged there is no deterioration because possibility is very small. After the 10000th step, although deterioration occurs, output of the proposed system hardly changes. It is due to the fact that the displacement is very small. It can be confirmed that when displacement becomes big around 20000step, output value of the proposed system becomes high. The proposed system shows the third story has deterioration.

5. Damage Assessment of Reinforced Concrete Bridge Decks Using AdaBoost

In order to establish a rational maintenance program for bridge structures, it is necessary to collect enough data about the material and structural characteristics and to evaluate the structural damage of existing bridges in a quantitative manner. However, it is often seen to lose the drawings or not to record the design specification applied. Moreover, it is difficult to avoid the subjectivity of inspectors when visual data are used for the evaluation of damage or deterioration. In this section, an attempt is made to develop a new system that can evaluate the damage condition of existing structures by using the visual information given by digital photos. The proposed system is based upon such new technologies as image processing, photo-grammetry, pattern recognition, and artificial intelligence. The damage of Reinforced Concrete (RC) bridge decks is evaluated with the aid of digital photos and pattern recognition. Using the proposed system, it is possible to automatically evaluate the damage degree of RC bridge decks and therefore avoid the subjectivity of inspectors. Several numerical examples are presented to demonstrate the applicability of the proposed system.

5.1 Damage Evaluation of RC Deck by Pattern Recognition

In this study, the damage of Reinforced Concrete (RC) bridge decks is evaluated with the aid of digital photos and pattern recognition[9][10]. In general, the procedure for extracting the characteristics of cracks showing up on concrete decks through digital images and the classification of the damage level based on the characteristics are used in the typical pattern recognition system.

To obtain the test material, digital images of concrete decks taken by a digital camera are used. If input data that can be acquired in low resolution by using a common digital camera is used, the costs for the assessment of integrity can be reduced and input data can be acquired easily. The total number of digital images is 47 and each image is scanned with the resolution of 360 pixels per inch in both directions. In this resolution, each image is normalized to a 768×480 pixel rectangle and converted to the grayscale image. The digital images used in this study are obtained by marking the cracks with white chalk. The damage levels for all digital images are classified into three categories by an expert.

In this study, characteristics are extracted based on such four criteria as continuity, concentration, directionality (unidirectional or bi-directional), and types (hexagonal or linear) of cracks. The crack pattern of thin lines can be considered a set of directional linear elements and hence characteristic extraction by the projection histogram would be effective. Because the characteristics of projection histogram of a crack pattern provide information on the positions and the quantities of cracks, they can be used as the quantitative characteristics representing the continuity and the concentration of cracks, for the classification of crack patterns. The histograms projected on two directions are computed for extracting a crack pattern; one is the horizontal direction and the other is the vertical direction. The projection histograms are data structures used to count the number of crack pixels when the image is projected on the vertical and horizontal axes.

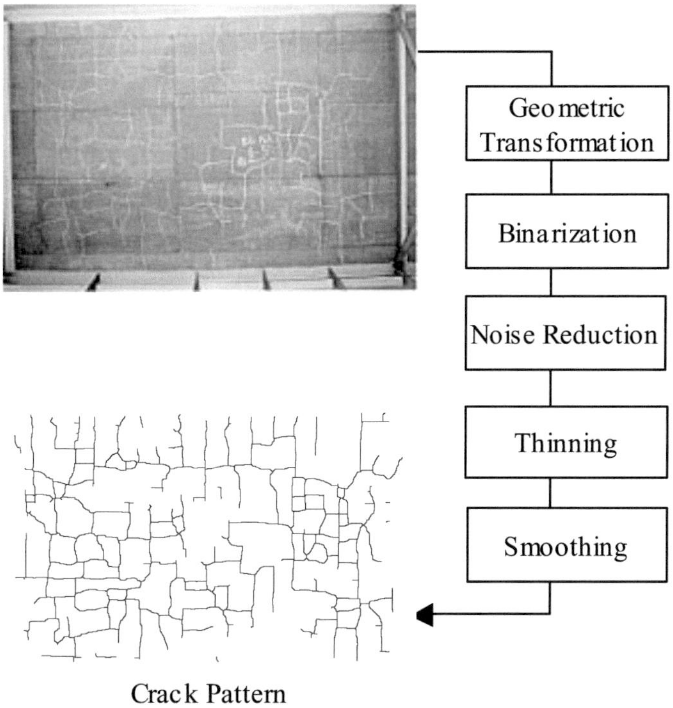

Fig. 21. Procedure of image pre-processing

The characteristic values in each dimension are the number of crack pixels in row for the horizontal histogram, in column for the vertical histogram, and are the quantum numbers in accordance with the dimensionality of characteristics vectors. Figure 22 shows an example of horizontal and vertical projection histograms extracted from a crack pattern.

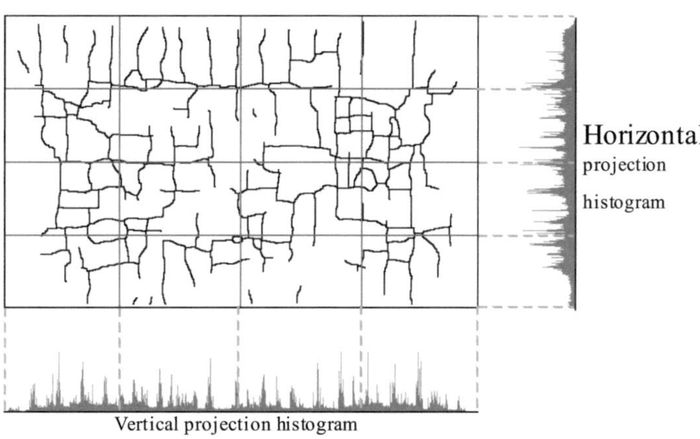

Fig. 22. Example of horizontal/vertical projection histograms extracted from a crack pattern

5.2 Experimental Results

The classification of the digital images of cracks is implemented by using the AdaBoost technique. In this study, neural network is used for weak learning system. 20 images of cracks are used for learning of AdaBoost and the remaining 32 images are used for evaluating the classification results. This implementation is repeated many times changing the learning data every times. In this learning stage, three damage levels judged by an expert for each image are used as the teaching signal. Also, the teaching data includes the same number of each damage levels data. In this numerical example, the effectiveness is evaluated by the recognition rate of non-learning data and by comparing with the results of neural network. The learning parameters of neural network using back propagation and AdaBoost are shown in Table 7 and Table 8.

Number of layer	3
Number of unit of input layer	512
Number of unit of hidden layer	64
Number of unit of output layer	3
Learning time	30000
Learning factor	0.3
Inertia factor	0.9 inertia

Table 7. Leaning parameters of neural network

Number of round	30
Learning Time of neural network	1000

Table 8. Leaning parameters of AdaBoost

The parameters of neural network used for the weak learning system of AdaBoost are the same as Table 7. The learning parameters are set up as the same for neural network and AdaBoost so as to compare their performances. Table 9 shows the classification results with the distribution of directionality. This result is the average of all trials.

Method	Recognition accuracy (%)			
	Rank A	Rank B	Rank C	Total
Neural network	60.0	38.5	87.5	68.1
AdaBoost	90.0	92.3	95.8	93.6

Table 9. Recognition accuracy

About 70 % recognition accuracy is obtained by using neural network. Especially, the recognition rate of Rank B is very low (38.5 %). It is caused by the fact that some digital images of Rank B are close to both Rank A and Rank C. Therefore, recognition rate of Rank B becomes low. On the other hand, by using AdaBoost, over 90 % recognition accuracy is obtained and the recognition rates of all rank are over 90%. Especially, the recognition rate of Rank B is improved. From this result, AdaBoost technique can recognize the complex classification problem that neural network cannot recognize. It is considered that the proposed system can classify similar digital images by using AdaBoost.

Table 10 shows several examples of classification by neural network. The classification is performed by the biggest value of output.

Output of system			Rank
A	B	C	
0.989	0.011	0.002	A
0.011	0.231	0.159	B
0.032	0.001	0.993	C
0.851	0.154	0.001	A
0.165	0.005	0.736	B
0.006	0.001	0.999	C

Table 10. Classification by neural network

From Table 10, it is seen that the classification of Rank A and Rank C can be performed in a clear manner. On the other hand, Rank B cannot be definitely classified. This implies that the classification of Rank B is complex and therefore difficult by using neural network. Table 11 shows the examples of classification by AdaBoost.

Output of system			Rank
A	B	C	
0.848	0.575	0.226	A
0.550	0.896	0.189	B
0.152	0.569	0.899	C
0.997	0.602	0.129	A
0.438	0.675	0.354	B
0.139	0.570	0.918	C

Table 11. Classification by AdaBoost

From Table 11, by using AdaBoost, all ranks are clearly identified. From this result, it is concluded that the AdaBoost technique is efficient even for complex problems like the problem treated here.
Table 12 shows a comparison of the recognition accuracies of learning data and checking data.

	Recognition accuracy (%)	
	Learning data	Checking data
Neural Network	65.0	68.8
AdaBoost	95.0	93.8

Table 12. Recognition accuracies by neural network and AdaBoost

From Table 12, by using AdaBoost technique the recognition accuracy is improved for both learning data and checking data, whereas neural network has no sufficient recognition accuracy even for the learning data. This implies that neural network has a possibility not to obtain the right rules for the case with complex learning data. On the other hand, AdaBoost technique has higher recognition accuracy for both learning data and checking data. Namely, AdaBoost technique can obtain right rules and recognize complex problems by combining several weak learning systems. From this, it can be confirmed that AdaBoost technique is quite efficient for the evaluation of damage condition of RC bridge decks.

6. Optimal Maintenance Planning Considering Health Monitoring Information

In order to establish a rational bridge maintenance program, it is inevitable to determine the deterioration curves of various components of bridges. However, it is quite difficult to identify appropriate deterioration curves because of various uncertainties involved in the prediction process and environment evaluation. Furthermore, it is necessary to take into account the effects of natural hazards such as earthquake, typhoon, flood, etc. Under the situation, although the existing bridges should be kept in a safety condition through inspection and maintenance works, it is not easy to maintain them in a satisfactory level, because of the financial constraints. In this study, an attempt is made to develop an optimal maintenance planning system that can account for the seismic risk. In the proposed system, an optimal maintenance scheduling is obtained with the aid of Genetic Algorithm (GA), in which the deterioration curve can be updated by using the data given from the structural health monitoring. Introducing the health monitoring information, it becomes possible to change the repair intervals or repair methods that can reduce Life-Cycle Cost (LCC) and seismic risk. The structural health monitoring is performed using fuzzy reasoning. Several numerical examples are presented to demonstrate the applicability and efficiency of the proposed method.

6.1 Problem of Maintenance Scheduling

The objective of bridge maintenance is to keep the bridge condition well and to lengthen its life. In order to establish an appropriate maintenance schedule for the bridge, it is very important to minimize the maintenance cost. However, there is a necessity to consider the risks of damage and failure caused by earthquakes. Then, since there is a trade-off relation between the maintenance cost and seismic risk, it is very difficult to satisfy both the objectives.

In the past researches, the trade-off has been treated by using the multi-objective optimization of the maintenance cost and seismic risk. However, the multi-objective optimization methods provide a lot of solutions so that it is not easy to choose a solution among the solution candidates. Also, there is a big problem at the prediction of the deterioration rate. Since the deterioration has uncertainties, the accuracy of the prediction is low. The low accuracy of the prediction may cause the increase of seismic risk. Namely, it is important to specify an appropriate deterioration rate.

6.2 Maintenance Scheduling Considering Seismic Risk

LCC of bridge structures consists of initial construction cost, maintenance cost, and failure cost (renewal cost, user cost, social and environmental costs and so on). In usual, LCC analysis considers the damage and deterioration of materials and structures. However, in the region that often suffers from natural hazards such as typhoons and earthquakes, it is necessary to account for the effects of such natural hazards.

Based on the seismic risk analysis, LCC is evaluated focusing on the effects of earthquakes that are major natural disasters in Japan. At first, LCC analysis is formulated to consider the social and economical effects due to the collapse of structures occurred by the earthquake as well as the minimization of maintenance cost. The loss by the collapse of structures due to the earthquake can be defined in terms of an expected cost and introduced into the calculation of LCC. A stochastic model of structural response was proposed, which accounts for the variation due to the uncertain characteristics of earthquake [11]. Then, the probability of failure due to the earthquake excitation is calculated based on the reliability theory. Furthermore, LCC evaluations are performed not only for a single bridge but also many bridges forming road networks [12][13].

In the past researches [14][15], both the maintenance cost and seismic risk were treated by using the multi-objective optimization technique. However, it is not easy to select an appropriate maintenance plan among a lot of candidates that the multi-objective optimization provides as a set of Pareto solutions.

As mentioned before, there is such another big problem that the prediction of the deterioration curve essentially involves various uncertainties. This implies that the accuracy of the prediction is low and insufficient, which may cause the increase of the seismic risk.

6.3 Maintenance Planning System Considering Seismic Risk

In this section, an attempt is made to develop a maintenance scheduling system that can consider the maintenance cost and seismic risk at the same time to achieve a rational maintenance program by using GA.

6.3.1 Objective function

In this research, the objective function is the maintenance cost.

6.3.2 Sub-objectives

There are a lot of efficient solutions when optimizing only the life cycle cost. Although the maintenance cost is equal, the characteristics of the maintenance schedule are different from each other. Therefore, when the maintenance cost is equal, the seismic risk is considered as a sub-objective. The seismic risk is defined in the following:

$$SeismicRisk = P_d \times P_h \times C_d \tag{25}$$

where P_d is the probability of seismic damage occurrence, P_h is the earthquake occurrence probability and C_d is the seismic loss.

6.3.3 Introduction of health monitoring

In this research, it is assumed that the health monitoring system can recognize the deterioration rate with accuracy. When the prediction error is large, the maintenance schedule is updated by GA. By updating the schedule, the seismic risk can be reduced. The flow of the proposed system is shown in Figure 23 and the updating process of the maintenance schedule is shown in Figure 24. By introducing the health monitoring, it is possible to reduce the maintenance cost and seismic risk.

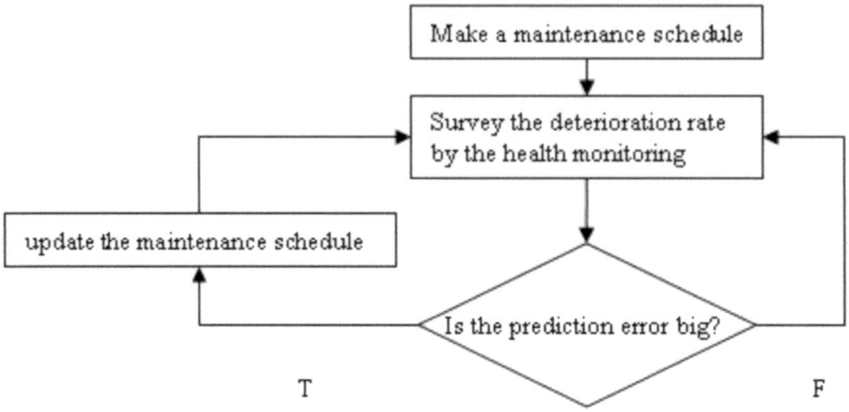

Fig. 23. Flow of the proposed system

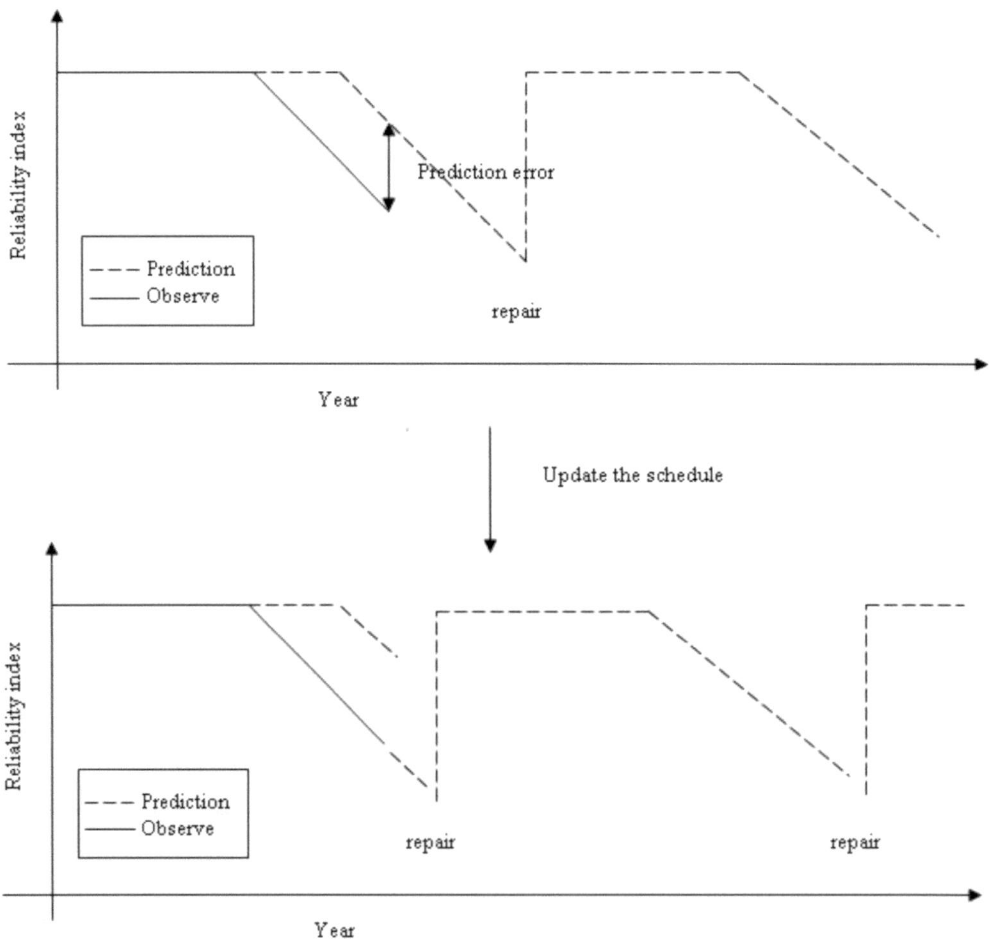

Fig. 24. Updating process of maintenance schedule

When the prediction error is large, the deterioration curve can be updated by using the data obtained from the health monitoring system and the optimal maintenance schedule is searched by GA based on the updated deterioration curve.

6.3.4 Uncertainty of deterioration

Figure 25 shows the deterioration curve of a member under the severe environment. The deterioration accelerates after 27 years. It is assumed that the preventive effects for corrosion lose after 27 years, the required safety level is prescribed as 0.8, and the service life is 100 years.

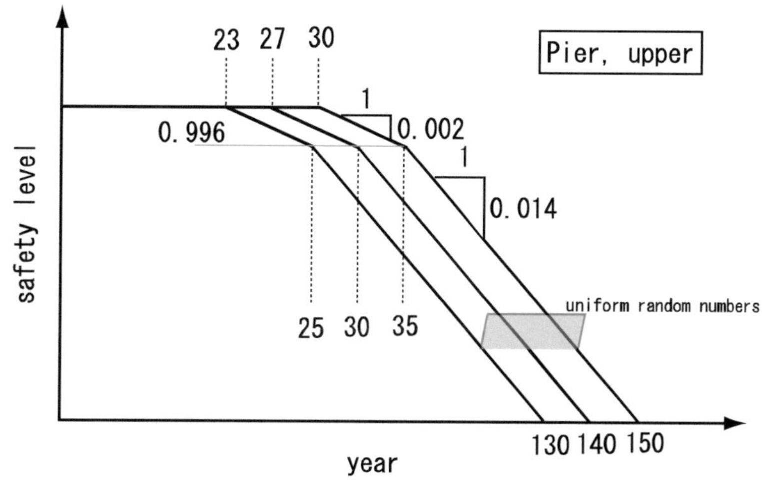

Fig. 25. Deterioration curve of RC member

6.4 Numerical Example

A numerical examination for a bridge is presented. The uncertainty of the deterioration curve is expressed by the normal distribution. In this numerical example, it is assumed that the health monitoring system can update the deterioration curve every year. The result of the proposed system with health monitoring system is compared with the systems without health monitoring. The simulation is done 100 times and the result is shown in Table 13.

Seismic Risk	Monitoring Without	With
Max	180477 (Yen)	155767 (Yen)
Min	169817 (Yen)	155272 (Yen)
Average	176872 (Yen)	155469 (Yen)

Table 13. Seismic risk

Table 13 shows that the proposed method with health monitoring can provide less seismic risk than that without health monitoring, by using Equation (25). In this table, Max, Min and Average mean the maximum seismic risk, the minimum seismic risk and the average seismic risk in 100 times simulation. This result shows the proposed system can adapt to the uncertainties of the deterioration by introducing the health monitoring system. Since the maintenance cost of the proposed system is almost the same, the effectiveness of the proposed system is verified.

7. References

[1] Sugimoto, H. & Katagiri, A. (1997): On Support System for Restoration Process of Disaster-Stricken Lifeline Network by GA, Vol. 43, No. 2. pp. 517-524. (in Japanese).

[2] Furuta, H. & Nakatsu, K. (2004): Optimal Restoration Scheduling for Earthquake Disaster by Emergent Computing, Proc. of IFIP WG7.5 Working Conference on Reliability and Optimization of Structural Systems, Kobe, Japan.

[3] Tamaki, H., Arai, T. & Abe, S. (1999): A Genetic Algorithm Approach to Optimization Problems with Uncertainties", Institute of Systems, Control and Information Engineers Journal, Vol. 12, No. 5, pp. 297-303. (in Japanese).

[4] Frangopol, D. M. & Furuta, H. (eds.), (2001). Life-Cycle Cost Analysis and Design of Civil Infrastructure Systems, ASCE, Reston Virginia.

[5] Ito H., Takahashi Y., Furuta, H., & Kameda, T. (2002): An Optimal Maintenance Planning for Many Concrete Bridges Based on Life-Cycle Cost. Proc. of IABMAS, Barcelona, Spain, CD-ROM.

[6] Furuta, H., Kameda, T. & Frangopol, D. M. (2004): Balance of Structural Performance Measures, Proc. of Structures Congress, Nashville, Tennessee, ASCE, May, CD-ROM.

[7] MLTI. (2001). Cost Estimation Standards for Civil Constructions, Ministry of Land , Transportation and Infrastructure, Japan.

[8] Furuta, H. & Sugimoto, H. (1997). Applications of Genetic Algorithm to Structural Engineering, Tokyo, Morikita Publishing (in Japanese).

[9] Yagi, N. (2000): Digital Image Processing, Ohmsha (in Japanese)

[10] Seul, M., O'Gorman, L. & Sammon, M. (2001): Practical Algorithms for Image Analysis, Cambridge University Press

[11] Furuta, H., Koyama, K., Dogaki, M., & Frangopol, D. M. (2004): Seismic Risk Evaluation and Life-Cycle cost Analysis of Bridge Structures in Japan, Proc. of 2nd ASRANeT Colloquium, Barcelona, Spain.

[12] Furuta, H., Kataoka, H., Dogaki, M. & Frangopol, D. M. (2005): Effects of Seismic Risk on Life-Cycle Cost Analysis for Bridge Maintenance, Proc. of 4th International Conference on Current and Future Trends in Bridge, Construction and Maintenance, Kuala Lumpur, Malaysia.

[13] Furuta, H., Koyama, K., Oi, M. & Sugimoto, H. (2006): Life-Cycle Cost Evaluation of Multiple Bridges in Road Network Considering Seismic Risk, Proc. of 6th International Bridge Engineering Conference, Boston, USA.

[14] Furuta, H., Koyama, & Oi, M. (2005): Life-cycle Analysis of Bridge Structures Considering Maintenance Cost and Seismic Risk, Proc. of IFIP WG7.5 Working Conference on Structural Reliability and Optimization, Aalborg, Denmark.

[15] Furuta, H., Nakatsu, K. & Frangopol, D. M. (2005): Optimal Restoration Scheduling for Earthquake Disaster Using Life-Cycle Cost, Proc. of 4th International Workshop on Life-Cycle Coast Analysis and Design of Civil Infrastructure Systems, Coco Beach, USA.

Forecasting Chaotic and Non-Linear Time Series with Artificial Intelligence and Statistical Measures

Aranildo Rodrigues L. J.[1], Paulo S. G. de Mattos Neto[2],
Jones Albuquerque[1], Silvana Bocanegra[1] and Tiago A. E. Ferreira[1]
[1]*Statistics and Informatics Department, Federal Rural University of Pernambuco*
Recife - Pernambuco
[2]*Center for Informatics, Federal University of Pernambuco*
Recife - Pernambuco
Brazil

1. Introduction

The most of the classical time series literature suppose that the series are stationary (or that the time series can be transformed in stationary series through some simple transformation, such as differentiation), and that the series phenomenon is a linear process. In this sense, all time series can be represented by linear models.
However, time series encountered in practice way not always exhibit characteristics of a linear process, then there is not any reason that generalizes the linearity supposition for a real world time series. In fact, the high complexity of the real world phenomena induce to think, more naturally, about non-linear and chaotic structures presents in the data of time series than linear structures.
Loosely speaking, a time series is a set of observations made sequentially in time. Examples of real world time series abound in such fields as economics, business, engineering, natural sciences (commonly in the meteorology, geophysics and biology), social sciences, etc (Lam, 1998). Phenomena like human breath rate, human electrocardiogram, earthquake, stock prizes are some examples of real world time series. A typical intrinsic feature of a time series is that the adjacent observations are dependent, where the nature of this dependence among time series observations is of considerable practical interest. The *time series analysis and forecasting* is concerned in mathematical and statistical (and more recently, computational) modelling for analysis of this dependence.
Mathematical and statistical methods are successfully used for time series analysis and forecasting (Box et al., 1994; Gooijer and Kumar, 1992; Kantz, 2004), but sometimes these approaches are not trivial to apply in practical sense, considering that some times series (mainly real world time series, as the financial or economical series, climatic series, etc) have a chaotic and non-linear behavior and many types of components, such as trends, seasonality, impulses, steps, model exchange and other uncontrolled features.
Alternatively, in the last two decades, the Artificial Neural Network (ANN) model have been widely used in order to solve the time series forecasting problem, presenting less mathematical complexity than the typical non-linear statistical methods. However, the ANN

approach has a critical point, the correct adjust of its parameters, since this adjustment is dependent of the problem. To solve this problem of adjustment, many Intelligent Hybrid Systems have been proposed to model a time series, where an ANN has the parameters automatically adjusted, with a problem dependent procedure. A very promising approach is to combine the ANN with others Artificial Intelligence techniques, as genetic algorithms, evolutionary strategies, simulated annealing, among others, for enhancement the final time series forecast.

In this chapter is presented some intelligent techniques as Artificial Neural Networks (Haykin, 1998), Genetic Algorithms (GA) (Goldberg, 1989), Particle Swarm Optimization (PSO) (Eberhart and Kennedy, 1995; van den Bergh and Engelbrecht, 2004), Greedy Randomized Adaptive Search Procedures (GRASP) (Feo and Resende, 1995; Resende and Ribeiro, 2003) and an Intelligent Hybrid method, composed of an ANN combined with GRASP procedure and Evolutionary Strategies, for chaotic and non-linear time series prediction, called GRASPES.

The GRASPES method is based on a multi-start metaheuristic for combinatorial problems to train, to tune and to adjust the structure and parameters of an ANN. The GRASPES is capable to evolve the parameters configuration and the weights in order to train the ANN, searching, in evolutionary sense, the minimum number of relevant time lags for a correct time series representation. It also looks for an optimal or sub-optimal predictive model. A detail experimental procedure, explained step by step, is shown, where an investigation is conducted with the GRASPES method with four different fitness function and with two time series. The results achieved are discussed and compared, according to five well-known statistical performance measures, like MSE, MAPE, POCID, Statistical of U Theil and ARV. Furthermore, in order to fill some lacks of experimental justified guidelines to help the practitioners to find good predictions using these techniques, an experimental analysis is made according to different types of fitness functions evaluations.

This document is organized as follows. In Section 3, some modelling strategies for non-linear times series analysis are presented. Intelligent methods for computational modeling are described in Section 4 and the problem of time series forecasting is defined in Section 2. The proposed method is developed in Section 5. The statistical performance measures and the fitness functions are presented in Section 6 and 7 respectively. Experimental results and some discussions are presented in Section 8. Finally, Section 9 provides the conclusion and a few remarks.

2. Time Series Forecasting Problem

In the branch of statistics, signal processing, or many other study fields, a time series is a set of data points, measured generally at successive times, spaced at (often uniform) time intervals, defined by,

$$X_t = \{x_t \in \mathbb{R} \mid t = 1, 2, 3 \ldots N\}, \tag{1}$$

where t is the temporal index and N is the number of observations. Therefore, X_t is a sequence of temporal observations orderly sequenced and equally spaced.

The objective of the forecast problem is to apply some prediction techniques for the time series X_t and to identify patterns presents in the historical data, building a model able to identify the next time patterns. This kind of problem is not always easy to solve, considering that a real world time series has a huge complexity.

In this context, a most relevant factor for a good forecasting performance is the correct choice of the time lags considered for a time series representation. For situations where there is a clear linear relationship among historical data of a phenomenon, the functions of auto-correlation

and partial auto-correlation are capable of identifying the important lags. Such procedure is usually applied in linear models, such as Box-Jenkins' models (Box et al., 1994).
However, when working with complex time series, which is the general situation in real world applications, the structures of relationship among historical data are actually non-linear, which makes the analysis procedure of the time lags based on those functions only a crude estimate.
Such relationship structures among historical data constitute a d-dimensional state space, where d is the minimum dimension capable of representing such relationship. Therefore, a d-dimensional state space can be built so that it is possible to unfold a time series in its interior. Takens (Takens, 1980) has proved that if d is sufficiently large, such built state space is homeomorphic to the state space which generated the time series. Thus, Takens Theorem (Takens, 1980) has provided the theoretical justification that it is possible to build a state space using the correct lags, and if this space is correctly rebuilt, guarantees that the dynamics of this space are topologically identical to the dynamics of the original system's state space.
In this way, it verifies that the main problem in the rebuilding of the state space is the correct choice of dimension d, i.e., the correct choice of the relevant time lags necessary for system dynamics characterization. In literature, can be found many methods used for the definition of the lags(Pi and Peterson, 1994; Savit and Green, 1991; Tanaka et al., 2001). Such methods are usually based on measures of conditional probabilities, which consider:

$$x_t = f(x_{t-1}, x_{t-2}, \ldots, x_{t-d}) + R_t \quad (2)$$

where $f(x_{t-1}, x_{t-2}, \ldots, x_{t-d})$ is a possible mapping of the pasts values to the facts of the future and R_t is a noise term. Generally, R_t decreases with the increase of d, and if the system is totally deterministic, R_t tends to zero when d exceeds the minimum embedded dimension necessary for the system description. With this kind of procedure, the objectives are to define the minimum embedded dimension capable of representing the series, to find the sensibility of x_t with respect to the time lags, and to estimate the size of the noise.
The exhibited method in this chapter does not discard any possible correlation that can exist between the series data, even higher order correlations, since it carries out an iterative automatic search for solving the problem of finding the relevant time lags using an evolutionary algorithm.

3. Computing and Mathematical Modelling

The term *model* is normally used for a structure which has been built purposely to exhibit the behavior of some other objects. Generally only some features and characteristics will be retained in the model depending upon the use.
Many models used for time series forecasting have standard forms, where they try to capture the time series features. One of these models is the popular ARIMA model (Box et al., 1994), which is the most common choice among the practitioners for time series prediction, but it is not the best choice for the case of non-linear time series forecasting problems (Rodrigues et al., 2008)
Furthermore, statistical parameters are obtained as a result of modelling uncertainty about problem data by specification of probability distributions over these data. The value of a statistical model stem from the ability to represent solutions that hedge against multiple possible future outcomes. In deterministic and linear model, optimal solutions tend toward extreme point solutions which rely on a limited set of activities (basic variables) and force a solution to meet critical constraints tightly. Thus, to model real problems, statistical parameters have

been used with Mathematical Programming, Differential Equations and Cellular Automata. Particularly, Kantz (2004) has been presented the most common strategies these approaches. As reported by Derek Holmes (Robert R. Mc Cormick school of Engineering and Applied Science - Northwestern University - `http://users.icms.northwestern.edu`), many decision problems can be modeled using mathematical programs, which seek to maximize or minimize some objective which is a function of decisions. The possible decisions are constrained by limits in resources, minimum requirements. Decisions are represented by variables. Objectives and constraints are functions of the variables, and problem data. Stochastic programs are mathematical programs where some of data incorporated into the objective or constraints is uncertain. Uncertainty is usually characterized by a probability distribution on the parameters. Although the uncertainty is rigorously defined, in practice it can range in detail from a few scenarios (possible outcomes of the data) to specific and precise joint probability distributions. It is possible to formulate a Stochastic Linear Program, as shown on the Argonne National Laboratory (Mathematics and Computer Science Division - `http://www.mcs.anl.gov`), like a task that seek to minimize the cost of the first-stage decision plus the expected cost of the second-stage recourse decision:

$$\textbf{Min} \quad c^T x + E_w Q(x,y),$$

subject to

$$Ax = b \quad \textbf{and} \quad x \geq 0,$$

where

$$Q(x,y) = \quad \textbf{Min} \quad d(w)^T y,$$

subject to

$$T(w)x + W(w)y(w) = h(w).$$

The first linear program(LP) minimizes the first-stage direct costs, $c^T x$ plus the expected recourse cost, $Q(x,y)$, over all the possible scenarios while meeting the first-stage constraints, $Ax = b$.
The cost Q depends both on x, the first-stage decision, and on the random event, w. The second LP describes how to choose $y(w)$ (a different decision for each random scenario w). It minimizes the cost $d^T y$ subject to some function, $Tx + Wy = h$. This constraint can be thought of as requiring some action to correct the system after the random event occurs.
One important issue to notice in stochastic programs is that the first-stage decision, x, is independent of which second-stage scenario actually occurs. This is called the *non-anticipativity property*. The future is uncertain and so today's decision cannot take advantage of knowledge of the future. In this way, we can treat the events as independent ones and approximations on expected values are mathematically possible as to convert the problem in a deterministic equivalent one, which is used in Kantz (2004).
Therefore, intelligent methods for computational modelling have been successful applied to capture the chaotic and non-linear behavior of *forecasting real time series* (Ferreira et al., 2005; Ghiassi et al., 2005; Rodrigues et al., 2008; Zhang et al., 1998).

4. Intelligent Methods for Computational Modelling

In the field of intelligent computing there are several approaches that can be used for computational modeling. The techniques to be used are determined by the problem at hand, for problems such as classification or recognition of patterns can be used RBF networks, Support

Vector Machines (SVMs), KNN (K-Nearest Neighbors Algorithm), Meta-Heuristics, among others. For optimization problems can be utilized Genetic Algorithms, Particle Swarm Optimization, among others. For forecasting problem, Neural Networks , Multi-Layer Perceptron, Jordan type or Elman type, are heavily used and generally are combined with others techniques as Evolutionary Algorithms (Genetic Algorithms, Evolution strategy, Evolutionary programming and Genetic programming) and others approaches as Particle Swarm Optimization or SVMs for example.
In the next sections will describe some techniques used to further the time series forecasting problem.

4.1 Artificial Neural Networks – Multi-Layer Perceptron

An Artificial Neural Networks (ANN) is a mathematical model inspired in a biological neural network which automatically extract useful patterns to represent the desired information. The ability to learn through examples and to generalize the learned information is one of the most attractive characteristics of the ANN.
The key element of this abstract model is the structure of the information processing distributed system. It is composed of a large number of highly interconnected processing units divided in layers, but working in union to solve a determinate problem. Through a learning process, where adjustments to the synaptic connections that exist between the neurones, the ANN seek the best possible solution, being a similar process to biological neurons.
Each ANN is create and configured for a specific application, such as data classification or forecasting problem. The ANN is used with successful in solving time series forecasting problems due to its characteristic of modeling complex non-linear relationships among data (Ghiassi et al., 2005), without any prior supposition of the data nature.

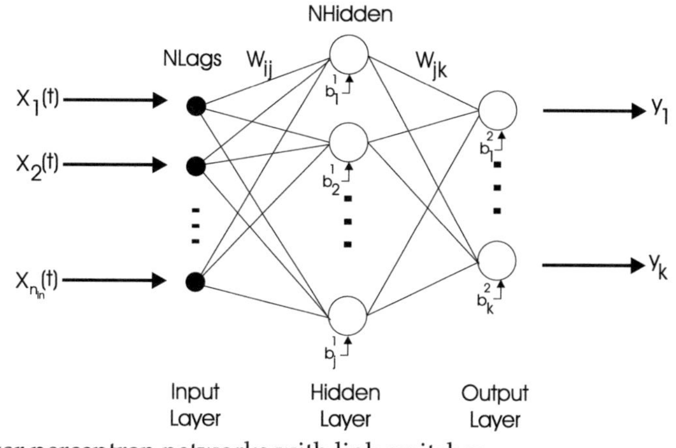

Fig. 1. Multi-Layer perceptron networks with link switches.

The possibility to improve the prediction performance of ANN can be achieved through the correct adjustment of its parameters. The main problem is to determine the optimal or sub-optimal values of these parameters. Whereas that all parameters are problem dependent, it is a very complex task to find them into a very wide universe of possibilities. However, a layer ANN just solve a set of linearly separable problems, so to solve non-linearly separable problems, it is necessary to use at least one hidden layer ANN, according to Cybenko(Cybenko,

1989), who also proved that an ANN is an universal approximate function since the ANN has at least one hidden layer.
As the goal of this work is to predict continuous functions, then a MultiLayer Perceptron (MLP) networks with three layers of type *i-j-k* should be used, where i denotes the number of time lags (processing units in input layer), j denotes the number of processing units in hidden layer (sigmoidal units) and k denotes the number of processing units in output layer (the chosen prediction horizon here is of one step ahead, so $k = 1$ should be used).
Three possible distinct forms of modeling the ANN are proposed ($NetMod = 1,2,3$), where each one is described below and its parameters are:

- W_{ij}, weight of connections of the input layer for the intermediary layer;
- W_{jk}, weight of connections of the intermediary layer for the output layer;
- b_j^1, bias of the intermediary unit;
- b_k^2, bias of the output unit,

where all these parameters are real values.
The first ANN model ($NetMod = 1$), uses the sigmoidal activation function for all hidden processing units. The output processing unit uses a linear activation function where a sigmoidal function is applied to its bias. The output of ANN is given by,

$$y_k(t) = \sum_{j=1}^{n_h} W_{jk} Sig\left[\sum_{i=1}^{n_{in}} (W_{ij} Z_i(t) - b_j^1)\right] - Sig(b_k^2), \tag{3}$$

where $Z_i(t)$ ($i = 1, 2, \ldots, n_{in}$) are the ANN input values, n_{in} denotes the ANN input number and n_h is the hidden units number. Since the prediction horizon is one step ahead, only one output unit is necessary ($k = 1$). The term Sig is a sigmoidal function,

$$Sig(x) = \frac{1}{1 + exp(-x)}. \tag{4}$$

The utilization of the sigmoidal function to the bias, in this model, is the assumption of the linear correlation between the delay and a possible non-linear behavior of the series.
The Second ANN model ($NetMod = 2$), consists of hidden units activated by a sigmoidal function with its output layer using a linear function, given by:

$$y_k(t) = \sum_{j=1}^{n_h} W_{jk} Sig\left[\sum_{i=1}^{n_{in}} (W_{ij} Z_i(t) - b_j^1)\right] - b_k^2. \tag{5}$$

The Third ANN model ($NetMod = 3$), applies the sigmoidal activation function to all processing units, given by:

$$y_k(t) = Sig\left\{\sum_{j=1}^{n_h} W_{jk} Sig\left[\sum_{i=1}^{n_{in}} (W_{ij} Z_i(t) - b_j^1)\right] - b_k^2\right\}. \tag{6}$$

These three MLP modeling ($NetMod = 1,2,3$) can be combined with other systems, and it will search by architecture that better describes the time series phenomenon.

4.2 Genetic Algorithm

Genetic Algorithms (GA) (Goldberg, 1989) are a technique of directed random search widely applied in complex optimization problems. They are particularly interesting for employment in situations where the number of parameters is very large and analytical solutions are very difficult, or impossible, to obtain. The modified GA (MGA) exhibited here was originally proposed by(Leung et al., 2003) where new genetic operations were introduced to improve its performance.

4.2.1 Population

The population is composed of individuals (chromosomes), where each of these individuals represents a possible model for time series prediction: an ANN and its parameters.
Initially, the first set of population, P, is generated randomly, $P = \{\mathbf{ind}_1, \mathbf{ind}_2, \ldots, \mathbf{ind}_{pop\_size}\}$, where $\mathbf{ind}_i$ ($i = 1, 2, \ldots, pop\_size$) are the individuals that make up the population and pop_size is the population size. Each individual, or chromosome, is composed of genes (the parameters of the solution) given by

$$\mathbf{X} = (x_1, x_2, \ldots, x_p) \tag{7}$$

where x_i ($i = 1, 2, \ldots, p$) are the solution parameters and p is the maximum parameters number.
Each chromosome in the population is evaluated (Section 7) and the better chromosomes return higher fitness values.

4.2.2 Selection

In each generation, two chromosomes in the population will be selected to undergo a genetic operation (crossover operation) by the fitness proportionate method. A popular selection method is the spinning the roulette wheel(Goldberg, 1989; Leung et al., 2003), where the chromosome having a higher fitness value should therefore have a higher chance of being selected (higher potential parents will produce better offspring).

4.2.3 Genetic Operations

After the selection process, two chromosomes (parents) are combined to generate new chromosomes (offspring) by genetic operations. The genetic operations include the crossover and mutation operations.
The crossover operation is the basic means for exchanging information from the two parents ($\mathbf{p}_1$ and $\mathbf{p}_2$). These parents will produce one offspring composed of four new chromosomes (four sons), according to the following mechanisms:

$$C_1 = [c_1^1 \quad c_1^2 \quad \cdots \quad c_1^{no\_Vars}] = \frac{\mathbf{p}_1 + \mathbf{p}_2}{2} \tag{8}$$

$$C_2 = [c_2^1 \quad c_2^2 \quad \cdots \quad c_2^{no\_Vars}] = \mathbf{p}_{max}(1 - w) + \max(\mathbf{p}_1, \mathbf{p}_2)w \tag{9}$$

$$C_3 = [c_3^1 \quad c_3^2 \quad \cdots \quad c_3^{no\_Vars}] = \mathbf{p}_{min}(1 - w) + \min(\mathbf{p}_1, \mathbf{p}_2)w \tag{10}$$

$$C_4 = [c_4^1 \quad c_4^2 \quad \cdots \quad c_4^{no\_Vars}] = \frac{(\mathbf{p}_{min} + \mathbf{p}_{max})(1 - w) + (\mathbf{p}_1 + \mathbf{p}_2)w}{2} \tag{11}$$

$$\mathbf{P}_{max} = [para_{max}^1 \quad para_{max}^2 \quad \cdots \quad para_{max}^{no\_Vars}] \tag{12}$$

$$\mathbf{P}_{min} = [para^1_{min} \quad para^2_{min} \quad \cdots \quad para^{no\_Vars}_{min}] \tag{13}$$

where $w \in [0 \ldots 1]$ denotes a weight to be determined by user, $\max(\mathbf{p}_1, \mathbf{p}_2)$ and $\min(\mathbf{p}_1, \mathbf{p}_2)$ denotes the vector with each element obtained by taking the maximum and minimum, respectively, among the corresponding element of $\mathbf{p}_1$ and $\mathbf{p}_2$, no_Vars denotes the number of variables to be tuned and $para^j_{min}$ and $para^j_{max}$ are the minimum and maximum values of the parameter $\mathbf{X}^j_i$ for all i, respectively.
According to the Equations 8 – 11, the potential offspring spread over the state space defined by $\mathbf{P}_{max}$ and $\mathbf{P}_{min}$. Equations 8 and 11 result in searching around the center region of the state space (if $w \to 1$ then $C_4 \to C_1$), whereas Equations 9 and 10 move the potential offspring near to the domain boundary (if $w \to 1$ then $C_2 \to \mathbf{P}_{max}$ and $C_3 \to \mathbf{P}_{min}$).
After the potential offspring are generated by the crossover operation, the best offspring is chosen, and if this offspring is better than the worst chromosome from the old population, then this offspring replaces the worst chromosome.
Each one of the four new chromosomes generated by the crossover process is cloned and its clones undergo the mutation operation, where three new chromosomes are generated by,

$$MC_{i,\alpha} = [c^1_i \quad c^2_i \quad \cdots \quad c^{no\_Vars}_i] + [\delta_1 mc^1_i \quad \delta_2 mc^2_i \quad \cdots \quad \delta_{no\_Vars} mc^{no\_Vars}_i] \tag{14}$$

where $\alpha = 1,2,3$ is the mutation index, $i = 1,2,3,4$ is the offspring index, δ_u ($u = 1,2,\ldots,no\_Vars$) can only take values 0 or 1, and mc^u_i ($u = 1,2,\ldots,no\_Vars$) are randomly generated numbers that satisfy the constraint $para^u_{min} \leq c^u_i + mc^u_i \leq para^u_{max}$. Small mutation are more likely than largest ones(Eiben and Smith, 2003) therefore a gaussian, with normal distribution, is used to perform the mutation operation .
The first mutation operation ($\alpha = 1$) is such that only one δ_u is 1 and all the others are 0 in Equation 14. The second mutation operation ($\alpha = 2$) is obtained by Equation 14, where some δ_u, randomly chosen, are set to 1 and others are set to 0. The third mutation operation ($\alpha = 3$) is obtained with all δ_u equal to 1 in Equation 14. A real number is randomly generated and compared to a user defined number $p_{Mut} \in [0 \ldots 1]$ (accepted mutational probability). If the real number is smaller than p_{Mut} then the mutated chromosome replaces the chromosome with the smallest fitness in the population. However, if the real number is larger than p_{Mut}, then the mutated chromosome replaces the chromosome with the smallest fitness of the population if and only if its fitness is greater than the fitness of the worst chromosome in the population.
The stopping criterion are: training progress, where the GA will stop when occurs a defined number of generations without a percentage increase the average of the population, and the maximum generations number.
The steps necessary for implementing the whole modified GA algorithm are shown below (Algorithm 2).

4.3 Particle Swarm Optimizer Fundamentals

The Particle Swarm Optimization (PSO) is an optimization technique based on a particle population of randomly solutions (i.e. individuals) to the optimization task at hand, where the population is referred to as swarm. At each iteration, each particle moves by the search space in the direction of its own personal best solution found so far, as well as in the direction of the global best position discovered so far by any of the particles in the swarm (van den

```
begin
  τ → 0; // τ:  Number of iteration
  initialize Pop(τ); // Pop(τ): population for iteration τ
  evaluate f(Pop(τ)); // f(Pop(τ)): fitness function
  while not termination condition do
    τ → τ+1;
    select two parents p1 and p2 from Pop(ø);
    perform crossover operation according to Equations 8 to 11;
    perform mutation operation according to Equation 14 to generate three new
    chromosomes MC1, MC2 and MC3;
      // Reproduce a new Population
    The chromosome generated by the crossover operation with the largest fitness
    value replaces the chromosome with the smallest fitness value in the
    Pop(τ − 1);
    for i=1 to 3 do
        // pMut: probability of Mutation acceptance
      if random number < pMut then
        MCi replaces the chromosome with the smallest fitness value in the
        Pop(τ − 1)
      else
        if f(MCi) > smallest fitness value in the Pop(τ − 1) then
          MCi replaces the chromosome with the smallest fitness value in
          the Pop(τ − 1)
    evaluate f(Pop(τ));
end
```

Fig. 2. Procedure of the Modified GA

Bergh and Engelbrecht, 2004). In this way, if any particle discovers a promising solution, the swarm is guided to the new solution in order to explore more thoroughly the found region. Assume that the swarm size is given by s. Each individual ($1 \leq i \leq s$) has a current position in search space (x_i), a current velocity (v_i) and a personal best position in the search space (y_i). Assuming that the function f is to be minimized, the swarm consists of n particles, and at each iteration, each swarm particle velocity is updated by

$$v_{i,j}(t+1) = wv_{i,j}(t) + c_1 r_1 [y_{i,j}(t) - x_{i,j}(t)] + c_2 r_2 [\hat{y}_j(t) - x_{i,j}(t)] \ , \quad (15)$$

where $j \in 1, 2, \ldots, n$, $\hat{y}_j(t)$ denotes the current position in search space (found by any swarm particle), $y_{i,j}(t)$ represents the personal best position in the search space (found by each swarm particle), $v_{i,j}$ is the velocity of the j-th dimension of the i-th particle, c_1 and c_2 represent the acceleration coefficients, which control how far a particle will move in a single iteration, and $r_1 \sim U(0,1)$ and $r_2 \sim U(0,1)$ are elements from two uniform random sequences in the interval [0,1]. The term w is referred to as inertia weight, in which this value is typically setup to vary linearly from 1 to near 0 during the course of the procedure. It is worth to mention that this is reminiscent of the temperature adjustment schedule found in Simulated Annealing algorithms(van den Bergh and Engelbrecht, 2004).

Thus, the new particle position is updated by

$$x_i(t+1) = x_i(t) + v_i(t+1). \tag{16}$$

The personal best particle position and the global best particle found by any particle during all previous iterations are updated by equations (17) and (18), respectively.

$$y_i(t+1) = \begin{cases} y_i(t) & \text{if } f(x_i(t+1)) \geq f(y_i(t)), \\ x_i(t+1) & \text{otherwise.} \end{cases}; \tag{17}$$

$$\hat{y}(t+1) = \text{argmin} f(y_i(t+1)). \tag{18}$$

```
begin
    initialize the particle population;
    while stop criterion not satisfied do
        for i = 1 to s of population swarm do
            if f(x_i(t)) < f(y_i(t)) then
                y_i(t) = x_i(t);
            end
            if (f(y_i(t)) < f(ŷ_i(t))) then
                ŷ_i(t) = y_i(t);
            end
        end
    end
    update the velocity and position of each particle according to equations (13) and
    (14);
end
```

Fig. 3. Particle Swarm Optimizer Procedure

The term v_i is normalized in the range $[-v_{max}, v_{max}]$ in order to reduce the likelihood of particles leaving the search space. It is worth to mention that this mechanism doesn't restrict the values of x_i in the range of v_i, it only limits the maximum distance that a particle will move during each iteration(van den Bergh and Engelbrecht, 2004). Figure3 illustrates the PSO procedure.

4.4 The GRASP Method

The GRASP (Resende and Ribeiro, 2003) method is a randomly interactive technique which each iteration consists of two phases: construction and local search.
The construction phase builds a feasible solution, whose neighborhood is investigated until a local minimum is found during the local search phase. The best overall solution is kept as the result. The general expectation is that, given a sub-optimal solution, closed to it there will be, with high probability, other sub-optimal (or optimal) solutions. The search will tend to look around of such solution, stopping when a local optimum model is found.
A problem of combinatorial optimization, is defined by the finite set of data $D = \{1, 2, \ldots, N\}$, the set of possible solutions $G \subseteq 2^D$, and the objective function $f : 2^D \to \mathbf{R}$. For minimization problems, searches for the excellent solution $S' \in G$ such that $f(S') =< f(S) \forall S \in G$. The ground set D, the cost function f, and the set of feasible solutions G are defined for each specific problem for example as described on Algorithm 4.

```
begin GRASP
    initialize MaxIter, Seed;
    Read Input();
    for i=1 to MaxIter do
        Solution ← Greedy Randomized Construction(Seed);
        Solution ← Local Search(Solution);
        UpdateSolution(Solution, BestSolution);
    end
    return BestSolution;
end
```

Fig. 4. Pseudo-code of the GRASP metaheuristic (Resende and Ribeiro, 2003).

5. The GRASPES Method

The GRASPES (Rodrigues et al., 2008) is basically a combination of Evolutionary Strategies(ES) and the GRASP method (Section 4.4).

For methods based on evolutionary computation (Evolutionary Strategies are a part of evolutionary computation), the process of biological evolution is mimicked. Population is composed by set of trial solutions of the problem, being each solution (individual) coded by a parameter vector (data structure, referred to as chromosome).

Let **X** be a chromosome defined by,

$$\mathbf{X} = (x_1, x_2, \ldots, x_p; \sigma_1, \sigma_2, \ldots, \sigma_p) \tag{19}$$

where x_i and σ_i are respectively the solution parameters and the mutation step size of each parameter with $i = 1, 2, \ldots, p$ and p is the maximum parameters number. The model represented by Equation 19, used to describe a three-layer ANN parameters, coded the chromosomes in the population.

The mutation operation is defined by Eiben and Smith (2003) ,

$$\mathbf{X}' = (x'_1, x'_2, \ldots, x'_p; \sigma'_1, \sigma'_2, \ldots, \sigma'_p), \tag{20}$$

with

$$\sigma'_i = \sigma_i \cdot exp(\tau' \cdot N(0,1) + \tau \cdot N_i(0,1)), \tag{21}$$

$$x'_i = x_i + \sigma' \cdot N_i(0,1), \tag{22}$$

where $\tau' \propto 1/\sqrt{2f}$, $\tau \propto 1/\sqrt{2\sqrt{f}}$, f is the degree of freedom and $N(0,1)$ is a normal gaussian distribution.

Each individual codifies a three layer Multilayer Perceptron (MLP) ANN, which represents a model for time series forecasting. An ES initialize one individual I, which is a potential solution, generated randomly. The individual will be evaluated by the fitness function, Equation 29 described on Section 7, where betters individuals will return higher fitness values. The ES clones the father's chromosome I_p and will then undergo a operation of mutation which changes the genes of the chromosome. For tuning the ANN structure (Leung et al., 2003), integer random numbers are generated to define the ANN number of time lags (processing units in input layer i), the number of processing units in hidden layer (sigmoidal units j) and the modeling of the ANN. For each weight of the optimal individual I the mutation is applied as

described in the Equations 20, 21 and 22. This new individual is evaluated and will be saved, if and if only, its solution quality (Section 7) is better than the actual father.
This steps will be repeated until the mutated individuals number criterium or the size of the population n is reached. When this fact occur, it will be said that a Parent's Generation (PG) occurs and if this PG has any offspring better than father it will substitute the father. The stopping criterion are: progress of PG evolution, where the method will stop if a PG iteration number occur without better individual generation (a individual is considered "better" when your fitness is greater, a percentage value, than the father), or a maximum PG number. The basic steps of the method are described in the Algorithm, 5.

```
begin GRASPES
    initialize parent;
    evaluate f(parent);  // f(·): fitness function
    while not PG criterium reached do
        clone parent;
        for w=1 to number of iteration per father do
            define the input layer i and hidden layer j;
            perform mutation operation on sons I_τ;
            evaluate f(I_τ);
            if f(I_τ) > parent's fitness value then
                save the offspring;
                if the size of n was reached then
                    break;
                end
            end
        end
        if (f(parent) - f(offspring)) > % of minimal fitness) then
            the individual will be the new parent;
        end
    end
end
```

Fig. 5. Pseudo-code of the GRASPES Method

6. Error Measure

For the forecasting problem, the natural measure of performance is the prediction error. However, there is no universal measure adopted (by the literature of the branch) to evaluate the prediction (Tashman, 2000). Error measures also play an important role in calibrating or refining a model so that it will forecast accurately for a set of time series (Armstrong and Collopy, 1992). The use of only one error for evaluate the model performance (*e.g.*, MSE), not shows the behavior of the predict (Clements and Hendry, 1993) in a clear way, for this reason more performance criteria should be considered for make robust the evaluation of the results and final desirable goals (Tashman, 2000).
Considering T the value to be predicted of the time series (target) and O the model output (prediction), five well known error measure are considered to evaluate the prediction performance:

MSE (Mean Squared Error):the most popular measure used for performance prediction,

$$MSE = \frac{1}{N}\sum_{j=1}^{N}\left(e_j\right)^2, \tag{23}$$

where N is the amount of the target points on the set and $e_j = (T_j - O_j)$.
MAPE (Percentage Average Error):

$$MAPE = \frac{1}{N}\sum_{j=1}^{N}\left|\frac{e_j}{X_j}\right| \tag{24}$$

where X_j is the point of the set in the instant j.
U of Theil Statistics: it is based in the predictor MSE, normalized by a random walk forecast error. A random walk model assumes that optimum value for the time $t+1$ is the value gotten in the time t, plus a noise term. Thus, the U of Theil Statistics can be given by:

$$Theil = \frac{\sum_{j=1}^{N}\left(T_j - O_j\right)^2}{\sum_{j=1}^{N}\left(T_j - T_{j+1}\right)^2}. \tag{25}$$

that associates the model performance with a random walk model. If the U of Theil Statistics is equal to 1, the predictor has the same performance of a random walk model. If the U of Theil Statistics is greater than 1, then the predictor has a worse performance than a Random Walk model, and if the U of Theil Statistics is less than 1, the predictor is better than a random walk model. So, the predictor is usable if its U of Theil Statistics is less than 1, and tends to the perfect model if the U of Theil Statistics tends to zero.
POCID (Prediction of Forecast the Alterations of Direction): measures the percentage of rightness with the trend of the series, if the future value will to go up or to go fall in relation to the current value.

$$POCID = 100\frac{\sum_{j=1}^{N} D_j}{N}, \tag{26}$$

with

$$D_j = \begin{cases} 1 & \text{if } (T_j - T_{j-1})(O_j - O_{j-1}) > 0, \\ 0 & \text{other case.} \end{cases} \tag{27}$$

ARV (Average Relative Variance): measures the relative performance model gain of the prediction of the series average,

$$ARV = \frac{\sum_{j=1}^{N}(O_j - T_j)^2}{\sum_{j=1}^{N}(O_j - \overline{T})^2} \tag{28}$$

where N, T_j, and O_j are the same parameters of the other evaluation measures, and $\overline{T}$ is the time series mean. If the ARV value is equal to 1, the predictor has the same performance as calculating the mean over the series, if the ARV value is greater than 1, the predictor is worse than simply taking the mean, and, if the ARV is less than 1, then the predictor is better than considering the mean as the prediction. So, the predictor is usable if the value of ARV is less than 1, and tends to the perfect model when the ARV tends to zero. In an ideal model, the POCID tends to 100% and all other error measures tends to zero.

7. Fitness Function

The first important feature about fitness computation is that it represents 99% of the total computational cost of evolution in most real-world problems. Second, the fitness function very often is the only information about the problem in the algorithm: any available and usable knowledge about the problem domain should be used (Eiben and Schoenauer, 2002). Basically, the fitness function (aptitude), assigns a fitness value to each point in the space, where this value can be seen as a measure of how good a solution, represented by that point in the landscape, is to given problem (Hordijk, 1996). The correct choice of the fitness function is fundamental for a good solution of the problem.
For the best ANN model choice (of each individual), it is calculated its fitness function through of error measure, which is:

$$fitness = f_n(I) \tag{29}$$

where the functions are:

$$f_1(I) = \frac{1}{1 + ARV} \tag{30}$$

$$f_2(I) = \frac{1}{1 + MSE} \tag{31}$$

$$f_3(I) = \frac{1}{1 + THEIL} \tag{32}$$

$$f_4(I) = \frac{POCID}{1 + ARV + MSE + THEIL + MAPE} \tag{33}$$

8. Experimental Results

There is no only and universal way adopted for define the cardinality of the data set, but one common example used is divide the series in three sets: training set with 50% of the data, validation set with 25% of the data and test set with the last 25% of data. In order to be able to concentrate on the effects of the methods, it makes sense avoid unnecessary complications due to effects of other much more components (Jansen et al., 2005). For this reason all series investigated were normalized to lie within the interval [0;1] and the MLP networks are not trained by any conventional algorithms like backpropagation (Haykin, 1998) for example, avoiding the possibility that the training method could interfere in the general search.
Conclusions about the accuracy of various forecasting methods typically require comparisons across some time series (Armstrong and Collopy, 1992). Two financial time series were used for evaluation of the GRASPES (Dow Jones Industrial Average Index and S&P500 Stock Index).
For each time series with a different fitness function, ten experiments were repeated and the results with the best individual according with the best value of the validation fitness function (of the test set) is chosen to represent the model. For the predictions (with 1 step ahead of prediction horizon), the methods automatically choose a window time with length between 1 lag and 10 lags for the time series representation and the size of the j-layer (between 1 and 10). In addition, experiments with two hybrid methods to training an ANN (one using a modified genetic algorithm -MGA- and another using particle swarm optimization -PSO) are used for comparison with the proposed method.

The termination conditions for the GRASPES are increase of 1% of the minimal population fitness average value better than the previous (in the case of GRASPES the population is only one individual), after 10000 generations or when the fitness function of the validation set decrease 1% with respect to last round.

8.1 Standard & Poor 500 (S&P500)

The S&P500 Stock Index is a index of market values of the most negotiated actions in the New York Stock Exchange (NYSE), American Stock Exchange (AMEX) and Nasdaq National Market System. The S&P500 series corresponds to the monthly records from January 1970 to August 2003, constituting a database of 369 points. In order to reduce exponential trend of the S&P500 Stock Index, the natural logarithm was applied to the original values of the series.

	MGA	PSO	GRASPES			
Measures	f_3	f_4	f_1	f_2	f_3	f_4
ARV	0.015	0.053	0.009	0.012	0.011	0.044
MAPE	0.012	0.240	0.009	0.010	0.010	0.020
MSE(10^{-4})	1.776	6.988	1.183	1.418	1.416	4.896
POCID	77.419	51.111	67.391	68.817	67.391	72.043
THEIL	1.760	9.704	1.166	1.407	1.395	4.871

Table 1. Results - S&P500 - Best Individuals

The table 1 shows the experiments results, where for the MGA (Modified Genetic Algorithm) methodology the best fitness function was the f_3, for the PSO methodology the best fitness function was the f_4 and for the GRASPES method all fitness functions were shown. The GRASPES has always a superior performance when compared with the hybrid method using PSO. The Table also shows that when the GRASPES uses the fitness function f_1, f_2 and f_3 the MGA beat only the POCID error.
Figures 6, 7, 8 and 9 show the results of the test set according with the target (solid lines) and the predict values (dashed lines).

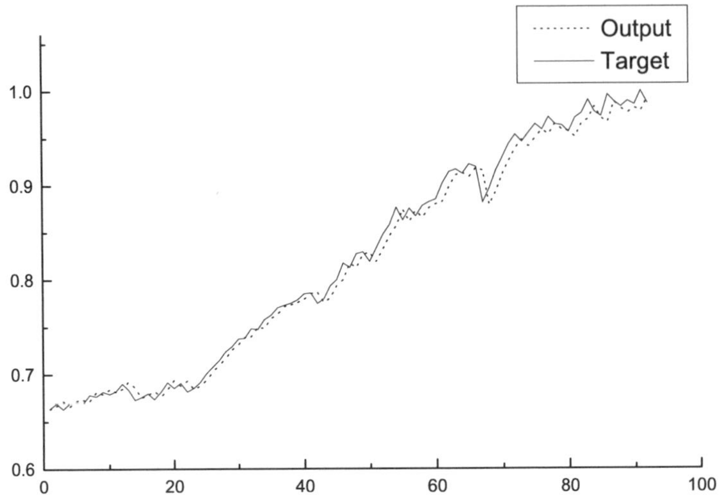

Fig. 6. Prediction os S&P500 series with Fitness Function f_1.

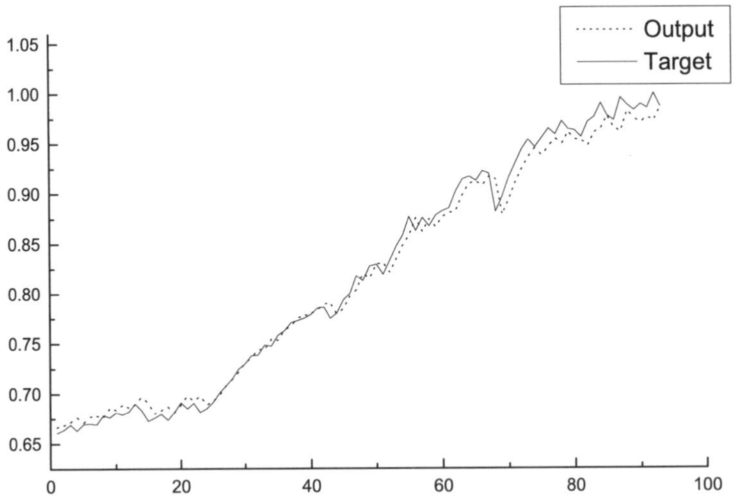

Fig. 7. Prediction os S&P500 series with Fitness Function f_2.

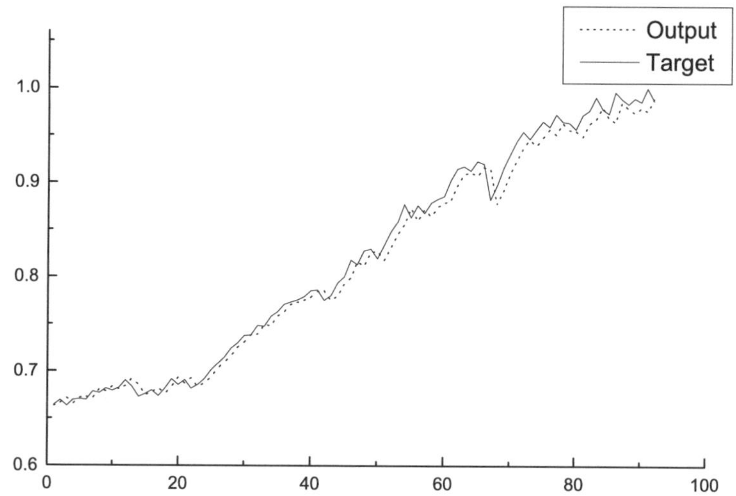

Fig. 8. Prediction os S&P500 series with Fitness Function f_3.

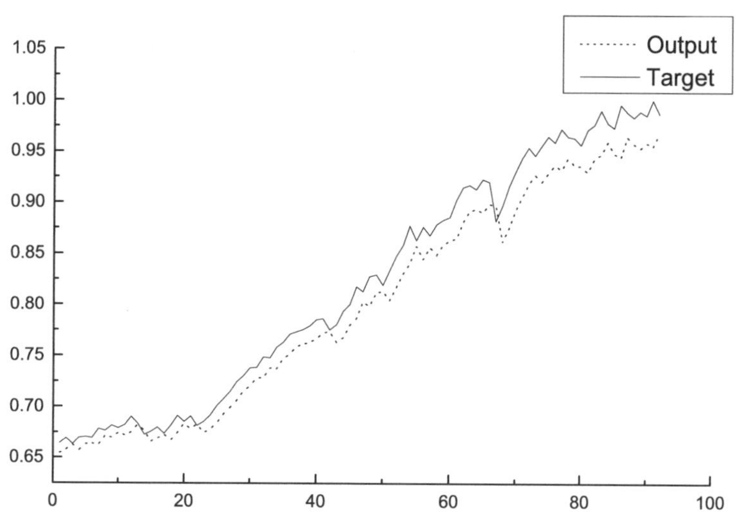

Fig. 9. Prediction os S&P500 series with Fitness Function f_4.

8.2 Dow Jones Industrial Average (DJIA)

The Dow Jones Industrial Average (DJIA) Index series corresponds to daily records from January 1st 1998 to August 26th 2003, constituting a database of 1420 points.

	MGA	PSO	GRASPES			
Measures	f_1	f_4	f_1	f_2	f_3	f_4
ARV	0.034	0.049	0.032	0.034	0.033	0.033
MAPE	0.098	0.143	0.095	0.098	0.096	0.097
MSE(10^{-3})	0.909	1.200	0.831	0.827	0.823	0.842
POCID	52.112	47.025	51.685	52.112	51.267	52.112
THEIL	1.087	1.986	0.998	0.991	0.986	1.009

Table 2. Results - DJIA - Best Individuals

Table 2 shows that the GRASPES has always a superior performance when compared with the hybrid method using PSO. The Table also shows that when the GRASPES uses the fitness function f_2 and f_3 the POCID error is the same as MGA and the others error are better. Figures 10, 11, 12 and 13 show the results of the test set according with the target (solid lines) and the predict values (dashed lines).

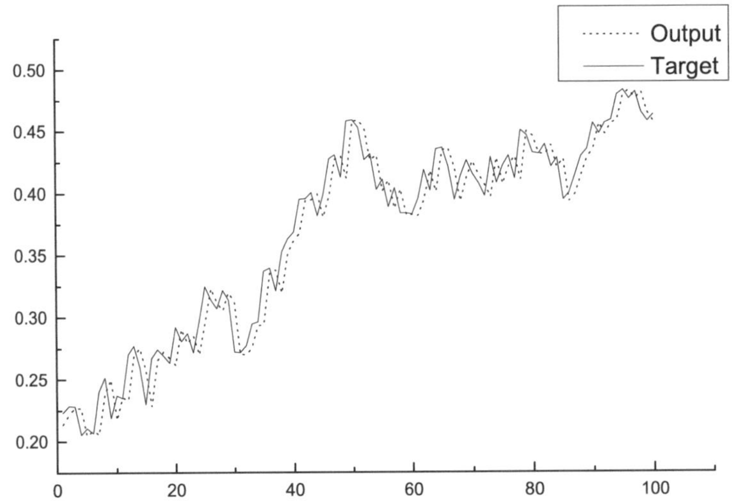

Fig. 10. Prediction os DJIA series with Fitness Function f_1.

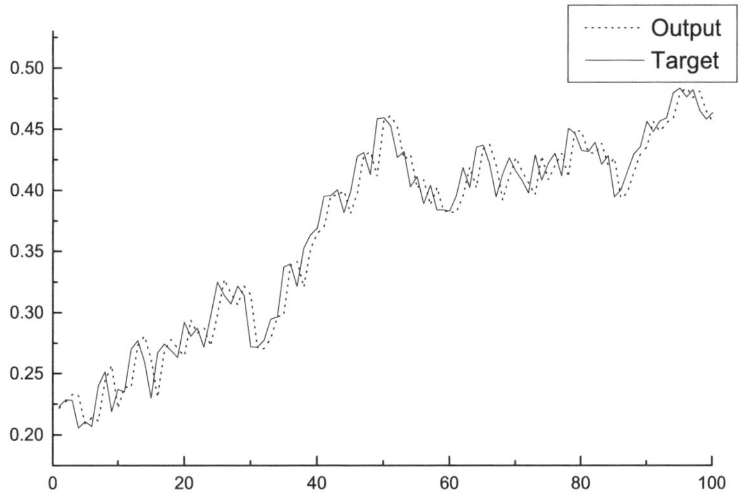

Fig. 11. Prediction os DJIA series with Fitness Function f_2.

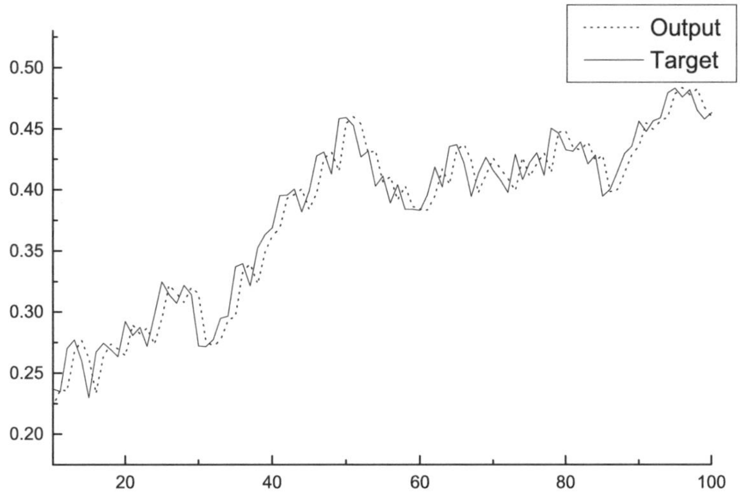

Fig. 12. Prediction os DJIA series with Fitness Function f_3.

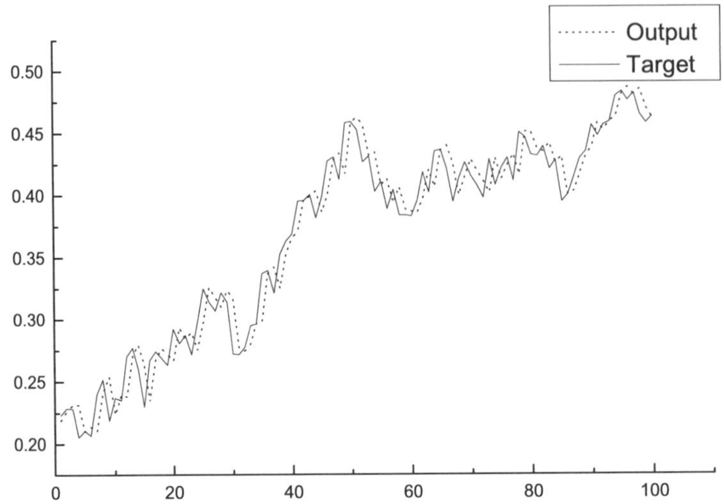

Fig. 13. Prediction os DJIA series with Fitness Function f_4.

9. Conclusions

In this chapter was presented a summary of how use the intelligent computational modelling for time series forecasting and the importance of the correct choice of the fitness function. Three methodology were employed for adjust the parameters of an ANN, a Modified Genetic Algorithm (MGA) (Section 4.2), a Particle Swarm Optimization (PSO) (Section 4.3) and the GRASPES Method (Section 5).

The success of evolution control is highly dependent of the optimization algorithm and the fitness function complexity (Buche et al., 2005). As affirmed in the Section 7, the fitness function assigns a fitness value to each individual in the population of Evolutionary Algorithm, at any time, measuring how good is a solution. This solution is represented by a point in the landscape. When an algorithm has a possibility to be guided by different fitness functions, each one will walk on the space, pointing in a different way. The experiments presented here show that the choice of the fitness function is also very important as the choice of the intelligent method employed for time series modelling.

The results reached with the MGA and PSO methods were developed in independent way and can be found at (de Mattos Neto et al., 2009; Rodrigues et al., 2009), respectively. In the Rodrigues et al. (2009) was employed eight different fitness functions, where the fitness function of Equation 32 achieved the best performance for the S&P500 index series and the fitness function 3 obtained the best result for the Dow Jones Industrial Average index series. However, in the (de Mattos Neto et al., 2009) the main goal was to develop the combination between the intelligent techniques ANN and PSO. For this reason, only one fitness function was applied (fitness function given by Equation 33)

Analyzing the S&P500 index results obtained here is possible to observe that the statistical error measures have a strong accomplished. These statistical measures present many times a competitive behavior. For example, observing the Table 1 for the GRASPES method, the fitness function f_2 (Equation 31) is directly based on MSE error, but f_2 has a inferior performance for the MSE error than the fitness function f_1 (Equation 30) which is based on ARV error. This observation shows that the choice of the fitness function is not a trivial decision.

According to the Table 2, where the experimental results for the Dow Jones Industrial Average are exhibits, it is possible to observe that the variation among the analyzed fitness functions are not significative. This observation shows that the sensibility of the choice of the fitness function for the Dow Jones Industrial Average is very low in comparison with the S&P500 index results, *i.e.*, small changes of the fitness function evaluation could lead to a significantly improved forecast performance.

10. References

Armstrong, J. S. and Collopy, F. (1992). Error measures for generalizing about forecasting methods: Empirical comparisons, *International Journal of Forecasting* **8**(1): 69–80.

Box, G. E. P., Jenkins, G. M. and Reinsel, G. C. (1994). *Time Series Analysis: Forecasting and Control*, third edn, Prentice Hall, New Jersey.

Buche, D., Schraudolph, N. and Koumoutsakos, P. (2005). Accelerating evolutionary algorithms with gaussian process fitness function models, *IEEE Transactions on Systems, Man, and Cybernetics, Part C: Applications and Reviews* **35**(2): 183–194.

Clements, M. P. and Hendry, D. F. (1993). On the limitations of comparing mean square forecast errors, *Journal of Forecasting* **12**(8): 617–637.

Cybenko, G. (1989). Approximation by superpositions of a sigmoidal function, *Mathematical Control Signals Systems* **2**: 303–314.

de Mattos Neto, P. S. G., Petry, G. G., Rodrigues, A. and Ferreira, T. A. E. (2009). Combining artificial neural network and particle swarm system for time series forecasting., *Proceedings of International Joint Conference on Neural Networks*, IEEE, Atlanta - Georgia.

Eberhart, R. C. and Kennedy, J. (1995). A new optimizer using particle swarm theory, *Proceedings of the Int. Symp. Micro Machine and Human Science*, Nagoya, Japan, pp. 39–43.

Eiben, A. E. and Schoenauer, M. (2002). Evolutionary computing, *Information Processing Letters* **82**(1): 1–6.

Eiben, A. E. and Smith, J. E. (2003). *Introduction to Evolutionary Computing*, Natural Computing Series, Springer, Berlin.

Feo, T. and Resende, M. (1995). Greedy randomized adaptive search procedures, *Journal of Global Optimization* **6**(2): 109–133.

Ferreira, T. A. E., Vasconcelos, G. C. and Adeodato, P. J. L. (2005). A new evolutionary method for times series ferecasting, *GECCO '05: Proceedings of the 2005 conference on Genetic and evolutionary computation*, ACM, New York, NY, USA, pp. 2221 – 2222.

Ghiassi, M., Saidane, H. and Zimbra, D. K. (2005). A dynamic artificial neural network model for forecasting time series events, *International Journal of Forecasting* **21**(2): 341–362. `http://www.sciencedirect.com/science/article/B6V92-4F011CS-2/1/6ada74e2310edd6e2a37a22516d28e63`.

Goldberg, D. E. (1989). *Genetic Algorithms in Search, Optimization, and Machine Learning*, Addison-Wesley.

Gooijer, J. G. D. and Kumar, K. (1992). Some recent developments in non-linear time series modelling, testing, and forecasting, *International Journal of Forecasting* **8**: 135–156.

Haykin, S. (1998). *Neural Networks - A Comprehensive Foundation*, second edn, Pearson Education.

Hordijk, W. (1996). A measure of landscapes, *Evolutionary Computation* **4**(4): 335–360. `http://www.mitpressjournals.org/doi/abs/10.1162/evco.1996.4.4.335`.

Jansen, T., De, K. A. J. and Wegener, I. (2005). On the choice of the offspring population size in evolutionary algorithms, *Evolutionary Computation* **13**(4): 413–440. http://www.mitpressjournals.org/doi/abs/10.1162/1063656057746669 21.

Kantz, H. (2004). *Nonlinear Time Series Analysis*, second edn, Cambridge University Press.

Lam, L. (1998). *Nonlinear physics for beginners: fractals, chaos, solitons, pattern formation, cellular automata, complex systems.*, World Scientific.

Leung, F. H. F., Lam, H. K., Ling, S. H. and Tam, P. K. S. (2003). Tuning of the structure and parametrs of the neural network using an improved genetic algorithm, *IEEE Transaction on Neural Networks* **14**(1): 79–88.

Pi, H. and Peterson, C. (1994). Finding the embedding dimension and variable dependences in time series, *Neural Computation* **6**: 509–520.

Resende, M. and Ribeiro, C. (2003). Greedy randomized adaptive search procedures, *Handbook of Metaheuristics*, Vol. 57, Springer, pp. 219–250.

Rodrigues, A., de Mattos Neto, P. S. G. and Ferreira, T. A. E. (2009). A prime step in the time series forecasting with hybrid methods: The fitness function choise, *Proceedings of International Joint Conference on Neural Networks*, IEEE, Atlanta - Georgia.

Rodrigues, A., Ferreira, T. A. E. and de A. Araujo, R. (2008). An experimental study with a hybrid method for tuning neural network for time series prediction, *Evolutionary Computation, 2008. CEC 2008. (IEEE World Congress on Computational Intelligence). IEEE Congress on* pp. 3435–3442.

Savit, R. and Green, M. (1991). Time series and dependent variables, *Physica D* **50**: 95–116.

Takens, F. (1980). Detecting strange attractor in turbulence, *in* A. Dold and B. Eckmann (eds), *Dynamical Systems and Turbulence*, Vol. 898 of *Lecture Notes in Mathematics*, Springer-Verlag, New York, pp. 366–381.

Tanaka, N., Okamoto, H. and Naito, M. (2001). Estimating the active dimension of the dynamics in a time series based on a information criterion, *Physica D* **158**: 19–31.

Tashman, L. J. (2000). Out-of-sample tests of forecasting accuracy: An analysis and review, *International Journal of Forecasting* **16**(4): 437–450.

van den Bergh, F. and Engelbrecht, A. P. (2004). A cooperative approach to particle swarm optimization., *IEEE Trans. Evolutionary Computation* **8**(3): 225–239.

Zhang, G., Patuwo, B. E. and Hu, M. Y. (1998). Forecasting with artificial neural networks: The state of the art, *International Journal of Forecasting* **14**: 35–62.

28

Fuzzy Pattern Modelling of Data Inherent Structures Based on Aggregation of Data with heterogeneous Fuzziness

Arne-Jens Hempel and Steffen F. Bocklisch
Chemnitz University of Technology
Germany

1. Introduction

Nowadays we are drowning in data but starving knowledge. In order to arise knowledgeable from the flood of data it has to be analysed. The goal of such an analysis is the creation of a model or the classification to a known phenomenon, e.g. modelling of the traffic flow in cities, medical or machine diagnosis (Herbst, 2008; Hempel, 2008a; Weihs, 2005).

Basically there are two main philosophies to deduce a model, namely theoretical and experimental modelling. In experimental modelling it is assumed that measurement data (objects) reflect a phenomenon by data-inherent structures. Unfortunately every observation is afflicted with inaccuracies such that the data might depict interesting phenomena characteristics just vaguely.

The knowledge about occurring imprecision is additional and valuable information. With the help of the fuzzy set theory it can be taken into account as a supplementary model feature (Zadeh, 1965). By understanding the whole modelling problem as a fuzzy classification task, where specific fuzzy sets referred to as fuzzy pattern classes form a model equivalent, the fuzzy pattern modelling method represents such a capable approach. Among several sophisticated solutions for such a task, which in general apply nonparametric fuzzy sets or a composition of different fuzzy sets (Bezdek, 2005) the main philosophy behind this work is the exclusive usage of a single specific parametrical fuzzy set to model data-inherent structures as well as the data itself.

Its key feature – a closed and uniform framework – provides the ability to incorporate occurring imprecision into the so called fuzzy pattern class model. The same framework allows an automatic deduction of fuzzy pattern class models based on a set of learning data with heterogeneous fuzziness.

The mission of the chapter is in the first place the introduction of the afore mentioned data-driven fuzzy modelling method to an audience applying experimental modelling (e.g. scientists, engineers, medical scientists or machine diagnosis specialists etc.). Another objective is to make a novel contribution to the field of experimental modelling. Consequently it is the concern of this work to provide a more general view onto the method.

In order to give an easy understandable survey about fuzzy pattern modelling the chapter will be organized in four main sections:

- Definition of the fuzzy pattern class model.

The second section will establish the fundamental terminology, the mathematics and the most general case of the multivariate fuzzy pattern class concept. Besides this definition part the application of fuzzy pattern classes as well as the representation of data with fuzzy pattern classes is introduced.

- Data-driven design of fuzzy pattern classes.

The automated design of fuzzy pattern models will be presented in section three step by step.

- Properties of fuzzy pattern class models.

In order to complete the survey, section four will provide information about advantages, disadvantages and limitations of fuzzy pattern models.

- State of the art research.

The last section will introduce ways to overcome the afore elaborated limitations of simple fuzzy pattern class models by sketching the state of the art research about networks of fuzzy pattern classes.

2. Definition of the Fuzzy Pattern Class Model

The multivariate fuzzy pattern class (FPC) is determined by set of basis functions. However, due to the here pursued type of modelling a basis function defines also a one-dimensional fuzzy pattern class model. Consequently a preliminary study of the one-dimensional class definition provides an easy access to derive the multivariate case.

In its most general form a one-dimensional fuzzy pattern class A is defined by the following unimodal side-specific parametrical prototype over a class specific reference system U, the so called class space.

$$\mu^A(u) = \begin{cases} \dfrac{a}{1+\left(\frac{1}{b_l}-1\right)\left|\frac{u}{c_l}\right|^{d_l}} & u < 0 \\ \dfrac{a}{1+\left(\frac{1}{b_r}-1\right)\left|\frac{u}{c_r}\right|^{d_r}} & u \geq 0 \end{cases} \tag{1}$$

With its graph illustrated by figure 1:

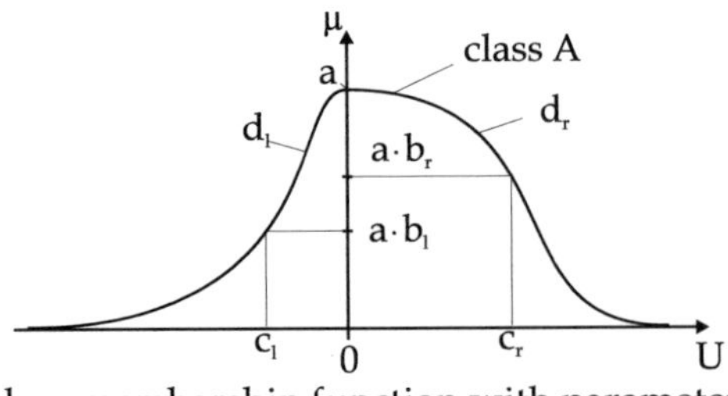

Fig. 1. One-dimensional class membership function with parameters

According to figure 1 it becomes obvious that the unidimensional function concept is based upon a set of seven parameters a and $\vec{p} = (b_l, b_r, c_l, c_r, d_l, d_r)$. The further specification of these parameters results from the fact that the parameter a characterises an entire fuzzy pattern class (FPC), whereas the parameters combined in $\vec{p}$ are related to a specific dimension of the class space (Bocklisch, 1987). Beyond their mere mathematical functionality all parameters possess the following semantic meaning:

- The parameter a represents the maximum membership value of the fuzzy pattern class $\mu^A(u)$. Regarding a structure of classes a expresses the weight of a specific class. Considering a dynamic classification process it embodies the topicality or authenticity of the information represented by that class (Hempel, 2005; Paessler, 1998).
- In the normalised case $a = 1$, the parameters $b_l, b_r \in [0,1]$ assign the left- and right-sided membership values at the class borders $u = -c_l$ and $u = c_r$.
- c_l, c_r mark the support of a class in a crisp sense. Both parameters characterise the left- and right-sided expansions of a fuzzy pattern class.
- The continuous descent of the membership function is specified by the parameters d_l, d_r. From a graphical point of view d_l, d_r determine the shape of the membership function, or in other words, the fuzziness of a class. From a modelling perspective this means that the d-parameters allow the incorporation of imprecision into a class model.
  The smoothest class shape is obtained for $d_{lr} = 2$, whereas the crisp case results for $d_{lr} \rightarrow \infty$. However for calculation purposes $d_{lr} = 20$ has proven to be a sufficient value to represent the crisp case.

Based on the introduced one-dimensional fuzzy pattern class model the multivariate fuzzy pattern class A derives from the intersection of such basis functions using the N-fold compensatory Hamacher intersection operator (2), where n denotes the index of the basis functions and N the total number of dimensions (Scheunert, 2001).

$$\cap_{Ham}\, \mu^A = \left(\frac{1}{N}\sum_{n=1}^{N}\frac{1}{\mu_n^A}\right)^{-1} \tag{2}$$

Regarding the main philosophy behind this paper, the key feature of this intersection is the conservation of the parametrical class concept for the multidimensional case, see (3).

$$\mu(\vec{u}) = a \cdot \left[\begin{array}{l} 1 + \dfrac{1}{2N}\displaystyle\sum_{n=1}^{N}\left(1 - sgn(u)\right)\left(\frac{1}{b_{ln}} - 1\right)\left(\frac{|u_n|}{c_{ln}}\right)^{d_{ln}} \\ + \dfrac{1}{2N}\displaystyle\sum_{n=1}^{N}\left(sgn(u) + 1\right)\left(\frac{1}{b_{rn}} - 1\right)\left(\frac{|u_n|}{c_{rn}}\right)^{d_{rn}} \end{array}\right]^{-1} \tag{3}$$

The definition of the fuzzy pattern class model is completed with the augmentation of the class describing set of parameters by a class space position $\vec{u}_0$ in the original feature space and a class space orientation $\vec{\varphi}$. $\vec{u}_0$ is also denoted as class representative since it determines the spot of the highest class membership.

Figure 2 depicts the influence of the additional parameters for a two-dimensional three class structure. The different location of each class results from the representatives

$\vec{u}_{c10} = (0.25\,,0.85)^T$, $\vec{u}_{c20} = (0.5\,,0.5)^T$ and $\vec{u}_{c30} = (0.75\,,0.25)^T$, whereas an additional class orientation φ of 50° has been applied to the middle class.

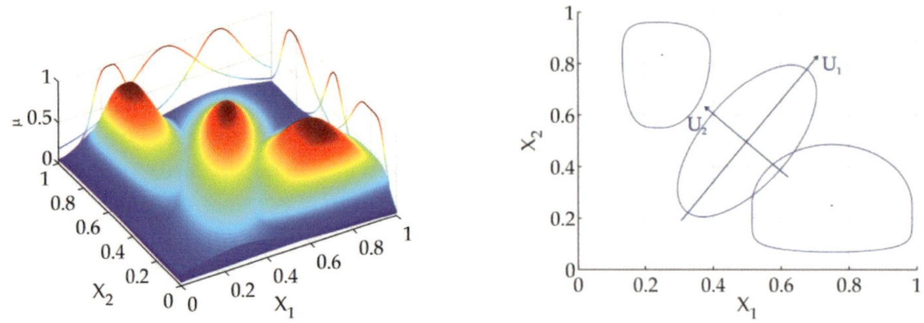

Fig. 2. complete representation left, border–curve representation right

As it can be seen there are two different ways of depicting fuzzy pattern class models a so called complete representation and a border–curve presentation. The complete representation is the most meaningful. It unifies the influence of all class parameters by mapping an N–dimensional class into an $N+1$ dimensional space, in particular the effects of the shape defining parameters d can be observerd. As a consequence a complete representation requires a lot of computational costs. On the contrary the border–curves of a class are defined by the geometrical locus with same class memberships. It follows naturally that the border–curve presentation based on equipotential membership lines can be computed with less effort while capturing a class's location, orientation and extension. The border–curve representation equates a mapping of an N–dimensional class into an N dimensional space. Figure 2 exhibits this border–curve mapping for the class membership $\mu(u) = 0.5$. Additionally it is pointing out the difference between the class space U and the feature space X. Due to the fact that U is a class specific reference system each point or object given in the feature space X has to be referred to U to be meaningful. The relation between both is given by transformation (4) where u_0 corresponds to the centre of a class space and the matrix T realises the class space rotation.

$$u = T(x - u_0)\ |u \in U, x \in X \tag{4}$$

2.1 Data Representation with the help of Fuzzy Pattern Classes

One outstanding feature of the here discussed method is the treatment of measured objects as fuzzy pattern entities. This means each object of a data set is considered to be a so called atomic fuzzy pattern class. The fuzzy perception of objects is justified by the fact that every observation (measurement) inheres an inaccuracy a so called elementary fuzziness (e.g. imprecision of a sensor), see figure 3.

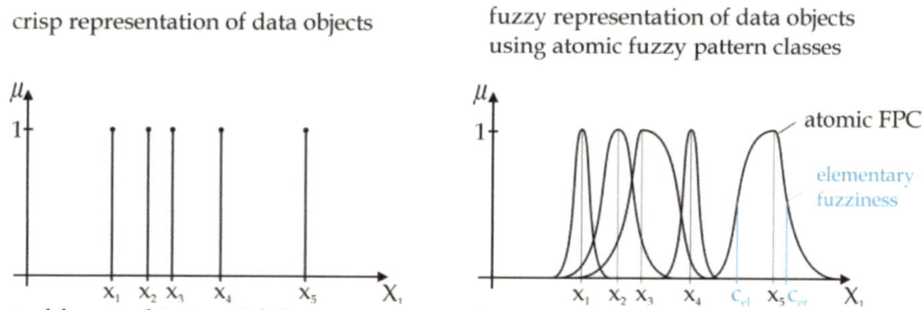

Fig. 3. Set of fuzzy objects with heterogeneous elementary fuzziness

The denotation atomic results from the fact that objects are the smallest informational unit available; they are the atoms of a data set. In order to signify that a fuzzy pattern class represents an object it is defined upon a specific set of parameters. Due to the fact that it is modelling the smallest informational entity the atomic class carries the weight $a = 1$ and its border memberships are set to $b_{lr} = 0.5$. Furthermore it is unlikely for objects to exhibit "internal" distributions therefore the class shape is assigned to $d_{lr} = 2$ leading to the atomic FPC description (5).

$$\mu^{Obj}(\vec{x}) = \begin{bmatrix} 1 + \dfrac{1}{2N}\displaystyle\sum_{n=1}^{N}(1 - sgn(x_n))\left(\dfrac{|x_n - x_{0n}|}{c_{eln}}\right)^2 \\ + \dfrac{1}{2N}\displaystyle\sum_{n=1}^{N}(sgn(x_n) + 1)\left(\dfrac{|u_n - x_{0n}|}{c_{ern}}\right)^2 \end{bmatrix}^{-1} \quad (5)$$

The only parameter that has not been specified yet is the expansion of a fuzzy object referred to as elementary fuzziness. The elementary fuzziness expresses the measuring accuracy of a sensor or the trust behind the position of the object in the feature space (if it is for example given verbally by an expert).

If there no such information available the elementary fuzziness is set symmetrically according to the given sensor inaccuracy (e.g. two percent of the measurement scale). If on the contrary there is access to such information the elementary fuzziness can take an asymmetrical or heterogeneous shape which consequently has to be imbued to the modelling process. Typical sources for elementary fuzziness are data sheets of a sensor, sensor characteristics as well as statements of experts. Figure 4 sketches the emergence of heterogeneous elementary fuzziness with the help of a nonlinear sensor characteristic (another example is diode characteristics).

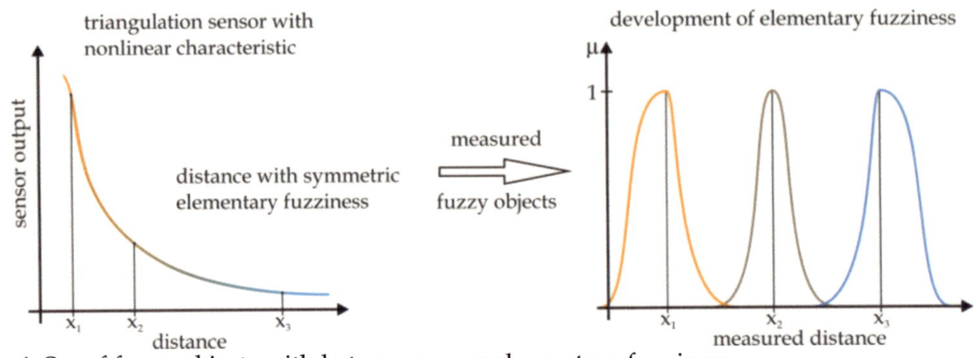

Fig. 4. Set of fuzzy objects with heterogeneous elementary fuzziness

Assuming a feature space spanned by two of such sensors it is likely to obtain the following exemplary set of fuzzy objects, see figure 5.
Especially when considering the border–curve ($\mu(u) = 0.5$) presentation, it can be imagined that the elementary object fuzziness might affect an experimental deduced model. The latter example motivates the reason to imbue elementary fuzziness into the modelling process. Hence the here introduced concept of fuzzy data will serve as foundation for the aggregation process.

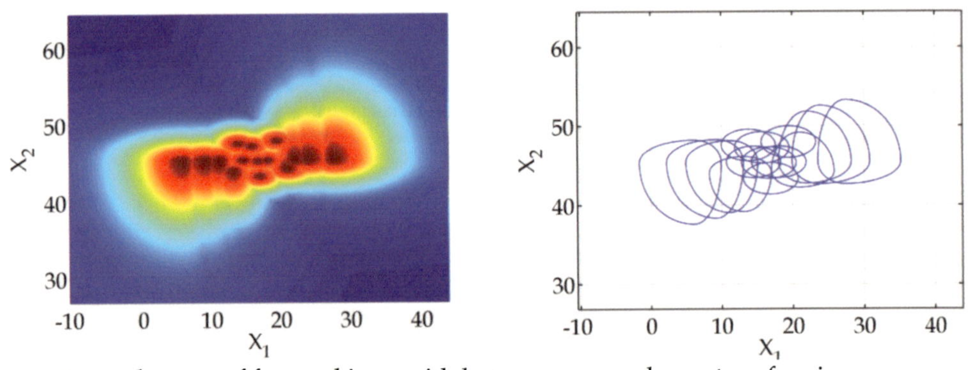

Fig. 5. Exemplary set of fuzzy objects with heterogeneous elementary fuzziness

2.2 Fuzzy Patter Classification

As introductorily alluded the entire modelling task is understood as a fuzzy classification task. In the framework of classification a more comprehensive model is characterised by a set of meaningful classes. For this purpose all model relevant fuzzy pattern classes are grouped together in a so called fuzzy pattern classifier. In operating mode the fuzzy pattern classifier then assigns unknown objects to this class structure. The results of the classification process are stored into a so called vector of sympathy $\vec{s} = (s_1, s_2, \dots, s_K)^T$. Each component of $\vec{s}$ denotes the membership of a classified object to the corresponding class, where K is the total number of classes.
The gradual membership of an object to a given class is calculated using (1).

$$s_k = \mu^k(\vec{x}) \text{ for } k = 1,2, \dots, K \quad (6)$$

According to the last section the objects to be classified are considered to be fuzzy entities. However the classification of fuzzy pattern objects goes beyond the scope of this work such that each object to be classified is denoted just by a vector of features $\vec{x} = (x_1, x_2, \ldots, x_N)^T$ where N represents the number of feature dimensions. All full review about the classification of fuzzy objects can be found in (Hempel, 2005)
Figure 6 illustrates the process of classification with the help of a one-dimensional three class structure and the alongside listed classification results.

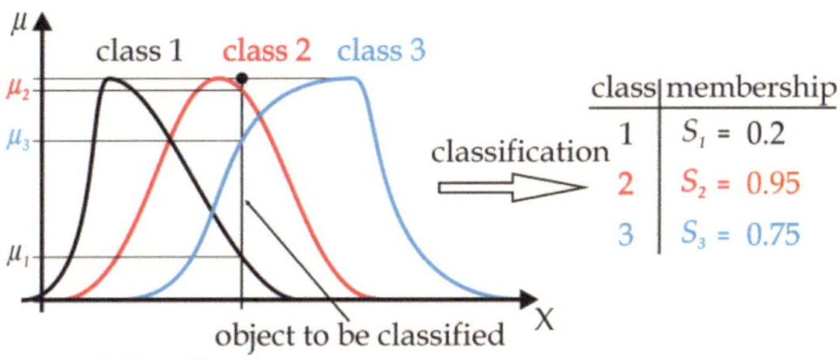

Fig. 6. One-dimensional classification process

The vector of sympathy describes an assignment of the object to the class structure with respect to its location in the feature space. Since the classifier comprises three fuzzy pattern classes it assigns three values of membership.

3. Aggregation of Fuzzy Pattern Classes from Data with Heterogeneous Fuzziness

As mentioned earlier the concept of classification embodies three subtasks: discovery of (data-inherent) structures, modelling of these structures and finally the usage or application of these models to classify unknown data.
At this point it is assumed that the first task, discovery of a structure within a set of data, has been resolved by a preliminary conducted cluster analysis or any other structure discovering algorithm (Bacher, 1996; Jain 1988). This section revolves around the question how to model an *already structured* set of data applying the afore introduced definition of fuzzy pattern classes as a modelling framework. Hence it is addressing the second task.
Basically fuzzy pattern class models can be obtained via two different ways (Bocklisch, 1987). First via definition by expertise, where an expert interprets the data at hand and determines all class parameters based upon task and domain specific knowledge. This approach is not pursued here.
The here featured second approach is a data-driven method, strongly advocating the goal to model known data-inherent structures. Based upon the class labelled set of "learning" data all class parameters are assigned automatically by a two step aggregation procedure, according to figure 7 (Hempel, 2005; Päßler, 1998).

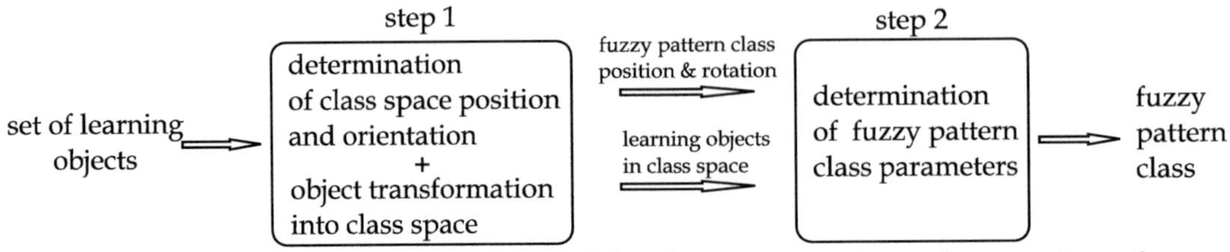

Fig. 7. Signal flow and general progression of the object aggregation to fuzzy pattern classes

As figure 7 indicates the class construction starts with the determination of the class location and rotation in the first step and is completed with assignment of the class parameters in the second step. The main features during this procedure are:

- consideration of the data fuzziness throughout the entire process,
- mapping of data distribution onto the class shape and
- data sequence independency.

Besides its specialisation on fuzzy data the class aggregation can also be applied to usual (crisp) data. In order to perform a congeneric aggregation the crisp learning dataset is just extended to a set of fuzzy objects, using the introduced function concept section 2.2.
Since the multivariate fuzzy pattern class model derives from its basis functions the task of deducing the class parameters can be performed in a dimension wise manner. Hence, for the sake of clarity all computations will be only shown for an arbitrary dimension, all further dimensions follow analogously.

3.1 First Step of Aggregation: Determination of the Class Space

As mentioned before the aggregation is based on a class labelled set of data being split up according to its class labels. Each subset is treated separately but in the same manner by the subsequent algorithm, resulting in different fuzzy pattern classes. Because of its uniformity the class construction will be shown with an exemplary subset x given in the original feature space, where N represents the number of object dimensions and M total number of objects.

$$x = \begin{pmatrix} x_{11} & \cdots & x_{1M} \\ \vdots & \ddots & \vdots \\ x_{N1} & \cdots & x_{NM} \end{pmatrix} \tag{7}$$

Origin of the class space

The origin $\vec{u}_0 = (u_{01}, \dots, u_{0i}, \dots, u_{0N})^T$ of the class space is referred to as class representative it marks the location of the highest class membership and is the reference point for all other parameters. It is calculated dimension–wise as the mean over all class supporting objects. In order to allow for heterogeneous elementary fuzziness each object representative is adjusted based on its specific elementary fuzziness, (see figure 8).

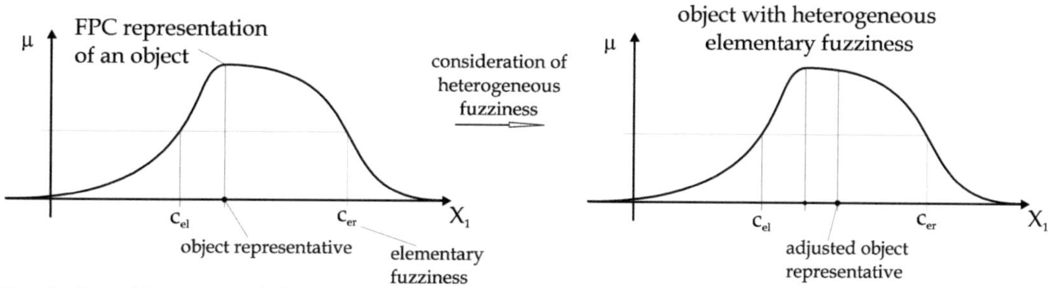

Fig. 8. Consideration of object specific elementary fuzziness via object representative adjustment

The above illustrated adjustment is realised by a weighted mean over the object representatives, the left-sided and right-sided elementary fuzziness in every dimension, see equation (8).

$$\tilde{x}_{i,j} = \frac{1}{1+2g}\left(x_{i,j} + g\left(2x_{i,j} - c_{eli,j} + c_{eri,j}\right)\right) \tag{8}$$

yielding:

$$\tilde{x} = \begin{pmatrix} \tilde{x}_{11} & \cdots & \tilde{x}_{1M} \\ \vdots & \ddots & \vdots \\ \tilde{x}_{N1} & \cdots & \tilde{x}_{NM} \end{pmatrix} \tag{9}$$

The weight of the object borders c_{el}, c_{er} is be specified by the parameter $g\epsilon[0,1]$, where $g = 0$ blanks out the influence of the elementary fuzziness and $g = 1$ values object representative and the elementary fuzziness equally. For the fully automatic class construction g is set according to the membership of c_{el}, c_{er} $(g = 0.5)$.
Figure 9 demonstrates the effect of the adjustment procedure for a two-dimensional object.

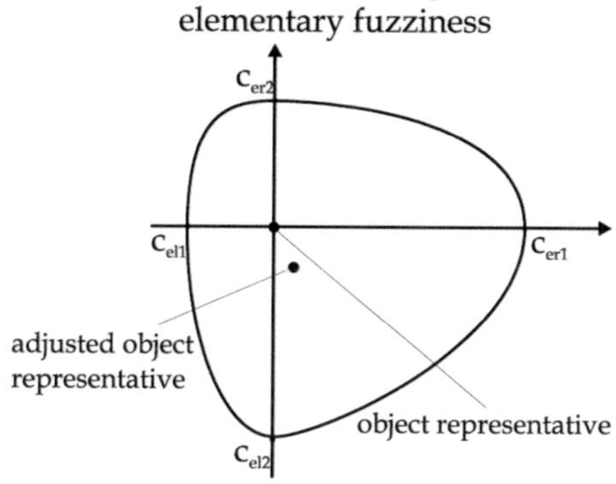

Fig. 9. Fuzzy induced representative adjustment for two-dimensional object

Rotation of the class space

In order to realise an optimal FPC-model of the data structure the class specific reference system U is rotated into the neutral axis of x. Thus the alignment of a class space U^N is defined by a set of $N-1$ rotation angles and stored in the parameter vector $\vec{\varphi} = (\varphi_1, \varphi_2, \ldots, \varphi_{N-1})^T$.

Dealing with fuzzy objects it has to be born in mind that the elementary fuzziness might affect the class orientation. Similar to the above considerations the elementary fuzziness is taken into account by the adjusted object representative (9).
The entire rotation can be denoted in matrix representation:

$$T = T_{N-1} \cdot T_{N-2} \cdot \ldots \cdot T_i \cdot \ldots \cdot T_1 \; where \; T_i \in \mathbb{R}^{N \times N}$$

$$T_i = \left(t_{i_1 i_2}\right) \left| t_{i_1 i_2} = \begin{cases} \cos\varphi_i & for\; i_1 = i_2 = 1 \; or \; i \\ \sin\varphi_i & for\; i_1 = 1, i_2 = i \\ -\sin\varphi_i & for\; i_1 = i, i_2 = 1 \\ 1 & for\; 1 \neq i_1 = i_2 \neq i \\ 0 & else \end{cases} \right. \tag{10}$$

3.2 Second Aggregation Step: Determination of the Class Parameters

After the determination of the class space U all class parameters can be deduced based on the position and fuzziness of the class supporting objects. Since the origin of the class space is the reference point for all class parameters it is also necessary to refer the class supporting objects to their class space.

Transformation of the objects into the class space

Such a reference is generated by an affine object transformation into the class space, see equation 11.

$$u = T(x - u_0) \; where \; u = \begin{pmatrix} u_{11} & \cdots & u_{1M} \\ \vdots & \ddots & \vdots \\ u_{N1} & \cdots & u_{NM} \end{pmatrix} \tag{11}$$

Due to the fact that the objects themselves are fuzzy pattern entities a mere transformation of the object representatives according to (11) is insufficient, as their elementary fuzziness has to be transformed into the class space as well. Figure 10 depicts this concern for the two dimensional case.

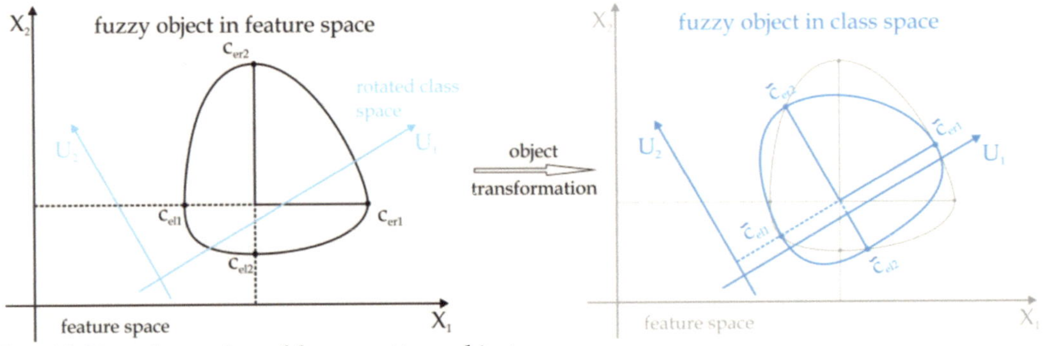

Fig. 10. Transformation of fuzzy pattern objects

Several methods to transform a fuzzy object have been reviewed considering interpretability, errors and computational costs (Hempel, 2005) The most promising method takes the heterogeneous elementary fuzziness into account using the back-transformed unity vectors of the class axis and their intersection points with the border curve ($\mu(u) = 0.5$) of the fuzzy object.

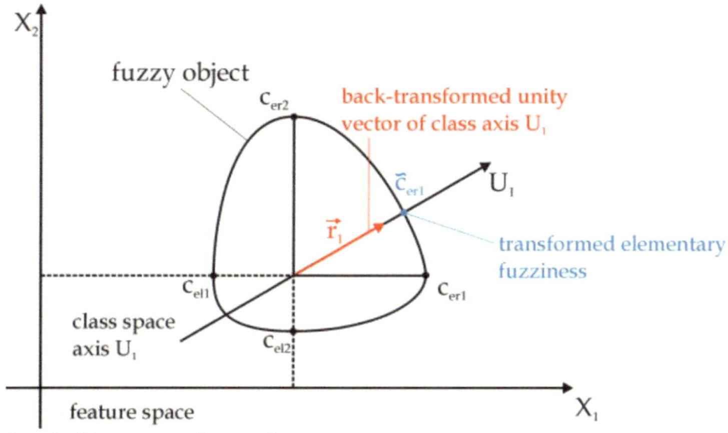

Fig. 11. Principle of object transformation

As figure 11 exemplifies, the values of the elementary fuzziness for a specific class axis (U_1) results from the dilation factor of its transformed unity vector $\vec{r}_1$. Due to the side specific modelling and the heterogeneous elementary fuzziness the significant ce-parameter are selected by quadrant discrimination during calculation.
After their transformation the set of objects is split up into two ordered sets of left-sided and right-sided objects O_{li}, O_{ri}.

$$
\begin{aligned}
O_{ri} &= \{u\} \ \left| u_{0i} \le u_{i,1} \le u_{i,2} \le \cdots \le u_{i,R} \right. \\
O_{li} &= \{u\} \ \left| u_{0i} \ge u_{i,1} \ge u_{i,2} \ge \cdots \ge u_{i,L} \right.
\end{aligned}
\tag{12}
$$

Specification of the class borders
In each class space dimension the extensions c_l, c_r of a class are determined by the outermost objects including the elementary fuzziness, (14)

$$
\begin{aligned}
c_{ri} &= \max_{s=1...R} \left(u_{i,s} + c_{eri,s} \right) \\
c_{li} &= \min_{s=1...L} \left(u_{i,s} - c_{eli,s} \right)
\end{aligned}
\tag{13}
$$

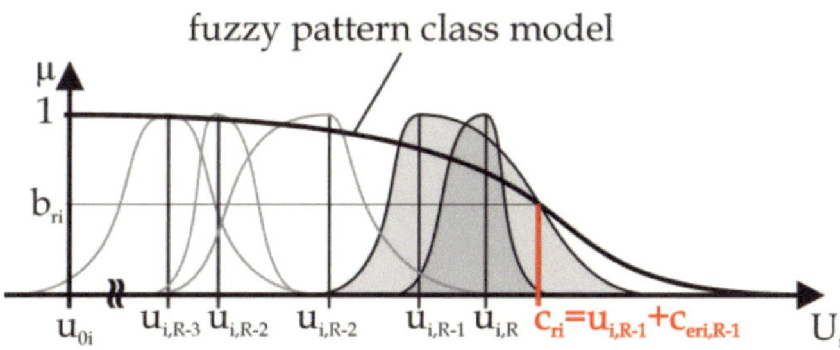

Fig. 12. Specification of the class borders in the ith dimension

Since the class parameters d_{lr}, b_{lr} are obtained analogously for each class space dimension as well as for the left- and right-handed function branch the following considerations are straitened to the right-sided function branch.

Determination of the class shape

The shape of a fuzzy pattern class (d_r) is assigned based on the agglomeration properties of the class supporting objects. The more the data resembles an agglomeration according to a geometric series the smoother the class shape. The rate of resemblance is determined by the mean distance alteration between two adjacent objects $q_{i,j}$.

Figure 13 depicts the calculation of this rate $q_{i,j}$ for an arbitrary class dimension.

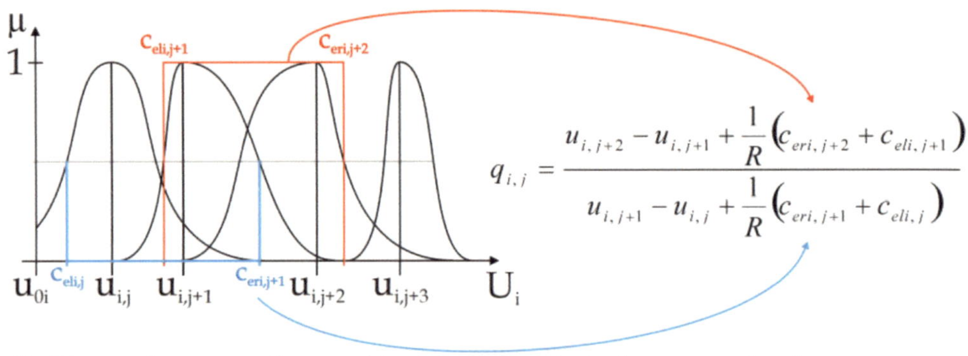

$$q_{i,j} = \frac{u_{i,j+2} - u_{i,j+1} + \frac{1}{R}\left(c_{eri,j+2} + c_{eli,j+1}\right)}{u_{i,j+1} - u_{i,j} + \frac{1}{R}\left(c_{eri,j+1} + c_{eli,j}\right)}$$

Fig. 13. Distance between adjacent objects including their elementary fuzziness

Based on the mean change of distance between two adjacent objects the class shape d_{ir} is determined in such a manner that the smoothest class shape $d_{lr} = 2$ is realised when the objects are cumulating in the centre of the class conform to a geometric series. On the contrary the crisp class shape $d_{lr} = 20$ is obtained when the objects are at least equally distributed over the class space.

The effects of the object specific elementary fuzziness $c_{eri,j}$, $c_{eli,j}$ is balanced out against the number of class supporting objects R. Correspondingly, the shape of classes being supported by a small number of objects is mainly characterised by the elementary fuzziness, whereas classes with a high number of class supporting objects experience a reduced influence of the elementary fuzziness onto their shape.

Assignment of the border membership

The value for border membership b_r is derived under the conservation of the object cardinality. This means that the sum of the area under all objects is required to be equal to the area under the fuzzy pattern class function, see figure (14).

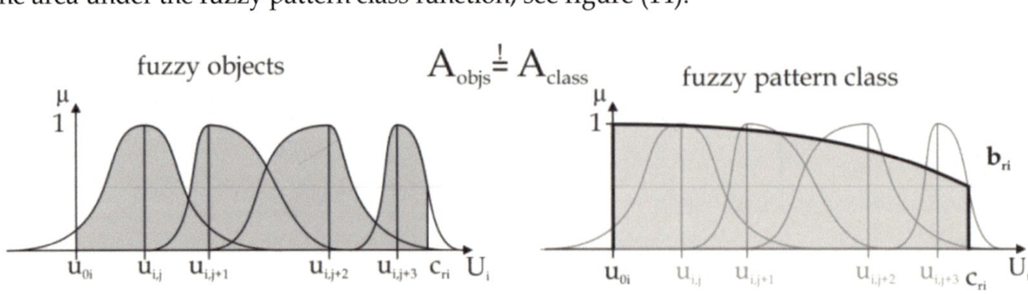

Fig. 14. Claim for the conservation of the object cardinality

The border memberships b_r are estimated over the unity interval $b_r \in [0,1]$ by (14) taking into account the prior results for c_r and d_r.

$$A_{class} = \int_0^{c_{ri}} \frac{du}{1 + \left(\frac{1}{b_{ri}} - 1\right)\left(\frac{u - u_{0i}}{c_{ri}}\right)^{d_{ri}}} = A_{objs} \; |b_{ri} \epsilon [0,1] \tag{14}$$

Assignment of the class weight

The weight of a class within a structure of fuzzy pattern classes depends on the total number of its class supporting objects M, $(a = f(M))$. Under the assumption of an evolutionary growing class weight a results from (15).

$$a(M) = a_{max}\left(1 - \left(\frac{a_{max} - 1}{a_{max}}\right)^M\right) \tag{15}$$

The assumption of an evolutionary growing according to (Peschel, 1986) is motivated by the fact that the emergence of a class from elementary observations is a structural transition from a quantitative growing to a qualitative one (classes are superordinate entities compared to objects).

4. Properties of Fuzzy Pattern Class models

The introduced fuzzy modelling concept is round off by having its major properties, advantages and drawbacks discussed subsequently.

The most characterising features of fuzzy pattern class models namely versatility, uniformity, treatment of fuzzy data and a closed modelling framework emanate from the unimodal, side-specific and parametric class membership function.

In its most general case fuzzy pattern classes offer multivariate fuzzy models with various asymmetric shapes, ranging from peak- over bell- to crisp forms (see figure 15). Together with the introduced data-driven design fuzzy patter classes allow to map class internal object distributions as well as correlative relations.

Besides all multi-dimensionality and flexibility the parameters of fuzzy pattern classes remain semantically motivated ensuring its the interpretability and transparency.

Furthermore the parametric class concept provides a good trade off between data compression, computational cost and generality. Especially for high dimensional models a sufficient level of data compression is reached since each fuzzy pattern class is defined upon a set of eight parameters per dimension. By connecting the basis function of every dimension exclusively on parameter level the chosen conjunction operator saves computational costs.

Both advantages are traded off for generality in so far as fuzzy pattern classes are convex models, specifying a convex area of the feature space. Consequently FPCs are most suited when it comes to model convex data-inherent structures.

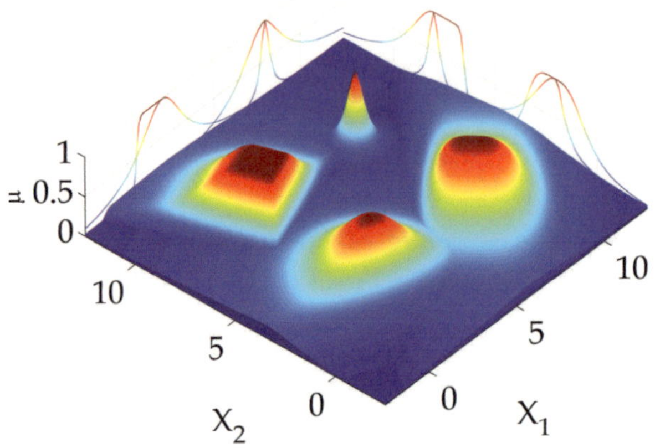

Fig. 15. Side-specific shape variety of fuzzy pattern classes

However when it comes to model nonconvex data-inherent structures fuzzy pattern class models are afflicted with errors. Figure 16 illustrates such an error by having an enclosed central object accumulation aggregated to a fuzzy pattern class.

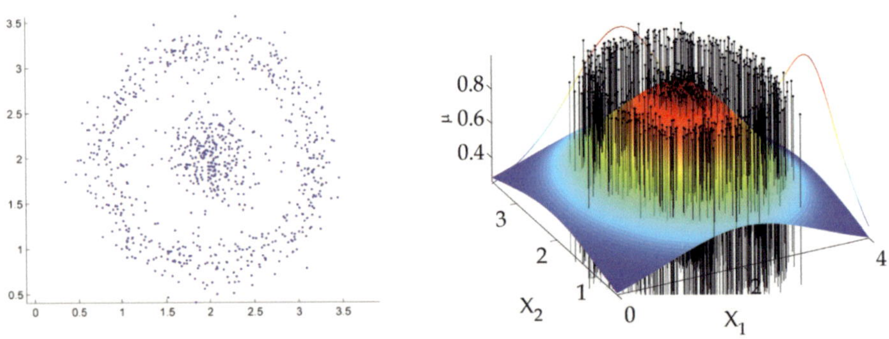

Fig. 16. right: data-inherent structure; left: associated fuzzy pattern class

The region between the ring shaped object arrangement and the central object accumulation does not belong to the given data structure. Nonetheless it will be associated with high grades of memberships by the corresponding fuzzy pattern model.

5. Networks of Fuzzy Pattern Classifiers

In order to circumvent this major drawback two possibilities have been thought of, leading to the state of the art fuzzy pattern research. The first way is a cluster based approach rendering a nonconvex describable by segmenting the data into convex subsets. The second access to dissolve the convexity drawback arises from the adoption of fuzzy pattern anti classes (FPAC) (negating fuzzy pattern models).

Both approaches lead to hereafter introduced networks of fuzzy pattern classifiers or so called fuzzy pattern classifier network. A Fuzzy Pattern Classifier Network (FPCN) consists of interconnected Fuzzy Pattern Classifier (FPC) nodes, representing its functional core. It is a modelling approach combining fuzzy set theory and network theory, as powerful and flexible tools of modelling.

5.1 Cluster Based Fuzzy Pattern Classifier Networks

In the cluster based approach the layout of the network structure and the configuration of classifier nodes, will be addressed by a hierarchical clustering and selection strategy. Aside from the fact that a mere clustering would work on every data-inherent structure it might create considerably large structures of fuzzy pattern classes at the expenses of model clarity. In order to maintain model clarity different layers of detail corresponding to a certain structural resolution have been introduced.

In its current implementation the cluster based fuzzy pattern network evolves from coarse to fine structures (Hempel, 2008a; Hempel, 2008b). Starting with the entire set of data a cluster analysis is conducted. Since each cluster method uses its specific strategy to discover structures some phenomena typical structures remain indiscoverable by a certain method (Jain, 1978). That is why at least an ensemble of sufficiently diverse cluster algorithms is applied (Strehl, 2005). Based on the clustering results (class labels) the data set is split into the most stable cluster configuration. All subset are modelled as fuzzy pattern class (see section 3) in an associated classifier node and subsequently treated separately but in the same manner, producing the next level of detail. As an overall result the cluster based approach leads to a network oriented hierarchical fuzzy pattern model.

An exemplary cluster based FPCN with the supporting set of data is given by figure 17.

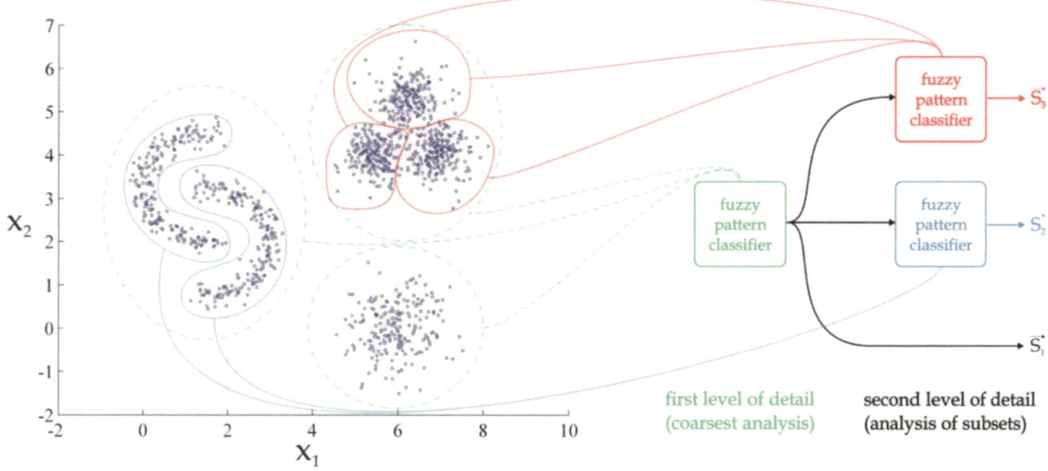

Fig. 17. cluster based fuzzy pattern network model

In the first level of detail (entire data set) the cluster analysis returned the highlighted (dashed lines) three class structure stored in the first fuzzy pattern classifier node. In the second level analysis each subset is treated separately generating a three class structure for the upper left subset summarised by the upper classifier node and a two class structure captured in the lower classifier node. Finally, each classifier is connected with its preceding node, eventually creating the tree-like FPCN. In detail the classifier nodes are connected with respect to the components of the sympathy vector that is originating from the fuzzy pattern classes of preceding node. This clear connection facilitates the information propagation throughout the network. The node activation is based on the highest component of the sympathy vector.

5.2 Fuzzy Pattern Classifier Networks with Anti–Classes

Instead of applying current clustering methods the fuzzy pattern anti–class (FPAC) strategy exploits the inverse of a data structure to create a fuzzy model. The principal idea behind this approach consists in the negation of a class assertion over its unsupported class space, see figure 18.

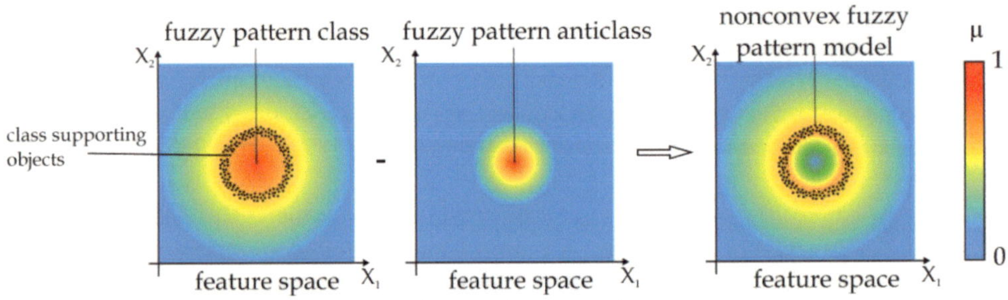

Fig. 18. Anti–class approach for a ring shaped data structure

Like it is depicted, the negation works on semantical level and from this point of view FPACs can be seen as a further specification of a preceding fuzzy pattern class. The repeated specification of fuzzy pattern classes and anti–classes can be interpreted as a network of such classes.

In order to conserve the modelling framework, the automated model generation and the model properties (such as flexibility, interpretability, computational efficiency, etc.) the negating anti–classes are defined upon the same membership function concept as the fuzzy pattern classes. Due to this definition it is also valid that FPACs, like usual fuzzy pattern classes, can be supported by objects, or better so called anti–objects, and that the before elaborated aggregation procedure can be applied on these anti–objects.

The crucial point of this approach lies in the determination of a set of anti–objects forming an inverse data–inherent structure. Unfortunately these anti–objects are unavailable prior to the design such that, they have to be generated and distributed over the class space. Concretely this generation and distribution process is driven by the policy that anti–objects will exclusively accumulate in the unsupported class space within the borders of an object modelling FPC.

Figure 19 illustrates the results of the above outlined anti–object generation with the help of the example given in figure 16. Similar to figure 16 original objects are highlighted in blue, whereas the constructed anti–objects are displayed in orange.

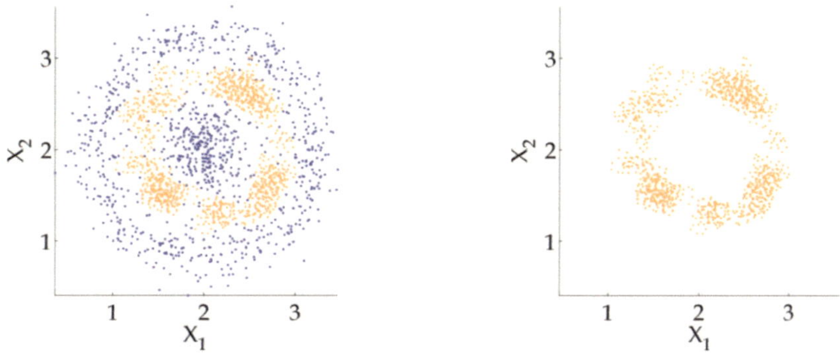

Fig. 19. Right: objects and generated anti-objects; left: anti-objects only

Due to distribution policy the anti-objects accumulate in the area between the ring and the central object agglomerations (see right side of figure 19) forming itself a ring-like anti or inverse data-inherent structure (see left side of figure 19). Because this ring-like anti-object structure is again a nonconvex structure the modelling fuzzy pattern anti-class will be inadequate and it might appear that the whole problem was just shifted to the anti-object structure. This is not the case since the entire procedure can be repeated on the anti-class yielding a convex set of anti-anti-objects and hence an appropriate anti-anti-class (see figure 18).
In sum the fuzzy pattern anti-class approach results in a sequence of three fuzzy pattern classifiers. The first one is a model over all given (original) objects it is further specified by the second classifier (anti-node) comprising all anti-objects being itself specified by the last classifier (anti-node). Figure 20 summarises the resulting fuzzy pattern model with the help of its memberships (right) and its network presentation (left).

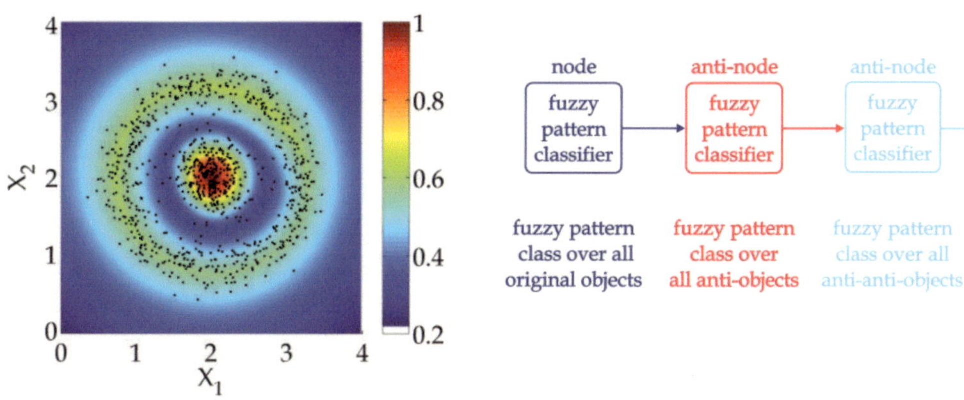

Fig. 20. Right: complete fuzzy pattern model; left: associated fuzzy pattern classifier network

The fuzzy pattern network works similar to its design. An unknown object is evaluated by the first classifier node ensuring a general membership to the data structure. Thereafter it is processed by the first anti-node, excluding a membership if it is situated in the centre. In the last step (third classifier node) this anti-class membership is negated for central located objects, ensuring that the region between centre and outer ring maintains a low membership.

6. Conclusion

This chapter dedicates itself towards the establishment of a closed fuzzy modelling framework for data-inherent structures. By and large the entire modelling process is conceived as fuzzy classification task, where superordinate fuzzy classes agglomerate structures of related data.

The closeness of this modelling framework is ensured by a *side-specific, parametric, basis function motivated, multivariate* membership function concept holding for data as well as for classes. Due to its central role the class membership function has been explicitly defined, its adoptions for objects of data have been motivated and its application has been sketched.

The main concern this chapter lies in the presentation of a data-driven algorithm to agglomerate fuzzy data to fuzzy class models without leaving the modelling framework. The innovation regarding this agglomeration is the treatment of data that exhibits heterogeneous elementary fuzziness (asymmetric measurement insecurities) and the consideration of these heterogeneous elementary fuzziness throughout the whole agglomeration process.

The resulting fuzzy pattern class model embraces advantageous properties like multi-dimensionality, shape diversity, semantic interpretability, transparency, unimodality and computational efficiency. The major drawback of the fuzzy class model arises from its convexity.

The patronage of fuzzy pattern classes for convex shaped data sets can be resolved with a network oriented design paradigm. In detail two state-of-the-art design approaches for networks of fuzzy pattern classifiers have been sketched. Their data-driven design and their combination are of particular interests for further research.

Another aspect of the here pursued type of structure modelling is that it works in the original feature space without a transformations applied for fuzzy support vector classifiers (Schölkopf, 2001; Li, 2008).

7. References

Bacher, J. (1996) *Clusteranalyse*, Oldenburg, 3-486-23760-8, München, Wien

Bezdek, J. C.; Keller, J.; Krisnapuram, R. & Pal, N. R. (2005), *Fuzzy Models and Algorithms for Pattern Recognition and Image Processing (The Handbooks of Fuzzy Sets)*, Springer-Verlag New York, Inc., 0387245154, New York

Bocklisch, S. F. (1987). *Prozeßanalyse mit unscharfen Verfahren*, VEB Verlag Technik, 3-341-00211-1, Berlin

Hempel, A.-J. (2005). *Aggregation und Identifikation von Fuzzy-Objekten mit unterschiedlichen elementaren Unschärfen*, Masterthesis, TU Chemnitz

Hempel, A.-J.& Bocklisch, S. F.(2008a) Hierarchical Modelling of Data Inherent Structures Using Networks of Fuzzy Classifiers *Tenth International Conference on Computer Modeling and Simulation 2008*, pp. 230-235, 0-7695-3114-8, Cambridge April 2008., IEEE, Cambridge

Hempel, A.-J. & Bocklisch, S. F. (2008b). Design of a Fuzzy Classifier Network Based on Hierarchical Clustering *9th international PhD Workshop on Systems and Control*, pp. 403-408, 978-961-264-003-3, Izola

Herbst, G. & Bocklisch, (ed.) Classification of Keystroke Dynamics - A Case Study of Fuzzified Discrete Event Handling. *9th International Workshop on Discrete Event Systems*, pp. 394-399, 978-1-4244-2592-1, Gothenburg 2008

Jain, A. K. & Murty, M. N.& Flynn, P. J. (1999). Data clustering: a review. *ACM Computing Surveys*, Vol. 31, 3, 264-323, 0360-0300

Li, X. & Shu, L.(2008).Fuzzy Theory Based Support Vector Machine Classifier Fuzzy Systems and Knowledge Discovery, *Fourth International Conference on Fuzzy Systems and Knowledge Discovery*, pp. 600-604, 978-0-7695-3305-6, 2008, IEEE Computer Society, Jinan, Shandong, China

Peschel, M. (1986). *The predator-prey model : do we live in a Volterra world?*, Springer, 0387818480, Wien ,New York

Päßler, M. (1998). *Mehrdimensionale Zeitreihenmodellierung und Prognose mittels Fuzzy Pattern Modellen*, TU Chemnitz, Chemnitz

Scheunert, U.(2002). Fuzzy-Mengen-Verknüpfung und Fuzzy-Arithmetik zur Sensor-Daten-Fusion, In: *Fortschritt-Berichte*, Reihe 8, VDI-Verlag, 3-18-394108-2, Düsseldorf

Schölkopf, B. & Smola, A. J.(2001). Learning with Kernels: Support Vector Machines, Regularization, Optimization, and Beyond,The MIT Press, 0262194759, Cambridge, MA, USA

Strehl, A.(2002). *Relationship-based Clustering and Cluster Ensembles for High-dimensional Data Mining* The University of Texas, Austin

Weihs, C. & Gaul, W. (2005), *Classification – the Ubiquitous Challenge: Proceedings of the 28th Annual Conference of the Gesellschaft Fur Klassifikation E.V., University of Dortmund*, Springer, 978-3-540-25677-9, Dortmund

Zadeh, L. A.(1965). Fuzzy Sets *Information and Control*, 8(3), 338-353

Efforts in Agent-based Simulation of Human Panic Behaviour: Reference Model, Potential, Prospects

Bernhard Schneider
University of the German Armed Forces Munich, Computer Science Department
Germany

1. Introduction: Challenges in Modelling Human Behaviour

Human behaviour and its modelling is one of the major challenges in state of the art modelling and simulation for a wide range of application areas, no matter if dealing with question sets in social, economic or even in a security or military context. Two major questions arise: what is the task of the modelling expert and what methods are suitable to tackle these tasks? To represent human behaviour in simulation models in an adequate fashion, the human being has to be perceived a psychosomatic unit with cognitive capabilities that is embedded in a social environment. Physiological and psychological factors together define the internal state of human being that unfortunately is not directly measurable or observable. Accordingly, the modelling expert has to address on determining and modelling relevant somatic characteristics and intangibles in the form of cognitive, emotional and social determinants of human behaviour, their dynamics, correlation, and impact on the concrete shape of human behaviour in specific situations.
In brief, a complex system has to be created, where the output at a certain point of time by means of observable domain dependent patterns of behaviour depends on the entirety of sensory inputs at that time and the current internal state. A system theoretical view on the modelling task seems to be appropriate to describe transitions of the system's state and interconnect the single factors.
In order to provide the capability to consider even highly realistic human behaviour and to obtain valid simulations, it is necessary to keep the conceptual model of a human being, strictly speaking the subset of relevant aspects of human behaviour to be simulated, as close as possible to reality. This can be achieved by theory driven modelling based upon the latest theories and findings in psychology and sociology.
On the technical side, agent-based methods proofed to be suitable for constructing simulation models including human factors. The paradigm of agent-based modelling proclaims the representation of human beings by autonomously deciding and acting software agents. The design process is supported by established agent architectures and reference models.
An application area where all of the mentioned aspects on modelling and technical side are of importance can be found in the modelling of human behaviour in large event security

scenarios where even the danger of a panic breakout during evacuation processes in public places like a station concourse or even in closed rooms, pedestrian tunnels or airplanes has to be taken into account. To analyze, assess and optimize the quality of security concepts and the system of systems approach, computer simulations can be a very helpful instrument, helping to increase quality and reduce risks in the design cycle and overall costs.
This chapter gives an overview about current research work related to modelling and simulation of human behaviour in panic situations and presents the new reference model SimPan as an innovation in this area. The research work is interdisciplinary in its nature and touches on research areas in computer science, especially modelling and simulation, systems theory and artificial intelligence as well as psychology with the main areas social psychology and cognitive psychology.

2. State-of-the-art in simulation of evacuation situations

Two different approaches to describe human behaviour in evacuation situations have been established in the last decade. Behaviour models on the one hand are theories about human behaviour in panic situations that are based upon empirical data and socio-psychological findings. Movement models on the other hand concentrate on detailed description of the dynamics of pedestrian movement. Dependent on the chosen degree of resolution, movement models can be subdivided into macroscopic, microscopic and mesoscopic models.
Macroscopic models as presented by Daamen (Daamen, 2002) and Helbing (Helbing et al., 2002) assume an analogy with the motion of pedestrians and the motion of gases and fluids and do not focus upon individual differences between human beings in a moving crowd. In microscopic models by contrast, human beings are represented as single simulation entities with individual features. Typical exponents of that approach are cellular automata as described by Kirchner (Kirchner & Schadschneider, 2002) and Muramatsu (Muramatsu et al., 1999) as well as agent-based models as developed by Becker and Schmidt (Becker & Schmidt, 2005), Banarjee (Banarjee et al., 2005) or Gipps and Marksjö (Gipps & Marksjö, 1985). Mesoscopic models as described by Vassalos (Vassalos et al., 2002) combine aspects of both approaches by situational conditioned employment of interconnected macroscopic and microscopic simulation parts.

3. SimPan as an innovation in the scope of modelling panic behaviour

In common to all of the mentioned approaches is the fact that psychological determinants of individual behaviour in evacuation situations are, if at all, just of marginal interest. In contrast to related modelling approaches, the SimPan reference model integrates established psychological theories and findings to model and simulate observable patterns of human behaviour in the course of panic situations. It contains modelling approaches for common environmental phenomena in context of panic, describes their impact on an individual's internal state and comprises corresponding patterns of human behaviour. The reference model SimPan serves as a conceptual basis for the construction of agent- based models to simulate human behaviour in panic situations but equally leaves space for individual adaptation to specific requirements defined by particular fields of application.

4. System-theoretical modelling principles

The human being can be seen as a complex system. A system in terms of system theory is characterised by a set of state variables. These state variables can change their value on the basis of their own dynamics or on the basis of a sensory input. Besides the state variables, dependent variables can be introduced and calculated by means of the state variables. The modified internal system state consisting of the new values for state variables and the new dependent variables will then lead to an output that can, in some cases, take on the form of an observable action executed by an agent.

The transfer function F describes how the system state variable z(tn) turns into the subsequent state z(tn+1), in the time-discrete case:

$$z(tn+1) = F(\ tn,\ z(tn),\ w(tn),\ x(t)\ ) \tag{1}$$

The following equation describes the state transfer in the time-continuous case:

$$z'(t) = F(\ t,\ z(t),\ w(t),\ x(t)\ ) \tag{2}$$

The algebraic function H describes the relation between the state variable z(tn+1) and the dependent variable w(tn+1):

$$w(tn+1) = H(\ tn+1,\ z(tn+1)\ ) \tag{3}$$

The output function G determines the manner in which the new internal state, which came about as a result of the input, shows itself as output y(tn+1) to the outside:

$$y(tn+1) = G(\ tn+1,\ z(tn+1),\ w(tn+1),\ x(tn+1)\ ) \tag{4}$$

The interplay between these functions to model the human information processing system is depicted in figure 1.

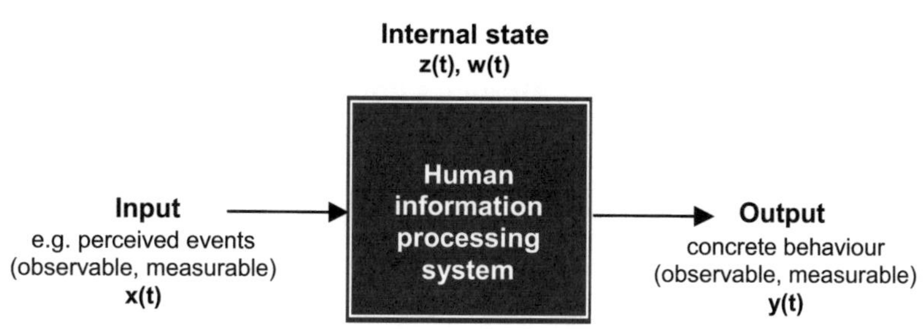

Fig. 1. System-theoretical modelling approach for a complex system

An example could be a state variable FearS representing the emotion fear. The value for that FearS can change by itself or through mental processing of inputs from the outside, e.g. the cognitive evaluation of a perceived event in the environment. Such a sudden frightening experience as input can lead to a sudden increase of the state variables value. By contrast, if

nothing happens in the environment, the value of FearS decreases continuously over time until it reaches a minimum value. It is the function F that describes both of these changes in time.
The dependent variable FearM is closely correlated to the state variable FearS. FearM is the corresponding strength of the motive to reduce that fear, e.g. by introducing a flight reaction. The stronger the fear state FearS, the higher the value for the motive strength FearM. The algebraic function H determines the dependency of FearM on FearS.

5. Reference Models

A reference model is a domain independent methodology-founded scheme of construction as proposed in (Klinger 1999) that describes a standard solution for modelling problems and serves as a blueprint for a class of real systems sharing a common deep structure. Major aim in using reference models is to reduce the complexity of design tasks and thereby reduce the effort in time and work concerning the development of simulation models. A reference models capacity depends on the size of its set of solvable problems.
In the modelling and simulation context, two different kinds of reference models can be distinguished. The first sort of reference models proposes a structure for simulation models similar to the addressed real system and addresses implementation issues. Hence, the proposed structure is defined by a set of abstract model components and different types of semantic connections between them: causal dependencies and discrete information flows. As an example the PECS reference model developed by Urban (Urban, 2007) can be named.
The inner life of abstract model components has to be specified by a second sort of reference models that contains comprehensive modelling approaches for domain dependent cause-effect relationships detached from structural or implementation issues. The second kind of reference models fills a given structure with concrete content. The reference model SimPan to be presented in this chapter belongs to the second class of reference models. It provides a comprehensive modelling approach for a specific problem area: human behaviour in evacuation situations. SimPan is inherently structured but does not give any recommendations on the structure of a SimPan- based simulation model. For this reason, SimPan can be supplemented by PECS.

5.1. PECS: A reference model for the structure domain in agent based models

With the PECS reference model as described in (Urban, 2000), a component-oriented hierarchical architecture for the agent-based simulation is proposed that applies to a wide range of systems where human behaviour plays a part. The principal architecture as depicted in figure 2 claims to be applicable for more than just special ad hoc cases.
In PECS the complex real system to observe is decomposed into a set of interacting components, where each component consists of a set of state variables and rules or equations, which describe the state transitions and output of that component. The overall structure of the PECS- world is shown in figure 1. Besides the PECS- agents, there are two global components, Environment and Connector, which represent and administrate the modelled environment and realise interaction between agents.

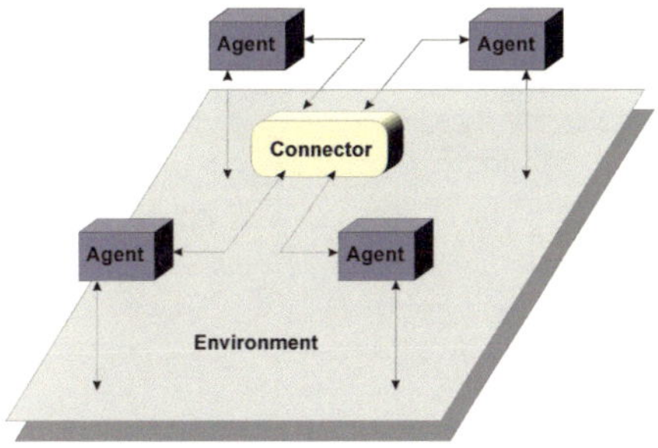

Fig. 2. The PECS- world

The internal structure of a PECS agent is based on a system-theoretic approach and on the usual architecture in robotics. PECS provides a network of abstract model components, organized in three layers: an input layer, an intermediate layer and an output layer. The input layer comprises components Sensor and Perception. The component Sensor is intended to encapsulate functionality for the reception of sensory input data from the environment of the agent. Sensory information is pre-processed in the component Perception, where information-filtering mechanisms or perception processes may be realised.
The intermediate layer describes the internal state of an agent and consists of components Social Characteristics, Cognition, Emotion and Physis. These components describe the internal state of the agent and contain the state variables and the associated state transition functions. The component Cognition, in particular, provides space to model a knowledge base as well as high level functionalities as a basis for realization of deliberative and reflective agent behaviour.
Finally, the components Behaviour and Actor belong to the output layer and describe the observable behaviour of an agent. The component Behaviour contains a set of condition-action rules to model the reactive behaviour of the agent and to co-ordinate the interaction of reactive, deliberative and reflective behaviour by means of determining the execution order of actions that derive from a specific behaviour. Execution orders are passed on to the Actor component that contains a repertoire of actions that the agent is capable of. These actions can be divided into external and internal actions. External actions may have an impact on the environment. Internal actions can have a direct effect on the agent's internal state. Figure 3 illustrates the overall structure of a PECS agent.

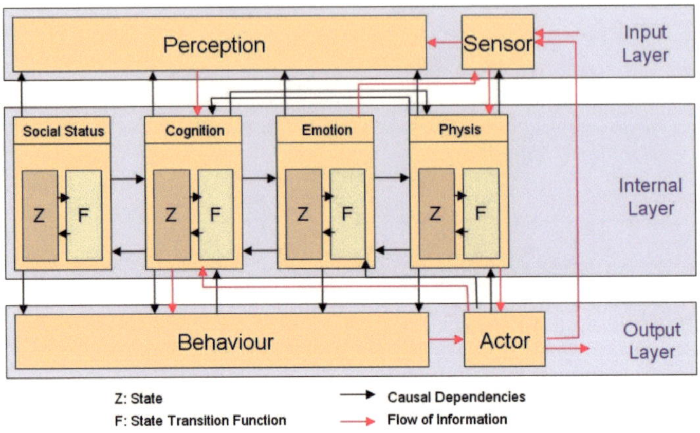

Fig. 3. The internal structure of a PECS Agent

5.2 PECS Component Cognition

As the PECS reference model is based on the component-oriented, hierarchical modelling principle, complex components can be functionally decomposed into a set of specialised, interconnected sub-components. Following this maxim, the component Cognition of the PECS reference model is subdivided into five components: SelfModel, EnvironmentModel, ProtocolMemory, Planning and Reflection. Each of these sub-components contains its own state variables and its own state transition function.

The component SelfModel contains the agent's knowledge about its own internal state and related operations. The component EnvironmentModel is construed for storing a mental representation of the agent's environment and mental processes designed to manipulate and extend this representation such as learning or reasoning. The idea for providing a component ProtocolMemory originally was inspired by the approach taken by Dörner (Dörner, 1999). ProtocolMemory is intended to gather information about executed action sequences, formerly pursued action plans and methods used to analyse them. Within the component Planning, planning process can be modelled. A planning process is responsible for the generation of action plans to reach the agent's intended goals, whereas a plan is considered a sequence of actions to be performed one after the other. To construct a plan, the component Planning can retrieve information from the components SelfModel, EnvironmentModel and ProtocolMemory. The basic idea of having a component Reflection was taken from Sloman, who proposed a three-layered architecture for human-like agents including a Meta-Management-Layer (Sloman, 2000). The function of the component Reflection is to monitor, evaluate and improve internal processes. In order to perform this task, reflective processes can exchange information with the components SelfModel, EnvironmentModel, Protocol-Memory and Planning. The component Reflection acts as a supervisor or manager within cognition. It is necessary if the agent should possess reflective capabilities. The internal structure of the component Cognition is shown in figure 4. A complete description of the PECS reference model is provided in (Urban, 2007).

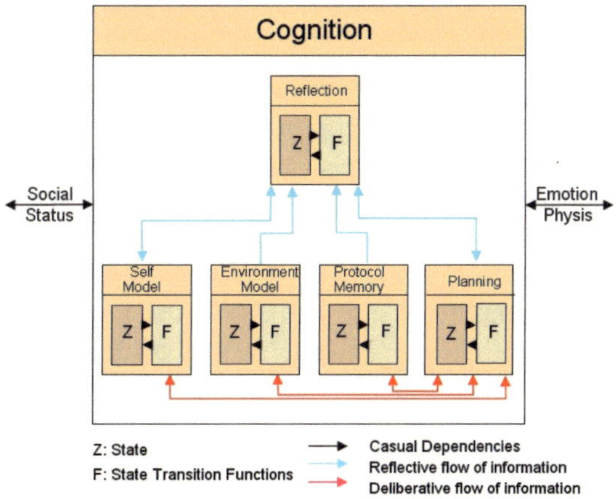

Fig. 4. The interior of component cognition

As PECS describes a structure and makes proposals how to distribute model parameters and functions in the structure, the challenge by employing the reference model is to fill its abstract components with life. Adopting the general reference model to individual peculiarities of a real system is possible by filling in the empty spaces provided by the architecture. This means, for example, that the number and the type of state variables, the dependent variables as well as the structure of the transfer function F, the algebraic function H and the output function G can be modified without difficulty. Similarly, the agent can be endowed with a diverse repertoire of actions that indicate the internal and external actions that the agent is capable of. As a result, very diverse agents and communities of agents can be described with the same reference model.

5.3 Agents as representatives for human beings

The application area for human-like agents is very wide. It comprises - among others - figures in games, robots which interact with humans, software agents meant to provide information to their clients as well as human beings in simulation models with social psychological background. Agents as model-representatives for humans are constructed using the filtering mechanisms of abstraction and idealisation. The application of these filtering processes is a necessary step in modelling but equally prevents the creation of a direct replica of real facts. Accordingly, the resulting model can only be a reduced version of its original and does not contain all the qualities which distinguish human beings as human beings. Nevertheless, agents can still have a purpose in science, technology and theory. The application area for agents in the research work to be presented is the modelling of human behaviour in evacuation situations.

6. The reference model SimPan

In this paragraph the basic theories and concepts to model scenarios in the context of security operations are presented.

6.1 Different conceptions of panic

In the context of security research regarding evacuation situations, it is important to have a clear understanding of the term panic, its emergence and dynamics. According to (Foreman, 1953), there are two basic conceptions of panic in the area of social psychological research. The first one comes from the area of economy and defines panic as a mass response to a real or imaginary collapse of the market. This mass response arises from the collective attempt to escape from a period of inflation and exhausting trade. Besides this economical conception for panic, the second one is based on a sociological point of view. This definition concentrates on individual emotional states and the resulting individual behaviour of a human being as reaction to a real or imaginary imminent threat to his own life. Panic is regarded as internal state, which is determined by demoralisation, confusion and fear or anxiety. This state may - besides other reactions - result in precipitous flight reactions.

According to Dombrowski and Pajonk (Dombrowski & Pajonk, 2005) there are also two different empirical approaches to explain panic behaviour. The first one bases on the classical crowd psychology, which emerged at the end of the nineteenth century and was mainly influenced by Gustave LeBon (LeBon, 1973). The main axiom of crowd psychology states, that in a crowd, the individual is subjected to the influence of the community (Heinz & Schöber, 1972). The term crowd is described by Kruse (Kruse, 1986) as the affiliation of individuals to a common spirit, which evens out the differences between individuals and enervates the intellectual abilities of the individuals. This state transition manifests itself in the loss of sense of responsibility (Reicher, 2001) and a tendency to impulsive, deviant and irrational behaviour (Mummendy & Otten, 2002).

The second empirical approach emanates from human science and was mainly influenced by Enrico Quarantelli (Quarantelli, 2001) in the mid of the twentieth century. The approach emphasizes mental processes of the individual. This socio- psychological approach tries to get insights into human behaviour during situations of crisis by analysing empirical material through comparative data analysis. Two motivationally determined distinctions in collective behaviour concerning panic can be made: the flight from a certain undesirable situation and the resolute trial to achieve something desirable. In each of these two modes of collective behaviour there exists a kind of competition, which cannot be controlled by social or cultural constraints any longer. Due to these theories, there are quite different suppositions for the development of panic: they reach from irrational behaviour, induced by fear and social influences to rational evaluation of effort and benefit as well as the emergence of normative support of self-serving behaviour.

6.2 Definition of the term panic

As a basis for the modelling work, the sociological conception of panic is referenced. Within the scope of SimPan development, panic is defined as an internal state of a human being, marked by the presence of the dominant emotional motive fear. Strong fear prevents an individual from showing highly-developed kinds of behaviour like conscious and planned behaviour, and reduces the range of available behavioural patterns to thoughtless flight reactions, instinct-guided behaviour and rigidity. This definition combines theories suggested by Quarantelli (Quarantelli, 1954) and Janis in (Schulz, 1964).

6.3 States, motives and motive selection

Motives can be seen as the mainsprings for human behaviour. According to Schmidt and Schneider (Schmidt & Schneider, 2004), motive is a psychological force deriving from an internal state of a human being. There is a close connection between states and the corresponding motives: motives are consciously experienced states. Motives like drives or emotions, and not physiological states, institute acting and direct it towards a certain target.
All motives appear with certain intensity and compete against each other. The motive with the highest motive-intensity at a certain point of time determines - possibly influenced by additional factors - the behaviour of the agent, in the sense that it gets action-leading (Dörner, 1999). Dependent on other internal influences like the current degree of self-control or availability of information about possible flight destinations, the action-leading motive determines the current behaviour and thus the performed action of an individual at that time. As the intensity of motives changes with time, different motives may be action-leading at different points in time. Hence, the agent may behave in a completely different way due to the changed action-leading motive. The interaction between states, motives and behaviour is depicted in figure 5.

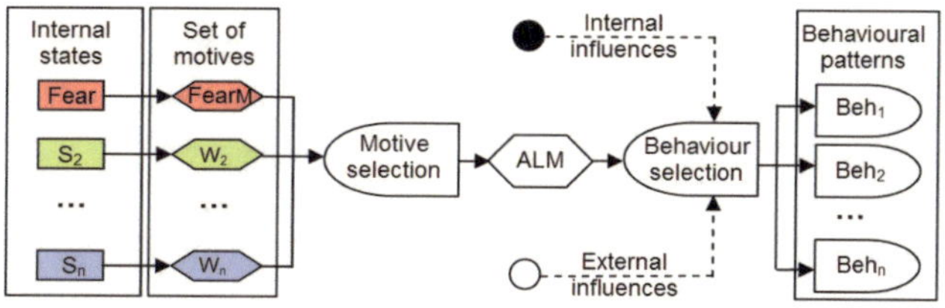

Fig. 5. Motives and motive selection

6.4 The state variable fear

Following the suggested conception of panic, the relevant motive to model is the emotion fear. The theory of cognitive appraisal for emotions as described by Cañamero (Cañamero, 1997), serves as a theoretical basis for modelling emergence and temporary course of individually experienced fear. Accordingly, individuals evaluate constantly perceptions concerning events taking place in the environment. Detection or assumption of a possible threat is considered to be responsible for arise of emotion in the sense of a sudden discrete increase of fear.
According to Schmidt (Schmidt, 2000), a single emotional state like fear can be modelled following the system- theoretical approach by a single state variable that does not depend on other internal states. The dynamics of the state variable FearS is supposed to have a continuous and a discrete part. The continuous part describes a permanent decay (eq. 7) and increase (eq. 6) of the state intensity over the time and is described by differential equations:

$$FearS' = FearInc - FearDec \quad (5)$$
$$FearInc = PC\_FearInc*FearS*SenP*Crow\_i*SForce\_i \quad (6)$$
$$FearDec = PC\_FearDec*FearS*Crow\_i*SForce\_i \quad (7)$$

The constant factors PC_Fear{Inc,Dec} determine the individual propensity to get anxious (eq. 6) and to return to a relaxed internal state (eq. 7). The dependent variables Crow_i and

SForce_i represent the individually weighted impact on the internal state of an agent ascribed by crowding and social forces. The parameter SenP reflects the individual sensation of physical pressure in the environment, while Sc is a constant factor acting as a scaling parameter.
Discrete decay of fear (eq. 8, 9) is modelled by simulation events. A decay of fear occurs if an agent realises calming stimuli emanating from direction signs (e.g. showing the way to an exit) or from loudspeakers (e.g. providing information about possible escape routes and appropriate behaviour in evacuation situations) reflected by the dependent variable FearInf (eq. 8, 10) or from other agents expressed by the dependent variable FearRefA (eq. 9, 11).

$$\text{FearS}^\wedge = \text{MAX}(\text{ C\_FearMin },(\text{FearS} - \text{FearInf}*\text{MAX}(0,(1-\text{SenP}*\text{Sc}+ \text{Crow\_i}*\text{Sc}- *\text{SForce\_i}*\text{Sc})))) \tag{8}$$

$$\text{FearS}^\wedge = \text{MAX}(\text{ C\_FearMin },(\text{FearS} - \text{FearRefA}* \text{MAX}(0,(1-\text{SenP}*\text{Sc}+ \text{Crow\_i}*\text{Sc}- *\text{SForce\_i}*\text{Sc})))) \tag{9}$$

$$\text{FearInf} = \text{PC\_CalmingInf} * \text{EffCalmingInf} \tag{10}$$

$$\text{FearRefA} = \text{PC\_CalmingRefA} * \text{EffCalmingRefA} \tag{11}$$

The dependent variables EffCalming{Inf,RefA} in equations (eq. 10, 11) represent the actual efficiency of calming attempts influencing an agent. It is suggested that the first attempt is the most successful one, later attempts have a smaller impact on the individual fear. This is expressed by equations (eq. 12, 13) where the constants C_Calming{Inf,RefA}Max represent the maximum efficiency achievable by calming stimuli. The corresponding graph is depicted in figure 6.

$$\text{EffCalmingInf} = \text{C\_CalmingInfMax}*(1/\text{NumAttemptsInf}+1) \tag{12}$$

$$\text{EffCalmingRefA}= \text{C\_CalmingRefAMax}*(1/\text{NumAttemptsRefA}+1) \tag{13}$$

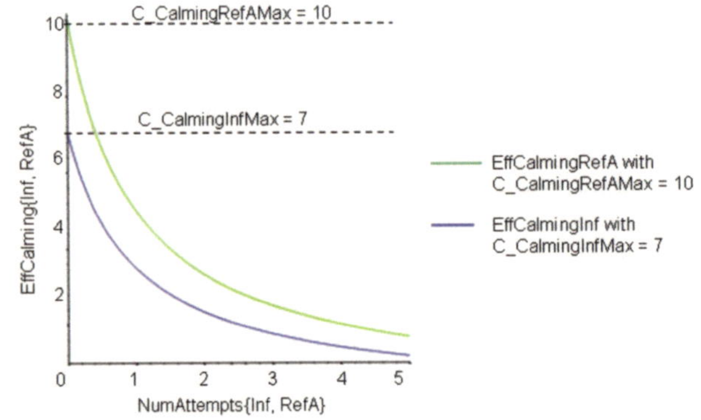

Fig. 6. Motives and motive selection

A discrete increase of the state variable FearS as expressed by equation (14) is triggered by the perception of a fear-inducing event.

$$\text{FearS}^\wedge = \text{MIN}(\text{C\_FearMax}, (\text{Fear}+\text{Threat}*(1+\text{SenP}+\text{Crow\_i}+\text{SForce\_i}))) \tag{14}$$

The variable Threat expresses the individually evaluated perception of a threat. Threat is a numerical value that depends on the type of perception modelled by the parameter Perception_type, which can hold the integral values 0 to 3, where the value 0 indicates no perception of the event at all, the value 1 describes a perception of the effects of the event with a certain delay in time, the value 2 stands for an immediate perception of the effects of the event and the value 3 defines a direct perception of the event itself, where the agent is located near the origin of the threat. These values can be used to evaluate the threat emanating from the perceived situation. The higher the value of Perception_type, the more dangerous the current situation is to be evaluated. This can be implemented using a tabular function as shown in table 1, which maps the value of Perception_type to a concrete value of the variable Threat. As the evaluation of a situation concerning threat depends on an agent's individual predisposition for fear and his experiences with critical situations in the past, this has to be expressed by the tabular function.

Table 1 shows a tabular function that correlates the type of perception with the Threat value. The third row insinuates a low predisposition for fear, the fourth one a high predisposition. Figure 7 elucidates these dependencies.

Attribute	Concrete value			
Perception_type	0	1	2	3
$Threat_1$	0	7	28	65
$Threat_2$	0	40	78	100

Table 1. Relation between type of perception, realized threat and predisposition for fear

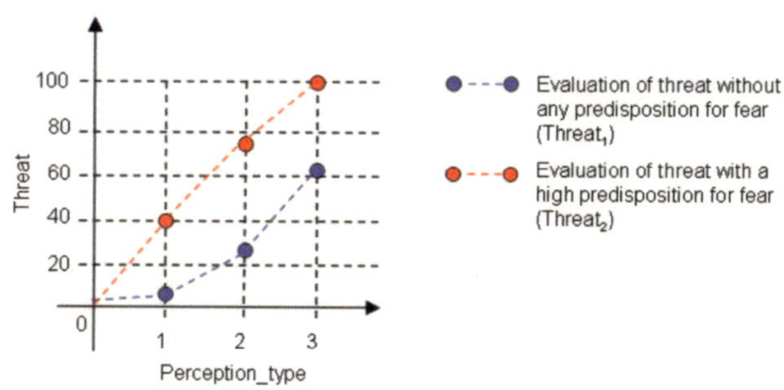

Fig. 7. Evaluation of threat

The course of the state variable FearS according to the equations (1, 8, 9, 14) is depicted in figure 8.

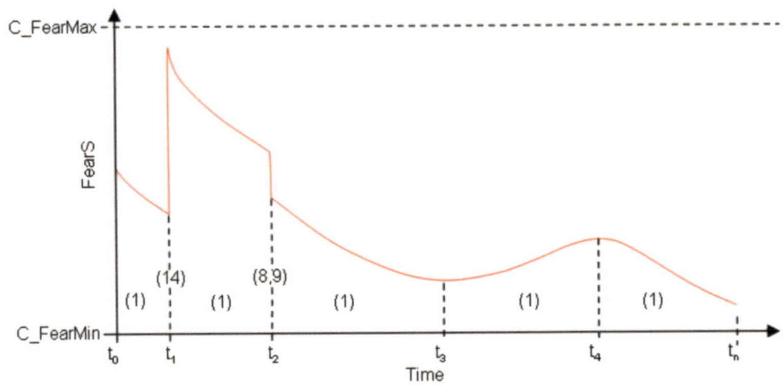

Fig. 8. Dynamics of the state variable FearS

6.5 Sensation of physical pressure

In panic situations, there is a physical factor that influences a human beings internal state: pressure. Pressure is caused by aggressive human behaviour that appears during competition for resources like space or flight opportunity. Pressure has the potential to attack infrastructure, to claim lives and also to cause panic situations. The sensation of physical pressure is supposed to increase fear. Further on, there is a relation between the objective amount of physical pressure affecting an agent and the individual experienced pressure. The later one is determined with the help of a set of individual thresholds as depicted on the left hand side in figure 9.

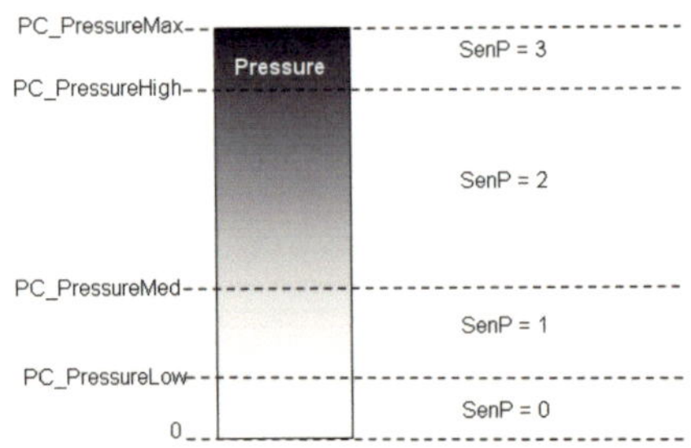

Fig. 9. Individual sensation of pressure

In addition to purely psychological processes, SimPan takes into account implications of physical pressure on the physical constitution of a human being in the sense of agents being crushed to death.

6.6 Crowding

Besides physical pressure, some less obvious quantities are supposed to influence the temporary course of individual fear. One among them is known as crowding. Stokols defines it as an "[…] experiential state in which the restrictive aspects of limited space are perceived by the individuals exposed to them." (Stokols et al. 1977). According to Langer (Langer & Saegert, 1977), crowding intensifies emotional responses to situations. As a decisive factor to express the individual feeling of being crowded, the dependent variable AgentDen to express the available space per agent and the individual suggestibility concerning crowding as constant value PC_Crow are getting introduced (eq. 15). Figure 10 shows different courses of the variable Crow_i dependent on the concrete value of the individual suggestibility.

$$\text{Crow\_i} = \text{C\_CrowMin} + \left(\frac{\text{C\_CrowMax}}{1 + e^{-\text{PC\_Crow}*(\text{AgentDen}-\text{C\_CrowIncMax})}} \right) \tag{15}$$

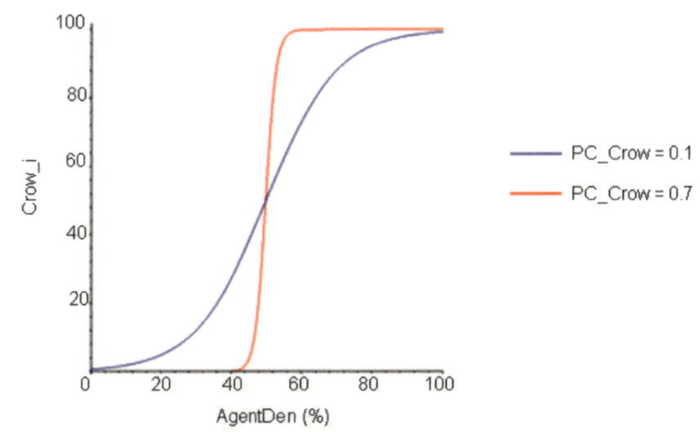

Fig. 10. Relation between crowding and available space per agent

6.7. Social forces

According to Latané (Latané, 1981), an individual's emotional state can be influenced by the mood of other human beings around. Latané suggests the intensity I of the influencing source, its proximity in time and space N and the number of influencing sources A as relevant parameters to describe the power of social influence.

This can particularly be applied to a crowd of human beings in panic which can confer the own fear on others. If strong social forces are acting on an agent, he can be infected by the predominant emotion in the crowd, dependent on his individual predisposition for social influences.

As fear is the only emotional state represented, social influence on fear is modelled by means of the dependent variable SForce_i. It represents the individually experienced degree of emotional charge in the environment. The modelling approach contains following interpretations of the parameters defined by Latané: A means the number of agents, I the average intensity of the motive FearM of all agents and N holds the size of the environment.

$$\text{SForce\_i} = \text{C\_SForceMin} + \frac{\text{C\_SForceMax} * (\frac{A}{N})}{1 + e^{-\text{PC\_SForce}*(I-\text{C\_SForceIncMax})}} \tag{16}$$

The course of the dependent variable SForce_i is depicted in figure 11. The value of the personality constant PC_SForce determines the gradient of the curve, the relation between number of agents and available space per agent determines the maximum strength of the suggestibility concerning social influence.

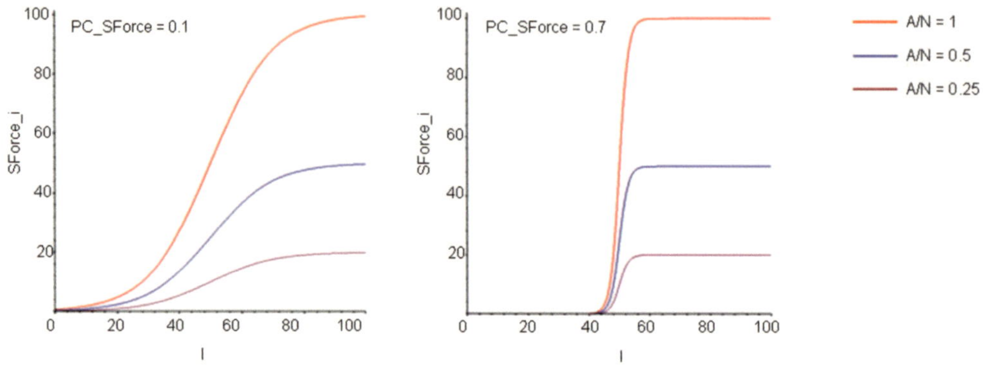

Fig. 11. The modelling of social force

6.8 Emotional Intelligence

To enable SimPan-agents to counteract against behavioural limitations caused by their own fear, they are provided with capabilities going along with emotional intelligence. The psychological concept of "Emotional Intelligence" introduced in 1990 by Mayer and Salovey serves as a modelling basis. Mayer and Salovey defined emotional intelligence as "the ability to monitor one's own and others' feelings and emotions, to discriminate among them, and to use this information to guide one's thinking and action" (Mayer & Salovey, 1997). Of special interest are the capabilities to observe and to monitor actual emotions and the act of will to replace emotion-induced actions by others, more suitable and sensitive ones.

The modelling of emotional intelligence is described in detail in (Schmidt & Schneider, 2004). Basic model elements are an agent's arousal, the emotional intelligence quotient EQ and the motive FearControlM. A high value for the motive FearControlM indicates the need to control the own emotional state. In the special case of simulating short time panic situations, the parameter EQ can be supposed not have any dynamic behaviour and thus is modelled as a constant parameter. Arousal is defined as sum of all motive intensities.

If, and only if, an agent's arousal is lower than an individual threshold ThresArousal that is influenced by the agent's EQ and the motive FearControlM is action-leading, the agent is given the chance to enter a reflective phase temporarily and thereby realise that it is the own fear that motivates the agent to execute inappropriate actions. A reflective phase is characterized by a modified computation of the state variable FearS. The related equation considers the agent's EQ in the following way: the higher the EQ the faster the fear state of the agent, and as a direct consequence, the intensity of the motive FearM decreases.

In the suggested modelling approach, the conscious control of emotion is not reserved to reflective agents, but the lower the motive intensity of FearM (and therefore the higher the degree of behaviour control), the more likely the motive FearControlM becomes action guiding. Therefore it is most likely that an emotional intelligent acting agent is a reflective or at least a deliberative one.

7. The motive FearM

The emotional state FearS is connected to the corresponding motive FearM (eq. 17).

$$\text{FearM} = \text{C\_FearMMin} + \frac{\text{C\_FearMMax}}{1 + e^{-\text{C\_FearMInc} * (\text{FearS} - \text{C\_FearMIncMax})}} \quad (17)$$

Figure 12 shows the relation between the motive FearM and the state FearS. The modelling of motives, based upon states, is described in detail in (Schmidt, 2001).

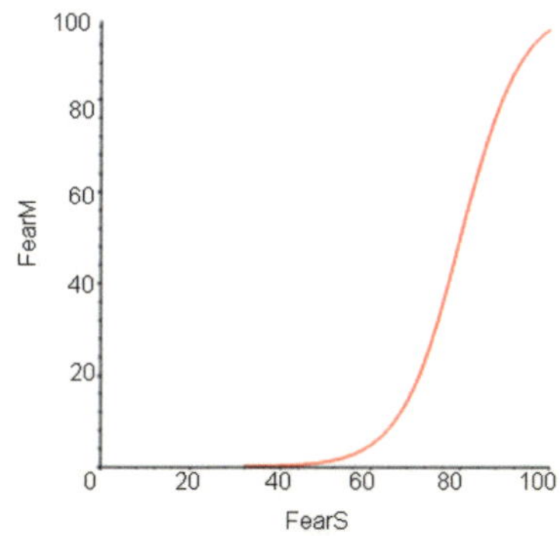

Fig. 12. Relation between FearM (motive) and FearS (state)

8. Gradual reduction and impairment of human behavioural control

The emotional motive FearM is supposed to exert a strong influence on human behaviour in panic situations. The modelling approach addresses this by introducing a fear-based reduction of an individual's ability to control the own behaviour, accompanied by a restriction of the spectrum of available behavioural patterns. Strong fear may prevent an individual from showing phylogenetically highly-developed kinds of behaviour like conscious and planned behaviour. Marked by strong fear, human behaviour is most likely guided by instinct, often expressed by thoughtless flight reactions of panic participants. The reference model encounters these aspects by classifying human behaviour into reactive, deliberative and reflective patterns and by suggesting a gradual reduction of the human behavioural potential in dependence of the intensity of the motive FearM and individual thresholds as depicted in figure 13 on the left hand side.

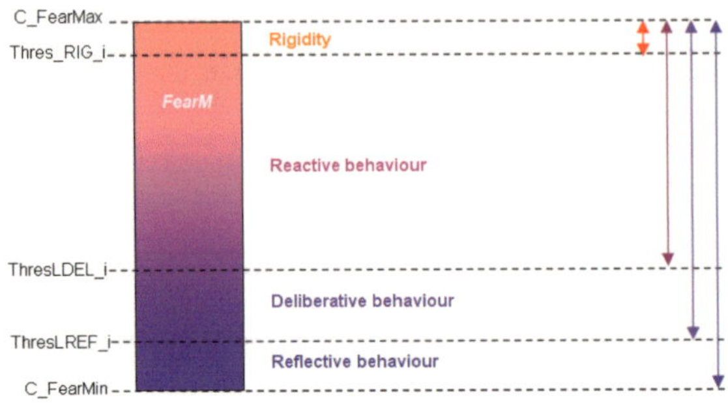

Fig. 13. Impairment of behavioural control

At a low value for the motive FearM (that means FearM ϵ [C_FearMin, ThresLREF_i[), the whole spectrum of behavioural patterns is available. An increase of the motive intensity goes along with a gradual reduction of the set of potential available behaviours from reflective to deliberative and finally reactive behaviour. Very strong fear causes an agent to fall into rigidity. The concrete shaping of behaviour is determined by an agent's personality, individual attitudes, experience, and quality of information about the exact situation as well as familiarity with the place.
The developed concept provides the opportunity to model a behavioural spectrum comprising rigidity, panic-stricken flight response coined by self- preservation, herding as well as cautious flight reactions and altruistic behaviour shown by less fearful or trained human beings such as enforcement officers.

9. Reactive behaviour

Reactive behaviour is to be characterised as instinct-driven or trained. People acting in the reactive spectrum of behaviour are expected to not being able to process complex information and to determine independent flight destinations. Therefore they are reliant on simple information for example visual stimuli like signs or the observation of a fleeing crowd. In the reactive range, SimPan offers modelling solutions for rigidity, wandering around and participating in a mass stampede.

9.1 Rigidity

If a human being suddenly gets very frightened or shocked due to the perception of a threat, it is possible that the ability to move and act is suspended temporarily. Such a state is referred to as rigidity. Accordingly, the modelling approach defines two preconditions (a, b) for rigidity, which must be satisfied by an agent: the intensity of the motive FearM must exceed the individual threshold ThresRIG_i (a) and a fear-inducing event was perceived by the agent recently (b). If both preconditions are satisfied, rigidity is activated. It is implemented as time-consuming internal action, which disables cognitive processes and the execution of external actions and lasts as long as FearM falls below the threshold ThresRIG_i. This can for example be due to the continuous decrease of fear or calming attempts by other agents or technical sources of information.

9.2 Wandering around

In panic situations it can be observed that people start moving in a certain direction without objectively identifiable destination, suddenly stop for a while to apparently realign and subsequently start moving in another direction. It is supposed that these people either have no information about possible flight destinations at all or are not able to process complex information like verbal directions to exits far away due to temporary non-availability of planning processes. To enable an agent to show a similar behaviour, SimPan defines two preconditions (c, d) to be satisfied: the intensity of motive FearM must be in [ThresDEL_i, ThresRIG_i[(c) and the agent possesses no information about a possible flight destination (d). If both preconditions are satisfied, the agent stays at his current position for an individual period of time. Afterwards it determines a preferred direction to move in this direction for a random span of time. The current cycle of movement ends, if the selected span of time is expired or the agent abuts upon an obstacle in the environment. In these cases the next cycle is started. The behaviour of wandering around is repeated as long as the motive FearM leaves the indicated range or an exit gets into the view of the agent. The consequent behaviour of the agent may then be modified in two ways. First, if the agent's fear decreased so that FearM < ThresDEL_i is now able to select a behaviour pattern out of the deliberative spectrum. Second, if the agent's fear increased so that FearM ≥ ThresRIG_i, and it perceived a fear-inducing event, rigidity is enforced.

9.3 Approaching an exit within eyespot and pushing

Reactive agents are supposed not to be able to process most of the information offered by technical sources of information. SimPan suggests that the only information they can handle is the information emanating from an exit within their eyespot. If a reactive agent recognised an exit, it will try to approach it. This can be achieved without employing explicit processes of planning. To initiate this kind of behaviour the strength of the motive FearM must be in the range [ThresDEL_i, ThresRIG_i[and an exit must be within eyespot of the agent. To reach the exit, the agent tries to reduce the difference between the position of the exit and the own position in each step it takes. A simple approach to realise such a strategy is to segment a two- dimensional environment in quadratic cells of different types (e. g. accessible and not accessible), where each cell can be occupied by one agent at a certain point of time. The decision of an agent, which cell next to enter is made anew after each step according to a set of rules. If it is not possible for the agent to come closer to the exit in one step, for example due to obstacles or other agents blocking its way, it tries to exert pressure towards other agents being located on cells which are closer to the exit. If two agents try to enter the same cell using pushing mechanisms, the stronger one is successful. The weaker one has to stay on the current position. If an agent pushes into a cell, which is already occupied by an agent that cannot stand the pressure, the two agents swap their cells. Since pushing is regarded as aggressive, less considerate action, only reactive and deliberative agents use this mechanism in contrast to reflective agents.

9.4 Participation in a mass flight

Reactive agents, not explicitly possessing any information about a concrete flight destination, but being surrounded by other agents that form some kind of flight mass, are carried along with the crowd and orient their movements toward that of their fleeing neighbours. A mass stampede is headed by a reflective or deliberative agent moving consciously towards an exit (or at least towards the coordinates it supposes an exit to be). An agent must satisfy two preconditions to participate in a mass stampede in a non-leading role: the intensity of the motive FearM is in the range [ThresDEL_i, ThresRIG_i[and the agent observes a fleeing crowd. Note that the reactive agents do not know the destination of the mass stampede; they can only use information concerning the direction in which they have to move to follow the deliberative agent. An agent once participated in a mass stampede may also lose track of the crowd again if he gets out of sight and consequently wanders around again.

10. Deliberative behaviour

Deliberative behaviour is characterised by individual and cautious flight reactions directed towards a specific destination. In order to show deliberative behaviour, the value for the dependent variable FearM must be in the range [ThresREF_i, ThresDEL_i[. In this case, an agent is capable of determining a flight destination independently and of developing an appropriate action plan.

10.1 Planning

To choose an appropriate flight destination, deliberative agents are both able to use information already stored in memory and to process new information received from external sources of information such as loudspeakers. If the agent knows about more than one flight destination, it may choose one of them considering some quality factors like distance between its position and the possible flight destination. To reach the target location as quick and unharmed as possible, the employed planning process (e.g. an implementation of the A*- search algorithm) has to account for obstacles and other disturbing factors. By executing a plan, a deliberative agent may start to lead a mass flight. Leading in the case is a passive and "accidental" process, as deliberative agents simply follow their own goals and thereby provide a behaviour pattern which can be emulated by observing reactive agents around. The related modelling approach described below is geared to the principle of wandering ants, where a small number of heading ants provide a "spoor" of pheromones and the remaining population of the ants simply follow this spoor. The intensity of the spoor may decrease depending on the time passed by and atmospheric conditions. SimPan emulates this phenomenon by introducing the capability of deliberative and reflective agents to generate temporary information spheres.

10.2 Construction and update of information spheres

An agent's active potential information sphere (APIS) is a square in the model environment with side length of n cells, where the centre is defined by the cell currently occupied by the deliberative or reflective agent. The APIS satisfies two conditions: $n > 1$ and $(n \bmod 2) = 1$. In the APIS, an agent can spread different kinds of information (e.g. its current flight vector). Other agents entering a sphere can access the information. The active valid information sphere (AVIS) defines a subset of the APIS, excluding cells located in front of the agent (in direction of the agent's movement) and cells belonging to the blind spot of the agent. These are cells in the APIS from which the agent himself cannot be seen – for example due to obstacles like walls or columns. Figure 14 shows the APIS of a deliberative agent.

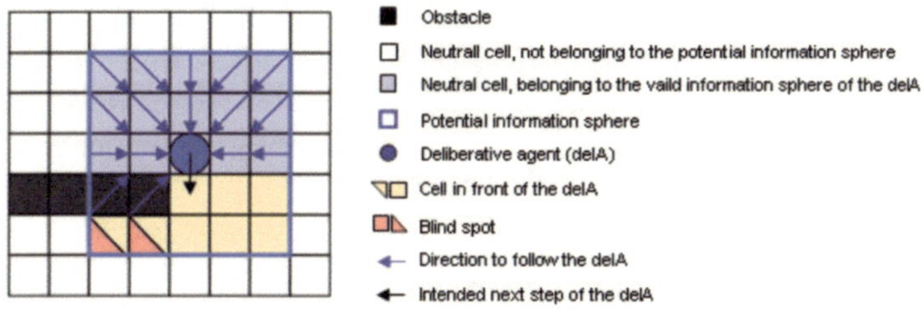

Fig. 14. The information sphere of a deliberative agent

Cells belonging to an agent's AVIS hold the information about which cell has to be entered next by a reactive agent to strictly follow the deliberative agent. By defining the AVIS it is ensured that reactive agents do not run towards the deliberative agent during a mass flight if located in front of it and are only able to join a mass stampede if they immediately observe agents already participating. A new AVIS is generated with each movement of the deliberative agent.

10.3 The Fading of former active information spheres

Just like the pheromone spoor of ants in nature, agent's former AVIS do not release their stored information immediately, but stay active for a period of time, which can be defined arbitrarily. As a consequence, there can be a set of AVIS at a certain point of time belonging to the same agent. If an AVIS expires, the related information stored in the cells is deleted.
Figure 15 shows the set of AVIS of a deliberative agent, where the transparency of the colour of the cells belonging to the AVIS indicates the time to its expiry. The more transparent a cell is, the nearer its time of expiration is.

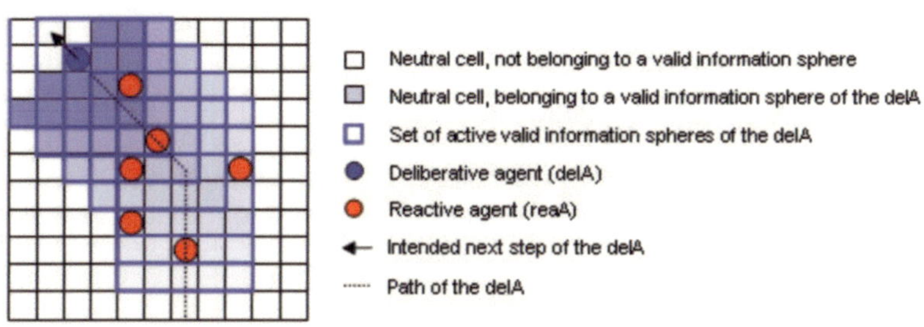

Fig. 15. Fading information sphere of a deliberative agent

10.4. Reflective behaviour

Reflective agents are capable of thoroughly controlling the own behaviour. Deliberative behaviour is therefore expanded by the ability to consciously leading, guiding and calming down reactive agents. An agent's reflective behaviour spectrum is enabled if motive intensity of FearM is in the range [C_FearMin, ThresREF_i[.
SimPan suggests introducing pacification spheres for reflective agents. The pacification sphere of a reflective agent equals the dimension as its information sphere and is not static but moves with the agent. As with the definition of an agent's active potential information sphere, an active potential (APPS) and a valid pacification sphere (AVPS) is defined. The

APPS is defined analogous to the VPIS, whereas just only cells in the blind spot of the agent are excluded in the AVPS. By excluding these cells it is ensured that a reflective agent cannot calm down agents, which are not in sight. A reflective agent does only possess one AVPS at a certain point of time. Figure 16 shows an exemplary pacification sphere of a reflective agent.

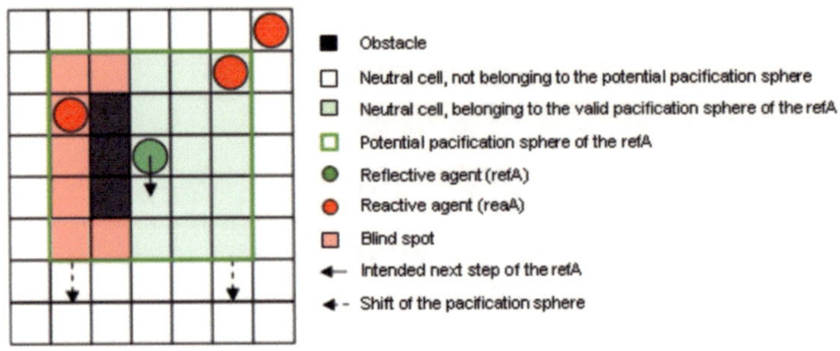

Fig. 16. Pacification sphere of a reflective agent

The fear state of a reactive agent that enters the pacification sphere of a reflective agent decreases discretely. The effect of a calming stimuli recognized by a certain reactive agent decreases with the number of attempts, as defined in equations (eq. 10-13).

11. Content and structure: interplay between SimPan and PECS

To implement the reference model SimPan it is recommended to specify the agent's model structure following the guideline given by the architectural pattern PECS. The reference model SimPan can easily be projected onto the PECS structure to fill its components with content. Internal states and state transition functions defined by SimPan can be assigned to specific PECS model components. Like that, the dynamics calculation of the state variable FearS (5-14) and the motive FearM (17) can be encapsulated in the PECS component Emotion. Further on, the influence of physical pressure on the continuous increase of fear (8, 9, 14) can be realised by employment of a predefined casual dependency between PECS components Emotion and Physis.

12. Potential and Prospects

The reference model SimPan has already been put into practice by integrating the developed modelling concepts into a prototypical agent-based simulation model. The simulation model was developed using the Simplex3- Framework, described in (Schmidt, 2001)

12.1 Case studies

First case studies were done to verify the suitability of the presented modelling approach. Characteristic elements of real panic situations like arching and clogging around exits and casualties due to high pressure exerted by a jostling crowd were observable. Figure 17 shows a screenshot taken from a simulation run with the prototypical simulation model involving 360 agents in an environment composed of 41 x 45 cells, each with a side length of 0.5 meters.

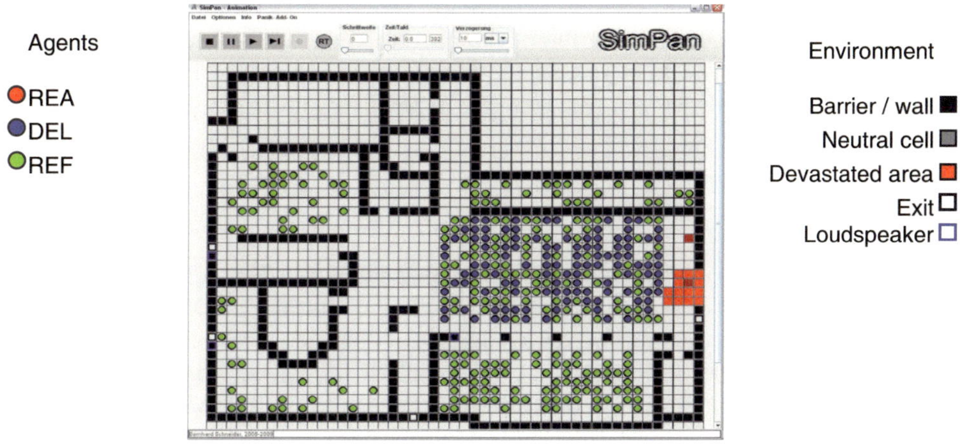

Fig. 17. Screenshot taken from a case study

The scenario is based on a real world panic event that took place on February 20, 2003 in the Station Nightclub in West Warwick, Rhode Island. A fire caused by pyrotechnics near the stage of the club triggered a panic flight towards the main entrance of the club. Egress from the night club was hampered by crowding at the main entrance. In the course of the panic event 96 people lost their lives, 87 were injured.

12.2 Propects

SimPan does explicitly not claim to replace established approaches in the context of evacuation simulations but to complement them and to open up new research areas in the given context. The development of a reference model for agent-based modelling of human behaviour in panic situation seems to be a reasonable step to address research questions that are not sufficiently manageable using existing models, for example where and when to initiate what kind of calming stimuli, how to proceed with panicking people in the crowd or how to detect emotional charge in the environment before it comes to a panic breakout.
The next steps to transfer SimPan from academia into practise are definition of a concrete real world use case (in the best case in cooperation with an external customer), adaptation of the reference model to the specific requirements of the use case, construction of a new SimPan- based simulation model using a high- performance simulation framework to be able to handle even large evacuations scenarios with thousands of people involved and finally calibration of the simulation model in respect of the use case scenario. The aim of calibrating the model is to reduce the set of assumptions to be made regarding initial values for model parameters (especially defining the internal state of a human being to be simulated).
It is important to mention that the success of calibration efforts, especially for simulation models including human factors, strongly depends on the availability of real world data. For this reason, plausibility considerations and face validations done by subject matter experts are often conducted to supplement calibration with "hard" comparison data. Additionally, "intelligent experimentation" by employing the Data Farming methodology can be used to

support the calibration process. Data Farming circumscribes selective generation of simulation data by conducting thousands and, if necessary, millions of simulation runs on a high performance computer cluster. Certain Designs of Experiment are employed to determine model parameters to be varied (and thus to define scenarios to be simulated). Analysis of the generated data with the help of distribution plots or regression trees can be done in terms of a sensitivity analysis and can help the analyst to gain important insights into the model dynamics.

13. Summary

In the chapter, the reference model SimPan was presented. SimPan provides as a comprehensive approach for psychologically based modelling of human panic behaviour and follows a system theoretical perspective on modelling of complex systems such as the human being. The reference model itself serves as a conceptual framework for the construction of agent- based models in the given context and offers space for individual adaptation to specific requirements defined by particular fields of application.

Panic is defined as an internal state, marked by the strong emotional motive fear. A high level of fear may prevent an individual from showing certain kinds of behaviour, among them conscious and planned behaviour. More critical, strong fear can additionally lead to thoughtless flight reactions of panic participants. The modelling approach addresses this by introducing a fear-based reduction of an individual's ability to control the own behaviour, accompanied by a restriction of the spectrum of available behavioural patterns.

Additionally, SimPan addresses motivation and mechanisms of motive dynamics and motive selection in particular, social influence on the emergence of emotion, attitude and action and emotional intelligence and the ability of consciously controlling emotion and different kinds of human behaviour, categorised as reactive, deliberative and reflective.

As a basis for modelling the concepts of human panic behaviour, the architectural pattern PECS was considered. The PECS reference model provides capabilities for object- oriented model specification. Its application area is settled in the field of agent- based simulation. PECS offers a modular but comprehensive view of human behaviour modelling, where a human being is considered an autonomous creature with physical conditions, emotional states and cognitive capabilities, embedded in a social environment.

Experiments with a simulation prototype based on the reference model SimPan reproduced characteristic elements of real panic situations like arching and clogging around exits, propagation of pressure in the environment and an increased the emotional charge of individuals during an evacuation situation. In a next step, model parameters should, as good as possible, be calibrated. This sophisticated task mainly depends on the availability of real world data concerning human behaviour in panic situation.

The model is intended for employment in the field of analysing and testing kinds of behaviour and strategies to avoid panic. Simulating the complexity of panic situations in an adequate way also includes emergent phenomena and gives the analyst the possibility to identify specific dangerous situations that could be avoided by changing the procedure of an operation or some parts of the infrastructure. Possible fields of application are hereby mass meetings of political kind, sporting events, fires in closed rooms, acts of terrorism in public places or air accidents. The intersection of all mentioned scenarios is the need to develop strategies to evacuate people from danger zones in a systematic manner without triggering panic behaviour. Figure 18 gives an overview about relevant parameters of the reference model SimPan.

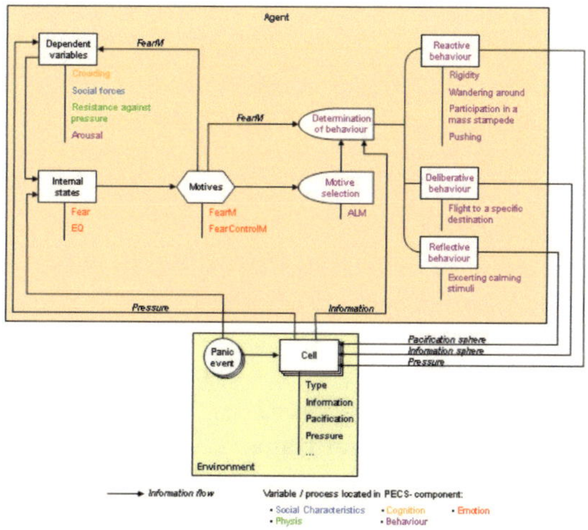

Fig. 18. Graphical representation of the reference model SimPan

14. References

Banarjee S., Grosnan C. & Abraham A. (2005). Modeling Crowd Behavior Using Emotional Ants. *Journal of Studia Universitatis Babes-Bolyai, Informatica*, Volume L, Number 1, 2005, pp. 37-48

Becker, C. & Schmidt, B. (2005)., Bewegung von Menschenmengen - Agentenbasiertes Simulationsmodell zur Untersuchung von Drängel- und Druckmechanismen. *Proceedings of the ASIM2005*, pp. 792-794, ISBN : 3-936150-41-9, Erlangen, September 2005, SCS Publishing House, Erlangen

Cañamero, D. (1997). Modeling Motivations and Emotions as a Basis for Intelligent Behaviour. *Proceedings of the First International Symposium on Autonomous Agents (Agents '97)*, pp. 148-155, Marina del Rey, February 1997, The ACM Press, New York

Daamen, W. (2002). SimPed: a Pedestrian Simulation Tool for Large Pedestrian Areas, *Proceedings of the European Simulation Interoperability Workshop 2002*, London, June 2002

Dörner, D. (1999). *Bauplan für eine Seele*, Rowohlt Verlag, ISBN : 3499611937, Reinbeck bei Hamburg.

Dombrowski, W. R., Pajonk, F. - G. (2005). *Panik als Massenphänomen*. Der Anaesthesist, 54, 2005, pp. 245-253

Foreman, P. B. (1953). Panic Theory, *Sociological and Social Research*, 37, 1953, pp. 295–304

Gipps P. G. & Marksjö M. (1985). A microsimulation model for pedestrian flows, *Mathematics and Computers in Simulation*, 27, 1985, pp. 95-105

Heinz, W. R., Schöber, P. (1972). Kollektives Verhalten – Alte Fragen, neue Perspektiven, In : *Theorien kollektiven Verhaltens Band 1*, Heinz, W. R. & Schöber, P. (Eds.), Hermann Luchterhand, 9783472611189, Darmstadt

Helbing, D., Illés F. & Vicsek T. (2002). Crowd disasters and simulation of panic situations, In :*Science of Disaster: Climate Disruptions, Heart Attacks and Market Crashes*, Bunde, A., Kropp, J., Schellnhuber, H. J. (Eds.), pp. 193–216, Springer, 3540413243, Berlin Heidelberg.

Kirchner, A. & Schadschneider, A. (2002). Simulation of evacuation processes using a bionic-sinspired cellular automaton model for pedestrian dynamics. *Physica A*, 312, 2002, pp. 260-276

Klinger, A. (1999). *Referenzmodelle für die Abbildung von Personalsteuerung in der Simulation*, SCS, 156555129X, Erlangen.

Kruse, L. (1986). Conceptions of Crowds and Crowding, In : *Changing Conceptions of Crowd Mind and Behavior*, Graumann, C. F. & Moscovici, S. (Eds.), pp 117–142, Springer, 9780387961873, New York

Langer E. J. & Saegert S. (1977). Crowding and Cognitive Control. *Journal of Personality and Social Psychology*, 35, 3, 1977, pp. 175-182

Latané, B. (1981). The Psychology of Social Impact. *American Psychologist*, 36, 1981, pp. 343-356

LeBon, G. (1982). *Psychologie der Massen*. Kröner, 9783520099150, Stuttgart

Mann, L. (1999). *Sozialpsychologie*, Beltz Verlag, 9783407220424, Weinheim, Basel

Mayer, J. D. & Salovey, P. (1997). What is Emotional Intelligence? In : *Emotional development and emotional intelligence*, Salovey, P. & Sluyter D. (Eds.), pp. 3-32, BasicBooks, 0465095879, New York

Mummendy, A. & Otten, S. (2002). Aggressives Verhalten. In: *Sozialpsychologie. Eine Einführung*, Stroebe, W., Jonas, K. & Hewstone, M. (Eds.), Springer, 9783540420637, Berlin

Muramatsu, M., Irie, T. & Nagatani, T. (1999). Jamming transition in pedestrian counter flow. *Physica A*, 267, 1999, pp. 487- 498

Quarantelli, E. L. (2001). The Sociology of Panic. In: *International Encyclopedia of the Social and Behavioral Siences*, Smelser, N. J., Baltes, P. B. (Eds.), pp. 11020-11030 , Pergamon Press, 9780080430768, Elsevier

Quarantelli, E. L. (1954). The Nature and Conditions of Panic. *The American Journal of Sociology*, Vol. 60, No. 3, Nov. 1954, pp. 267-275

Reicher, S. (2001). The Psychology of Crowd Dynamics. In: *Blackwell Handbook of Social Psychology : Group Processes*, Hogg, M. A. & Tindale, S. R. (Eds.). pp. : 182-208, Blackwell, 9780631208655, Oxford

Schmidt, B. (2000). *The Modelling of Human Behaviour*, SCS-Europe BVBA, 1565552113, Ghent

Schmidt, B. (2001). *The Art of Modelling and Simulation - Introduction to the Simulation System Simplex3*. SCS- Europe BVBA, 1565552288, Ghent

Schmidt B. & Schneider, B. (2004). The Reflective Control of Cognition and Emotion, *Proceedings of the 2004 Operational Research Society Simulation Workshop*, Birmingham, May 2004

Schulz, D. (1964). *Panic Behavior. Discussion and Readings*. Random House, New York

Sloman, A. (2000). Architectural requirements for human-like agents both natural and artificial. (What sorts of machines can love?), In: *Human Cognition and Social Agent Technology, Advances in Consciousness Research*, Dautenhahn, K. (Ed.), pp. 163-195, John Benjamins, 1556194358, Amsterdam

Stokols, D., Rall, M., Pinner, B. & Schopler, J. (1973). Physical, social and personal determinants of the perception of crowding. *Environment and Behaviour*, Volume 5, 1973, pp. 87-115

Urban, C. (2007). *Der Mensch im Simulationsmodell*, VDM Verlag Dr. Müller, 9783836420532, Saarbrücken

Urban, C. (2000). PECS: A Reference Model for the Simulation of Multi-Agent Systems, In : *Tools and Techniques for Social Science Simulation*, Ramzi S., Troitzsch, K. G. & Gilbert, N. (Eds.), pp. 83-114, Physica-Verlag, 379081265X, Heidelberg

Vassalos, D., Kim, H., Christiansen, G. & Majumder, J. (2002). A Mesoscopic Model for Passenger Evacuation in a Virtual Ship-Sea Environment and Performance-Based Evaluation, In : *Pedestrian and Evacuation Dynamics*, Schreckenberg, M. and Sharma, S. (Eds.), pp. 369-392, Springer, 3540426906, Berlin

Effective agent-based geosimulation development using PLAMAGS

Tony Garneau, Bernard Moulin
Département d'informatique et de génie logiciel, Université Laval
Québec, Canada

Sylvain Delisle
Département de mathématiques et d'informatique, Université du Québec à Trois-Rivières
Québec, Canada

1. Introduction

During the past decade, the technology based on Software Agents (SA) has been applied to a large number of domains such as computer games, entertainment movies involving animated characters, virtual reality, user interface design involving personal agents, web-based interfaces and tutoring systems using virtual avatars, to name a few. Since the SA technology is now mature, new fields may benefit from it as, for example the field of Geographic Information Systems (GIS) applied to decision support, and more specifically the domain of geo-simulation. During the past decade, the number of software using digital geographic data has increased a lot, being popularized by applications such as web-mapping, assistants for route planning and monitoring using GPS (Global Positioning System), exploration of virtual cities and geographic territories using tools such as MapQuest and Google Earth. Besides these popular applications, GIS have been used for a long time by governmental and private organizations whose activities deal with the geographic space in a way or another. Most of these applications, however, are complex since they deal with spatial dynamic phenomena and usually involve large populations of individuals (persons, animals, insects, plants, etc.) and their interactions (Courdier et al. 2002).

There are numerous situations that decision makers from various sectors (governmental, economics (Fagiolo et al. 2007), military, industrial (Gnansounou et al. 2007), medical, social) need to monitor in order to insure human security (Foudil and Noureddine 2007) (in case of flood, earthquake or wild fire), the respect of public order (crowd monitoring, evacuation of people, peace-keeping activities) or the adequate use of infrastructures (i.e. monitoring of people and households transportation and shopping habits to better plan urban infrastructures). In such situations, GIS are very useful to gather data about geographic phenomena and to carry out spatial operations on it in order to generate various thematic maps that provide decision makers with an overview of the situation and its evolution.

However, GIS should be enhanced with other techniques in order to provide an enhanced support to decision makers. Geo-simulation (Beneson and Torrens 2004) is such an approach which became popular in geography and social sciences in recent years. It is a useful tool to integrate the spatial dimension in models of interactions of different types (economical, political, social, etc.) and is used to study various complex phenomena (CORMAS 2009), especially in the domain of urban dynamics and landcover planning.

Using Multi-Agent in Geo-Simulation

Since these phenomena usually involve large populations in which individuals behave autonomously, several researchers thought to take advantage of multi-agent simulation techniques (d'Aquino et al. 2003; Guyot and Honiden 2006; Gnansounou et al. 2007; Papazoglou et al. 2008), which resulted in the creation of the new field of Multi-Agent Geo-Simulation (Koch 2001; Moulin et al. 2003). However, most geosimulation applications deal with very simple agent models, mainly expressed in terms of simple behavior and decision rules, either attached to spatial portions (i.e. cells in cellular automata) or to simple agents moving around in a virtual geo-referenced space (Beneson and Kharbash 2005; Müller et al. 2005). Indeed, the degree of sophistication of agent models depends on the scale of the simulation. For example in the traffic simulation domain, different kinds of simulations are developed at macro-, meso- and micro-scales in order to respectively study traffic flows in regions of different extent (macro- or meso-level) or to create micro-models based on individual vehicles behaviors (Helbing et al. 2002; Bourrel and Henn 2003). Nevertheless, most models that drive such simulations of agents' movements in geographic space are either based on mathematical models (usually systems of differential equations) or on simple rules (Torrens and Benenson 2005; Levesque et al. 2008).

However, there is a large variety of phenomena in which individuals need to make informed decisions, taking into account the characteristics of the geographic environment as well as the effects of other agents' actions. Hence, there is a need for more sophisticated agents' models, akin to intelligent software agents' models, in order to carry out autonomous behaviours within geographic virtual environments (Crooks et al. 2007). Such a model was proposed by Moulin and colleagues (Moulin et al. 2003) in which agents have several knowledge-based capabilities: 1) perception (of terrain features, objects and other agents); 2) navigation (autonomous navigation with obstacle avoidance coupled with perception); 3) memorization (of perceived features and objects), communication (with other agents)); and 4) objective-based behaviour (based on interrelated goals and activity plans).

However, whatever the sophistication of the models, specifying agent behavior models is a difficult task and designers need efficient and user-friendly tools to support them. Some existing tools for agent-based simulations, such as CSF, GASP (GASP), HPTS (Donikian 2001), AI.Implant (AI.implant 2003; AI.implant 2009) and PathEngine (PATHEngine 2009), deal with the spatial aspects of agent behaviors by providing good navigation mechanisms for the characters. Unfortunately, they tend to neglect the proactive aspects of agents and their interactions with the environment. Other tools such as SimBionic (Fu et al. 2002) and SPIR.OPS (SPR.OPS 2009) offer sophisticated specification means for objects/agents behaviors based on models inspired by finite state machines (Fu et al. 2003). But, the use of finite state machines leads to complex graphs to represent relatively simple reactive behaviors. Behaviors developed using these tools lead to reactive agents or "navigation driven" agents (Cutumisu et al. 2006). Hence, they are not sufficient for the development of geosimulations of social phenomena in which agents need to implement knowledge-based capabilities in relation with the space in which they evolve. In both cases, resulting agents do not have decision-making capacities. Moreover, since most of these tools do not provide perception mechanisms, agents cannot apprehend the virtual environment (act in the environment and interact with the object/agent contained in it).

To help solve these problems, we claim that software agents with space-related capabilities should be introduced in the virtual spatial environments associated with geo-simulations. We call these agents "spatialized SAs" (SSAs for short) and they are characterized by the following properties:

- Autonomous and individual perception mechanism
- Decision-making in relation to a geo-referenced virtual environment
- Proactive and autonomous behaviors taking into account their knowledge about the world (the virtual environment).

The specification of this type of agents is a difficult task and, to our knowledge, no existing simulation environment enables designers to specify SSAs. In the context of the PLAMAGS Project (Programming LAnguage for Multi-Agent Geo-Simulations), we have developed a high-level language and a complete development environment allowing a designer to quickly develop and execute multi-agent geo-simulations. The PLAMAGS toolkit was motivated by the need to provide a complete and real programming language dedicated to the specification and the execution of multi-agent geo-simulations.

Section 2 introduces the architecture and the main concepts on which the PLAMAGS language is based. Section 3 presents the main characteristics of the language. Section 4 is an overview of the IDE. Section 5 presents miscellaneous PLAMAGS features and Section 6 concludes the paper with a discussion and some future work.

2. Main models provided by the PLAMAGS architecture and language

This section aims to introduce the overall design we propose for MAGS' development. Section 2.1 presents the principles that guided PLAMAGS' development as well as how they are interrelated to form a coherent whole. Section 2.2 further describes the different models that PLAMAGS supports with respect to MAGS' specification and implementation.

2.1 The PLAMAGS architectural model

A fact that greatly contributes to make MAGS' development a challenge is the inherent necessity to work with two very distinct sets of concepts, GIS and Multi-Agent Based Simulations, which share neither the same problems nor the same concerns. Thus we have to conciliate these differences in order to allow the fruitful interactions necessary to the synergy we seek.

As a matter of fact, Figure 1 presents an overview of the model upon which PLAMAGS is based. As it can be noticed, the main components of a PLAMAGS simulation's model are: 1) a VGE (Virtual Geographical Environment) that renders the simulation environment; 2) the agents and objects located in this environment (which are characterized by behaviors); 3) the simulation scenario and, ultimately 4) the results of the simulation. These four elements are in constant interaction and constitute the core of the system. However, on a more global level, PLAMAGS' architecture can be seen as two distinct parts; first the programming language for the MAGS, and, second, a set of tools to facilitate its use. These tools are bundled into an IDE (Integrated Development Environment) that simplifies as much as possible the language's usage. The IDE also provides the user with a development framework.

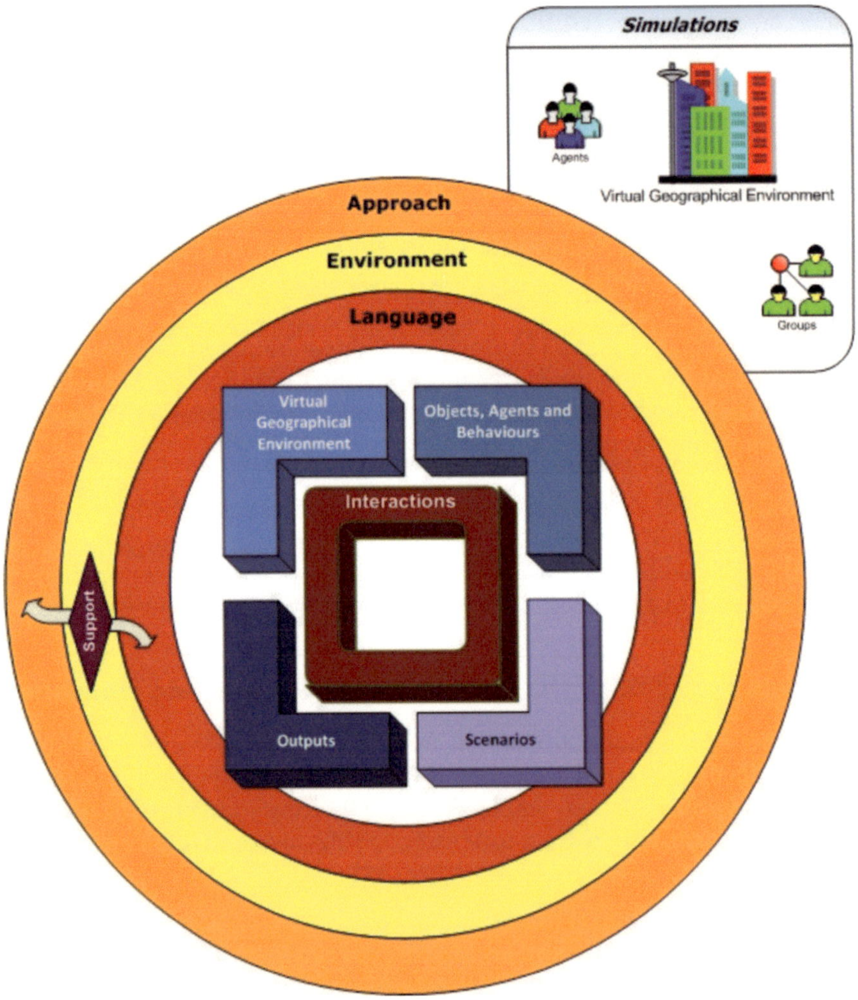

Fig. 1. PLAMAGS' architecture

Since we cannot present PLAMAGS' architecture in details in this chapter, we will briefly present an overview of the most important elements, such as the VGEs and scenarios, as well as the specification of objects, agents and their behaviors. We will also present the main tools of the IDE, and we will show how the language can be used to retrieve and manipulate spatial information.

2.2 Objects and agents

Independently of their specific characteristics (be they passive objects, reactive agents or proactive/cognitive agents), SSAs participating in geo-simulations have common important characteristics: they are situated in a virtual geo-referenced space (they actually move in it), they must apprehend its content (they perceive the objects and agents located in the virtual space), and they must interact with the elements (objects and agents) contained in the virtual space.

As an illustration, we developed a simulation of a demonstration (see figure 2). In such a simulation agents need to perceive tear gas and to react to them. Agents also need to distinguish different types of agents such as police, rioter and demonstrator agents and to behave according to their perception of the other agents' actions. As another example, pedestrians participating in a peace walk must be able to perceive and follow the group walking along a planned route, adjust their own pace to the crowd's pace, avoid cars and other obstacles. We distinguish three categories of SSAs, depending on the complexity of their behaviors, reasoning and interactions with the virtual space: passive SSAs, reactive SSAs, and cognitive SSAs.

Fig. 2. Distant view of a hot spot of the event.

2.2.1 Static object (passive SSA)

In a simulation, numerous components are still objects having a physical presence in the VGE, but no behavior. These objects may have various properties such as a color, a weight and a dimension, but they do act. We may also need other types of objects that are data structures without any physical representation as for example, the representation of a position in the virtual environment.

In our model, we use a specific language structure to represent passive SSAs. This structure is called a *static object type* which is equivalent to an object-oriented (OO) class in an object-oriented language enhanced with a visual representation and a spatial/physical definition (if necessary). As for OO classes, a static object type has properties (which can be constant or modifiable) and methods. Methods can be used to attach processes to static objects as for example to change their location, their visual representation and change their properties as a result of the actions applied by agents on the objects. In addition to standard OO classes' capacities, static objects can own a visual representation and a spatial/physical definition and description (bounding volume, mass, etc.). In the demonstration simulation, fences are defined as static objects since they only have some properties and a physical presence, but no behavior (see figure 3).

Fig. 3. Confrontation between the police and demonstrators.

2.2.2 Active object (reactive SSA)

Reactive SSAs have relatively primitive behaviors that can be efficiently represented using a reactive agent approach. We represent reactive SSAs thanks to a specific language structure that we call active object. Active objects are equivalent to reactive agents in classical agent models. Their capabilities are similar to those of static objects' (properties, methods and visual/spatial/physical definition) but are augmented with a set of lists of rules used to specify their behaviors. Reactive SSAs have no elaborate decision-making capabilities: they only react to their inputs (most of the time obtained from their perception mechanism) thanks to the aforementioned lists of rules which are automatically triggered by the simulation engine. Using these rules, the reactive agent has the possibility to interact with its environment and other SSAs during the simulation (Levesque et al. 2008).

In our simplified demonstration simulation (see figure 4), considering that squad members 'blindly' obey to the instructions of their squad leaders, we chose to specify them as reactive SSAs, using an active object type called *squad-member*.

Fig. 4. Formation line of squad members.

Figure 5 presents some parts of the *"squad-member"* type and the list of rules defined to represent its reactive behavior. In Figure 2, the method *"moveToward"* is a "managed action" (also called "perform"), a structure provided by PLAMAGS and explained in Section 3.

```
246  public active object Squad
247    attribute: ....
248        rules SquadRules trigger when [newDestination() == true]
249    method: ...
250
251  private rules SquadRules mode disjunctive
252    rule WP_1 mode conjunctive         ...
253    rule FL mode conjunctive
254        lhs IS_FL [operation] == [Commander.FORMATION_LINE] // other lhs...
255        rhs GO_FL call moveToward(destination.x, destination.y, 1, true) // other rhs...
256        ...
```

Fig. 5. Line 248 declares that "squad" objects use a list of rules called "SquadRules" (defined at line 251) which will be automatically triggered by the simulation engine.

2.2.3 Agent (cognitive SSA)

We consider cognitive SSAs as agents that behave autonomously. Such agents must be able to interact with their environment (virtual geographic environment, objects and other agents), make decisions with respect to their own states and preferences and act accordingly. A reactive approach is not sufficient to represent these behaviors. We thus defined cognitive SSAs thanks to a specific language structure that we call agent.

In addition, to all the attributes of an active object, an agent is characterized by a number of static and dynamic variables whose values describe the agent's state at any given time. Using these variables, the system can simulate the evolution of the agents' dynamic states and trigger the relevant objectives. An agent is also associated with a behavior which is represented by a set of multi-layered directed graphs, each one composed of a set of objectives that the agent tries to reach (see Figure 6).

2.3 Behaviors

Behavioral graphs are the most powerful and expressive behavioral data structures existing in PLAMAGS. They are used to define complex agent's behaviors of simulations' agents. The power of these graphs lies in their high flexibility, customizability and their ability to represent behaviors in different ways.

A behavioral graph in PLAMAGS is a multi-layered graph in which nodes represent objectives which can be either atomic or composed of sub-behaviors. The objectives are organized in hierarchies such that elementary objectives (called simple objectives) are associated with actions that the agent can execute (i.e. objectives "PresenceAct" and "CheckAround" in Figure 3). Each agent owns a set of objectives corresponding to its needs (Moulin et al. 2003). An objective is associated with rules containing constraints on the activation, execution and completion of the objective, called activation rules, execution rules and completion rules (Moulin et al. 2003; Garneau et al. 2008). Constraints are dependent on time, on the agent's state, and on the environment's state. Objectives are also linked to resources that must be either acquired or already owned for them to be executed. The selection of the current agent's objectives relies on the graph structure, on previously executed objectives, on the missing required resources and on priorities and activation/execution/completion rules related to the agent's objectives. The execution of an objective is always conditional to its execution rule being triggered and the required resources being available. An objective's priority is primarily a discriminating function or expression used to choose between potential future objectives. It is also subject to modifications brought about by the opportunities that the agent perceives in the environment and by the temporal constraints applying to the objective. Resources are agents' assets that can be assigned exclusively to an objective's execution. The allocation of resources between objectives for iteration is dictated by the objectives' priorities.

The structure of the multi-layered directed graph allows us to define a behavior at different levels of abstraction and to divide behaviors into sub-behaviors. An abstraction level can be added by inserting a compound or an aggregate objective in the behavior. A compound objective can be thought of as a decomposable structure representing a sub-behavior (its structure is similar to a behavior structure), see Figure 7. Aggregate objectives are also decomposable structures, they are composed of a set of objectives, but those one are not interrelated. These objectives allow us to represent goals (or composite objectives) where neither a hierarchical structure nor a predefined sequence of objectives is needed. Compound and aggregate objectives are perfectly suitable to regroup an agent's objectives by goal. Since "non-simple" objectives are composed of other objectives, any number of abstraction levels can be specified. The decomposition stops when an objective is composed of actions (corresponding to simple objective). At this time, it is considered to be the "execution level" of the behavior.

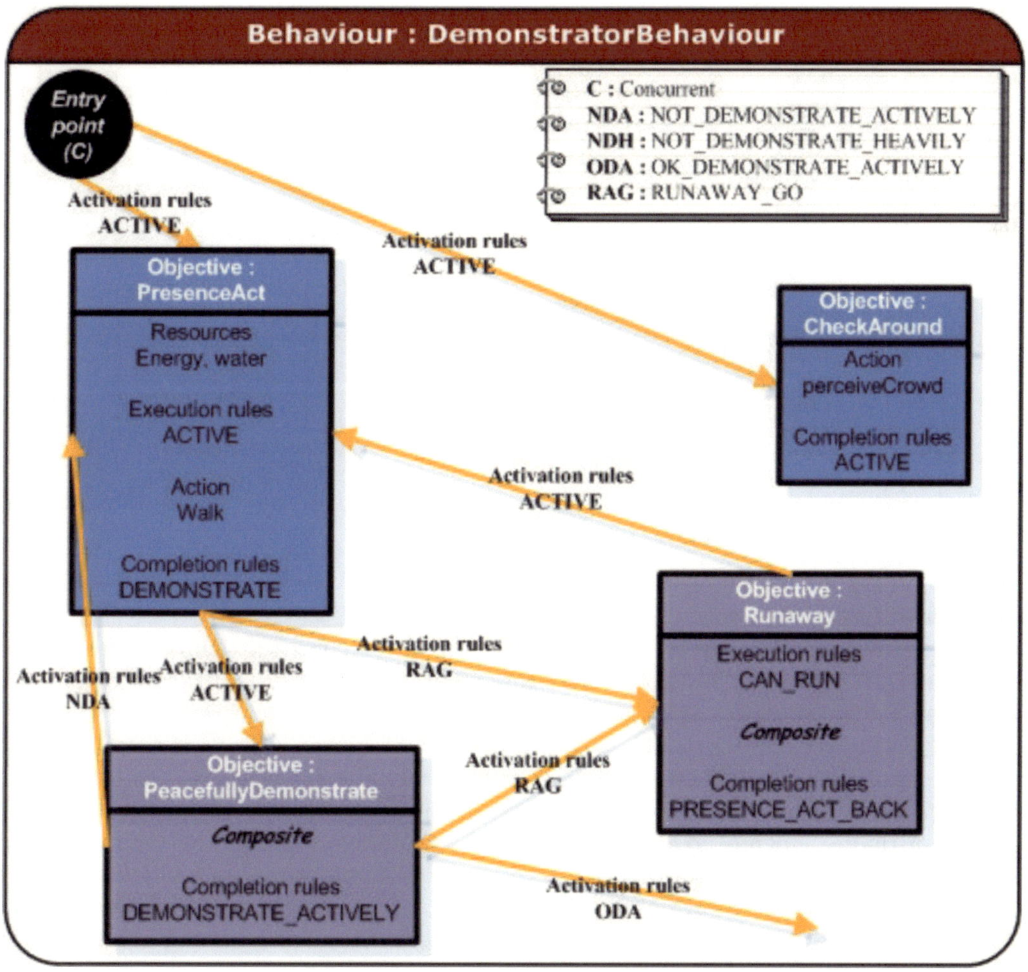

Fig. 6. A part of the demonstrator's behavior (in the demonstration simulation) similar as those displayed through PLAMAGS's graphical interface.

Since agents often need to simultaneously achieve more than one objective, we provide an execution mode allowing to concurrently activate several objectives. The "mode" declaration is specified for each objective because concurrent activation is not desirable everywhere in a behavior graph. This allows to locally control the activation of parts of the behaviour graph. For example, in Figure 6 the behaviour entry point (a special simple objective) declares "C" as an indicator to specify that successor objectives (PresenceAct and CheckAround) can be activated concurrently (if their respective activation rules are correctly triggered). But, everywhere else, only one successor of an objective will be executed at a given time (note that when "C" is not specified, the execution is considered to be single).

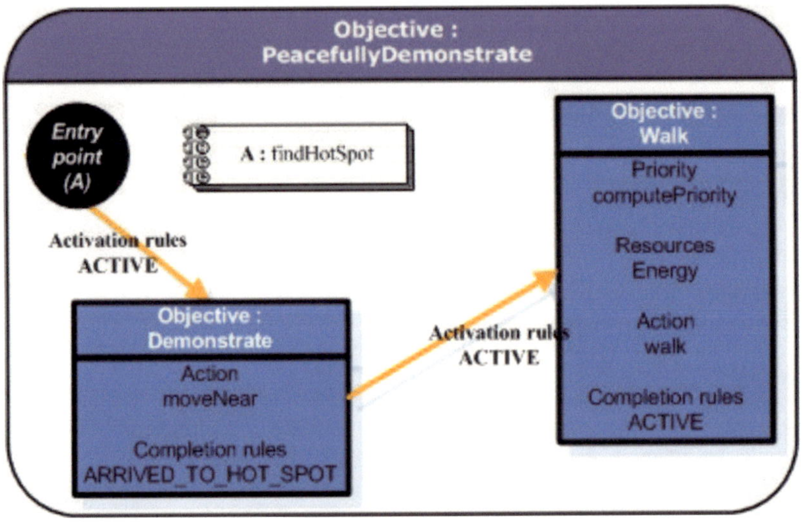

Fig. 7. Internal view of the PeacefullyDemonstrate objective used in the demonstrator agent's behaviour (in the demonstration simulation).

2.4 Other PLAMAGS models

Objects, agents and the agents' behaviors are the main concepts defining simulations' dynamism in PLAMAGS. However, there exist other concepts that further define a MAGS simulation namely scenarios and agent groups. On the one hand, *scenarios* allow specifying the VGE (including the 3D model, textures, coordinate system, elevation maps, collision matrix), simulation parameters (cycles per time unit, time unit to use), and the initial characteristics of agent populations. On the other hand, *agent groups* allow to describe the complex attributes inherent to a group such as the individual relations between members, influence of the group on its member (and conversely). Agent groups are perceived by the agents, objects and other groups of the simulation. A last simulation influencing type exists, but it is limited to model clouds of smoke (although thoroughly) using attributes like perceptibility, particles density, speed and acceleration of solid particles.

In this section, we presented the different types of SSAs and how to represent an agent's behavior. Section 3 will show how these concepts are defined and usable in the language.

3. The PLAMAGS language

This section presents the PLAMAGS language, a complete and expressive agent-oriented language providing standard procedural and object-oriented (OO) features. One of the main advantages of this language is that it facilitates the transformation of simulation designs into executable code. The data structure and features of this language are thus well adapted to the needs of MAGS developers.

In order to stay as close as possible to concrete needs for the development of MAGS, the language syntax includes all the tools required to easily create the VGE, to specify agents and scenarios. It is not possible to present all the language elements in this paper. We will mainly focus on the structures implementing the SSAs' characteristics presented in the previous section. Let us now define some technical aspects of the language.

3.1 Interpreted procedural, descriptive and declarative language

In essence, PLAMAGS is an interpreted language with a Java-based interpreter. This interpreter is included in a complete IDE. The language is used to write specifications, to implement and execute MAGS. Its syntax makes explicit all structures and parameters and is easily readable.

We can thus sum up this language as: i) easy to use for simulation descriptions; ii) within reach to non programming experts; iii) intuitive and easy to master for experts and developers.

In addition to its MAGS-oriented features, PLAMAGS also offers the syntactical structures found in mainstream structured and object-oriented programming languages such as Java, C++ and C#. Such structures must to be present in any programming. Unfortunately, there seems to be a trend in MAGS-oriented specification languages that provide adequate functionalities to specify MAGS, but lack the basic constructs of programming languages that are needed to develop complete systems. Breaking with that trend, PLAMAGS offers: 1) built-in data types; 2) user-defined data types (closely related to OOP classes); 3) ability to define methods and constructors; 4) support for overloaded and recursive functions; 5) control and loop structures; 6) set of logical and mathematical operators as well as a casting operator; 7) a set of access modifiers (inspired from OOP); 8) package-based modularity infrastructure; 9) instance, class-wide and global variables; 10) support for object composition.

3.2 Integrated support for MAGS

Notwithstanding the fact that the language supports structured programming much like general-purpose programming languages, either object-oriented or procedural, the appeal of PLAMAGS obviously comes from its integrated support for MAGS. This support is directly embedded into the language's basic structures and keywords and allowing for a simple specification of the simulation's attributes and components. All the main components of MAGS are mapped to keywords that are used to declare and define them: this facilitates the usage of the language in a purely descriptive way. Hence, a user can easily set up a simulation by completing some templates using only keywords and simple expressions.

The next two sub-sections present these language-embedded structures and the mechanisms offered by the language to retrieve and manipulate data related to the geo-spatial environment, as well as information generated by agents' interactions. These mechanisms are integrated in the language, thus enabling a completely seamless transition from specification of a MAGS to its implementation.

3.2.1 Simulation description

This section presents and justifies the structures chosen to implement the three types of SSAs introduced in Section 2.

Passive and reactive SSAs (i.e. static and active objects)

Since passive SSAs are inanimate components of the simulation having various properties or structures representing properties of other components, OO classes could be used to define such SSAs. However, our static object structure also provides the means to specify behaviors in the form of rules.

Reactive behaviors expressed by rules, allow a component to respond to stimuli (applying functions to these stimuli, to modify internal states, to carry out actions, etc). We implemented a rule list model that is directly inspired by traditional reactive approaches in which a rule is made up of a set of conditions. These conditions must satisfy certain constraints; and when these constraints are satisfied, a series of actions is triggered. In PLAMAGS' active objects (or reactive SSAs), the rule's conditions are relational operators that can be applied to both object properties and function calls. Most of the time, these function calls return computed data obtained from the perception. Whenever the rule conditions are satisfied, actions (method calls and spatialized actions) and properties modification are triggered. Figure 2 shows the definition of an active object and its rule list.

Rule list multiple usages

In PLAMAGS, rule lists are used in different situations. As we saw above, they are used as behaviors for active objects, but they can also be used to verify conditions when activating, executing and completing agents' objectives. However, independently of their use, they always have the same structure and the same execution logic. A PLAMAGS rule list contains one or several rules. Each rule is composed of a list of preconditions known as LHS (Left Hand Side) and a list of consequents known as RHS (Right Hand Side). A rule must have at least one LHS and one RHS. A precondition is always evaluated to "true" or "false". A consequent can result in a property modification or a method call.

Agents and their behaviors

As mentioned in Section 2.2.3, a cognitive SSA is characterized by a behavioral component which is represented as a layered graph composed of a set of objectives that the agent tries to reach (nodes). This sub-section introduces the main structures of the language implementing behaviors in PLAMAGS. The code presented in this sub-section represents the behavior and objectives of Figure 6 and Figure 7. An interesting feature of the behaviors is that they are directly transferable from the visual representation to PLAMAGS code. It allows for the modeling of the behavior in an intuitive way using a graphical representation. Thereafter, this model can quickly and easily be transferred into PLAMAGS executable code. We will illustrate the various concepts by referring to the code specifying a demonstrator agent (Figure 8).

```
688 public agent Demonstrator
689    attribute: ...
690    behaviour DemonstratorBehaviour // optional : trigger every [...] or when [...]
691    method: ...
692 end agent
693
694 private behaviour DemonstratorBehaviour
695    entry execute concurrent
696          successor CheckAround activation rules ACTIVE
697          successor PresenceAct activation rules ACTIVE
698    end entry
699    exit .... end exit
700 end behaviour
```

Fig. 8. The "behavior DemonstratorBehaviour" declaration specifies that the demonstrator type will use a behavior called "DemonstratorBehaviour".

The behavior

The "behavior" is the global structure representing the whole behavior graph. It allows for identifying the "entry point" (see top left in Figure 3 and line 695 in Figure 8) of the behavior which can be viewed as the initialization of the behavior (this one will be executed only once). It also specifies that after the execution of the entry point, objectives "CheckAround" and "PresenceAct" will be executed concurrently thanks to the "execute concurrent" declaration (each one will be executed at each behavior execution).

The objectives

Objectives are the main components of the behavior. They are used to manage goals that an agent tries to reach. These behaviors can take different forms and they can be divided into three categories: simple objectives, compound objectives and aggregate objectives. Each objective has some basic elements. This section describes common elements to all objectives.

Basic objective elements

Whatever its type, an objective is characterized by some basic elements: a state (implicit), a list of successors (optional), required resources and priority (optional), an execution rule list (optional) and a completion rule list (mandatory). This section quickly describes these elements.

Objective states

The state of an objective is an implicit attribute representing the current context of an objective for a certain agent. This attribute can be consulted or modified using activation, execution and completion rules (the rule list example will show how to access this attribute). The runtime engine uses objective states to determine which actions it must undertake: to change the current running objective, to add or withdraw an objective from the execution process, etc.

Successors

A successor links an objective to a potential objective (its successor) that may be activated if the execution of the behavior of the first objective is successfully completed. A successor is composed of a destination objective (mandatory), an activation rule list for the destination objective (mandatory) and a priority function (optional) to discriminate objectives when necessary. Lines 696 and 697 of Figure 8 declare two successors named "CheckAround" and "PresenceAct" (these objectives must be defined elsewhere).

Activation rules

Activation rules are used to influence the state of a potential successor objective. For example, after the execution of the entry point in the demonstrator's behavior (see Figure 8), the behavior runtime engine has to choose the next objective to execute (in the next iteration). In this case, since the execution of the entry point's successors is specified to be concurrent, the behavior engine will have to execute all active successors. But, to check if an objective must be activated, the engine triggers the activation rules of each successor. Thereafter, the engine checks the state of each successor and it will schedule for execution all successors whose state is "active". Figure 9 shows an activation rule list used to verify if the objective "Runaway" must be activated. It checks whether some properties (anxiety, bravery and formation level of the crowd) satisfy certain levels. If it is the case, the state of the "Runaway" objective is set to "ACTIVE".

```
private rules RUN_AWAY_GO
   rule CHECK_STATES
        lhs S_1 [anxiety] >= [Crowd.ANXIETY_LEVEL]
        lhs S_2 [bravery] < [Crowd.BRAVERY_LEVEL]
        lhs S_3 [Crowd.getFormationLevel()] >=
                [Crowd.SCARING_FORMATION_LEVEL]
        rhs K set objective.this.STATE = [objective.ACTIVE]
end rules
```

Fig. 6. Rule list called "RUN_AWAY_GO" used in the "PresenceAct" and "PeacefullyDemonstrate" objectives.

Execution rules

The execution rules of an objective are rules which are automatically triggered immediately before each execution of an objective. These rules are used to control the execution of an objective by modifying its state. Once the rule list is triggered, the behavior engine uses the state value of the objective to determine if the objective needs to be executed at the current iteration, or if the system needs to wait and reevaluate them at the next behavior execution.

Completion rules

The completion rules of an objective are rules which are automatically triggered immediately after each execution of an objective. These rules are used to control the execution of an objective by modifying its state. Once the rule list is triggered, the behavior engine uses the state value of the objective to determine the action to be carried out: either re-execute the objective, or choose a successor, or stop the branch's execution (this graph's section). Note that the completion rules are only used to determine the action to perform on the currently executed objective. If the action consists in choosing another objective (if the objective's state is set to "successfully terminated"), then the activation rules of successors will be used to determine which successor will be chosen.

Resources and priorities

Resources and priorities are used to automatically monitor the exclusive execution of concurrent objectives at any iteration.

Objective types

As previously mentioned, objectives are divided into three types: simple, compound, and aggregate. Simple objectives are the most basic objectives. Their body is composed of a list of actions that are iteratively triggered when the objective is executed. In the demonstrator's behavior (Figure 6), "PresenceAct" and "CheckAround" are two simple objectives. Figure 10 shows the code of the "CheckAround" objective.

```
private simple objective CheckAround
        action perceiveCrowd()
        completion rules ACTIVE
end objective
```

Fig. 10. The "CheckAround" simple objective implementation.

Compound and aggregate objectives

A compound objective is a decomposable structure representing a sub-behavior. Figure 4 shows the internal view of the "PeacefullyDemonstrate" compound objective. The implementation and the execution of a compound objective are similar to a behavior. It consists in executing the sub-graph (the sub-behavior). An aggregate objective is another decomposable structure. But, contrary to a compound objective in which the inner objectives are linked together by successors, an aggregate objective is composed of a set of objectives without any direct relation between them. The execution of an aggregate objective triggers the execution of the objectives composing it which are in the active state.

3.2.2 Interactions between objects/agents and the VGE

Typically in a MAGS, the interactions between the objects/agents and the VGE are very frequent since an interaction is required every time an agent needs to query or act upon its environment. PLAMAGS includes various mechanisms, structures and an appropriate syntax to facilitate these interactions. Let us now present the main interactions.

Sending commands to the 3D environment

PLAMAGS provides a simple mechanism to send commands to the 3D environment that is which looks a classical method call. Collectively, these commands are called "perform" functions. The majority of the "performs" are what we call "managed actions" that are provided to ensure the spatial coherence of the virtual environment. The language offers movement and displacement actions such as "moveToward", moveNearAvoidObstacles", etc., allowing the displacement of components without worrying about the spatial constraints.

Information retrieval (feedback) from the 3D environment

We can specify many more interactions between simulation components and the VGE than just sending commands. Indeed, the agents and objects must also be kept aware of their situation in the environment so that they can behave as expected by the designer. Two types of information are generally required by an agent or an object from the VGE: its "spatial situation" within the VGE (its location, orientation, elevation, etc.) and its current perception of the environment.

Object/Agent spatial situation

The language introduces the keyword "percepts" whose sole purpose is to query the VGE regarding the "space related" attribute (position, orientation, elevation angle, etc.) whose name follows the keyword. This technique very effectively hides the complexity of the underlying operations.

Perception information retrieval

Agents and active objects are not only aware of their situation but are also aware (possibly partially) of the situation of other agents/objects located within the range of their senses. Retrieving this kind of information from the VGE is taken care of the keyword "references". Processing massive quantity of perceived facts can be a relatively inefficient and costly task. Hence, we split the perceived facts are into categories: i) agents and objects; ii) perceived gases; iii) groups; iv) projectiles. Retrieving perceptions by categories limits the number of facts passed to the simulation engine, and also coarsely filters facts that are obviously not relevant for an agent in its current context.

Configuring physical and spatial capabilities

In Section 1, we insisted on agents' space-related capabilities that a MAGS tool must automatically handle (perception, collision detection, obstacle avoidance, etc.). Most of these capabilities are directly integrated and configurable in the PLAMAGS language using what we call "*mapped items*".

Mapped items are simple language declarations specifying spatially/physically/visually related characteristics of agents and objects. Once these characteristics are specified, they are automatically managed by the simulation engine. Figure 8 shows how to specify some mapped items: the bounding volume and the field of view of the agent.

```
map boundingVolume : "automatic"
map fieldOfView : "20, 180, 0"
...
private void perceiveCrowd()
        local r : references = [references.Sight]
        for [i : int = 0;i < r.size(); i = i + 1] ... end for
end method
```

Fig. 11. Two "mapped items" and a method recovering perceived objects/agents.

In the demonstration simulation example, demonstrator agents have their own perception mechanism. To assign perception capabilities to a reactive or cognitive SSA, we only need to add a property "*fieldOfView*" with a radius and an angle in degrees to specify the angular extent of the visual field. Once the *fieldOfView* property is set, it is possible to recover the elements perceived by the agent any time. Figure 11 shows the code to recover perceived elements.

The language offers more than 90 different features corresponding to most of the basic capabilities needed to easily and automatically handle the agents' physical interaction with the spatial environment. It is easy to use these features, and consequently the user can pay attention to the specification of the cognitive aspects of the SSA's behaviors without the burden of programming them and verifying their coherence at the spatial level. For instance, with the four properties of figure 12, we define 1) the 3D model to be used for the EVG (i.e. the site); 2) the system of coordinates of the environment (0-500 units on the X axis, 0-500 units on the Y axis, and 0-125 units on the Z axis); 3) the file in which the height map of the 3D model will be saved; and 4) the initial position of the camera. Figure 13 shows the resulting view.

```
map mapModel : "res/models/quebec_city.3ds"
map coordinates : "0, 500, 0, 500, 0, 125"
map heightMap : "res/maps/heightMap.map"
map camera : "106, 26, 85, 27, -88"
```

Fig. 12. Definition of four essential properties of the EVG.

Discussion

The keywords « perform », « percepts », « references » and « map » are powerful tools that allow simple and seamless interactions between the simulation's components (agents/objects) and the 3D environment. Using these keywords (and their associated functions), a component can send commands to the 3D engine, retrieve information about its own situation and about other component it perceives. Developers thus have all the required tools to integrate geographic information into the decision-making process of the agents.

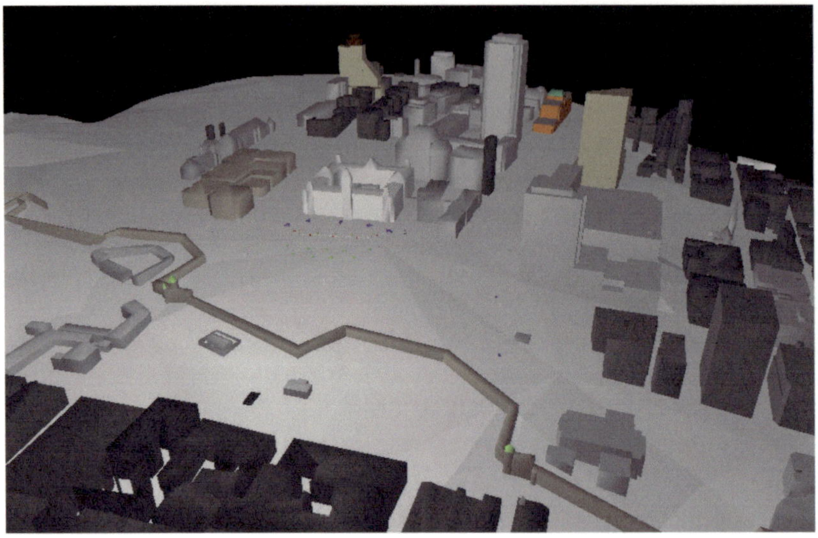

Fig. 13. View of Quebec City obtained using the properties of figure 12.

4. The PLAMAGS IDE

PLAMAGS IDE is an application that aims to help developers in using PLAMAGS by combining all the tools required to design, implement and execute a PLAMAGS program into a single piece of software. Figure 14 shows a global view of the PLAMAGS IDE when a project is loaded. In "A", we can see the built-in text editor displaying *Commander.bdl,* a PLAMAGS source file. In "B", there is the Project Manager which allows browsing the project's files and opens them into the text editor. In "C", we have the context tree of the currently editing file which sums up the attributes, object and other structures defined in the file. The component in "D" is a tabbed pane showing the output of the compiler and the execution engine (when either is loaded).

4.1 Integrated Development Environment

The IDE provides all the tools that are necessary to allow developers to create applications efficiently using the PLAMAGS language. Features are: i) a project manager; ii) a text editor; iii) a visual file structure navigator; iv) a real-time syntax checker; v) a Java classes browser; vi) a graphical configuration tool (sets, for instance, the JDK, fonts, etc.); vii) a built-in versioning system. Figure 9 shows some of these features in action.

Type creator (using stubs)

The MAGS related structures can be defined with stub files that enable the instantiation of objects of the corresponding type. The *Type Creator* provides stub files' templates for static objects, active objects, agents, behaviors, atomic objectives, complex objectives, compound objectives, aggregated objectives, rule lists, as well as scenarios. These templates accelerate the development by sparing the developer the tedious and error prone part of writing a stub file.

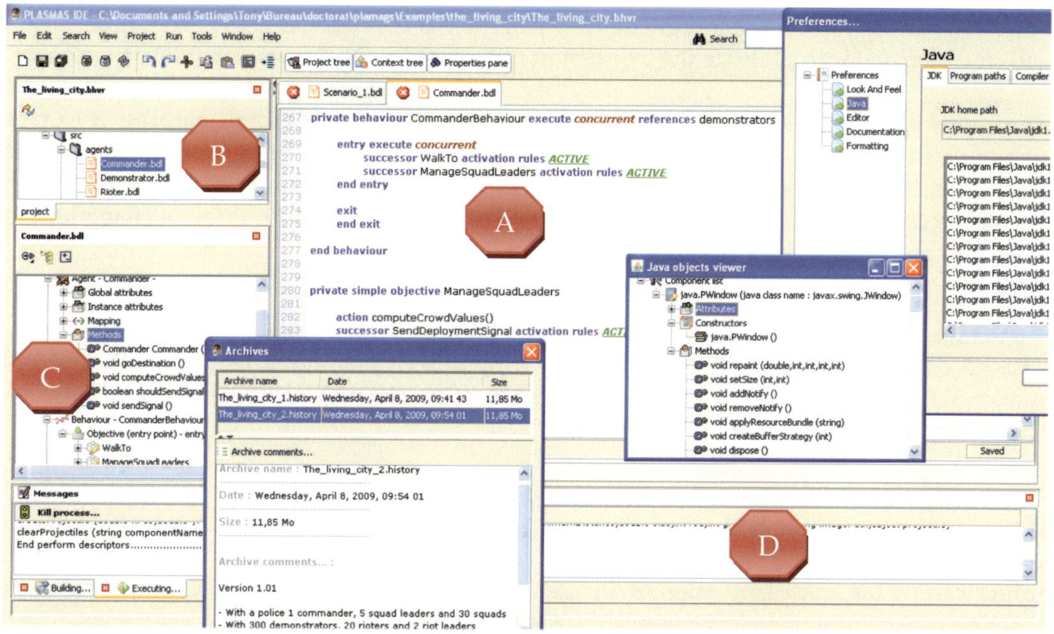

Fig. 14. Global view of the PLAMAGS IDE.

4.2 Language Support Suite

In addition to the development tools, PLAMAGS also provides tools to verify and execute the source files written in the language. These tools are either integrated in the IDE or provided as stand-alone applications.

Syntactic and Semantic Language Checker

As previously mentioned, the IDE includes language checker that verifies the content of every file of the current project in real-time and detects both syntactic and semantics errors.

PLAMAGS Language Interpreter

The Language Interpreter allows translating in real-time a PLAMAGS program into a set of Java instructions. The Java Runtime then takes over and evaluates each expression and executes the associated code when needed. The interpreter is responsible for the main following tasks: i) to evaluate the mathematical, boolean and relational expressions; ii) to create the structures specified using the language; iii) to evaluate and to dereference of attributes; iv) to execute method calls; v) to open the channels between Java and the execution engine; vi) to route the attribute query toward the requested object. However, when a behavioral structure has to be executed, the interpreter delegates this task to the Behavior Execution Engine.

Behavior Execution Engine

An execution engine might sound quite the same as an interpreter, but it is not the case. The main difference between the two is that the interpreter analyzes and evaluates conditional expressions whereas the execution engine executes pre-built structures such as rule lists and behaviors. In fact, if the execution engine encounters a conditional expression, it halts and calls the interpreter to evaluate the expression and recovers the control afterwards.

The execution engine is totally separated from PLAMAGS behavioral features: it can be thought of as a plug-in that handles several tasks. It executes instructions, handles the transitions between components taking into account the constraints and maintains each agents' structures sound. This separation would allow for modifying or even changing the execution engine without any coupling problems.

4.3 3D Engine

The 3D engine bundled with PLAMAGS is a module whose main responsibilities are to render 3D scenes and to manage the consistency of spatial and physical relations between the objects which are part of the simulation.

For instance, it must ensure that agents and active objects do not go through buildings' walls or another agent body that the laws of physic prevail in the virtual world when collisions occur, etc. The computation of available perceptions and other properties influenced by the spatial situation of an agent are also handled by the 3D engine since such tasks require computing a large number of spatial constraints.

Considering that the visual 3D rendering and the management of spatial constraints and physics are complex tasks and often computationally demanding, the engine relies on two specialized external libraries, JPCT (JPCT 2009) to accelerate the computations and PhysX (PhysX 2009) to manage the physics in the virtual world.

4.4 Simulation's Control and Visualization Interface

In order to simplify the execution of MAGS, the IDE includes a tool to visualize and to control the execution of the simulations.

4.4.1 Direct Control

As we can see in Figure 15, the user interface allows a user to control a running simulation. The simulation can run continuously (launched by the 'Run' button) or step by step. These steps are: i) loading the 3D map on screen; ii) instantiate the scenario; iii) initialize the scenario; iv) start the simulation; v) pause the simulation; vi) continue the simulation; vii) execute next step, etc.

4.4.2 Custom Interfaces for Agents

PLAMAGS also offers the possibility to have a personalized execution interface by cfrating a personalized window in which the simulation can be displayed. It is also possible to add *listeners* that are used to interact with the simulation by exchanging 'events' with the simulation.

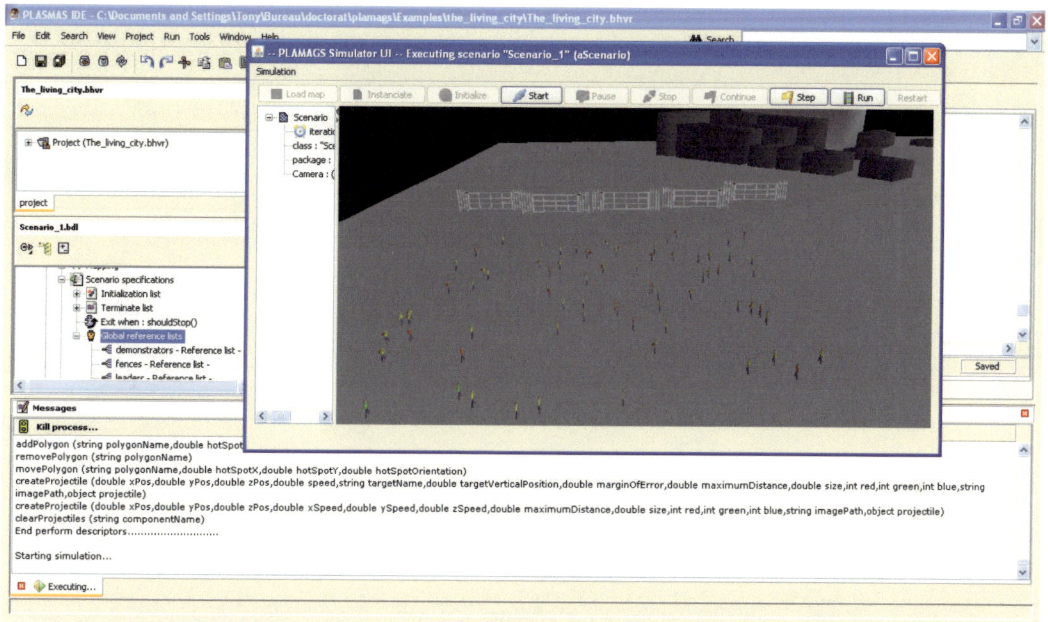

Fig. 15. Simulation interface running through the IDE.

Let us emphasize that the language checker, the interpreter, the execution engine, the libraries (3D and physics) and the visualization interface are all integrated in the IDE, but that they all can be used outside of it as well.

5. PLAMAGS features

In this section we discuss some features that contribute to the expressiveness, the simplicity and the effectiveness of PLAMAGS.

5.1 Graphical specification of graph and translation into PLAMAGS

The last component of PLAMAGS IDE which is still under development is an interface that will allow to greatly simplify the development and understanding of behavioral graphs (Figure 16). The Behavior Creator will allow a user to visually create and bind the various objects that together constitute a behavioral graph, as well as to specify the properties of an objective and the rules used by this objective.

When finished, the Behavior Editor will allow users to define agent behaviors in a simple, intuitive and visual way, thus effectively avoiding the syntactic and structural complexity that underlines the definition of multi-layer directed graphs. Furthermore, users will be allowed to shift back and forth between the source code and the visual representation instantly.

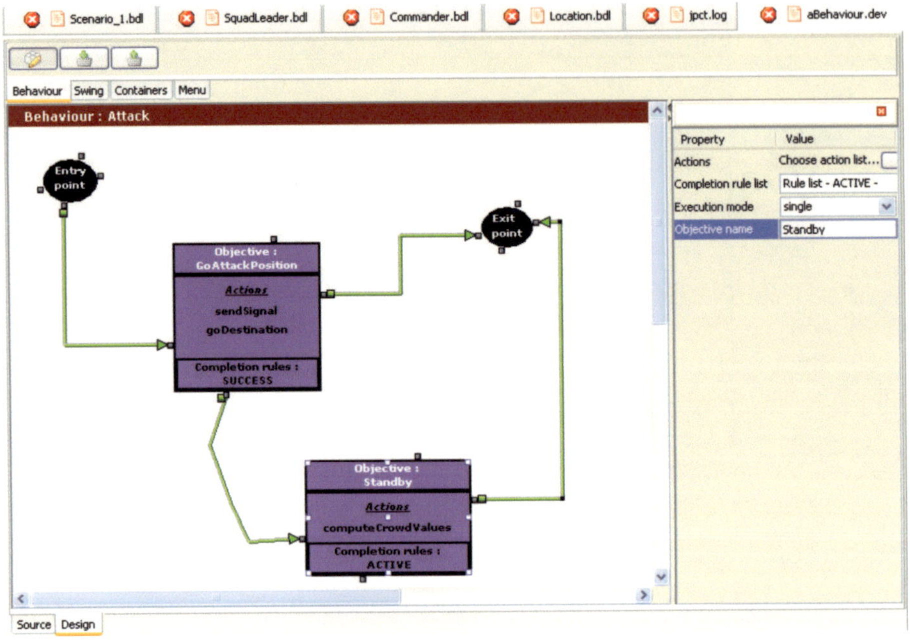

Fig. 16. Visual tool for behaviour creation.

It seems rather obvious that the visual representation of a behavioral graph is easier to understand than its textual equivalent since the visual part, the graph, even blank, carries semantics that one should write in a textual context. The difference with respect to complexity only grows as the size of this graph rises.

5.2 Compiled execution Mode

As we previously mentioned, PLAMAGS was originally designed as an interpreted language, which proved to be too inefficient for development and execution of large MAGS. This motivated the decision to add to the IDE a tool that compiles the interpreted code and then executes it. This tool is not completed yet; it currently supports simulations in which the user can specify active objects, scenarios and the use of gas. The part which would compile agent specifications is still under development.

The compiling technique that this tool implements is composed of three steps: first, the Java source code is generated from the PLAMAGS definition; second, the Java code is compiled; and third, the compiled code is executed using an execution engine. Splitting the technique in such steps enables the user to verify and modify the Java code before it is complied. This technique is a definitive solution to any eventual shortcomings of the language since the injected instructions are not subject to any limitations or restrictions. We empirically compared the interpreted and complied execution engines: the compiled engine was over 300 times faster than the interpreted one.

5.3 PLAMAGS' extensibility

Although in most situations, it is possible to develop simulations using PLAMAGS as a stand-alone development tool. However it might be sometimes desirable, if not necessary, to interact with external software such as external libraries or to use some code written in Java. We now introduce the techniques to so in both directions.

Using external Java classes and libraries

From the onset of the PLAMAGS Project, we designed the system so that communication between Java and PLAMAGS would be bidirectional. However, accessing PLAMAGS from Java should be allowed in specific cases.

PLAMAGS allows the use of any Java class and the technique is the same regardless of where the class comes from (JDK, libraries, folders). Each external class used in PLAMAGS requires to be assigned a name specified in a dedicated section of its source file. This name is used to reference the class in the PLAMAGS source code. Nothing prevents the use of the actual name of the class as its PLAMAGS name. Then these "new" types of static objects (along with their java properties and methods) are directly usable in the language, seamlessly using PLAMAGS syntax.

Accessing the simulation from Java

It is also possible to reference a PLAMAGS simulation from a Java application. To ensure a simple and safe interaction, the communication must go through what we call an *Externalizor* which exposes the relevant functions while preventing reckless interactions. The externalizor allows for sending "perform" commands to the 3D engine, accessing the components and the scenario of the simulation. This feature is used to carry out any operation outside PLAMAGS, as needed.

6. Conclusion

To sum up, the PLAMAGS environment provides: 1) a program editor (with real-time error checking); 2) a project management tree; 3) a contextual tree (describing the components of the file); 4) a language validation engine (similar to a compiler); 5) a runtime engine (an interpreter); 6) a 3D engine to visualize the simulations; 7) a visual programming tool (to graphically develop behaviors). In addition, it provides a Java objects browser for mapped types, an integrated help mechanism, a simulation start-up and a Java runtime configuration. It is executable both under Windows and Linux.

As previously mentioned, most of the multiagent geosimulation tools used to specify agents' behaviors are either strongly centered on the specification of behaviors' spatial aspects, or based on models inspired by finite state machines, which usually leads to create reactive agents. Similarly to tools which have "navigation or spatialized driven" behaviors, PLAMAGS offers a lot of predefined navigation actions. Although we consider spatialized and navigation behaviors as an important part of a geosimulation, they do not suffice to develop advanced multiagent geosimulations where agents possess cognitive capacities. To address this need, we introduced behaviors using multi-layered directed graphs. Contrary to other models inspired by finite state machine, PLAMAGS behavior's graphs manage concurrent execution and multiple concurrent, infinite decomposition of agents' goals (sub-behavior layers), expressive and powerful transitions between nodes proceeding into two phases: activation and completion (using rule lists and priorities), execution control of objectives using resources, priorities and execution rules. Behavior-related structures are at the very heart of PLAMAGS' architecture and language.

In addition to offering a language and an IDE, PLAMAGS provides a configurable tool allowing tracing the execution of simulations. The tool even allows a designer to inspect step by step the execution of the behavior runtime engine and to get details about its decision choices.

We used PLAMAGS in several simulation projects and have identified three main shortcomings for which we intend to find solutions in our short term future work. First, the definition of a simulation's initial properties, VGE, objects and agents, for a specific scenario, is a demanding task when performed at the programming level. A graphical specification tool would facilitate the task from the user's perspective. Second, the JPCT library seems to reach its performance limits when confronted with complex 3D models. Indeed, such models require too much time for graphical rendering and tend to use too much memory. This is why we use very simple models for the representation of objects and agents. We may try to find a replacement library. Third and last, our numerous experiments involving various simulations have shown that it would be very convenient to add a "save simulation state" function in order to save a simulation, modify one or more elements of its structure, and then resume the simulation in the state saved before the changes.

We are currently developing the visual specification interface for behaviors. Once this module will be completed, the user will be able to specify agent behaviors in a visual programming mode. Thereafter, it will be possible to automatically generate the corresponding PLAMAGS code. The user will also be able to do the opposite operation and go from the textual programming mode to the visual one. We are currently extending the compiled version of PLAMAGS so that it can support agents and their behaviors. We are also investigating the possibility to integrate some behavior validation mechanisms using graph theory.

Acknowledgements: Parts of this project have been financed by Geoide, the Canadian Network of Centers of Excellence in Geomatics. The first author also benefited from a scholarship from the Natural Sciences and Engineering Council of Canada.

7. References

AI.implant (2003). AI-implant: A game-AI derived general scalable model for life-form simulation in MOUT-based applications.

AI.implant. (2009). from http://www.presagis.com/.

Beneson, I. and V. Kharbash (2005). Geographic Automata Systems:From The Paradigm to the Urban Modeling Software. AGILE 2005 and GISPlanet 2005, Estoril, Portugal.

Beneson, I. and P. M. Torrens (2004). "Geosimulation: Automata-Based Modeling of Urban Phenomena."

Bourrel, E. and V. Henn (2003). Mixing micro and macro representations of traffic flow: a hybrid model based on the LWR theory. 82nd TRB Annual Meeting (Transportation Research Board), Washington, USA.

CORMAS. (2009). from http://cormas.cirad.fr/.

Courdier, R., F. Guerrin, F. H. Andriamasinoro and J.-M. Paillat (2002). "Agent-based simulation of complex systems: application to collective management of animal wastes." Journal of Artificial Societies and Social Simulation **5**(3).

Crooks, A., C. Castle and M. Batty (2007). Key Challenges in Agent-Based Modelling for Geo-Spatial Simulation. Geocomputation 2007, National Centre for Geocomputation (NCG), National University of Ireland, Maynooth, Co. Kildare, Ireland.

Cutumisu, M., D. Szafron, J. Schaeffer, M. McNaughton, T. Roy, C. Onuczko and M. Carbonaro (2006). "Generating Ambient Behaviors in Computer Role-Playing Games." IEEE Intelligent Systems **21**(5): 19-27.

d'Aquino, P., C. Le Page, F. Bousquet and A. Bah (2003). "Using Self-Designed Role-Playing Games and a Multi-Agent System to Empower a Local Decision-Making Process for Land Use Management: The SelfCormas Experiment in Senegal." Journal of Artificial Societies and Social Simulation **6**(3).

Donikian, S. (2001). HPTS: a behaviour modelling language for autonomous agents. International Conference on Autonomous Agents, fifth international conference on Autonomous agents, Montréal, Québec, Canada, ACM Press.

Fagiolo, G., A. Moneta and P. Windrum (2007). "A Critical Guide to Empirical Validation of Agent-Based Models in Economics: Methodologies, Procedures, and Open Problems." Computational Economics **30**(3): 195-226.

Foudil, C. and D. Noureddine (2007). "An autonomous and guided crowd in panic situations." Journal of Computer Science & Technology **2**(2): 134-140.

Fu, D., R. Houlette and S. Henke (2002). "Putting AI in Entertainment: An AI Authoring Tool for Simulation and Games." Intelligent Systems **17**(4): 81-84.

Fu, D., R. Houlette, R. Jensen and S. Henke (2003). A Visual Environment for Rapid Behavior Definition. 2003 Conference on Behavior Representation in Modeling and Simulation, Scottsdale, Arizona.

Garneau, T., B. Moulin and S. Delisle (2008). PLAMAGS: A Language and Environment to Specify Intelligent Agents in Virtual Geo-Referenced Worlds. Proceedings of the 19th IASTED International Conference on Modelling and Simulation., Quebec City, Canada.

GASP. (2009). from http://www.irisa.fr/prive/donikian/behavioral_programming_environment.html

Gnansounou, E., S. Pierre, A. Quintero, J. Dong and A. Lahlou (2007). "Toward a Multi-Agent Architecture for Market Oriented Planning in Electricity Supply Industry." International Journal of Power and Energy Systems **27**(1): 82-91.

Guyot , P. and S. Honiden (2006). "Agent-Based Participatory Simulations: Merging Multi-Agent Systems and Role-Playing Games." Journal of Artificial Societies and Social Simulation **9**(4).

Helbing, D., A. Hennecke, V. Shvetsov and M. Treiber (2002). "Micro- and Macro-Simulation of Freeway Traffic." Mathematical and computer modelling **35**(5-5): 517-547.

JPCT. (2009). from http://www.jpct.net/.

Koch, A. (2001). Linking Multi Agent Systems And GIS - Modeling And Simulating Spatial InterActions –. Angewandte Geographische Informationsverarbeitung XII, Beiträge zum AGIT-Symposium.

Levesque, J., F. Cazzolato, J. Perron, J. Hogan, T. Garneau and B. Moulin (2008). CAMiCS: civilian activity modelling in constructive simulation. SpringSim 2008.

Moulin, B., W. Chaker, J. Perron, P. Pelletier, J. Hogan and E. Gbei Fonh (2003). MAGS Project: Multi-Agent GeoSimulation and Crowd Simulation. Conference on Spatial Information Theory (COSIT'03), Ittingen, Switzerland, Springer-Verlag.

Müller, J.-P., C. Ratzé, F. Gillet and K. Stoffel (2005). Modeling And Simulating Hierarchies Using An Agent-Based Approach. MODSIM05 : International Congress on Modelling and Simulation. Advances and Applications for Management and Decision Making Melbourne, Australia.

Papazoglou, P. M., D. A. Karras and R. C. Papademetriou (2008). On the Multi-threading Approach of Efficient Multi-agent Methodology for Modelling Cellular Communications Bandwidth Management Agent and Multi-Agent Systems: Technologies and Applications. **4953/2008**.

PATHEngine. (2009). from http://www.pathengine.com/.

PhysX. (2009). 2008, from http://www.nvidia.com/object/physx_9.09.0408_whql.html.

SPR.OPS. (2009). from http://www.spirops.com/.

Torrens, P. M. and I. Benenson (2005). "Geographic Automata Systems." International Journal of Geographical Information Science **19**(4): 385-412.